Mythologies

Tungus shaman. Nerchinsk, Transbaikal, USSR. Paris, Musée de l'Homme collection. Photo Kobizett-Angarski.

Mythologies

Compiled by

YVES BONNEFOY

A Restructured Translation of

Dictionnaire des mythologies et des religions des sociétés traditionnelles et du monde antique

Prepared under the Direction of

WENDY DONIGER

Translated by Gerald Honigsblum,
Danielle Beauvais, Teresa Lavender Fagan, Dorothy Figueira,
Barry Friedman, Daniel Gold, Louise Guiney,
John Leavitt, Louise Root, Michael Sells, Bruce Sullivan,
and David White

Volume Two

The University of Chicago Press • *Chicago and London*

YVES BONNEFOY,
a scholar and poet of world renown, is
professor of comparative poetics, Collège de France.
Among his many works to have appeared in English, two
have been published by the University of Chicago Press—a
volume of poetry, *In the Shadow's Light* (1991), and a work
of criticism, *The Act and Place of Poetry* (1989), both
translated by John T. Naughton.

WENDY DONIGER
is the Mircea Eliade Professor in the
Divinity School, and professor in the Department of South
Asian Languages and Civilizations, the Committee on Social
Thought, and the College, at the University of Chicago.
Under the name of Wendy Doniger O'Flaherty she has written,
among other books, *Women, Androgynes, and Other Mythical
Beasts* (1980), *Dreams, Illusion, and Other Realities* (1984),
and *Tales of Sex and Violence: Folklore, Sacrifice, and
Danger in the Jaiminīya Brāhmaṇa* (1985), all published
by the University of Chicago Press.

The University of Chicago Press, Chicago 60637
The University of Chicago Press, Ltd., London

Printed in the United States of America

00 99 98 97 96 95 94 93 92 91 5 4 3 2 1

Originally published as *Dictionnaire des mythologies
et des religions des sociétés traditionnelles et du monde antique,*
sous la direction de Yves Bonnefoy, publié avec le
concours du Centre National des Lettres,

This book is printed on acid-free paper.

Library of Congress Cataloging-in-Publication Data
Dictionnaire des mythologies et des religions des sociétés
traditionnelles et du monde antique. English.
Mythologies / compiled by Yves Bonnefoy.
p. cm.
"A restructured translation of Dictionnaire des mythologies et des religions des sociétés traditionnelles et du monde antique prepared under the direction of Wendy Doniger."
Includes bibliographical references and index.
ISBN 0-226-06453-0
1. Mythologies—Dictionaries. 2. Religion, Primitive—Dictionaries. I. Bonnefoy, Yves. II. Title.
BL311.D513 1991
291.1'3'03—dc20 90-46982
CIP

Contents

VOLUME TWO

PART 6
WESTERN CIVILIZATION IN THE CHRISTIAN ERA

The Survival of Myths in Early Christianity 649
Christian Judgments on the Analogies between Christianity and Pagan Mythology 655
The Euhemerism of the Christian Authors 666
Christianity and Mythology in the Greek Church 671
The Naassenes' Use of Pagan Mythologies 675
The Gnostics and the Mythologies of Paganism 677
The Perates and their Gnostic Interpretation of Paganism 680
Eros among the Gnostics 682
Hecate in Greek Esotericism 685
Justin the Gnostic: A Syncretistic Mythology 686
The Medieval West and "Mythic Thought" 688
The Survival of the Ancient Gods in the Middle Ages and the Renaissance 692
Alchemy and Mythology 701
Cabala and Mythology 704
Pan among the Cabalists and Alchemists of the Renaissance 705
Fables and Symbols from Sixteenth- and Seventeenth-Century Hermeticism 706
Hercules in Alchemy 711
Orpheus in the Renaissance 712
King Arthur, the Romances of the Round Table, and the Legend of the Grail 713
Tristan and Isolde 717
Gypsy Myths and Rituals 718
Fable and Mythology in Seventeenth- and Eighteenth-Century Literature and Theoretical Reflection 722
The Mythology of Ancient Switzerland 733
Mythic Elements in French Folklore 734
French Fairy Tales, Folktales, and Myths 738
Folk Beliefs and Legends about Fairies in France 743
Popular Customs and Rituals in France 746
Romanticism and Mythology: The Use of Myths in Literary Works 752
Romanticism and Myth in Blake, Nerval, and Balzac 756
The Mythology of European Decadent and Symbolist Literature 758
The Androgyne 764
The Androgyne, the Double, and the Reflection: A Few Myths of Romanticism 765
Romantic Myths of the Rebel and the Victim: Satan, Prometheus, Cain, Job, Faust, Ahasuerus, Don Juan, and Empedocles 767
Spirits of the Elements in the Romantic Period: Sylphs, Water Sprites, Salamanders, Gnomes, and Elves 771
Orpheus and the Poetic and Spiritual Quest of Romanticism 772
The Isis of Romanticism: The Myth of the Wife-Mother—Helen, Sophia, Mary 774
Julian the Apostate in Romantic Literature 775

Napoleon as Myth 777
Modernity's Challenge to Myth, in the Poetry of Hölderlin, Heine, Baudelaire, Mallarmé, T. S. Eliot, and Rilke 778
Hölderlin's Dionysus 781
Myth in Twentieth-Century English Literature 783
The Survival of Ancient Myths in Modern Greek Poetic Consciousness 787
Imagination and Mythology in Contemporary Literature (Tolkien, Lovecraft) and Science Fiction 790
Myth and Political Theory: Nationalisms and Socialisms 793

PART 7 SOUTH ASIA, IRAN, AND BUDDHISM

The Religion and Mythology of Vedic India 799
Soma as Sacrificial Substance and Divine Figure in the Vedic Mythology of Exchange 803
Vedic Cosmogony 806
The Mythologies of Hindu India 808
The *Yūpa* (Sacrificial Post) in Hindiusm 811
Rudra/Śiva and the Destruction of the Sacrifice 813
Purāṇic Cosmogony 817
The Hindu God with Five Heads (*Pañcamukha*) 824
Deva/Asura: Celestial Gods and "Demons" in Hinduism 826
Vasiṣṭha/Viśvāmitra and the Separation of the Priestly and Royal Functions 827
The Main Myth of the *Mahābhārata* 829
The *Rāmāyaṇa* 834
Viṣṇu and Śiva, the Supreme Gods of Hindu Bhakti 839
Popular Hinduism 842
Avatars 849
Nara/Nārāyaṇa 852
Matsya: The Fish and the Flood in the Work of the Mythic Imagination 853
Narasiṃha, the Man-Lion 854
Paraśurāma 856
Vāmana, the Dwarf 858
The Childhood and Adulthood of Kṛṣṇa 859
Gaṇapati 864
Skanda, a Great Sovereign God of South India 866
Devī: The Goddess in India 869
Kāmadhenu: The Mythical Cow, Symbol of Prosperity 873
Symbols of the Earth in Indian Religion 873
Ganges and Yamunā, the River of Salvation and the River of Origins 875
Pre-Islamic Iran 877
Ahura Mazdā (or Oromazdes, Ohrmazd) 890
Anāhitā (or Anahid) 891
Mithra (or Mihr, Mihir, Meher) 891
Vayu (or Vay, Vai) 892
Verethraghna (or Varahran, Bahram) 893
Buddhist Mythology 893
The Guardian of the Gate: An Example of Buddhist Mythology, from India to Japan 896

PART 8 SOUTHEAST ASIA

Austroasiatic, Vedic, and Brahmanic Myths of Southeast Asia 913
Southeast Asian Origin Myths and Founding Myths 916
Earth Spirits in Southeast Asia 918
Southeast Asian Myths and Rituals of the Moon 924
The Acculturation of the Divinities of Hinduism in Southeast Asia 926
The Mythic Themes of Theravāda Buddhism in Southeast Asia 929
The Religions and Myths of Insular Southeast Asia 931
Divine Totality and Its Components: The Supreme Deity, the Divine Couple, and the Trinity in Indonesian Religions 937
The Origin of Humanity and the Descent to Earth of the First Human Beings in the Myths of Indonesia 940
Culture Heroes of Insular Southeast Asia 941
Communal Festivals in Insular Southeast Asia 947
Indonesian Rites of Passage 949
A Myth of the Origin of Grains: Hainuwele in Ceram, Indonesia 952

The *Wayang* (Ritual Theater) and Its Myths in Java and Bali 953
The *Rāmāyaṇa* in Indonesia 957
Recent Forms of Eschatology and Messianism in Insular Southeast Asia 958
Desacralization from Myths to Tales in Java 959
The Mythology of the Highlands of Madagascar and the Political Cycle of the Andriambahoaka 961
The Mythology and Ritual of the Indigenous Populations of the Southern Part of the Indo-Chinese Peninsula: Orientation of Research 976
The History and Function of Indo-Chinese Myth: Change and Permanence 979
Indigenous Indo-Chinese Cosmogony 981
The Functions and Methods of Mediators and Intermediaries among the Indigenous Indo-Chinese 985
The Number Seven, Even and Odd, among the Indigenous Indo-Chinese 988
The Ambiguous Notion of Power among Austroasiatic and Austronesian Peoples: The *Potao* of the Jarai 990
Yang: The Sacred Connection, Sacrifice, and the Ritual of Counting among the Austroasiatic and Austronesian Ethnic Groups 992
Vietnamese Mythology 995
The Origins and the First Ages in the Major Structures of Vietnamese Mythology 996
Civilizing Heroes and the Organization of the First Vietnamese Kingdom 1001

PART 9 EAST ASIA AND INNER ASIA

Chinese Mythology 1007
Chinese Cosmogony 1008
Sky and Earth, Sun and Moon, Stars, Mountains and Rivers, and the Cardinal Points in Ancient China 1010
Ancient Chinese Goddesses and Grandmothers 1015
Mythical Rulers in China: The Three Huang and the Five Di 1018
The Great Flood in Chinese Mythology 1024
Myths and Legends about the Barbarians on the Periphery of China and in the Land of Chu 1026
Chinese Demons 1028
The Mythology of Smelters and Potters in China 1032
Caves and Labyrinths in Ancient China 1033
Some Legends about Laozi and the Immortals in Daoist Mythology 1034
Remarks on Japanese Religions and Mythological Beliefs 1037
The Vital Spirit and the Soul in Japan 1041
Japanese Conceptions of the Afterlife 1044
Buddhism and Archaic Beliefs in the Shinto-Buddhist Syncretism of Japan 1049
Mountains in Japan 1051
Magic in Japan 1053
Japanese Divination 1055
The *Yamabushi,* Mountain Ascetics of Japan 1056
The *Tengu* Demons of Japan 1059
Japanese Shamanism 1062
Japanese Festivals and Seasonal Rites: *Matsuri* and *Nenchū Gyōji* 1063
Korean Mythology 1070
Introduction to Tibetan Mythology 1075
The Importance of Origins in Tibetan Mythology 1077
Cosmogonic Myths of Tibet 1079
Anthropogonic Myths of Tibet 1082
Divine Sovereignty in Tibet 1086
The Religion and Myths of the Turks and Mongols 1089
Turkish and Mongolian Cosmogony and Cosmography 1095
Turkish and Mongolian Demons 1096
The Turkish and Mongolian Ancestor Cult 1097
The Importance of Animals in the Religion of the Turks and Mongols: Tribal Myths and Hunting Rituals 1097
The Tree of Life and the Cosmic Axis among the Turks and Mongols 1101
The Mountain as Cosmic Axis among the Turks and Mongols 1102
Turkish and Mongolian Shamanism 1103
The Sky God and the Stars among the Turks and Mongols 1105
Water among the Turks and Mongols 1107

Turkish and Mongolian Eschatology: The End of the World and the Fate of Man after Death 1107
Turkish and Mongolian Master Spirits (Ejen and Izik) 1108
The Cult of Fire among the Turks and Mongols 1109
Turkish and Mongolian Funerary Customs 1109
Heroes of the Turks and Mongols 1111
The Turkish and Mongolian Ritual of the Blood Oath 1112
The Earth among the Turks and Mongols 1112
The Personification of Thunder among the Turks and Mongols 1113
Gods and Myths of the Abkhaz, the Cherkess, and the Ubykh of the Northern Caucasus 1113
Souls and Their Avatars in Siberia 1116
The Sky, the Great Celestial Divinity of Siberia 1119
Siberian Master Spirits and Shamanism 1120
Siberian Religion and Myths: The Example of the Tungus 1128
Finno-Ugrian Myths and Rituals 1132

PART 10 THE AMERICAS AND THE SOUTH PACIFIC

The Mythology of the Inuit of the Central Arctic 1145
Native American Myths and Rituals of North America 1152
The Creation of the World in Native American Mythology 1160
The Sun Dance among the Native Americans: The Revival of 1973 1163
Mesoamerican Religion 1165
Mesoamerican Mythic and Ritual Order 1169
Mesoamerican Creation Myths 1173
Mesoamerican Religious Conceptions of Space and Time 1176
The Sky: Sun, Moon, Stars, and Meteorological Phenomena in Mesoamerican Religions 1180
The Earth in Mesoamerican Religions 1184
Fire in Mesoamerican Mythology 1187
The Mesoamerican Image of the Human Person 1188
Cosmic Disorder, Illness, Death, and Magic in Mesoamerican Traditions 1189
Myths and Rituals of the South American Indians 1192
Indians of the South American Forest 1194
Religions and Cults of the Societies of the Andes 1201
Religious Thought and Prophetism among the Tupi-Guarani Indians of South America: The Land Without Evil 1206
Religions and Mythologies of Oceania 1208
Papua New Guinea 1224

Epilogue: The Contemporary Need for Myths—a Testimonial 1231

Index 1237

SUMMARY OF CONTENTS OF VOLUME ONE

Part 1 Africa
Part 2 The Ancient Near East
Part 3 Celts, Norse, Slavs, Caucasians, and Their Neighbors
Part 4 Greece
Part 5 Rome

PART

6

Western Civilization in the Christian Era

The Survival of Myths in Early Christianity 649
Christian Judgments on the Analogies between Christianity and Pagan Mythology 655
The Euhemerism of the Christian Authors 666
Christianity and Mythology in the Greek Church 671
The Naassenes' Use of Pagan Mythologies 675
The Gnostics and the Mythologies of Paganism 677
The Perates and their Gnostic Interpretation of Paganism 680
Eros among the Gnostics 682
Hecate in Greek Esotericism 685
Justin the Gnostic: A Syncretistic Mythology 686
The Medieval West and "Mythic Thought" 688
The Survival of the Ancient Gods in the Middle Ages and the Renaissance 692
Alchemy and Mythology 701
Cabala and Mythology 704
Pan among the Cabalists and Alchemists of the Renaissance 705
Fables and Symbols from Sixteenth- and Seventeenth-Century Hermeticism 706
Hercules in Alchemy 711
Orpheus in the Renaissance 712
King Arthur, the Romances of the Round Table, and the Legend of the Grail 713
Tristan and Isolde 717
Gypsy Myths and Rituals 718
Fable and Mythology in Seventeenth- and Eighteenth-Century Literature and Theoretical Reflection 722
The Mythology of Ancient Switzerland 733
Mythic Elements in French Folklore 734
French Fairy Tales, Folktales, and Myths 738
Folk Beliefs and Legends about Fairies in France 743
Popular Customs and Rituals in France 746
Romanticism and Mythology: The Use of Myths in Literary Works 752
Romanticism and Myth in Blake, Nerval, and Balzac 756
The Mythology of European Decadent and Symbolist Literature 758
The Androgyne 764
The Androgyne, the Double, and the Reflection: A Few Myths of Romanticism 765
Romantic Myths of the Rebel and the Victim: Satan, Prometheus, Cain, Job, Faust, Ahasuerus, Don Juan, and Empedocles 767
Spirits of the Elements in the Romantic Period: Sylphs, Water Sprites, Salamanders, Gnomes, and Elves 771
Orpheus and the Poetic and Spiritual Quest of Romanticism 772
The Isis of Romanticism: The Myth of the Wife-Mother—Helen, Sophia, Mary 774
Julian the Apostate in Romantic Literature 775
Napoleon as Myth 777
Modernity's Challenge to Myth, in the Poetry of Hölderlin, Heine, Baudelaire, Mallarmé, T. S. Eliot, and Rilke 778
Hölderlin's Dionysus 781
Myth in Twentieth-Century English Literature 783
The Survival of Ancient Myths in Modern Greek Poetic Consciousness 787
Imagination and Mythology in Contemporary Literature (Tolkien, Lovecraft) and Science Fiction 790
Myth and Political Theory: Nationalisms and Socialisms 793

The Survival of Myths in Early Christianity

The Old Testament

I. Hellenistic Judaism

The Old Testament is no less important to Christianity than it is to Judaism, although each does a different reading of it. It follows that any inquiry into the mythical foundation that may have persisted in early Christianity must take into account early Christianity's view of the Law and the Prophets. When it comes to biblical hermeneutics, we know that the Church Fathers were often influenced by the Hellenized Jews who lived just before the Christian era. This is what makes the testimony of the most prominent of these Hellenized Jews, Philo of Alexandria, so interesting.

Philo evokes a contemporary trend which he himself condemns—that of reducing certain biblical episodes to the level of Greek myths that were deemed comparable. The identity of these comparativists is not certain, but it is hard to know who they could have been if not those free-thinking Jews, a few examples of whom are known to us. At all events, Philo has them say to the pious Jews: "The Books that you claim to be sacred also contain those myths that you are accustomed to laugh at when you hear others tell them." By way of proof, they offered the Homeric myth of the Aloadae piling up mountains to reach the sky (Homer, *Odyssey* 11.305–20), "in place of which Moses introduces" the construction of the tower of Babel, although the biblical episode of the confusion of languages (Gen. 11.1–9) may have been "similar to the [pagan] myth" of the original community of language among all living beings (*De confusione linguarum* 2.2–4, 9). Shortly before the Christian era, therefore, some exegetes were convinced of the mythical quality of at least a few pages of the Old Testament. Philo reports concurrent examples that probably illustrate the same orientation: when Moses speaks of giants (Gen. 6.4), he is alluding to myths by poets on the same subject (*De gigantibus* 13.58); systematic detractors minimize the sacrifice of Isaac and Abraham's consent to it (Gen. 22.1–19) by comparing it to the practice among Greeks, private citizens or even kings (here one can discern a reference to Iphigenia sacrificed by Agamemnon), of sacrificing their children in the hope of gaining military success (*De Abrahamo* 33.178–34, 183); Philo finally points to certain demented slanderers of the Scriptures who claim that the story of the various animals cut in half by Abraham (Gen. 15.9–17) actually describes an act of divination, with a sacrificial victim and the inspection of its entrails (*Quaestiones in Genesin* 3.3). Such information was recognized as historically significant by H. A. Wolfson[1] and J. Daniélou.[2]

The adjectives and other qualifiers that Philo uses show that he does not support this tendency. But he does admit that a number of passages from the Bible are mythical, provided, he insists, that they are taken literally—a restriction which, though his adversaries had no use for it, greatly changes the perspective. He gives examples of biblical texts of this type: the planting of paradise by God (Gen. 2.8), imagined as the work of a careful gardener arranging a place in which to relax, is a "mythopoeisis" which would not occur to anyone (*Legum allegoriae* 1.14.43); the creation of Eve out of a rib taken from the sleeping Adam (Gen. 2.21–22), taken literally, "resembles a myth" (*Legum allegoriae* 2.7.19–20); if one stops to think about them, the anthropomorphisms that Moses applied to God in his pedagogic endeavor (such as Gen. 6.7: God regrets having created man and thinks of destroying him; Deut. 8.5: like a man, God educates his son) become absurd in themselves and in their consequences, for they are the "mythopoeses" of impious men (*Quod deus sit immutabilis* 12.59).

This last text suggests that there were literalists among the exegetes who, probably unintentionally, went so far as to call certain pages of the Bible myths, thereby objectively joining the cause of the aforementioned comparativists, although their intentions and methods were quite different. To avoid the risk of seeing the Bible concede part of its territory to myth, one merely had to renounce extreme literalism: by the miracle of allegory, mythical appearance dissolves and makes way for a more respectable theoretical meaning. Such is the rejoinder with which Philo responds to the threat of the mythicization of Scripture. Take, for instance, the two biblical serpents, the serpent in paradise, who speaks and seduces the woman (Gen. 3.1–5), and the bronze serpent, who procures the welfare of anyone who merely looks at him (Num. 21.9). On the face of it, "They look like wonders and monsters, . . . but if one explains them by allegory, the resemblance to myth vanishes, and the truth reveals itself

The baptism of Christ. Mosaic in the nave of the church of Daphni, ca. 1100. Photo Hans Hinz—Skira.

with all clarity": the mortal knots of the first serpent are the knots of pleasure; the bronze of the second serpent is the strength of the soul that nothing can attack (*De agricultura* 22.96–97). So the myth that one might on occasion be tempted to suspect in the Bible is just an illusion that vanishes in the light of allegory. The *De opificio mundi* (56.157) repeats this idea with an example close to the preceding one: the passage of Genesis that refers to the planting of paradise with two trees, the enticing serpent, the fall, the punishment—despite all appearances (Gen. 2.7–3, 24), these "are not the mythical fictions dear to the race of poets and Sophists, but rather examples of figures that invite one to allegory, in accordance with implied meanings." These are some of the ideas about myth in Philo's hermeneutics that have been discussed by G. Delling,[3] and by me in a previous work.[4]

II. Patristic Christianity

As P. Heinisch[5] has pointed out (along with many other scholars), Philo had an enormous influence on the exegesis of the Church Fathers. Among the teachings that were handed down in this way are his views that although certain biblical texts appear to be mythical, such an appearance is shattered by the allegorical interpretation, which virtually exercises a demythologizing function, as J. Daniélou has wisely observed.[6] Another way of formulating this principle is to say that without allegorical exegesis, one remains unarmed before all the appearances of myth. That is how Gregory of Nyssa dealt with the verses from Genesis (2.16–17) concerning the tree of knowledge; without actually naming the allegory, he designated it in no uncertain terms: "If one does not contemplate the truth in the narrative by means of philosophy, the unsuspecting reader will find the narrative inconsistent and similar to myth" (*Commentary on the Song of Songs*, prologue, ed. Langerbeck, pp. 11, 5–7).

Origen had previously given yet another presentation of the same concept. He claimed that the Old Testament was both myth and truth (or, following the classical dichotomy, *mythos* and *logos*) depending on the quality of its readers: it was myth for the Jews, who perceived only its surface, but it became truth for Christians who through allegory penetrated to its deep meaning. The following are two texts taken from Origen that typify this way of seeing things. First from *Contra Celsum* 2.4 and 5.42: Christians "bestow greater honor on the Books of the Law by showing what depths of wise and mysterious teachings are enclosed in these texts, whereas their meaning has escaped the Jews, whose contact with them is too superficial and mythical." "To Jews, children with the intelligence of children, the truth was still proclaimed in the form of myth; but now, for the Christians who seek instruction and wish to make progress, what were formerly myths, to call them by their name, are now metamorphosed into those truths that were hidden in the myths." (The Bible read by Jewish eyes is still described as "myth" and "mythology" in 2.5–6, and 52 of the same treatise.) We can see how these various authors solved the problem of myth in the Bible by subjectifying it: myth that was nothing but myth could not be found in the Holy Scriptures, which is why the comparativists' illusion was false; Scripture merely contains apparent and provisional myths destined to wither away under the effect of the allegorical reading. This is precisely the ideology that was held in common by many Hellenized Jews and by the Church Fathers. Origen took a step forward where Philo obviously could not follow him when he made the appearances of myth the lot of the Jews and profound truth the privilege of Christians.

III. The History of Religions

The tendency toward comparativism that Philo denounced nevertheless continued, in a slightly different form. For it is not Greek myths that today provide us with counterparts to the Old Testament (although there are plenty of examples of those); rather, we turn to more ancient cultures, Babylonia and Phoenicia, where we pick up striking parallels, notably between biblical narratives of the creation and the flood, and the Babylonian poem of the *Enūma eliš* and the epic of Gilgameš. It used to be accepted without argument that this coincidence could be explained by an influence exerted on Israel; this view was championed by H. Gunkel[7] among others. Since then, scholars have become more circumspect; see, for example, the works of A. Heidel[8] and E. O. James.[9] People still resort to analogies that indicate the presence of considerable mythical segments in the Old Testament. But these episodes are marked by a particular coloration because of the monotheism basic to the the Jewish tradition.

We shall not attempt to give an inventory here of all the episodes with mythical dimensions in the Bible, but rather limit ourselves to a typical example, myths of water, referring the reader for more details to the work of P. Reymond.[10] Hebrew cosmology rests essentially on the myth (not exclusively Jewish) of a primordial ocean that surrounds the dry earth boundlessly, threatens its existence, and gives birth to all the waters on earth, below (rivers and springs) and above (rain). The origin of time is marked by Yahweh's struggle with this hostile element, often personified by the sea monsters Rahab

(Job 26.12) and Leviathan (Isa. 27.1; Ps. 74.13–14, etc.). The primordial struggle of God against the forces of the sea also develops against the Nile and its incarnation the Pharaoh, himself assimilated to the crocodile of Egypt. This amalgam is admirably depicted in Ezekiel 29.3–4: "These are the words of the Lord God: I am against you, Pharaoh king of Egypt, you great monster, lurking in the streams of the Nile. You have said, 'My Nile is my own; it was I who made it. I will put hooks in your jaws,' " etc.

The mythical ocean of the Bible is not only liquid; it is also dark. This dual quality excellently describes the formlessness of original chaos. Yahweh's creative action consists in his victory over the dark ocean; this victory is marked at the beginning of Genesis (1.2, 6–7) by two important features of domination: the spirit of God prevails over the waters by hovering over them (or is it perhaps that he watches anxiously over the nascent world which the waters still threaten?), and God divides the waters in two by interposing the firmament. The sea is henceforth "held back with two doors" (Job 38.8). The mythical water is domesticated by God, who uses it to punish men (the flood, Gen. 6–9) or to serve them (the water that springs forth from the cleft rock during the exodus from Egypt, Ps. 78.15–16, 105.40, etc.). Numerous analogies to this sequence of grandiose depictions occur outside of Israel: Yahweh's victorious struggle with the ocean evokes Marduk's struggle against Tiamat in the *Enūma eliš;* the sea monster Leviathan also appears in the Canaanite legend of Ba'al and Anat known through texts excavated at Ras Shamra-Ugarit. But, as before, we should not hasten to infer an influence on biblical authors; rather, we should think of parallel roots going down into a common mythical background.

The New Testament

I. Keeping Myth at Bay

> For we did not follow cleverly devised myths (*sesophismenois muthois*) when we made known to you the power and coming of our Lord Jesus Christ, but we were eyewitnesses of his majesty.

Such is the profession of faith by which the Second Epistle of Peter (1.16) defines the antimythical position of the New Covenant. Nothing could be clearer, even if the word "myth" does not have there exactly the same meaning that we have seen until now. The designation "eyewitnesses" (*epoptēs*) applied to the beneficiaries of a revelation is in the context all the more peculiar since it comes from the technical language of the Greek mysteries. Saint Paul's hostility toward myth is equally well known: his precept to Timothy is to "have nothing to do with those godless myths, fit only for old women" (1 Tim. 4.7), to warn the Ephesians "to give up . . . studying those interminable myths . . . which issue in mere speculation and cannot make known God's plan for us, which works through faith" (1 Tim. 1.3–4), for the time will unfortunately come when "they will stop their ears to the truth and turn to mythology" (2 Tim. 4.4). He asks his other disciple Titus to insist that the Christians of Jewish origin in Crete not "lend their ears to Jewish myths and commandments of merely human origins, the work of men who turn their backs upon the truth" (Titus 1.14). These are the only five passages in which the New Testament refers to myth by that name. They consistently define a wholly negative attitude. In particular, the last two Pauline texts cited pose myth and truth as opposites, such that any belief in one constitutes a denial of the other.

The theologian's reflection on Christian specificity moves in the direction of these biases. The Greek philosophers who lived during the period of Christian expansion defined myth by its ability to give a temporal appearance to the timeless. Plotinus thus said that "myths, in order to be truly myths, must parcel out their content over time and separate from one another many beings who are together and can only be distinguished by virtue of their rank or their powers" (*Enneades* 3.5 [50] 9.24–6). A similar view may be found in the philosopher Sallust, a friend of the emperor Julian, when he interprets the myth of Cybele and Attis. A strikingly different approach is taken by Christianity, which, particularly in the first few centuries, placed at the very heart of faith the reality of time and newness in historical progress. No one has more accurately described the contrast between these two mentalities than H.-Ch. Puech (in a lecture[11] that I unfortunately did not know about when I wrote my own study of this subject).[12]

Because the content of myth is indifferent to temporality, myth presents itself as a model capable of indefinite repetition. By contrast, the redemptive incarnation and passion constitute a single and nonrepeatable fact. The Jewish high priest who once a year entered into the most secret sanctuary of the Temple or the Holy of Holies foreshadowed the sacrificed Christ. Christ in turn accomplished what the high priest had only begun, offering himself up, not once a year, but once and for all in the totality of history. This is the lesson of chapter 9 of the Epistle to the Hebrews (see also 1 Peter 3.18), where there is a recurrence of the adverbs *hapax, ephapax,* (Latin *semel*), marking the absolute singleness of the sacrifice. It must be added that this conviction surely rested in large measure on the eschatological perspective of a nascent Christianity: since the end of time was expected in the near future (Paul thought he would be a witness to this event; we shall return to this below), there was no room for an eventual repetition of the passion.

One might object that Christianity itself provides the setting for a certain repetition of previous situations, and to this extent it is allied to the world of myth. For instance, the liturgical cycle annually reproduces the principal events in the life of Jesus (his conception, his birth, various episodes of his public life, his passion and death, his resurrection, and his ascension). Furthermore, the ritual celebration of the sacraments often recalls either the episodes of sacred history that prefigure them—what Saint Paul called its "types" (thus the flood and the crossing of the Red Sea are recalled in memory by the ceremony of baptism)—or the scenes from the life of Jesus during which they were instituted (the celebration of the Eucharist somehow reactualizes the Last Supper). One may therefore discern, notably in the conception of sacramental practice as a reactivation of the founding elements, a phenomenon not without analogy in the mysteries of the Hellenistic East, in which the ritual reenactment of original myths allowed the initiate to relive, through participation, the destiny of the deity. Baptism, for instance, is conceived by Saint Paul as a burial with Christ, an assimilation into his death and resurrection, the privilege of putting on Christ as a garment (Rom. 6.3–5; Gal. 3.27), whereas Johannine theology sees as the effect of the Eucharist the mutual dwelling of the faithful in Jesus and of Jesus in the faithful (John 6.56). But we should not lose sight of the fact that, unlike myths, biblical "types" and scenes of institution are regarded by Christianity as historical events. Moreover, anyone who hesitates to admit to the necessarily temporal nature of this religion and, hence, its nonmythical character has at his disposal some evidence to the contrary, which H.-Ch. Puech has brilliantly demonstrated, namely, the confrontation with Christian Gnosticism, which conceived time as essentially bad and salvation as deliverance from time: by thus severing Christianity from any temporal and historical perspective, Gnosticism, unlike the Church, fully embraced myth.

II. New Testament Mythology and Demythologization

This is not to say that early Christianity is free of any mythical factor, however steeped in history it is supposed to be. There is convincing evidence to that effect in the New Testament itself, despite the denials we have mentioned. For the sake of continuity, let us return to the example given above with respect to the Old Testament. There is little doubt that myths of water lie in the background of the Gospels. Thus, the scene described in the synoptic Gospels (Mark 4.35–41, etc.) when Jesus quells the storm on Lake Gennesaret must be viewed as yet another episode of the struggle between God and the primordial ocean, which persists in rebelling despite its defeat. In the fourth Gospel, the most level-headed exegetes, such as A. Jaubert,[13] detect several fairly well developed references to the original mythical water. The same would apply to the water flowing from Jesus' side on the Cross (John 19.34), and especially to the idea of "living water" mentioned in the dialogue with the Samaritan woman (John 4.6–15) and in Christ's comparing the gift of the Holy Spirit to the streams of living water flowing out from within him (John 7.37–39).

In the 1950s the surviving mythical elements in the New Testament were brought to light by the brilliant exegete Rudolph Bultmann in a series of remarkable scholarly works.[14] Bultmann discovered many mythological elements (he preferred "mythological" to "mythical") in the teaching of Christ. Among them is the conception of the "Kingdom of God" as an eschatological reality about to come. "There are some of those standing here who will not taste death before they have seen the Kingdom of God already come in power," said Jesus (Mark 9.1), and Saint Paul was convinced he was among those whom the coming of the Lord would find still living (1 Cor. 15.51–52; 1 Thess. 4.15–17). Other similar depictions include the splitting up of the universe into three storeys (which explains Christ's descent into hell and his ascension into heaven; see Acts 1.9–11, Eph. 4.9–10), the belief in miracles and in the intervention of supernatural forces, the idea that Satan and the demons rule the world and men's souls, and so forth. All these conceptions are thought to be mythological insofar as they differ from scientific conceptions.

No less mythological, in Bultmann's eyes, is the picture that the early Christian community had of its founder. At issue are not miracles like virgin birth but two major images applied to Jesus. First, he is proclaimed the "Son of Man" who at the end of time is supposed to come back on the clouds of heaven to judge the world in a thunderous cosmic blaze (see for instance Matt. 25.31–32; Thess. 4.16–17; 2 Pet. 3.10–12). But this is a title, usage, and setting that are usual in late Jewish apocalyptic, as is seen, for example, in the Book of Daniel (7.13–14). Second, Jesus is presented as the preexisting Son of God who abandons the divine pleroma, becomes man, descends on earth by breaking down the dividing wall, accomplishes his mission of reconciliation and salvation, and finally reascends into heaven. Those are the categories of Pauline christology (for example, Eph. 2.13–16; Col. 1.13–22 and 2.9–15) and Johannine christology (John 1.1–18). But they are also the categories of the Gnostic myth of the primordial man who is a savior; from him too, as from Jesus, flows the living water that revives the universe, according to the Naassenes, the Gnostics described by Hippolytus (*Refutatio omnium Haeresium* 5.9, 19). This double kinship of the christology of the New Testament with apocalyptic and Gnosis seems to Bultmann to be the very signature of its mythological nature.

Such cosmological and religious representations belong to their own time; we cannot expect today's believer to hold them to be true; even if he wished to do so, he would not willingly choose a defunct image of the world. Similarly, the truth of Christian preaching is to be found not in these mythologies but in the fact that it is fundamentally a *kerygma*, a personal message to the human conscience, a universalist challenge which cannot be compromised by the necessarily contingent and now outgrown cultural context in which it was heard. This is the definition of *kerygma* that Bultmann finds formulated precisely in Paul's statement to the Corinthians: "Only by declaring the truth openly do we recommend ourselves, and then it is to the common conscience of our fellow men and in the sight of God" (2 Cor. 4.2). We must not, however, deny that mythological statements have any function, for they do contain a meaning, which they also hide, that is deeper than they are themselves. To discover this meaning, we must accomplish the work for which Bultmann coined a word that has since then come into general usage: "demythologization" (*Entmythologisierung*).

The appropriate function of mythology in general is to bring divine reality down to the human level, and to endow transcendent subjectivity with "worldly" objectivity. According to Bultmann's famous definition, "the mode of representation in which the nonworldly, the divine, appears worldly and human, the beyond as the here below, is mythological."[15] Furthermore, this misconstruction through mythology is more or less the lot of all religion, which, in its attempt to express the divine, can only resort to a language and categories that are incapable of expressing it. J. Sperna Weiland[16] rightly believes that Bultmann is reiterating in his own way the rationalist criticism which, in the early stages of Greek thought, denounced the anthropomorphic theology of the poets. The task of demythologization must therefore be to identify behind the screen of an outdated cosmology the religious intention from which it emerged. For science, it is absurd to speak of a top and a bottom of the universe; but if the biblical assertion that God resides in heaven is devoid of immediate meaning, it does endeavor to translate divine transcendence indirectly. Similarly, to situate hell under the earth is a way of depicting the terrifying character of evil, and so forth. If the image of "heaven" thus serves as the spatial expression of God's transcendence, then the idea of the "end of the world" is its temporal expression. Behind the apparent content of eschatological preaching can be heard an exhortation to the availability by which human beings open themselves up to the future of God. New Testament mythology also speaks to human beings about themselves. As we have seen, the function of the cosmological myth is not to define an objective image of the universe but to shed light on the divine nature; its function is also to reveal the way in which people experience their condition in the world—in other words, to express a certain understanding of human existence. This is an existential interpretation, and Bultmann does not attempt to conceal the fact that he has borrowed it from Heidegger.

These theses of Bultmann on demythologization and its premises have awakened considerable interest and won many disciples. It matters little that some of them, like R. A. Johnson,[17] have tempered the originality of his positions by demonstrating the philosophical roots and historical anticipations of *Entmythologisierung.* But Bultmann's arguments have also met with much resistance. More recently, the *religionsgeschichtliche* perspective adopted by Bultmann—that the preexisting Son of God was a category predating Pauline christology, which then borrowed it—has been strongly and cogently criticized by M. Hengel.[18] But it was not the assertion of the presence of mythical elements in the New Testament that upset exegetical scholars. H. Schlier,[19] who is not a Bultmann exponent, has no difficulty in recognizing the double influence of Jewish apocalyptic and the Gnostic primordial man, to which he even adds the influence of Hellenistic mysteries; but this triple concession is clearly equivalent to abandoning to myth a considerable portion of the Gospels and the Epistles. No, what is really disturbing is that Bultmann does not contain mythology within any limits, however broad, but rather absorbs into it everything in the New Testament that is not specifically kerygmatic. Thus O. Cullmann, in an important book,[20] first endorses the way Bultmann applies demythologization to the entire history of salvation and not just to its extremities. But later he begins to fear that this history, in which we can see the essence of early Christianity, may be totally dissolved in the process.[21] We should add to this major objection our own sense of the importance of the notion of an irreversible unfolding of time in the definition of Christian reality. The same challenge is expressed, sometimes colored by confessional preoccupations, by L. Malevez[22] and R. Marlé,[23] the latter with the additional interest of having prompted a response from Bultmann himself.[24] The controversy is probably not over, but Bultmann's contribution thus far has been to draw attention, more than anyone else before him, to the reality of a mythical component in the New Testament. We can and must discuss the dimensions of this component; we can no longer deny its existence.

The good shepherd. Rome, catacombs.

Liturgy

I. Myths of Water in Baptism

It is widely recognized that the mythical function of consciousness operates even more freely in liturgical practice than in literature or in the realm of speculation. G. P. Zacharias[25] has shown that Christian liturgy is an excellent testing ground for Jung's analyses of the workings of the psyche. Mythical elements could probably be detected behind many liturgical gestures or formulas of early Christianity. To avoid spreading ourselves too thin, we shall focus on two fairly representative examples, the first one connected to the Jewish myth (mentioned earlier) of the primordial ocean as the enemy of god.

Baptism, as it is practiced in the New Testament (for example, Matt. 3.13–16: the baptism of Jesus in the Jordan River; Acts 8.38–39: the baptism of the Ethiopian eunuch), involves descending into water and rising out of it. Pauline theology (Rom. 6.3–9) sees baptism as a double assimilation, first to the death and burial of Christ, then to his resurrection and his victory over death. The two pairs of acts can be perceived as parallel: the baptismal candidate both immerses himself in, and escapes from, a mythical water, a sea of death.

Two observations support this contention. First, in the earliest form of Christianity there is a connection between baptism and Christ's descent into hell immediately after his death. According to the Jewish cosmology that was still powerful at that time, to go underground among the dead leads to the realm of the original Ocean. Second, the theology and liturgy of the first centuries A.D. claimed to discern figurative interpretations or "types" of baptism in episodes in the Old Testament. Among these, the three principal ones were the flood (Gen. 6–8), the crossing of the Red Sea by the Israelites in the flight from Egypt (Exod. 14.15–31), and the crossing of the Jordan into the Promised Land (Josh. 3.9–17). We can see that all three of these accounts illustrate the confrontation between the primordial ocean and Yahweh, and the latter's victory over the former. We are led to conclude that baptism too, in the unfolding of its ritual, is regarded as the last skirmish in this mythical struggle, which is as old as history. In the liturgical and doctrinal texts of the patristic era, numerous indices can be found of this conjunction of baptism with the *descensus ad inferos* and the three episodes in the Old Testament; they have been admirably collected by P. Lundberg.[26] But we must also realize that the New Testament bears witness to the same phenomenon. The first Epistle to the Corinthians (10.1–2) is a clear example: "Our ancestors were all under the pillar of cloud, and all of them passed through the Red Sea; and so they all received baptism into the fellowship of Moses in cloud and sea." The first Epistle of Peter (3.19–21) is more obscure; but in these few lines we can recognize the descent into hell, the flood, and baptism: "In the spirit he [Christ] went and made his proclamation to the imprisoned spirits. They had refused obedience long ago, while God waited patiently in the days of Noah and the building of the ark, and in the ark a few persons, eight in all, were brought to safety through the water. It is the 'antitype' of this water, baptism, that now will save you too."

II. Orientation and Solar Myths

Early Christians prayed facing east, where the sun rises. This differs from the custom of the Jews, who pray facing Jerusalem, as Daniel does in the biblical book that bears his name (6.11); so important is this difference that Elkesai, the

Orpheus Christ. Sabbartha alabaster. Tripoli Museum. Photo Baudot-Lamotte.

founder of a Judeo-Christian sect, dissociated himself from Christianity by prescribing that his followers face Jerusalem and forbidding them to face east. The Scriptures contain many details confirming each in its own way the special position of the east: the earthly paradise was planted "to the east" (Gen. 2.8); it is believed that Christ's ascension took an eastward course, for the Latin version of Psalm 68 (67), verse 34, applies to the Lord the phrase *qui ascendit super caelum caeli ad orientem* ("who ascended above heaven, to the east of heaven"), and his return is also expected to come from the east; the angel in the Revelation of John (7.2) rises out of the east, and so forth.

These coincidences result not from mere chance but from the early assimilation of Christ to the sun, in particular the rising sun. The classical work on this subject remains that of F. J. Dölger.[27] Already in the hymn of Zachariah (Luke 1.78–79), Jesus is called "the morning sun from heaven [who] will rise upon us, to shine on those who live in darkness, under the cloud of death." This has the ring of a prophetic naming of Christ as the "sun of righteousness" referred to in Malachi (4.2); Tertullian summarizes an entire past and future tradition when he writes (*Adversus Valentinianes* 3.1): *orientem, Christi figuram* ("the east, the figure of Christ"). The metaphor was already well implanted when, at the end of the third century, it became even more firmly rooted and was used to thwart the cult of *Sol invictus* imposed by the Emperor Aurelian. Thus, the pagan festival of the *dies natalis Solis invicti* ("the day of the birth of the unvanquished Sun"), celebrated on 25 December when the exhausted sun is reborn, made way for the nativity of the solar Christ.

One can understand how such grandiose imagery could not work its way into early Christianity without bringing in with it a fringe of mythical cosmology. Here again, it may be in certain details of the liturgy and worship that the contamination can most easily be identified. For example, in the ritual of baptism, between the renunciation of the devil and the profession of faith in Christ, the catechumen would suddenly turn around, pivoting from west to east; for the west was taken to be the realm of darkness ruled by the Prince of Darkness, and so the baptismal candidate looked in that direction to repudiate Satan, but he turned to face east at the moment he joined Christ. This ceremonial detail, commented upon by several ancient authors and also studied by F. J. Dölger,[28] may certainly be regarded as a vehicle of the mythical mentality. On the other hand, as J. A. Jungmann[29] has demonstrated, the depiction of the solar Christ required an eastward orientation not only for prayer but, consequently, for church building and even for the layout of cemeteries; Greek and Roman temples also faced east. It was finally concluded that this orientation of the church, when added to that of the Christians inside, made it difficult both for the congregation and for the celebrant to position themselves. As a result, starting in the fourth century, church builders turned the apse rather than the facade of the church toward the east, probably without awareness of the ancient images that prompted these architectural concerns from afar.

J.P./g.h.

NOTES

1. H. A. WOLFSON, *Philo: Foundations of Religious Philosophy in Judaism, Christianity and Islam* (Cambridge, MA, 1948), 1:82–84 and 124.

2. J. DANIÉLOU, *Philon d'Alexandrie*, Les Temps et les Destins (Paris 1958), 107–10.

3. G. DELLING, "Wunder-Allegorie-Mythus bei Philon von Alexandreia," *Wissenschaftliche Zeitschrift der Martin-Luther—Univ. Halle—Wittenberg*, Gesellschafts- und Sprachwiss. Reihe, 6 (1956–57): 727ff., and 737ff., n. 139ff. The article is reprinted in *Gottes ist der Orient*, Festschrift für O. Eissfeldt (Berlin 1959).

4. J. PÉPIN, "Remarques sur la théorie de l'exégèse allégorique chez Philon," in *Philon d'Alexandrie*, Actes du colloque de Lyon de 1966 (Paris 1967), 143–46.

5. P. HEINISCH, *Der Einfluss Philos auf die älteste christliche Exegese (Barnabas, Justin und Clemens von Alexandria)*, Alttestamentl. Abhandlungen, 1, 1–2 (Münster 1908).

6. J. DANIÉLOU, "La démythisation dans l'école d'Alexandrie," in E. Castelli, ed., *Il Problema della demitizzazione, Archivio di Filosofia* (Rome 1961), 45–49.

7. H. GUNKEL, *Schöpfung und Chaos in Urzeit und Endzeit: Eine religionsgeschichtliche Untersuchung über Gen 1 und Ap Joh 12* (Göttingen 1895).

8. A. HEIDEL, *The Babylonian Genesis: The Story of Creation* (2d ed., Chicago 1951); *The Gilgamesh Epic and Old Testament Parallels* (2d ed., Chicago 1949).

9. E. O. JAMES, *Myth and Ritual in the Ancient Near East* (London 1958).

10. PH. REYMOND, *L'eau, sa vie et sa signification dans l'Ancien Testament*, Supplements to *Vetus Testamentum* 6 (Leiden 1958), 123–24, 182–98.

11. H.-CH. PUECH, "Temps, histoire et mythe dans le christianisme des premiers siècles," in C. J. Bleeker et al., eds., *Proceedings of the 7th Congress for the History of Religions* (Amsterdam 1951), 33–52.

12. J. PÉPIN, "Le temps et le mythe," *Les études philosophiques* 17 (1962): 55–68, reprinted in *Mythe et allégorie: Les origines grecques et les contestations judéo-chrétiennes* (2d ed., Paris 1976), 503–16.

13. A. JAUBERT, *Approches de l'Évangile de Jean,* Parole de Dieu (Paris 1976), 58–63, 140–46. See also C. H. DODD, *The Interpretation of the Fourth Gospel* (2d ed., Cambridge 1970).

14. R. BULTMANN, "New Testament and Mythology," in H. W. Bartsch, ed., *Kerygma and Myth* (London 1953), 1–44; "Zum Problem der Entmythologisierung," in H. W. Bartsch, ed., *Kerygma und Mythos* (Hamburg 1952), 2:177–208; *Jesus Christ and Mythology* (New York 1958); "Zum Problem der Entmythologisierung" (bis), in *Glauben und Verstehen* (Tübingen 1965), 4:128–37. These are the principal works of R. Bultmann on New Testament myth.

15. BULTMANN, "New Testament and Mythology."

16. J. SPERNA WEILAND, "La théologie de la démythisation est-elle une idéologie?" in E. Castelli, ed., *Démythisation et idéologie* (Paris 1973), 180.

17. R. A. JOHNSON, *The Origins of Demythologizing: Philosophy and Historiography in the Theology of Rudolf Bultmann,* Studies in the History of Religions 28 (Leiden 1974).

18. M. HENGEL, *Der Sohn Gottes: Die Entstehung der Christologie und die jüdisch-hellenistische Religionsgeschichte* (2d ed., Tübingen 1977), 32–93; English translation, *The Son of God* (Philadelphia, 1st ed. 1975).

19. H. SCHLIER, *Essais sur le Nouveau Testament,* Lectio divina, 46 (Paris 1968), chap. 5, pp. 97–112: "Le Nouveau Testament et le mythe."

20. O. CULLMANN, *Christ and Time: The Primitive Christian Conception of Time and History* (rev. ed., Philadelphia 1964), "The Connections between History and Prophecy."

21. O. CULLMANN, "Le mythe dans les écrits du Nouveau Testament," in K. Barth et al., *Comprendre Bultmann: Un dossier* (Paris 1970), 15–31.

22. L. MALEVEZ, *Le message chrétien et le mythe: La théologie de Rudolf Bultmann,* Museum Lessianum, section théol., 51 (Brussels and Paris 1954).

23. R. MARLÉ, *Bultmann et l'interprétation du Nouveau Testament,* Théologie, 33 (Paris 1956).

24. R. BULTMANN, "In eigener Sache," in *Glauben und Verstehen* (Tübingen 1960).

25. G. P. ZACHARIAS, *Psyche und Mysterium: Die Bedeutung der Psychologie C. G. Jungs für die christliche Theologie und Liturgie,* Studien aus dem C. G. Jung–Institut, Zürich, 5 (Zurich 1954).

26. P. LUNDBERG, *La typologie baptismale dans l'ancienne Église,* Acta Seminarii Neotestam, Upsaliensis, 10 (Leipzig and Uppsala 1942); see also J. DANIÉLOU, *Bible et liturgie: La théologie biblique des sacrements et des fêtes d'après les Pères de l'Église,* Lex orandi, 11 (Paris 1951), 97–155.

27. F. J. DÖLGER, *Sol salutis: Gebet und Gesang im christlichen Altertum,* Liturgiegeschichtliche Forschungen, 4–5 (Münster 1925).

28. F. J. DÖLGER, *Die Sonne der Gerechtigkeit und der Schwarze: Eine religionsgeschichtliche Studie zum Taufgelöbnis,* Liturgiegeschichtliche Forschungen, 2 (Münster 1918).

29. J. A. JUNGMANN, *The Early Liturgy, to the Time of Gregory the Great* (South Bend, IN, 1959).

Christian Judgments on the Analogies between Christianity and Pagan Mythology

I. The Problem

1. *Insertions and dissimilarities.* When nascent Christianity had to define itself in the face of Greek culture, especially of pagan theology, it hesitated between two contrary responses. As A. J. Festugière has demonstrated,[1] both responses were offered by the apostle Paul. In his Athenian discourse, of which the Acts of the Apostles (17.16–34) describes the setting and preserves the outline, Paul manipulated the language and ideas of the philosophers of the time, who were his listeners, and showed how the new religion had come to fulfill their expectations: the place that paganism held vacant for the "unknown god" was claimed for the Christians' God, whom Paul introduced by leaning heavily on Stoic stereotypes. But this attempt at harmonization ended in almost total failure; so when Paul left Athens for Corinth, he chose a quite different method, which is echoed in the beginning of the First Epistle to the Corinthians (1.17–25; 2.1–5). No longer is there any attempt to fit the new religion into a continuity with pagan theology; instead, pagan earthly wisdom and pagan logical and rhetorical knowledge are brutally confronted with the scandal of the Gospel and the folly of the Cross.

It can be claimed, without exaggeration, that this two-sided approach in Pauline preaching gave rise to two opposing currents which run through the whole of Christian history. These are recognizable from the time of the Church Fathers; certain authors strive to present their belief as the realization of what was best in pagan theology, while others, by contrast, accentuate the antagonism between the two. This cleavage is no doubt due to several circumstances: the diversity of temperaments, which is the first thing one thinks of, was not all-determining; one should also take into consideration the historical situation as well as political and social conditions. Minds tended in different directions as persecution became rife, or as tolerance reigned, or as the Christian empire triumphed. For whatever reasons, this duality of attitudes is undeniable, though some defend one or the other position while many hesitate between the two or temper the one with the other.

In the pages which follow we shall apply this schema to a particular problem—the existence and import of characteristics common to Christianity and to preceding theologies. The intransigent attitude would be to deny, in the name of Christian transcendence, the very fact of such analogies; Tertullian, for example, is content to contrast the purity associated with the virgin birth of the Son of God to the squalor in which the sons of Jupiter were born: "The Son of God was not born in such a way that he had to blush at the name of son or at his paternal lineage; he did not have to submit to the affront, through incest with a sister or the debauching of a daughter or of another man's wife, of having a divine father covered with scales, horned or feathered, or changed into a shower of gold like the lover of Danaë. The human infamies that you commit are Jupiter's infamies! But the Son of God does not have a mother as the result of unchastity; and even the mother that you see him to have was not married" (*Apologeticus* 21.7–9).

Contrary to what one might expect, however, such a flat refusal is not the prevailing attitude among the Fathers. More often, they admit that certain intersections are possible between the gods and heroes of paganism (including their myths and ceremonies) on the one hand, and the figures and events of biblical history (including Christian beliefs and life) on the other. They are led to make such a concession for varied reasons: for one, their pagan adversaries, as we shall see more than once in this context, had drawn their attention to many of these similarities, and it was safer to admit to them in order to defuse them than to close one's eyes to them. Indeed, the uses to which the Christians put these intersections with paganism, the explanations they give for them, and the importance they accord to them vary greatly, ranging from a simple figure of speech to the Christianization of a pagan element. We must attempt to distinguish between these different styles of comparative thought, starting from the most superficial, which are of no consequence, and progressing toward those which bring into play an entire view of history. Here, then, is the bottom rung of the ladder.

2. *Comparisons without theological intent.* An example of such comparisons is the one that the earliest Christian apologists made between the Noah of Genesis (5.29–9.29) and the Deucalion of classical mythology (cf. among others Ovid, *Metamorphoses* 1.313–415). It is, in fact, less a comparison of these two figures than the reduction of the latter to the former. Theophilus of Antioch rejects the legend of Deucalion and Pyrrha surviving the flood and throwing stones behind them, which turn into men; but he retains the name of Deucalion as one that the pagans, by means of a bizarre etymology, gave to Noah (*Ad Autolycum* 3.18–19; see also 2.30, and the earlier Justin Martyr, *Second Apology* 7.2). This amounted to an admission of a certain homogeneity between the two cultures. It would be two centuries before Christian specialists in chronology, Eusebius of Caesarea and his translator Jerome, would distinguish between the localized flood of Deucalion and the older, universal flood of Noah, which was completely unknown to pagan history. This new outlook is described and adopted in Augustine's *City of God* (18.8, 10).

On other occasions, in the case of Christian authors raised on Greek culture, a biblical episode spontaneously evokes a mythic episode, or vice versa. In an attempt to stir the hardened hearts of the idolaters, Clement of Alexandria compares them to Niobe (turned into a rock, cf. *Iliad* 24.602–17), then catches himself and, "in order to speak more in the language of our mystery," replaces Niobe by Lot's wife (who became a pillar of salt, Genesis 9.26) (*Protrepticus* 10.103–4). The pagan Platonist Celsus wanted to keep only the blameworthy traits in the story of Joseph, and forgot that this person preferred prison to the burning passion his master's wife had for him (Genesis 39.7–20); the Christian Origen reproaches Celsus for his omission, while the virtue of Joseph reminds him of the quite analogous, yet to his eyes inferior, virtue ascribed to Bellerophon (who rejected, at the peril of his life, the advances of Anteia, wife of his protector King Proetus, cf. *Iliad* 6.155–70) (*Contra Celsum* 4.46). Such parallels, which today continue to strike us with their pertinence, came automatically to the minds of the Christians of Alexandria, though hardly above the level of free association.

A comparison of the same order, destined to endure for a long time, was established by Eusebius between Heracles and the Samson of the Book of Judges (13.24–16.31); he claimed he collected it from the Jewish tradition. The comparison is naturally based on the physical strength common to both individuals, who were, Eusebius adds, almost contemporaries, close to the time of the fall of Troy (*Chronica*, preface, in the translation by Saint Jerome; and again in *Praeparatio Evangelica* 10.9.7). The art and literature of the Middle Ages and the Renaissance would popularize the analogy, retaining in particular the episode of Heracles slaying the Nemean lion, since this has a homology in the biography of Samson (Judges 14.5–6). Medieval sculpture would similarly metamorphose Heracles into Saint Christopher and Heracles slaying Geryon into Saint George slaying the dragon. On the medieval Christianization of Heracles, which remains superficial throughout, we may refer to a study by M. Simon,[2] and, with respect to pictorial representations of Heracles, a book by J. Adhémar.[3] This concern to provide a biblical figure corresponding to the Greek hero continues down to Dante: David's combat with Goliath (1 Samuel 17.4–51) finds its replica in that of Heracles with Antaeus (cf. Ovid, *Metamorphoses* 9.183–84; Lucan, *Pharsalia* 4.597–660) (Dante, *De Monarchia* 2.9.11; cf. 2.7.10, and *Convivio* 3.3.7–8).

II. Rhetorical Uses

1. *The language of the mysteries.* The preceding parallels may be imputed to mere reminiscences, natural to authors at the crossroads of two cultural traditions. Others are more premeditated, responding to the need felt by certain Christian apologists to address themselves to pagan listeners in the religious language of pagans.

Such a design is perhaps nowhere better expressed than at the end of the *Protrepticus* (12.119.1), when Clement of Alexandria announces to his pagan interlocutor: "Come . . . and I shall show you the Word and the mysteries of the Word by transposing your own imagery (*kata tēn sēn diēgoumenos eikona*)." Following this resolution, which Hugo Rahner[4] rightly considers an exemplary statement, Clement presents the essence of Christianity in the technical language of the Dionysian mysteries: baptism and eucharist thus lend themselves to a description in which the *dadouchoi* (torch bearers), the *epoptia* (supreme revelation), the initiation, the hierophant (in this context the Lord), the *muste* (initiate), the seal, the lighting, etc., all play a part (12.120.1–2). Christian authors, from Saint Paul to Pseudo-Dionysius the Areopagite and Maximus the Confessor (sixth and seventh centuries), indulge freely in these borrowings from the vocabulary and notions of the Greek mysteries; the reader may consult E. Hatch's classic work and a more recent work by Arthur Darby Nock.[5]

There is yet another way of speaking to pagans in the language of their own religion. It consists in extracting some of the more popular episodes from the mythical biographies of pagan gods or heroes, and transposing their meaning in such a way as to render more accessible a given aspect of the Christian mystery. This procedure assumes a recognition on the part of the Christian authors of parallels between their own religion and classical mythology. Such parallels remain quite superficial, and their manipulation does not essentially differ from the point-for-point comparisons treated above. The procedure may, however, be extended into a rhetorical orchestration, in which different episodes from the mythological account take on a meaning determined by the principal theme. This assertion may be verified in a famous example.

2. *The Christian Odysseus.* As A. Wifstrand[6] has noted, the New Testament is still quite restrained in its use of *exempla* borrowed from Greek culture; second-century Christian apologists use a few of these, but most often with hostile intentions. A much more hospitable attitude appears in the third century with Clement of Alexandria—perhaps because the Gnostics had, in the meantime, taken the Christian amalgam with Greek mythology as far as it could go. We could go on citing forever the rhetorical uses of paganism

made by Clement and his successors in order to formulate Christian ideas; rather, we shall take a particular case—to wit, the legend of Odysseus and the Sirens—and follow it through part of the tradition. This too has been masterfully studied by Hugo Rahner,[7] as well as by P. Courcelle[8] and Jérôme Carcopino.[9]

Shortly before the passage we just examined on the reemployment of the language of the mysteries, Clement of Alexandria evokes the famous episode of Odysseus's encounter with the Sirens and with Charybdis (*Odyssey* 12.39–123, 154–259). In his eyes, the Sirens symbolize the misdeeds of habit and the appeals of pleasure, and Odysseus, when he thwarts them by tying himself to his mast, is the image of the Christian who triumphs over perdition by embracing the wood of the Cross (*Protrepticus* 12.118.1–4). A little later than Clement, Hippolytus of Rome draws attention to a detail, neglected by his predecessor, in the same account and endows it with meaning: before having himself tied up to the mast, Odysseus plugs his companions' ears with wax; here we are to understand that faithful Christians are to remain deaf to the insidious propaganda of heretics, and become one in body with the wood of the Cross so as to conquer agitation and remain firm (*Refutatio omnium Haeresium* 7.13). Toward the end of the third century, Bishop Methodius of Olympus was nourished on Homer, as V. Buchheit has shown;[10] his principal work, *The Symposium*, not only imitates that of Plato but, starting in the prologue (§ 4), refers to the banquet of the Olympians in the *Iliad* (4.1–4). In another work, a *Treatise on Free Will* (1.1–3), the same author contrasts the fatal song of the Sirens to the salutary chorus of the Prophets and Apostles, in the presence of whom one need not plug one's companions' ears with wax nor gird oneself with ropes. Methodius nevertheless abstains, unlike his two predecessors, from comparing the mast of Odysseus with the tree of the Cross. A century later, however, Saint Ambrose renews these ties with tradition: for him, the sea is the deceitful world, the Sirens the sensuality that enthralls the soul, the rocky shore the body; far from blocking one's ears, one should open them to the voice of the Christ; one should attach oneself, not like Odysseus to a mast with material bonds, but to the wood of the Cross with spiritual bonds. Ambrose is not loath to innovate on several points: among the circumstances that delay the voyage of Odysseus he cites, apart from the Sirens, the sweet fruits of the Lotus Eaters and the gardens of Alcinous (*Odyssey* 7.112–32; 9.82–104). As is natural for a Latin author, he mixes his Homeric memories together with certain recollections of the voyage of Aeneas according to Virgil (*Aenead* 1.536; 2.23). Especially important for the viewpoint under consideration here is the fact that Ambrose himself notes traffic between Greek mythology and the Bible when he observes that the Bible speaks of Giants and the Valley of the Titans (Genesis 6.4; 2 Samuel 5.22; 23.13), and that the prophet Isaiah (13.21) names the Sirens. (This whole passage from Saint Ambrose is found in his *Exposition of the Gospel According to Saint Luke* 4.2–3.)

The last important representative of this tradition was the fifth-century bishop Maximus of Turin, who probably took his inspiration from the passage from Ambrose just cited. The term-for-term correspondence between the episode in the *Odyssey* and its Christian application is now carried to its extreme: the sea is a representation of the hostile world, the pleasures of which are represented by the Sirens; Ithaca is the celestial land where the true life will be lived; the means to enter it is the Church, whose image has traditionally been the boat; here, as in Neoplatonist allegory, Odysseus incarnates the human condition; secured to his mast, which symbolizes the Cross, he naturally stands for the Crucified, but also for every Christian, and even all of humanity; his companions evoke the more distant adepts who nevertheless are within the shadow of the Cross, such as the penitent thief: finally, even the wax stuck into their ears is given a meaning—it is the Scriptures. In this detailed paralleling, Maximus capitalizes on nearly all of the contributions of his predecessors; his personal appetite for rhetoric makes him the ideal representative of this mode of using myths. Unlike the writing of Clement, Hippolytus, Methodius, and Ambrose, his text has never been translated into French. For these varied reasons, he is worth presenting in translation here, in spite (or because) of his inflated and prolix style. He begins with an account of the danger threatening Odysseus and of the hero's expedients for protecting himself against it:

> The pagan fables relate the story of the famous Odysseus who, tempest-tossed upon a wayward course over the sea for ten years, could not reach his homeland; his navigation had brought him to a place in which there arose, in its cruel sweetness, the suave song of the Sirens; they charmed those who came there with a melody so seductive that instead of taking in this sensual delight, they threw away their lives in shipwreck; such was the seduction of this song that hearing the sound of their voices was enough to make a man a prisoner to their magic charm: he would stop steering toward his desired port and rush into undesired ruin. Odysseus, it is said, having come to the brink of this exquisite shipwreck and wishing to escape from the perils of its sweetness, filled the ears of his companions with wax and then tied himself to the mast of his ship; thus his men would be deaf to the fatal charm, and he would deliver himself from the danger of changing his ship's course.

Then follows the Christian application:

> If, then, this fable relates that for this man Odysseus to tie himself to the mast was to be delivered from peril, how much more necessary it is to proclaim what truly came to pass; to wit, that today it is the whole of the human species that has been wrested from the threat of death by the tree of the Cross! Indeed, from the moment Christ the Lord was nailed to the Cross, from that very moment, we have been able to traverse with closed ears, so to speak, those critical points at which the world unfolds its seductions; for we do not stop to listen to the fatal messages of this world, nor do we deviate from our path toward a better life and fall astray upon the reefs of pleasure. For not only does the tree of the Cross allow the man who is nailed to it to see his homeland once again, but it also protects, by the shadow of its might, his companions who are grouped around him. That the Cross returns us to our homeland after much wandering is proclaimed by our Lord when he says to the crucified thief: "Today shalt thou be with me in paradise" (Luke 23.43). This thief, who had for so long been wandering and shipwrecked, certainly could not have returned to the homeland of paradise, which the first man had left, other than tied to the mast. For the mast on the ship is, in a sense, the Cross in the Church, which alone keeps itself safe and sound amid the seductive and mortal shipwrecks which shake the world from one end to the other. Thus anyone who, in this ship, attaches himself to the tree of the Cross or whose ears have been closed by means of the Holy Scriptures does not fear the sweet tempest of lust. For the comely features of the Sirens may be said to be the

cowardly cupidity of the pleasures, a cupidity which by its pernicious seductions softens the firmness of the spirit that has become its prisoner.

The beginning of the next paragraph is important from a methodological standpoint: in his Christian preaching, the author does not refrain from drawing on the imagery of myths in the same way that he draws on the *exempla* of the Old Testament; but he takes care to contrast the pure fiction of myths to the historical context of the biblical accounts: "Thus Christ the Lord was hung on the Cross to free the entire human race from the shipwreck toward which the world is heading. But let us forget the fable of Odysseus, which is an invention without reality; let us see if we can find in the Holy Scriptures some similar example, which Our Lord, before accomplishing it himself, first initiated through his prophets!" (These passages from Maximus of Turin may be found in his *Sermon* 37.1–3, in vol. 23, pp. 145–46, of the Mutzenbecher edition in the *Corpus christianorum;* and in *Homily* 49 in vol. 57, col. 339B–340B of the *Latin Patrology* of Migne.) The last sentence cited offers a remarkable definition of the relationship between the person of Jesus and the figures who announce him in the Old Testament: this is the typological perspective, which is clearly distinguished from the allegorical exegesis of myth. When it comes to substituting a biblical "type" for the fable of Odysseus, whose rhetorical use he has exhausted, Maximus cites the bronze serpent: affixed by Moses on the top of a pole (Numbers 21.6–9), this apotropaic object was seen, from New Testament times onward (John 3.14), as an image of the salvation procured by the Crucified. Here it is contrasted, in an equally traditional way, to another biblical serpent—that of Paradise, who is also wound around a tree.

III. The Chronological Quarrel

1. *Newness and oldness.* It is according to these categories, need it be said, that the New Testament defines itself with regard to the Old. This antithesis is not absent from the Gospels (the old skins and the new wine of Matthew 9.17, etc.); but it is with Paul that it takes on its true dimension: the Christian is invited to take off the "old man" to put on the "new man" (Colossians 3.9–10; Ephesians 4.22–24); he shall serve in the newness of the spirit and no longer in the oldness of the letter (Romans 7.6); he shall be a new creature in Christ, for whom *vetera transierunt, ecce facta sunt omnia nova* ("the old things are passed away; behold, all things are become new"; 2 Corinthians 5.17. Taking its cue from this Pauline theme, one of the earliest documents of noncanonical Christian literature, the *Epistle of Barnabus* (5.7; 7.5), twice calls Christians "the new people" (*ho laos ho kainos*).

Saint Paul defined Christian newness with regard to Judaism. Next came the tendency to cast Hellenism together with Judaism as two parallel expressions of oldness. This is what we find in a second century apocryphal text, the *Kerygma Petri:* "It is in a new way that you worship God through the Christ. . . . The Lord has laid down a new covenant for us; for the ways of the Greeks and Jews are old, but we Christians worship him in a new way in a third generation." Clement of Alexandria, citing this text, accentuates this ternary aspect immediately afterward: "(Peter), it seems to me, clearly showed that the one and only God is known by the Greeks in pagan fashion, by the Jews in Jewish fashion, but by us in a new and spiritual fashion" (*Stromateis* 6.5.41.4–7). In the *Protrepticus,* which is addressed to the Greeks, Clement retains only the Greeks and omits the Jews: "Today, even your myths seem to have aged. . . . But where is Zeus himself? He has aged, like his wings," and lost the ardor and cleverness which marked his amorous exploits (*Protrepticus* 2.37.1–3). Paganism, Clement says further, has fallen into superstition in its old age: it may find youth, and even innocent childhood, if it comes to worship the true God (*Protrepticus* 10.108.3).

This glorification of Christian newness must have grated on many followers of traditional paganism. Some of them said so themselves: the Platonist Celsus, cited by his adversary Origen (*Contra Celsum* 7.53), lets slip, in an address to the Christians, a "you who are so taken with innovation"; earlier, the historian Suetonius had identified Christianity as a *superstitio nova* ("new superstition"; *Nero* 16.3). Judgments of the same sort may be inferred through the retorts of the Christian apologists; the latter defended themselves against being considered as "newcomers," *hesterni,* as may be seen in A. Casamassa's classic article.[11] The unknown Christian author of the *Letter to Diognetes* asserts that people would ask such questions as: "Why do [the Christians] not accept the gods recognized by the Greeks, nor keep the religious observances of the Jews? . . . And why has this new race of men (*kainon genos*), this new way of life, come into the world only now and not earlier?" (1.1). The arguments exchanged between Christians and pagans on this theme have recently been studied once again in N. Zeegers-Vander Vorst's work.[12]

Perhaps it was to silence this objection that the Christians, without tempering their claims to newness, also attempted to connect themselves with ancestors of indisputable antiquity, who were none other than the Jews. This connection was difficult to make, not only because the Christians professed themselves to be the "new people," but also because the Gospels and especially the Pauline writings strove to dissociate them from a Judaism that was judged to be outdated. A passage from Tertullian, himself somewhat of an anti-Semite, conveys this ambiguity: "But since we have stated that our religion is founded upon the documents of the Jews, which are so old, though it is generally known (and we ourselves agree) that our religion is itself comparatively new, belonging as it does to the time of Tiberius, perhaps one might on this ground discuss its nature and say that, under the cover of a religion that is very illustrious and certainly authorized by law, our religion conceals certain new ideas that are its own, for aside from the question of age we do not agree with the Jews about abstaining from certain foods, or about the sanctity of festival days, or about their distinctive bodily mark, or sharing their name, which would of course be our duty if we were the servants of the same God" (*Apologeticus* 21.1–2). Nor did the false situation in which the Christians found themselves escape their adversaries; this is the reproach put in the mouth of the Jew in Celsus's *True Discourse:* "How can you trace your beginnings back to our sacred texts and yet, in doing so, scorn them, while you have no other origin to claim for your doctrine than our Law?" (in Origen, *Contra Celsum* 2.4).

2. *Antiquity and truth.* Given that the Christians could validly claim their antiquity through Judaism, just as a young grafted branch acquires the age of the old stock of the wild olive (a metaphor that Tertullian, in *De Testimonio Animae* 5.6, takes up, not without alterations, from Saint Paul in Romans 11.17–24), the Church Fathers increased their efforts to prove that Jewish prophecy was older than Greek culture. They concentrated on the person of Moses, who was regarded as the most outstanding figure of early Judaism: they

had to show that he, more than all others, preceded the earliest representatives of pagan tradition. As for the pagans, the dominant tendency was to take Homer as exemplary, so that the chronological debate often took the form of a man-to-man combat between these two individuals; I have attempted to show this in another work.[13] It was for this reason, among others, that Christian authors became so closely interested in the Greek poet, as may be verified in the works of Jean Daniélou[14] and G. Glockmann.[15]

In fact, the way had been opened by late Judaism itself, at least among those of its representatives who were the most influenced by Hellenism—for example, the historian Josephus at the end of the first century (*Contra Apionem* 2.2.14). Among Christians themselves, this theme appears briefly in Justin (*First Apology* 59.1). Even more concerned with it was his disciple Tatian, who inaugurated a demonstrative schema that was to become classic: in the opinion even of historians who adhered neither to Judaism nor to Christianity, Moses was the contemporary of the Argive king Inachus, who preceded the Trojan War by four centuries (*Oratio ad Graecos* 31.35–36, 38–41). The same argumentation may be found in the long chapter (*Stromateis* 1.21, especially §§ 101–2) which Clement of Alexandria, in acknowledging his debt to Tatian on the point, devotes to a comparative chronology of the Hebrew people and the neighboring civilizations. His conclusion is peremptory: "Moses was at the height of his powers even before the date at which the Greeks place the creation of man"; or, "It is thus proved that Moses preceded not only the Greek sages and poets, but also the majority of their gods" (ibid. §§ 106.2 and 107.6). At about the same time, Tatian's schema makes its appearance in the Latin world with Tertullian (*Apologeticus* 19.1*–2* and 3; the whole of chapter 19 wrestles with the problem). In the first half of the fourth century the historian Eusebius, a specialist in chronology, places so much value in the debate that he puts together an entire dossier with the texts we have just seen in Tatian, Clement, Josephus, and others (*Praeparatio Evangelica* 10.9.12–13.13). Eusebius adopts the now classic demonstration of Tatian and inserts complementary elements derived from other sources: Moses was earlier than the Phoenician historian Sanchuniathon of Beirut, who was himself a contemporary of Queen Semiramis and, like her, much earlier than the Trojan war (ibid., 10.9.13–17).

What was it that motivated the Christians to forget temporarily the prerogatives of their newness and to link themselves, at whatever cost, to the early age of Judaism? What made their adversaries determined to deny Judaism this anteriority with regard to their own history? Surely it was the conviction, which reigned everywhere at the time, that the antiquity of a doctrine guaranteed its truth. It is striking that, in the space of a few pages, Theophilus of Antioch associates these two notions four times in the same terms: our Scriptures and our beliefs, he repeats, are "older and truer" (*archaiotera kai alēthestera*) than those of every other people (*Ad Autolycum* 2.30; 3.16, 26, 29). The Latin Fathers had their own formula to lend authority to that which is connected with antiquity: *auctoritas vetustatis* (Minucius Felix, *Octavius* 20.2; Lactantius, *Divinae Institutiones* 2.6.7; Ambrose, *Exameron* 1.1.3; etc.)—a formula that Tertullian, better than anyone else, developed when speaking of the Jewish and Christian Scriptures: "The authority of these documents is assured them first of all by their extreme antiquity. Among you also the credibility of something is proved by its antiquity, which is as respectable as religion. Authority is given to the Scriptures by their extreme antiquity" (*Apologeticus* 19.1 and 1*.

By claiming, to their advantage, the chronological priority of the Jews over the Greeks, the Christian authors also conformed to the spirit of the time in another respect. There was a belief, maintained by Plato and Aristotle, that became more and more deeply engrained in the Hellenistic and Roman periods, as many works have shown:[16] that barbarian wisdom preceded and inspired Greek culture. Tatian (*Oratio ad Graecos* 35) and Clement of Alexandria (*Stromateis* 1.15.71.3; 1.29.180.5) shared this outlook of the period; but they put it to a use that was quite uncommon (outside of Christian and, naturally, Jewish circles): they held that the prophets of Israel themselves were to be counted among those barbarian sages, of whom they were the earliest and most eminent. Tatian thus calls Moses "the initiator of the whole of barbarian wisdom" (ibid., 31), while Clement, after enumerating the prophets of Egypt, the Assyrian Chaldeans, the Gallic Druids, the Persian Magi, the Indian Gymnosophists, and various others, notes that the Jewish people are by far the oldest of all (ibid., 1.15.71.4–72.4). Furthermore, the two authors are not afraid to treat Christianity as a "barbarian philosophy," nor to speak of themselves as "we Barbarians" (Tatian, ibid. 42; Clement, ibid. 1.29.180.3, etc.). The famous article by J. H. Waszink should be consulted on these various points.[17]

IV. The Explanation by "Theft"

1. *Borrowing, theft, adulteration.* We have dwelled on the confrontation of comparative chronology since it seems to have weighed heavily on the Christians' evaluation of the features they shared with classical paganism. From the moment they thought that, by virtue of their connection to the Jewish people, they preceded Greek history, they were able to consider resemblances to their adversaries only as cases of plagiarism committed against them by the latter. The direction of influence seemed beyond all doubt; as Justin unambiguously puts it, "It is not we who think like the others, but all of them who imitate us in what they say" (*First Apology* 60.10). Tertullian would recall the determining role played by chronology: "That which first existed is necessarily the origin of what followed. And this is why you have things in common with us or things that resemble ours"; so it is, he continues, that our Wisdom (*sophia*) gave you your philosophy, and our prophecy your poetic divination (*Apologeticus* 19.1.5*–6*). This slide from posteriority to dependence, in Judaism as well as in Christianity, has been studied by K. Thraede.[18]

Such an overview is susceptible to subtle variations, according to the polemical temperament. When this becomes heated, the pen is moved to write the word "theft" (*klopē*). Thus Theophilus of Antioch: "These tortures were predicted by the prophets, but later poets and philosophers stole them from the Holy Scriptures in order to make their own teaching seem trustworthy" (*Ad Autolycum* 1.14; 2.37, trans. Robert M. Grant, Oxford 1970). But the true theoretician of this sort of explanation--as A. Méhat[19] and R. Mortley[20] have suggested—was Clement of Alexandria. Here is one of his programmatic texts on this point, in which he attempts (in rather unconvincing fashion) to found the accusation of "theft" upon a verse from John (10.8) and asserts that the plagiarism committed by paganism extended beyond the miracle accounts to a large part of their theology and ethics:

> Let us now see, since the Scriptures treat the Greeks as "thieves" who stole barbarian philosophy, how we may briefly prove that they were indeed thieves. Not only shall we establish that it was by copying the miracles of our

history that they described their own, but we shall also convict them of digging up and falsifying the most important of our dogmas—our Scriptures are older than theirs and we have shown this—concerning faith, wisdom, gnosis, and knowledge, hope and charity, repentance, continence, and in particular the fear of God. (*Stromateis* 2.1.1.1)

This page introduces, with one word, another important notion: that the supposed theft perpetrated by the Greeks is at the same time a falsification. Clement had already observed that they had not understood all of the Hebraic doctrines which they had purloined and coopted as being their own: some of these they altered, while they applied an indiscreet and incompetent sophistry to others (*Stromateis* 1.17.87.2). In the same period, the same accusations of unwarranted appropriation, of curiosity, of incomprehension, and of adulteration are leveled against the same "men of glory" by Tertullian (*Apologeticus* 19.1.6*; 47.3). The resemblance between the two authors undoubtedly derives from the fact that both were dependent upon Tatian, who explains the formation of Greek mythology as follows:

> With much indiscretion, the sophists of Greece applied themselves to altering all that they borrowed from Moses . . . , first in order to appear as if they were making a personal statement, and, second, in order that, in camouflaging by I know not what false rhetoric all that they had not understood, they might bring truth down to the level of mythology. (*Oratio ad Graecos* 40)

Justin had also expressed the same idea in a more summary fashion, and saw the fact that the pagans contradicted each other as proof that each had, in his own way, misunderstood Moses (*First Apology* 44.10).

2. *Greek and Latin examples.* The Fathers furnished these general views with a plethora of illustrations, often taken by one author from another, so that it is difficult to select samples. According to Justin (*First Apology* 69.3,6), the darkness of Genesis (1.1) is the source of the Erebus of the poets (Hesiod, *Theogony* 123). The creation account recorded by Moses is, in the eyes of the Christians, one of the Jewish texts most impudently pirated by the Greeks: the notion of the seventh day; the falling out between Ocean and Tethys; the Greeks reduced by Menelaus to the water and earth from which they were made; the cosmic ornamentation of the shield of Achilles—all that these scattered disparate traits of epic poetry have in common, according to Clement of Alexandria (*Stromateis* 5.14.99.4–107.4), is that they came from a distorted reading of the beginning of Genesis. We have seen the same author challenge the originality of the Greeks not only on points of doctrine, but also in the accounts of miracles: Clement holds that the famous prayer of the pious Ajax, which brought rain during a catastrophic drought (Apollodorus Mythographus, *Bibliotheca* 3.12.6, 9–10), merely plagiarizes a prayer (of very different inspiration, it must be said) of Samuel (1 Samuel 12.17–18) (*Stromateis* 6.3.28.1–29.3).

In the same line of thought, Origen saw the episode of the Tower of Babel (Genesis 11.1–9) as the source of the Homeric narrative of the scaling of heaven by the Aloidae, who threatened the gods (*Iliad* 5.385–91 and *Odyssey* 11.305–20), and the burning of Sodom and Gomorrah (Genesis 19.1–29) as the starting point of the legend of Phaethon (Euripides, *Hippolytus* 735–41, etc.) (*Contra Celsum* 4.21). It is undoubtedly the same Alexandrian milieu that produced, about the same time, an *Exhortation to the Pagans,* spuriously attributed to Justin. In this unknown author, we again encounter several examples of the sort we have seen in Clement and Origen and in others as well—thus the wonderful garden of Alcinous (*Odyssey* 7.114–26) manifestly imitates the Paradise of Genesis (2.8–9), while the fall of Lucifer in Isaiah 14.12 gave rise to the punishment of Ate, who was thrown down from Olympus in *Iliad* 19.126–31 (§ 28).

Further removed from Greek culture, Latin patristics takes less pleasure in accumulating illustrations of this sort; yet these are not rare. Serapis, the Hellenized Egyptian god whose head is crowned with a modius, is really the Jew Joseph, the judicious counselor to the Pharaoh on matters concerning wheat (Genesis 41.25–57) and the object of a cult inspired by gratitude for this advice; but Joseph was the great grandson of Sarah, Abraham's wife, from which his name of "child of Sarah," *Sarras paîs* in Greek, became Serapis. The reduction of a Greco-Egyptian divinity to a biblical personage, with the aid of etymology in the finest tradition, is found in the fourth century in the works of the Christian apologist Firmicus Maternus (*De errore profanarum religionum* 13.2). It had begun earlier with Tertullian, who undoubtedly drew on a Jewish source (*Ad nationes* 2.8.9–19). We saw at the beginning of this article that Samson, the hero of the Book of Judges, evoked, in the eyes of certain Fathers, the figure of Heracles; at that time Heracles was certainly not seen as a true *copy* of Samson. By the end of the fourth century, with the heresiologist Filaster of Brescia, it was a foregone conclusion that by drawing on the figure of Samson the pagans had come to call valiant men "Heracles" (*Liber de Haeresibus* 8.2).

3. *A widespread accusation.* The thesis of theft appears less extraordinary if it is recalled that late Judaism had pointed early Christianity in this direction. In the second century B.C. the Jewish historian Artapanos makes Moses the inspiration for Orpheus (Eusebius, *Praeparatio Evangelica* 9.27.4); his contemporary and coreligionist Aristobulus had preceded Clement of Alexandria in postulating that the celebration of the seventh day in Homer and Hesiod had been taken from the Scriptures (Eusebius, *ibid.* 13.12.13). N. Walter argues strongly for this view.[21] An influence so stubbornly asserted was bound in the end to convince a few Greek philosophers; such a conviction was undoubtedly behind the well-known statement by the Neophythagorean Numenius of Apamea, who regarded Plato as none other than "a Moses speaking Greek" (cited by Clement of Alexandria, *Stromateis* 1.22.150.4).

On the other hand, it must be realized that the Christian apologists, in alleging such seemingly incongruous examples of "theft," were often just replying to their adversaries, who proffered the same examples—naturally in support of the reverse lineage. Thus, the pagan Celsus saw the Tower of Babel and the burning of Sodom and Gomorrah as mere caricatures of the Greek legends of the sons of Aloeus and of Phaethon, and Origen (*Contra Celsum* 4.21) merely reverses the argument. As I have attempted to show elsewhere,[22] Celsus similarly held that Christian views regarding the devil are nothing but counterfeits of various Greek myths. But we know from the works of C. Andresen[23] that the positions taken by Celsus had the opportunity to reply to Justin's *Apology;* so a great polemic arose between successive generations, who did not dispute the proposed analogies but drew their arguments from them in opposing fashions.

Furthermore, wholly analogous controversies are to be found even within Greek culture. For example, Herodotus (*History* 2.53) echoes a debate on the question of whether or not Homer and Hesiod had preceded, i.e., informed, the ancient poet-theologians. Elsewhere, certain philosophers were accused of plagiarizing poets who were their compatriots, as the biblical authors would be accused by Celsus; "Epicurus is caught red-handed in the act of stealing; he has taken his most solid theories from the poets"; such is the grievance formulated by Sextus Empiricus (*Adversus Grammaticos* 273).

V. The Thesis of Demonic Imitation

1. *The intercession of demons.* Clement of Alexandria presents an important variant of the theory of theft: the theft was committed not directly by the Greeks but by a disobedient angel for their benefit. Here is a very clear text: "Philosophy . . . comes to us stolen or given to us by a thief. Some Power, some Angel, learned a shred of truth, without himself remaining faithful to the truth, and he breathed this knowledge to men, teaching them the fruit of his theft" (*Stromateis* 1.17.81.4).

Tertullian also implicates demons in this theft, calling them "spirits of error," but he attributes much subtler intentions to them: by falsifying the true doctrine, demons established fables similar to it and offered these to poets and philosophers; since they would not be believed by the public, these fables would discredit the Christian faith, which was similar to them—but when doubt would thus have destroyed the faith, there would be a return to the poets' and philosophers' fables, which are the alternative to faith. This truly diabolical calculation is made clearer through the examples which follow: if there is general mirth when Christians predict the judgment of God, Gehenna for the punishment of souls and paradise for their recompense, it is because people are laughing about the pagan replicas—the tribunal of hell, the Pyriphlegethon, and the Elysian Fields. But Tertullian is able to throw back these arguments and defuse their malice: "Where, I pray you, did the poets and philosophers get these things that are so like ours? Only from our mysteries. Now, if they got them from our mysteries because these are more ancient, then our mysteries are more reliable and more to be believed, for even what is nothing but a copy of them finds credence." As for supposing that they might have been taken from their own soil, how then could our mysteries, which preceded them, be a copy of them (*Apologeticus* 47.11–14)?

2. *The counterfeiting of Christian prophecies.* Demons held an important place in the theology of the apologist Justin. In agreement with a thesis that was current in the first centuries of the common era, he holds the false gods of paganism to be demons: it was these demons who committed the horrors which poets and mythologists ignorantly assign to the king of the gods and to his brothers Pluto and Poseidon (*Second Apology* 5.3–5).

Another misdeed on the part of the demons was, according to Justin, to travesty the Scriptures so as to supply mythology with traits that have perceptible parallels with the Christian and Jewish faiths. For example, the reason people place the image of Kore, the daughter of Zeus, over springs is that demons imitated the verse from Moses (Genesis 1.2) about the spirit of God moving upon the face of the waters. The demons, furthermore, knew that God had conceived in his thought the world that was to be created; from this primordial thought, with equal perversity, they had Athena, another daughter of Zeus, born without sexual intercourse. Justin formulates an unexpected grievance against this supposed perversion: he holds that it is ridiculous for thought to be represented by a female form. He seems to ignore the fact that, starting with the Presocratics, Athena had never ceased to be regarded as an image of thought, and even of divine thought, as F. Buffière has demonstrated.[24] In any case, Justin has no difficulty in showing that the behavior of Zeus's other children can be explained in the same way (*First Apology* 64.1–6).

Justin had used such an explanation not long before for some of these gods. In his eyes, demons find a choice ground for their manipulations in particular pages of the Scriptures: in the messianic prophecies, inspired visionaries mysteriously described the Savior long before his coming. So the demons, in order to deceive and mislead the human race, took the offensive and suggested to the poets who created myths that they give Zeus many sons and attribute monstrous adventures to them, in the hope that this would make the story of Christ appear to be a fable of the same sort, when it came. We recognize in this strategy imputed to the demons the very strategy Tertullian had imputed to them, no doubt in following Justin's analyses. The only problem, continues Justin, is that the demons did not exactly understand these prophecies, which they wished to realize in their own way—and the imitations they made of them are filled with errors, as Justin undertakes to show with some highly interesting examples (*First Apology* 54.1–4).

Moses (Genesis 49.10–11) relates a prophecy of Jacob that the Messiah would bind his foal to a vine and wash his garments in wine. The demons made two imitations of this: on the one hand, Dionysus, the son of Zeus and Semele, the inventor of the vine, who was cut into pieces and resuscitated and then ascended into the sky, and whose mysteries involve an ass; on the other, Bellerophon, the son of a man, who ascended into the sky on the horse Pegasus. This duality alone demonstrates for Justin that the demons had not entirely understood the prophecy, which did not specify whether the Messiah would be the son of God or of a man, nor whether he would ascend on the foal of an ass or of a horse. They did know from Isaiah (7.14; 52.13) that he would be born of a virgin and would ascend into heaven by his own power; they then inspired the story of Perseus, born of the virgin Danaë, and of Zeus, who had transformed himself into a rain of gold. When it is said that Heracles, the son of Zeus and of Alcmene, valiantly traveled over the world and ascended into the sky after his death, how is it not possible to see this as an imitation of the Christian prophecy of Psalm 19, (verse 5): "rejoiceth as a strong man to run a race"? Finally, having learned from the same source (Isaiah 35.5–6) that the Messiah would heal the sick and raise the dead, the demons staged the story of Asclepius (*First Apology* 54.5–10; a parallel and sometimes more complete development of this is found in Justin's other work, the *Dialogue with Trypho* 67.1–2; 69.1–5; 70.5, in which the demons give way to the devil, called the "serpent of error"; on Heracles, see M. Simon's[25] excellent commentary).

There is nevertheless in the prophecies, Justin continues, an episode that the demon imitators never credited to a single son of Zeus because it was announced in a purely symbolic fashion, which made it unthinkable for them: it is the crucifixion (*First Apology* 55.1). All the same, the evil-doing of the demons was not limited to inventing sons of Zeus before the coming of the Christ; when he had come, they recognized him as the prophesied Messiah, and set magicians against him (ibid. 56.1).

No other Christian author would take up in such breadth this sort of explanation for the resemblances which come to light between the person of Christ and certain mythological figures. But there are various resurgences of such argumentation. In the fourth century, Firmicus Maternus announced his intention to "review successively all the formulas of pagan religion, to prove that the worst enemy of the human race borrowed them from the holy and venerable predictions of the prophets to serve his filthy crimes" (*De errore profanarum religionum* 21.1). These "formulas," which Firmicus calls *symbola,* are those of the mysteries, of which he gives a few examples. He also considers some pagan rites, which he denounces as misleading imitations of prophecies; contrary to Justin, according to whom the demons had in no way penetrated the prophets' allusions to the Cross, Firmicus holds that it was in order to counterfeit the material of the Cross that the devil had wished to make wood the instrument of rites of renewal (citing the pine in the cult of Cybele and Osiris, the tree trunk in that of Proserpine, etc.) (ibid. 27.1–2).

3. *Mithra and Jesus.* Among the formulas of profane worship, Firmicus Maternus cites the following: "the god born of stone," which, as we know from other sources, designates Mithra. In his eyes, this stone evokes another stone—that by which God promises to strengthen the foundations of the future Jerusalem (according to Isaiah 28.16), and which prophetically designates the Christ. In the perspective that we have just seen, the first of these elements could only have come from the second by theft, fraudulent transfer, adulteration of the faith—and this is, indeed, the author's judgment (*De errore profanarum religionum* 20.1).

Justin had preceded him on this precise point: the initiators into the mysteries of Mithra speak of the god "born of a stone" and call the place of initiation a "cave" because, under the influence of devils, they are imitating the prophecies of Daniel (2.34: the stone that was hewn from the mountain in the dream of Nebuchadnezzar) and of Isaiah (33.16: the righteous one in a cave of solid rock). Justin counters this satanic counterfeiting of Isaiah's prophecy by pointing out the true symbolic import of the verse, which, he contends, refers to the cave of the Nativity at Bethlehem (*Dialogue with Trypho* 70.1–3; 78.5–6).

According to the same verse from Isaiah, the righteous one will receive an inexhaustible supply of bread and water in his cave, which is, Justin continues, a clear prophecy of the eucharist in its two forms (ibid. 70.4); but initiation into the mysteries of Mithra also entails the presentation of bread and a cup of water, accompanied by certain formulas. This coincidence too comes from an imitation imputable to perverse demons (with the difference that here the object of their counterfeiting is no longer prophecy but the actual Gospel accounts of the institution of the eucharist) (*First Apology* 66.4). The same resemblance would be recorded, and explained in identical fashion, by Tertullian: the office of the devil is to pervert the truth and imitate the divine sacraments in the mysteries of idols. The devil too has his baptism, through which he promises the expiation of misdeeds, and Mithra marks the foreheads of his soldiers, celebrates the oblation of bread, gives an idea of the resurrection, crowns his martyrs, etc. (*De praescriptione haereticorum* 40.2–4).

VI. An Apologetic Starting Point

1. *Homogeneity constituted as an argument.* In the writings of Tertullian (*Apologeticus* 47.11–14), we have encountered the idea that paganism had manufactured myths similar to Christian doctrines in order that the obvious falsity of the former should cast doubt, by reason of their similitude, on the latter. The African priest skillfully defused this calculation without relinquishing the presupposition: if the pagan myths inspired belief, how much more should our mysteries, of which theirs are copies, do so! These two arguments, which run in opposite directions, both rely on certain analogies between the two beliefs. More than once, Christian apologists used the same assumption for the same advantage, in various ways. Tertullian himself, in treating of the incarnation and the virgin birth, requires that the pagans first accept them simply because of their resemblance to the myths which they themselves had forged out of the corresponding prophecies: "For the time being accept this 'fable,' which is like your own, until I show you how he is proved to be Christ and who they are among you who have previously circulated fables of this genre, to destroy this truth" (*Apologeticus* 21.14); shortly thereafter (ibid., 21.23), the same author would have them admit that the Christian ascension is "much truer" than (which implies "comparable to") those of Romulus and other Romans.

But this sort of argument goes back farther than Tertullian, for Tatian, wishing to substantiate the incarnation, evokes certain mythic metamorphoses (of Athena as Deïphobus [*Iliad* 22.226–27], of Apollo as the cowherd of Admetus, of Hera as an old woman in the presence of Semele), and authorizes himself, on the basis of this parallel, to take the Greeks to task: "You who insult us, compare your myths to our accounts. . . . Considering your own legends, accept our teachings, if only on the basis of their being myths similar to your own" (*Oratorio ad Graecos* 21). Furthermore, the last passage cited from Tatian turns out to be based, almost word for word, on Justin. Justin has just cited a mass of practices, events, authors, and texts, all borrowed from Greek tradition, which imply a belief that souls remain sentient after death. He refers, for example, to necromancy, the conjuring of the dead, possession, the great oracles of Dodona and of Delphi, philosophers favorable toward the idea of reincarnation, Homer's trench and Odysseus's descent to the underworld (*Odyssey* 11.24ff.), and so forth. After enumerating these pagan testimonies to a belief also held by Christians, Justin demands an at least equal adherence to the Christian version: "If only on the basis of its resemblance to this teaching, accept ours" (*First Apology* 18.3–6).

A comparable attitude appears in Origen, although with a slightly different application. His adversary Celsus refused to accord any meaning other than the literal one to the biblical pages on the creation of woman from the rib of the sleeping Adam (Genesis 2.21–22) and on the garden of different trees planted by God, with its serpent who rebels against the divine commands (ibid., 2.8–9; 3.1–5). In both accounts, Origen opportunely cites as parallels the Hesiodic myth of Pandora (*Works and Days* 53–98, most of which he cites); the first woman, given by Zeus to men as "an evil thing and the price paid for fire" (the comparison with Eve, who alone has a historical reality, had already been instituted by Tertullian, *De corona militum* 7.3); and the Platonic myth (*Symposium* 203b–204c, also cited in great part) of the birth of Eros, who was conceived in the garden of Zeus (the importance of this last text to the Platonist tradition, both pagan and Christian, was revealed by J. M. Rist).[26] Confident of this convergence, Origen feels justified in demanding that the two biblical accounts and the two Greek myths be read in the same light. If, as one would be correct in doing, one recognized a doctrinal import hidden in the depths of the Greek myths, it would be unreasonable to deny such an import to the biblical accounts and merely to retain their surface meaning (*Contra Celsum* 4.38–39). We recognize here the procedure of using analogies with paganism as an authorization to demand at least the same treatment for Christian beliefs. The reality of this argument stands out even more in the two examples that we are about to look at.

2. *The Christ and the sons of Zeus.* We have recalled how the Christians of the first generations insisted that the "newness" of their religion be recognized. A passage from Justin that speaks of the most miraculous aspects of the person and life of Jesus is therefore surprising: "We offer nothing new with respect to those among you who are considered the sons of Zeus." What follows shows that this declaration is to be taken literally: if Jesus is the Word of God, it must be known that this is something he holds in common with Hermes, the Word of Zeus; if he was born of a virgin, so was Perseus; if he healed the sick and raised the dead, it must be admitted that Asclepius did the same; if he was crucified, the sons of Zeus too had their passions (Asclepius struck by lightning, Dionysus dismembered, Heracles throwing himself into fire); and finally, if he ascended into heaven, such was also the case with Asclepius, the Dioscuri, Perseus, Bellerophon on the back of Pegasus, and Ariadne who was placed among the stars—to say nothing of the deceased emperors (*First Apology* 21.1–3; 22.2–6).

Further pages in the *Apology* as well as the *Dialogue with Trypho* again take up many of these episodes pertaining to the sons of Zeus, as we have seen; but in these instances their purpose is to illustrate the fraud perpetrated by the demons who travestied the messianic prophecies because they misunderstood them. Justin's purpose here is quite different and even more surprising: he appears to be overcome by a comparativist frenzy at which even the most reductionist historians of religions would balk. He sets himself to taking the edge off the most salient points of Christology in order to dissolve them in their assimilation to the mythological biographies. No doubt his strategy is an apologetic one: by maximizing the parallels between Christ and the Greek gods, he may legitimately claim the same welcome among the pagans for Christ as for the Greek gods. A little later, Justin clearly declares his aspirations—and his chagrin at failing to see them realized—when he says: "While we say the same things as the Greeks, we alone are hated!" (ibid., 24.1). Naturally, this desire to gain a foothold, even at little cost, among the pagan masses, can only represent an initial and minimal phase in the apologetic enterprise. As Justin himself notes, Christ has arguments other than this in his favor: "All of our teachings received from Christ . . . are alone true . . . , and if we judge them worthy of being welcomed by you, it is not because of these resemblances but because we speak the truth." As for explaining the analogies in question, the chapter ends with the thesis dear to this author: "Before the Word became man among men, some took the initiative under the influence of evil demons and, through the intermediary of the poets, presented as reality the myths they had invented" (ibid., 23.1, 3).

3. *Heracles and Jonah.* A short branch of the tradition concerning Heracles, first represented in the third century B.C. by the Alexandrian poet Lycophron (as noted by M. Simon),[27] credits the hero with having spent three days in the belly of a fish with no harm done except for the loss of his hair. Apart from this last detail, the parallelism with the prophet Jonah is striking; several Christian commentators on the Book of Jonah (2.1–11) referred to it, and used it in the service of an argument which closely follows those we have just seen. Here, in the first half of the fifth century, is the conclusion of Cyril of Alexandria: "It is out of the question for us to give credence to divine prodigies on the basis of the Greek fables, but we retain them to our benefit, to convince the incredulous that the scope of their own legends does not allow them to reject such elements in our accounts" (*Commentary on Jonah* 11; *Patrologia Graeca* 71.616C–617A). In other words, coincidences such as those between Heracles and Jonah, which are unimportant for Christians in their own practice, are useful for making an impression on the incredulity of the Greeks. In the eleventh century the same conclusion is reached through the same comparison by the Byzantine exegete Theophylact, archbishop of Achrida: the story of Jonah is apparently incredible, especially to minds steeped in Greek errors, but the parallel from Heracles creates a dilemma for them: "Either they will also accept our miracles, or they will also reject their own. But we must not use the decay of their myths to reinforce the solidity of our own truth" (*Exposition on the Prophet Jonas* 2.1; *Patrologia Graeca* 126.932 BC).

VII. A Propaedeutic to Christianity

1. *Providential Greek culture.* At the beginning of this study, we saw various Church Fathers refer to certain mythological situations which were more or less comparable to Christian truths, in order, they thought, to speak to their pagan interlocutors in their own language; they were taking advantage of these parallels on a merely rhetorical level, without dealing with underlying questions. But to base an apologetic procedure on such parallels, even at the level we have just described, was to imply recognition of a certain reality in them. There is, however, a third Christian view of the analogies with paganism, which invests them with eminent value since it gives them a foundation that is nothing less than a design of Providence. This perspective must at least be noted in conclusion; it is part of a far broader view, that of the function of Greek culture in the economics of Christian salvation.

This function might be said to be propaedeutic—the word used by Clement of Alexandria, the principal representative of this theology of history. Saint Paul, he says, gives the "rudiments of the world" (Epistle to the Colossians 2.8) as a symbol of Greek philosophy because that philosophy is, so to speak, "elementary," and because it is a "propaedeutic" (*propaideia*) of the truth (*Stromateis* 6.8.62.1). But the function that fell to Greek philosophy is to be understood in two very different ways, neatly distinguished by Clement in an earlier passage: in a more banal sense, philosophy is today a "propaedeutic" (*propaideia*) in the direction of the true piety for minds desirous of reaching faith through demonstration; in a more profound and fundamental sense, it was given to the Greeks in the beginning, before the Lord extended his call to them, "because it was, itself, the educator of Hellenism, just as the Law was that of the Jews, for moving toward the Christ" (*Stromateis* 1.5.28.1, 3).

Several pages of the *Sixth Stromatis* are devoted to this vision of history. In discussing the consciousness of Christian newness we cited a sentence on the three modes—Greek, Jewish, and Christian—of the knowledge of God. Clement accentuates the strict parallelism between the two kinds of "evangelical preparation": on the one hand, the Law and the Prophets were given in their time to the barbarians (i.e., the Jews); and, on the other, philosophy was given to the Greeks, in order to habituate the ears of both to the Good News (6.6.44.1). Here, "philosophy" takes on a broader meaning than it has today, extending to the whole of culture.

Clement is bold enough to conceive of a Greek prophetism corresponding to the Jewish: "Just as God, wanting to save the Jews, gave them prophets, he also inspired among the Greeks the most prominent personalities to be their own prophets in their language, according as they were capable of receiving the gift of God, and he distinguished them from ordinary people" (6.5.42.3). Concurrent texts by the same author have been cited by J. Daniélou.[28] It is easy to understand, within this very particular perspective, how any intersection, however approximate or superficial, between the Greek religious corpus on the one hand and Jewish or Christian beliefs on the other would stand out and assume meaning in a way quite unlike those we have previously seen.

2. *Heiliger Homer* ("holy Homer"). The proof that Clement includes both poetry and mythology in his understanding of "Greek philosophy" is to be found first of all in the fact that he considers Homer primarily a Greek prophet. In his *Paedagogus,* in which he gives a commentary on the numerous scriptural texts in which milk is introduced as a symbol of spiritual nourishment, Clement first thinks of the beginning of book 13 of the *Iliad* (lines 5–6) in which the righteous (in fact, the noble Scythian tribes) are called "milk eaters" (*galactophagoi*), and he infers from this that Homer "prophesies involuntarily" (ibid. 1.6.36.1). There also appears to be a distinction, in the *Odyssey* (9.275, 410–11), between a "Zeus with the aegis," about whom the Cyclops hardly concern themselves, and a "great Zeus," whom they dread. In this god, of whom there are apparently two persons, Clement sees an allusion to the Christian duality of the Father and the Son, and he again concludes that Homer "was favored with an authentic gift of prophecy" (*Stromateis* 5.14.116.1; this feature was pointed out by F. Buffière).[29]

It seems as if, parallel to the Hebraic tradition, which of course remains the privileged channel, part of the Revelation had flowed into Greek culture; it is to the reality of this double current arising from a single source that we must relate—both in their indices and in their consequences—the coincidences that leave the present-day reader skeptical, though they impressed Clement. Homer, the principal prop for this demonstration, emerges from it as sacralized as the Jewish prophets—a canonization that H. Rahner[30] characterized so well with the formula he borrowed from Goethe: *Heiliger Homer!* It should also be noted how, under different guises, comparing Homer with the Holy Scriptures was a favorite pastime of certain humanists and scholars of the modern era; the works of N. Hepp[31] are persuasive on this point.

To return to the first centuries A.D., it would appear that this Christian Homer was more attractive to marginal currents of thought than to the orthodox tradition. The Gnostic Naassene sect is said to have founded itself upon a harmonization between the Homeric poems and the Jewish Scriptures, a harmonization made possible in both cases through the application of a highly inventive allegorical exegesis. This is what Hippolytus had to say in their regard: "Following the new method of interpretation of literary works which they have invented, they attribute to Homer, their prophet, the glory of having first, in a mysterious way, revealed these truths, at the same time as they mock those who have not been initiated into the Holy Scriptures, in pressing such ideas upon them" (*Refutatio omnium haeresium* 5.8.1). Among the many examples of this amalgamation, here is another, which long held the attention of H. Leisegang[32] and, later, J. Carcopino:[33] at the beginning of the last book of the *Odyssey* (24.1ff.), we see the souls of the dead suitors of Penelope being conducted to the Mead of Asphodel by the golden wand of Cyllenian Hermes. Now, the Naassenes not only identify this god with the Logos, which is unremarkable, but they identify him precisely with the Christian Word; his golden wand is none other than the iron rod of Psalm 2 (verse 9); it awakens the drowsing souls, conforming to the role reserved for the Christ in the Epistle to the Ephesians (5.14); as for the suitors, they are really men who, awakened from sleep, recall the bliss from which they have fallen and hope for their redemption, according to the Christian perspective (Hippolytus, *Refutatio omnium haeresium* 5.7.29–33).

3. *The Sibyl and Virgil.* The *Sibylline Oracles,* to which our attention has been drawn anew by V. Nikiprowetzky,[34] are today regarded as a highly composite work, in which elements that are very diverse in both date and source are found side by side. A basic corpus of pagan oracles was augmented between the second century B.C. and the second century A.D.—in imitation of primitive literary patterns, for purposes of propaganda to paganism—by a Jewish contribution (not without Christian interpolations) and then by a fully Christian contribution. But the Fathers of the second and third centuries, who often cite this collection (sometimes associating the Sibyl with the name of Hystaspis, the Iranian pseudo-magus, as do, for example, Justin, *First Apology* 20.1, 44.12, and Clement of Alexandria, *Stromateis* 6.5.43.1), conceived of it quite differently. For them it was an exclusively pagan work in which they admiringly discovered a mass of Jewish and even Christian parallels, whence their conviction that here once again they were dealing with a manifestation of the Revelation, and their habit of paralleling its testimony with Jewish prophecy. On this line of thought, which continued to perpetuate itself in the Middle Ages in the first strophe of *Dies irae: Teste David cum Sibylla,* see the works of K. Prümm.[35]

Their very title suggests that the *Sibylline Oracles* should not be considered without recalling the celebrated Virgilian *Fourth Eclogue,* for Virgil there makes reference to a prophecy by the Sibyl of Cumae, and the two texts are, in the eyes of many other Christians, to be placed in a somewhat comparable situation. The content of this short poem is well known; the salient points are as follows: the Virgin returns, a new generation descends from heaven, a child is born who will receive the divine life and will govern the globe pacified by his father, the golden age begins in spite of the fact that there remains in the hearts of men something of the ancient malice, etc. As J. Carcopino[36] has shown, this is a work adapted to circumstances, in which all of these traits are fully explicable through reference to the historical situation; that is, to local history.

But, especially if one believes that these verses date from 40 B.C., such a concentration of details charged with evocation for the Christian consciousness could only lead to reading it as a non-Christian but true prophecy. In fact, as has been shown by P. Courcelle's scholarly investigation,[37] a number of authors—often, it must be admitted, second-rate ones—identified the Virgilian child with the Infant Jesus, the new generation with the Christian people or with the incarnated Word, and so forth. Some nevertheless hesitated to bestow the title of prophet upon Virgil because it was totally without understanding it that he conveyed the annunciation of the Christ, which he received from the Sibyl, herself a true prophetess. Virgil, the unconscious prophet: this, roughly, is how Saint Augustine and the grammarian Philargyrius thought of the author of the eclogue, just as Clement of Alexandria saw Homer as an "involuntary prophet."

In spite of their appeal, these harmonizing interpretations

met with resistance among the Christians themselves. The most famous, and most severe, was that of Jerome: "These are puerilities, like charlatans' tricks, teaching what one does not know; even worse—to use an unpleasant expression—than not even to know what one does not know" (*Letter* 53, to Paulinus, 7). The partisans nevertheless remained more numerous than the adversaries, and would continue to be so down to the Middle Ages, when Abelard and then Dante were the most celebrated defenders of the messianism of the eclogue. Both of these writers, in line with Augustine's thought, also see Virgil as having announced the incarnation without realizing it, and therefore without believing it himself. Abelard compares him in this regard to Caiaphas; Dante, as I showed in another study,[38] expresses the same conviction by the compelling image of a man walking while holding behind his back a torch that sheds light upon those who follow him but leaves the man himself in darkness (*Purgatorio* 22.67–69). It matters little whether these authors made Virgil a conscious or merely an "objective" prophet, since, in the latter case, the prophetic function in the full sense of the word belonged to the Sibyl. What is significant is that the existence of analogies such as those we have discussed—some of them real, but most of them superficial or even illusory—fueled the conviction that classical paganism, from Homer to Virgil, never ceased to lead toward Christianity.

J.P./d.w.

NOTES

1. A.-J. FESTUGIÈRE, "Saint Paul à Athènes et la Ire Épître aux Corinthiens," *L'enfant d'Agrigente* (Paris 1941), 88–101; on the Athens discourse, see the classic thesis by B. GÄRTNER, *The Areopagus Speech and Natural Revelation* (Uppsala 1955).

2. M. SIMON, *Hercule et le christianisme* (Paris 1955), 170–73.

3. J. ADHÉMAR, *Influences antiques dans l'art du Moyen Age français: Recherches sur les sources et les thèmes d'inspiration* (diss., Paris; London 1937; 2d ed., 1975), notably 221–22 and pl. XXIII 72. For pagan survivals in primitive Christian art, see also W. ROTHES, "Heidnisches in altchristlicher Kunst und Symbolik," in *Festgabe A. Ehrhard* (Bonn and Leipzig 1922), 381–406.

4. H. RAHNER, *Griechische Mythen in christlicher Deutung* (Zurich 1945; 2d ed., 1957), p. 21, etc.

5. E. HATCH, *The Influence of Greek Ideas on Christianity;* 2d ed. by F. C. Grant (New York and Evanston 1957), 283–309; A. D. NOCK, *Early Gentile Christianity and Its Hellenistic Background* (New York 1964), 116–45.

6. A. WIFSTRAND, *L'église ancienne et la culture grecque,* trans. from Swedish (Paris 1962), 107–34.

7. RAHNER, *Griechische Mythen in christlicher Deutung,* 414–86. See also the well-documented articles that the same author published in the *Zeitschrift für Katholische Theologie* from 1941 through 1964 under the general title of "Antenna crucis"; these studies have been conveniently reassembled in H. RAHNER, *Symbole der Kirche: Die Ekklesiologie der Väter* (Salzburg 1964), 237–564; titles include: "Odysseus am Mastbaum," "Das Meer der Welt," "Das Schiff aus Holz," "Das Kreuz als Mastbaum und Antenne," "Das Mystische Tau," "Der Schiffbruch und die Planke des Heils," "Das Schifflein des Petrus: Zur Symbolgeschichte des römischen Primats," "Die Arche Noe als Schiff des Heils," and "Die Ankunft im Hafen."

8. P. COURCELLE, "Quelques symboles funéraires du néo-platonisme latin: Le vol de Dédale; Ulysse et les Sirènes," *Revue des études anciennes* 46 (1944): 65–93; "L'interprétation evhémériste des Sirènes-courtisanes jusqu'au XIIe siècle," in *Mélanges L. Wallach* (Stuttgart 1975), 33–48.

9. J. CARCOPINO, *De Pythagore aux Apôtres: Études sur la conversion du monde romain* (Paris 1956), 192–221. It is now known that one of the Gnostic Copt writings discovered at Nag Hammadi, *L'Exégèse de l'âme,* also exploits the legend of Odysseus, in concurrence with biblical texts; cf. M. SCOPELLO, "Les citations d'Homère dans le traité de *L'Exégèse de l'âme,*" in M. Krause, ed., *Gnosis and Gnosticism* (Leiden 1977), 3–12.

10. V. BUCHHEIT, "Homer bei Methodios von Olympos," *Rheinisches Museum* 99 (1956): 19–36.

11. A. CASAMASSA, "L'accusa di 'Hesterni' e gli scrittori cristiani del II secolo," *Angelicum* 20 (1943): 184–94.

12. N. ZEEGERS-VANDER VORST, *Les citations des poètes grecs chez les apologistes chrétiens du IIe siècle* (Louvain 1972), 184–86 and 272. For Christian attitudes in the first three centuries toward the part of pagan authors, see more generally W. KRAUSE, *Die Stellung der frühchristlichen Autoren zur heidnischen Literatur* (Vienna 1958).

13. J. PÉPIN, "Le 'challenge' Homère-Moïse aux premiers siècles chrétiens," *Revue des sciences religieuses* 29 (1955): 105–22.

14. J. DANIÉLOU, *Histoire des doctrines chrétiennes avant Nicée,* 2: *Message évangélique et culture hellénistique aux IIe et IIIe siècles* (Tournai 1961), book 1, pp. 73–101, "Homère chez les Pères de l'Église."

15. G. GLOCKMANN, "Das Homerbild der altchristlichen Literatur in der Forschung der Gegenwart," *Klio* 43–45 (1965): 270–81; by the same author, *Homer in der frühchristlichen Literatur bis Justinus* (Berlin 1968).

16. For example, A. J. FESTUGIÈRE, *La révélation d'Hermès Trismégiste,* 1: *L'astrologie et les sciences occultes* (Paris 1944), 19–44; H. DÖRRIE, "Die Wertung der Barbaren im Urteil der Griechen: Knechtsnaturen? Oder Bewahrer und Künder heilbringender Weisheit?" in *Antike und Universalgeschichte, Festschrift H. E. Stier* (Munster 1972), 146–75.

17. J. H. WASZINK, "Some Observations on the Appreciation of 'The Philosophy of the Barbarians' in Early Christian Literature," in *Mélanges C. Mohrmann* (Utrecht and Anvers 1963), 41–56.

18. K. THRAEDE, "Erfinder," part 2, in *Reallexikon für Antike und Christentum* (1962), cols. 1242–61.

19. A. MÉHAT, *Étude sur les "Stromates" de Clément d'Alexandrie* (Paris 1966), 356–61.

20. R. MORTLEY, *Connaissance religieuse et herméneutique chez Clément d'Alexandrie* (Leiden 1973), 162–66.

21. N. WALTER, *Der Thoraausleger Aristobulos: Untersuchungen zu seinen Fragmenten und zu pseudepigraphischen Resten der jüdisch-hellenistischen Literatur* (Berlin 1964), 44–51 and 150–71.

22. J. PÉPIN, *Mythe et allégorie: Les origines grecques et les contestations judéo-chrétiennes* (2d ed., Paris 1976), 448–52.

23. C. ANDRESEN, *Logos und Nomos: Die Polemik des Kelsos wider das Christentum* (Berlin 1955), 352–55.

24. F. BUFFIÈRE, *Les mythes d'Homère et la pensée grecque* (Paris 1956), 279–89.

25. SIMON, *Hercule et le christianisme,* 111.

26. J. M. RIST, *Eros and Psyche: Studies in Plato, Plotinus and Origen,* "Phoenix," supplement vol. 6 (Toronto 1964).

27. SIMON, *Hercule et le christianisme,* 174–75.

28. DANIÉLOU, *Histoire des doctrines chrétiennes avant Nicée,* 2: *Message évangélique et culture hellénistique aux IIe et IIIe siècles,* book 1, pp. 53–55.

29. BUFFIÈRE, *Les mythes d'Homère et la pensée grecque,* 361 and note 86.

30. RAHNER, *Griechische Mythen in christlicher Deutung,* 357.

31. N. HEPP, "Les interprétations religieuses d'Homère au XVIIe siècle," *Revue des sciences religieuses* 31 (1957): 34–50; *Homère en France au XVIIe siècle* (Paris 1968).

32. H. LEISEGANG, *La gnose,* trans. from German (Paris 1951), 89–90.

33. CARCOPINO, *De Pythagore aux Apôtres,* 180–81.

34. V. NIKIPROWETZKY, *La troisième Sibylle* (Paris and The Hague 1970).

35. K. PRÜMM, "Das Prophetenamt der Sibyllen in kirchlicher Literatur mit besonderer Rücksicht auf die Deutung der VI. Ekloge Virgils," *Scholastik* 4 (1929): 54–77, 221–46, and 498–533.

36. J. CARCOPINO, *Virgile et le mystère de la VIe Églogue* (2d ed., Paris 1943).

37. P. COURCELLE, "Les exégèses chrétiennes de la quatrième Églogue," *Revue des études anciennes* 59 (1957): 294–319.

38. J. PÉPIN, *Dante et la tradition de l'allégorie* (Montreal and Paris 1970), 103–5.

The Euhemerism of the Christian Authors

I. Euhemerus and His Doctrine

We have very little precise information about Euhemerus, a Greek known only from a small number of testimonies which often disagree with one another (these may be found in the collections of G. Némethy[1] and G. Vallauri[2]). He is most often said to be a native of Messene in Peloponnesos, or Messina in Sicily, but he is also said to come from Agrigento, or Tegea, or Chios. According to Diodorus the historian, it was King Cassandra of Macedonia (316–297) who sent Euhemerus on an expedition to the Red Sea; on the other hand, Euhemerus seems to be cited by the poet Callimachus in works that must date from 275–270. It can thus roughly be estimated that Euhemerus went on his travels as early as 300–298, and wrote about them around 280. On these data, see Jacoby's 1907 article, which is still valuable.[3]

In Euhemerus, the author is always identified with the voyager. Returned from his exploration, he draws from it a geographical novel in which real memories rub shoulders with affabulation; this combination is given free reign in the description of Panchaia, an imaginary island off the coast of Arabia. Euhemerus would have it that he found there "a temple of Zeus Triphylian, in which a golden column stood whose inscription indicated that it had been erected by Zeus himself; on this column, the god had inscribed the details of his greatest deeds, in order that posterity be informed of them" (fgt 23 Nemethy = *testim* 4 Vallauri = Lactantius, *Divinae Institutiones* 1.11.33). It is this testimony by the gods about their own exploits that Euhemerus comments on in a *Sacred Record* (*Hiera Anagraphē*), a clever title that reminds one that what is being treated is mainly an "inscription." Nothing remains of this work, but some Greek authors mention it, especially Diodorus of Sicily. The Roman poet Ennius translated (or adapted) it into Latin, and the Christian Lactantius preserved fragments of that translation, whose title was probably *Sacra Historia*.

This is enough to yield a rough idea of the theology of Euhemerus. The central idea is connected to the inscription in the temple of Zeus: it is that the gods of mythology were at first men, who were divinized *post mortem* in recognition of eminent services that they had rendered to humanity. As Lactantius also says (*De ira dei* 2.7.8 = *testim* 15N = *testim* 5mV), "It is beyond doubt that all those who receive worship as gods were men, and that the first and the greatest among them were kings; but that by virtue of the courage with which they had served the human race, they were gratified with divine honors after their death; or else following the good deeds and inventions with which they had embellished the life of humankind, they ensured for themselves an imperishable memorial. Who does not know this? . . . Those who hold to this teaching are primarily Euhemerus and our Ennius." But the popular pantheon also included gods of lesser morality who were, according to the preceding principle, difficult to identify with public benefactors; they too, however, could be explained by the same principle, provided that violence and deceit were substituted for good deeds and gratitude. On this subject, Sextus Empiricus (*Adversus Mathematicos* 9.17 = fgt 1N = *testim* 5c5) seems to have preserved the express formulations of the *Sacred Record:* "Euhemerus, known as 'the Atheist,' says this: 'When men lived in disorder, those whose superiority in strength and intelligence permitted them to make everyone carry out their orders, wishing to receive more admiration and respect, falsely attributed to themselves a superhuman and divine power, which caused the masses to regard them as gods.'"

In reducing the shimmering of mythology to the more prosaic realities of history, Euhemerus joined the current of rationalist criticism applied to popular religion, a current that has been studied by P. Decharme[4] and A. B. Drachmann;[5] this is why he was known as "the Atheist." He was an innovator; the Sophists, especially Prodicus, are sometimes considered his predecessors. But Prodicus, although he explained divinization in terms of utility, was thinking mainly of the benefits offered by the great natural realities—the sun, rivers, springs, fruits of the earth, etc.—which men turned into gods; it was only at a later point that he extended this principle to the inventors of beneficial crafts themselves, and this thesis was not as well documented as the first. On the other hand, as G. Vallauri has shown,[6] Euhemerus was not a sniper. His great idea incontestably corresponds to the spirit of his age; it is clearly related (and we shall see that the Christians were not mistaken about this) to the cult of sovereigns which was instituted in the Hellenistic period. Several authors or currents more or less contemporaneous with Euhemerus (the uncertainty of our chronology does not permit us to say whether he influenced them or was indebted to them) offered, as he did, a theory of the gods as former great servants of humanity. We do not know the exact moment at which ancient Stoicism adopted this explanation for certain gods—or, more accurately, for certain heroes, such as Heracles, Castor and Pollux, Asclepius, Dionysus. It is in any case a foregone conclusion with Zeno's student Persaeus of Citium (certainly posterior to Euhemerus by a few years), whose thesis was formulated by Cicero (*De natura deorum* 1.15.38) as follows: "Those who had devised something of great usefulness were honored as gods." There was another author, Hecataeus of Abdera (or of Teos), probably slightly earlier than Euhemerus, who proposed altogether analogous views on the origins of the Egyptian gods, if in fact he was, as is generally asserted (but see the counterargument of W. Spoerri),[7] the source, in the Egyptian domain, of the historian Diodorus of Sicily.

Euhemerus, therefore, was certainly not the only person of his time to defend the thesis we have just described. But it was his name that remained coupled to it for posterity, notably for the Christian writers of the first centuries. For these writers broadly explored the possibilities Euhemerism offered, and we shall see why and how they did so. Works on this subject are rare, but we should at least point out the articles by F. Zucker[8] and K. Thraede,[9] and the dissertation by J. W. Schippers,[10] to which we might add my own earlier studies;[11] we should also add that the works of J. D. Cooke[12] and of P. Alphandéry[13] on the medieval developments of Euhemerism, and by J. Seznec[14] on survivals of ancient theologies down to the Renaissance, contain much data on their use in the patristic age.

II. Christian Formulations

1. *Defense and illustration of Euhemerus.* The pagan gods are false gods; but what are they really? Christian theologians could not evade a response to this question. This response often takes the form, as with Saint Augustine, of describing the gods of the nations as "foul demons who wish to pass as gods": *deos gentium esse inmundissimos daemones . . . deos se putari cupientes* (*City of God* 7.33). Euhemerism, however, offered an alternative, which Christians hurried to adopt. In spite of the atheism attached in classical tradition to the name

of Euhemerus, Theophilus of Antioch (*Ad Autolycum* 3.7 = *testim* 19–20N = *testim* 5IV) was perhaps the only Christian who noted his impiety. Many Church Fathers, on the other hand, absolve him along with other supposed "atheists," and compliment him on his clairvoyance. The African Arnobius of Sicca (late third to early fourth century) illustrates this outlook: "We surely cannot show here that all those whom you introduce under the name of gods were men: it suffices to open Euhemerus of Agrigento—whose books Ennius translated into an Italic language that everyone understands—or else Nicagoras of Cyprus, or Leo of Pella, or Theodore of Cyrene, or Hippo and Diagoras, both of Melos, or a thousand other authors who, attentive to scrupulous accuracy and as the free men that they were, brought to the light of day facts that had been left in shadow" (*Adversus nationes* 4.29 = *testim* 14N = *testim* 5iV). Elsewhere, Clement of Alexandria (*Protrepticus* 2.24.2 = *testim* 13N = *testim* 5hV) makes a very similar comment, which may have been Arnobius's model. At the beginning of the third century, Minucius Felix (*Octavius* 21.1 = *testim* 9N = *testim* 5fV) counts Euhemerus among historians and sages; Saint Augustine (*City of God* 7.27 = fgt 20N = *testim* 5n2V), calling history to the aid of poetry, associates his name with that of Virgil, who is also taken as a witness to the fact that Saturn was a mere dethroned king (*Aeneid* 8.319ff.). This last text shows that the Christian author was at pains to find Euhemerism in texts other than those of its founder; he would see another of his partisans in the person of the Egyptian Hermes Trismegistus, who, he says, "testifies that the gods of the Egyptians are men who have died" (*City of God* 8.26, using as an illustration the Hermetic *Asclepius* § 24).

The haste with which Christian authors adopted the theses of Euhemerus may be explained in part by the fact that they found similar theses in some of their scriptures. Such is the case with the Wisdom of Solomon, to which attention has been drawn by J. D. Cooke (see note 12); here are the terms in which the genesis of idolatry is traced in it: "For a father, consumed with grief at an untimely bereavement, made an image of his child, who had suddenly been taken from him; and now he honored as a god what was once a dead human being, and handed on to his dependents secret rites and initiations. Then the ungodly custom, grown strong with time, was kept as a law . . . and the multitude, attracted by the charm of his work, now regarded as an object of worship the one whom shortly before they had honored as a man" (*New Oxford Annotated Bible*, Wisdom of Solomon 14.15–20). This development (undoubtedly from the first century B.C.) on the origin of the gods is incontestably linked to Euhemerism, from which it probably takes its inspiration. Eight centuries later, Isidore of Seville would recall it, perhaps in order to describe the same kind of retrogression: after the death of certain great men, their friends represented them by means of an effigy simply as a means of consoling themselves and honoring their memory; it was only the following generations which, with the help of demonic influences, fell into the error of making gods of these men (*Etymologiae* 8.11.4).

In their portrayal of Euhemerism, the Christians accentuated particular aspects of it. The original humanity of the gods is less striking to them than the death through which they have passed, which continues to cling to them; more than divinized men, they are "corpses": "we, who are alive, do not sacrifice to corpses who are gods, and we do not worship them," is what we read in the Second Epistle (3.1), attributed (wrongly) to Saint Clement, one of the first bishops of Rome; "You have ended up as corpses yourselves, for having put your trust in corpses," is the warning given to the pagans by Clement of Alexandria (*Protrepticus* 3.45.5); "They never manufacture gods except from corpses," writes the historian Eusebius (*Praeparatio Evangelica* 3.3.17), echoing the same idea. They fear beings that are twice dead, "more dead than the dead": such is already the statement attributed to the Apostle Peter in the *Clementine Homilies* (10.9).

In explaining by what error men came to worship those who had previously been their peers, Clement stresses the aura of prestige with which the distant past is so easily endowed, while the present remains ignored for its banality. The historian Thucydides (*Peloponnesian Wars* 1.21.1) had earlier observed that "with the passing of time, most historic facts pass into the region of myths that no one can believe." Clement again takes up this idea of the complicity of time and myth: "Those whom you worship were once men, who afterwards died. But myth and time have loaded them with honors . . . For the past, being cut off from immediate control by the obscurity which time brings, is invested with a fictitious honor . . . That is how the dead men of old, made venerable by the authority that time concedes to error, are believed to be gods by those who come after" (*Protrepticus* 4.55.2–3). It was, moreover, a Jewish explanation before it became Christian; we find it on the lips of another Clement, a cultivated Greek converted to Judaism and the protagonist of the *Clementine Homilies* (6.22); these homilies themselves belong to a Jewish apologetic tradition which may go back as far as the beginning of the second century. It takes time to forget that the gods were once men; but too much time results in a weakening of the legend. As Clement of Alexandria says (*Protrepticus* 2.37.1–3), the myths and gods of paganism "have aged" today, and Zeus himself is no longer the intrepid lover he once was (Tatian, *Oratio ad Graecos* 21, already spoke in a like fashion: "Why does Hera no longer bear children? Has she grown old, or does she lack someone who might announce it to you?"). But it is the discovery of Euhemerus that consummates this decadence, described by Clement by means of a metaphor familiar to ancient theories of myth, that of "laying bare" (the verb *gumnoun*)—the truth "lays bare" the mass of gods by tearing away their masks (*Protrepticus* 2.27.5); the myth of Zeus is "laid bare" before the eyes of the pagans (2.37.3)—which is all another way of saying that the Euhemerist explanation strips the Greek pantheon of its finery and reduces it to its mere human expression.

Thus Christian thought tried to accredit Euhemerus's hypothesis by analyzing the process of divinization. Other authors offer equally enlightening examples. Lactantius, the principal witness to the Latin adaptation of Euhemerus, reduces the classical pranks of Jupiter to purely human dimensions: the golden rain with which the god showered Danaë's breast was nothing more, in a concrete sense—if one subtracts from it all the poetic amplification—than the wages of a common courtesan, just as "rain of iron" is used for a volley of arrows; the eagle of Ganymede was originally simply the insignia of the legion sent out to kidnap the young shepherd; as for the bull of Europa and the heifer into which Io metamorphosed herself, we are to understand these ruminants, in a more prosaic way, as figureheads on the prows of the ships used to transport the two maidens (*Divinae Institutiones* 1.11.17–22; in the same vein, *Epitome divin. instit.* 11; certain of these explanations are taken up again by Augustine, *City of God* 18.13).

2. *The divinization of emperors and pharaohs.* We have seen that the appearance of Euhemerism was probably not uncon-

nected with the cult of the Hellenistic sovereigns. This *Sitz im Leben* could not escape the Christian authors, who associated the theses of Euhemerus with the apotheoses of princes which were taking place before their eyes or had occurred recently. This is what Athanasius of Alexandria does, for example, in a *Discourse against the Pagans*. His Euhemerist convictions are well established: the gods are very ancient leaders, upon the loss of whom (along with their relatives) there was lamentation—such was the case with Zeus, Hermes, Osiris, etc. (*Contra Gentes* 10, *Patrologia Graeca* 25.24A). Thus was constituted the antique pantheon, its principal author being Theseus, the legendary king of Attica (10.21BC). Athanasius clearly refuses to take such divinities seriously; as he says in a well-turned phrase, "Their mythology is not a theology" (19.40C). For him, the process of divinization unveiled by Euhemerus evokes the apotheosis bestowed upon emperors and claimed by some of them for third parties (as by Hadrian for his favorite Antinous) (9.20CD). Against such pretensions, Athanasius simply observes that, since the worker should be superior to his work, mortal men are incapable of making gods (9.21A; an analogous argument had previously been more amply developed by Tertullian, *Apologeticus* 11.1–3).

The passages from Athanasius are undoubtedly the most synthetic, but they are not the only ones to be found in patristic literature on the subject. The author of the *Clementine Homilies* (6.23) bases his arguments on Euhemerism, recalling that down through the Ptolemaic period the Egyptians had made gods of their pharaohs even while they were still alive. As for Saint Augustine, he would note that Euhemerus's explanation is rendered probable by the spectacle of different episodes in Roman history: "What then is surprising in the fact that the earliest men did for Jupiter, Saturn, and the rest the very thing that the Romans did for Romulus and wanted to do, in a more recent time, for Caesar himself?"(*De consensu evangelist*. 1.23.32).

This pretension to legal apotheosis on the part of great individuals naturally rankles the Christians, who are sometimes presented as adversaries of Euhemerism; we have seen that such is not the case, except to the extent that Euhemerus might have appeared to them as being partial to aspirations to divinization on the part of sovereigns. Whatever the case, it must be said that, in their rejection of apotheosis, the Christian authors, as often happened, followed in the footsteps of certain Greek philosophers. We saw above that the Stoic Persaeus of Citium, regarding the phenomenon of heroization, held a doctrine related to, and probably dependent upon, that of Euhemerus. And Cicero, describing the thesis of Persaeus in his dialogue *De natura deorum* (1.15.38), puts his account in the mouth of an Epicurian philosopher named Velleius, who no sooner formulates the doctrine than he condemns it with great verve: "What could be more absurd than . . . to raise men to gods once death has destroyed them?"

3. *The "letter of Alexander to Olympias."* Even though Euhemerus never, properly speaking, founded a school, his theses were exhibited in works other than his own. Among the latter, a text should be noted here for the echo it finds among Christian listeners; that is, a so-called letter from Alexander of Macedonia to his mother Olympias, discussed in an article by F. Pfister.[15] Various Christian apologists (Tertullian, Minucius Felix, Cyprian, Augustine) believe that the author really was Alexander, to whom the Euhemerist theory was thought to have been revealed in Egypt. Here, for example, is how Athenagoras, the earliest among them, associates the Macedonian king with the historian Herodotus, who precedes him by a century: "Herodotus and Alexander, the son of Philip, in his letter to his mother, say that they have learned from the priests that these gods were once men. Each of them is said to have had conversations with the priests in Heliopolis, Memphis, and Thebes" (Athenagoras, *Supplication to Marcus Aurelius* 28).

Other Fathers of the Church (Tatian, Tertullian again, Clement of Alexandria, Eusebius, Arnobius), commenting on the same subject, evoke a certain Leo. That all of these writers had the same text in mind is demonstrated by the fact that Augustine (*City of God* 8.5, 27; *De consensu evangelist*. 1.23.33) makes Leo the Egyptian priest from whom Alexander received the revelation of the original humanity of the gods. Such divergencies lead one to believe that this was a document of which the Christians had only heard tell, and that its author was neither Alexander nor Leo but an unknown individual whose ideas and lifetime were close to those of Hecataeus of Abdera and of Euhemerus; he was probably later than they and influenced by them. Of all of the Christian writers, only Arnobius, in a passage cited above, speaks of Leo *of Pella;* this geographical detail might lead one to believe that he was a real individual; but this does not accord with the testimony of Augustine, who sees Leo as a *sacerdos Aegyptius*. The situation being so confused, especially if one remembers that Pella was the capital of the kingdom of Macedonia and the birthplace of Alexander, one is tempted to subscribe to F. Pfister's hypothesis, that Arnobius's "Pellaeus Leon" was merely a metaphor designating Alexander, the "lion of Pella!"

III. The Arguments Set Forth

1. *The "synonymy" of the gods.* Accepting Euhemerism, the Christian authors muster various arguments in favor of this doctrine; some were their own, but most had been formulated before them. So it is that Clement of Alexandria, in order to "refute the imaginations" that presided over the constitution of the pagan pantheon, invokes what he calls the "synonymies" (*Protrepticus* 2.27.5), and what today we would call homonymy: the fact that the names of the greatest gods refer to several distinct divinities. By way of illustration, he recalls that there were three Zeuses, five Athenas, six Apollos, and many an Asclepius, Hermes, Hephaestus, and Ares (2.28.1–29.2). Many other Christian authors made sport of the fact that several would-be gods could bear the same name, especially that of Zeus (Theophilus of Antioch, *Ad Autolycum* 12.10; Minucius Felix, *Octavius* 22.6; Arnobius, *Adversus nationes* 4.14, etc.); but none could exploit these circumstances to the advantage of the Euhemerist thesis as well as Clement did. The way had nevertheless been opened by the pagan philosophers themselves; Cicero, for example, in the third book of his dialogue *De natura deorum,* borrows from Cotta, the spokesman for skepticism in the New Academy, a long elaboration on the plurality, not only of Jupiters, but also of Vulcans, Mercuries, Apollos, etc. (*Nat. D.* 3.21.53–23.60). This fact had already been interpreted there as an argument in favor of the human origin of these gods, as the first sentence of his declamatory passage shows: "We ought also to fight those who argue that these beings who came from the human race and were transported to heaven are not really, but only by convention, the gods whom we all honor with our most devout veneration" (3.21.53).

2. *The traces left by the gods.* It could have been predicted that the bodily peculiarities of the gods would be seen as

indices of their human origin. In his treatise *On Isis and Osiris* (chap. 23), Plutarch shows himself to be personally hostile to Euhemerism; he nevertheless notes (chap. 22) that, according to the Egyptians, Hermes had short arms, Typho was red-headed, Horus blond, Osiris brunette; and he gives voice to the following conclusion: "This is because, by nature, they were men." The Christian Eusebius makes no mistake; in searching in his *Praeparatio Evangelica* (3.3.15–16) for confirmations for his Euhemerist convictions, he sees how he can make good use of Plutarch's text on the bodily characteristics of the gods. He cites that text as "witness to the fact that they were mortal men." The details of their physical appearance are just part of the picture, and Clement of Alexandria invokes other concrete data that point in the same direction: "May the lands they dwelled in, the arts they practiced, the record of their lives, yes, and even their tombs, convince you that they were only men" (*Protrepticus* 2.29.1).

In drawing out this argument, Clement and Eusebius followed Euhemerus's lead directly, as several sources show: "Euhemerus and our Ennius show the birth, marriage, progeniture, power, exploits, death, and tomb of all the gods" (*testim.* 15N = *testim.* 5mV = Lactantius, *De ira dei* 2.7.8; cf. on the same *testim.* 9N = *testim.* 5fV = Minucius Felix, *Octavius* 21). The last element mentioned, the tomb as an attestation of death, is the most important of all; it is the only one retained by Cicero (*Nat. D.* 1.42.119 = *testim.* 2N = *testim.* 5dV): *ab Euhemero autem et mortes et sepulturae demonstrantur deorum* ("Moreover, both the deaths and the tombs of the gods are demonstrated by Euhemerus"). Euhemerus was especially concerned with Zeus, narrating his death in Crete, the funerary rites performed by his sons the Curetes, and the placing of the body in the sepulcher in Cnossos (fgt 29N = fgt 24V = Lactantius, *Divinae Institutiones* 1.11.46). Thus the poet Callimachus, wishing to dismantle nascent Euhemerism, would choose to refute it on this ground (*Hymn to Zeus* 8–9 = *testim.* 1bV): "The Cretans are always liars; for the Cretans even built your tomb, O king, but you did not die, for you exist forever."

The Christian authors take care not to side with Callimachus; several of them expressly rebuke him and say that the Cretans are right rather than he, as shown in the texts brought together by N. Zeegers-Vander Vorst.[16] Tatian (*Oratio ad Graecos* 27) and Clement of Alexandria (*Protrepticus* 2.37.4) took this line. The interpellation of Athanagoras, which comes at the end of three chapters on the human origin of the gods, merits a citation; it points out the contradiction of the poet, who denies that the god is dead but recognizes that he was born, without realizing that he who is born must die: "You believe, Callimachus, in the birth of Zeus but you do not believe in his tomb. And thinking to conceal the truth, you proclaim his death, even to men who are unaware of it; if you see the cave you recall Rhea's giving birth, but if you see the funerary urn you throw darkness over the death of the god, not knowing that the only eternal being is the God without a beginning" (*Supplication* 30). Origen took up the same argument—that death necessarily follows birth—but his text is notable in that he gives the floor to his adversary, the pagan Celsus, who says to the Christians: "You mock those who worship Zeus, giving as a reason the fact that his tomb is displayed in Crete, and yet you honor Him who came out from the tomb, without knowing how and under what authority the Cretans act in this way" (*Contra Celsum* 3.43). It is a sentence exceptionally rich in information: this Platonist of the second century knew the Christian argument derived from the tomb of Zeus; he found little coherence between it and faith in a resurrected God; and he knew (unfortunately without making it known) an allegorical justification of the myth of the sepulcher of Zeus. Whatever the case, Origen maintains the historicity of the tomb of Zeus while alleging that the learned Callimachus was ignorant of any allegory of this kind.

Aside from the reference to Callimachus's *Hymn to Zeus*, which seems to be limited to the four authors we have just seen, there is no end to the list of Christians who advance the argument of the tomb. The *Clementine Homilies* nevertheless are worth singling out for the fact that they do not merely turn the tomb of Zeus in Crete to their account, but feel that their Euhemerist convictions will be more widely shared if they add the tombs of Kronos in the Caucasus, Ares in Thrace, Hermes in Egypt, Aphrodite in Cyprus, Dionysus at Thebes, Asclepius in Epidaurus, etc. (5.23 and 6.21; the theses are proposed by the Jewish or Judeo-Christian Clement). A passage taken from Tertullian is of interest because it adds to these sepulchers the consideration of other "monuments of antiquity" from which we learn about the gods, the cities in which they were born, the lands in which they left traces of their activities: Tertullian hopes that the pagans will succumb in the face of such proofs and recognize that all their gods were formerly men (*Apologeticus* 10.3–4). This conclusion leads to Euhemerism, which Tertullian next develops (10.6–11) by using Saturn and Jupiter as illustration. After much hesitation over which one of the two contemporaneous authors influenced the other, it is generally thought today that it was Tertullian who served as model for Minucius Felix. In fact, the latter offers an elaboration on Saturn and Jupiter very similar to the one we have just seen (*Octavius* 23.9–13). With admirable clarity he mobilizes Jupiter—to whose tomb he adds, as we have seen Athenagoras do, the cave of Ida—to the cause of Euhemerism: "Even today people visit the grotto of Jupiter and show his tomb, and the very sites that he consecrated prove his human nature (*ipsis sacris suis humanitatis arguitur*)" (23.13; M. Pellegrino's edition of *Octavius* is valuable for its copious annotation, especially on the chapter in question).[17]

3. *The existence of rites.* Many historians of religions today conceive of the relationship between myth and ritual in such a way that myth appears to justify ritual a posteriori. An example of these etiological myths is provided by M. Eliade: "Preconjugal ceremonial unions preceded the appearance of the myth of the preconjugal relations between Hera and Zeus, the myth which served to justify them."[18] This is a point on which the Fathers of the Church were not very "modern." For they believed in general that the cultic activities of paganism bore witness to the historical reality of myths, in other words, to the human origin of the gods.

The argument begins with Tertullian, who parallels the names of the gods, which are an element of their civil status as mortals, with their histories, which are confirmed by rites: "With regard then to your gods, I see only the names of certain dead men of the past, about whom I hear tales, and I identify their sacred rites from the tales (*sacra de fabulis recognosco*)" (*Apologeticus* 12.1; we have just encountered the word *sacra*, "sacred rites," in the work of Minucius Felix—*ipsis sacris suis*—who invokes the cave and tomb of Jupiter while thinking of the rites that were performed there). The same reasoning would soon become more explicit with Arnobius, as we see in this passage: "How then, do we prove that all these stories are records of actual events? From the solemn rites, of course, and the mysteries of initiation, either those which take place at stated times and days or those which the people hand down in secret, preserving the perpetuity of their special customs. For it must not be believed that these practices are without their origins, that they take place without rhyme or reason, that they do not submit to motives that link them with primitive institutions." Here Arnobius offers examples of the way in which today's sacred liturgies are rooted in yesterday's human episodes, thus rendering them incontestable: the pine introduced in procession in the sanctuary of Cybele is the image of the one under which Attis emasculated himself; the annual phallophoria reflect the castrating mission of Liber; the secret ceremonies of Eleusis contain the memory of the wanderings of Ceres in search of Proserpina and some of her stopping places. Whether or not they are correct, Arnobius continues, these examples leave no loopholes: "If these mysteries have another cause, that is nothing to us, so long as they are produced by some cause. For it defies belief that these practices were all undertaken without antecedent causes; or we must judge the people of Attica to be crazy for having forged a religious rite that has no motive. And if our conclusion is clearly established, if the causes and origins of the mysteries derive from actual events (*e rebis actis mysteriorum causae atque origines effluunt*) . . ." (*Adversus Nationes* 5.39; cf. 5.5–7 for the development of his examples; on this passage, as well as for the whole of Arnobius's apologetic treatise in general, see the commentary by George E. McCracken).[19]

4. *The dilemma of Xenophanes.* While they are the principal index of the original humanity of the gods, the tombs also become the favored place for their worship. In a text of Jewish apologetics from the end of the second century or the beginning of the first century B.C., introduced into the Greek Bible under the title of the *Letter of Jeremiah,* we read that the offerings presented to the pagan gods are assimilated to those placed on tombs (verse 26).

A saying that gained great currency in the first Christian centuries was that the temples of false gods were tombs, their own tombs. Athenagoras (*Supplication* 28) attributes this saying to the Euhemerist theologians of Egypt, and also to a Greek grammarian of the second century B.C., Apollodorus, the author of the treatise *On the Gods,* which was known, perhaps directly but more likely indirectly, to several Christian authors (on this last point, see the works of Zucker[20] and Geffcken[21]). "They despise the temples as if they were tombs" (*templa ut busta despiciunt*), says Cecilius, the pagan interlocutor in Minucius Felix's dialogue (*Octavius* 8.4), of the Christians; in the fourth century, Firmicus Maternus, another apologist, found these words to his taste and put them to his own use: *Busta sunt haec, sacratissimi imperatores, appellanda, non templa* ("These should be called tombs, most sacred emperors, not temples"; *De errore profanarum religionum* 16.3). It was primarily Clement of Alexandria who gave credence to this theme: "These temples . . . are euphemistically called temples, but they are really tombs . . . Be ashamed to honor these tombs" (*Protrepticus* 3.44.4); and later, with regard to the temple of Antinous, which was consecrated by the emperor Hadrian: "Just like temples, so also tombs, pyramids, mausoleums, and labyrinths seem to be objects of reverence; they are temples of the dead, just as temples are tombs of the gods" (4.49.3).

This parallel was not pushed any farther. But it has an important corollary: if it is true that the temples are nothing but tombs, then it follows that the mourning connected with tombs should invade and alter the worship offered in temples. This critique had been formulated by Greek philosophy itself; we find it in Cicero's *De natura deorum* in the mouth of the spokesman for Epicureanism, Velleius, who addresses it to the Stoic Persaeus, having just described the latter's theory on divinization, which is close to Euhemerism: by thus introducing deceased men among the gods, "the whole cult of the gods becomes an expression of mourning" (*quorum omnis cultus esset futurus in luctu,* 1.15.38; here, as elsewhere, we may read this Ciceronian dialogue, a fundamental document in the religious philosophy of antiquity, in A. S. Pease's edition,[22] which is irreplaceable, especially for its fabulous wealth of notes).

This incompatibility, strengthened by the similarity in sound of the Latin words *cultus* and *luctus,* led Christian authors to argue in the form of a dilemma. Once again, they do not reject Euhemerism; they continue to be indebted to it for having shown them the human origin of the pagan gods; but, like Velleius, they clearly spurn the idea that gods so conceived could be anything but false gods. It is in this sense that they exploit the principle whereby an authentic cult could not be exclusively funerary: if your gods are gods, do not mourn for them; if you mourn for them, admit that they are men.

This schema is first established by Athenagoras, when he writes of the gods of Egypt: "If they are gods, they are immortal; but if they are wounded and if their sufferings constitute their mysteries, they are men" (*Supplication* 28; the dilemma is veiled by the fact that the author passes from the notion of mortality to that of suffering, which the mysteries perpetuate). Earlier (14), Athenagoras had similarly referred to the incoherence of the cults celebrated in Egyptian temples, in which everyone beats his breast in unison as if at a funeral, and everyone offers sacrifices such as are made to gods. The same reasoning attains its greatest limpidity in Clement of Alexandria: "If you believe they are gods, do not lament them, nor beat your breast; but if you mourn for them, stop thinking that they are gods" (*Protrepticus* 2.24.3). Among Latin authors, the memory of the Ciceronian antithesis between *cultus* and *luctus* persists. After recalling the demonstration of grief which colors the legend of Isis and governs her annual mysteries, Minucius Felix asks: "Is it not ridiculous to mourn what one worships or to worship what one mourns?" (*vel lugere quod colas vel colore quod lugeas*) (*Octavius* 22.1). In the fourth century, this dilemma takes a plainly scholastic turn with Firmicus Maternus: "If they are gods whom you worship (*colitis*), why do you mourn them (*lugitis*)? Why do you celebrate annual ceremonies of mourning for them? If they deserve tears, why do you heap divine honors on their heads? Do either one thing or the other: either do not weep for them if they are gods, or, if you think they deserve grief and tears, do not call them gods any longer, lest your lamentations and tears should defile the majesty of the divine name." (*De errore profanarum religionum* 8.4; on this apologetic treatise, the author of which is a converted pagan, see the commentaries of the editor A. Pastorino,[23] as well as that of the French translator G. Heuten[24].)

This consensus of the Christian apologists on the incompatibility of worship and mourning may be surprising, coming as it does from the followers of a religion in which the central figure of the cult is precisely that of a man-God who has been put to death. The explanation may derive from the fact that these authors could not themselves define the dilemma in question, but had merely borrowed it unsuspectingly from a Greek philosophical tradition. Clement of Alexandria makes no mystery of this source; for he does not offer the formula we have just seen as his own, but cites it as a warning addressed to the Egyptians by someone he does not name. He does imply that it is one of those philosophers reputed to be "atheists" because of the insight with which they brought to light the errors concerning the gods; to this end he cites some names, including that of Euhemerus (*Protrepticus* 2.24.2, as indicated at the beginning of this study).

In fact, the author of this dilemma is the pre-Socratic Xenophanes of Colophon, well known for his biting critique of the theology of Homer, a critique that the Christians would also use to their advantage. It was an apothegm to which the earliest witness was Aristotle, who saw it as an illustration of a certain rhetorical procedure: "To the people of Eleus who asked whether or not they should offer a sacrifice to Leucothea and mourn her death, Xenophanes counseled that if they thought her a goddess, they should not mourn her, but, if they thought her a woman, they should not sacrifice to her." We are certainly in the presence of the antithesis between divinity and humanity and, in parallel fashion, between a religious cult and mourning; lacking, however, are two elements which are characteristic of the text cited by Clement—i.e., that there the remark is addressed to the Egyptians, and that there the dilemma is altered by a form of chiasmus. But these differences disappear in another tradition of the sayings of Xenophanes, attested by Plutarch: "Xenophanes of Colophon was thus right to judge that the Egyptians, if they believed in the gods, should not mourn their death, but that if they did mourn them, they should not believe them to be gods" (the texts of Aristotle and Plutarch—and two other analogous texts, also by Plutarch—may be found in H. Diels and W. Kranz, *Die Fragmente der Vorsokratiker,* 6th ed. [Berlin, 1951], vol. 1, p. 115; see also p. 180, in which the same apothegm is attributed by an ancient author, aberrantly, to Heraclitus). So it was in the version known to Plutarch that the saying of the pre-Socratic reached Clement of Alexandria and his successors. This episode illustrates the skill with which the Christian apologists often use the Greek philosophers themselves to refute the theology of paganism: they hasten to Euhemerus for demonstration that the gods are deceased men, in other words, they think, false gods. And if anyone should be tempted to take this kind of divinization seriously and to believe that those lamented dead have become real gods (it is improbable but not impossible that such was the personal opinion of Euhemerus), then the apologists call on Xenophanes to support their assertion that one cannot mourn a dead man and worship a god in the same person.

J.P./d.w.

NOTES

1. G. NÉMETHY, *Euhemeri reliquiae* (Budapest 1889).

2. G. VALLAURI, *Evemero di Messene* (Turin 1956).

3. F. JACOBY, "Euemeros," 3, in Pauly-Wissowa, *Real-Encyclopädie,* vol. 11 (1907): 952–72. Jacoby also compiled a collection of *testimonia* concerning, and fragments of, Euhemerus (in which, unfortunately, many of the texts are mentioned instead of being cited in full) in his monumental work *Die Fragmente der griechischen Historiker* (Berlin 1923), under no. 63, vol. 1:300–313.

4. P. DECHARME, *La critique des traditions religieuses chez les Grecs, des origines au temps de Plutarque* (Paris 1904); on Euhemerus and Euhemerism, 371–93.

5. A. B. DRACHMANN, *Atheism in Pagan Antiquity* (London, Copenhagen, and Christiania 1922), 111–13.

6. G. VALLAURI, *Origine e diffusione dell'evemerismo nel pensiero classico* (Turin 1960).

7. W. SPOERRI, *Späthellenistische Berichte über Welt, Kultur und Götter: Untersuchungen zu Diodor von Sizilien* (Basel 1959).

8. F. ZUCKER, "Euhemeros und seine *hiera anagraphē* bei den christlichen Schriftstellern," *Philologus* 64 (1905): 465–72.

9. K. THRAEDE, "Euhemerismus," in *Reallexikon für Antike und Christentum* (1966), 6:877–90.

10. J. W. SCHIPPERS, *De Ontwikkeling der Euhemeristische Godencritiek in de Christelijke Latijnse Literatuur* (diss., Utrecht; Groningen 1952). For the euhemerism of the Latin Fathers, essentially Arnobius and Lactantius, see G. L. Ellspermann, *The Attitude of the Early Christian Latin Writers toward Pagan Literature and Learning* (Washington 1949), 58–59 and 72–74.

11. J. PÉPIN, *Mythe et allégorie: Les origines grecques et les contestations judéo-chrétiennes* (2d ed., Paris 1976), index I, see "Evhémère."

12. J. D. COOKE, "Euhemerism: A Mediaeval Interpretation of Classical Paganism," *Speculum* 2 (1927): 396–410.

13. P. ALPHANDÉRY, "L'evhémérisme et les débuts de l'histoire des religions au moyen âge," *Revue de l'histoire des religions* 109 (1934): 5–27.

14. J. SEZNEC, *The Survival of the Pagan Gods: An Essay on the Role of the Mythological Tradition in the Humanism and Art of the Renaissance,* Studies of the Warburg Institute, 11 (London 1940; Paris 1980), especially 13–18.

15. F. PFISTER, "Ein apokrypher Alexanderbrief: Der sogenannte Leon von Pella und die Kirchenväter," in *Mullus, Festschrift Th. Klauser* (Münster 1964), 291–97.

16. N. ZEEGERS-VANDER VORST, *Les citations des poètes grecs chez les apologistes chrétiens du IIe siècle* (Louvain 1972), 103–4.

17. M. MINUCII FELICIS, *Octavius,* con introd. e commento di M. Pellegrino (Turin 1947).

18. M. ELIADE, *The Myth of the Eternal Return, or Cosmos and History* (Princeton 1954), 27.

19. ARNOBIUS OF SICCA, *The Case against the Pagans,* translated and annotated by G. E. McCracken, 2 vols. (Westminster, MD, 1949), 2:583–84.

20. E. ZUCKER, *Spuren von Apollodoros peri theōn,* bei christlichen Schriftstellern der ersten fünf Jahrhunderte (diss., Munich; Nuremberg 1904).

21. J. GEFFCKEN, *Zwei griechische Apologeten* (Leipzig and Berlin 1907), pp. XVII and 225–26; on the dilemma of Xenophanes in Athenagoras, p. 225.

22. M. TULLUS CICERO, *De natura deorum,* A. S. Pease, ed., 2 vols. (Cambridge, MA, 1955; 2d ed., Darmstadt 1968), 1:263–64.

23. JULIUS FIRMICUS MATERNUS *De errore profanarum religionum,* a cura di A. Pastorino (Florence 1956), 116.

24. JULIUS FIRMICUS MATERNUS, *De errore profanarum religionum,* G. Heuten, trans. (Brussels 1938), 64 and 161–62.

CHRISTIANITY AND MYTHOLOGY IN THE GREEK CHURCH

By the year 313, when the Edict of Milan marked a decisive rapprochement between the Roman Empire and the Church, the Church already had behind it two centuries of existence at the heart of a Hellenism which had itself been drawn into the flow of history during that time. To be sure, that ancient religious system was still in place, under the benevolent aegis of the reigning power and elites and in the collective conservation of tradition. The place and times of rites persisted, with their developments, their mythic justifications punctuated by major or minor names from the classical pantheon. This picture, however, needs some important retouchings. The first is the increasing attraction of sources of wisdom attributed to the East. These initiate one into paths to a happy personal and stellar immortality, founded on terrestrial asceticism, and are placed under the patronage

Saint George killing the dragon. Sculpture on two panels of pine. Nicosia, Cyprus Folk Art Museum. Museum photo.

of long adopted exotic gods and goddesses such as Isis, or, at least, gods renewed by exoticism such as the Egyptian Thoth-Hermes. Next, there is the flowering, on various levels, of symbolic speculations fueled by the Greek myths, portrayals of episodes invested with new hope (such as the labors of Hercules on sarcophagi, or the flight of the Dioscuri on the subterranean vault of the Porta Maggiore in Rome), as well as the extensive philosophical constructions of a Plotinus in the third century. In such a perspective, one is confronted less by the continuity of ancient mythology than by the fabrication of a contemporary mythology in the second and third centuries, produced by imperial Hellenism in response to the questions of the time. The ancient traditions and their symbolic interpretations are combined with borrowings of varying antiquity from cultures bearing little or none of the stamp of Hellenism from the Roman or Persian East. Among these cultures is Judaism in its diverse currents, which at that time was elaborating its theory of angels and defining the figure of Satan, itself undergoing influences from Persia. This was also the time when an obsession with demons, invisible and omnipresent assailants, was developing, an obsession that Christianity would claim for its own from the very start. Finally, the myths taught in the Gnostic sects, of which some existed within Christianity itself, are perhaps the most striking monument to the powers of invention that were manifesting themselves at the time. These would have a medieval posterity of their own.

It was in this cultural context that the young Christian Church had to find its place. An Origen or a Clement of Alexandria were deeply imbued, on a philosophical level, with the very culture they found so easy to combat on a literally narrative or naively ritual level. This leads to an essential, secular ambiguity. The Byzantine elite, whether or not it was of the Church, would not abandon the philosophical approach, the rhetorical discipline, and the literary baggage of ancient Hellenism: the teaching it received assured its cultural preservation, with greater or lesser success from one period to another, and its distinctive social value remained intact as a result. On the other hand, Hellenic Christianity as a whole integrated into its new faith those traditions whose function remained necessary, such as the annual cycle of festivals. As a result, the encounter of the Eastern Church with the complex mythology that existed around the year 313 is not an encounter between a scholarly culture and a popular culture, but rather the beginning of a thousand-year coexistence of cultural practices at different levels of society and different levels of consciousness, levels whose respective scope and depth would vary according to the efficacy of the official repression imposed upon the ancient religion.

We may thus pass quite quickly over the well-known dates and facts that serve as landmarks in the battle against the old gods carried out publicly in the fourth century by the Church, which was associated with the ruling power except during the short restoration under Julian (361–363). The repression that had begun with Constantine reached its official end with the general prohibition against the ancient religion proclaimed by Theodosius I in 392. Nevertheless, the reign of Justinian I (527–565) was still marked by the confiscation of sanctuary properties and the prohibition of teaching by pagans. And although Bishop Porphyry tore down the sanctuary of Marneion of Gaza at the end of the fourth century, the last internal missions, notably those in the mountains of Asia Minor, were established around 542, and the last matters involving personalities of the capital, including the patriarch himself, occurred around 570. The whole of the sixth century is still marked by skirmishes that erupt in the cities on the days on which the old festivals, the *Vota* and *Bromalia,* provoke excitement. The seventh century marks the real threshold, for in Byzantium this was the period of invasions perpetrated by peoples who were in every way non-Christian—Arabs, Avars, and Slavs. The result is a definitive identification between the Christian cause and that of the political Roman-ness of Hellenic culture. In 626, the Virgin appears on the walls of the capital under siege by the Avars and their troops, and saves it. The historical data of Christian Hellenism are complete thenceforth and for all time.

The realm of Christian Hellenism would be immense if it were defined as that of churches born, directly or indirectly, of the Eastern Roman Empire, from Alexandria to Kiev and Moscow, from the Caucasus to the Balkans. We thus focus on lands which remained, for all intents and purposes, Hellenic in language and, at least predominantly, Hellenic in culture—for to venture further, especially into Slavic lands, would be to pursue the identical Christianization of too different a substratum. Delimited in this way, the history of Christian Hellenism presents three great continuities on three cultural levels: the elite, the Church, and the Christian people.

Most manifest is the great secular culture of an elite in which service to the State is closely associated with service to the Church: both are taught at the same desks, and in a language whose mythological allusion remains a sign of recognition all the more appreciable for the fact that it is scholarly. To be sure, the formalism of an Agathias, in the century of Justinian, is not the scholarship of a Photius in the ninth century, nor the classical mastery of Psellus and his friends in the following period. But literary references to mythology adorn even sacred speeches, even episcopal correspondence, and even a Life of a saint of the eleventh or twelfth century that likens the struggle of the missionary saint Nikon in the region of Sparta to the labors of Hercules. In the same way, though to a lesser degree, the iconographic setting of secular life draws on the ancient repertory. The Neoplatonist current flows without interruption from Plotinus, from Proclus and the Athenian Academy of the fifth century, to the philosophers of the capital of the eleventh century, and finally to Mistra and the person of Georgius Gemistus Plethon as the empire dragged to its close and the Renaissance dawned. There was always a very fine line, right down to ideas which were suspect and subject to prosecution, as in the case of John "The Grammarian" and of Leo the Philosopher in the ninth century, the difficulties experienced by Michael Psellus, the accusations he himself made against the patriarch Michael Cerularius, and the trials of John Italos in the eleventh century. It is difficult to plumb the depth of the temptations thus denounced. But it must not be forgotten that people like Psellus and, it would seem, Cerularius drew from ancient Hellenism more than merely the forms and ideas of that great cultural tradition. They were also nourished with its obscure and dangerous curiosities, and recovered from it the magical or divinatory practices which the end of antiquity had developed against demons—for demons continued to offer the same face to people of the eleventh century, arousing in them the same obsession.

The greatest source of information on the relations of the Greek Church and its people with Hellenic mythology is to be found not here but in the documents written by clerical or monastic scribes. Such information thus has a twofold application, to the practices of the Christian people but first and foremost to the clerics themselves. We find it in accounts of martyrs (increasingly flamboyant in more recent periods), in the Lives of the saints (which range from quite fictional works of spiritual edification to biography), in the observations and interdictions of Church councils (of which the most significant takes place in 692), and in the commentaries of later canonists. Finally, liturgical books, notably those of southern Italy, like the collections of magic formulas that continue an earlier tradition, throw light on the marginal areas in which the Church accepts and absorbs the practices of its people, and in which Christianity imprints its own forms on ancient responses. With the end of the Middle Ages, ordinary ecclesiastical culture ceases to constitute a distinct and significant stratum, and the distance between the observer and the observed collectivity reaches its present dimension. Such is the case with Leo Allatius (1586–1669); a Uniate Greek born on Chios who settled in Rome, he left an important testimony within the framework of his work in favor of a union of the churches. In the nineteenth century, with the national self-reassertion of Greece and the general renewal of the study of ancient Hellenism, Christian Greek culture was scrutinized in a search for continuity. Information collected at the end of the nineteenth century and the beginning of the twentieth century is thus attributable to Greek or foreign scholars, who came for different reasons to a single path, the quest for the ancient stratum of contemporary Greek culture. The first of these scholars were mobilized by the fundamental debate provoked by the assertions of Fallmerayer (1842) on the historical rupture inflicted upon the populations of Greece by the medieval influx of Slavs. The next group left their libraries and universities to search in the field for still living traces of ancient Hellenism. All of these enterprises put together a mass of data in which the survival of ancient Hellenism naturally occupies an important position. Although marred by an overly vertical penetration downward through historical strata, the data nevertheless make possible a better method for analyzing the religious system into which Christianity and the vestiges of the ancient cults were integrated. We thus remain in the direct line of our medieval sources, and can verify their correctness.

There is certainly a continuity between the medieval sources and contemporary observations, and its course may be traced back to antiquity. Yet the true extent of this continuity must be appreciated. The most immutable grounding, and undoubtedly the oldest even with regard to the ancient religion, is that of the calendar, the annual cycle of festivals. The council held in 692 in the capital to extirpate the heretical contagion, whether Judaizing or Hellenic, still fully recognizes the ancient rituals in the traditional festivities that mark the year: the Calends of January 1st, the *Vota* of the 6th, the *Bromalia* of November-December, and March 1st. The council condemns the wild dancing that drives women out into the streets, encourages costumes and masques, and is performed, according to the Fathers, in the name of the false gods of the Greeks (i.e., the pagans). The Fathers refrain from naming these gods, with one exception: their explicit prohibition against proclaiming the name of the "infamous Dionysus" while trampling grapes in the press. The hagiography of Steven the Younger, martyred in 764 for his defense of icons, gives his date of death as November 28th—the day on which the iconoclastic emperor, by his own testimony hardened in his Hellenism (i.e., paganism), celebrates the *Bromalia,* proclaiming the names of Dionysus and Bromius, the fathers of seed grains and wine. Commenting on these canons in the twelfth century, Theodorus Balsamon asserts that the practices they condemn have not yet disappeared. Demetrius Chomatianus, archbishop of Achrida at the beginning of the thirteenth century, mentions the same festivities while also giving details about the *Rousalia* carnival, which Balsamon indicated as a practice found on the borders of the Empire. This immemorial cycle, in which the dead and living take part in the succession of the agrarian seasons, persists in the Greek islands today. Its culminating periods are the Twelve Days that separate Christmas from the Epiphany, the three weeks of Carnival (during which the pantomimes of the Kalogheroi reproduce an archaic Dionysian ritual of death and resurrection), Saint George's Day in April (a festival of shepherds, like the ancient Parilia), Pentecost in its connection with the dead, and the night of Saint John in June. The sites bear witness to the same permanence, especially the sanctuaries dedicated to Christian saints to which people still come in search of healing, most often through the ancient ritual of spending the night there (incubation): the practice is attested to without a break through the medieval and modern periods.

This victorious perenniality was bought at the price of the almost total obliteration of the names of the gods themselves. At the beginning of the Greek Middle Ages, a lesser power, often malevolent, doomed to defeat in the end but uncontested in the present, was the lingering sign of the old gods in the Hellenic Christian consciousness (starting with that of the clergy itself). But the names of those gods were quickly repudiated, which is equally significant; the council of 692 passed over their names in silence in reference to their festivals, but also in the important and oft-renewed prohibition against ancient forms of oath-taking and especially of divination. In the stories of martyrs composed after the triumph of the Church, the gods are named wrongly, or driven into anonymity. These tales recount the victory of their hero over the Hellenic gods his persecutor has ordered him to worship, gods whose statues crumble to dust at the invocation of a Christian. The designation of the gods shows to what extent their memory had become blurred in the mind of the ordinary cleric. Sometimes a single god, such as Apollo, is designated as superior to all the others. Sometimes they are degraded collectively as anonymous "demons." In the same vein, the Lives of the saints up to the sixth century relate militant episodes of destruction of local sanctuaries. But in the same period, and even later, they also evoke victories over demons of the countryside, phantoms without name or any semblance of a condemned past (as pagan gods), who perch in trees or lurk in isolated tombs or ancient ruins. The action taken by the Church thus represented the other side of a general belief that it shared, and with which it was imbued, at both a popular and a local level, even in its own ritual: an example is the late repertory of Italo-Greek prayers preserved in a sixteenth-century manuscript, which continues to place demons that are to be avoided in trees and ancient tombs, as well as at crossroads—while references to names drawn from the ancient repertory remain insignificant, especially in proportion to those of a Judaizing tinge, such as are found especially in amulet texts. Dionysus constituted a lasting exception. One should not, however, succumb to the nineteenth-century authors' obsession with explicit ancient lineages, such as the story of Saint Diony-s(i)us who brought the first vine stock to Naxos, or the story of Saint Demetra, honored at Eleusis, and of her daughter ravished by a Turkish magician, and of the young man who would go to her rescue. Whatever interest these tales may hold, they are perhaps less significant than the survival of Charon, of the bogey-woman Gyllu, or of the troop of Nereids. It should be noted that the aquatic and sylvan seductresses recur in Slavic folklore, and that the Slavic presence or influence in Hellenic territory is hardly taken into account by Fallmerayer's adversaries.

Elijah in his chariot of fire. 1655. Amberg-Herzog collection. Geneva, Musée d'Art et d'Histoire de Genève. Museum photo.

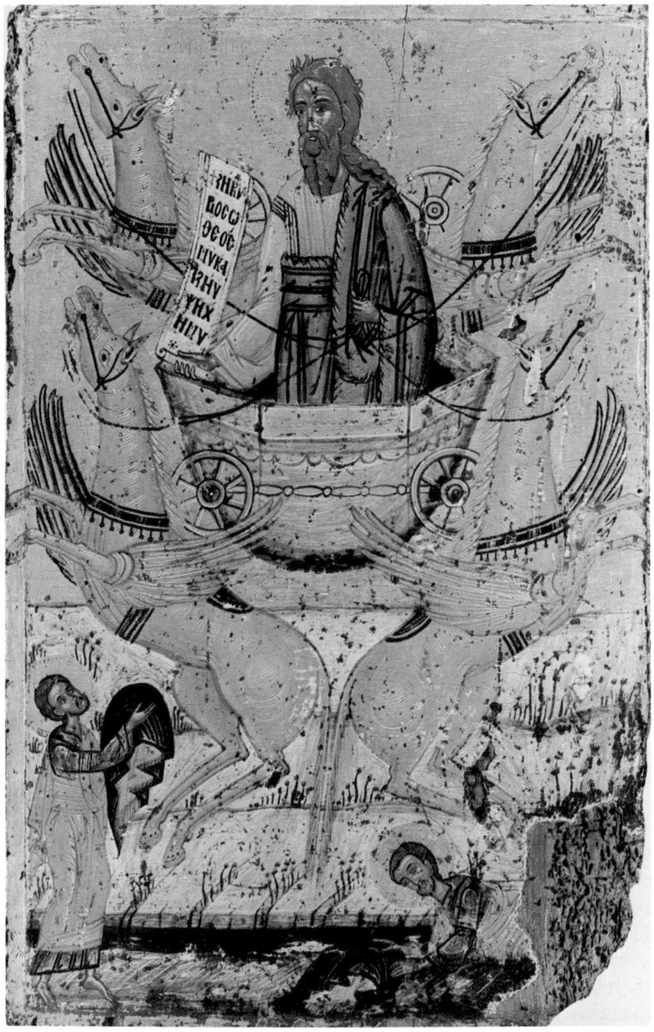

Christian Hellenism, then, did not forget the ancient religious strand but eclipsed the names of the gods under whose patronage the old rituals were performed and, by that act, dissolved the mythic accounts that explained those rituals. Does this mean that Christian Hellenism was bereft of a mythology? The question primarily involves a portion of the ancient heritage which is not that of classical or Romanized Hellenism, but that of Gnosticism. Its medieval posterity in Byzantium—the Paulicians and Bogomils—preserve or enrich the myths about Creation, the first man, and the role of Satan in the created world. The cults of the saints and of the Virgin are more difficult to analyze.

The first answers, formulated at the turn of the twentieth century, proposed direct and simple identifications, of the "Mithra = Saint George" type. But such identifications do not stand up to examination. First of all, they can never be justified by an exhaustive and point-for-point coincidence; their authors tied them hastily to various partial similarities, places of worship, attributes, and festival dates. Next, and more important, this collection of facts, however interesting it may be, has never accounted for the initial and major innovation developed by Christianity, which is the cult devoted to the saints, to their living person, to their tomb, to their images, and, in a comparable fashion, to the Virgin. Hence, the temple of Athena Parthenos became a church of the Virgin; shepherds celebrated Saint George's Day on a date which was more or less that of the Parilia; Saint Elijah, whose festival day falls in July, exercises from the heights of the hills an atmospheric power that justifies his biblical assumption but also recalls that of Zeus and of Helios; Saint Michael took Hermes' role as conductor of souls to the afterworld. But all of this is secondary. What must first be analyzed is the constitution of a network of supernatural mediators—nearly all, reputedly, of human birth, but of whom the most widely honored nevertheless have no history, nor even any legend, apart from the collection of their miracles; it is a repertory of rites of supplication, of the motifs and mechanics of these miracles. Research needs to be undertaken starting from local data. It will thus be found that the saints offer no myths, new or old—if the term "myth" is taken to mean an account which is at once explanatory and reversible—but merely fragments of earlier myths, as well as fragments of rituals, some more coherent than others. To go beyond this would mean questioning the whole history of the Christian religion.

E.P./d.w.

BIBLIOGRAPHY

1. General History

K. S. LATOURETTE, *A History of the Expansion of Christianity* (London 1947), vols. 1–2. G. OSTROGORSKY, *A History of the Byzantine Empire* (Oxford 1968). A. PIGANIOL, *L'Empire chrétien,* new ed. by A. CHASTAGNOL (Paris 1972). E. STEIN, *Histoire du Bas Empire,* vol. 1: *A.D. 284–476* (Paris 1959); vol. 2: *A.D. 476–585* (Paris 1949). A. E. VACALOPOULOS, *The Greek Nation, 1453–1669: The Cultural and Economic Background of Modern Greek Society* (New Brunswick, NJ, 1976).

2. History of Culture

a) General Studies

H. G. BECK, *Kirche und theologische Literatur im byzantinischen Reich* (Munich 1959). J. GOUILLARD, *Le Synodikon de l'Orthodoxie,* Centre de rech. d'hist. et civil. byzant., Travaux et mémoires 2 (1967): 1–316. J. M. HUSSEY, *Church and Learning in the Byzantine Empire, 867–1185* (Oxford and London 1937). P. LEMERLE, *Le premier humanisme byzantin: Notes et remarques sur enseignement et culture à Byzance des origines au Xe siècle* (Paris 1971).

b) The End of Antiquity

J. CARCOPINO, *La basilique pythagoricienne de la Porte Majeure* (Paris 1927). F. CUMONT, *Recherches sur le symbolisme funéraire des Romains* (Paris 1942). A.-J. FESTUGIÈRE, *La révélation d'Hermès Trismégiste,* 4 vols. (Paris 1944–54). J. GEFFCKEN, *Der Ausgang des griechisch-römischen Heidentums* (Heidelberg 1920). H. JONAS, *The Gnostic Religion* (2d ed., Boston 1963; reissued 1970). W. E. KAEGI, "The Fifth-Century Twilight of Byzantine Paganism," *Classica Medievalia* 27 (1966): 243–75. M. MESLIN, *La fête des Kalendes de janvier dans l'Empire romain: Étude d'un rituel de Nouvel An* (Brussels 1970). A. MOMIGLIANO, ed., *The Conflict between Paganism and Christianity in the Fourth Century* (Oxford 1963). A. MOMIGLIANO, "Popular Religious Beliefs and the Late Roman Historians," *Studies in Church History* 8 (1971): 1–18. R. REITZENSTEIN, *Poimandres: Studien zur griechisch-ägyptischen und frühchristlichen Literatur* (Leipzig 1904).

c) Aspects of Byzantine Neoplatonism

A. H. ARMSTRONG, ed., *Cambridge History of Later Greek and Early Medieval Philosophy* (Cambridge 1967). A. CAMERON, "The Last Days of the Academy at Athens," *Proceeds. Cambridge Philol. Society* 145 (1969): 7–29. J. GOUILLARD, *La religion des philosophes,* Centre de rech. d'hist. et civil. byzant., Travaux et mémoires 6 *(Recherches sur le XIe siècle)* (1976): 305–24. F. MASAI, *Pléthon et le platonisme de Mistra* (Paris 1956).

d) Myths of Heresy

G. FICKER, *Die Phundagiagiten* (Leipzig 1908). M. LOOS, "Certains aspects du bogomilisme byzantin des XIe et XIIe siècles," *Byzantinoslavica* 28 (1967): 39–53; "Satan als erstgeborener Gottes: Ein Beitrag zur Analyse des bogomilischen Mythus," *Byzantino-Bulgarica* 3 (1969): 23–35.

3. Beliefs and Rituals

a) Sources Mentioned

Council of 692: text in F. LAUCHERT, *Die Kanones der wichtigsten altkirchlichen Concilien nebst den apostolischen Kanones* (Freiburg and Leipzig 1896), 97–139; comm. of Theodore Balsamon, *Patrol. Graeca,* vol. 137 passim.

Life of Stephen the Younger, in *Patrol. Graeca,* vol. 100, 1069–1186. DEMETRIOS CHOMATIANOS, J. Pitra, ed., *Analecta* 6 (1891): 509–10ff. MICHEL PSELLOS, "Accusation du patriarche Michel Cérulaire devant le synode," L. BRÉHIER, ed., *Rev. Et. Grecques* 16 (1903): 375–416; 17 (1904): 35–76.

Prayers, amulets, exorcisms: F. PRADEL, *Griechische und süditalienische Gebete, Beschwörungen und Rezepte des Mittelalters* (Giessen 1907). A. A. VASILIEV, *Anecdota graeco-byzantina,* vol. 1 (Moscow 1893).

b) Studies

S. P. KYRIAKIDES, *Two Studies on Modern Greek Folklore* (Salonika 1968). J. C. LAWSON, *Modern Greek Folklore and Ancient Greek Religion: A Study in Survivals* (1910), reprint with foreword by A. N. OIKONOMIDES (New York 1964). G. MEGAS, *Greek Calendar Customs* (Athens 1958). N. G. POLITIS, *Meletē epi tou biou tōn neōterōn Hellēnōn* (Essay on the life of the modern Greeks) (Athens 1871–74). B. SCHMIDT, *Das Volksleben der Neugriechen und das hellenische Altertum* (Leipzig 1871). K. SVOBODA, "La démonologie de Michel Psellos" (diss., Brno 1927).

4. Cult of the Saints

a) General Studies

P. BROWN, "The Rise and Function of the Holy Man in Late Antiquity," *Journ. Rom. Studies* 61 (1971): 80–101. P. E. LUCIUS and G. ANRICH, *Die Anfänge des Heilgenkults in der Christlichen Kirche* (Tübingen 1904); also in French.

b) Particular Studies

G. ANRICH, *Haghios Nikolaos,* 2 vols. (Berlin 1913). J. B. AUFHAUSER, "Das Drachenwunder des Hl. Georg in der griechischen und lateinischen Überlieferung," *Byzant. Archiv.* 5 (1911). A. D. DE GROOT, *Saint Nicholas: A Psychoanalytic Study of His History and Myth* (The Hague 1965). S. GEORGOUDI, "Sant'Elia in Grecia," *Studi e Materiali di Storia delle Religioni* 39 (1968): 293–319. K. KRUMBACHER, *Der heilige Georg in der griechischen Überlieferung* (Munich 1911). *Millénaire monastique du Mont Saint-Michel,* 3: *Culte de Saint Michel et pèlerinage au Mont,* M. Baudot, ed. (Paris 1971). W. VON RINTELEN, *Kultgeographische Studien in der Italia Byzantina: Untersuchungen über die Kulte des Erzengels Michael und der Madonna di Costantinopoli in Süditalien* (Meisenheim 1968).

The Naassenes' Use of Pagan Mythologies

Known only from the account in the *Elenchos* (V, 6, 1–10, 2), the Naassenes never went by that name, which was invented by some polemicist who wanted people to believe that they were worshipers of the snake (*naḥaš* in Hebrew), like those who were called Ophites in Greek and *Ḥēwē* in Syriac. They referred to themselves as Gnostics, as we learn from several passages (V, 2, p. 77, 4–5 Wendland; V, 6, 4, p. 77, 30–78, 1; V, 11, p. 104, 4–5). Two of the sacred writings they used were the *Gospel according to the Egyptians* (V, 7, 9) and the *Gospel according to Thomas* (V, 7, 20), the first belonging to the pagan branch of Gnosticism, the second to a primitive literary form of Christian Gnosis. That they were connected, as has also been pointed out (V, 7, 20), with the apostolic tradition of James, "brother of the Lord," transmitted to Mariamme (Mary Magdalene), is a conventional argument added by the Christian editor of the pamphlet used by the polemicist in composing his account of the Naassenes. The document of pagan Gnosis that underlies it may go as far back as the waning of the first century B.C. The title of this earlier document as well as that of its reinterpretation, which has come down to us, remain unknown. In the eyes of the Eastern author of the *Elenchos* compilation, the absurdity of this particular form of Gnosis comes from the systematic use of "Greek and barbarian" pagan mythology (V, 7, 1, p. 79, 3–5), these two denominations designating a Gnostic interpretation—through the language of mysteries—of myths that Greek esotericism attributed to the Assyrians, Egyptians, and Phrygians.

In this type of pagan Gnosis, reinterpreted in the Christian manner, the primordial man, Adamas, defined the principle of the universe as one because it was male, and as triple because it was composed of breath (spirit), soul, and earth. Breath and earth have a precise status, above and below, male and female. But what is this soul, which occupies the intermediary position? The essence of Gnosis was to answer this question. The median position of the soul, the passage that each being had to make, descending toward existences and rising again toward being, makes the soul the principle of becoming; it is Phusis, the universal cosmic nature, the Gnostic replica of the Platonic Soul of the world.

The Naassenes' interpretation of the three myths of Adonis, Endymion, and Attis allows us to determine the soul's status precisely. Because Adonis means both the desire of the soul to tend toward generation and its withdrawal toward death through its inability to procreate, the soul is at once fertile and infertile, Aphrodite and Persephone (Kore). Endymion, the beloved of Selene (the moon), expresses the desire of the beings from above to unite with the male beauty of the soul. Rhea, the mother of the gods, castrating her lover Attis, shows symbolically that the spiritual part of the soul, the object of Selene's desire, is the original and heavenly element that comes from Adamas and is thus intellectual and male because it rejects the perceptible, which is both inferior and female. The three myths complement each other and must be read together. The sterility of the soul—its Persephone side—is what relates it to the material of the bodies in which it is held prisoner; the fertility of the soul—its Aphrodite side—is what allows it to initiate the chain of life of those who exist and, after that, to rejoin and conjoin its origin.

All that is retained from the myth of Isis and Osiris, the "Egyptian" version of the "Assyrian" myth of Attis, is the sequence dealing with Isis's search for the sexual organ of Osiris. Isis is dressed in seven black robes, for which there is a triple interpretation. The first is astrological: the seven robes of Isis designate the realm of nature (*phusis*) and of generation (*genesis*), governed by the world of planets in a state of perpetual movement and change. The second is cosmological: Osiris is the symbol of water or "the seminal substance," the first element of life and of becoming. And the third is liturgical: the sexual organ of Osiris, lost and found again, henceforth naked, erect, and crowned with fruit in temples and on streets and paths, evokes the initiation ritual of the soul, which is first abandoned and then returned unto itself, made fertile through identification with its original male principle.

Hermes with his erect sexual organ, interpreter of the gods, psychopomp, holding sway over time, in opposition to the dividing and separating word of the demiurge Ialdabaoth, represents the function of a Logos that succeeds in achieving communication, a Logos of revelation because it allows a descent from above to the realm below, a Logos of redemption because it achieves the passage of the souls from the country of death—Egypt or the Ocean—to the mother earth of the living—Jerusalem or Jordan—that is, from the mixed world, which is inferior and material, to the unified world, which is superior and spiritual.

This passage marks the end of the soul's wandering, the moment when "the unfortunate one [the soul] whose wanderings have led it into a labyrinth of ills" (V, 10, 2, p. 103, 10–11) has reached its celestial homeland. Its primitive unity restored, the soul belongs henceforth to the "kingless race" of those who have definitively broken with the world of forms and appearances. This state of beatitude, characteristic of the perfect possessor of Gnosis, is described in a series of images borrowed from the hierogamic ritual of the mysteries of Cybele: the drunkenness from the cup of Anacreon, a cup filled with wine from the wedding at Cana; statues from the temple of Samothrace, with hands raised and sexual organ erect, symbolizing the plenitude of the inner kingdom where all androgyny disappears in the identification with the primordial being; an allegorical interpretation, in the homiletic style, of a hymn in which all the names of Attis are proclaimed: Adonis, Osiris, Mene-Selene, Adamna, Corybas, Papas, the corpse (*nekus*), the god, the fruitless one (*akarpos*), the goatherd, the harvested ear of corn, and the fluteplayer born of an almond. Each of these terms is explained in detail and is applied to the Gnostic, who has in a sense become initiated into the mysteries and is the seer of his own essence. In this Eleusis of the world above, the Gnostic regards himself as an initiate and as Demeter's husband, stripped of all his clothes and then reclothed, at once virginal, because the hemlock made him into a eunuch, and fertile, because he wears the yellow, harvested ear of corn, in other words because he has assimilated the immeasurable fertility that comes from the castration of Attis: "I will sing of Attis, the son of Rhea, not to the thin sound of little bells, nor to the languishing flute of the Curetes of Mount Ida, but with the song of Phoebus's lyres I will mingle my cries of Evoe Evan! For he is Pan, he is Bacchus, he is the shepherd of the shining stars."

Such language harks back to a liturgical practice in the tradition of Greek mysteries that was in active use in an ancient pagan form of Gnosis, and was later reused in a purely fictitious way by the Christian author of the Gnostic pamphlet attributed to supposed Naassenes.

M.T./g.h.

BIBLIOGRAPHY

R. REITZENSTEIN, *Zwei religionsgeschichtliche Fragen* (Strasbourg 1901), 95–96; *Poimandres* (Leipzig 1904), 81–102. W. BOUSSET, *Hauptprobleme der Gnosis* (Göttingen 1907), 183–86. R. REITZENSTEIN and H.-H. SCHAEDER, *Studien zum antiken Synkretismus aus Iran und Griechenland* (Leipzig and Berlin 1926), 104–73. R. P. CASEY, "Naassenes and Ophites," *Journal of Theological Studies* 27 (1926): 374–87. A. D. NOCK, "Iranian Influences in Greek Thought," *Journal of Hellenic Studies* 49 (1929) = *Essays on Religion and the Ancient World*, Z. Stewart, ed. (Oxford 1972), 200–201. M. SIMONETTI, "Qualche osservazione sulle presunte interpolazioni della Predica del Naasseni," *Vetera Christianorum* 7 (1970): 115–24. TH. WOLBERGS, *Griechische religiöse Gedichte der ersten nachchristlichen Jahrhunderte* (Meisenheim 1971), 1:37–82; to be completed by A. Kehl, *Jahrbuch für Antike und Christentum* 15 (1972): 95–101.

The Gnostics and the Mythologies of Paganism

At first sight, the pagan heritage of the Gnostics appears less monolithic than their Christian adversaries would have it. The constant accusation brought against them of having systematically transposed the gods and myths of the Greeks with the help of "barbarian names" is an all-purpose argument that proves nothing. To show, for example, that Valentinus is nothing but a vulgar imitator of Hesiod, Epiphanius points out the parallels between the ordering into syzygies of the set of thirty aeons of the Valentinian pleroma, which are born of the Abyss (Bythos), and a series of entities of the *Theogony* born of Chaos, which are also set up in opposing pairs and reduced for practical purposes to thirty in number (see *Panarion* 31.2.4–4.9). In fact, only the parallel between the Valentinian Bythos and the Hesiodic Chaos is operative; all the rest is artificial.

From their self-proclaimed proofs that Gnosticism was merely camouflaged paganism, searching, according to the formula of Irenaeus, to "adapt to myths the sayings (*logia*) of God" (*Adversus Haer.* 1.8.1 = Epiphanus, *Panarion* 31.24.6), the heresiologists drew the conclusion that the practices of the Gnostics were as contrary to the ethos of Christianity as their thought was to the "orthodoxy." And now the Gnostics are accused pell-mell of eating meat consecrated to idols, of participating in the festivals and games of the pagans, of practicing adultery and incest (Irenaeus, *Adversus Haer.* 1.6.3 = Epiphanius, *Panarion* 31.21.1–6), of organizing, under the cover of sacred rituals, carousings, drinking parties, orgies, abortions, and manducations of sperm, menstrual blood, and fetuses (Epiphanius, *Panarion* 26.4.3–5.8)! These facts were manifestly evoked to prove that deliquescent thought and dissolute practice go hand in hand.

In fact, the paganism of the Gnostics is not to be found where the Church Fathers placed it. It does exist, but elsewhere. Documents on the subject, which came to Europe in the eighteenth and nineteenth centuries or were discovered after the Second World War near Nag Hammadi, show it to be subtler than what was presented by the authors of heresy catalogs, who were eager to drive out those who contested from within, and more compact than is admitted by modern critics, whose knowledge is clouded by Jewish sources alone, following a long, fruitless search in the direction of Babylon or Iran for an explanatory frame-myth. As it appears to those who read the Gnostics' texts today and are familiar with what the Gnostics themselves read, the paganism of the Gnostics, who were more or less Christianized, is linked to the powerful influence exerted on their thinking by the literary, ideological, and practical models of the magical papyruses, of Hermeticism, of Middle Platonism, and of the Mystery religions.

As for the gods of paganism themselves, those who were taken back and integrated by the Gnostics into their own pantheon were adopted in order to feed the Gnostic astrological demonology and Platonizing panallegorism. They were transformed in both cases, either into planetary categories of fate as among the Astrologers, or into figures of the wandering and saved soul as among the Platonists. The Gnostic interpretation of the gods and myths of paganism is thus founded upon the interpretation that was operative in the popular and scholarly philosophy of their time. But only rarely did they reproduce it as such; most often they brought to it an increase of signification, even as they tried to compress myth to the utmost. The Gnostic reading of the myth of the phoenix remains a good example of this method (see *Revue de l'Histoire des Religions* 183 [1973]:117–42).

Another example is the Gnostic habit of attributing to the planetary entities of paganism the status and role of the angels in the Jewish demonology of the apocalypses. Already reduced to an astral function by the Mathematicians, the Greek god as reused by the Gnostics gains a renewal of personality as the archon of intermediate space. In the description of the sphere of destiny that ends the *Pistis Sophia,* the five gods—Kronos, Ares, Hermes, Aphrodite, and Zeus—are appointed by Ieu to oversee all the archons of the cosmic system. Each of them bears a double name and is connected to a consort power; the one that belongs to Zeus, who is good, has the duty of holding the tiller of the world (p. 356, 2–357, 17 of the Coptic text, ed. Schmidt, Copenhagen 1925). This primary function of the guardians of the circular celestial motions enables the five planetary gods to be guides to souls after their death. Under the guidance of Hermes as psychopomp, they cause the soul to circle the earth three times, so that it can rejoice in the spectacle of creation; next they make it descend into the Amentos (Hades), so that it can be afflicted by the sight of the infernal fire; then they cause it to rise again to the "middle way," the sphere of destiny, in which the flame of punishment also burns; and finally it is led up to the Virgin of Light to be judged. Zeus and Aphrodite stand in front, Kronos and Ares behind. If the soul is needful of supplementary purification, it is then thrown into the water below the sphere, which is a boiling fire. Only after this ordeal may it drink of the cup of forgetfulness and the cup of sobriety, which cause it to enter a new and luminous body (p. 381, 24–383, 11 of the Coptic text). Among the Manichaeans, too, the luminaries become vehicles for souls, and Hermogenes makes the sun a refuge for resurrected bodies.

Paganism, while providing the soul with its escorts in the particular otherworldly zone in which they exert their authority, also provides it, more generally, with the images of its condition as a traveler who has left a far distant land to fall to this world below. In order to describe the fate of the wandering soul in search of its true homeland and delivered in this existence into the seductions and tribulations of the world, the Gnostics took up some of the allegories used by the Platonists in their own time. Two characters from Homer, Helen and Odysseus, were used as motifs for allegorical transpositions.

Held prisoner in Ilion (= matter), where she appears as a reflection (*eidōlon*) of the beauty of Hellas, her homeland, which is the intelligible world (see Hermias, *In Plat. Phaedrum,* p. 77, 13–78, 1 Couvreur), Helen incarnates, in a type of Christian Gnosis attributed to Simon Magus, the splendor of the first thought (*Ennoia-Epinoia*) of the intellect (*Nous*) of the Father. But she is also the lost lamb of the Gospel (Luke 15:4), wandering among the angels and the luminaries—her own creatures, who have forced her to live successive lives in the bodies of women. It is she who caused the Trojan War. The poet Stesichorus, who attacks her in his verse, goes blind; he recovers his sight while writing his *Palinodia.* Helen ends her long transmigration in a brothel in the city of Tyre in Phoenecia. It is there that Simon discovers her, and by means of a ransom he frees her from her bonds and marries her. They thus form, as a couple, "the perfect love," "the Holy of Holies," procuring salvation for humans through the revelation of Gnosis. The myth, told by Irenaeus (*Adv. Haer.* 1.23.2–3, pp. 191–93 Harvey) and his continuators (among others, *Elenchos* VI, 19, 1–7), rests upon a traditional mystic interpretation, from the late period, of the *Iliad* and the Trojan War: the kidnapping of Helen (= the divine part of the soul), torn from her own people and nostalgic for them, provokes a combat of powers, as a result of which this soul will be restored to its original homeland.

In a non-Gnostic work read by the Gnostics, which was discovered at Nag Hammadi (II, 6) and entitled *Exegesis on the Soul*, the tears of Odysseus, whom Aphrodite has deceived and brought to Calypso, express this same nostalgia for one's lost homeland: "No one is worthy of salvation if he still loves the place of his wanderings. This is why it is written by the poet, 'Odysseus sat on the island, prey to his tears and his sorrow; he turned his face from the words of Calypso and from her impostures; he wished to see his homeland and the smoke of its hearths and, above all, wished for the assistance of heaven to return to his homeland.' The soul, in turn, says, 'My man has turned away from me; I want to return once more to my homeland.' For the soul groaned, saying, 'It is Aphrodite who deceived me; she made me leave my homeland; I left my firstborn behind me, along with my husband who is good, wise, and handsome' " (p. 136, 25–137, 5). As a prisoner in a world subjected to the heavenly bodies and to fate (= Calypso, the daughter of Atlas) and trapped inside a body enslaved by sex (= Aphrodite), the soul will seek to "flee" and to free itself from the double bond of microcosm and macrocosm to reach its "true place," which is Gnosis, as quickly as possible.

In the *Apophasis Megalē*, a treatise placed under the authority of Simon Magus and related in the *Elenchos*, the *molu* plant with the black root and the milk white flower (*Odyssey* 10.304–6), the magical herb given by Hermes to Odysseus to protect him from the enchantments of Circe, is an allegory on the transformation made by Moses (= the Logos) when he turned the bitter water of the desert into fresh water (Exodus 15:22–24). It is thus the image of the metamorphosis of the wandering soul, restored to itself by Gnosis, which has been brought to it by the Logos and brings it to the knowledge of life in its movement (exodus) through the desert of the difficulties and bitter things of this world (VI, 15, 3–4). The *molu* procures the knowledge of all things and restores the soul to its primal "character," which properly belongs to it (VI, 16, 1). The Stoic philosopher Cleanthes associated the *molu* of Odysseus with the logos, that is, with reason, whose role is to calm the ecstatic leaps and passions of the soul (*SVF* 1.526 Arnim). For Porphyry, the *molu* represents the virtue of prudence and wisdom (*sōphrosunē*), which allows the soul that is thrown into the "*kukeōn* of generation," the mixture that is this world, to escape from its "miserable and bestial form of life" (Stobaeus, *Anthologion* 1.49.60 Wachsmuth).

The allegorical interpretation of the tale of Eros and Psyche, transmitted by Apuleius, is connected with the mystic exegesis of the *Iliad* and the *Odyssey*. Eros draws Psyche into the machinations of existence: sensuality, marriage, procreation, and death (*Nag Hammadi Coptic* II/5, p. 109, 19–25). For Justin the Gnostic, Psyche is under the power of Naas the serpent; incited by him, she sows corruption among the beings (*Elenchos* V, 26, 26). But the blood that flows from Psyche after her intercourse with Eros, which then spreads over the earth, gives birth to roses "for the joy of the light" (*Nag Hammadi Coptic* II/5, p. 111, 8–14). This twofold aspect of the dark and light soul is connected, in the same work, with the ambivalence of an Eros established in the middle of paradise, at the origin of all life and all death.

Heracles also becomes a Gnostic hero as the traditional figure of the Stoic sage before he comes to symbolize in

The zodiac. Rome, Biblioteca apostolica vaticana, MS gr. 1087, folio 310v. Library photo.

(Right) Gnostic papyrus from Nag Hammadi (Codex II, no. 10544, p. 136). Cairo, Coptic Museum, Museum photo.

(Far right) Hermaphrodite. Rome, Capitoline Museum. Photo Oscar Savio.

Plotinus the fate of the double soul divided between the darkness of Hades (= the body and the world) and the light of the gods (= the intelligibles), a reflection (*eidōlon*) that is separated yet remembers its true being, which is "above" (*Enneads* 1.1.12.31–39; 4.3.27.7–23). In the mythology of Justin's *Book of Baruch*, he appears as a link in a chain of prophets sent by Elohim to try to recuperate the divine element—breath (*pneuma*)—that dwells in men (see *Elenchos* V, 26, 27–28). Following the messengers Baruch and Moses, the one sent to Adam and the angels of heaven and the other to the circumcized (the Jews), Heracles is portrayed as the "prophet coming from the uncircumcized peoples" (p. 131.5); the pagans will be the object of his mission. His twelve labors are allegories of the battles he fought against the twelve planetary angels of the Earth called Edem. Seduced by Omphale, however, whom Justin assimilates to Babel and to Aphrodite, he puts on the robe of Edem, which shuts him into the universe of lesser powers. "It is in this way," the myth concludes, "that the prophecy and works of Heracles had no effect." The Heracles of Justin the Gnostic, as savior and then prisoner, and the divided Heracles of

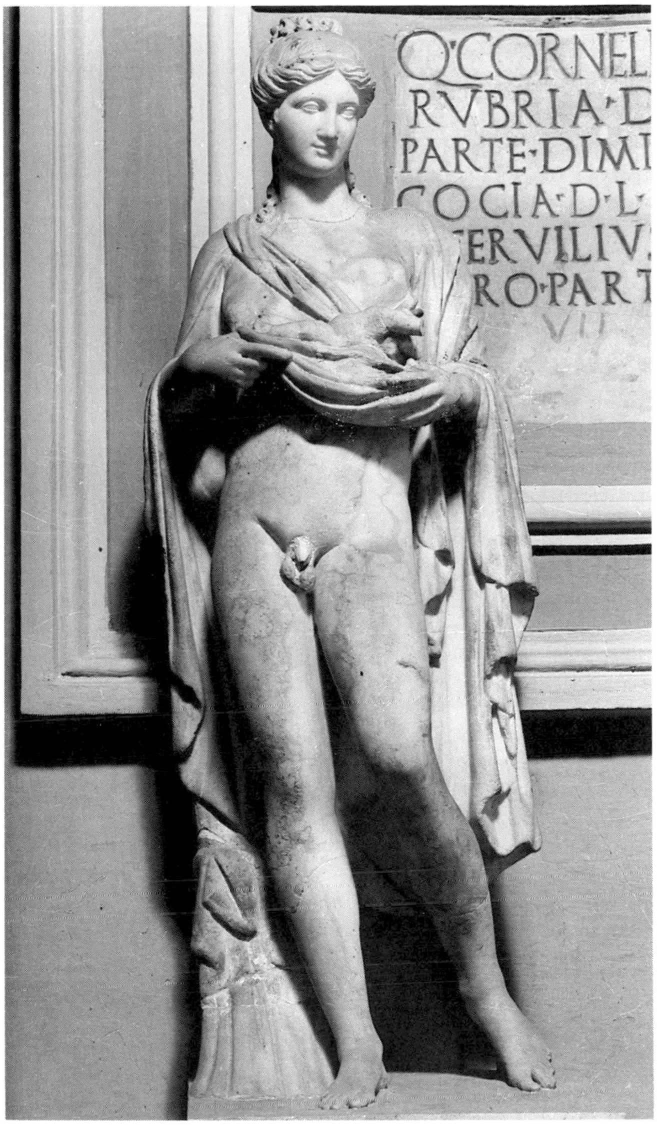

Plotinus, the reader of Homer, belong very much to the same period in the history of ideas.

The Egyptian myth in its Greek reinterpretation of the wanderings and tears of Isis, who is searching for her twin brother and lover Osiris (Plutarch, *Moralia* 356a–358b), served as the starting point for the Valentinian myth of the wanderings and tears of Sophia, abandoned to the sorrows and passions of this world, "a supplicant to the Father," because she has lost the unity of her origin and suffers from love of her twin (Irenaeus, *Adv. Haer.* 1.2.2 = Epiphanius, *Panarion* 31.11.4). Similarly, in the version of the myth presented in the *Elenchos,* the offspring of the Sophia above, himself called the "external" or "lower Sophia," overcome by sorrow and anxiety, looks for his twin everywhere and begs that he who has abandoned him return to him; it is then that the "common fruit of the pleroma," Jesus, who makes the sadness of Sophia into the "material substance" of the universe (*Elenchos* VI, 32, 3–6), is sent to him. Transformed by the creative Logos of Osiris and rendered capable of "receiving all bodily and spiritual forms," Isis incarnates, by her nature, the female principle of the universe; it is she who contains the whole (*pandechēs*) and who presides over all of generation (see Plutarch, *Moralia* 372e). Hence she is assimilated to Platonic matter, as the support and recipient of all things (*Timaeus* 49a; 51a). In the same way, among the Gnostics, the Valentinian Sophia, having surrendered to passion, becomes the principle of the constitution and essence of matter, out of which the world is born (Irenaeus, *Adv. Haer.* 1.4.2 = Epiphanius, *Panarion* 31.16.7). The child of Isis, Horus (= Harpocrates), "debased by matter through the bodily element" (*Moralia* 373b3–4), corresponds to the deformed offspring of the Valentinian Sophia, and is described as a "substance disorganized and without form," analogous to the primordial earth of Genesis and called "the runt" (*Elenchos* VI, 30, 8–31, 2). But just as the Isis of the Platonic tradition has an innate love for the first principle, which is the Good (Plutarch, *Moralia* 372e), so the Valentinian Sophia feels passion and desire for the Father (Irenaeus, *Adv. Haer.* 1.2.2 = Epiphanius, *Panarion* 31.11.4). Just as Isis is called "the seeking of Osiris," *zētēsis Osiridos* (*Moralia* 372c20), Sophia is "the seeking of the Father," *zētēsin tou Patros* (*GCS* 25, p. 403, 13). The joy of Isis, who carries in her the seeds of the world (Plutarch, *Moralia* 372e13–14), corresponds to the laugh of Sophia, who gives birth to light (*GCS* 25, p. 410, 22). The prostrate and weeping Isis, whose tears fecundate the soil of Egypt with floodwaters (Pausanias, *Periegēsis* 10.32.18), corresponds to the sorrow of Sophia, whose tears are the source of the sea, springs, and rivers, from which all the elements of the world come (Irenaeus, *Adv. Haer.* 1.4.2–4 = Epiphanius, *Panarion* 31.16.7–17.8). Last, the sequence of the myth about Isis's search for the phallus of Osiris (*Moralia* 358b) becomes the object, in Naassene Gnosis, of a triple interpretation, which is astrological, cosmological, and initiatory.

The portrait of Isis "of manifold names," *muriōnumos* (Plutarch, *Moralia* 352e), who is hermaphroditic by nature because of her identification with the moon (368c), underlies the portrait of this universal Mother of living creatures, who among the Gnostics is called Sophia, Eve, or Barbelo. Following the pattern of aretalogies which enumerate the titles and virtues of Isis, the Gnostics composed hymns, of which certain fragments have been found at Nag Hammadi (II/4, p. 89, 16–17; II/5, p. 114, 8–15); an entire treatise was even constructed upon this literary genre (*Nag Hammadi Coptic* 6/2; see, for example, p. 13, 27–14, 14). After the fashion of Isis, the mother goddess of the Gnostics encompasses what for humanity are opposites; she is at once virgin and mother, father and mother, prostitute and virgin, male and female, whole and part, self and other: "My husband is he who engendered me, and I am his mother and he is my father and my lord." The soul of each is henceforth engulfed in this soul of the world. With the Gnostics as with their contemporaries, the myth of the soul that wanders across the multiplicity of this world has for its corollary the myth of the repose of this soul in the fullness of the transcended division. The dispersion (*diaspora*) of the soul that is in submission to the planetary god is answered by the coming together (*sullexis*) of the Isian and sovereign soul.

The gods of paganism thus served the Gnostics merely as a means to illustrate this dialectic. In the same way that they are used by their contemporaries who are magicians, philosophers, and astrologers, so the Gnostics use these henceforth supernumerary entities of a drama, whether classifying them in catalogs of demons or dissolving them in allegorism. With the exception of Eros, none of the pagan gods that pass into Gnosis provides a new myth. Mythos and logos are no longer balanced. On the other hand, the fact that certain Gnostics, such as the Perates, the Naassenes, and, to a lesser extent, Justin, chose this very field of Hellenism to satisfy their appetite for allegory made possible the efflorescence of surprising systems of thought—the truly original and most successful forms of the Gnostic interpretation of the gods of paganism.

M.T./d.w.

BIBLIOGRAPHY

A. DIETERICH, *Abraxas: Studien zur Religionsgeschichte des späteren Altertums* (Leipzig 1891). H. USENER, *Götternamen: Versuch einer Lehre von der religiösen Begriffsbildung* (Bonn 1895; 3d ed., Frankfurt 1948). W. BOUSSET, "Die Himmelsreise der Seele," *Archiv für Religionswissenschaft* 4 (1901): 136–69, 229–73. R. REITZENSTEIN, *Poimandres: Studien zur griechisch-ägyptischen und frühchristlichen Literatur* (Leipzig 1904). E. NORDEN, *Die Geburt des Kindes* (Warburg 1924). R. P. CASEY, "Two Notes on Valentinian Theology," 1: "Valentinian Myths," *Harvard Theological Review* 23 (1930): 275–90. A. TORHOUDT, *Een onbekend gnostisch systeem in Plutarchus' De Iside et Osiride* (Louvain 1942). M. TARDIEU, *Trois mythes gnostiques* (Paris 1974).

The Perates and Their Gnostic Interpretation of Paganism

In the first half of the second century A.D., some Christian Gnostics were connected with the Ophite branch of Gnosticism by virtue of the important role of the serpent (Greek *ophis*) in their system of symbols. Known only from the account of them in the *Elenchos* (V, 12–18), the Perates are presented as adepts of the Chaldean science, devoting themselves to "allegorizing the order of the astrologers" (V, 15, 4, pp. 110, 29–30 Wendland) and to "transforming the names" (V, 13, 9, p. 107, 9–10; V, 15, 2, p. 110, 22) of Chaldean categories of stars into entities for their own pantheons. We are also told that they called themselves Perates because they alone, being aware of the laws that fix the "necessity of becoming" and the "ways by which man came into the world," were "able to cross over and go beyond (*perasai*) corruption" (V, 16, 1), in other words the planetary spheres that determine the fate of any individual that is subject to generation. Only the names of their founders are known: Euphrates the Peratic (a surname added by the heresiologist) and Celbes of Carysta, also known as Acembes or Ademes (V, 13, 9; IV, 2, 1; X, 10, 1). In the *Contra Celsum* (VI, 28, 31–2), Origen points out that "those who call themselves Ophites (*Ophianoi*) boast of having a certain Euphrates as the instigator of their ungodly doctrines." As this comment comes right after the refutation of the astrological chart that Celsus attributed to some Christians, we may surmise that Euphrates and Celbes represented the primitive layer of what the heresiologists called "Ophitism." In fact, "Ophitism" was nothing more than a form of theological reflection within Christianity itself; it used astrological terminology just as Bar-Daisan did, and the Peratic system was to become one of its later variants, marked by a specifically Gnostic character.

The books that the Perates read were the "Book of Moses" (V, 16, 8, p. 112, 14)—that is, Genesis, Exodus, and Numbers—in the Old Testament, and the Gospel according to John in the New Testament. Among the books they drew from "ignorance" (a Gnostic term for Hellenism) to support their theses, the Perates used Homer, Heraclitus, Aratus, and the Sibylline oracles among other "poets" and "sages." They also used short astrological treatises analogous to those recorded on magical papyruses. By way of example, the author of the *Elenchos* cites a long excerpt (V, 14), purposely chosen for its particular obscurity, from one of the books "held in high esteem among them," which was entitled *Hoi Proasteioi heōs Aitheros* ("The Suburbanites up to the Ether") (IV, 14, 10, p. 110, 12–13). As the content of the treatise reveals, such a title designates the gods and demons assigned to each of the planetary spheres that in some way constitute the periphery (*proasteion*) of the ethereal realm in which the first principle resides. Each god is introduced with his various names, consorts, functions, and signs. The first among them, Kronos, "tied in ropes after having locked up the dense, nebulous, obscure, and dark network of Tartarus," is assimilated to the power of the sea, Thalassa, who came from chaos and the slime of the abyss and is the mother of the Titans. Chorzar, the androgynous daughter of the sea, guardian of the waters, which she soothes by playing twelve small flutes, corresponds to Poseidon. The Curetes are associated with the rising of the sun; Ariel is chief of the winds; Osiris and Isis, the latter identified with the constellation of the Dog, designate the keepers (Archons) of the hours of night and day. Rhea, Demeter, Mēn, and Hephaestus, presiding over food, fruit, and fire, represent the dual movement, upward and downward, right and left, of the signs of the Zodiac on the ecliptic. The Moirai, cause of generation, are three powers of the middle air. Finally, at the lower extremity of the circles, and therefore the closest to us, is Eros, "forever a child" and androgynous, the "principle of beauty, pleasure, freshness, youth, concupiscence, and desire"; he brings to a close the catalog of the gods who are rulers (*toparchai*) of the planets.

The content of such a document has nothing Gnostic about it and can in no way be considered the source of the whole account of the Perates in the *Elenchos*, as the critics unanimously claim. The Christian polemicist in fact used two separate books. The first was the *Proasteioi* of the fragment summarized above, which was read by the Perates and belonged to the pagan literature of magic and astrology. The second, the title of which is not given (citations being always introduced by "said he"), was a document of genuinely Peratic revelation, an apocryphon placed under the name of an Old Testament revelatory figure, perhaps Moses, by virtue of the place it occupies in the excerpts cited in the *Elenchos* as well as in late Greek esotericism in general.

The world according to the Perates, like that of the Valentinians, is a triadic emanative system but, unlike the Valentinian world, does not fit into any syzygies. The triad forming the unity of the whole includes the first principle, the Perfect (*teleion*), which is the Good or the Unbegotten, followed by the Unlimited (*apeiron*), constituting the self-begotten world (*autogenēs*) of the powers of the intermediary space, and finally, in third place, the Particular (*idikon*), that is, our own world, begotten by flow (*kata aporroian*) originating in the stars, the causes of generation.

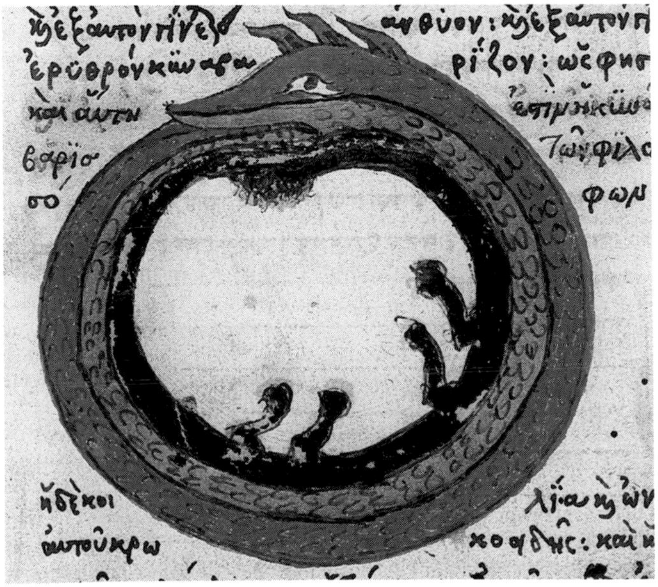

The serpent Ouroboros (ms. gr. 2327, fol. 196). Paris, Bibliothèque nationale. Photo BN/S.R.D.

Unlike the third, the first two worlds are essentially incorruptible and imperishable. Furthermore, each part of the triad defines a class of gods, of logos, of intellect, of man, of nature, of the body, of power, and therefore of Christ, who, "starting with the three parts of the world, possesses within him all compounds and all powers" (V, 12, 4). His function will be to "cause to go back upward what had come down from on high" (V, 12, 6), that is, to restore to its fullness the original unity of being.

For the Perates, this basic outline corresponded to the triadic models used by the Astrologers (center or monad, a universe of powers subject to declination and ascension, generation), by Physicians (brain, cerebellum, spinal cord), and by Platonists (Father, Son, matter).

Matter (*hulē*), defined as having no quality (*apoios*) and no shape (*aschēmatistos*), is the work of the homicidal demiurge, the Archon of this world, "an aborted being who was born in the night and will perish in the night" (V, 17, 6). Because water is the fundamental constituent of matter, matter is identified with the Kronos of astrology, the consort of Thalassa. Thalassa is the power of disorder and mud that has come from the eternal humid element, always in motion and in convulsions, mistress of becoming and of death, analogous to Thalatth-Omorka (Homoroka) in the cosmogony of Berossos (FGrH III C no. 680 F 1[6] Jacoby) or to the Gūḥra' of Qūq, the gaping cavern of the waters of death swallowing the seven virgins who are the companions of the Mother of living creatures (cf. Theodore bar Konai, p. 334, 20–25 Scher).

Precisely by virtue of the position that he occupies in the triad, the Autogenēs, identified with the Johannine Son and Logos, is declared to be in "perpetual movement," attracted simultaneously upward by the immobile Father and downward by moving matter (V, 17, 2), like Hermes ferrying "downward all that belongs to the Father" (p. 114, 34) and "from here below to points beyond" (p. 115, 17). From the Father he receives powers, impressions, and ideas, which he transmits to matter, somehow channeling their flow, like a painter mixing on his tablet (= matter) forms and colors, that is, that which comes from the Father (V, 17, 5). This same function is described with the help of another "proof" (*apodeixis*, p. 116, 1) drawn from the nature of the cerebellum, the intermediary between the encephalon and the spinal cord; the cerebellum "attracts through the pineal gland the spiritual and life-giving substance that flows from the brain" (V, 17, 12), and from there directs it into the spinal cord, where it is changed into semen and at the end of its flow is expelled through the phallus.

The character of this second principle, defined as "always in motion" and analogous to the serpentine cerebellum (*drakontoeidēs*), connects it with the bronze serpent in Numbers 21.6–9, trained by Moses in the desert, that is, on the other side of the Red Sea (= Thalassa), which stands for the water of corruption and death (= Kronos) of this world, in which "little Egypt" (= the body) swims. The soteriological function of this serpent, which is called "universal" (p. 112, 18), "true and perfect" (p. 112, 7–8), is described with a remarkable profusion of allegories. It is the rod of Moses, the vanquisher of the rods of the magicians of Egypt, and it stands for the power within the very person of Moses. It is

Brass serpent. Milan, Basilica of Saint Ambrose. Photo Segre.

Eve, universal distributor of Logos, wisdom, and life, the "common nature" (*koinē phusis*, p. 113, 6) of the world above, as opposed to the particularity (*idikon*) of our world. It is the very mystery of Eden, whose river carries the waters of life. It is the emblem of the victims of the God of the Old Testament: Cain, the just slayer of a brother sullied by a bloody sacrifice; Esau of the blessed robe, who saw the face of God; Nemrod the builder of the Tower of Babel, "giant and hunter before the Lord"; and finally Jesus, "betrayed by his brothers" and "raised up" on the wooden cross. It is the constellation of the serpent-bearer (Ophiuchus, Serpentarius), which "shines eternally in the sky" and was described by Aratus as holding east and west, merged together, near its head (V, 16, 15). Finally, it is identified with the motionless *ouroboros*, closed upon itself, holding its tail in its mouth and thus symbolizing the completeness of the Father, the conjunction of the beginning and the end. It is thus the supreme anti-Kronos, countering the bond of death, which holds the world in its grip, with the bond of knowledge (*gnōsis*) and of the vision of the first unity: "By gazing up at the sky, someone with blessed eyes will see the splendid image of the serpent coiled up at the great beginning (*archē*) of the sky, becoming the principle (*archē*) of all movement for all who are born" (V, 16, 14). Thus there are three serpents corresponding to the three elements that make up the triad: the *ouroboros* for the Father; the bronze serpent for the Son; and the burning and venomous serpents of the desert for matter. The first two evoke life and Gnosis; the third evokes the ruin that is bound up with this world.

Peratic mythology drew from the thought of Egyptian astrologers and magicians. It took the possibility of multiple allegorical combinations, which the Jewish Platonistic current of Alexandria offered it, and made that possibility its own. But unlike other Gnoses, which chose one side or the other, proceeding by way of selective elimination or retrieval, Peratic mythology simultaneously had recourse to Judaism by way of anti-Judaism, to astrology by way of anti-Chaldaism, to Greece by way of anti-Hellenism, and to the Gospel by way of anti-Christianity. In this, it is Gnostic. It is highly unlikely that it was the expression of a school or a church. Between Valentinus and Bar-Daisan, Heracleon and Qūq, its inventor occupies a profoundly original position in the history of thought.

M.T./g.h.

BIBLIOGRAPHY

A. HILGENFELD, *Die Ketzergeschichte des Urchristentums* (Leipzig 1884), 263–67. FR. BOLL, *Sphaera: Neue griechische Texte und Untersuchungen zur Geschichte der Sternbilder* (Leipzig 1903), 309–10. W. BOUSSET, *Hauptprobleme der Gnosis* (Göttingen 1907), 124–25. H. LEISEGANG, *Die Gnosis* (4th ed., Stuttgart 1955); K. PREISENDANZ, "Ostanes," in PAULY-WISSOWA, *Real-Encyclopädie*, vol. 18 (Stuttgart 1942), cols. 1625–26.

Eros among the Gnostics

The sole writing that speaks of the mythic itinerary traveled by Eros (*Nag Hammadi Coptic* II 5, p. 109, 1–111, 28) concentrates, as do most descriptions of the period, on the genealogy and function of the god. Eros is the son of Pronoia, the *paredros* (consort) of the demiurge Ialdabaoth. Upon seeing the beauty of the angel of light, still called the primordial Adam or Light-Adam, that creature arisen out of the splendor of the ogdoad—i.e., from the Father, who is the principle of all things—Pronoia ardently wishes to unite with him. But the angel refuses, and she herself is too weighed down by her tenebrous element to be able to mount up to him. So she tears the luminous particles away from the angel, mixes them with her blood, and spreads them over the earth. By this act Pronoia responds, in kind, to that of her husband, who had flung his sperm "into the center of the earth's navel," whence the terrestrial Adam of the Garden of Eden had arisen. It is in the very middle of paradise that Eros is born as the fruit of the moist desire of his mother and the astral fire of the angel: he is thus androgynous by nature. "His masculine nature is Himeros, because he is a fire that comes from the light. The femininity within him is a soul of blood and comes from the substance of Pronoia" (p. 109, 3–6).

Because he unites in himself the two antagonistic forces of the primal Adam and of Pronoia, and because he is the place in which the union of love-desire (Himeros) and the beloved soul (Psyche) is realized, Eros produces sensual pleasure (*hēdonē*), which will lead to marriage, procreation, and death (p. 109, 20–25). Apart from the discrete allusion to the popular tale of Amor and Psyche, the Gnostic myth of the origin of Eros refers especially to the hermaphroditic conception of the Orphic Eros, whom the *Pseudoclementine Homilies* assert to have been formed "by Pronoia of the divine breath (*pneuma*)": "This living being Orpheus calls Phanes, because, when he appeared, the whole universe was illuminated by his splendor, Phanes having been brought to perfection in the womb of the liquid element by the brilliance of fire, the most magnificent of the elements; and there is nothing incredible about this, for in glow-worms, for example, nature has given a watery light for us to see" (6.12.4). Born of the mingling of the dry and the wet, of male fire and female blood, under the aegis of a Pronoia who was the bearer of light and of the divine breath, the Gnostic Eros governs the fusion of the primordial elements. According to an expression in the *Oracles,* he is their bond and their unifier, he who by projecting all things unifies them (pp. 25–26 Kroll). But, at the same time, this role of the conjoiner of opposites played by Eros does not give him in the Gnostic pantheon the eminent status which he enjoyed among the Orphics. He remains at the very source of the death that is transmitted by his daughter, sensual pleasure. Like the Eros of the Platonic myths of the *Symposium,* who is shared between heaven and earth, Poros and Penia, and gods and men, the Gnostic Eros is halfway between the light of the Father and the darkness of chaos, a daemonic intermediary being, situated neither above in the ogdoad nor below on earth, but in a space described by Plato as the garden of the gods (203b6); the Gnostic author specifies that this place is "in the center of the navel of the earth," in Eden, which is the garden (*paradeisos*) of the biblical god, beyond the sun and the moon.

Installed in paradise, Eros inaugurates his function as intermediary by stimulating all beings by the sight of his splendor: "He is very handsome in his beauty, having more loveliness than all the creatures of chaos. When all the gods and their angels saw Eros, they became enamored of him. But when he appeared to them all, he set them on fire. Just as many lamps are kindled from a single lamp, and the light is one light, and the lamp is not diminished, so Eros was scattered in all the creatures of Chaos, and he was not diminished. In the same way that he appeared in the midpoint (*mesotēs*) between light and darkness, so Eros appeared between angels and men" (p. 109, 6–19). Here we find a series of themes common to the whole period. In the *Poimandres,* personified Nature "smiles with love" upon seeing the "inexhaustible beauty" of the primordial man reflected in the water (§ 14). As a means to express the idea of the nondepletion of the primal energy of a God who gives his knowledge, Numenius would employ the same terms as the Gnostic author: "It is in this way that one can see a lamp lit from another lamp, bearing a light which did not deprive its source of light: only its wick was lit by that fire" (fr. 23 Leemans = 14 Des Places). Justin too uses the same image to describe the inexhaustible character of the Logos, which communicates itself: "Just as we see that from a first fire another fire is produced, without diminishing the fire from which the other was lit, the first fire in fact remaining the same, even so the new fire too which is lit here is seen to be entirely real without having diminished the one from which it was lit" (*Dialogue with Trypho* 61.2). Furthermore, by placing Eros between light and darkness, the Gnostic author brings together, in an erudite syncretism, the Greek genealogy of Eros, who is born of the night and is a transmitter of fire, and the activity of the God of Genesis, who separates light from darkness and night from day. Like a lamp that makes visible what is indistinct in darkness, Eros illumines beings submerged in the confusion of chaos. By allowing the elements to be distinguished, he is a reference mark and a center (*mesotēs*). As a sign of recognition and a principle of order, he is also that being who transmits the fire and blood from which he comes, and from which the disorders of the world are born. Born of the night, he remains a child of the night, communicating to beings and things the irrationality of his mother.

The luminary function of Eros was linked to his dependence on light and fire, and his sexual function to his connection with the "blood of the virgin" (p. 109, 1–2), by virtue of which Eros would govern all of the watery sphere, in the fecundated woman as much as in the fertilized ground: "Thus the intercourse (*sunousia*) of Eros was accomplished. The first sensual pleasure sprouted upon earth, woman followed earth and marriage followed woman, procreation followed marriage and death followed procreation. After that particular manifestation of Eros, the grapevine sprouted up from the blood which was poured upon the earth. Therefore those who drink it (the vine) engender in themselves the desire for intercourse. After the grapevine, a fig tree and a pomegranate tree sprouted up on earth, together with the rest of the trees, according to their kind, having their own seed within them derived from the seed of the powers and their angels" (p. 109, 19–110, 1). As principles of fertility and destruction, earth and woman represent the two aspects of the ambivalence of Eros. This is nothing new to the Greek world. Yet the way in which our Gnostic draws a correspondence between the three consequences of the sensual pleasures of woman (marriage, procreation, and death) and the three trees (vine, fig, pomegranate)—all three connected with Eros and possessed of a precise sexual symbolism—is entirely original. Wine, the drink of Aphrodite and Dionysus, composed like Eros of fire and boiling blood, leads man to the "desire for coitus" (p. 109, 29). The fig tree, a tree that is always green because it provides, according to Pliny, four harvests each year, is the phallic symbol par excellence; Dionysus uses a branch of the fig tree as a substitute for a phallus in a myth told by Clement of Alexandria (*Protrepticus* 2.34.3–4). Later Judaic writings would designate the fig tree as the tree of the forbidden fruit. Its leaves would serve to cover the nakedness of Adam and Eve. The pomegranate, which is filled with a multitude of grape seeds that ferment beneath its skin, contains a wine that is particularly recommended for the pleasures of love. Like his mother Aphrodite, Eros is portrayed holding pomegranates in his hands. But this fruit is also associated in the Greek world with Hera, the goddess of marriage and of procreation. Thus, the ancient myths still have their say when the Gnostic author wishes to name three plants associated with the sexual function of Eros. And it is not by mere chance that the mythic horticulture of Eros is built upon these three trees alone, for each one, within a single semantic field, portrays a particular aspect of the sexual function (fig tree–phallus–Dionysus; wine–sensual pleasure–Aphrodite; pomegranate–fecundity–Hera) and recapitulates through the perspective of the vegetal code the semantic totality of the cosmogonic and anthropological manifestation of Eros. It is thus in a very coherent fashion that the Gnostic author constructed, by reusing traditional schemata, the picture of an Eros who rules over both woman and earth.

While the cosmogonic epiphany of Eros, which separates light from darkness, remains positive, that of the Eros who

Androgynous winged Eros. Vienna, Kunsthistorisches Museum. Museum photo.

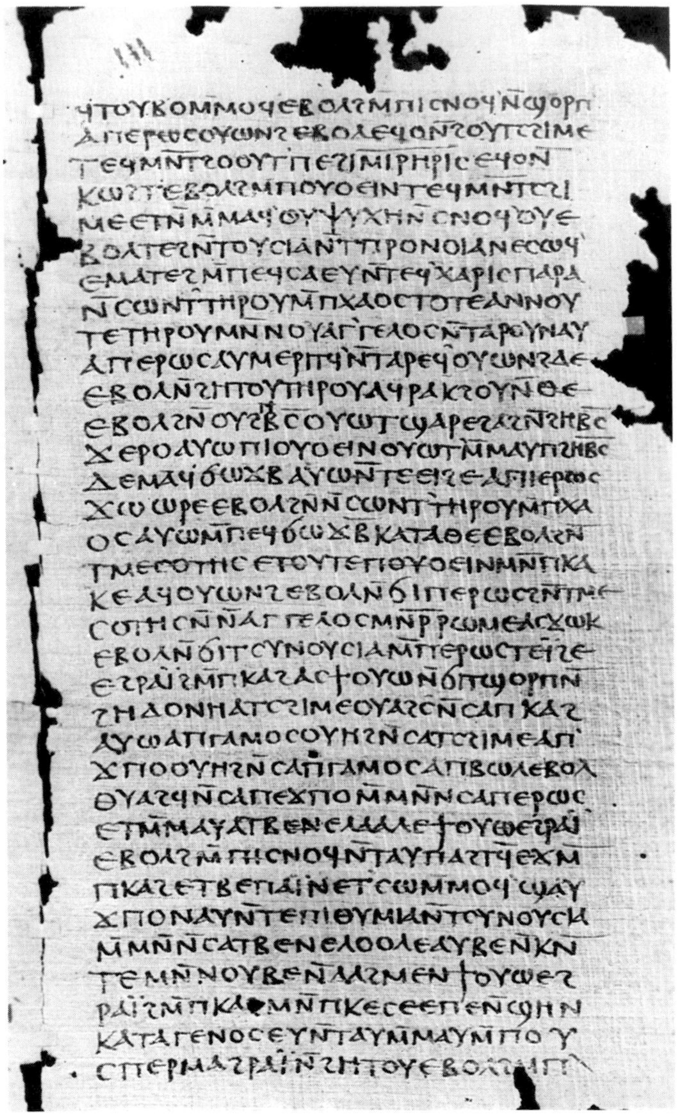

Gnostic papyrus from Nag Hammadi (Codex II no. 10544, p. 109). Cairo, Coptic Museum. Museum photo.

appeared "between angels and men" would, through recourse to woman, cause a principle of death to enter the world. The Coptic Gnostic text calls this death a dissolution of beings, a *bōl ebol* (p. 109, 24; the term is also found in *The Dialogue of the Savior, Nag Hammadi Coptic* III, 5, p. 122, 3). One consequence of this manifestation was the expulsion of Adam and Eve from paradise. But if, by reason of his fundamental duplicity, Eros is the most dreaded of the gods, he is also the most beautiful and most desirable, since his ambivalence, composed of fire and blood, expresses the totality of the primordial elements, the dry and the wet, from which the world was born. At once a principle of the dissolution of things and a principle of their reintegration, he both originates the sensual pleasure of copulation and, at the same time, according to the elegant formula of the *Pseudoclementine Homily,* "realizes the culmination of the beauty of the world" (p. 111, 16–17 Rehm). After the description of Eros's function as source of the madness that carries away the world, there is a description of this same function organizing what is beautiful in the world: paradise.

The Eden of Eros was created by Justice, an entity belonging to the ogdoad of the Father, "outside the circuit of the moon and the circuit of the sun in the luxuriant earth, which is in the east in the midst of the stones. And desire (*epithumia*) is in the midst of the trees that are beautiful and tall" (p. 110, 2–7). Paradise is situated beyond the time determined by the luminaries of day and night, in a mythic east of the Age of Gold in which precious stones abound. Because they are made up of the antagonistic elements of the wet and the dry, solar fire and river waters, precious stones belong to the biological and sexualized world, as do animals and plants, and consequently, just like trees, enter the semantic field of Eros. The plants of paradise, named by the Gnostic author, conform to the data of Jewish and apocalyptic tradition: to the north is planted the tree of life and immortality, which has a solar brilliance and is identified with the cypress-olive pair; near it is the tree of knowledge, which has a lunar brilliance and is identified with the fig-palm pair (p. 110, 6–11, 8). The relationship between Eros and paradise is also illuminated by the threefold reference to Eden as the land of beauty, of delights, and of desire—three titles that are eminently related to the god of Love. The description of paradise ends with an interpretation of the myth of Amor and Psyche. Just as Pronoia had spread her blood over the earth, from which Eros was born, so Psyche unites with Eros in paradise and spreads her blood over the earth, from which roses and lilies will be born (p. 111, 8–12). And then each of the daughters of Pronoia, one at a time, comes to unite with Eros, to give birth to all of the plants (p. 111, 14–24). By a skillful, harmonious syncretism, the editor of the Gnostic text seeks to present symmetrically the two universes—or rather the two gardens (*paradeisoi*)—in which the beauty and the desire of Eros dwelled: first the biblical Eden, from which evil powers are excluded and where, consequently, all the trees and fruits are beautiful and desirable; then the Greek paradise of Eros, in which the powers connected with sexual defilement appear. These two paradises, the Judaic and the Greek, constitute the two faces of an ambivalent Eros, whose androgyny, made of blood and fire, implies that his work will itself be ambiguous, being male and good on the one hand (fire = biblical Eden) and female and evil on the other (blood = Greek garden).

Eros is the only Greek god to have escaped an astrological and daemonological reduction among the Gnostics because he remained omnipresent and in fashion during this period—the end of the second century B.C.—when the system of which this treatise speaks was being constructed. Romances, oracles, and epigrams take possession of him; depictions of him abound in sarcophagi as well as in private homes as a companion at every moment in this life and the life beyond. Plotinus commented on him in his lectures as tending toward the beauty of the One, and the *Chaldean Oracles* proclaim him to be the son of the paternal intellect and the unifier of the totality of being. So it is not surprising that this god, familiar in the popular and scholarly mythology of Roman Egypt, should have furnished Gnostic thought with one of its least obscure and most brilliant pages. From the Eros of the ancient theogonies, who arose out of the earth, from chaos, or from an egg, to the beautified Eros of Gnosticism, placed in the midst of the stones and trees of paradise, we can trace the history of a single idea: that this world bears within itself the force that makes it survive.

M.T./d.w.

BIBLIOGRAPHY

M. TARDIEU, *Trois mythes gnostiques: Adam, Éros et les animaux d'Égypte dans un écrit de Nag Hammadi 2, 5* (Paris 1974).

HECATE IN GREEK ESOTERICISM

To the Christian Gnostics, who believed that magic had been brought to the earth by fallen angels, Hecate represents one of the five Archons appointed to rule over the 360 demons (or daemons) of the "Middle," the aerial place below the zodiacal sphere or the circle of the sun, which fixes the Heimarmene. She has three faces and twenty-seven demons under her command. She occupies the third level in the hierarchy of the "Middle," between two female demons, long-haired Paraplex and Ariouth the Ethiopian, and two male demons, Typhon and Iachtanabas (*Pistis Sophia*, chap. 140; Coptic text: p. 363, 8–364, 6 Schmidt).

During the same period, this secondary figure of Gnostic daemonology is also an omnipresent personage in the pantheon of magical papyruses, because of the range of meanings attributed to her emblems and because of the system of associations which link her to, and even identify her with, other gods and goddesses.

Her three forms (*trimorphos* PGM XXXVI, 190) and her three faces (*triprosōpos*, IV, 2119, 2880) make her, as in classical Greek tradition, the goddess of crossroads (*triodites*, IV, 27, 2962) and the protectress of roads; but they express above all the "abundance of all magical signs" (XXXVI, 190–191), possessed by the "sovereign" goddess (*kuria*, IV, 1432) "of many names" (*poluōnumos*, IV, 745). The three-faced Hecate of the love charm of Pitys, contained in the magical Greek codex of Paris, has the head of a cow on the right, the head of a female dog on the left, and the head of a girl in the center (IV, 2120–2123). The Hecate engraved in a magnetized rock (IV, 2881–2884) also shows three faces: a goat on the right, a female dog on the left, and in the middle a girl with horns.

Her mouth exhales fire (*puripnoa*, IV, 2727); her six hands brandish torches (IV, 2119–2120). Hence, engraving her name with a bronze styletto on an ostracon (XXXVI, 189) or on a lead tablet (IV, 2956) will have the effect of a fire "burning" and "consuming" the beloved woman (XXXVI, 195, 200), so that she is deprived of sleep forever (IV, 2960, 2965–2966). Furthermore, the fire that inhabits Hecate, as the most subtle of the four elements, characterizes her keen intelligence and the extreme sharpness of her perception (*puriboulos*, IV, 2751). Her whole being radiates with the brilliance of the fire from the stars and from the ether. The *Chaldaean Oracles* made this Hecate "of the breasts that welcome storms, of resplendent brilliance" into an entity "descended from the Father," associated with the "implacable thunderbolts" of the gods, with the "flower of fire," and with the "powerful breath" of the paternal Intellect (p. 20 Kroll). Because she carries and transmits fire from above, she is the supreme goddess of vivification. The reason Hecate's womb is so remarkably "fertile" (*zōogonon*, p. 19 Kroll) is that she is filled with the fire of paternal Intellect, the source of life or the strength of thought, which it is her duty to communicate and to disseminate.

Through her emblems and her triadic conception, Hecate is associated with another goddess of time and destiny, Mene or Selene, the goddess of the moon. The prayer to the moon of P IV, 2785 invokes them as one and the same entity; epithets and attributes of the two goddesses are interchangeable. Hecate/Selene also has three heads, carries torches, presides over crossroads: "You who in the three forms of the three Charites dance and fly about with the stars . . . You who wield terrible black torches in your hands, you who shake your head with hair made of fearsome snakes, you who cause the bellowing of the bulls, you whose belly is covered with reptilian scales and who carry over your shoulder a woven bag of venomous snakes" (IV, 2793–2806). She has the eye of a bull, the voice of a pack of dogs, the calves of a lion, the ankles of a wolf, and she loves fierce bitches: "This is why you are called Hecate of many names, Mene, you who split the air like Artemis, shooter of arrows" (IV, 2814–2817). She is the mother (*geneteira*) of gods and men, Nature the universal mother (*Phusis panmetōr*): "You

Hecate. Paris, Bibliothèque nationale, Cabinet des Médailles. Photo BN.

come and go on Olympus and visit the vast and immense Abyss: you are beginning and end, you alone rule over all things; it is in you that all originates, and in you, eternal, that all ends" (IV, 2832–2839). Another hymn in the Paris codex used as a love charm shows the same joy in piling up titles of the goddess, who has this time become Aphrodite, the universal procreator (*pangennēteira*) and mother of Eros (IV, 2556–2557), at once below and above, "in the Hells, the Abyss, and the Aeon" (IV, 2563–2564), chthonic (IV, 1443), holding her feasts in tombs (IV, 2544) and associated with Ereskigal, the Babylonian queen of Hells (LXX, 4), but also the "celestial traveler among the stars" (IV, 2559), nocturnal, but also the bearer of light (IV, 2549–2550).

Her ring, scepter, and crown represent the power of the one who, possessing the triad, embraces all. Above and below, to the right and to the left, at night as during the day, she is the one "around whom the nature of the world turns" (IV, 2551–2552), the very Soul of the world, according to *Chaldaean Oracle* "the center in the middle of the Fathers" (p. 27 Kroll), occupying, according to Psellus, an intermediary position and playing the role of the center in relation to all the other powers: to her left the source of virtues (p. 28 Kroll), to her right the source of souls, inside, because she remains within her own substance, but also directed to the outside with a view to procreation.

Whether invoked in love charms to bring to oneself the woman one desires (the *agōgai* of the magic papyruses) or evoked by the "constraints that subdue the gods" (the *theiodamoi anankai* of the Chaldaen philosophers, p. 156, v. 190 Wolff), Hecate is henceforth inscribed in a table of correspondences and combinations which go far beyond her proper function as a goddess of enchantment and magic. It is from this Hecate, the product of the syncretism of the papyruses, that the tradition of the Hecate of the Neoplatonic commentators on the *Oracles* takes shape.

M.T./t.l.f.

BIBLIOGRAPHY

R. GANSCHINIETZ, *Hippolytos' Capitel gegen die Magier,* TU 39/2 (1913): 64–70. TH. HOPFNER, *Griechisch-ägyptischer Offenbarungszauber,* SPP 21 (1921): 259 d; "Hekate-Selene-Artemis," in *Pisciculi . . . Franz Joseph Dölger dargeboten,* T. Klauser and A. Rücker, eds. (Münster in Westf 1939), 125–45. M.-P. NILSSON, *Die Religion in den griechischen Zauberpapyri* (1947), reprinted in *Opuscula selecta,* 3 (1960): 143–45. H. LEWY, *Chaldaean Oracles and Theurgy: Mysticism, Magic and Platonism in the Later Roman Empire* (Cairo 1956), 47–56, 83–98, 269–73, 292–93, 353–55, 361–66. TH. KRAUS, *Hekate: Studien zu Wesen und Bild der Göttin in Kleinasien und Griechenland* (Heidelberg 1960); "Alexandrinische Triaden der römischen Kaiserzeit," *Mitteilungen des Deutschen Archäologischen Instituts,* 19 (1963): 97–105.

JUSTIN THE GNOSTIC: A SYNCRETISTIC MYTHOLOGY

Justin the Gnostic is artificially linked by heresiology to the Christian Gnostics through a triadic system superficially analogous to that of the Sethians or the Perates, and through the very secondary role that Jesus plays in the final phase of the soteriology. In the single account by the Christian polemicist who speaks of him (*Elenchos,* V, 23–28), he is described as the author of a treatise on revelation entitled *The Book of Baruch,* written in the second half of the second century A.D. Nothing is said of the individuality of the author, but the passages cited from his book lead one to believe that his was a personality that remained profoundly Oriental, closer to Qūq, to Monoïme, or even to Elchasaï than to the representatives of the schools of Platonizing Gnosticism.

Three principles (*archai*), roots (*rhizai*), or sources (*pēgai*) dominate the universe, all three of them uncreated (*agennētoi*). Above is the innately good being, male, endowed with foresight (*prognōstikos*) and identified with Priapus. His ithyphallic symbol, in charge of guarding the ripe autumn fruit (*opōrai*), represents all of creation, which he protects. From then on, according to one of those etymologies of which the Gnostics were very fond, he becomes "the one before (*prin*) whom there was nothing," "the one who created whereas nothing existed before" (*priopoein*), the source of the inexhaustible fertility of the universe (V, 26,

33). In the middle of the triad is the Father, identified with the Jewish Elohim, endowed with will (*thelēsis*) and split between the extreme limits of the triad. As in the Valentinian myth of the ignorance of the demiurge, he at first has no idea of the existence of the first principle and believes himself to be the only God (V, 26, 15). In the third place is a young girl who is a goddess, half earth, half snake, to whom is given the Hebrew name of paradise, Edem, land of origins where the snake lives, also called Israel, endowed with anger (*orgē*), deceitful and perverse, jealous and evil. With a double intelligence and a double body (*dignōmos* and *disōmos*), she incarnates the duplicity of all women, simultaneously drawn toward men, whom she pollutes, and attracted by Elohim, whom she makes her lover. But, unlike the Valentinian Sophia at the boundaries of the two worlds, the origin of evil but also of salvation, the unique function of Justin's sly and lubricious Edem is to be forever responsible for all misfortunes that befall men; this perfidious goddess of the earth is the "prostitute" (V, 27, 4, p. 133, 13) who chains everyone she approaches, both God and men, to his destiny of death. The three principles being outside of time and without any descendants, the sole object of the myth is thus to explain how one of the divine elements—the breath (*pneuma*) of Elohim—escaped from the control of its owner (the fall) and was then restored to him (salvation).

In Justin's mythology, the story of the fall does not describe, as does the Valentinians' version, a second time frame for the process of organizing the universe; it takes place not outside the triad of the principles but inside it, coextensive with the primordial order itself. Indeed, the demiurgic scenario takes place at the beginning of things through the desire that instantaneously carries the second principle (= the Father, or Elohim) toward the young girl Edem, a union that is allegorically represented by the two loves of Zeus, in the form of a swan for Leda and of golden rain for Danaë (V, 26, 34–35). It is thus a metamorphosed Elohim who unites with Edem. But the account of the Christian polemicist does not indicate the particular form of metamorphosis undergone by virtue of the will to dissimulate, since desire (*epithumia*) and will (*thelēsis*) are the Gnostic constant at the origin of all faults. Thus smitten with each other, Elohim and Edem unite and give birth to twelve angels, who form the astral structure of the universe, or the paradisiac land of origins. Thus the paradise of Genesis is merely an allegorical interpretation proposed by Moses for those angelic seeds planted in Edem by Elohim (*Genesis* 2.8). The two trees in paradise allegorically designate the two angels which appeared in the third rank of the zodiacal entities: Baruch, the tree of life, on the side of the father; Naas (= the snake), the tree of the knowledge of good and evil, on the side of the mother. Similarly, the four rivers in paradise are an allegory used by Moses to describe the tetradic organization of the angels: "These twelve angels, which are intertwined with the four parts of the universe, surround and rule the world, holding it in a kind of satrapic power which they derive from Edem; they do not always stay in the same places, but surround the world as in a dancing circle, moving from place to place, and gradually leaving to others the places that were established for them" (V, 26, 11–12). The first consequence of Elohim's reciprocal love for Edem is the installation of the Heimarmene, an uninterrupted torrent that rolls its stream of distress and vice around the world, chaining all beings to "the necessity of evil" (p. 129, 1). The Valentinians had responded to the problem of the origin of evil by adopting the Platonic solution; Justin adopts the determinism of the astrological conception, whose materialism he radicalizes by transferring it to ontology: evil is nothing but the product of a movement in the very center of the triad. The evil being, engendered by nature and materialized by the astral sphere, comes directly from the unbegotten themselves, Elohim and Edem, under the indifferent eye of Priapus.

The emergence of the sphere of planetary angels will set the entire anthropogonic process in motion. The angels of Elohim pull an animal body, heavy and lifeless, out of the earthly part of Edem—a variant of the Valentinian myth of Sophia's abortion. Elohim and Edem then undertake to make it the "seal and memorial of their love, the eternal symbol of their union" (p. 128, 4). Edem gives it a soul (*psuchē*), the principle of existence (*bios*); Elohim gives it breath (*pneuma*), the principle of life (*zōē*). Thus arises the primordial couple, Eve and Adam, each "in the image" of their model. The centripetal mobility of the astral angels, circling around the world, corresponds to the centrifugal force of the human microcosm trying to escape the circle of destiny in order to rejoin the point of origin.

The myth of the fall, which opens with the union of Edem and Elohim, ends with the story of their separation. Curious to know the secrets of the universe, and by nature drawn toward the heights (*anōpherēs*, p. 129, 5), Elohim climbs with his angels into the upper reaches of the sky, where he discovers the perfect light of Good. Without his angels, since they are Edem's sons, he then enters into the luminous depths of the supreme principle, and sits down on its right. But from that moment it is no longer possible for him to regain his breath (*pneuma*), which is trapped in humans. Sad to have been abandoned, Edem attempts one last time to seduce Elohim, and surrounds herself with all the cosmic beauty of her angels. All is in vain. Furious, she avenges herself by striking at what remains of Elohim in humans, the breath-spirit. In order to make Elohim experience in his turn the torture of separation and sadness, she enjoins Aphrodite-Babel, the first of her demons, to inspire in humans the dramas of love—broken hearts, adultery, and divorce. She then commands Naas (the snake), the third of her angels, to unite with Eve and then with Adam, as a result of which the spirit of Elohim in man is brought to lewdness and pederasty.

As in all the systems of the time, a corollory of the myth of the fall states that salvation will consist in seeing to it that the breath-spirit of Elohim, which resides in humans, is detached first from the multiple degradations, mutilations, and humiliations that it underwent through the power of the inventor of sexuality, Edem-Israel of the double and earthly body, so that it can then reascend, pure and light, to its originating principle. To this evil action of Edem—striking, through her intervening angels (Aphrodite-Babel and Naas), the breath of Elohim inherent in the human spirit—Elohim will set up a counteroffensive of salvation in four stages, each marked by the dispatch of a prophet and dominated by the antagonism of Psyche (on Edem's side) and Pneuma (on Elohim's side)—the anthropological version of the antagonism inherent in the macrocosm (the angels of the father against the angels of the mother).

Elohim first sends Baruch, the third of his angels (= the anti-Naas), to the children of Edem-Israel, the Jews. The voice of Baruch, calling the people of the circumcised to conversion, is stifled by the hissing of Naas. Elohim sends Baruch off a second time, but this time only to the Jewish prophets. They are seduced by Psyche, who is manipulated by Naas, and make a mockery of Baruch's words. Two dispatches, two failures. For the third mission, Elohim chooses Heracles, whom he sends among the uncircumcised (= the pagans) to fight the twelve angels of Edem. In twelve gigantic battles, Heracles triumphs over the lion, the hydra, the boar, and so forth, allegorical names of the mother's angels. Seduced by Omphale, however, who is none other than Aphrodite-Babel, Heracles is stripped of his strength, that is, of the orders transmitted to Baruch by Elohim, and puts on Edem's own robe. Unsatisfied by this partial victory, Elohim sends Baruch off once again, "in the days of King Herod," to a boy of twelve, Jesus of Nazareth, the son of Joseph and Mary, who is busy tending sheep. He reveals to him the Gnosis—the knowledge of the past (the loves of Edem and Elohim, and the repentance of the latter), the present (Naas's fight against Baruch), and the future (the return of Pneuma to the Good). Furious at seeing Jesus resist all his attempts at seduction and remain faithful to Baruch, Naas has him crucified. But Jesus, "abandoning on the wood the body of Edem" (p. 131, 31–32), "gives back the spirit (*pneuma*) into the hands of the Father (= Elohim) and rises up to the Good" (p. 132, 23). The death of Jesus thus marks the end of the antagonism of Psyche and Pneuma and the definitive victory of Elohim over Edem. Justin's tritheist system is therefore a camouflaged dualism: above, the male universe of good, the domain of Priapus-Elohim; and below, the female universe of evil, the domain of Edem. To classify such a Gnostic system among the Christian Gnostics, as the author of the *Elenchos* followed by later criticism has done, is not acceptable.

The anti-Judaic bias of a Justin so taken by Jewish Scriptures is obvious. On the other hand, when Christian heresiology accuses Justin of "following word for word the myths of the Greeks" (p. 125, 8) by simply applying the myth of the union of Heracles with the young girl/snake "to the generation of the universe" (V, 25, 1–4), this constitutes a polemical argument invented for the sake of the cause. The myth of the half-earth/half-snake woman associated with the biblical Edem was not borrowed from Herodotus, as is said in the *Elenchos;* according to Van den Broek, it emerged from speculations that are connected with the cult of Isis-Thermouthis in Hellenistic Egypt. But it is more likely that the goddess of the earth, described by Justin as a young girl or a young virgin (*korē*, p. 127, 4), the wife (*suzugos*, p. 129, 6) of an astral god, comes from the esoteric tradition of the "Hellenized Magi," according to whom the earth is a young virgin betrothed to Parnsag (Theodore bar Konai, *Liber scholiorum,* 11, p. 297, 12–14 Scher). Moreover, the chain-of-prophets theory recalls the theory that is found in pseudo-Clementine writings or among the Elchasaites. Unlike the latter, Justin lacks the essentially Christian element almost entirely; at the same time, the uncreated and eternal character of the elements of the triad appears incompatible with the "Judeo-Christian" theses in the strict sense. However, the importance given to water symbolism (stagnating waters below the firmament; living waters above) is connected with Eastern baptist trends. Finally, Justin's Christological Docetism recalls that of the *Apocalypse of Peter,* in which Jesus "the carnal" is nailed to the cross while Jesus "the living" is joyful and laughs (*Nag Hammadi Coptic* VII, 3, p. 81, 10–22), just as his diatribe against the Jewish prophets is related to that of the *Second Logos of the Great Seth* (*Nag Hammadi Coptic* VII, 2, p. 62, 27–64, 12). This pagan-dominated Elchasaism, which is Justin's system, is the response to a desire for synthesis between a syncretist mythology stemming from the Chaldean astrologers and a baptist practice impregnated by Gnosticizing Docetism.

M.T./t.l.f.

BIBLIOGRAPHY

W. VÖLKER, *Quellen zur Geschichte der chrislichen Gnosis* (Tübingen 1932), 27–33. E. HAENCHEN, "Das Buch Baruch: Ein Beitrag zum Problem der christlichen Gnosis," *Zeitschrift für Theologie und Kirche* 50 (1953): 123–58; reprinted in *Gott und Mensch: Gesammelte Aufsätze* (Tübingen 1965), 299–334. M. SIMONETTI, "Note sul Libro di Baruch dello gnostico Giustino," in *Vetera Christianorum* 6 (1969): 71–89. A. ORBE, "La cristología de Justino gnóstico," *Estudios Eclesiásticos* 47 (1972): 437–57. R. VAN DEN BROEK, "The Shape of Edem according to Justin the Gnostic," *Vigiliae Christianae* 27 (1973): 35–45. W. SPEYER, "Das gnostische Baruch-Buch," *Jahrbuch für Antike und Christentum* 17 (1974): 190.

THE MEDIEVAL WEST AND "MYTHIC THOUGHT"

The conjunction of the terms "Christianity" and "mythology" was not at all shocking to the *philosophes* of the eighteenth century: on the contrary, analogous to their unfavorable judgments on the myths of other civilizations, the "great minds" saw in Catholicism a tissue of errors and affabulations that strained the limits of Reason, a "Christian mythology" relegated by the Enlightenment to the dark centuries of the Middle Ages.

In the nineteenth century, this "Christian mythology" entered the fields of study of historians and folklorists. But, though it partially avoided polemic in order to become an object of knowledge, it was still not apprehended through a unified vocabulary and precisely defined concepts: each author, it seems, could furnish his own definition of myth. Agreement was reached on one point: no one questioned the use of the word "myths" and "mythologies" when treating of the Middle Ages.

A primary procedure, which is generally recognized as outmoded today, was the search for the *origins* of "myths" spread by medieval Christianity. In his *Essays on Christian Mythology* (1907), Paul Saintyves was especially concerned with the Greco-Roman origins of the "Christian mythology" of the Middle Ages. More recently, Henri Dontenville has connected "French mythology" with an ancestral Celtic mythology, which he claims to have recovered from eleventh- to sixteenth-century documents and from more recent folklore.

Commenting on the title of his great work *The Saints as Successors to the Gods,* Saintyves strongly asserts that "the cult of martyrs and saints is of pagan origin," though he does go on to say more precisely that "this does not mean that they are not Christian." Churches have been built on numerous sites of pagan cults, and the pagan festivals yielded to the great Church festivals (Christmas, All Saints', etc.) on the same days. Similarly, the gods or heroes of antiquity were transformed into saints of the Church, and ancient myths are found to lie at the origin of certain hagiographic legends. For example, the legend of Saint Julian the Hospitable seems to reproduce the myth of Oedipus (page 269). It is true that the same might be said of the apocryphal legend of Judas, who was never—far from it—assimilated to a saint; but Saintyves never explains this contradiction in his thesis. His hypotheses nevertheless have the merit of being applied to long periods of time, necessary in the study of narrative traditions, and of taking account of an important part of the cultural heritage from which Christianity progressively arose. But these merits should not obscure the fact that the function of the saints who interceded with God was, simply because of the central presence of God, radically different from that of the pagan gods.

On the other hand, Dontenville's reconstitution of a "French mythology" bears the stamp of the "Celtic school": this is organized around the "mythic" giant Gargantua, to whom are connected the great legendary characters of the Middle Ages—Merlin, Morgan Le Fay, King Arthur, the serpent woman Mélusine, the horse Bayard, Tarasca, etc. One may wonder about the validity of a method which rests more on phonetic analogies than on a genuine scientific etymology. Elsewhere, though it is true that these narrative traditions were quite widespread, it is doubtful that they operated on a "national" or even a pan-European scale: it is likely that no narrator, let alone any listener, was ever aware that Gargantua could have been connected both to Mount Gargan in Italy and to Mont Saint-Michel in Normandy. The perspective that time and the scholarly work of Rabelais offer to the modern Celticist should not make him forget that the social context in which these folkloric traditions functioned was certainly much narrower. Our opinion is that this framework should be brought back to the scale of village or urban communities, or even to lineages such as that of the Lusignans, who explain their origins by reference to the legend of Mélusine.

A second methodology tends to reserve the expression "Christian mythology" solely for those medieval narrative traditions that were concerned with the world beyond. This is the implicit procedure followed by Sabine Baring-Gould in his *Curious Myths of the Middle Ages* (1866–88), and especially by Arturo Graf in his great book *Myths, Legends and Superstitions of the Middle Ages* (1892): myths, and not mere legends, were those accounts which, in the twelfth century, placed in the East the earthly Paradise to which Seth, the son of Adam, went to ask in vain for his father's pardon. In the same period, other "myths" relate that Morgan Le Fay carried the wounded Arthur to the Isle of Fortune (according to Geoffrey of Monmouth); if we are to believe Gervase of Tilbury, this Arthurian court was in Sicily in the depths of Mount Etna, where purgatory was located.

Graf sees a connection between these representations of the world beyond, which is nevertheless located on earth, and the "myth" of the land of Cockaigne. Cockaigne is also situated on earth, but it is made for the living, for people who enjoy good living, in fact, since it spares its inhabitants from eating the overly delicate food of paradise, "where it is prohibited to eat anything other than fruits or to drink anything other than water," according to a fourteenth-century German poem. Cockaigne—whose name evokes cakes (the German *Kuchen* or the English *cake* have the same root)—is the world of the carnival inversion of rules about eating and of the Church calendar, signifying the definitive triumph of "Carnage" over "Lent." Thus Lent is only observed once every twenty years, while the festival of Easter is repeated four times each year! As František Graus (1967) has shown so well, Cockaigne, essentially conceived as a village region or, less often, as a manor, is one of the

Paris, Bibliothèque de l'Arsenal. Photo Giraudon.

three great forms of the medieval utopia. Another is the pursuit of the ancient utopian traditions, which continue to be known in literate circles; the third, by contrast, is "popular," and represents the medieval version of the Golden Age. This is pushed back into a past that is never as distant as that of the earthly Paradise before the fall, and is generally connected with the name of a more or less legendary saint-king whose reign remains the symbol of peace and opulence. Cockaigne is thus the expression neither of the most scholarly culture nor of folkloric culture; it is associated with the intermediate milieu of Goliards and students, who were aware of both village traditions and the Latin culture of the clergy. It expresses the utopia of a world in which, thanks to the fountain of youth that is at the center of this land, sensual pleasure and youth are perpetually renewed.

We must dispute Graf's use of the word "myth," but we should recognize that the author did not devote himself to the traditional quest for "origins." On the contrary, he grounded his research in history, demonstrating—with regard to the image of the devil, for example—how these representations are the product of a constantly evolving society, and are not reducible to "origins" containing all of their future developments in advance. If, however, he seems to have sensed the need for a typology of narrative genres, he was never explicit about it; if he distinguished "myths" from "legends," he never really gave his reasons for doing so. He assimilated utopia into myth, which, as we shall see, is unjustifiable.

The word "myth" is also employed by historians of medieval heresy when they speak of a "Cathar myth." Here the observer is presented with a body of structured and apparently autonomous beliefs (some have even spoken of "another religion" rather than a heresy, which is merely a deviation from Christianity) which express essential truths about the origin of the world, of evil, of man, and about the fate of the soul after death. The principal theme of this "Cathar myth," such as it appeared in the south of France and in northern Italy from the twelfth to the fourteenth centuries, is the rivalry between the two principles of Good (God) and Evil (Satan). This opposition underlies the story of the origin of souls: by means of the charms of his creature, Woman, Satan succeeds in seducing the majority of the spirits of God, who leave Paradise through a hole. When the Father notices what is happening, he puts his foot over the hole, but in vain; it is too late and nearly all of the spirits have gone away. These spirits, however, in the presence of Satan, remain nostalgic for the celestial glory they once knew. To make them forget it, Satan gives them a carnal envelope, the body, which is thus a creation of Evil; upon the death of the body, the soul leaves it and goes to dwell within another body, that of an animal or a man. This transmigration of souls is the only hell that exists, and here too it is situated on earth. When a soul eventually enters the body of a Cathar Perfectus, it is assured its salvation, for the death of this man will allow it to return to the Father. And when all of the souls have returned to God, it will be the end of the world. Legends were grafted upon this basic narrative, and those concerned with the migration of souls play an important role. One of these relates that a Perfectus found in a ravine a horseshoe that he had lost in that very spot when he was previously a horse. All of these accounts have multiple functions: they offer an explanation for the history of the world, from its beginning to the end of time, and a unified representation of this world and the world beyond. At the same time, they justify the internal divisions between the heretical groups, between Perfecti and Believers, and the alimentary and sexual taboos of the Cathars, for whom all that concerns the flesh is diabolical. This group of narratives, organized into a coherent whole, does resemble what might be understood as a "mythology." But first the illusion of its autonomy must be dissipated: Like orthodoxy, this body of narratives was constituted out of an interpretation of the Scriptures. Furthermore, it would be a mistake not to see it as a complete theology, seeking, through the same rational avenues as does the theology of the Church, arguments it might use to counter the Church. Under these conditions, is it legitimate to speak of "myths"?

Although historians of medieval Christianity have not hesitated to use the words "myths" and "mythologies," they have given them widely varying contents. Beyond these divergences there is the basic question of whether it is legitimate to speak of "myths" with reference to medieval Christianity, regardless of the particular meanings one might give the word. This question demands that the word be given as clear a definition as possible, to ensure its applicability to the Middle Ages. The clarification demanded of the medievalist is all the more urgent for the fact that the analysis of myths has constituted one of the most dynamic branches of research in the human sciences for at least thirty years.

Myth defines itself at the heart of a structured narrative system according to its own logic, constituting the sole form of articulation and reception for the essential truths of a given society: myth tells what is known about the world, the cosmos, human society, animals, and gods. The logic of myth is that of "savage thought," which keeps reorganizing the same elements ("mythemes") according to symbolic codes of affinities, in the same way, according to Lévi-Strauss, that a *bricoleur* (a kind of professional scrap collector and fix-it man) assembles given materials already at hand. Furthermore, myth, as opposed to legend, does not claim to be the account of a historical tradition; nor does it express, as opposed to a utopia, an aspiration for a different society: on this subject, the reader may refer to Pierre Vidal-Naquet's pertinent remarks. We should also note, along with Jean-Pierre Vernant, that mythic thought, which is the totality of the thinking of a society at a given moment of its historical development, may yield its place to another kind of thinking, as occurred in ancient Greece, when political reason and philosophy came to birth at the same time as the polis.

These definitions seem to exclude from the outset any evocation of a medieval "Christian mythology." In fact, the essential verities of medieval Christianity were uttered not by the voice of myth but by the Book, which reproduces the revealed and immutable Word of a unique God and is interpreted by the clergy. Far from engaging in a discussion that was closed on itself and founded on combinations of ever-repeated images, the clergy found, in the very distance they placed between their reason and the Word of God, the possibility of a continuous transcendence of their thought. As faith in quest of understanding (*fides quaerens intellectum*), and as a refusal to take pleasure in the play of oppositions or in the opposing will to reduce all contradictions (the meaning of Abelard's *Sic et Non*), theological reason excludes myth.

Paris, Bibliothèque des Beaux-Arts. Photo Giraudon.

Of course, medieval Christianity did inherit myths, starting with the Semitic myths of Genesis, the Flood, etc., which the Bible had bequeathed to it. Deposited as they were in the Bible, however, and spread and explained by the Church, these myths were not lived as such: they constituted the *historia* par excellence, sacred History, and Moses, as the Dominican Vincent de Beauvais stated in the thirteenth century, "was the first among us to write the history of the beginning of the world" (*Speculum Doctrinale* 3.127). What has elsewhere been stated by myth is now attested to by the historian.

Historia, which enumerates in chronological order those events which in fact took place (*res factae, res gestae*), is set against *fabulae,* the artifices of language—that is, according to Saint Augustine, against the myths of pagan antiquity (known to the authors of the Middle Ages through the mythographers of late antiquity, especially through the *Mythologiae* of Fulgentius), against entertaining fables (those of Aesop above all), and against the false beliefs of the Manicheans (*Contra Faustum Manichaeum,* ed. Migne, *Patrologia Latina,* vol. 42, col. 374). Here we can see just how much the "Cathar myths" of the modern historians are in fact inherited from the clerical tradition of the Middle Ages. Thus, not only is it impossible to assimilate medieval Christianity to a "Christian mythology," but medieval Christianity itself took its distance from all the accounts that it perceived as myths (*fabulae*) in order to pass judgment on them.

Medieval Christianity is not to be identified, however, with the religion of the clergy alone. The clergy designated as *fabulae* the oral traditions of the *illiterati,* that is, all persons—long including the lay members of the aristocracy—who had no access to writing, to the Latin language, in a word, to the culture of the clergy. Is it appropriate, at least at this level, which by convention we call folkloric, to speak of "mythology" and "myths"?

Historically, it is true, the roots of medieval folklore are to be found in a pre-Christian past, which at that time had until quite recently been on the fringes of Christianity for the Slavic, Scandinavian, Celtic, and Germanic populations who had just been Christianized or were being Christianized. This pagan past was more complex in the case of Gaul, where Romanization had preceded Christianization. But here the collapse of the social structures of the Late Empire may have favored a Celtic "revival" with which Christianity, still not firmly established, would have found itself in brutal confrontation. Whatever the case, folkloric culture is not reducible to these "origins": it was perpetually taking shape and transforming itself in symbiosis with the scholarly culture of the clergy; it became Christianized even as it folklorized official Christianity.

These reciprocal borrowings were not, however, the products of chance; nor were they at all symmetrical. We know that hagiography borrowed heavily from folkloric legends. In the same way, even if the Church had a definite view of the Creation and of the origin of time, it was less comfortable about concrete descriptions of the last things: here there was a certain deficiency or at least a perceptible rift between the account of Genesis, which was realistic but set in the past, and the eschatological symbolism of the Apocalypse, set in the future. Thus it was particularly with regard to the last things that a need was felt to complete and render more concrete the beliefs and even the dogma of the Church: whence the success of the resulting commentaries on the Apocalypse, elucidations that were scholarly but which, quickly vulgarized, fueled a popular millennialism from the thirteenth to the fifteenth centuries that easily slipped into heresy (Spirituals and Beguines, Hussites, etc.). There was a consequent pressure for folkloric depictions, soon assimilated by the clergy, which A. Graf calls "myths." Jacques LeGoff has shown that from the twelfth century onward, under pressure from folk culture, the Christian afterlife became definitively organized, and purgatory took its place between hell and paradise. An analogous deficiency could also be found in the case of the figure of the devil; to be sure, Satan is present in the New Testament, where he comes to tempt Christ himself; and antiquity also had its demons. But it is only with the high Middle Ages that the devil becomes ever-present, obsessive, and tyrannical, which had never previously been the case. It should be further noted that one of the reasons for this medieval diabolical proliferation is the attribution, from the time of Christian antiquity, of a demonic character to certain pagan divinities. It must be clearly recognized, Saintyves to the contrary, that the devil too, and not only the saints, succeeded the gods.

Inversely, what was the effect of Christianization on folk culture? Clerical culture was not content with vulgarizing its topics, baptizing legends, and informing traditional rites. It had especially dispossessed folk culture of its preeminent knowledge: knowledge of the other world, an ear for supernatural beings, and the interpretation of visions, the control of which the clergy meant to reserve for itself alone. The constitution of a "white magic" domesticated by the Church and the increasing repression of all folk demonology followed the same pattern.

Under these conditions, it is difficult to see how medieval folklore could have spoken through myths, for it is the function of myths to constitute and transmit such knowledge. Since this function was monopolized by the Church, the clergy could no longer speak of myths, for their efforts tended in the opposite direction, toward a rational explanation of the Word of God.

Folklore, then, was left with the other narrative genres, which, though far from negligible in importance and function, do not go to the heart of the matter as myth does. Specialists in the study of popular narrative genres strove to give them definitions, which were sometimes too rigid: folktale, whose function is to offer a "naive ethics" (A. Jolles); legend, which has a familial thematization and is anchored to a particular topography and history (H. Bausinger), etc. These narrative genres were allowed to develop freely, and it is they rather than myths that are revealed to us in the written documents of the Middle Ages.

At the same time, although we should not speak of "mythology" or of "myths" in this connection, we may perhaps find "mythic thought" in these folktales and legends. The originality of medieval folk culture resides not only in its contents but also in the way it has organized those contents. Current studies on the narrative traditions of medieval folklore all show that this folklore operated according to a logic that was different from the theological reasoning of the clergy, at least of the most scholarly fraction of the clergy. The structural transformations revealed by the variants of a single account also allow us to speak here, like the ethnologists, of "savage thought" and, like the historians of ancient Greece, of "mythic thought." It is in this sense, we believe, that medieval studies can and should take their place in the now open field of the analysis of myths and oral traditions.

The prudent position we are adopting is also dictated by the state of the documents with which we are constrained to work: it is on the local scale, as we have shown, that one must reconstitute the narrative system of a thirteenth-century village community, for example. But through the written texts of the scholarly culture we can grasp only dispersed shreds of oral traditions, rescued from oblivion by the zeal of an inquisitor or the curiosity of an "intellectual" of the Middle Ages. We are also unable to restore narrative systems, and without them it is difficult to speak of "mythology" and "myths"; Dontenville's attempt is too ambitious in its geographical scope to be convincing. However, sometimes the documentation seems more favorable: using the inquisition register of Jacques Fournier, bishop of Pamiers, Emmanuel Le Roy Ladurie recently brought back to life an entire village community of the upper Ariège in the early fourteenth century. This case is a peculiar one in many regards: at Montaillou, the Cathar heresy had, so to speak, restored to the laity the knowledge of the essential truths, and the "Cathar myth," unlike the interpretations of the Perfecti in the twelfth century, who were so well versed in theological debates, had been reinterpreted in the light of local folklore and inserted into the narrative traditions of the village. In this way, the respect that the Perfectus of the time inspires in the simple Believer is compounded by the attractiveness of his eternal word, for he knows all about Good and Evil, the Creation and the end of the world, and the fates of the souls of deceased family members who, in the ravines close to the villages, search for a body to enter. He knows all about the social order, too. In the beginning was incest: brothers and sisters married freely. Today, on the contrary, the village is a collection of neighboring "*domus*," familial groups which are at once rivals and relatives since they practice the exchange of women between them. The marriage of dowried girls threatens the material equilibrium of each "*domus*." It creates a permanent danger and inspires nostalgia for a bygone day when girls were not expected to leave their homes, and gave themselves to their brothers. But that primordial incest set brother against brother, and had to be put to an end: by imposing exogamy and marriage, the Church instituted the present social order, which, for the sake of peace, sacrifices these peasants' ideal of self-sufficiency. One would like to find other versions of this account, so as to compare it with all of the parallel accounts that must have been circulating at that time. One may at least ask a question: on the inner fringes of Christianity, where folklore and heresy were intermingled and the ascendancy of the Church was less strong, is it not possible that the medieval West also knew myth?

J.-C.S./d.w.

BIBLIOGRAPHY

1. For a general introduction to the history of medieval Christianity: J. LE GOFF, *La civilisation de l'Occident médiéval* (Paris 1964). K. THOMAS, *Religion and the Decline of Magic: Studies in Popular Beliefs in Sixteenth and Seventeenth Century England* (London 1971); all of part 1 concerns the Middle Ages.

2. On the theoretical problems posed by the analysis of myths: CL. LÉVI-STRAUSS, *The Savage Mind* (Chicago 1966). J.-P. VERNANT, *Mythe et société en Grèce ancienne* (Paris 1974), especially 195–250, "Raisons du mythe"; *Les origines de la pensée grecque* (Paris 1969). P. VIDAL-NAQUET, "Esclavage et gynécocratie dans la tradition, le mythe, l'utopie," *Recherches sur les structures sociales dans l'Antiquité classique* (Paris 1970), 63–80.

3. On narrative genres: A. JOLLES, *Einfache Formen: Legende, Sage, Mythe, Rätsel, Spruch, Kasus, Memorabile, Märchen, Witz* (Tübingen 1930). H. BAUSINGER, *Formen der Volkspoesie* (Berlin 1968).

4. Ancient mythology in the scholarly culture of the Middle Ages: J. SEZNEC, *La survivance des dieux antiques: Essai sur le rôle de la tradition mythologique dans l'hymanisme et dans l'art de la Renaissance* (Paris 1939). A. RENAUDET, *Dante humaniste* (Paris 1952). F. SAXL and E. PANOFSKY, *Classical Mythology in Medieval Art* (New York 1933).

5. Mythology and folklore: N. BELMONT, *Mythes et croyances dans l'Ancienne France* (Paris 1973), which is justly critical of H. DONTENVILLE, *La mythologie française* (Paris 1948). The opposite is true in the case of the Tarasque: L. DUMONT, *La Tarasque: Essai de description d'un fait local d'un point de vue ethnographique* (Paris 1951).

6. Hagiography and "mythology": P. SAINTYVES, *Les saints successeurs des dieux: Essais de mythologie chrétienne*, 1 (Paris 1907); *En marge de la Légende Dorée. Songes, miracles et survivances. Essai sur la formation de quelques thèmes hagiographiques* (Paris 1931). Suggestive in a different way: B. DE GAIFFIER, "Mentalité de l'hagiographe médiéval d'après quelques travaux récents," *Analecta Bollandiana* 86 (1968): 391–99. See especially: F. GRAUS, *Volk, Herrscher und Heiliger im Reich der Merowinger* (Prague 1965). J. LE GOFF, "Culture cléricale et traditions folkloriques dans la civilisation mérovingienne," *Niveaux de culture et groupes sociaux* (Paris 1968), 21–32; "Culture ecclésiastique et culture folklorique au Moyen Age: Saint Marcel de Paris et le dragon," *Ricerche storiche ed economiche in memoria di Corrado Barbagallo* (Naples 1970), 2:53–90.

7. The world beyond and utopias: A. GRAF, *Miti, Leggende et superstizioni nel Medio Evo* (Turin 1892); *Il diavolo* (Milan 1889). S. BARING-GOULD, *Curious Myths of the Middle Ages* (New Hyde Park and New York 1866–88). A. MAURY, *Croyances et légendes du Moyen Age* (Paris 1896). C. G. LOOMIS, *White Magic: An Introduction to the Folklore of Christian Legends* (Cambridge, MA, 1948). F. GRAUS, "Social Utopias in the Middle Ages," *Past and Present* 38 (1967). J. LE GOFF, *The Birth of Purgatory*, trans. Arthur Goldhammer (Chicago 1984). Finally, on the millenarian movements of the low Middle Ages: N. COHN, *The Pursuit of the Millennium* (London 1957). And especially: B. TÖPFER, *Das kommende Reich des Friedens: Zur Entwicklung chiliastischer Zukunftshoffnungen im Hoch mittelalter* (Berlin 1964).

8. On the "Cathar myth": A. BORST, *Die Katharer* (Stuttgart 1963), also in French. *Cathares en Languedoc*, Les Cahiers de Fanjeaux 3 (Toulouse 1968). E. LE ROY LADURIE, *Montaillou, village occitan de 1294 à 1324* (Paris 1975).

9. Folklore and oral traditions in historical studies today: besides the above cited studies by J. Le Goff, see: J. LE GOFF and E. LE ROY LADURIE, "Mélusine maternelle et défricheuse," *Annales E.S.C.*, 1971, 587–622. J. LE GOFF and P. VIDAL-NAQUET, "Lévi-Strauss en Brocéliande," *Critique* 326 (June 1974): 541–71. J. C. SCHMITT, "Religion populaire et culture folklorique. A propos d'une réédition: La piété populaire au Moyen Age d'Etienne Delaruelle," *Annales E.S.C.*, 1976, 5. On the particular relations between folklore and learned literature in the vernacular: E. KÖHLER, *L'aventure chevaleresque: Idéal et réalité dans le roman courtois*, French trans. (Paris 1974). Outside the period and in a different context see also: C. GINZBURG, *Il formaggio e i vermi* (Turin 1976). M. BAKHTIN, *Rabelais and His World* (Cambridge, MA, 1968), trans. from Russian.

The Survival of the Ancient Gods in the Middle Ages and the Renaissance

I. The Middle Ages

Before inquiring how mythology was interpreted in the Middle Ages, we should remember that it had survived on different levels, mainly in folklore. It was among the *pagani*, in rural areas, that polytheism had most tenaciously persisted. With the advent of Christianity, the cult of sylvans and nymphs was not annihilated along with the temples knocked down by the first apostles in Gaul. "Immutable at the depths of rivers, in the eternal twilight of forests, the spirit of the old days lived on." Regarding this tenacity we have the testimony of the capitularies and the councils who up to the Carolingian period denounced superstitious practices and condemned as sacrilegious those who continued to light flares and fires near trees, rocks, and fountains. Their anathemas remained powerless. Gregory the Great had already recognized the impossibility of extirpating the layers of beliefs rooted "in such stubborn minds"; the only way to fight superstition was to assign the pagan vestiges to the new cult, to put pious images on trees, to carve crosses on menhirs, to place fountains under the invocation of the Virgin—in a word, to cover the ancient venerations with a cloak of orthodoxy. Indeed, strange assimilations had made the saints the successors of the gods. Saint Christopher, for example, had become the heir of Mercury, Hercules, and even Anubis. Having lent him their attributes and practices, they continued to be honored under the saint's name. These amalgams and avatars were further means of survival. But demons, too, took over guard duty from the gods, so to speak. "It was foolishly said: the great Pan is dead; then, seeing that he lived, he was made into a god of evil." The pagan origins of the sabbath were denounced by the Council of Aix-la-Chapelle, which found Diana, *panagorum dea* ("goddess of the pagans"), among the wicked women straddling animals, along with Satan. Michelet describes sorcery, a pact with the powers of instinct, as a rebellion, a revenge of nature oppressed by Christian asceticism.

But it was the Christians who, paradoxically, preserved mythology and even taught it. For it remained well above rustic superstitions; it was an integral part of classical culture, a culture adopted by the Church in the first centuries. The Church Fathers, who were imbued with it, were aware of the difficulty and the danger of preserving in education a literature and an art indissolubly linked to polytheism; but they accepted the necessity of permitting their youth to be instructed in schools of the Greco-Roman type. Tertullian himself recognized this necessity. In the fourth century, Christian children and adolescents were raised as pagans; despite the immorality of fable, they entered with Virgil into a familiarity with the gods, for the essence of the grammarian's schooling remained the explication of the poets; it was, moreover, from the list of the gods' names that one learned to read. The last generation to receive this instruction was the one raised by Ausonius. With the invasions that destroyed the ancient school, an eclipse began which lasted until the eighth century. In the middle of the sixth century, scholastic life was perpetuated in Rome and in Africa, and then came the collapse of culture and the decadence of letters. However, the ancient sources had not dried up; beyond the barbarian rupture, seeds of renewal survived. The Carolingian "renaissance," to which the name of Alcuin is linked, flourished in the twelfth century, when Chartres and Orleans became the great seats of classical studies. But each renewal was accompanied by a rise in neopaganism—witness the popularity of Ovid in the twelfth century (the preeminent *aetas Ovidiana*). The correspondence of monks is full of mythological allusions, and the goliards, who resuscitated paganism even in their mores, dedicated poems to Narcissus, to Philomela, and to Pyramus and Thisbe. At the end of the century, Alexander of Villedieu complained that old gods were being worshiped in Orleans, that Venus,

Deianira being abducted by Nessus. Fragment from a small column in Chartres Cathedral. Photo Giraudon.

Bacchus, and Faunus had their altars and their festivals there: the path to Paradise was lost.

Medieval art shows signs of these "renaissances." Here, too, antiquity once again became inspirational. When the first churches rose from the ruins of pagan sanctuaries, and oratories replaced shrines to the Lares, the vestiges were incorporated into new constructions and were put to use for the new religion. Sarcophagi were transformed into altars, their fragments into stoups or baptismal fonts; diptyches and ivory cases served as reliquaries; images of the Olympians were encrusted in the ambo of Aix-la-Chapelle. The sculptors who copied these pagan relics looked to them first for decorative forms and formulas, for lessons in technique and style—but also for profane themes, which they would combine with sacred representations. In decorating Christian tombs, the sculptors of Arles had already introduced mythological motifs on the covers of their sarcophagi: Castor and Pollux, Eros and Psyche, and so forth. In Roman art, ancient allegories of the Earth and the Ocean, and of the Moon and the Sun on their chariots, accompanied the crucifixion and the apparition of Christ in his glory. Sirens and centaurs reappeared on tympana, lintels, and capitals. Chiron's education of Achilles is depicted at Vezelay. The same scene was formerly depicted at Chartres, together with the abduction of Hippodamia. And on a column of the western portal one even sees Deianira carried away by Nessus. The end of the twelfth century offers one of the most unexpected examples of a pagan monument in the interior of a cloister—the famous fountain that was constructed to serve as a washbowl for the monks of Saint-Denis. Its mutilated basin stands today in the courtyard of the École des Beaux-Arts in Paris; the rim is decorated with medallions, perhaps copied from cameos, on which about thirty heads are sculpted in relief. Among the heroes and allegories one can distinguish Jupiter, Neptune, Thetis, Ceres, Bacchus, and pastoral divinities. Gothic art, which abandoned ancient forms, seemed to retain from antiquity only its prophetic prefigurations: antiquity is scarcely represented in cathedrals except by the Sibyl. However, at the base of the portal of Auxerre there is a sleeping Eros.

In the last analysis, the survival of the gods through the Middle Ages, up to the dawn of the *Rinascimento*, can be explained by an important and general reason: they were protected by the interpretations that antiquity itself proposed for their origin and nature. These various interpretations, corresponding to various representations, can essentially be reduced to three.

The first is Euhemerism, popularized by Ennius: the gods were only humans, raised from the earth to heaven by the idolatry of their contemporaries. Christian apologists and the Church Fathers willingly adopted this interpretation and used it as a weapon against paganism—a two-edged sword, for though it relegated the gods to the level of mortals, it confirmed their existence and allowed them a place in history. Paulus Orosius, Isidore of Seville, and their successors would later attempt to assign them a place in time. Going back to the primitive ages in Egypt, Assyria, Greece, and Rome, Isidore discovered mythological dynasties; every single chronicler after ranked the gods among ancient kings and heroes, and at the same time sought to connect them with the great figures of the sacred History in lineages parallel to those of the patriarchs, judges, and prophets. As a result of these synchronisms, the prestige of the gods was restored. Moreover, to make a place for characters of fable in the annals of humanity was to recognize that they had been its benefactors. They had earlier obtained the honors of apotheosis because they had destroyed monsters, built cities, invented arts. Prometheus, Atlas, Hercules, Theseus, Isis who taught writing, and Minerva who taught women weaving were the venerable precursors of civilization.

In the twelfth century, the *Historia Scholastica* of Petrus Comestor codified the parallelism between profane history and the history of the people of God. In its translation by Guyart des Moulins it became a sort of scholastic manual of mythology, providing Vincent de Beauvais with the essence of what he wrote about the gods in his *Speculum Historiale*. Iconography illustrates this diffusion, and this direction, of Euhemerism. In Florence, Giotto's bell tower, on which the prophets are represented, depicts on the first section of the bas-reliefs, near Daedalus the first aeronaut, Orpheus the father of Poetry, and Hercules the conqueror of Cacus.

On the other hand, pride of race prompted scholars of the Middle Ages to seek ancestors and forebears for their people in the fabulous past. Thus the Franks claimed to be descended from the Trojan Francus, as earlier the Romans had claimed to have been from the Trojan Aeneas; the Italians had Janus and then Saturn and his sons for their first kings. The prodigious success of the *Romance of the Rose* is explained in part by its ethnogenic character. Mythological characters became the patrons of such and such a people, the stock from which it was born. They were also founders of dynasties; princes discovered ancestors for themselves among them, and boasted of having at least a demigod as the originator of their house. Thus Brutus, the Trojan hero, became the ancestor of the kings of England; and that is why the abduction of Helen is portrayed in a thirteenth-century genealogical scroll illustrating that royal lineage. The chronicles and world histories thus became vehicles of a mythographic tradition that would flourish in the Renaissance.

The physical interpretation, according to which the gods were heavenly bodies, perpetuated another tradition. Anyone discerning a governing intelligence behind the movement of the spheres is inclined to place divinity in the sky; but astronomical nomenclature, which attached each planet, each constellation, each sign of the zodiac to a character from fable, had encouraged the Greeks and the Romans to identify celestial bodies with gods. This "mythologization" of the sky was the result of a long evolution, complicated by the intrusion of exotic "signs" from Egypt or Chaldea: the *sphaera graecanica* was rivaled, or fed upon, by a *sphaera barbarica*, whose elements became mixed up with classical elements.

The definitive fusion of astronomy and mythography shows the influence of the Stoics, who were satisfied with a rationalist interpretation that seemed to legitimize and purify the gods by reducing them to cosmic symbols; but the major influence was that of Oriental cults (particularly the cult of the Sun, in Persia, and the Babylonian cult of the planets), which were prevalent in the Greco-Roman world. Not only was the belief in sidereal gods confirmed; it took on an extraordinary religious intensity. Indeed, the stars were alive; they had a face, a gender, a personality, and their power was awesome, for they were the arbiters of destiny: they determined the fate of men and of empires. Thus, toward the end of the pagan era, the gods who were dethroned on earth became all-powerful once again, thanks to astrology, in the sky. But here, too, Christians preserved what they wished to abolish. Astrology, which they ought to have abhorred, maintained its partisans and supporters among them; even its adversaries made important concessions to it. Neither Lactantius nor Saint Augustine questioned the influence of the stars; but they maintained that the will of man and the grace of God could conquer this

Monks' wash basin in the Abbey of Saint-Denis. Thirteenth century. École des Beaux Arts. Photo Giraudon.

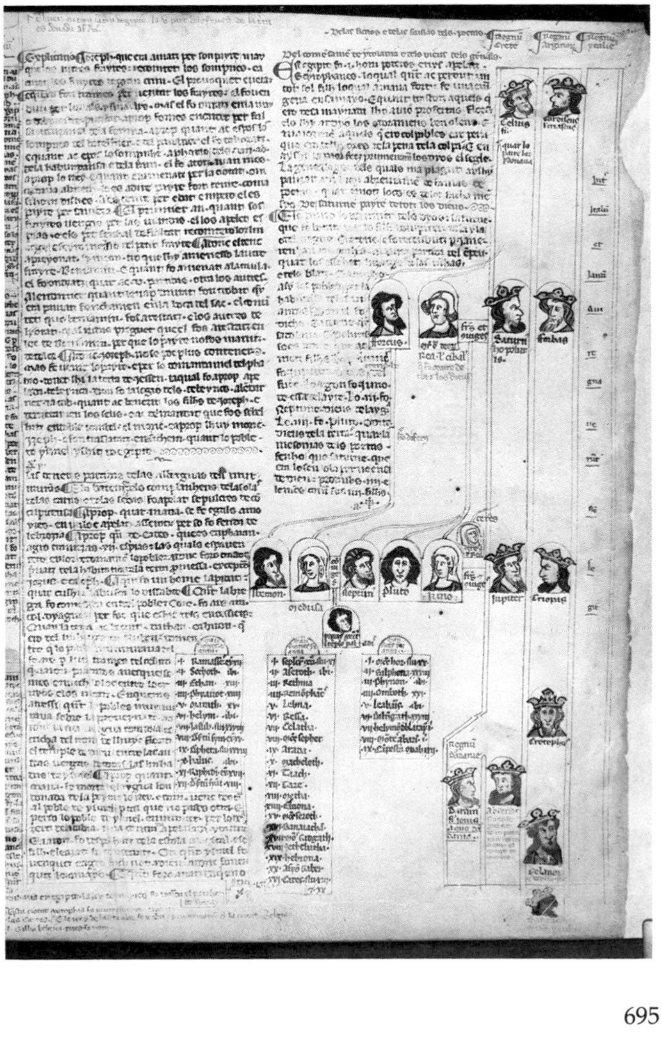

Caelus and his descendants (Ms. Egerton, 1500, fol. 6). London, British Library. Library photo.

influence. Others saw the coercion of the stars as merely an expression of the doctrine of predestination, or at least as the intermediary through which God manifested his immutable decrees. Indeed, even when they condemned astrology, the apologists and the Church Fathers kept its deep root intact; the fear of demons and their evildoing haunted the popular imagination, but the astrological conception of causality dominated the greatest minds.

After the twelfth century, the influx of Arabic science into the West gave astrology a renewed virulence. The *Ghāya*, a manual of practical magic composed of Oriental and Hellenistic materials, was translated into Spanish at the court of Alfonso X; about twenty Latin manuscripts of it are known under the title of *Picatrix*—"the Reverend Father Picatrix, rector of the Diabological Faculty," as Rabelais would call him. This manual taught how to conjure up celestial powers and render them favorable; it taught formulas of prayer and invocation and prescribed instruments for the purpose: images of Jupiter, Venus, Mars, and Saturn, engraved on rocks, gained the influence of the corresponding divinities. As we have seen, gemstones bearing effigies of the gods had never ceased to be used; now they served as amulets and talismans; this time it was in the lapidaries that the gods found refuge.

The third system of interpretation consisted of discovering a spiritual meaning in the figure of the gods, and a moral lesson in their adventures. This sort of allegory had been applied by the first critics of Homer, such as Heraclitus, and, at the end of the pagan era, by Stoics such as Cornutus, to justify the apparent impiety of the myths by distinguishing

Juno-Memory (Vat. ms. Palat. lat. 1066, fol. 223v). Vatican, Biblioteca apostolica vaticana. Library photo.

their literal meaning from their deep or secret meaning. Since that time, the old legends had gradually been elevated: in the *Aeneid* the Olympians regained their dignity; with his genius for deifying moral ideas, Virgil moralized the gods. But in the hands of the Neoplatonists, allegory became a means of sanctifying them. They studied fable in depth as if it were a sacred text. In his treatise, *On the Gods and the World,* "a veritable pagan catechism," Sallust, a friend of the emperor Julian, chose the most shocking myths in order to reveal a philosophic content in them—accessible, it is true, to initiates alone. Julian himself applied the method in his hymns to Helios and to the Great Mother, with the intention of contrasting the mythology thus regenerated to the Christian cult.

The Church, for that reason alone, should have been hostile to allegory. But the apologists and the Church Fathers themselves applied the method to holy books; and they employed it in education. Having conserved profane poetry in their own education, they were inevitably led to moralize mythology in their turn. In the sixth century, the *Moralia* of Gregory the Great, biblical allegories, had their counterpart in the *Mythologiae* of Fulgentius, profane allegories. In the Middle Ages, the fable as a whole became a *philosophia moralis.* Thus the three goddesses between whom Paris had to choose were, according to Fulgentius, symbols of the active life, the contemplative life, and the amorous life. In the Carolingian period a poem by Theodulf, bishop of Orleans, explained how wise men could turn the lies of poets, beginning with Ovid, into truths.

Beginning in the twelfth century, this type of exegesis reached stunning proportions. It was then that Bernard de Chartres and John of Salisbury meditated on pagan religion, "not out of respect for false divinities, but because they disguised sacred teachings, incomprehensible to the common man." It was above all the time when the rehabilitation of Ovid—who was proclaimed *Ethicus* and even *Theologus*—was affirmed. Arnolphe d'Orleans and John Garland rigorously demonstrated the edifying nature of the *Metamorphoses.* In the first years of the fourteenth century the immense *Moralized Ovid* appeared, whose author distinctly declared that if one knew how to read the poems, "everything is for our edification." The eyes of Argus on the tail of Juno's peacock are the vanities of the century; Phaethon is Lucifer; Ceres searching for Proserpina is the Church beckoning the souls of sinners. To the same century belonged (among other commentaries) Robert Holkot's *Moralia super Ovidii metamorphoses* and Thomas Waleys's *Metamorphosis Ovidiana moraliter explanata.* Rabelais would mock the allegorizers who claimed to discover "the Sacraments of the Gospel" in Ovid; Luther, who denounced allegory as a seductive courtesan, would thunder against those who "turned Apollo into Christ, and Daphne into the Virgin Mary." But they would not halt the popularity of these aberrations.

Allegories and conventional moralizations are again found in the works of Dante, where mythology holds a place that is at first sight surprising. With Dante, too, fable, a repertory of passions, is full of edifying meanings. In the *Purgatorio,* the stories of Aglaurus, Progne, Midas, Meleager, and Pasiphaë become so many examples of human deviation. But Dante's attitude toward pagan divinities is profoundly original. He treats them seriously, even with reverence. Not only does he accept the reality of these supernatural beings, but he suggests that between the Fall and the Redemption they played a premonitory role, so that they sometimes elucidated the lessons of the Old Testament. In the "Bible of the Gentiles," the great gods, the *superi,* veiled intelligences, were instructed to make the world aware, in a disguised form, of the authority of the true God. Through the sanctions that Jupiter or Apollo inflicted on sinful mortals they gave human creatures a presentiment of the absolute submission owed to the Creator. Hence the importance, in the *Commedia,* of the "titanic" theme of insubordination, revolt, and the punishments for these transgressions. Dante confirms the judgment by condemning to hell the rebels struck down by the gods. As for the demons that torment them, the most notorious—Charon, Pluto, Minos—are taken from among the *inferni.* Whereas the *superi,* the heavenly spirits, acted for a yet hidden God, these fallen spirits were invested with infernal functions; they passed into the service of Satan.

In the following century, the most extravagant and systematic monument of Christian allegory applied to mythology is a revised version of a treatise by Fulgentius—the *Fulgentius Metaforalis* by the Franciscan John Ridewall. The order of the chapters is governed by the identification of the gods with virtues, an identification stretched by analysis to the most minute subtleties. Thus Saturn is Prudence; the elements that compose this virtue are Memory, Intelligence, and Foresight. Ridewall examines these children of Saturn one by one: Juno ("Memoria"), Neptune ("Intelligentia"), and Pluto ("Providentia"). The respective attributes of these gods are explained precisely by the ideas they represent. Juno's veil is meant to hide the shame of sin, fostered by Memory; the rainbow that crowns her is the sign of her reconciliation with

God, obtained through remembrance and repentance; the scepter she holds indicates that the pardoned soul has regained control of itself, another benefit of Memory.

It was through these three systems of interpretation that the gods ultimately survived. The three systems, however, were not mutually exclusive. At the risk of proposing contradictory explanations, scholars of the Middle Ages frequently applied all three of them to the same character or to the same fable. Pierre d'Ailly, who affirmed the concord between astronomy and history, maintained that the gods were both stars and rulers. On the other hand, there were points of contact as well as of interference between the three cycles. When mythological heroes were taken as examples, morality came to the aid of history. Each planet had its temperament; it determined not only the destiny but the character and the abilities of those born under its influence, who, through this transmission from the physical to the moral, truly became its "children." The ambition of medieval culture, its concern with embracing the totality of knowledge, confined within the *Summaries* the *naturale,* the *morale,* and the *historiale.* In this reduction to unity, numerals played a primordial role: by reason of their number, the planets, the signs of the zodiac, and the elements were placed in concord with the virtues, the months, and the humors, in order to establish the interdependence of all parts of the cosmos and all forms of knowledge. Scholasticism further develops these tables of concord. In his *De natura rerum,* Alexander Neckham codified the relationship, established in the ninth century, between the planets and the virtues. In the *Convivio,* Dante compares these same planets "by reason of their properties" to the liberal arts: the Sphere of the Moon corresponds to Grammar; that of Mercury, to Dialectic; that of Venus, to Rhetoric; that of Jupiter, to Geometry, etc. As for the sphere of fixed stars, it showed "manifest" resemblances to Physics, Metaphysics, Morals, and Theology.

Venus, Juno, Pallas (ms. fr. 143, fol. 198v). Paris, Bibliothèque nationale. Photo BN.

Diagrams graphically express these relationships, by circles containing smaller circles that form a tracery of symmetrical compartments. At the center of these microcosms is written the name of Man, himself an abridgment of the Universe. But the gods have their role in these correspondences, which is why they are first found in the miniatures in encyclopedias, before reappearing in Italian monumental art. In Florence they are seated on Giotto's bell tower with the Sibyls and the prophets, in the same row as the virtues, the sciences, and the sacraments; they dominate the entire cycle of figures that recount the creation of man and the invention of the arts. At the Trinci palace in Foligno, frescoes painted around 1420 also developed the great encyclopedic theme; the gods are once again in evidence, and once again historic and cosmic traditions intersect; mythical characters and stellar powers make an essential contribution to this decorative whole.

The Renaissance gathered together and developed these various interpretations; when the gods reappeared in full daylight, it was first in one of these frameworks. In this matter the Renaissance is greatly indebted to the Middle Ages. The reason the continuity long remained unsuspected is that the classical form of the gods was lost in the meantime; they had become unrecognizable. The history of their metamorphoses can nevertheless be followed from the Carolingian period up until the fifteenth century, mainly because of the extremely rich documentation furnished by miniatures in astrologic-mythological manuscripts. These illustrations can be divided into two groups, according to whether they had a visual model as a prototype or were derived from a simple descriptive text.

The "visual" tradition may be further broken down into several families. The first had a purely Western origin and character and flourished until the thirteenth century or thereabouts. Essentially it included the *Aratea,* that is, the manuscripts of that poem (translated by Cicero), the *Phaenomena,* in which Aratus describes the constellations as a mythographer rather than as an astronomer. The Carolingian copies of the *Aratea* restored the ancient model with striking fidelity. But new and strange versions appeared at the end of the Middle Ages, which came from the Orient. They are found in two contexts—first, in Arabic astrological manuscripts, where Hellenistic figures had been profoundly altered by the transcribers who were ignorant of mythology. Hercules, for example, is dressed as a Turk, with a scimitar and a turban; Medusa, decapitated by Perseus, becomes a bearded demon. Second, they are encountered in illustrations in Michael Scot's treatise, composed in Sicily around 1250. This treatise, of which we have more than thirty manuscripts, shows the strangest constellations, borrowed from the "barbaric sphere." The drawings of the planets are even more bizarre: Jupiter is represented as a scholar, Saturn as a warrior, and Mercury as a bishop. This last series of figures goes back, by way of the *Ghāya,* to a Babylonian tradition. It, too, played a role in fourteenth-century Italian monumental art: in the Spanish Chapel in Florence, in the Eremitani of Padua, on the capitals of the Doges' Palace—it is in this extraordinary iconography that the Olympians were disguised.

Apart from astronomical manuscripts, examples of the "visual" tradition are rarely found outside of Byzantine art, though miniatures of profane manuscripts and ivory caskets with mythological motifs still remain very close to Hellenistic models. There is, however, a surprising Western illustration of Raban Maur's *De rerum naturis* in the copy by Montecassino. However crude the divinities represented may be, an ancient model can still be detected behind each one of them.

The types derived from a descriptive text, a "literary" source, constitute a distinct group. Here the Byzantines were privileged; they had the "Library" of Apollodorus, and perhaps even an illustrated manuscript of the work that served as a mythographical manual from the ninth to the fourteenth century. In the West, this family of gods is found in allegoric treatises. These treatises contained two parts, the first descriptive and the second moral. The descriptive elements were generally taken from early mythographers and scholiasts such as Macrobius, Servius, Lactantius Placidus, Martianus Capella, and Fulgentius: it was their erudition that served as a basis for the medieval compilers. After 1100, illustrations appeared in the margins of treatises of this kind. A manuscript of Remi d'Auxerre's *Commentaries* on Martianus Capella shows a series of gods: Cybele, Apollo, Saturn, Mercury, and others; but they are difficult to identify, for the miniaturist had only one text to guide him, and this text, slavishly followed, engendered only barbaric images. This also applies to Ridewall's *Fulgentius metaforalis,* whose illustrations are grossly anachronistic caricatures.

The *Liber imaginum deorum* of Albricus deserves special attention, for it was to have a lasting influence on iconography. Albricus, who has been identified with the *Mythographus Tertius,* may have been Alexander Neckham, who died in 1217. His work, called the *Poetarius* or the *Scintillarium poetarum,* enjoyed great popularity as an aid to reading the profane poets; but it is encumbered by a heavy allegorical critical apparatus, and there is no illustrated manuscript of it available. Two centuries later an abridgment, the *Libellus de imaginibus deorum,* would become a useful aid to artists. Between the *Liber* and the *Libellus* came an eminent intermediary, Petrarch himself, who in describing the images of the gods decorating the palace of Syphax, in his *Africa,* followed Albricus step by step, though retaining only his pictorial elements. In this pared-down form, the *Libellus* was taken up again in 1340 by a friend of Petrarch's, Pierre Bersuire, who put it in the Fifteenth Book of his *Redictorium morale.* This Fifteenth Book, in which Bersuire "moralizes" Ovid, includes a series of "portraits" of the gods, borrowed, says the author, from Petrarch, "for I was unable to find images of the gods themselves anywhere else." It was Bersuire's "portraits," collected and rid once again of their commentaries, that finally, around 1400, constituted the *Libellus.* This time the result was pure iconography, and the same formula kept recurring: *pingebatur* ("it is painted"). The Codex Reginensis 1290 of the Vatican, which contained the text of the *Liber,* also contained that of the *Libellus,* illustrated with ink drawings executed around 1420. The images were lively and charming, but they showed only a distant kinship with the ancient forms, for they were only "reconstructions" of the gods following a text, or rather a mosaic of texts; indeed, as we have seen, all the descriptions come from disparate sources.

Nonetheless, these composite figures in the *Libellus,* which "codify" the gods' traits and fix them in an immutable attitude, were to establish a lineage in art. The *Libellus* was to become a repertory, as is attested not only by a rich series of Italian, Flemish, and French miniatures but by representations of all sorts: tapistries, enamels, and sculptures. On a capital at Autun on which Luxuria is depicted, Vulcan, Venus, and Eros appear as they are described in the *Liber.* The illustrated book, as we shall see, helped propagate the *Libellus,* which, while it continued to serve as a source for mythographers and as a reference for humanists, was to furnish artists with guiding examples during the entire Quattrocento, and even after.

In sum, by the end of the Middle Ages the "visual" and "literary" traditions had profoundly altered the classical forms of the gods. Unfaithful copies, substitutions, disguises, or naive reconstructions—it is hard to tell from which procedure they suffered most, not to mention the mistakes, blunders, and misconceptions that further aggravated this corruption and that can be explained by their peregrinations from east to west, and from north to south.

The gods were gradually to regain their shape. By examining certain series it is possible to follow the stages of this restoration. Some factors delayed it, however, of which the most important were the influence of the printing press and the illustrated book. The printing press first published only the mythographers that the Middle Ages had drawn from (aside from the *De natura deorum*), and medieval compilations

Microcosm (ms. lat. 13002, fol. 7v). Munich, Bayerische Staatsbibliothek. Library photo.

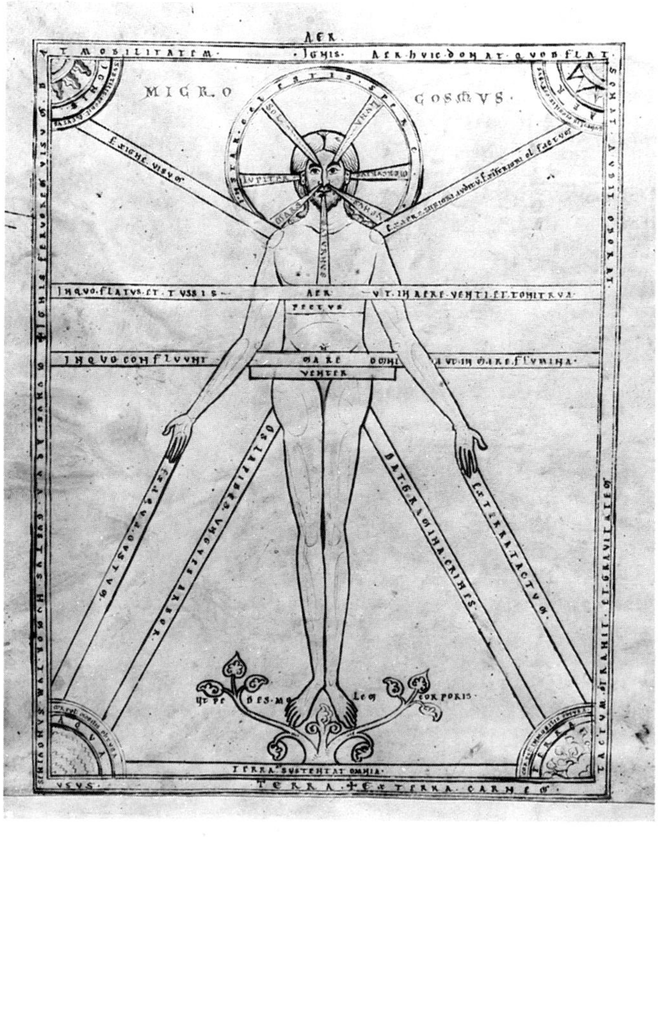

themselves, beginning with the *Liber* of Albricus. Boccaccio's *Genealogia deorum,* heir to this tradition, would be the great repertory during the first half of the Cinquecento. It underwent eight printings between 1473 and 1532, whereas Apollodorus's *Library* (used, as we have seen, by the Byzantines) was not published—in Greek and Latin—until 1555. Above all, the illustrated book served to disseminate an iconographic tradition that was still completely medieval. The great mythological incunabula were Boccaccio's *De Casis* (Ulm 1473) and his *De la ruyne des nobles hommes et femmes* (Bruges 1476). During the same period there appeared, in Anvers and Paris, the *Recueil des Histoires de Troie,* the *Faits et Prouesses de Jason,* and the *Destruction de Troie la Grant,* which had nine printings from 1484 to 1526. The tradition that was perpetuated through these books was that of the *Libellus*—a Norse tradition, not a classical one—and the woodcuts could just as well have illustrated romances of chivalry. It was these woodcuts, however, that first assured the graphic diffusion of the favorite themes of the Renaissance: the abductions of Europa and Proserpina, and so forth. Toward the end of the fifteenth century these models, still Gothic in appearance, could be found everywhere, whereas the archaeological discovery of antiquity had begun long before. The unique role of the Renaissance would be to restore to ancient subjects their ancient forms.

II. The Renaissance

Collectors, among whom the prototype was Cyriacus of Ancona, brought together copies of medals, inscriptions, and fragments of sculpture and architecture. And two camps were formed in elegant society and among patrons: admirers of courtly romances, and antiquarians. The *Hypnerotomachia Poliphili,* published by Aldo Mannucci in 1499, is a compromise combining a love story—a story which also conceals an initiation into the most serious mysteries—with a repertory of classical archaeology. This strange book, magnificently illustrated, was to have a deep and lasting influence not only on the appearance and the decoration of books to come, but also on architecture and painting. It can be compared to Petrarch's *Triumphs,* another great book, which underwent several printings before 1500 and whose illustrations were inspired by classical sculpture, such as Mantegna's "Triumph of Caesar."

Another category of illustrated books, the *Emblemata,* engendered a long tradition. Their principal sources were old medals—especially the reverse sides (from whose figures Pisanello drew his inspiration)—as well as hieroglyphics engraved on obelisks. Scholars had believed that they could decipher them ever since Cristoforo de Buondelmonti had returned from Andros, in 1419, with the manuscript of the *Hieroglyphica* by Horus Apollo. Their influence exploded in the *Hypnerotomachia.* Aldo printed them in 1505, and Piero Valeriano provided them with a monumental commentary in 1556. The humanists, who believed them to be the key to a sacred language, fabricated cryptograms in turn. The first collection of *Emblemata* was the one by Alciat, in 1531, which underwent more than fifty printings in all languages. And mythology had an important place in works of this genre; the countenances and attributes of the gods in them were interpreted as signs concealing truths or moral maxims. In turn, these alleged hieroglyphics (which drew from several sources in addition to Horus) introduced a curious deviation into figurative mythology, a deviation with major consequences. For the time would come, toward the end of the sixteenth century, when it would once again be necessary to reconcile the pagan fable with Christian teachings, and the *Emblemata* were to become the ideal instrument for this compromise.

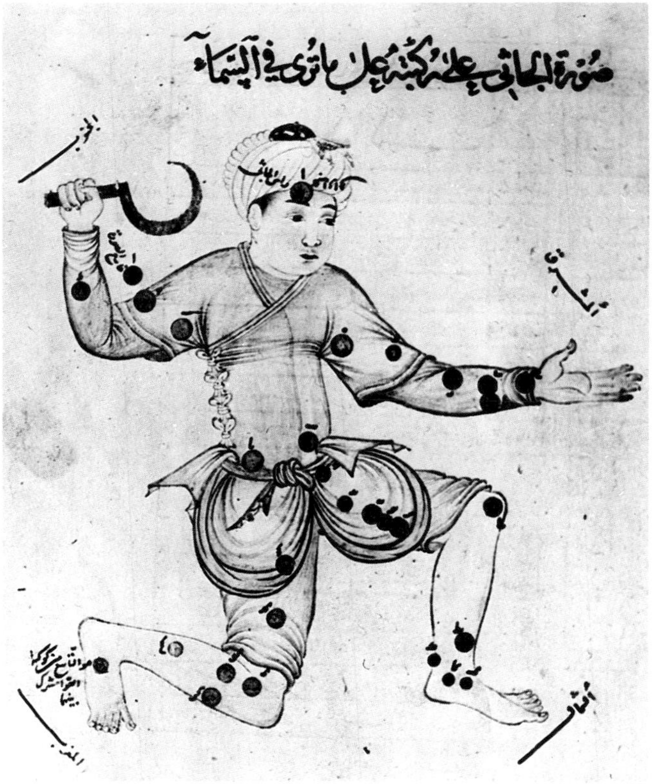

Hercules (ms. arab. 5036). Paris, Bibliothèque nationale. Photo BN.

Around 1500 in Italy the gods seemed omnipresent: they were on the ceilings of palaces, sometimes on the cupolas of churches, on marriage chests, almanacs, and suits of armor; they participated in the ceremonial entrances of rulers and in carnival processions; they presided over fountains in public squares and haunted garden grottos. But their role was not always purely decorative. They often reappeared, as we have said, in particular frameworks, systems of ideas elaborated in the Middle Ages, whose encyclopedic spirit still breathed in works such as the Malatesta temple and the Stanza della Segnatura. Raphael's "Parnassus" can be fully understood only as an element of a design in which all parts are connected even in their details: Poetry combines with Philosophy, Theology, and Justice to compose the four human understandings; on the ceiling the four elements are represented by episodes arranged in pairs: in each, a mythological scene is combined with a historic scene, and these diverse cycles are intertwined. The elements are attached to the sciences by way of the virtues, according to a diagram which at the same time makes apparent the relationship between the sciences: Theology and Philosophy have the same relationship as fire and water; Jurisprudence and Poetry have the same relationship as the earth and the sky.

But fable also played a part in real life: certain programs allied politics with morality. Aside from their edifying intentions—the triumph of Reason over the passions, of mind over matter—they contained (and always under a

Venus and the Graces. "The Tarots of Mantegna."

mythological cloak) allusions to contemporary events. In the decoration of the Palazzo del Te, Jupiter whipping the Giants illustrated the punishment of those who rebel against divine authority; at the same time it was a tribute to the efforts of Charles V for having reestablished imperial power in Italy. Likewise, in the Doges' Palace, Mercury and the Graces, Bacchus and the Ariadne of Tintoretto sing the praises of the Most Serene Republic, of its prosperity, and of the wisdom of its government. In the ballets given at the French court for Catherine de Medicis, Circe represented the horror of civil wars, and Minerva the return of order and peace. The Renaissance assigned a pagan demeanor even to Christian themes. On a candelabra in the basilica of Saint Anthony of Padua, Riccio portrays the pascal sacrifice of the lamb in front of an altar on which an Olympian Christ is standing; conversely, the *Sacrifice to Priapus* by Jacopo de' Barbari utilizes the elements of a Presentation to the Temple. These overlappings are not blasphemous; rather they express a sense of harmony and continuity. While Bellini's Redeemer pours his blood into a chalice, behind him, on a bas-relief, a drinking scene is taking place. The famous example of the Maenad transformed into a holy woman at the foot of the Cross reminds us that the Renaissance employed ancient models not only in a different context but also with a meaning totally different from the original.

Nor should the omnipresence of the gods be regarded as the boasting expression of liberated instinct and joy of life. With their beauty, certainly, they recovered their power of heroic or sensuous contagion. But at the same time they regained a singular dignity. This restitution of form is also a reconsecration, for fable is theology as much as it is poetry. It is no longer bound by a lying religion; for the pagans it was true. Such is Boccaccio's argument; and it followed that the poetry of the ancients, like their philosophy, maintained its legitimacy even in a Christian century. Hence the attitude of the humanists toward pagan beliefs. The fervor of their mythological erudition, like the archaeological and philological fever that consumed them, was a form of piety, *docta pietas*. They pursued the dream of a syncretism or a universal theism, with Platonism for a gospel; and they elaborated a religion of initiates.

Nothing is more expressive of this ambition than the great mythological creations of the Renaissance, many of which are enigmatic—such as Botticelli's "Primavera" and "The Birth of Venus," Piero di Cosimo's "Mars and Venus," Michelangelo's "Leda" and "Bacchus," and Titian's "Sacred and Profane Love." To clarify these works completely it is not enough to indicate their immediate sources; one must find a spirit, a climate—that of the humanists among whom they were born. The iconological studies by Panofsky and Chastel, and Wind's *Pagan Mysteries of the Renaissance*, have proved the worth of this method. The Neoplatonists of the Quattrocento, Pico della Mirandola, and Marsilio Ficino, who saw Plato through the eyes of the final representatives of paganism—Iamblichus, Proclus, Porphyry, and Plotinus—borrowed their notions about the mysteries and the rites of initiation; and they elaborated a theory of cryptic expression, which was applied to the visual arts. The artists whom they counseled, or who came under their influence, deliberately clouded the profound meaning of their works: the works only become fully intelligible when one is aware of the intentions and secret "doctrines" that they contained in abundance.

The principal key is to be found in the "Orphic theology," to which Plato, according to Proclus, was the heir. It was a Trinitarian system, a philosophy of transmutation. The development of the unity into a triad; the coincidence of opposites in the unity; *discordia concors*—these maxims were the clue to the mythological compositions that were the most hermetic in appearance; they formed their hidden structure. For mythology, too, has its triads of the Parcae and the Charites, illustrating procession, conversion and return; and Paris sees perfection divide into three goddesses. Every god was ambiguous, encompassing two extremes: the eloquent Mercury was the god of silence; Apollo inspired both madness and moderation; Minerva was peaceful and warlike; and Pan was hidden in Proteus. Their duplicity engendered infinite combinations, for they were alternately divided and united by a dialectical movement. As for Marsyas and Psyche, their stories, illustrated by Raphael, hide essentially the same lesson: purification through trial. The terrestrial Marsyas is tormented so that the celestial Apollo may be crowned; the misfortunes of Psyche are merely stages of a mystical initiation and redemption.

Raphael. *Apollo and Marsyas.* Rome, Vatican. Photo Anderson-Giraudon.

Other nuances remain inexplicable as long as one fails to appreciate the role of paradox and irony in the intentions of the artist and his advisers. The Neoplatonists learned from Plato himself how to speak of sacred subjects playfully; Apuleius and Lucian taught them the art of *serio ludere*. The facetious note is evident in Bellini's "The Feast of the Gods"; and Mantegna himself, serious as he was, created his "Parnassus" in a spirit less heroic than mocking. The unique accent of the great mythologies of the Renaissance, their singular splendor, may reside in what radiates through the veils, the soothsaying, and the smiles.

J.Se./t.l.f.

BIBLIOGRAPHY

For the essential bibliography on the subject, see J. SEZNEC, *The Survival of the Pagan Gods* (New York 1953). The present list, which follows the order of the questions treated in the article, includes the most important among recent publications.

H. MARROU, *Histoire de l'éducation dans l'Antiquité* (Paris 1948). E. MÂLE, *La fin du paganisme en Gaule et les plus anciennes basiliques chrétiennes* (Paris 1950). P. FRANCASTEL, *L'humanisme roman* (2d ed., Paris 1970). R. PFEIFFER, *History of Classical Scholarship from 1300 to 1850* (Oxford 1976). H. WADDELL, *The Wandering Scholars* (new ed., New York 1961). J. HUBERT, J. PORCHER, and W. F. VOLBACH, *Carolingian Art*, chap. 3 (London 1970). W. OAKESHOTT, *Classical Tradition in Medieval Art* (London 1959). R. RENUCCI, *Dante, disciple et juge du monde grégo-latin* (Clermont-Ferrand 1954). K. WEITZMANN, *Greek Mythology in Byzantine Art* (Princeton 1951). G. BOAS, *The Hieroglyphics of Horus Apollo* (New York 1950). D. C. ALLEN, *Mysteriously Meant: The Discovery of Pagan Symbolism and Allegorical Interpretation of the Renaissance* (Baltimore 1970). E. PANOFSKY, *Renaissance and Renascences in Western Art*, chap. 4 (Stockholm 1960). E. GOMBRICH, *Botticelli's Mythologies*, Warburg Institute Studies 26 (London 1945). E. WIND, *Bellini's Feast of the Gods* (Cambridge, MA, 1948); *Pagan Mysteries in the Renaissance* (London 1958; new ed., 1968).

ALCHEMY AND MYTHOLOGY

"It is easy to be a poet among the gods."

All other things being equal, it might be said of history, especially the history of the Renaissance, what the Cabalists, uncovered by the Phoenix of that period, said of the book of Revelation, that each of its letters presents seventy faces, meaning by that number the inexhaustible totality of the words of God.[1] One after the other, various modes of thought of that time, rejected by a history that based itself on a science rendered still darker in the occultist night,[2] have been studied by historians of science,[3] of art, of religions: magic, astrology, hermetism, lapidary, the science of numbers, physiognomy, in a word, the cabala. And although the history of these strange researches has not always escaped the frowns of the historian for such an episode of "menschlichen Narrheit,"[4] people have nonetheless discovered in it the poetry that makes all things new.

Though alchemy scarcely appears in works on the Renaissance,[5] historians of alchemy[6] have long made room for it in the *Mytho-Hermetic Dictionary in which One Finds the Fabulous Allegories of the Poets, the Metaphors, the Enigmas and the Barbarous Terms of the Hermetic Philosophies Explained*, the complement and table to the *Egyptian and Greek Fables* of Antoine Joseph Pernety (1716–1801), and in several other works of his predecessors. The most famous, because of the beauty of Matthäus Merian's engravings, is Michael Maier (1568–1622), physician to Rudolph II and friend of the Rosicrucian Robert Fludd, whose entire program is displayed on the title page of the *Arcana arcanissima, hoc est Hieroglyphica Aegyptio-Graeca vulgo necdum cognita, ad demonstrandam falsorum apud Antiquos Deorum, dearum heroum, animantium et institutorum pro sacris receptorum originem, ex uno Aegyptiorum artificio, quod aureum animi et corporis medicamentum peregit, deductam, unde tot poetarum allegoriae, scriptorum narrationes fabulosae et per totam encyclopaediam, errores sparsi clarissima veritatis luce manifestantur, quaeque tribui singula restituuntur, sex libris exposita* (The most secret secrets, i.e. the Greco-Egyptian hieroglyphics not yet widely known, are here set forth in six books, in order to show the origin among the ancients of the false gods, goddesses, heroes, and living beings, and the received institutions for sacred matters, deduced from the art of the Egyptians, which produced the golden remedy of the body and the soul, whence come so many allegories of the poets, the fabulous narratives of the ancient writers, and the errors that are scattered through the entire encyclopedia, and which are here shown in the clearest light of truth and are individually restored in order to be assigned). There is also the fabulous Salomon Trismosin, author of the *Vellus aureum* (the *Golden Fleece*); Jacob Tollius, author of the *Fortuita, in quibus praeter critica nonnulla, tota fabularis historia graeca, aegyptiaca ad chemiam pertinere asseritur* (Chance occurrences: in which, in addition to several critical

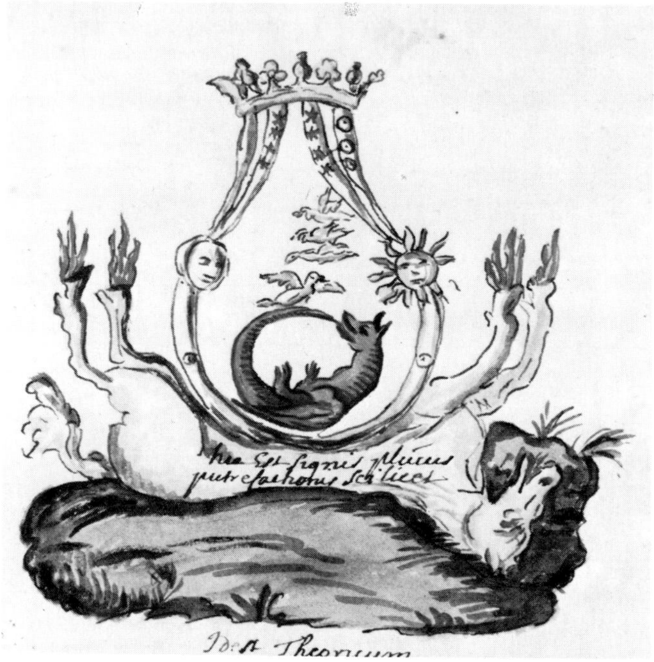

Treatise on alchemy, *La clef de la grande science* (MS Ars. 6577, fol. 8v). Paris, Bibliothèque de l'Arsenal. Photo BN.

matters, the entire Greek, Egyptian history of fable is asserted to pertain to alchemy); and, in the sixteenth century, Giovanni Bracesco, Cesare della Riviera. It is nevertheless important to know the history of the interconnections between alchemy and mythology.

The first witnesses to alchemical mythology cited in the Renaissance[7] are medieval authors: Suidas, whose *Lexicon* mentions alchemy, notably the Golden Fleece, three times; Eustathius, the commentator on Homer; Albert the Great, whose *De mineralibus* alchemicizes the myth of Pyrrha and Deucalion and the myth of the Gorgon; and the *Pretiosa novella margarita*, written around 1330 A.D. by Petrus Bonus Lombardus,[8] which allegorizes the *Bucolics*, the *Georgics*, and the *Aeneid*, as well as the *Metamorphoses*. It is the same fire that hardens clay and melts wax; it is Proteus, the golden bough, Phaethon, the Labyrinth, Medea, the Dragon whose teeth Jason sows, Pyramus and Thisbe. Nicolas Flamel evokes[9] "those serpents and dragons that the ancient Egyptians painted in a circle . . . they are those dragons that the ancient poets set to guard, never sleeping, the golden apples in the gardens of the Hesperidean nymphs. They are those upon whom Jason, in the adventure of the Golden Fleece, poured the potion prepared by the beautiful Medea . . . they are the two serpents sent by Juno, who is metallic by nature, which the mighty Hercules, that is, the sage, must strangle in his cradle." Or:[10]

. . . These of Mythology
In whom the ancient knowledge shines,
As seen in Jason, Cadmus,
Hercules, Aesacus, Achilles,
Then in the two monsters of Perseus.

Giovanni Aurelio Augurelli (ca. 1454–ca. 1537) was the first Renaissance poet to extol alchemy under the veil of fables. He is supposed to have been imitated by Gianfrancesco Pico della Mirandola (1469–1533), if we may judge by the poems included in the *De auro libri tres*, long suspect because of the late date of its publication. With the testimony of Lilio Gregorio Giraldi (1479–1552), who took refuge in the castle of Mirandola after the sack of Rome, we can no longer neglect valuable information about the readings: Giraldi, who had brought with him a manuscript of Psellus on the royal art, read the *Argonautics* with his friend, who had an alchemical eye.

About the same time in France, a Norman alchemist, Vicot, who worked in Flers like Nicolas de Grosparmy and Nicolas Valois, composed in verse, unfortunately rather prosaic, *The Great Olympus, or Poetic Philosophy Attributed to the Much Renowned Ovid*. The "initiated," who claim that this work dates from the time of Flamel, have not read, among other things, a precise reference to the French translation of Alciat's *Emblemata*, of which it constitutes, moreover, the first alchemical interpretation. Moreover, one of the numerous copyists of these works by the Flers alchemists, another Norman, Jean Vauquelin des Yveteaux (1651–1716), proposed—well before Pernety—a mytho-hermetic dictionary that remains in manuscript: *Fabulous Truths, a Curious Treatise on the origin of the Sciences and on the Progress of their Communication, with the Exposition and Explanation of the Fictions of the First Savants. The Whole for the Comprehension of Ancient and Modern Authors Who Treat of Theology, Morality, Philosophy, Physics, Alchemy, History, Fables, Romances, Stories and Poetic Fictions, Magic and the Early Sciences, Divine Cults*.[11]

Meanwhile, in the realm of dictionaries more properly alchemical, Giovanni Bracesco da Iorci Novi in *La espositione di Geber* of 1544 supplied the alchemical meaning of several important fables. Another Norman, Robert Duval, recopied the whole, sanctioning these interpretations with the examples of Pico della Mirandela and Flamel, whose enigmas he had seen at the cemetery of the Innocents. Most of the symbols of the period are found in two folios published in 1591 by Antonio Ricciardi (ca. 1520–1610), a friend of P. Bongo, the author of *Mysticae numerorum significationis liber: Commentaria symbolica in duos tomos distincta, in quibus explicantur arcana pene infinita ad mysticam, naturalem et occultam rerum significationem attinentia, quae nempe de abstrusiore omnium prima adamica lingua: tum de antiquissima Aegyptiorum coeterarumque gentium orphica philosophia, tum ex sacrosancta veteri mosaica et prophetica, nec non coelesti nova christiana, apostolica et sanctorum patrum evangelica theologia depromta sunt. Praeterea quae etiam celeberrimorum vatum fragmentis et denique in chymistarum secretissimis involucris continguntur* (The book of the mystical meaning of numbers: symbolic commentaries separated into two volumes, in which are explained almost infinite secrets pertaining to the mystical, natural, and secret meaning of things, which are derived from the more abstruse, first Adamic language of all peoples; both with relation to the most ancient Orphic philosophy of the Egyptians and other peoples; then from the time of ancient Mosaic and prophetic theology; and especially from the heavenly new Christian Apostolic and evangelical theology of the holy fathers. Besides which, these matters are also touched upon in fragments of the most celebrated prophets and finally in the encased and most secret beliefs of the chemists).[12]

Jacques Gohory Parisien (ca. 1520–76) added to these interpretations those from the romances of the Middle Ages. In dedicating the translation of the thirteenth book of *Amadis of Gaul* to the duchess of Nevers, Gohory, who published a translation of the *Poliphilus*, wrote: "But it is not to be forgotten in connection with Poliphilus (whose lover Polia is said to have been born in the Trevisane border region), and with the goldsmith Augurel, who also throws light on the matter, and with Count Bernard Trevisan, that Merlin tells among his prophecies how at Tarvis a person is to be born who will make gold and silver." And Gohory, who also published *The Perilous Fountain . . . Containing the Cryptography of the Secret Mysteries of Mineral Science,* added: "It is not a ridiculous absurdity that princesses are carried away by Magicians, Giants, and Giantesses, at the beginning of this book, in an azure chariot conducted by four harpies, and the fortunate virgin in the chariot of swans, nor that Medea of Colchis is mounted on her chariot that is yoked to two dragons, nor that Juno the goddess of wealth goes in her chariot drawn by two peacocks. For the preceding wonders are set forth by the Englishman Bacon in the book *On the Admirable Power of Art and Nature.*" Gohory was well-read, because in the preface he states: "Here you see the infernal Rock on which Jason's rich weapons are found, and the terrible serpent like the dragon of Columna and his dark cavern, things also treated by our authors François Guillaume de Lorris and Jean de Meun, the poet of the *Amorous and Perilous Fountain,* and Nicholas Flamel, who has left notable signs of them in his pictures in Paris at various temples in the form of dragons and angels of certain colors. Two gilt leaves from that work have lately been carried off by curious people, from the two ossuaries of the town's public cemetery."

Blaise de Vigenère (1523–96), who was in the service of the Gonzagues de Nevers (who were kindly disposed toward alchemy) and who praised the romances of the Middle Ages, has added many digressions on alchemy in a work of a translator likened at that time to Amyot. And we must set in its proper place *The Images or Pictures from the Flat Painting of Philostratus,* which Michael Maier knew, Goethe appreciated, and Tollius cited. Clovis Hesteau de Nuysement (ca. 1560–ca. 1624) is our greatest alchemical poet, but we will have to make room at his side for Nicolas Barnaud (ca. 1538–ca. 1607), who gave an alchemical interpretation to the famous inscription from Bologna of Aelia Laelia Crispis, as well as to the *Enigmas* of C. Symposius, which François Bérolade de Verville included in *The Voyage of the Fortunate Princes, a Cryptographic Work,* but which he criticized in his *Palace of the Curious.* Let us not forget Claude Barthélémy Morisot (1592–1661), a friend of Rubens, who dedicated his alchemical romance *Peruviana* to Gaston d'Orléans. It was about the same time that Pierre Jean Fabre de Castelnaudary (1588–1658), whose *Hercules Piochymicus* became part of Pernety's *Dictionary,* dedicated to the same prince and his adepts his *Summary of Alchemical Secrets.*[13]

Title page of *Arcana Arcanissima* by Michael Maier. Paris, Bibliothèque nationale. Photo BN.

Another figure in this history was one Angelo Ingegneri,[14] who published at Naples, in 1606, *Contra l'Alchimia e gli Alchimisti, paliodia dell'Argonautica, con la stessa Argonautica dichiarata da copiose postille del proprio autore.* A friend of Cesare della Riviera, the author of the *Mondo magico degli Heroi,* and of an ambassador for Charles V, Giacom' Antonio Gromo surnamed Ethereo, who had composed a *Medea ricamata,* an alchemical work illustrated with drawings, Ingegneri had at first extolled alchemy in the myth of Jason and Medea, through which a symbolism often difficult to grasp could be assessed. Giving an account of the *Fortuita* of Tollius, one of the collaborators of the *News from the Republic of Letters* noted:[15] "To tell the truth, I might never have believed that an idea of alchemy could be extracted from the speeches of Sophocles, . . . but everything changes in the hands of a clever man," while one of the admirers of Tollius in our time,[16] who presents himself as an "adept," could write: "The mythologies of the gods and heroes, like the religion of Christ, the Apostles, and the evangelical annals, have solid meaning and real value only in the undeniable and numerous connections that they show with alchemy, its materials and its operations."

F.S./b.f.

NOTES

1. G. G. SCHOLEM, "La signification de la Loi dans la mystique juive," G. Vajda, trans., *Diogène* 15 (1956): 14.
2. F. SECRET, "Du 'De occulta philosophia' à l'occultisme du XIXe siècle," *Revue de l'histoire des religions,* 1975.
3. It suffices to mention the Warburg Institute studies: L. THORNDIKE's *History of Magic and Experimental Science,* published in 8 vols. beginning in 1923; *Ambix, the Journal for the Study of Alchemy and Early Chemistry,* founded by F. Sherwood Taylor; *Isis,* founded by George Sarton; etc.
4. Cf. review by J. DE BALTRUSAITIS, "La quête d'Isis," *L'oeil* 161 (1968): 38.
5. One need only consult the bibliography in the English translation of J. SEZNEC's classic work, *The Survival of the Pagan Gods: The Mythological Tradition and Its Place in Renaissance Humanism and Art* (New York 1953); M. TURKER, *Bibliographie zur Symbolik, Ikonographie und Mythologie* (Baden-Baden 1960); and *Bibliographie zur Symbolkunde* from 1964.
6. See, among others, the bibliography in J. VAN LENNEP's *Art et alchimie* (Paris and Brussels 1966) and the preface to the Italian edition of PERNETY's *Dictionary* (Milan 1971) (this dictionary was reissued in the *Bibliotheca hermetica,* under the direction of R. Alleau, who wrote the article "Alchimie" in the *Encyclopaedia universalis*).
7. F. SECRET, "Notes sur quelques alchimistes italiens de la Renaissance," *Rinascimento* 23 (1973); "Gianfrancesco Pico della Mirandola,

Lilio Gregorio Giraldi et l'alchimie," *Bibliothèque d'humanisme et Renaissance* 38 (1976).
8. L. THORNDIKE, *A History of Magic and Experimental Science* (New York 1934), 3:155.
9. *Bibliotheca Hermetica* (Paris 1970), 104; cf. 110.
10. Ibid., 144.
11. F. SECRET, *Annuaire de l'École pratique des Hautes Études* (Sciences religieuses) 83 (1974–75).
12. *Annuaire* 79 (1971–72).
13. F. SECRET, "Claude Barthélemy Morisot, chantre de Rubens et romancier chymique," *Studi francesi* 40 (1970).
14. "Littérature et alchimie au XVIIe siècle: L'écusson harmonique de Jacques Sanlecque," *Studi francesi* 47 (1972).
15. *Nouvelles de la République* (April 1687), 400.
16. E. CANSELIET, *Les douze clefs de la philosophie* (Paris 1971), 18, and *Mutus Liber*, 79.

CABALA AND MYTHOLOGY

It is well known that the Cabala was much in vogue[1] after the scandal of Giovanni Pico della Mirandola's *Conclusiones* and after the publication of *De arte cabalistica*, when secretive men were in open dispute. Equally well known are the relationships that were established between this current of new ideas and astrology, alchemy, etc. Consequently, it is hardly surprising that mythology was "Cabalized," in other words, that fables born among the Gentiles were interpreted with the help of a tradition peculiar to the Chosen People. Nor is it surprising that the Church Fathers had been able to interpret paganism, and that Peter the Venerable,[2] alerted by the denunciations of the Karaites, had judged the Talmudists, who read their fables literally, to be more foolish than the Ethnics. After the *Apologia* and the *Conclusiones*, the Orphic Hymns, "fables and pure nonsense" in appearance, took on meaning, thanks to the mysteries of the Cabala, which were not "imaginary nonsense or tales of charlatans" but more deeply rooted meanings hidden under the outer crust of the Law.[3] The same can be said for the Curetes in the service of Orpheus, for the Powers in the service of Dionysus, for Orpheus and Night, and for *Ensof* in the Cabala.[4]

The *Theologia poetica*, which was supposed to interpret the *Graecia mendax* (Greek lie) according to the purest *veritas Hebraica* (Hebrew truth) and the principle of correspondences hailed by the *Heptaplus*, was never written. Circumstances were such that the work of Egidio da Viterbo (1469–1532),[5] who tried to bring the *Theologia poetica* to fruition in his own way, remained in manuscript form.

Indeed, this hermit from Saint-Augustin, general of the order at the time of Luther's revolt, left a work that should not be too hastily judged as clashing with the religious reform brought about by Luther, but should be closely studied in order to be understood. Egidio da Viterbo became a cardinal and preached the urgent need for reform at the Lateran Council; according to him, it was up to *homines per sacra immutari, non sacra per homines* ("men to be changed through sacred things, not sacred things through men"). After the sack of Rome, he wrote that God had not permitted sacred things to be profaned, but the profaning of sacred things was to be avenged. Recalling that it was on hearing the cardinal preach on the Virgin that Jacopo Sannazaro conceived the idea for his *De partu Virginis*, a historian insisted with Erasmus that Sannazaro should have sacrificed less to paganism when treating an altogether Christian subject. The historian, however, quoted the cardinal as saying to the poet, "When I received your divine poem, I wanted to become better acquainted immediately with this marvelous creation. God alone, who inspired it with his breath of life, can reward you worthily, not by giving you the Elysian fields, the fabulous retreat of the likes of Linus and Orpheus, but by giving you blessed everlasting life."[6]

It is still unclear how Egidio da Viterbo, perfect Hellenist that he was, became the most erudite Christian scholar of Hebraic literature. Yet from *De Ecclesiae incremento*, written in 1507 on the occasion of the discoveries made by Portugal, to his last work, the *Scechina*, in which the last of the Sephirot reveals to Clement VII and Charles V the mysteries of the Aramaeans (whose language was that of the *Zohar*), Egidio da Viterbo seems to have followed a path opened by his compatriot, the Dominican Giovanni Nanni, known as Annius of Viterbo (1432–1502). This Etruscan bard maintained that the Greeks had corrupted not only the true origins of the Latins, but also the truths that had been transmitted by the offspring of Noah or Janus, which in Aramaic means wine. It seems that one of the parties responsible for Annius's etymological delirium was a physician to Alexander VI by the name of Samuel Zarphati. Annius had projected a *Historia hetrusca pontificia a Pontifice Noa qui est Janus in Vaticano coepta* (The Pontifical Etruscan history from the Pontifex Noa, who is Janus, begun in the Vatican). This is the theme of the *Historia XX saeculorum* (History of Twenty Centuries) that Egidio dedicated to Leo X, in which knowledge of the Cabala informed an Etruscan subject matter. We do not possess the promised treatises—*De symbolis* (On Symbols) and *De Etruscorum arcanis* (On the Secrets of the Etruscans)—but we do have a rich corpus of themes barely sketched in completed works preserved in the series of glossaries *Glossarium chaldaicae linguae et Cabalae vocabula* (The Glossary of the Chaldean Language and the Words of the Cabala), or *Caldea Babylonica et Aramaea fratris Aegidii* (The Babylonian Chaldean and Aramaean of Brother Aegidius).[7] Even Aegidius Viterbiensis, who sometimes signed his name Aegidius Palaeologus, followed in the footsteps of Annius, who claimed that Palaeologus was the Greek translation of Viterbiensis or Lucumo. These *arcana* (always called *cana* following Solon's apostrophe to the Greeks, who remained children) are worthy of study.[8] Among them are the Sibyl; *semita Dei* (the footpath of God)[9]; Cybele, wife of the Etruscan king Jasius, whose nuptials Isis[10] attended and who was named for the Hebrew word that means Cabala; Camilla,[11] who in Virgil's *Aeneid* (7.803) moves ahead of the advancing winds and is so named for the Chasm of Ezekiel, where holy animals moved with the velocity of thunder; and Paris,[12] so called by Priam, the descendant of Dardanus, because he would break the reign, since his name means "to burst in," according to Hebraic etymology. There are also interpretations of fables according to their biblical models or the great themes of Plato, Homer, and Virgil. Father de Lubac, after describing as "a strange polyphony" a sermon in which Egidio "calls on Minerva, Odysseus, Venus, Juno, Paris, Helen, Pallas, Ajax for help," went so far as to assert that the fifth book of the *Scechina* "ends on a few lines that are perhaps one of the most beautiful poems of renascent Christian humanism."[13]

Drawing on common sources but proceeding along different paths and in an altogether different setting, Guillaume Postel (1510–81) systematized a craze of which the *Cratylus* is the masterwork and invented the word *emithology* to characterize it. The usual term *etymology* is in fact a metathesis of the word *emithology*,[14] craftily effected by the Greeks. In the language of creation and revelation, its root *emeth* means truth (*veritas*), which Postel, according to his method, wrote as *Berritas*, meaning "a well."

Being an admirer of the etymologies of Annius of Viterbo and, like him, dead set against the *Graecia mendax* (Greek lie) and in favor of Etruria, Postel undertook to eliminate fables from calendars, geography, and astronomy. He made his purpose clear in the title: *Signorum caelestium vera configuratio aut Asterismus, stellarumve per suas imagines aut configurationes dispositio, et in eum ordinem quem illis Deus praefixerat restitutio et significationum expositio, sive Caelum repurgatum* (The true configuration of the celestial signs, or Asterism, or the disposition of the stars through their images and configurations, both restored in the very order in which God previously established them and explained in their meanings, or, finally, Heaven Recleansed). Cleansing this heaven of Greek fables and restoring the order willed by God, Postel expressed ideas he discovered by translating the *Sefer Bahir*,[15] which ridiculed the theme of the thirty-six decans. When Postel was not measuring his sky, he was busy rediscovering in Capricorn the scapegoat sent to Azazel and in Taurus the bull that Adam sacrificed (according to the Cabalists) or the bull that is the fourth leg of the Merkabah.[16] In 1572, when a new star appeared in the constellation of Cassiopeia, Postel inflated ancient mythology with the emithology of Cassiopeia that comes both from Cush, the firstborn conceived by Ham in the ark in violation of the law of abstinence,[17] for which he stole the books of magic composed by Adam; and from Aph, the face. The new star heralded the coming of Christ "in us," and the end of the black faces of tyrants. Determined to refer to Africa as Chamesia, Asia as Semia, and Europe as Japetia, in order to abolish the fable of the cow and the "abominable ne'er-do-well,"[18] Postel occasionally indulged in altering the spelling of the word Asia[19] in the holy tongue, in order to recapitulate his sermon. With aleph and samekh, Asia means remedy, for God instituted in Asia the mysteries of salvation. With aleph and shin, Asia means founding, for the world was peopled by colonies that had come from Asia. With ayin and shin, Asia further means realization, for everything will be brought about through the mystery of Christ contained in Asia, spelled with a samec and a hain, meaning the bread of the Eucharist, which the firstborn of the Restitution consecrated at Venice for the whole world.

Postel multiplied these emithologies in his *De Etruriae originibus*, included them in the *Galliade*, and sprinkled them throughout his works, which he signed at the end of his life with the name of Pos-tel or Rorisperge, which in the holy tongue means distributor of dew.

Postel was not the last to play with the ways of Cabalistic art set forth in *De arte cabalistica*. Cesare della Riviera, who mixed the Cabala with his alchemy, found in Diana[20] *Diem, cioe lucem afferens naturae* ("Bringing the day, namely, the light of nature"). At the very least a new world, endowed with the genius of the Hebrew language and with the amazing parables of the Rabbis, had been opened up, and poetry flowed from it. One need only open *De harmonia mundi* by Franciscus Georgius Venetus (1460–1540), later translated by the poet Guy Le Fèvre de la Boderie; the *Scechina* by Egidio da Viterbo; the wonderful digressions of Blaise de Vigenère, who was an astrologer, an alchemist, and a Christian Cabalist; and, last but not least, the reveries of Athanasius Kircher as found in the *Iter extaticum*, which is at the heart of J. Baltrusaitis's fine book on the quest of Isis.

F.S./g.h.

NOTES

1. F. SECRET, *Les kabbalistes chrétiens de la Renaissance* (Paris 1965).
2. H. DE LUBAC, *Exégèse médiévale*, IV, II (Paris 1964), 187. This fine book has a whole chapter on symbolism; cf., by the same author, *Pic de la Mirandole* (Paris 1974).
3. *Conclusiones* (Paris 1532), 12.
4. *Conclusiones*, ed. B. Kieszkowski (Geneva 1973), 81, 82.
5. J. W. O'MALLEY, *Giles of Viterbo on Church and Reform: A Study in Renaissance Thought* (Leiden 1968). Cf. *Annuaire de l'École pratique des Hautes Études* 83 (1974–75).
6. M. AUDIN, *Histoire de Léon X* (Paris 1846), 513.
7. Ms B.N.F. *lat. 596 et 597*.
8. *Historia*, fol. 198 v.
9. Ibid., fol. 229.
10. Ibid., fol. 223.
11. *Scechina* (Rome 1959), 2:229.
12. *Historia*, fol. 42 v.
13. H. DE LUBAC, *Pic de la Mirandole*, 102 and 306.
14. F. SECRET, *L'émithologie de G. Postel, Umanesimo e Esoterismo* (Padua 1960).
15. *Notes sur G. Postel, B.H.R.*, 1977.
16. *Signorum . . .* (Paris 1552).
17. F. SECRET, *De quelques courants prophétiques et religieux sous Henri III, R.H.R.*, 172 (1967).
18. *De universitate* (ed. 1635), 31.
19. M. S. BRIT, *Sloane 1409, Commentarius in Apocalypsim*, fol. 238.
20. *Il mondo magico*, ed. J. Evola (Bari 1932), 47.

Pan among the Cabalists and Alchemists of the Renaissance

There have been many reproductions of the hieroglyphic representation of Jupiter or of Pan as put forward by Athanasius Kircher in his *Oedipus Aegyptiacus*.[1] He may have taken the idea from the *De harmonia mundi*, a wonderful work, which Guy Le Fèvre de la Boderie translated. We shall cite the passage from his great poem *La Galliade* in which the theme of Pan is Cabalized:[2]

To show a Whole that bounds all things,
He depicts a Pan who has two horns
On his head, designating by this obvious sign
Both the channel of the east and the channel of the west.
A large deerskin bespeckled with stars
He wears on his back; it is the vaulted tent
Of the glittering firmament wherein shine brightly
More eyes than ever-watchful Argos had.
From his chin his beard hangs down to his belt,
Which radiates influence upon the heart of nature:
He plays a flageolet with seven pipes,
Which are the seven pitches of the seven glowing lights

That make the world dance round and round,
All the different feet falling into step.
He delights in hearing, from the caves and the woods,
The answering voice of Echo repeating his own seven voices,
Because the influence of each part
Harmonizes with the Whole of which it is a part.
From his waist to his cloven-hoofed feet
He is all covered with thick-layered hair
To show that the bottom of the round machine
Under his cloven hooves is made of earth and water
And that the elements, mingling into one another,
Seem to be unequal, hairy and bristly,
And Syrinx who feigned to be his friend
Was Nature organized in sweet alchemy.
Because he had read on Chaldean monuments[3]
That wines were kept within grapes
Ever since the seven days when the world was created,
And that we are intoxicated by the wine abounding
In the house of God who pours his liquors
Into the vessels of hearts through nine pure pipes,
Therefore he invented nine Bacchuses and nine Muses
Who with their sweet infusions go about intoxicating
The divine poets who have drunk of them.

And Clovis Hesteau de Nuysement, who, like La Boderie, was in the service of François d'Alençon, was able to alchemize this theme by citing Orpheus. After he had presented his Demogorgon,[4]

Virgil, perfectly well versed in all these mystic secrets, gave to this Spirit or soul of the world the name of Jupiter, whom he has his shepherd Damete invoke for the sake of his songs since, he claims, all things are filled with him. This god of the forests, Pan, worshiped by shepherds, may be taken to be the same thing. For, aside from his name, which means "all," he is also made into the lord of the forests because the Greeks considered him the priest of Chaos, which they otherwise called Hile, meaning a forest. In his hymn, Orpheus calls on him as follows:
Pan the strong, the subtle, the whole, the universal;
All air, all water, all earth, and all immortal fire,
Thou who sittest upon the same throne with time,
In the lower, middle, and upper kingdom,
Conceiving, begetting, producing, guarding all;
First in all and of all, thou who comest to the end of all,
Seed of fire, of air, of earth, and of the waves,
Great spirit enlivening all the limbs of the world,
Who goest about from all to all changing natures,
Lodging as the universal soul within all bodies,
To which you give existence and movement and life,
Proving by a thousand effects thy infinite power.

F.S./g.h.

NOTES

1. *Oedipus,* tomus secundus, pars prima (Rome 1653), 204.
2. *La Galliade ou de la révolution des arts et des sciences* (Antwerp 1578), 115. Cf. F. SECRET, *L'ésotérisme de Guy Le Fèvre de la Boderie* (Geneva 1969), 136.
3. The wine kept in its grapes since the six days of creation (Talmud, *Berakot* 34 b) symbolizes the delights of the world to come; cf. G. VAJDA, *Le commentaire d'Ezra de Gérone sur le Cantique des cantiques* (Paris 1969), 262, n. 40.
4. Ed. Matton, p. 279.

Fables and Symbols from Sixteenth- and Seventeenth-Century Hermeticism

I. The Mytho-Hermetic Dictionary

Henri de Linthaut's *Commentary on the Treasure of Treasures of Christophe de Gamon* glosses this brief outline of the main Hermetic fables, following G. Bracesco:[1]

"I know (a) that we must cover up, as our Poems,
This heavenly secret with a heap of allegories.
I know that this scholarly knowledge of Nature
Wants soundlessly to encircle her sacred forehead with laurel,
To maintain her greatness in secret silence
And to admire the excellences of her high secrets.

"(a) The ancient philosophers were admirable for their ability so dexterously to cover over all their science with the pleasant veil of poetical fables. For if we believe Empedocles, the entire practice and matter of this art is hidden under the fable of Pyrrhus and Deucalion, and, in particular, the preparation of Sulphur is hidden under the story of Hercules and Anthea. The conversion of Jupiter into a shower of gold hides the distillation of philosophical gold; the eyes of Argus converted into a peacock's tail hide sulphur changing its color. Under the fable of Orpheus is hidden the sweetness of our quintessence and drinkable gold. With the Gorgon turning those who look at her to stone they have covered the fixation of the Elixir, and have hidden philosophal sublimation under Jupiter converted into an eagle, carrying Ganymede off to the heavens. Under the fiction of the golden tree that grows a new branch when a branch is cut off they have hidden the distillation of philosophers' gold, which they have also covered with Jupiter cutting off his father's genitals. They called Mercurial water the chariot of Phaethon. By Minerva armed they meant this distilled water, which has in itself very subtle portions of Sulphur. By Vulcan whom Minerva follows, they have hidden the Sulphur following this same water, and its salt in putrefaction. By the cloudy cover with which Jupiter surrounded Io, they meant the little skin that appears at the beginning of the congealing of the Elixir: and it is said that the black particles that follow are the black sails with which Theseus returned to Athens. By the flood and the generation of animals, they meant the generation and distillation of Sulphurs. By Mars our Sulphur, by Juno the air, and sometimes the element of earth. Under Vulcan hurled down to Lemnos for his deformity they depicted the preparation of our first black Sulphur. With Atalanta they covered our Mercurial water, quick and fugitive, whose race is arrested by the golden apples thrown by Hippomenes, which are our fixing and coagulating Sulphurs. And that with which Theseus anointed the mouth of the Minotaur are the different kinds of Labyrinthine Sulphurs, that is the Mercurial water of our limed vessel, which is the true Minotaur, being both mineral and animal and thus sharing two natures.

"Here is a part of the fictions of poets that hide the main points of our science. If you desire a fuller interpretation of them, consult Bracesco in his Dialogue of Demogorgon and Geber. . . ."[2]

One can in any case consult the little "Dictionary" that we have put together here; Hercules, Orpheus, and Pan, however, are treated in other parts of this work.

II. The Chariot

Giovanni Piero Valeriano Bolzani (1477–1558), who dedicated to Cardinal Egidio da Viterbo, his protector, the hieroglyph of the stork, the symbol of piety chosen by the Cabalist,[3] echoes, in the *Hieroglyphica seu de sacris Aegyptiorum aliarumque gentium literis commentarius* (Hieroglyphics, or commentary on the sacred writings of the Egyptians and other peoples), one of the main themes of the successor of Annius of Viterbo:[4] "The sovereign Majesty (so majestic and great that it is seen in the celestial regions) is borne in a chariot, not a Platonic chariot in which the great Jupiter, constructor and sovereign governor of heaven, rides lightly about, but a chariot that we can see in the venerable old monuments of the Tuscans, a chariot of which Giles of Viterbo, a figure strong in doctrine, has drawn out the deepest secrets or mysteries of the Aramaeans and made us see it in our day in a public form. The Aramaeans said that one and the same book had two ordinances or laws: one written, the other delivered from God to Moses: the former is for the people, the latter for the wise: the former represents human things in common shapes, while the latter represents the luminous forms of divine things: and the former reveals the history of the creation of the world and the way to rule it, the latter the instrument, even the image of divinity drawn from life. Plato seems to mention the two kingdoms of Jupiter and Saturn as the happiest and most perfect, in that by Jupiter he means human life and action, but by the kingdom of Saturn he means the contemplation of divine things. . . ."

Then, after citing the *Georgics* (1.125) on Jupiter and *Metamorphoses* (1.89) on the Golden Age, he continues: "To return to our theme, Hebrew has two different names for these two: the first is Bresit, that is, the work of creation: the latter is called chariot, that is, secret knowledge. So this secret second law, which must be unveiled by the Messiah and by his own, is hieroglyphically described by them in the figure of the chariot. This is Ezekiel's chariot in his vision of the four images by which, like precious pearls and seals, the Lord created four leading angels and princes of all the heavenly intelligences. The first pearl is on the right hand, whence come beautiful, pleasant things, and is called Michael. On the left hand is another pearl from which things of strong, austere complexion come, and which is called Gabriel. Raphael is like a medicine mixed and tempered by these first two. In the fourth place is Uriel, the closest to the earth as dispenser of the three above-mentioned. Thus Michael and Gabriel are taken for the two wheels, Raphael for the seat, which is in the middle, and Uriel for the axle. The Greek theologians call the power of Michael in God Venus, Gabriel Mars, Raphael Jupiter, to whom the seat is dedicated. The fourth, the sun, which has the power of the male and the female, source of all generation, in Hebrew is called Uriel and Adonim. Orpheus cites all four of these in a verse calling him male/female, geniture and Adonis; it is thus not so fabulous that Plutarch should have remarked on the honor and service the Jews pay to Bacchus . . . for he holds that they solemnize their feast of the Tabernacles in honor and praise of Bacchus, and that Adonis and Bacchus are the same. . . ."

The chariot is one of the themes most often evoked by Egidio da Viterbo. In the Golden Age, the Tyrrhenians, the Etruscans, who were not fixed to one place like trees or mollusks, had chariots for houses, acorns for food, springs and brooks for drink, and the sky for a roof. The patriarchs of Etruria devoted themselves to contemplation, despising wealth, and it was to those who practiced contemplation that the *sella currilis*[5] was reserved, which the Romans, who for a long time sent their children to learn among the Etruscans, borrowed from them. The chariot, which symbolizes the contemplation of divine realities, is contrasted to the horse, which symbolizes the arrogant philosophy of the Greeks,[6] as is witnessed in one of the last lines of the first *Georgic,* echoing the considerations of the *Pheadrus: "Fertur equis auriga, neque audit currus habenas"* ("The driver is carried away by the horses, and the chariot does not heed the reins").

The chariot theme is linked to the four mysterious letters F A V L, which were earlier deciphered by Annius of Viterbo and designate the sacred wood where the Lucumons taught the doctrine proclaimed by Ezekiel for the fourth age, when he saw a human Face (*Facies*), an Eagle (*Aquila*), a Calf (*Vitulus*), and a Lion (*Leo*); and he saw these initials, which designated—with the names of the tribes of Faluceres, Arbanos, Vetulonios, and Longolanos—the Fountain (*Fons*) of sovereign good, whose Dawn (*Aurora*) it announced, which heroic Virtue (*Virtus*) loved in order to receive Light (*Lux*) from it.[7] And because of the arcane nature of its transmission, they gave it the name of "Faulas" or fables.[8]

Two centuries later, a French Jesuit, Joachim Bouvet (1656–1730), rediscovered the Mercava in the Chinese tradition.[9] This missionary, who presented Louis XV with the portrait of the Emperor Kangxi, whose envoy he was, and who corresponded with Leibniz, was called the father of the symbolic system, who discovered in Chinese traditions—particularly in the *Yi Jing,* "the Book of Changes,"—the mysteries of Christianity. In a magnificently illustrated text of 1724, *Pro expositione figurae sephiroticae Kabalae Hebraeorum, et generatim*

Page from a manuscript by the Jesuit priest Joachim Bouvet in which he shows concordances between Cabala and the *Yi Jing.* Chantilly, Archives of the Society of Jesus, MS Fonds Brotier.

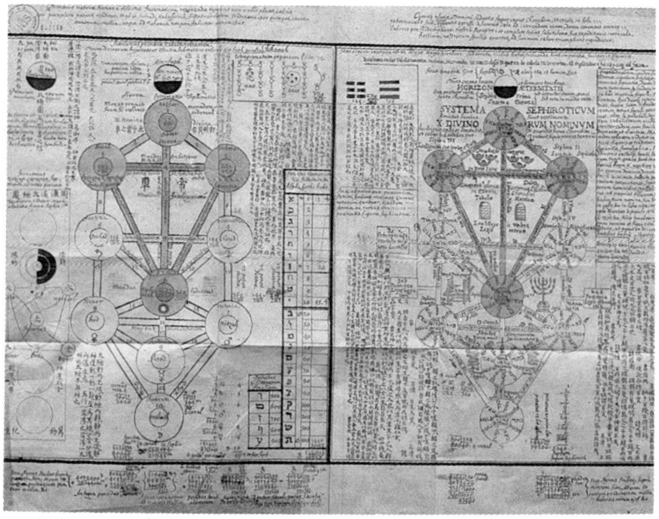

demonstranda mira conformitate primaevae Sinarum sapientiae hieroglypicae cum antiquiore et sincera Hebraeorum Kabala ab ipso mundi primordio, per sanctos Patriarchas et Prophetas successive propagata (Through the exposition of the figure of the sephirot in the cabala of the Hebrews wondrous things are demonstrated, in general, by the conformity of the ancient hieroglyphyic wisdom of the Chinese with the ancient and true cabala of the Hebrews from the very beginning of the world, propagated successively by the holy fathers and the prophets), he uncovered, masked under the figure of the monarch Huang Di on his chariot drawn by six winged spirits or six dragons, the Lord of the Mercava of Ezekiel and the Cabala.[10]

III. Demogorgon

The word Demogorgon appears in the *Mytho-Hermetic Dictionary,* but Pernety attributes to Raymond Lull a treatise on operations on stone, entitled *Demogorgon,* in the form of a dialogue in which Demogorgon is one of the interlocutors. In fact, it was Giovanni Bracesco degli Orsi novi who in 1544 published *La Espositione di Geber filosofo,* in which Geber, in a dialogue with Demogorgon, recounts the meaning of this ancestor of the gods according to the "genealogia delli Dei de Gentili."[11] And Jean Seznec,[12] following Carlo Landi's book,[13] which is extremely rare in France, has summarized the fortunes of this invented god. Also to be noted is some later research, since Landi forgot Leo Ebreo[14] in his list of vulgarizers of Demogorgon, and since citation of Demogorgon can upon occasion help us to date a work which "initiates" situate a century earlier.[15] I am referring to the *Five Books, or the Key to the Secret of Secrets*[16] of Nicolas Valois, who speaks of the calcination of the body, "which the Ancients symbolized by a Dragon asleep in the fire, guarded by an old man who is the virtue of sulphur retained in the soul, which Demogorgon awakens from the earth by our Mars." And among those who followed Bracesco we may note Clovis Hesteau de Nuysement, who, repeatedly citing Bracesco, was not shy about returning to this new character several times.[17]

"But in order for me to tell my portion of the meaning hidden under these Mythologies, do we not see clearly that the ancient Demogorgon, father of all the gods, or rather of all the members of the world, who is said to live at the center of the earth, covered with a green and iron-bearing cloak, feeding animals of all sorts, is none other than the universal Spirit who from the womb of Chaos, obeying the voice of the Lord, lights up the heavens, the elements, and all that is in them, which he has since then always maintained and quickened; for he truly does live in the middle of the earth, as I have amply declared at the beginning of this book, that is, at the center of the world, where he is placed as on his throne, and whence like the heart of this great body and seat of universal life, he produces, animates, and nourishes all. But this green and ferruginous coat in which he is dressed can hardly be anything but the surface of the earth which envelopes him, blackish and iron-colored, enameled and painted with grasses and flowers of all sorts."

And Nuysement ends up by assimilating him to Pan.

IV. Memnon

Memnon, who made harmonious sounds at the break of day, does not figure in the *Mytho-Hermetic Dictionary,* but Raymund Minderer (ca. 1570–1621), a doctor from Augsburg as unknown as his contemporary Michael Maier is famous, did not fail to produce an alchemical exegesis of him. Minderer, who is neglected in Ferguson's *Bibliotheca chemica* but who discovered ammoniac acetate, did not claim that the ancients intended to teach alchemy under a veil. In the *De calcantho seu vitriolo . . . disputatio iatrochymica* (in which he studies, in turn, Proteus, Hercules, and Memnon), the Memnon of the *Theogony,* of the *Aeneid,* of the *Metamorphoses,* and of Tzetzes' *Chiliades,* is connected with vitriol.[18] This black king of the Ethiopians shows the power of vitriol over the black fumes of atrabile, as does the fact that he is the son of Dawn. Memnon's expedition to Troy and the struggle against Achilles allow us to glimpse the battle of vitriol against the worst enemies of the human race, and Achilles is the Hermetic artisan who by fire and his alchemical art kills the calcanthum. The fight also demonstrates the weapons of Memnon, who like Hercules vanquishes monsters. His sword, hanging in the temple of Asclepius, completes the proof. His metamorphosis into a bird on the pyre perfectly illustrates the transformation of vitriol into volatile spirit. And the funeral column that made sounds at the break of day evokes, for those familiar with alchemical operations, the droplets tinkling at the beaks of retorts, which require the operator to keep watch lest there be an explosion.

V. The Phoenix

The phoenix has its place in the Hermetic bestiary,[19] but its place in the illumination of Guillaume Postel seems all the more worthy of note in that it appears only in manuscript works, which illuminate, along with the profound myth of the firstborn son of Mother Jeanne, a totally Gnostic way of thinking, based particularly on certain monuments of Hebraic literature.

It is in the form of a prophecy of the Venetian Virgin that Postel presents the Palma or Thamar, explaining only that [20] "since among the elementary things there is no thing living that lasts longer than the Palma while producing such fruits, perfect in sweetness and nutritive value, the Lord desired to be recognized here in this world in the substance of this Palma not only as the supreme example of sweetness and nutrition, temperament and long life, but also for the sake of perfect love. For nothing better shows the disposition of the upper world toward the lower than the nature of the palm tree, which is made in such a way that it is impossible that it be found or survive in any place unless both male and female are found there . . ." Now, at the time when Postel met Mother Jeanne at her hospice in Venice, he was translating a certain number of texts from Hebrew literature. This is where he found, after the current etymology of Jehochanna, the grace of the Lord, the theme of the "god with a human face," interpreted as Tipheret, the Messiah who has a dual character as both male divinity and female humanity. Then he discovered the story of the bird[21] as immense as its egg, the Bar Yukne, which with Leviathan and the Ox will be served at the feast of the just. Postel, who himself was the egg laid by this "advice," rejected the reading Bar Iucneh, and, sure that it was really his own Jehochanna, he immediately interpreted it as the Gan Eden, the garden that God planted, which he rediscovered in the word "Wecanah" in Psalm 80, verse 15: "that which your right hand has planted." From here on we must follow Postel's glossed translation of the passage from the *Commentary on Genesis:* "Rabbi Simlai said: Chavah (Eve) (after she had eaten the fruit of the tree) came to Adam and said: Do you think that I am dead? Behold, another Chavah has been created for thee (she was predicting the Mother of the World for the new Adam) for there is nothing new under the sun (everything returns) [and Postel uses the word 'revolvuntur,' which translates 'Gilgul,' the recirculation of souls]. If I were dead, you would remain alone. But as Isaiah writes [but Postel replaces 'the earth' in the text with 'woman']: It is not in vain that I have created even woman, I formed her so that she might endure (so that, restored, she might remain inseparably with Adam and her sons). The masters said: She began to say, 'There is an abundance of food.' Domestic and wild animals and all the flying things heard her, with the exception of one bird (*avem unam*) called Chul, as it is written in Job: I will have days as many as Chul." Postel, who translated this text twice, points out that literally the word means sand, and that it may thus be read as the Canah from which all Israel came, without noting that the Vulgate translated it "*sicut palma*" ("as if it were a palm"). In the other translation he claims that this Chul is the Phoenix, a bird imagined on the basis of the genius of the province of Phoenicia, whence everything comes and to which everything returns, but that here the Phoenix really seems to be, not a "chimeric goat-stag" bird, but a unique intelligence which rises above all other creatures, and Postel finishes the translation: "Rabbi Inai said: This bird lived for a thousand years. And at the end of the thousand years, a fire came out of its nest and burned it up. An egg remained in this fire, and the bird came back, grew up, and lived (thus under the image of the phoenix they represent what I have called Jochana, who comes back to life from the dust and gives life to the whole human race). Rabbi Iodan, son of Rabbi Simeon, said: It has lived for a thousand years; at the end of the thousand years its body is consumed and its wings come off its body; what remains of it is like an egg, which produces new limbs."

And Postel concludes: "All things, but men above all, are restored by this bird in every age, for it is similar to the Chul or Phoenix, who for this reason is called Chaliah, which means 'revolution.'"

VI. Sagittarius

Fulcanelli's *Mystery of the Cathedrals* does not mention the representation that Pierre Jean Fabre de Castelnaudary (1588–1658) was still able to see at Saint-Sernin in Toulouse, for which he offered an alchemical interpretation in the *Alchymista christianus*:[22] "A centaur, or a Sagittarius, armed with his bow, fires an arrow against a monster whose face is that of a woman, the body that of an eagle, the feet and tail those of a dragon. An enigma which could receive a Christian interpretation, but which should be interpreted chemically and alchemically because it is such, allowing us to contemplate under the surface the admirable correspondence of the natural and divine arcana. Chemically the Sagittarius represents mercurial water. As in the Sagittarius, in this volatile piece of rock one can distinguish two natures: one igneous and sulphurous, overcoming other natures and essences by its power, just as human nature overcomes all others; and the Mercury of the philosophers, which like the equine nature of the centaur is characterized by the rapidity of its movement. And just as the horse is consecrated to the celestial sun, mercurial water is consecrated to the terrestrial sun. As for the bow and arrows, they represent the effects of mercurial water, which through putrefaction poisons and kills the metallic substance or chemical chaos represented by the monster, who contains three natures: sulphur, mercury, and salt, or animal, vegetable, and mineral natures. The animal nature, which has the color of fire, is indicated by the human face. The vegetable or mercurial nature is indicated by the eagle's body. This nature the alchemists call eagle, which is of the nature of air, for in air is hidden the greatest abundance of the vital spirit. The mineral nature or salt of the philosophers is represented by the lower part of the monster, which is that of the venomous and murderous dragon. Just as the dragon dwells in the bowels of the earth, where it feeds and grows, so does the mineral nature or salt of the philosophers occupy the bowels of the earth, where it feeds and grows, and like the dragon devours everything and renews itself. This is the secret of the chemical art: chemical chaos or the metallic nature must be destroyed, put to death, and putrefied by the deadly poisoned arrows of mercurial water, so that everything may convert itself into an eagle and finish as a dragon, that is, be completed in earthy matter, fixed and permanent, which is the fixed salt of the philosophers, which converts everything into itself, as is said in the Table of Emerald: it is the strength of all strength, the strong strength, when it has been converted into earth. This can also be mystically understood of Christ and his Church, who should constitute one body, strong to resist tempests, as is said in the two verses carved in marble:

Juncta simul faciunt unum duo corpora corpus,
Sic est in toto fortius orbe nihil,

the two bodies joined together make a single body and there is nothing stronger in the world."

VII. The Scarab

Athanasius Kircher (1602–82), the hero of the quest of Isis,[23] even while attacking alchemy magnified its purely spiritual doctrine, finding it in concord with the true Cabala, which he did not condemn along with the Cabala of the rabbis. Dazzled by John Dee's discovery, copied by Cesare della Riviera, of the hieroglyph of Mercury, Kircher perceived the hieroglyph of the scarab as the key to the chemical art, in perfect concordance with the famous exegesis of *bereshit*, the first word of the Hebrew Genesis, at the end of the *Heptaplus*.

The scarab signifies the raw material of the metallic art: rolling up the bodies of the whole world, it produces an egg, visible above its tail. The seeds of all the metals that hide there eventually rise up to the seven spheres of the planets: besides the five spheres of the minor planets, the head of Horus designates the sun, and the segment of a circle above it designates the moon, and inside it is the cross, natural symbol of the elements. Between its forelegs the scarab holds a tablet bearing (in Greek script) the word *phulo* which signifies love. If like doctors we dissect this hierogrammatism into its parts, we obtain this phrase: The soul of the world or the life of things is hidden in the machine of this lower world, where rests the egg fertile in seminal reasons, which, exercising its power over the spheres of the metallic planets, animates them with its heat and makes them act, so that Horus, that is, the sun and the moon, emerges through the dissolution of the elements and the separation of pure from impure things. When this is done, each thing is linked to every other thing by a natural and sympathetic love, and this is the completion of the work.

Kircher, before explaining a discourse too obscure for novices, referred to his *Prodomus Coptus*, in which, after analyzing the hieroglyph of the scarab, he connected it with Pico della Mirandola's analysis of the first word of Genesis:[24] "The father to the Son or by the Son, beginning and end or rest, created the head, the fire, and the foundation of the great man by good accord or alliance." "What can the winged

Scarab. In Kircher, *Oedipus Aegyptiacus.* Paris, Bibliothèque nationale. Photo BN.

globe in the hieroglyph signify other than the famous circle whose center is everywhere and whose circumference is nowhere, to speak with Trismegistus, which is the supermundane abstract Intellect, first Intelligence, celestial Father. What could the body of the scarab signify other than the Son whom his Father has constituted principle, rest, and end of all things, by whom all was made and without whom nothing is made. Lest someone be angered at seeing God himself, who surpasses all admiration, being compared to the most vile, the most horrible, the most stinking of all beings, let us hear what Saint Augustine, the great light of the Church, has said of the admirable humanity of Christ in his *Soliloquies:* 'He is my good scarab, not so much because he is the only son of God, author of himself who took on our mortal form, but because he rolled in our filth, whence he sought to be born a man.' By this son, then, eternal Wisdom and true Osiris, the world was created, this great man, whose head is the angelic world, source of knowledge, whose heart is the sun, source of movement, life, and warmth, and whose foundation is the sublunary world. What could the character signifying love designate but this Spirit, who, '*meharephet peney ha-maym,* floating on the waters,' gives life to all things by the fire of his most fertile love, and ties all together in a good alliance.''[25]

VIII. The Sirens

Egidio da Viterbo dealt with this theme a number of times, in the *Sententiae ad mentem Platonis* (Opinions According to the Mind of Plato), the *Historia XX saeculorum* (History of Twenty Centuries), and in the *Scechina.* In the *Sententiae,*[26] the Sirens represented the three powers of the soul—memory, intelligence, and will—since, according to Cicero, they are teachers of knowledge. Indeed, in the *De finibus* (On the Ends), Cicero, after translating the passage from the *Odyssey* about the Sirens, adds: ''Homer could see that his fable would be without value if the Sirens sang nothing but little songs to catch a man like Ulysses in their net: it is, then, knowledge that the Sirens promise.'' In the *Historia XX saeculorum,*[27] speaking of Naples, ''ornament of the Tyrrhenian sea, which breathes the sweetness of the sky and the winds, which blossoms with the wealth of the sea and the land, born for leisure, the fine arts and the pursuit of wisdom,'' Egidio da Viterbo evokes Virgil who, though from Mantua, sang of Parthenope, one of the Sirens, whose body, when cast up on the shore, marked the birth of Naples. And he repeats Cicero's judgment, but in order to specify that the true knowledge is arcane wisdom, which was cultivated by the ancient Tyrrhenians. At that time it was forbidden to divulge this knowledge to the people, who, by hearing talk about several degrees of the divine realities, would have been separated from the Unity. This is what was taught by the Hebrews in their Cabala, by Pythagoras in his Symbols, Plato in his Epistles, Virgil in the fourth book of the *Aeneid,* and the Romans when they forbade disclosure of the Books of Numa. But if divine wisdom is salutary, why were Ulysses' sailors drowned? What is good for the wise harms those who are not. It is like the sun, pleasant to our eyes, unbearable for the sick. The same is true of the Sirens' song, heard only by Ulysses and not by his troop of companions, like a warning given by the son of God not to cast holy things before dogs. He wanted to be the rock of foundation for some, but for others, according to the word of the Apostle, a rock of scandal. Or, as Paul says (2 Corinthians 2.16): ''To the one we are the savor of death unto death; and to the other the savor of life unto life.'' A signification that Egidio picks up again in the *Scechina*[28] concerning the Talmud's interdiction, in the treatise *Haghiga,* against revealing this divine wisdom to the vulgar, ''neither to several nor to two, but only to the single pious, wise, and full-grown man,'' and he sees as a parallel to the Sirens' reefs the mysterious stones, *lapides Bohu, mephulot,* plunged into the abyss,[29] which represent the desires of the body.

IX. Vesta

In the *Treatise on Fire and Salt,* published after his death, Blaise de Vigenère evokes Vesta, along with Pallas, as follows:[30]

''These two deities, Pallas and Vesta, both virginal and chaste, as is fire, represent to us the two fires of the sensible world: Pallas, that is, is the celestial, and Vesta the elemental fire of this lower world: which, although cruder and more material than that of the upper world, nevertheless always tends contrariwise, as if it sought to separate itself from the corruptible substance to which it remains attached, to return free and exempt from all these hindrances to its first origin whence it came, like a soul imprisoned in the body:

> *Igneus est ollis vigor, et caelestis origo*
> *Seminibus, quantum non noxia corpora tardant,*
> *Terrenique herbetant artus, moribundaque membra.*
> (Fiery energy is in these seeds, their source is heavenly; but they are dulled by harmful bodies, blunted by their own earthly limbs, their mortal members).[31]

''The other, on the contrary, while more subtle and essential, throws itself toward the earth here below, as if these two ceaselessly aspired to meet and come before each other, like two pyramids, the upper one with its base firmly in the Zodiac, where the sun completes its annual journey through the twelve signs. From the peak of this pyramid, all that is born and has its being drops down here below, according to the doctrine of the ancient Astrologers of Egypt; therefore nothing appears on earth or in the water that is not sown there from heaven, which is like a laborer who cultivates it. And marking this world below with its warmth, with the efficacy of its influences, it leads the whole to its complete perfection and maturity: which is also confirmed by Aristotle in his books *De ortu et interitu*.[32] But the fire of this lower world, on the other hand, has the base of its pyramid attached to the earth, making one of the six faces of the cube, to which the Pythagorians attribute its form and figure because of its form and invariable stability: and from the point of this pyramid arise contrariwise the subtle vapors that serve to nourish the sun, and all the other celestial bodies; according to what Phurnutus, following others,[33] has written: an inextinguishable fire, he says, is attributed to Vesta, because the fiery power that is on earth takes from its nourishment from Vesta; and on this the sun sustains itself and consists. This is also what Hermes implied in his Table of Emerald: *'Quod est inferius, est sicut quod est superius; et e converso, ad perpetranda miracula rei unius'* ('What is below is just like what is above; and the reverse, for the sake of accomplishing the miracles of the one world'). And Rabbi Joseph, son of Carnitol, in his *Gates of Justice*:[34] 'The foundation of all lower edifices is placed on high; and their peak or their summit here below, like a tree inverted. As if man were nothing but a spiritual tree planted in the paradise of delights, which is the earth of the living, by the roots of his hair, according to what is written in the *Canticles* 7: *Comae capitis tui sicut purpura Regis juncta canalibus*.'

"These two fires, the high and the low, which in this way recognize each the other, were not ignored by the Poets, for Homer in book 18 of the *Iliad*[35] put Vulcan's forge in the eighth starry heaven, where he is accompanied by his artisans, endowed with a singular prudence, who know all sorts of works, which have been taught them by the immortal Gods in whose presence they labor. In book 8 of the *Aeneid*, however, Virgil put this workshop here below on earth, on an island called Vulcanian,

Vulcani domus, et Vulcania nomine tellus[36]

to show that fire is in both of these regions, the celestial and the elementary, but in diverse ways."

F.S./j.l.

NOTES

1. *Commentaire de H. de Linthault de Mont-Lion sur le Trésor des trésors* (Lyon 1610), 97.
2. *La espositione di Geber* (Venice 1544); Latin translation in 1548; cf. "Notes sur quelques alchimistes italiens de la Renaissance," *Rinascimento* 23 (1973): 203.
3. F. SECRET, "Le symbolisme de la kabbale chrétienne dans la Scechina d'Egidio da Viterbo," *Archivio di filosofia* (Rome 1958), p. 150.
4. Trans. J. de Montlyard (Lyon 1615), 579.
5. *Historia XX xaeculorum* (ms. Naples IX.B.14), fol. 208 v: "Domos urbesque aspernente curru contenti vitam traducerent ut currum semper ad decus currulis contemplationis allicerentur. Quare Chabala quae de divinis agit a Talmudistis doctoribus: et veterum sapientibus Maase Mercava: opus currule assidue nuncupatur. Statuas vero tam equestres: quam currules ab Ethruscis accepisse Romanos."
6. Ibid., fol. 244 v: "Graccus philosophus superbiam philosophiam indicat equo: italicam Tyrreni plaustro curruque significat."
7. Ibid., fol. 55 v, 181, etc.: *De Ecclesiae incremento, Traditio*, 25 (1969).
8. *Historia*, fol. 231 v "illis occultis narrationibus: quas a Faul faulas vocabant."
9. Cf. *Annuaire École pratique des hautes études (sci. religieuses)*, 86 (1977–78).
10. Ms. Fonds Brotier of the archives of the Society of Jesus (Chantilly), fol. 183 "de mystico ipsius curru, super nubes et alas sex spirituum (quales spectantur in ipsa figura sephirotica) seu sex draconum, qui sunt spirituum seu angelorum typi."
11. *La espositione*, p. 71 v.
12. *The Survival* (Harper, ed. 1961), 221.
13. *Demogorgone, con saggio di nuova edizione delle Genealogie deorum gentilium del Boccacio e silloge dei frammenti di Teodonzio* (Palermo 1930) (an. VIII).
14. *Dialoghi d'amore*, S. Caramella, ed. (Bari 1929), 106ff.
15. N. VALOIS, *Les cinq livres*, Bernard Roger, ed. (Paris 1975).
16. Ibid., p. 265.
17. *Traictez du vray sel secret*, Matton, ed. (Paris 1974), 278.
18. *De calcantho* (Augsburg 1617), 44.
19. PERNETY, *Dictionnaire*, s.v.; J. VAN LENNEP, *Art et alchimie*, p. III; bibliography in M. TARDIEU, *Trois mythes gnostiques, Adam, Éros et les animaux d'Égypte dans un écrit de Nag Hammadi*, II, 5 (Paris 1974).
20. *Le prime nove del altro mondo . . . inititulata La Vergine Venetiana* (Padua 1555), French trans. (Paris 1928), 42.
21. *Sloane 1411*, fol. 388 v: "Quare in psalmo 80 scripta est faeminea vox Canah et hortum"; *Sloane 1409* (translation of the *Beresith Rabba*), fol. 133, 135 v; *Sloane 1411* (*Commentaire du Recanati*, fol. 84, 98 v; cf. on the sources, J. BUXTORF, *Lexicon Chaldaicum talmudicum et rabbinicum* (Basel 1639), fol. 720 Hwl, and 952; cf. G. SCHOLEM, *Les origines de la kabbale* (Paris 1966), s.v. Palmier and M. Tardieu.
22. Cf. *Alchymista* (Toulouse 1632), 232; cf. *Littérature et alchimie*, B.H.R., 35 (1973): 520.
23. J. BALTRUSAITIS, *La quête d'Isis*.
24. F. SECRET, "Beresithias ou l'interprétation du premier mot de la Genèse chez les kabbalistes chrétiens," in *In principio: Interprétation des premiers versets de la Genèse* (Paris 1973).
25. *Œdipus Aegyptiacus* (Rome 1654), 3:405. *Prodromus coptus* (Rome 1636), 263.
26. Cf. text in E. MASSA, *I fondamenti metafisici della Dignitas hominis* (Turin 1954), 86.
27. *Historia*, ms. Naples, IX.B.14, fol. 148 v; see also fol. 53 v.
28. *Scechina* (Rome 1959), 2:83.
29. Ibid., 1:178; on these stones see G. SCHOLEM, *Les origines*, s.v.
30. *Traicté* (Paris 1617), 69.
31. *Aeneid* 6, c. 730, trans. Allen Mandelbaum (New York 1961).
32. This is the title of the translation by J. PERION (Paris 1552).
33. Cf. CORNUTUS (L. Annaeus) in *C. Julii, Augusti liberti fabularum liber* (Paris 1578), 164 v (in Teubner, ed., 1881, p. 53).
34. *Cant.* VII, 5; cf. JOSEPH IBN GIQATILIA, *Sha'arey Tsedeq* (Riva 1561), f. 18 v; cf. on the theme G. VAJDA, *Le commentaire d'Ezra de Gérone sur le Cantique des cantiques* (Paris 1969), 301.
35. *Iliad* 18.370.
36. *Aeneid* 8.423.

HERCULES IN ALCHEMY

One of the last historians of the theme of Hercules,[1] Marc René Jung, offered a note on Hercules in alchemy. He cited[2] Michael Maier and Pierre Jean Fabre, whose *Hercules piochymicus* was summarized by Pernety. It is enough to observe that Hercules appears to be everywhere for alchemists who are eager to find Diana under veils. Blaise de Vigenère, quite unjustly neglected, spoke a lot about it in his *Philostrate*: "If we want to apply this fantasy or poetic fiction to natural philosophy, we have already said in the preceding portrayal that Hercules is none other than the Sun, which by its heat and its rays, acting as arrows, exterminates the Hydra with all of its reborn heads, that is, the cold, the quality proper to water, of which this serpent is born and whose name it bears."[3] But it was Nuysement who dealt with all of the labors:

The labors of Hercules that are regarded as vain fables
Are by this secret art true symbols.
Geryon with his three bodies, terrifying and powerful,
Is the triple quicksilver embracing the ground and the moon.
The giant born of the earth, the indestructible Antaeus,
Whose power no one could supplant
As long as he touched his mother the Earth,
Is the spirit, living and hot,
Of our gold, which our water draws out and raises on high.
The Hydra that is constantly reborn, with seven horrible heads,
Is water, mother of gold and of all fusible bodies,
The water that never dampens, nor extinguishes the fire,
The serpent that the sun must kill little by little.
The monstrous species of the light Centaurs
Are the hideous matter of the two joined seeds.
The treacherous Diomedes with his cruel horses
Is the Artist hiding his cache of metals
In the secret room where his water devours it.
The shield of the Amazon Hippolite is Iris who decorates
This water with a hundred colors. The sickening dung
Of the Augean stable is the stinking blackness
That covers corpses after their putrefaction.
The birds of Stymphalus that ravage the pasture
Of the ill-fated Phineus, coming to defile him,
Are the strong vapors that come out of bodies.
The pursuit and capture of the wild boar
Is when matter enters the color grey
And leaving its darkness in order to become white
Gives a sign for the worker of its good fortune.
The skin of the great lion that this demigod wears
Is the red color that puts on the whiteness.

The bull he subdues is the body that is fixed.
The stag with golden horns is the yellowing fixed body.
Cerberus with the three throats is the newborn child, who asks
That someone feed it with new meat.

F.S./d.w.

NOTES

1. Cf. H. DE LUBAC, *Exégèse médiévale* 4, 2, p. 228, on Hercules and the theses of M. Simon, R. Trousson, and Pierre Sage.
2. *Hercule dans la littérature française du XVIe siècle* (Geneva 1966), p. 202.
3. *Poeme philosophic de la vérité de la phisique minerale,* Matton, ed., p. 95, v. 1600.

Orpheus in the Renaissance

Orpheus was so much in vogue during the Renaissance that a number of chapters could easily be added to the studies[1] already devoted to the subject. One Joannes Goropius Becanus (van Gorp, 1518–72), who was a friend of Christophe Plantin and Benito Arias Montano, both artisans of the Royal Polyglot of Philip II, and who is generally derided for having found that Flemish was more ancient than Hebrew in his bizarre *Origines Antwerpianae sive Cimmeroriorum Becceselana* (1568), accumulated in his *in-folios* the substance of an Orphic theology, which revealed the meaning of poetry to the Bishop of Antwerp, Laevinius Torrentius.[2] We should at least recall that the sixteenth century opens with a *Vellus aureum* by G. A. Augurelli, who in his *Chrysopoeia* evoked the *Argonautica*[3] which Lilio Gregorio Giraldi later read by the fireside in the company of Gianfrancesco Pico della Mirandola:

And in this place the most happy Nymphs
Through these treasures lush and rich
Untangle with a beautiful ivory comb
The Golden Fleece. There,
To acquire glory,
Prince Jason came first, by boat,
With his men, to carry off this fleece.
The noble youths did not fear,
Under Hercules and Jason,
Skillfully to wend their course
Through so many ocean waves
To reach the wealthy isle of Colchis.

According to the Reverend Vicot, chaplain to the lord alchemists of Flers, in the commentary to his *Grand Olimpe,*[4]

Some believed that this fleece was a book made of a sheepskin, so named for that reason, a book in which this noble secret was inscribed. Others allegorizing more subtly believed that the reference was to the first lord of this work, namely, Aries. Still others speak about a potent medicine consisting of fine wool gathered and fleeced from the back of a sheep. But whatever the case, at least we know that some time ago a brave young person, who by means of this divine powder had faithfully served one of our neighboring states, was rewarded by having an Order established in memory of him in this present state, which is still today called the Order of the Golden Fleece.

It is to a knight of the Golden Fleece that the Doctor from Antwerp, Guillaume Mennens, dedicated his *Aurei velleris sive sacrae philosophiae vatum selectae ac unicae mysteriorumque Dei, naturae et artis admirabilium libri tres* (Three books, of the golden fleece or the sacred philosophy, unique and chosen by the prophets, and of the mysteries of God, and of the nature and art of wondrous things), in which there are many references to the *De harmonia mundi* (On the harmony of the world) of Franciscus Georgius Venetus, who like many of his contemporaries was as much interested in astrology and alchemy as he was in the Cabala. Nor should we overlook the *Aureum Vellus, oder Güldin Schatz und Kunstkammer* by the great Salomon Trismosin, translated by Pierre Victor Palma Cayet (1525–1610), known as Petrus Magnus because he was interested in alchemy and the Cabala, and because he introduced Doctor Faustus to France.[5]

Orpheus, in whom Guy Le Fèvre de la Boderie found the "Mouth of Light" according to his teacher's emithology, is enthroned right in the middle of the temple of Intelligence engraved by Bartolomeo del Bene in his *Civitas veri,* which was published by his nephew Alphonse del Bene, bishop of Alby (1538–1608).[6] Del Bene attacked the alchemists in this

Orpheus. From Bartolomeo del Bene, *Civitas veri* (1609). Paris, Bibliothèque nationale. Photo BN.

Orpheus. From Bartolomeo del Bene, *Civitas veri* (1609). Paris, Bibliothèque nationale. Photo BN.

work and wrote a poem in Italian in which he showed that it was because of their longing for the divine poets David and Orpheus, the bards of immortality, that the Furies invented the alchemists, who boast of making men immortal during their own lifetimes.[7]

It is, moreover, for the same reason that Jean de Sponde (1557–95) praised Paracelsus, actually "Aureolus," for having resumed the conquest of the Golden Fleece in his own time. Jean de Sponde mentions this in *Homeri quae extant omnia,* dedicated to Henri III in 1573, in which he expounds on alchemy, having come to study this science at Basel, notably with one Theodor Zwinger.[8]

F.S./g.h.

NOTES

1. Cf. D. P. WALKER, "Orpheus the Theologian and Renaissance Platonists," *Journal of the Warburg Institute* 16 (1953), reprinted in *The Ancient Theology* (London 1972); F. JOUKOVSKI, *Orphée et ses disciples dans la poésie française et néo-latine du XVIe siècle* (Geneva 1970).
2. F. SECRET, *Annuaire de l'École pratique des hautes études* (sciences religieuses), 82 (1973–74): 257ff.
3. F. HABERT DE BERRY, trans., *Les trois livres de la Chrysopée* (Paris 1550), 69.
4. Ms. F. FRANC, 12299, fol. 115, cf. *Notes sur quelques alchimistes italiens,* p. 209.
5. *Alchimie et littérature,* in *Bibl. d'Hum. et Ren.* 35 (1973): 516.
6. *Civitas,* p. 249, "In medio intelligentiae templo suo . . . Statua est Orphei vatis theologi"; the attack on the alchemists is on p. 153.
7. Le Mans, ms. 7, fol. 94 v; cf. M. E. COUDERC, "Les poésies d'un Florentin," *Giornale storico dell. Let. ital.,* 1891.

"Poi che dal ciel la bella donna et pia
Qual manna o mele hybleo
Di Liban piovve infra gran cedri pria
Et detto il carme al pastorello Hebreo
. . .
Et con la Tracia poscia, et dolce lyra
Mosse le piante, e sassi . . ."

8. F. SECRET, "Notes pour une histoire de l'alchimie en France," *Australian Journal of French Studies* 9 (1972): 222.

KING ARTHUR, THE ROMANCES OF THE ROUND TABLE, AND THE LEGEND OF THE GRAIL

I. The Arthurian Legend

The term "Arthurian legend" has existed in scholarly French usage only since the publication of Edmond Faral's famous work by this title dealing with the genesis of certain Latin texts from the Middle Ages. The title is somewhat paradoxical, for according to Faral these texts, rather than

King Arthur. Vision of the holy grail. Paris, Bibliothèque nationale, MS fr. 112. Photo Bibliothèque nationale.

recording a legend, fabricate one from bits and pieces, and stem from no particular folk tradition. Such is the case of the *Historia Regum Britanniae* composed by Geoffrey of Monmouth in 1137, the earliest date for the imaginary chronicles of the reign of King Arthur, from his great conquests to his heroic death on the battlefield in 542. This chronicle and its adaptation in French verse by Wace (1155) were already part of the Arthurian stories that had as their protagonist the fabulous king surrounded by his knights, who owed him, according to feudal custom, their homage and faith. In order to explain the appearance of these texts and their many derivatives, need we hypothesize the existence of a true legend transmitted orally from generation to generation? The theory of folk origins has never been anything more than a succession of postulations which are often contradictory and almost always unverifiable, since no positive proof can be summoned in favor of the existence of a preliterary Arthurian myth. This does not mean that Celtic or Scandinavian folklore lacks parallels and analogies to certain narratives which are connected with the legendary figures of King Arthur and his knights. The point is, however, that none of these parallels is recorded within the Arthurian framework, none is linked to the characters or themes as the literary texts of the Middle Ages present them, and so none can be properly called "Arthurian." Literary scholarship has persisted in cultivating this type of speculation because it has been unable to propose an alternative explanation which would even begin to do justice to the texts. Such an explanation was not possible until the day that the narrative literature of the Middle Ages gained the right to be treated as a body of work subject to the laws of literary creation. Before giving up the search for the myth, however, we must be convinced that the blossoming of stories grouped around the character of King Arthur and his Round Table can explain one another, as so many other analogous traditions do, through the autonomous and spontaneous effort of the authors of our texts, and notably through the use of two distinct and yet complementary procedures. One consists of gathering together all the elements already in existence, which until now have appeared only in isolation. Like a magnetic field, the work thus becomes the locus where, once reunited, these elements form a new structure, acquiring an original significance. This procedure underlay the formation of epic and fictional cycles that dominated all French narrative literature in the thirteenth century. The other procedure, a term used here in no pejorative sense, is a timeless one. It consists of rethinking a given body of work to give it a new meaning, more profound, more subtle, or simply more in keeping with the tastes of the public to whom it is addressed. The pseudo-chronicle of Geoffrey of Monmouth was only the beginning of the myth of the greatness and the fall of the Arthurian monarchy, a myth that was elaborated over the course of the last three centuries of the Middle Ages through the successive contributions of French and English writers. According to Geoffrey, as in all the chronicles derived from his *Historia* (Wace's *Brut,* Layamon's *Brut,* and the fourteenth-century English poem *Morte Arthure*), Arthur dies a victim of the treachery of Mordred. This is a fortuitous incident which is unexpected and unjustified. French prose writers of the thirteenth century, authors of the great Arthurian cycle (1220–25), applied themselves to creating a motive for this major event, making it the culmination of a whole series of intelligently developed themes. This process continued until the third quarter of the fifteenth century, in the hands of the greatest of the Arthurian prose writers, Sir Thomas Malory. We move from a single episode in a chronicle to the tragic drama of *Morte Arthur saunz guerdon,* just as, in a work of romantic fiction, we move from a single fact to a structured work. Insofar as the main Arthurian themes have undergone this evolution, it may be said that Arthurian mythology as a whole springs from the dual movement that forms wholes and continuously renews their meaning. This mythology is found in English-speaking countries at all levels of oral and written culture, from stories still told aloud today in Wales and Cornwall to the works of poets and prose writers of our times.

At what precise moment was the idea of the great king's survival and eventual return to the country he had once made the most beautiful kingdom on earth added to this already rich and fertile collection of romantic themes? Here again we encounter a very general belief, which appears in the folklore of many other countries: the refusal to accept as final the disappearance of a savior, a liberating hero, who must return to ensure the salvation of his people. It is in the logic of things that tales of the glorious exploits of a great king lead to the hope for his return, and there is nothing to contradict the view that, in the British tradition, this hope itself was also of literary origin. Its first expression is found in the chronicles based on the work of Geoffrey of Monmouth and those of Wace and Layamon, and the Latin formula *Rex quondam rexque futurus* ("the Once and Future King") continued to appear even in the fourteenth-century *Morte Arthure.* In the fifteenth century, Malory described this belief, while at the same time indicating that he did not share it: "This," he said, "is what some think; all we really know is that in this world the great king changed his life."

Two other themes developed in an analogous manner: the theme of the Grail and that of the romance of Lancelot and Guinevere. Clearly, it is within an Arthurian framework—in the stories of Chrétien de Troyes—that they appear for the first time, one in the *Conte de Graal* (*Story of the Grail,* ca. 1181), and the other in the *Conte de la Charrette* (*Story of the Cart,* ca. 1172). But these stories are actually foreign to the Arthurian "legend" proper. The King Arthur to whom they refer is no longer the fabulous warrior of Geoffrey of Monmouth and Wace. The King Arthur of Chrétien de Troyes does not even remember the exploits attributed to that warrior. His role consists solely in encouraging the adventures that take place around him; he has no thoughts of becoming involved himself. It was not until the thirteenth century, in the great Arthurian cycle in prose attributed to Walter Map, that the epic of Arthur's kingdom, the Grail, and the passionate love affair of Lancelot and the queen all came together. In this context, the latter two themes acquired new meaning and depth. From that moment on, their true value appears as a chance phenomenon born of the imagination of remodelers and adapters rather than deriving from the mysterious depths of popular traditions. Sequences created in this manner sometimes seem to be preliterary myths, such as the theme of the kingdom transformed into a wasteland (*terre gaste*). Recent research has shown that this story was formed through the agglutination of diverse elements originally independent of one another; so we cannot regard them as parts of a single original myth. Simply by respecting the chronology of our texts from the twelfth and thirteenth centuries, we see how the true architects of the legend of the *terre gaste* worked their material. And this work did not cease with the vogue of French Arthurian novels; it continued through the work of Thomas Malory in the fifteenth century right up to one of the greatest poems of the twentieth: Eliot's *The Waste Land.* If Chrétien de Troyes had lived to see the extraordinary development of the Grail motif, he might have asked himself, like Boaz: How could this have come from me? Such a question would remain unanswered if we forgot to take into account the creative imagination of the writers of the thirteenth-century prose cycle, who used the Grail as a symbol of divine grace without asking what it meant.

II. The Grail

We do not even know the meaning of the Grail in the poem by Chrétien de Troyes that bears its name (ca. 1181). The pageant of the Grail as he described it has caused rivers of ink to flow in our time. For the young knight Percival who saw it, as well as for all readers of this passage, it provides an opportunity to look in wonder at two mysterious objects: the Grail itself, that is, the sacred vessel carried by a maiden, and the bleeding lance in the hands of a young man who leads the procession. If, when that procession passed before him, Percival had only asked its significance, the *méhaigné* king, the wounded king who lived in the castle, would have been cured of his wounds. But Percival, interpreting too literally the advice given him by a wise man named Gornemant, was careful not to ask that question. If he had asked it, who knows what the people of the castle would have told him? Did Chrétien de Troyes himself know the exact meaning of the object he introduced into his poem? We do not know, just as we do not know whether a Grail legend ever existed before Chrétien de Troyes. The evidence suggests that if there was a legend, it was of strictly literary origin like the Arthurian legend, created and propagated by writers. Chrétien de Troyes was followed at the end of the twelfth century by Robert de Boron, the author of a poem called *Estoire du Graal* (*The Story of the Grail*) or *Joseph of Arimathie.* According to Robert de Boron, the Grail was the vessel in which Joseph had collected a few drops of Christ's blood after the crucifixion, and which Joseph's brother-in-law Bron, and his son Alan, were to carry to England—a symbol of the faith which would spread through the Western world. Did Robert de Boron compose a *Percival* as well? No record remains of such a work, but it is possible that the *Perlesvaus,* a prose text from the beginning of the thirteenth century, was an adaptation of a lost poem of Robert de Boron.

The main event in the evolution of the Grail theme in the thirteenth century is the substitution of Galahad for Percival in the role of the hero of the Grail. Galahad, the pure knight and natural son of Launcelot, appears for the first time in the great Arthurian cycle composed between 1220 and 1225, where he seems to play the role of a liberator charged with delivering the Arthurian kingdom from the sin of lust. He alone would be able to see the Grail clearly and openly and to achieve his quest. He alone, because of his character and his behavior, would be able to give human incarnation to the magic light which emanated from it. Furthermore, the Grail here has a very specific meaning, as Etienne Gilson has demonstrated in a famous study (*Romania,* 1925). Before this symbol of divine grace, the knights of King Arthur are somehow ranked according to their degree of perfection or imperfection. Galahad attains the highest knowledge of the divine mystery, which can be obtained through a pure mind (*pura mens*). At a lower level are Percival and Bohort, who arrive at this knowledge through their senses, while Launcelot reaches it only through dreams: three mystic states admirably described in the preceding century by Saint Bernard of Clairvaux. The cycle in which Galahad's quest first appeared was followed by a composition almost as extensive as what is now called the *Roman du Graal* (1235). While the quest for the Grail was only an episode of relatively limited scope in the great Arthurian cycle, in the *Roman du Graal,* Arthur's kingdom, "the adventurous kingdom," is destined from the beginning to face this magical object, whose mere presence seems to condemn the kingdom as much as the ideology of chivalry it embodies. In the same period, Wolfram von Eschenbach in his *Parzival* reestablished the eponymous hero in the role of knight of the Grail and transformed the Grail itself into a magical stone with a profoundly moral significance. Wagner was visibly inspired by Wolfram, whose source seems to be none other than Chrétien de Troyes. This had a curious consequence: for most modern readers, the Grail legend is a legend of Percival, while for readers in the last three centuries of the Middle Ages the Grail legend was essentially that of Galahad, inseparably linked to the prose poem about Lancelot. Because this story survived to modern times only through Sir Thomas Malory's adaptation (published in 1485 by William Caxton), only English-speaking countries retain the memory of the pure knight Galahad. As with the Arthurian legend or the legend of Tristan and Isolde, the Grail legend became diversified according to the various forms and interpretations given to it by the poets and prose writers of the late Middle Ages. As a poetic theme, or as a religious or moral symbol, the Grail has never been anything but the product of their imagination.

We have no reason to search elsewhere for the secret of its emotional power and its prodigious and widespread influence.

III. *Terre Geste* (Wasteland)

In its most complete and latest form, this theme includes four elements: a miraculous weapon, a serious wound suffered by a great man (king or knight), the devastation of a kingdom, and the healing of the wounded man. The blow that inflicts the wound—the "dolorous stroke"—is almost always given by the miraculous weapon, while the other elements of the narrative are often separated from one another. They are found together for the first time in one of the branches of the *Roman du Graal,* sometimes called the *Suite du Merlin* and dating approximately from 1230–35.

The four elements of the theme of the wasteland in this work form a continuous narrative whose protagonist is Balain, an unfortunate knight who seems destined to bring sorrow to all he meets. The "dolorous stroke" which causes the devastation of the country is dealt by him while he is defending himself against the powerful king Pelles, a king mysteriously linked to the theme of the Grail, since it is the Grail in the hands of the pure knight Galahad that will heal him. The architects of the legend of the *terre gaste* not only constructed a perfectly coherent and well-balanced scenario; they knew how to enhance in a new way the theme of the Grail within the Arthurian cycles, as the hapless knight was contrasted to the fortunate knight Galahad. The one plunges Arthur's kingdom into gloom and misfortune, while the other floods the kingdom with a new light and shows it the way to salvation.

E.V./d.b.

BIBLIOGRAPHY

1. Texts

GEOFFROI DE MONMOUTH, *Historia Regum Britanniae,* Acton Griscom, ed. (New York 1929); *Historia Regum Britanniae: A Variant Version,* J. Hammer, ed. (Cambridge, MA, 1951).

WACE, *Le roman de Brut,* Ivor Arnold, ed., 2 vols. (Paris 1938–40).

LAYAMON, *Brut,* G. L. Brook and R. F. Leslie, eds. (London 1963).

CHRÉTIEN DE TROYES: two editions: (1) W. Foerster, *Sämtliche erhaltene Werke nach allen bekannten Handschriften,* 4 vols. (Halle 1884–99); Wörterbuch (1914). (2) An edition based on Guiot's copy (Bibl. Nat. franç. 794): *Erec et Enide,* Mario Roques, ed. (1955); *Cligés,* A. Micha, ed. (1957); *Le Chevalier de la Charrette,* M. Roques, ed. (1958); *Le Chevalier au lion (Yvain),* M. Roques, ed. (1960); *Le conte du Graal* (Perceval), F. Lecoy, ed., 2 vols. (1975); *Le conte du Graal et les continuations: Der Percevalroman,* Alfons Hilka, ed. (Halle 1932); *Le Roman de Perceval ou le Conte du Graal,* W. Roach, ed. (2d ed. revised and augmented, 1959); *The Continuations of the Old French Perceval of Chrétien de Troyes,* W. Roach, ed., 4 vols. (Philadelphia 1949–71); GERBERT DE MONTREUIL, *La continuation de Perceval,* Mary Williams, ed., vol. 1 (1922), vol. 2 (1925); vol. 3, Marguerite Oswald, ed. (1975); *The Elucidation: A Prologue to the Conte du Graal,* A. W. Thompson, ed. (New York 1931); *Bibliocadran,* L. D. Wolfgang, ed., *Beihefte zur Zeitschrift für romanische Philologie,* 150 (1976).

ROBERT DE BORON, *Le roman de l'estoire dou Graal,* W. A. Nitze, ed. (Paris 1927).

Der Prosaroman von Joseph Arimathia, G. Weidner, ed. (Oppeln 1881); *The Modena Text of the Prose Joseph d'Arimathie,* W. Roach, ed. *Romance Philology* 9 (1955–56): 313–42.

The Didot Perceval, According to the Manuscripts of Modena and Paris, W. Roach, ed. (Philadelphia 1941).

Perlesvaus: Le haut livre du Graal, W. A. Nitze and T. Atkinson Jenkins, eds., 2 vols. (Chicago 1932–37).

La queste del Saint Graal postérieure à la Vulgate, Critical Ed., F. Bogdanow, ed., forthcoming.

WOLFRAM VON ESCHENBACH, *Parzival,* text (after Lachmannschen's 5th ed., 1891; narrative and glossary by Werner Hoffman), Gottfried Weber, ed. (Darmstadt 1967).

The Vulgate Version of the Arthurian Romances, H. O. Sommer, ed., from *Manuscripts in the British Museum,* vol. 1: *L'estoire del Saint Graal;* vol. 2: *L'estoire de Merlin;* vols. 3–5: *Le livre de Lancelot del Lac;* vol. 6: *Les aventures ou la Queste del Saint Graal: La mort le Roi Artus;* vol. 7: *Supplement: Le livre d'Artus, with Glossary* (Washington 1908–16). Partial editions: *La Queste del Saint Graal,* A. Pauphilet, ed. (1924); *La mort de Roi Artu,* J. Frappier, ed. (1936; 4th ed., 1968).

G. PARIS and J. ULRICH, *Merlin, roman en prose du XIIIe siècle publié avec la mise en prose du poème de Merlin de Robert de Boron d'après le manuscrit appartenant à M. Alfred H. Huth,* 2 vols. (Paris 1886).

La folie Lancelot, F. Bogdanow, ed. (Tübingen 1965).

SIR THOMAS MALORY, *The Works,* Eugène Vinaver, ed., 3 vols. (2d ed., Oxford 1967).

La demanda del Sancto Grial, Primera Parte: *El Baladro del sabio Merlin con sus profecias;* Segunda Parte: *La demanda del Sancto Grial con los maravillosos fechos de Lanzarote y de Galaz su hijo, Libros de Caballerias,* part 1 of *Ciclo arturico,* by ADOLFO BONILLA Y SAN MARTIN (Madrid 1907). *El Baladro del sabio Merlin segun el texto de la edicion de Burgis de 1498,* Pedro Bohigas, ed., 3 vols. (Barcelona 1957–62). *A Demanda do Santo Graal,* Augusto Magne, ed., 3 vols. (Rio de Janeiro 1944).

2. Critical Studies

J. D. BRUCE, *The Evolution of Arthurian Romance from the Beginnings Down to the Year 1300,* 2 vols. (Göttingen and Baltimore 1923); 2d ed. (1928, 1958), with a bibliographic supplement by A. Hilka. E. K. CHAMBERS, *Arthur of Britain* (London 1927); reprinted with bibliographic supplement (Cambridge 1964). E. FARAL, *La légende arthurienne,* Études et documents, 3 vols. (Paris 1929). J. FRAPPIER, *Chrétien de Troyes* (Paris 1957; 2d revised ed., 1971); *Étude sur la mort le Roi Artu, roman du XIIIe siècle, dernière partie du Lancelot en prose* (Paris 1936; 2d ed. revised and augmented, 1961). R. S. LOOMIS, ed. *Arthurian Literature in the Middle Ages: A Collaborative History* (Oxford 1959).

F. LOT, *Étude sur le Lancelot en prose* (Paris 1918); reprinted with a supplement (1954). J. S. P. TATLOCK, *Legendary History of Britain* (Berkeley and Los Angeles 1950). E. VINAVER, *A la recherche d'une poétique médiévale* (Paris 1970); *The Rise of Romance* (Oxford 1971). P. ZUMTHOR, *Merlin le Prophète: Un thème de la littérature polémique de l'historiographie et des romans* (Lausanne 1943).

F. BOGDANOW, *The Romance of the Grail* (Manchester and New York 1966). A. C. L. BROWN, "The Bleeding Lance," *Publications of the Modern Language Association* 25 (1910): 1–59. K. BURDACH, *Der Graal* (Stuttgart 1938); reprinted (Darmstadt 1974). R. S. LOOMIS, *Arthurian Tradition and Chrétien de Troyes* (New York 1949); *Celtic Myth and Arthurian Romance* (New York 1927); *The Grail, from Celtic Myth to Christian Symbol* (Cardiff and New York 1963). *Lumière du Graal. Etudes et textes présentés sous la direction de René Nelli* (Paris 1951). W. GOLTHER, *Parzival und der Gral in der Dichtung des Mittelalters und der Neuzeit* (Stuttgart 1925). J. MARX, *La légende arthurienne et le Graal* (Paris 1952); *Nouvelles recherches sur la littérature arthurienne* (Paris 1965). A. PAUPHILET, *Études sur la queste del Saint Graal attribuée à Gautier Map* (Paris 1921). *Les romans de Graal dans la littérature des XIIe et XIIIe siècles* (Paris 1956).

E. VETTERMANN, *Die Balen-Dichtungen und ihre Quellen,* supplement to *Zeitschrift für romanische Philologie,* 60 (1918). J. WESTON, *From Ritual to Romance* (Cambridge 1920).

Tristan and Isolde

We have many texts pertaining to the legend of Tristan and Isolde, among them fragments of two great French poems of the twelfth century, one attributed to Béroul, the other to Thomas; a German poem of the same period composed by Eilhart von Oberg; a Norwegian saga; a German poem of the thirteenth century by Gottfried von Strassburg; an English poem entitled *Sir Tristrem;* a prose version in Italian; and finally a prose romance in French preserved in a very large number of manuscripts as well as in a few printed editions of the late fifteenth and early sixteenth centuries. In an attempt to explain both the origin and the vast diffusion of this legend, scholars first applied to the legend of Tristan the general theory of the mechanical formation of epic, just as they had done for other literary traditions including the Homeric poems and the French *chansons de geste.* This theory, conceived and developed by the great German romantic thinkers, was tinged by the mystique of the spontaneous and the primitive, which saw poetry as an impersonal product of popular genius created by virtue of an immediate intuition, presumably the manifestation of the divine in man. According to the theory, all narrative poetry was originally a tradition of short songs, each devoted to an isolated event. These songs were not frozen by writing. Rather, expert singers peddled their wares, so to speak, on street corners, and the songs thus passed on from generation to generation by simple word of mouth. Finally, collectors gathered them, set them down in writing, and developed them with the view toward putting together vast collections of narratives. According to this hypothesis, what was preserved of the legend of Tristan may well be just such a series of assemblages. Behind it all was a theme of singular strength and vitality, namely, the illegitimate and guilty love of Tristan for Isolde, a love whose fatal and indestructible nature was symbolized by the love potion that Tristan and Isolde drink by mistake during their voyage from Ireland to Cornwall. According to Gaston Paris, to this basic theme were added progressively the various components of what we now call the romance of Tristan: the dangers met by the lovers, the attempts by their enemies to destroy them, the episode of their joint exile and their life in the forest, then their summons by the king to return, their renewed indiscretions, their forced separation, Tristan's exile in Brittany, his futile effort to forget Isolde the Fair by marrying Isolde of the White Hands, the poisoned wound that he suffers in combat and that Queen Isolde alone can cure, her own departure for the distant land where Tristan is dying, her arrival at the moment after his death, and finally her own sudden death on the dead body of her lover. According to the romantic canon, this theme did not take shape in its overpowering simplicity inside the soul of a single poet. Separate poems joining together and breaking up into various groups may have made up the first phase of the life of the legend. During the next phase, an attempt may have been made to group into one coherent story the adventures of Tristan and Isolde until their deaths. A late nineteenth-century German scholar by the name of Golther described the poem of Eilhart von Oberg as a "conglomerate of disparate scenes and episodes artificially linked together." In the same period, Novati, an Italian scholar, was writing: "Béroul's poem, although it can be said that it is rather solidly constructed, at every moment reveals the solderings between the pieces from which it was made." Against the background of this doctrine, the great

Le roman de Tristan et Yseult (ms. fr. 103, fol. 1). Paris, Bibliothèque nationale. Photo BN.

medievalist of our century, Joseph Bédier, put forward his findings with all the strength of his talent and erudition. He claimed that the basis of the whole poetic tradition has always been a single poem, the common archetype of all the known romances that speak of Tristan and Isolde. This archetype is not an aggregate of collected pieces, but a spontaneous work of art resplendent in the unity of its creation. Few people seriously challenge this hypothesis today. There are of course divergent views regarding the content of the common archetype. Again it was Bédier who first attempted to reconstruct the archetype by adopting a very simple method that he explained in the following terms. First, one compares the four "primary" versions derived from the original romance, i.e., the poems of Béroul, Eilhart, and Thomas, and the prose romance. When these versions yield differing accounts, one must ask by what criteria the antiquity of a particular feature may be determined: its archaic "turn," its intrinsic value, its conformity to the overall work? We are aware of how precarious such determinations may be. Nonetheless, Bédier's work led him to make the following statement:

> Every time the comparison could apply to at least three of the texts, the features which, for reasons of taste, feeling, and logic, we deemed original were features attested by three versions or by at least two of them. Conversely, the features which for reasons of taste, feeling, and logic we deemed to have been revised and of more recent date, appeared to be isolated in a single version of the ones compared.

Bédier was able to make the important claim that the compared versions were independent from one another for the following reason: since each time two or three of them were in agreement, they were faithful to their source, whereas each time that they were not in agreement, they were at variance with the source. Hence, our texts allow us simultaneously to establish the existence of an archetype and to reconstruct it in its broad outlines. Béroul and Eilhart, according to recent investigations, were probably the most faithful to the archetype. Their adaptations most clearly assert the essential theme of the original romance, namely, the juxtaposition, forever unresolved, of the two irreconcilable powers, that of the love potion and that of the social law which the lovers never repudiate. This does not alter the fact that if we are to understand the evolution of the legend into the modern period, we must consult Thomas's version and the French prose version, which implicitly or explicitly proclaim the sovereign rights of love. Thomas inspired, among others, the German poet Gottfried von Strassburg, from whose work, in turn, Wagner learned the legend of Tristan. The prose romance (1230), itself widespread in medieval Europe, made the legend of Tristan into one of the romances of the Round Table. In a collection of English prose romances published in 1485 by William Caxton under the title of *Le morte d'Arthur,* Sir Thomas Malory gave us an abridged version of the romance that serves as the source for most modern English versions.

Should we assume that a popular legend, predating the first Tristan romance, was disseminated by the Celts from across the Channel and passed on by Breton bards, as certain French poets claim? The existence of a legend featuring Mark, his wife, and his swineherd Tristan in love with the wife is attested in a very ancient Welsh triad, a plain, unpolished story in which there is talk neither of a love potion nor of the social order that the lovers are destined simultaneously to violate and to respect. It is not of this story that one thinks when postulating an original Celtic Tristan, but of something as complete and as profoundly poetic as the French archetype of our earliest romances. But we have no proof that such a work ever existed. A romance of Tristan composed in France toward the middle of the twelfth century is, outside of our texts, the sole tangible reality. Given the current state of our knowledge, we cannot deny the most compelling poem of the French Middle Ages its profound and startling originality.

E.V./g.h.

BIBLIOGRAPHY

1. Texts

Béroul's *Tristan:* E. Muret, ed., 4th ed., revised by L.-M. Defourques (Paris 1970); A. Ewert, ed., *The Romance of Tristan* by Béroul (Oxford 1939), introduction and commentary, vol. 2 (1970).

Thomas's *Tristan:* J. Bédier, ed., *Le roman de Tristan par Thomas,* 2 vols. (Paris 1902–5); B. H. Wind, ed., *Les fragments du Tristan de Thomas* (Paris 1960).

Folies Tristan: J. Bédier, ed., *Les deux poèmes de la Folie Tristan* (Paris 1907); E. Hoepffner, ed., *La Folie Tristan de Berne,* 2d ed., revised and corrected (Strasbourg 1949); *La Folie Tristan d'Oxford,* 2d ed., revised and corrected (Strasbourg 1943).

EILHART VON OBERG, *Tristrant,* ed. fr. Lichtenstein (Strasbourg 1877).

GOTTFRIED VON STRASSBURG, *Tristan und Isolt,* F. Ranke, ed. (Berlin 1930); idem, G. Weber, ed., with G. Utzmann and Werner Hoffmann (Darmstadt 1967).

The Romance in Prose (partial editions): R. L. Curtis (Munich 1963); J. Blanchard, *Les deux captivités de Tristan* (Paris 1976).

Tristram saga, E. Kölbing, ed. (Heilbronn 1878).

2. Critical Studies

Arthurian Literature in the Middle Ages, R. S. Loomis, ed. (Oxford 1959), chaps. 12–14, 26. EMMANUÉLE BAUMGARTNER, *Le Tristan en prose: Essai d'interprétation d'un roman médiéval* (Geneva 1975). DANIELLE BUSCHINGER, *Le Tristan d'Eilhart von Oberg* (Paris 1975). M. DELBOUILLE, DENIS DE ROUGEMONT, and E. VINAVER, *Tristan et Iseut à travers le temps* (Brussels 1961). A. FOURRIER, *Le courant réaliste dans le roman courtois en France au Moyen Age,* 1: *Les débuts* (12th century) (Paris 1960). W. GOLTHER, *Tristan und Isolde in den Dichtungen des Mittelalters und der neuen Zeit* (Leipzig 1907). P. JONIN, *Les personnages féminins dans les romans français de Tristan au XIIe siècle,* Publ. de la Faculté des Lettres (Aix-en-Provence 1958). J. KELEMINA, *Untersuchungen zur Tristansage* (Leipzig 1910); *Geschichte der Tristansage nach den Dichtungen des Mittelalters* (Vienna 1923). E. LOESETH, *Le roman en prose de Tristan, le roman de Palamède et la compilation de Rusticien de Pise, analyse critique d'après les manuscrits de Paris* (Paris 1891); reprinted by B. Franklin (New York 1970). W. RÖTTIGER, *Der heutige Stand der Tristanforschung* (Hamburg 1897). G. SCHOEPPERLE, *Tristan and Isolt: A Study of the Sources of the Romance* (Frankfurt and London 1913); reprinted by B. Franklin (New York 1958). A. VAVARO, *Il roman di Tristan di Béroul* (Turin 1963). E. VINAVER, *Études sur le Tristan en prose, les sources, les manuscrits, bibliographie critique* (Paris 1925).

GYPSY MYTHS AND RITUALS

Of all the ethnic minorities scattered throughout the world, Gypsies are perhaps one of the most original by virtue of their life-style and their adherence to tradition. In the heart of our developed and urbanized countries, this wandering people manifests a profound will to survive despite all attempts to assimilate it and despite the countless harassments and persecutions of which it have been the target. The last such attempt resulted in the extermination of nearly five hundred thousand Gypsies in Nazi concentration camps.

One of the basic factors of this resistance is the Gypsies' religious sense. We say religious sense rather than religion, because it is above all a general state of mind and a specific ethical and religious behavior rather than a system of dogmatized beliefs and institutionalized ritual practices. This kind of religious life is closely tied to the history of the Gypsies and to their culture, which it nurtures and endows with meaning. We therefore begin with a brief overview of the origins of the Gypsies and the originality of their nomadism.

I. Nomadism and Gypsy Life

In order to understand the Gypsy soul, we must never lose sight of the close link between the history of this people and the type of nomadism within which it has preserved its identity to this day. Gypsy myths and rites may then be perceived in the context of their true nature and of their functioning.

Originally from India, Gypsies reached Europe at the beginning of the modern era (fifteenth and sixteenth centuries), after long wanderings through the Near East. Many invasions have swept over Europe and shaped its population. The Gypsies constitute the last such invasion, the most peaceful and by far the least numerically significant. They came too late into a world already organized politically, so that there was no place left for them, and no hope of occupying some vacant territory. They were compelled to scatter throughout all civilized countries, cornered as they were by two necessities: first, they had to be accepted by native populations despite the suspicion they aroused by the alien character of their ethnic type, language, and customs, marking them as intruders or undesirables; second, they had to live. They did so by preserving their originality and continuing in the path of nomadism that had always worked for them, which we have elsewhere called "parasitic nomadism" (without any pejorative overtones). Whereas most nomadic people are largely self-sufficient, hunting or raising cattle on lands that they know, such could not be the case for the Gypsies. To survive, they had to establish a trading pattern with settled populations, often by limiting their nomadism to a single country. To make such commerce possible, Gypsies learned many small trades compatible with their wandering life and incorporated them into the old rural world: tin-plating of kitchen utensils, basket weaving, pot and pan making, saddlery, handicrafts, door-to-door retailing, horse trading, metal scrapping, circuses, bear training, popular and veterinary medicine, musical entertainment for festivals and country weddings, fortune-telling, etc.

Needless to say, such trades have become less and less profitable. The advent of industrial and urban society has brought about considerable change in the rural world with which the Gypsies lived in a symbiotic relationship. The rural world has shrunk quantitatively; industrialization has reached the farmer; the standard of living has increased; and widespread education and the pervading influence of the mass media have transformed needs and made obsolete the small-scale trading (except for metal scrapping and the secondhand market) which allowed Gypsies to survive while continuing to practice their ancestral nomadism. This has led to the crisis of acculturation that now threatens the very survival of this people's cultural identity (see my article, "Les Tsiganes face au problème de l'acculturation," *Diogène*, 1976, no. 4).

II. Christianity and Animism

When speaking of the religion of the Gypsies, we should distinguish clearly between two things. On the one hand, Gypsies officially profess a particular religion, usually the Christian faith. On the other hand, a backdrop of animistic religion survives tenaciously in an abundance of ancient myths and in the practice of magic rites, more or less integrated into the official religion.

Gypsies have usually adopted the faith of the country in which they wandered, be it Islam or Christianity (Eastern Orthodoxy, Roman Catholicism, Protestantism, and today Pentecostalism in many instances). Here again, it has been a question of survival. On arriving as aliens in the Christian West, to take one example, where being a pagan was the worst of all disgraces (the same may be said of the Muslim areas in the Balkans, where the Gypsies adopted Islam), Gypsies saw that adopting the local religion was in their best interest, especially in view of the fact that baptism constituted the only real form of identity. Insecure as Gypsies were and uncertain of the welcome they might receive, they were afraid of being expelled or persecuted (even today the precariousness of camping zones reserved for nomads perpetuates this form of racism), and of being unable to practice their indispensable trades. Belonging to the local religion thus became a basic guarantee for the Gypsies. It alone could confer on them the minimum of credibility that they needed to be accepted by the settled populations. We should not, however, think that joining the official religion was merely a superficial act. Though initially an act of self-interest, it was most often incorporated into the Gypsy religious mentality, which, as we shall show below, was of an animistic type.

Gypsies reinterpreted Christian beliefs and rites from a more primitive and fundamental religious structure. This animistic base indicates an overarching religious mentality that pervades all of Gypsy life, even while leaving it open to other religious beliefs experienced in an original style. To summarize this basic religious sense, we could say that for the Gypsies there are not two realms—that of everyday, secular life, and that of far-off, extraterrestrial deities. Rather, the world in which the Gypsies lead their daily existence is peopled with mythical and supernatural beings—kindly and evil spirits, demons, fairies—who bear various names and assume all sorts of bodily features and appearances.

At every moment of their life, Gypsies feel that they are in contact with those beings on whom their personal fate rests, beings who are hidden behind the most familiar events, persons, and things. This attitude is a form of the "law of participation" that characterizes people who live close to nature, who feel that they have a special bond with the cosmos and are subject to the influence of the mythical beings that control the generally menacing cosmic forces. Knowing that they are in communication with this supernatural universe, the Gypsies try to make it work on their behalf by performing specialized rites (of purification, exorcism, prophylaxis, healing, divination, etc.). This religious element has played a major role in the Gypsies' resistance to a hostile environment, as it is the soul of their very own nomadism. Openly despised by sedentary populations, under constant threat of persecution, the Gypsies could reach deep inside themselves for the strength of their conviction that they are part of a superior world dominating the real world. Moreover, the pride they experience in their destitution and the mystery with which they shroud their magic rites make them respected and feared, and thus encourage others to accept their meager services.

III. The Gypsy Religious Sense

It is difficult to isolate the original religious elements of the Gypsy world from the successive contributions of religions adopted at a later time. Certainly, with the progress of evangelization the earlier elements have gradually become blurred or, at best, have survived within a kind of reinterpretation of Christain dogmas that they themselves have influenced. Ethnologists of the previous century, H. von Wlislocki among them, who managed to live in close touch with Gypsy groups in central Europe, collected a number of mythical narratives, especially cosmogonies. With respect to the creation of the world, we can observe a basic dualism, conceivably of Iranian origin (after leaving India, the Gypsies stayed in Persia for a long time), whereby God opposes the devil in a kind of contest, but with a clearly Christian tone, for the devil ultimately submits to God. This cosmogony contains many elements common to most such accounts, including primeval waters, the tree as the source of life, and the separation of heaven and earth.

Underlying the Gypsy religious mentality, one thing we know for certain: Gypsies believe in the existence of a benevolent God (Del, Devel) who is a creator-god. Far from any pantheistic concept, he is very much a personal god, the almighty whom Gypsies often invoke for his kindness in connection with every event, even in the midst of magic rites.

Specifically Christian elements seem to coexist happily with the older, animistic core. In particular, belief in Jesus Christ (Baro Devel) is hardly distinguishable from belief in God the creator and protector of mankind. In their quest for a happy existence, Gypsies have a great cult of the saints and particularly of the Virgin Mary (see § V below, on the mediating importance of femininity). Accustomed as they are to believing in a myriad of superior beings, benevolent or malevolent, they are comfortable with devotion of the saints (hence the success of pilgrimages, such as that of the Saintes-Maries in Provence). They are likewise serious about exorcising the devil; hence the importance attributed to Christian baptism, understood to fall under the general rubric of exorcism.

Two features of Gypsy religiosity seem to be carryovers of a pre-Christian stage: the problem of death and salvation, and the existence of numerous spirits that influence daily life.

The god of the Gypsies may be God the Creator, Providence, who loves mankind, but he is by no means the God who redeems from sin (little importance is given to this redemptive aspect of the mission of Christ), nor is he the God who rewards or punishes after death. The absence of the idea of repayment in the afterlife is connected with a fatalism characteristic of Gypsy psychology. It is undeniable that the Gypsies believe in the immortality of the soul, the soul being conceived of in a rather material way. This afterlife, however, is not the salvation that concludes existence in the Christian sense. It is not an immortality capable of bringing about total happiness (or the misery of hell). It is, rather, a kind of painful peregrination of the soul in a mysterious world full of terror and fright. This bodily soul or vital principle remains in death until it reaches putrefaction. Accordingly, numerous funerary customs assume that the dead person slumbers and that the living have the obligation to help him in his laborious peregrinations in the Kingdom of the Dead, particularly through libation, meals, and festivals. The best known funerary festival is the famous Pomana, celebrated a year and six weeks after the burial. Whereas the meal that is eaten in the presence of the deceased before his burial takes place in an atmosphere of jubilation, of licentiousness even, the meal of the Pomana assumes a certain dignity and takes place in accordance with a precise ritual. The deceased who is being celebrated is represented by a living being, of approximately the same age, who is washed and dressed in new clothes and assumes the role of the deceased by imitating his or her tastes and mannerisms. The objective of the Pomana is twofold. On the one hand, it is an act of solidarity toward the deceased, who is thought to be still living elsewhere and who needs help and consolation in his painful new roaming. But the Pomana also has a prophylactic purpose (and here we are introduced into the real mythological universe of the Gypsies), namely, to protect the living from the harmful influences that every dead person releases in the form of evil spirits.

IV. Gypsy Mythology

Gypsies indeed believe in a multitude of supernatural beings, good and evil spirits, who exercise their influence throughout the course of life. This belief comes across in numerous tales and magic rites.

The importance of these numerous spirits would lead us to believe in a kind of polytheism among the Gypsies, one that stands out against the background of monotheism referred to above, which it does not contradict. Adopting an official monotheistic religion (Christianity or Islam) kept Gypsies from seeing these spirits as "gods" in the classical sense. These beings, however, participate no less in the divine absolute, for they influence the existence of mortals. Their functional character further explains their multiplicity. The general acculturation of Gypsies today makes it difficult to pinpoint the origins of these mythical beliefs, strata of a layered religious consciousness that bears the traces of influences of various populations among whom Gypsies once lived.

Among these countless spirits, all of whom have more or less physical features, we can distinguish several groups that are often confused even by modern Gypsies themselves. The main group is made up of the famous goddesses of fate, the Oursitori (or Ursitory, called Ourmes by certain tribes) or "white women," because they wear white dresses. Their descriptions and life-styles vary greatly from tribe to tribe. In general, they are connected with the plant kingdom and regarded as kinds of souls of trees. They go in groups of three and intervene mainly at the birth of a Gypsy, determining the child's fate. One of these fairies is good, another is bad, and the third plays an intermediary role. Some historians see a link between this belief and that of the ancient Parcae. Most magic rites prescribed by this belief aim to influence these goddesses of fate on the occasion of a birth by offering them the appropriate food and by invoking them with numerous prayers whispered by a magician at the entrance to the house in which the delivery has taken place. A contemporary Gypsy has written a novel (Mateo Maximoff, *Les Ursitory,* Paris 1946), later produced as a movie, which popularized this belief.

Beside these goddesses, the Gypsy world of the supernatural is peopled by many other spirits whose actions are revealed mainly at the time of illness or death. Convinced that they live symbiotically with all of these spirits, Gypsies see them in all natural phenomena. Accordingly, they explain illness as the invasion of a pathogenic spirit struggling against the vital spirit that every man bears within him.

Gypsies generally believe in the existence of an individual protective spirit, a sort of guardian angel, which is often difficult to distinguish from the breath of life (what we might call the soul), and which the Gypsies of southeastern Europe call Butyakengo (etymologically, "he who has many eyes," to be better able to spot dangers threatening his protégé). This protective spirit helps to unite the generations. Every person who dies leaves on earth part of his vital or protective spirit, which goes on to live in the body of a descendant (generally the oldest). The other descendants are not shortchanged, however, because the protective spirit of the departed remains on earth and continues to protect the descendants. In so doing, this spirit acts as a portion of the soul of the departed which generations pass on to one another. Each individual, whose body is enlivened by his own spirit or soul, is also visited by a portion of the spirit of his descendants. Herein lies a fine point: to the extent that this portion is distinct from the spirit that belongs strictly to a given person, it constitutes within him a protective spirit, which can leave him for a while.

The protective spirit actually watches over the man in whom it dwells, even though it leaves his body while he sleeps in order to protect him from impending danger. Whereas a dying man gives up his soul (his individual vital spirit) through the mouth, it is through the ears that the protective spirit inherited from the ancestors moves in. It warns its protégé by a ringing in the ear. If it should leave the body momentarily, it does so out of the right ear, the left ear being the port of entry; hence the care Gypsies take in cleaning their left ear with their little finger, also known as the auricular finger because it is small enough to be introduced into the ear. For that purpose, Gypsies carefully file the fingernail of their auricular finger. It is essential to facilitate the return of the protective spirit and its warning messages on which the protégé's life may depend. Since the deceased has no more need of a protective spirit (being destined to roam in a parallel and mysterious world), certain Gypsy tribes break the little finger of the corpse and tie a coin to it with a red thread.

Many such beliefs and rites must have been borrowed from the prevailing folklore in a more or less distant time. Traces of some have come down to us in popular language, for example, in the French expression *Mon petit doigt me l'a dit* ("My little finger told me," equivalent to "A little bird told me" in the English-speaking world). Such borrowings are undeniable even if the demands of Gypsy life have resulted in the integration or reinterpretation of these alien elements. We could find many other examples in beliefs in evil spirits as causes of illness and misfortune. Among them, we can cite those spirits who are freed by death and who explain why, for Gypsies, death is laden with curses and taboos that affect those who remain. Though often mixed together, these evil spirits are of two sorts, the Moulo and the vampires.

The Moulo, synonymous with "ghost" or the "moving dead," designates the spirit of a dead person that can make itself manifest and reincarnate itself in another person or animal. It is often translated as the "living dead." The origin of the Moulo is revealing. Not every dead person becomes a Moulo, only a stillborn child. For some Gypsy tribes, the Moulo has no bones, and both hands lack the middle finger, which he left in the tomb. He lives in the mountains and often visits houses to steal what he needs. He can become visible to the eye, which is always a bad sign.

In other tribes where belief in the Moulo is less pronounced, it is more or less subsumed into the belief that the souls of the dead transmigrate to animals—a dog, a cat, a frog—in the form of evil spirits.

This brings us to the other kind of spirits freed by death, the vampires. The myth we are encountering here is not endemic to Gypsies but is found in the folklore of many Indo-European branches (especially Slavs and ancient Germans). Historians have established a clear link between the *lukanthropos* of the Greeks, the *versipellis* of the Romans, the werewolf of the ancient Germans, and the Gypsy vampire, an evil spirit that possesses the body of a deceased man. Hence the precautions taken by Gypsies when one of their own dies, lest such a harmful spirit escape and bring misfortune. This further explains certain libations during the funerary meal, particularly the Pomana (see above): to ward off evil spirits from the tomb, wine or aquavita is poured over it.

Also widespread among the Gypsies is the belief in witches, conceived of as women endowed with evil powers rather than as supernatural beings, fairies or goddesses, like the Oursitori. A woman turns into a witch after having sexual relations with a demon that causes disease. (Etymologically, the Gypsy word for witch means a woman who becomes irritated by the delight of her human brothers.) Their special feature is that they can transmit this demoniacal spirit to a man or an animal, for instance, to a worm or a small snake, which in turn may transmit the spirit to a man sleeping with his mouth open.

In their great variety, these beliefs have also often been borrowed from the prevailing, even Christianized folklore. Accordingly, many Gypsy tribes schedule their great annual festival of the witches during the night of Whitsunday. Similarly, the connection between many dietary taboos and the belief in witches is probably attributable to a reinterpretation of ancient taboos, the meaning of which has been lost. Incorporating these taboos into the mythology of witches gave them a new vitality. This carryover was in fact made within a context dominated by sexuality. For example, the broad bean is a forbidden food because it looks like a testicle. Besides the sexual origin of the witch's powers (relations with demonic spirits), the renewing of such powers takes place in a similar context, namely, the blood vow. In classical Christian demonology, this vow can be made by a man or a woman, and involves giving the devil a little blood taken from one's arm after inflicting a wound on oneself. In the case of the witch, she revives her power by giving the devil her menstrual blood to drink. Obviously, the Christianization of many Gypsies often eliminated these older mythical elements. But belief in the power of witches, in their capacity to cast spells, to cause misfortune by giving someone the evil eye or by breathing on someone, was bound to create an aura of mystery surrounding the Gypsies, especially among gullible people, susceptible to superstition and thereby more likely to respect these strange nomads and to supply them with a few resources.

V. Magic Rites and Femininity

Myths condition rites. The multiplicity of myths and their highly varied origins explain the variety of ritual practices, some examples of which we have already seen. We should now look at the major place occupied by women in Gypsy mythology. On the one hand, we have the intermediaries between evil spirits and men, namely, witches. On the other hand, the benevolent Oursitori are goddesses. The intermediaries between the supernatural world and the human world are mostly women performing a magic function, be it divination, healing, or propitiation. Although the Gypsy world knows no priestly function (not even in the person of the tribal chief), sorceresses perform the functions that are ordinarily relegated to the priestly castes in most religions (telling fortunes, exorcising, invoking the gods, healing, etc.).

A Gypsy woman usually becomes a sorceress by inheriting such powers and the knowledge of the rites from an ancestor. Some Gypsies compare sorceresses with witches (for example, when the sorceress has sexual relations with water spirits), but the connotation of sorceress is less pejorative and does not involve the blood vow.

Living in a symbolic universe peopled by evil forces and taboos, Gypsies know that their fate is controlled by the random alternation of good luck (*Bacht*) and bad luck (*Bibacht*). They therefore engage in more and more rites in an effort to know what their fate may be and to redirect it to the extent that they can. Hence the rites of purification performed against the impurities carried by a woman at the time of her period or by a child at birth, or at the moment of death when numerous impure spirits are freed. This impurity is not ethical. It is mostly involuntary and connected with an existential situation. The rites of divination that have popularized fortune-tellers reflect the need to scrutinize inexorable fate. Best known is the use of Tarot cards, but other more esoteric techniques also apply, for instance, the use of an animal's scapula. For healing rites, various dialectics are used, the best known being "signs," in which the apparent properties of an animal or plant designate that animal or plant as a remedy for a given sickness. For instance, a stiff joint is wrapped in the supple skin of an eel. Other rites refer to Christian symbolisms: the ass that had the privilege of carrying Christ may show up in certain therapeutic techniques.

All these myths and rites certainly suggest a syncretising of religious elements that originated in very different sources. But from a more phenomenological point of view, we should rather be talking of symbiosis. For these borrowings are not purely artificial, nor have they been artificially preserved. Once incorporated into the mythical universe of the Gypsies, they took on new life, allowing this marginalized people to preserve its identity to this day.

F.C./g.h.

BIBLIOGRAPHY

In general, see F. COZANNET, *Mythes et coutumes religieuses des Tsiganes* (Paris 1973), which contains all the desired references.

There are many monographs, most of which are to be found in two specialized journals: *Journal of the Gypsy Lore Society* (Edinburgh) and *Études tsiganes* (Paris).

See also the analyses in the following general works: J. BLOCH, "Que sais-je?" *Les tsiganes* (3d ed., Paris 1969). M. BLOCH, *Mœurs et coutumes des tsiganes* (Paris 1936), originally in German. F. BOTEY, *El Gitano* (Barcelona 1970). J.-P. CLEBERT, *Les tsiganes* (Paris 1961). A. COLOCCI, *Gli Zingari* (Turin 1889). C. DUFF, *A Mysterious People: An Introduction to the Gypsies of All Countries* (London 1965). E. FALQUE, *Voyage et tradition: Les Manouches* (Paris 1971). R. LIEBICH, *Die Zigeuner in ihrem Wesen und in ihrer Sprache* (Leipzig 1883). J.-P. LIÉGEOIS, *Les tsiganes* (Paris 1971); *Mutation tsigane* (Brussels 1976). W. IN DER MAUR, *Die Zigeuner, Wanderer zwischen den Welten* (Vienna 1969). P. SERBOIANU, *Les tsiganes: Histoire, ethnographie, linguistique,* trans. from Romanian (Paris 1930). W. SIMSON, *A History of the Gypsies* (London 1961). F. VAUX DE FOLETIER, *Les tsiganes dans l'ancienne France* (Paris 1961); *Mille ans d'histoire des tsiganes* (Paris 1971). G. E. C. WEBB, *Gypsies, the Secret People* (London 1961).

The following vocabularies are also very useful: M. COLINON, *Les Gitans, vocabulaire, tradition et images* (Manosque 1975). S. A. WOLF, *Grosses Wörterbuch der Zigeunersprache* (Mannheim 1960).

Fable and Mythology in Seventeenth- and Eighteenth-Century Literature and Theoretical Reflection

For anyone who hopes to define the status of ancient myths in the seventeenth and eighteenth centuries, there are two extremely dissimilar domains for consideration. One domain includes all the events of culture (poetry, theater, ballet, painting, sculpture, decorative arts) in which mythological motifs are recognizable; the other comprises the historical, critical, and speculative texts that attempt to elaborate a knowledge of myths, a science of myths. In the period in question, this distinction was clearly expressed by terms that demarcated to the fullest extent the difference established by contemporaries between the free use of mythological motifs and the studied knowledge of myths: for the former, *fable,* and for the latter, *mythology.*

I. The Function of Fable in Classical Culture

Fable is the body of received ideas about the gods of paganism. Largely founded on Hesiod, Ovid, Apollodorus, and more recent popularizers (such as Natale Conti), it is a repertory of genealogies, adventures, metamorphoses, and allegorical correlations. And as the motifs of fables are omnipresent—among the ancients read in secondary schools, in the tragedies seen at the theater, in historical presentations, in decorations and dwellings—fable is an obligatory discipline in the education of a respectable man. Thus a circle is formed: it is necessary to know fables in order to understand the works offered by recent and ancient culture; and, because fable is learned, and the ancient model remains alive, new works that are composed go back to fable either to borrow its subject matter or to use its ornamentation—in depictions, emblems, and phrases.

Rollin, in the sixth book (part four) of his *Treatise of Studies* (1726), which remained authoritative for more than a century, mentions fable and justifies its study in a subtle way:

> There is hardly a subject in the study of belles lettres that is either of a greater utility than that of which I speak here, or that lends itself better to profound scholarship. . . .

Without knowledge of fable, there can be no knowledge of literature:

> It is (an advantage) of great application . . . for the understanding of authors, be they Greek, Latin, or even French, in the reading of whom one is stopped short if one does not have some tincture of fable. I am not only speaking of poets, of whom we know this to be almost the natural language: it is also often employed by orators; and it sometimes furnishes, through favorable application, the liveliest and most eloquent touches. . . . There are other kinds of books to which everyone is exposed: paintings, engravings, tapestries, and statues. These are so many enigmas to those who are ignorant of fable, which often serves as their explanation and their key. It is not rare for people to speak of such matters in conversation. It seems to me not at all agreeable to remain silent and to appear stupid in a group for lack of instruction in a matter that may be learned in youth at little expense.

Knowledge of fable is the very condition for the legibility of the entire cultural world. It is one of the prerequisites for participation in the "conversations" in which an educated man is called on to play a part. Fable, for Rollin, is indispensable to anyone who would understand the aesthetic milieu in its entirety, and who would be accepted into a chosen "group." It thus serves a double function; it is an imaginal language offering access to a certain type of organized speech, and this language functions as a social sign of recognition between individuals who can decipher in the same fashion the universe of mythic fictions.

Jaucourt, in his *Encyclopedia* article on "Fable," is in emphatic agreement:

> This is why knowledge, at least superficial knowledge, of fable is so common. Our plays, both lyric and dramatic, and every genre of our poetry allude to it perpetually; the engravings, paintings, and statues that adorn our cham-

Oedipus. From Mme. de Genlis, *Arabesques mythologiques* (1810–11), vol. 2, pl. 4. Paris, Bibliothèque nationale. Photo BN.

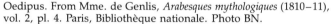

Perseus. From Mme. De Genlis, *Arabesques mythologiques* (1810–11), vol. 2, pl. 2. Paris, Bibliothèque nationale. Photo BN.

> bers, our galleries, our ceilings, and our gardens are nearly always drawn from fable: finally, it is so widely used in all of our writings, our novels, our pamphlets, and even in our ordinary conversations that it is impossible to be unaware of it at least to a degree without having to blush at one's lack of education.
>
> . . . Fable is the heritage of the arts; it is a source of ingenious ideas, of humorous images, of interesting subjects, of allegories and emblems whose use—whether more or less favorable--responds to genius and taste. Everything is active and endowed with breath in that enchanted world where intellectual beings have bodies, where countrysides, forests, and rivers have their particular divinities: I know that these are chimerical characters, but the role they play in the writings of the ancient poets, and the frequent allusions made to them by modern poets, have almost made them real for us. Our eyes are so accustomed to them that it is difficult for us to see them as imaginary beings.

The author of an *Elementary Encyclopedia*, which appeared in 1775, betrays irritation with fable but nevertheless maintains its necessity. His way of recommending Chompré's *Dictionary of Fable* (which Rollin had already hailed) clearly shows that this work, being at once an allegorical iconology and a repertory of fabulous heroes, aims not so much to examine the substance of myths as to decipher the *attributes* used by artists: at most, it is a semiological code that serves to express an "intention" in a consecrated language:

> It is an assemblage of puerile tales bereft of verisimilitude, which would be worthy of scorn were these chimeras not absolutely necessary in order to understand the ancient authors, to be moved by the beauties of poetry, of pictures and allegories, and even to make use of an infinity of conventional expressions, such as "She's a Megara, a Fury, a Muse." . . . I invite my readers to equip themselves with the small portable *Dictionary* by M. Chompré. It is very useful to young people and, indeed, to everyone. Whether one is looking, for example, for the subject of a tapestry, a picture, or an allegorical piece, with this book one is certain of finding it.
>
> If there is an eagle, look up this word, and it will refer you to *Jupiter*, to *Periphas*, and to *Ganymede*. If it is a scythe, you will find *Saturn* or *Time*. If a figure is holding a trumpet, the word trumpet will refer you to *Fame*. . . . Through the attributes you will come to know the subjects: and with a little judgment you will come to guess the artist's intention.[1]

This dictionary enables one to slip from one language into another; it is a translation tool, permitting artists and poets to find the appropriated "figures" and, furthermore, ensuring that readers will be able to go back from the figure to the original idea. Recourse to the dictionary postulates a disjunction between appearance and meaning, which is immediately nullified by a system of fixed correlations, a system that makes all possible strangeness vanish from allegory. For this reason, the use of mythological figures is reduced to a stylistic procedure: the reader or spectator is to translate the image of trumpet by the concept of Fame; and if a particular image of the trumpet holds our attention by the elegance of its form or the shine of its brass, an informed reading will avoid tarrying over this literalness whose only function is to be temporary, to indicate the "elevated" or "noble" register of the expression.

Reduced to this sort of lexicon, fable—even as it refers back to a fictive past located in Greco-Latin space—takes on an ahistorical appearance: in it, everything becomes simultaneous, even genealogies. Fable develops its networks synchronically, as if it were the vocabulary of a single state of language. The internal chronology of fable is not inscribed in the historical passage of time. From the moment that the gods, their names, their cults, their connections with people and places, etc., become the object of historical research, fable becomes an object of scholarship, and is no longer the closed and self-sufficient system we have described. It then becomes a matter for "antiquaries" (if they restrict themselves to inventories of exhumed documents: statues, altars, medals, side by side with written sources such as inscriptions, literary texts, etc.) or for mythologists (if they develop hypotheses on the origin of fables, and on the differences or resemblances between the religious beliefs of various peoples, etc.). This is a difficult and dangerous domain, and Rollin advises educators to halt at its threshold: "It would be best, it seems to me, to avoid what is related only to scholarship and would render the study of fable more difficult and less agreeable; or, at least, to relegate reflections of this kind to brief notes."

Jaucourt ends his *Encyclopedia* article on "Fable" by drawing up a program of mythological knowledge that goes beyond a mere familiarity with the figures of fables:

> But to carry one's curiosity to the point of attempting to pierce the diverse meanings or the mysteries of fable, to understand the different theological systems, and to know the cults of the pagan gods is a branch of learning reserved for a small number of scholars; and the branch of learning that constitutes a very large part of belles lettres, and is absolutely necessary in order to have an understanding of the monuments of antiquity, is what is called *Mythology.*

It is thus a matter of interpreting the figures of fable according to the exigencies of a historical, genetic, and systematic understanding. Whereas fable itself, in a vulgarized and facile form, is a universal means for "poetizing" everything, "mythology" questions it about its origins, its intellectual import, its revelatory value, and its ties with institutions and customs. In short, the semantic opposition between fable and mythology may be enunciated as the difference between a generalized and stabilized interpretive system, and a rational type of reflection that makes this interpretive system an object to be interpreted according to other criteria of validity.

The renewal of myth at the end of the seventeenth century arose from this type of scholarly reflection, which applied itself to understanding mythic inventiveness in a new way since stereotyped recourse to fable had revealed itself to be sterile and tedious. Nevertheless, before reviewing the development of mythological theories, we must define, more clearly than we have done thus far, the function of fable in the "classical" European—especially French—culture of the seventeenth and eighteenth centuries.

In a culture that tolerates the coexistence of the domains of the sacred and of the profane, fable clearly occupies the profane area: it inhabits the world of mundane diversions. We may even go so far as to say that, by its avowed absence of truth value, fable is the very index of the futility of mundane existence. Fable desires to be nothing more than fiction or ornament, or, at most, scholarly remembrance. Its authority is declared to be nil vis-à-vis religious authority from the very start. As aestheticized paganism, claiming no more than beauty or grace, it is not a dangerous rival to the Christian orthodoxies—unless souls allow themselves to be unduly controlled by it and to become inflamed by the impure examples of the pagan pantheon.

Let us return to Rollin, the perfect spokesman for the religious institution at the beginning of the eighteenth century. When he includes fable in his educational program, it is not only in order to enhance the understanding of literary or pictorial works. It should also serve as a warning, as a counterproof to Christian truth:

> This study, when followed with the caution and wisdom that religion demands and inspires, may be of great utility to the young.
>
> First, it teaches them what they owe to Jesus Christ their liberator, who freed them from the powers of darkness and allowed them to move into the admirable light of the Gospel. What were men before him . . . ? Fable gives us the answer. They were blind worshipers of the devil who knelt before gold, silver, and marble; who offered silver to deaf and dumb statues; who recognized gods in animals, reptiles, and even plants. . . . Every story told in fable, every circumstance in the life of the gods, should at once fill us with confusion, admiration, and recognition. . . . A second advantage of fable lies in the fact that, in disclosing the absurd ceremonies and impious maxims of paganism, it inspires in us a new respect for the august majesty of the Christian religion, and for the sanctity of its morality.

Belief is thus to be reserved for the sole legitimate authority, revealed dogma; whereas these pagan figures are to be censured, even though in everyday life—as Rollin recognizes—their visual images, ever-renewed, surround us. At the very least, and in spite of its power to seduce, the unreality of fable leaves no doubt about the vanity of worldly existence. The presence of fable is a sure indication that worldly desires lead one astray into "false" objects. Thus the necessity of directing one's love toward its true object—God, Christ—becomes all the more urgent.

But the demarcation between the sacred and the profane has its own legitimacy, for it is postulated by religious authority itself. By way of determining the exact domain of its own jurisdiction, religious authority tolerates the existence of an external domain, which it watches over without forcing it to comply with its strictest rules. In order not to break the ties with the sacred order, human life is permitted to unfold, in part, in a profane time and space; and the figures inherited from a sacred order that has come to an end—the order of paganism—may innocently serve as ornaments to a part of existence that is not directly governed by the truths of the faith. Certainly, the imaginary is dangerous, and the images of desire constitute a grave peril to Christian souls: but in one way—in the form of a pantheon to which no one could try to attach any serious belief—orthodoxy permits a *superficial* survival of what is, in another way, censured and repulsed by Christian ethics. Hence, in a more or less balanced compromise, Christianity (and especially the Catholicism of the Counterreformation) allowed the entire universe of polytheistic drives and undercurrents—which it had historically supplanted and which its true believers were invited to deny and surpass—to coexist by its side, though in the form of a gratuitous image and a defused fiction. This compromise authorizes a certain duplicity: "worldly" people (including the king himself) could taste of profane diversions, surround themselves with pagan scenes, and even become actors in mythological ballets, but they had to listen to the preachers and receive the sacraments.

Love and ambition—the two great provinces in which worldly concupiscence operates (*libido sentiendi, libido dominandi*)—celebrate their triumphs in the disguise of fable. In love poetry, recourse to the code of fable is a part of a system of distancing which, in transposing feeling into heroic or pastoral fiction, allows desire to be made manifest, while giving it a glorious, purified expression which is detached from trivial contingency. In this sense, fable ensures a displacement of all of the elements of discourse in the direction of a register that is entirely ludic and "polite"—which is exactly what defines the "gallant" attitude. When we recall that the principal corpus of myths—Ovid's *Metamorphoses*—already has a strong ludic component, it is obvious that in order to satisfy the taste for novelty, for the "piquant," which held sway in cultivated circles, artists and poets strove to outdo one another in playing this game. This competitive bidding is particularly perceptible in the art of the European rococo, with its proliferation of the decorative, its supple sinuousity, and its ornamental use of miniatures. But this element of the intellectual game, at times combined with more authentically experienced components, is already apparent in mannerism and in the vogue for literary conceits (as, for instance, in the *Adonis* of Marini); we find it again in the affectation of the seventeenth century, and it is still present in the badinages of the end of the eighteenth century. Benserade and his *Metamorphoses of Ovid Set in Rondeaux* are an excellent example of this excess of affectation: the work was seen as "piquant" because it was a well-tempered paraphrase that made use of a small, regular form to abridge and rework a Latin text whose mythic content had itself already been made the object of playful levity. The game is thus doubled. The rondeau is a miniature in comparison to the model it imitates: all is made to turn in a tight circle of twelve verses, of which the first four syllables reappear two more times—concluding the poem in their final appearance. At the end of the ancien régime, in C. A. Demoustier's *Letters to Emilie about Mythology,* the mythic narrative is reduced to banter interspersed with verse: the versified elements are sometimes episodes or commentaries from the narrative, sometimes gallant compliments to the person addressed. This form, inherited from the seventeenth century, becomes so light as to be meaningless. Here again, the mythology, which is told letter by letter, undergoes a paring down, an attenuation, turning it into the minimal substance of an adventure story and the excuse for a facile pedagogy whose aim is merely to please. It is only one step away from that work patronized by Madame de Genlis, in which all that remains of the gods is their names, represented by calligraphy in the form of an emblem.

Yet the mythic repertory that is capable of transcribing current events or feelings in a fictive register may also serve to magnify and celebrate them in a triumphant mode. Miniaturization is just one of the propensities of the joyous imagination, the one in which play seeks to ally itself with the conquest of innocent levity. When play, on the other hand, becomes charged with glorifying intentions, it magnifies without allowing itself to be restrained by the regulations of the real world. The mythological fiction makes possible the laudatory hyperbole, which would otherwise be unpronounceable within the bounds of Christian order. For a victory in battle, the Christian festival culminates in the adoration of the God of armies: *Te Deum laudamus.* But the Christian festival has as its double a profane and thus mythological festival, which exalts the prince himself: he is compared with Mars or Hercules, he is the favorite of Bellona, and so forth. For a princely birth, Christian baptism has its double in ceremonies or poems of fabulous inspiration, in which announcements are made of nothing less than the imminent return of Astraeus and the Golden Age. The apotheosis of the prince may set the stage for his lawful representatian within a system of divine figures, the validity of which is established, from the start of the game, as belonging to the past and which is now pure appearance. This "white" divinization allows the energies of celebration to blossom; and while these powers remain captives of the Greco-Roman model, they allow for every sort of extravagance, for they pretend to be nothing but pure show. The Sun King is allowed to dance in the costume of Apollo. Jupiter can descend from the sky, in a stage machine, to announce to future centuries an illustrious lineage of sovereigns.

Although the conventional system of Greco-Roman mythology favors a purifying or glorifying transmutation, it is no less vulnerable for this, since the authority upon which it is founded is nothing more than an aesthetic habit. There is nothing to protect it against parody, or against the ebb of tastes, which would abandon mythic embellishment to return to the ordinary reality of desire.

The direction taken by satire and comedy in the seventeenth century was to remove the masks, to reverse the trajectory of the mythological enterprise with its purifying trends (affectation) or glorifying trends (the ideal of the nobility), and to return to literalness all that the mythological code had previously transferred into the metaphorical dimension. In contrast to the tableaux in which desire is exalted and divinized, satire brings us down again into the world of everyday life and into the reality of instinct in its brutal state. The following episode from the *Discourse on the Journey of Saint-Germain in Laye,* which figures in the *Satirical Cabinet* (1618), is exemplary in this regard: the mythic decor is read as an erotic stimulant:

Mais faisons, je vous pry, pour saouler nostre veuë,
Dans la chambre du Roy encore une reveuë.
Voyez, en cest endroit, comme Mars et Venus
Se tiennent embrassez, languissans et tous nuds;
Voyez les à ce coing, en une autre posture:
Avez-voux jamais veu si lascive peinture?
Haussez un peu les yeux, et voyez les encore
En une autre façon, dessus ce plancher d'or;
Voyez les ici pres, tous deux encore aus prises.
Quoy! tout est plain d'Amours et de flames éprises,
Dans ceste belle chambre! Allons, fuyons ces lieux:
Sortons-en, je vous prie, ou bien faisons comme eux!

But I pray you, to proclaim our vows,
Let us meet again in the bedroom of the King.
Look over there, as Mars and Venus
Embrace, languishing and entirely nude;
Look at them over here, in a different position:

Have you ever seen such a sexy painting?
Raise your eyes a bit, and look at them again
In a different form, above this golden floor-board;
Look at them close by here, the two of them still locked together.
O my! Everything is full of love-making and heated passion,
In this beautiful bedroom! Come on, let's get out of here:
Let's leave, I beg you, or else do what they are doing!

One may be sacrilegious with impunity when dealing with the pseudo-sacred. Burlesque plays freely upon such license. The great mythic images that are used to ennoble the circumstances of public and private life are the means of transmutation and travesty. By disfiguring and caricaturing them, one realizes a return to their trivial reality: to travesty what was a means of travesty is to nullify its depicted purity and glory, and to return to the grit and smell of the world as it exists for those who have lost their illusions. Dassoucy's *Ovid in a Good Mood,* Scarron's *Virgil Travestied,* the young Marivaux's *Homer Travestied,* and Blumauer's late *Virgil's Aeneas Travestied* (Vienna 1732–94) constitute more than attacks on the most highly respected literary models. Through those models, they assault the very virtues that were exalted by the epico-mythic tradition: warlike exploits, the sacrifice of one's life for country and glory. Their mockery, which took aim at the heroes and gods of antiquity, was more generally directed against the heroic ideal. The simple pleasure of living is of far greater value. What is denounced, then, is fictive immortality, a deal offered to fools, counterfeit money whose mythic celebration pays those who shed their blood on the field of battle. Following the wars of Louis XIV, parody, as employed by Marivaux, attacked not only the ancients and their partisans but, even more, the illusions of military glory. Verses such as these (addressed by Andromache to Hector) are demobilizing. They "demystify" the common ground of the undying memory:

Oh! great gods! when I contemplate
The afflicted state of widowhood,
I find a bed to be quite fearsome,
When in that bed we are no longer two!
Once the bloody Achilles
Killed my father in a town . . .
Well then! What was its name?
I do not remember its name.
He buried him himself, it is said,
With great sumptuousness:
But when a body is buried,
What is the good of honoring it?
No matter what glory one is buried with,
One has nothing but the earth for cover.

This resolutely worldly confession of faith (which reduces death to mere interment), in challenging a "pagan" image of immortality,[2] implies disbelief in Christian immortality. We might even say that parody is a burlesque of mythic narratives and pastoral or warlike fables which does not limit its destructive effect to the aesthetic dimension alone, or even to the hierarchy of "official" values: indirectly it directs itself against the highest authority. For, even though fictive, the world of fable nonetheless offers images of a sovereignty that is homologous to the ruling sovereignty but is, so to speak, legal tender. To attack Jupiter and the gods of fable is, according to one's insinuations, to attack in *effigy,* and with impunity, the king and the powerful, the holiness of God, of the Pope, and so forth. Since the world of fable is, by the decree of the spiritual powers that be, a profane world without any true sacred content, there can be no blasphemy or lèse-majesté in disfiguring it. The critique leveled by libertinism against religion or against the centralizing monarchy can thus be effected obliquely by attacking (in appearance) only those powers which the least suspect Christian tradition had never ceased to condemn. As may be seen, the duality of the (Christian) sacred and the profane (placed in its "mythological" setting) is arranged in such a way as to make it possible to play sometimes upon their separation and their mutual exclusion and sometimes upon their parallelism and their isomorphism. If pagan and Christian sovereignty are considered in their formal similarity (an identical structure in which all is dependent upon a supreme divinity; an identical presence of the miraculous), then a polemic against Christianity (or against the superstitious aspects of Christianity) may be developed in total safety by directing its darts only against what at first sight appears to be the gods of paganism (for example, the article "Jupiter" in Bayle's *Dictionary*). If Christianity and paganism are viewed as incompatible, hos-

Louis XIV as the Sun God in the ballet *La nuit,* 1653. Anonymous watercolor. Paris, Bibliothèque nationale. Photo Giraudon.

tility to Christianity may be manifested by the more dangerous means of resolutely favoring the world of fable. Under the cover of an aesthetic tradition that had become acclimated to mythological fiction and had given it its noble pedigree, the rebellious mind would proclaim its preference for the pagan fable over the doctrine imposed by the Church, which was no less fabulous and lying but was a thousand times less agreeable. This was the time when anti-Christian feeling first showed its face unveiled: that open antipathy recurred several times after the Renaissance, but especially in the seventeenth century. In the case of a Voltaire, the option of paganism—in his *Apology for Fable*—does not so much attest an authentic sentiment in favor of the world of myth as it attests the opportunism of a method of propaganda that is capable of putting barbs on anything:

Savante antiquité, beauté toujours nouvelle,
Monument du génie, heureuses fictions,
Environnez-moi des rayons
De votre lumière immortelle:
Vous savez animer l'air, la terre, et les mers;
Vous embellisez l'univers.
Cet arbre á tête longue, aux rameaux toujours verts,
C'est Atys, aié de Cybèle;
La précoce hyacinthe est le tendre mignon
Que sur ces prés fleuris caressait Apollon. . . .

Wise antiquity, beauty always new,
Monument of genius, happy fictions,
Surround me with the rays
Of your immortal light:
You know how to animate the air, the earth, and the seas;
You embellish the universe.
This tree with the high head, with branches always green,
It is Atys, loved by Cybele;
The precocious hyacinth is the tender darling
Whom Apollo caressed in these flowering meadows. . . .

Another series of examples follows, and Voltaire continues:

Tout l'Olympe est peuplé de héros amoureux.
Admirables tableaux! séduisante magie!
Qu'Hésiode me plaît dans sa théologie
Quand il me peint l'Amour débrouillant le chaos,
S'élançant dans les airs, et planant sur les flots!
Vantex-nous maintenant, bienheureux légendaires,
Le porc de saint Antoine, et le chien de saint Roch
Vos reliques, vos scapulaires,
Et la guimpe d'Ursule, et la crasse du froc;
Mettez la Fleur des saints à côté d'un Homère:
Il ment, mais en grand homme; il ment, mais il sait plaire;
Sottement vous avez menti:
Pour lui l'esprit humain s'éclaire:
Et, si l'on vous croyait, il serait abruti.
On chérira toujours les erreurs de la Grèce;
Toujours Ovide charmera.

All of Olympus is peopled with amorous heroes.
Admirable scenes! Seductive magic!
How Hesiod pleases me with his theology
When he depicts Love disentangling chaos,
Bounding in the air and soaring on the waves!
Praise us now, you fortunate creatures of legend,
The pig of Saint Anthony, and the dog of Saint Roch,
Your relics, your scapulars,
And the wimple of Ursula, and the squalor of the monk's robe;
Put the Flower of the saints next to a Homer:
He lies, but like a man; he lies, but he knows how to please;
You have lied stupidly:
With him, the human mind is enlightened:
But if anyone believed you, he would be made stupid as a brute.
People will always cherish the errors of Greece;
Ovid will always charm.

Voltaire appears less inclined actually to enter the world of fable than to make an ally of it in his battle for the Enlightenment and for a civilization of earthly happiness. His *Apology for Fable*, far from taking him out of his own element, only confirms his choice—in favor of an urban civilization and the pleasures to be had through the arts—which is proclaimed in his famous poem *The Man of the World*. Voltaire's Homer, through whom "the human mind is enlightened," has nothing "primitive" about him. Fable, as sung by Voltaire, comes down to a modern, profane diversion, in clear contrast to religious practice. The dichotomy of the sacred and the profane, to which we have alluded from the start, is nowhere more noticeable than in the final verses of the poem:

Si nos peuples nouveaux sont chrétiens à la messe,
Ils sont païens à l'Opéra.
L'almanach est païen, nous comptons nos journées
Par le seul nom des dieux que Rome avait connus;
C'est Mars et Jupiter, c'est Saturne et Vénus,
Qui président au temps, qui font nos destinées.
Ce mélange est impur, on a tort; mais enfin
Nous ressemblons assez à l'abbé Pellegrin,
"Le matin catholique, et le soir idolâtre,
Déjeûnant de l'autel, et soupant du théâtre."

If our new peoples are Christians at Mass,
They are pagans at the Opera.
The almanac is pagan, in which we measure our days
Only with the name of the gods that Rome knew;
It is Mars and Jupiter, it is Saturn and Venus,
That preside over time, that make our destinies.
This mixture is impure, it is wrong; but in the end
We resemble rather closely the Abbé Pellegrin:
"Catholic in the morning, and idolatrous in the evening,
Lunching at the altar, and dining at the theater."

Up to this point we have considered myth only in its formal and most general aspect; that is, as the agent of an aesthetic transformation on the profane level, under the assumption that the starting point of myth was regularly presented in a circumstance of life that one wished to celebrate, to purify, or to magnify. But the mythological code, with its variants and its multiple branches, also exists for itself, independent of those embellishments to which it might serve as a vehicle. It presents a broad canvas abounding in passionate connections, extreme situations, and monstrous acts. Upon this preexisting material, imagination and desire may freely project their most authentic energies by making use of its choices and scenarios. Certain seventeenth- and eighteenth-century works may be regarded as reinterpretations of great mythical themes—with the proviso that these artists were less interested in modifying the meaning of myths than in using them as a field for the free play of their faculties. In its received form, of course, myth remains a "subject" that demands respect. But in an aesthetics which, contrary to our own, did not place a premium on the kind of "originality" that could produce content, subject, and style (i.e., the entirety of a work's constituent parts) ex nihilo, the freedom of expression left to the artist in treating a known fable in whichever way he desired was enough to liberate, in certain cases, some very deep-seated forces. Even the most apparently frivolous narrative or tragedy can be intensely seductive in its hidden meanings. As told by LaFontaine, the story of Psyche, in its playful and free form, is charged throughout with symbols that are piled upon the primary data and revolve around the themes of the secret and of instant recognition. *Andromache, Iphigenia,* and *Phaedra* are plays in which the mythic element is psychologized, thus allowing for the free play of the dark forces of passion. The abandoned Ariadne or Dido present lyricism as well as music with an occasion for the melodious *lamento,* the mournful lament. Under the safeguard and the cover of an existing myth, which offers it a form of reception, desire is allowed to live out its imaginary satisfaction impersonally. The traditional mythic structures are perceived as obstacles only from the time when the exigencies of personal expression are to prevail. The role played by the mythic universe as foundation for and receiver of projections of desire is complemented by a more intellectual function, which may build pedagogical, political, or ethical constructs upon the epico-mythical schemata. The mythic framework allows for the embellishment, enlargement, and "detemporalization" of moral lessons for the edification of young princes. Fénelon's *Telemachus* is at once a prose poem, a "Bildungsroman," and a political utopia. The Odyssean setting, with its foam-capped sea, its apparitions of Amphitrite, and its nymphs lying under verdant arbors, ensures a harmonious fusion of these composite elements. Mentor, who is Minerva, in the guise of a profane fable lavishly distributes a lesson of wisdom in which the most rigorous precepts of Christian doctrine are protected, decanted, universalized, and rendered agreeable.

Furthermore, in examining the choices made by seventeenth- and eighteenth-century writers and artists working within this mythic complex, one cannot help but observe the emphasis on certain themes, according to the period in question, that point to a common anxiety often related to the preoccupations to which that particular time was sensitive. It is fair to say that the baroque, haunted by the changeableness of appearances, enjoyed fables of metamorphosis (Bernini's *Daphne* is one case among many). *Pygmalion*s abounded in the eighteenth century, not only because that century posed the question of the animation of matter, but also because its artists dreamed of an imitative perfection for which they might be rewarded by a loving embrace from their own work come to life. It is no coincidence that the sole writing of Jean-Jacques Rousseau on a mythical subject is a *Pygmalion,* in which the writer's fundamental narcissism is given free play: the artist's desire is paid back by the being formed by him as the image of his ideal. A limit has been reached here. The fable of Pygmalion represented, in a language that was still mythic, a demand for self-expression whose next manifestation would consist of a rejection of any mythic mediation, any recourse to preexisting fable. Similarly, in a later period (around 1800), certain heroic myths (Prometheus, Heracles, Ganymede) would be called upon to express hope and revolt: the apotheosis of the human hero makes it possible to glimpse a future in which the rule of the ancient gods will have collapsed, giving way to man. Here again, mythic language tends toward its own abolition, to the extent that the disappearance of the authority of the gods carries with it the fall of traditional imagic discourse as this was organized around them. This would lead, ultimately in Wagner's *Twilight of the Gods,* to recourse to a total myth culminating in the fall of the mythic universe, conceived as a now inoperative expression of an ancient law of the world.

But this tendency, far from being the only one, is mirrored—as we shall see—by an exactly opposite tendency.

II. The Growth of Mythological Theories

Fable, stabilized in the form of a body of fixed accounts and symbols which are indefinitely repeatable, can thus, in the most favorable cases, be relived, reanimated, and given presence by a fiery imagination capable of projecting its dream upon a preexistent image. A musician or painter (more often than a poet) could at times, in the eighteenth century, breathe new life, a passionate shiver, a seemingly invented strangeness, into the theme of a fable.

But the renaissance of mythic material took place via a more circuitous path which, paradoxically, at first sight seemed to be leading to the death and final expulsion of fable. It was mythology—that is, scholarly discourse applied to myths—that put the world of fable to death, but even in doing so it gave it the grounds, in an unexpected way, for a new, enlarged, and rejuvenated efflorescence.

It was a case of a progressive evolution, whose stages are not difficult to trace.

The mythology of the eighteenth century fuses, in variable proportions, the learning of the antiquarians (concerning the attributes of the gods, places of worship, written sources, coins, etc.) and the conjectures of the theologians: the convenient hypothesis, which goes back to Clement of Alexandria, is that the pagan gods are the pluralized and degenerate reflections of the true God of which Genesis speaks, or of the kings of the sacred scriptures. For infidels and sinners, primordial Revelation has been progressively obscured. After the dispersion of Babel, when people had forgotten the first and only God, nothing held them back from divinizing their princes, their rivers, their animals. But, in the same way that the pagans' languages, in the eyes of the etymologists, are corrupt derivatives of the Hebrew, so one can divine in their deities, though falling short, the holy religion of which they are the distorted reflection. The Abbé Banier perfectly summarizes this common view:

> In the earliest times, men worshiped one God. Noah preserved in his family the devotion his fathers had offered to the creator; but it did not take his descendants long to corrupt its purity. The crimes to which they abandoned themselves soon weakened the idea of the Divine, and people began to associate it with perceptible objects. What appeared to them to be the brightest and most perfect in nature moved them to homage; and for this reason the sun was the first object of their superstition. From sun worship, they moved to the worship of other celestial bodies and planets, and the entire heavenly troop . . . attracted a religious cult to itself, as did the elements, the rivers, and mountains. Things did not stop there; nature itself was regarded as a divinity, and under different names she became the object of worship for different nations. Finally, great men were seen as meriting, either by their conquests or by their invention of the arts, honors due only to the Creator of the Universe: and this was the origin of all the gods adored by paganism.

Such a mythological system places the various traditional theories of the origins of myths (Euhemerism, astral symbolism, etc.) on an equal footing in order to explain the false religions even as it indicts them, all the while maintaining, intact, the authority of a primary Revelation, of which the Church has remained the depository.

But this orthodox mythology, in developing a psychological explanation for the cause of the crimes and the impiety of the infidel nations, engendered an even bolder line of thought directed at the very motives of every faith and every form of devotion: the skeptics would use it to undercut the authority that orthodoxy thought to preserve and reinforce. The weapons used by the Church against superstition could easily be turned against the Faith, and the most common ruse was to attack Church dogma itself, in the guise of carrying on the fight led by the defenders of the Faith against idolatry. From this point on, the God of the Hebrews was to be submitted to a causal interpretation analogous to the one that the theologians reserved for the pagan gods. The explanation given by Lucretius, "inborn dread" (*insitus horror,* 5.1160–1239), would hold for every cult without exception. (The "libertine" current of the seventeenth century had widely cultivated this return to the Epicurean doctrine.) Fable, instead of being secondary and derivative, would appear as the primary response of men to the terrors of dreams, to great natural events, to all that amazed them.

Fontenelle's short dissertation *Origin of Fables* connects myths and polytheism with simple causes: ignorance, wonder, terror in the face of the powers experienced everywhere in nature, and the propensity to explain the unknown by the known. Fables offer us "the history of the errors of the human mind." It follows that one should not hesitate to learn every aspect of fable; mythology is to be practiced as Fontenelle does it in order that we may be set right: "To fill one's head with all the excesses of the Phoenicians and the Greeks is not a science, but to know what led the Phoenicians and the Greeks to these excesses is indeed a science. All mankind is so alike that there is no people whose idiocies should not make us tremble."

Here we see the meeting between scorn for fable and the affirmation of the great epistemological value of reflecting on the beginnings of our relationship to the world and on the errors committed by the mind when it was first left to its own devices. Everything began, for the savage as well as for the infant, with a deplorable propensity for false explanations, up to the time when our intelligence, as it was slowly and progressively disabused, became capable of laughing at its childish beliefs, and even of knowing why it allowed itself to be drawn into the world of fable. The cultivated mind sees a warning here too: the "primitive" errors into which every people has fallen are also errors of every period, and nothing is easier than falling back into error. One must always be on one's guard against yielding to the ever-renewed temptation of myth. Our imagination ever remains receptive to myth even when our reason denies it: "While we may be incomparably more enlightened than those whose crude minds invented the Fables in good faith, we all too easily return to that same way of thinking that made Fables so agreeable to them. They passed them on because they believed them, and we pass them on with just as much pleasure even though without belief; all of which proves that imagination and reason can have little to do with one another, and that matters of which reason has been disabused from the start lose nothing of their attractiveness as regards the imagination." The dichotomy of the sacred and the profane, which allowed fable to subsist on the periphery of sacred history, is thus replaced by the dichotomy of reason and imagination. Once again, fable is regarded as stripped of all truth, all authority; it is reason (and not revelation) that is master. But the imaginary and the pleasure that attaches to it are not branded with any moral reprobation: they are perfectly legitimate so long as they do not usurp the prerogatives of reason. Illusion has the right to enchant us as long as we know that we are in the realm of poetry and not science: when we give in to the seductions of myth, by playing its game we tarry in a world that we were capable of leaving behind forever. The poets of the childhood of the world—Homer and Hesiod—are certainly admirable, but their great images are nothing but the reverse side of their ignorance. In the perspective of a progressive becoming in which reason perfects itself from one century to the next, myth is the innocent witness to the first babblings of the mind, starting from the time when the soul could speak only in metaphor to voice its terrors and its wonders. This general theory of myth places all faiths on an equal footing: it makes an exception for the "true religion" only as a precaution and for the sake of style. The intellectual education of men should lead them to shed all prejudices, all errors, all cults. (Such disillusionment leads to poetry that makes use of fable without admitting to it, in a cold, spiritual, and mocking tone: the entire antipoetic eighteenth century defines itself in this way.)

But not everyone bore witness to the same confidence in the powers of cultivated reason. Hume, who interprets the birth of fables more or less in the way of Fontenelle, betrays doubt about the constructs of reason. It is possible that these constructs are no more solid than the polytheistic cosmogonies—in which case our "progress" becomes precarious, and the pleasure that we derive from ancient myths is less childish than it might appear. In our uncertainty regarding the true, myth can at least claim the privilege of beauty, without being any more of a lie than the things we take to be reasonable. Reason that is divested of illusions about its own powers can still show indulgence for the first creatures produced by the imagination.

The complete rehabilitation of myth would soon follow in this vein. But in order for this to occur, the primary experience of the mind, instead of being assigned the mark of imperfection, had to become endowed with the character of plenitude, the prerogative of unity. In this reevaluation of myth it is easy to see a return of theological thought, which would come to be combined with the psychological explanation of the production of primary ideas and primary feelings. *Genesis* reappears behind (or in) the simple impulses of the mind, which constitute the first stage of the genetic reconstruction of the intellectual faculties of the human race. However "stupid" we may call the child, the savage, or early man, they nevertheless lived in immediate contact with the world: they were like Adam in paradise. Revelation was not given to them from the outside like a doctrine; it ruled from within. Their knowledge consisted not in reflection but in participation: they lived in familiarity with the world and its forces. In this image of primordial community (which is itself based in myth), a primary role falls to those powers attributed to primitive language: it is at once speech and song (Strabo says this; Vossius and Vico repeat it;[3] Rousseau and Herder develop its theoretical consequences). It carries in itself the "almost inevitable impression of passion seeking to communicate itself" (Rousseau). Speech and feeling are not dissociated; expressive fidelity is absolute; there is no longer any place for lying or abstraction. The heart and speech of humans no longer make two. As for the gods that humans imagine, in the grip of terror or in a playful spirit, they are but the face of a living nature that turns toward them—a nature to which they are not strangers. Immediate to themselves, immediate to nature, humans manifest, in early lyricism and in the first great epics, the impulse in which the

Bernini, *Apollo and Daphne*. Rome, Villa Borghese Museum. Photo Alinari-Giraudon.

greatness and the limits of their mortal condition are inscribed. Such is the new conviction which restores to myths a legitimacy at once ontological and poetic, and which lends equal attention to the testimonies of every primitive literature. As if in response to this new attention, entire mythologies come to light or are partially invented: the Edda, Ossian, the sacred books of the East, the songs of the American Indians. These works reveal an art that preceded art, a poetry anterior to any rule of composition. And people took delight in recognizing, in this "barbarism," a grandeur and an energy no longer possessed by the civilized languages.

The result was not only a broadening of the field of mythological knowledge, nor a mere increase in the repertory of epic or naive texts made available to people of good taste who were weary of the frivolities of their own century. For those who experienced the power of these texts, the idea of a regenerated poetry, a language restored to its primitive vigor, inevitably prompted the desire for a new way of living and feeling which would recover the fullness of primitive times. In its nostalgia for the high language that has been lost, the mind turns toward the beginnings of societies in the hope of drawing out an enthusiasm that will give birth to songs capable of restoring to peoples, in the immediate future, the boiling impetus and the unanimous soul that have deserted them. The resurrected notion of genius is an invitation to listen to the voice which speaks out of the depths of nature and the collective consciousness. In a project of this sort, the poet, having recognized that all of the peoples of the world, at the time of their first self-affirmation, glorified themselves in their gods and heroes, felt himself drawn toward a past which he could offer to his fellow citizens in order to unite them in the state of mind of the reinvented community. Thus, it is once again toward the Greek and Roman (and, subordinately, Celtic or "Gallic") models that the French poets turned: but the traditional models themselves—after the revelation of the Nordic and Oriental antiquities—now offered a new face. Now it was no longer bad taste that was to be found in Homer, Aeschylus, Pindar, or even Virgil, but a gigantic, savage sublimity, contact with which could only be revivifying. Marked by an idealistic conviction of Neoplatonist inspiration, the Neoclassical system aspired not only to bring together the atemporal forms of the Beautiful, but also, following Winckelmann, to affirm that the archetypes of "beautiful nature" could only manifest themselves by virtue of the flowering of political liberty in the Greek city-states. At the cost of certain displacements and condensations, the deities presented in Greek statuary appear as the incarnation of this ideal, as it was fashioned by free citizens. To be sure, this perspective causes the primitive world to lose much of its harshness and ferocious savagery: the all too smooth serenity celebrated by Winckelmann as the reflection of an intelligible heaven cannot be the vehicle for energies that are meant to erupt from the mysterious depths of living nature. But for an André Chénier there is no contradiction in seeking the juxtaposition, in the Hellenic past as a whole, of a formal harmony, the heat of young desire, and, especially, the great breath of freedom. This to the extent that the imitation of the ancients amounted to more than a mere repetition of names or images: it was to be a second conquest of fire, a transfusion of energy. "Let us light our torches at their poetic fires." Herder, about the same time, hoped that the poetry of the ancients, without being made the object of a servile imitation, could become the source for a modern "heuristic poetry" which would allow for the invention of "an entirely new mythology." But he quickly recognized the difficulty there would be in reconciling "the spirit of reduction with the spirit of fiction," the "dismembering of the philosopher" with the "ordered reassembling of the poet."

The appeal is thus addressed to the poet, who is expected to awaken the collective impulse by exalting the hearts of men and restoring the presence of forgotten divine forces. At stake is society itself, people's search for renewed awareness of the bond that unites them. The figure of the ancient gods becomes charged with a political significance here. They are witnesses to what the popular soul needs in order to recognize itself; they must again become what they were: respondents and guarantors whom the social group imagined in its own image, and in whom it discovered its truth, its own nature. The privileged theater for the return of the gods as evoked by the poets is human celebration (national or universal celebration, according to whether one generalizes or particularizes its scope).

We see here the formation of a "myth of mythology" (H. Blumenberg), which makes the uncertain origins of myths coincide with the origin of the nation (or of humanity), and shows the people in a world in crisis their duty to reunite themselves with their lost origins (with lost nature) lest they lose their souls and perish. No sooner is this new myth formulated and this duty enunciated than questions are raised. Is it possible for the people of an age of science and of reasoned reflection to recover the naive wonderment of a young humanity that peopled nature with deities that were changeable and not slaves to the principle of identity (K. Ph. Moritz)? In the ode entitled *The Gods of Greece,* Schiller evokes at length the ancient host of gods: but they were banished and will never return; nature is thenceforth *entgöttert,* bereft of gods. Our poetry can only live by coming to grips with this absence, by saying that we miss them: "What must live immortally in song must perish in life." Incapable of recovering naive simplicity, modern poetry devotes itself to sentimental nostalgia. Jean-Paul would restate it in his own way: "The beautiful, rich simplicity of the child is enchanting not to another child but to someone who has lost it. . . . The Greek gods are but flat images for us, the empty clothes of our feelings, and not living beings. And while there were no false gods on earth at that time—and every people could be received as a guest at the Temple of another people—today we hardly know anything but false gods. . . . And whereas in the old days poetry was an object of the people, just as the people were the object of poetry, today we sing only while going from one office to another. . . ."

Falconet, *Pygmalion and Galatea*. Baltimore, Walters Art Gallery. Museum photo.

The impossibility of bringing ancient mythology back to life (not because we no longer admire it, but because we admire it too much and because the present time has become incapable of accepting it) merely accentuates the desire to see the birth of a new mythology. We find this idea at the end of a text (copied in Hegel's hand in 1796, but perhaps the work of Schelling, and certainly inspired by Hölderlin) known as "the oldest systematic program of German idealism": "We need a new mythology, but this mythology should be placed in the service of ideas, it should become a mythology of *reason.* Those ideas which do not present themselves in an aesthetic form—that is, a mythological form—are without interest for the people; and conversely, a mythology that is not reasonable is an object of shame for the philosopher. Thus the enlightened and those who are not enlightened will end up joining hands: mythology must become philosophical in order to make the people reasonable, and philosophy mythological, in order to make the philosophers sensitive. Then will we come to see the establishment of an eternal unity between us." In many of his writings (*Bread and Wine, Archipelagus,* etc.), Hölderlin chose to speak of the intermediate moment, the time of anxious waiting, between the irreversible disappearance of the ancient gods and the rise of a new god, a Dionysus or a Christ of the final hour. In 1800, Friedrich Schlegel in turn called for a new mythology, arising not, as had the old, from a contact with the perceptible universe, but "from the most profound depths of the spirit," just as harmonious order unfolds "when chaos is touched by love."

Though it may have been disappointed, this expectation of a new flowering of myth (a myth which would once again become the kingdom of unifying imagination, but also the triumph of sensible reason, and which would no longer borrow the face of the ancient gods) attributes to the future, to history that is to come, a function whose equivalent may be found only in religious or gnostic eschatologies. And even when myth seems still to be lacking, both human time and history as made by humans are profoundly mythicized by this hope. In awaiting the coming of a new mythology as if it were to be a veritable Parousia, this thought was already mythically defining the present as the deaf gestation of a new Adam, as the nocturnal examination of the point from which the universal dawn would shine forth: the present was a time of working and testing, moving forward, forced halts, attempts at new beginnings. Human history, the object of the new mythopoesis, reveals an intelligible meaning; it is the reconquering, under a still unknown appearance, of the lost wholeness, the collective reintegration into a unity, the return to the oldest truth, at the cost of bringing an entirely new world into being. Conceived in this way, myth, which at the beginning of the eighteenth century had been purely profane ornamentation, becomes the sacred par excellence, the ultimate authority—a sacred that imposes its laws in advance and judges human values in a final tribunal. Having never come to pass, it is nevertheless the judge of all that comes to pass. Such a change is but the corollary of another change: what had been the sacred at the beginning of the eighteenth century—written revelation, tradition, dogma—is submitted to a "demystifying" critique which reduces it to a mere human work, a fabulous work of the imagination. The sacred is reduced to a psychological function, while certain human faculties (feelings, consciousness, imagination) or certain collective acts (the common will) become endowed with a sacred function. In the intellectual history of this century, the sacralization of myth is closely associated with the humanization of the sacred. It is no longer sufficient, as has so often been done, to see the philosophy of the Enlightenment as a process of "secularization," in which human reason laid claim to prerogatives which had previously belonged to the divine *logos.* A reverse movement is also apparent, whereby myth, at first cast aside and held to be absurd, was now seen as having a deep and full meaning, and valued as revealed truth (Schelling). This double transformation effects a redistribution of the contrasting elements of the profane and the sacred. The old sacred sheds its skin and the profane order becomes charged with a mythic hope for a liberating progress. In the expectation of a ruling myth which will invent the humanity of the future, the old myths are taken up again as prefigurations—myths of Prometheus, Heracles, Psyche, and the Titans—but now they are used to designate rebellion, desire, and the hopes of those who aspire to become masters of their destiny. The myth that is to come, as sketched in advance by a diffuse expectation, will not only be imagined by man (by the poet-prophet, the people-poet, or humanity at work), but will also have man himself as its hero. The awaited Myth—born neither of the truth of history nor of the truth of poetry—is no longer a theogony but an anthropogony. It is one that will celebrate in song, in order to assemble the peoples, the Man-God who produces himself from his own song or by the work of his hands. All the mythologies of the modern world are but the substitutes and small change of this unfinished Myth.

J.St./d.w.

NOTES

1. Revised, amplified, transformed, Chompré's *Dictionnaire* became F. Noël's *Dictionnaire de la fable* (1801), which was used by artists and poets of the nineteenth century. Noël's *Dictionnaire de la fable* includes the mythologies of the Norse, Asia, etc.; the Greco-Roman world, while remaining predominant, ceased then to be the sole purveyor of imagery.

2. Of course, it is not a matter of the afterlife as the Homeric poems present it, but rather as it is promised by the mythological convention current in the seventeenth century.

3. Vico proposes a false etymology according to which *muthos* is related to *mutus* (mute), indicating that fable appeared in silent times and was the earliest form of speech, which came to be joined with an earlier language consisting of gestures and mute signs.

BIBLIOGRAPHY

Seventeenth- and Eighteenth-Century Authors (in Chronological Order)

G.-J. VOSSIUS, *De gentili theologia . . .* (Amsterdam 1668). A. VAN DALE, *Dissertationes de progressu idolatriae et superstitionum et de prophetia* (Amsterdam 1696); *De oraculis veterum ethnicorum* (Amsterdam 1700). P. JURIEU, *Histoire critique des dogmes et des cultes, depuis Adam à Jésus-Christ* (Amsterdam 1704). W. KING, *A Discourse concerning the Inventions of Men in the Worship of God* (5th ed., London 1704). J. TOLAND, *Letters to Serena* (London 1704). J. TRENCHARD, *The Natural History of Superstition* (London 1709). B. LE BOVIER DE FONTENELLE, *De l'origine des fables* (Paris 1724). C. ROLLIN, *Traité des études,* 4 vols. (Paris 1726); *Histoire ancienne,* 13 vols. (Paris 1730–38). S. SHUCKFORD, *The Sacred and the Profane History of the World Connected . . . ,* 2 vols. (London 1728). A. RAMSAY, *The Travels of Cyrus, to Which Is Annexed a Discourse upon Mythology of the Ancients* (London 1728). T. BLACKWELL, *An Enquiry into the Life and Writings of Homer* (London 1735). T. BROUGHTON, *Bibliotheca historico-sacra, or an Historical Library of the Principal Matters Relating to Religion Ancient and Modern, Pagan, Jewish, Christian and Mohammedan,* 2 vols. (London 1737–39). A. BANIER, *La mythologie et les fables expliquées par l'histoire,* 3 vols. (Paris 1738). N. PLUCHE, *Histoire du ciel . . . ,* 2 vols. (Paris 1739). G. VICO, *La scienza nuova* (3d ed., Naples 1744). R. LOWTH, *De sacra poesi Hebraeorum praelectiones* (London 1753). P. H. MALLET, *Introduction à l'histoire de Dannemarc . . .* (Copenhagen 1755); *Edda . . .* (3d ed., Geneva 1787). D. HUME, *The Natural History of Religion* (London 1757). A. PERNETY, *Les fables égyptiennes et grecques dévoilées* (Paris 1758). P. CHOMPRÉ, *Dictionnaire abrégé de la fable* (Paris 1759). C. DE BROSSES, *Du culte des dieux fétiches . . .* (1760). A. COURT DE GÉBELIN, *Le monde primitif . . . ,* 9 vols. (Paris 1773–83). R. WOOD, *An Essay on the Original Genius and Writings of Homer* (London 1775). J. BRYANT, *A New System or an Analysis of Ancient Mythology* (London 1775–76). J.-S. BAILLY, *Lettres sur l'origine des sciences* (Paris 1777); *Lettres sur l'Atlantide de Platon* (Paris 1779). J. G. LINDEMANN, *Geschichte der Meinungen älterer und neuerer Völker im Stande der Roheit und Kultur, von Gott, Religion und Priesterthum* (Stendal 1784–85). C. G. HEYNE, *Opuscula academica* (Göttingen 1785–1812). C. A. DEMOUSTIER, *Lettres à Émilie sur la mythologie* (Paris 1786–98). R. P. KNIGHT, *A Discourse on the Worship of Priapus . . .* (London 1786). J.-P. RABAUT DE SAINT-ÉTIENNE, *Lettres à M. Bailly sur l'histoire primitive de la Grèce* (Paris 1787). P. C. REINHARD, *Abriss einer Geschichte der Entstehung und Ausbildung der religiösen Ideen* (Jena 1794). C. F. DUPUIS, *Origine de tous les cultes,* 12 vols. (Paris 1796). W. JONES, *Works,* 6 vols. (London 1799). F. NOËL, *Dictionnaire de la fable,* 2 vols. (Paris 1801). K. P. MORITZ, *Götterlehre . . .* (3d ed., Berlin 1804). J. A. DULAURE, *Des divinités génératrices, ou des cultes du phallus chez les anciens et les modernes* (Paris 1805). F. CRUEZER, *Symbolik und Mythologie der alten Völker, besonders der Griechen* (Leipzig and Darmstadt 1810–12). F. C. BAUR, *Symbolik und Mythologie, oder die Naturreligion des Altertums,* 3 vols. (Stuttgart 1824–25). J. G. HERDER, *Sämtliche Werke,* 33 vols. (Berlin 1877–1913). W. BLAKE, *Complete Poetry and Prose* (London 1948). JEAN-PAUL, *Vorschule der Aesthetik* (Munich 1963). F. HÖLDERLIN, *Sämtliche Werke,* 6 vols. (Stuttgart 1943–61), *Œuvres,* edited by P. Jaccottet (Paris 1967). F. SCHLEGEL, *Kritische Schriften* (Munich 1970).

Modern Studies on the History of Mythology (in Chronological Order)

F. STRICH, *Die Mythologie in der deutschen Literatur von Klopstock bis Wagner* (Halle 1910). O. GRUPPE, *Geschichte der klassischen Mythologie und Religionsgeschichte* (Leipzig 1921), important. R. SCHWAB, *La renaissance orientale* (Paris 1950). W. REHM, *Götterstille und Göttertrauer* (Berlin 1951); *Griechentum und Goethezeit* (Bern 1952). F. E. MANUEL, *The Eighteenth Century Confronts the Gods* (Cambridge, MA, 1959), important. J. DE VRIES, *Forschungsgeschichte der Mythologie* (Freiburg and Munich 1961). R. TROUSSON, *Le thème de Prométhée dans la littérature européenne* (Geneva 1964). J. BALTRUŠAITIS, *La quête d'Isis* (Paris 1967). Y. F.-A. GIRAUD, *La fable de Daphné* (Geneva 1968). P. ALBOUY, *Mythes et mythologies dans la littérature française.* M. FUHRMANN, ed., *Terror und Spiel: Probleme der Mythenrezeption* (Munich 1971), important. B. FELDMAN and R. D. RICHARDSON, *The Rise of Modern Mythology* (Bloomington and London 1972), an important anthology of documents, commentaries, and bibliographies. K. KERENYI, *Die Eröffnung des Zugangs zum Mythos: Ein Lesebuch* (Darmstadt 1976), a collection of texts on myth, from Vico to W. F. Otto.

The Mythology of Ancient Switzerland

Despite occasional hypercriticism, archeological discoveries made in Switzerland lead us to conclude that there was a ritual life in the area even in Paleolithic times.[1] But it is not until the Bronze Age that we find evidence of a mythology, of which certain vestiges are reflected even in contemporary Switzerland.

With the Roman presence on Helvetian soil, documents bearing on native beliefs or on great Celtic deities multiplied: Lugh, Sucellus, and Epona all had their devotees, as did local deities such as Artio, Mars Caturix, Genava (protectress of Geneva), and Aventia (patron goddess of Avenches). An inscription from this last locality mentions the "Lugavi"; this inscription is analogous to the one at Uxama (Osma) in the Spanish province of Soria and supports the view that Lugh was a "multiple" god, perhaps triple. An Irish story alludes to triplicity. Like Danaë, Ethnē—Lugh's mother—is locked up in a tower. McKineely, the owner of a blue cow, disguises himself and manages to rescue the young woman. From that union triplets are born; two die by drowning, and Lugh is the sole survivor.[2]

The great Celtic myths have not left clear traces on Swiss folklore; yet a curious coincidence should be mentioned. The city of Bern, founded in 1191 by the Zaehringen family following a successful bear hunt, is adjacent to a site called Muri, where in 1832 a votive statuette dedicated to the goddess Artio was discovered: she is depicted sitting, facing a large bear, which seems to be climbing down from a tree. To this day, the city of Bern raises bears in pits, but the present inhabitants' affection for their ursine heraldry cannot be connected with the goddess Artio or with any kind of totemism. Yet various popular traditions, of which some are still alive and others disappeared during the past few centuries, must have connections with myths of ancient Switzerland, though it is not possible to establish whether these myths are Celtic or Germanic. There are carnival customs common to youth groups that existed among both the Celts (for example, the Irish *feinid*) and the Norse (for example, the Scandinavian *berserkir*). The "Punchiadurs" of Grisons indulged in ritual combats analogous to those that took place on the occasion of the Roman Caprotine Nones. The Roitschegetten of Lötschental (Valais) or the Klausen of Appenzell still indulge in a kind of wild hunt in carnival season.

A custom still observed in Sursee (Lucerne) on Saint Martin's Day, 11 November, consists of decapitating, blindfold, a goose hanging from a string; this custom cannot merely be connected with a memory of the days of the tithe.[3] Each competitor must wear a blindfold in the shape of the sun and a loose-fitting red cape. In other places, "wild men" appear, whether at carnival time, in tales and legends, or on inn signs. Sometimes they wear bear costumes. This ancient heritage was formerly neglected because of its popular character, and the related mythical stories were treated with contempt like old wives' tales.[4] In central Switzerland and in Valais, legends have been recorded that correspond to the story of the death of the great Pan told by Plutarch in his treatise on the disappearance of the oracles. Since Switzerland is hardly an isolated case, Plutarch may have recorded the Greek version of an ancient popular European theme.[5]

Stories about giants and dragons also show how arbitrary it often is to speak of French or German mythology. Gargantua has left his traces in French-speaking areas, whereas in German-speaking Switzerland the giants have a rather Norse look about them. All these giants really look alike. Similarly, the legendary dragons of Switzerland remind us of Tarasques or Mélusines as much as monsters from the Germanic epic stories. Celtic and Norse sources, similar in background, interpenetrate and cannot be told apart.

The bear goddess Artio. Votive statuette. Bern, Historisches Museum. Museum photo.

One Swiss theme, however, the best known by far, has origins that must be sought in northern Europe—the theme of William Tell.

Several historians of religions have recently demonstrated that certain Indo-European heroes, formerly considered historical characters, in fact belong to mythology. A striking case, and probably the most recent, is that of William (Wilhelm) Tell. It had long been noted that the stories about Tell, Toko, Puncker, William of Cloudesly, and others were very much alike, and it was agreed that the theme of the remarkable archer came from a Scandinavian source. But this case study had generally been limited to the episode of the apple placed on the head of a child and hit with a shot from a crossbow.[6]

Skill in archery was thought to have a supernatural quality. The *Malleus maleficarum* devotes several pages to this subject, and if he had actually lived, the skillful crossbowman would certainly have brought down upon himself the thunderbolts of the Inquisition.[7] Fairies and witches were credited with the power of unleashing magic, harmful arrows. The esoteric symbolism of the bow and arrow may also be at play here.

Shadows also obscure the episode of Tell's escape as a prisoner navigating a lake. Norse heroes comparable to Tell have also escaped, but on skis. Such is the case of Toko, Heming, and Geyti Aslaksson. Toko ends up at sea, but the two Scandinavian deities famous for their bowmanship, the god Ullr (Ollerus) and the goddess Skadi, move about on skis. Furthermore, Ullr navigates on bones as well as he does in a boat; a picture in the *Historia de gentibus septentrionalibus* by Olaus Magnus illustrates the practice of supernatural waterskiing.

Sucellus. Viège bronze. Geneva, Musée d'Art et d'Histoire. Museum photo.

The very name Wilhelm (*helm* means helmet) and the episode of the hat shows that the headdress plays a significant role—its magic value in several myths is well known—and also that Tell (or Toll, i.e., crazy) by his very name belongs to a troublesome category, that of madmen. Tell's refusal to take off his own hat to a piece of headgear hooked onto the end of a pole is interpreted as the political gesture of a madman, that is, of an individual quasi-ritualistically authorized to express popular sentiment and unpleasant truths. This interpretation takes no account of ethnographic or religious facts such as the worship of the symbol of a deity placed on top of a pole (a fact mentioned by Olaus Magnus, book 3, chapter 2), or belief in magic arrows. In this realm of ideas, we should also mention the rock engravings of northern Europe that depict horned or masked skiers and a remarkable sorcerer shooting numerous arrows at another figure.[8] Nor should we forget that the fool and the archer have played a prominent role in the British Morris dances and mystery plays.

The story of Tell is a composite of several stories, one of which, the skier-archer, might be of Paleo-Finnish origin. In the nineteenth century, the historian Jean de Müller wrote that Tell's male line of descent ended in 1684 with Jean Martin's death, and his female line ended in 1720 with Vérena's death. Today, this Swiss national hero has left the bounds of history and entered, full-grown, the realm of myth.

R.C./g.h.

NOTES

1. For the cult of the bear, see CHRISTINGER and BORGEAUD, *Mythologie de la Suisse ancienne* (Geneva 1963), 29ff. The excavations of the Petit Chasseur at Sion (Valais) and those of the Carschenna (Grisons), for example, have brought to light important documents on cultural life prior to the Roman occupation or the arrival of the Celts, but these documents cannot be linked to particular myths.
2. Ibid., p. 88.
3. Another game played in Switzerland, *marelle* (hopscotch), is probably connected to ancient initiatory rites and to the myth of the labyrinth (ibid., 2:107ff.).
4. This is, for example, the attitude of Apuleius with regard to the tale of Psyche and Cupid (*Metamorphoses*, 4.27).
5. PLUTARCH, *De defectu oraculorum*. J. MULLER, *Sagen aus Uri* (Basel 1969), 3:207–10. L. COURTHION, *Les veillées des mayens* (Geneva), 197–201.
6. *Quellenwerk zur Entstehung der schweizerischen Eidgenossenschaft III Chroniken*, Band 1 (Aarau 1948). H. DE BOOR, *Die nordischen, englischen und deutschen Darstellungen des Apfelschussmotivs*. M. DELCOURT, "The Legend of Sarpedon and the Saga of the Archer," *History of Religions* 2, 1 (1962).
7. H. INSTITORIS and J. SPRENGER, *Le marteau des sorcières (Malleus maleficarum)* (Paris 1973).
8. H. KÜHN, *Die Felsbilder Europas* (Stuttgart 1952). W. J. RAVDONIKAS, *Les gravures rupestres des bords du lac Onega et de la mer Blanche* (Moscow 1938), vol. 2.

Mythic Elements in French Folklore

It may appear surprising, if not paradoxical, that France is covered in this book. France does not have, and probably never has had, its own mythology in the sense of an organized system of narratives about origins and supernatural beings. The mythology of France is not really French, for it is an emanation and complement of the Christian religion. First, therefore, we must demonstrate the historical absence of a "French mythology" while at the same time justifying its presence in this work.

I. The Absence and Presence of a French Mythology

Historians caution us against any temptation to make Celtic or, later, Roman Gaul the prefiguration of modern France, which would thus be the end of a linear evolution. It took many centuries for the political, linguistic, cultural, and religious differences between the diverse ethnic strata to be effaced and for a certain national cohesion to develop. Popular French consciousness nevertheless tends to place the Gauls in a special position as the ancestors of the French, but this Gallic "myth" is of scholarly origin and does not appear before the sixteenth century. Gallic religion, mythology, and culture left very few material traces, and we know that the political structures of Gaul were replaced by those of the Romans after the conquest, and then by those of the Franks. Latin was quickly imposed over all of the Gallic territory, both because it was the language of the conquerors and because it could be written. The invasions and implantations of the barbarians finally drove out all that may have remained Celtic in Gaul. It is not our purpose here to explain the Celtic vestiges: that subject is treated in other articles in the present work.

The instrument that turned out to be most effective in concealing a potential and precocious French mythology was incontestably Christianization. Its action was twofold, positive on the one hand and negative on the other. It was negative when, over several centuries, it strove to condemn, combat, and extirpate those beliefs and practices which the Church held to be pagan. This struggle changed the two known forms of such belief, through the organic processes of rejection and assimilation. In 452 the Council of Arles condemns worshipers of rocks; in 538 the Synod of Auxerre stigmatizes those who worship fountains, forests, and rocks. In 567 the Council of Tours recommends that all those who, before rocks, do things unrelated to the ceremonies of the Church be driven from the Church. In the seventh century, Saint Eligius, in the homilies related in his *Vita,* written by Saint Owen, stigmatizes the practices denounced as pagan. The continuing struggle was apparently quite ineffective, since the Church was obliged to pursue it until well after the Council of Trent. The assimilative method met with much greater success, but it was a success that sometimes turned against the victor. It consisted in Christianizing practices that were—or were considered to be—of pagan origin. "It is the same with sacred forests as with the Gentiles," declared Saint Augustine; "one does not exterminate the Gentiles but one converts them, changes them; in the same way one does not cut down sacred groves; it is better to consecrate them to Jesus Christ." In the same way, local deities that watch over springs and fountains are replaced by the names of missionaries and local saints (Sébillot, 1904–7). From the texts of the councils and synods that have come down to us, the essential objects of persistent paganism appear to have been water, rocks, and forests. We may thus speak of survivals, even though the forms of the beliefs and practices may have changed considerably over the centuries.

Christianity acted much more positively, however, when it offered the Gallo-Roman peoples a self-sufficient mythic and religious system. Here we find the main reason for the absence of a French mythology, since the needs of the majority of the people were satisfied by the Christian system. But because not all of the people were completely satisfied, a number of beliefs, stories, and practices managed to slip through the cracks of the Christian religion, while others thrived independently, parallel to Christianity. Whether grasped in its state of syncretism with Christianity or in an independent state, this ensemble belongs to the domain known as folklore. In comparison with "authorized" mythologies which are learned as relatively well organized systems, folklore, by its very nature, often appears in pieces. To anyone first encountering it, folklore presents itself in the form of crumbs, debris, and fragments, in which it conceals its mythic nature. Folklore thus carries forward those mythic

Festival of the Tarasca at Tarascon (1946), a good example of a popular festival inserted into the Christian liturgical calendar. Paris, Musée des Arts et Traditions populaires. Museum photo.

materials to which Christianity and later scholarly culture refused to give a noble expression, so that they had to appear in seemingly harmless forms—tales, legends, beliefs, and "popular" practices—although the inoffensive appearance of such forms did not always shelter them from the condemnation of the Church or the dominant culture.

This is, in all likelihood, the only mythology France has known—although it does not belong to France alone in all of its expressions, since European folklore is divided not according to strict national boundaries but into broader areas. An attempt has nevertheless been made to bring to light a French mythology, by attributing Celtic origins to it: we are referring to Henri Dontenville's work (1948). The central character of this recovered mythology is Gargantua—not so much Rabelais's hero as the Gargantua of a great number of stories and beliefs which are essentially topographical. To Gargantua is attributed the creation of numerous mountains, hills, buttes, menhirs, lakes, swamps, etc. (Sébillot, 1883). According to Dontenville, Gargantua is the son of the Celtic god Belen (Bélénos), but this divine origin is demonstrated by an etymological elaboration that lacks rigor. Other supernatural personages, such as the fairies Morgana and Mélusine, also gravitate around this mythology. It is incontestable that Gargantua was a popular character before becoming a literary figure thanks to Rabelais. On the other hand, it is quite difficult to make him the hero of a French mythic system postulated through beliefs and accounts called survivals and vestiges. Mythology has not reached the scientific level of linguistics, which is able to reconstruct with some accuracy the earlier state of a language. According to Émile Benveniste's formulation, linguistics has succeeded "in restoring the wholes that evolution has broken up, in bringing buried structures to light" (Benveniste, 1969, 1:9). The science of mythology, unlike the science of etymology, is not ready to produce reconstructions of an earlier stage on the basis of present-day elements: it does not have laws that direct the evolution of mythic systems, for the evolution is the function of too many variables for all to be studied at the same time.

The theory that folklore consists of the vestiges of vanished mythologies is not a new one. Set forth more or less explicitly earlier, the theory did not spread until the beginning of the nineteenth century, when it became the foundation of the vast undertaking of the brothers Grimm. The folktales that they collected and published under the title of *Kinder- und Hausmärchen* (1812–15) were thought to have preserved the beliefs and customs of the ancient Germanic peoples, after they had given them a poetical form which was the product not of scholarly poetry but of "natural" poetry which, through the intermediary of creative people, was of divine origin. In Jacob Grimm's *Deutsche Mythologie* (1835), the theory becomes more explicit. It surmises that a mythology and a pantheon which were highly developed in the pre-Roman era were destroyed by the medieval Church and survive only in the form of the fragments found in folklore.

While the brothers Grimm gave this theory the fame and influence that are so well known to us, they did nothing but express—albeit in a work of great importance—a current of European ideas which was to be found in France from the first quarter of the nineteenth century. The first systematic collection of what was not yet called folklore was undertaken by members of the Celtic Academy—transformed after 1815 into the Society of the Antiquarians of France—whose expressed goal was to collect dialects, patois, and jargons, place names, monuments, usages, and traditions, in order to "explicate ancient times by modern times." It was the same doctrine—which we will call the ideology of survivals—that governed both the French venture (which declined after 1825–30) and that of the brothers Grimm, which was more abundant and prolonged.

It should be noted that this current of ideas in the Europe of the first half of the nineteenth century was characterized by strong nationalism, as it was in France in the second half of the century, after the research was temporarily eclipsed between 1830 and 1860–70. This nationalism would seek its foundation in the camp of the Gauls and the Celts, so it was natural that the historians and archaeologists should determine its theoretical foundation. The foundation is accepted without discussion by folklorists such as Paul Sébillot and all those who worked on the *Review of Popular Traditions,* while the Celticists, archaeologists and historians such as Henri Gaidoz, Alexandre Bertrand, and Alfred Maury, turn into folklorists the better to affirm their thesis. As far as Henri Gaidoz is concerned, refer to the article "Popular Customs and Rituals in France," in which one of his studies is presented and discussed. As for Alexandre Bertrand, in his book *The Religion of the Gauls* (1897) he writes the following lines, which the brothers Grimm themselves could not have disavowed:

> There exist, or there existed in human memory, in our country, as in Ireland, Germany, and the Scandinavian countries, old customs, old traditions, and old superstitions, which are faint but still recognizable echoes of primitive times. "Driven from their temples," H. Gaidoz could write, "the Gallic gods took refuge in our countryside"; we shall go in search of them. The very care taken by the Church very early to stigmatize the old beliefs, to anathematize them, or to Christianize them by changing their spirit—most often without visibly modifying their form—in its inability to uproot them, strongly attests to the important role that they played in the country before Christianity and to the people's lively attachment to them. (Bertrand, 18–19)

In order to elucidate the problems arising from the connections between mythology and folklore, we must criticize the notion of survivals. Despite its fragility, it has constituted the founding principle of folklore studies until recent times, for in France it was only with the works of Arnold van Gennep that the notion was abandoned, even though his contemporary Pierre Saintyves continued to use it. Note that van Gennep was a man of the soil and Saintyves was not. Ethnology has taught us that a belief or custom can never be a pure survival. It may sometimes be an archaism with respect to the dominant culture, but it is never an anachronism. In order to be maintained, traditions must have a function in the culture of which they are a part. Claude Lévi-Strauss expresses this very clearly concerning the beliefs and customs of Christmas:

> Explanations by survivals are always incomplete; for customs neither disappear nor survive without reason. When they persist, the cause is to be found less in the viscosity of history than in the permanence of a function which modern analysis should be able to disclose. . . . We are, with the rites of Christmas, in the presence not only of historical vestiges, but also of forms of thinking and of behavior which reveal more general conditions of life in society. The Saturnalias and the medieval celebration of Christmas do not contain the final ground for a ritual otherwise inexplicable and devoid of meaning; but they do offer comparative material which is useful for drawing out the deep meaning of recurrent institutions. (Lévi-Strauss, 1952)

Even assuming that a practice might have been preserved without much change from Gallo-Roman antiquity to the nineteenth century, its meaning could not be exactly the same, since its cultural context is fundamentally dissimilar, and the greatest differences are found in the diversity of the religion and the economy.

Although it is inadmissible that popular beliefs, practices, and narratives are pure vestiges or survivals of an earlier state, they should not be divested of all reference to the past. The past is essential not as an explanatory principle but as a given in the material. It is a constant in folklore, at whatever historical time one observes and collects, to be at once caught in the present moment and reflected into a more or less distant past. The term "popular traditions," which is sometimes used for folklore, is a good indication of the nostalgic component of these materials. A reality observed *hic et nunc* always refers to a tradition; that is, to a past. But this past is

Steps of the ages. Gangel, Metz. Paris, Musée des Arts et Traditions populaires. Museum photo.

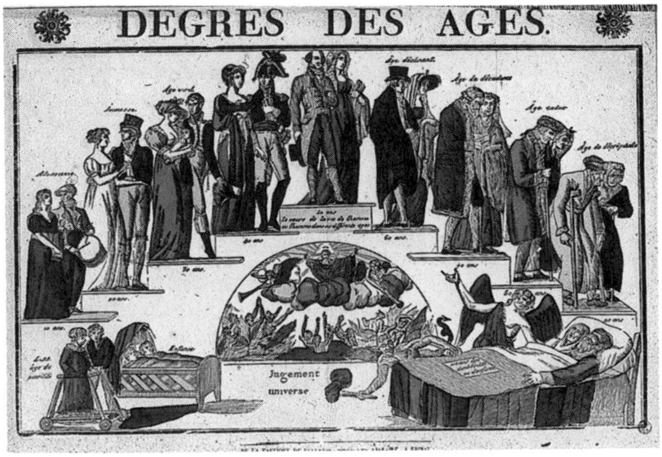

The twelve months of the year. Calendar from Epinal, Pellerin. Paris, Musée des Arts et Traditions populaires. Museum photo.

not truly historical: it is reflected from generation to generation back to distant origins which are difficult to inscribe in history. But the quest for origins is by definition not historical but mythic. In this sense folklore, by its very nature, includes mythic fragments whose importance varies according to the form and technique by which it is expressed. Clearly, popular beliefs, practices, and stories are likely to serve as vehicles for mythic fragments. These are the three forms we have chosen to study.

It is thus evident what separates us from the early folklorists of France and Europe, but also what we hold in common. They regarded folklore as the vestiges of ancient mythological systems altered, mutilated, and even corrupted by the wear of time, as archaeological monuments may be. As with such monuments, it became necessary to submit them to reconstruction, a mental reconstruction that would invest them with meaning. Failing this reconstruction, "survivals" were regarded as freaks, curiosities, if not aberrations. Throwing them back into the past provides them with a meaning, a meaning that cannot always be restored to them, but which exists because it did exist: this kind of meaning may be called retrospective.

On the other hand, we believe—without denying the phenomena of transmission—that folkloric acts are bearers of a *present* mythic component, even if this component is viewed as ancient and archaic both by observers of the acts and by those who practice them. It is not possible for depictions and practices bereft of a current meaning, and thus of a function, to continue to exist: in the case of folklore the current sense and function are constituted by a throwback into the past. Curiously, this throwback is accompanied by a feeling of extreme precariousness. All folklorists, regardless of the age for which they gather folklore, insist on the urgency of their work and on the inevitability of the disappearance of what they collect. The same fragility is attributed to the collected folklore as is attributed to archaeological fragments which are freed from their earthly gangue and thus likely to crumble because of their great age.

II. Popular Beliefs, Rituals, and Narratives

The forms of folklore from which we will attempt to extract the underlying mythic forms are popular beliefs, rituals, and narratives. It is not that folklore is manifested only in these three forms, but they are easier to decipher than popular art, dress, or dance, whose apparently greater technical material and social function mask their mythic component even more.

In their techniques, popular narratives are obviously closest to myths, yet are not myths, since this "fluid oral literature" involves only folktales and legends. The folkloric taxonomy which distinguishes them is useful from a formal point of view inasmuch as it introduces terms of reference. This taxonomy is certainly less clear-cut on the level of meaning. The legend is an account which appears to be inserted into time or space, and usually into time *and* space. It presents real places and a cast of characters which are supposed to have existed. This historico-topographical insertion essentially occurs through the presence of proper names: personal names and place names. An example is the Charlemagne of epic legends, who is imagined to be the king of the Franks who was crowned emperor of the West at Aix-la-Chapelle in 800. The folktale, by contrast, appears as a purely fictional account; people and places are impersonal, and its temporality is not historical but narrative, i.e., internal to the account. Although popular legends and folktales are narratives, as opposed to beliefs, rituals, and practices, we will not examine them all together. Legends have a more fundamental relationship with beliefs than with folktales, in the sense that the relationship between them is generative: beliefs generate legends in forms of varying complexity. As for popular folktales, we will treat only those which are elegantly, and rightly, called *contes merveilleux* ("supernatural stories" or "fairy tales"), i.e., numbers 300 to 749 in the Aarne and Thompson classification (1961).

Of all of the folkloric expressions, the most difficult to comprehend are undoubtedly folk beliefs, since these offer the least material support. They are also often apprehended under a form other than their own: i.e., that of the legends they engender, or of the practices and rituals they underlie. These practices are characterized by the fact that they exclude—or try to exclude—language, and only use objects and actions. Of course, no practice or ritual has ever totally eliminated language, but the words or formulas used in them are to be assigned to what Claude Lévi-Strauss calls implicit mythology.

Formally, these diverse expressions are distinct from one another. From the point of view of their contents, this is not completely the case. There are slippages from one form to another. A motif from a popular folktale may be found in a legend. A practice refers to a belief. Another belief may have been collected as a legend in another time or place or from another informant. But the most developed form of the legend allows for the identification of a generative or contracted core, reduced to its most basic expression by a reverse movement. In the schema of a ritual, one may recognize the theme of a popular folktale, to which this form clearly gives a much greater freedom.

These movements, these shifts, these comings and goings have at least two causes. We know from the works of Lévi-Strauss that "mythic thought is essentially transformational," as testified by the mythic fragments that are carried in this way. The other cause is the particular nature of this mythology "in crumbs," which could not be expressed in the form of a coherent whole because Christianity occupied, and not without a certain aggression, almost the entire authorized field of expression. Forced to be fragmented in order to be expressed, this "implicit" mythology became perhaps even more fluid than the others.

In spite of its fundamental fluidity, we will attempt to grasp its most important aspects under the following rubrics: "French Fairy Tales, Folktales, and Myths"; "Folk Beliefs and Legends about Fairies in France"; and "Popular Customs and Rituals in France."

N.B./d.w.

BIBLIOGRAPHY

A. AARNE and S. THOMPSON, *The Types of the Folk-Tale: A Classification and Bibliography* (Helsinki 1961). A. AUDIN, "Les rites solsticiaux et la légende de S. Pothin," *Revue de l'histoire de religions* 96 (1927): 147–74. N. BELMONT, *Mythes et croyances dans l'ancienne France* (Paris 1973). E. BENVENISTE, *Le vocabulaire des institutions indo-européennes*, 2 vols. (Paris 1969). A. BERTRAND, *La religion des Gaulois: Les druides et le druidisme* (Paris 1897). J. F. BLADÉ, *Contes populaires de la Gascogne*, 3 vols. (Paris 1886). P. DELARUE, "Les caractères propres du conte populaire français," *La pensée*, no. 72 (March–April 1957), 39–62. P. DELARUE and M. L. TENEZE, *Le conte populaire français*, 2 vols. (Paris 1957–64). D. DERGNY, *Usages, coutumes et croyances*, 2 vols. (Abbeville 1885–88; 2d ed., Brionne 1971). H. DONTENVILLE, *La mythologie française* (Paris 1948). G. DUBOIS, *Celtes et Gaulois au XVIe siècle: Le développement littéraire d'un mythe nationaliste* (Paris 1972). G. DUMÉZIL, *Légendes sur les Nartes* (Paris 1930); *Mythe et épopée*, 3 vols. (Paris 1968–73). L. DUMONT, *La Tarasque: Essai de description d'un fair local d'un point de vue ethnographique* (Paris 1951). C.-M. EDSMAN, *Ignis divinus. Le feu comme moyen de rajeunissement et d'immortalité. Contes, légendes, mythes, rites* (Lund 1949). P. FORTIER-BEAULIEU, *Mariages et noces campagnardes dans le département de la Loire* (Paris 1937). H. GAIDOZ, *Études de mythologie gauloise: Le dieu gaulois du soleil et le symbolisme de la roue* (Paris 1886), published first in the *Revue archéologique* (1884–85). C. GAIGNEBET, *Le carnaval: Essais de mythologie populaire* (Paris and Payot 1974). J. GRIMM and W. GRIMM, *Kinder- und Hausmärchen*, 2 vols. (Berlin 1812–15); the 3d ed. (1856) includes a third volume of commentaries; often translated into English, e.g., M. HUNT and J. STERN, trans., *Grimm's Fairy Tales* (New York 1944). J. GRIMM, *Deutsche Mythologie* (Berlin 1835); in English as *Teutonic Mythology* (London 1882–88). H. HUBERT, "Étude sommaire de la représentation du temps dans la religion et la magie," in H. Hubert and M. Mauss, *Mélanges d'histoire des religions* (Paris 1909). A. LE BRAZ, *La légende de la mort chez les Bretons armoricains*, 2 vols. (Paris 1923). C. LÉVI-STRAUSS, "Le Père Noël supplicié," *Les temps modernes*, no. 77 (1952); "L'analyse morphologique des contes russes," *Cahiers de l'Institut de science économique appliquée* 9 (March 1960): 3–36; reprinted in *Anthropologie structurale* (Paris 1973), 2:140–73, under the title "La structure et la forme." A. MAURY, *Croyances et légendes du Moyen Age* (Paris 1896). E. MÉLÉTINSKY, "Marriage: Its Function and Position in the Structure of Folktales," in P. Maranda, ed., *Soviet Structural Folkloristics* (The Hague and Paris 1974), 61–72. M. MONNIER, "Vestiges d'antiquité observés dans le Jurassien," *Mémoires de la Société des Antiquaires de France*, 4 (1823). V. PROPP, *Morphology of the Folk-Tale* (Bloomington, IN, 1958), original in Russian. P. SAINTYVES, *Essais de mythologie chrétienne: Les saints successeurs des dieux* (Paris 1907); *Les contes de Perrault et les récits parallèles* (Paris 1923); *En marge de la Légende dorée* (Paris 1931); *Corpus du folklore des eaux en France et dans les colonies françaises* (Paris 1934); *Corpus du folklore préhistorique en France et dans les colonies françaises*, 3 vols. (Paris 1934–36); *L'astrologie populaire* (Paris 1937). P. SÉBILLOT, *Le paganisme contemporain chez les peuples celto-latins* (Paris 1908); *Gargantua dans les traditions populaires* (Paris 1883); *Le folklore de France*, 4 vols. (Paris 1904–7; reprinted Paris 1968). M. TEISSIER, "Recherches sur la fête annuelle de la roue flamboyante de la Saint-Jean, à Basse-Kontz, arrondissement de Thionville," *Mémoires de la Société des Antiquaires de France* 5 (1823): 379–93. A. VAN GENNEP, *The Rites of Passage* (Chicago 1960; originally Paris 1909); *Le folklore* (Paris 1924); *Le folklore de la Bourgogne: Côte d'Or*, Contributions au folklore des provinces de France (Paris 1934); *Manuel de folklore français contemporain* (Paris 1937–58); in books 3 and 4 there is a systematic and critical bibliography on the folklore of France. A. VARAGNAC, *Civilisation traditionnelle et genres de vie* (Paris 1948).

Journals

Mélusine: Recueil de mythologie, Littérature populaire, traditions et usages. Founded by H. Gaidoz and E. Rolland in 1877 (10 vols. between 1877 and 1912).

Revue des traditions populaires. Founded by P. Sébillot in 1886 (32 vols. through 1918).

Revue d'ethnographie et des traditions populaires. Founded by M. Delafosse in 1920 (10 vols. through 1929).

Revue de folklore français et de folklore colonial. Edited by P. Saintyves (13 vols., 1930–42).

Arts et traditions populaires. Journal of the Société d'ethnographie française (1953–70).

Ethnologie française. Journal of the Société d'ethnologie française. Founded in 1971.

FRENCH FAIRY TALES, FOLKTALES, AND MYTHS

Vladimir Propp's contribution to the study of the folktale, especially to the study of the tale as myth, is both important and unsatisfying. His well-known analysis of the functions of the folktale provided the fundamental schema for the folktale but at the same time constituted a reductionist approach. And while Propp is convinced that the fairytale derives from myth, he sees this process as what could be called devolutionist. Propp's works on this problem are not sufficiently known in France, but what he says here and there in his *Morphology of the Folktale* is explicit enough. "If we define these tales from a historical point of view, they deserve the old, now abandoned, name of mythical tales" (p. 122, alluding to Wilhelm Wundt's terms *Mythusmärchen* and *Märchenmythus*). The tale derives from the myth through the intermediary of an historical evolution: "It is quite possible that there is a relationship, governed by laws, between the archaic forms of culture and religion on the one hand, and between religion and folktales on the other hand. A culture dies, a religion dies, and their content is transformed into a folktale. The traces of archaic religious representations that are preserved in folktales are so obvious that they can be isolated before any historical study" (pp. 131–32).

Once more we find the historical problematic as the theoretical foundation of folklore. Unfortunately, there is nothing to indicate that French fairy tales are derived from ancient religion and mythology, either Celtic or Gallo-Roman. We know, on the other hand, that they are variants of tales found throughout the Indo-European domain, so their origin goes back much earlier, perhaps to the beginning of the Neolithic—in which case we cannot say anything about them at all. On the other hand, if one is willing to admit that fairy tales include still-meaningful mythical fragments within a structure that has lost its coherence, then an attempt at decoding becomes possible.

Another Russian formalist, E. Meletinsky, sees the opposition between myth and folktale as based on an opposition between the collective and the individual: the myth is concerned with the collective fate of the universe, of humanity, of the local community, while the folktale is concerned with the fate of individuals. This remark is very helpful and does not contradict Claude Lévi-Strauss's proposition that the difference between myth and folktale is a difference of degree. On the one hand, "folktales are built on weaker oppositions than those of myths: not cosmological, metaphysical, or natural, but more often local, social, or moral ones"; on the other hand the folktale "is less subject than the myth to the triple exigencies of logical coherence, religious orthodoxy, and collective pressure. . . . The folktale's permutations become relatively freer and progressively acquire a certain arbitrariness" (1960). Folktales may be considered myths that are weakened in their structure and expression, but this does not make the meaning of their content any less mythic. It is only harder to grasp.

In this analysis of the contents of French fairy tales, which represents only a preliminary outline, we will make use of a remark of Propp's. In the *Morphology of the Folktale* he says "The voyage, one of the main structural foundations of the folktale, is the reflection of certain representations of the voyages of the soul into the other world" (p. 132). The motif of the voyage, particularly the voyage into the other world—but is it just one motif among others, or is it rather the very essence of the fairy tale?—sometimes appears quite explicitly, sometimes more obscurely, and sometimes in an insignificant guise. It certainly reflects an eschatology which, in spite of sometimes having a Christian appearance, has little to do with Christianity.

One tale type (T471, *The Bridge to the Other World* in the Aarne-Thompson classification) has the French name of the *Voyage dans l'autre monde* (journey into the other world). Its distribution in France is uneven: sixteen of the twenty-six known versions are from Brittany, seven others are from Gascony, and the others from Alsace and Nevers. The initial motif makes it possible to divide them into two groups. The young hero's journey is provoked either by an unknown person who asks him to bear a message to the other world or by his decision to visit his sister, who is married to a foreigner who took her to a distant land. We will summarize what seem to be the richest versions from the second group.

Wedding party leaving a church. Lithograph, Laruns. Paris, Musée des Arts et Traditions populaires. Museum photo.

"Mardi Gras is dead; shrovetide follows without regret." Paris, Musée des Arts et Traditions popularies. Museum photo.

A girl who does not want to get married finally marries a foreigner, who appears in different guises depending on the version: a young man dressed all in white and as handsome as an angel; a beggar, when she is the king's daughter; the *Ankou*, death personified, in a Breton version; a magnificently dressed lord who turns out to be a dead man; a young man as bright as the sun; a man with red teeth, or simply the Sun in person. After the wedding he takes her far away to his kingdom. Her brother decides to visit her, but his journey turns out to be long, difficult, and full of challenges and strange spectacles. When he arrives at the castle where his sister lives, she tells him that her husband is gone all day long, leaving early in the morning and only coming back in the evening. The husband agrees to let his brother-in-law go with him on this daily trip, on condition that he remain completely silent while they travel. In some versions it is during this journey that he sees strange spectacles whose

Mardi Gras procession. Woodcut (Second Empire). Paris, Musée des Arts et Traditions populaires. Museum photo.

meaning is revealed to him only when he comes back in the evening: these are always Christian allegories, the main one being that he visits Heaven and sees Purgatory and Hell as he goes by them. He returns to his village; certain versions indicate that his voyage seemed short to him but really lasted several hundred years. He dies soon after his return.

The archaic appearance of this tale is especially striking in the least-Christianized versions. It readily evokes cosmogonic myths, since we understand that the husband of the hero's sister is the Sun, even in the most Christianized versions in which he is not designated as such: his daily trip is sufficiently explicit in this respect. The Christianization of the story has caused a shift in the axis of the narrative: it is no longer centered on the marriage with the Sun, which now serves as a subsidiary motif to the Christian journey of the hero.

This fairy tale, perhaps better than any other, gives the impression of being the result of a complex labor of stratification. Around its archaic kernel (the motif of the Sun, his wife, and his daily journey) Christian allegorical motifs have been assembled, most of which were probably created in the Middle Ages, at the time of the formation and fixing of the representations and images concerning the triple localization of the world beyond, in Heaven, Purgatory, and Hell. The form proper to the fairy tale has included all of these motifs within a single narrative.

Among the other archaicizing traits of the story, note the motif of the journey itself, which is used to express a temporal problematic. The voyage to the other world, that is, a spatial displacement, has the function of translating a temporal category, that of eternity. We have said that in certain versions the time the hero spent in the other world seemed very short to him, but in fact he had spent several centuries there. No one recognizes him when he comes back to his village: "They looked in the old record books and found that about three hundred years earlier there had been a family of that name which had since completely died out." This way of expressing time by space and the unfolding of time by displacement in space are used a second time in the tale. For the husband, the Sun (whether he is named as such or not), goes on a daily journey which requires him to leave early in the morning and return only in the evening. The story rarely justifies these regular absences; if it does so, it says that he goes around the world, or that he goes to Heaven. The daily displacement thus expresses a daily periodicity, while the hero's long and laborious journey conveys, by contrast, a long duration, covering several generations, which is too much for human memory to master

Handing on the distaff to the new bride. Sketch by Jules Lecoeur in *Le Monde illustré* of 1865. Paris, Musée des Arts et Traditions populaires. Museum photo.

and which is revealed only in written documents (inscriptions in record books or on tombstones), the image of eternity. The time of a human life lies in between these two times, one of which is periodic and the other, by definition, not periodic. It shares something of the qualities of both: it is periodic in the sense that generations follow one another but is of a longer periodicity than the succession of days and nights, though its prolongation never lasts until its abolition, that is, for eternity. In most of the versions, the end of the hero's journey and (sometimes) his return home are followed by his death, which is the promise of the eternal joys of Heaven for him—since at this point Christianity takes over the narrative again.

The mythic character of the principal motifs of the tale is beyond doubt. If necessary, we can confirm this by comparing the tale with a story collected among the Ossets, a population of the northern Caucasus, among whom a piece of ancient Indo-European mythology has survived in the form of legends about people called the Narts (Dumézil 1930 and 1968–73, and "Popular Customs and Rituals in France"). Sozryko, the hero of the story, is equally well known among the populations neighboring the Ossets, the Chechens and Kabardinians. The tale possesses obvious solar traits.

One day while hunting, Sozryko pursues a hare and shoots all his arrows at it, but it vanishes before his very eyes. The hunt leads him into the Black Mountains, to a black castle of iron, where the daughter of the Sun dwells, guarded by her seven brothers. He immediately asks for her hand, which is granted to him on two conditions: he must bring a hundred deer, a hundred wild sheep, and a hundred head of various kinds of game; and he must fill the four quarters of the castle with leaves from the Aza tree, a tree of heaven. His mother advises Sozryko to go first to the Master of Game and then to his own first wife, now dead, who will ask the Master of the Dead for the leaves. He sets out for the land of the dead; on his way he sees strange spectacles whose meaning he does not understand: a man and a woman lying under the skin of a bull which, although it is enormous, cannot cover the one without uncovering the other, while farther along he sees another couple who fit comfortably under the skin of a hare; he sees two shoes, one of goatskin, the other of pigskin, fighting and jumping on one another. When he finally reaches his late wife she explains the meaning of the strange visions: they are the punishments and rewards for actions on earth. But other encounters are allegories for the future: the puppies lying on a heap of rags who barked at him were announcing the coming insolence of the young. In addition, his wife gives him the leaves from the tree of heaven. To shake off the dead who try to follow him back, Sozryko shoes his horse backward and bursts through the gates of the infernal kingdom. With his game and his leaves he returns to the castle of the seven brothers, who give him their sister, the daughter of the Sun, in marriage (Dumézil, 1930, no. 28).

Despite a great deal of remodeling, this narrative is highly evocative of the French folktale version of the "journey into the other world." The same characters appear, although their distribution is different: a girl, sister, wife or future wife, a brother or brothers, a hero who is clearly solar in the French story, who has solar traits if we consider the whole set of Caucasian stories about him. All of these characters are involved in a voyage to the world beyond. In both cases the journey is crowded with strange spectacles which are only explained afterward in the form of allegories. The allegories are not at all the same in the French folktale and the Caucasian legend, although there are elements common to both, such as the couple united or divided on the ground, or the battle of the two shoes, which is worth comparing with one of the encounters in the French tale. Most versions of that tale say that the hero finds his way blocked by two goats violently butting their heads together, ravens fiercely fighting, two trees banging together with such fury that pieces of wood shoot out of them, and two stones smashing each other brutally. According to the explanation at the end of the story, these are generally two brothers who were enemies during their lifetimes, or two quarreling spouses. The motif of two objects that crash together violently, and through which the hero must pass—the rocks of the Symplegades—is found in a great number of mythologies and designates the perilous entrance to the other world. In what is certainly a weakened form, we find it both in the French folktale and in the Caucasian legend.

Both of these narratives, then, bring together comparable or similar motifs to tell the story of a voyage to the other world, while each orders the motifs in a somewhat different way. While the Caucasian legends have probably undergone less remodeling than the folktales in relation to the ancient stock of Indo-European mythology, they probably do not represent an archaic, original, and primitive state in comparison with the folktales: the Caucasian stories have at least undergone a considerable change in form, since they have passed from myth to legend. But the comparison shows that the common theme and motifs of the two stories are indeed mythic, even if their form is not.

The theme of the voyage to the other world occupies the whole narrative space of this particular story. But it also appears frequently in other French fairy tales, where it does not present the same irreversible character and is often linked instead to the quest for, or a reconquest of, a husband or wife.

In *The Love of Three Oranges* (T408), the initial explicit motif is the quest for a wife.

A young prince breaks a container that belongs to an old woman; she puts a curse on him: he will never be happy until he finds and marries the Love of Three Oranges; or else he desires to marry a girl who is "rosy, black, and white"; or else he simply wants to get married. He goes off on his search; he walks for months or years and finally meets one or more supernatural beings (the Mother of the Winds, for example) who advise him to arm himself with certain objects: their usefulness will be revealed at the castle where the old woman with the three oranges lives. He arrives there after an exhausting voyage, and thanks to the objects, which are exactly right for the job, manages to get to the old woman's room; he steals the three oranges from her and runs away. On the way back he cuts one of the three oranges in two, and a marvelously beautiful girl comes out of it, asks him for something to drink, and dies, since he has no water to give her. The same thing happens with the second orange, so he waits until he finds a fountain to open the third. This time the girl quenches her thirst and survives. But he leaves her by the fountain in order to go and find clothing and ornaments for her worthy of the rank she is going to have. During his absence a witch, black woman, or Moorish woman takes her place after turning the girl into a dove or a fish. The prince, surprised to find her so ugly, marries her anyway, or gets ready to marry her, since she blames her transformation on her long wait. But the dove attracts the prince's attention, and he breaks her enchantment.

This lovely tale is typical of the stories of the quest. That it is a journey into the other world is hardly in doubt: the great length of the journey, its difficulties, and the meetings with supernatural characters mark it clearly, as does the marvelous origin of the girl whom he desires. Indeed, the very motive of the journey is desire, desire for a woman without even knowing whether she exists, desire inflicted on the hero by an old woman. In this sense we can speak of a journey of initiation, if initiation consists of the adolescent's tearing himself away from the influence of his mother to become integrated into the society of men. Success in this transitional passage is rewarded with the possibility of marriage. In so-called primitive societies, this passage takes place by means of rituals that are often demanding, long, and complex. European societies, on the other hand, in which initiation rites as such have never existed or have not existed for a very long time, nevertheless maintain the idea of an initiation, a purely imaginary one, since it appears more or less clearly in folktales. The initiation essentially consists of a journey, beginning with a departure from home in which can be seen the symbolic rupture of the Oedipal ties. The voyage leads to another world which is not necessarily conceived of as a world of the dead: strictly speaking, it is a world that lies beyond the human world. A young Ojibwa Indian leaves his family and village to retire to a deserted place where he fasts and meditates until a supernatural being appears to him and becomes his guardian spirit. In fact, all initiation rituals have a phase in which the initiate is supposed to be dead, that is, they always include a passage to the world beyond.

The theme of the voyage in fairy tales thus represents, on the one hand, the adolescent's flight from and break with his Oedipal feelings and, on the other hand, the winning of magical objects and a beautiful bride who brings gifts; she is often the daughter of a king. The journey is thus charged with the possibility for him to become a hero, often by triumphing over his own brothers: thus in the version of *The Love of Three Oranges* from Guyenne, only the youngest of the three brothers receives from an old woman the fruits (here they are apples) containing the marvelous young women, since only he was kind to her; his two older brothers, who set off with him "to seek their fortune as if it were something you could pick up along the side of the road," come back empty-handed, since they refused to help the old woman in distress.

In all these tales the hero is male. Are there any in which he is replaced by a heroine, and do they show the same narrative pattern? There are, of course, stories in which the main character is a girl or a young woman, but while they too contain the motif of the voyage to the world beyond, their lesson is quite different. The most important of these tales in terms of the number of versions and the beauty, variety, and richness of the story is entitled *The Search for the Lost Husband* (T425). The ancient story of Psyche as told by Apuleius in *The Golden Ass* is one of its European forms, although it is not the prototype. *Beauty and the Beast* is another of its forms. Here is the version from Gascony collected by J. F. Blade (1886).

A Green Man with one eye has three daughters, each more beautiful than the next. One evening the King of the Ravens comes to ask for one of the daughters in marriage, and to force him to agree he puts out the Green Man's one eye. The youngest daughter accepts him in order to restore her father's sight; the marriage is celebrated and the bridegroom carries her off to his castle, which lies three thousand leagues away, "in the land of cold, in the land of ice, where there are no trees or greenery." At midnight, in the darkness, the King of the Ravens reveals that he and his people were changed into ravens by a sorceror. His penance must last for seven more years, and until then his bride must not try to see him at night when he takes off his feather clothing and lies down next to her, separated by a sword. In the morning before daybreak he gets up and goes out. During the day the poor bride wanders around, always alone, in the ice and snow; but one day she comes to a poor hut; next to it a wrinkled old woman is washing linens as black as soot and singing a refrain that says she is waiting for the "married virgin" to come. The girl helps her wash her clothes, which become as white as milk. The old woman foretells trials for her, but promises to help her in the day of her greatest need. Seven years, less one day, pass, and that night the girl decides to see what her husband looks like. He is as beautiful as the day. She brings the candle closer, and a drop of wax falls onto him; he wakes up and sadly tells her that since she has violated the prohibition, he has fallen back into the power of the sorceror. The sorceror chains him to the peak of a high mountain on an island and sets two wolves to guard him: one is white and keeps watch during the day; the other is black and keeps watch at night. The young wife leaves the castle and goes back to the old washerwoman's cottage. The washerwoman tells her where her husband is being held prisoner and gives her magical objects: an inexhaustible sack and an inexhaustible gourd, iron slippers, and a golden knife for cutting "the blue grass, the grass that sings night and day, the grass that breaks iron." When her slippers break, it will be almost time for her to rescue her husband. She walks for one year through the land "where there is neither night

"Fairy tales." Cover of a chapbook. Woodcut. Épinal, Pellerin. Paris, Musée des Arts et Traditions populaires. Museum photo.

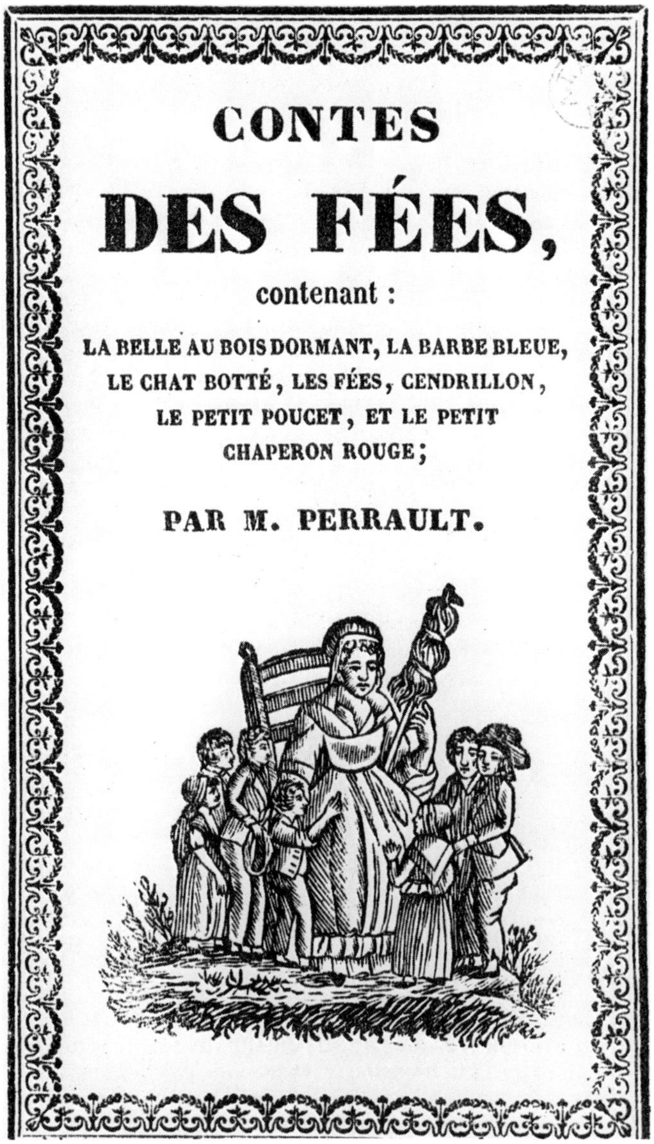

nor moonlight, where the sun always shines"; then for another year in the land "where there is neither day nor night, where the moon always shines"; finally for a third year in the land "where there is neither sun nor moon, and it is always night." There she finds the grass that cuts iron: her iron slippers are broken. She gathers the grass and sets off again, walking until she finds the sun. At the edge of the sea she takes a boat, disembarks on the island where her husband is being held prisoner, puts the wolves to sleep with the singing grass, kills them with the golden knife, breaks the chain of seven hundredweight with the grass that breaks iron, and frees her husband and all his people, who had been turned into ravens.

In this story, then, it is the young girl who must undertake the journey to the world beyond, characterized in this version by cold, ice, darkness, emptiness, and great distance. But unlike what we see when the hero is male, marriage is not the result of the adventure, its crown and reward: marriage represents, rather, something already given at the beginning of the narrative. For the heroine the marriage is acquired almost from the start, but it appears to be an unhappy union with a repulsive creature, a monstrous animal, whom she agrees to marry through filial piety to free her father from a terrible evil or even to save him from death. By overcoming a terrible trial she succeeds in transforming the monstrous marriage into a happy union with a prince "as beautiful as the day." But first she violates a prohibition, and this greatly delays her final happiness.

We see then that the lesson of this story is different from those in which the hero is male. The adolescent boy must undergo an initiation before he can find a bride and accede to the married state; the girl undergoes the same kind of initiation during marriage and through her own fault, because she violates the taboo laid down by her husband. While the nature of the initiation may be the same for both—a voyage full of difficulties to the other world—its meaning is different in the second case: it seems that for girls it is marriage itself that constitutes the initiation. The *Laws of Manu,* the early collection of texts from ancient India compiled between the second century B.C. and the second century A.D., confirms this hypothesis: "For a woman, marriage replaces initiation. Her zeal to serve her husband is for her what study and discipline under the Brahman are for a man, her care in keeping house is equivalent to his maintenance of the sacred fire." For the woman must transform the attachment she has to her father into affection for and devotion to her husband, who appears to her, in a patriarchal society like that of the ancient Indo-Europeans and the cultures that developed from it, as a horrifying monster. One of the forms of the prohibition laid down by her husband consists, in a fairly large number of versions, of not staying too long with her family when she goes to visit them, as she is permitted to do after her marriage. She obeys this rule once, twice, but the third time she goes she forgets the time. That is, the taboo the heroine transgresses is that against remaining too attached to her natal family. As punishment she must suffer a long trial to win her husband back and so to prove her devotion to him. In patrilineal societies, such as Indo-European societies past and present, brides are usually foreigners: they come from a different family, a different lineage. They are introduced into a family that is not their own to fulfill a duty that is essential to the future of this family, i.e., to bear children. It is thus necessary to test their loyalty, devotion, and zeal toward their husbands; this trial constitutes their initiation which, unlike that of the boy, takes place at the time of marriage. This initiation, which has disappeared from the rituals of the Indo-European peoples (assuming that it ever existed), is no longer present except in the popular realm of the imaginary, in the myths underlying their fairy tales. The motif of the voyage to the world beyond, which thus goes back to the initiation of young people, girls or boys, is not, of course, the only mythical motif that appears in these stories, but it is certainly the most important, the richest, and the most persistently fascinating.

N.B./j.l.

BIBLIOGRAPHY

See "Mythic Elements in French Folklore," above.

Folk Beliefs and Legends about Fairies in France

Although they are different in form, beliefs and legends are comparable in their modes of production and their functions. It has often been observed that beliefs engender legends through a process of narrative development: a belief may be expressed in a sentence or unfolded in an account. Such an account always includes specific information about time and place, which are often nearby. Anatole Le Braz, who had noted this phenomenon in his investigations, states it very clearly in the introduction to his book, *The Legend of Death among the Armoricain Bretons* (1923):

> The legend is a local product: we have seen it take root, grow, and flower. It is perpetually in the course of formation and transformation: it is alive. The actors that it brings into play are known or have been known to all. They are the people of the canton, of the parish; they are your neighbors, they are you yourselves. . . . The setting is also real: it lies before your very eyes, at your door. It is the sunken road you have passed over a hundred times, the moor that you see here made fuzzy by gorse, the cemetery enclosed in the dark greenery of great yew trees; it is the sea.

In his book, one can see clearly how the mechanism functions by which belief engenders legend. For example, Le Braz relates the following belief (which is not peculiar to Brittany, since it is certainly found throughout all of France): "As long as a dead person is lying out on the funeral platform, it is an offense to him to send the people of the house out to work in the fields, as if nothing had happened" (1, p. 220). After setting forth this prohibition, he goes on to cite the account of one of his female informants, an account which she had related as a personal reminiscence:

> While she was a servant girl at Kersaliou, the master of the house died. It was the beginning of July, and the eldest son was out haying with the household staff. They

Farmhouse mill and raised stone. Saint-Pierre, Morbihan. Photo Musée des Arts et Traditions populaires.

heard the news at the three o'clock collation. When this was over, the eldest son sent the servants back to work, in spite of being told that such was not the custom. Returning to the field, they perceived a man trampling down the hay, whom they recognized to be their deceased master. The vision disappeared. They finished their work and brought in the hay. The time came a few months later to begin using that hay as forage for the animals. But within a few days all the animals in the stable died, and the veterinarian was unable to do anything for them. The ruined son began drinking, and hanged himself on Christmas night: his failure to respect his dead father had brought about his misfortune.

We can see very clearly in this account the narrative development which has the initial belief for its object. This belief, far from being fixed like a dogma, plays a part in everyday experience and produces its events, which only take on their meaning when they are reconstituted in a narrative form. Here we encounter once again what Henri Hubert affirmed in his study "The Representation of Time in Religion and Magic" (1909): "Myths are rejuvenated in history. They draw out from it elements of reality which serve to consolidate the belief of which they are the object as myths. . . . The rejuvenation of myths is not a phenomenon that is different from the general phenomenon of their localization in the past, but a particular form of the same phenomenon."

"Myths rejuvenated in history" are nothing but legends. It is precisely by virtue of this phenomenon of renewal in and through history that legends are diverse, unstable, and abundant. As the collection of Anatole Le Braz so clearly shows, the same belief may give rise to a great number of different accounts. But one nevertheless always finds in them the generative mythic core that is the belief.

The same phenomenon of the engendering of legends from beliefs is also found in what may be called the topographic mythology of France, in which the principal protagonists are fairies, supernatural beings characterized by their small or Gargantuan size.

Beliefs about fairies are an excellent example of the interpretation of folkloric facts in terms of survivals. A. Maury forcefully declares that "fairies appear to us to be the last and most persistent of all of the vestiges that paganism left imprinted on peoples' minds" (1896). For him, fairies are the inheritors of the characteristics and functions of the Parcae and of the name of Fatum or the Fata, these being no more than the Roman designation for the Parcae. The etymology from *fatum, fata* is certain. As for the attributes of fairies, it cannot be denied that they greatly overlap those of the Parcae.

Like the Parcae, fairies preside over childbirth and decide the fate of the newborn child. They are, as was once said, "wombmates." In Brittany, they were served a meal in a room next to that of the mother who had given birth, as a means of conciliating them. They are also spinners. Van Gennep reports in his *Folklore of Burgundy* (1934, p. 175) that at Clamerey, a fairy named La Beuffenie formerly came to thread her distaff at midnight in a secluded place, on a crag that dominated Armançon. It is sometimes said that menhirs or rocks are distaffs planted in the ground by fairies. The association made about the Parcae between their function as dispensers of fate and their character as spinners is not found explicitly for fairies, although such an association may be postulated on the basis of the great importance of the symbol of the thread of destiny in Europe. But fairies have characteristics that the ancient Parcae do not have. Fairies are connected with the megaliths. The relationship is sometimes only toponymic, resulting in the appellations of the Rock of the Fairies, the Stone of the Fairies, the Cabin of the Fairies, the Cave of the Fairies, etc., to describe menhirs, dolmens, and shady walks throughout France. At times the designations are accompanied by legends:

> Long ago, a fairy traveling through Sainte-Colombe (Landes) carrying the Peyre-Lounque (a rock located in the region) attached to her distaff, met an unknown old man who said to her: "Where are you going?" "To Dax." "You will, if you say, 'And may it please God.'" "Whether or not it pleases Him, the Peyre-Lounque is going to Dax." The old man, who was none other than God himself, ordered her to abandon her rock at that very place, which she had to do, and he added, "Until it pleases God, it will not leave this place." (Sébillot, 1904–7, vol. 4, p. 6)

Sometimes they carry these enormous rocks in their aprons: a rockslide near Ailly in the Vosges is called the Burden or the Fairies' Load—it fell from their aprons. But they are not content merely to spread megaliths around: they are also builders. Near Remiremont, a causeway built with Cyclopean masonry which joins Saint-Mont to the mountain of Morthome bears the name of the Bridge of the Fairies. The amphitheater of Cimiez is called the "Tub of the Fairies." In Poitou, the fairy Mélusine constructed the old roads of the region, as well as the arenas and aqueducts of Poitiers and a great number of chateaux: one night was sufficient for her to build the castle of Lusignan.

This role of builder is totally unknown among the Parcae. It is thus incorrect to see fairies as the heirs of the Parcae merely on the basis of two shared characteristics. The other characteristics of fairies should connect them on the one hand with the popular figure of Gargantua, and on the other with the supernatural and innumerable populations of goblins, elves, sprites, imps, etc.

In French topographical beliefs and legends, Gargantua shapes the countryside, particularly irregularities in terrain.

> In the canton of Châtillon-sur-Indre, people give the name of "foot scrapings of Gargantua" to large mounds, of which the largest is the Footstep of Bourges, located near Clion. It is maintained that once, when Gargantua had one foot in Bourges and the other in this place, he shook one of his shoes, and thus flung his foot-scraping (the mass of clayey soil that sticks to the bottom of the shoes of people who walk in the rainy season) next to the church of Murs, two leagues from Clion, while the other shoe dropped another scraping in the vineyards of Château, close to Bourges, which has been called Mottepelous from time immemorial. (Sébillot, 1883, p. 197–98)

Gargantua is the source of the elevation upon which the city of Laon is built: finding his basket to be too full, he emptied part of it onto the plain, which became a mountain. But it was not only by unloading that he shaped the irregularities in the terrain; it was also, as Rabelais himself said, "en fyantant et compissant (in shitting and pissing)." "In the Chartreuse range, the Aiguille de Quaix is known in

Mélusine returning to suckle her child. Couldrette, Bibliothèque nationale MS fr. 12575, folio 89. Photo BN.

the area by the name of l'Etron de Gargantua (Gargantua's Turd). The giant, needing to stop to satisfy a bodily need, placed one foot on the helmet of Nero and the other on Mount Rachais. The needle (Aiguille) does seem to resemble this object from a certain angle. Gargantua pissed at the same time, which is what produced the cascade of Vence." His appetite is not described as any less formidable in popular tradition than it is in Rabelais. He is a glutton who swallows, without noticing them, enormous boats, which he takes to be small flies. But he is sometimes nauseated and vomits them, thus forming the rock of Bé near Saint-Cast, for example.

All of these beliefs and the accounts that develop them are to be found in nearly identical form throughout France, in which Gargantua mythically modeled not so much the landscape in its totality as the most remarkable accidental landforms. The means he uses for this are of an oral and anal nature, so that a mythic character may be seen in him that comes from those two stages of infantile development. His gigantic size has its source in the inverted projection of the disproportionate view that children have of adults and the world.

Tradition often stresses, on the other hand, fairies' diminutive size. They manipulate—it is said—materials which, if they are not always construction materials, are nevertheless hard and resistant. They sometimes carry them in the form or manner of distaffs, or else in their aprons: Gargantua carries malleable materials in his basket or in his stomach (earth, excrement). These characteristics of fairies are clarified if, in opposition to the character of Gargantua, one sees in them phallic figures which would thus belong to the following stage of infantile sexual development.

In their contacts with humans, fairies manifest a certain ambivalence, just like the numerous populations of various goblins, who resemble them in their diminutive size. They render services to humans, but it is difficult to have social ties with them because of their sensitive and skittish character. In the Alps and Pyrenees, those supernatural beings of small stature who help the herders are called servants; in exchange, they are left small offerings in kind, such as the first skimming of the best cream. If one neglects to leave them their share, they may take cruel vengeance, for example, by leading the herd over a cliff and leaving the region forever.

Sometimes the relations between fairies and humans extend to marriage: the legend of Mélusine is the best known of these, but there are a great number of others which always include a prohibition which the husband must scrupulously respect. The nature of the prohibition is quite varied: not to see his fairy-wife while she is bathing, not to see her on Saturday, not to look at her naked shoulder, not to call her a "bad fairy," etc. The union brings prosperity, but one day the husband violates the prohibition and the fairy disappears forever. It is striking to note the frequency of this denouement in accounts which relate the variety of relationships between humans and the small supernatural beings. They disappear, leave the country, and never appear again. The pattern is so marked that one cannot help but wonder whether the etiology of these accounts does not reside precisely in this matter: they exist to explain the disappearance of fairies, goblins, and other sprites, which is due to a fault of men who are unable to maintain good relations with them over long periods of time, in spite of the advantages of such associations. What we see here is a schema similar to that of the great origin myths of primitive peoples, which place at the beginnings of humanity a golden age in which all things were realizable and death did not exist. As the result of a sin, the violation of a taboo, all of the advantages enjoyed by humanity are withdrawn, and relations with the supernatural beings are interrupted or grow difficult. This is a particularly good example of the process of weakening from mythology to folklore: it is no longer a question of the fate of humanity or the social community, but of the fate of an individual and the outcome of his conjugal union and prosperity.

These legends also manifest, more or less explicitly, a symbolic teaching: the world of fairies and sprites disappeared in the face of Christianity because they belonged to paganism. Once again the ideology of survivals is at work: legends about fairies and their relations with humans are very much of the present, but they tell of a past regarded as finished. The past nevertheless remains inscribed in various places which thus serve as the basis for remembering it.

N.B./d.w.

BIBLIOGRAPHY

See "Mythic Elements in French Folklore."

Popular Customs and Rituals in France

In the preface to his book *Les Saints successeurs des dieux* (The saints: successors of the gods) (1907), P. Saintyves let it be known that his work would be followed by another volume entitled *La Mythologie des rites* (The mythology of rituals), in which he intended to examine the pagan rites that persisted in the cult of the saints and led to the development of certain hagiographic legends. This work never saw the light of day, but its suggestive title raises the question of whether it is proper to speak of a mythology of rituals.

For Saintyves, the transition from myth to ritual was never in question. Referring to the tales of Perrault, he maintains that "a myth is but the exegesis of or the commentary on a ritual," which allows him to regard the stories as the narrative relics of ancient seasonal or initiation rituals that have fallen into disuse. Cinderella is thus the Bride of the Cinders, paraded around on Shrove Tuesday and promised to the young sun, while her stepmother is the old year, and the stepmother's daughters are the months preceding spring. Tom Thumb is the young boy who must undergo initiation rites; he is led by his father into the initiation enclosure, the forest, where he must undergo a number of trials.

I. The Popular Rituals of Marriage

This theory assumes a historical process of degeneration and argues that the evolution proceeds from ritual to myth. If we make an effort to avoid this historicizing point of view, and if we consider the materials of ritual and myth to be coupled in an ongoing relationship, we may then argue that myths and rituals are, in the words of Claude Lévi-Strauss, "different transformations of identical elements." We shall attempt to show this by taking as an example a popular ritual of marriage that was quite widespread in France at least until the end of the nineteenth century, a ritual that is called the "hidden bride," the "false bride," or the "substitute bride." The following description was published in 1823, but its author observed the ritual in Bresse before the Revolution (Monnier, pp. 355–56).

> The day set for signing the contract is commonly the eve of the marriage celebration. Before supper, a peculiar scene unfolds among the Bressans: the bride-to-be invites several of her girlfriends to her house where they put on one another's clothes and move into a separate room. The groom-to-be then shows up with his friends and his brothers and finds the house locked up. They knock at the door and ask about a ewe they have lost. They are told that there is no ewe there that belongs to them, but they are persistent and finally gain entry into the house and search every room. When they get to the door to the room with the girls in it, they knock, ask again, and receive the same answer as before. Finally, one person comes out and, after asserting that he has just checked to see that there was no strange ewe in his flock, makes all the young maidens file out one by one. The husband-to-be makes them dance successively, and if he fails to recognize his bride-to-be, he becomes the object of banter for the rest of the evening.

There are many parallels to this amusing description, among them one that George Sand recounts in the appendix to *La Mare au Diable,* and another, more recent one that originated in the province of the Loire and was in practice until about 1920 (Fortier-Beaulieu).

The young men on the groom's side show up at the door of the bride's house on the morning of the wedding. Everything is locked. They climb over the wall and sing in the courtyard so that the door may be opened for them. They finally get in, but the bride-to-be hides in the hayloft, behind her grandmother's bed, in the kneading trough, or in the covered tipcart, or else she is disguised as a pipe-smoking beggar sitting by the fireplace or as an old woman. In some villages, they used to throw down a dummy called "the ghost," or "the first bride," to the young men assembled in front of the house and then burn it in the farmyard.

These scenes surely have a playful element, but they could not have been enacted for the sole purpose of entertaining the wedding guests, especially the young men. An apparently insignificant clue suggests that this ritual was so important that just as it was disappearing a new element came to pick up a part of the meaning of the former practice. At the time when the custom was waning in the country in France, i.e., between 1870 and 1880, the bridal gown as we know it today came into fashion: the white dress and veil. The function of the veil may have been to conceal the bride temporarily, when the ritual of the hidden bride was no longer performed; for the veil harkens back through the centuries to the custom in ancient Rome, where *nubere* meant both to veil and to marry.

The symbolism of this ritual may first be deciphered on the social level. It is meant to express and play upon the reservations felt by the "wife givers," which is what at that moment the parents and friends of the bride happen to be, toward the "wife takers," the groom's party. This can only be a game, since it takes place at a moment in the long process of betrothal and marriage when the marriage agreement has

Peasants carrying firebrands in the fields on Christmas Eve. Tonneins (Lot-et-Garonne). Drawing by Gustave Janet. Photo Musée des Arts et Traditions populaires, Paris.

The lamb cart at Christmas. Les Baux. Photo Musée des Arts et Traditions populaires, Paris.

long since been concluded and would be very difficult to undo.

But the ritual has a deeper symbolic level that reaches down to the underlying myth. To bring it to light, we must call on a set of supernatural stories known in the international typology as the substitute bride (T403). One of the finest versions in French was collected by J. F. Bladé in 1886 and is entitled *Le Drac*.

By his first wife, a man has two strong, brave sons and a daughter as beautiful as the morning. His wife dies, and he marries a wicked, ugly widow who has a daughter who resembles her in every way. She persecutes her stepchildren until the two exasperated brothers leave for the war in order to distinguish themselves; they promise to find a husband for their sister, and they take a little statue with them made in her likeness (in other versions, it is a portrait). They demonstrate such courage in war that the son of the king of France summons them. He sees the statuette, falls in love with their sister, and orders them to fetch her so that he may marry her. The jealous stepmother, with her daughter, escorts the two brothers and the bride-to-be, who is dressed in her wedding gown. On the way, the stepmother intercepts the communication between the brothers and the sister and forces the sister to take off her wedding clothes. She puts them on her own daughter and throws the bride-to-be into a mud pit. The king's son, furious to see such an ugly girl arrive, sends the two brothers, the stepmother, and her daughter to their deaths. (In other French versions the prince marries the homely girl because he falls victim to the stepmother's magic spell.) The true bride-to-be is first rescued by a gardener's wife and then carried off by the Drac into his underwater kingdom. He ties her to a long gold chain that allows her to reach the shore. For three days she sings a riddling song that intrigues the prince's servants. The prince is alerted, breaks the chain, and recognizes the girl as his promised bride. (In the versions in which the prince kept the false bride and the stepmother, he expels the intruder and punishes her mother severely.)

In this story as in the ritual, a bride is temporarily hidden from her groom and replaced by a false bride. This thematic core is enriched in the tale with important imaginary developments that the ritual cannot afford. The theme, however, is the same. What is its meaning?

If we accept Claude Lévi-Strauss's contention that men exchange women in the same way that they exchange words, it is easy to recognize in the tale of the substitute bride the transfer of a woman to a man, the prince, her future husband, a transfer brought about by another man, her brother; the transfer is interrupted by the stepmother and then reestablished. The interruption of the transfer is achieved by the interruption of communication between the brother and sister. Coming as an intermediary between them, the stepmother alters the brother's words and is thus able to eliminate the sister and to substitute her own daughter, the false bride-to-be. But if women stopped circulating among men, marriages could only be incestuous. The false bride-to-be of the ritual and the tale is a representation of the imaginary incestuous bride-to-be and is substituted in play for a brief moment in place of the true bride-to-be, the one whom it is socially permissible to marry.

This interpretation of the tale, and later of the ritual, is confirmed by a story that is not French but most certainly belongs to the Indo-European mythical heritage. We are referring to a story that is part of the Nart epic that was made known to us by G. Dumézil (1930, 1968–73). This collection of popular epic legends is characteristic of some populations of the northern Caucasus, from the Black Sea to the Caspian Sea, and most particularly of the Ossets, the probable descendants of the ancient Scythians, among whom the narrative tradition has proved to be the most long-lived, though their neighbors, the Chechen-Ingush, Cherkess, and Abkhaz have sizable fragments in the form of variants. The saga of the Narts, fabulous heroes who lived in very ancient times, is of considerable interest: in a "folklorized" form, it has preserved to this day features of ancient Indo-European mythology, particularly the trifunctional organization of society identified by Georges Dumézil.

This epic presents an extremely popular female character, remarkable for her birth, beauty, and intelligence: the Prin-

The new fire of Holy Saturday. Copperplate. Paris, Picard, 1724. The rekindling of the fires is prescribed by the Roman rite, but it is also a ritual found in a large number of religious systems and carries a cosmological meaning and function. Paris, Musée des Arts et Traditions populaires. Museum photo.

cess Satana. The story of her wedding may be viewed as a parallel to the ritual and tale of the substitute bride. This reading of the story is much more direct, much cruder, but all the more interesting in that we are dealing with a tradition that originates in Indo-European mythology and is better preserved, less worked over and altered, than the French tradition.

Satana is the sister of the two high-ranking heroes from one of the three principal families of the Nart epic, the Äxsärtägkats, characterized by valor and strength; one of the other two families is distinguished by abundant cattle and the other by intelligence. When she is old enough to marry, Satana asks herself who is the man most worthy of her and concludes that only her own brother, Uryzmäg, is bold and intelligent enough for her. She sees only one obstacle to this project: he is already married. Nevertheless, she shares her project with him: "No one gives away his finest possession as a gift. Would it not be a pity for me to go over to another family? So I can marry only you." He repels her indignantly; she must therefore practice deceit. Some time later, Uryzmäg sets out on an expedition for a year and orders his wife to prepare food and drink for his return. When the year has nearly elapsed, she dutifully proceeds to prepare the intoxicating beverage of the Narts. Try as she may, she cannot make the liquid, because Satana has prevented this by a magic spell. The desperate wife asks her sister-in-law to come to her aid. Satana consents on condition that her brother's wife will lend her her wedding gown and veil for one night. The wife agrees and soon the drink is ready. Uryzmäg comes home; a great feast takes place and at night Satana dressed as the wife takes the wife's place in the conjugal bedroom. Through magic she prolongs the wedding night beyond its normal duration. When the legitimate wife dies of a broken heart, Satana reveals her true identity to her brother, who is at first horrified and then resigned.

Carnival in Paris. Woodcut by Gangel in Metz. Photo Musée des Arts et Traditions populaires, Paris.

It would be hard not to see in this account one of the primitive forms of the French tale and ritual despite the alterations they have undergone, alterations that change the reading but not the meaning. The tale and the ritual show that in all marriages there is the risk and temptation of incest, which is conjured up and played out in this manner to make it easier to avoid it. The Ossetic account shows this incest as having been realized, but it is realized by supernatural heroes and not by human beings, since the narrative form is that of a legend: this is another way to avoid incest.

This example of the deciphering of a ritual through a story need not imply that the myth predates the ritual and serves as its basis. These are two different forms of expression, one of which, myth, enjoys greater freedom in the realm of the imaginary and thus allows us to register a greater number of elements that may lead to an interpretation. On the other hand, what ritual loses in the imaginary realm, it gets back in the form of the considerable affective impact of enactment. In this light, the old debate about the priority of one of the forms or the other is no longer at issue.

This popular ritual of marriage, which seems to stem from

a common Indo-European source, may be classified in the very important category of rites of passage. The inventor of this heuristic concept, Arnold van Gennep (1909), placed under this rubric not only the rituals that mark the course of a human life from the cradle to the grave but also those that mark the passage of time, that is, periodical and cyclical, seasonal and calendrical ceremonies. Among the first kind, marriage was certainly the most important and the most developed. Baptism, which marked the newborn child's entrance into the social and religious community, long remained a ceremony restricted to a very small number of individuals. And although funerals sometimes brought the entire local community together, the authority of the Church acted as an obstacle to any significant development of popular rituals on these occasions.

II. Bonfires, Stakes, Firebrands, Fire Wheels, Christmas, Lent, and Midsummer Day

Among the numerous periodic rituals, those that involve the use of fire, whether bonfires or firebrands, are particularly noteworthy because of the mythical content one is tempted to see in them. In France, as in most European countries, rituals of fire were performed during the cycles of Christmas, Lent, and Midsummer Day (24 June). The dates of Christmas and of Midsummer Day fall close to those of the winter and summer solstices (21 December and 21 June). As a result, authors have viewed these holidays as Christianized forms of pagan solar cults. Despite the denials by van Gennep, who insisted that these were *not* solstitial ceremonies, the near coincidence of the dates is striking, though it does not fully explain the content of the rituals as they were performed.

The bonfires of the cycle of Shrove Tuesday–Lent are, within the general schema, related to those of Midsummer Day. In fact, in most instances they are mutually exclusive: wherever fires are made during Lent, they are not made on Midsummer Day, and vice versa. The rule is not absolutely general, since there are some folkloric zones where the practice takes place at both times of the year. Such places, however, are rare and are situated mostly at points of contact between areas of Midsummer Day bonfires (northwestern, western, southwestern, southeastern France) and areas of Shrove Tuesday–Lent fires (eastern, central-eastern France). The general schema of ceremonies of bonfires and firebrands calls for a celebration at each solstice except when the summer celebration is replaced by another one scheduled halfway through the cycle, at around the time of the equinox. This very general arrangement shows that the part of the year that is ceremonial in this respect begins at the moment when the day begins to grow longer and ends when it stops growing longer; the beginning of the period is marked by a bonfire ritual at home and the end—or the midpoint—by a communal bonfire ritual.

During the Twelve Days of Christmas, that is, the period from Christmas to Epiphany, there were few localities where bonfires or firebrands were lighted. The custom practiced at Pertuis in the Vaucluse is therefore noteworthy because of its rarity. The feast of the Beautiful Star, fully described in the eighteenth century by the Abbé Achard, was celebrated on the eve of Epiphany. This is how an observer at the beginning of the twentieth century described it: "The star is nothing but a cart with its rear carriage loaded with flammable material. In front sits a man who seems to drive the team. The cart is drawn by ten or twelve animals and crosses the town at full gallop to the acclaim of all the people. Buckets of water are poured at every moment over the firebox so as to prevent the flame from reaching the driver. If the fire flares up, it is a sure sign of a good crop. . . . But if the fire goes out or does not rise in a spiral, the crop will be poor, and everyone goes home unhappy. After the ride, the cart is unloaded in the town square and whoever gets hold of a burning firebrand first and carries it home to his hearth will bring good fortune there" (van Gennep, 1937–58, p. 3043). This curious moving bonfire, which represents the star followed by the Magi, thus determines whether crops will be good or bad, while its firebrands protect the house.

In some festivities in the Christmas cycle, firebrands are carried as individual torchlights. In and around Dreux, the processions of the Flaming Coals took place on Christmas Eve. The torches were pieces of wood dried in an oven and split lengthwise down the middle. The children's torches were mullein stems dipped in oil. All the townspeople would gather by neighborhoods around five in the afternoon and assemble at the Town Hall, where the clergy and the magistrates would join them. From there they would all walk three times around the covered market and the Church of Saint-Pierre, shouting "Noël, nolet, nolet." Upon returning to their neighborhoods, the people would lay down their torches to form a bonfire with the nonburning ends facing outward. They would then bring the remainder of that end piece back home with them to ward off misfortune. "This procession would take place in surprising order and with great respect, considering the size of the crowd." It was also said that the fire from the torches did not scorch or hurt. The circumambulation of the market and the presence of shepherds who had brought lambs with them from nearby farms suggest that the ritual was meant to attract prosperity.

The custom of the Yule log, though not practiced everywhere, was nevertheless much more widespread than the custom of the firebrands. The earliest description of this ritual comes from a student from Basel who was working on a doctorate in medicine at Montpellier. It dates back to 1597.

> On 24 December, Christmas Eve . . . a large log is placed on the andirons in the fireplace, over the fire. When it starts burning, the entire household assembles around the fire and the youngest . . . is supposed to hold a glass full of wine, a piece of bread, and a little salt in his right hand and a lighted candle in his left hand. Then all the boys and the men remove their hats and the youngest (or his father in his place) speaks thus: "Wheresoever the master of the house comes and goes / may God grant him much good / And no evil at all / And may God grant him childbearing women / kidding goats / lambing ewes / foaling mares / kittening cats / rat-bearing rats / And no evil at all, but plenty of good." It is said that the live coals cannot burn through a tablecloth on which they are placed. The people carefully keep the coals the year round. . . . When this has been done, they sit down to an ample meal, without fish or meat, but with excellent wine, preserves, and fruit. The table is set and left overnight, and on it are placed half a glass of wine, bread, salt, and a knife. (van Gennep 1937–58, pp. 3101–5)

This precise description requires only a few additional bits of information that are easily furnished by the accounts of countless regional witnesses. It is sometimes said that the log must be big enough to burn for three days (in which case it is called *Tréfoué*), or even for all twelve days of the cycle. Usually it is supposed to come from a fruit-bearing tree; in this connection, it is not hard to understand the choice of a log from an oak tree, since acorns once were human and animal food, and oak is a hard and slow-burning wood.

The half-burned logs are kept and used in often well-defined magical ways: they protect people and animals from illness; they keep harmful animals away from the house and the fields; they forewarn against the evil spells of sorcerers. Like the fire of Midsummer Day, the fire of the Yule log does not cause burns, nor do its sparks. Sometimes people would hit it with a firebrand in order to make as many sparks fly as possible, while uttering the following formula of prosperity: "So many bushels of wheat, so many jugs of wine" (Auvergne); "As many sparks as little chicks" (Poitou); "As many sheaves and sheaflets as sparks and sparklets" (Côte d'Or). The children would also hit it with a stick to get out the preserves and dried fruits that had been hidden in it for them. People would then say in Burgundy and in Franche-Comté that the log was "vomiting," "pissing," "shitting," or "giving birth."

The ritual of the Yule log is designed to promote prosperity, human, animal, and agricultural. The ritual is in most cases celebrated inside the home and within the family circle. Furthermore, it does not appear as if the Church tried to eradicate it as being superstitious, nor did it try to Christianize it. The few observable Christian embellishments seem to have been added spontaneously and rather late in the process without altering the essence of the ritual. In all of these matters, the fires of Midsummer Day differ from the Yule log. The Church fought long and hard against the Midsummer fires and, unable to eradicate them, tried to give them a Christian veneer through the presence of the clergy and through a process of rationalizing the ritual by assimilating it to the feast of Saint John the Baptist. Moreover, the fires are lighted by the whole local community and out of doors, in the most public way possible: the site is often chosen so that the fire can be seen from a great distance. Thus, not only do the Midsummer Day bonfires differ from the Yule logs in a number of characteristics, but they also have a much more highly developed and much richer ritual. A great number of descriptions of the Midsummer fires are listed in a bibliography in the *Manuel* by van Gennep (1937–58). The following one comes from the marshlands of Poitou; it was published at the beginning of the nineteenth century.

> The eve of Midsummer Day is a great festival throughout the countryside. After sunset, each brings his piece of firewood to the square; the firewood is shaped into a pyramid; the priest then comes forward in a solemn procession and lights the fire. The crackling fire thrills every heart; everyone looks joyful. Young men and women hold hands and are eager to start dancing around the new fire. But the heads of the families are there, and before they give way to the impatient young people, everyone must pass through the salutary flame the thick clump of mullein plants and walnut tree branches which, before the following dawn, must be placed above the door of the main cattleshed. Finally the ceremony is over, the young people remain in possession of the arena, the silence is broken, the groups spring forward, shouts of joy are heard, and there is dancing and singing. In the meantime, the old people warm themselves and place cinders in their clogs to ward off a multitude of ills.

From these descriptions, a certain number of general features of rituals can be identified that are pertinent to this particular ceremony. First, the entire local community participates in the preparation of the bonfire, and each person, even the poorest, contributes a piece of firewood. Sometimes, but more rarely, all the young people are charged with collecting the wood. Second, the lighting is performed by the clergy so that the Church may appear to be in control of what it could not prevent. Third, there is a procession around the fire, sometimes once, sometimes repeatedly, either before, or more often after, the lighting. The procession may make three, nine, or, rarely, fourteen (as in Bresse) full circles around the fire, or it may last until the fire dies out. Rounds are danced by "young people of both sexes" according to the reports of almost all observers. In some localities, the dances predicted and assured a prompt marriage. Fourth, the people made the fire give off as much smoke as possible by throwing herbs and green branches (sometimes bones) on the fire, and people and animals would be exposed to the smoke. Finally, when the fire began to die down, there were still two ritual acts to be performed. The participants, especially the young men and women, would jump over the bonfire once or several times, in order to get certain benefits: to protect themselves from illness, to get married within the year, to enjoy general prosperity. Then the half-burned pieces of firewood would be retrieved and kept in the house throughout the year so they would protect all those who lived in the house, human and animal alike, against lightning, fire, thieves, and sickness. The remains of the Yule log had the same power, and the fire of Midsummer Day, like that of Christmas, is not supposed to scorch.

The other forms of the ritual fires of Midsummer are relatively rare but all the more noteworthy. The most beautiful description, published in 1822, recounts the festival of the fire wheel of Basse-Kontz, in the district of Thionville (Teissier). This village is built halfway up the slope on the left bank of the Moselle River. The top of the slope forms a plateau called the Stromberg. The men and boys of the village go to the top at nightfall, while the women and the girls remain halfway up by the fountain. The wheel is on top; it is a straw cylinder "weighing four to five hundred pounds with a pole going through its center and sticking out three feet on either side. The pole is the rudder which the two drivers of the wheel hold on to." Every inhabitant has willingly provided a bale of straw: refusal to do so would bring certain misfortune in the course of the year. The surplus straw is used to make firebrands. As soon as the wheel is set on fire, two young men grab the ends of the pole and send it rolling down the slope. The goal is to dive into the Moselle river and extinguish what is left of the flaming wheel. But they rarely manage to do it. Success means that there will be a good crop. During this time, the men light straw firebrands, hurl them into the air, and relight them as long as the wheel continues to roll. Some run alongside the wheel. When it passes by the women assembled halfway down, they greet it with shouts.

This ritual clearly reveals an agrarian magic. The proper guidance of the wheel and its immersion in the river are the guarantors and omens of a plentiful harvest in the vineyard. This feature is also present in the bonfires of Midsummer Day, but often more diffusely and less explicitly.

Authors have identified these festivals as the remnants of a pagan cult of the sun. In this regard, the most interesting study was Henri Gaidoz's work on the Gallic sun god (1886). Some Gallic statues represent an individual often naked, bearded, with a full head of hair, and carrying a six-spoked wheel in his hand. More highly Romanized in southeastern Gaul, he seems to have been assimilated to Jupiter. For Gaidoz, the wheel is the image of the sun. There is no shortage of evidence in Indo-European (particularly Indian) mythologies to convince one of this. Furthermore, "the principal Christian festivals were substituted," he claims, "for festivals predating Christianity by quite some time, and for dates that for many centuries had already been devoted to popular cults." Since the two solstices were the most striking dates in popular imagination, the two great festivals of the year must have been scheduled at these times. In fact, we know of only one, the great feast of Mithra, the *Sol invictus,* which was celebrated on December 25. We must not forget, however, that Mithraism, which came from the East, was adopted by the Roman legions at the beginning of the Christian era and was not firmly established among the populations among whom they were camping. As far as the feast of Midsummer Day is concerned, Gaidoz is content to assert that it is "the continuation, under a Christian label, of the feast of the summer solstice, that the wheel, the symbol of our Gallic god, played a major role in these rites, and that our memories of it are not yet lost, though they are becoming fainter every day." This course of development is difficult to prove, for there is no known ancient ceremony celebrated on the summer solstice. Moreover, the first reference to the feast of Midsummer Day dates from the seventh century and appears in a homily of Saint Eloy, who says: "Let no one on Midsummer Day or on certain solemn occasions honoring the Saints practice the observance of the solstices, dances, carols, and diabolical songs." A survival of Germanic paganism is excluded from this, since the oldest reference to the fires of Midsummer Day in Germany dates from 1181. What remains is the problematic Celtic origin. No document indicates that solstitial fires existed in Gaul. Nothing proves that the god of the wheel, most likely a solar deity, was indeed associated with rituals of this kind. To account both for the Gallo-Roman deity and for the popular rites of Midsummer Day, it is enough to see in the wheel and particularly in the flaming wheel an Indo-European symbol of the sun.

It is, however, difficult to exclude totally from the data concerning the popular festivals of Midsummer Day the fact that at this time in the solar year the sun is at its apogee and that it is about to wane. In certain communities of the Auvergne, Bourbonnais, Languedoc, the Vosges, and the Bouches-du-Rhône, people would climb to the top of a hill during the night of June 23–24 to watch the sun rise and to greet it, often with shouts of joy. In this way, they would topographically mark the most extreme point of the sun's summer rising. Curiously, the Church in its efforts to Christianize these moments of rejoicing rationalized their connection with the summer solstice through the hallowed character of John the Baptist. In John 3:30, Saint John the Baptist, speaking of Jesus and introducing himself as his precursor, says, "He must increase and I must decrease," while Saint Augustine, making an error of a few days, says, *"In Johannis nativitate dies decrescit"* (on John's nativity the day decreases). We can see in this an example of the complex process by which French folklore was formed, probably mostly during the high Middle Ages according to the repeated claims of van Gennep. This formation, this invention, is by and large the result of the encounter, sometimes even the collision, between the Christian tradition, well established by that time, and popular mythical creativity.

Symbolically, the fires of Midsummer Day thus represent the sun at the height of its strength, just before it starts decreasing. The symbolism is quite clear in the case of the flaming wheels, since many mythologies represent the sun in this form. But the French rituals of the summer solstice are neither the reflection nor the relic of an improbable solar mythology. They can only really be explained if we consider

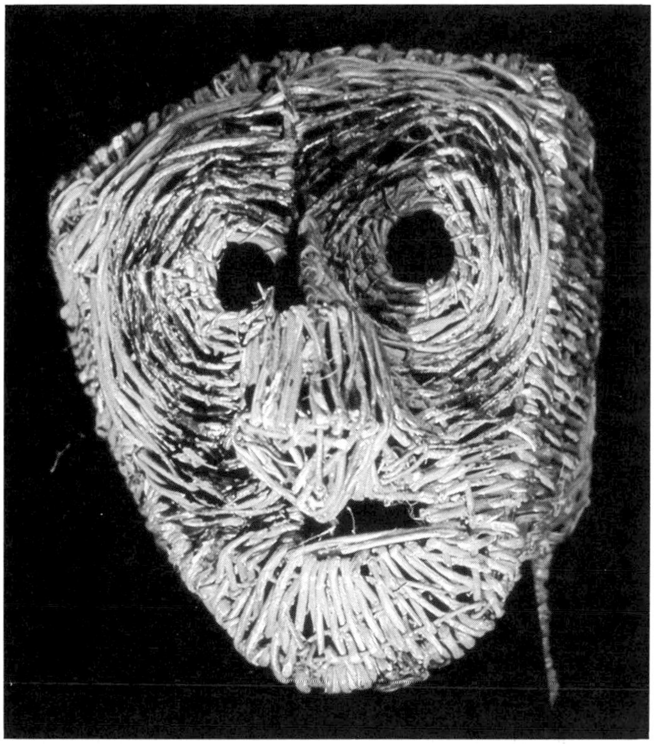

Mask. Aubrac. Photo Musée des Arts et Traditions populaires, Paris.

Midsummer Day bouquet above a cowshed door (Doubs). Photo Musée des Arts et Traditions populaires, Paris.

the general annual system of fires and bonfires: at Christmas, Shrove Tuesday–Lent, and Midsummer Day. It has been said that these rituals defined, in a way, one-half of the ceremonial year. Not that the second part of the year has no calendrical festivals, but they are much rarer and of lesser importance. As a result, the ritual organization of the year does not follow the Celtic calendar that divided the year into two parts in terms of two great festivals: Samain (November 1) and Beltaine (May 1), to which were added two other divisions determined by the festivals called Imbolc (February 1, Feast of Saint Bridget) and Lugnasad (August 1). This calendar did not follow the movement of the sun like the French popular calendar, the key to which rests not so much in solar symbolism as in the accompanying agrarian magic. The increasing sun, represented and supported by fire rituals, is the symbol, the guarantor, and the omen of the growth of plants, the propagation of domestic animals, and the prosperity of human beings. As the youngest in the family in Montpellier would say after the lighting of the Yule log: "And may God grant him childbearing women / kidding goats / lambing ewes / foaling mares / kittening cats / rat-bearing rats / And no evil at all, but plenty of good." All the fires that were lighted between Christmas and Midsummer Day, including Shrove Tuesday and Lent, involved formulas and rituals with an agrarian function. Within this general frame of reference, the rituals of Shrove Tuesday–Lent are partly the doublets of those of Midsummer Day. Of course, they also involve other elements, which the reader will find described in Gaignebet's book on the subject, a book full of erudition, but sometimes questionable from the theoretical point of view.

In the underlying mythology of the calendar ritual system, bonfires and firebrands represent the sun increasing from the winter solstice to the summer solstice, not as the symbols of a forgotten pagan deity but because the nature of fire enables it to materialize the idea of growth and the irresistible burgeoning of plants. Like the plant kingdom, fire moves upward and defies gravity. The Church accorded only a limited place to agrarian rituals (ember days and Rogation Days), but popular mythical thinking spontaneously created those forms of ritual for which it felt the need.

N.B./g.h.

BIBLIOGRAPHY

See the article "Mythic Elements in French Folklore."

Romanticism and Mythology: The Use of Myths in Literary Works

I. In France

According to Schelling, the products of mythology "by their depth, their endurance, and their universality are comparable only to nature itself." Nineteenth-century French literature sought a grand epic synthesis, philosophical and social; this is evident in Balzac's *Human Comedy,* the works of Ballanche, Lamartine's *Visions,* Victor Hugo's *Legend of the Centuries* and *God,* Michelet's *History of France,* and Auguste Comte's *Course of Positive Philosophy.*

Moreover, myths, as Mircea Eliade has pointed out, "reveal the structures of the real and the multiple modes of being in the world." Archaic myths are generally simplifications, designed to facilitate the understanding of the real, whereas later myths, by contrast, complicate forms and relations. The myths elaborated by nineteenth-century writers generally fall into the second category, whether they consciously modified an old myth to give it a new meaning or created a wholly or partially new myth.

At the beginning of the nineteenth century, a debate was launched between supporters of Greek and Roman mythology and partisans of the Christian supernatural. In Germany (see references to Herder below) and in France, many pondered over the origins of mythologies and over the meaning that they should be given.

For our purposes, the century begins with Goethe and Schiller in Germany, with William Blake in England, and in France with Chateaubriand's publication of *The Genius of Christianity* in 1802. This date, a milestone, also happens to be the year of Victor Hugo's birth. From then until 1825 there was a veritable war of mythologies. In a work entitled *On Literature,* which appeared before 1800, Madame de Staël called upon the Olympian Zeus, also known as the celestial Jupiter, to make way for Óðinn. She proposed to replace the fables of the Greeks and Romans with fables by Scottish, Icelandic, and Scandinavian bards, which she mixed together, designating them under the general rubric of Norse Mythology. In fact, as early as 1756, Paul-Henri Mallet had published his *Monuments of the Mythology and the Poetry of the Celts, particularly of the Ancient Scandinavians [sic].* In this work he brought to French readers the poems of the *Edda,* which he introduced as the "Bible of the Norse God Odin." In 1760, James MacPherson published his *Fragments of Ancient Poetry,* which inspired the pseudo-Ossian fashion. According to Madame de Staël, again in *On Literature,* "the shock to the imagination that the Ossianic poems cause inclines one's thought toward the deepest meditations." She thought that this mythology prepared the way for the acceptance of Christianity among the Norse peoples, because she did not understand the violent and bloody character of most of the gods in the *Edda.* It was not by chance that Ossian was one of Napoleon's favorite readings and remained in vogue throughout his reign.

In England, people never stopped reading the Bible. In France, Chateaubriand in the *Genius of Christianity* (1802) took up the defense of the Christian supernatural and recommended that poets seek inspiration in the Bible, in Milton, and in Tasso. It was partly through his influence that the Old Testament was rediscovered and became one of the bedside books of the French romantics.

Germanic influences helped to give the Christian supernatural its full vigor. Among these influences were Gessner's *Idylls* and Friedrich Klopstock's *Messiah* (1758–73). Vigny owed his "Jewish poems" to them, and by 1823 he was ready to institute in France a "Christian theogony" modeled, he claimed, on that of Hesiod. During the Empire, Edward Young's *Night Thoughts* (1742–45) made the Last Judgment a fashionable subject. Milton's *Paradise Lost* was translated into verse by Delille in 1804, and into prose by Chateaubriand in

1836. But Chateaubriand's theories led poets on a false trail. Chateaubriand criticized the epics of Dante, Milton, and Klopstock, condemning any poem in which religion constituted the central subject and not the subordinate theme, "where the supernatural is the *basis* of rather than incidental to the image." In his pamphlet *The Literary Scruples of the Baroness Mme de Staël* (1814), Alexandre Soumet opposed this theory; he wrote: "Could it be that subjects almost entirely based on the supernatural such as *The Messiah* and *Paradise Lost* are the only ones that can henceforth be apprehended by the stern imagination of the moderns? Our epic concepts must touch throughout upon the mysteries of another world." When in 1840 he published *The Divine Epic,* he stated in his preface that he had turned the Muse into a "mystical initiate," adding: "The supernatural, which is only incidental in ancient epics, almost always becomes the very subject of the songs of a modern epic poet. A wholly spiritualist religion commands him."

In order to avoid the sublime monotony that such a conception of an epic might engender, writers resorted to national traditions, fairies, magicians, and witches for the sake of variety. From 1813 to 1817, Marchangy published his eight-volume *Poetic Gaul,* devoting a large part of it to Scandinavian mythology and to an enchanting supernatural derived from Tasso. He claimed that the French national epic was organized around the figure of Charlemagne and that France's national epics might well rival Homeric literature. Charles Nodier emerged as the promoter of this "national" supernatural. In the *Journal of Debates* of 27 November 1817 (an article collected in book 2 of the *Mélanges de littérature,* pp. 317–24), he enthusiastically hailed the completion of the publication of *Poetic Gaul,* and he wrote:

> Look at your fables, your mythology, your old customs, poems, and tragedies: sublime subjects among which we merely have to make a choice, to give the seal of genius, so that in the empire of drama and epic they can take the place of the lamentable and eternal stories of Troy, Argos, Thebes, and Mycenae.

Nodier himself later illustrated the mythology of superstitions with *Trilby* and *The Crumb Fairy.*

The coexistence of Christianity with popular beliefs, some of which go back to prehistoric times, can be astonishing. Nonetheless, Madame de Staël pointed out in *De l'Allemagne* (1810) that popular superstitions are always analogous to the dominant religion, and she added: "A host of beliefs ordinarily attach themselves to religion and history alike." Joseph de Maistre went even further: "Man's worth can only be measured by what he believes. That does not mean that one should believe in nonsense, but it is always better to believe too much than to believe nothing." Moreover, in the tenth homily in the *Soirées in Saint Petersburg* the same author declares that superstition, as the term implies, is something beyond legitimate belief, and that, as such, it is "an advanced work of religion that must not be destroyed." This is a kind of paraphrase of the Gospel parable of the good and bad seed. Notes published by E. Dermenghem argue: "Superstition is the excess of religion . . . We must not believe that religion is one thing and superstition another, rather we should seriously ask ourselves if superstition might not be a necessary advance post of religion" (*Joseph de Maistre the Mystic,* p. 28).

Nodier always claimed that the supernatural answered a fundamental human need, the need to believe. He was later saddened to see popular beliefs on the wane, and would take great pains to preserve their memory. He showed clearly how the frenzied supernatural and the fantastic were born of the decadence of faith. Several works present the confrontation of mythologies. In *The War of the Gods* (1797), Evariste Parny burlesqued the confrontation of gods from various regions. Curiously, this mythological hodgepodge foreshadowed the parades of divine characters in Flaubert's *Temptation of Saint Anthony.* Chateaubriand, looking back with irony on his early work, *The Natchez,* later said, "It shows the supernatural in all its forms—the Christian supernatural, the mythological supernatural, the Indian supernatural: muses, angels, demons, spirits." In *The Martyrs* (1809), too, episodes associated with the religions of the Gauls and the Norse are added to the central struggle between Greco-Roman mythology on the one side and Christianity on the other.

Marchangy suggested as a subject for an epic the reestablishment of the empire by Charlemagne, precisely because it offered an opportunity to depict the gods of various religions. This is what the Vicomte of Arlincourt referred to in the second canto of his epic *Charlemagne, or the Caroleid* (1818), in which the gods Teutates, Óðinn, and Irminsul foment a rebellion against Charlemagne for his role in the spreading of Christianity. Throughout the epic (which has no less than twenty-four cantos), many mythologies are brought together. One step farther and it would be syncretism. This can already be found in Fabre d'Olivet, the author of *The Loves of Rose and Ponce de Meyrueis* (1803), who wrote a poem entitled *The Troubadour,* made up of five cantos and written in the archaic French of the langue d'oc. In this last work, the angel Gabriel is assimilated to Cupid, and Mary to Juno; Mary Magdalene becomes a figure of Mylita-Astarte as well as Aphrodite-Venus, and the deadly sins bear Hebrew names.

Vico's *New Science* appeared in 1725, although its influence in France was not felt until Michelet's translation in 1827. According to Vico, myths could be viewed as a kind of summary of primitive history. He saw in Homer a collective being, a symbol of the Greek people chanting their own story in national epics. In eighteenth-century France, Vico had a heterodox disciple in Nicolas Boulanger, who in his *Antiquity Unveiled by Customs* (1766) claimed to have found the source of all mythologies in the revolutions in nature, especially in the memory of the great geological catastrophes.

The nine-volume *Primitive World* of Court de Gébelin (1773–84) exerted a considerable influence. In this work, all myths were endowed with a historical meaning, often closely related to the history of agriculture. But the etymological dictionaries included in this work also engage in a deep meditation on language, an extension of some of the speculations of Father Athanasius Kircher.

In year III of the First Republic (A.D. 1794), Charles-François Dupuis published his *Origin of All Cults,* which set forth the thesis that the adventures of the gods describe the phenomena of nature, primarily celestial phenomena, such as the revolutions of the sun and the moon, their movements with respect to the constellations, etc. Although these theories have a measure of truth, they cannot account for the totality of all myths.

The idea of a universal revelation, which already appears in Lafitau's work in the eighteenth century, was quite widespread in the nineteenth century. With the development of secret societies and Illuminism, some authors claimed to recognize a prefiguration of Masonic rituals in the mysteries of Egypt and Eleusis. They traced the universal tradition step by step, and in their view myths had multiple and deep meanings. One work was particularly representative: *Freemasonry Traced to Its True Origin, or the Antiquity of Freemasonry*

Proved by the Explication of the Ancient and Modern Mysteries, by Alexandre Lenoir (1814).

Joseph de Maistre shared with these authors the belief in a primitive revelation identical with Hebrew and Christian monotheism. In his *Essay on Indifference in the Matter of Religion* (4 volumes, 1817–23), Lammenais later claimed to have rediscovered the original monotheism hidden behind the gods of polytheism. Baron Eckstein later introduced Hindu mythology into France in his newspaper *The Catholic,* and Lamartine then used his translations from the Sanskrit in his *Plain Course in Literature.* According to Eckstein, paganism was nothing but a corrupted and degenerate Catholicism, and he searched everywhere for the old sources of beliefs, doctrines, and symbols that could make up what might be called "the catholicism before Catholicism." He laid the groundwork for the comparative history of religions by comparing the myths of India, Iran, Greece, Scandinavia, and ancient Germany. Some of these studies foreshadow astoundingly the works of George Dumézil.

Eckstein's role was considerable. He introduced into France the ideas of his master, Frederick Kreuzer, the author of the celebrated *Symbolism and Mythology of Ancient Peoples* published in 1810–12. In 1824, Benjamin Constant, who had read the work in German, predicted in the first volume of his book *On Religion* the triumph of Kreuzer's book over "the narrow and arid system of Dupuis," and Constant added, "It will be a triumph for the imagination and in certain ways a gain for science." In fact, Kreuzer's work marked the dawn of the science of myths; Joseph-Daniel Guigniaut would later devote his life to translating him, to completing and rectifying him, and thus he became in France the true founder of religious studies, as Michelet pointed out. The French edition of Guigniaut's work, thus enriched, appeared in ten volumes between 1825 and 1851, with an extremely suggestive volume of plates. Entitled *Religions of Antiquity Considered Principally in Their Symbolic and Mythological Forms,* it fascinated the poets because it supplied them with a whole repertory of symbols and analogies. Drawing upon Schelling's philosophy of nature, Kreuzer claimed that the symbol is "the primitive form of human intelligence" and that it makes it possible to give finite intelligences an image of the infinite. By this means the priestly caste in the Orient received the primitive revelation and transmitted it to still uncultivated peoples. The symbol, which is "the idea made palpable and personified," gives birth to the myth, which explains and illustrates the idea through a narrative. Primitive revelation is preserved in mysteries. The Neoplatonists alone were able to penetrate the real spirit of paganism and the meaning of its secret rites.

The notion of a language of nature, of the primitive spoken word, formulated by Kreuzer, is related to certain speculations of Court de Gébelin, Claude de Saint-Martin, and Fabre d'Olivet.

In the December 1823 issue of *The French Muse* (thus before Guigniaut's publication), Alexandre Soumet echoed these doctrines. He claimed that poetry "explains and completes the work of the Creator." Everything is symbolic in the eyes of the poet. Through a continuous exchange of analogies and comparisons, he seeks to rediscover some traces of the primitive language, revealed to man by God, of which modern languages are but a flimsy shadow. Thus the faith in the truth of the imagination arose. Pierre Leroux, and later Charles Baudelaire, took this doctrine as far as it could go; Baudelaire went on to speak of the inexhaustible depths of the universal analogy.

This led to the flowering of epics, mentioned earlier, which owed as much to Vico as to Kreuzer in their conception.

The proponents of syncretism—Thalès Bernard, Gérard de Nerval, and Louis Ménard—must also be counted among the disciples of Kreuzer. They could claim to belong simultaneously to all religions (Nerval is said to have espoused seventeen) because they interpreted them symbolically. In their eyes, the symbol redeemed both religion and poetry. Beginning in 1828, Victor Cousin developed his brand of syncretism, which was thoroughly imbued with Neoplatonism and would later influence Quinet, Vigny, and Nerval. In *The House of the Shepherd, The Death of the Wolf,* and *The Bottle in the Sea,* Vigny appeared as the creator of modern myths. In *Daphne,* he reproached Christianity for having adulterated pure ideas, but after he had dreamed of a religion without images, he came to realize that he was dreaming an impossible dream.

French romanticism essentially fed on myths. This is especially true of the work of Victor Hugo, who dominated this period.

II. In Germany

Goethe deserves special attention here because his work served in many respects as a prelude to romanticism in Germany. A large number of great mythic themes gravitate around *Wilhelm Meister* and *Faust.* In his dramatic works, Goethe treated such subjects as Pandora and Iphigenia, which go back to classical antiquity. *The Green Serpent* is an allegory of human life inspired by *The Alchemical Wedding of Christian Rosencreutz* by Johann Valentin Andreae.

With *The Robbers* (1781), Schiller made current a modern myth with an extraordinarily promising future, the myth of the "noble bandit." Works like *Maria Stuart* (1800) and *Wilhelm Tell* (1804) give a mythical dimension to historic characters. Finally, his *Letters on the Aesthetic Education of Man* (1793) reflect on the proper use of mythology.

Although Bonald, Fabre d'Olivet, Joseph de Maistre, Saint-Martin, and Ballanche exerted a great deal of influence on literature in France, German Romanticism was imbued with occult doctrines to an even greater extent than was French romanticism. The loftiest ideas of Neoplatonism had been reintroduced in Germany by Meister Eckhart, Paracelsus, Agrippa von Nettesheim, and finally Jakob Böhme. Such poets as Ludwig Tieck and Novalis, and after them the storyteller E. T. A. Hoffmann, were deeply marked by their reading of Böhme.

For Johann Georg Hamann, the "magus of the north," all of creation is "a discourse addressed to the creature by means of the creature." Another great stimulus was Johann Gottfried von Herder, who took an interest in popular traditions and who in his quest for syncretism arrived at immanentism (the perception of God in the universe). The German romantics conceived of nature as an animate being. One of their fundamental myths is the quest for the primitive language from which all languages were differentiated and for the original religion which was at the origin of multiple beliefs.

Herder began his essay *On the Germano-Oriental Poets* by condemning all imitation of Oriental poetry, by which he meant imitation of the Old Testament. Converted for a time to Eastern aesthetics between 1769 and 1774, while he was preparing his *Oldest Document of the Human Race,* he returned to the idea of the supremacy of the language, mythology, and poetry of Greece. Later both Friedrich von Schlegel and his brother August Wilhelm Schlegel helped to acquaint Europe with Hindu literature. Numerous German scholars, among them J. A. Kanne, F. Majer, Görres, Karl Ritter, and Gottfried Müller, took myths seriously and encouraged others to do so.

But from the standpoint of our concern, the most important statement comes from Friedrich Schelling's *On the Philosophy of Art* (1802–3), in which he asserts that "the gods are the absolute itself seen through the particular and considered as real," that mythology "is the necessary condition and raw material of all art," and, further, that

> mythology is the universe in holiday dress, in its absolute state, the true universe per se, the image of life and supernatural chaos in divine imagination, already poetry by itself and in turn poetic matter and poetic elements. It is the world and in a sense the earth, the only place where works of art can flourish and live. Only in a world of this kind are immutable and determined forms possible, the only forms through which eternal ideas may be expressed.

Herder's ideas came to be known in France primarily through Edgar Quinet. Since works by Goethe, Schiller, and E. T. A. Hoffmann were also translated and discussed, their influence became, oddly enough, more significant than that of Sir Walter Scott and James Fennimore Cooper. Novalis, Tieck, Arnim, and Kleist were also translated and appreciated, but only later.

III. In Great Britain

With regard to the gradual swing into romanticism that took place in England—a writer like William Blake (1757–1827) may already be identified with romanticism—Louis Cazamian spoke of the phenomenon of collective paramnesia. Indeed, the English merely discovered within themselves latent tendencies that had already prevailed in their literature during the Elizabethan era. This explains why sensational statements or manifestos were almost entirely absent. The preface that Wordsworth and Coleridge wrote for the anonymous *Lyrical Ballads* (1798), or Shelley's *Defense of Poetry* (1821), cannot really be compared with Stendhal's *Racine and Shakespeare* let alone with Hugo's *Preface to Cromwell*.

Endowed with an exceptional imagination, William Blake was a prophet and visionary who elaborated a whole mythology in which he objectified the powers of his mind. He associated the imagination with the sun in the air and the ego, and called it *Los-Urthona;* sentiment, connected with fire, was *Luvah-Orc;* sensation and water were *Tharmas;* cold reasoning, connected with the earth, was *Urizen*. A throng of secondary figures, no sooner noticed than named, came to make up a personal mythology parallel to the Old Testament and Greek mythology. Blake was convinced that he was the reincarnation of Milton. His Gnosticism persuaded him that Satan was man's true friend, and he identified Christ with the human Imagination.

The most vigorous mind of the first generation of romantics was Samuel Taylor Coleridge, but since he was addicted to opium, he completed virtually nothing of what he began. In both of his most successful poems, *Kubla Khan* (1791) and *The Rime of the Ancient Mariner* (1798), he assumed the role of a maker of myths. Poe's *Adventures of Arthur Gordon Pym* later derived partly from *The Rime of the Ancient Mariner.*

In Byron's sizable oeuvre, *Manfred* and *Cain* were conceived according to the system of philosophic symbolism. Shelley transmuted his ideas into poetry and traversed a brief trajectory that allowed him to pass from anarchistic individualism to the meaning of human brotherhood and the meaning of the authority of sages. He disavowed rationalism and affirmed intuitive truths, finally espousing an idealistic pantheism. Like Vigny's *Moses,* his poem *Alastor* is devoted to the theme of the solitude of the superior individual. John Keats, in his majestic though unfinished masterpiece *Hyperion,* sought to rival Milton by describing the heavenly revolutions of pagan mythology, as Milton had described the Christian cycle of paradise lost and regained. Even the imagination of Thomas Carlyle, eloquent prose writer though he was, was of a mythicizing nature, and he was imbued with German idealism. His *Sartor Resartus* (The tailor retailored) (1833–34), based on a philosophy of clothes reminiscent of Balzac, is a transposed autobiography in which he expresses his contempt for his time by setting appearances in opposition to essences.

IV. A New Renaissance?

The return to myth that characterizes romanticism in France, Germany, and Great Britain appeared in all the countries of Western Europe in the nineteenth century. In Spain, José Zorilla y Moral gave the Don Juan myth its definitive form with *Don Juan Tenorio* (1844); Leopardi, who treats Prometheus with irony in *The Wager of Prometheus,* also wrote *Sappho's Last Song*. This poem may explain the mental leap that poets always make, the step that binds them to myths: "The happiest days of our lives are the first to wither away."

The glance backward constituted by the recourse to myths may well be at the same time the quest for a lost happiness, for a golden age when the young gods revealed themselves to humans. Maier later defined Sanskrit poems as "the dreams of children of our own species." The nineteenth century was for Europe the period of a true "Oriental Renaissance." In 1841, Edgar Quinet entitled a chapter of his *Genius of Religions* "The Oriental Renaissance." The following year, L. Dussieux, the author of the remarkable *Essay on the History of Oriental Erudition,* published in *The New Encyclopedia,* emphasized the fact that this renaissance had its roots in the previous century and was complementary to the first Renaissance.

In 1800, Friedrich Schlegel wrote, "It is in the Orient that we should look for the supreme romanticism," and before the end of the century, the inquiry of the elite takes on a planetary character. The goal of all the great Western poets was to rival the Hindu epics, the *Rāmāyaṇa* and the *Mahābhārata,* which explains in part the immense though only partially complete projects to which we alluded at the beginning of this article.

An oneiric text by the English writer De Quincey (translated into French successively by Musset in 1828 and Baudelaire in 1860) gives a probing account of the way in which Oriental mythologies, largely conflated and mixed together, invaded Western consciousness. In his book *The Oriental Renaissance* (p. 215), Raymond Schwab cites a passage from *The Confessions of an English Opium Eater* (chapter 4, "Pains of Opium," originally published in 1822): "I ran into pagodas, and was fixed for centuries at the summit or in secret rooms; I was the idol; I was the priest; I was worshipped; I was sacrificed. I fled from the wrathe of Brahma through all the forests of Asia; Vishnu hated me; Seva lay in wait of me. I came suddenly upon Isis and Osiris: I had done a deed, they said, which the ibis and the crocodile trembled at" (*The Collected Writings of Thomas de Quincey,* vol. 3, London: A & C Black, 1897, p. 412).

For all the poets of this time, the knowledge of Egyptian religion, Zoroastrianism, Hindu mythology, the Vedanta as expressed in the *Upaniṣads,* and Buddhism informed their work and supplied points of reference and comparisons. Such references, even when they remain implicit, help us to understand not only Lamartine, Vigny, Hugo, Nerval, and Michelet, but also Wordsworth, Coleridge, Shelley, Goethe, and Novalis.

J.Ri./g.h.

BIBLIOGRAPHY

P. ALBOUY, *La Création mythologique chez Victor Hugo* (Paris 1963). R. AYRAULT, *Heinrich von Kleist* (Paris 1966); *Genèse du romantisme allemand,* 4 vols. (Paris 1961–76). A. BÉGUIN, *L'ame romantique et le rêve* (Paris, repr. 1946). J. BUCHE, *L'école mystique de Lyon* (Paris 1935). N. BURTIN, *Un semeur d'idées au temps de la Restauration: Le baron d'Eckstein* (Paris 1931). R. CANAT, *L'Hellénisme des romantiques,* 3 vols.(Paris 1951–55). P.-G. CASTEX, *Le conte fantastique en France, de Nodier à Maupassant* (Paris 1951). L. CELLIER, *Fabre d'Olivet, contribution à l'étude des aspects religieux du romantisme* (Paris 1953). J.-A.-S. COLLIN DE PLANCY, *Dictionnaire infernal,* 4 vols. (Paris 1825–26). A. COURT DE GÉBELIN, *Monde primitif analysé et comparé avec le monde moderne,* etc., 9 vols. (Paris 1773–84; repr. Paris 1787). F. CREUZER, *Religions de l'Antiquité, considérées principalement dans leurs formes symboliques et mythologiques,* trans., partly recast, completed, and developed by DANIEL GUIGNIAUT, 10 vols. (Paris 1825–51). É. DERMENGHEM, *Joseph de Maistre mystique* (repr. Paris 1946). M.-J. DURRY, *Gérard de Nerval et le mythe* (Paris 1956; reissued 1976). E. EGGLI, *Schiller et le romantisme français,* 2 vols. (Paris 1927; index 1928). E. ESTÈVE, *Byron et le romantisme français, essai sur la fortune et l'influence de l'œuvre de Byron en France de 1812 à 1850* (Paris 1907). A. FABRE D'OLIVET, *Histoire philosophique du genre humain,* 2 vols. (Paris 1824). E. FRENZEL, *Stoffe der Weltliteratur* (2d ed., Stuttgart 1963). R. GÉRARD, *L'Orient et la pensée romantique allemande* (Paris 1963). F. GERMAIN, *L'imagination d'A. de Vigny* (Paris 1962). B. D'HERBELOT DE MOLAINVILLE, *Bibliothèque orientale* (Paris 1697). A. KOYRÉ, *La philosophie de Jacob Boehme* (Paris 1929). A. H. KRAPPE, *La genèse des mythes* (Paris 1938). J. LARAT, *La tradition et l'exotisme dans l'œuvre de Charles Nodier* (Paris 1928). M. MARACHE, *Le symbole dans la pensée et l'œuvre de Goethe* (Paris 1960). A. MONCHOUX, *L'Allemagne devant les lettres françaises de 1814 à 1835* (Paris 1953). H. PEYRE, *Bibliographie critique de l'hellénisme en France de 1843 à 1870* (New Haven 1932). M. PRAZ, *The Romantic Agony* (New York 1956). J. F. RICCI, *E. T. A. Hoffmann, l'homme et l'œuvre* (Paris 1941). J. RICHER, *Gérard de Nerval et les doctrines ésotériques* (Paris 1947); *Nerval, expérience et création* (2d ed., Paris 1970). J. ROOS, *Aspects littéraires du mysticisme philosophique* (W. Blake, Novalis, Ballanche) (Strasbourg and Paris 1951). R. SCHWAB, *La renaissance orientale* (Paris 1950). VAN TIEGHEM, *Le Romantisme dans la littérature européenne* (Paris 1948). A. VIATTE, *Les sources occultes du romantisme, 1770–1820* (Paris 1928).

N.B.: This bibliography is complemented by those of the individual articles listed and by references to a number of works in the text.

Romanticism and Myth in Blake, Nerval, and Balzac

For the second time, the gods have deserted the earth. Almost two thousand years ago, a cry went out, "The great Pan is dead." A second cry that proclaims that God is dead now answers that first cry. How are we to think about the world, to give meaning to our individual histories, to the history of mankind, to the history of the universe? We must somehow attempt to recover from the shock caused by the brutal challenge to a conception of the world that made it possible for everything to have meaning, from suffering to war, from birth to death, from individual fate to collective destiny. Suddenly it all collapses. What are we to do in such times of anguish? It is not a matter just of believing, but of thinking, of living. But it is no longer possible to believe or think for others: "I must create a system, or be enslaved by another man" (Blake). And all of these systems can be constructed only with the debris of the lost gods.

Some people limit themselves to acknowledging the absence of the gods and try to live in remembrance of the times when the gods were here. Others stand still, waiting for a new epiphany on the edge of the promised land which they herald but will not see. Still others become hardened in a refusal that rejects all possible forms of myth; but the refusal is coupled with a pathos that owes everything to struggle and to the minerality of absence. Nietzsche still struggles with the gods and is unable to get beyond the point where the struggle against the gods is also a struggle among the gods, Dionysus against Christ on the Cross. The deniers are not so far from the prophets. The downfall of mythology and religion assures that they will be diffused everywhere and inscribed within everyone's vision. The great Christian schemata that until now constituted a place forbidden to mythical elaboration are freed through the power of religious criticism and come to merge with the schemata of all other mythologies; the Christian religion lends all of its underground strength to the reactivation of the old myths. And the great figures of the denying prophets who arise are the figures of giants, who, worn out from fighting the gods in their attempts to replace them, can only be recognized in the dark forms of Satan, Prometheus, or Dionysus. Among these figures are not only Byron, Blake, and Hugo, but also Marx and Nietzsche.

Still others choose to hear Nerval when he asks, "Will I see myself compelled to believe everything just as our fathers the philosophers felt compelled to deny everything?" But whether they refuse myth or want to believe in it at any cost, they all confront the same problem: we must, by whatever means, respond to the threat of seeing all meaning disappear. And the poet responds by asserting the omnipotence and omnipresence of meaning. To ward off the advent of a disenchanted and empty world, he constructs a wholly meaningful nature, and two thousand years later he renews the bonds with the pre-Socratic world in which myth is possible. For myth cannot develop from a desacralized nature; it demands a new way of conceiving what exists. Nature is not inanimate matter. It is energy: "Attraction and Repulsion, Reason and Energy, Love and Hate, are necessary to Human existence" (Blake). Thus invested with productive power, nature is all activity and movement. The materialist Engels seeks to rediscover in matter the dynamism that produces history and gives it meaning. We must go beyond the dualism that separates body and soul: "Man has no Body distinct from his Soul" (Blake). The body is nothing but a degenerate, heavy form of energy, which is, in contrast, wholly spiritual. The body is only an envelope, below which acts the dynamic essence that informs it. If Balzac believes in phrenology, it is because he sees at work everywhere the traces left by energy in its incessant activity, in man's brain as well as in social organization. Energy is present everywhere, in the inanimate world as in the human world: "A pure spirit grows larger under the outer crust of stones" (Nerval).

There are two worlds, a corporeal world and a spiritual world, that correspond point for point and make up the outer and inner components of whatever exists. Between the two worlds gates are erected that open to all who have the courage to cross the threshold: the gates of dreams, the gates of revelation, the gates of madness, the gates of artistic creation. These are the gates crossed by Milton and Blake, Louis Lambert and Balzac, Nerval and Aurélia. On this now animated world supernatural beings can multiply, beings who are nothing but the various shapes taken by various aspects of nature and history. There is no longer any break between the history of the earth and the history of humanity: once again, the universe is full of gods. In reading Buffon like a theogony, Blake and Nerval unfold the mythical stages in the life of the earth, and Balzac sees the gods and heroes in the street, in the office, in the store, and in jail. He does not enlarge the stature of his characters to make them closer to the gods; he makes them great only because he sees myths and gods in them. Balzac does not proceed from the fantastic to realism; he embodies myths progressively in the raw material offered to him by history and society. Esther Gobseck is an incarnation of Seraphita, and together with Lucien de Rubempré they reconstitute the couple Seraphitus-Seraphita; Vautrin is the devil, he is Cain, he is part of an infernal family whose demons are named Attila, Charlemagne, Robespierre, and Napoleon. The big city—Blake's London or Balzac's Paris—is a myth only because one projects upon it the vision of infernal cities that make it bear witness to the Apocalypse.

Nor is there a break between the history of humanity and individual history. Since the explanatory model is that of the organism, of the Great Animal, there is a direct relationship between ontogenesis and phylogenesis: simultaneous lives, successive lives, reincarnations, parallelisms of existences weave the fabric of historical and social events. If Vautrin is Cain, if Lucien de Rubempré is Abel, why should Nerval not be Lusignan or Napoleon? Once again, everything has meaning, right down to the slightest incidents, or perhaps the most fortuitous encounters in the life of an individual. The soldier who comes into Blake's garden and makes him stand trial is also a character of universal history, like the soldier of Africa whom Nerval meets and who becomes the sublime interpreter, the predestined confessor, the mediator between man and the supernatural. Each encounter has a meaning just as, for Balzac, each facial feature, each idiosyncrasy, each habit of the body and the mind carries a determined meaning. And these are the same mythical schemata that regulate the rhythm of individual existence and social life: masculine and feminine poles, grandeur and decadence, the descent into hell and the ascent back into the light, condensation and diffusion, separation and reconciliation; dualist schemata in which two opposite terms introduce the contradiction in being while awaiting the synthesis that is to reconcile them. This explains the importance of the Double, which haunts all creators: for Blake, all personalities are divided into Emanation and Specter, the feminine and masculine parts of the soul, which one day will rediscover their fruitful unity, in opposition with the hermaphroditic horror of Satan. Nerval sees himself threatened with dispossession by a Double who takes his place: "Am I the good one? Am I the bad one?" Balzac, also threatened by his own Double, gets rid of him and has all the characters into whom he put much of himself die: Louis Lambert, Valentin, Savarus, Z. Marcas. An obsession with the Double, but also a writing technique to overcome it.

William Blake, *The Eternal*. Etching. Manchester, Whitworth Art Gallery. Photo Manor, Kay, and Foley.

In this world animated by mythical forces, in this figurative history, the poet and the artist—double beings—occupy a central place. The poet is the seer, one who, like Blake, perceives the soul of beauty in the forms of matter; one who, like Balzac, penetrates deep into the soul of a stroller, to recover his share of the gift of life; one who, like Nerval, sees once again the unknown relatives that make up his genealogy. Knowledge through sensation is deceptive; it is the result of the contraction of a human being reduced to the state of opaqueness (Blake) and made insensitive to supernatural realities. Beyond the realm of knowledge through sensation, knowledge of another order flashes like lightning; this is the knowledge that Blake awaited for twenty years before he recovered the intellectual vision which intoxicated him. Within the scope of this exceptional experience, "objects and bodies are luminous in themselves" (Nerval). Then contact is established between the two parts of the universe, the material part and the supernatural part. The artist knows how to read and understand the signs of the language that is spoken by nature and that guarantees the existence of correspondences between microcosm and macrocosm. The poet is the intermediary between these two worlds, and his dwelling place is "the house of the Interpreter," the name that Blake's friends gave to his house. The paths of the communication may vary: Blake enters directly into contact with supernatural beings: "I am under the direction of heavenly Messengers day and night." Nerval can only see the gates of the Great Beyond open through the converging experiences of dream and madness. Balzac creates intermediaries who ensure passage to the two realms or who, like Seraphita, themselves participate in both realms. It is essential that these moments of contact leave enduring traces, for what is transmitted must be set down. The revelation must be inscribed on the page—by drawing or writing—both to allow the poet to ensure the vision for himself and to bear witness before men of the presence of the gods. "I wanted to have a material sign of the vision that had consoled me" (Nerval). Blake, Nerval, and Balzac rediscover what Swedenborg did when he gave the name of *Memorabilia* to the story of his mystical inspirations. Nerval edited the *Memorabilia,* which he placed at the culmination of *Aurélia;* Blake inserted "memorabilia" ("A Memorable Fancy") in the *Marriage of Heaven and Hell,* and "memorabilia" would be a fitting word for the Sibylline phrases recorded from the mouth of Louis Lambert, who had gone mad in the eyes of the world. A special intermediary with the world Beyond, the poet is himself a maker of myths. Thus he shares responsibility for creation, before which he experiences the anxieties of the demiurge, anxieties and agonies that are recapitulated in Blake's *Milton, Aurélia,* or *Unknown Masterpiece.*

Blake, Balzac, and Nerval faced a common spiritual dilemma, and many others could have appeared beside them: Hölderlin and later Nietzsche, to mention only two. Clearly it would be illusory to expect to understand them solely on the basis of the particular conditions of their visions, on the basis of their peculiarities, excesses, or madness. What matters is not excessiveness or madness in itself, but this excessiveness or that madness. Both date from a time of crisis when myth alone, both in reason and in madness, could respond to the anxieties of someone who sought and asked.

J.M./g.h.

The Mythology of European Decadent and Symbolist Literature

Nothing could be more baffling than the history of decadence and symbolism. Of symbolism, Valéry said that it was "a certain region of the literary universe, that is, in France between 1860 and 1900." This says too much if we define symbolism strictly; too little if we mean decadence and symbolism taken as a whole that extends in space beyond France and in time beyond 1900. Valéry finally became aware of this and stated that "nothing in what has been written, nothing within the memory of those who experienced this period ever went by that name at any given date." Symbolism is therefore just "a myth."

Introducing the new term "myth" only adds to the general state of confusion. It can be invoked only if its full meaning is restored and if a study of the myths in symbolist and decadent literature replaces the vain attack on some ill-defined "myth of symbolism." This new alliance of decadence and symbolism under the sign of myth should be more enlightening than the quarrels and reconciliations of tiny groups within the literary arena.

I. The Glamour of a Word

Ancient, vague, inevitably the bearer of a potentially negative nuance and yet offering access to the fullness of the sacred, the word "myth" could not help but fascinate the men of that time. It swept their imagination into a dream of universality. "Myth is a tree that grows everywhere, in any climate, under any sun, spontaneously and without cutting," wrote Baudelaire in his article "Richard Wagner and *Tannhaüser* in Paris." "Religions and poetry from the four corners of the world provide us with overwhelming proof on this subject." But precisely because myth is in essence religious, it also contributed to this "vague sort of aesthetic spiritualism," which is, according to Valéry, the main characteristic of symbolism.

The great variety of mythological flora bears witness to the universality of myth. Although the Greco-Roman pantheon and its appendages have the lion's share, poets did not hesitate to make their contributions with Hebrew mythology (Herod, Salome) and national mythologies (Celtic myths in Yeats, Maeterlinck, and Apollinaire; legends of the *Kalevala* in Leino; the Cid in Manuel Machado; Indian myths in Rubén Darío), when they were not forging personal myths, such as Stefan George's Maximin or Blok's Beautiful Lady. It was no longer a matter of collecting myths in the manner of Leconte de Lisle or gathering up "all the gods the world has known" in the manner of Louis Ménard, but rather of molding them into boldly synthetic figures. Baudelaire had already noted that Wagner's Elsa was none other than "the ancient Psyche, who was also the victim of demonic curiosity, and who was also unwilling to respect her divine spouse's anonymity; she too lost all her happiness upon penetrating the mystery." For Gabriele d'Annunzio the "royal Herodias" was at the same time "the ancient Gorgon with her full head of hair . . . Circe, Helen, Omphale, and Delilah, the courtesan with a horrible laugh" (prelude to the *Intermezzo di rime,* 1884).

The sampling might be deemed superficial and the mix ornamental. They are, however, indicative of a quest that can be said to be spiritual. The Monsieur de Phocas of Jean Lorrain left society and abandoned the salons and the boudoirs of young women in order to find in the solitude of his townhouse on the rue de Varenne, in the contemplation of the jewels of Barruchini, or in Oriental self-annihilation, the gaze that he sought: it was "the gaze of Dahgut, daughter of the king of Ys, the gaze of Salome too; but especially the limpid and green clarity of the gaze of Astarte, of Astarte who is the demon of lust and also the demon of the sea." Similarly, J. K. Huysmans's des Esseintes thinks he has discovered in Salome, as Gustave Moreau represented her, "the ancient Helen," "Salammbô," Isis, Kālī, in other words, always "the deity symbolic of indestructible lust, the goddess of immortal Hysteria, the cursed Beauty," the one that Swinburne had celebrated under the name of Dolores.

Symbolic? Allegorical rather—allegory being only a "chilled symbol," as Hegel pointed out. The mythological syncretism of Jean Lorrain or Huysmans seems to have but

Gustave Moreau, *L'Apparition*. Paris, Musée Gustave Moreau. Photo Giraudon.

one aim, the triumph of a single deity, or better still, the triumph of a principle identified with the obsession of the decadent individual. When Tédor de Wyzewa stressed in *La Revue wagnérienne* of 8 June 1886 that for moderns, legends and myths are "nothing but symbols," he meant "allegories." And when Baudelaire defined his wretched swan which escaped from its cage as a "strange and fatal myth," he made it an allegory of fate that compelled man to exile. The exile of a mythological character (Andromache) and of a paradigmatic figure (the consumptive Negress) confirms this all the more, and confirms as well the compulsion that acts upon the poet himself, exiled from the ideal and immersed in the world of the spleen. The myth of the swan is indeed his myth—and the myth of himself—since he takes from it only one meaning, his own, identifying it with himself. Baudelaire wastes no time in recognizing it: "everything for [him] becomes allegory."

Such is the jeopardy into which decadent and symbolist literature casts myth, reducing it, as Henri de Régnier said, to "the conch shell that resounds with *one* Idea." For Yeats, Helen represents the fatal power of all beauty. In this respect, no example is more characteristic than Henri de Régnier himself. He made the birds of Lake Stymphalis into an allegory of passing time (*Epigram* in *Les Jeux rustiques et divins* [Rustic and divine games]), and he made the trials of Ulysses into the poet's martyrdom (*L'Homme et la Sirène* [The man and the siren]). Symbolic rather than symbolist, this treatment of myth is not new. It recalls Vigny's Moses, Shelley's Prometheus, Leconte de Lisle's Niobe, and Victor Hugo's Satyr, all of whom also embody an idea. And for Ballanche the ultimate meaning of all myths could be reduced to a single idea. Baudelaire treated the issue no differently when he discovered the universal meaning of sin in the Wagnerian myths and, more generally, in the "allegory created by the people," which is myth.

To ward off this danger, the "overly precise meaning" condemned by Verlaine in his famous *Art poétique* had to be erased. The use of myth becomes truly symbolic when the writer attempts to apprehend a mystery that is never completely discovered and must never be solved. "The perfect use of the mystery constitutes the symbol" was Mallarmé's answer to Jules Huret's question. And in the Manifesto of 18 September 1886, Jean Moréas took care to point out that "the essential character of symbolist art consists in never going as far as conceiving of the idea in and of itself." Mallarmé's faun and Mallarmé himself hesitate among diverse interpretations of the nymphs that appear to them. Everything begins with questions about a myth. Doubt, "heap of ancient night," is the very reason for the length of the discourse which will try in vain to exhaust the bulk of the mystery: "I, proud of my repute, I will long speak of goddesses."

The result is a fondness for ambiguous mythological figures—monsters, sphinxes, chimeras; a fondness also for the central and ever-dissolving figures of mystery cults (Orpheus, Isis, Dionysus) or of the celebration of mystery (the Grail); a fondness for myth to the extent that, more mysterious than discourse, myth gropes its way tentatively closer and closer into the zone of the unknowable.

The danger this time is that myth will express nothing but the quest itself. For Cavafy, for instance, the trials and tribulations of Odysseus are no longer, as they were for Henri de Régnier, merely the sufferings of the martyr-poet. They are the stages of an Orphic initiation through which the poet must pass:

> You will never meet the Lestrygonians,
> the Cyclopes and the fierce Poseidon,
> if you do not carry them within your soul,
> if your soul does not raise them up before you.
> (Trans. Rae Dalven, *The Complete Poems of Cavafy*, New York: Harcourt Brace Jovanovich, 1976, p. 36)

For Mallarmé, myths of the voyage to the world beyond play an essential role that can only be explained by such an imaging of the poetic quest. Although in *Le Guignon* (Bad luck), the *Mendieur d'azur* (The azure beggar), the *Martyrs de hasards tortueux* (Martyrs of tortuous perils), and the vultureless *Prométhée* (Prometheus), there are still the romantic mannerisms of Odysseus, we are on the other hand dealing with an Odysseus who faces the mystery of death and nothingness, the Odysseus of the *Nekuia* (The journey to the dead), when we deal with the poet of the *Tombeaux* (The tombs) or "the one who went to draw tears from the river Styx." A flash of union between decadence and symbolism, the "Prose pour des Esseintes" emerges as the annihilating evocation of another voyage, seemingly more Platonic than Homeric, toward the isle of Ideas. But the inquiry about myth makes room this time for the negation of a Utopia (the land of Pulcheria) where myth itself self-destructs.

II. The Rebirth of Myth

In July 1885, after Baudelaire and before Claudel, Mallarmé dedicated to Richard Wagner his *Rêverie d'un poète français* and thereby found himself led by his very subject to return to myth. To avail himself of another mythological motif dear to him, namely, the Phoenix, he established for his own time and in his country a death and resurrection of myth. In fact, "the French mind, strictly imaginative and abstract, therefore poetic . . . , loathes legend, and as such is at one with art, the inventor, in its integrity." And yet "this century or our nation which extols it have dissolved myths through conceptions only to make new ones."

The model which the French mind was supposed to spurn was Wagnerian drama. In giving preference to myth over history, Wagner fulfilled the vow of the first German romantics, Schlegel, Arnim, and Brentano. "Myth is the primitive and anonymous poem of the people," he wrote. "In myth, human relations shed their conventional form almost completely . . . and reveal what makes life truly, eternally, understandable." At issue, therefore, is not an ascent into the increasingly thick mists of the unknowable, but the revelation of what could be termed the essence of life. Baudelaire, who thoroughly understood that Wagner's poems "borrowed in large measure from the romantic spirit," also saw clearly that the ambition of the German master was to discover "the universal heart of man," and all this through myth.

The rebirth of myth did not happen without major modifications, which significantly transformed mythological figures, as in the case of *Tannhäuser.* "Radiant ancient Venus, Aphrodite born of white foam, has not crossed the horrifying shadows of the Middle Ages with impunity. She no longer dwells on Olympus nor on the shores of a fragrant island.

Odilon Redon, *Brunehilde,* "Twilight of the Gods," final scene. Lithograph. Illustration for *La Revue wagnérienne,* 8 August 1885. Photo Martine Pont.

She has withdrawn deep inside a magnificent cave, to be sure, but one illuminated by fires that are not those of kindly Phoebus. By going underground, Venus draws close to Hell, and with certain loathsome ceremonies is undoubtedly about to pay steady homage to the archfiend, prince of the flesh, and lord of sin." It is as if, after the death of Venus (her disappearance from Cythera in *Les Fleurs du mal* [The flowers of evil], her corpselike stillness in Swinburne's *Laus Veneris*), one could witness the weird spectacle of her resurrection (the Venus in furs of Sacher-Masoch), the birth of an ambiguous deity, simultaneously statue and woman, hetaera and goddess, Greek and barbarian.

The use of mythology in theater also changed. Wagnerian drama sought to reinstate the mythic force of Greek tragedy. Nietzsche wrote his famous book *The Birth of Tragedy* in order to hail the rebirth of tragedy thanks to Wagner, tragedy in the post-Euripidean and post-Socratic sense of the term. For Nietzsche, myth remained a temporary and necessary concession to the Apollonian, since society would not tolerate the eruption of the purely Dionysian. Between music and our musical feelings carried to their utmost, "myth and the tragic hero arise, both being fundamentally nothing but symbols of universal realities of which music alone can speak directly. If we could feel as purely Dionysian beings, myth as symbol would have no effect on us; we would pay it no heed and would not stop lending an ear to the echo of the universals *ante rem.* But it is at this point that the Apollonian force erupts and, restoring our almost annihilated individuality, brings to it the balm of a delightful illusion." Jean Lorrain felt free to create a pretty vignette from the love of Tristan and Isolde (*Yseut,* in *Le Sang des dieux* [The blood of the gods]). Gabriele d'Annunzio felt free to turn the cup of tea, which had become as ritualistic in Rome as in London, into the modern avatar of Tristan's love potion. According to Nietzsche, Wagner introduced the mythical couple only to bring us to the moment when the image fades out, when the phenomenal world reaches its limit, and when Isolde's song of the love-death rises like a "metaphysical swan song." Myth proceeds on its course of self-destruction. Yet, curiously enough, this self-destruction cannot be articulated without recourse to mythological language. The paradox of Wagner's *Tristan* is renewed with Nietzsche's commentary, a vast fresco of Apollo and Dionysus which must nonetheless suggest that what exists beyond these images is as illusory as the others.

One would like to believe that Mallarmé understood the difficulty. Instead of indulging in philological erudition, as Nietzsche did, instead of bantering heavy-handedly, as Claudel did over that *gros édredon d'Isolde* ("stout eiderdown of Isolde"), he favored an abstract concept of myth, as if it had become disembodied, a mental myth stripped even of the prop of a name. At the very most, one will see "awaken" in this setting "the Figure which is None," and art admiring itself in the empty space it has opened up for itself.

III. The Myth of Decadence

People often compare the *Néant* (Nothingness) of Mallarmé to Stefan George in *Algabal* (1892), particularly where the Roman emperor Heliogabalus represents the despotic and inhuman soul which in its omnipotence can find only loneliness and sterility. This figure is very characteristic of what can be called the myth of Latin decadence or simply the myth of decadence.

Since for quite some time Edward Gibbon, Montesquieu, and others had applied the word "decadence" to the degradation of the Roman Empire, the switch to the empire of Badinguet and to the years which followed its collapse was easy. When the Sâr Péladan (Joséphin Péladan, 1859–1918) entitled his vast epic novel, his "éthopée," *Latin Decadence,* he meant to represent and condemn modern customs that had been corrupted by materialism. We all know Verlaine's famous statement, so characteristic—considering its date (1883)—of a general state of mind:

Je suis L'Empire à la fin de la Décadence
Qui regarde passer les grands Barbares blancs
En composant des acrostiches indolents
D'un style d'or où la langueur du soleil danse.

I am the Empire at the end of Decadence
looking at the great white Barbarians passing through
All the while composing indolent acrostics
In a golden style in which the languishing sun dances.
(*Langueur* in *Jadis et naguère*)

Often explicit, as in this sonnet by Verlaine, the comparison with the decadence of the Roman Empire is a constant. Baudelaire, in his study of the painter Constantin Guys, had already spoken of "decadences," i.e., troubled, transitional times "when democracy is not yet all-powerful, when the aristocracy is only partially tottering on the edge and degraded." The decadence he lived was of just such a kind, and he recognized himself just as easily in the Apulean era, the second century A.D. Toward this century and those that followed, which were even gamier, were drawn men like des Esseintes in Huysmans's *A Rebours* (Against the grain) (1884): "Stormy times, jolted by horrendous troubles, . . . while the Roman Empire shook at its foundations, while the lunacies of Asia, the filth of paganism, overflowed its bounds."

Many writers of the decadent and symbolist era felt surrounded by barbarians. For Huysmans, it was "the new generations, those hotbeds of hideous boors who feel the need to speak and laugh loudly in restaurants and cafés; who without apologizing push you around on the sidewalk; who without even excusing themselves or even addressing you, stick a set of baby carriage wheels between your legs." For Maurice Barrès, it was other people, those who surround Philippe (his double in *Le Culte du moi* [The cult of me]), people who have a conception of life diametrically opposed to his (*Sous l'oeil des Barbares,* [Under the eye of the barbarians]) (1888). In act 2 of *Tête d'Or* (The head of gold) (1889), Claudel's first masterpiece, Simon Agnel triumphs over the redheaded barbarians. The helpless watchmen who were supposed to guard the palace show up again, ten years later, in *Le Poème des décadences* (The poem of decadences) by Milosz, in which courtesans discuss precious stones to the roar of "the ocean of barbarian hordes from afar." Some people resist, withdraw into their splendid solitude, or declare themselves ready for the supreme fight. Others, however, accept, or even with loud cries call the barbarians liberators. There is the new aristocracy of Nietzsche, the Pleiades of Gobineau; there are also the patrician dandies of Milosz and the d'Annunzio of the *Intermezzo di rime,* who does not answer the call of cohorts fighting against the barbarians and who would rather forget his happy fate in idleness, "amidst mad or treacherous pleasures."

Simple imagery of the time, one might claim; but it is more than that. The myth of decadence, the myth of the barbarians, betrays the haunting obsession that the doomsday myth (or at least doomsday for a certain kind of world) imposed on the imagination of turn-of-the-century writers. As early as 1866, the Goncourt brothers spoke of "the end of societies." In *Le Crépuscule des dieux* (The twilight of the gods) (1884) of Elémir Bourges, the duke, attending a performance of *Götterdämmerung* in Bayreuth, sees in it the symbol of the end of the world as he knows it: "All the signs of destruction were visible on the old world, like angels of wrath, above a condemned Gomorrah." A critic praising Marcel Schwob writes, "Magically you evoke antiquity, this Heliogabalesque antiquity toward which flow the imaginations of thinkers and the brushes of painters, these decadences and these doomsdays, mysteriously perverse and macabre."

But the modern age is just as Heliogabalesque. Must we condemn it, or must we, on the contrary, delight in it? The same hesitation recurs. Despite the "pagan school," myth, in any case, is not an opportunity for a return to "naked eras," for a "renewal of resources"; it proclaims a forthcoming *eschaton* for which setting suns are the decor. In "a world worn threadbare where the most beautiful things on earth seem to fall into pieces by themselves," as Walter Pater writes in *Marius the Epicurean* (1884), is there any possible hope of starting over beyond chaos or mere exhaustion?

IV. Back to Basics

To answer this question after the fact, we will deliberately set aside the revival of Christian literature and aesthetic consolation and for the moment concentrate on the way in which the decadent and symbolist period conceived myth. Mallarmé's *Les Dieux antiques* (The ancient gods) happens to be an extremely loose adaptation of a manual attributed to the Reverend George William Cox and published in 1867: *A Manual of Mythology in the Form of Question and Answer.* But the manual and its French adaptation are inseparable from the school of comparative mythology, which ever since the mid-nineteenth century posits a so-called naturalist conception of mythology. The assumption made by Ludwig Preller is that "nature was the maternal foundation and the starting point for the representation of gods." The names of the principal exponents of this school—Preller, Bréal, Adalbert Kuhn—figure prominently in the foreword to *Les Dieux antiques.* The only name missing is that of Max Müller, the most important of all.

The great merit of the naturalistic conception of myth is to pull it away from an allegorical system and give it back to an archetypal system. For the aforementioned scholars and for the popularizers who came later, mythology reenacted the spectacle of the primordial elements. These are the elemental forces of nature and its dazzling manifestations—sun, rain, lightning, the flow of rivers, the growth of plants, all "represented as the varied actions, the changing states of living beings" and expressed "in narratives full of imagery" in the great divine myths. The foreword to *Les Dieux antiques* further states: "What pleasure is added to our sense of surprise at the sight of familiar myths slowly evaporating in water, light, and elemental wind, through the very magic that analysis of the ancient word implies!" Hence a new task that might well be assigned to the poet: to reenact the great spectacles and permanent conditions of life that stand behind mythological figures and to reveal in them elemental symbols.

Adalbert Kuhn preferred the archetype of the storm. Max Müller, G. W. Cox, and after him Mallarmé inclined rather toward the sun. For Cox, "the epic poems of the Aryans are merely versions of one and the same story, and this story originates in the phenomena of the natural world and in the course of each passing day and year." In a more concise and striking form, Mallarmé presents the same idea. The poems "are never anything but one of the numerous narrations of the great solar drama performed under our eyes each day and each year." Zeus is the pure sky; Athena, dawn; Hermes, the wind accompanying daybreak; Paris, the dark power of night that robs the western sky of the beautiful twilight. The desertion of Ariadne, and of Brunhild, means nothing but the fact that the sun cannot be delayed in the east by dawn. And if "Oedipus proves to be overcome by a power he cannot resist," it means that "the sun cannot rest in its course: the heavenly body does not act freely; in the evening, it must join the dawn from whom it was separated in the morning."

In Claudel's first drama, the parallel between the fate of Tête d'Or (Head of gold) and the course of the sun is too clear to conceal a new paraphrase of what Mallarmé would call "the solar act." (Claudel was one of Mallarmé's audience on the rue de Rome.) The victorious hero attempts in vain to forget that sun "whose first rays would in olden times make him sing / like a stone cast against bronze," and he attempts instead to see in it nothing but a "cow's lung floating at a butcher shop door." He comes back to fetch it, however, to take it with him finally on his expedition toward the gates of Asia, toward the land of the dawn. The death of Tête d'Or takes place at the end of a long death struggle, which is also the dying of the sun in the sky.

Ô soleil! Toi, mon
Seul amour! ô gouffre et feu! ô sang! ô
Porte! Or, or! Colère sacrée!
. . .
Je meurs. Qui racontera
Que, mourant, les bras écartés, j'ai tenu le soleil sur ma poitrine comme une roue?

O sun, Thou, my
Only love! O abyss and fire! O blood! O
Gate! Gold, gold! Holy wrath!
. . .
I die. Who shall tell
That, dying, arms outstretched, I held the sun on my chest like a wheel?

Reappearing quite explicitly this time is the myth of Memnon, the famous black statue that sings under the influence of the sun's first rays.

Many other examples could be cited: Odysseus appearing as the "avenging sun" in *Anciennetés* (Antiquities) by Saint-Pol Roux ("Le Palai d'Itaque au retour d'Odysseus métamorphosé en mendiant" [The palace of Ithaca on the return of Odysseus disguised as a beggar]) (1885); the inspiring sun in *The Seventh Ring* (1907) by Stefan George; the murderous sun in Bély's "A mes amis" (To my friends) (1907); the Herculean sun in Rubén Darío's "The Optimist's Greeting" in *Cantos of Life and Hope* (1905); the menstrual sun in Apollinaire ("Merlin et la vieille femme" [Merlin and the old woman] in *Alcools* [Alcoholic spirits]) (1913); the sun of "light and life" which the Jewish poet Chernichovsky in his indefatigable hope sought in an extraordinary collection of the most diverse myths leading up to a "face-to-face encounter with the statue of Apollo."

The end point of this solar quest through myths might well be the astonishing *Cantique de la connaissance* (Hymn of knowledge) by Milosz, in *La confession de Lémuel* (The confession of Lémuel) (1922), fruit of "the teaching of the sun-bright hour of the nights of the Divine." Here again the sun is the primal element; from it "gold draws its substance and its color; man draws the light of his knowledge." The sun

Alexandre Séon, *Le sar Mérodack Joséphin Peladan,* Catalogue of the Salon de la Rose-Croix, 1892. Photo Martine Pont.

Frontispiece for the Androgyne, from the cycle "la décadence latine" ("Ethopée"), 1891, by Alexandre Séon. Catalogue of the Salon de la Rose-Croix, 1892. Photo Martine Pont.

makes it possible for the new poet to reach the knowledge of archetypes: "being of the nature of our mind," they "are situated, as he is, in the consciousness of the solar egg." This immediate knowledge must lead to the abolition of symbols, instruments of a mediating knowledge:

> The poets of God saw the world of archetypes and described it piously through the precise and luminous terms of the language of knowledge.
> The decline of faith is manifest in the world of science and art by a growing dimness of language.
> The poets of nature sing the imperfect beauty of the world of the senses according to the ancient sacred mode.
> However, struck by the secret discordance between the mode of expression and the subject,
> And powerless to rise up to the only special place, I mean Patmos, the archetypes' land of vision,
> In the night of their ignorance, they imagine an intermediary world, floating and sterile, the world of symbols.

We pass from what Gilbert Durand calls the "numinosity" of myths to the luminosity of archetypes. The "Idea" sought by the symbolist mystique descends from heaven to return to earth, less ideal than "surreal," or perhaps even just simply real. For deep down, Milosz seems to be dreaming of the abolition of the dualism phenomenon/noumenon, and with him all those poets who are referred to as "naturistic" and who were often nothing but repentant symbolists. This milestone in literary history, for which the turn of the century could easily be made responsible, is more likely explained by the ambiguities of symbolism. There is no better example of this than a poem from *Chants de pluie et de soleil* (Songs of rain and sun) (1894) by Hugues Rebell, in which the poet persists in speaking of the "Idea" when he really means "things":

Je ne m'occuperai point de ces petites agitations
qui commencent sur un vagissement,
Et se terminent par un râle,
Mais de l'Idée qu'elles révèlent.
Je regarde les larmes, je regarde les sourires,
Ainsi que la pluie et le soleil;
Et les rugissements, les cris, les clameurs joyeuses,
les appels désespérés,
Passent en moi comme le vent dans les branches
d'un grand chêne.
Je n'étudierai point une passion, une âme, un visage,
Mais je monterai sur la Tour qui domine l'horizon,
Pour découvrir les peuples en marche,
Voir la forêt, la plaine et la mer
Et entendre des milliers de voix célébrer l'harmonie.

I will no longer busy myself with these trifling agitations
that begin with a wail
and end with a death rattle,
but with the Idea that they reveal.
I regard tears, I regard smiles,
like rain and sunshine;
and the bellowings, the cries, the joyous outcries, the desperate calls,
are to me like wind in the branches of a great oak tree.
I will no longer study a passion, a soul, a face,
but I will climb the Tower that dominates the horizon
in order to discover the peoples on the march,
to see the forest, the plain, and the sea,
and to hear the thousands of voices celebrate harmony.

After Whitman, writers like André Gide and Vicente Huidobro came to an agreement in their appeal to the things of the earth. In a famous mythological poem, *Les Muses* (The Muses) (the first of the *Cinq Grandes Odes* [The five great odes], 1900–1905), Claudel assigned to the second creator, namely, himself, the task of discovering the gold buried in the heart of each element, the gold of divine presence hidden by the Wagnerian myths. As if in accordance with the wish of Saint-Pol Roux, the renewal of the Word corresponded to "l'Age du Soleil" (The age of the sun), "the star bursting like a ripe fruit whose seeds of sensitive and moral clarity must be welcomed."

A decadent art could easily be accused of being epigonal, of giving too much attention to works and traditions of the past. Thus, at the end of the nineteenth century a mythology of the times, mythological bric-a-brac, emerged. It went against the grain of a modernity deemed vulgar; but curiously enough, it also went hand in hand with it. Nietzsche had a brilliant explanation for this phenomenon: deprived of myths, modern man is starving for myths, and he "rummages in all past eras to find his roots, even if he has to rummage back to the farthest reaches of antiquity." Accumulation is not the only characteristic of the turn-of-the-century use of myth. Ornamental, allegorical, symbolic, it tends to cut itself off from its archetypal roots, at least among second-rate writers. The Rimbaud of *Illuminations* constitutes a remarkable exception. And Nietzsche proposed for the myth of Prometheus simultaneously an allegorical interpretation (the need for crime that is imposed on the titanic individual) and an archetypal interpretation: "the hyperbolic value which a naive humanity attributes to fire as it does to the true palladium of a nascent civilization." The poets of life, the "naturists," whom literature textbooks present as the gravediggers of symbolism, benefited nevertheless from a current that was not interrupted during the second half of the nineteenth century, namely, comparative mythology, with an original attempt to return to the elemental meaning of myths. Was this the finish or the rebirth of myths? The end has all the makings of a renewal. The poetic quest, seemingly reaching out to a "beyond," reverts to a "here below." It remains, like the myth in what is alive, the locus of a contradiction.

P.Br./g.h.

BIBLIOGRAPHY

General Works on Decadence and Symbolism

Symbolism: A Bibliography of Symbolism as an International and Multi-Disciplinary Movement, ed. D. L. Anderson (New York 1975). A. BALAKIAN, *The Symbolist Movement: A Critical Appraisal* (New York 1967). G. MICHAUD, *Message poétique du symbolisme* (Paris 1954).

General Works on Mythology in the Period

P. ALBOUY, *Mythes et mythologies dans la littérature française* (Paris 1969). M. PRAZ, *La carne, la morte e il diavolo nella letteratura romantica* (Milan 1930; new ed., Florence 1976). P. BRUNEL, "L'au-delà' et l''en-deçà': Place et fonction des mythes dans la littérature 'symboliste'," *Neohelicon* 3–4 (1974).

Works on Mythology

L. PRELLER, *Griechische Mythologie* (Leipzig 1854). G. W. COX, *The Mythology of the Aryan Nations* (1870). S. MALLARMÉ, *Les dieux antiques* (Paris 1880); reprinted in Mallarmé's *Œuvres complètes*, ed. H. Mondor and G. Jean-Aubry (Paris 1945).

Texts

C. BAUDELAIRE, "Richard Wagner et *Tannhaüser* à Paris," in *La revue européenne*, 1 April 1861. C. P. CAVAFY, *Poiemata* (Ikaros 1952); English trans., K. P. Kabaphes, *Poems* (New York 1952). P. CLAUDEL, *Tête d'or*, Librairie de l'art indépendant (1890); reprinted in *Théâtre*, ed. J. Madaule and J. Petit, vol. 1 (Paris 1967). G. D'ANNUNZIO, *Intermezzo di rime* (1883), in *Tutte le Opere di Gabriele D'Annunzio*, ed. E. Bianchetti (1950–64). J. K. HUYSMANS, *A Rebours, new ed., U.G.E., coll. 10/18, no. 975.* J. LORRAIN, *Monsieur de Phocas*, new ed., Le Livre Club du Libraire (1966); *Le sang des dieux* (1882), new ed., Édouard-Joseph (1920). O. V. DE L., MILOSZ, *Poésies*, new ed., A. Silvaire (1960), 2 vols. H. REBELL, *Chants de pluie et de soleil*, Librairie Charles (1894). L. VON SACHER-MASOCH, *Venus im Pelz* (Stuttgart 1870); English trans., *Venus in Furs* (Boston 1925). P. VALÉRY, "Existence du symbolisme" (Maestricht 1939), reprinted in vol. 1 of *Œuvres*, ed. J. Hytier (Paris 1962). W. B. YEATS, *The Collected Poems* (London 1933).

The Androgyne

There is no one myth of the androgyne, but rather a family of myths. Should these be considered different variants of the same original or fundamental myth? Probably not. It is better to speak of a mythic theme, whose actual unity we cannot affirm but which functions as an exemplary case. All the constitutive elements of myth are encountered in this theme, as in a microcosm, and all the explanations, all the patterns of analysis of myth, find their justification in it.

The androgyne theme is extremely widespread, one might almost say universal: it is recognized everywhere, from Greece to China, from Egypt to pre-Columbian America, from Africa to Oceania. It does not occupy the same position everywhere and almost never takes the same shape; but there is hardly a mythical construction in which a trace of the androgyne is not found. The theme is extremely polymorphous and appears not only in the form of mythical narratives: it is a complex in which the observation of nature, rituals, personal fantasies, the figures of gods, and narratives are blended. The point of departure is surely the consideration of an essential given of human existence: there are distinct sexes with corresponding physical and psychological characteristics. But nature everywhere offers to observation the presence of beings of uncertain sex, bisexual beings, the whole gamut of intersexual states. The recognized limits and forms of the states may vary from culture to culture, as the characteristics of each sex vary: their presence poses a problem and requires an explanation, since the irreducible presence of the two sexes demands it.

Thus a combination of three terms is formed—masculine, feminine, androgynous—which appears in the form of a myth that is lived and represented, a myth in action. A whole series of rituals, in particular those that are called rites of passage, give ample place to bisexuality: disguises in which one sex assumes the dress and attributes of the other, and operations such as subincision by which a man is symbolically endowed with the sexual organs of both sexes. Ceremonies of initiation, marriage rites, mourning ceremonies, fertility festivals, agrarian rites, and carnivals play upon the inversion of the sexes, mingling them in order to institute, if only for an instant, a symbolic androgyny. Multiplying and perhaps explaining the effect of these rites, almost everywhere there are fantasies of bisexuality, which belong to the most archaic foundation of our representations. For each sex, the presence of the other constitutes a source of anxiety, a threat, and a complement at once desired and feared. Accordingly, having both sexes is a recurrent fantasy, present in dreams, stories, works of art, and alchemy: simultaneously *animus* and *anima*, a human being is double and oscillates between the two poles of a totality that he seeks to reconstitute.

The androgyne also appears in the form of gods, double deities who have both masculine and feminine powers. These gods may be the origin of cosmologies, representing the primordial confusion before beings separate, divided according to the categories of the organized world as we know it, but also incarnating the double aspect of power and fertility, Zeus Labraundos, bearded and with six breasts on his chest, or Dionysus the man-woman. Besides the gods there are androgynous heroes, such as Tiresias, who passes successively through the two sexes; and something of a mythic fascination endures in the interest taken in an Aeonian knight. The priests themselves may be androgynes: devotees who castrate themselves in order to reconstitute the bisexuality of their god, shamans who dress and live as women in order to incarnate the cosmic totality. The rites and gods are associated with mythical accounts, in which the androgyne serves to explain the birth of the world and its development. More or less elaborate, the accounts are gradually transformed into mythical allegories or explicit philosophico-religious systems (the myth of Plato's *Symposium*, Orphism).

Can the mythological complex of the androgyne be explained by a single schema? People have claimed to account for it by ritual, by the psychology of archetypes, by a function of mediation: between the two poles of masculine and feminine there is a mediating category, androgyny, that makes it possible to pass from one pole to the other and to reflect at the same time on both terms of the opposition; might not the serpent of Genesis be the hermaphroditic intermediary between Adam and Eve, as the androgynous shaman is the intermediary between earth and heaven? It is certainly imprudent to reduce a mythical complex to its formal surface structure: the semantics of a myth is richer than its basic combinatory organization, as is demonstrated by the diverse forms of its preservation and its revivals in occidental tradition.

Although polytheistic religions everywhere grant androgyny an important place, the situation is completely different with the monotheistic religions of salvation: androgyny is not only put aside, it is systematically concealed. And we can understand why: the one god, refusing the empirical determinations of the gods of polytheism, cannot participate in one sex or the other without contradiction. As the object of a negative theology, he can be neither masculine, nor feminine, nor androgynous. But, concealed by the orthodoxies, androgyny continued to live on their margins, in the esotericisms of the Jewish, Christian, and Muslim traditions. Recurrent themes circulated in these traditions, in which Gnosticism, Neoplatonism, cabala, alchemy, and mysticism came to meet: an androgynous god, a god of origins, the product of an unbegotten forefather, the primary celestial power that gives birth to a series of aeons symmetically distributed in male and female pairs; the first androgynous human, who possesses both sexual powers and is thus truly

Khnopff. *The Sphinx*. Brussels, Musées royaux des Beaux-Arts de Belgique. Museum photo.

made in the image of god; the fall of man, who finds himself separated from the universal life and for whom the division of the sexes marks the origin of evil, which is separation; finally the ascension toward the light that at the end of time must reconstitute the androgyny of the origins. Androgyny thus marks the beginning and the end of history, to which it gives a meaning.

At the end of the eighteenth century, esoteric traditions emerged from the shadows and converged with two other movements to reactivate the theme of androgyny. On the one hand, with Winckelmann artistic neoclassicism accorded a central place to the hermaphrodite, regarded as the incarnation of ideal beauty, in which the partial beauties of the two sexes are harmoniously merged; and, after the heroic nudity of David and his school, plastic arts from the turn of the century offered a new type of nude: the clear-cut opposition between the male and female canons of beauty is succeeded by a beauty in which sexual contrasts are subdued, in which the body assumes the uncertain forms of the androgyne (Girodet, J. Broc, Granger, Dubufe). From another quarter, nascent biology lent a new force to the masculine-feminine pair, which became one of the fundamental categories of the romantic *Naturphilosophie:* the pair of terms, separated and tending to reconstitute an original unity, constitutes a polarity, a model particularly able to account for the physical and social world. At the same time, scientific observation multiplies the cases of intersexuality that exist now with all the force of scientific affirmation, while literature takes an interest in homosexuality or ambiguous sexuality. In this way, physical hermaphroditism and psychological androgyny reconstitute the double effect produced by mythical androgyny—horror and the holy, repulsion and adoration—reactivated by scientific understanding of living forms.

Throughout the nineteenth century, the theme of androgyny assumed greater prominence. Two types of androgyny succeeded one another and intermingled. In the first half of the century, the androgyny of synthesis and totality was theorized by F. von Baader and appeared in the works of Michelet, Balzac, and Wagner. In the second half of the century, the androgyne became a central figure of literature and the arts, from Swinburne and Peladan to G. Moreau and Stefan George: this was a more ambiguous androgyne, who lives only on the hesitation and indecision between the two poles, while adorning himself in the glamours of erotic or even satanic provocation. Does this revival of androgyny involve a real myth or only a fantasy reserved for a few creators? But the diffusion of the fantasy is itself a sign, the sign of a reflection on identity and sexual roles, thus proclaiming that mutation which leads us to question the masculine-feminine duality in our culture. Androgyny became again a myth; after Fliess, Freud affirmed the existence of a primal bisexuality: the human being is, at at least one moment in his development, woman-man and man-woman (Groddeck). And if, as Freud has said, the theory of instinct is our mythology, it was reserved to psychoanalysis to restore to the androgyne his function as myth, that is, as the paradigmatic narrative that makes sense of the world for a whole culture.

J.M./b.f.

The Androgyne, the Double, and the Reflection: A Few Myths of Romanticism

I. The Androgyne

Nineteenth-century writers generally accepted the dogma that the original Adam or "Kadmon Adam" of the Hebraic tradition was androgynous—the Platonic myth of the first androgyne furnishing, moreover, confirmation from a different tradition.

Fabre d'Olivet made Isha, the wife of Adam, a representation of human will, a notion that Ballanche was to take up again. Ballanche saw the descendants of Seth as the Orientals, representing the male, active, and initiating principle, in opposition with the Cainites or Occidentals, associated with the female, passive, and initiated principle. From another point of view, in which he followed Vico, he held that the patrician principle must regenerate the female and plebeian principle through initiation.

Father Enfantin saw himself as representing only half of the revelatory couple, while his imitator Ganneau ("the one-who-was-Ganneau") claimed to be Mapah (father and mother), the perfect androgyne. In 1829, H. de Latouche published *Fragoletta,* a clever and rather vulgar romantic treatment of the theme of a creature who is both man and woman. The heroine of *Mademoiselle de Maupin* (1836) of Théophile Gautier is an ambiguous being, a woman nevertheless, whose androgyny is chiefly mental. A late story from the same author, *Spiritist* (1865), describes a search for the union of souls that results in the creation of a new being, according to the doctrine of Swedenborg, who had also inspired Balzac's *Seraphîta* (1835).

Novalis, who always dreamed of total fusion with the loved one, found the image of the hermaphrodite prominent in the works of J. Boehme. But in both Balzac and Novalis, the process of angelization takes place through carnal ecstasy, which assumes absolute monism, the identity of body and spirit.

Though Balzac clearly describes "two creatures reunited in an angel, lifted by the wings of pleasure," the writer's degree of sincerity in *Seraphîta* poses a problem. He badly wanted to seduce Mme Hanska, and it is somewhat disturbing to note that in the same period he described a case of lesbianism in *The Girl with the Golden Eyes.* The invention of the character of Seraphîtus-Seraphîta suggests a misunderstanding of Swedenborg. For Swedenborg had not imagined that such a hypostasis could assume human form and become incarnate.

II. The Theme of the Double

The theme of the Double, in its various aspects—the Dioscuri, the Menechmes, Narcissus, and Amphitryon—has close connections with the theme of the Androgyne, but nevertheless gave rise, in the nineteenth century, to a whole series of works which must be mentioned separately. In a sense, the link between the theme of the Double and the recollection of a primordial Androgyne, or the myth of Narcissus, is established through the Gnostic belief that Adam lost his celestial nature because he became enamored of his own image. But in the Occidental conscience, at least, every work is born at first from the author's interest in himself, and it is with good reason that A. W. Schlegel saw Narcissus as an image of the poet.

In the foreground of romantic works pervaded by the theme of the Double must be placed the work of Jean-Paul Richter. In *Siebenkäs* he had defined the *Doppelgänger* (or *Doppeltgänger*): "It is what people call those who see themselves." Of course, a psychic phenomenon so exceptional (and one to which alcoholics seem especially inclined) has given birth to a modern myth, illustrated by numerous and important works. In Jean-Paul's novel *Siebenkäs,* the protagonists Leibgeber and Siebenkäs are "a single soul in two bodies," which is the very definition of the mystic androgyne. The same conception is found in *Titan* (1800), by the same author; however, in this work Albano commits the fatal error of believing that the demonic Roquairol is his soul brother. In this story, there are no less than five pairs of doubles, several women have the same appearance and are substituted for one another, and, in this gratuitously complicated plot, Jean-Paul finally also introduces the Menechmes of his *Siebenkäs. Flegeljahre* (The mad years, 1804) depicts the twins Walt and Vult, whose personalities are portrayed as complementary.

Goethe, in book 11 of *Poetry and Truth,* relates the vision of his double that he had after he had left Frederica Brion. In *Wilhelm Meister,* he multiplied the family resemblances and the doubles. He approved the analysis of J. J. Ampère, who saw in Faust and Mephistopheles the complementary aspects of his self.

In *Isabelle of Egypt* (1812) Achim von Armin introduced an original variant of the Double: Bella Golem, a magical double of the protagonist. In *Peter Schlemihl* (1814) Chamisso told the story of the man who sold his shadow. The theme of the double, in all its aspects, is a fundamental idea in the work of E. T. A. Hoffmann, whose stories abound in split personalities, transfers of personality, and malevolent doubles, in keeping with the interest of the times in "magnetism" and somnambulism. Especially characteristic is *The Devil's Elixirs* (1814), which was influenced by the theories of G. H. Schubert; there the storyteller produced counterparts who also serve as doubles. The hero is a young Capuchin friar, Médard, whose double is his half brother Victorin. Beside the satanic woman, Euphemia, is Aurelia, who is eventually identified with Saint Rosalie. In *Princess Brambilla* (1820), the protagonists suffer from "chronic dualism." Finally, it is striking to see Hoffmann, in *The Adventure of the Night of Saint Sylvester,* introduce Schlemihl, who no longer has a shadow, bringing him together with Spikher, who abandons his reflection.

The underlying idea throughout is that madness is a form of wisdom, that dream and fantasy alone may permit us to connect the external aspects and the mysterious aspects of our existence. In many respects, the character of Kreisler, the genial musician and fool, the hero of *Kater Murr,* is the double of Hoffmann himself.

Hoffmann's work (especially *The Devil's Elixirs* and *The Night of Saint Sylvester*) exerted a profound influence on Gérard de Nerval. The memory of the *Elixirs* reappears in *The Chimeras,* especially in *Aurelia* (1855). Moreover, the theme of the double also intrudes repeatedly in this story; Neval gives it the Oriental name of *ferouer* (*farvāsis*). Previously, in "The Story of Raoul Spifame," from the *Illuminati,* and in "The Story of Caliph Hakem," from the *Voyage to the Orient,* Nerval had treated several aspects of the theme of the double. For him, the obsession with resemblances is linked to paramnesia and the quest for personal identity; *Corilla* and the scenario of *Polygamy Is a Hanging Matter* are equally characteristic. For both Hoffmann and Nerval, the problem of the double is associated with the problem of literary creation. It is by looking at his self in a crystal with multiple facets that the creator brings forth his characters, who themselves nearly always appear in pairs, the laws of the human spirit being in this respect consistent with those of biology: Balzac and Dostoyevski, for example, conceived their characters both in twos and in fours. Dostoyevski treated the theme in his early novel *The Double* (1846), and in *The Brothers Karamazov* (1880) he depicts Ivan conversing with the Devil, an objectification of the obscure part of his being, before coming to grief in madness. The counterpart, the real person, should not be confused with the double, a projection or reflection that has only a potential existence; on the literary plane, however, the two themes are closely connected. It is the double that is treated in Heinrich Heine's poem *The Double* ("I am the fruit of your thoughts"), Coleridge's poem *Transformation,* Musset's *The Night of May* (1835); in Edgar Allen Poe's *William Wilson* (1839), somewhat as in the work of Hoffmann, the theme of the double is combined with the theme of the counterpart.

Heinrich von Kleist wrote of "tragic somnambulism"; his characters are subject to the absence of their selves (as was their creator). His *Amphitryon* (1807) depicts Jupiter endeavoring to make Alcmene understand that there are two distinct selves in her husband's personality. The principal characters of his great plays *Penthesilea* (1808), *Catherine of Heilbronn* (1810), and *The Prince of Homburg* (1821, posth.) contain two antagonistic personalities, and the conflict between the conscious personality and the suppressed tendencies plunges them at times into a sort of hypnosis, at which point they lose consciousness of their actions.

Ralph Tymms has pointed out that Zacharias Werner, at about the same time, created characters subject to similar divisions of consciousness in *Attila, King of the Huns* (1808) and *Wanda, Queen of the Sarmatians* (1810), and Grillparzer saw in Zacharias Werner an image of Narcissus. In a different vein, Charles Nodier told the *Legend of Sister Beatrice:* this is a pious story from the work of Abraham Bzovius, according to which the Virgin was supposed to have assumed, for some years, the appearance and the place of a nun unfaithful to her vows, while awaiting the return of the nun to the convent from which she had fled.

In the background of all these literary works lurks, transposed onto the plane of individual consciousness, the long Indo-European and biblical tradition of legendary twins, one of whom is usually inferior to the other: Pollux must assign half of his immortality to Castor, Zethus dominates Amphion, Romulus kills Remus, Cain slays Abel. Always one is sacrificed and the other becomes a founding hero. All of these myths express the same truth, conveyed in parallel terms by novels and stories: that the resolution of antagonisms is necessary for survival.

But, in another formulation, the image of the soul is conceived as a double (on the same scale or smaller). Thus, in several ways, the myth of the Double appears to be quite fundamental, and there is no reason to be surprised that this myth assumed such importance in the nineteenth century.

J.Ri./b.f.

BIBLIOGRAPHY

I. The Androgyne

P. ALBOUY, "Le mythe de l'androgyne (à propos de *Mademoiselle de Maupin*)," *Mythologiques,* 1976, 324–33. A. J. L. BUSST, "The Image of the Androgyne in the Nineteenth Century," in Jan Fletcher, ed., *Romantic Mythologies* (London 1967), 1–95. M. ELIADE, *Méphistophélès et l'androgyne* (Paris 1962). H. EVANS, *Louis Lambert et la philosophie de Balzac* (Paris 1951). T. GAUTIER, *Mademoiselle de Maupin,* Marcel Crouzet, ed. (Paris 1973). M. PRAZ, *The Romantic Agony.*

II. The Double

J. LHERMITTE, "Clinique et physiopathologie," *Les hallucinations* (Paris 1951), chap. 4. J. PERROT, *Mythe et littérature sous le signe des jumeaux* (Paris 1976). O. RANK, *Don Juan: Une étude sur le double* (Paris 1932). A. STOCKER, *Le double: L'homme à la rencontre de soi-même* (Geneva 1946). R. TYMMS, *Doubles in Literary Psychology* (Cambridge 1949).

Romantic Myths of the Rebel and the Victim: Satan, Prometheus, Cain, Job, Faust, Ahasuerus, Don Juan, and Empedocles

In his *Introduction to Universal History* (1830), Michelet in a strange mixture of ideas placed Prometheus at the origin of a wholly romantic lineage: "Liberty without God, impious heroism, in literature, the satanic school that was heralded in Greece in Aeschylus's *Prometheus Bound,* and was revived by Hamlet's bitter doubts, is idealized in Milton's Satan and with Byron falters into despair" (*OEC,* vol. 35, pp. 457–58). A "titanic" tradition flourished in nineteenth-century Europe in numerous works: next to the Titan Prometheus, Satan, as remodeled by Milton, participates as chief of the rebels and, curiously enough, is identified with Pan.

We have long known that the romantics never ceased to draw from the ancient well, which explains the parallel development of myths borrowed from Judeo-Christian books (the Bible, the *Book of Enoch*) and of Greek and Latin myths. In an attempt to assess the contemporary, apparently fallen, condition of man, myths of the fall develop along several parallel tracks, with the oppressor god sometimes called Jehovah and sometimes Zeus-Jupiter.

I. Satan

In the aftermath of Milton's *Paradise Lost* (book 1), Satan's successors go in several directions. One of his descendants, Karl Moor in Schiller's *The Robbers* (1781), was to be the original model for the "noble bandit," whose extraordinary literary posterity included Vautrin and Jean Valjean. Another track consists of mysterious and domineering men, rebels of high caliber such as Montoni in Ann Radcliffe's *Mysteries of Udolpho* (1794), Schedoni in *The Italian, or the Confessional of the Black Penitents* (1797) by the same author, Ambrosio in Lewis's *The Monk* (1796). In Germany, the figure of the mysterious bandit inspired Heinrich Zchokke's *Abellio* (1794), which in turn inspired Charles Nodier's *Le Voleur* (1805) and *Jean Sbogar* (1818). These are all dual characters, so that the theme of the noble bandit is tied to that of the dual personality, of which we shall speak later.

But it was probably Byron who carried the type of the rebel to its peak of perfection by conceiving a whole series of gloomy heroes, all prey to a mysterious fate, in works that bear their names: *Lara, The Corsair, The Giaour.* Byron wanted to be like his heroes, which led him to playact his life and to waste it away sedulously. We may recognize the debased forms of the Byronic hero in the protagonist of Alexandre Dumas's *Antony* and in certain characters created by Eugène Sue or Paul Féval, late incarnations of the noble bandit who, in Satanic disguise, represent the Good and aim to save the state. But Médard, the hero of E. T. A. Hoffmann's *The Devil's Elixirs* (1816), had great trouble in distinguishing good from evil. Moreover, Paul Féval puts Byron himself on stage in *The Mysteries of London* (1844), where he appears under the name of the Marquis de Rio Santo.

Hugo's Satan has an intense dramatic presence, and yet he is by definition the one-who-does-not-exist, since the poet does not really believe in the existence of the Devil and identifies evil with matter. All the incarnations of Evil in the work of Hugo, as Pierre Albouy has shown, are envious or jealous before they are wicked.

II. Prometheus

Resorting to an ancient image, Byron (*Prophecy of Dante*) and Hugo (*The Genius, Odes and Ballads,* IV, 6) turn

Prometheus into the image of the misunderstood genius, bringing men the fire from heaven, that is, inspiration. According to P. S. Ballanche (*Orpheus*, book 8), man, thanks to Prometheus, "has acquired the capacity for good and evil." The romantic Prometheus is the foremost example of Titanism; he protests and rebels against the state of things imposed on earth by the Deity, which strikes him as neither rational nor moral. This rebellious posture directed against the apparent reign of evil on earth often involves writers in a kind of Neognosticism that leads to the rehabilitation of beings heretofore considered guilty, such as Cain and, more particularly, Satan, who are then depicted as man's helpers (Byron, *Cain;* Vigny, *Eloa*).

With Lamartine, the pendulum swings constantly from revolt to resignation and back. Resignation seems to be an idea formulated in *The Desert* to mean a God conceived as unknowable. In the piece entitled *Man*, the second of the *Poetic Meditations* (1820), dedicated to Byron, he takes a position with regard to the English poet, saying to him: "Leave doubt and blasphemy to the son of night." But the significant inversion of the roles of God and Satan had already appeared in William Blake, who finally identified himself with Milton, pointing out that Milton "was on the devil's side without realizing it," and who saw Jesus Christ as representing the human imagination.

The romantics' misinterpretation, in part deliberate, of Aeschylus's *Prometheus* was further encouraged by the fact that only the first part (*Prometheus Bound*) of the Greek playwright's trilogy has survived. Of *Prometheus Unbound,* which showed the Titan's reconciliation with Zeus, we have only fragments, and on *Prometheus the Fire Bringer* we can merely conjecture.

In his preface to *Prometheus Unbound,* Shelley explains that reconciliation was inconceivable: the sufferings and endurance of Prometheus, and his opposition to a tyrannical god, seemed to Shelley to constitute the very essence of the myth. Shelley's *Prometheus Unbound* is a lyric masterpiece; in it, the Titan simultaneously represents the human spirit and, in certain respects, Christ. Jupiter appears as the objectification of man's base desires, an incarnation of evil. To free himself from oppression, it is enough to will it by depending on reason and science; this is what makes the work a hymn to human freedom. Demogorgon, a complex character difficult to analyze, seems to represent Necessity seen as a chain of events. The fourth and final act reaches the cosmic dimension; its last verses express recurring optimism in the face of sufferings and evils:

> To suffer woes which Hope thinks infinite;
> To forgive wrongs darker than death or night;
> To defy Power which seems omnipotent;
> To love and bear; to hope till Hope creates
> From its own wreck the thing it contemplates;
> Neither to change, nor falter, nor repent;
> This, like thy glory, Titan, is to be
> Good, great and joyous, beautiful and free;
> This is alone Life, Joy, Empire, and Victory.

In thus expressing his hope in man, Shelley, as M. Raymond Trousson has shown, established the prototype of the romantic Prometheus. In *The Bible of Humanity,* Michelet makes Prometheus the first democrat and extends the inspiration of the English poet. Edgar Quinet summarized his own conception of Prometheus in the preface to his trilogy *Prometheus,* after indicating that in his opinion this hero "is the image of religious humanity." He goes on to say: "But not only does he have this historical character, he also encompasses the inner drama of God and man, of faith and doubt, of creator and creation; because of that, this tradition can be applied to all times and this divine drama shall thereby never end." In accordance with Herder's philosophy of history, whereby each form is born of the one preceding it, Edgar Quinet makes Prometheus the pagan forerunner of Christ. Such a conception of the religious evolution of humanity clearly implies that religions are mortal, as are all things human ("as the eagle grows old, so will the dove"). Quinet never lacked inspiration, but his power of expression was never quite commensurate with his ideas, which explains why he is seldom read.

In *God* (4, *The Vulture*), Hugo contemplates the character of Prometheus at length, and sees him as the awakener of consciousness and reason, the man of progress, who pushed back superstitions and ignorance. In a short early poem entitled *Prometheus* (1816), Byron had already hailed the Titan who rebelled against the deity, the Titan whose "divine crime was to be good." Louis Ménard's early work *Prometheus Unbound* (1843) is also the apotheosis of progressive faith: "The Ideal is within you: Behold the supreme God." As M. R. Trousson pointed out, what attracted the romantics to the character of Prometheus is the fact that he was not content to limit himself to an egocentric revolt, but managed to be regarded as a philanthropist, building a new world with the help of reason and knowledge. With the exception of Nerval, the theme of Pandora disappears almost entirely, since Prometheus is no longer considered guilty. The romantic *Christ* becomes a Promethean figure. But it was Madame de Staël who provided an incomplete translation of Jean-Paul Richter's *The Dream* in her *On Germany* (1810), and who must surely be held chiefly responsible for the fact that Vigny (*The Mount of Olives,* 1843) and Nerval (*Christ among the Olive Trees,* 1844) almost simultaneously made Christ a purely human figure, rebelling against the ruthless Jehovah.

III. Cain

The romantics place Cain among the great rebels or great victims, and in 1821, Byron devoted to him the "mystery" that we have already mentioned. This character, interpreted within a more traditional framework, inspired Hugo to write his celebrated *Conscience* in *The Legend of the Centuries. Conscience* was first intended for *Chastisements,* because Hugo was identifying the accursed Cain with Napoleon III, as is evident from the piece entitled *Sacer esto* (Let it be holy) in *Chastisements* and from numerous fragments that have been preserved.

IV. Job

In the Bible, the Book of Job raises the problem of divine justice and the relation of man to the divine (who takes the form of a hurricane). It inspired Edward Young's *Night Thoughts on Life, Death, and Immortality,* and was widely commented upon during the nineteenth century. Chateaubriand spoke of Job in his *Genius of Christianity,* Pierre Baour-Lormian includes in his *Poetic Evenings* a *Job, a Lyrical Poem.* In 1842, P. Christian prefaced a new edition of a translation of Young's *Night Thoughts* and Hervey's *Graves* with an "Essay on Jobism." In 1851, Isidore Cahen states in his *Sketch on the Philosophy of the Poem of Job:* "Job is more modern and timely than Prometheus himself because he better expresses the bitter disenchantment that is the fruit of a more advanced civilization." In his *Book of Job* (1826), William Blake had explained the sufferings of Job through an exhausting literal interpretation of the text. Only upon accepting his misfortunes and understanding that the spirit alone brings life will Job again find grace in the eyes of Jehovah.

In Ballanche's *Orpheus,* the story of Job runs parallel to that of Prometheus. Whereas Prometheus inaugurated the mode of revolt, Job was the first to raise the moral problem of evil. Ballanche sees the doctrine of the immortality of the soul as emerging from the very despair of Job. Quinet in turn says that Job heralds Christianity (*The Genius of Religions,* V, 4); he does, however, consider that Job "stops at doubt" and contrasts him with Prometheus, "who goes so far as to curse." According to P. Leroux (*Job,* 1866; prologue published in 1860), God answers the plea of his creature with the theory of progress. Lamartine put Job among his "faithful books"—whenever he feels sad and evokes the problems of suffering and death, an irresistible propensity leads his inspiration back to the Book of Job, as we see in some of the most famous poems in *Poetic Meditations* (The Vale, *Despair, Providence for Man,* and *Autumn*). In *Harmonies,* the poem *Why Is My Soul Sad?* is in the same vein; other examples can easily be found. All of this culminates in the magnificent pages on Job in the *Familiar Course of Literature* in 1868.

Hugo's Job is sometimes seen as an actual character and sometimes perceived from within. According to Hugo, Job is superior to Prometheus; we read in *The Unfortunates* (from *Contemplations*): "Even when Prometheus is there, it takes only you, Job, / To make the manure heap higher than the Caucasus." Everywhere one looks one finds this gigantic manure heap or "homo humus." In *William Shakespeare,* in which Hugo articulated his *ars poetica* most explicitly, he stresses the fact that "Job's resignation completes Prometheus's revolt," but he also emphasizes Job's titanic character and power: "Fallen, he becomes gigantic. He crushes the vermin on his open wounds, while calling out to the stars." And, like Quinet, Hugo concludes, "Job's manure heap, once transformed, will become Christ's hill of Calvary."

As P. Albouy has rightly asserted, one might expect Hugo to come up with a wretched but pugnacious character who would embody both Job and Prometheus—and this he did in *The Laborers of the Sea* (1866), with Gilliatt: "A struggling Job, a fighting Job, who faces scourges squarely, a conquering Job, and if such words were not too lofty for a poor fisherman of crabs and crawfish, a Promethean Job." As Hugo intended, Gwynplaine in *The Laughing Man* is a thunderstruck Titan, part Job and part Prometheus. He represents the misshapen people ripe for liberation and rebellion. After Villequier, moreover, Hugo relived Job's drama for himself, and an entire part of his poetry may be deemed "Jobian." This holds true particularly for *Contemplations,* book 4 (*Pauca mea*).

The same inspiration can also be found in numerous poems. It was already evident in *Interior Voices* (1836) with the poem *Sunt lacrymae rerum* (Things Have Tears), for example, and it can still be seen in *Lux* (in *Chastisements*), in *All of the Past and All of the Future* (in *The Legend of the Centuries*), in *The Donkey,* and, in fact, every time Hugo takes up the theme of the Almighty overwhelming his human creature. The Jobian theme of God's unfathomable grandeur also appears in *At the Window through the Night* (in *Contemplations*). Among the fragments published by René Journet and Guy Robert under the title *Things of the Bible,* which appear in P. Albouy's second volume of *Poetic Works* (Bibliothèque de la Pléiade, 859–63), many lines translate or paraphrase passages from the Book of Job. These fragments are sketches for *Contemplations.*

V. Faust

Faust is one of the rare modern myths. For many French romantics, the first reading of Goethe's *Faust* in Gerard de Nerval's translations of 1828 and 1835 was a kind of initiation. And when in 1840 the second part of *Faust* began to be known in France, it became apparent to what extent writers were projecting their hopes and dreams on this one work. Faust as a character took his place beside Hamlet among the heroes of knowledge and understanding and was considered to be a typical representative of the conscience of the Western world as it had been affirmed since the Renaissance. The profound remarks formulated in 1840 by Nerval in his preface to the new edition of *Faust,* parts I and II, had endless repercussions: of particular significance were Nerval's comments on the Helen episode, which he saw as an attempt to reconcile the ancient and modern worlds.

Parallel to Goethe's version of the story of Faust, a popular version of the legend was evolving. This version was preserved by Friedrich von Klinger, who wrote a novel based on it, in which the protagonist travels in many countries and meets with one disaster after another, trying to use the power of Mephistopheles to good ends. Klinger's account inspired Byron's unfinished work *The Deformed Transformed* (1822) as well as Méry and Nerval's joint work *The Image-Maker of Harlem* (1851), which they complicated with ideas about reincarnation. Many other works and characters owe more than one element to Goethe's *Faust.* They include William Beckford's *Calif Vathek* (1786) and numerous rebellious characters: Byron's Giaour mentioned above, the hero in *Manfred* (1817), and Ambrosio in M. G. Lewis's *The Monk.*

Next to Quinet's *Ahasvérus* belongs George Sand's *The Seven Strings of the Lyre* (1839), a symbolic drama in which Albertus, Mephisto, and Helen encounter one another around a lyre, whose strings embody man's noblest inspirations. Honoré de Balzac parodied the theme of the pact with the devil in *Melmoth Reconciled,* which superimposed the memory of Maturin on that of Goethe; but he treated it seriously in *Lost Illusions* (1842), in which Vautrin proposes the diabolic pact to Lucien de Rubempré. And Nikolaus Lenau wrote a lyric and pessimistic *Faust* (1835, definitive edition 1840) in which the hero, like Lucien, commits suicide. This last example represents what one might call a contamination of the character of Faust by that of Werther. The Faust theme was also taken up by composers: Berlioz produced his *Eight Scenes from Faust* in 1828 and *The Damnation of Faust* in 1846. Gounod's *Faust* is dated 1859. To his credit, Robert Browning chose a character closer to the legendary Faust than to the historical Faust (if we are to believe Trithemius and Melanchthon's contention that Faust was an imposter and a sodomite) in his *Paracelsus* (1835).

VI. Ahasuerus, the Wandering Jew

In his youth, Goethe had sketched the outline of an epic poem on Ahasuerus, but the extant fragments have no direct bearing on the character himself. In the seventh canto of Shelley's *Queen Mab* (1813), Ahasuerus speaks out: he curses Jehovah and the priests and derides Jesus. Shelley's Wandering Jew prefers "the liberty of Hell to the servitude of

William Blake, *Job.* London, British Museum. Photo Fotomas.

Heaven"—a good demonstration of juvenile illusions. Friedrich Schubert also chose this character to express his own pessimism.

Perhaps because it was written in his youth, Edgar Quinet's *Ahasvérus* (1833) remains one of this writer's most readable works, characterized by a kind of fresh, youthful inspiration not always evident in his later writings. The principal character is the Wandering Jew, and in the first part there are numerous literary echoes and imitations of the first part of Goethe's *Faust.* Many of Quinet's characters speak with voices unfamiliar to us: Leviathan, the great serpent, the Vinateya bird, the Ocean, the rivers, the Valley of Josaphat, the desert, the stars, sphinxes, and griffins, but also mules, chariots, and birds, not to mention angels and demons. The interweaving sometimes becomes forced when not only Strasbourg Cathedral but even the characters on its stained glass window (including the symbols of the Evangelists) are endowed with the ability to speak! This may well be a poetic idea applied too systematically, although some of the curious dialogues show real strokes of inspiration.

As for doctrine, Quinet begins with Herder's philosophy of history; he then places at the center of his concerns the phenomenon of religion and ends by refuting God and deifying man. Ahasvérus is saved by the love of Rachel, a fallen angel, because she took pity on him and became a servant of Mob (death). In the scene of the Last Judgment, which precedes the conclusion, Ahasvérus is forgiven and becomes the image of mankind to come, whereupon the Eternal Father says to Christ the Judge: "Ahasvérus is the eternal man. All the others are like unto him. Your judgment of him will serve us as the judgment of them all. Our work is now ended, as is the mystery. Our city is closed. Tomorrow we shall create other worlds." The last word is given to Annihilation and Nothingness. The conclusion as a whole must be interpreted within the framework of a pessimism for which, on a cosmic scale, the sum total of all human lives constitutes but a brief moment in time before man makes way for a better-endowed or different species or else Nothingness. In this regard, Quinet never wavered, for he wrote at the end of his *Genius of Religions:* "In the rapid course of our lives, we are barely granted a moment to get to know this universe, and then we must die. Let us then take a hurried glimpse at the spectacle of what people have thought, invented, believed, hoped, and worshiped before our time. By tying all this past to our brief existence, it will seem that we ourselves grow in scope and that, starting from an imperceptible point, we too are making an infinite line."

These words help us to understand why writers, particularly eighteenth-century writers, have so often chosen to express themselves through myths. For myths give the individual a feeling of belonging to a long tradition and thus of overcoming solitude.

VII. Don Juan

Faust is in search of both love and knowledge. The romantic interpretation of the character of Don Juan, formulated in a tale by E. T. A. Hoffmann (1813), tended to turn Don Juan, the mythical hero, into a hero in quest of love and thirsting for the infinite, which went beyond the explicit intentions of Mozart and his librettist Da Ponte. Henceforth, parallels and comparisons between the two heroes recur everywhere, notably in Hugo's *Preface to Cromwell* (1827), in Musset's *Rolla* (1833), and in Théophile Gautier's *Comedy of Death* (1838). It was Christian Dietrich Grabbe who wrote a *Don Juan and Faust* (1829), which superposed two plots and tied together, without actually mixing them, Da Ponte's libretto and Goethe's *Faust.* The main idea was to contrast two heroes who aspired to be superhumans, one typical of the Latin temperament, and the other representing the Germanic mind and soul ("I would not be Faust if I were not German").

Meanwhile the figure of Don Juan, born in Spain, continued his career in the various literatures. Byron used him as a transparent mask for his ironic, sometimes burlesque, and largely autobiographical epic *Don Juan* (1819/1824), which he said he wrote "without any plan but with materials." It is often regarded as his masterpiece; in any case, it is the only work in which Byron succeeded in casting an almost lucid gaze upon himself. In the same year, 1830, Don Juan was the subject of Pushkin's *The Stone Guest* and of Balzac's *The Elixir of Longevity.* In *Namouna* (1832), Musset made him an artist in search of beauty, and in the following year, in *The Morning of Don Juan,* he focused on the confrontation between reality and life. In 1834, Blaze de Bury in *The Commandant's Dinner Party* created a single character combining Don Juan Tenorio and Don Juan Mañara, and absolved the sinner.

In 1834, Prosper Mérimée published his narrative *Souls in Purgatory;* in 1836 Alexandre Dumas staged *Don Juan de Mañara or the Fall of an Angel.* In Lenau's play of 1844, Don Juan, grown old, is killed by the Commander's son; it is really a suicide in disguise. We should also mention Levavasseur's *Don Juan the Graybeard* (1848); J. Viard's *The Old Age of Don Juan* (1853); and Baudelaire's 1846 poem, *Don Juan in Hell* (1846, in *The Flowers of Evil,* 15).

As might be expected, Spain is where the play that established the theme was written, *Don Juan Tenorio* by José Zorilla y Moral (1844), acted communally on All Soul's Day. It is a large-scale play in two parts, in which Don Juan is saved through the intercession of Doña Inés.

VIII. Empedocles

Among the pre-Socratic philosophers, Empedocles was probably the one whose life lent itself most readily to a romantic interpretation. That explains why several nineteenth-century authors counted him among the heroes of knowledge. Like Hamlet, about whom Hugo wrote substantially in *William Shakespeare,* he is a victim of the constant replay of melancholy thoughts. Unlike Faust, he does not succeed in freeing himself through pleasure and action and finally throws himself into the crater of Mount Etna. Hölderlin persistently lends this character some of his own fundamental questions. The successive versions of his *Empedocles,* unfortunately never finished, are strikingly beautiful. The character is depicted as unable to resign himself to having lost the direct contact with the divine which he once possessed and which deified him. "He through whom the spirit has spoken, must depart on time," we read in the first version in 1798. The third version (1799) features a moving dialogue with his disciple Pausanias. The ode that the poet dedicates to the death of Empedocles starts as follows: "Searching and searching for life, you see / A divine fire shooting forth in brilliance deep beyond the earth."

In 1829, Count Jean Labensky (whose pen name was Polonius) published in French a poem of a thousand lines, entitled *Empedocles,* in which he states: "But man chose error over ignorance. / He was meant only to love, but he wanted to know." Louis Ménard, in a poem bearing the same title published in 1851, endows Empedocles with a belief in metempsychosis.

If only because of its romanticism, Matthew Arnold's "Empedocles on Etna" (1852) may well be his masterpiece; after its completion he reverted to a kind of neoclassicism. Arnold's character has read *Hamlet, Faust,* and *Manfred,* as well as Obermann and Amiel. He is a lonely man because of his very superiority. His philosophy is borrowed from Lucretius and Epictetus. He is nothing but knowledge; a particularly beautiful line captures the sense of the poem: "Nothing but a devouring flame of thought."

In Hugo's *God* (*The Ocean from Above*), a spirit challenges him in these admirable terms: ". . . curious about the abyss. Empedocles from God."

J.Ri./g.h.

BIBLIOGRAPHY

1. Satan

M. MILNER, *Le diable dans la littérature française de Cazotte à Baudelaire,* 2 vols. (Paris 1960).

2. Prometheus

A. PY, *Les mythes grecs dans la poésie de Victor Hugo,* P. B. SHELLEY, *Prometheus Unbound* (London 1820). R. TROUSSON, *Le thème de Prométhée dans la littérature européenne,* 2 vols. (Geneva 1964). See also the works by P. ALBOUY and M. PRAZ cited in the text.

3. Cain

C. GRILLET, *La Bible dans Victor Hugo* (Lyon 1910).

4. Job

P. ALBOUY, *La création mythologique chez Victor Hugo* (Paris 1963). C. GRILLET, *La Bible dans Victor Hugo* (Lyon 1910). A. WRIGHT, *Blake's Job: A Commentary* (Oxford 1972).

5. Faust

E. M. BUTLER, *The Fortunes of Faust* (Cambridge 1952). A. DABEZIES, *Le mythe de Faust* (Paris 1972). C. DÉDÉYAN, *Le thème de Faust dans la littérature européenne,* 6 vols. (Paris 1954–67).

6. Ahasvérus

G. VABRE PRADA, *La dimension historique de l'homme ou le Mythe du Juif errant dans la pensée d'Edgar Quinet* (Paris 1960–61).

7. Don Juan

M. BERVEILLER, *L'éternel Don Juan* (Paris 1961). G. GENDARME DE BÉVOTTE, *La légende de Don Juan,* 2 vols. (Paris 1911). L. WEINSTEIN, *The Metamorphoses of Don Juan* (Stanford 1959).

8. Empedocles

M. ARNOLD, *Empedocles on Etna* (London 1852). F. HOLDERLIN, *Empedokles* (Zurich 1949), in many editions and translations. V. HUGO, *Dieu,* R. Journet and G. Robert, eds., 2 vols. (Paris 1960), with a valuable index of proper names. The line cited, in the volume *L'Océan d'en haut,* is no. 3426.

Spirits of the Elements in the Romantic Period: Sylphs, Water Sprites, Salamanders, Gnomes, and Elves

At the confluence of popular traditions with Neoplatonism and the cabala is situated the belief, at least a poetical belief, in the spirits of the elements, which appeared in the writings of numerous nineteenth-century authors. The relevant texts include the writings of certain Fathers of the Church (Lactantius, Cyprian, Clement of Alexandria), Neoplatonists, and cabalists such as Macrobius and Philo, and the Byzantine Michael Psellus (eleventh century), the restorer of Neoplatonism. In 1566, Paracelsus published a *Liber de nymphis, sylphis, pygmaeis et salamandris et de caeteris spiritibus* (Book of nymphs, sylphs, pygmies, and salamanders, and of various spirits); various Christian cabalists of the Renaissance, such as Pico della Mirandola, R. Fludd, G. Postel, and Thomas Heywood in England, also spoke of the spirits of the elements.

In 1670, the Abbé of Villars, in a humorous tone, set out in the *Comte de Gabalis* the theory of elementary spirits, thus constituting what would come to be called the "philosophy of the Rosacrucians": this distinguished the ondines, water sprites; salamanders, spirits of fire; sylphs, associated with the air; and gnomes or elves, connected with the earth. But in narratives, these inventions become superimposed upon the fairy wonderlands of folktales or upon the belief in other beings of the intermediate world, ghosts, spirits, and demons.

Superimposed upon the influence of the various authors

already mentioned was the influence of Jacques Cazotte's novel, *The Amorous Devil* (1772), in which the incarnation of a demon, Biondetta, in order to seduce and tempt Alvare, pretends to be a sylph who needed to be loved by a man in order to attain immortality. Schiller left an unfinished work, *The Visionary* (1786–89), which was inspired by this theme. La Motte-Fouqué published *The Mandragore* in 1810 and *Ondine* in the following year. In order to be reunited with Eros, Psyche must become immortal; the love of Huldbrand of Ringstetten can immortalize Ondine.

But Huldbrand falls in love with Bertelda, with disastrous results. As early as 1812, Achim von Arnim, in *Isabella of Egypt*, develops the theme of the Mandrake, a wicked little magician born from the tears (or the sperm) of an innocent man who is hanged. From La Motte-Fouqué's Ondine is directly derived the White Lady of Avenal in *The Monastery*, by Sir Walter Scott (1820); the very idea of a "white woman" may have come from one of the bedside books of the romantics, Collin de Plancy's *Infernal Dictionary*, which says that this is a name given to certain sylphs or nymphs. In Scott's *Peveril of the Peak* (1822), there is a Fenella who seems to be a caricature of Goethe's Mignon. Finally, *Anne of Geierstein* (1829) tells the story of a complex being, Hermione, who partakes simultaneously of the nature of the sylphs and that of the salamanders.

In 1821, Alexis-Vincent-Charles Berbiguier de Terre Neuve du Thym published his astonishing work *The Elves, or All the Demons are not in the Other World*. Charles Nodier, in *Trilby* (1822), set in the Scotland of Sir Walter Scott, creates an enigmatic being who is something of a synthesis of the spirits of the elements since, depending on the episode that he is in, he is connected with air, fire, or water. E. T. A. Hoffman, who had read *The Amorous Devil* and *Gabalis*, both of which were translated into German, introduced references to the spirits of the elements into his narratives, which are directly influenced by La Motte-Fouqué and also by Louis Tieck, the author of the *Runenberg* and *The Elves* (1811). In this way the archivist Lindhorst in Hoffman's *The Golden Pot* is the incarnation of Oromasis, the prince of igneous substances (who duly added to the repertory of Collin de Plancy). *The Mines at Falun* (1819), the subject of which was hinted at in a story by Jean-Pierre Hebel (*The Unhoped-for Meeting*, 1808), combines the theme of the mines, evoked by Novalis in *Henry of Ofterdingen*, and the influence of the *Runenburg* of Tieck; the great Venus of Tieck corresponds to the Queen of Metals in Hoffman.

Finally, it is appropriate to connect the spirits of the elements with the figure of the queen of Sheba. In *The Crumb Fairy* (1832), by Charles Nodier, the hero, Michel, is protected in his waking state by the Fairy, who has singular powers. But he also lives a kind of dream from one night to the next, in which the Crumb Fairy, so wise in the daytime, at night becomes the wife of Solomon, the radiant Makeda. This can be traced back to the Platonic concept that identifies Wisdom and the Good with Beauty. And it is said that Michel becomes "the emperor of the seven planets." Nerval's queen of Sheba in his *Voyage to the Orient* (1851) is an authentic "daughter of fire," who also commands the spirits of the air through the mediation of the Hudhud hoopoe bird.

One wonders about the deep motivations of all these authors, who depicted the spirits of the elements as representations of a cruder creation relative to human beings, but with an element of purity that is associated with their very nature. A detailed study of each author would make possible an exposition of the compensatory mechanisms or projections that came into play. A study of the group as a whole remains to be done.

J.Ri./d.w.

BIBLIOGRAPHY

ACHIM VON ARNIM, *Isabelle d'Égypte*, introduction, translation and notes by René Guignard (Paris), translation reprinted in book 2 of *Romantiques allemands* (Paris 1973). A. CHASTEL, "La légende de la Reine de Saba," *R.H.R.*, 1939. F. CONSTANS, "Deux enfants du feu, la Reine de Saba et Nerval," *Mercure de France* (April–May 1948). F. DE LA MOTTE-FOUQUÉ, *Ondine*, appears in a translation by Jean Thorel in book 1 of *Romantiques allemands* (Paris 1963), Maxime Alexandre, ed. In the same volume are: TIECK, *Le Runenberg et Les Elfes; Le vase d'or* by HOFFMANN; LA MOTTE-FOUQUÉ, *La mandragore*. E. T. A. HOFFMANN, *Le vase d'or*, Paul Sucher, ed. (Paris 1942). GÉRARD DE NERVAL, *Œuvres*, vol. 2 (contains *Le voyage en Orient* and *Les illuminés*). C. NODIER, *Contes*, P. G. Castex, ed. (includes *Trilby* and *La fée aux miettes*). O. PARSONS COLEMAN, *Witchcraft and Demonology in Scott's Fiction* (Edinburgh and London 1964).

Orpheus and the Poetic and Spiritual Quest of Romanticism

In the romantic period, the figure of Orpheus shone with particular intensity. All the great poets referred to the singer and magus of Thrace, and Brian Juden could with good reason place much of the literature produced in France from 1800 to 1855 under the patronage of Orpheus. But in fact, all of European romanticism corresponds to a rebirth of Orphism, understood in a broad sense, insofar as religious aspirations were expressed in terms of lyricism. And in many respects the romantics joined the spirit of the Renaissance when, for them, the figure of Orpheus served to support the expression of a spiritualist philosophy that allowed the poet to be affirmed as both a magus and a leader of peoples. Indeed, each episode of the myth of Orpheus—the loss of Euridice, the descent into the underworld, the death of Euridice, Orpheus dismembered by the Maenads—is apt to receive diverse interpretations, and as a whole these exemplary situations form something like the breviary of the existential condition of the poet in the world. In other respects it was understood, from the time of Kircher, Dupuis, and Kreuzer (translated by J. D. Guigniaut), that the Orphean Lyre represented not only the constellation of that name, but planetary harmony, and even the entire universe, while the animals charmed by Orpheus represented the constellations (as Lucian of Samosata had already stated in his treatise, *On Astrology*).

Saint-Martin and Fabre d'Olivet made Orpheus a great theosophist. According to Fabre d'Olivet, the love of Orpheus for Euridice represented the love of true science, and the loss of Euridice was associated with a collapse in personal and descriptive lyricism when the first inspiration, prophetic and philosophical, had become inaccessible. In his *Orpheus* (1829), P. S. Ballanche turns the character into a pontiff and a theologian, whose teaching prefigures Christianity. Orpheus is a northerner and a plebeian by choice. In his misfortunes Ballanche sees above all the pain of a failure in love (which results in giving the myth a personal meaning), and the descent into the underworld seems to him to represent an initiation. Generally, Orpheus expresses "universal lamentation." Nevertheless, through suffering, the magus reaches the transcendent vision, the fullness of knowledge, and his gaze acquires the power to transfigure Nature.

Victor Hugo, in the preliminary passage of the *Odes* (*The Poet in the Revolutions*), saw a modern Orpheus in André Chénier ("Who knows how to love, knows how to die"), and he regrouped all the aspects of the myth—the social role of the poet, prophecy, purity, sublime love, the martyr—all the abysses. In *The Satyr* he put the great cosmic lyre into the hands of the main character, turning him into a complete Titan, simultaneously Pan and Orpheus. And in the Idyll of *The Legend of the Centuries* dedicated to *Orpheus* one reads: "I am the human soul that sings / And I love." In poem 50 of the third book of the *Four Winds of the Spirit, Sacred Horror,* Hugo has this phrase: "The serene poet contains the obscure prophet / Orpheus is black." And in *God,* he depicts Orpheus releasing Prometheus, whereas according to the traditional story Heracles was the author of this deed. This means that the poet represents the spirit triumphing over matter and tyranny. The character of Orpheus is often, for Hugo, the pretext for fruitful comparisons with Job, Jacob, Moses, and Dante.

Indeed, one could establish a long list of characters who, in the works of this period, represent the poet. We should add at least Amphion, Arion, Homer, Pythagoras, and Faust.

In the *Voyage to the Orient* Nerval took too seriously the episodes of the *Sethos* by the Abbé Jean Terrasson (followed also by A. Lenoir) who, claiming to tell of the initiation that Orpheus received in Egypt, described the trials by the elements, also present in the libretto of Mozart's *Magic Flute* by Emmanuel Schickaneder. But exhuming, in *The Illuminated,* the *Thrace* of Quintus Aucler, a title that refers to the *Threicius vates* ("Thracian prophet," the name given to Orpheus, not by Virgil, but by Ovid, *Metamorphoses* 11.2), he cited numerous pages from it, which summed up the complete doctrine of the *Orphica.* In *El Desdichado,* identifying in turn with the poet-magus, he would use the expression "constellated lute" for the human element subject to celestial influences (a meaning that he had found in the *Three Books on Life* by Marsilio Ficino, and in Guy Le Fèvre de La Boderie, the translator of the Florentine Neoplatonist). Orphism and neo-Pythagoreanism nurtured the best of the inspiration of the author of the *Chimeras.* Finally, *Aurelia* describes a modern "descent into Hell"; the second part has the epigraph: "Euridice! Eurydice!"

In Germany the theories of J. G. Hamann and J. G. Herder laid the foundations for a new Orphism. The theme of the hero's descent into hell was taken up and developed in *Heinrich von Ofterdingen* by Novalis (Friedrich von Hardenberg) and in Goethe's *Faust,* part 2. Hölderlin was truly spellbound by ancient and modern Greece, and most of his work is essentially Orphic. The titles of some of his poems

Delacroix, *Eurydice Picking Flowers.* São Paulo, Museu de Arte. Photo Giraudon.

Gustave Moreau, *Dead Poet Being Carried by a Centaur.* Paris, Musée Gustave Moreau. Photo Musées nationaux.

Gustave Moreau, *Orpheus on Eurydice's Grave.* Paris, Musée Gustave Moreau. Photo Musées nationaux.

are revealing (*To the Heavens; To the Parcae; To the Morning; The Poet's Vocation; To Mother Earth*). Recall the surprising beginning of *Patmos:* "So near. And difficult to grasp, the god!"

Shelley, author of *Hymn to Apollo* and *Hymn to Pan,* also, in 1820, dedicated a poem to *Orpheus.* In it he depicted plants forming a natural sanctuary around the singer who mourns Eurydice and whose lament imposes silence even on the nightingale. Finally, John Keats was the author of *Ode to Apollo, Hymn to Apollo,* and *Endymion.* His most ambitious work, *Hyperion,* remained unfinished. In order to celebrate the Greek gods it was truly something of Orphic inspiration that the poet, in his Miltonic lines, was trying to recapture.

The Orphic vision of the universe should be connected with certain prose poems by Alphonse Rabbe and Maurice de Guérin. The former, in *The Centaur,* describes the loves of the Centaur and of Cymothoë. Visits to the antiquities in the Louvre, in the company of Trébutien, are the source of Maurice de Guérin's prose poem *The Centaur* (1836), upon which his posthumous glory long rested. *The Maenad* came shortly afterward. Guérin relived something of the pagan intuition of the ancient poets; he juxtaposed in himself two irreconcilable traditions, and at the last moment he chose Christianity. But in his *Journal* he had noted on 10 December 1834: "I live with the interior elements of things." And in a text of the same year he evoked the fable in which the forests departed in Orpheus's footsteps, seeing in it the memory of a time when nature understood the language of man and obeyed him. His prose poems, inspired by statues, have a Dionysian rather than a truly Orphic character. One may say the same of Keats's *Endymion* and of Kleist's striking *Penthesilia.*

J.Ri./t.l.f.

BIBLIOGRAPHY

QUINTUS-NANTIUS AUCLER (for: GABRIEL-ANDRE AUCLERC): *La Thréicie, ou la seule voie des sciences divines et humaines, du culte vrai et de la morale* (Paris, year 7). M BESSET, *Novalis et la pensée mystique* (Paris 1947). L. CAZAMIAN, *Histoire de la littérature anglaise* (Paris 1929), part 2; part 1 is by Émile Legouis. L. CELLIER, "Le romantisme et le mythe d'Orphée," *Cahiers de l'association internationale des études françaises,* no. 10 (1958). B. JUDEN, *Traditions orphiques et tendances mystiques dans le romantisme français,* 1800–1855 (Paris 1971).

The Isis of Romanticism: The Myth of the Wife-Mother—Helen, Sophia, Mary

In the works of many writers, especially poets, of the nineteenth century, a great female character, mother or wife or both, appears. Many, even if they are detached from Christianity, retain an attachment to the Virgin Mary. Goethe introduces into the *Faust* of 1824 the descent to the Mothers, who have preserved the essence of Helen, who represents the archetype of Beauty. Helen contributes to Faust's reconciliation with fate. In Faust's dream, the feminine ideal moves from Margarethe to Helen and then to the Virgin Mary. The final chant of the celestial choir says: "The eternal feminine leads us upward." George Sand, in her anti-Faustian novel *The Seven Strings of the Lute* (1840), gives the name Helen to the character who represents human love.

At the root of the importance of Isis to the romantics is the romantic interpretation of the Egyptian mysteries proposed by various scholars and writers of the eighteenth century, as well as the Masonic rituals (often derived from the works in question), which gave importance to the figure of the goddess, making her a representation of Nature. The libretto of Mozart's *Magic Flute* by Schikäneder was derived from the *Sethos* of the Abbé Jean Terrasson (1731) and from Liebeskind's Hindu story, *Lulu, or the Magic Flute;* the tests by the elements which are described there represent what was believed at the time to have constituted the Isiac mysteries. Goethe was so interested in them that in 1798 he wrote a *Second Part of the Magic Flute.* It was in 1798 as well that Novalis began his *Disciples of Saïs,* in which we read: "To understand Nature, one must recreate Nature within oneself in her complete cycle."

In the philosophy of Jakob Böhme, Sophia represented not only Wisdom, the mystical spouse, half of the androgynous Adam, but also the Virgin of Light, identified with Logos. Poets such as Novalis explored both the Masonic tradition and Boehme, combining Isis and Sophia. After the death of his young financée, Sophie von Kühn, Novalis recorded in his journal the phrase "Christ and Sophia." His *Hymns to the Night* (1800), with their stunning sensuality, represent the triumph of the nocturnal and feminine side of being, much like the famous sonnet *Artemis* in Nerval's

Chimeras. In both cases, the love object is identified not only with Nature but also with Night and Death ("C'est la Mort ou la Morte . . . [It is death or the dead woman]," wrote Nerval). In Novalis's *Henri d'Ofterdingen* (1800), the central moment of the novel is marked by the love of Henri and Mathilde, and Mathilde can be identified with both Sophia and the Virgin of Saïs.

An important episode in Ballanche's *Orpheus* (1829) retraces the initiation of Thamyris—a disciple of Orpheus—into the mysteries of Isis. Alfred de Vigny's extremely maternal conception of the character of Kitty Bell in *Chatterton* (1835) corresponds to this same search for the feminine ideal. His great poem *The House of the Shepherd* (1844) deals with the whole problem of man's relationship with Nature ("On me dit une mère et je suis une tombe [They call me a womb, and I am a tomb]"), which is well described by the two fundamental aspects of the Earth (Demeter and Persephone), while Eva, the companion of man, is seen as a mediator between him and nature. Even in the posthumous poem *The Anger of Samson,* we read: "L'homme a toujours besoin de caresse et d'amour / Sa mère l'en abreuve alors qu'il vient au jour [Man always needs caresses and love; his mother drenches him in them when he comes into the world]." In the poem *Helen* (1821), as well as in the narrative *Daphne* (1837), Vigny applauds the feminine incarnations of the divine: the Virgin, Venus, the houris in the case of Helen and Thea in the case of Daphne, Ceres-Deo, Minerva-Pronoë, and Venus-Ourania, who correspond to the religious orientations of the poet even more than to those of his hero, Julien.

It would be possible to include many excerpts from Alphonse de Lamartine here too, since his entire life was colored by the memory of his mother. One excellent example is *The Tomb of a Mother* (circa 1829–30) in *Harmonies.* And the force of the maternal image in Lamartine's work is responsible for the grandeur of his admirable poem *The Vine and the House* (1857).

J.Ri./d.b.

Isis. From Kircher, *Oedipus Aegyptiacus,* 1652. Photo X.

BIBLIOGRAPHY

See the bibliography of the article "Orpheus and the Poetic and Spiritual Quest of Romanticism" and also: J. BALTRUŠAITIS, *Essai sur la légende d'un mythe. La Quête d'Isis: Introduction à l'Egyptiomanie* (Paris 1967). J. CHAILLEY, *La flûte enchantée, opéra maçonnique* (Paris 1968). P. NEWMAN-GORDON, *Hélène de Sparte, la fortune du mythe en France* (Paris 1968). NOVALIS (F. DE HARDENBERG), *Petits écrits,* trans. Geneviève Bianquis (contains *Les Disciples à Saïs*), Paris 1947; *Hymnes à la nuit,* Paris 1943. A. ROLLAND DE RENÉVILLE, *L'expérience poétique* (Paris 1938; reprinted 1965), chap. 4: "Le sens de la nuit."

JULIAN THE APOSTATE IN ROMANTIC LITERATURE

The mythic transfiguration of the emperor Julian II, also called Julian the Apostate, is a remarkable case in the history of ideas. For after he had been, for a dozen centuries, associated with Satan and the Antichrist, he was to become from the sixteenth century onward a model of tolerance and good government, mainly because of the influence of Erasmus, Bodin, and Montaigne. Two historic traditions, parallel and contradictory, explain these differing viewpoints—that of the Fathers of the Church (with Saint Gregory of Nazianze and Saint John Chrysostom), who accused him of all possible crimes, and that of the witnesses and panegyrists Ammianus Marcellinus and Libanius. By giving credence to the testimony of one group of witnesses or to the other, it is possible to arrive at diametrically opposed conclusions, which explains how Julian, over the centuries, could serve as a pretext and support for the expression of the most diverse ideologies.

In 1817 Charles Nodier, in an account published in the *Journal of Debates,* made Julian an image of Bonaparte, a tyrant without religion, and himself the image of the Antichrist. But twenty years later, in the *Dictionary of Conversation,* he used a portion of the same text to make him into a kind of Voltaire: "There was a certain affinity of character and intention between these two men, the most violent enemies that hell could raise against Christ." Thus, by a clever shifting of the scales, Nodier returned to the image of Julian which had prevailed for so long.

In 1822, Aubrey De Vere Hunt wrote a dramatic poem whose main character was Maximus of Ephesus, the magician and theurgist, who appears throughout the work and is presented as the "emperor's evil genius." Julian, bereft of personality, is but a puppet in his hands: his only free act, in the end, is to kill Maximus. Maximus, seeing luck turn against him, passes over to the Persian camp. The best scenes of the play are lyrical, as when the genie of the empire appears to Julian. Victor-Joseph Étienne de Jouy (en-Josas) in 1827 wrote *Julian among the Gauls,* a classical tragedy in five acts in verse; this play recalls one of Voltaire's tragedies because it has all the qualities of a pastiche by Corneille, to the point of textual borrowing. Julian and the Gallic prince Bellovese are both in love with the beautiful Greek slave Theora. She dies by poison at the end of the play. The chauvinism of the author is given free reign in his conception of the character of Bellovese, who has all the noble virtues of his race.

In the first two discourses of his *Historical Studies,* a late work (1831), Chateaubriand discusses Julian at length, and the second discourse is entirely devoted to him. Documentation is plentiful and the author seems to force himself to judge equitably this emperor who "brought his erudition into his life." But in fact, Chateaubriand proceeds without much critical spirit, by an accumulation of evidence of very uneven worth, and collects, without objection or reservation, the commentaries of Christian historians—detractors of the emperor—and the tales of persecution that they invented.

In his youth Alfred de Vigny (1816) wrote a tragedy about Julian which he later destroyed. Beginning in 1832 he dreamed of writing a *Second Opinion of Dr Black,* which, like the first play, would consist of three narratives, dealing, respectively, with Julian, Melanchthon, and Rousseau, each ending with a "suicide." The general problem envisioned was to have been the influence of religion on ethics. The plan was reworked several times, but the definitive work never took form. The part of the work that was written was entitled *Daphne,* from the name of the region near Antioch, and dates essentially from 1837.

Vigny introduces Julian in this work, although the main character is Libanius, the Old Sage of Antioch (known in history for having been Julian's friend and panegyrist). In *Daphne,* Julian comes to ask Libanius's advice and, surprisingly, the philosopher discourages his efforts to restore paganism: one cannot go back in history. Julian's longest speech is a summary of his treatise *On Helios the King.* When he has come to understand the futility of his efforts, Julian, despairing, leaves for his Persian campaign. His death is presented as a disguised suicide (which, in fact, it may have been). For years Vigny meditated on the character of Julian, and a great deal of material for his unfinished work can be found in his *Journal.* In 1833 he confessed to the process of identification in these words: "If metempsychosis exists, I was this man. He is the man whose role, whose life, and whose character would have suited me best of any in history."

In 1853, the German poet Eichendorff wrote an epic poem on Julian, focusing on his wars against the Germans. In his posthumous poem *The Dove* (*Last Songs,* 1872), L. Bouilhet depicted Julian mourning the death of paganism, and he himself announced the impending end of Christianity. Louis Ménard's *Dreams of a Mystic Pagan* (1876) contained *The Last Night of Julian;* in his poem the genie of the empire exhorts Julian to resign himself to the inevitable.

Henrik Ibsen first planned a trilogy on Julian, but then replaced the whole section about the battle of Strasbourg with a narrative and divided his work, published in 1873, into just two parts. The general title was *Emperor and Galilean: A Drama of World History.* Each part had five acts; the first part was *Caesar's Apostasy* and the second *Emperor Julian.* Among the primary sources, Ibsen had read only Ammianus Marcellinus and the *Life of Maximus* by Eunapius of Sardis. For the rest he turned to modern historians—first, the Germans Neander, J. E. Auer, and David Strauss, then to Albert de Broglie, author of *The Church and the Roman Empire in the Fourth Century* (1856). Ibsen put whole pages copied from these sources into the mouths of his characters, but at the same time he invented the character of Helena, the wife of Julian, a cruel and sensual woman who reveals to Julian at the moment of her death by poison that she has been the mistress of his brother Gallus.

Ibsen was unaware of the fact that Julian was raised in Arianism, nor did he seem to know, although it was indicated by all his sources, that Julian quickly returned to paganism and had hidden the fact for ten years, not proclaiming it publicly until he became emperor. A passage written by Neander on the Cainites probably inspired the major scene of evocation, in act 3 of *Caesar's Apostasy:* Maximus of Ephesus causes Cain and Judas to appear and indicates that Julian is the reincarnation of the same principle. Another possible source for this scene was the memory of canto 34 of Dante's *Inferno,* in which Judas, Brutus, and Cassius are crushed by the three mouths of Lucifer. The Manichaean schema which Ibsen implicitly proposes is the following:

Cain—Abel (and his "substitute" Seth)
Judas—Christ
The pagan Julian—the Christian Jovianus

Maximus is presented as the apostle of the "third reign"; he respects Christ because he is a prophet, but he announces the arrival of a religion superior to Christianity. This is where we must look for the philosophy of history which underlies the work. Ibsen had been very much affected by the Franco-Prussian war and by the Commune. He adopted the belief that events and men are directed by a "will," the agent of a rigorous determinism. According to him, the advent of the "third reign" would be the reconciliation of the spirit and the flesh, of paganism and Christianity.

The second part of the work, *Emperor Julian,* was perhaps written too rapidly. It covers the eighteen months of Julian's reign, while the first part dealt with a period of ten years. Only the negative side of Julian is developed here; he is shown as a personal enemy of the Galilean; he pursues the Galilean's disciples in his hatred and cruelly persecutes them, all the while remaining unable to detach himself completely from Christianity. He is reduced to bad temper, hypocrisy, and vanity, to the point where one wonders if he is really the same character as in *Caesar's Apostasy.* Ibsen modifies the historical order of events in order to make Julian's order to burn his fleet on the Tigris appear an act of madness. The play ends with an inquiry about predestination and the fact that some people can be "damned by obedience," an idea that is already present in the poem *Judas* ("And if Judas had been refused?").

Whatever point of view is adopted and unless only one specific episode in the life of the emperor is treated (as was done by de Jouy), every romantic writer who told the history of the emperor was forced to end in a stalemate: Julian was out of step with history.

J.Ri./d.b.

BIBLIOGRAPHY

E. FRENZEL, *Stoffe der Weltliteratur* (2d ed., Stuttgart 1963), article "Julian Apostata." H. IBSEN, *Œuvres complètes,* P. G. La Chesnais, trans., vols. 9 and 10 (Paris 1937). A. DE VIGNY, *Stello, Daphné* (Paris 1970).

Napoleon as Myth

Napoleon, who had a keen sense of propaganda, was the architect of his own legend. During his reign, the press, literature, and painting were systematically placed under his control and gave a glorious and embellished image of him that tended to present him as a pacifist and the restorer of Catholicism and, outside France, as the liberator of oppressed peoples. As soon as Napoleon fell, there was a change. Caricatures of the emperor dominated for a while, making him the Corsican Ogre; they were circulated far and wide by his opponents. Satirical drawings thus joined the anti-Bonapartist propaganda that was already present among German nationalist poets such as Arndt, Theodor Körner, and Rückert. The condemnation is blatant in Chateaubriand's *De Buonaparte et des Bourbons* (1814) and also in Byron's *Ode to Napoleon* (1814). The same year Senancour protested openly in his "Letter from an inhabitant of the Vosges," and was one of the first to depict Napoleon as the man who, after conquering fate, was in the end overcome by it. This eventually became the essential idea behind the romantic myth.

The transition to the level of myth finally came with his death on Saint Helena on 5 May 1821, making the emperor a victim, which accounts for his frequent identification with Prometheus. His death occasioned Manzoni's poem *Il cinque maggio* (The fifth of May) and Grillparzer's *Ode to Napoleon.* Lamartine's *Bonaparte,* in his *Nouvelles Méditations* (New meditations) of 1822, is a poem that coldly questions Bonaparte and his fate and that echoes Manzoni. There is also Béranger's poem *Le Cinq mai,* in his *Souvenirs du peuple* (Memories of the people) (1828), and his famous *Parlez-nous de lui, Grand-mère* (Tell us about him, Grandmother). The *Mémorial de Sainte Hélène* (Memorial of Saint Helena), published in 1823, went on to enrich the legend. In it, Bonaparte poses as the liberator and unifier of the people, whereas in reality he had fought against liberalism and nationalism in all their forms.

There was then a progressive turnabout by certain writers. Hugo's mother may have taught her son to hate Napoleon and his crimes; but with his poem *Les Deux Iles* (The two islands) (1826), resentment gave way to pity, and the life of Napoleon was compared to the sun in its passage from east to west. The *Ode à la Colonne* (Ode to the pillar) (1827) was Hugo's response to an affront directed at four marshals of the empire during a reception at the Austrian Embassy.

Nerval, the son of a military doctor of the Grand Army, thought of himself as (or wished he had been) a "Napoleonite." He was sixteen years old when he wrote his own "Cinq mai" (The fifth of May, 1824), and in 1827 he published *Napoleon et la France guerrière, Elégies nationales* (Napoleon and France at war, national elegies), dedicated to Napoleon and for the most part written before 1825. The memory of the emperor haunted numerous texts by Nerval, particularly the six sonnets known by the title of *Autres Chimères* (Other fancies). Stendhal is known to have "fallen with Napoleon"; the heroes of his novels refer constantly to the emperor. Julien Sorel in *The Red and the Black* (1831) reads the *Mémorial,* and Fabrice in *The Charterhouse of Parma* (1839) is present at the battle of Waterloo. Balzac helped reinforce Napoleonic legend by the place he gave the emperor in *The Human Comedy.* Moreover, he conceived his opus as an imitation of Napoleon in which he intended "to achieve with the pen what he began with the sword." Already in *The Country Doctor* (1833), he presented an unforgettable "Napoleon seen by the people."

After the Return of the Ashes to Paris on 15 December 1840, the infatuation became widespread. Napoleon appeared in Balzac's work again: *The Vendetta* (1830), *A Shadowy Affair* (1841), *The Thirty-Year-Old Woman* (1844). Balzac admired Napoleon as a remarkable example of energy and of the sublime. In 1835, Vigny published *Military Servitude and Greatness,* in which a hovering presence of the emperor appeared. In *Memories from beyond the Grave* (1818), Bonaparte became "the colossal man," and Chateaubriand described his epoch as though it had consisted of a long dialogue between Napoleon and him. In 1844, Carlyle devoted a chapter of his *Cult of Heroes* to Napoleon. In 1845, Thiers began to publish his *History of the Consulship and the Empire,* completed in 1862.

A day in the reign of Napoleon, or the sun personified. Paris, Bibliothèque nationale. Photo D.R.

Franque, *La France dans l'attente du Retour d'Egypte.* Paris, Musée du Louvre. Photo Musées nationaux.

The first history of what was then a recent period, it was to have great success. Hugo sang the praises of the Return of the Ashes; in *The Chastisements* he included the *Expiation* (1852), in which he exalted Napoleon in order to humiliate his nephew. In his novel *Les Misérables* (1862), he chose to reenact Waterloo. Although Tolstoy in *War and Peace* (1864) made the emperor into a kind of soulless marionette, its strings pulled by fate, and although Proudhon, Littré, Erckmann, and Chatrian (*The Conscript of 1813,* 1864) saw Napoleon as a *condottiere* without scruples, Goguelat's account in *The Country Doctor* already suggested the deification of Napoleon, who was identified with the messiah. As early as 1816, Wendel Wurtz had given the black legend a mythical extension by identifying Napoleon with Appolyon, the destructive genie of the apocalypse. Mickiewicz, in *Pan Tadeusz* (1834), paid Poland's respects to Napoleon; later, under the influence of Towianski, he would make him the new messiah. Nerval took J. B. Pérès's hoax seriously: Pérès, in *How Napoleon Never Existed* (1827), satirized the theories of Dupuis and turned Napoleon into the new Apollo.

One problem remains that has never received a satisfactory solution. The objectively verifiable elements of Napoleon's career—the names of individuals, the general course of events—spontaneously organized themselves according to the structure of the solar myth. Although Napoleon is not entirely identified with the sun, it is nevertheless true that the myth built around his historical personality is of a complexity seemingly born of the resolution of certain opposites. He represents both liberty and authority; the messiah and, at the same time, the antichrist; warrior and also legislator. And if one tries to understand how, after his death, many of his contemporaries changed their attitudes toward him from hostility or resentment to admiration, one reaches the conclusion that they subconsciously made Napoleon into an image of the father bigger than life—at the same time simple and mysterious, kindly and terrifying. Since many of their fathers or paternal uncles had fought in Napoleon's armies, this image is not hard to explain.

The extension of the myth over the whole world came later and goes beyond the limits of this essay.

J.Ri./g.h.

BIBLIOGRAPHY

J.-B. PÉRÈS, *Comme quoi Napoléon n'a jamais existé,* 1827. See the reprint in *La Tour Saint-Jacques* (July–August 1956), with a study by Robert Amadou. J. TULARD, *Le mythe de Napoléon* (Paris 1971). R. WHATELY, *Historic Doubts Relating to Napoleon* (1st ed. anonymous, 1819), presents Bonaparte as a collective being representing the "better part" of the people and the army of France and insists on the *improbable* character of his life.

Modernity's Challenge to Myth, in the Poetry of Hölderlin, Heine, Baudelaire, Mallarmé, T. S. Eliot, and Rilke

Hölderlin

Two-thirds of the way through *Patmos* (1803), one of his last great hymns, Hölderlin, who has just evoked the disappearance of the evidence from the mythic time of Christ, the destruction of the temples, and the invisibility of the gods both in heaven and on earth, abruptly interrupts his evocation to ask about the meaning of these deficiencies that he has identified with his own time. The question, "What is it?," with which the tenth stanza of the poem ends, is answered by some lines as simple as they are essential in their attempt to repossess the truth of a historic becoming:

It is the cast
Made by the sower when he scoops
Wheat into the shovel and sweeps it
In an arc
Toward the clear
Void over the threshingfloor,
The husk falls at his feet, but
The grain does reach its goal,
And no bad thing it is, if
Some disappears, the live sound
Of speech
Fades, for divine work too is akin
To ours, the Highest does not want
All things at once. . . .

(Translated by Christopher Middleton from Friedrich Hölderlin and Eduard Mörike, *Selected Poems,* Chicago: University of Chicago Press, 1972, pp. 83–85.)

The reader will have recognized in this response the condensation of at least three biblical passages: the image of the preaching of John the Baptist (Matthew 3:12): "Whose fan is in his hand, and he will thoroughly purge his floor, and gather his wheat into the garner; but he will burn up the chaff with unquenchable fire"; the story of Ruth and Boaz (Ruth 2:2–17); and, perhaps especially, the passage from the Gospel (John 12:24): "Verily, verily, I say unto you, Except a corn of wheat fall into the ground and die, it abideth alone: but if it die, it bringeth forth much fruit."

What should nevertheless arrest us even more than this syncretism is the use that is made here of a parabolic language on the level of poetry. The question posed at the end of the preceding stanza bears fundamentally upon the meaning of a history whose upheaval Hölderlin could indicate as few others could. The night of the absence of the gods, in the writing of this poet, is far more than a simple metaphor: it is the declaration, the sharp act of perception, of a historical and metaphysical reality, which seems at first to lack the support of a transcendence that might assure its redemption. Nothing could be more serious, less "metaphoric," for Hölderlin, than this declaration.

It is precisely this seriousness that makes the lines we have cited so interesting. What the poetry achieves here is nothing less than a mythical repossession of the real. Just as the grain dies in order to be reborn as wheat, after failing to reach its goal, so too we are to understand that this night of history is called upon to cut across the proof of its negativity so that, in the end, the day will dawn that will mark the return of the gods. The concrete image, invested with the authority of the sacred text, makes it possible to signify the historical process by anchoring it in a natural rhythm. Existence and its meaning are one: we are in the poetic universe of myth.

What Hölderlin succeeded in affirming once more in 1803, at the price of great tension and an unequaled dialectic force, constitutes the model—at once dreamed of and inaccessible—of what has since been called modern poetry. Whoever inclines to the history of the poetic texts of the last 170 years or so cannot help but be struck by the progressive movement by which the gesture of confidence in the use of a mythic model loses if not its validity at least its force of credibility. The few remarks that follow certainly do not aim to exhaust the subject, but propose to illustrate this movement.

Heine

In his poem, *The Gods of Greece,* composed in 1825–26, Heinrich Heine reverses the order of the certainties that we saw at work in Hölderlin. In Heine, myth no longer serves as a foundation for history, but rather submits to history. The gods of Greece, which the imagination identifies in clouds at night, in this poem are made "suppressed and defunct" figures; Zeus appears here with "extinguished lightning" in his hand and with his face marked by "unhappiness and sorrow"; Aphrodite, "once golden, now silver," here has no more than an "appalling" beauty and is said to be the "goddess of corpses," "Venus Libitina." The founding nature of the gods in Hölderlin is succeeded here by a series of figures born of history and subject to its finitude: "For even the gods do not reign forever; the young ones take the place of the old ones." The relativization of mythic beings leads them to become no more than the supports for an entirely immanent vision of history, in which the struggle of antagonistic forces, far from representing a metaphysical confrontation, has taken a clearly political turn: man, in this poem, becomes morally superior to the gods because, unlike them, he does not side with those who are strongest, but joins in solidarity with those who are conquered.

Baudelaire

This feeling of a lost mythic integrity is found again, though in a rather different sense, at the beginning of the work of the one who, together with Georg Büchner in the medium of theater, could be said to be the founding poet of modernity: Charles Baudelaire. From his earliest poems, Baudelaire seems to long for the "naked epochs / When Phoebus amused himself gilding statues," and when "Cybele, fertile in generous fruits, / Did not find her sons too heavy a weight"; yet he does not hesitate to point out the contemporary truth of myth in those "poor twisted bodies, thin, pot-bellied, or flaccid," which "the god of Utility, implacable and serene, / swaddles as children in their bronze diapers," in other words, we understand, in the allegorical vision of a reality dispossessed of its mythic fullness.

In *The Swan,* for example, Baudelaire evokes the "strange and fatal myth" of the animal "that has escaped from its cage," in which he sees the image of the human condition of exile. But, except for the fact that this poet does not distinguish the term "myth" from the term "symbol," or "emblem," or even "allegory," his use of the swan does not so much reactualize a sphere of meaning or a mode of being that belongs to myth as it transforms the creature—just like Andromache, to whom it is compared—into a sign of the loss of or separation from myth. Baudelaire's swan is not an identity whose presence is sufficiently solid to suggest, if not to found, a poetic order in which signs are organized according to their own essence—which would be the very definition of a poetry of myth; on the contrary, it marks a division that allows only divided realities and the image of that division to become linked to it. And it is precisely in this division that Baudelaire deciphers the modernity with which, in opposition to romanticism, to pantheism, or to metaphysical Manicheanism in the style of Hugo, he will identify his poetry.

One could argue that some of his poems, some of his essays (on Poe, on Hugo, on Gautier), express the idea of a "shadowy and profound unity" that is able to bring together and to integrate the whole of reality into a network of "correspondences" which assure it of meaning in the manner of a myth. The importance accorded to the imagination, to the dream, is a sign of this meaning. But though these tendencies are incontestable, they do not go beyond the stage of intention. The only genuine figure that can really claim the status of a unifying locus of the real in Baudelaire is, paradoxically, death. The Baudelairean One is the unity of what perishes; death, moreover, is the only absolute that can measure itself against the absolute of the exigency of infinity. And if certain poems in the *Flowers of Evil* seem to reach a mythic dimension, despite everything—notably the great passages in the *Parisian Pictures*—they do so precisely because their repossession of finitude raises death to the level of a necessity that is visibly constitutive of what is real.

This recognition of death as a presence that is simultaneously intimate and universal is also what leads Baudelaire to attempt to make the work of art the only place the other side of death. Beyond his macabre Petrarchism, this view of death underlies a poem such as *A Piece of Carrion*—even though, against the avowed intention of the author, it could also be read as the expression of the triumph of a poetics designed to speak of the perishable part of existence (cf. the letter from Rilke to Clara of October 7, 1907). The architectural will of the poet of *Flowers of Evil,* his insistence on the independence and immanent logic of form, constitute an extension of and a response to the consciousness of a reality that could formulate no other myth than finitude. What ultimately characterizes the poetics of the *Flowers of Evil* is a tension—the tension between a palpable reality accepted in its opacity, its irreducibility to any idealization, and a (formal) dream in which the imaginary is able to recompose the network of identities that are as much material as they are spiritual.

Mallarmé

It might be supposed that the thinking of the greatest French disciple of Baudelaire, Stéphane Mallarmé, developed from a tension of the same kind. At least his early poems, as well as certain documents dating from his formative period, suggest such a connection. But, unlike his master, Mallarmé was to situate his place of choice in the realm of dream: "Yes, I know," he wrote to Henri Cazalis in April of 1866,

> we are nothing but vain forms of matter, but quite sublime for having invented God and our soul. So sublime, my friend, that I want to give myself this spectacle of matter, being conscious of it and nevertheless rushing passionately into the Dream that matter cannot be, singing of the Soul and all the parallel divine impressions that have accumulated in us since the earliest times, and proclaiming before the Nothing, which is truth, these glorious lies! Such is the plan of my lyric volume, and such perhaps will be its title, the Glory of the Lie or the Glorious Lie.

As one can see in these lines, the degenerating structure of Mallarmé's vision, which affirms in the same stroke the idealistic orientation of matter and the unreality of that orientation, hardly lends itself to a mythical apprehension. Moreover, even when Mallarmé did resort to mythic motifs in his poems, his use of myth remained marked by his vision of the real as a fiction. This is certainly true of the two great poems sketched during those years, the "Herodiade" and "The Afternoon of a Faun."

Mallarmé's Heriodiade is not the temptress that Flaubert would describe ten years later, in a dazzling page of his *Three Tales,* in the act of seducing Herod Antipas. She is the figure of a poetry dedicated to reflexivity, a poetry incarnate in his image of a woman looking at herself in a mirror. Her narcissism, her fierce refusal of any nubility (cf. "Yes, it is for me, for me, that I have blossomed, alone!"), are the image of Mallarmé's (mythic) desire for a language restored to its purity of a musical essence. A "dyad," in that her concern for herself determines her both as the desiring subject and as the image of her own desire, this "heroine"—even in her name—suggests the recoiling inward in which Mallarmé sought the salvation of language through poetry.

The mythic subjugation of the Faun is still more subtle. Since for Mallarmé the solar and musical figure of this fabulous creature is manifestly nothing but the image of the poet, or of poetic power, this poem too reveals the desire for reflexivity that was already at work in the "Herodiade." At the same time, however, the artifice by which the Faun feigns possession of the nymphs, whom he really has only desired, ends with the evocation of a reality which, for being fictive, is no less endowed with a charge of concretion and even of a sensuality of which there are few other examples in French poetry:

> As for me, proud of my voice, I'll speak at length
> Of those divinities and by idolatrous
> Depictions strip yet more veils from their shade.
> Thus, when I've sucked the brightness out of grapes,
> To chase regret deflected by my feint,
> I lift the empty cluster to the sky,
> Laughing, and, wild to be drunk, inflate
> The shining skins and look through them till night.
> (Translated by Patricia Terry and Maurice Z. Shroder, in *Stéphane Mallarmé, Selected Poetry and Prose,* ed. Mary Ann Caws, New York: New Directions, p. 37.)

The use of a mythical figure (a Faun) makes it possible to question what is immediately real ("Did I dream that love?") but leads here to the emergence of a poetic reality all the more absolute for being manifestly more fictive.

The gesture by which fiction was identified with the very site of reality, this absolute poetic idealism—which Mallarmé himself later went beyond by transforming his negative theology into a kind of theology of the twenty-six letters of the alphabet—set off one of the two currents which, following the turn-of-the-century symbolism, were to fertilize the poetry of the twentieth century and notably its use of myth: a Valéry, a Saint-John Perse, in France, a Stefan George, a Rilke, in Germany, would tap into that current, each in his own way.

Eliot

But this would not happen without the close parallel development of another current, which should be identified here. The end of the nineteenth century set the stage for an exacerbated and mythicizing idealism in the realm of literature; yet it also saw the development of works which, following the upheaval stirred up by Schopenhauer and Nietzsche, manifested a kind of renaissance of materialism. Starting in 1896, Freud wrote his *Interpretation of Dreams* (published in 1899), which is practically contemporary with the first volumes of Sir James George Frazer's *The Golden Bough,* the pioneering work in the field of mythic ethnology. Significantly, once Freud's fundamental concepts had been developed, the interest of psychoanalysis was to shift into the field of myth (*Totem and Taboo* dates from 1913, one year after Otto Rank's great book *The Incest Motif in Literature and Folktale*), that very myth whose historical origin and nature Frazer, after others, had demonstrated. Despite the general crisis of values in European society and civilization that led to the first World War—a crisis that was expressed in art by an impressive spate of inventiveness (cubism and futurism in painting, the Vienna school, Stravinsky in music)—writers were strongly stimulated by this challenge to their range of choice. This helps to explain how the great poem that would attempt to draw up the double balance sheet of civilization and literature, once the war was over, at the same time presents itself as a profound questioning of mythic speech.

We refer to T. S. Eliot's *The Waste Land,* published in 1922. *The Waste Land* signifies any barren land, ravaged land, but the title is also a direct reference to the land stricken with sterility in the legend of the Grail, in which Eliot, influenced by a book by an English medievalist who was a disciple of Frazer, learned to recognize a medieval, Christianized transposition of certain myths of fertility borrowed mainly from Egyptian and Mesopotamian antiquity. At its simplest level, use of the Grail myth tends to establish an equivalence between the medieval symbol of a land awaiting its deliverance and the ruined condition of postwar Europe. Such was, one might say, the mythic analogy of this text.

But this analogy constitutes only one of the levels of meaning in this poem—the most apparent, perhaps, but not the most profound. Aside from the fact that the mythic narrative is borrowed only in a most discontinuous manner (and is used much less closely, for example, than the myth of the *Odyssey* in Joyce's *Ulysses,* which had appeared in the previous year), *The Waste Land* is concerned less with the theme of mythic desolation than with questioning an entire series of previous poetic discourses, which are themselves quite often connected with a myth, for which this poem constitutes a kind of museum.

As Eliot himself indicated in the notes that accompany his poem, and as has often been remarked since, *The Waste Land* is largely made up of quotations. These quotations, borrowed from sources as diverse as Dante's *Inferno,* the *Satyricon* of Petronius, Elizabethan drama, the Bible, the *Upaniṣads,* the *Confessions* of Saint Augustine, and the *Flowers of Evil,* actually have less to do with a unified way of thinking—in this case a way of thinking about desolation—than they signify, through the often ironic or parodying use that is made of them, the decrepitude of the mythic design of their original context. "I had not thought death had undone so many," says one of the speakers of this poem (quoting Dante), as he watches a crowd of resigned pedestrians file over London Bridge—people who are so many metaphors for speech. As much as it is the enactment of a myth, *The Waste Land* is the properly Babelian actualization of the impossibility of a founding speech. The "death" of the inhabitants of the waste land, a synonym for the spiritual collapse of Europe of 1920, here also prefigures the end of the demiurgic period of poetry. Or, to put it differently, the figures who speak in the poem are not the only ones stricken by death, but through them the integrity of the poetic source or realm of which they have been made the symbols is also stricken.

Rilke

The fact that death is necessarily connected with the very possibility of myth is something few poets, after Eliot, have failed to realize. Rilke, for example, though he rejected Eliot's method of collage and fragmentation, in that same year 1922 could let his Orpheus emerge only by specifying in characteristic fashion that "Only one who has lifted the lyre / among shadows too, / May divining render / the infinite praise" (*Sonnets to Orpheus,* translated by M. D. Herter Norton, New York: W. W. Norton and Company, 1942, p. 33). When one turns to the poets of France, Italy, the United States, or Latin America, it seems that this is a universal experience, one that World War II made even more oppressing.

The historic relativization of spiritual horizons and social ideals, the affirmed will of a critical attitude of the mind, combined with the collapse of the sacred rhetorics and orders of speech, contributed more than a little to take apart what Western poetry since Homer had never ceased to put together. Belief in myths, as Paul Ricoeur has remarked, has for many people ceded its place to the interpretation of myths and of modes of belief that connect us with myth. Is it not time to close this chapter of our history, even if it is a principal chapter?

For two reasons, beyond all the skepticisms and all the rationalizations, it may be too early to do so. First, despite the immense deployment of efforts to objectivize, formalize, and grasp the origin and the nature of language, language continues, in the final analysis, to refuse to reveal its essence other than in a movement of the invention and creation of images which, while integrating ever more extended levels of reflexivity, keep their metaphoric essence. Nor must we forget that this growing reflexivity has come to be joined, by a kind of necessary counterpoint or compensation, with a simultaneous liberation of the unconscious which, while ruining certain conventional poetic forms, has not stopped and still does not stop formulating its truth by the creation of new structures that find in myth one of their most profound resources. The averred impossibility of a metalanguage that could formalize the essence, in the last analysis a metaphoric essence, of language returns dialectically to a consciousness of the mythic founding of that metaphor. As a result, in the connections that unite (and disunite) man with his human environment, earthly or cosmic, the need for the fiction through which the first connections with the world are avowed and formulated remains perceptible.

Despite all the impasses of literature today, at least the hope of giving voice, through the language of myth, to the always difficult harmony of an enchanted flute beyond all disenchantments may thus continue to affirm itself.

J.E.J./g.h.

BIBLIOGRAPHY

B. HEDERICH, *Gründliches mythologisches Lexicon,* 1770. J. FRAZER, *The Golden Bough: A Study in Magic and Religion,* 12 vols. (London 1890–. J. WESTON, *From Ritual to Romance* (Cambridge 1920).

F. SCHELLING, *Philosophie der Mythologie* (Stuttgart 1856). F. NIETZSCHE, *The Birth of Tragedy* (New York 1967). S. FREUD, *The Interpretation of Dreams* (New York 1927); *Totem and Taboo* (New York 1927), trans. from German. H. VON HOFMANNSTHAL, "Ein Brief," 1901–2, in *Gesammelte Werke,* Prosa I (Frankfurt 1959). S. MALLARMÉ, *La musique et les lettres* (Paris 1894). O. RANK, *Das Inzest-Motiv in Dichtung und Sage* (Leipzig 1912). P. VALÉRY, "Sur Phèdre femme," in *Variétés IV* (Paris 1944). T. S. ELIOT, "Tradition and the Individual Talent," *Selected Essays* (London 1932). M. BLANCHOT, *L'espace littéraire* (Paris 1955).

E. CASSIRER, *The Philosophy of Symbolic Forms,* 3 vols. (New Haven 1953–57). W. BENJAMIN, *Ursprung des deutschen Trauerspiels* (Berlin 1928). P. RICOEUR, *The Symbolism of Evil* (Boston 1969). *Terror und Spiel: Probleme der Mythenrezeption,* H. R. Jauss, ed. (Munich 1971).

Hölderlin's Dionysus

Dionysus became the god of poetry at the very moment when poetry itself analyzed its own status with the greatest precision, namely, in Germany in the work of Friedrich Hölderlin (1770–1843). In answer to Klopstock, who was content with rather superficial identifications, Hölderlin proposed a much more finely tuned connection between poetry and the god of wine, who in his eyes was also the god of joy, as attested by his translation of the last great chorus of Sophocles' *Antigone.* He writes:

The banks of Ganges heard how the god of joy
Was hailed when conquering all from far Indus came
The youthful Bacchus, and with holy
Wine from their drowsiness woke the peoples.
And you, our own day's angel, do not awake
Those drowsing still?
("The Poet's Vocation," 1800, translated by Michael Hamburger, from *Friedrich Hölderlin: Poems and Fragments,* Cambridge: Cambridge University Press, 1980, p. 173)

"Day's angel" is the mediator between the gods and men in the sphere of temporal action where contemporary history is made. He is the poet who, like Dionysus, stirs the soul of people by reinterpreting the moments when, according to tradition, God has revealed himself, seeing these moments in the light of great movements of the present, such as the French Revolution. But while he renewed the sacred chant of the Old Testament prophets and of the Greek poets, and made his own poetry the equivalent of the Revolution, Hölderlin must indeed have feared that he was not on the level of his god, since in the same ode he reminds us of the humiliating scene in Euripides' *Bacchae* when Dionysus, in bonds, is dragged about by the servants of Pentheus "like a captured wild animal," a "tame beast." The poet is almost tempted to take advantage of the god's docility to gain control over him, thus usurping the authority of the divine message. He would then have used the innocence and purity of the god for the benefit of his own arbitrary and idle humors, and would not have listened to him. Hölderlin is thus compelled to create an equivalent of the ancient song, but one that is renewed by modern-day events so that it might keep alive the fire that glows in the countenance and actions of Dionysus.

Hölderlin is the only modern poet who attempted to conform scrupulously to the Pindaric and Sophoclean modes, not by imitation, which would be a reduction, but *a fundamento*. Since Dionysus was no longer the god of a large community, his re-creation could be achieved only by song, or, to put it more precisely, he would be the fruit of the components of song, that is, a metaphor of song itself. In the quasi-Pindaric hymn "As on a holiday" (1800), the poet's attention was called to "the signs and deeds of the world"—the Revolution and the coalition wars that resulted from it. He is struck by the thunderbolt of Zeus as if, in Hölderlin's language of mythical metaphors, he were himself Semele, the mother of Dionysus. The thunderbolt engenders his poem, which is therefore identical with Dionysus, the synthesis of heavenly fire and maternal earth. In this frame of reference, the god appears both as the sign reverting to the pure elements of father and mother, and as the shelter offered by the earth against the danger of paternal fire. He is the god of encounter, exchange, of the mutual appeasement of two powers that men cannot receive without something to mediate between them; and this mediation comes about through language, which has a dual character: it reveals the burning immediacy of the spirit, but it also reveals the structuring and legislating form produced by word order and the laws of syntax and rhythm.

Dionysus may thus be the model for the union of opposites. But he is also the mediator between the origin and the developments which are indicated throughout the tradition right up to the threshold of a future not yet realized. Wine, the sign of his double birth, is a promise. Friends are seen feasting together—something Hölderlin frequently evokes, as in the *Stuttgart* elegy, which is thoroughly imbued with the spirit of Dionysus; the friends not only recall with rapture the presence of Zeus but also express ardent hope for a return of his presence in a new form. The French Revolution initiates a movement that could renew the times to the point at which community spirit would again be possible, the spirit of brotherhood of an entire people. This future heralded by wine, by Dionysus, is in keeping with the festivities that Dionysus inspired in ancient times. "Bacchus is the spirit of community"; here we have a renewal of what the Greeks knew. Hence the poem, Dionysus, and the wine which is his sign, are all three at the pivot where the past is called upon to transmute itself into the future. All three both recall and announce the mediation that they ensure between spirit and language, heaven and earth, masculine and feminine, ancient and modern, north and south, east and west, ancient community and future community. All told, Hölderlin bestowed on Dionysus the same status as that of his poem. He is a demigod always moving between Hellas and Hesperia, who sweeps his disciples along in his voyage "from land to land in the holy night."

In the elegy "Bread and Wine" (1800), Dionysus appears as someone who attracts creatures that have fallen prey to holy delirium, leading them beyond all bounds. He also appears as the conciliator of night and day, guiding the stars upward, downward, eternally joyful, "like undying verdure . . . because he remains." This god of awakening is the dynamic principle that pushes its devotees beyond all finitude, but it is also the principle of stability that resists the night of forgetfulness through the firmness of its attachment to the fullness of life past or to come.

In this period, Hölderlin charges the poet with the mission of delivering the German spirit from the torpor of its wintery slumber, which makes Dionysus above all the incarnation of the heavenly fire. Later, starting in 1803 when he began to be debilitated by illness, Hölderlin thought that he could see hovering over the world the threat of total collapse, anarchy, a new reign of the Titans; he then saw Dionysus in a very different aspect, as a guide capable of restraining nations intoxicated with death, of keeping them in shape, helping them curb their elemental forces. His fear of imminent universal dissolution inspired a Dionysus of stability and bounds, henceforth brother to two other demigods, Heracles and Christ. Their three labors forge, in heroism, a new permanence in the relation between man and the earth, which becomes habitable again by virtue of the institution of an order and of its law ("Unique," 1803). This Dionysus, guarantor of the people's stability through the grace of the rites and words born of his fire—tragedies, for instance—is finally merged into Christ, the founder of religious orders and communities.

Here is a dual dimension, already hinted at in the hymn "The Rhine" (1801), in which Rousseau is first interpreted in the light of the "divine delirium" of the god without law but later appears as the man in the background, like the recluse who prefers obscurity to profusions of joy, in order to relearn a weak song. This second dimension, the aspect of moderation, aspires to the security of a refuge and goes hand in hand with Hölderlin's belated image of the god who recovers from his perilous birth in the shade of German forests among the flowers, but who at the same time brings to the Northmen the virtues of the children of the sun.

B.B./g.h.

BIBLIOGRAPHY

1. Ancient Mythology in German Literature

F. STRICH, *Die Mythologie in der deutschen Literatur von Klopstock bis Wagner* (Halle a.S. 1910). J. G. ROBERTSON, *The Gods of Greece in German Poetry* (Oxford 1924). A. BECK, *Griechisch-deutsche Begegnung: Das deutsche Griechenerlebnis im Sturm und Drang* (Stuttgart 1947). R. BENZ, *Wandel des Bildes der Antike in Deutschland* (Munich 1948). W. REHM, *Götterstille und Göttertrauer* (Bern 1951); *Griechentum und Goethezeit* (3d ed., Bern 1952). W. F. OTTO, *Die Gestalt und das Sein* (Darmstadt 1955). K. REINHARDT, *Tradition und Geist* (Göttingen 1960). W. SCHADEWALDT, *Hellas und Hesperien* (Zurich and Stuttgart 1960). K. ZIEGLER, "Mythos und Dichtung," in *Reallexikon der deutschen Literaturgeschichte* (2d ed., Berlin 1962), 2:569–84. K. HAMBURGER, *Von Sophokles zu Sartre: Griechische Dramenfiguren antik und modern* (Stuttgart 1962). W. EMRICH, *Protest und Verheissung* (2d ed., Frankfurt am Main and Bonn 1963), 67–94. H. HATFIELD, *Aesthetic Paganism in German Literature: From Winckelmann to the Death of Goethe* (Cambridge, MA, 1964). W. KOHLSCHMIDT, "Die

Antike in der modernen Dichtung," in *Dichter, Tradition und Zeitgeist* (Bern 1965), 112–27. H. J. MÄHL, *Die Idee des goldenen Zeitalters im Werk des Novalis* (Heidelberg 1965). M. FUHRMANN, *Terror und Spiel: Probleme der Mythenrezeption* (Munich 1971).

2. Dionysus in Germany

M. MOMMSEN, "Dionysos in der Dichtung Hölderlins," *Germanisch-Romanische Monatsschrift*, n.s., 13, 4 (1963): 345–79. M. DIERKS, *Studien zu Mythos und Psychologie bei Thomas Mann* (Bern and Munich 1972). J. SCHMIDT, *Heinrich von Kleist: Studien zu seiner poetischen Verfahrensweise* (Tübingen 1974). B. BÖSCHENSTEIN, "Die *Bakchen* des Euripides in der Umgestaltung Hölderlins und Kleists," in *Aspekte der Goethezeit* (Göttingen 1977), 240–54; *Leuchttürme* (Frankfurt am Main 1977), 44–63.

Myth in Twentieth-Century English Literature

The problem of myth, of how we should deal with it and how it might deal with us, has troubled English-language writers in this century, as it has troubled writers everywhere. It is not a problem that will go away; it has at least been given several new twists. It would seem appropriate to begin considering it by looking at Yeats, the writer who appeared, at times, the most willing to allow myth to persuade him.

Yeats turned first to the mythology of Ireland, participating in the Celtic Revival of the end of the last century, which followed from several decades of work on the old Irish legends by scholars and translators and which coincided with a general renewal of interest in myth and folklore. He was twenty-five years old when Frazer's *The Golden Bough* appeared in 1890. Myth represented for him a kind of hygiene of the spirit. It was a means of seeing, utterly opposed to science, to materialism, and to Anglo-Saxon abstraction. The illuminist tradition of the eighteenth and nineteenth centuries relives in his work, offering to the imagination a universe saturated with dream and symbol, and allowing a return to origins, "to the roots of the Trees of Knowledge and of Life." Yeats even entertained the hope at one point that Celtic mythology would spread with the same force as the Germanic mythology of Wagner and others, being convinced that "every new fountain of legends is a new intoxication for the imagination of the world." It is true that, at first, he distorted Irish legends by assimilating them to a fin-de-siècle revery and to the melancholy of an infinite longing, reliving in a way that earlier Celtic revival that had penetrated European romanticism via the writings of Chateaubriand and Goethe, having been launched by Macpherson's so-called translations from Ossian.

Myth was also the possibility of recreating the Irish nation. Yeats desired to nourish the memory of his compatriots with the tales of Cúchulain, Ossian, Deirdre, and also of the fairies, witches, and ghosts of popular belief that he celebrated in *The Celtic Twilight*. He claimed that the Irish had a particular aptitude for myth: that stories of meetings with supernatural creatures were more numerous in Ireland than in the whole of the rest of Europe, that peasant and nobleman alike, to the end of the seventeenth century at least, respected those legends, and that even in his own day country people spoke with the dead "and with some who perhaps have never died as we understand death." The aim was in part political: in its myths, legends, and folklore could be discovered an Ireland utterly free of English contamination, at a moment when the relationship between the two countries was intensely at issue. But the aim above all was to discover place. By speaking "out of a people to a people," Yeats endeavored to reunite the Irish nation to the Irish land. Mythology, he believed, bestows on a race its first unity, "marrying" it "to rock and hill," and so giving birth, one might say, to a meaningful geography and to a geography of meaning. Even Christianity was not to be excluded. Although in "The Wanderings of Oisin" he opposed the druidic Ireland of Ossian to the Catholic Ireland of St. Patrick, he recognized elsewhere that the "places of beauty or legendary association" had also been impregnated for centuries with the Christian faith.

Mythology also provided a place for his own poetry, preserving it from what he saw as a false subjectivity, a fragmentary individualism inherited from the Renaissance. One of the deep aspirations of modern poetry expresses itself in a passage like the following: "I filled my mind with the popular beliefs of Ireland . . . I sought some symbolic language reaching far into the past and associated with familiar names and conspicuous hills that I might not be alone amid the obscure impressions of the senses." Nevertheless, despite this belief in locality, Yeats combined Celtic myths with others in the gradual elaboration of a cosmology that in the end was heterogeneous and personal. A member of the Theosophical Society and an initiate of the Order of the Golden Dawn, he studied Oriental religions, occult systems, magic, astrology, alchemy, the cabala, Neoplatonism, the "correspondences" of Swedenborg and Blake, and out of this eclectic brew produced *A Vision*. This preposterous and unforgettable book, whose concepts and images feed into many of his greatest poems and plays, emerged, according to Yeats, from revelations communicated to him by certain spiritual masters through the automatic writing of his wife. They taught him that everything was governed by the twenty-eight phases of the moon, which could be represented by a geometrical construction of wheels and "gyres." Each period of history had its phase, as did each individual, and as the whole of history passed again and again through all the phases, so each individual followed the same sequence in a series of reincarnations. Hence the existence of an *anima mundi*, a great general memory of the race, a notion that is clearly related to the collective unconscious of Jung.

Rather than delving further into this intriguing "phantasmagoria" (the word is Yeats's own), it is worth noting the attraction of a cyclical, lunar system for other writers of the period—it is to be found, in one form or another, in Joyce's *Finnegans Wake*, Pound's "Pisan Cantos," and Graves's *The White Goddess*—and also the apocalyptic nature of Yeats's version, since he worked out the cycles of history in such a way that the moment of his own life would correspond to a cataclysm. Around 1927 our period of civilization, founded by Christ, was to encounter, in war and terror, its antithesis, the Antichrist, the "rough beast" slouching toward Bethlehem to be born. Yeats's thinking here corresponds to that of his age. From Mallarmé ("the trembling of the veil") to Spengler's *Decline of the West*, Eliot's *The Waste Land*, and D. H. Lawrence's *Apocalypse*, apocalypse became the myth of an

W. B. Yeats. Photo BBC/British Council.

epoch. In the imagination of many, of course, the myth was actually lived through.

So myth also represented a possiblity of order, when "Things fall apart; the center cannot hold." Hence Yeats's preoccupation with the "unity of being" and "unity of culture." Yet to meditate on the unity of culture is arguably to recognize that such unity no longer exists; and to meditate on myth is surely to reduce it to an object of culture, to a series of objects exhibited in the imaginary museum. The irony is that Yeats, who could not endure "an international art, picking stories and symbols where it pleased," exploited mythologies for his poems and other works with the same cosmopolitan and skeptical erudition as Joyce, Eliot, or Pound (or Thomas Mann, for instance, since the phenomenon was not exclusive to writers in English). It is true that Yeats believed that the parallelism between Celtic and, say, Indian mythology was not fortuitous, and that every symbolic system derived from a single original belief. The result is nonetheless a mythology blatantly synthetic. As Eliot wrote, in *After Strange Gods:* "Mr. Yeats was in search of a tradition, a little too consciously perhaps—like all of us."

With Eliot too the exploitation of myth is a late-cultural phenomenon, and our distance from myth is suggested in his work even more decisively. The theme of *The Waste Land* could be seen as the sterile multiplicity of mythologies that we find at our disposal, fragments of an excessive and shattered past that we no longer know what to do with. The notes added to the poem refer to two works of anthropology, Frazer's *The Golden Bough* and Jessie Weston's *From Ritual to Romance. The Golden Bough,* which exerted a profound influence on Eliot's generation, derives religion from sympathetic magic, studying the persistence, in the Middle Ages and even in modern folklore, of ancient fertility rites, whose purpose was to ensure the rebirth of spring after the death of nature in winter, and whose focus was the death and resurrection of a vegetation god such as Adonis, Attis, or Osiris. Eliot's poems may be read in this perspective. At the beginning the vegetation god is buried, and there is talk of his dog, that is to say, Anubis, the jackal-headed god who aids Osiris's restoration, and of the hyacinth that is associated with him. In the fourth part Adonis is submerged in water in accordance with a parallel rite, in the person of a sailor who shares his Phoenician nationality, while at the end the rain falls, and it does so by the Ganges, the source of the most ancient of all vegetation myths. The poem is also a descent into Hades, like that which the golden bough made possible for Aeneas.

Jessie Weston sees in this fertility cult the origin of the Grail story, with even the miraculous cup itself representing a cultic object. She also associates the four symbols of the Grail: cup, lance, sword, stone or dish, with the four suits of the Tarot pack (having, as it happens, consulted Yeats). In *The Waste Land,* accordingly, the quest of the Grail and the laying down of Tarot cards become further spectral paradigms of the narrative. The place of the poem is a land laid waste and infertile partly by the sexual inadequacy of its inhabitants, like the Fisher King's territory in the Grail stories, where the vegetation fails because of his mysterious wound. At the end of the voyage, Eliot's reader finds himself, like the Grail knight, in the Perilous Chapel and the Perilous Cemetery, so as to be initiated into the mysteries of physical life (the rain falls) and spiritual life (the thunder speaks). It is the Tarot which predicts the entrances of a hanged god, of Adonis, and of the Fisher King.

These readings, however, are inexact, because of the dysfunctioning of the various narratives. The Tarot pack, for example, is interpreted by a charlatan who has "a bad cold." The reference to Parsifal's ritual purification occurs in a line quoted from the "Parsifal" of Verlaine, a poem which duly celebrates a man who has "overcome Women" but which is dedicated to a notorious homosexual. The reference is followed in Eliot's poem by another homosexual encounter. This derision of narrative can be partly explained by the fact that the modern victims of sterility, and the "hypocritical reader" who observes them, do not desire the regeneration promised by the myth. But the derision is also internal: narrative itself, as well as its "content," is in question. The narration breaks down. The rain falls, yet the plain remains arid; the quester's voyage is accomplished, yet he seems to lose his reason. The quest is even rendered null in the very first line of the poem, since April, the month which in Chaucer's *Canterbury Tales* encourages people by its sweet showers to go on pilgrimages, has become "the cruellest month."

The derision is clearest in the famous assembling in the text of juxtaposed and contradictory fragments. The quester is the reader himself who, confronted by these impenetrable objects, must ask their meaning. In another mythical perspective, the fragments are also the leaves of the Sibyl, who appears in the epigraph and elsewhere—shards of an oracle blown about by the wind. One might argue that traditional narrative is a kind of Grail quest, since it seeks its accomplishment in its ending. *The Waste Land,* on the contrary, mocks linear and teleological narrative in a text deliberately incoherent, a kind of waste land of writing. And at the deepest point of the poem another myth, of dispersal and confusion, is being recreated: the myth of Babel. Babel is present in the poem through a number of allusions—above all, its tower is "abolished" in the ending, precisely at the moment when the text crumbles into five different languages—and its effect is everywhere. A variety of languages seethes disquietingly throughout the text; the notes employ as many, and not always the same ones; the short epigraph and dedication contrive to use Latin, Greek, English, and Italian; and the translation of the *Upaniṣads* that a note recommends is in German. Even within individual languages, syntax dislocates and words fall apart.

If there is a derision of narrative, in fact, there is also derision of language. Language is one of the themes of the poem (the most *superficial*) so that cultural and psychological alienation are accompanied by a linguistic alienation, a fall of language that reflects the fall of man. In the Babel of the poem everything is dispersed: mythologies, places, historical moments, literary works quoted in fragments. According to this text built from the ruins of other texts, the Great Memory is a plethoric jumble, and historical consciousness a "heap of broken images." The last part of the poem, it is true, seeks a remedy for Babel. The thunder pronounces a restorative syllable, "Da," and the three words of salvation which derive from it are taken from Sanskrit, the oldest Indo-European language and the one which might serve to gather the scattered tongues. Yet the last lines are fixed in a definitive ambiguity, a juxtaposition of the rain of Sanskrit and the aridity of the numerous dialects.

The myth of Babel is at the center of *The Waste Land,* as of the whole of Eliot's work. And isn't Babel, a language myth, the fundamental myth in modern literature? Polyglot writing is one of its signs, in *The Waste Land* but also in the *Cantos* of Pound and, among more recent works, in *Renga,* a quadrilingual poem preoccupied with languages, texts, myths, composed by three Europeans of different nationalities and a Mexican. Above all, writers since Mallarmé ("languages imperfect through being several, there lacks a supreme one") recognize in one way or another the failure of language, and aspire to its renewal. Hence, in so many poets, novelists, and dramatists, a voluntary dilapidation of writing and the elaboration of new idioms.

This effort to recreate language is even more striking in Joyce, whose use of a multivariety of myths seems an attempt at an encyclopedic complexity. *Ulysses,* a rewriting of the *Odyssey,* has its main characters—Stephen-Telemachus, Bloom-Ulysses and Molly-Penelope—travel through a storyworld abounding in other reminiscences of the Homeric tale, while also involving them in numerous further myths of Greek, Jewish, Christian, and other origins. *Finnegans Wake,* a *summa* patient of a plurality of readings, enacts the myth of universal fall and resurrection, centering it on the original fault of the hero, H.C.E., on his dream and his awakening. The book also uses the theory in Vico's *The New Science* of the three phases of history and their eternal recurrence. It relives the dream of the whole of humanity, which at the end begins anew, and more particularly the dream of Finn MacCool, a mythical Irish hero asleep on the banks of the Liffey in Dublin, whose awakening or return is the awakening of all the heroes of the past. One finds in *Finnegans Wake* a use of Irish mythology quite different from that of Yeats, and one sees above all the oneiric nature of the narrative, dream being the natural domain of myth, for Jung as for others.

One also sees that the mythology is accompanied by a topography. Mythographer of the city of Dublin, Joyce makes the Irish capital a kind of *omphalos;* as the author of novels at once intensely realist and densely symbolic, he furnishes universal myths with a quotidian site. This concentration on Dublin distances him again from Yeats, and links him with that wider literary opening of the modern City to the insinuation of myth, other major expressions of which are the Paris of Baudelaire and the London of Eliot.

Joyce was far from considering myth as an initiation to knowledge, or a form of being. According to Eliot, the presence of myth in *Ulysses* is "a way of controlling, of ordering, of giving a shape and a significance to the immense panorama of futility and anarchy which is contemporary history." (This comment dates from the year following the publication of *The Waste Land.*) "It is a method already adumbrated by Mr. Yeats . . . It is, I seriously believe, a step toward making the modern world possible in art." Certainly, *Ulysses* offers itself as a kind of cosmos, where Joyce has endeavored to transpose myth *sub specie temporis nostri* (under the vision of our time), and where he has articulated a single story through several "stories" in parallel series: episodes of the *Odyssey,* organs of the body, Jewish rites, colors, etc. In the same way, the abundant material of *Finnegans Wake* is organized in a highly concentrated cyclic order (which recalls Yeats's *A Vision,* about which Joyce said, moreover: "What a pity he did not put all this into a creative work"). Nevertheless, the order that myth imposes upon a refractory world is far from secure. *Ulysses* even seems as problematic in this respect as *The Waste Land,* and its symbolism of lost keys suggests our distance at once from the novel and from a common mythology that reader, author, and characters might share. Its relations with the *Odyssey* are in any case in part burlesque, and the entanglement of mythic and literary reminiscences—Bloom is a rerun of Ulysses, Moses, the Wandering Jew, Sinbad the Sailor, Rip Van Winkle, and God the Father, among others—is as much a marvelous hotch-potch as an encyclopedic order. As for *Finnegans Wake,* it describes itself explicitly as "Chaosmos" and "Microchasme."

Parody and self-parody would seem to be a sure sign of a troubled relation to myth. A possible resolution, for a modern mind assailed by knowledge, is the comedy which, at the deepest level of the works, maybe absorbs that irony; and another, in terms of the myth itself, is in the heroines of the two novels, Molly Bloom and Anna Livia Plurabelle. These women are also, with due allowance for mirth, goddesses, feminine principles, who absorb everything into themselves. Molly "is" *Gea Tellus* or Cybele, the Earth and the universal mother; Anna Livia, the river, the sea, the maternal waters.

Like Eliot, Joyce also uses myths of language, as of art, and his use is equally ironic. Stephen, the future writer, is associated in *A Portrait of the Artist as a Young Man* with the Egyptian god Thoth, who was accused of theft and impiety for having invented writing. In both *A Portrait* and *Ulysses* he also represents Icarus, son of Daedalus. His father is not only the architect of the labyrinth—the labyrinth of Dublin, of Ireland, of his own past, and perhaps of the book itself, where Stephen wanders in search of a way out—but a forger, and thereby, according to the paronomasia which presides over Joyce's writing, a maker of false coin, a fabricator of texts and of stories. One finds in Joyce, as in Eliot, the same persistent and uneasy mockery of one's craft.

This irony too, however, seems resolved in *Ulysses,* by the fact that all the characters, events, symbols, and so on, are united by metempsychosis in language, "metempsychosis" being a word that actually circulates in the book; while *Finnegans Wake,* which is set "by the waters of babalong" and

Khnopff, *The Silver Headdress.* Pencil sketch. Private collection. Photo Dulière-Skira.

which, to return to another myth, is a kind of apocalypse of language, nevertheless finds its beginning, like Proust's *In Search of Lost Time,* in its end: the last word of the book is a definite article which seems to introduce the sentence-ending that opens the book. The Egyptian serpent bites its own tail, Vico's eternal recurrence is enacted by the story itself, and the whole book becomes a noun.

Other writers have explored various strata of the land's mythology. David Jones in particular, a poet and painter of both English and Welsh extraction, was preoccupied with "the Island of Britain" and with King Arthur, "the central figure of our island myth." Like Yeats, and like the Joyce of *Finnegans Wake,* he explored "the Celtic cycle that lies, a subterranean influence as deep as water troubling, under every tump in this Island, like Merlin complaining under his big rock." Also like them he founded his myths on a topography. The body of the hero in *The Sleeping Lord,* who is in part Arthur, is also the landscape, as are the bodies of Finn, and of the giant Albion in Blake.

In *The White Goddess,* Robert Graves excavated the prehistoric mythologies of Britain, examining the conflicts that existed among them and speculating on the cults that existed at Avebury and Stonehenge, in quest of the White Goddess, who gave to the island, he surmised, its early names of Samothea and Albion. In her capacity of goddess of the moon and the universal mother, he claimed to trace her worship from the Mediterranean to northern Europe, before her displacement by male gods and by the logic of Socrates. To rediscover the White Goddess, with whom Molly Bloom and Anna Livia Plurabelle are not unconnected, would be, for Graves, to recover the possibility of myth and also of poetry. For the goddess is equally the Muse (she was ousted in this role too by the male Apollo), and the center of the most widespread myth to do with literature. In Graves's version, however, she is creative and yet destructive, the goddess of death as of inspiration, demanding from her adept total sacrifice, and what she recalls most in modern times is the "belle dame sans merci" of the romantic agony.

Lawrence too was concerned with pre-Olympian mythologies, in his search for the openness to the cosmos, the veneration of the body of the universe, which he saw as chronologically prior to the cult of gods. It is true that, before Graves, he referred to the White Goddess, "the great cosmic Mother crowned with all the signs of the zodiac," and to "the great dark God, the ithyphallic, of the first dark religions"; and that *The Plumed Serpent* envisaged the return of a pre-Columbian Mexican god. Yet this further attempt to recover a mythic consciousness in a way bypassed the gods, whom, at the deepest level of his conviction, he "refused to name." He studied rather a kind of cosmic sensitivity, among the Etruscans, among the American Indians, and in what he considered the primitive and pagan substratum of the *Apocalypse* of Saint John. Inspired by a cyclic conception of time, he even foresaw a return to the living cosmos, via the apocalyptic crisis through which our civilization was passing, by means of certain ancient rites that mime a descent into the underworld followed by rebirth. It may be that *Lady Chatterley's Lover* enacts the seven phases of a rite of initiation in the domain essential to Lawrence, that of sexuality.

During a period covering about two generations, writers questioned mythology with something like fear and trembling. Their readers are bound to ask, as they asked, whether it is still possible, and vitally useful, for a modern European to place himself in contact with mythic sensibility, and it is not surprising to find among certain contemporary writers an impatient hostility to myth. Myth continues, however, in the work of a writer like Ted Hughes, who turns to mythology and folklore to make contact with "the bigger energy, the elemental power circuit of the Universe," and who also refers to "the great goddess of the primeval world." In *Crow* he creates a mythology, yet without overtly deploying myths drawn from a diversity of times and places: his poem does more or less without history and anthropology. He has declared that he wanted to produce "something autochthonous and complete in itself . . . with the minimal cultural accretions of the museum sort . . . hoarded as preserved harvests from the past." The words could be aimed at many of the texts we have considered, especially *The Waste Land* and *Ulysses.* A whole period of literature seems to be concluded when he demands that his myth should be the springing of "essential things . . . from their seeds in nature . . . after the holocaust and demolition of all libraries."

M.Ed.

BIBLIOGRAPHY

I. Texts

T. S. ELIOT, *Collected Plays* (London 1962); *Collected Poems, 1909–1962* (London 1963). ROBERT GRAVES, *The White Goddess* (London 1961). TED HUGHES, *Crow* (London 1972). DAVID JONES, *In Parenthesis* (London 1937); *The Anathemata* (London 1952); *The Sleeping Lord* (London 1974). JAMES JOYCE, *A Portrait of the Artist as a Young Man* (London 1916); *Ulysses* (Paris 1922); *Finnegans Wake* (London 1939). D. H. LAWRENCE, *The Plumed Serpent* (London 1926); *Mornings in Mexico* (London 1927); *Lady Chatterley's Lover* (London 1928); *Apocalypse* (London 1931); *Etruscan Places* (London 1932). EZRA POUND, *The Cantos of Ezra Pound* (London 1964). W. B. YEATS, *Collected Poems* (London 1950); *Collected Plays* (London 1952); *A Vision* (New York 1956); *Mythologies* (London 1959).

II. Critical Studies

MICHEL BUTOR, *Répertoire* (Paris 1960), chapters on Joyce and Pound. EDMUND WILSON, *Axel's Castle* (New York 1931), chapters on Eliot, Joyce, Yeats. MICHAEL EDWARDS, *Eliot/Language* (Skye 1975). HUGH KENNER, *The Invisible Poet: T. S. Eliot* (New York 1959). F. O. MATTHIESEN, *The Achievement of T. S. Eliot* (New York 1935). D. E. S. MAXWELL, *The Poetry of T. S. Eliot* (London 1952). MICHAEL KIRKHAM, *The Poetry of Robert Graves* (London 1969). JOHN PRESS, *Rule and Energy* (london 1963), chapter on Hughes. KEITH SAGAR, *The Art of Ted Hughes* (Cambridge 1975). BERNARD BERGONZI, *Heroes' Twilight* (London 1965), chapter on Jones. HARRY BLAMIRES, *David Jones* (Manchester 1971). UMBERTO ECO, *L'oeuvre ouverte* (Paris 1965), chapters on Joyce. STUART GILBERT, *James Joyce's Ulysses* (London 1930). CLIVE HART, *Structure and Motif in Finnegans Wake* (Evanston 1962). HARRY LEVIN, *James Joyce* (Paris 1950). JEAN PARIS, *James Joyce par lui-même* (Paris 1957). GRAHAM HOUGH, *The Dark Sun: A Study of D. H. Lawrence* (London 1956). FRANK KERMODE, *Modern Essays* (London 1971), chapter on Lawrence. DONALD DAVIE, *Ezra Pound: Poet as Sculptor* (London 1965). GEORGE DEKKER, *Sailing After Knowledge: The Cantos of Ezra Pound* (London 1963). DENIS DONOGHUE and J. R. MULRYNE, *An Honoured Guest: New Essays on W. B. Yeats* (London 1965). RICHARD ELLMANN, *The Identity of Yeats* (New York 1954). T. R. HENN, *The Lonely Tower: Studies in the Poetry of W. B. Yeats* (London 1950). KATHLEEN RAINE, *Yeats, the Tarot and the Golden Dawn* (Dublin 1972). PETER URE, *Towards a Mythology: Studies in the Poetry of W. B. Yeats* (London (1946).

The Survival of Ancient Myths in Modern Greek Poetic Consciousness

Though modern literature frequently refers to and uses ancient myths, in modern Greece such practices are, understandably, matters of special concern. The Greek spirit, naturally disposed to create myths, continues to use, maintain, and illustrate legends that belong to the national heritage, and it sometimes does so in the simplest aspects of everyday life. Frequent visits to sites where mythological events occurred and habitual contemplation of the heights on which a particular hero performed his exploits help make legends familiar. When a Greek names his child Athena or Dionysus, when a vine grower from Nemea refers to his wines as the "blood of the lion," he does not feel that he is adopting elements of culture. There is no intellectual search, no artifice, no affectation in those choices. Their lives are simply imbued with an idea that is not acquired but passed down from ancestors, with subconscious memories and with a tradition as old as the memory of their country. That is why myth, rather than being an object of metaphor, is the essential element and building block of Greek literary thought.

Prior to the rebirth of the Greek state in the early nineteenth century, popular Greek song, the constant expression of the thought of the Hellenic people, included legendary subjects, although its content was often based on current reality, that is, on the misfortune of the enslaved Greek people. In many different versions, one can discern the recollection of a minor mythological act or references to great legends. In a song portraying the rape of a woman by the Saracens (Isle of Symi version), the sun goes to warn the husband, Yannakis, of his misfortune, thus playing the role of the "guardian of gods and men" who warned Demeter of the abduction of Persephone (in the *Homeric Hymn to Demeter*). The exploits of the heroic frontier guardian Digenis Acritas are sung all over Greece. When Digenis kills a snake or, by the command of his king, stands up to a monstrous and ravaging crab, the song refers to the legend of Saint George and, further back, to an adaptation of the Labors of Heracles or an exploit of Apollo. The theme of the sacrifice of a woman, necessary for the success of a human enterprise, inspired by the legend of Iphigenia, is developed in numerous versions of the Panhellenic song of the "Bridge of Arta." The bridge can be built only if the master mason immures his wife in its foundation. The adventure of the husband returning after a long absence and bent on testing his wife's faithfulness before he is recognized is also widespread throughout Greece, on the islands as well as on the mainland. In versions from the Aegean islands of Zante and Thessaly, the meeting occurs at a fountain where the wife is washing clothes. Here the song alludes to two episodes in the *Odyssey:* Odysseus coming back to Ithaca and Odysseus discovered by Nausicaa on the beach. In a popular song, most likely from mainland Greece but widespread from Corfu to the Pontus, a murderous mother serves her husband the liver of their son, who had discovered the mother's infidelity. This recalls the feasts of Atreus and Tantalus. Yet, true to the very nature of popular songs, the ancient inspiration is never obvious but always implicit.

Modern Greek poetry, which was born with the independent Greek state, reserves a rather large place for ancient myths, elements of a national wealth that the newly freed Greeks had their hearts set on illustrating and developing. The way legends are treated varies both with the individual temperament and situation of each author and as a function of the evolving new Hellenism.

Andreas Kalvos (born 1792 on Zante, died 1867 in London; author of twenty *Odes* that appeared in 1824 and 1826) wrote a work, often compared to that of Pindar, in which he celebrates the high points of the War of Independence by simulating a war of antiquity through the use of ancient terms and forms, and through constant recourse to allusions and comparisons that create an intensely mythological climate. In the *Odes,* he often uses allegory and invokes the Muses, Graces, Friendship, Wealth, Wisdom, Virtue, Victory, and Liberty, "brilliant daughters of Zeus." By personifying them, the poet commemorates the sites of martyrdom: Chios, Psará, Samos, Souli. He evokes mythological traditions: the feasts of the gods (*To the Muses*), the nourishment of immortals whose mouths have the fragrance of ambrosia (*To Parga*), and the dwellings of Olympus (*To Liberty*). Deities and heroes appear: Kypris, whose touch was so sweet (*To Psará*); Icarus, whose wings freed him (*To Samos*); the Maenads and Eros, who made way for Ares on the devastated island (*To Psará*); but also the Erinyes summoned to punish the Turk (*To Chios*). The constant intention of Kalvos was to ennoble the act of war by applying to the modern event the meaning and the symbolic value of the ancient myth and to restore to the newly freed land the poetic beauty that legends had conferred upon it.

Konstantinos Kabaphēs (Cavafy) (born 1863, died 1933 in Alexandria; author of nearly 150 short published pieces, *Poems*) wrote a scholarly work, often difficult, in which ancient history and mythology occupy a major place. Allegory is there too. In *Dionysus and His Crew* (trans. Rae Dalven, *The Complete Poems of Cavafy,* New York: Harcourt Brace Jovanovich, 1976, p. 23), seated next to the god are License, Drunkenness, Song, Feast, as well as Telete, goddess of rituals; Sleep and Death take part in *The Funeral of Sarpedon* (ibid. p. 21). Sometimes the poet's intention is essentially aesthetic, in specific scenes such as the description of the handsome young man, the son of Zeus, killed by Patroclus (see Homer *Iliad* 16.665–83) in *The Funeral of Sarpedon.* From another perspective, starting with the experience of life, of the eternal human problems that arouse his pessimism, the author conceives his poem as a recollection and transposition of a moral premise or a philosophical universal into the world of mythology. In *Ithaca* (ibid. p. 36), the poet invites man, the new Odysseus, to face courageously the assaults of the Laestrygones, the Cyclops, and Poseidon. Sometimes he develops the theme of man abandoned by the gods: in *Infidelity* (ibid. p. 20), Thetis, who has been assured of Apollo's protection for her child, Achilles, learns that it was this god himself who killed her son; the original version of the poem bore in epigraph an excerpt from Plato's *Republic* that refers to this incident as recorded in Aeschylus's *Tragic Iliad.* When the hour has come, Antony loses the protection of the gods, and the poet invites him to resign himself to his fate in *The Gods Forsake Antony* (ibid. p. 30). In *Footsteps* (ibid. p. 15), when the Furies enter Nero's home, the "wretched" Lares hide. The sadness of death is illustrated by the grief of the immortal horses pulling the body of Patroclus in *The Horses of Achilles* (ibid. p. 24: see *Iliad* 17.423–55). The impotence and ignorance of mortals are very briefly and laconically illustrated in *Interruption* (ibid. p. 12), a poem that shows Metanira preventing Demeter from making her child immortal and Peleus terrified by the exploits of Thetis when she is trying to make Achilles invulnerable (cf. Apollonius of Rhodes *Argonautica* 4.865–79 and Apollodorus *On the Gods* 3.13). The notion of opposition can be expressed at another level, namely, that of the relationship between a dying paganism and a rising Christianity, illustrated by the seven poems devoted to the Emperor Julian, but also by isolated works such as *Supplication* (ibid. p. 5) or *Kleitos' Illness* (ibid. 133), in which the meaning and the image of the myths more or less disappear behind the historical antagonism of the two religions. Whether it is a philosophical thought, an invitation to Stoicism, or the mere description of an aesthete, the use of the mythological element in Cavafy's work, sometimes allusive, sometimes explicit, sometimes intimately tied to historical recollection, is never based on an overarching view, but on the analysis of a particular fact or of an exact detail.

The often scholarly aspect of the expression of myth and its occasionally artificial application are characteristics common to Kalvos and Cavafy, perhaps due to the same cause: their lack of contact with Greek soil. When he published his *Odes,* Kalvos had lived mostly abroad (in Italy and England). Cavafy spent his life in Alexandria.

Wholly different is the inspiration of Kōstēs Palamas (born 1859 in Patras, died 1943 in Athens; author of numerous collections of poems, two epics, a drama, etc.), who always lived in Greece and took part in the political and social evolution of the young state. This was a time when events and intellectual movements were causing a global dread of Hellenism and of the traditions of Hellenism, which follow one another without conflict. In the *Hymn to Athena,* a long poem, the author evokes the bond that in his mind ties the ancient world to the modern world. Indeed, Palamas treats myths as did the romantics who influenced him, but he also often expresses the strictly Hellenic attitude that takes possession of the indivisible elements of the whole Greek domain. In the poem *My Fatherlands* from the collection *Life Immovable,* Palamas projects allegorical forms of beauty onto the landscape of Missolonghi, where he grew up, and later onto the site of Attica. He presents a personified Pentelicus and Olympus, and he sings of the sites "where Homer's Phaeacians still live" and of the bliss that the specter of Solomos finds in the Elysian fields. In a single burst and in the same poem, he aims to celebrate the works of Digenis and the exploits of the heroes of the Independence, and then to evoke the maidens with baskets on the Acropolis, carrying Athena's cloak to the temple; thus he gathers together the immortal beauties from the history of Hellenism. He draws another parallel, rather unusual in the eyes of a Western reader but natural to the mind of a Greek artist, which goes beyond apparent distinctions to link notions common to paganism and Christianity, especially Eastern Orthodoxy. In *Sibyl,* after a reference to Virgil's *Aeneid* 6.65, he compares the prophetess to the *Panagia Odigitria* or "Guiding Virgin," a type of Byzantine virgin frequently found in religious iconography.

Assimilations on the same order were to be widely developed by Angelos Sikelianos (born 1884 in Leneade, died 1951 in Athens; author of a massive poetic work, *Lyrical Life* [trans. Edmund Keeley and Philip Sherrard, *Selected Poems,* Princeton: Princeton University Press, 1979], and of tragedies). He was an intellectual, an author exceptionally sensitive to the spirit and meaning of myths, a man for whom the gods had never left Greece. He told the story that, as a young child, during an earthquake he was filled with joy at the thought that the earth was speaking to him. Sikelianos's eagle eye saw through material appearances and was able to reach down to the deep meaning and eternal value of each scene. The spectacle—so common—of a he-goat in the midst of a herd of she-goats grazing by the shore of the Aegean Sea is for the poet the pure and simple materialization of a myth, so obvious that only the title, *Pan,* makes an explicit reference to the legend. He makes *The Greek Funeral Banquet,* inspired by a ceremony to which he was invited, an occasion to evoke the libations and banquets of initiation; with the "blood of Dionysus" he calls forth the souls of the dead and invokes the protection of Dionysus-Hades. Sikelianos's imagination exalts ordinary moments of life, finding a hidden meaning for them that links them to the most ancient traditions. In *Sacred Way* (ibid. p. 99), the showman's she-bear who stands erect on the Sacred Way at Eleusis in front of her cub suffers at the sight of his young nostrils wounded by the iron ring, and becomes the symbol of the weeping mother in the poet's consciousness:

> One of them,
> the larger—clearly she was the mother—
> her head adorned with tassels of blue beads
> crowned by a white amulet, towered up
> suddenly enormous, as if she were
> the primordial image of the Great Goddess,
> the Eternal Mother, sacred in her affliction,
> who, in human form, was called Demeter
> here at Eleusis, where she mourned her daughter,
> and elsewhere, where she mourned her son,
> was called Alcmene or the Holy Virgin. (Ibid. p. 101)

The kinship of faiths and religions and the hidden unity of symbols—marked by a number of titles: *Conscience of My*

Fresco from the facade of the refectory of the Great Laura, Mount Athos. Upper righthand corner: Artemis withdraws at the moment of the Annunciation. Photo Paul Huber, Bern.

Land, Conscience of My Race, Conscience of Faith—such were the convictions that animated Sikelianos when in 1926 he established the Delphic Feasts and attempted to create a center, a spiritual "omphalos," at Delphi, where he also had the tragedies staged in interpretations that allowed room for the neo-Hellenistic tradition.

George Seferis (born 1900 in Smyrna, died 1971 in Athens; author of *Poems* and *Essays*) lived through the painful experience of the catastrophe of Asia Minor. Endowed with a nature easily inclined toward melancholy, he was twenty-two when the Greeks were expelled from Ionia, and he lost his native land forever. Like all the Greeks born at the turn of the century in Turkey, he was to remain deeply marked by this misfortune; a significant part of his work is colored by melancholy, nostalgia, and the sentiment of parting, loss, frustration, shipwreck, and death. In this framework, he uses many mythological themes to illustrate the permanence of their symbolic value and the endurance of the Greek spirit. In *Mythistorema* (trans. Rex Warner, *Poems,* London: Bodley Head, 1960), allusions to myths are numerous, sometimes expressed in subtitles such as *Argonauts* (ibid. p. 13), *Astyanax* (ibid. p. 27), and *Andromeda* (ibid. p. 29), sometimes very discreetly indicated by a single proper name: Odysseus, Adonis, Orestes, the Symplegades. The collection ends with a wish borrowed from Homer's *nekuia* (journey to the dead):

> Those who one day shall live here where we end,
> If ever the dark blood should rise to overflow their memory,
> Let them not forget us, the strengthless souls among the asphodels.
> Let them turn towards Erebus the heads of the victims.
> We who had nothing shall teach them peace. (Ibid. p. 31)

In a long mythological poem from *Log Book 3, Helen* (bearing inscriptions of verses from Euripides' *Helen*), the heroine reveals that only her shadow went to Troy and that the war was a snare:

> Great pain had fallen on Greece.
> So many bodies thrown
> To jaws of the sea, to jaws of the earth:
> . . .
> That so much suffering, so much life
> Fell into the abyss. (Ibid. pp. 115–16)

Through these lines, it is easy to see the memory of another Ionic war, the massacres at Smyrna in September

1922. Numerous references to the tragedies and to Homer could also come from a more purely intellectual attitude. In *The Thrush* (ibid. p. 15), a man—simultaneously Odysseus and Seferis—seized by the dizziness of imagination and dreams, recalls "the lustful Elpenor." In *The Light,* Seferis evokes the fate of Oedipus deprived of the sight of the sun before the Nereids and the Graiae who "come running at the sight of scintillating Anadyomene" Aphrodite. A poem written in the Transvaal in 1942, *Stratis the Sailor among the Agapanthi,* from *Log Book 2,* is in a most significant way thoroughly permeated with mythological memories and traditions: the Agapanthi; "asphodels of the Negroes," who demand silence and prevent the author from speaking to the dead; and the goatskin bottle of the winds, which deflates itself (the author tries in vain to fill it); the memory of the house and of the old dog who waits until the voyager returns to die—all these are so many separate elements that illustrate an idea expressed by Seferis in *In the Manner of G.S.,* included in *An Exercise Book:* "Wherever I travel, Greece keeps wounding me" (ibid. p. 51).

But in modern Greek literature, all the genres use myths. Nikos Kazantzakis (born 1883 in Heraclion, died 1957 in Fribourg-en-Brisgau; author of novels, essays, dramas, and poems) wrote a drama in three parts, *Prometheus,* in which the gods appear on stage; also a tragedy, *Theseus,* or *Kouros,* directly inspired by the legend; and a very long epic of 33,333 lines, *The Odyssey,* which begins at the moment when the hero returns to Ithaca, an epic that can be interpreted as the adventure of modern man.

George Theotokas (born 1905 in Constantinople, died 1966 in Athens; author of essays, novels, and plays) narrated the venture of ambitious young idealists in his novel *Argo.* In his drama *The Bridge of Arta,* he takes up the theme of the popular song. In a brief tragedy, *The Last of the Wars,* he deals with the departure of the captive women after the Trojan War. He also wanted to create a "myth of Alcibiades" in his long play *Alcibiades.*

Pandelis Prevelakis (born 1909 in Rethymnus; author of essays, novels, plays, poems), without borrowing his title from tradition, created in his novel *The Sun of Death* the character of Aunt Roussaki, a deeply Christian Cretan peasant woman who serenely adopts and embellishes legends such as that of Demeter and Persephone, and the exploits of ancient heroes (by a device similar to that of Sikelianos), and whose daily life is illuminated by a familiar, intimate, and intuitive knowledge of the meaning and value of each plant, animal, and heavenly phenomenon. In her world where all is spirit, Roussaki lives out in utter calm both the pagan myth and the orthodox Christian myth. She creates them and maintains them and deserves to be regarded as a feminine image of Hellenism.

In their attempts to become part of world literature, modern Greek authors since World War II have had a slight tendency to withdraw gradually from traditional Greek fields, and thus from the world of mythology, in order to devote themselves instead to the universal problems of twentieth-century man.

R.R./g.h.

BIBLIOGRAPHY

In French

S. BAUD-BOVY, *La chanson populaire grecque du Dodécanèse* (Paris 1936). C. CAVAFY, *Poèmes* (Paris 1958). And on Cavafy: M. YOURCENAR, *Présentation critique de Constantin Cavafy* (Paris 1958, 2d ed.). C. DIMARAS, *Histoire de la littérature néo-hellénique* (Athens 1965). D. HESSELING, *Histoire de la littérature grecque moderne* (Paris 1924). N. KAZANTZAKIS, *L'Odyssée* (Paris 1968); *Théâtre I* (Paris 1974). And on Kazantzakis: C. JANIAUD-LUST, *Nikos Kazantzaki* (Paris 1970). P. PREVELAKIS, *Le soleil de la mort* (Paris 1966). And on Prevelakis: A. CHAMSON, "Prévélakis et la Crète," *Mercure de France* 1148 (April 1959): 579–88. G. SEFERIS, *Poèmes* (Paris 1963); *Trois poèmes secrets* (Paris 1970).

In Greek

G. THEOTOKAS, *Argō* (Athens, 2 vols.); *Theatrika Erga* (Athens 1965–67, 2 vols.). A. KALVOS, *Ōdai* (Athens 1970). K. PALAMAS, *Hapanta* (Athens, 16 vols.). A. POLITH, *Historia tēs Neas Hellēnikēs Logotechnias* (Thessalonika 1972). A. SIKELIANOS, *Lyrikos Bios* (Athens 1946–47, 3 vols.).

Imagination and Mythology in Contemporary Literature (Tolkien, Lovecraft) and Science Fiction

Every human being has two umbilical cords: one, made of flesh, is cut at birth; the other, even before conception, weaves a person into language. But not only can this second cord never make up for the cutting of the first, it is itself an ambiguous, or paradoxical, umbilicus: it connects only by keeping apart; it plunges each person into the immense universe of meaning only at the price of an irrevocable break (marked particularly by the proper name), a gulf that forever separates every subject from what would fulfill him. Moreover, the object of fulfillment, of completion, is constituted only within the universe of meaning (although the body is always determinative for its elaboration). And language thus comes between the object that it has itself helped to create and the subject who desires this object.

Fictional narratives are one of the forms of compromise (sexual life is another, and the most basic) which seek to reduce this paradox. They portray a thousand figures of fulfillment, figures which external reality would find it hard to provide; but the narratives offer the possession and full enjoyment of the figures only on condition of raising a symbolic barrier, which they announce: "This is a story, it's not true."

Fictional narratives, like myths and religions, are responsible for producing a link with fulfillment for man: an umbilicus of replacement. There is, however, a wide gap between a discourse, presented as fiction, that aims to produce wonder and a sense of pleasure, and another, presented as true, that regulates the individual's relations with the social body and writes his destiny on a register whose absolute points of reference are established and expressed by myths or religions.

The symbolic barrier in this second type of mythic discourse is marked above all by the fact that nothing can be changed by an individual: the truth is believed to escape the grasp of any particular person. Furthermore, one cannot possess and use the truth as one likes, but only according to the order of particular rituals and institutions, within the limits which the doctrine assigns to human beings. In the fictional narrative, by contrast, everything is permitted, since "it's not true." Someone who renounces telling the truth gains in return the right to make worlds out of the materials that language and symbolic representations provide for him.

Subjection to verisimilitude is not much of a constraint: quite simply, the fictional narrative must not maintain a discourse that is more unlikely than religious discourse. This is the limit within which it must remain (even if it sometimes narrows this limit to align itself with a positive discourse—psychological observation, history, the sciences, etc.—as, for example, in the classical novel). The literature that is called imaginative always stays the closest to its function as a pseudo-umbilicus, and thus to the broadest of its conditions of verisimilitude: it invents myths.

But this type of literature does not, any more than any other, escape the necessity to give some density to the representations evoked by the words of the narrative. To this end, one convenient procedure consists in dipping into the vast storehouse of already existing religious discourses, with the reservation that these discourses must cease to be taken as true, or rather as true for everyone; religions that have come to be considered beliefs, representations labeled folklore or superstitions, myths reduced to the level of fables or fairy tales, all these materials are able to provide grist for imaginative narratives. The narratives do not take up these materials as such: they acclimatize them to their new function; they use the pieces to make something different; they parody them, betray them, disown them (in brief, they use them), and this both to make them function in conformity with the representations in force among the category of readers to which they are addressed and to give the texts the character of a creation, to make the reader share in the pleasure of mastery: the reader must always be able to see that he is dealing with a created work, even when its artificiality is elaborated by the author so as to be "true to life."

Thus, while all narratives can be considered, in one way or another, to be bearers or creators of myths, only some, by the expedient of borrowing or parody, are linked with already existing beliefs, religions, or myths. But even a category limited in this way remains far too vast to cover here. I will therefore touch on only a few points to mark certain of the most representative directions of this use of mythology; with J. R. R. Tolkien first of all (a British author who died in 1973), whose work is addressed both to children (*The Hobbit*) and to adults (*The Lord of the Rings,* a long narrative in an archaic style, reminiscent of a medieval saga). We will then look at H. P. Lovecraft, the American author of horror stories who wrote between the two world wars. I would like, finally, to sketch the position of the gods in the problematic of the narratives of science fiction (or futuristic fiction).

I. *The Hobbit* by J. R. R. Tolkien

With *The Hobbit,* Tolkien joins the tradition of J. M. Barrie, whose hero Peter Pan is still famous; but Tolkien differs notably in that his fantasies are systematically based on beings whose names, at least, come from folklore (although he adds characters of his own invention, such as "hobbits"): dwarfs (with beards and hoods, naturally), giants (ferocious ones), elves, goblins, a sorcerer (old and wise, with a long white beard), a dragon (who, of course, breathes fire), raven messengers, etc.

With a cast like this, a setting made up of vast regions with varied landscapes, the wondrous possibilities provided by spells, enchantments, a ring of invisibility, and an attractive goal (a well-guarded treasure), Tolkien has the makings of a story with innumerable ups and downs—but a story that offers pleasure of what kind? In other words, where in this tale are the figures of fulfillment? According to what modalities do narratives like Tolkien's put their readers into some sort of relationship with fulfillment?

For the beginnings of an answer to this question, I will first note the following: the writing in *The Hobbit* supports the consistency of characters and plot by basing itself essentially upon the recollection of a convention, and the establishment of a connivance, between reader and author. To read *The Hobbit* is to enter into a game in which you enjoy a kind of guarantee: that however horrible certain episodes may be in themselves, they will not impose, they will never absorb the reader completely. For the author is constantly reminding us that he is there, in the wings of the story that he is telling; although his commentaries to the reader can be called humorous, it is precisely in this sense: although they are presented as serious and useful explanations of particular points in the narrative, they really have the effect of placing in the foreground the author's connivance with the reader, indicating that "at bottom, none of this is really true," and that the only ground on which the characters are standing is precisely that of the complicity between the author and the reader.

In this narrative mode, the fact that the names of many characters, along with some of their semiological traits, have been taken from a tradition external to the narrative itself is important and effective. For dwarfs, elves, and goblins constitute a set of representations shared by the author and his readers (since they know that these representations exist outside them). To introduce them by name is to ask the reader more or less explicitly to place himself within the frame of a convention. This procedure is the inverse of the one that consists of introducing a character through the weight of his (pseudo-) reality, i.e., through the multiplicity of semiological traits which engage him in a discourse of verisimilitude. It is as if at the moment of bringing a new character into play, Tolkien announces: "What about an elf—that suggests something to you, doesn't it? Here is my variation on the theme of an elf's traditional descriptive traits. Now here are the modifications entailed in this new element's entry into the current conjecture of the story."

Alongside these shared representations, explicitly introduced as such, the author calls upon others, which act as if there were nothing out of the ordinary about them and so come to portray reality. For example, while Bilbo the Hobbit is a being of pure fantasy (that is, the fruit of an accepted convention), he nevertheless presents the "reality" of a child. Not that he objectively displays the same types of motivations and feelings as children; rather, he evinces the same reactions of pleasure and fear as those which the child reader can suppose are characteristic of his own nature. This, then, is a bridge which connects not the reader to the author but the subject of the enunciation (the reader in the act of consuming the narrative) to the subject of the enunciated (Bilbo, for example). This link is not the register of connivance, but of analogy, identification. It is reinforced by all the indications that surround the daily life of the hero: Bilbo's lodgings, for instance, with all that a comfortable life re-

Elric the Necromancer. Drawing by Philippe Druillet. © Dargaud éditeur, Paris, 1975.

Dead Gods. Drawing by Philippe Druillet. Photo D.R.

quires, like the house of the three bears in the fairy tale, and especially with all the fixings for breakfasts and teas that leave nothing to be desired. The indications of comfort (or, by contrast, of insecurity) used in the narration function as an echo and amplification of the comfort felt by the child in the very act of consuming the narrative (especially when the story is read to him by an adult).

The connection with fulfillment which narratives like *The Hobbit* establish is thus nothing but the deployment, in the imaginary space of the enunciated, of the connection that is the basis of the very possibility of their enunciation. The voice of the storyteller, or the very pages of the book, are the concentrated site of a possibility of comfort; they establish the reader or listener in a position where all reality calls a truce; it lets him suck the milk of a story (a story of hidden treasure, for instance) at the breast of the storyteller. Elves and dwarfs, goblins and dragons—precisely because everyone knows that they have no existence other than their names—help to maintain this truce by reminding us that here (in the enclosed space of the enunciation of the narrative), the linguistic convention is law and has the power to suspend the dangers and privations that a confrontation with reality involves.

II. H. P. Lovecraft

Of all the authors classed in the genre of fantastic fiction or science fiction, Lovecraft is the one who has had the most systematic recourse to a pantheon. A pantheon purely as a parody: Lovecraft speaks of his gods as if they were generally recognized as gods. He carefully respects his own conventions, the same pantheon being common to all of his fiction (here too, as with Tolkien, we find that dimension of play by which the author simultaneously creates a universe and explicitly marks its conventional character, based on language).

At the apex, at the deepest level of the hierarchy, Azathoth, the unbounded, the sultan of demons, dwells in Primal Chaos. Among the mute gods who surround him are Nyarlathotep, the Crawling Chaos; in Outer Chaos, Yog-Sothoth, the Protoplasmic, also from the stars; Cthulhu, emprisoned inside a submerged city. Less horrific than Cthulhu is Dagon, another marine divinity. Minor gods include Umr-Attawil, Tsathoggua, Ghatanothoa, Hastur, and the Shub-Niggurath mentioned in an undiscoverable book of black magic, the *Necronomicon:* for along with these deities there are secret books that perpetuate their worship, as well as worshipers, dark and deviant personalities or degenerate human groups.

Maurice Lévy has called this effort at consistency the "myth of Cthulhu." But any kinship of Lovecraft's work with a myth or a religious system is entirely external. Defined as they are by their names and descriptions, the gods of the Lovecraftian pantheon are not differentiated like those of a genuine religious mythology: they repeat one another in a redundant way; all are representatives of more or less unfathomable regions of Chaos.

Lovecraft's knowledge of mythology may have helped him to enrich the description of his deities: Cthulhu, for instance, has many traits in common with Typhon, who is, like him, akin to the powers of Chaos, to "those who came before" (Hesiod's formula, but it could have been Lovecraft's), those cut off from the orderly world by a gate forever sealed (although for Lovecraft this gate opens often enough).

These imaginary deities are of a type with whom human beings cannot connect themselves by any symbolic and institutional mediation. Contact with them is a transgression, a short-circuit, an encounter which "normally" should not take place (Lovecraft's narrative is always the story of an exception). They are sacred pollution, the omnipotence of a glutinous and eternal matter; in brief, Lovecraft evokes a sense of the religious that overflows any symbolic inscription, and tongue-ties the universe of signs. Phrases such as "daemon activity," "shocking rituals," "outlaw sect," and "devilish exchange" are frequent and are used to amplify the word "blasphemous" (one of the author's favorite adjectives). In their constant repetition, these stereotyped phrases themselves become elements in a litany of incantation that reactivates a holy terror for each story, the evocation of powers which, like the pagan deities attacked by Christianity, come from the register of the diabolical.

Lovecraft's mythological base thus presents a very different sense from that of an author like Tolkien. The representations that Lovecraft gathers around his nonhuman entities are supported more by a paradoxical use of language than by the simple conventions of play: here language seeks to point out its own insufficiency in the face of the ineffable, the unnameable. Lovecraft portrays (by means of language, of course) various figures of the power that overflows and silences all language and all convention. Far from extending and illustrating the cozy fulfillment created by the reader's position in the enunciation (the reader, reading, lives only events of language), the sites of fulfillment in Lovecraft are those where, eluding the grasp of language, the real bursts forth.

For those who reach them, these forbidden places offer a restoration of the umbilicus of flesh; but this time it is an umbilicus whose circulation, to be restored, must be reversed: no longer nourishing and constructive, it is now a destructive suction, going toward the mother, toward the hero's absorption into flesh and into a lineage of the dead (from which he has only temporarily emerged). The power of Lovecraft's gods thus lies not in their science, laws, or wisdom (since for this they would have to recognize their subjection to some symbolic instance): it lies in their monstrous flesh, their power of contagion, a result of their crushing disproportion to any human order.

If Lovecraft abundantly, repetitiously, portrays sites of fulfillment, the subject of those that he has enunciated, the narrator, is plunged into these sites, to benefit from the experience. In these tales the author never marks himself as the subject of the enunciated: the reader must be alone in his confrontation with the site of fulfillment, for the goal of the narrative is to produce dread, not comfort. Here, language wants to restore conditions in which it would not have existed, but does so, and can do so, only from the moment that it exists. The enterprise is thus simultaneously serious (fascinating, extreme) and not serious, since it plays tricks and knows that it is playing them. Although in the enunciated no barrier now separates the hero from the divine (which, *by this fact,* is transformed into the diabolic), the reader is nevertheless in contact with the abyss of fulfillment only through the mediation and the screen of the narrative.

III. On Mythologies in Science Fiction

In science fiction, fulfillment is signified primarily in the form of the mastery of the immeasurable, the domination and spanning of enormous distances of space and time. Scientific discourse comes in, on the one hand, to connect reality (as well as it can) with the elaborations which otherwise would remain simply phantasmic. On the other hand, the presence of scientific discourse also serves to affirm the power of symbolic activity over what tends to go beyond it.

The introduction of fragments of discourse that parody the discourse of the exact sciences is thus never a sufficient reason to discount the presence of the divine. One need only peruse the titles of works of science fiction to be convinced of this: the struggle for omnipotence, faced with the obstacles of immensity and death, calls for the use of the vocabulary of religion and the cosmic.

The theme of a disproportion to be surmounted is everywhere present in science fiction, sometimes depicted in a problematic close to that of Lovecraft: the awesome omnipotence of the aliens, masters of vast distances in space and time, a diabolical invasion by creatures of flesh dominated by eyes or tentacles, threatening the measured universe of men. But, more specifically, the gods in science fiction are large-scale human beings, freed from the limits of death, possessing science and power on a universal scale; and yet never quite certain of having the last word in the struggles and rivalries that oppose them to other gods. Men become gods (in the work of Roger Zelazny, for example), or gods with a human face (in the work of A. E. Van Vogt), must keep up a constant outbidding for symbolic mastery: they must constantly be foiling plots, inventing machines that outclass those of the enemy, defeating the totalitarian rationality of a power (religious, political, technological) that bears all the earmarks of a fulfillment against which the hero must measure himself. Thus the figures of fulfillment presented to the reader are based on the disproportion between the reader himself and the material universe of which he is part, and *inseparably,* on discourses that, in their totalizing vocation, offer simultaneously the means of portraying this disproportion and the means of measuring up to it.

F.Fl./j.l.

BIBLIOGRAPHY

J. R. R. TOLKIEN, *The Hobbit* (Boston and New York 1938); *The Lord of the Rings,* 3 vols. (Boston 1954–56). H. P. LOVECRAFT, *Dagon; The Shadow out of Time; The Outsider; The Color out of Space; Beyond the Wall of Sleep.*

Science Fiction

Gods and god-men are frequently employed by authors such as O. STAPLEDON (the first one to tackle this theme), P. J. FARMER, M. MOORCOCK, A. E. VAN VOGT, D. F. GALOUYE, and R. ZELAZNY.

Among the numerous works on science fiction, I suggest *63 auteurs, bibliographie de science-fiction,* by A. VILLEMUR (Paris 1976); and the work of D. WOLHEIM, *Les faiseurs d'univers* (Paris 1974), who stresses more than others the theme of gods in science fiction.

General

The most general work on fantasy literature is no doubt that of P. VERSINS, *Encyclopédie de l'Utopie, des voyages extraordinaires et de la science-fiction* (Lausanne 1972).

On ghost stories, see the book by M. LEVY, *Le roman "gothique" anglais, 1764–1824* (Toulouse 1972). On fantasy literature in general see *Introduction à la littérature fantastique,* by T. TODOROV (Paris 1970).

Myth and Political Theory: Nationalisms and Socialisms

Although the nineteenth century is the century of the rebirth of myth and of mythology, this is a renaissance only of the myths of pagan antiquity and the mythologies revealed by the curiosity of travelers and the discoveries of scholars. Poets and artists use these mythologies to construct their own symbolic universe and to restore meaning to a world from which the gods seem to have retired. But many do not stop at a purely individual perspective, and attempt to build collective myths. Since the beginning of the nineteenth century, the poet, and more generally the intellectual, has felt that he was invested with a mission that is situated at the crossroads of two traditions: the tradition of the *philosophes* of the eighteenth century, who assert that they are fighting for enlightenment and progress, and the tradition of unknown prophets, those obscure interpreters of history who read the characters of the divine tongue in the symbols of the world and comment on its revelation (Hamann, Saint-Martin, Court de Gébelin, Fabre d'Olivet). The intellectual picks up where the disqualified clergy left off and claims a capacity to create myths and religions. When waiting for the gods—old or new—ends in disappointment, an ersatz mythology appears: the myth of religion as art and revelation as art. Thus, for the first time, the great literary and artistic works of the tradition are regarded as myths: Faust, Don Juan, and Don Quixote become the bearers of a universal and sacred meaning of which their creators were unaware. This religion of art may take all forms, from the artistic socialism of William Morris to the lofty and hopeless religion of Mallarmé. But more often the writer seeks to take on a social responsibility and perceives himself as being invested with authority; this involves intervening in social struggles, bringing the judgment of history to bear on events, and pointing out the just course of action. The intellectual has just discovered a new territory over which he seeks to become an expert, namely, political territory: "Political Science, which is the Science of Sciences," writes Blake. The new gods will be the gods of political struggle.

It is on the political terrain that truly collective myths arise; not the personal myths of poets and writers, but the myths of social prophets, which are born of a cross between the ambitions of the intellectuals and the new social entities that appeared at the beginning of the nineteenth century. These entities include on the one hand the nation, in the modern sense of the term, of which all the inhabitants are at least by right equal citizens, and on the other hand, the social classes, the distant legacy of the Estates of the ancien régime. The situation of both protagonists is quite comparable. Just as the classes struggle for power within the nation, so the nations fight for the conquest of the universal empire. The two entities are thus inseparable, by virtue of their birth and their meaning. History explains the development of nations by the struggle and the oppression of peoples (A. Thierry), just as Karl Marx explains it by the struggle and the oppression of classes. But the two new actors are the ones in whose hands the fate of all is played out: these new fighters need new conceptions of the world. Moreover, the very appearance of these actors and their awareness of their roles are symbolic facts, the result of a mythological construction as well as of the material evolution of societies. Heroes of new struggles, the people and the social class need narrative paradigms to define their function and remind everyone of their significance. Naturally they need myths. An enormous effervescence of ideas is thus produced, the creators of which are the intellectuals, but also the marginal intellectuals, the semiliterate and the self-taught, as well as established writers and ideologues. We are dealing with something like a "primitive soup" of modern ideologies, comparable to the flowering of philosophical and religious sects at the beginning of the Christian era, out of which a selection of ideas unfolded, similar to the natural selection of species: the fittest survived in the end.

Out of the period of ideological creation that spans the years between 1800 and 1850, two great mythical complexes emerged, the complex of the people and nationalism and the complex of the class and socialism, with a largely identical structure. To begin with, myth includes actors: on one side, the people (as described by Michelet or Hugo), and, on the other, the social class—whether the captains of industry of Saint-Simon or the proletariat of Marx. This mythical actor, who is not individual but collective, becomes incarnate in a series of mythical heroes: the Grand Ferré, Joan of Arc, or Gavroche as seen by Michelet and Hugo, or Spartacus and Thomas Münzer regarded as the martyrs of the oppressed classes. What matters is that the actors are aware of their lives and their roles: on the one hand, *Volksgeist*, the spirit of the people, in which the profound vocation of a culture is crystallized (Herder, Humboldt, Hegel); on the other hand, class consciousness, as a result of which the proletariat can see itself as the bearer of an exemplary fate. The fact is that the actors, people and class alike, have a mission to accomplish, which they carry within themselves and which historical development must let them bring to fruition. This realization is revealed in an ambiguous and contradictory form. It is the result of a struggle (the people's war, the class struggle) and at the same time aims for a universal reconciliation. Each country believes that it is invested with a providential mission, just as each class believes that it is destined to triumph over the others in the end; but in the universal fatherland, individual countries will find a "melting pot," just as the classes will all disappear in the classless society. It is thus a matter of bringing about peace, but peace can be achieved only at gunpoint. The transition to the final state must take place in a sudden mutation, conquest, or revolution by which all values are transmuted. Thus a new form of government is set up, an unprecedented era that inaugurates the end of history, the end of separate nations and classes. The linear time of human history is broken; the rupture puts an end to it and at the same time goes beyond it without recourse to transcendence.

In order to recognize the movement of history and hasten its development, a man of knowledge and action is needed, a prophet-theoretician, heralding the change to come. The moment he appears, he founds a school around him, with disciples and institutions that guarantee the spread of the doctrine (Saint-Simonists, Fourierists, positivists, Marxists). The party is only the organized and conscious form of this militia of disciples.

This myth rests on a scientific component (largely pseudoscientific at that) whereby the prophet-theoretician is a man of science, a historian, a geographer, a sociologist, an anthropologist, an economist, or a politician, and his theoretical construction is seen as scientific, science being the only orthodox model of knowledge. To the scientific component a technical component is added, the one already inscribed in the myth of Faust: science can make us the absolute owners and masters of nature. This technique of domination must also be exercised on society and history: the myth of the real Utopia, according to which a complete and coherent organization of the social world is possible. There is, however, a difference between the two mythical complexes. Originally the socialist complex favored the technical and scientific models, and the nationalist complex favored organic models; but in both cases, the concern for organization and coherent domination is the same. Gradually the two types of models tend to combine, as can be seen in today's nationalisms and socialisms. In the same way, the two complexes and the two great mythical actors tend to overlap thanks to notions such as imperialism (Lenin) and proletarian nations (Mussolini): the relations between nations are the exact equivalents of the relations between classes.

Thus a new kind of myth arose, which came to take its

place next to the traditional myths in the repertory of the historian of religions and which led to a new conception of mythology. For the correct understanding of myth had been blocked by two obstacles: the refusal to consider revealed religions as myths and the affirmation of modern rationality, which would empty heaven of its gods. In fact, there are three kinds of myths. First there is the traditional myth of polytheistic religions, sacred history that took place in a primordial time and space and that ritualistically guarantees the creation and preservation of man and the world. Next there is a myth characteristic of religions of salvation with a universalist vocation. This is a historical myth, anchored in the history of men by the presence of a prophet or a founder who has perforated human time with transcendence; the relationships between time and myth are thus transformed. The historical time of the founder partakes of the sacred time that he exemplifies, but it simultaneously introduces into sacred time the linear dimension of a time divided up between before and after, between creation, annunciation, and salvation. Finally there is the myth of modern ideologies, not what is incorrectly called modern myths, but mythic history in which it is no longer gods but ideas that guide the movement of the real and guarantee the second coming. Here again the essential dimension is the organization of human, individual, and collective time; this is why it is better to speak of ideological myth than ideology—which is a confusing and misleading notion—when one wishes to designate the third form of myth. In any case, myth is defined as a specific organization of time.

At the end of each mythical cycle, some people have believed that all mythical thought had to be effaced before the splendor of what is true: each time the myth has begun anew, but in a guise in which no one could recognize it any more. If we are at the end of the age of ideological myth—and nothing could be less certain—then surely somewhere, unbeknownst to anyone, the myth of tomorrow is already crystallizing.

J.M./g.h

PART

7

South Asia, Iran, and Buddhism

The Religion and Mythology of Vedic India 799
Soma as Sacrificial Substance and Divine Figure in the Vedic Mythology of Exchange 803
Vedic Cosmogony 806
The Mythologies of Hindu India 808
The *Yūpa* (Sacrificial Post) in Hinduism 811
Rudra/Śiva and the Destruction of the Sacrifice 813
Purāṇic Cosmogony 817
The Hindu God with Five Heads (*Pañcamukha*) 824
Deva/Asura: Celestial Gods and "Demons" in Hinduism 826
Vasiṣṭha/Viśvāmitra and the Separation of the Priestly and Royal Functions 827
The Main Myth of the *Mahābhārata* 829
The *Rāmāyaṇa* 834
Viṣṇu and Śiva, the Supreme Gods of Hindu Bhakti 839
Popular Hinduism 842
Avatars 849
Nara/Nārāyaṇa 852
Matsya: The Fish and the Flood in the Work of the Mythic Imagination 853
Narasiṃha, the Man-Lion 854
Paraśurāma 856
Vāmana, the Dwarf 858
The Childhood and Adulthood of Kṛṣṇa 859
Gaṇapati 864
Skanda, a Great Sovereign God of South India 866
Devī: The Goddess in India 869
Kāmadhenu: The Mythical Cow, Symbol of Prosperity 873
Symbols of the Earth in Indian Religion 873
Ganges and Yamunā, the River of Salvation and the River of Origins 875
Pre-Islamic Iran 877
Ahura Mazdā (or Oromazdes, Ohrmazd) 890
Anāhitā (or Anahid) 891
Mithra (or Mihr, Mihir, Meher) 891
Vayu (or Vay, Vai) 892
Verethraghna (or Varahran, Bahram) 893
Buddhist Mythology 893
The Guardian of the Gate: An Example of Buddhist Mythology, from India to Japan 896

The Religion and Mythology of Vedic India

Of Vedic India we know nothing but the language and the religion. The only documents that this culture has left are texts, and the texts are religious in inspiration, tone, and destination. Here no object remains for the archaeologist's gaze; there is no external testimony to give the historian a point of support, a chronological reference. Between the end—a violent end, it is generally thought—of the Indus civilizations (whose dating is uncertain, and of which nothing is left but material remains) and the beginnings of Buddhism, followed by the first Greek accounts, what we know about India comes down to what we can learn from the Vedas. The Vedas, however, are sacred books that speak only of the sacred. It has been possible to identify certain hymns out of this mass which are secular in tone (such as the hymn "to the frogs," *Ṛksaṃhitā* 7.103). But these are only isolated cases; and while it is true that in these cases the playful element of religion carries more weight than its serious side, it is nonetheless true that the rare poems that can be termed profane emanate like all the others from sacerdotal sources.

The texts that Indian tradition groups under the name of *Veda,* "knowledge," form as a set what the same tradition designates as *śruti,* "revelation," literally "hearing": extraordinary figures, human beings, yet endowed with virtues and powers that place them above the gods, the *ṛṣis* (Louis Renou translates this term as "prophet") had a vision, in the time of origins, of particular portions of this knowledge and transmitted this vision to mankind. (One should note the succession of metaphors: the *ṛṣis saw* the Vedas, but they bequeathed them to posterity in the form of a text to be heard—and repeated.) Where did this revelation come from? Two types of answers to this question have been offered: for followers of certain Indian doctrines, the Vedic texts are the work of a divinity, and even the work of a personal god. For others—and notably for followers of the *Pūrva-mīmāṃsā*—the Veda is *apauruṣeya:* it has no personal author; what is more, it is uncreated, eternal, and unalterable, notwithstanding the fact that particular mythic events were the occasions for the *ṛṣis'* discovery of the different parts and different versions of the Vedic text. An idea that came to be accepted in the post-Vedic period is that the whole of the original Veda was concentrated into certain syllables, or even into a single syllable, and that the task of Vyāsa, the prototype and patron of all the *ṛṣis,* was to unfold and explicate (but at the same time to dilute) the Veda by giving it the form in which the world knows it.

The *śruti* is also called *trayī vidyā,* the "triple science." For Indian tradition, the Vedic text is made up of three vast collections: the *Ṛgveda,* "Veda of Verses"; the *Sāmaveda,* "Veda of Melodies"; and the *Yajurveda,* "Veda of Ritual Formulas." To these has been added a fourth Veda, perhaps a more recent one, and in certain respects of lesser dignity: the *Atharvaveda* (its name comes from the *ṛṣis* to whom it was revealed), which for the most part contains prayers and incantations of a specifically magical character. Verses, melodies, formulas, incantations: this division really applies only to the oldest layer of these three-plus-one Vedas. Each of them in fact consists of several strata which correspond to distinct "literary genres."

a. The *Saṃhitās.* Each Veda has as its original kernel one or more collections of "composed" poems which consist almost entirely of hymns and prayers. The *Saṃhitā* of the *Ṛgveda,* or *Ṛksaṃhitā,* is a collection of more than a thousand poems grouped into ten books or "circles" (*maṇḍalas*). On the basis of formal criteria and, more arbitrarily, content, modern exegetes distinguish an earlier part (*maṇḍalas* 2 through 7) and a later part within the *Ṛksaṃhitā* itself. It is now generally agreed that the earliest poems of the Veda are contemporary with the entry of the *ārya* invaders into India, that is, these poems took on the form in which they have been fixed around the fifteenth century B.C. But comparison with the Avesta (to mention only the Iranian domain, which is extremely close) shows that many traits of this archaic poetry have been inherited from a period before the separation between the *āryas* who were to become the Iranians and those who would move into India. On the other hand, the work of elaborating and fixing the Veda took place on Indian soil over many long centuries, until roughly the middle of the first millennium B.C. The *Saṃhitā* of the *Sāmaveda* consists mainly of verses drawn from the *Ṛksaṃhita* and adapted for recitation in song. The *Saṃhitā* of the *Yajurveda* (divided into the White and Black *Yajurvedas*) includes formulas, in prose or in verse or in mixed prose and verse, directly connected with the ritual and arranged in the order in which they were used in the ceremonies. Finally, the *Saṃhitā* of the *Athar-*

vaveda, quite composite in content, contains on the one hand, as noted, spells for long life, against sickness, against possession by demons, for gaining love or wealth—but also some long hymns in which the exaltation of a particular detail of the ritual is the point of departure for grandiose cosmic evocations.

b. To each of these *Saṃhitās* is assigned one or several *Brāhmaṇas*. The object of these prose treatises is *brahman*, that is, sacred knowledge. They are presented as kinds of theological observations on the rite: they describe the main articulations of the rite (whose different modalities they present and sometimes discuss), provide its mythological justification, and reveal its symbolic implications. The descriptive or prescriptive part of the *Brāhmaṇas* is made up of *vidhis*, "injunctions"; the rest consists of *arthavādas*, "explications," developments meant to stimulate the desire and imagination of the person performing the *vidhi*. The richest and most voluminous of the *Brāhmaṇas* is the *Śatapatha Brāhmaṇa*, "*Brāhmaṇa* of the Hundred Paths." It belongs to the White *Yajurveda*.

c. The *Āraṇyakas*, "forest (books)," follow the pattern set by the *Brāhmaṇas*, to which they form appendixes of a sort. But the rites that provide their theme lend themselves more specifically to a symbolic interpretation. The "*āraṇyaka*" reading of the rite leads directly into truths about the nature of man and the correspondences between macrocosm and microcosm—truths judged to be so charged with meaning that they belong to the domain of *rahasya*, the "esoteric." Too dangerous, in a way, to be pronounced or studied within the village community, they can be uttered only in the solitude of the forest.

d. Finally, the *Upaniṣads*. This term, which properly signifies "showing equivalences," designates a class of texts that are also extensions of some *Brāhmaṇas* or *Āraṇyakas*. The *Upaniṣads*, at least the oldest among them (which are in prose for the most part, unlike the later *Upaniṣads*), develop and systematize the speculative implications of the earlier texts. The ritual point of departure is often lost sight of or reduced to a mere pretext. What is aimed at is a "metaritualism," which, drawing the ultimate conclusions from the correspondence between the human person and the world, leads ultimately to the identification of *ātman*, the individual soul, and *brahman*, which from this point on will be none other than the Absolute: an identification presented both as a truth to be discovered and a goal to be attained.

e. To the Vedas strictly speaking, whose components have just been listed, are added the *Vedāṅgas*, (auxiliary) "limbs" or appendixes of the Vedas: technical treatises composed of *sūtras*, extremely concise aphorisms on how in practice to perform the *vidhi*. This definition particularly fits the *Kalpasūtras*, aphorisms on the rite, which are divided into *śrautasūtras*, instructions on the public ritual, and *gṛhyasūtras*, instructions on the domestic ritual. Another part of the *Vedāṅga* is made up of the *sūtras* of phonetics (*śikṣā*), which teaches the proper articulation of the Vedic text; the *sūtras* of grammar (*vyākaraṇa*); *sūtras* that analyze the metrical structures of Vedic poetry (*chandas*); those that formulate the etymology of Vedic words (*nirukta*); and, finally, *sūtras* on astronomy (*jyotiṣa*).

The *Saṃhitās*, the *Brāhmaṇas*, the *Āraṇyakas*, and the *Upaniṣads* together make up the *śruti*; the auxiliary limbs of *Vedāṅga* belong to *smṛti*, "remembered tradition." But what forms the most essential part of *smṛti* is the imposing ensemble of *dharmasūtras* and *dharmaśāstras*, prose aphorisms or more lengthy verse treatises on dharma, the religious, juridical, and social "law" (among the *dharmaśāstras*, the most famous is the collection of the "Laws of Manu"). Dharma is in principle eternal, but the texts that reveal it, unlike those that constitute *śruti*, belong to human culture: thus *smṛti* is not the object of the same reverence as is *śruti*. But the two are closely connected: a *smṛti* text is necessarily assigned, more or less artificially, to a particular Veda; indeed, a *smṛti* teaching is not fully valid unless it is based on an authority depending on *śruti*.

Together *śruti* and *smṛti* serve, even today, as the reference for Brahmanical orthodoxy. To be within the fold of Brahmanism means, on the level of doctrine, to recognize the truth of what is taught in these two classes of texts. We should add that the lineages of Brahmans are defined not only by the ancestors from whom they are descended, but also by the Vedic "branch" or school (that is, the subdivision of the Veda), and so the founding *ṛṣi*, with which they are associated: a man should marry within his caste but outside his *gotra*, the community which by family tradition is identified with the same *ṛṣi* as himself. But we must not think that the Vedic texts, passed down over the centuries from generation to generation with remarkable exactitude and fidelity, and used in ceremonies to this day, continued to be understood throughout this entire period, nor even that their text was studied. By the end of the Vedic period, the hymns of the *Ṛksaṃhitā* in particular had become for the most part a dead letter; this is understandable considering the archaism of the language of these texts, their extraordinary poetic violence, their morphological and semantic exuberance, the boldness of their syntax and rhetoric, and finally their deliberate hermeticism. In the fourteenth century, at Vijayanagar, in Mysore, a group of learned exegetes led by Sāyana prepared commentaries for nearly the whole of the Veda: these glosses, infinitely precious for the more recent parts of the Veda, were an unquestionable aid to the first Western Vedists. But once this stage was passed, they found themselves able to progress only through a critique of Sāyana. It has been repeated many times, and the arrogance of the claim does not make it any less true: it was Western philology that restored an understanding of the Vedic hymns to India.

Within the *śruti* itself, we have seen that a first distinction is called for by the very form of the texts: there is first of all the initial burst of the *Saṃhitā*—and then all the rest, which in one way or another is commentary or secondary development. For the Indian tradition, however, the dividing line is somewhat different: on the one hand it recognizes *mantras*, hymns, parts of hymns, or isolated formulas, in verse or prose, which have the common characteristic of being uttered in the rite and so constitute a part of the rite; and on the other hand what the tradition encompasses under the general rubric of *brāhmaṇa* (the word being used here in a broader sense); didactic and discursive rather than directly performative texts, these are commentaries or meditations on the rite but not elements of the rite itself. There is also another classification, this one also proposed by the Indian tradition, with the doctrinal content of the texts as its criterion: it distinguishes the *karmakāṇḍa*, the "section of acts," which mainly covers the *Brāhmaṇas*, from the *jñānakāṇḍa*, the "section of knowledge," which coincides with the *Upaniṣads*, understood as *Vedānta*, "completion of the Veda" (the *Āraṇyakas*, which occupy an intermediate position between the *Brāhmaṇas* and the *Upaniṣads*, are generally classed with the *jñānakāṇḍa*). The *Brāhmaṇas* are indeed oriented toward the "act" par excellence, the rite (and more precisely the sacrifice); they teach us how to perform it correctly, how it is to be understood, and the immediate or deferred boon that will be its result. The *Upaniṣads*, on the other hand, teach us that knowledge relegates action to the background; more, that knowledge (of the connections that may be glimpsed through meditating on the rite) is itself a means for us to free ourselves from the chain of births and deaths into which the act (including the ritual act) necessarily locks us. In this way the *Upaniṣads* are the source of inspiration to those who seek deliverance (*mokṣa*), whereas the *Brāhmaṇas* guide those who wish to follow the path of the meritorious act, which leads to heaven (*svarga*).

For any historian who is interested in mythology and ritual and who wonders about Vedism as a unity rather than about the relations between Vedism and the religious forms that followed it, what counts, of course, is not so much the articulation of the *jñānakāṇḍa* and the *karmakāṇḍa* as the relation between the hymns of the oldest part of the *Ṛgveda* on the one hand and the *Brāhmaṇas* on the other. At the time that the most archaic hymns were taking form, the *ārya* population occupied only the northwestern part of the subcontinent, Kashmir and the Punjab. The landscape of the *Brāhmaṇas*, on the other hand, is the Doab between the Ganges and the Yamuna, and the Gangetic Plain up to and past Banaras. In the *Brāhmaṇas* the social structure has changed, the distribution of activities, functions, and statuses among the different classes (*varṇas*) and castes (*jātis*) has become more complicated and at the same time more rigid. Even the language has changed. The Sanskrit of Vedic prose is extremely close to classical Sanskrit, and in the new conditions the culture as a whole, particularly the religion, had to be transformed through its contact with conquered populations (although it is a dangerous temptation, which has been yielded to all too often, to attribute all innovations, real or apparent, to the influence of non-Aryan populations—about which, after all, we have no definite knowledge).

As for the pantheon, the myths, and the theory and practice of the ritual, the chief difficulty in any attempt to write history or in any evaluation of historical shifts is not so much our ignorance of the events as the fact that the documents for the beginning of the period (the archaic kernel of the *Ṛgveda*) and the mass of later *Saṃhitās* and *Brāhmaṇas* are completely different in both character and significance.

The *Ṛgveda* consists of poems whose religious matter is not strictly speaking exposed but is rather evoked in a staggering web of metaphors. How much is stereotyped formula, how much topical description, and how much personal invention in the poet's eulogy to the divinity? The formulas that seem to sketch the characteristic and differential traits of a god melt into one another or collapse into others that are applied without distinction to any divine figure: a Vedic god, whatever his function and mythology, is always celebrated as a supreme, all-powerful god, the source or motive force of all cosmic processes. The myths, which provide the framework for the poems, figure in them only as fragments or allusions. Enigma is a procedure which not only Vedic poetics but also Vedic theology makes use of frequently; the obscure text is the symbol of the mystery of the cosmic reality to which it refers. The rite is an essential theme of these poems, in the sense that the moments and aspects of the sacrifice, the human participants, the utensils, and the material of the offering are exalted with the same ardor and the same refinement as the divinity itself (indeed, Bergaigne could claim that everything in the *Ṛksaṃhitā*, down to the tiniest detail, was based on the rite: the Vedic poem interweaves cult and myth, both of which have the function of representing, making explicit, and thus perpetuating the great phenomena of nature). But while in these texts the *ṛṣis* give us an idea of the eminent value that they attributed to the rite, they do not make it possible for us to visualize the concrete performance of a ceremony. In the *Ṛgveda*, the discourse on the rite is subject to the same ellipses, the same symbolizations, and the same transfigurations as is mythical discourse; and, as we might expect, myth and rite symbolize each other. Thus the work of understanding the Veda consists not only of deciphering the text but of reconstructing from the fragments that it offers us the totality—mythology, ritual, and the system of correspondences between the two—from which these fragments seem to have been detached or diverted. What materials can we use to fill in the enormous gaps that remain?

Three schools of Vedists (at least) confront one another: for some the *Ṛksaṃhitā* can be explained by what precedes it; for others, by what comes after it; for yet others, it can be explained only by itself. Members of the first school of thought see a profound break between the religion of the *Ṛgveda* and Brahmanism (and even more between the *Ṛgveda* and Hinduism): conceived, if not composed, by *ārya* bards before they settled in India, the older part of the *Ṛgveda* bears witness to the religion and world view of the Indo-Iranians; comparison with the earliest attested forms of the religions of other Indo-European peoples permits a kind of etymological reconstruction of the religion of the Veda. For the adversaries of these comparativists, on the other hand, the *Ṛgveda* is already a totally Indian work: the fauna and flora are those of India; and in the same way the religion should be treated as the point of departure for a tradition which becomes more explicit as it develops. If not going so far as to accept the *Brāhmaṇas'* claim to be a direct commentary on the *mantras*, one should at least consider the religious conceptions of these two parts of the *śruti* as homogeneous. A third group, finally, sees the Vedic hymns as a solitary block; light must be sought, they maintain, in an unflagging analysis of the text itself, and the text alone (and there is no doubt that it is this truly ascetic doctrine that has been behind the most decisive advances in Vedic philology, if not in our understanding of Vedic religion).

Problems of an entirely different nature confront someone who wishes to study the religion of the *Brāhmaṇas*. This is a very dry prose which, while far from limpid, at least aims at didactic clarity: the purpose of the *Brāhmaṇas* is not to use all the resources of poetry to evoke various divinities and powers toward whom human rites and prayers ascend; it is rather to explain to men why and how they should say these prayers and celebrate these rites. Here what is most disconcerting is the overabundance of explanations or, more precisely, of justifications. The rite required of men is always to some extent the consequence of a mythical event: it reproduces it, commemorates it, or seeks to rectify or limit an evil that came into being in the time of origins. And this causal connection, over and above the analogy between the cosmos and the sacrificial ground, concerns not only the major rituals as wholes: every detail of the rite is founded in mythology, and in such a way that their explanations frequently overlap and entangle one another.

The question that arises is this: how old and how authentic are these stories that come in at a certain point to give a reason for some ingredient or moment of the sacrifice, then disappear never to be heard of again? Take, for instance, the rule forbidding Kṣatriyas (members of the *varṇa* whose privilege is military and political power) to drink the soma that they are enjoined to offer to the gods—while the Brahmans who participate in the same sacrifice are entitled to a share of the drink (cf. *Aitareya Brāhmaṇa* 7.27ff.). Why this exclusion? It is, the *Brāhmaṇa* teaches, because the god Indra, as punishment for his numerous misdeeds, was himself denied the soma (a drink he coveted) by the other gods; this is why the Kṣatriyas, who in a sense have Indra as their patron, must also abstain from soma; later the interdiction was lifted for the god but not for the human group, which continues to serve, and by this very fact to commemorate, the sentence that the gods pronounced long ago against the fiercest and most powerful of their number. The myth appears in this form only in connection with this ritual prescription. In the developed, autonomous version of the myth, it is not the other gods who inflict this punishment on Indra; instead, the father of one of his victims excludes him from the soma sacrifice in which he is involved. This narrative, at least, can be connected with a well-attested set of myths. But what status can we attribute to the story's sequel? Deprived of soma, the Kṣatriyas have as their special sacrificial food the boughs and fruit of the *nyagrodha* tree, whose branches grow toward the earth. Why is this? As is often the case, the origin myth is really the story of a rite performed in the time of origins: when, thanks to their sacrifice, the gods became able to ascend toward the sky, their movement knocked over some cups of soma set out on the ground. These cups became the *nyagrodha,* and the thin streams of liquid that poured out of them became its branches.

These weak legends, which Bergaigne says "seem to have been made up after the fact to explain formulas that were no longer understood" (*La religion védique,* 3, p. 280), and which Dumézil (*Mythe et épopée,* 1, p. 150) calls pseudomyths, appear not only to justify ritual practices and the social organization and values which it is the explicit purpose of the rites to make known. They are also invoked when it is necessary (a common digression in discussions of the rite) to tell why the human body is made the way it is and why the rite must be performed if we want the body to be maintained harmoniously in its state. For what reason, in the *agnihotra* ceremony, must an offering of milk be made first to Agni (the god of fire) and only afterwards to Sūrya (the sun god) and Vāyu (the wind god)? Because it was Agni whom Prajāpati created first of all, making him come out of his own mouth. But also because (1) milk naturally belongs to Agni, since the milk of the cow is Agni's sperm—this is why it comes warm out of the cow's udder; and (2) it is thanks to this offering that Agni reproduces his own seed; and on the model of Agni, the man who offers the *agnihotra* is reproduced from his own seed. Why is it that human embryos survive and develop when no one feeds them? It is because "the sun, when it sets, enters like an embryo into the womb of fire . . . and along with the sun, all creatures become embryos: they lie down and are satisfied. If night wraps up the sun, it is because embryos are also wrapped up (in the womb). And if the *agnihotra* is offered in the evening, after sunset, this is for the sake of the sun when he is in an embryonic state: it is because of this that embryos survive without having to be fed . . ." (*Śatapatha Brāhmaṇa* 2.3.1.1ff.).

The rite and its mythic justification also explain why the nasal septum separates man's two eyes; why his palms and forehead are smooth and hairless; why his skin has no fur; his feet no hooves; why his fingers are both interdependent and independent. The myths also deal with speech: the form of nouns is always "motivated"; either their etymology is transparent, i.e., the object that they designate got its name because when it was created it was the origin, result, or site of an action designated by the verbal root from which the noun is derived; or else the etymology is opaque, and the myth explains by what malicious decision of the gods a phoneme was modified or displaced in such a way that the link between the derived form and the root ceased to be apparent.

What is interesting in this invention of mythic motifs that are ceaselessly returned to, reshaped, and accumulated (one could hardly list all the variants of the creation of the world—each quite different from all the others—that the *Brāhmaṇas* propose when the need arises) must be sought, we suggest, not principally in the myths thus fabricated, but rather in the ends that they serve. What is it that requires explanation and justification? It is man's relations with his own body, his language, and the fundamental constraints (physical or social)—so obvious that one forgets to notice them—that inform even his smallest movements.

There is thus a considerable difference between the inspiration, goals, and style of the hymns and those that can be observed in the *Brāhmaṇas.* But is the difference so great as to make pointless any comparison between the mythological contents of these two parts of the *śruti?* Certainly not. The same gods, after all, are in both. But the importance of each and their configuration has changed. While it is true that in the *Brāhmaṇas* Indra maintains the primacy that was his from the beginning (in the older part of the Veda, Indra is the greatest of the gods, the largest number of hymns are dedicated to him, and the most glorious feats are attributed to him), and while it is true that Soma and Agni, being both gods and elements of the sacrifice (soma, the matter of the oblation; fire, the vehicle of the offering), remain at the center of the religious structure, other divine figures nonetheless become blurred or altered. Varuṇa, originally the guardian of cosmic order, is now the punisher of ritual faults and the guardian of oaths. A more serious transformation affects the notion of *asura.* In the earlier parts of the *Ṛgveda,* the most powerful gods are called *asuras:* Mitra, Varuṇa, Aryaman, Agni, Rudra, the goddess Uṣas ("dawn"), Indra, the whole group of the Ādityas. What these divinities have in common is the possession of *māyā,* the art of fabricating forms, of creating wonders or spinning illusions. In the *Brāhmaṇas,* on the other hand, the *asuras* are demons, the perennial adversaries of the gods: gods and *asuras* battle one another for the possession of heaven and the control of the sacrifice. But the gods and the *asuras* are both sons of Prajāpati: here again is the main innovation of the later Vedas: the emergence of a primordial divinity who, from his own body, creates living beings, the sacrifice, the articulated pattern of time.

As an example we will present myths concerning Soma as they appear in connection with the ritual in various texts of the later part of the Veda.

C.Ma./j.l.

BIBLIOGRAPHY

Publications on various aspects of Vedic studies are listed and classified in L. Renou's *Bibliographie védique* (Paris 1931) and continued according to the same principles in R. N. Dandekar's *Vedic Bibliography,* 1 (Bombay 1946), 2 (Poona 1961), 3 (Poona 1973).

A. BARTH, *Les religions de l'Inde* (Paris 1879), in *Encyclopédie des sciences religieuses,* by Lichtenberger; reprinted in *Quarante ans d'Indianisme,* the works of Auguste Barth, vol. 1 (Paris 1914). A. BERGAIGNE, *La religion védique d'après les hymnes du Rig-Veda,* 3 vols. (Paris 1878–83). M. BLOOMFIELD, *The Religion of the Veda: From Ṛg-Veda to Upanishads* (New York 1908). W. CALAND and V. HENRY, *L'Agniṣṭoma, description complète de la forme normale du sacrifice de "Soma" dans le culte védique,* 2 vols. (Paris 1906, 1907). G. DUMÉZIL, *Aspects de la fonction guerrière chez les Indo-Européens* (Paris 1956); *Les dieux souverains des Indo-Européens* (Paris 1977); *The Destiny of the Warrior* (Chicago 1970), originally in French (Paris 1969); *Mythe et épopée,* 1–2 (Paris 1968, 1971). P.-E. DUMONT, *L'Agnihotra* (Baltimore 1939); *L'Aśvamedha* (Paris 1927). K. F. GELDNER, *Vedismus und Brahmanismus* (Tübingen 1928). J. GONDA, *Change and Continuity in Indian Religion* (The Hague 1965); *Die Religionen Indiens,* 1: *Vedismus und älterer Hinduismus* (Stuttgart 1960), also in French; *The Savayajñas* (Amsterdam 1965). J. C. HEESTERMAN, *The Ancient Indian Royal Consecration: The "Rājasūya" Described according to the Yajus Texts and Annotated* (The Hague 1957). V. HENRY, *La magie dans l'Inde antique* (Paris 1904). A. HILLEBRANDT, *Ritual-Litteratur* (Strasbourg 1897); *Vedische Mythologie,* 1–2 (2d ed., Breslau 1927–29). A. B. KEITH, *The Religion and Philosophy of the Veda and the Upanishads* (Cambridge, MA, 1925); *Vedic Index of Names and Subjects,* 2 vols. (London 1912). S. LÉVI, *La doctrine du sacrifice dans les Brâhmaṇas* (Paris 1898; 2d ed., Paris 1966, with preface by L. Renou). H. LOMMEL, *Altbrahmanische Legenden* (Zurich 1964). H. LÜDERS, *Varuṇa,* 2 vols. (Göttingen 1951–59). A. A. MACDONELL, *Vedic Mythology* (Strasbourg 1897). A. A. MACDONELL, A. B. KEITH, and J. MUIR, *Original Sanskrit Texts,* 5 vols. (London 1872–74). H. OLDENBERG, *Die Religion des Veda* (3d ed., Stuttgart 1923); *Vorwissenschaftliche Wissenschaft: Die Weltanschauung der Brāhmaṇa-Texte* (Göttingen 1919); "Zur Religion und Mythologie des Veda," Nachrichte von der Kgl. Gesellschaft der Wissenschaften zu Göttingen, Philosophische-historische Klasse (1915), 167–235, 361–403. R. PISCHEL and K. F. GELDNER, *Vedische Studien,* 3 vols. (Stuttgart 1889–1901). W. RAU, *Staat und Gesellschaft im alten Indien nach den Brāhmaṇa-Texten dargestellt* (Wiesbaden 1957). L. RENOU, *Anthologie sanskrite* (Paris 1947); *Les écoles védiques et la formation du Veda* (Paris 1947); *Études védiques et pāṇinéennes,* 17 vols. (Paris 1955–69); *Hymnes et prières du Veda* (Paris 1938); *Hymnes spéculatifs du Veda* (Paris 1956); *Les maîtres de la philologie védique* (Paris 1928); *Poésie religieuse de l'Inde antique* (Paris 1942); *Religions of Ancient India* (London 1953). L. RENOU and J. FILLIOZAT, *L'Inde classique, manuel des études indiennes,* 1 (Paris 1947), 2 (Hanoi 1953). B. SCHLERATH, *Das Königtum im Rig- und Atharvaveda* (Wiesbaden 1960). H. P. SCHMIDT, *Bṛhaspati und Indra: Untersuchungen zur vedische und Kulturgeschichte* (Wiesbaden 1968); *Vedisch vratá und avestisch urvāta* (Hamburg 1958). P. THIEME, *Der Fremdling im Ṛgveda: Eine Studie über die Bedeutung der Worte ari, arya, aryaman und ārya* (Leipzig 1938); "Mitra und Aryaman," *Transactions of the Connecticut Academy of Arts and Sciences* 41 (New Haven 1957). J. VARENNE, *Mythes et légendes extraits des Brāhmaṇas* (Paris 1967); *Le Veda* (Paris 1967), an anthology. M. WINTERNITZ, *History of Indian Literature,* 3 vols. (Calcutta 1920–33), originally in German.

Translations

Ṛgveda: K. F. GELDNER, *Der Rig-Veda aus dem Sanskrit ins Deutsche übersetzt und mit einem laufenden Kommentar versehen,* 4 vols. (Cambridge, MA, 1951–57).

Atharvaveda: D. W. WHITNEY, *Atharva-Veda saṁhitā: Translated with a Critical and Exegetical Commentary,* 2 vols. (Cambridge, MA, 1905).

Taittirīyasaṁhitā: A. B. KEITH, *The Veda of the Black Yajus School Entitled Taittirīya Saṁhitā Translated from the Original Sanskrit Prose and Verse,* 2 vols. (Cambridge, MA, 1914).

Śatapathabrāhmaṇa: J. EGGELING, *The Śatapatha-Brāhmaṇa according to the Text of the Mâdhyandina School,* 5 vols. (Oxford 1882–1900).

Aitareyabrāhmaṇa and Kauṣītakibrāhmaṇa: A. B. KEITH, *Rigveda Brahmanas: The Aitareya and Kauṣītaki Brāhmaṇas of the Rigveda, Translated from the Original Sanskrit* (Cambridge, MA, 1920).

Aitareya-Āraṇyaka: A. B. KEITH, *The Aitareya Āraṇyaka Edited . . . with Introduction, Translation, Notes, Indexes . . .* (Oxford 1909).

Soma as Sacrificial Substance and Divine Figure in the Vedic Mythology of Exchange

The sacrificial substance called soma and the divine figure Soma together form indissolubly the theme of a mythology that reveals its full meaning only in connection with the ritual that corresponds to it.

The sacrifices that use as the material of their oblations the plant called soma are the most prestigious form of the Vedic ritual. A considerable number of texts are devoted to the minute description as well as the glorification of the soma ceremonies (notably all of book 9 of the *Ṛksaṃhitā*). Despite all that has been said about it, we know very little about the nature of this plant. Its botanical identity remains uncertain, and controversies have surrounded it since the beginnings of Indian studies (see Wasson 1968), but have led to nothing but hypotheses. The plant seems far more important for what can be made of it in the cult and for what can be said of it poetically in the hymns than for what it actually is. Several species have probably borne the same name and served the same ends, and a text as early as the *Śatapatha Brāhmaṇa* lists the plants that can be used as substitutes for soma per se. The typical soma is above all a plant, *the* plant par excellence, that grows wild in mountainous regions, "in the north," whence it is brought with great difficulty. The part of the soma plant that is used in rituals consists of its stems, from which, when they are crushed, a brownish juice flows. When filtered ("clarified"), the juice is called soma too; it provokes in the men (and gods) who drink it a kind of euphoric exaltation that the texts take great pains to distinguish from ordinary intoxication and that in certain ways suggests the effects of hallucinogenic substances (as, for instance, in Ṛgvedic hymn 10.119).

The ritual of the soma plant is thus the history of the transformation that it undergoes between the time when it is picked and the time when its juice is squeezed out and consumed. The consequences of the ritual are twofold: immediate effects on the psyche of individuals, men and gods alike, who have the right to partake of this delicious beverage, whence they draw strength and exhilaration; and cosmic effects: the soma that flows in the sacrificial vats is the image and in a way the cause of all liquids, of all saps that carry life throughout nature. The earthly soma has a celestial counterpart whose receptacle is the moon: this is the *amṛta,* the liquor of immortality that the gods drink when the moon is full and the dead drink at the new moon (Gonda 1962, p. 84; Keith 1925, p. 166).

From the time of the *Brāhmaṇas* it has been taught that soma and the moon are one and the same, and the word soma later becomes one of the usual names for the moon in classical Sanskrit. What facilitates this close correspondence, to the point of identification, is the way in which both the planet and the plant are characterized by changes in their form and volume. The stems of soma that swell when they are immersed before being crushed are analogous to the crescent moon.

In the series of changes that the successive phases of the ritual impose on the soma plant, the Ṛgvedic hymns to the god Soma refer mainly to operations ranging from pressing (the stems are crushed with stones, and the stones themselves are glorified in hymns) to decanting and then to final clarification. The juice thus extracted is collected in vats and filtered in woolen sieves, and the melodious din of the soma splashing against the walls of the containers and the noise of the drops falling one by one through the filter are also constantly repeated poetic themes. The *Brāhmaṇas* go back farther into time and develop at great length what might be called the prehistory of the *soma pavamāna,* or the soma "in process of clarification." They discuss the ceremonies that precede or constitute the introduction of the soma into the sacrificial apparatus, notably the rite known as "the purchase of the soma." The mythology of the soma is essentially connected with the preliminary part of the ritual. The basic theme of the mythology is the "abduction" of the soma, or of Soma, by the gods. Men's efforts to obtain the soma and make it come to the sacrifice are presented in the *Brāhmaṇas* in such a way as to assign a symbolic function to them: to commemorate and transpose to the world of men the stratagems that the gods resort to in their attempts to secure soma for themselves. Each of these sequences, the mythical sequence and the ritual sequence, has its own coherence; in addition, the two sets cannot be superimposed on one another. Certain elements of the myth (of the different variants of the myth) are not translated in the ritual, and the ritual contains sections that are not found in the myth.

But the facts that are especially worth noting are the complexity of the mechanism of transposition and the mythical function (the function of a myth of origin) that the ritual assumes in connection with the actions of profane life: the myth justifies the ritual, and the ritual justifies the social institutions and behavior. In the myth, (the) Soma while already on his way toward the camp of the gods is diverted, somehow, by the Gandharvas, and the gods must repurchase him by paying a ransom that is none other than Speech (*vāc*). But the most dramatic moment of the rite of the introduction of the soma is a mock purchase: a strange dramatization requires the celebrants, already in possession of the soma stems, to hand them over to a man of low caste who assumes the role of "soma merchant." They "buy" the soma from him at the end of a violent but carefully orchestrated session of bargaining. This ritual transaction is overdetermined in the sense that several reasons for its existence are clearly indicated in the text:

1. It commemorates the myth: the soma merchant plays the part of the Gandharva; the cow that will eventually be the purchase price represents Speech which the gods gave to the Gandharva to regain possession of Soma, etc.

2. The soma obtained by the men is destined to be pressed on the sacrificial site. This pressing is a murder, the murder of a god: "Truly, they kill the Soma when they press him" (*Taittirīya Saṃhitā* 6.6.7.1; see S. Lévi 1898, p. 170). Just as one must take all sorts of precautions in order to circumscribe and reject the evil inherent in killing the victim of a blood sacrifice, so one must attribute to a stranger the crime of introducing Soma, simultaneously a god and an oblatory substance, into the system that will ultimately result in his killing. The soma merchant is wicked on two scores: first because he "represents" the Gandharva who retains Soma, and second as the scapegoat whom the celebrants and the sacrificer saddle with the sin of having procured the soma that they are about to offer.

3. The purchase of the soma, the purchase of a god, and a divine king at that, because once it is bought, the soma is welcomed as a royal guest, and Soma is frequently designated as a king, the only king that the Brahmans recognize (see Heesterman 1957, p. 75ff.), is in turn the prototype of the eminently profane social practice known as commerce. More precisely, the texts that deal with this connection between the purchase of and bargaining for the soma and commerce in general use the poetic figure of the a fortiori: "because one bargains to buy King Soma, everything is for sale here on earth" (*Śatapatha Brāhmaṇa* 3.3.3.1) . . . "Because the celebrant and then the seller first bargain and then come to an agreement, people here on earth do the same whenever anything is for sale; they too begin by bargaining and then come to an agreement" (ibid. 4).

The purchase of the earthly soma by the celebrants is an imitation of the repurchase of the celestial soma. The *Brāhmaṇas* show that between the mythic repurchase and the ritual purchase that repeats it and results from it there is a connection that is precisely the one that Benveniste points out in the history of Indo-European institutions: the repurchase, whose objective is the recovery of a living person, is the original form of purchase, the acquisition of material goods (see *Vocabulaire des institutions indo-européennes* [Paris 1969], vol. 1, p. 129ff.). But the transaction itself is a deception in two ways. The soma merchant is artificially incited by the celebrants, who pretend to buy from him what they in fact already have. And even this fiction is not fully carried out, since according to certain texts at least (among them *Āpastamba Śrauta Sūtra* 10.27.6ff.), all the negotiating ends with a brawl, or a mock brawl, during which the soma merchant is beaten with a bludgeon and the cow given to him in exchange for his soma is brutally taken back from him (see Gonda 1962, vol. 1, p. 185). This dramatization, quick dialogue, dramatic progression, and final reversal may have resulted in the notion that the origin of Indian theater is to be found in this part of the soma liturgy (see Hillebrandt 1927, vol. 1, p. 258). A rather fragile hypothesis, and an answer to a question that may not have any meaning; but one cannot help but be struck by all the "representation" that this ritual contains.

This set of preliminary actions constitutes what we might call the *dīkṣā* of the soma: wrapped in linens, the packets of soma stems are like fetuses surrounded by their membranes. This embryonic phase also characterizes the sacrificer during the *dīkṣā,* that is, the consecration that gives him the new body that he will use during the sacrifice per se. (For details on the *dīkṣā* of the soma which, however, is prepared to be not the sacrificer but the victim, see *Śatapatha Brāhmaṇa* 3.3.3.12.) The ritual actions performed during this preparation and this introduction of the soma serve not merely as the model or condition for the possibility of commerce; the Brāhmaṇa commentary goes further into abstraction and into the search for the basis of any activity that implies a comparison between a model and its replica. There comes a time in the course of these operations when the soma stems, displayed on a piece of linen, must be measured with one's fingers, alternately stretched and folded. "It is because one measures King Soma that measuring exists both among men and in general" (*Śatapatha Brāhmaṇa* 3.3.2.9). Exchange, simulation, measurement: here as in so many other examples, what establishes the elementary actions of men and gives them meaning is the fact that the actions first had to be performed in the ritual.

The following are the principal articulations of the myth in which the gods take possession of the soma, as it is told in the *Taittirīya Saṃhitā* 6.1.6.1ff., the *Aitareya Brāhmaṇa* 3.25, and the *Śatapatha Brāhmaṇa* 3.6.2.2ff.

1. In the time of the origins, Soma was in the celestial world, and the gods were here on earth. They wanted to have him come to them so that they could offer him in sacrifice. To that end, they produced two female creatures (protagonists of a separate mythology, who appear here as two "fictions"), two *māyās,* Kadrū and Suparṇī. Kadrū is the Earth; Suparṇī is Speech.

2. Kadrū and Suparṇī are rivals. "Whichever one of us," they decided, "has the best eyesight will triumph over the other and take over the other's person (*ātman*)." Suparṇī says, "I see on the other side of the ocean a white horse tied to a post." "I," replies Kadrū, "can see the wind moving the horse's tail." Kadrū and Suparṇī rush forward to see: Kadrū was right; she wins and takes over the *ātman* of her rival.

3. But Kadrū gives Suparṇī a chance to repurchase herself: "Go and seek Soma for the gods. Soma is in heaven. If you bring him back, I shall return your *ātman* to you." Suparṇī had children, the metric forms (*chandas*) of the Veda. She says, "This is why parents have children, to repurchase their *ātman*" (a reference to the theory that man is indebted to his ancestors and repays this debt by engendering descendants). She therefore charges her children with this task.

4. The metric forms are transformed into birds (their mother Suparṇī has a name meaning "well-winged"), and the *jagatī* is the first to take flight. (The *jagatī* is a stanza with twelve syllables in each line. But the narrative is also a myth of the origin of the metric forms: how did the stanzas come to have their present form? In the version in the *Aitareya Brāhmaṇa,* these metric forms are originally identical, although they bear different names: their differences are potential, and it is because of the events of the myth that the differences are actualized. The *jagatī,* like the other meters, is thus conceived as having originally been made of four-syllable lines.) After covering half the distance, she grows tired and sheds three syllables. After becoming monosyllabic, she is unable to reach Soma and returns to the gods, bringing back two elements that are essential to the sacrifice, the *dīkṣā,* the preliminary consecration of the sacrificer, and *tapas,* ascetic energy. (In the *Taittirīya Saṃhitā* version, the meters are from the beginning different both from one another and from what they will become later. When the *jagatī* takes flight, she consists of fourteen syllables. On the way she loses two syllables, but brings back the *dīkṣā* and the *paśus,* the animal victims.)

5. Now it is the turn of the *triṣṭubh* (a stanza with lines of eleven syllables; but originally, according to the *Aitareya,* the lines had four syllables.) The *triṣṭubh* must also shed a syllable—but only one—retrace her steps, and bring back the *dakṣiṇā,* that is, the sacrificial honoraria. (In the version in the *Taittirīya Saṃhitā,* she has thirteen syllables when she sets out and she loses two.)

6. The gods turn to the *gāyatrī* stanza, with eight syllables in each line. (The *gāyatrī* is the noblest meter because it is the metric formula of the *sāvitrī,* i.e., the prayer to the god Savitṛ, who is considered the quintessence of the Veda.) She reaches the soma, succeeds in frightening the guardians, and seizes the soma with her claws and her beak. She also takes possession of the two syllables dropped by the *jagatī* and the one syllable abandoned by the *triṣṭubh:* she thus becomes octosyllabic, the form we know today. (The same narrative is told in the *Taittirīya Saṃhitā,* which adds that the *gāyatrī* succeeded where the other meters had failed because she was accompanied by a female goat, *ajā.* But the *Śatapatha Brāhmaṇa* 3.3.3.9 says that *ajā* means "she who fetches," and the form *ajā* was originally the esoteric name of the goat. The *Taittirīya Saṃhitā* also says that because of this exploit the *gāyatrī,* the smallest of the meters, is also the most glorious meter.)

7. The part of the soma that the *gāyatrī* squeezes in her right claw is what later becomes in sacrifice the morning pressing; the part that she squeezes in her left claw is the noon pressing. But on the return flight, she sucks up the share of soma that she carries in her beak. Emptied of its juice, this part of soma is inferior to the previous ones. To cancel this difference, the gods decide to add "cattle" to the third pressing; and, in addition, the evening soma is mixed with milk, and the offering is followed by an offering of butter and an immolation of animal victims.

8. The meters that had failed in their attempts claim from the *gāyatrī* the lost syllables that she acquired. The *gāyatrī* refuses: the syllables belong to her because she found them. This judgment is confirmed by the gods: and that is why, even today, one can claim to be the owner of something one has found. The line of the *gāyatrī* thus has eight syllables, that of the *triṣṭubh,* three, and that of the *jagatī,* one. The *gāyatrī* reserves for herself the privilege of helping with the morning pressing and entrusts this task to the other two meters for the pressings of noon and evening. Unable to fulfill her duty, the *triṣṭubh* asks the *gāyatrī* for help. The *gāyatriī* intervenes in the noon pressing, joins the *triṣṭubh,* and from this combination is born a new *triṣṭubh* with eleven syllables. The process is repeated for the *jagatī,* which had become monosyllabic: adding the eleven syllables from the new *triṣṭubh,* she assumes her definitive form with a line of twelve syllables.

9. But before these adjustments take place among the meters, one event interrupts Soma's voyage toward the gods. The soma is intercepted by the Gandharva Viśvāvasu (this phase of the myth is told by the *Taittirīya Saṃhitā* and the *Śatapatha Brāhmaṇa*). The gods plot to take back Soma. "The Gandharvas," they say, "love women. Let us send them Speech, who is a woman." According to the *Taittirīya Saṃhitā,* the gods transform Speech into a one-year-old woman. Speech returns with the soma, but the unhappy Gandharvas follow her to the gods and complain: "Take back the soma, but let us keep Speech." The gods propose to let Speech decide. The gods and the Gandharvas enter into a competition to seduce Speech: the Gandharvas try to please her by reciting the Veda, but the gods, better advised, invent the lute and make music. They win, and Speech returns to their camp. That is why to this day women love music, dance, and frivolous songs. So goes the *Śatapatha Brāhmaṇa* version. The *Taitirīya Saṃhitā* version differs only in one detail: after serving as ransom for the soma, Speech takes the form of a gazelle and flees from the Gandharvas but does not return to the gods. The Gandharvas and the gods agree to compete to attract her. The *Taittirīya Saṃhitā* specifies that in the ritual the cow with which the soma is bought from the merchant represents Speech, and that it must be one year old, just like the Speech woman whom the gods gave to the Gandharvas to repurchase Soma from them. And the text also adds that Speech was one year old, and that is why humans speak when they reach the age of one. Moreover, just as the gods sought to please Speech, so the sacrificer and the celebrants must try to please the cow destined first to pay the soma merchant. They make an appropriate offering to him. And just as Speech chose the side of the gods, so the soma cow chooses the side of the sacrificer and the celebrants, who take her away.

With Speech and the soma at their disposal, the gods and men—each of these groups on the level appropriate to it—can now proceed to the immolation of their royal guest. But men do not limit themselves to a pure imitation, nor even to a transposition, of what the gods do; for, although the gods have given men the model of the quest for the soma, men give the gods the substance of the sacrifice. It is in drinking the soma prepared by men and transformed by the ritual into ambrosia that the gods are immortal.

C.Ma./g.h.

BIBLIOGRAPHY

In the bibliography at the end of the article "The Religion and Mythology of Vedic India," the following works refer particularly to Soma: BERGAIGNE, 1878, especially pp. 148–235. CALAND-HENRY, 1906–7. GONDA, 1962, especially pp. 81–86 and 184–91; 1965, pp. 38–70. HEESTERMAN, 1957, passim, especially pp. 69–90. HILLEBRANDT, 1927–29, especially 1:193–498. See also H. LOMMEL, "König Soma," *Numen* 2 (1955). L. RENOU, *Études védiques et pāṇinéennes* 9 (Paris 1961). U. SCHNEIDER, *Der Somaraub des Manu, Mythus und Ritual* (Wiesbaden 1971). R. G. WASSON, *Soma, Divine Mushroom of Immortality*, Ethnomycological Studies 1 (New York 1968).

Vedic Cosmogony

The Vedic hymns provide a great quantity of cosmogonic themes, but most are in the form of allusions or dispersed fragments, in which images recur of unfolding space, of the prop that holds earth and sky apart, etc. The myth of Indra is perhaps the only exception to this, and it is not by chance that it is taken up again in classical Hinduism, and in an interesting way, since in the intervening time the relations between Indra and Viṣṇu had changed. The Brāhmaṇas, by contrast, present myths with greater continuity; among these are accounts of cosmogonic value, more or less inchoate, which are related to some sacrificial rite. The principal myths were later taken up under the form of the avatars of Viṣṇu: the Fish, the Turtle, the Boar, and the Dwarf. These will be dealt with in the article on the avatar, for it is not by chance that these incomplete cosmogonic accounts could realize their callings by becoming transformed into myths of avatars, with their heroes becoming forms of Viṣṇu.

There is nevertheless a Vedic hymn that must be placed on a level completely distinct from all others, as much for its form as a well-articulated cosmogony as for its simultaneously diffuse, omnipresent, and highly structured posterity: this is the *Puruṣa Hymn* (RS 10.90), which we must cite in its entirety here (after the translation by Louis Renou, *Hymnes speculatifs du Veda*, Paris 1956):

> The Man has a thousand heads; he has a thousand eyes, a thousand feet. Completely covering the earth, he overflows it by ten fingers.
>
> The Man is none other than this universe, that which is past and that which is to come. He is the master of the immortal domain, because he grows beyond food.
>
> Such is his strength, and even more vigorous than this is the Man. All of the beings are one-quarter of him; the Immortal in the sky, the (other) three-quarters.
>
> With three-quarters the Man placed himself on high; the fourth had his birth here below. From there he spread in every direction, toward things that eat and things that do not.
>
> From him is born the (creative) Energy, from the (creative) Energy the Man was born. Once born, he stretched himself beyond the earth as far to the front as to the rear.
>
> When the gods performed the sacrifice with the Man as oblatory substance, the spring served as (ritual) butter, the summer as firewood, the autumn as offering.
>
> On the (sacred) palanquin they sprinkled the Man (that is,) the sacrifice that was born in the beginning. Through him the gods performed the sacrifice along with the Saints and the Seers.
>
> From this sacrifice offered in its total form, the speckled (ritual) fat was drawn off. From this were made the animals of the air, those of the desert, and those of the clusters.
>
> From this sacrifice offered in its complete form were born the verses, the melodies; the meters were also born from this, the (liturgical) formula was born from this.
>
> From this (sacrifice) were born the horses and all beasts with two rows of teeth. The bovines were also born from it, and from it were born the goats and the lambs.
>
> When they had dismembered the Man, how did they distribute his parts? What became of his mouth? What became of his arms? His thighs, his feet, what name did these receive?
>
> His mouth became the Brahman, the Warrior was the product of his arms, his thighs were the Artisan (better: "the man of the land" M.B.), from his feet was born the Servant.
>
> The moon was born from his consciousness, from his gaze was born the sun, from his mouth Indra and Agni, from his breath was born the wind.
>
> The atmospheric region came from his navel, from his head evolved the heaven, from his feet the earth, from his ear the celestial quarters: thus the worlds were determined.
>
> Seven were the planks of the palings, three times seven were made the burning logs, when the gods performed the sacrifice, having bound the Man as victim.
>
> The gods sacrificed the sacrifice by the sacrifice. Such were the first institutions. These powers had access to the firmament, in which are found the Saints, the original gods.

The poet is less concerned with a proper cosmogony, i.e., with an explanation of the universe that tells a story beginning with a chaos or a zero point, than with the organization of all that exists around two key ideas that are well identified: the Puruṣa and the sacrifice. The Puruṣa is above all the Male, but this is a Male whose form is undoubtedly human: in the same way *puruṣa* would become the common word designating man, but specifically the immortal aspect of transmigrating man, which is promised deliverance. But *puruṣa* would also become one of the names for the Absolute, and particularly of Viṣṇu, and this name would be given to a more "personal" Absolute than that of the *brahman*. The Puruṣa of the hymn is at once identified with our world and with the universe that envelops and transcends it, with the mortal and with the immortal. Its function as the origin of everything is accentuated by the reciprocal engendering that takes place between it, the Male, and the Female Energy: there is an implicit refusal to claim a precedence of one over the other, even if the Puruṣa is clearly the more essential principle. But a couple is thus formed that would become the Puruṣa and the Prakṛti—or Śakti—the original Male with the female energy which he projects outside of himself to produce the world. These two principles would give Hinduism its god/goddess opposition, in which the goddess, closer to the world, if only by her essential nature, would always exist as the active hypostasis of the god; she would be the god in action, whereas the god himself would always tend toward inaction, not by virtue of a "natural tendency" that he had from the start, but in order to incarnate those values that appeared in Hinduism.

Nevertheless, the creation of the world is not carried over into a sexual engendering. It is not a question of Energy—unless it is precisely the energy of the sacrifical activity, or the fertile female aspect of the sacrificial activity that is above all identified with the Puruṣa. The sacrifice lies at the base of everything; the Puruṣa is the sacrifice and also the sacrificial victim. Nothing is said about the person who offers the sacrifice (the gods generally serve as technicians, or officials), but to say that the Puruṣa is the sacrifice is also a way of identifying him with the person who sacrifices. Here we touch on what was undoubtedly the most profound intuition of the Vedic poets, one that would be at the root of innumerable mythic or other speculations in Hinduism: there is never a sacrifice that is not of one's self; if one sacrifices something to the gods, it must be something of oneself, something of value. In other words, the victim offered in sacrifice is nothing other than a substitute for the sacrificer. Thus each time that we see a man (or his son) appear in the position of sacrificial victim, in a myth or symbolically in a rite, one must not jump to the conclusion that this was originally a human sacrifice: in each case this is a reminder of the symbolic equivalence of the sacrificer and the sacrificial victim.

The emphasis thus placed upon the sacrifice in the Vedic hymn can mean only one thing: what it tells us about the Vedic state of the religion is centered upon the sacrifice. It is through the sacrifice that not only the organization of the human world but also the establishment of the rest of the universe is to be realized, including the forest animals and all that lies beyond this earth. This organizing principle would never be questioned—even when the Vedic sacrifice became outmoded in practice—but it would reappear transformed and relativized in the interior of the Hindu world.

Let us recall the four great "classes"—*varṇas*—of human beings born from the Puruṣa and the way in which they are connected to him. The Brahman, priest and cleric, is his mouth. The warrior-prince—Kṣatriya—is his arm. The Vaiśya—whose name indicates a close relationship with the land, with the earth that he inhabits, and whose class includes the agriculturalist, the pastoralist, and the merchant—comes from his thigh. And the Śūdra, the whole group of the service castes, is his feet. There is thus an implied hierarchy in this choice that goes from the head to the feet of the Puruṣa: note that, on the level of the Vedic gods who are later enumerated, Indra and Agni are his mouth. The sacrifice is first of all the food of the gods, a nourishing stream that constantly rises from the earth to the sky and that Indra, the king of the gods, causes to return to earth in the form of beneficent rain. Indra is both the king of the gods and the regulator of the rains that fall upon the earth, two apparently disparate functions that cannot be understood unless they are taken together. Agni is Fire, and above all the sacrificial Fire who is also called "the mouth of the gods," because he is charged with bringing to the gods, with his smoke, the sacrificial food that men feed to him: melted butter, the fat of the victim. But the Brahmans themselves are the gods of the earth, whom other men are required to feed. Feeding Brahmans—sacrificial priests and others—is part of the sacrificial rite, and this even comes to take the place of the whole of the rite, of the sacrifice itself. The Brahman is thus, like Agni or Indra, the mouth of the Puruṣa. His place in the cosmos as ordained by the sacrifice consists in part of receiving gifts, above all gifts of food: this becomes a part of the classical definition of the Brahman.

The Warrior is the arm of the Puruṣa: the arm as symbol of strength is obvious, but it may have a more complex significance, since the Kṣatriya is at once prince and warrior, warrior because he is prince. His arm is an arm of punishment, which is the essence of the prince, who carries out military campaigns on the exterior and polices the interior for the general peace. It is in these ways that the warrior exercises his classical function of protecting his subjects. The authority of his arm allows him, among other things, to collect taxes, which is essential to his administration and especially to his religious role: the protection of his subjects requires an abundance of sacrifices interspersed with general gifts to Brahmans.

If the Vaiśya is the thigh of the Puruṣa, this is probably by virtue of a play on words that was to be exploited for all it was worth. The man of the Viś is the man of the soil, the inhabitant of the country whose activity produces wealth, the preeminent royal subject on whom the king assesses taxes to cover his ritual and nonritual obligations. He thus has an essential connection with the earth, the ground of the kingdom, which is the source of all wealth. One of the names for the earth is *urvī*, "the wide," "the extended" (the feminine of *uru*), whereas the thigh is called *ūru*. In fact classical mythology pays little attention to the Vaiśyas, and the thigh as a symbol of the earth reappears sometimes in connection with Brahmans (like Aurva) and sometimes with Kṣatriyas (like Duryodhana).

As for the Śūdra, the lower castes whose sole duty is to serve the three higher *varṇas*, the only part of the Puruṣa which he could possibly be is the feet. The foot is the lowest part of a person: for this reason to place one's foot on someone's head is the most extreme humiliation, but to touch another's feet with one's head is an act of total submission and a recognition of one's own inferiority. The Śūdra is excluded from any participation in the sacrifice, and it is remarkable that the cosmic Puruṣa, the Puruṣa-sacrifice, nevertheless includes this group. This is an implicit recognition of the fact that the sacrificial system could not exist if the Śūdra refused to fulfill his functions, and for this reason he is incorporated into a cosmic order centered upon the sacrifice.

Indra, Agni, Sūrya the Sun, Candramas the Moon (masc.), and Vāyu the Wind are among the most important Vedic gods. With the exception of Indra, they are not individualized in complete myths. Classical Hinduism would convert them into guardians of the cardinal points, but here they are essentially recipients of sacrifice. Inhabitants of heaven, they occupy the highest level of a world in which earth, atmosphere, and the sky are superimposed.

Whatever may have been the concrete reality of the society of castes in the period in which this cosmogony was composed, every Hindu can recognize in it what for him constitutes the order of the world and can find in it the place assigned to him alone: what would come to be called dharma.

M.Bi./d.w.

BIBLIOGRAPHY

F. B. J. KUIPER, "Cosmogony and Conception: A Query," *History of Religions* 10, no. 2 (1970).

The Mythologies of Hindu India

This study of Indian mythologies will be restricted to Hinduism: Buddhism emigrated from India about ten centuries ago, and its Indian mythology owes a great deal to Hinduism. The same can be said about Jainism, a branch of Brahmanism that diverged at about the same time as Buddhism, and that survives in India to this day. We will leave aside tribal religions which, from north to south and from east to west, are all embedded within Hinduism: they are the religions of populations living apart from Hindu society, but are strongly influenced by this encompassing presence.

Hindu mythology is certainly one of the lushest and most complex that humanity has produced. At first glance it defies any attempt to order it, as well as any attempt to describe it exhaustively. But the various dictionaries and indexes have always emphasized monographic descriptions of divinities and rites, giving preference to enumeration and seeking exhaustivity. They have thus risked increasing the impression of extreme diversity, of gratuitous and uncontrolled fantasy. Our position will be the opposite of this: we will sacrifice exhaustiveness in favor of intelligibility, positing both a deep unity beneath the diversity and the possibility of grasping this unity through an appropriate method. This is why, in particular, this new collection is not meant to be a simple addition to the others, and does not hesitate to turn to the others for information (see bibliography). In most cases we will rather try to illuminate mythic data, not to speak of a new light.

We will not be dealing with myths *and* rituals, which would be an almost infinite task, but will use rituals as one of the sources for our understanding of myths (not the only one, for there is far from a one-to-one correspondence between myth and ritual). On the other hand, we will focus on the myth as the unit of study rather than its characters, motifs, or phases of composition: it is the myth that bears the meaning that engendered it, and it is therefore the myth that can provide the keys to interpretation, if we ask the right questions. We must, given the limits of brief articles, leave our preliminary work to some extent in the dark, and, in particular, almost completely ignore any comparison between different versions of the same myth. Yet all the great Indian myths present a multiplicity of versions, which we refuse to dissect according to the pseudohistorical principle of interpolation: for it is often the confrontation of these versions that provides us with the single global meaning of all of them, or of some obscure detail in its specific context, or that allows us to distinguish the basic myth from some sectarian inflection. The story that is chosen for presentation carries along with it the understanding attained by this preliminary labor: it is never just an innocent summary. References to the different texts will allow the reader to discover at least partially the elements of the interpretation. Such a method presumes that we leave the historical dimension out of consideration, and that all the versions of a single myth be taken ideally as synchronic. Mythic data is in fact neither dated nor datable, since its fixation in writing presupposes a more or less long oral tradition. When we can perceive an evolution it is usually so superficial that we can safely ignore it.

Nevertheless, India presents itself to us, through its texts, its monuments, and its still living practices and beliefs, with a historical depth of more than three thousand years. In spite of the lack of precise dates and in spite of the explicit will to

immutability, decisive changes have certainly taken place in the course of these three millennia, changes that myths can register in the absence of datable events. Moreover, a complex social organization, hierarchical in principle, adds a sociological density to this historical depth, a density that is bound to be refracted in the myths in which the society expresses itself: the myths and rituals must in one way or another take account of a hierarchical principle that is always at work. Finally, this complex and stable society, whose unity has never been realized politically or linguistically, stretches over an extremely vast geographical area: though Hinduism appears unified in its deep structure, it is evident that we must find, alongside pan-Indian myths and cults, complex local allegiances which are also inscribed in the deep structure and belong to it just as fundamentally as aspects that are geographically coextensive with Hindu society. We will then, even before considering the specifically religious values around which the myths are organized, note three kinds of division that in themselves give them a characteristic form, if not a particular content. On this level we already know, without any possible hesitation, that we are within the Hindu fold, since the forms, while not equivalent to the contents, are themselves translations of more or less conscious values that are found again on the level of content.

The first division particularly concerns classical Hinduism in its most Brahmanical form, the form explicated by the Brahmans, agents of the transmission of all normativity. It is,

Nartamalei. Photo M. Biardeau.

(Left) Lingarāja (early twelfth century). Photo by Jarrige.

paradoxically, historical in nature, in a universe that privileges atemporal unity, and is expressed entirely in the opposition between Revelation, *śruti* (literally, "hearing"), and Tradition, *smṛti* (literally, "remembering"). For classical Hinduism, i.e., the religious state that is found already constituted in the two great Sanskrit epics and in the socioreligious law codes, the Veda is considered the supreme norm, the basis of all else. Yet not only do the Vedic texts, from the earliest to the most recent, present states of the language that differ greatly from classical Sanskrit, compelling us to assume their historical anteriority; in addition, the state of the religion that they describe cannot be viewed as if it had an unbroken linear development in classical Hinduism, which nevertheless claims the Veda as its basis. There is a real break between the two, and it is likely that the received canon has been constituted as such largely because of this break: Revelation has been endowed with distance, strangeness, even unintelligibility, and at the same time absolute superiority. The canon consists entirely of texts that have left no trace on the ground: collections of hymns in verse, *saṃhitās;* mythico-ritual texts, *brāhmaṇas,* in which the hymns are broken up and scattered, transformed into formulas, and incorporated in the rite; and more or less esoteric speculations on the rites and myths, *upaniṣads* and *āraṇyakas,* which diverge widely from the rites and myths while at the same time maintaining them as intangible points of departure. When the oldest texts of Tradition—the *sūtras*—comment on the *brāhmaṇas,* one already has the impression of a great distance between the two types of texts. We are no longer dealing with quite the same state of the religion; the two may even be incompatible. But the intangibility of the Revelation—the real raison d'être of the Brahmans—means that the Vedic universe will continue to exist in an integral, if not perfectly intact, form within the new universe that is coming into being. Certain myths are privileged witnesses to the transcendence of the Veda in classical Hinduism. Better than any datable event, they help us to understand the enormous transformation of Hindu consciousness, a transformation partly contemporaneous with the birth of Buddhism and Jainism and therefore the expression of a period of intense socioreligious vitality. Several of the myths presented in this collection have been chosen precisely for the way that they mutually articulate Revelation and Tradition: cosmogonic narratives in the first place, the foundation myths of the religion; but also the story of Indra, which takes on a new dimension in its passage from the Veda to the epic; or the story of Dakṣa's sacrifice, whose classical posterity cannot be predicted from its Vedic origins.

The sociological division corresponds to the self-image of a hierarchical society. The high castes are recognized in certain values, precisely those that distinguish them from the lower castes. The lower castes, for their part, unabashedly express their subordination to the superior castes by elucidating their own values, held to be inferior. As a first approximation we can say that the high castes are characterized by practices that are considered pure (vegetarianism), while the lower castes follow the contrary practices (meat eating). But here we must be on guard against taking the formal opposition as a unidimensional one; the myths show that it is pervaded by the most diverse meanings: it is at work in particular in the innumerable narratives that bring together Brahmans and royal castes, the two components of the superior society who cannot live without one another. The pure practices of the Brahman, as opposed to the impure practices of the king, have a hierarchical connotation, since the king must submit to the Brahman's advice in all things; but it is the impurity of the king that makes it possible for the Brahman to do his own duty, that is, to stay pure. In the same way it is the serving castes, at the bottom of the social scale, whose impure practices make it possible for the supposedly superior castes to fulfill their own requirements. The myth does not stop there: there is no "impure-in-itself." Hinduism redeems impurity, and even transforms it into purity, by introducing a new variable into the social hierarchy, a sort of outsider who relativizes everything inside society with regard to his own values. Thus the hierarchical division is no longer anything but a formal aspect of a complex discourse in which all the values of Hinduism are at play—the very values that allow the articulation of Revelation and Tradition. It is not a question of opposing a superior to an inferior religion, even if the gods of some are not to the same extent the gods of others: Hinduism is the whole within which the small and the great of this world have their place and their chance for salvation, in which all are assured of finding the divinity appropriate to their heart, status, and lineage. From the point of view of the organization of research, this means that we must abandon the traditional opposition between the classical Indianist and the field ethnologist. Neither of these can do without the problematic of the other. What is really involved, in fact, is a single problematic, at work both in normative texts, mythical or otherwise, and in religious practice as it has been observed for almost two hundred years.

Collaboration between the specialist in classical religion and the ethnologist, whose experience is highly localized, is equally indispensable for the third division that Hindu mythology reveals: the great gods Viṣṇu and Śiva are found everywhere in the Hindu area, whereas other divinities, equally important in the devotion of the worshipers, are much more limited in extent. Sometimes we find gods whose sovereignty is recognized over an entire region—these may also be goddesses—and this territorial sovereignty takes material form in a regional pilgrimage site. Sometimes we find divinities linked to the locality itself, to the village; although the same names are found from one village to the next, as in the case of the "village deities"—*grāmadevatās*—of Andhra Pradesh, the worshipers associate them with the protection of their village alone and do not worry about whether two *grāmadevatās* with the same name are identical. On this level, we speak of "popular" religion, but in a sense that does not confine it exclusively to the lower castes, as was possible with the sociological division: for the local divinities group around themselves all the local castes, just as the sovereign divinity of a larger territory protects the territory's population as a whole. The annual festival of this divinity is really everyone's festival. This is why we will not oppose what has sometimes been called the "great" and "little traditions." The same people worship Viṣṇu and/or Śiva, and the sovereign god of their region, such as Subrahmaṇya, Narasiṃha, or Khaṇḍobā, and the local guardian deity. This geographical distinction provides yet another form to which the myths give a religious content and which reappears in the structure of the pantheon. Reference to classical texts may not be sufficient for the correct articulation of these different levels of the divine, for the geographical organization of forms of the divine takes on other meanings. This is why we have tried to give at least one localized example of the mythico-ritual complex that makes up the religion of a village. It would have been better to have many soundings of this kind, to reveal the enduring framework on which infinite variations are worked. The problem of the god-goddess relationship, for instance, arises particularly from the geographical register. There seem to be no "pan-Indian" goddesses apart from the consorts of Viṣṇu and Śiva, and in this case the role of the consort is not dissociated from that of the god. Yet on the regional or local level there seems to be a rivalry between god and goddess (sister, mother, or wife) which can be resolved in complementarity. The myth must also account for this reality, inscribed as it is in the religious geography of India.

Without the organizing principles that we have just enumerated, Hindu myths would remain discourses floating in the air without any directly intelligible connection with the people who have elaborated them. Yet these principles never appear as such in the myths themselves. To facilitate the understanding of the myths without having to repeat these principles of decipherment, we will present them in three types of articles. Some, dealing with the most fundamental myths, will stress the great structures of Hinduism. In these cases we will not hesitate to supplement the mythical narrative with data of various sorts that can bring the meaning to the surface. Other articles will use the myths to explicate the symbolic value of a particular object or, in contrast, the symbolic substitutes for an object that is highly charged ideologically: these articles should help the reader to penetrate the coded text that is a myth. Finally, we will discuss important myths in which these structures and symbols are at work, reducing the interpretation to a minimum. Here the goal, which must probably remain an ideal, is to make available for any reader the instruments for a rational decipherment of any Hindu myth: but decipherment remains an infinite task, which always leaves a residue behind it.

M.Bi/j.l.

BIBLIOGRAPHY

M. BIARDEAU, *Clefs pour la pensée hindoue* (Paris 1972). M. BIARDEAU and CH. MALAMOUD, *Le sacrifice dans l'Inde ancienne* (Paris 1976). C. DIMMITT and J. A. B. VAN BUITENEN, *Classical Hindu Mythology* (Philadelphia 1978). J. DOWSON, *A Classical Dictionary of Hindu Mythology and Religion, Geography, History and Literature* (10th ed., London 1961). L. DUMONT, *La civilisation indienne et nous* (1964); *Homo hierarchicus: Essai sur le système des castes* (Paris 1966). E. W. HOPKINS, *Epic Mythology* (1st Indian reprint, Varanasi and Delhi 1968; originally Strasbourg 1915). S. LÉVI, *La doctrine du sacrifice dans les Brâhmaṇas* (reprint, Paris 1966). A. A. MACDONELL, *The Vedic Mythology* (1st Indian reprint, Varanasi 1963). A. A. MACDONELL and A. B. KEITH, *Vedic Index of Names and Subjects*, 2 vols. (3d reprint, Delhi 1967). E. MOOR, *The Hindu Pantheon* (reprint, Varanasi and Delhi 1968). J. MUIR, *Original Sanskrit Texts on the Origin and History of the People of India, Their Religion and Institutions*, 5 vols. (reprint, Amsterdam 1967). W. D. O'FLAHERTY, *Hindu Myths* (Baltimore 1975). V. R. RAMACANDRA DIKSHITAR, *The Purāṇa Index*, 3 vols. (Madras 1955). L. RENOU, *Hymnes spéculatifs du Veda* (Paris 1956). Y. P. TANDON, *Purāṇa-viṣayasamanukramaṇikā: A Concordance of Purāṇa-Contents* (Hoshiarpur 1952). J. VARENNE, *Mythes et légendes extraits des Brâhmaṇa* (Paris 1967); *Le Veda, premier livre sacré de l'Inde*, 2 vols. (Paris 1967), an anthology; *Upanishads du Yoga* (Paris 1971). VETTAM MANI, *Purāṇic Encyclopaedia* (Delhi and Varanasi 1975).

The *Yūpa* (Sacrificial Post) in Hinduism

Sacrifice is a form of ritual so universal that Hubert and Mauss once devoted an entire *Essay* to it in an attempt to identify its common mechanism across various religious systems. It is at the core of the oldest form of Indian religion, what we call Vedic literature. Although the practice of Vedic sacrifice became increasingly rare very early, and although it was preserved only in a few great royal rituals, the notion of sacrifice has never stopped controlling the organization of the Hindu world and was actualized in renewed sacrificial forms still observable in India today.

In a world like that of Hinduism, where the polarization between the pure and the impure reaches a maximum tension, speculation on sacrifice can only bring out the internal contradiction of this ritual: designed to ensure the prosperity of everyone, it can do so only by including a harmful element of execution, the destruction of the victim. Moreover, it ensures the prosperity of the world that practices it only by opposing it to the wild, disorganized, and hostile world and by controlling the connections between the two worlds. It is therefore not surprising that there was much speculation about the *yūpa,* the sacrificial post. For the *yūpa* is situated on the edge of an altar of the sacrificial arena, half inside, half outside, thus symbolizing its function as frontier guard and communicator with the outside. It is the place where the victim is tied before being put to death. Finally, its verticality gives it the obvious role of a cosmic pillar. A hymn in the *Atharvaveda* (10.8) associates it closely with the *araṇis,* the two pieces of wood that ritually produce sacrificial fire by friction. It is fitting that this Veda, the least prestigious because its hymns have no connection with the solemn Vedic ritual, is the one that brings us one of the earliest speculations on the sacrificial post as a symbol of the totality of the sacrifice: the post embodies the very principle of all sacrificial activity, along with the essential tension that dwells in it. But it is also possible that its mythical fertility was a direct result of its ritual devaluation. We do not know when it stopped being actually functional: a Vedic hymn shows it soiled with the victim's blood, but the descriptions of the Vedic ritual imply the opposite: that the victim is not killed at the sacrificial post, though it is first tied to it. The *yūpa* could perhaps all the better play its role as a symbol: Hindu mythic thought has expounded at length on this theme, on the myth itself, the ritual, and the iconography. On the other hand, the *yūpa* is designated by all kinds of substitutes, mythical, iconographical, and linguistic (almost every term referring to a post or pillar in classical Sanskrit may be used symbolically to evoke the sacrificial post). All the variations on the sacrificial post are of course perfectly integrated into the Hindu universe of *bhakti* without ever losing sight of its original Vedic meaning. That is, it is associated first with Rudra-Śiva, since the Vedic Rudra is identified with the *yūpa,* but also with the Trimūrti, the trinity that the supreme deity divides into when it turns to the creation of our universe at the dawn of a new cosmic era. At this level, Rudra-Śiva has as his partners Brahmā and Viṣṇu, each of whom has his own function, complementary to that of the other two. Brahmā, the personification of Vedic knowledge and practice, the fertile aspect of the sacrifice, is the agent of creation. Viṣṇu, who is the sacrifice itself insofar as he is inseparable from the prosperity of the world (Śrī or Lakṣmī), is the guarantor of cosmic order. And Rudra-Śiva, because of his identification with the sacrificial post, the

Lighting the sacrificial fire by rubbing two pieces of wood. Photo M. Biardeau.

Linga in disuse, showing its three component parts—square, octagonal, and round. Photo IFI 33–7.

symbol of destruction, controls the destruction of the world when the moment for it comes (the indispensable complement of this sacrificial structure is provided by the renunciation of the world of sacrifice: Rudra-Śiva is thus *simultaneously* the preeminent yogi and the sacrificial post).

There is no question of exhausting the subject here. But we will limit ourselves to emphasizing the main variations on the theme of the sacrificial post. The most important and the most obvious, although perhaps the most ignored, variation is that of Śiva's linga, the virtually exclusive ritual representation of the god. The classical linga was mounted on a rounded or sometimes square pedestal called a *yoni*, "womb" or "vulva," depending on the context. It is therefore perfectly legitimate to see in the linga a phallic symbol. From there it is just a short step to making it the Indian version of a primitive phallic cult, a step that was taken with alacrity and is still taken, viewing Rudra-Śiva as a primitive, "non-Aryan" god, a latecomer into the Hindu constellation, where he encountered difficulties in being accepted. But, in the first place, the idea of a non-Hindu or non-Vedic Rudra-Śiva is a pure fiction that would be hard to support with archaeological evidence (even if we take into account one seal from the Indus civilization that might represent this figure); indeed, his connection with the Vedic world is as clearly defined as that of Viṣṇu and neither more nor less ancient than that connection. Beyond that, there have been attempts to misrepresent as history, in the Western sense of the term, stories that sought to explain a structure in the narrative mode. Therein lies the most common error in the interpretation of myths in general. Rudra-Śiva is not an upstart in Hinduism; rather, he is the part of the danger and impurity that Hinduism had to integrate as part of its system starting with the Veda, in order to make it viable. He is the requisite complement of Viṣṇu, the negative side of whatever Viṣṇu is the positive side of.

If, instead of reconstructing a hypothetical history based on data that are by definition ahistorical, we start from the Rudra-Śiva that is given by the oldest Vedic testimony, we see in the linga first a transposition of the sacrificial post. The problem is then how we moved from the meaning "post" to the meaning "phallus," or, more exactly, "copulation." But we are guided here by two factors: first, the profusion of myths, too long a subject to examine here; and second, the fact that this is a general problem in Hinduism: the sacrificial post is perceived as a "terrible" and impure representation of the god, of Rudra rather than Śiva. The devotion of a high-caste Hindu—and the frequenting of Śivaite temples by Brahmans is in itself a sign of nobility—seeks a benevolent and placated god, one who dispenses favors and brings deliverance, preferably a pure god who does not allow murder in his vicinity. The terrible function of Rudra, which cannot be annulled, goes back to the subordinate gods who surround him or to the Goddess with her bloody ritual, whom the lower castes more often worship. In a pure Hindu temple (with a vegetarian ritual), the sanctuary per se is the *garbhagṛha*, the "house of the embryo," in other words a womb, a place where the world is in its germinal state, where it constantly creates itself, whether the deity is Viṣṇu or Śiva. In the case of the representation of Śiva, the transition from post to phallus—meanings that remain, both of them, largely subconscious for most Hindus—seems to have resulted in a double iconographic modification. The oldest lingas that have been found are cylinders, which probably had no yoni as a pedestal. The classical linga, on the other hand, is found only in association with its yoni. Furthermore, nothing emerges but a portion of a cylinder, the upper part of the linga, which specifically represents Śiva. Immediately below and at the level of the yoni, and therefore not visible, is a portion of an octagonal section that represents Viṣṇu (the royal Viṣṇu watching over the eight cardinal points), while the square base (the four Vedas as well as the four cardinal points delimiting the world) is Brahmā. The phallic representation of Śiva thus embodies the very structure of Hindu divinity turned to the creation of the world. The linga-yoni combination presupposes that Śiva in this case is the supreme god, and no one else (to the extent that the linga is still a transposition of the sacrificial post). But it is represented at the level where it appears to be triple, the level of the Trimūrti that is tied to the creation of the world.

It is thus not by chance that one of the best-known myths about the linga features the three gods of the Trimūrti for the greater glory of Śiva. It is the myth of the "apparition of the linga," or *liṅgodbhava*, of which there are many Purāṇic versions (*Vāyu Purāṇa* 1.55; *Brahmāṇḍa Purāṇa* 1.26; *Śiva Purāṇa, Rudra Saṃhitā Sṛṣṭi Khaṇḍa* 15; *Liṅga Purāṇa* 1.17; *Skanda Purāṇa* 1.16.131–32, 1.3.9–15, 3.1.14, etc.). It is of particular interest since it brings out in all of its versions the meaning of the sacrificial post without emphasizing the phallic meaning, aside from attributing to Śiva the function of supreme creator. The narrative describes Brahmā and Viṣṇu disputing the question of who came first and who has the function of creating the world. The function of creator is understood here as meaning the function of the supreme deity and not the function attributed to Brahmā at the level of the Trimūrti. The quarrel therefore turns on the question of who is the supreme deity. Brahmā has no claim to this, and some versions of the myth stress Brahmā's incapacity. On the other hand, the Śivaite sects proclaim the absolute primacy of Śiva, in opposition to the claims both of the nonsectarian Hindu tradition and of the Vaiṣṇava sects.

Potu Raju from Mallavaram in front of a temple of the goddess. Photo M. L. Reiniche.

While Brahmā and Viṣṇu boast of their respective merits, a flaming linga appears, with no visible base or top. Brahmā then takes on the form of a *haṃsa* (the bird that symbolizes him because of a Sanskrit play on words) to go to find the top, and Viṣṇu transforms himself into a boar so that he may dig into the ground in order to try to find the base. Brahmā goes toward the sky, toward deliverance; Viṣṇu reverts to the role of sacrificial boar that he plays in Purāṇic cosmogony or else to one of the avatar forms that allow him to retrieve the earth from the bottom of the ocean of the flood. When both of them fail to achieve their ends, they worship the greatness of Śiva, whom the iconography depicts in all his glory inside the linga bursting open in a diamond-shaped split. Several versions pit the humility of Viṣṇu (who bows down with no resistance) against the deception of Brahmā, who claims to have reached the top of the linga. It is this lie that excludes Brahmā forever from the right to be worshiped by devotees.

Śiva's linga here is able to give a deliverance higher than Brahmā's and, at the same time, represents the salvific sacrifice more fundamentally than Viṣṇu. The linga is simultaneously the cosmic pillar, with no beginning or end, the sacrificial post (whose meaning is reinforced by its fiery nature, fire being the other destructive element of sacrifice, the one by which Rudra destroys the worlds), and the abstract representation of the Great Yogi. No single value is stressed because it embodies them all, wherein lies its transcendence. When Brahmā and Viṣṇu have failed in their active quest, they attain knowledge of Śiva through meditation.

We can therefore distinguish two principles with regard to the symbolism of the sacrificial post which allow us first to identify it and then to interpret it. We must of course handle these principles with care, in context, and not apply them mechanically. First: in a mythical narrative or in a visual representation, when an element, preferably unitary, is asserted through its verticality (there is even a unicorn Śiva), one can see in it a sacrificial symbol. Here are a few examples, which we cannot analyze further here: the lotus stem that comes out of the navel of Viṣṇu as he rests on the ocean or on the serpent Śeṣa and that bears an open lotus flower in which the four-faced Brahmā is enthroned; the tusk of the sacrificial boar on which he retrieves the earth; the single tusk of Gaṇapati; Viṣṇu's club; the palace pillar from which Narasiṃha emerges. One could go farther than this: the left leg of Vāmana-Trivikrama is raised to the point of verticality starting from a certain date in the history of art (eighth century?), as Śiva's leg is raised when he dances the *ūrdhva-tāṇḍava* (the "terrible" dance). This may well happen because the meaning of the "sacrificial post" is not far away. Finally, on a more down-to-earth level, we may decipher this same notion in the *daṇḍna,* the staff that symbolizes royal power.

Second: if in fact this vertical element—often in a totally anecdotal and trivial aspect—is the outcropping of the meaning "sacrificial post," we should attribute to it a function that we might call "Rudraic," after the "terrible" name of Rudra-Śiva. In every circumstance it manifests the inescapable part of violence, of murder and impurity, that is implicit in the very existence of the cosmos, and it impresses upon its bearer the Rudraic function that it signifies.

M.Bi./g.h.

BIBLIOGRAPHY

J. FILLIOZAT, "Les images de Śiva dans l'Inde du Sud. 1: L'image de l'origine du liṅga (*liṅgodbhavamūrti*)," *Arts Asiatiques* 8, fasc. 1 (1961).

Rudra/Śiva and the Destruction of the Sacrifice

I. Vedic Revelation

Sacrifice

The most ancient texts of the Veda are grouped into collections called *Saṃhitās* and include especially hymns to the many deities of the pantheon. On the level of the texts that came next, the *Brāhmaṇas,* the entire religion is organized around the sacrifice. The gods, to whom the invocations and oblations are addressed, are no longer the center of attention. Rather, the process (the "course") of sacrifice, the mechanism of sacrifice, has become the main point, and sacrifice has become an end in itself. It produces and organizes the cosmos. It is identified with Prajāpati, the author and master of all living creatures, a rather abstract Lord, beyond the deities of the pantheon. The focus shifts from the gods to the ritual. The *Brāhmaṇas* describe the rites, explain their hidden meaning, and shed light on their supposed origin and the meaning attributed to them in connection with etymologies, legends, and fragments of myths.

Sacrifice, an object of speculation by the Brahmans, is the foundation of the universe, the guarantor of good order and cosmic and social harmony, and the source of all prosperity. But it brings into play hidden and dangerous forces that must be handled carefully, that only the learned Brahman ("he who knows . . .") knows how to handle because he is a specialist in rituals and formulas and holds the key to their meaning. Even if it is performed correctly in full awareness of the facts, sacrifice always involves a portion of violence, of contact with death, and therefore a portion of danger and impurity. The animal victim is slain, the stalks of soma are crushed, and the seeds are pounded. During these violent but necessary operations, it is the sacrifice itself that is put to death: "Indeed, one kills the sacrifice when one lays it out" (*Śatapatha Brāhmaṇa* 2.2.2.1). It is therefore hardly surprising that they attribute to the sacrifice the intention to escape. It must be approached with all the wiles of a hunter: "The sacrifice has the nature of game" (*Pañcaviṃśa Brāhmaṇa* 6.7.10–11). Is it to ensure control over it that the *dīkṣita,* the one who submits to the preparatory consecration of the sacrifice (*dīkṣā*), wears a black antelope skin (*Śatapatha Brāhmaṇa* 1.1.4.1; see also 6.4.1.6)?

The Role of the Brahman

Since the animal is put to death by suffocation or strangulation with a noose, bodily lacerations and other damage to the victim caused during the offering are kept to a minimum. It is agreed that the necessary violence, evil, and danger are concentrated in a tiny part of the animal (*Śatapatha Brāhmaṇa*

1.7.4.5, 10). It is sometimes explicitly stated that the damaged part of the animal is the size of a grain of barley (*Taittirīya Saṃhitā* 2.6.8.4). But this minuscule morsel of meat is potentially quite dangerous. The imprudent gods discover it to their peril. "When these gods laid out the sacrifice, they offered the first separated share to Savitṛ; it cut off his hands . . . they offered it to Bhaga; it destroyed his eyes . . . They offered it to Pūṣan; it broke his teeth . . ." (*Kauṣītaki Brāhmaṇa* 6.13). How shall it be disposed of? What place, what priest will be able to neutralize this threat? For some, this task is incumbent upon Indra. He alone is able to absorb the shock. "'Indra is the strongest and mightiest of the gods; therefore offer it to him,' they said to one another; and so they did. He appeased it with the ritual formula" (*Kauṣītaki Brāhmaṇa* 6.14). Indra is the most vigorous of the gods. But his power, as has been noted, is not that of the warrior but of one who knows the ritual formulas (*brahman*). It is therefore no surprise that in other versions of the myth, Bṛhaspati (or Brahmaṇaspati), the "master of the formula," is mentioned in place of Indra: "They brought it to *Bṛhaspati;* it did him no harm; and thenceforth it was appeased" (*Śatapatha Brāhmaṇa* 1.7.4.8; see also *Taitirrīya Saṃhitā* 2.6.8.5).

Bṛhaspati is the priest of the gods. His counterpart or representative on earth, on the sacrificial site, is the priest called the Brahman (*Kauṣītaki Brāhmaṇa* 6.13). He is the most discrete but in a sense the most important of the officiants. He alone conducts half of the sacrifice (ibid. 6.11). The other priests recite formulas, sing, move about continuously, and perform all the operations of the ritual. The Brahman is immobile and virtually silent. He observes and oversees all that is said and done on the sacrificial site. Being the one who knows the texts and rites best, he intervenes when an error has been committed. As a physician, he "heals" the sacrifice (ibid. 6.12). He does this by resorting to Viṣṇu, because "Viṣṇu is the sacrifice" (*Śatapatha Brāhmaṇa* 1.7.4.20). The Brahman priest is therefore the one who, on earth and in the image of Bṛhaspati, harmlessly consumes the wounded part of the victim (1.7.4.13–17). To protect himself, he does this "through the mouth of Agni," fire.

The Slaying

The Brahman priest abolishes the wound, heals the sacrifice, and neutralizes the danger. Who then was responsible for the actual slaying? The sacrificer (*yajamāna),* the patron of the sacrifice, is not involved in the slaying, nor are any of the principal celebrants in charge of killing the animal. It is the *śamitṛ,* the executioner, of whom virtually nothing is known (does he belong to the caste of Brahmans?), that is charged with this vile and dangerous chore. One of the explanations of his name is that he must "appease" (*śamayati*) the victim, after obtaining its consent or at least without letting the animal moan audibly.

The Origins of Rudra

In the myth, Rudra is the one to whom the gods appeal to do their dirty work. Rudra is represented as living on the margin of the civilized world, as one coming from outside, as an intruder. He comes from the mountain; he emerges from the forest. He is a hunter. He stands for what is violent, cruel, and impure in the society of gods or at the edge of the divine world. The following is an account of the "birth" of Rudra. He is associated with fury and born of the tears of Prajāpati. "This is why the *Śatarudrīya* (oblation) is made. When Prajāpati was dismembered, the deities went away from him. Only one god did not leave him: Manyu, Fury. He felt himself stretched out inside. He (Prajāpati) wept (*rud-*) and the tears that poured from him landed on Manyu. He became Rudra . . . Rudra with a hundred heads, a thousand eyes, a hundred quivers, arose, his bow bent . . . looking for food. The gods were frightened" (*Śatapatha Brāhmaṇa* 9.1.1.6). To appease him, one offers him the *Śatarudrīya,* while reciting this litany: "We bow before your fury, O Rudra, before your arrow, your two arms . . . ! (*Vājasaneyī Saṃhitā* 16).

According to the *Kauṣītaki Brāhmaṇa,* Rudra is the product of a particularly dangerous and reprehensible union, an act of incest. "Prajāpati, desiring offspring, practiced intense austerities. As he became ardent, five were born from him: Agni (fire), Vāyu (wind), Āditya (the sun), Candramas (the moon), and Uṣas (dawn) as the fifth . . . Uṣas took the form of an *apsaras* (nymph) and appeared before them. Their spirits all flew out of their bodies toward her. Their seed fell" (ibid. 6.1). Prajāpati made a golden cup and collected the seed in it. Out of it came a creature with a thousand eyes and feet, bearing a thousand arrows. Prajāpati gave him eight terrible names: Bhava, Śarva, Rudra, Paśupati . . . (ibid. 6.2–9). Similarly, in the *Śatapatha Brāhmaṇa* (6.1.3.7–8), incest produces a young boy (*kumāra*) who is born weeping (*rud-*). This Kumāra is fire. The first of his eight names is Rudra: "Rudra is indeed Agni" (ibid. 6.1.3.10).

According to other versions, it is Prajāpati himself who commits incest with his daughter. Taking on the form of a male antelope, he mates with his daughter turned female antelope. The gods seek someone who can punish him, but find none among themselves. They pool the most terrible parts of themselves to produce "this god," that is, Rudra, but people avoid naming him. In exchange for dominion over domestic animals (*paśus,* see below), he pierces Prajāpati with his arrow (*Aitareya Brāhmaṇa* 3.33; see also *Maitrāyaṇī Saṃhitā* 4.2.12; *Jaiminīya Brāhmaṇa* 3.261–62). The theme recurs in the *Śatapatha Brāhmaṇa,* where the gods condemn Prajāpati's incest. They ask that "the gods who rule over the *paśus*" pierce Prajāpati. When the wrath of the god has been appeased, they heal him: "Prajāpati is indeed the sacrifice" (ibid. 1.7.4.1–4).

In the eyes of the gods, Prajāpati's incest is a sin or an evil, but a necessary evil, since Prajāpati-Sacrifice is the origin of the world and its inhabitants. Rudra is always associated with this dangerous moment in the career of Prajāpati (or of his sons). Sometimes he appears as the product of incest, and at other times the gods use him or even produce him in order to "punish" Prajāpati.

Mṛga/paśu

Rudra is a game hunter (*mṛga-vyādha,* meaning "one who pierces wild animals") and master of cattle (*paśu,* designating both domestic animals and sacrificial victims). This double qualification of Rudra is indeed important for understanding the myth, but it is not easy to follow all of its implications. By committing incest, Prajāpati places himself outside (or on this side of?) the norms. By becoming a male antelope, a wild animal (*āraṇya*) and no longer *paśu,* he ceases to be a normal sacrificial victim (since only *paśus* are used for sacrifice; *Śatapatha Brāhmaṇa* 13.2.4.3: *apaśur . . . āraṇyaḥ*); he enters a realm that is beyond the control of the gods, who must resort to Rudra, the god who regulates the outside world, the game hunter. The wound that Rudra inflicts on Prajāpati-Sacrifice corresponds to the wounded part of the animal victim, that damaged and dangerous part that the Brahman priest alone may consume (*Śatapatha Brāhmaṇa* 1.7.4.9). Rudra thus maintains ambiguous ties with the sacrifice. His presence is indispensable but dangerous. He represents the violent,

Bhairava. Private collection. Photo Dominique Champion.

unappeased aspect of fire and presides over the slaying of the victims. According to certain texts (*Aitareya Brāhmaṇa* 3.33; *Maitrāyaṇi Saṃhitā* 4.2.12), he obtains from the gods control over the *paśus* in exchange for his services. An ambiguous force, he has power over life and death, and since he exercises this right when the *paśu* is the sacrificial victim, it is necessary to keep him auspicious (*śiva*) so that he will spare and protect the cattle (and even humans, for man is also a *paśu* and Rudra may strike men as well as cattle).

The theme of incest expresses two ideas: one is the cosmogonic value of sacrifice, the first creative act, in which the "lord of living creatures" (*prajā-pati*) has no recourse other than to project out of himself a female creature, hence a daughter, and to mate with her; the other is the dangerous character inherent in all sacrifice, since it implies killing. Incest is reprehensible, and sacrificial killing is an impurity that one must rid oneself of. Precisely because life (of the cosmos) comes from death (of the victims and of all the substance of the oblations), the sacrifice (in which the sacrificer, the victim, and rite itself are identified) seeks to flee in the form of a game animal that is not suitable for sacrifice (see above) in order to escape from the gods. This can be translated: the sacrifice is what imposes order on the cosmos by opposing it to the world of the forest, uninhabited, hostile to man, and always menacing. If it is not properly performed, if its dangerous character is not overcome, the humanized space is taken over by savage space, and the world of the gods dissolves into disorganization. The gods must therefore resort to Rudra because his connection with the forest and with game makes him fit to circumscribe the limits of the two worlds, to neutralize the harmful aspects of sacrificial violence.

Rudra's Share

The *Śatapatha Brāhmaṇa* teaches that one must appease Rudra by granting him his share of the offering, without which he is liable to destroy the entire sacrifice: "The gods, by means of sacrifice, ascended into heaven" (ibid. 1.7.3.1); but the god who rules over cattle (*paśu*) was left behind. Seeing that he was excluded from the sacrifice (see *Gopatha Brāhmaṇa* 2.1.2; *Pañcaviṃśa Brāhmaṇa* 7.9.16), he pursued the other gods and threatened them with the weapon he was brandishing: "Reserve a share of the oblation for me!" The gods agreed and assigned him a supplementary offering, with what was left of the sacrifice (see *Aitareya Brāhmaṇa* 3.34.3). In the ritual, this is the last offering, the oblation to Agni Sviṣṭakṛt, fire that "makes good oblations." Again there is the association between Rudra and fire: "Agni is indeed this god (Rudra)" (*Śatapatha Brāhmaṇa* 1.7.3.8). Just as one says, "Viṣṇu is indeed the sacrifice," so one says, "Rudra is Agni" (e.g., *Śatapatha Brāhmaṇa* 1.7.3.8; 6.1.3.10; 9.1.1.1). This simply means that Rudra is the destructive and terrifying aspect of fire. Agni conveys the offerings to the gods, but precisely by destroying them and consuming them. The devouring fire frightens Prajāpati himself (*Śatapatha Brāhmaṇa* 2.2.4.1–6). All of Rudra's names are terrible when unappeased; only Agni is his propitious and appeased name. This may be why the offering to Rudra Paśupati, the terrible hunter who threatened the gods, is made in the name of Agni Sviṣṭakṛt. And care is taken that this supplementary offering to Rudra should not come into contact with cattle (*paśu*,) for fear that they may fall under the harmful power of Rudra (ibid. 1.7.3.21; see also 1.7.4.12; 12.7.3.20; *Pañcaviṃśa Brāhmaṇa* 7.9.18).

Rudra's Function

The myth from the *Śatapatha Brāhmaṇa* has more than once been presented as the reflection of a historical conflict. In this view, Rudra was a deity alien to the Vedic world, a deity whose origin was tribal, Dravidian, or even Hamitic, whose supporters were only able to introduce him into the Brāhmaṇic pantheon and ritual at the price of a lengthy struggle. But the absence of historical documents makes it virtually impossible to verify such hypotheses. How necessary are they? According to Vedic literature, Rudra represents one of the aspects and dimensions of all sacrifice. "Viṣṇu is the sacrifice." He embodies its harmonious process, its continuity, its promise of prosperity. Rudra, the hunter, the savage god, stands on the edge of the sacrifice. He is called *Sthāṇu*, from the name of the post to which the sacrificial animal is tied, situated at the border between the liturgical terrain and the outside world. But for all his marginality, Rudra(-Śiva) is no less indispensable to the proper function of the sacrificial mechanism. No sacrifice without killing, without violence, without impurity. Rudra is the catalyst for this dangerous side of sacrifice; he limits and controls it. If anyone forgets to offer him the share in the sacrifice that belongs to him, if anyone refuses to "give the fire its share" (sacrificing something to save the rest), the violence that he represents, far from being controlled and circumscribed, would invade the entire sacrificial site and destroy it.

II. The Epic Revivals

Rudra's threatening but indispensable presence continued to impose itself on later literature, both epic (*Mahābhārata*) and Purāṇic. The *Mahābhārata* (MBh) is the story of an eighteen-day war between the incarnations of the *devas* (gods) and *asuras* (antigods). Roughly speaking, this merciless war symbolizes the opposition between *dharma* and *adharma,* law and anomie, the order of the world and chaos. What is more, the MBh places this epic story within the framework of a cosmic cycle. The extermination at the end of the war is the image of the dissolution (*pralaya*) of the world at the end of time.

The Story

In this vast epic, we find at least four versions of a myth that might be called "the destruction of the sacrifice (of Dakṣa) by Rudra." Two of these versions have virtually no direct connection with the central story: the one in book 12, close to the *Vāyu Purāṇa,* and the one, in book 13, that echoes the narrative in book 7. For example, this is a summary of the version in book 10: The gods decide to offer a sacrifice and determine the distribution of the offerings. Unaware of Rudra's true nature, they do not assign any share to him. But "he" (Rudra), dressed in an antelope skin and with a bow in his hand, arrives furious on the site of the sacrifice. The earth trembles; the sun and fire lose their brilliance; the gods are terrified. Rudra aims an arrow at the Sacrifice and pierces it; it is transformed into a *mṛga* and takes flight. As if in play, he breaks Savitṛ's arms, destroys Bhaga's eyes and Pūṣan's teeth, and reduces all the gods to impotence. The gods and the Sacrifice beg for Rudra's protection, hoping to propitiate him. Rudra agrees to cast the fire of his wrath into the water. He heals the gods who were mutilated and restores the integrity of the Sacrifice and the harmony of the universe. The gods assign all the oblations to him.

A few preliminary remarks are in order. Depending on the version, the Sacrifice is offered by "the gods" or by Dakṣa. Dakṣa's name connotes the active mind, the ability to accomplish, the efficacious will, and finally sacrificial competence. The *Śathapatha Brāhmaṇa* identifies Dakṣa with Prajāpati (2.4.4.2). Later tradition makes him one of the sons of Brahmā, who is in many ways the heir of Prajāpati. The epic narrative has some abridging and displacements. Rudra, excluded from the oblations (see *Śatapatha Brāhmaṇa* 1.7.3), pierces the Sacrifice (ibid. 1.7.4) and himself mutilates the gods who in the *Brāhmaṇas* are wounded by the *prāśitra,* the damaged part of the victim. There is no longer anything about Prajāpati's incest, but the sacrifice continues to escape in the form of a *mṛga.* During the sacrifice in book 7, Rudra is given "a special share"; in book 10, the gods assign him "all the oblations."

How do these new versions of the myth fit both into the framework of the epic and into the extension of Vedic literature?

Book 7: The Sacrifice of Battle

Arjuna, the hero of the camp that represents the interests of the gods and dharma, has a vision that he alone is privileged to see. An individual shining with energy runs through the battle camp. The weapon that he brandishes does not leave his hand, but out of it come a thousand arrows that strike the enemy; Arjuna only strikes warriors that are already slain. The *ṛṣi* Vyāsa explains that this mysterious person is Rudra. He urges Arjuna to pay homage to this god and to sing praises from the *Śatarudriya* hymn. He recalls two or three myths about Rudra, especially the myth of the destruction of the sacrifice.

Arjuna's vision is certainly not a mere transposition of the myth of the destruction of the Sacrifice. There are certain constants in the role of Rudra. In countless passages the MBh lets it be known that war is a sacrifice in which any warrior—but especially the king—is simultaneously the sacrificer, the priest, and, if he dies in combat, the victim. In the MBh, Arjuna is not the titular king, but more than any other character in the epic, he represents the image of the ideal king. The vision that closes book 7 makes him discover that, in the sacrifice of war, it is not he who kills the enemy victims. The perfect warrior is only an instrument in the hands of the deity: Rudra does the slaying before him and for him. The Vedic texts made a connection between the damaged part of the victim and the arrow with which Rudra pierced Prajāpati-Sacrifice. Here, in a martial context and a martial language, Rudra performs the office of executioner. And the text suggests that victims who have fallen on the battlefield are "Rudra's share."

Book 10: The Eschatological Sacrifice

The war is over. After eighteen days of combat, Arjuna and his brothers, guided by Kṛṣṇa, the avatar of Viṣṇu-Nārāyaṇa, have achieved victory. In the enemy camp only three survivors remain. But one of them is of such size that the final outcome is not yet settled: Aśvatthāman, a warrior Brahman, a partial incarnation of Rudra, whose composite birth naturally evokes the Vedic myths of the origin of the god. Aśvatthāman was born "of the combination of Mahādeva (Rudra-Śiva) and Antaka (death), of Krodha (wrath) and Kāma (desire)" (MBh 1; see *Śatapatha Brāhmaṇa* 9.1.1.6 for Manyu; *Aitareya Brāhmaṇa* 3.33 for the combination of the terrible forms of all the gods). This Rudraic patrimony is reflected in a nocturnal ceremony during which Aśvatthāman offers himself up to Rudra-Śiva by immolating himself in the sacrificial fire. Rudra enters him and possesses him. Aśvatthāman then attacks the camp of the victors at night when they are asleep. He kills his principal adversaries not with the sword or arrows, but "like Rudra who personally strikes the *paśu.*" His two acolytes light three fires and burn down the entire camp, transforming it into a vast sacrificial area with its three great liturgical fires. The only survivors of this total destruction are Arjuna and his brothers, whom Kṛṣṇa had the foresight to bring to shelter. And when Aśvatthāman puts the finishing touch on his masterpiece of death by killing all the embryos in the dynasty of the victors, in the lineage of dharma, it is once again Kṛṣṇa who gives life back to the stillborn heir, Arjuna's grandson. Viṣṇu, of whom Kṛṣṇa is the avatar, must represent the continuity of the sacrifice and the stabilization or reestablishment of dharma. When Aśvatthāman is finally neutralized and condemned to exile and wandering (in the image of Rudra, the hunter, the savage god), Kṛṣṇa asserts that this warrior Brahman owes to Rudra his ability to unleash such destructive power. Kṛṣṇa then concludes with two myths, including the myth of the destruction of the sacrifice.

What connection is there between this last myth and book 10 of the MBh? A detailed study of the nocturnal carnage perpetrated by Rudra's Brahman incarnation, by the warrior possessed by Rudra, would clearly show many points of contact with the story of the destruction of the sacrifice, particularly in its epic and Purāṇic versions. Does this mean that the myth of the destruction of the sacrifice served as a model for book 10 of the MBh? The truth of the matter is more complex than that.

We must return to what was suggested above: the epic is not just a heroic story; it is also an image of the dissolution (*pralaya*) of the world at the end of a cosmic cycle. When the time of death approaches, Rudra destroys the world by fire, dissolves it, and reabsorbs it. The supreme deity in this phase of destruction is both sacrificer and yogi. Destruction by fire is interpreted as a sacrifice of cosmic dimensions for which Rudra-Śiva is both sacrificer and performer. But in this destructive enterprise with all its violence and death, the divine yogi acts with detachment and even indifference. The ideal king, to whom the message of the MBh and of the *Bhagavad Gītā* is addressed, finds in him the model of his own action, often cruel and violent, but indispensable for the good of the world. For the king and the warrior who act as yogis, detached from the fruit of action, war is a sacrifice that, rather than making them impure and prisoners of their passions, becomes a school of detachment and a way to deliverance.

Rereading the Vedic Myth

The entire context of epic and Purāṇic mythology sheds light on Aśvatthāman's intervention in book 10 and his connection with the sacrifice of Dakṣa. Despite all its sacrificial symbols, the story of the night massacre and the destruction of the camp is not merely the transposition of the myths of Rudra and Prajāpati in the *Brāhmaṇas*.

The myths or fragments of myths from the *Brāhmaṇas* were intended to justify certain liturgical rules that assured the correct functioning of the sacrifice by carefully delimiting the dangerous part, that is, Rudra's share. The destruction of the sacrifice and the mutilation of the gods here appeared to be a threat or a hypothesis: without Rudra, the sacrifice is impossible or destroys itself; if Rudra is not given his share, if he is willfully excluded from the sacrifice, then impurity, violence, and destructive fire take over the sacrificial site and the whole sacrifice.

Within the epic context, it is no longer merely a threat or hypothetical destruction in the event of a mistake during the ritual. It is a real and inevitable destruction. The myth of the destruction of Dakṣa's sacrifice takes on all of the symbolism of the periodic dissolution of the cosmos. The myth has in common with the burning of the camp of the victors an eschatological meaning that it did not have in the Vedic context: war ends with a universal conflagration that allows the survival only of the minimum number of creatures needed to ensure the start of a new era. The earthly crisis—a framework chosen to teach the king his duty—is a miniature of the cosmic crisis. War is the sacrifice appropriate to the warrior-king, just as the dissolution of the world is a monstrous cosmic sacrifice placed under the aegis of Rudra-Śiva. The theme of the destruction of Dakṣa's sacrifice by Rudra thereby logically takes on eschatological connotations that give the holocaust of Aśvatthāman its nobility and make explicit its true meaning in the epic drama.

The Purāṇas

This inquiry could be extended into Purāṇic literature. Many of the *Purāṇas* contain a version of the destruction of Dakṣa's sacrifice. The setting has become wider: all classes of beings and all the worlds are present. Rudra-Śiva duplicates himself by sending before him Vīrabhadra, the expression of his fury, and multiplies himself in troops (*gaṇas*) of cruel and repulsive creatures. The Goddess in the form of Kālī participates in the punitive expedition. Elements of this dramatization have influenced the composition of book 10 of the MBh. As for its global importance, a few brief remarks will have to suffice. Several versions tend to oppose Śiva to Viṣṇu in a sectarian way, either to ridicule Viṣṇu or to make him recognize the superiority of Śiva. Dakṣa becomes the model of the man who refuses, or shows that he is unable, to recognize that superiority. But what certain versions criticize in Dakṣa is at a deeper level the blind confidence in ritual (*karman*), whereas salvation is the fruit of knowledge (*jñāna*) and especially of devotion (*bhakti*). The questions that the myth attempted to answer in the *Brāhmaṇas* are progressively lost from sight. But the myth pursues its forward thrust.

J.Sc./g.h.

Purāṇic Cosmogony

The Purāṇas are a class of texts belonging to the *smṛti* tradition in India. They were transmitted over a long period of time and were established in a fixed form only after centuries of changes, additions, and omissions whose history is quite impossible to reconstruct. If we include in this group, besides the eighteen "great Purāṇas," the secondary and sectarian Purāṇas, the caste Purāṇas, and those Purāṇas connected with pilgrimage sites, they constitute an enormous body of literature, which has retained up to the present its capacity to be enriched. As their name indicates, they deal first, although not exclusively, with things of the past, and the account of the origins of the world figures in most of the "great Purāṇas." It is surprising that these texts, as diverse as they are, share a single account of creation, in which textual variations are almost insignificant. This must therefore be a fundamental narrative, which expresses the stability of a structure in which the Hindu world recognizes itself.

There is another surprise: one must both remember the Puruṣa hymn in which Vedic cosmogony is expressed, because its elements recur, and forget it, because a totally new organization emerges, sustained by new elements, in which the old elements are reinterpreted. This discontinuity constitutes a primary testimony to the impossibility of passing linearly from the Vedic world to the universe of classical Hinduism.

The essential difficulty in explaining the Purāṇic cosmogony is that it cannot be done solely in terms of myths. This is not only because of the complexity of the whole and the interpretive work that it demands, but also because this cosmogony sets up the fundamental values of Hinduism, many of which resist being cast into mythic or ritual forms of expression. Within the Vedic world itself, and within those higher castes that had the greatest interest in the sacrificial religion, a debate developed about the ritual. We find this is formulated in the Upaniṣads and the Āraṇyakas—texts that still belong to the *śruti,* to Revelation. It appears in the form of esoteric speculations on the ritual or, within the ritual itself, in the form of debates between Brahmans and kings, in teachings made by a husband to his wife (BAU), a father to his son (ChU), the Vedic god of death Yama to the obstinate Naciketas (KU), etc. The ensemble of values that emerge from this contention become mythologized in the restructuring of Purāṇic cosmogony. This results in a narrative of a type which, although it is somewhat unusual, especially in the first part, is easy to decipher. In addition, the Upaniṣadic debate itself and the values that flow from it are expressed through a certain number of concepts that the myth never explicates as such, even when they are its ultimate referents. These include yoga, renunciation, dharma, and bhakti, terms that must be introduced into the mythic account but defined without the aid of that account. Such is the price that must be paid for a culture that, although it is rich in myths, is only so by virtue of having developed a complex ideology in a complex society, an ideology that is clearly expressed in codes of laws or conceptual treatises parallel to the myths. One could almost say that mythic symbols and narratives are rich only in their conceptual richness, even if their uncommon language lends them another function, more didactic or "popular."

Cosmogony is thus composed of two quite distinct parts. We shall call the first "primary cosmogony or creation," in opposition to the other which will be called "secondary." Neither constitutes an absolute beginning, since this is a cyclic time that has two different levels of eternally recurring cycles (and there is even a third). The two accounts of creation correspond to temporal cycles of different lengths, and each period of creation has a corresponding period of the dissolution of the world, or of cosmic night, of equal duration, which itself gives rise to two separate accounts. The perfect logic of the whole makes it necessary to treat cosmic nights as inseparable segments of the cosmogonies. It is the same myth, unfolding in several episodes.

Primary Creation

At the beginning of a primary creation, we again encounter the Vedic Puruṣa, who is now known either as the supreme Puruṣa, *puruṣottama,* or as the supreme Ātman, *paramātman,* or as the supreme Brahman *parabrahman*—all three significant designations. But he is also called *mahāyogin,* the great yogi, which is for this period the most important aspect of the primal divinity, who is no longer a sacrificial victim: it is by an act of yoga that he will first set the universe in motion, in placing outside of the Male the primal Energy, the original nature—the *avyakta* (nondifferentiated), *pradhāna* or *prakṛti*—which draws all of its being from him. Once this first jolt in the immobility of Being has taken place, Nature will evolve through a prescribed series of forms, but her evolution is possible only through the immanent presence of the Puruṣa at each stage, even though that Puruṣa remains immutable and inactive, a yogi, detached from the world.

At this point, we may place the stages of primary cosmogony in a pattern, along with the corresponding stages of the "ascension" that the yogi undergoes, turning away from the world in order to rise up to the supreme Puruṣa, according to the *Kaṭha Upaniṣad* (3.10–11 and 6.7–8, with the variants indicated):

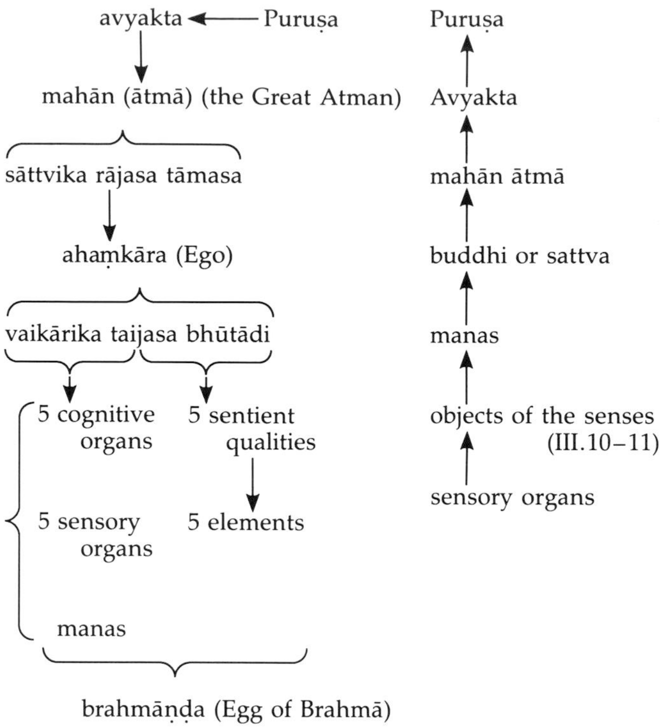

On one side we have the stages of a cosmic manifestation beginning with the Puruṣa and the Avyakta or Prakṛti, until the formation of an Egg of Brahmā; on the other side, the stages of ascension of the individual yogi toward the identification with the Puruṣa (who in the KU is named Viṣṇu). The direction of movement is inverted, but the stages are comparable, especially if we reduce the differences that might exist: the sensory organs and the objects of the senses are placed on an upward-tending line in the KU, whereas they constitute two parallel descending lines of evolution in the Purāṇas. This is in keeping with the role played in the Purāṇas by the three components of being, *sattva, rajas,* and *tamas,* below the Great *Ātman:* they are too functional to be left out of a description of the manifestation of the cosmos. The *rajas* is the active component, which, agitating itself, creates a disequilibrium in the whole and allows evolution to follow in a more linear fashion. The *sattva* (a term that designates being in general) is the pure, luminous, transparent, peaceful component, while the *tamas* ("darkness") is its opposite, all that is heavy, opaque, obtuse, and that represents the heaviness of Nature. The Puruṣa lies beyond these components, but its pure light (or consciousness) can be reflected in the transparency of the *sattva.* The *Avyakta* holds them in equilibrium, so long as none of the components becomes excessive. Starting from the *mahān* (*ātmā*), the triplicity of Nature permits the formation of a knot that is decisive for further evolution. The Great Ātman should not be taken as the universal Ātman (only the Puruṣa is worthy of this title), but rather as an Ātman, a "Self," who has not yet been limited by a sense of self. The *mahān ātmā* of the KU must be understood in the same way: as the stage at which the yogi crosses the limits of his empirical individuality. For this reason, the following stage in the cosmogony is the constitution of an ego, of a sort of cosmic individual who, drawing on his three components, will form on the one hand the equivalent of a human psyche and on the other the (objective and subjective) material world, sentient bodies, and impressions. The Great Yogi is at first Puruṣa in name only, but in the course of the evolution that will lead to the cosmos, he recovers the form of the cosmic man that he had in the hymn to Puruṣa. This is the inverse of the movement of the KU yogi through his human determinants to the Great Ātman, then to the Nondifferentiated, and finally to the supreme Puruṣa who is Viṣṇu.

On the other hand, if in the creative process we do not encounter the three stages mentioned in the yogic ascension (*manas, buddhi, mahān ātmā*), it is because the Purāṇic account in fact identified *mahān* (*ātmā*, the term *ātman* being generally omitted), *buddhi* ("Intellect"?), *sattva*, and even *manas*. In Hindu psychology, the *manas* plays the role of a "communal sense." It is through it that all the internal and external sensory elements pass, in order that they may be communicated to the *ātman*, that Self in which the equivalent of our "soul" may be seen, if it were not impossible for it to say "I" about itself. The Purāṇas thus treat the *ātman* either as the direct emanation of the *avyakta* or as an eleventh sense. There is no point in wondering what these stages could represent for the yogi. It is, however, significant that the process of the emanation of the cosmos passes over some of them and introduces an ego in their place. This is not an invention of the Purāṇas; it is to be found in the oldest Upaniṣads. It orients itself totally toward evolution as it reconstitutes the cosmic man.

What does this cosmogony mean? In the beginning was yoga, and no longer the sacrifice. The Absolute is that of the yogi, that is, the man who has renounced society, the sacrifices that ensure his prosperity, and all the activities of men. To renounce the world is first of all to contest the sacrificial rite, the idea that that rite, performed in order to obtain well-being in this world and in the beyond, binds man into a cycle of rebirths that is endless because its results are always produced in the future. Renunciation is thus release from rebirths. But it is not enough to leave the society in which one is living in order to reach that end: renunciation has its own logic, which draws man ever further away from the conditions of all empirical life; and yoga is offered itself precisely in order to help the renunciant to leave behind his concrete humanity, to turn his attention away from desirable objects, from desire itself, to turn toward what is beyond all things, which will release him.

Yoga thus becomes the supreme value, and the Absolute is that of the yogi.

Cosmogony itself is not the creation of renunciants; it can only be the discourse of men searching to explain the existence of this world and to ensure its essential parts. But these men knew of the yogi and of his speculations. The starting point for everything, the ground zero of cosmogony, thus takes the form of a projection of the yogi into the absolute. The cosmogonic Puruṣa is first of all the Great Yogi. It is more difficult to understand the cosmogonic inversion of yogic ascension, since the end of yoga is to extricate oneself from the world. But the KU itself says that "yoga is surging and disappearing"; it is a recurrent, and not continuous, experience. The yogi passes through phases of concentration in which the universe disappears from his senses, and phases of return into ordinary empirical consciousness. He does not deny the existence of the world; he merely alters his interest in it, reabsorbing his senses and their objects into himself to turn himself toward the interior world. Hence the transposition: the Great Yogi, in his state of concentration, reabsorbs the whole universe into himself, whereas he causes it to emanate outside of himself when he engages in the conditions of empirical life and makes himself into an ego. The alternation of cosmic days and nights is the same as the alternation of the yogic phases of the supreme Puruṣa. This also enables us to understand why cyclic time is necessary in Hinduism: the universe is perpetually tied to the perpetual yoga of the Puruṣa, who creates only for the good of creatures, as he is himself perpetually released. He could remain collected into himself and nothing would happen. But he agrees to return to ordinary life, to be reborn as it were, in order that beings might exist and strive for release.

The Trimūrti

The moment in which the *Avyakta* begins to evolve is regarded as the birth of Brahmā into a new life. Until this point, it has been as if the Puruṣa sacrifice of the Puruṣa hymn were placed in parentheses. The creation of a cosmic ego that causes the Puruṣa to recover a human form is a hint that the sacrifice has not completely disappeared. The account of the primary creation stops when an Egg of Brahmā has been constituted. This is a further step in the same direction.

Who is this Brahmā, who is now said to be reborn for a new life of one hundred years (the ideal duration of life in India, but Brahmā's years are not the same as human years)? The most elevated social category is that of the Brahmans: the Brahman, who is in theory a priest, is in charge of the Vedic sacrifice and is an expert in Vedic knowledge. He is so called because he knows the formulas—*brahman*—and their manipulation. The term *brahman* in the neuter comes to designate all of the Veda and all Vedic knowledge. It is also the name given to the function and power of Brahmans. In the masculine, the term designates the Vedic sacrificial priest who oversees the whole of the rite without doing or saying anything. The Brahmā (masc.) who is born in the primary creation in order to inaugurate a period known as a *mahākalpa* is apparently connected with this *brahman:* that is, with the Veda and the sacrifice for which it stands as charter. The proof of this will emerge in the secondary cosmogony. For the moment, it is the connection between the *brahman* and the supreme Puruṣa that must be defined. It has been stated that the Puruṣa was present and immanent at each moment of cosmic emanation. At the level of the Egg of Brahma, from which the world will emerge, it is he who takes the name and the form of Brahmā. But this is only one of the three forms that he takes on at this level, for there is a triplicity in which we again encounter the three components enumerated previously. Brahmā is the creative aspect, because knowledge and Vedic practices are the mover of the world in which we live; because he is eminently active, he is composed of *rajas*. At the same time, the Puruṣa is Viṣṇu, he who preserves and conserves the world by virtue of the *sattva* that is dominant in him; and he is Rudra(-Śiva), the destroyer, he who is charged with *tamas*. The ensemble makes up the Trimūrti ("Triple Form"), and each of these aspects operates in the myth.

There is a source of confusion at this point, because the supreme Puruṣa may also, according to the Purāṇas, be called Viṣṇu or Śiva, or even the supreme Brahman (neuter): the levels must be kept separate. In his nonmanifest, ultimate form, the Puruṣa is never Brahmā (masc.), and to be the supreme Brahman (neuter) does not prevent him from being called Viṣṇu or Śiva. Those are the only two proper names for the supreme Puruṣa.

Curiously, the Egg of Brahmā concludes the account of primary creation. We are told that the worlds are contained in it and that the Puruṣa resides in its center, but we never see this egg hatch, because secondary cosmogony follows a completely different set of rules. The chaos-egg is an Upaniṣadic image. The choice of this form, which is also found in other myths, seems to be connected with the fact that the Sanskrit word for bird is *dvi-ja,* "he who is twice born," because it is oviparous. This is also the name of the members of the three highest *varṇas,* because they are born a second time during the initiation ceremony, but it comes to be especially applied to Brahmans. It is thus normal to have the birth of Brahmā take place from an egg.

Secondary Creation

Secondary creation does not take up where the primary left off: it takes place, not at the beginning of a life of Brahmā, but at the beginning of a day of Brahmā or a *kalpa,* and explicitly presupposes the night that preceded it, of equal duration. There are 360 days in a year of Brahmā, and he lives for 100 years: there will thus be 36,000 cycles of the world or *kalpas* repeating secondary creation within a *mahākalpa* or life of Brahmā. Beyond this, the *kalpa* or day of Brahmā contains 1,000 *mahāyugas* or *yugas* of the (Vedic) gods, which are themselves separated, no longer by cosmic nights, but by "twilights." Knowing that a *mahāyuga* is made up of 12,000 divine years, and that one divine year is equal to 360 human years, we may conclude that the edifice of the Purāṇic double cosmogony with its symmetrical dissolutions of the world carries only the weight of theory, with no practical consequence for contemporary man, who has moreover taken care to situate himself at a comfortable distance from any cosmic catastrophe. Man occupies the center of a cosmic period, just as he is the center of creation.

The narrative is brief: Nārāyaṇa awakens on the one ocean, into which the earth, and even the triple world (hell, earth, heaven), have disappeared. He is described (*Viṣṇu Purāṇa* 1.4–5, *Kūrma Purāṇa* 1.6–7, *Vāyu Purāṇa* 1.6) in the terms that the Puruṣa hymn uses for the cosmogonic Puruṣa. Nārāyaṇa is the form of the Puruṣa during the cosmic night that separates two *kalpas.* When he awakens, he becomes Brahmā, who becomes Vāyu (Wind, but also the vital breath) in order to move and then transforms himself into a Boar to go to search for the Earth at the bottom of the water and to put it back on its supports.

Here ends the colorful part of an account that draws upon a cosmogonic theme found in the Vedic texts (notably *Taittirīya Saṃhitā* 7.1.5.1, *Kāṭhaka Saṃhitā* 8.2), in which it is Prajāpati who transforms himself successively into Wind and Boar and then unites with the Earth that the Boar has pulled out of the water. It is Brahmā who in the Trimūrti inherits the functions of the Vedic Prajāpati. It is important to specify this, because each of the three aspects of the Trimurti is, in its own way, identified with the sacrifice: thus Brahmā is a "Lord of Creatures," *prajā-pati,* while Viṣṇu is the guarantor of cosmic order, dharma, and of general prosperity, *śrī.* Śiva is identified with the fire that consumes victims and with the post to which they are bound when they are put to death. He is thus allied with the fatal and somber aspects of the sacrifice. We can already see that the cosmogony and dissolution that take place at the level of the Trimūrti are assimilated into a sacrificial act.

It is for this reason that every Purāṇic text identifies the Boar, who plunges into the ocean of the flood (see below) to pull out the Earth, with the sacrifice. There can no longer be any doubt that in moving from the primary cosmogony to the secondary cosmogony we have moved from the realm of yoga to the realm of the sacrifice. But the same Puruṣa is at work in the cosmic manifestation, which is another way of saying that the sacrifice occurs in the interior of yoga, and no longer as its antagonist but as its subordinate. The Hindu universe has grown by inserting the Vedic universe into the universe that the renunciants know and teach.

Brahmā—whose four faces evoke his identity with the four Vedas—continues the work of creation, once the earth has been set at the center of the triple world. But the character of the second part of the account, which is once again completely charged with ideology but with minimal detail, reconciles it with the primary cosmogony. Immediately after the completion of the two accounts follows an obligatory recapitulation of the stages of creation from the *mahān* (*ātmā*) to the final stage of secondary creation, without any interruption. This recapitulation does away with the imagery of the two accounts: the Egg of Brahma, Nārāyaṇa who awakens on the ocean and becomes Brahma, Vāyu, the Boar. It must be admitted that without such imagery the cosmogonic accounts lose much of their intelligibility. The images may be omitted only after their meaning has been acquired in the context of the whole. Even so, not everything in the second part is clear, as will be seen.

Brahmā begins by creating the quintuple *avidyā,* metaphysical Ignorance, which makes the creation of individual beings possible, because it allows them to be unaware of their identity with the Puruṣa. The creation of Ignorance by Brahmā is explicitly connected with his desire to create beings of every kind. After this a primary creation follows, in which the predominance of *tamas* is such that beings are immobile and unconscious and do nothing (*asādhaka*): these are the plants. Brahmā, unsatisfied, begins again. This time the four-footed animals appear, but they still have too much *tamas,* so if they move, it is generally to follow an evil path. Brahmā, discontented with his work, then creates the (Vedic) gods who live in the skies, that is, the uppermost part of the triple world. But the gods have such a predominance of *sattva* that they are completely satisfied with their lot and do nothing. Brahmā is pleased with this creation, but pushes his work further in order to obtain "effective" beings—(*sādhaka*). These are men, who have within them *tamas, sattva,* and *rajas* in such abundance that they are subject to suffering and must act to escape it. The following stage of creation seems to describe the kind of help, of "grace," that each category of beings receives; but the text is obscure, and one has the impression of confronting realities that are as inaccessible to us as were the yogic stages of ascension of the *Kaṭha Upaniṣad.*

Significantly, it is at the human level that *rajas,* the active component of which Brahmā himself is made, reappears. *Rajas* is connected with those activities that characterize men, the only creatures who are capable of studying the Vedas and sacrificing. This is the secret complicity between Brahmā and men: men are the sole agents of what Brahmā represents, the sacrificial act—*karman.* But—and this point changes everything—the ritual activity of men has as its sole motivation the suffering that must be escaped, and no longer the positive search for terrestrial happiness. Their goal becomes the same as that of the yogi when he wants to escape the world of rebirths conceived as a world of suffering. To be a *sādhaka,* according to Brahmā and according to all of classical Hindu thought, is to take the path that leads to the attainment of the Absolute; that is, release from all suffering: it is to take the path of yoga, for which the term is *siddhi,* "realization" of the Absolute. But the *sādhaka* is the one who, from the beginning, undertakes the ritual activity patronized by Brahmā. Instead of being an obstacle to release, ritual becomes a means to it, and metaphysical Ignorance becomes a precondition for access to the supreme Knowledge. Thus, ritual seems already to belong to the world of yoga. The cosmogonic account is not further explained with regard to these implications, though they allow us to glimpse an integration of yoga with ritual that leaves neither one nor the other wholly intact. This interpenetration of these two sets of values constitutes what in Hinduism is called *bhakti,* the religion of devotion. It is essentially around *bhakti* that the whole of classical mythology is composed, whether it be sectarian or nonsectarian. But the symmetrical account of the dissolution of the world will help make the structure and meaning of the whole more precise.

The Dissolution of the World

At the end of a day of Brahmā (*kalpa*), the world enters a period of night, the sleep of creatures. This period is inaugurated by a cosmic catastrophe—*pralaya,* "dissolution," "reabsorption"—of which the account includes two principal phases and an introduction. This account, which, like that of creation, is actually based in Purāṇic literature (*Viṣṇu Purāṇa* 6.3, *Agni Purāṇa* 368–69, *Kūrma Purāṇa* 2.45, *Bhāgavata Purāṇa* 12, *Matsya Purāṇa* 165, *Vāyu Purāṇa* 1.7.18ff.), has so deeply structured Hindu thought, right up to the present, that it is important to set it forth in all its complexity and discuss the different levels of interpretation that it offers.

a) The Cosmic Fire

In the "picturesque" account that describes the *pralaya* in most of the Purāṇas, it all begins with a prolonged drought that progressively weakens all the creatures. Then the sun burns more brightly, is divided into seven, and draws all of the moisture out of the triple world before setting it on fire. The fire rages from the earth to the hells and then to the sky, until the whole becomes a mere incandescent ball, and resembles the back of a tortoise once again. The monstrous sun that sets fire to the worlds is called by diverse names: it is Kāla-Agni, the Fire of Time, or Kāla-Agni-Rudra, Rudra the Fire of Time, or Agni-Saṃvartaka, the destructive fire. The *Viṣṇu Purāṇa* clearly states that Viṣṇu (here the supreme Puruṣa) takes the form of Rudra, because he wants to reabsorb the world into himself.

mahākalpa (= life of Brahmā)	Supreme Purusa: Viṣṇu or Śiva	
		Brahmā (*rajas*) (day) + Brahman (night)
kalpa (= day of Brahmā)	Trimūrti	Viṣṇu or Puruṣa (day) + Nārāyaṇa (*sattva*) (night)
		Rudra, (*tamas*)

Note: Rudra is the "terrible" name of Śiva (= "the Beneficent")

Translation: the Puruṣa—who in the great Vaiṣṇava Purāṇa is called Viṣṇu—takes the *tāmasic* form of Rudra in the Trimūrti in order to burn up the world. The destructive role of Rudra is thus connected with his Vedic character: identified with the fire that consumes the victims, he is qualified to burn up the worlds, but at the same time he makes the fire into a sacrifice in which the three worlds are the victims. On the other hand, one must take literally Viṣṇu's desire to reabsorb the world into himself: at the level of the *mahākalpa* (the life of Brahmā), the rhythm of cosmic days and nights was assimilated to the rhythm of the yoga of the Puruṣa. The same holds on the level of the *kalpa:* it is by virtue of his yoga, but at a lower stage of yogic experience, that the Puruṣa periodically reabsorbs the worlds into himself and emits them. This lower stage is limited to the contents of the Egg of Brahmā, but these contents are more complex than they at first appear. The burning of the world is thus as much an effect of the *tapas* of Śiva as it is a sacrifice. The yogic character of the cycle of the *kalpa* (day of Brahmā) is irrefutably confirmed when it is further understood that the sleep of Nārāyaṇa on the cosmic ocean, from which secondary creation arises and with which it terminates at the end of the account, is really a yogic sleep, during which all of creation is reabsorbed into him. The dissolution of the world that the fire inaugurates is thus both a sacrifice by Rudra and an act of yoga by the divinity.

This double interpretation of the first act of the *pralaya* becomes more specific with respect to the fate of creatures in this catastrophe. In all the variants, the sky is emptied of its inhabitants when the fire reaches it: either they betake themselves to the higher spheres of their own will, or the heat of the fire drives them there. Those who inhabit the sky are primarily the gods, the great Seers of previous ages, the Perfected Ones—*siddhas,* those who have reached the culmination of the yogic experience, i.e., the renunciants—but also the members of the higher *varṇas* of normal human society who have fulfilled their dharma, along with their retinue. There is a logic here: renunciants no longer have any right to a special fate, because yoga and the sacrifice are no longer regarded as being in opposition. They are thus associated in the sky with all those who are there at the moment of *pralaya* and are promised release. Among these are the heads of high-caste families and apparently those who have served them properly and have thus properly fulfilled their duty, their own dharma. In the perspective of the renunciant at odds with the ritual world, the sky was a world into which one was reborn, a transmigratory world like all the others, a fruit of the ritual. It remains so to a certain extent, outside of the moment of *pralaya,* but at the same time it becomes an obligatory stage on the way to release, even for the renunciant. There is another transformation: in the original perspective, release applied only to members of the upper castes—because to become a renunciant was to renounce one's sacrificial fires—but in the Purāṇic view, release seems to include all of the world. Salvation is promised to all. Finally, release is not an individual process, even if the merits of each person continue to play a role. It takes place collectively for all those who happen to be located in the sky at the desired moment.

All of the inhabitants of the sky at the moment of *pralaya* are thus destined for release: they will not be reborn again. Their ascent above the sky results in the appearance of other spheres: *maharloka* (here *loka* means "world" and *mahas* means "strength, power," and irresistibly evokes for the mythographer the *mahān ātmā*), *janaloka* (the world of those destined for rebirth, if one derives *jana* from the root *jan-,* "to be born"), *tapoloka* (the world of ascetic heat—*tapas*), and the *brahmaloka.* This is the highest sphere, the end of the odyssey of creatures liberated at the end of a *kalpa.* But this ascension is far from immediate and linear: creatures oscillate between two of these spheres situated beyond the transmigratory cycle for ten *kalpas* before they are able to reach the Brahmaloka. When they finally arrive there, they enjoy absolute independence, all are equal, and they have perfect happiness.

The arrival at Brahmaloka is the part of this account that is the most clearly stated. This world of Brahmā or of Brahman (neuter) is a reminder of the fact that release takes place within the Egg of Brahmā—in the terminology of the primary cosmogony—that is, in the part of the universe where the sacrificial values hold sway. The universe of *bhakti,* which up to this point has had a temporal structure, now unfolds spatially. But the Brahmaloka, the site of release, cannot merely be the world of Brahmā, if Brahmā is first of all the god of the sacrifice. Its description—the absolute equality between all who have been liberated, the absence of a ruler, that is, the reverse of the terrestrial world—appears to be the mythic transposition of release as it is conceived by the "orthodox" renunciant. This is the high-caste renunciant who withdraws from a world governed by ritual to effect his own salvation, the renunciant at odds with the ritual world: the solitary *sannyāsin* ("renouncer"). For him, release from rebirths is the final stage of a process more "gnostic" than yogic: he is to reach an intuitive, experiential consciousness, the total identity of his *ātman*—of his Self, of his own being divested of an ego—with the Brahman. It is possible for the supreme form of the divinity to receive the name of "supreme Brahman," but this is merely a secondary designation for him, given as a reminder of the fact that he has within himself the Brahman of the *sannyāsin.* The Absolute that is defined by its being beyond the rite, that repudiates it by presupposing it, is by preference given the name of Brahman (or Ātman, since the two terms are interchangeable): the best that may be said is that the terrestrial Brahman is a projection of this, and that this Absolute cannot be dissociated from the *brahman* that it renounces. But contrary to the Brahman of the *sannyāsin,* the Brahmaloka is not the supreme level: it is situated at the level of the Trimūrti.

If Brahmaloka is truly the mythic "place" of release according to the conception of the *sannyāsin,* then it is possible to decipher step by step the rest of the odyssey of those who are released. Note first that they escape the cosmic fire: but in a society where the higher castes have recourse to the burning of the dead—a rite conceived as a sacrifice, the last in which the fire is ignited with the sacrificial fire of the deceased—the fact of being spared the cosmic fire evokes the treatment given to *sannyāsins* alone. Not only are they inhumed and not burned, but their death involves no impurity for those near them. That is, they are at no time associated with the dangerous world of "the departed"—*pretas*—not only because they no longer have a sacrificial fire in which to be burned, but because they have already observed their funeral rites by entering *sannyāsa.* At the same time, like all who die, they are subject to an intermediate period, which usually ends on the eleventh day, between inhumation and the final rites. This could well be the explanation for the curious oscillation of those who have been released, between two spheres above the world of transmigration, but below the Brahmaloka, over a period of ten *kalpas* (ten days of Brahmā).

Before taking up the fate of transmigratory creatures, we may quickly complete our description of the second phase of release, which takes place at the level of the *mahākalpa,* thus at the end of a life of Brahmā. From the point of view of the cosmos, reabsorption into the Puruṣa takes place in exactly the opposite order from that of cosmic emission, and thus tells us nothing more. As for those who are released from the Brahmaloka, they too are reabsorbed with Brahmā into the Puruṣa, where they will remain forever. No account specifies what they gain from this ultimate stage of release in relation to the first. But other myths describe this final residence of the released in the supreme Puruṣa as the paradise of Viṣṇu, Vaikuṇṭha, or Śiva, Kailāśa, according to the name that they give to the supreme divinity.

An account of the cosmic fire would not be complete if it did not specify the fate of those who are to be reborn. These are those who were living in the two lower spheres of the triple world at the moment of the fire. The fire of Rudra or Kāla reduces them, as well as the three worlds, to ashes, but their *ātmans,* the transmigratory part of them, escape in order to pass the cosmic night in a place where they are to be reborn with their *karman:* their refuge is the Janaloka. The name of the sphere that shelters them is a good indication of what awaits transmigratory beings, even if it is itself beyond transmigration.

It is evident, from all this symbolism, that the fire is a sacrifice, a sacrifice in which the fire is Rudra, i.e., in which the destructive aspect is primary. But the cosmic fire is also conceived as the funeral pyre of ordinary beings, of those who have not been promised release. The *ātmans* of these beings have to be conserved somewhere. The Janaloka is thus chosen for them.

Whatever their origins are, and by whatever means these cosmic spheres that appear only in the account of *pralaya* came into being, it seems clear—according to a process that recalls the stages of the primary cosmogony—that these are cosmological transpositions of seven ritual exclamations, of which the first three, in common usage, had a cosmological import from the start. The *Vāyu Purāṇa* (2.39.18b–27, 31b–34) attributes the creation of the seven worlds (*bhūr, bhuvas, svar, mahas, jana, tapas, satya* = *brahman*) to seven words of Brahmā. The three lower worlds form the "triple world," that of transmigration, even after the Purāṇas have replaced the intermediary space—*bhuvas*—with hell in order to lodge there the antigods, the *asuras.* When they are used on numerous ritual occasions, they are obviously meant to designate the three worlds. The rest is less clear, but we may note certain rituals in which the seven exclamations take the place of the three. These are the texts of the tradition (*smṛti*) that appear to be the most direct commentaries on the Vedic ritual that discuss these terms; it is thus nearly certain that the Purāṇic authors were aware of this, and that their account is an intended transposition. Whether or not they invented the cosmic spheres corresponding to the last four exclamations, the seven exclamations were never used together except in the ceremony of entry into *sannyāsa* and in the burial of *sannyāsins.*

This also confirms the hypothesis that the first phase of *pralaya*—the one that, moreover, determines the fate of transmigratory as well as released beings—follows a pattern inspired by the world of the orthodox *sannyāsin,* of the high-caste renunciant who regards the Absolute as Brahman rather than as Viṣṇu or Śiva. We must now complete the lesson taught by the account of secondary creation: henceforth yoga would regulate not only sacrificial values but every form of renunciation that proceeded from it directly. Release as defined by the *sannyāsin* becomes no more than a first stage toward final release. The Brahman of Brahmaloka is not the ultimate resting place of the one who is released, and, correlatively, the one who is released is not necessarily the *sannyāsin* in the strict sense of the word. The latter loses his prerogatives and is forced to allow into his company those he thought he had left behind for all time when he renounced his worldly existence. It is for this reason that the expanded universe developed in the primary creation and its corresponding reabsorption must be characterized as the universe of bhakti, of the religion that broke through the bonds of brahmanical orthodoxy decisively (in technical terms, the bonds of the *varṇāśramin*) to offer salvation to all. However, the continued use of "orthodox" categories at the same time shows that these have been not abolished but more safely preserved within that which encompasses them.

b) The Flood

When the three worlds have been consumed by the fire fanned by the breath of Rudra—or by the breath of the serpent Śeṣa (*Viṣṇu* 6.3.24) whom we will encounter again—the breath once again comes into play, that of Viṣṇu Janārdana (the "Oppressor of Creatures"), or more simply, the Wind, in order to pile up the clouds and start the rain that extinguishes the fire and submerges the rest of the three worlds in the one ocean. When the deluge has finished the work of the fire, the Wind appears again, this time to dissipate the clouds and end a rain that has continued for over one hundred years (like the initial drought). Then, on the ocean where everything else has disappeared, Viṣṇu lies asleep. He has the name of Vāsudeva or Nārāyaṇa, the two names that make him the container of all of the creatures: it is thus in him that, in the account of the *pralaya* between two *kalpas,* one must imagine the existence of the four spheres that lie above the triple world of transmigration. He either sleeps directly on the cosmic ocean (*Viṣṇu* 6.37–41) or on the serpent Śeṣa (*Vāyu* 2.4.4). All is plunged into darkness, but this Nārāyaṇa is none other than Brahmā, the god who at the dawn of a new day recreates everything.

The flood narrative (see *Matsya* for a different account) thus brings the universe back to the state from which secondary cosmogony began. The cycle of the *kalpa* is thus completed, and the cycle of the *mahākalpa* is also seen coming full circle with the completion of a life of Brahmā and the end of the journey of those who have been released. In the world of the narrations of the destruction of the world, sometimes the theme of the cosmic fire predominates and sometimes the theme of the flood. Both themes are used here: the first, corresponding to the first phase of the dissolution of the world, serves to determine the fate of the creatures; the second would be unexpected if it did not make it possible to return the cosmos to the state from which secondary creation began. Should this simple superposition of two themes be seen as a redundancy or as a mythic necessity?

The first part of an answer is given by the change in the divinity who controls the scene. Rudra disappears with the Fire, as does Janārdana (which is a "terrible" name of Viṣṇu-Kṛṣṇa). From this point on it can only be Nārāyaṇa or Vāsudeva, who is none other than Brahmā the creator but who for the time being sleeps on the cosmic ocean. The god made of *tamas* has given way to the god made of *sattva.* When Viṣṇu is associated with the preservation of the worlds, we think of his association with the sacrifice that ensures the prosperity of the three worlds; but he is also the one who preserves the worlds, or more exactly the creatures, during the cosmic night. To say that he is made of *sattva* is to restore to *sattva* its proper meaning of being in general, or the totality of beings (the Sanskrit abstract noun has both senses). Viṣṇu in the form of Nārāyaṇa (or Vāsudeva) thus carries all of the creatures in himself, both those awaiting rebirth and those who are released to the level of Brahmaloka. As already noted in connection with the *mahākalpa* and the ultimate form of the Great Yogi, the emission and reabsorption of the worlds are tied to the rhythm of divine yoga. We find this same pulsation on the level of the *kalpa.* The sleep of the god on the ocean is a yogic image, mentioned in the Purāṇic account (for example, *Kūrma* 45.55; *Viṣṇu* 6.4.6), and its most famous mythic use occurs when the Goddess appears, at the time of his awakening, as the personification of his yogic sleep, *yoganidrā* (a feminine noun, luckily). It is sufficient to specify that this yogic repose is not so deep as the sleep of the god between two *mahākalpas,* since it allows the creatures to survive as a trace in the divine consciousness. The theme of yogic sleep occurs again at another level—in which the image does not reveal its meaning so easily—with regard to the epic Kṛṣṇa: each time that he is called upon for a crucial appearance, he is found asleep on his couch. He thus seems to be not only an avatar of Viṣṇu but also a reincarnation of the *ṛṣi* Nārāyaṇa.

A second part of the answer is that the ocean of the flood is a universal image of the return of the world to chaos. But the most commonly described scene puts the serpent Śeṣa between the ocean and Nārāyaṇa: the great coiled serpent is another image of the unformed, of chaos, but this serpent is named Śeṣa, "the remainder," which gives him a much more precise meaning. Śeṣa is most precisely what remains of the cosmic sacrifice, the incandescent ball that the breath of Viṣṇu and the clouds save from total annihilation. The meaning of this remainder lends itself to two complementary interpretations. Every Brahman knows that he should eat only the "remainder" of the sacrifice: in practice all food to be consumed should be sacrificial food. Thus it is necessary for a portion of it to be offered to the gods, who may also be represented by any guest who might have arrived unexpectedly. The remainder of the sacrifice is thus the condition for all pure life, for all prosperity. Here, in the context of the *pralaya,* it is the promise of a future rebirth. The sacrificial circle continues, and on the cosmic level where we exist it merges with the cycle of the *kalpa.* Nārāyaṇa the yogi sleeps on the sacrificial remainder of the world. Yoga and sacrifice join to ensure the continuity of the world, and the sacrifice is once again subordinated to yoga.

The meaning of the serpent—*nāga*—which echoes the cosmic sacrifice, also requires a more precise interpretation of the ocean. The *nāgas,* in Hindu mythology, live in a subterranean aquatic world. There is thus a connection between Śeṣa and his natural milieu, the ocean. Beyond this, however, we are reminded of funerary rites, for an aspect of these rites is transposed in the cosmic fire. After incineration, the ashes of the dead are collected and at least some of them are thrown into the Ganges to ensure a heavenly rebirth or release for the dead (the waters of the river mingle with those of the ocean at its mouth, just as the individual *ātmans* melt into the Brahman): the heavenly resting place (the Vedic world beyond) and eternal release, as we have seen, are no longer placed in opposition, and the Ganges is the river of salvation, of all salvation. Every river becomes the Ganges or is mysteriously connected to the Ganges, and the cremation grounds of India are always put on the bank of a river. The theme of the flood is thus put to another logical use. The disappearance of the residue of the cosmos in the ocean—the symbolic meaning of the sacrificial residue is borne here by the serpent Śeṣa—corresponds to the phase of the immersion of the ashes and promises a happy future for everyone: heavenly rebirth, in the popular consciousness, is merely the collateral for good future rebirths, and this is all that is asked of the Ganges for the individual, as it is asked of the flood for the three worlds.

M.Bi./d.w.

BIBLIOGRAPHY

M. BIARDEAU, "Études de mythologie hindoue," parts 1–3, *BEFEO* (1968–71). CH. MALAMOUD, "Observations sur la notion de 'reste' dans le brâhmanisme," *Wiener Zeitschrift für die Kunde Südasiens* (1972).

Abbreviations

BAU	*Bṛhad-āraṇyaka-upaniṣad*
ChU	*Chāndogya-upaniṣad*
K	*Kūrma-purāṇa*
KU	*Kaṭha-upaniṣad*
V	*Vāyu-purāṇa*
Vi	*Viṣṇu-purāṇa*

The Hindu God with Five Heads (*Pañcamukha*)

The number five is one of the most widely used numbers in classical Hinduism. It would probably be impossible to bring all of its uses together into a single pattern of meaning. It is nevertheless a recurring theme in both classical and modern iconography, in which its meaning is clear and its structure well defined. The theme is a representation of divinities with five heads or five faces—*pañcamukha*—though the mythology gives no account of this fivefold multiplication of the heads of divinities and generally assumes that divinities have only one head. Among the gods of the sanctuary proper, we find the multiplication by five only for the linga of Śiva, which becomes curiously transformed into a *pañcamukha-liṅga:* Śiva is the only divinity whose mythology includes the mention of five heads (see below). On the other hand, five-headed figures can be found on processional images and frequently on the reliefs that adorn walls and pillars. Thus we have Gaṇapatis, Hanumāns, Bhairavas, Goddesses, Viṣṇus, and Narasiṃhas with five heads. But we must exclude from this list Brahmā, who never has more than four heads (see below), Dattātreya, who often has three as the incarnation of the Trimūrti, and Skanda, who has either one or six. Most of the time the five heads are not on the same plane. The most frequent arrangement is of four heads placed according to the four cardinal directions around a central pivot (the linga, for example) with a fifth placed on top. When the five heads are on the same plane, the central head marks the highest point of the curve formed by their crowns. The five heads thus become (with some exceptions) four heads plus one.

This representation would seem to be the generalization of a theme that has its basis in a specific myth, or rather in two myths that are connected to one another, but of which the first may have come into existence only because of the second. The first concerns Brahmā exclusively. The classical Brahmā, heir to the Vedic Prajāpati, is still associated with the theme of incest that quite logically characterizes the progenitor of all creatures. But the theme is used in a new way. The account that the *Matsya Purāṇa* (3.30–41) gives of this is very clear in its brevity: Brahmā, wanting to create beings, divided in two so as to form a couple, but the woman who issued from this division appeared to be his daughter because she was born from his body. As soon as he sees her, he falls in love with her beauty and desires her violently, despite the protests of the *ṛṣis* (led by Vasiṣṭha) who are born of him and consider her their sister. The woman has the

Five-headed Bhairava. Chariot wood. Madras Museum special collections. Photo IFI 298–51.

name of Sāvitrī, Sarasvatī, Gāyatrī, Brahmāṇī, and Śatarūpā ("having one hundred forms"), and it is she whom we meet again as the consort of Brahmā: the *gāyatrī* (or *sāvitrī*), for example, is only a Ṛgvedic verse that the Brahman must recite each day at sunrise, but it ends up, like all the other names of this series, designating the Vedic Speech personified and the feminine energy that ensures Brahmā's fertility, the energy through which Vedic knowledge may be expressed and communicated. Without her there would be no ritual, and thus no viable creation.

Sāvitrī, once created, shows her respect for her father by walking around him to the right (*pradakṣiṇa*, i.e., clockwise). Brahmā, ashamed but overwhelmed with desire—*kāma-ātura*, "sick with desire," the text says—so badly wants to follow her with his eyes that a new head appears to the right, then another to the rear, and then a fourth to the left. His incestuous desire makes him lose all the merits he acquired by the asceticism that he had practiced to create beings. Then he grows a fifth head on top, which he covers with an ascetic's topknot, and he orders his sons to create beings (in his place?).

Brahmā thus has four heads plus one. The first four are absorbed in watching and desiring the beauty of Sāvitrī, with whom he would create the world; for does not everything arise from the Veda and thus from Brahmā? But because of this desire he has exhausted the merits of his asceticism and his creative capacity. The fifth head, with its ascetic's topknot and its gaze turned upwards, returns to its earlier austerities and leaves the work of creation to Brahmā's sons. The symbolism of this account is complex: in it we find first of all the Vedic idea of the exhaustion that is provoked by the creative act and the ritual act—always identified—and that calls for a regeneration of lost powers. But Hinduism greatly enriched this theme, which meanwhile had passed through Upaniṣadic reflections: between the Brahmā who is sick with desire and the fifth head with its ascetic's topknot there is clearly the same tension that is found between the sacrificial values that underlie all of creation and the renunciation of the world that is the final end of creation. The religion of ritual is henceforth assimilated to the world of desire: one performs a ritual only out of a desire for a certain result, and Brahmā is sometimes identified with Kāma, the god of love. But the Upaniṣads were very quick to make the distinction between the inferior *brahman*—the Veda, the science of ritual, the Vedic Speech—and the supreme Brahman, that which transcended ritual and word, the absolute of the renunciant. Here apparently the first four heads of Brahmā operate on the level of ritual—the driving desire behind the ritual act becoming the desire for the beauty of Sāvitrī, for creative Speech, and for creation as a whole. There are four heads because there are four Vedas, and because the terrestrial world, the world of desire and the world of acts—*karmabhūmi*—is symbolized by the four cardinal points. As for the fifth head, this is the symbol of the supreme Brahman, the one in which the renunciant seeks his ultimate deliverance from rebirths, and which is found again in Hindu cosmology as Brahmaloka, "the world of Brahmā," but also "of the Brahman."

Five-headed Viṣṇu seated on five Brahmās. Temple of Sattanadar at Nagapattinam (South India). Photo IFI 6680–3.

Yet Brahmā is never represented with anything but the first four heads. We know, on the other hand, that he is the only one of the three divinities of the Trimūrti who is not considered to be a god of *bhakti;* that is, who has not been raised to the supreme level of cosmology, as Śiva and Viṣṇu have been. He remains closely tied to the sphere of the Veda and of the ritual, even in his renunciant dimension, which is an effective way to take account of the relationship that the high-caste renunciant retains with the ritual world that he has left behind. Brahmā is not the god of grace, as a god of bhakti should be. All he knows how to give is favors—*vara*—which reward the ascetic efforts of an individual, preferably of an *asura* or an evil prince with suspect motives: he never leaves the circle of retribution of *karman,* even when the *karman,* "ritual action," becomes *tapas,* "austerities," "ascetic heat." He is not the god of the unearned boon.

This is what the second myth undertakes to explain, in permanently depriving Brahmā of his fifth head. It is Śiva, or one of his terrible emanations, who takes charge of the execution, which gives the myth the misleading appearance of being a Śaiva sectarian myth: to cut off one of Brahmā's heads, in short, to sacrifice it, is automatically to commit Brahmanicide, one of the most detestable crimes of Hindu dharma. Who but Śiva could undertake such a task in the world of bhakti? The myth is recounted many times (*Vāmana Purāṇa* 2; *Kūrma Purāṇa* 2.31, etc.), with multiple variants and more or less disastrous consequences for Śiva, whose sufferings we shall here summarize. The outline of the account is very simple: Rudra-Śiva and Brahmā quarrel. Brahmā believes in his own superiority and angers Rudra with remarks made by his fifth head. Rudra then gives himself five heads so as to be equal to Brahmā, but Brahmā's fifth head still refuses to recognize Rudra's superiority, until Rudra cuts it off with a stroke of his fingernail (or commands Bhairava to do this). Rudra goes away, but because this head remains stuck to his hand—where it becomes his begging bowl (the begging bowl of his Kāpālika devotees, the men "with a skull")—he has to make a long pilgrimage to rid himself of it.

What is interesting here is that Śiva gives himself five heads to become the "physical" equal of Brahmā: the five heads are as widely known in Hinduism as the four heads of Brahmā. Each head has a name that is attested in the *Mahā-nārāyaṇa Upaniṣad* (which can hardly be suspected of Śaiva sectarianism), and they are also designated by the generic term of *pañcabrahma,* "the five *brahmans,*" "the five ritual formulas," as the five names are given in ritual invocations transmitted by the Upaniṣads. As for the *pañcamukhaliṅga,* its most widespread form is that of a linga with an anthropomorphic face on each of its four sides, oriented to the cardinal directions, while the fifth is simply the upper extremity of the linga, rising above the four faces. It is evident that the five faces of Śiva are not of the same order as the five faces of Brahmā in the first myth. The end of the linga symbolizes the supreme form of the god, unmanifested, the form related to release, while the four faces recall the bond that unites Śiva with the world of Vedic ritual (as well as Śaiva ritual, which is merely a continuation of the Vedic ritual).

We also know representations of Viṣṇu with four or five heads, but here the lateral heads are generally the heads of animals that recall the theriomorphic avatars of Viṣṇu: boar, lion, fish. On the other hand, the sectarian Vaiṣṇava concept of the four *vyūhas*, the four "unfoldings" of the god, which, through successive levels, allow him to pass from the supreme nonmanifest state to the manifest state (the names of the *vyūhas* are borrowed from the mythology of Kṛṣṇa and appear in the MBh), remained sectarian and was not translated into iconography. This may be a supplementary confirmation of the nonsectarian character of the myth of the decapitation of the fifth head of Brahmā. Given the position of Viṣṇu with regard to sacrificial values, he naturally takes the title of the supreme Brahman, and no one dares to contest his title. He has no need to debate with Brahmā over a superiority that is recognized to be his from the start (except for the exigencies of Śaiva mythology).

The generalization of the iconographic theme of five-headed divinities is not a chance occurrence: it expresses the fact that every Hindu god, no matter what his level in the pantheon, represents for his devotee the totality of bhakti, the impossible summation of prosperity in this world: *bhukti,* and deliverance in the other world: *mukti.* If it is a relatively secondary divinity like Bhairava or Hanumān (who have the function of "guardians of the territory" of the superior god), he more or less implicitly takes on the role of intermediary to the higher god on behalf of the devotees who appeal to them.

M.Bi./d.w.

Deva/Asura: Celestial Gods and "Demons" in Hinduism

The opposition between the *devas*—celestial gods—and the *asuras* (is "demons" the correct translation?) is less a myth than an omnipresent motif in Indian mythology, a motif that merits a clarification of meaning.

The theme is already present in Vedic literature, although it is difficult to tell how the two were originally distinguished from one another, since the god Varuṇa, for example, is often considered to be an *asura.* The *devas* and *asuras* have the same father: Prajāpati, the primordial Progenitor, but the *asuras* are the older and stronger sons. They would invariably be victorious in the conflicts in which they fight the gods if the gods did not resort to a ruse or a benefactor (such as Viṣṇu, with his three steps) to defeat them. But it is clear that, in spite of the strength of the *asuras,* it is the gods who are to receive the sacrifice, who are the keepers of sacrificial knowledge, and whose place in the ritual assures the order of the world. Yet on the Vedic level, where *deva* and *asura* seem to be associated with the sky, their opposition is limited to the ritual domain. This fundamental relationship will not vary; it will become more detailed through various types of oppositions, but these oppositions will leave intact the neutral "nature" of the *devas* and *asuras* when they are taken individually. If *deva* is translated as "god," it is tempting to translate *asura* as "demon," but this opposition has for us a moral connotation that is not appropriate in the Indian context.

This becomes even clearer in classical Hinduism, where the war between the *devas* and *asuras* is a recurrent theme (avatar myths, epics). Their relationship thus remains, collectively, one of hostility. The gods become the sole legitimate occupants of heaven—*svarga*—while the *asuras* inhabit the infernal regions. The space that divides the higher luminous sphere from the kingdom of darkness is occupied by the earth inhabited by men—which logically becomes the place where the hereditary enemies meet in battle. The society of the gods is organized like the society of the *asuras,* after the model of human society: there is no mention of castes, but there is a king of the gods—always Indra—and a royal chaplain, Bṛhaspati ("the master of the ritual formula"), of the Aṅgiras family. Similarly, there is a king of the *asuras* whose name varies from one myth to another, and a chaplain of the *asuras*—who is as much a Brahman as the chaplain of the gods—named Śukrācārya, of the family of the Bhṛgus, to whom are attributed powers that exceed those of Bṛhaspati and who is the real source of the might of the *asuras.* When the triple world—*trailokya*—is in order, the celestial gods receive the sacrificial offerings of men: this is the state of dharma in which the hierarchy of beings is respected. When the *asuras* defeat the gods, they drive them out of heaven and receive the sacrificial offerings in their place. The normal order is reversed, and catastrophe is inevitable, for the triple world cannot continue under these conditions. At such times Viṣṇu "descends" to reestablish dharma and to return everyone to his proper place, with the *devas* above and the *asuras* below. But Viṣṇu is no longer a simple Vedic god of the sacrifice, a *deva* in the ordinary sense. His divinity is of the highest order, and it is to him that the oblations that men offer to the *devas* ultimately go. Correspondingly, the *devas* have lost their role as the models of human sacrificial activity. Meanwhile, on earth the Vedic sacrifice has practically disappeared, and sacrifices (*yāga* and no longer *yajña*) are offered in temples to the gods of bhakti: to Viṣṇu, Śiva, the Goddess, and all the great regional gods connected with Viṣṇu or Śiva.

There is a new element in the *deva/asura* conflicts that expresses this new universal dimension: even when the king of the *asuras* succeeds in occupying the throne of Indra, it is possible for a particular *asura,* preferably his heir, to refuse the fait accompli, more from devotion to Viṣṇu and to dharma than devotion to the *devas.* The gods become mere terms of a series which also includes Brahmans, cows, and the Vedas—that is, they become parts of the dharma of which Viṣṇu is the sole guarantor. Prahlāda, son of Hiraṇyakaśipu, king of the *asuras* and a great devotee of Viṣṇu, was to reign over the underworld after his father was killed by Narasiṃha and Indra was reinstated on his throne. Vibhīṣaṇa, the brother of Rāvaṇa, was to rule over Laṅkā, the kingdom of the *rākṣasas* (a variant of *asuras* in the classical mythology: Rāvaṇa is the reincarnation of Hiraṇyakaśipu), when Rāma killed Rāvaṇa and won back Sītā. Prahlāda and Vibhīṣaṇa are good *asuras-rākṣasas.*

The strength of the *asuras* may be connected with that of their chaplain (as in the myth of Yayāti), but the most frequent theme is that of the boon that Brahmā gives to the king of the *asuras* which guarantees him nearly total invulnerability; yet Viṣṇu will continually rely on trickery to strike the heel of this Hindu Achilles. Śukrācārya and Brahmā are clearly equivalent terms here. They establish a connection between the power of the *asuras* and the ritual, since Śukra is the Brahman priest of the *asuras,* whereas Brahmā represents precisely the knowledge and power of the ritual. They thus illustrate the possible deviation from the ritual order (and from retribution for actions) that is not integrated into the order of bhakti—in which Viṣṇu is all-powerful—and the necessity to integrate the ritual order into the comprehensive order of bhakti. The triple world is no more than a small part of the universe, even if it is the only part in which anything actually happens, but the dharma that guides it becomes finely tuned with the rest of the universe.

On the level of popular mythology, i.e., the one that is current and locally diversified, the theme of the opposition of the *devas* and the *asuras* has an application that also presupposes the intervention of bhakti: the king of the *asuras* can transform himself into a *bhakta* at the moment when he is killed by the great local god (a form of Śiva or Viṣṇu) or by the Goddess. His death in battle with the god becomes a warrior's sacrifice that assures him of his salvation. He thus becomes the guardian of the great god in his temple. This is a motif that makes it possible to integrate an inferior, impure divinity (the king of the *asuras* has by definition the rank of a Kṣatriya, is carnivorous, and requires blood sacrifices) into a pure temple; to transpose in the temple the hierarchical relationship that unites the pure and impure castes. And this is not the only mode of articulation of the pure and the impure within the Hindu pantheon.

M.Bi./d.w.

BIBLIOGRAPHY

G. DUMÉZIL, *Mitra-Varuna: Essai sur deux représentations indo-européennes de la souveraineté* (4th ed., Paris 1948); *The Destiny of the Warrior* (Chicago 1970). J. GONDA, *The Vedic God Mitra* (Leiden 1972). F. B. J. KUIPER, "The Basic Concept of Vedic Religion," *History of Religions* 15, no. 2 (1975); *Varuṇa and Vidūṣaka: On the Origin of the Sanskrit Drama* (Amsterdam, Oxford, and New York 1979). H. LUDERS, *Varuṇa*, 2 vols., 1: *Varuṇa und die Wasser* (Göttingen 1951); 2: *Varuṇa und das Ṛta* (Göttingen 1959). A. A. MACDONELL, *Vedic Mythology* (Indian reprint, Varanasi 1963).

VASIṢṬHA/VIŚVĀMITRA AND THE SEPARATION OF THE PRIESTLY AND ROYAL FUNCTIONS

Vasiṣṭha and Viśvāmitra are two *ṛṣis* that a very rich mythology usually portrays as two enemies. From the Vedic period, one of them was known as the best Brahman priest (one of the celebrants of the Vedic sacrifice, the one who presides) and the other as a *ṛṣi* of royal origin who is nevertheless accepted as the chaplain of a king, and a great number of Vedic hymns are attributed to him. The Vedic information is fragmentary and does not form a coherent whole. But in classical Hinduism, beginning with the epics, Vasiṣṭha is a symbol of the pure Brahman, son of Brahmā himself or of the Vedic gods Mitra and Varuṇa. Viśvāmitra, on the other hand, is the "upstart," who, born a Kṣatriya, sought to acquire the quality of a Brahman, which is normally acquired only by birth. The confrontation between the two individuals has consequently been interpreted for a long time as one of the echoes of a historical conflict between Brahmans and Kṣatriyas, when the Kṣatriyas rebelled against the superiority of the Brahmans. The meaning of these mythic stories is mainly ideological, even if Vasiṣṭha and Viśvāmitra did once exist. The confrontation, which is found elsewhere, is the expression of a very particular balance that regulates the relationship between Brahmans and Kṣatriyas. Although they are deprived of all material power, Brahmans are superior because they are the experts in the Vedic sacrifice, the source of all wealth in this world, and because they have a very pure way of life. What the Kṣatriyas have is strength, but even that strength would be denied them if the Brahmans did not sacrifice on their behalf and receive their gifts, thereby sanctifying the obligatory impurity of Kṣatriya customs. The equilibrium of society rests on the strict separation of the priestly and royal functions, which involves a parallel separation of the social categories performing those functions: a Brahman can only be a Brahman and cannot rule over a kingdom; a Kṣatriya can only be a king and warrior and cannot be his own priest or keep his wealth for himself. It is characteristic that the alleged revolt by the Kṣatriyas expressed in the myths consists, not in denying the power appropriate to Brahmans, but in envying it and claiming it, in other words, in combining the two powers. The sacrosanct separation is thus removed and there is chaos.

We know that the (historical?) exception represented by Viśvāmitra led to an abundant literature. His confrontation with Vasiṣṭha is concretized in several different accounts that are generally given in isolation. There are many epic and Purāṇic versions, and they are rather divergent, though the message seems to be always the same. We have chosen here the version of the *Rāmāyaṇa,* which has the advantage of giving in a single account the principal episodes of the struggle between the two *ṛṣis* by joining them with a common thematic thread. In the *Rāmāyaṇa,* Vasiṣṭha is the chaplain and counselor of King Daśaratha, the father of Rāma. Daśaratha receives a visit from Viśvāmitra (1.18), who asks him to entrust Rāma to him for a brief period of time, but Vasiṣṭha must intervene to secure Daśaratha's consent. At this point the two *ṛṣis* are at last reconciled. A few chapters later (1.51–65), however, their quarrels are reported to Rāma.

Viśvāmitra, the son of King Gādhi, goes around the world with his army. He arrives at Vasiṣṭha's hermitage, where he is received with hospitality. They strike up a conversation. Vasiṣṭha asks his guest if his kingdom is prospering. He then insists on feeding the entire army. To do so, he calls his cow Śabalā, who provides him with all that he needs for a sumptuous feast. The dazzled Viśvāmitra offers Vasiṣṭha one hundred ordinary cows in exchange for Vasiṣṭha's cow. Vasiṣṭha refuses, because all of his activity as a Brahman depends on the cow, since he cannot sacrifice without her. Viśvāmitra makes an even better offer, which is still rejected. Viśvāmitra then tries to take the cow away by force, but at Vasiṣṭha's bidding she emits warriors who proceed to destroy Viśvāmitra's army. Viśvāmitra's hundred sons attack Vasiṣṭha, who reduces them to ashes in a fit of rage.

Viśvāmitra then leaves his kingdom to his only surviving son, withdraws into the forest, and practices austerities in honor of Śiva, who appears to him and asks him what he wants. Viśvāmitra replies that he wants the knowledge of all weapons, including magic weapons. Armed with this panoply, he presents himself at Vasiṣṭha's hermitage more boastful than ever and begins by setting it on fire. All Vasiṣṭha has

Ascetic among his five fires. Photo P. Amado.

to do is counter with his Brahman's stick—the *brahmadaṇḍa*—to annul the effect of Viśvāmitra's weapons. Viśvāmitra realizes that the power of the Kṣatriya is nothing next to that of the Brahman. He must purify himself in order to become a Brahman. He goes south with his principal wife and devotes himself to great austerities. At the end of a thousand years, Brahmā appears to him and bestows on him the title of royal *ṛṣi*. Viśvāmitra is not satisfied and begins a new period of asceticism.

At this moment, the pious king Triśaṅku takes it into his head to offer a sacrifice in order to ascend to heaven with his human body. Vasiṣṭha, his chaplain, tells him this is impossible. Vasiṣṭha's sons are asked and also refuse to perform this sacrifice, which their father has declined to undertake. Triśaṅku threatens to go to see another priest. Vasiṣṭha's sons then condemn him to be a *caṇḍāla* (untouchable). He is abandoned by all. Triśaṅku calls on Viśvāmitra, who is moved by compassion when he sees him. The fallen king protests his innocence and asks for his help. Viśvāmitra agrees to undertake the sacrifice and to summon other *ṛṣis* to help him: Triśaṅku will ascend to heaven in his human form. Viśvāmitra dispatches his sons to search for the other *ṛṣis* and bring them back. They all come except for Vasiṣṭha's sons, who consider the sacrifice even more impossible now, with a Kṣatriya celebrant and an untouchable sacrificer. Viśvāmitra reduces them to ashes (with the fire of his anger) and condemns them to be reborn seven hundred times as untouchables. His curse is effective. He then undertakes the sacrifice, but when he invites the gods to receive their share, they abstain. Then, confident of the power that he was given for his ascetic ardor (*tapas*), Viśvāmitra interrupts the sacrifice and sends Triśaṅku to heaven by his own power. Triśaṅku ascends, but Indra sends him away, because he has been cursed by his teacher (Vasiṣṭha and his sons) and does not merit the rewards of heaven. Triśaṅku calls on Viśvāmitra to help. Viśvāmitra breaks Triśaṅku's fall and sets out to create another heaven for his protégé, beginning with another Big Dipper to the south. The gods intervene and stop him from pursuing his work. Viśvāmitra explains that he has promised Triśaṅku and he cannot go back on his word. He convinces the gods to let the constellation he has created remain in the sky and to let Triśaṅku live in it, shining like a star. The sacrifice is completed, and they all return to their respective dwelling places (another version of the story of Triśaṅku appears in *Harivaṃśa* 1.12–13).

Viśvāmitra leaves the south, where his austerities have been prevented from achieving their purpose. He settles in Puṣkara and begins to practice *tapas* again. At that moment, King Ambarīṣa of Ayodhyā begins to perform a sacrifice. But the sacrificial victim is stolen by Indra. The celebrant directs the king to replace the victim quickly, for the disappearance of a designated victim is a serious sin. The king searches for a victim and is ready to buy one at the price of thousands of cows. He encounters the *ṛṣi* Brahman Ṛcīka with his wife and children and offers to buy one of his sons for one hundred thousand cows, in order to make the child into the sacrificial victim. Ṛcīka does not want to sell his oldest son, and his wife does not want to be separated from her youngest son. The middle son, Śunaḥśepa, volunteers to be the victim, and his father receives the one hundred thousand cows and a pile of gold coins. Ambarīṣa takes Śunaḥśepa with him. On the way, he stops at Puṣkara to rest. There Śunaḥśepa meets Viśvāmitra, his maternal uncle, and asks him to free him and to allow Ambarīṣa to achieve his desires in another way. Viśvāmitra asks his sons to take Śunaḥśepa's place. The sons refuse. The father curses them and condemns them to be reborn on earth as untouchable dog eaters for one thousand years, like Vasiṣṭha's sons. He advises Śunaḥśepa to let himself be tied to the sacrificial stake and to sing praises to Indra and Viṣṇu. He will then be freed. He does so and Indra grants him a life of one thousand years and Ambarīṣa is rewarded for his sacrifice. Viśvāmitra resumes his austerities for another thousand years (another version of the story of Śunaḥśepa appears in *Aitareya Brāhmaṇa* 7.13–18).

One thousand years elapse and Brahmā and all the gods come to reward Viśvāmitra by giving him the title of *ṛṣi*. Viśvāmitra continues his austerities because this does not satisfy him. After a long time, the nymph Menakā comes to bathe in the lake at Puṣkara. The *ṛṣi* falls in love with her and lives with her for ten years, thus wiping out all the fruits of his austerities. Viśvāmitra realizes that this is a trick that the gods have played on him. He dismisses Menakā and sets out for the mountains in the north.

The gods are frightened by his new austerities. They ask Brahmā to reward him with the title of *maharṣi* (great *ṛṣi*). Viśvāmitra asks Brahmā if this means that he has finally mastered his senses. The answer is no; he will have to prolong his *tapas* once again. During the summer, he sits between four fires, under the sun that acts as the fifth fire; he remains unprotected during the monsoon rains and lives in the water during the winter. This goes on for a thousand years. The gods and their king Indra are worried. They send the nymph Rambhā to Viśvāmitra, but because she fears the wrath of the ascetic, Indra promises her help in the form of a cuckoo with a spellbinding song. Viśvāmitra senses a trap; he angrily curses Rambhā and turns her into a stone statue, but he promises her that a very glorious Brahman (Vasiṣṭha) will free her. Yet he has once again consumed all the merit of his *tapas* in the fire of his anger.

Viśvāmitra resolves never to get angry again and not to speak or eat or even to breathe for hundreds of years, until he has reached the status of Brahman. To that end, he settles in the east. This time he does not allow himself to be distracted from his vow, even by Indra who comes to tempt him, disguised as a Brahman. Smoke comes out of his head, which disturbs the three worlds. All the inhabitants of heaven ask Brahmā to put an end to his *tapas* for fear that he will set the worlds on fire. He must be granted his wish. Brahmā therefore goes to inform him that he has now become a Brahman and grants him long life. Viśvāmitra then asks that Vasiṣṭha recognize him as a Brahman. Vasiṣṭha accedes to the gods' request and proclaims that Viśvāmitra is a *brahmarṣi*. That is how Viśvāmitra became a Brahman and the greatest ascetic of them all.

The exception proves the rule: Viśvāmitra had to spend thousands of years practicing harsh austerities to attain the status of a Brahman. He was delayed when, not fully master of himself—which is supposed to be the virtue of a Brahman, on the model of the yogi—he was on several occasions tempted to abuse the power acquired through his *tapas* to perform remarkable feats or else simply yielded to the temptation of love or anger. He covered the entire spectrum of possible downfalls before attaining perfect mastery of himself. The slow ascension described in the *Rāmāyaṇa* did not win everyone's approval, for Viśvāmitra appears in a less flattering light in other myths. See, for example, the story of Hariścandra in *Mārkaṇḍeya Purāṇa* 1.7–9, in which Viśvāmitra is depicted as merciless; the story of King Kalmāṣapāda in *Mahābhārata* 1.174–76; and the story of the river Sarasvatī, ibid. 9.42, in which Vasiṣṭha is the paragon of all virtues, especially patience, in the face of the odious Viśvāmitra. In every way, this upstart Brahman retains something of his Kṣatriya origin.

M.Bi./g.h.

The Main Myth of the *Mahābhārata*

The *Mahābhārata* (MBh), the longer of the two Sanskrit epics, has been translated or adapted into several of the modern languages of India and plays an enormous role in the traditional education of the Hindu consciousness even today. There is a single myth that unfolds throughout the course of its eighteen sections. But it is filled with secondary myths meant to illustrate a point of doctrine or to bring consolation. There are also many didactic discourses, and books twelve and thirteen consist essentially of the teaching given by Bhīṣma to Yudhiṣṭhira.

Only the principal myth in its most significant articulations will be discussed here, with an emphasis on what it shares with the myth of the *Rāmāyaṇa* (R); for there is a clear parallelism between the two epics. Both give an account of the duties of a perfect king devoted to Brahmans—and from this, the duties of all categories of human beings—and have as their narrative theme the myth of an avatar: Rāma in the R, and Kṛṣṇa in the MBh. However, whereas the R presents the story of the exploits of Rāma, the perfect prince and incarnation of Viṣṇu, the MBh has a much more complex narrative plot, duplicating the avatar Kṛṣṇa in himself and in Arjuna, the ideal prince. The MBh is far less the tale of the epic deeds of Kṛṣṇa than the tale of the epic deeds of the five Pāṇḍava brothers; Kṛṣṇa is present only to guarantee by his presence and by his advice the ultimate victory of the Pāṇḍavas and its profound import for the triumph of dharma. The *Harivaṃśa*, the supplement to the MBh, traces the epic deeds of Kṛṣṇa beginning with his birth.

The simplified account that will be given here necessarily refers to the complicated genealogical ties that unite heroes and heroines, ties that contribute to the originality of the MBh in relation to the other epic. Bear in mind that the system of kinship in the epic involves preferential cross-cousin marriage (a man's marriage to the daughter of his mother's brother or his father's sister). Cross-cousin marriage has as a corollary the importance of the relationship between brothers-in-law (and cross-cousins), a very close relationship indeed, and of the role of the mother's brother and (eventually) the father's sister: two brothers-in-law (the husband and the brother of the same woman) are allies and can count on one another in all circumstances. Normally a man and his mother's brother also give mutual assistance; failure to do so implies a serious disorder. This system of kinship, sketched here only in broad terms, is still known and practiced in South India.

From the myth of the avatar the MBh gets its "date," at the juncture between two yugas, but this chronological framework is very loose and has no effect on the unfolding of the plot, which mainly takes place on earth. In fact, the two yugas, the Dvāpara and the Kali (the two worst), are transformed into *asuras* who become incarnate, one (Kali) as the usurping prince Duryodhana, the son of the blind Dhṛtarāṣṭra, and the other as his mother's brother Śakuni, who will be his tool. Duryodhana has ninety-nine brothers, all *rākṣasas* (demonic and cannibalistic beings) who have become incarnate. He challenges the kingship of the five Pāṇḍava brothers, who represent dharmic kingship. Though the five brothers are regarded as the sons of Pāṇḍu, when a curse prevented Pāṇḍu from uniting with his two wives, Kuntī and Mādrī, the first three sons were actually engendered in Kuntī by the gods Dharma, Vāyu, and Indra (the king of the gods), while the last two, the twins Nakula and Sahadeva, were engendered in Mādrī by the twin gods called the Aśvins. These are thus divine incarnations. When Pāṇḍu dies young and his second wife, Mādrī (the sister of an incarnate *asura*, Śalya), ascends his funeral pyre, the Pāṇḍavas are raised at the court of Hāstinapura, the capital of the dynasty of the Kurus, with their cousins, the Kauravas, the hundred sons of Dhṛtarāṣṭra. Their mother, Kuntī, also takes shelter in Hāstinapura. Dhṛtarāṣṭra, the older brother of Pāṇḍu, must take the place of his dead brother, but he assumes a kingship for which he is not qualified because of his blindness. Furthermore, he is placed under the moral authority of his uncle Bhīṣma, the Kṣatriya who renounced both throne and marriage and whose complete detachment assures his perfection, and of Bhīṣma's younger brother Vidura. Bhīṣma is the incarnation of Dyaus, the sky, whereas Vidura, whose status is inferior because his mother is a Śūdrā, is the incarnation of Dharma.

From the very start, the situation is explosive. The tutelary presence of Bhīṣma (associated with the name of the capital, Hāstinapura, "the elephantine city"—which could also be the heavenly capital, since King Indra has an elephant for his mount) seems to create a heaven on earth. Thus, Hāstinapura could be heaven, normally inhabited by the gods and placed under the sovereignty of Indra. But there, next to the gods who are incarnate in the Pāṇḍavas and Vidura, are the one hundred demonic sons of Dhṛtarāṣṭra, placed in a position of superiority because of the role assumed by their father. At first Dhṛtarāṣṭra exercises an

Memorial to a warrior killed in combat in the company of his wife. Hampi Museum (Karnataka). Photo M. Biardeau.

impartial rule, with the help of Bhīṣma and Vidura, but the appetites of his elder son, Duryodhana, soon cause him to deviate from his course. This, if we have deciphered it correctly, sets the scene for a war between the *devas* and the *asuras* in which the *devas* will inevitably be routed from their domain, heaven, but which will ultimately end in their favor, thanks to the intervention of the avatar.

However, the other theme dear to the myths of the avatar, the confrontation between Brahman and Kṣatriya, is not absent. When Prince Drupada and the Brahman Droṇa study the Veda together under the watchful eye of Droṇa's father, they become friends. When Drupada becomes king, Droṇa the Brahman, who is so poor that he cannot find milk for his son, comes to ask Drupada for help on the basis of their former friendship. Droṇa is also ambitious and would really like to be called the king's friend. To this end, he obtains arms and becomes proficient in their use under the tutelage of the Brahman warrior Paraśurāma. But a Brahman cannot be a warrior. In addition, Drupada refuses to remember the former friendship, which became impossible as a consequence of their insuperable differences. Droṇa appears to have no intention of serving the king as chaplain or minister, which would have been appropriate for a Brahman, and the friendship that he claims would exclude such subordination. The problem is posed in such a way that it is no more Droṇa's fault than Drupada's. Rather, it is the divine order that from behind the scenes uses men to play its own game. It was the divine order that made Pāṇḍu disappear and placed the Pāṇḍavas at the mercy of their paternal uncle.

Droṇa, repulsed and still poor, goes to take refuge with his brother-in-law, the Brahman warrior Kṛpa (another symptom of a crisis situation), who is the master-at-arms of the cousins at the court of Dhṛtarāṣṭra. Droṇa in turn becomes their master-at-arms and quickly singles out the Pāṇḍava Arjuna as his best student. As his honorarium, he makes the princes promise to make a secret vow come true on the day when their military education is completed. Droṇa's vow is that the cousins wage war on Drupada to avenge him. The promise is fulfilled; the victory over Drupada is effected mainly by Arjuna, who brings Drupada to his master, bound hand and foot. Droṇa, magnanimous in his way, sets Drupada free and gives him half the kingdom, keeping the better half for himself. His dream of equality thus comes true, and he offers Drupada his friendship a second time. But Drupada can think only of vengeance; he will perform a sacrifice to get a son who can defeat Droṇa. He knows that the power of a Kṣatriya alone cannot get the better of a Brahman who combines his own power with that of a warrior. From Drupada's sacrifice is born not only a son, Dhṛṣṭadyumna, the incarnation of the sacrificial fire (the god Agni), but also a daughter, Kṛṣṇā Draupadī, the incarnation of Śrī or of Śacī, the wife of Indra. From that time on, Drupada dreams of having Arjuna himself for his son-in-law. And indeed Draupadī becomes the wife of the five Pāṇḍavas.

Finally the avatar himself becomes one of the protagonists, although he explicitly delegates his tasks to the Pāṇḍavas, depending on the circumstances. His special tie with the Pāṇḍavas is expressed in terms of kinship: Kuntī, the mother of the three elder sons, is his father's sister; she is also known as Pṛthā, a name that makes her related to the earth—Pṛthivī. But Kṛṣṇa has a much closer tie with Arjuna, the third Pāṇḍava, since the two of them are incarnations of the two inseparable *ṛṣis,* Nara and Nārāyaṇa. Since Nārāyaṇa is a name of Viṣṇu, of whom Kṛṣṇa is the avatar, it was necessary to work through the creation of these two *ṛṣis* (ascetic "visionaries," assuring communication between the world of men and the invisible world) in order to forge the profound unity of the pair Arjuna/Kṛṣṇa. In times of crisis, it is not only Viṣṇu-Nārāyaṇa who becomes incarnate, says the MBh; it is Nārāyaṇa who divides himself into Nara and Nārāyaṇa in order to come down among men when it is time to fight. Arjuna is the incarnation of Nara, whereas Kṛṣṇa is the incarnation of Nārāyaṇa. Since they are incarnations of *ṛṣis,* the asceticism of the renunciant is never far from them: Kṛṣṇa remembers that he is a yogi and Arjuna is associated with this yoga. To seal this tie in terms of kinship, it is logical for Kṛṣṇa to give his sister Subhadrā to Arjuna in marriage. Thus they that were cross-cousins become brothers-in-law.

This ontological identity between Kṛṣṇa and Arjuna clarifies the relationship between the first three Pāṇḍavas: the eldest, the son of the god Dharma, is normally the king at the explicit level of the narrative. But it is clear that his sovereignty is of a special type: a mediocre warrior who leaves the most difficult tasks for his brother, he is always tempted to renounce power and retire into the forest. His sovereignty is the sovereignty of the value that he represents, dharma. Together the five brothers constitute a sovereignty that is subordinate to dharma. This is symbolized by the fact that Yudhiṣṭhira, also known as the Dharmarāja, "the king of dharma" or "King Dharma," is at their head. It is also significant that Dharma and Dharmarāja are names of Yama, the god of death. The group of Pāṇḍavas is on earth for the sole purpose of making sure that the earth and the Kuru dynasty weather the crisis that threatens to sink them. The entire group is there to wage war, even if Arjuna is more specifically in charge by virtue of his relation to the avatar. The second brother, Bhīma, the son of Vāyu, is in radical opposition to his older brother. Vāyu, the wind, is characterized by strength, and so is Bhīma. But Vāyu is also the breath of life, the first and last manifestation of all life. And Bhīma is the advocate of all that allows the world to remain alive and well. He can be brutal if this is necessary to dispel a threat, and he believes in the value of desire as a motive for action, whereas his brothers preach detachment. His qualities of violence and blindness are such that he readily gives in to Draupadī's every whim (she is the common wife of the five brothers). He is as close to the interests of this world as Yudhiṣṭhira is removed from them, but he always submits to his older brother and even to Arjuna.

If Arjuna comes third in line, though he appears to be the most important, it is because his role assumes submission to the opposed values represented by his older brothers. For therein lies the role of the king, to make it possible for all his subjects to live in peace according to their dharma and their wishes (including the renunciants in the forest). For that purpose, he must be perfectly disinterested but an invincible warrior. Arjuna, who is not the king in the epic, actually represents the ideal of the king.

Everything makes the twins, Nakula and Sahadeva, inferior to their older brothers, even though they identify themselves with them in all of their undertakings and serve them, Sahadeva being closer to Yudhiṣṭhira, and Nakula being closer to Arjuna and Bhīma. The hierarchical structure of society requires the existence of faithful executors without a will of their own. The twins at the same time represent all that in the society of the three worlds is inferior to the Brahmans and the Kṣatriyas (and, hence, the gods). It is not by accident that the twins have a mother's brother who is an *asura.* This recalls that the *asura* is evil, not by nature, but only if he refuses his inferior position.

Open animosity between the cousins soon breaks out, all the more because Yudhiṣṭhira wins the affection of everyone and Dhṛtarāṣṭra quickly designates him crown prince: as the eldest son of Pāṇḍu, the deceased king, Yudhiṣṭhira has a legitimate claim to the throne. But Pāṇḍu, while he was still alive, went to the forest in order to let his blind older brother, despite his handicap, take power in his name. Duryodhana does not give up. He is all the less resigned because he has a ferocious appetite for power that he pits against the detachment of Yudhiṣṭhira. Childish pranks are soon followed by criminal outrages. When, thanks to Vidura's warnings, the Pāṇḍavas escape from the burning house of lac, they undergo an initial period of clandestine life in the forest. Bhīma kills his first *rākṣasas,* and he even inherits a *rākṣasa* son after living for a while with the sister of one of his victims. This is a valuable alliance. The five brothers and their mother take refuge with a Brahman. Dressed as young Brahman students, they do not leave until they have liberated the area from a *rākṣasa.* On the way they join a troop of Brahmans who are heading for the celebration of the *svayaṃvara* of Draupadī: the princess is called upon to "choose" a husband for herself, and Drupada, her father, has designed a test that he believes only Arjuna can pass. The winner of the contest is the one that Draupadī must "choose." As expected, Arjuna wins the contest while still disguised as a Brahman and without being recognized. This Kṣatriya, whom Droṇa had equipped with a *brahmāstra* (a magical weapon that symbolizes the power of the Brahman), thus claims to possess a power superior to that of an ordinary Kṣatriya. He combines within himself something of the power of the Brahmans and something of the power of the Kṣatriyas, which must assure his invincibility and at the same time make him the privileged defender of the Brahmans and the Brahmanic order, in other words, of dharma.

It is on the occasion of the *svayaṃvara* that Kṛṣṇa appears for the first time in the narrative, along with his older brother Balarāma. It is also at this point that the mysterious Karṇa appears among the competitors, the adopted son of a Sūta (an inferior caste, "mixed," from the union of a Brahman and a Kṣatriya). He is really the son that Kuntī bore to Sūrya, the sun god, before her marriage and that she abandoned after she gave birth to him in secret. He will not know his origin until after he has firmly committed himself to the faction of Duryodhana. Nor will the Pāṇḍavas find out that he is their brother until after his death on the battlefield. On the day of the *svayaṃvara,* Draupadī refuses to let him try his luck because he is not a Kṣatriya. Duryodhana makes him a king on the spot, but this kingship in itself is not sufficient to give him the quality of a Kṣatriya: this is a violation of dharma and Draupadī will not be satisfied with such an artifice.

Arjuna therefore wins Draupadī, the incarnation of Śrī or Śacī, and she will always secretly favor him. But as a result of an involuntary decision made by Kuntī, Draupadī must marry all five brothers, an anomaly that the myth must justify in several ways, but that also underscores the unity of the five brothers. The brothers from then on possess the woman who is the incarnation of Śrī, the prosperity of a kingdom governed according to dharma, and they have as a brother-in-law the incarnation of Agni, the sacrificial fire. They have also already chosen a Brahman chaplain, so they are in a position to assume power, at least in normal times. A supplementary dimension takes account of the time of crisis, the time of the avatar, which is the time of the epic. In the course of a solitary pilgrimage around India, Arjuna meets Subhadrā, Kṛṣṇa's sister, with whom he immediately falls in love. Kṛṣṇa gives him permission to take his sister away, and Arjuna persuades Draupadī to accept this secondary wife by introducing her as his servant, dressed as a cowherd, a *gopālikā.* After this marriage, Draupadī bears a son to each of her five husbands, and Subhadrā also has a son by Arjuna.

Yudhiṣṭhira celebrates his coronation with the solemn sacrifice of the *rājasūya* (the consecration of the king). The sacrifice is preceded by the more or less compulsory submission of all the surrounding peoples and also by the death of King Jarāsandha, an enemy of Kṛṣṇa whom Kṛṣṇa had reserved as a victim for Bhīma. At this point the two parts of the biography of Kṛṣṇa are joined in the *Harivaṃśa.* Yudhiṣṭhira is at the height of his splendor, and Duryodhana's jealousy is at its peak. In order to obtain through deceit what he cannot get in any other way, Duryodhana plots with his mother's brother Śakuni, with Karṇa, and with his brother Duḥśāsana. A dice game is organized at the court of Dhṛtarāṣṭra (the ritual of the *rājasūya* itself includes a dice game) in which Yudhiṣṭhira must play against Śakuni, who plays on behalf of his nephew Duryodhana. Yudhiṣṭhira is inexperienced, and Śakuni, a clever and dishonest player, is sure to win. During the first round, the Dharmarāja loses all his possessions, including his brothers, himself, and their common wife. But she refuses to become Duryodhana's slave: Did Yudhiṣṭhira have the right to gamble her away? No one dares to answer her question, and tension is high in the assembly, when suddenly ominous noises are heard, which make Dhṛtarāṣṭra, Duryodhana's father, decide to free Draupadī and to grant her a wish. She quickly asks for freedom for her husbands. But a second round of dice is organized immediately, and this time the stakes are victory or a twelve-year exile in the forest, followed by a year-long period during which the five brothers and their wife would have to live completely incognito. If they should be recognized, they would have to leave for the forest for another twelve years. Śakuni wins again, and Duryodhana fervently hopes never to allow Yudhiṣṭhira the opportunity to seize power again. This day marks the beginning of his reign. In fact, the crucial turn is at the end of the first round of dice when Draupadī annuls its results: after this, her fate remains tied to that of her five husbands. She goes into exile with them, scorning Karṇa's suggestions and Duryodhana's advances. Śrī—the prosperity of the kingdom, inseparable from dharma—goes away with the Pāṇḍavas, thus signifying that they have lost power only temporarily and that Duryodhana will be unable to rule. The narrative could not express Draupadī's personal choice: it is she who saves the Pāṇḍavas by deciding to follow them.

So they depart for the forest, the long sojourn into the wilderness assigned to the renunciant (but also to the hunter-king), in which the Pāṇḍavas live a life that is a mixture of the life of ascetics (in particular, they live in sexual abstinence despite the presence of their wife) and the life of hunter-kings. It is a sojourn marked by significant events, among them an attempted abduction of Draupadī by the brother-in-law of the enemy cousins, during which each of the brothers affirms his own role and prepares himself for what is to follow: it is clear that the exercise of kingship cannot do without this renunciation, even if in reality it does not necessarily include living in the forest but takes more inward forms. The main event is the five-year period that Arjuna spends in heaven with Indra, his father, after he has gained access to heaven through harsh asceticism and the grace of Rudra-Śiva. In *svarga* (heaven), Arjuna prepares himself for his earthly role by triumphing over the *asuras,* the enemies of the gods, with the weapons given him by the gods: this is the role of an avatar. Everything moves toward a war between the cousins, in which the fate of dharma is at stake.

The thirteenth year is the crucial one, since, if they are recognized, the five brothers and their wife will have to go back into the forest again. But they have the promise that they will overcome this trial. All six of them appear at the court of Virāṭa, king of the Matsyas ("fish"), in various disguises that serve to hide them and at the same time reveal their individual characters: Yudhiṣṭhira has become a Brahman proficient at dice, and the whole court of Virāṭa spends the entire year playing dice, to the great triumph of Yudhiṣṭhira. Bhīma is a cook, a butcher, and a wrestler. As for the twins, one cares for horses and the other, cows. Draupadī is the queen's maid in charge of hairdressing and the preparation of perfumes and ointments. The most important disguise is that of Arjuna, who presents himself as a eunuch. Eunuchs could not be warriors—and in any case the brothers hid their weapons before they arrived, separately, one by one, at the court of Virāṭa. Arjuna has a woman's name (through which his true identity is transparent: Bṛhannalā, under which can be read Bṛhan-nara, "the great Nara"); he has long, flowing hair; and he is the dancing and singing master to Virāṭa's daughter Uttarā. But Uttarā will become the wife of Abhimanyu, the son of Arjuna and Subhadrā; thus Abhimanyu is Kṛṣṇa's nephew, and the son born to him and Uttarā will inherit the dynasty. As a eunuch, Arjuna maintains a relationship with the princess that will make it possible to weather the crisis; he becomes a symbol of the world that keeps on living and is reborn, a world that is identical with divine play—*māyā* or *līlā.* Arjuna dances and causes the world to dance, like the divinity itself; and it is through this that his royal role becomes apparent.

This entire period, during which Duryodhana's efforts to discover his cousins are all in vain, is a preparation for the war that will follow. The language is that of sacrifice: the war will be a sacrifice of warriors, and the sojourn in disguise at the court of Virāṭa is the requisite period of consecration —*dīkṣā*—during which the sacrificer acquires a divine body for the period of the sacrifice. The *dīkṣā* is conceived as a return to the womb and a rebirth. The period of living in hiding is the passage through the womb, as the narrative notes on two occasions. The year ends with the brilliant reappearance of Arjuna as a warrior. Virāṭa, after losing his general (whom Bhīma secretly killed for pursuing Draupadī too assiduously), is attacked by the Trigartas and the Kauravas. While Virāṭa takes four of the Pāṇḍavas to fight against the Trigartas and wins thanks to them, the Kauravas attack his deserted capital, where Virāṭa's son, Uttara, has been left behind with the eunuch Bṛhannalā (Arjuna). Thus, Arjuna soon finds himself the lone warrior—with Uttara as his charioteer—facing all the great Kaurava warriors: Duryodhana and Karṇa, as well as Droṇa and Bhīṣma. He routs them and takes back the herds of Virāṭa, which they had taken. But now he must reveal his true identity, since the year of probation has just come to an end. At this point, all the Pāṇḍavas acknowledge who they are, and Uttarā marries Abhimanyu.

Duryodhana does not want to relinquish even the smallest part of his kingdom to Yudhiṣṭhira. After last-minute negotiations, war breaks out. The Pāṇḍava side raises seven armies, and Dhṛṣṭadyumna, the brother of Draupadī and the incarnation of Agni (the deified sacrificial fire), serves as commander-in-chief on all fronts, although Arjuna remains technically above him. On the Kaurava side are eleven armies (11 + 7 = 18; there are 18 sections in the MBh, 18 chapters in the *Bhagavadgītā,* and the battle lasts 18 days), and Bhīṣma is the first commander-in-chief. At the end of the tenth day, Bhīṣma is disabled and is replaced by Droṇa, who is killed five days later, after he has killed Drupada. Bhīṣma and Droṇa have never stopped hoping that the Pāṇḍavas will win, but since Bhīṣma is the incarnation of Heaven, and Droṇa is the incarnation of the chaplain of the gods, they must appear in the Kaurava camp in order to symbolize the occupation of heaven by the *asuras.* Both consider themselves Duryodhana's prisoners. When Karṇa, the third commander-in-chief, is killed by Arjuna, he is replaced by Śalya; although he is an incarnate *asura,* Śalya is the mother's brother of the twins; he has contributed to Karṇa's defeat and wants to help his nephews. The victory is won at the cost of some infractions of dharma, the most famous one being the lie that Yudhiṣṭhira must tell to bring about the death of Droṇa, the invincible Brahman warrior: he tells him that his son Aśvatthāman has been killed. The infractions are always either suggested or approved by Kṛṣṇa as being necessary in the crisis of dharma. Kṛṣṇa himself does not fight: he is Arjuna's charioteer and does what Arjuna asks him to do. It is in this capacity that he preaches the *Bhagavadgītā* at the dawn of the first day of battle. The charioteer—*netṛ*—is not only the driver of the chariot but also a guide and counselor. The avatar has delegated his violent function to Arjuna and teaches him spiritual matters. Symmetrically, he has granted Duryodhana the support of his troops (magical?), whom Arjuna annihilates in a great carnage.

Just as the war is thought to be over—only three warriors are left of the Kauravas: the Brahman Kṛpa; the Brahman Aśvatthāman, the son of Droṇa and nephew of Kṛpa; and the Kṣatriya Kṛtavarman, since Duryodhana has died on the battlefield—a last bloody episode ensues. Aśvatthāman, with the aid of Kṛpa and Kṛtavarman, goes to set the Pāṇḍavas' camp on fire during the night and to kill all the survivors. With foresight, Kṛṣṇa had already made the

Bhīṣma on his bed of arrows. Temple of Halebid (Karnataka). Photo Michel Defourny.

Pāṇḍavas leave, but among the victims are Dhṛṣṭadyumna, the murderer of Droṇa, and Draupadī's five sons. Aśvatthāman takes his vengeance. The role of Kṛṣṇa (who withdraws) and of Rudra (who "possesses" Aśvatthāman); the apparition of a hideous black woman, the "Night of Time"; the fire; the holocaust of all the occupants—all of this evokes the end of the world. The episode makes the war the symbolic transposition not only of a conflict between the *devas* and the *asuras* but also of an end of the world at the end of a cosmic cycle. Total annihilation is just barely avoided, but there must be a "remnant" of the sacrifice: with a magic weapon, Aśvatthāman kills all the embryos carried by the women of the Pāṇḍava camp. He also kills Abhimanyu's son, whom Uttarā is carrying in her womb and who now represents the only hope of the dynasty. Kṛṣṇa promises to revive him when Uttarā gives birth to the dead child, thus playing the role of Viṣṇu in the destruction of the world. All lamentations are in vain in the face of so many disappearances. There are not even any guilty parties; the divine order had willed it since the beginning.

The narrative is then interrupted for a long time to make room for the teachings of Bhīṣma—who never seems to finish dying—teachings directed at his grandnephews on kingship, deliverance, and other subjects crucial to dharma. The MBh is a veritable *summa* of Hindu ideology.

The narrative resumes with the great horse sacrifice celebrated by Yudhiṣṭhira, immediately preceded by the birth of Parikṣit, the stillborn child whom Kṛṣṇa, his great-uncle, revives. A penance for sins committed (but they are not really sins), a ritual reprise of the war-sacrifice, and a reaffirmation of Dharmarāja's kingship—the sacrifice is all of these things. Yudhiṣṭhira's brothers reappear beside him with their common spouse and their mother; the others are there too: the blind Dhṛtarāṣṭra and his wife; Kṛpa, the Brahman who also had to fight on Duryodhana's side (probably the incarnation of the Rudras, the celestial host in which Rudra-Śiva is duplicated, and thus closely tied to Aśvatthāman, his nephew, an incarnation of Rudra, of Death, of Anger, etc.); and Vidura, who did not fight. Order is restored, and Parikṣit must grow up (the chronology surrounding the final events fluctuates, to say the least). But the characters of the drama leave the stage one by one. First, Dhṛtarāṣṭra, his wife, Kuntī, and Vidura retire into the forest. Vidura (an incarnation of dharma) dies during a strange encounter with Yudhiṣṭhira where he pours himself out, so to speak, into his nephew, the Dharmarāja. The other three then die in a forest fire accidentally ignited by the sacrificial fire of Dhṛtarāṣṭra. This is once again the theme of fire as a reprise of the funeral pyre. Then comes the turn of Kṛṣṇa and his brother, Balarāma. The members of the clan kill one another at Dvārakā, where they had retreated to be among their own people. Both die as yogis: Balarāma reassumes his form as a serpent (he is the reincarnation of the serpent Śeṣa), while Kṛṣṇa is killed by a stray arrow shot by the hunter Jara ("old age"). Dvārakā is flooded by the waters of the ocean. Arjuna then notices that his weapons have no strength left; his role is finished along with Kṛṣṇa's. This is a signal. After setting the affairs of the kingdom in order and giving the kingship to Parikṣit, the Pāṇḍavas set out together, along with Draupadī, on the road to heaven. Draupadī and four of the brothers die one after the other on the way. Yudhiṣṭhira alone reaches the gate of heaven, accompanied by a dog who has been following him since the beginning of his journey and from whom he refuses to be separated in order to enter heaven. This dog turns out to be the form taken by Yudhiṣṭhira's father, Dharma, in order to put his son's virtue to a final test. In heaven, Yudhiṣṭhira is reunited with all of the warriors killed during the battle, after a brief vision of hell to make him expiate his few sins.

M.Bi./g.h.

BIBLIOGRAPHY

Translations

The Mahābhārata of Krishna-Dwaipāyana Vyāsa, translated by P. C. Roy and K. M. Ganguli, 12 vols. (Calcutta 1883–96). *The Mahābhārata,* translated and edited by J. A. B. van Buitenen (Chicago 1973–78), 3 vols. = Parvans 1–5; also *The Bhagavadgītā in the Mahābhārata* (Chicago 1981).

Studies

M. BIARDEAU, "Études de mythologie hindoue IV et V," *Bulletin de l'École française d'Extrême-Orient,* 1976 and 1978. G. DUMÉZIL, *Mythe et épopé,* 1: *L'idéologie des trois fonctions dans les épopées des peuples indo-européens* (Paris 1968); *Mythe et épopé,* 2: *Types épiques indo-européens: Un héros, un sorcier, un roi* (Paris 1971). H. GEHRTS, *Mahābhārata, das Geschehen und seine Bedeutung* (Bonn 1975). A. HILTEBEITEL, *The Ritual of Battle: Krishna in the Mahābhārata* (Ithaca, NY, 1976).

Abbreviations

MBh *Mahābhārata* (edition of Citrashala Press, Poona)
R *Rāmāyaṇa* (edition of Gita Press, Gorakhpur)

The *Rāmāyaṇa*

Shorter than the *Mahābhārata* (MBh), the *Rāmāyaṇa* (R) is attributed to the *ṛṣi* Vālmīki, although the various Sanskrit versions known to date are sufficiently divergent for the oral tradition to have had an impact on it, as it has on the MBh. It has been adapted or translated into several modern Indian languages. The most widely known non-Sanskrit versions in India are the version of Tulsīdās in Hindi and the version of Kamban in Tamil.

The R seems to be older than the MBh, which mentions the adventure of Rāma on several occasions and gives a summary of it. This is not the case the other way around. However, the story of Rāma Jāmadagnya, the oldest versions of which appear in the MBh, is well known to the *Rāmāyaṇa.* It is true that Paraśurāma appears in the first section of the R, which is thought to be of more recent date than the rest. But it would be difficult to set this section aside in order to bring out the basic structure of the poem—which constantly refers back to it—and we will here consider it as significant as the rest. The same principle guides the analysis of the MBh. In any case, it is more fruitful to compare the two epics than to wonder which came first, since we know that they were both composed over a span of several centuries. The fact that the MBh deals with the lunar dynasty and the R deals with the solar dynasty expresses the complementarity of the two works: the two dynasties together represent the traditional and theoretical division of the Kṣatriyas.

The R is far less didactic in form than the MBh, and the symbolism that it uses emphasizes much less the typical structure of an avatar myth: notably, there is no allusion to the point at which two yugas join to "date" the narrative, as is expected of a descent of Viṣṇu to the earth. This does not mean that the epic ignores this structure, since the account of the fall of Laṅkā and the death of Rāvaṇa makes ample use of images of the end of the world identical to those of the MBh, and since the narrative as a whole is ordered with respect to that moment, but the conception as a whole may have a less powerful and less carefully detailed symbolism. There is no doubt, however, that the ultimate purpose of the R, besides the amusement that it provided for the princes, is the same as that of the MBh: to teach what a good king should be.

The R is the story of Rāma, the perfect prince, the model of a king, and to this day, *rāmarājya,* "the kingship of Rāma," is the highest reference to good government (the term was notably part of Gandhi's vocabulary). But the prince is also an avatar of Viṣṇu. Therein lies the first major difference from the apparent structure of the MBh. Whereas the MBh puts the entire weight of the action on the five Pāṇḍava brothers and gives the avatar Kṛṣṇa the role of counselor to Arjuna, the R features the Rāma avatar as the central character. And the avatar is himself a king, while Kṛṣṇa is not. This is not, however, a simple avatar. The story of his birth at the same time as the birth of his three brothers heralds a well-known theme of later Viṣṇuism and provides an example of an omnipresent motif in Hindu mythology.

King Daśaratha of Ayodhyā, who has three wives but no descendants, celebrates a great sacrifice in order to obtain offspring. At the same time, the gods are harassed by the *rākṣasa* Rāvaṇa, king of Laṅkā. Laṅkā (Sri Lanka) represents the far south as opposed to Ayodhyā, Daśaratha's capital, north of the Ganges, not far from the Himalayas. Since the north is always superior to the south, this particular north-south structure is the substitute for the heaven-hell opposition when the adversary of the gods is the king of the *asuras.* The epics do not make a strict distinction between *rākṣasas* and *asuras.* The first are cannibalistic, but there are good *rākṣasas* just as there are good *asuras,* as long as they enter into the service of dharma in their legitimate place, which is inferior to that of the gods. The gods therefore address Brahmā, the cause of their plight, since it is he who made Rāvaṇa invincible. However, Rāvaṇa in his contempt for men did not include them in the list of creatures who are not to be capable of killing him. Brahmā and the gods therefore ask Viṣṇu to become incarnate among men in order to deliver them from Rāvaṇa. Viṣṇu accepts, and when Daśaratha's sacrificial fire blazes up, an extraordinary creature rises from it and hands the king a bowl of magic porridge, which he must give to his wife to obtain a son. Daśaratha apportions the porridge among his three wives. The first, Kauśalyā, gets half of it; she will give birth to Rāma, the rightful heir. Of the remaining half, he gives one half (that is, a quarter of the whole) to his second wife, Sumitrā, and half of what is left (i.e., one-eighth of the total) to his third wife, Kaikeyī, and the remaining eighth to Sumitrā again. Kaikeyī gives birth to Bharata, and Sumitrā gives birth to twins, Lakṣmaṇa and Śatrughna (the births take place in that order). Since they are all "portions" of Viṣṇu, it is known right away that they will form a unified block, despite the bad queen Kaikeyī; but the theme of twins, which is also found in the MBh, recalls a familiar structure: Rāma and Bharata will occupy positions in the forefront, with Bharata totally devoted to Rāma, whereas the twins will serve Rāma and Bharata, respectively, in the capacity of confidants, devotees, and assistants. This is in keeping with the principle that in India a man, particularly a man of high standing, cannot alone fulfill the totality of the role given him. The hierarchical relationship must appear in one way or another. If there are only four forms of Viṣṇu,

Offering to Hanumān. Katmandu. Photo Catherine Jarrige.

and not five, as there are five Pāṇḍavas, it means that the supreme form of Viṣṇu, which makes up the fifth comprehensive term, remains unmanifested. There are four brothers, just as later there are four *vyūhas* ("deployments") of Viṣṇu, the number four recalling the four Vedas as well as the four cardinal points, that is, the realm of human action.

While in the MBh the five Pāṇḍavas are sons of different celestial gods and Kṛṣṇa is Viṣṇu's avatar (doubled also by the Brahman *ṛṣi* Vyāsa, and also consubstantial with the Pāṇḍava Arjuna), the R has recourse to what seems to be an altogether different assignment of roles. Indeed, Viṣṇu is not the only one in the R to become incarnate, but this time the gods become incarnate not among men but among monkeys (and secondarily bears, but these may be dismissed for our purposes since their role is not distinct from that of the monkeys, and they are never in the forefront). The divine incarnations are ultimately more numerous than in the MBh, but Rudra is missing (Purāṇic mythology turns Rāvaṇa himself into a devotee, a *gaṇa* of Rudra-Śiva). Bṛhaspati, Kubera, Viśvakarman, Agni, the Aśvins, Varuṇa, and Parjanya are explicitly said to be the fathers of different monkeys, but the essential roles, those that require special attention, are incontestably those of Hanumān, the son of Vāyu, Vālin, the son of Indra, and Sugrīva, the son of Sūrya. Here we recognize deities whose incarnations play prominent roles in the MBh. They will appear later as the action unfolds (*Kiṣkindhā kāṇḍa*, or book 4). Some thought must be given to the need for these divine partners and to the choice of monkeys as their incarnations. But the conjunction of the worlds of men and of monkeys precludes the well-informed ties of kinship that, in the MBh, symbolically fuse alliances and solidarities.

Vasiṣṭha, Daśaratha's chaplain, performs the traditional rites for all four sons as they grow up in such a way as to confirm their hierarchy and accentuate the primacy of Rāma. They are already adolescents, experts in arms as well as in the Vedas, when the *ṛṣi* Viśvāmitra arrives at the court of Daśaratha. Viśvāmitra asks Daśaratha to lend him his son Rāma, who alone will be able to rid him of the *rākṣasas* who keep him from completing his sacrifice by defiling it. These *rākṣasas* are to no one's surprise minions of Rāvaṇa, and the incapacity with which Viśvāmitra is struck is only one aspect of the insults that the all-powerful Rāvaṇa inflicts on the three worlds. According to Viśvāmitra, only Rāma can kill the *rākṣasas* and make possible the fulfillment of the sacrifice. This is the first trial of Rāma in his role of defender of the Brahmanic order and proves his quality as an avatar. The express approval of Vasiṣṭha is required for Daśaratha to consent to let his son leave with Viśvāmitra, accompanied by Lakṣmaṇa. On the way, Viśvāmitra teaches them magic formulas that will make them invincible. This is also the occasion for their apprenticeship in living in the forest; they spend one night in a hermitage that was occupied by Rudra, the very spot where Rudra reduced the god Kāma ("love") to ashes. They must also kill Tāṭakā, the mother of one of the *rākṣasas* who are oppressing Viśvāmitra. Then Viśvāmitra equips them with an impressive array of magic weapons, some of which evoke the destruction of the world. When Rāma reaches Viśvāmitra's hermitage, he has no trouble ridding it of the *rākṣasas* while Viśvāmitra himself performs his sacrifice.

This is only a preparation for what is to follow. Instead of returning home, Rāma and Lakṣmaṇa are invited by Viśvāmitra and his entourage of *ṛṣis* to continue their journey to Mithilā, where King Janaka has an extraordinary bow. This bow is the one that Rudra used previously to threaten the gods during the sacrifice of Dakṣa, because he had been forgotten in the distribution of the shares in the sacrifice. But the gods had propitiated him in time, and he had given them his bow. No one can string the bow. In fact, Rāma, escorted by powerful Brahmans, has to go to a *svayaṃvara* analogous to that of Draupadī in the MBh, because Janaka has decided to give his daughter in marriage only to a prince who can string and bend Śiva's bow. The comparison with the MBh is relevant especially in view of the fact that Sītā's birth is just as marvelous as that of Draupadī. Her father Janaka ("the begetter") saw her rise from the furrow (*sītā*) that he was digging with his plow to prepare the sacrificial area. She was thus born, like Draupadī, not from a human womb but from the earth sanctified for the sacrifice. Rāma, who has been well prepared by Viśvāmitra, easily bends the bow to the point of breaking it. He obtains Sītā's hand in marriage. At the same time, Lakṣmaṇa also gets a wife, Sītā's sister, and the other two brothers marry the two daughters of Janaka's younger brother. All four weddings are therefore celebrated by Vasiṣṭha at the same time in Mithilā in the presence of

Viśvāmitra, who then disappears from the epic, never to appear again.

It is apparently important that the alliance with Janaka be solidly established, although this plays virtually no part in the rest of the narrative. The king, already well known in the Veda for his piety, is sometimes referred to as the king of Mithilā (in the northeast of the Indus-Ganges plain, on the border of the Himalayas) and sometimes as the king of Videha. He is also called the Videha ("the bodiless"), and he is in possession of the bow with which Rudra-Śiva, contrary to the most commonly known versions of the myth, refused to destroy the sacrifice of Dakṣa. Before he gets home Rāma stops at the hermitage where Rudra, engaged in the austerities of a yogi, reduced to ashes Kāma, the god of love, who had come to seduce him. The text explicitly cites this episode as the reason for Kāma's other name, Anaṅga ("the bodiless"). The two facts invite comparison. Janaka's daughter is born of the sacrificial area of "the bodiless" one who had become the "begetter." Is it possible that Śiva allowed this sacrificial act to become fertile in anticipation of the crisis of the world, just as Draupadī was born of a dangerous sacrifice that her father had performed in order to get a son who could kill his enemy Droṇa? The role of Viśvāmitra, the Brahman born a Kṣatriya, helps to load the situation with hidden and disquieting meanings, while Vasiṣṭha's presence makes it certain that dharma is observed. Sītā is not explicitly given as the incarnation of Śrī, but she is described as such, and all throughout the epic she is compared or assimilated to Śrī (for instance when Hanumān finds her in the *aśoka* woods at Laṅkā, 5.16.6ff.).

Another trial: on the way back to Ayodhyā, the retinue of Daśaratha and his family encounters Paraśurāma. This Brahman, a great destroyer of Kṣatriyas, challenges Rāma (could he be the new avatar?) by challenging him to bend Viṣṇu's bow, which he is holding in his hands. Rāma bends it with such ease that Paraśurāma admits defeat and bows to Rāma as if he were Viṣṇu in person.

Rāma earns the affection and admiration of all. In the absence of his brother Bharata and of Śatrughna, Daśaratha decides to anoint him crown prince. Everyone agrees except of course Queen Kaikeyī, Bharata's mother, who seeks to ensure the kingship for her son. The preparations for the ceremony of consecration are quickly completed, and on the eve of the event Rāma must undergo rites of purification. Meanwhile, Kaikeyī reminds Daśaratha that she had once saved his life and that he had then promised her a reward of her choice. The time has come to grant her wish. Daśaratha must send Rāma into exile in the forest for fourteen years and consecrate Bharata as crown prince. Kaikeyī believes that in fourteen years the people will have forgotten Rāma. After a night of vain supplications, Daśaratha is forced to yield so as not to go back on his word, given so long ago. If he refused, Kaikeyī would commit suicide. The day when Rāma was to be consecrated turns into the day of his departure for exile. Disinterested and virtuous, he submits with joy, seeking above all to allow his father to keep his word. But Sītā, whose exile was not expected, refuses to remain in Ayodhyā. She determines to follow her husband into exile, for she cannot live without him. She imposes her decision on her husband. They leave in the company of the faithful Lakṣmaṇa, and Daśaratha dies of a broken heart soon after. Bharata is summoned to be consecrated as king, since the kingdom cannot remain without a king. When he arrives, Bharata learns of his mother's scheming at the same time as he learns of his father's death. He refuses to rule in place of Rāma, whom he considers the rightful heir to the throne. So he goes off to the forest in search of his brother to tell him of their father's death and to persuade him to return to Ayodhyā and assume the throne; Bharata asserts that he will refuse the kingship in any case. But Rāma is of the opinion that his father's death does not invalidate his promise. He will therefore spend fourteen years in exile with Sītā and Lakṣmaṇa. Bharata then pledges to carry on the administration of the kingdom while awaiting the return of his brother, and he enthrones Rāma's sandals to symbolize his brother's reign. He will venerate them and ask them for orders every day, and he will live the life of an ascetic for the entire period.

The differences from the plot of the MBh are obvious. The wicked queen's plan fails, and there are not two camps fighting over the throne of Ayodhyā. During Rāma's absence, the royal function will be reduced to a minimum, and its ascetic component will be dominant. This will be a time of latency, of waiting and trial, the meaning of which will become more precise but once more will shed light on the importance of detachment and renunciation for the perfect exercise of kingship. Bharata's asceticism symbolizes his refusal to "enjoy" ruling the kingdom in his brother's place. Another crucial fact is Sītā's departure with Rāma. Like all princesses of royal rank, she symbolizes the kingdom and its prosperity. Because she is Śrī, she can only be on the side of dharma, and her departure from Ayodhyā signifies both the period of latency about to befall the kingdom and the future return of Rāma. As a result, the reign of the wicked Duryodhana in the MBh and the regency of the virtuous Bharata in the R are symbolically identical. The presence of Draupadī and Sītā in the forest is a sign of that. The ensuing events will place Sītā at the center of the drama much more clearly. Looming on the horizon are the threat posed by Rāvaṇa and the role given to Rāma, the avatar of Viṣṇu. Along with the obvious differences between the MBh and the R at the most superficial level, there is also a strict parallelism in the construction of the first three books of both epics. The first book gives the myth of the births, the first ordeals, and marriage; the second, in the MBh, is the royal consecration of Yudhiṣṭhira followed by the disastrous dice game and the departure for the forest; in the R, the second book describes how the consecration of Rāma as crown prince is replaced by his condemnation to exile in the forest. Finally, the third book of both epics corresponds to the time of exile in the forest. From that point on, the structural differences noted up to this point at the level of the narrative will bring about differences in the development of the plot.

The forest where Rāma settles is called the Daṇḍaka (forest of punishment); the use of power to punish the wicked outside as well as inside the kingdom is, for Brahmanic ideology, the very essence of royal power. Rāma finally sets up his hermitage at Pañcavaṭī (the site of "the five banyans") near the source of the Godāvarī River (the site of modern Nasik in the state of Maharashtra). But from the moment that he enters the forest, it becomes clear that he will not live the life of an ascetic like the others. All the *ṛṣis* who live in the hermitages that he visits count on him for protection from the *rākṣasas* who threaten their peace and their ascetic practices. He will therefore keep some of what, in a manner of speaking, constitutes the essence of the royal function, as the very name of the forest foreshadows. Sītā does not understand. Should he not be giving himself over wholly to asceticism and nonviolence? No, answers Rāma, he is a Kṣatriya, and he cannot refuse the *ṛṣis* (Brahmans) the protection that they ask for. His dharma has not changed. In the MBh, the period of exile in the forest is marked by the death of some *rākṣasas* too, but Bhīma is always the one to take charge of it; Yudhiṣṭhira devotes himself more willingly to asceticism, while Arjuna prepares for war in the heaven of Indra. And Draupadī too reminds Yudhiṣṭhira of his dharma as a Kṣatriya, which he seems to forget. Here Rāma alone is king, and his function cannot completely disappear. It is even asserted in this period of exile, which also will be the time of struggle against the enemies of dharma.

The first serious skirmish with the *rākṣasas* is the result of the visit to the hermitage by Śūrpaṇakhā, Rāvaṇa's sister and a terrible *rākṣasī*, who has the power to take on a seductive form. She falls in love with Rāma, wants to take him away from Sītā, and promises him all sorts of delights that will make him forget his dreary ascetic life. We recognize here the theme of the temptation of ascetics in order to subvert their virtues and the power that the virtues confer upon them. Rāma is, however, unshakable. He is as faithful to Sītā as Sītā is to him. The perfect king and Śrī are inseparable. Lakṣmaṇa rids his brother of the bothersome demoness by cutting off her nose and ears. Disfigured, she goes to complain to Khara ("rude," and also "ass"), another one of her brothers who is camped nearby with fourteen thousand *rākṣasas*. War breaks out and Rāma kills all the *rākṣasas* including Khara. Śūrpaṇakhā's love has turned to hatred, and she goes to seek vengeance in a highly feminine form heavily laden with symbolic implications.

Śūrpaṇakhā goes to Laṅkā to see her brother Rāvaṇa, not so much to speak to him about Rāma, who killed their brother Khara, and about the danger that he represents for them, as to extol Sītā's incomparable charm. Śūrpaṇakhā is so eloquent that Rāvaṇa is seized with an intense desire to take Sītā for himself and searches for a way to do this. With some difficulty he convinces his friend Mārīca (whose name evokes a "mirage") to accompany him to Pañcavaṭī in order to put his plan into action. The plan calls for Rāvaṇa to hide and for Mārīca to take the form of a golden deer so splendid that Sītā will covet it and Rāma will pursue it eagerly. The deer will have to carry Rāma a suitable distance away, and then it will imitate Rāma's voice to call Lakṣmaṇa to the rescue and thus force Lakṣmaṇa to leave Sītā by herself in the hermitage. Rāvaṇa will then take advantage of Lakṣmaṇa's absence to carry Sītā away. Everything goes according to plan. When Rāma finally kills the deer, it reverts to its *rākṣasa* form. Lakṣmaṇa, hearing his call, is not taken in: this cannot be Rāma's voice. Unfortunately, Sītā, ignorant like all women and given to momentary impulses, thinks that she recognizes Rāma's call and forces Lakṣmaṇa to run to his rescue. Rāvaṇa wastes no time in appearing. He tries in vain to seduce Sītā and then carries her off into the air, dragging her by the hair. He must first mortally wound the vulture Jaṭāyu, who tries to prevent the abduction and warns Rāvaṇa that he is making a serious mistake. Before he dies, Jaṭāyu has just enough time to tell Rāma and Lakṣmaṇa what has happened. This is the beginning of the wanderings of the two brothers in their touching quest for Sītā, which will take them first to the kingdom of monkeys and then to Laṅkā.

The abduction of Sītā by the king of the *rākṣasas* has no counterpart in the MBh. It is, however, clear that his desire to take for himself the princess who represents Śrī on earth is analogous to Duryodhana's desire for Draupadī during the dice game. The differences between this successful abduction and the scorned propositions of the Kaurava usurper are practically nonexistent. Rāvaṇa will imprison Sītā on Laṅkā in a garden of his harem and will each day attempt to seduce her, alternating between threats and promises but resolved not to use force. Sītā's absolute faithfulness is her only safeguard, but every Hindu knows that there is nothing that a faithful woman cannot obtain. Her character as a *satī*, or perfect wife, is her most inviolable protection. At a deeper level, it is impossible for a nondharmic king to possess Śrī.

Rāma and Lakṣmaṇa have therefore left Pañcavaṭī in search of Sītā. They leave in a southward direction on Jaṭāyu's instructions. On the way, they meet the monkeys Hanumān and Sugrīva and quickly become friends with them. Each tells his story. Sugrīva's story is not absolutely transparent. He was the king of Kiṣkindhā, but he was dispossessed of both his throne and his wife (they go together, as we know) by his brother Vālin. Sugrīva is the younger brother of Vālin, and Vālin was king quite legitimately. However, one day in the forest Sugrīva came in good faith to believe that his brother had disappeared and would never return. He therefore returned to their capital and succeeded his brother on the throne, fully enjoying the privileges of his new high position: feasts, banquets, women, nothing lacking, until the day when Vālin unexpectedly reappeared, drove Sugrīva out, and reclaimed the power; he kept his brother's wife at the same time. With the last detail, Vālin is of course at fault, but can he really be regarded as a usurper? The situation is not very clear. But the two monkeys are in possession of jewels that Sītā had dropped from the air on her way to Laṅkā, and Hanumān, Sugrīva's favorite advisor, immediately demonstrates great devotion to Rāma and gets along splendidly with Lakṣmaṇa. A pact is concluded: Rāma will help Sugrīva recover his kingdom while Sugrīva will place his troops of monkeys at Rāma's disposal in order to retrieve Sītā from Rāvaṇa.

Sugrīva's cause is not altogether just, and we may see in this equivocal situation one of those bendings of dharma from which the MBh does not recoil whenever it turns out to be necessary for the final victory. But the episode has another dimension. We know that Vālin is Indra's son, while Sugrīva is Sūrya's son, and Hanumān is Vāyu's son. We thus find in the monkeys the divine incarnations that the MBh puts among the Pāṇḍavas and Karṇa, Kuntī's secret elder son. Arjuna is Indra's son, Bhīma is Vāyu's son, and Karṇa is Sūrya's son. We may recognize in Arjuna the figure of the ideal king—as his father Indra is king of heaven—while Bhīma has inherited from his father his strength and lust for life. As for Karṇa, he embodies the sun when it deviates from its normal course and burns the world at the end of a cosmic period. He is the enemy of Arjuna, who can only rule over a world ordered by dharma. Karṇa-Sūrya has been made king on the spur of the moment by Duryodhana-Kali, while Arjuna-Indra is not a king at all in the MBh. This is what brings us to the narrative structure of the R: to be sure, Rāma's exploits have not yet spoken explicitly of the end of the world, of the cosmic crisis; the overall setting has not insisted on this framework peculiar to the myth of the avatar. But the respective positions of the two kings of the monkeys could be a transposition of that framework: the sovereignty is denied to Indra's son, who would otherwise have a rightful claim to it, and is given to Sūrya's son, whose legitimacy is doubtful and who will lead his army into great carnage. This son of Sūrya has the son of Vāyu at his service. Sūrya and Vāyu are closely associated in the myth of the dissolution of the world at the end of a cosmic period; the wind fans the fire set by the sun. It is logical that it should be Rāma, the avatar dedicated to destruction for the sake of dharma, who kills Vālin-Indra to make room for Sugrīva-Sūrya.

But why monkeys? Rāma and Lakṣmaṇa needed an army to help them retrieve Sītā, without whom they could not reenter Ayodhyā (the period of exile was drawing to a close).

Hanumān. Private collection. Photo Dominique Champion.

The monkeys, headed by Hanumān, turn out to be excellent and humble devotees and elucidate the bhakti that must be addressed to the human king as well as to the avatar of Viṣṇu that he represents. However, to this day Hanumān has countless shrines almost everywhere in India, which make him the protector of the places where he is worshiped. There he is not the ecstatic devotee that is represented in Rāma's temples, hands joined before the god, but rather an unarmed monkey running with a mountain in one hand and trampling on a demon. If one is to judge by what Hanumān says about himself to his half-brother Bhīma in the MBh, what Hindu consciousness remembers about monkeys is above all their vegetarianism, synonymous with nonviolence (Hanumān reproaches Bhīma for his unreasoned violence). The most frequent name applied to monkeys in the R is that of *vānara,* evoking the forest—*vana.* These swift and strong creatures fight with no weapons, using only rocks and uprooted trees (as Bhīma does on occasion). We may therefore advance the hypothesis that monkeys (and probably bears for the same reason) were chosen to form Rāma's troops because they also evoke the values of self-denial and self-sacrifice that are required of the perfect warrior. Their bhakti is merely the expression of these values and of the link that they necessarily imply with the supreme divinity.

Hanumān is the first to set foot on the island of Laṅkā after crossing the sea in one leap. He finds Sītā and promises her an early rescue. All by himself, he could undoubtedly abduct Sītā and even defeat the *rākṣasas,* but Sītā persuades him to save this glory for Rāma. Vāyu's son therefore contents himself with setting a fire in Rāvaṇa's capital so as to leave signs predicting the impending disaster, taking pains to spare the palace of Vibhīṣaṇa, a brother of Rāvaṇa, in whom he has discovered a good *rākṣasa.* Indeed, Vibhīṣaṇa, unable to convince Rāvaṇa to surrender Sītā to Rāma and to make an alliance with him, leaves the island and puts himself at Rāma's service with full devotion. From this moment on, it is certain that he will be chosen to succeed Rāvaṇa on the throne of Laṅkā after Rāvaṇa's death. Starting with this first fire of Laṅkā, the evocation of the Fire of Time or of the end of a yuga becomes as frequent in the R as it is in the MBh. This is not a simple poetic image; it is the entire symbolism of the myth of the avatar that is once again developed. Viṣṇu becomes incarnate only when a crisis of dharma makes inevitable a bloody war in which the good and the wicked must perish in the sacrifice of battle so that dharma may be restored. The war is a reduced form of the end of the world.

After forewarning Rāvaṇa of what to expect, Hanumān reports on his mission to Rāma and Sugrīva. They immediately decide on an expedition during which many monkeys will meet their death, as will Rāvaṇa's older son, Indrajit, even though he had been strong enough to defeat Indra; and finally Rāvaṇa himself will be killed by Rāma. Laṅkā is again set on fire, but this time from top to bottom. Rāvaṇa, before the power of his enemy, sees the truth: Rāma may well be Nārāyaṇa in person. Vibhīṣaṇa is immediately installed on the throne of Laṅkā, having abundantly proved his devotion to Rāma, to the point of making war against his own brother.

The reunion of Rāma and Sītā is less touching than one would have expected from the scenes where they lament their separation. To keep dharma safe, Rāma consents to take Sītā back only after she has undergone an ordeal of fire, from which she emerges victorious: she entered the fire and it refused to burn her, a sure sign that Rāvaṇa did not touch her and that Śrī is intact. Only then can the couple return to Ayodhyā, their period of exile completed, and Bharata arranges a triumphant welcome by the entire population.

Thus, unlike the MBh, in which war follows the period of exile because Duryodhana refuses to return his kingdom to Yudhiṣṭhira, the R includes the war in the period of exile. Because the overall setting is symbolically less clear (Bharata awaits his brother's return to the position of head of the kingdom), the war Rāma must wage has a more subtle symbolic meaning. On the level of narrative, it is not his kingdom that Rāma must wrest from the *rākṣasas,* but his wife, Śrī incarnate, without whom he cannot be king. By taking Sītā away from him, Rāvaṇa takes away the one who symbolizes the kingdom along with the prosperity ensured by good government, carefully performed sacrifices, and respect for Brahmans. Sītā's abduction is like the duplication of the theme of exile, both being signs of the disorder embodied in Rāvaṇa's power, and reveals its meaning, because a good king must be like a yogi in the world, a prince capable of complete detachment with regard to his reign, and at the same time capable of self-sacrifice in the service of his kingdom. Rāma's return to Ayodhyā had to go by way of Laṅkā, the kingdom of the *rākṣasas*. The ordeal saved the cause of dharma (as the fire's refusal to burn Sītā shows), and Rāma has fulfilled the duties of an avatar.

The last part of the R, like the first, is considered to be a later addition. Whereas the first part seems indispensable for understanding the work as a whole, the last part is disconcerting in content. Our inability to account for it is what makes us think of it as a false conclusion. But let us guard against those pseudohistorical reconstructions designed to account for an apparent difficulty in the narrative.

After his return to Ayodhyā, Rāma is again seized with doubts about Sītā, and he sends her into exile in the forest, where she finds refuge in the hermitage of Vālmīki (the presumed author of the R). This is where she gives birth to twins, Kuśa and Lava, the sons of Rāma. When, after a long separation, Rāma is led by his sons to recognize Sītā's innocence, she is summoned back from exile and asks the earth, from which she was born, to take her back. The earth opens and swallows her. Many Vaiṣṇava devotional texts assert that Rāma reigned for one thousand years after his return to Ayodhyā, which seems to run counter to the sense of this tragic end.

A comparison with the MBh may help to reconcile this ending of the story with the "authentic" R, despite everything. In any case, simply to regard it as an extra piece tacked on is a sure way to deprive it of any meaning. The last books of the MBh are not the most successful. Obviously, the epic authors had to solve a difficult problem on the narrative level. The Pāṇḍavas, and similarly the pair Kṛṣṇa and Arjuna, came down to earth for the time of the crisis and to save dharma. Once their task is accomplished, they must withdraw. This is how the population of Dvārakā kills itself off, Balarāma and Kṛṣṇa die, and Dvārakā is soon after submerged under the ocean. This first catastrophe, which concerns the avatar himself, is the signal for the Pāṇḍavas to depart for heaven. The *Uttara Kāṇḍa* (section 7) of the R probably tries to solve the same problem. Rāma has rid the world of the *rākṣasas* and reestablished dharma. He must then withdraw. Just as the rest of the R is centered on Sītā's fate, so the disappearance of the heroes, once their task is accomplished, is symbolized by the disappearance of Sītā, who simply returns to her place of origin. The Śrī whom she embodies—just as Draupadī embodies Śrī in the MBh—is not the Śrī of peacetime. Not only must she put up a superhuman resistance to the demon who wishes to possess her, but she must also insist that the act of killing the demon be reserved for her husband alone. Rather than accept an abrupt intervention by Hanumān who would materially resolve the problem, she unmistakably chooses war, being a true princess. She came to earth for that purpose, like Rāma himself. The surest signs of this, from the beginning, are her birth from the sacrifice of Janaka and the role Śiva's bow plays in the choice of her husband. The R does not say, as the MBh says of Draupadī, that she was born to destroy many Kṣatriyas, but the entire epic implies that she was born to destroy the evil *rākṣasas* and many good monkeys. Hanumān sees in her the cause, and indeed the worthy cause, of all that has happened. When she disappears, the continuity of the dynasty is assured. Thus the last section of the R may be awkward; it may even be surprising at first sight, but it is not as devoid of meaning as one might believe. *Exeunt omnes.*

M.Bi./g.h.

BIBLIOGRAPHY

G. COURTILLIER, trans., *La légende de Rama et de Sita extraite du Ramayana de Valmiki* (Paris 1927). M. N. DUTT, trans., *The Ramayana*, trans. into English prose from the original Sanskrit of Valmiki, 4 vols. (Calcutta 1891–94). T. H. GRIFFITH, trans., *The Ramayan of Valmiki*, trans. into English verse (Varanasi 1963). C. RAJAGOPALACHARI, *Ramayana* (Bombay 1976). M. L. SEN, trans., *The Ramayana*, a modernized version in English prose, 3 vols. (Calcutta). H. P. SHASTRI, trans., *The Rāmāyaṇa of Vālmīki*, 3 vols. (London 1952–59).

Abbreviations

MBh *Mahābhārata*
R *Rāmāyaṇa* (Gita Press, Gorakhpur)

Viṣṇu and Śiva, the Supreme Gods of Hindu Bhakti

Viṣṇu and Śiva are the two supreme gods of Hindu bhakti. All the other gods that one finds in myth and ritual are related to them as avatars or sons. There are two essential reasons for treating them together here: the first is that they are usually seen as mutually exclusive, supreme gods of different and antagonistic sects. Without ignoring either the historical and still current reality of the sects or their mythical creations, we must note the limits of their influence on most devotees (we must distinguish the major Vaiṣṇava and Śaiva sects from the more limited groups of disciples of a spiritual master or guru, who adopt their chosen deity), and we must also reverse the order of logical priority: sects are understood only as choices made within a system of beliefs in which Viṣṇu and Śiva are given together, which we shall designate by a term borrowed from the Sanskrit: the Hinduism "of the Tradition." Within this system, each god has a place and a set of characteristics that define him and are found in all myths, even in sectarian concepts.

The second reason is that the emergence of the two gods out of the Vedic pantheon has often been regarded as entirely contingent: two minor gods at the level of Vedic sacrifice, they appear as the great gods of the yogi starting with the Upaniṣads (Viṣṇu in the *Kaṭha Upaniṣad* and Rudra-Śiva in the *Śvetāśvatara Upaniṣad*), and later as the great gods of bhakti, or Hindu devotion, starting with the epics. But the contingency is greatly reduced when we note that ever since Vedic literature the two gods have had a basic connection with sacrifice, and that this connection, different for the two, is what determines their later promotion. The Vedic Viṣṇu can be seen in the epic and Purāṇic Viṣṇu, just as the Vedic Rudra can be seen in the Hindu Rudra-Śiva.

The Vedic literature on the subject is too vast and too dispersed to give exact references here. Basically, all the mythical data mentioned here can be found in the *Śatapatha Brāhmaṇa*, which may serve as a starting point for more intensive study. It should be remembered that at this level the myths are more fragmentary than they are in Hinduism, and that one must juxtapose them and seek their unity in the meaning rather than try to reconstitute a narrative unity that may never have existed.

Almost everywhere in the *Brāhmaṇas*, Viṣṇu is identified

Pool of the Temple of Mahākuteśvara (Karnataka). Photo M. Biardeau.

(Right) Ardhanārīśvara, Temple of Kodumbalur (South India). Photo M. Biardeau.

with the sacrifice as a global operation with all its agents and instruments but above all with the sacrifice as the source of all prosperity in this world, with the glorious and triumphant sacrifice. In this respect he is associated with Śrī, that shining glory and prosperity that sacrifice, and sacrifice alone, can give to the earth.

It is also because he is identified with sacrifice, which in the Vedic hymn to Puruṣa takes on a human form, that the gods make him stretch out on the ground to delimit with his body the sacrificial area: Viṣṇu is the creator of liturgical space, consequently of all ordered space, of all the cosmos. This second feature led to the idea of associating him with Indra, the king of the gods, in order for him to open the space for his strides; he takes three strides, as there are three worlds, one on top of another, with the sky as the highest level. This creation of ordered and sanctified space expresses Viṣṇu's general connection with the cosmic order that will be called dharma. The order is controlled by sacrifice.

Another aspect seems surprising at first: the gods are united against Viṣṇu and cut off his head with the tip of his bow. Within a ritual context in which the victim is not decapitated but suffocated, the meaning is not immediately obvious. But whatever the contemporary practice may be, Vedic ritual attaches great importance to the heads of the victims, without saying explicitly how one is to procure the heads (indeed, without even saying that they are victims): they are placed in the fire altar (the head of a goat, a horse, etc., and even of a human). Although nothing is known of the practice that preceded the suffocation of the victims, it is known that blood sacrifice in later Hinduism is always performed through decapitation and that the head is generally the only part of the victim that is offered to the deity. It is therefore not unreasonable to propose that Vṣṇu, beheaded by his own bow, is there identified with the victim of the sacrifice. The cosmogonic Puruṣa supplies the model for such identifications (sacrificer-victim-sacrifice), and Viṣṇu has a vocation to become this Puruṣa, which he will indeed become when Puruṣa becomes the supreme god and the Great Yogi.

But it is not known how he became the Great Yogi at the same time as he became the supreme Puruṣa, unless the two meanings—the meaning of the yoga embodied in the Great Yogi and the meaning of the sacrifice symbolized by the Puruṣa—were inseparable very early. The name of Puruṣa Nārāyaṇa, which appears in the *Śatapatha Brāhmaṇa* with no reference to Viṣṇu, bears witness to this coalescence of the two aspects; the *Kaṭha Upaniṣad,* however, merely calls Puruṣa Viṣṇu. Whereas the Absolute also takes on the name of Brahman, which evokes the totality of knowledge and of Vedic practices, this epithet is also often coupled with the name of Viṣṇu (or Śiva), reverting to the image of the cosmogonic Puruṣa (the Man-Sacrifice). Viṣṇu is the supreme Brahman, the god of deliverance that is promised to the yogi.

Conversely, Rudra remains from one end of Vedic literature to the other the terrible god whom one must render propitious (*Śiva*) by an appropriate ritual. We shall not stress here his terrible aspect, which comes to him from his essential association with the deadly and dangerous aspects of sacrifice: the stake to which the victim is tied and the fire that consumes him. We must, however, note the connection that causes so many apparent contradictions, the connection between the dreaded aspect of the god and his nature as the Great Yogi. In fact it is easier to grasp what predisposes the Rudra of the sacrifice to become Rudra-Śiva who is the Great Yogi than it is to understand the transformation of Viṣṇu into the Great Yogi. Rudra is the mountain dweller, the god of the wild places that are uninhabited or are inhabited by outlaws or wild animals. In the *Śatarudrīya,* for instance, he is represented as accompanied by all sorts of unsavory characters, humans or animals or unclassifiable creatures, who together catalyze all that Hindu consciousness finds most disturbing. But the renunciant is also at least in theory one who left the village for the forest, and when he abandons life in society, he draws closer to the life of the wilderness. That is why there are in the forest both hunters (impure, since they kill animals)—Rudra is a hunter—and renunciants. At the present time the temples of great regional divinities located on mountains accommodate both the hunter-god and the yogi god. The mountain partakes of the same symbolism as the forest. Rudra-Śiva, the terrible god who looks with "favor" on his devotees, is logically associated with the yogi and becomes a yogi himself.

This has important implications for the connection with Viṣṇu: because he is the luminous god-sacrifice and the dispenser of all prosperity, his yoga must add something more to the purity required of the man in the world who sacrifices. When a man becomes a yogi, he makes a meticulous search for anything that keeps him from impurity: he keeps a vegetarian diet, he filters his water to avoid swallowing tiny animals, he abstains from using fire, which also kills insects, etc. The renunciant of the Brahman caste, the only one who has the right to be called a *sannyāsin,* has as his deity Nārāyaṇa, the yogic form of Viṣṇu most often represented in the great Vaiṣṇava temples. The Śaiva ascetic or the sectarian Śaiva may also seek a rigorous purity; such is the case, for instance, in the Śaivasiddhānta in South India. But the attitude toward the pure and the impure is rather that of someone who has placed himself outside these categories for good. Since the pure and the impure are distinctions that govern the society of castes, the renunciant places himself beyond the pure and the impure. He shows this by representing Śiva in his impure aspects (hunter, god of cremation grounds, etc.), and by adopting practices considered impure. The Kāpālikas used to drink from and receive alms in a human skull; they used to dress in rags that they picked up from the cremation grounds. The Śaiva renunciant is more a yogi than a *sannyāsin* (literally, renouncer); he may also come from non-Brahman castes and generally does.

When Viṣṇu and Śiva appear as gods of bhakti (which they are in the Hindu Tradition as well as in the sects), these differential features appear too. Viṣṇu is at the head of the ordered world. He therefore logically has a royal aspect that never leaves him. Even the reclining Viṣṇu of the great temples who presents the theme of the yogic sleep of Viṣṇu during the cosmic night, or, more precisely, his reawakening at the dawn of a new day of the world, wears a royal diadem. The cosmogonic myth of the Purāṇas is taken up by the cultic iconography with a visual variant (given particularly in the *Mahābhārata* 3.272): Viṣṇu lies on the serpent Śeṣa who is coiled on the ocean. Out of his navel comes a long-stemmed lotus that holds in its petals a four-headed Brahmā, who represents the first stage of the creation of the world. At his feet is Śrī, who has become his wife.

There is no doubt that in nonsectarian Hinduism Viṣṇu is the supreme god. He appears in both epics which, to be sure,

Inside the shrine of Śiva at Mahākuteśvara (Karantaka). Photo M. Biardeau.

do not ignore Rudra-Śiva. That is why it is he—the pure god, both yogi and king, the symbol of the union of the two highest *varṇas,* Brahman and Kṣatriya—who according to the theory must descend to earth. The classic list of avatars connects them solely with Viṣṇu. Another consequence of the primacy of Viṣṇu is his essential connection with the Goddess, who is generally and too hastily considered to be Śaiva. Although she is Śiva's wife, she is Viṣṇu's sister, and this double connection, formulated especially in South India, is in itself a denial of sectarianism, since it makes Viṣṇu and Śiva brothers-in-law. Finally, Viṣṇu's wife, Śrī or Lakṣmī, often splits into Śrī and Bhū (the Earth), and the Earth, which cannot exist without Śrī, needs the Goddess to watch over her.

As for Śiva, in his great temples he is both the terrible god of sacrifice and the yogi. His ritual representation in the form of a linga is the source of much incoherent writing about the primitive aspects of this phallic god. There is no doubt about the sexual interpretation of Śiva's linga: the male organ is inserted in the yoni, the female organ, in an act of procreation. This is for Śiva the symbolic equivalent of the reclining Viṣṇu, whose awakening causes a lotus to emerge from his navel, a lotus that bears Brahmā. We may even safely assert that the lotus stem has the same symbolism as Śiva's linga. Clearly the deity of the shrine is the one that brings the worlds to the seminal state and makes them blossom each in its own way. During his cosmic sleep, Viṣṇu carried the creatures within him, and he emits them in the form of a lotus that reveals Brahmā among its petals. For Śiva, it is his connection with the sacrificial post that serves as the theme: the *sthāṇu* ("erect pole," one of Śiva's names) is also, in the "terrible" mode, a promise of fertility for the world at the same time as it is a threat of death for the victim that is tied to it. Moreover, through the simplicity of its structure, it gives a representation of the god as close as possible to the unmanifest, as unanthropomorphic as possible. When Śiva is represented in human form (in shrines where he is in a subordinate position, or on mural decorations), he always wears his hair in a bun, like an ascetic; he is always the yogi, the form of the deity that is in charge of the dissolution of the worlds, who sacrifices the world at the end of a cosmic period in a great conflagration. All of this is what is echoed in the linga. The most ancient lingas that have been found do not seem to have been associated with a yoni. The yoni must have been added to make the sacrificial post tolerable as a ritual form in order to eliminate any deadly connotation and to assert the improbable fertility of a god who is a yogi. The sexual symbol thus formed is the solution to the double contradiction that haunts Rudra-Śiva and that his devotees remain aware of: a contradiction between the deadly aspect associated with impurity and death, and the consecrated fertility of the creator (for in his great temples Śiva is considered to be a supreme god, and the worlds emanate from him); and a contradiction between the chaste ascetic and "procreation" necessary for the birth of the worlds. We could not understand this choice if we did not go back first to the Vedic sacrificial post and then to the role played by Rudra-Śiva in the myth of the dissolution of the worlds, in which it is as a yogi that he burns up the three worlds. In the final analysis, all of this was possible only from the perspective of Vedic conceptions, in which the god who presides over the death of sacrificial victims (Rudra is Paśupati, "master of the cattle" and/or "master of sacrificial victims") must be alien to the inhabited world, living as he does in the forest like the yogi.

M.Bi./g.h.

BIBLIOGRAPHY

J. GONDA, *Viṣṇuism and Śivaism: A Comparison* (London 1970). W. D. O'FLAHERTY, *Asceticism and Eroticism in the Mythology of Śiva* (London 1973).

Popular Hinduism

By popular Hinduism is meant the religion as it can be observed in the representations and practices of the whole Hindu population of a given region of India. Briefly, what is involved is a transition from myth to ritual: in the context of the religion of a great civilization like that of India, this means a transition from the Hinduism of the texts—originally and generally in Sanskrit, but often translated as so many versions in an orally transmitted or even written corpus in the various vernaculars of the subcontinent—to its expression as it is actualized in the cults and the pantheon specific to a region. Here we touch on one of the first problems in the observation of Hinduism: the diversity and variety of religious practices from one region to the next, in spite of many common traits and a social system characteristic of all Hindus, i.e., the caste system, based on, among other things, the essentially religious principle of the distinction between pure and impure.

Regional diversity combines with another source of difficulty for an understanding of the whole: some of the religious practices of the middle and lower castes, generally nonvegetarian, seem very different from and incompatible with Hindu orthodoxy and the practices of the upper castes, generally vegetarian, especially with those of the Brahmans. The divinities of the lower castes, served by non-Brahman priests, receive meat offerings and demand blood sacrifices; their cult seems to reveal principles opposed to the Brahmanical ideals of nonviolence and purity.

This apparent contradiction was systematized and transformed by an entire current of thought into a dichotomy whose terms were irreconcilable because they were explained on the basis of a pseudohistorical origin that linked Hinduism with the Aryans alone and attributed any practices judged deviant to the indigenous peoples whom the Aryans conquered. While anthropological studies of recent years have helped us to go beyond this historicism, they have still not entirely broken with the old dichotomous view of popular religion. Yet the study of the organization of the pantheon and the cults in a particular region, as well as the study of the representations expressed in myths locally associated with them, reveal a global structure whose fundamental principles are those of classical Hinduism. This proposition will be illustrated on the basis of a general study done in Tamil Nadu in the district of Tirunelveli, a region at the southern end of the Indian subcontinent.

I. Inferior Divinities (or Deified "Demons")

Divinities of low status are innumerable; they are found throughout India under the most varied names; they are of both sexes, but male divinities, always associated with a barely personalized feminine principle (sister or consort), are dominant in Tirunelveli. In this region their sanctuaries are very distinctive: they are made up of groups of little columns in the shape of truncated pyramids, each of which is the seat and representation of the divinity; a statue in the god's image completes, or sometimes replaces, them. No matter how many seats form it, any sanctuary is supposed to include twenty-one gods, an expression of wholeness. In Tamil this type of holy place is called *pēy-kōvil,* "sanctuary of demons" (from the Sanskrit *preta,* "deceased"). This name tells us something about this category of divinities: they are malevolent creatures, sharing as a group characteristics that hardly distinguish them from demons (among whom are classified the unsatisfied dead); they are transformed into gods and made benevolent from the moment when, after their seat is erected, they are worshiped.

A *pēy-kōvil* can be located either inside or outside the village; sometimes there are two of them; in any case, the divinity who presides over it has a sanctuary of localized reference somewhere in the district. This may be situated within the grounds of one of the main temples of the god Śāstā. Generally speaking, each of these lower divinities can be found in a subordinate position either in a temple of Śāstā or in a temple of the Goddess (see § III below, "Śāstā and the

Amman koḍai of the untouchables of Pallar: those possessed by Pallar walk around the whole village. Photo M.-L. Reiniche.

Goddess"). In this way their sanctuaries are connected in a kind of network across Tirunelveli.

The sanctuary of a lower god belongs in principle (for there are extensions and exceptions) to the kin group descended patrilineally from the ancestor who contracted the relationship with the divinity and built his seat. This relationship, called *aḍimai* ("being at the feet," devotion, slavery), is woven from extremely particular but quite stereotyped circumstances, whose history is sometimes connected directly to the myth of the divinity concerned. In most cases the cult develops following an accidental death or an occasion (a mistake) which allowed the divinity to "follow" the ancestor and impose himself on him and his family by bringing evil (sickness, death), until he is recognized and worshiped.

The various stories telling how the *aḍimai* relationship was contracted reveal two important points. On the one hand, the divinity in his demonic form always comes from somewhere else; it is what is not one's own. Evil is the other, and otherness is expressed in different ways: the demon is generally the god of another group of a different caste; he is also a haunter of open spaces—external and opposed to the special space of the village—and especially the forest and cremation grounds; it is in these places that he attacks the wretch whom he has chosen and whom he pursues (in normal times, the *extra muros* sanctuaries of these divinities are always dangerous places to frequent).

On the other hand, the notion of sacrifice, which keeps returning in various forms, seems essential. A tragic death at the hands of a demon is the sacrifice necessary for a foundation: in giving the cult its basis, it gives the worshiping group the indispensable base that, in circumstances and social contexts that are specific to each case, allows it to define its own identity and develop. (In other regions of India it may be the unsatisfied dead person himself who, by being worshiped, becomes a protective divinity.)

The demon, transformed into a benevolent divinity, continues to manifest his presence on certain occasions through possession. For a given kin group, to possess a god, that is, to have a sanctuary that belongs to him and to worship him there periodically, also means to be possessed: while the

A *pēy-kōvil* outside a village, shown eight days after the *koḍai,* Photo M.-L. Reiniche.

One possessed by the "demon" Çudalai MāḍaN. A temple outside the village of Minkulam (South India). Photo M.-L. Reiniche.

Mariyamman koḍai. One of the possessed and a *Kaniyar.* Photo M.-L. Reiniche.

term *aḍimai* puts the accent on subordination, it also expresses an identity between the group and its god, as well as a relationship of reciprocity from which bargaining is not excluded. Possession, like the ritual, is transmitted from father to son.

The festivals, called *koḍai,* "gift," that celebrate these divinities generally take place once a year, at dates fixed according to each sanctuary's custom, mainly in the hot, dry season from January to August. The *koḍai,* which lasts for three days, is a highly institutionalized affair in Tirunelveli and requires a large number of specialists. Even though it concerns lower gods, in all cases except for untouchables a Brahman priest consecrates and purifies the sanctuary. But the culminating point of the festival is the offering of meat and the sacrifice of male goats. The possessed, those who by heredity "dance the god," are present at all the main stages in the festival, but especially during the sacrifices. Under the effect of a fast begun eight days earlier and in a state of extreme purity, they keep themselves apart from village life for the whole time of the festival, living outside the village;

they are temporarily compared to renouncers. Since they become the god whom they dance but continue to be members of the group offering the sacrifice, they express the identity of the divine and the human and are at the same time indispensable intermediaries for an effective sacrifice. During these festivals specialists sing the story of the god who is being celebrated.

II. Myths

Among all the lower divinities, there is one category particularly in evidence in Tirunelveli: the *māḍaN*. The local myths of two of them are significant in showing how the cults described above should be understood within the larger context of Hinduism.

1. The Story of Takka RājaN

King TakkaN (the Tamil form of the Sanskrit name Dakṣa, a well-known figure in the classical myths) performs *tapas* to obtain a daughter. Śiva, won over by his asceticism, sends Pārvatī to be his daughter; but when the goddess reaches the age of sixteen, he comes to take her back just as TakkaN is about to give her in marriage to a king. TakkaN, enraged, makes a great sacrifice (*yāga*) which so heats up Kailasa, where Śiva and Pārvatī reside, that they cannot stand it any longer. Pārvatī sends her first two sons, Subrahmaṇya and Gaṇeśa, to plead with her father, but to no avail. Śiva then creates VērvaiputtiraN—the "son (born) of sweat"—(in the classic myth, Vīrabhadra) and sends him to destroy TakkaN's sacrifice. In his carnage, VērvaiputtiraN cuts off TakkaN's head and replaces it with the head of a bovine (*māḍu*). When TakkaN is expelled from heaven, he descends to earth to a mountainous place in the west of Tirunelveli district near the source of the Tambraparni, where there is an important regional temple of Śāstā (see § III below, "Śāstā and the Goddess"), the temple of Sorimuttu. TakkaN, now the god Taḷavāy MāḍaN, has a sanctuary there; he then goes on a pilgrimage the length of the valley. Wherever he stops, there is now a place of worship. He finally arrives at another Śāstā temple; this Śāstā keeps him near himself, on the bank of the reservoir: Taḷavāy MāḍaN, the "war chief" of Śāstā, splits in two and becomes Karaiyadi MāḍaN as well, "he who is at the foot of the bank."

After this the story becomes more specific and tells how the god, through a series of crimes against men, is able to impose his worship on one or more local groups.

The following story has many points in common with the preceding one. In both cases, the reference to Dakṣa lays more or less explicit stress both on the destruction of the sacrifice and on the destructive sacrifice, and the rest of the story can be understood as a development of the same theme. In addition, both of the stories include both an extraterrestrial episode and a terrestrial one; it is thus clear that we are dealing with a form of the descent of the divinity, which reproduces at a certain level—that of the immediate interests of man and local society—the function of the avatar.

2. The Story of Çuḍalai MāḍaN

Pārvatī, after doubting the omnipotence of her husband Śiva, is condemned to become the daughter of Dakṣa until Śiva comes to reclaim her and marry her. Pārvatī, also called Brahmaśakti, asks for a child. Śiva sends her to the infernal regions, where the fire of final destruction is kept, to gather a spark from a sacred lamp in the hem of her clothing. The spark then turns into a shapeless mass (*muṇḍam*, "[shaved] head" or "trunk without a head"). When Pārvatī complains, Śiva makes the lump into a child, but instead of feeding him on milk the goddess gives him nectar; the starving child goes and eats from a corpse that is being burned at the cremation ground (*cuḍalai*).

The corpse eater, henceforth called *çuḍalai māḍaN* or *çuḍalai muṇḍaN*, cannot remain in Śiva's paradise and goes down to earth. But before leaving, he imposes conditions: he asks to be given a female counterpart, and he wants a cult (*bali*). The gods prepare this on the cremation ground, and the MāḍaN demands meat offerings, animal victims, and alcohol; he also asks for a *narabali* (human sacrifice). Śiva causes the birth of the Kaniyar singers and dancers, who are ready to offer their blood in place of, or as if it were, a *narabali* (here the myth describes a *koḍai;* the Kaniyar sometimes offer their blood at them). MāḍaN, satisfied, goes to earth to receive the offerings of men.

The first part of the myth is full of reminiscences of more classical texts and elements that in various ways stress the notion of sacrifice. By his birth MāḍaN is associated with the fire of destruction, and logically he is a corpse eater like the cremation fire: he is comparable to Śiva in his terrible form. On the other hand, it is not insignificant that Çuḍalai MāḍaN is first born as a *muṇḍam* (on the level of the sanctuary, the split *māḍaN-muṇḍaN* is often represented by two divinities). *Muṇḍam* can refer both to the ball of food offered to the divinity and to the severed head of the sacrifice. The presence in the sanctuary of *muṇḍaN* next to Çuḍalai MāḍaN, like the "bovine" head (*māḍu*, which may be the source for *māḍaN*) on the shoulders of Taḷavāy MāḍaN—alias Dakṣa—tells us that each of these divinities symbolizes the sacrifice in the double sense of the one who offers the sacrifice and the sacrificial victim. Also note MāḍaN's relation to the goddess as *śakti*, which sometimes, in the text, goes so far as to identify them.

The second part of the myth describes the demon's wanderings on earth. He descends at Kāśi (Banaras), the holy city of Hinduism on the Ganges, and from there goes to Madurai, formerly the political and religious capital for the whole of the far south of India. He worships the goddess of the great temple of the city, becomes known to the local Brahmans, and then departs for Tirunelveli. He crosses the district and even pays a visit to Kerala country, which borders the district to the west. While on the one hand he worships the higher divinities of the great sanctuaries, at the same time he oppresses the people at every step of his journey until they worship him: he possesses the women as if he were their husband, feeds on the fetuses of pregnant women, kills men, burns down houses, and uses disguise and illusion to spread confusion.

Then Çuḍalai MāḍaN goes to Śāstā's sanctuary in Sorimuttu, which is situated near the source of the Tambraparni in the Ghats. He settles near there on the finest tree in the forest, a *vaNNi maram*, the "fire" tree; Brahmaśakti is on top of it and the demons are all around it. At this point carpenters come to cut down the tree for the great temple of Subrahmaṇya at Tiruchendur, in the eastern part of the district. They are supposed to turn it into a "flag tree," the pole at the entrance to the sanctuary, on which the divinity's banner is hoisted at festivals to be carried in processions. As soon as the carpenters start their work, MāḍaN makes them all kill one another in a great bloodbath. After thus forcing recognition of his hegemony, he demands worship, and the tree cannot be cut down until he gets it. Finally there is a processional return to Tiruchendur; MāḍaN is celebrated in blood sacrifices, including sacrifices of buffaloes, and Subrahmaṇya grants him the right to receive offerings in this world because he has the power to subdue evildoers.

Çuḍalai MāḍaN in human form, at Gopalasamudram (South India). Photo M.-L. Reiniche.

The various episodes of this tale simply repeat over and over again the necessity of the destructive sacrifice whose victim is, finally, man. The necessity is accompanied by a mutual and hierarchical acknowledgment between the higher values represented by the great gods and the values of blood sacrifice demanded by the deified demons.

The myth's geographical frame corresponds more or less to Tirunelveli and highlights the east-west axis of the Tambraparni River with Sorimuttu and Tiruchendur—Śāstā and Subrahmaṇya—as its two poles. On the regional level, the main sanctuaries of the divinities are spatially opposed. The sanctuary of Sorimuttu, located both in the mountains and in the forest, is the ideal place to polarize all the values associated with *kāḍu*, open space, the "forest," in opposition to *grāma*, inhabited space. The forest tree, the "fire" tree that is the dwelling of both the demon born of the fire of the sacrificial lamp and the goddess, slayer of powers that disturb the world order, must be transported from its wild place to the pure and separate place of the great temple of Subrahmaṇya. Made into the "flag tree," it becomes the symbol of the manifestation of divinity and of the positive sacrifice that must be performed for the good of the worlds. But the passage from one place to the other, which can be understood as a separation between the negative (dangerous) and positive aspects of the sacrifice, cannot be accomplished without a consecration of the destructive aspects: these ground and make fertile the positive sacrifice of the great temple, since this cannot take place until the values represented by the inferior divinity have been recognized.

This separation, on the level of representation and worship, between the ideals of nonviolence and purity and the recognition that any act required for the maintenance of life is indissociable from violence and impurity, is transposed to the society itself. As in the myth, it is primarily non-Brahmans, and especially members of the lower castes, who are the demons' prey; in relation to the higher castes, their vulnerability is indissociable from their impurity, and their ignorance makes them "stupid beings" (*māḍaN*), which assimilates them to the divinity of the same name. Individually all men (including Brahmans) are impure and stupid because they are composed of both life and death. In this system, nevertheless, the Brahmans are the guardians of the positive sacrifice because of their knowledge and the purity that they are in a position to preserve. The ignorance and impurity attributed to the lower castes makes them the exact antithesis of the Brahmans; they are the preeminent agents and victims of the destruction and negation of life, as well as of its fertility. Just as the positive and negative aspects of the sacrifice are complementary, the lower castes are as indispensable as the Brahmans for the maintenance of society and the prosperity of the world.

All of the inferior divinities are connected more or less explicitly with Śiva (or with the Goddess). This is to be understood in connection with the destructive aspects of the god, and more precisely with his relation to the sacrifice, especially its impurities and dangers: there is an equivalence between MāḍaN and the terrible form of Śiva; both of them haunt cremation grounds, and the villagers do not hesitate to identify them. There is also a distance between them. Çuḍalai MāḍaN is born as a shapeless mass, evoking either the severed head of the sacrifice or the ball of food of the offering, but in either case it is the symbol of the sacrificial victim. Furthermore, he is not essentially different from Taḷavāy, MāḍaN, or Dakṣa, sacrificed by Śiva with the help of Vīrabhadra, who comes forth out of Śiva. MāḍaN is both Śiva and Śiva's sacrificial victim; at the same time he is an intermediary between Śiva and men, the manifestation of the god (in his terrible aspects if they are not properly recognized) on this earth.

The splitting in two of Śiva and his delegate reflects another splitting: that which takes place during the festival between those who offer the *koḍai* and those who are possessed. Both of these belong to the same kin group, but the possessed person is separated from the group and, going outside the dwelling area to seek a state of abstinence and purity, finds himself temporarily in a situation of renunciation. During the principal moments of worship, he dances the god, and, like Śiva's dance, the dance of possession is a dance of destruction, and its presence is particularly necessary at the moment of blood sacrifice. It is as if the possessed person's particular state of purity and identification with the god made it possible for him to handle the dangerous aspects of the sacrifice, and consequently to make its benefits fall back upon the group of which he never ceases to be a member.

III. Śāstā and the Goddess

The hierarchically superior position of Śāstā and the Goddess, to whom the inferior divinities are subordinate, serves to express a different, more general, level of religious and social reality. Throughout the south of Tamil Nadu, the god Śāstā (also often known under the name of AiyaNār) and the Goddess, while they have separate places of worship, are always associated, to the extent that locally they are complementary from various points of view.

We can take the example of a village of Tirunelveli: depending on its importance, it will have at least one, and usually several, sanctuaries of goddesses. One or two may be common to the village as a whole; the other belongs to the area of a local group of a caste or subcaste. With their different names, the various goddesses are always forms of the great Goddess, and their equivalence is expressed by saying that they are eight sisters. Two of them, however, are distinguished. She who dwells at the "north gate" is supposed to be responsible for the foundation of the village: as such, she is considered the eldest of all the sisters, and she is also called *brāhmacāriṇī:* the notion of celibacy gives her a dimension of renunciation. The other goddess is the figure of the supreme wife, the wife of the great god, here Śiva, and she has all the auspicious traits of female destiny. Both of these, the one because she is a renouncer, the other because she is a wife, receive only vegetarian offerings. In this they are opposed to all the other goddesses of the locality, closer to the terrible form of Durgā or Kālī, who demand blood sacrifices during festivals that, like those of the inferior divinities, are called *koḍai.* In one of their sanctuaries, shared by the entire locality, the first male goat sacrificed to the goddess is offered in the name of the community as a whole by the most important person in the village in terms of authority and wealth, generally a non-Brahman, but always a member of a high caste in which the rules of orthodoxy and vegetarianism can be strictly followed. Finally, these goddesses have their hereditary possessed mediums, members of the group to whom the sanctuary principally belongs.

Festival at the temple of Śiva. Photo M.-L. Reiniche.

In this region of Tamil Nadu, the Goddess appears above all as a goddess of the locality, as closely connected to the habitat itself as to the people who live there. Her functions are connected with the prosperity and well-being of the group, and above all its health: as is the case elsewhere in India, the Goddess both gives and cures illness in general and smallpox in particular. The myths associated with her are not especially distinctive. They echo the main theme of the *Devī Māhātmya:* the Goddess's struggle against the *asura.* On the popular level, sickness is directly associated with her: because the Goddess rid the world of *asuras,* they say, the Lord granted her the boon of spreading smallpox. The myth expresses, not without paradox, the fact that all forms of evil are interconnected.

The cult of the local goddess is sometimes associated with the cult of Śāstā in the same cycle of festivals. This is rarely the case in Tirunelveli. However, at the time of the Goddess's *koḍai* (as well as during the festivals of the lower divinities), the story of Śāstā is always sung before the story of the divinity who is being celebrated.

The preeminence of Śāstā over the Goddess is due both to his status as a male divinity and to the fact that he is generally a vegetarian god—although there remains a certain ambiguity on this point, to which we shall return. Moreover, in Tirunelveli it is explained by saying that he always receives the first homage because he is the god of the *kula.* This term, which designates a corporate group, has a greater or lesser extension depending on the context. In this case it means the patrilineal descendants of a distant ancestor, and every *kula* of whatever caste is supposed to celebrate the Śāstā of the ancestor's place of origin, thus associating the origin of what may be called a clan or a lineage with a given locality and territory. Elsewhere in India such a divinity is usually found only among the high castes, Brahmans or aristocratic Kṣatriya lineages; it goes with status, prestige, and a certain form of authority, none of which the middle and lower castes have; among middle and lower castes in Tirunelveli, genealogical memory is short and the lineage structure relatively weak. In this context, the extension of which Śāstā is the object as the *kula* god probably results from historical factors that are difficult to account for, but also from certain characteristics of the god and his cult.

Śāstā's sanctuaries are innumerable; generally situated outside the locality, they are often found on the bank of a reservoir: the god has something to do with the arrival of water and the fertility of the fields; as a result, every Śāstā is the god of those who hold traditional rights over the land irrigated by a reservoir. At the same time, he is a hunting god; he commands the beasts and demons and rules over the wild space that is in opposition with the inhabited space of the village. More locally, one or more Śāstās are associated with the territory that depends on and defines an agglomeration. Their sanctuaries are usually only of local interest, with the exception of a small number of them, including the sanctuary of Sorimuttu for Tirunelveli and that of Sabarimalai in Kerala; both are located in the mountains.

In Tirunelveli the festival of Śāstā is celebrated in March on Panguni Uttaram, a date of the Hindu calendar reserved for Subrahmaṇya in other parts of Tamil Nadu. In Tirunelveli district this is the occasion for a displacement of the population: everyone goes to worship his ancestral Śāstā; on this occasion every sanctuary brings together people not only of different castes but from different localities. A distinction is nevertheless maintained, among both the devotees and the divinities of a sanctuary, between vegetarians and nonvegetarians. The services on the morning of the festival are strictly vegetarian; Śāstā is honored above all others and receives honors from everyone, including the Brahmans and the orthodox high castes. But with the approach of night Śāstā seems to be forgotten in favor of the inferior divinities who are subordinate to him. The festival starts to look like a *koḍai* offered by non-Brahmans, with meat offerings, blood sacrifice, and dances of possession.

Every Śāstā sanctuary is thus the site for the operation of one of the fundamental principles of Hinduism, that of the distinction between vegetarian and carnivorous (gods and men); this overlaps with other essential oppositions: nonviolence-violence, pure-impure, etc. At the same time, Śāstā, chief of the demons, sanctions blood sacrifices, but not without ambiguity, since while every devotee says that he is raising a male goat to offer to his Śāstā on Panguni Uttaram, when the time comes he will dedicate it to an inferior divinity. In this sense, a Śāstā sanctuary is also the site where the relationship between inferior and superior is symbolically expressed: just as the deified demons are subordinate to Śāstā, who at the same time guarantees them a certain legitimacy, so the great majority of non-Brahmans are subordinate to the traditional holders of status, authority, and superior rights over the land. These non-Brahmans are devotees of the inferior divinities, and it is these who are their *kula* gods; but they always refer to the superior power, in this case to Śāstā.

The relationship that unites Śāstā to the inferior divinities can be specified in at least one case. The divine personality of the god is not easily defined, and there is a certain diversity in his iconography, his attributes, etc. Sometimes he seems to resemble Vīrabhadra, who was produced by Śāstā to destroy Dakṣa's sacrifice; this trait is confirmed in Tirunelveli at a certain number of sanctuaries: whenever Talavāy-Karaiyaḍi MāḍaN, alias Dakṣa, the divinity with a bovine head, is near Śāstā, the god, even if not recognized as such by his devotees, is basically Vīrabhadra. We can surmise that at least in this particular case (although it is likely that the attribution can be generalized to a certain extent) Śāstā assures the functions of Vīrabhadra—and so of Śiva-Rudra—in connection with the sacrifice.

Although Śāstā has often been taken for a modest village divinity of Dravidian origin, and although his cult is restricted to South India (Kerala and part of Tamil Nadu), he must not be confused with the inferior divinities: he is their master but does not belong to their category. Among his names, *aiyaN, aiyaNār, aiyappaN,* from Sanskrit *ārya,* "Lord, master," and *śāstā,* from Sanskrit *śāstṛ,* "he who punishes, governs, teaches," all refer to both the Brahman and the king.

The myth of his birth, well known among the villagers, is taken directly from various Purāṇic versions. A *rākṣasa* performs *tapas,* and through his asceticism he obtains from Śiva the ability to burn or cut whatever he touches with his finger. Hardly has he received this gift when he wants to try it out on Śiva himself, who is forced to flee. Viṣṇu intervenes in his seductive female form of Mohinī and gets the *rākṣasa* to destroy himself. Śiva wants to see Viṣṇu in the form of a young woman; he lets himself be seduced in turn, and from his seed AiyaNār is born.

The Purāṇa tells nothing more than this; in its relative simplicity, the symbolism of this myth—and notably the complementarity of the two great gods in a single act of creation—is probably sufficient in itself. Yet the story is continued in regional texts. As in the case of the inferior divinities, the second part of the story takes place on earth: Śāstā is also a form of divine descent.

One of the versions, the one that is sung during festivals in Tirunelveli, does not explain the descent; but the version presented in the myth of Śāstā from Sabarimalai is entirely Purāṇic and takes up a well-known mythic theme: Śāstā is sent to earth as the adopted son of a king of Kerala country, for he is the only one who can kill the female buffalo-*asura, mahiṣi.* From this point on, the two stories are comparable: the god is both literate and expert in the use of arms. In the Tirunelveli version he presents himself to the king of Madurai and stands out among all the king's warriors (this recalls Tirunelveli's political dependence on Madurai). As the result of a plot hatched by the king's entourage, he is sent to the forest to get tiger's milk to cure the queen's pretended headaches. In the Kerala version, Śāstā takes advantage of this opportunity to kill the female buffalo *mahiṣi.* Then in both versions he returns to the royal city with tigresses; he sows terror, confounds the wicked, and reveals his divine nature. After this he withdraws to a mountain—to Sabarimalai or Aryankavu—where he has his sanctuary: here he is represented as a yogi (whereas in the plain he is usually accompanied by two wives).

The myth simultaneously affirms Śāstā's royal characteristics and his Brahmanic ones (he is literate and a renouncer). Everything takes place on the level of a particular kingdom. The divinity imposes himself through his warlike and superhuman aspects, but he does not reign directly over society; it is the territory as a whole that he protects. Śāstā is associated more with external space; he is a hunter and yogi: hunting and renunciation are both associated with the forest; since he dominates the wild world, he commands the demons, but he is also concerned with the fertility of the fields and with the water that they need. He embodies the potentialities of external space in relation to the socialized space of the village.

Although on the cosmic level Śāstā is the destroyer of the *asura,* on the earthly level of the kingdom he restores order, and he does this by introducing the values of the forest (since in the last analysis the ultimate value is renunciation) into the organized world of the royal city. The struggle against the *asura* remains the model and justification for divine intervention among men, as well as the means of transmitting the message of Hinduism: salvation through devotion and renunciation.

In a way the complementarity of Śāstā and the Goddess is what unites the two spaces and the values associated with them. While the goddess of the locality (she can also have other dimensions) is connected with the habitat, Śāstā is connected with the territory as a whole, which includes the village. This is also a complementarity in function with regard to the different needs of the group, more or less comparable to the complementarity of men and women in Indian society.

We must not, however, be too rigorous in defining the spheres of influence of the two divinities. We have seen that the legend of Śāstā from Sabarimalai, in giving a mythical reason for the birth, takes up a theme that is generally associated with the Goddess: the destruction of the buffalo *asura*. While the goddess battles the buffalo demon *mahiṣa*, Śāstā deals with the feminine form, *mahiṣi*. This is probably a case of the appropriation of a well-known theme by the followers of the famous AiyappaN of Sabarimalai. Nevertheless, the use of this theme, with its reversal of masculine and feminine roles, is not without significance and tends to suggest a certain functional equivalence of the forms of descent of the god and those of the goddess. On the level of the manifestation, the masculine and feminine aspects of the divine vary by complementing one another.

IV. Divine Hierarchy and Social Hierarchy

Both Śāstā and the Goddess, like the inferior divinities on another level, can be regarded as forms of descent of the supreme divinity; even the goddess, the personalized and projected "energy" (*śakti*) of the god, is viewed in this way in local myths. In the context of rural life, these forms of descent are closer to human interests in their main aspects: the complementary functions of Śāstā and the Goddess are more closely connected with the territory and its prosperity, as well as with the health and well-being of the resident group; those of the inferior divinities are connected with the fertility of the kin group.

Every village has these two categories of divinities. If the agglomeration is important enough, moreover, the supreme form of the god (Śiva or Viṣṇu) is also present in a great Brahmanic temple. On this level, too, the cult and the festivals concern the general prosperity of the locality, especially the maintenance of the sociocosmic order of which the local order is the projection. In Tirunelveli, in sum, simplifying the complexity of the pantheon a bit, we can distinguish three categories of temples corresponding to three main categories of divinities.

On the local level of each of these sanctuaries, we are in the universe of the ritual, of either vegetarian or blood sacrifice, that is, of the effective act, whose goal is the good of the worlds, and so of man; the universe of the ritual corresponds to that of society. But it is also important to note that no divinity is limited to this universe; each of them participates in the ultimate values of renunciation, which lie beyond specifically social values. The demonic dimension of the inferior divinities has in it something comparable to the values of renunciation, if only in a negative sense; and this whole set of values (renunciation, danger, something beyond the pure and the impure) is associated in Hindu symbolism with the same space, that of the outside, the world of the forest, opposed to the social space of the village, the space of the strict separation of pure and impure and the distinction of castes. While in the end it is the values of renunciation and devotion that orient the religion of the ritual, in a parallel way the values associated with the demonic forms of the divine (violence, impurity) seem in the last analysis indispensable for making the ritual fruitful and gaining the goods of this world that are necessary for the reproduction of any life and any society.

The dichotomous series introduced by the opposition of vegetarian and carnivore, pure and impure, etc., is reproduced both in the pantheon and among men; in a way the vegetarian divinities are those of the Brahmans and the other high castes, whereas the meat-eating divinities are those of the lower castes. This overly one-sided view must, however, be qualified. To meet a crisis, even a Brahman will occasionally offer (vegetarian) worship to an inferior god; on the other hand, the superior divinities are the objects of everyone's devotion. But the multiplicity of representations is definitively resolved in the affirmed unity of the divine.

Similarly, the relationship between pantheon and society is complex and cannot be reduced to a vague reflection. The three divine categories of the local pantheon correspond to the three main divisions of the society, more or less assimilable to the *varṇas* of the classical tradition; this equivalence operates on the level of the functions that each category, divine and social, assumes. On the one hand, the Brahmans hold the knowledge of the world order as it is and should be, and therefore also purity; by their status, they are close to the superior form of divinity. By contrast, the population of the non-Brahmans, the Śūdras, is entirely involved in tasks of service for the higher *varṇas*. Between these two extremes, those who have both wealth and authority over men take on, locally and regionally, the functions of the Kṣatriya *varṇa*—whether or not they really come from it. On the one hand, they compete with the Brahmans in maintaining the social order according to dharma; on the level of the great temple, they are the ideal practitioners of the function of sacrificer, reproducing in this way the function of royalty. On the other hand, because of their authority and the protection that they are supposed to provide, they work with the Śūdras to maintain local prosperity; it is they who order blood sacrifices to the local goddess. Their intermediate position and their functions correspond to those of Śasta and the Goddess.

It is on this level that the various oppositions are resolved, in particular the opposition between nonviolence and blood sacrifice. The function of power sanctions the necessity of this always violent act for the prosperity of the world and, in the last analysis, for the preservation of the Brahmanic ideals of nonviolence and purity. The structure of the local pantheon involves a complete construction of the world that includes a model for society and its reproduction.

M.-L.R./j.l.

Avatars

Classical mythology knows only of avatars (*avatāras*) of Viṣṇu, but there are also local avatars of Śiva. And alongside the avatars of Śiva and of Viṣṇu, the two sons of Śiva also appear on the scene, and one of them at least, Skanda-Subrahmaṇya, seems to have a function in South India that is quite similar to that of an avatar, namely, the function of a great god who is sovereign over a given territory. By contrast, nowhere is there a son of Viṣṇu. But classical mythology, even if it introduces Gaṇapati only quite late, knows Skanda very well from the time of the epics. It is important to pay attention to these differences, and this is one of the problems that the myths of avatars should help to resolve.

On the other hand, at least on the mythic level, the avatar of Viṣṇu is always related to a cosmic period, the yuga. The Supreme Puruṣa emits the world for the period of one *mahākalpa* (one life of Brahmā or one hundred years of Brahmā), and within one *mahākalpa* there are one hundred times three hundred sixty days of Brahmā or *kalpas,* which are so many cycles in which the triple world, under the guardianship of the Trimūrti, undergoes a period of emission and a period of reabsorption, a cosmic day and night. Each *kalpa* is measured by one thousand *mahāyugas* or "divine" yugas, each *mahāyuga* being composed of a series of four yugas in decreasing order: the Kṛta Yuga, in which dharma, the sociocosmic order, is in a perfect state, is measured by four thousand "divine years" and is flanked by two "twilights" (but not "nights," as are periods of greater duration) of four hundred years each; the Tretā Yuga, in which dharma is reduced by one-fourth, has a length of only three thousand divine years and two twilights of three hundred years; during the Dvāpara Yuga, dharma is cut in half, and the duration is two thousand years, with twilights of two hundred years. Finally, the Kali Yuga, the most evil yuga and the one in which we live—as it should be—retains only one-fourth of dharma and one thousand years of duration, with twilights of one hundred years. When these are added up, a *mahāyuga* lasts for twelve thousand divine years, a figure that must be multiplied by three hundred sixty to get the corresponding number of human years. Here we are in a temporal unit which concerns us more than the *kalpa,* not only because of its duration, but also because it involves dharma, for which man is responsible above all. Also, the yuga (and the *mahāyuga*) is operative only in our triple world, and the cosmic crises that constitute the twilights affect only the three worlds between which the creatures transmigrate. Whatever may have been the origin of the yugic structure, it is not insignificant that in Hindu mythology the four yugas borrow their names from the game of dice.

According to the theory—which was already taking form in the epic—an avatar is a "descent" of Viṣṇu into the triple world when, at the end of a yuga, dharma is in such a bad state that a divine intervention is needed to reestablish it. They go so far as to say that Narasiṃha, the half-man, half-lion avatar, appeared at the end of the last Kṛta Yuga, that Rāma was the avatar at the end of the Tretā Yuga, and that Kṛṣṇa was the avatar of the end of the Dvāpara. This attractive ordering is not without its problems: it is difficult to understand how Viṣṇu intervenes in order to reestablish dharma when the following yuga is in fact inferior in dharma to the one that preceded it. Devotion to Kṛṣṇa cannot tolerate the idea that Kṛṣṇa could have remained in the world during the Kali Yuga, and has this yuga begin with the death of Kṛṣṇa: but Kṛṣṇa descended to earth at the end of the Dvāpara with the precise purpose of restoring dharma. On the other hand, it would be hard to find an account of a cosmic twilight like those given in the Purāṇas for the creation and dissolution of the cosmos. There are various accounts, for each avatar, but although they all bear witness to an identical deep structure and make use of stereotyped characters, one would still be hard-pressed to speak of *the* myth of the avatar or of *the* twilight between two yugas in the same way as we spoke of *the* Purāṇic cosmology and *pralaya.* In short, although we can conceive of a temporal cycle on the order of a *kalpa,* it would be on the level of the *mahāyuga,* of the group of four yugas, rather than that of the yuga: at the end of the Kali Yuga, a catastrophe permits the passage to a new Kṛta Yuga and reestablishes the integrity of dharma. And this eventuality is foreseen for the end of our Kali Yuga, when Viṣṇu will intervene in the form of the Kalkin avatar. But in any case, this temporal cycle—which must be essential, since it is the unit by which the greater cycles were determined—no longer corresponds to a rhythm of divine life or divine yoga. There is thus a rupture between the cycles of Purāṇic cosmogony and the yugas, with which epic mythology seems more preoccupied than with *kalpas.*

Another difficulty arises from the ambivalence that the universalism of bhakti introduces with regard to dharma: the Kali Yuga is the preeminent age of bhakti, because with dharma disappearing, devotion to Viṣṇu must compensate for it; thus Śūdras and women, those forgotten by high-caste society, may find salvation during this yuga by means of devotion—including performance of their duties as women and Śūdras. Divine grace does the rest. Is it so necessary, then, to reestablish a Kṛta Yuga, the age in which salvation is most difficult to obtain? Apparently divine grace allows sin to flourish, since even the wicked can obtain salvation if their last words are for Viṣṇu. They even tell the story of the evil man who, in his hour of death, called to his son just before dying; his son was named Nārāyaṇa, which is also the name of the god, and this was enough to save him. But the salvation of individuals does not prevent social disorder from increasing, so one must wait for the inevitable return of a golden age. The confusion is increased when one remembers that devotion is preferentially given to the avatars of Viṣṇu who come to reestablish dharma: Rāma and Kṛṣṇa are the principal objects of Vaiṣṇava bhakti (at least in northern India). This is simultaneously the reinforcement of dharma by bhakti and the mutual opposition of the two.

What then is the meaning of the divine intervention, of the new form taken by the supreme Puruṣa? The classic list of the ten avatars—which even today allows certain variants—does not tell us much more. The list contains an anomalous assemblage of themes, of which some are cosmogonic themes taken from the Veda (the Fish, the Tortoise, the Boar, the Dwarf), while others are much more enigmatic, and since they occur today as the ruling divinities of certain regions, we may well imagine that it was their cultic position which made them avatars. In any case, this sidesteps the question that remains to be resolved, for this incarnating god had the gift of inspiring theologico-comparative innovations.

If we bear in mind that it is the epics that speak to us of these divine descents for the first time (in stories in which Viṣṇu is accompanied on earth by a certain number of heavenly gods, the ancient Vedic gods, or other superhuman beings) and center their story around these descents, we may expect them to throw some light upon the problem. The main difficulty then becomes the enormity of the works to be dealt with, the MBh especially; yet it is the MBh, in which didactic passages are constantly mingled with the narrative, that is the most apt to give us the answer to our question. It strikes us immediately that the narrative is explicitly located at the junction between the Dvāpara Yuga and the Kali Yuga, but that two of its characters are, also explicitly, incarnations of Dvāpara and Kali, who have become *asuras* to fit the demands of the myth. The chronological framework of the junction between the two yugas is quite fuzzy, and there continues to be debate today about the point in the narrative where one yuga gives way to the other. On the other hand, the fact that the incarnation of Kali becomes the usurping king who, in order to take control of the royal house, goes to war against the five brothers who represent righteous kingship, thus precipitating the catastrophe foretold from the start, is fundamental. This is because at several points the epic does not hesitate to call a bad king a Kali, and this epithet develops into the more formal idea that it is the king who makes the yuga (MBh 5.132; 12.69–70) or, as is said in the *Laws of Manu* (9.301–2), that it is the king who is the

The wild-boar avatar of Viṣṇu saving the earth. The Temple of Alagarkoil (Madura). Photo M. Biardeau.

Rāma, the avatar of Viṣṇu and the hero of the *Rāmāyaṇa*. Private collection. Photo Dominique Champion.

yuga. In other words, the state of the world, that is, the state of dharma, depends essentially upon the governing king.

But in the *Rāmāyaṇa*, the Rāma avatar is the legitimate king. When he is exiled he recovers his kingdom only after the conquest of Laṅkā; that is, after a war in which the enemy must be killed at any cost. In the MBh the intrigue is more complex, for the Kṛṣṇa avatar acts as though his past as an avatar were behind him and offers himself as a model for the representative of the ideal king, who also stands as his own double. The avatar thus recovers in himself something of the yogi Puruṣa when he contents himself with counseling and guiding without engaging in battle, yet he ensures the victory of his close friend Arjuna when he takes the initiative in all the twisting of dharma, i.e., of the code of battle, that he makes in order to win: what matters here above all else is making war and winning the victory in order to save the world. Avatar and king are undoubtedly connected, and they are on earth to make war; the MBh says this explicitly.

If Hindu mythic structures have reserved such an important place for the avatars of Viṣṇu, it is not only because the character of the king is pivotal to Hindu society. It is also and especially because his role and the ethic that it presupposes are opposed on the one hand to those of the Brahman and on the other to those of the renunciant. To express it in religious terms, it is because he is excluded from salvation. The fact that it is the epic genre that introduces us to the avatar is sufficient proof that war is central to the debate. The king is considered to be above all the possessor of power and the one who uses power to administer punishment within the kingdom. This is not his only role, but it is this role that concerns the ideology.

Without repeating the whole debate on *ahiṃsā*, "nonkilling," we may summarize what appears to have been the fundamental approach of the Hindu tradition, which was based on a revelation that centered on the sacrifice *and* on its negation: the sacrifice, of which the Brahman is the officiating priest, implies by definition the destruction of the oblatory substance, either animal or vegetable (every great Vedic sacrifice includes both kinds of oblation). Every destruction is a death, every death a stain, a sin of impurity that constitutes a danger to the sacrificer as well as to the officiating priest. The ritual takes account of this and takes every precaution to wipe out the stain inherent in sacrifice and even all impurity: since it is possible to say "killing in sacrifice is not killing" (*Manu* 5.39), it then suffices to transform every activity into a sacrifice in order for every killing, even the most insignificant and the most inevitably joined to life, to be expiated. The renunciant who refuses the sacrifice also refuses this facility and becomes fastidious about the canons of ahiṃsā. Apparently we owe to the renunciant the adoption of a vegetarian diet by the Brahman and his imitators and correlatively the very rapid abandonment of official Vedic sacrifices, for which purely vegetable offerings were substituted. The ideal of the renunciant commanded the attention of the man of the world at the same time as the Absolute became the Great Yogi. Conceived as superior, he evidently first made his mark on the Brahman, who became and remains to the present day the champion of *ahiṃsā*. Within the bhakti tradition, the Brahman is no more than the one who must live under the shelter of royal protection and can practice the trade of officiating priest only by keeping himself pure of all "violence." In particular, he may not defend himself.

But the Hindus—whom we mistakenly imagine to be forever lost in contemplation and unable to deal with material necessities—did not, for all this, shut out the Kṣatriya, the king and warrior, from the realm of values. They are too convinced of the need for strong government. Only the Kṣatriya can encourage, and if necessary constrain, each individual to follow his dharma (even the renunciant, who became a role model for society). The distinction and complementarity of the two superior *varṇas,* Brahmans and Kṣatriyas, already mentioned in the Puruṣa hymn, becomes all the stronger for this. The more the Brahman becomes "nonviolent," the more the king must be able to make war. And since the Supreme Puruṣa, as the Great Yogi, is the guarantor of Brahmanic values (in which the sacrifice becomes subordinated to yoga), he must also have a form that guarantees royal values: this is the avatar. The avatar has not forgotten that he was a yogi, but he also knows that he has descended into a world in which the sacrifice is the sole driving force, a world whose cyclic renewal is conceived as a total sacrifice. It is easy to see how war could become the warrior's perfect form of sacrifice, a sacrifice in which he would have only a marginal need for the Brahman officiating priest and in which he might offer himself as victim with the hope of substituting the person of the enemy in the course of battle. And if this sacrifice, as murderous as any other, is performed with indifference, "for the good of the worlds," it carries with it no pollution because it requires no attachment.

The epic conceptions are accompanied by a complete transformation of the doctrine of *karman*—of action, notably of ritual action. The renouncer of the Revelation (*śruti*) is first of all the one who condemns all action, particularly ritual acts, because they produce results in an indefinite number of rebirths. The *Bhagavad Gītā*—whose inclusion within the MBh is all too often forgotten—disputes the validity of this form of renunciation: Kṛṣṇa (the avatar) explains to Arjuna (the figure of the ideal king) how it is impossible to live without action and consequently to live without killing, if only imperceptible animalcules. But the counterpart of this is that it is not the act that pollutes but attachment to the results of the act, the fact that the act is wanted in order to produce a desired fruit. If one suppresses this attachment and substitutes for it concern for the good of the worlds, which may be termed a royal concern, then not only does every act become good and productive of deliverance, but the man who performs it imitates the divinity who, while a yogi and insofar as he is a yogi, perpetually "acts" in order to keep the worlds in existence. When the warrior kills enemies who threaten dharma, he is the image of the yogi god who reabsorbs the worlds into himself: this is the meaning of the terrible vision of himself that Kṛṣṇa gives to Arjuna in the *Gītā* (11). The avatar, the warrior form of the divinity, is only an image of the Great Yogi who reabsorbs the worlds into himself at the end of the *kalpa* or the *mahākalpa*. Similarly, the king who is at war against evil enemies, and who kills them for the good of the worlds and through his adherence to the order of the worlds desired by the divinity, is the replica of the avatar and thus the lesser image of the Great Yogi whose yoga produces the sacrifice of the worlds.

In practice, the myths of the avatars are generally placed in opposition to the divine incarnation of one or many *asuras* who, under one form or another, try to take control or have taken control of a power which does not belong to them and by which they establish in the world a state of disorder—*adharma*. A typical scenario is that of the battle of the *devas* and the *asuras,* in which the *asuras* are victorious and dislodge the *devas* from heaven. The inhabitants of the infernal regions, occupying heaven, receive in the place of the gods the oblations coming from the earth: the cosmic order is turned upside down, and the gods go to ask the help of Viṣṇu, who "descends" to restore the only viable order. Often the story includes a favor bestowed by Brahmā upon the king of the *asuras,* the baneful consequences of which he finds he is unable to control. Another scenario sets the stage on earth, where the fate of the three worlds (heaven, earth, hell) unfolds: here it is a Kṣatriya, a king, who fails to make dharma reign in his kingdom. Whatever the nature of his bad conduct, the result is always that the Brahmans are wronged, and this harms even the gods, who need harmony between Brahmans and kings in order to receive their portion of the sacrifice and to be nourished with it. The evil Kṣatriya is always finally considered an incarnate *asura,* and the disorder always takes the form of the encroachment of royal power upon the power of the Brahmans.

M.Bi./d.w.

BIBLIOGRAPHY

M. BIARDEAU, "Études de mythologie hindoue," part 4, *BEFEO* (1976).

Abbreviations

MBh *Mahābhārata* (Poona 1930: Citrashala Press edition)
R *Rāmāyaṇa* (Gorakhpur edition)

NARA/NĀRĀYAṆA

Nārāyaṇa is well known as a name of Viṣṇu. He seems to appear in the form of the *ṛṣi* Nārāyaṇa and is thus inseparable from the *ṛṣi* Nara. The *ṛṣi,* an omnipresent character in Hindu mythology, is a man of bygone times (the seven great *ṛṣis* of the origins are Brahmā's first creatures) whose ascetic life in the forest and extreme purity (connected with a scrupulous practice of daily rituals) developed his knowledge and power in an extraordinary way. Simultaneously an ascetic in the forest and a householder with his wives and his sacrificial fires, he provides the mythic model for the *vānaprastha,* the one who has settled in the forest, the theoretical stage in every human life between the stage of the householder and that of the total renunciant. He is the watchful intermediary between gods and men. Among the best known *ṛṣis* are Nārada, Vyāsa (the other incarnation of Nārāyaṇa, the one who brought the Veda to men, as well as the MBh and the Purāṇas), Agastya, Vasiṣṭha, and Viśvāmitra. It is, however, unusual to see the supreme god himself take the form of an *ṛṣi*, and we must still take into account the way he splits into Nara and Nārāyaṇa. Because it is truly a splitting: the *Śatapatha Brāhmaṇa* (a text of the Vedic canon) contains what may have been the basis of this mythic creation. In 13.6.1, in the context of the (human) sacrifice to the Puruṣa, the Puruṣa is referred to as Puruṣa Nārāyaṇa. We know that *puruṣa* and *nara* are synonyms (meaning "man"), and it seems clear that *Nārāyaṇa* is the mythical transformation of the expression *puruṣāyaṇa*, which occurs in one Upaniṣad. Puruṣa Nārāyaṇa—who at this stage is still not explicitly Viṣṇu—is the proper name of the supreme deity associated with *Nārāyaṇa*, a name that is patronymic in form. One only has to cut this name in two and put *nara* back in place of *puruṣa* to obtain two characters, one of whom will be called Nara and the other Nārāyaṇa.

This creation seems to be tied to the MBh: it may have been motivated by the splitting of the avatar into Kṛṣṇa and Arjuna, the avatar himself (Nārāyaṇa) and the ideal human king who must play the role of the avatar on earth (Nara). Since it was impossible to read this dichotomy directly into Nārāyaṇa the supreme god, it was hypostasized in a pair of inseparable *ṛṣis*. But these two *ṛṣis* merely constitute the intermediate stage that makes it possible to pass from Viṣṇu to Kṛṣṇa and Arjuna. So their mythology, though rich, is fragmentary.

The epic (7.201.86) tells us that Nara was born of the asceticism of Nārāyaṇa, who is the son of Dharma. In 12.334.8–9, it speaks of Nārāyaṇa, the son of Dharma, who has taken a quadruple form: Nara, Nārāyaṇa, Hari (another name of Viṣṇu), and Kṛṣṇa. Purāṇic literature makes Ahiṃsā (Nonviolence) the mother of both *ṛṣis*. Invariably their hermitage is in Badarī, in the Himalayas, which is identified with modern Badrinath, a pilgrimage site dedicated to Viṣṇu and located on the upper Ganges.

These two *ṛṣis*, of such a special nature, maintain a privileged position among all the others, a position that evokes their ties to the supreme Puruṣa: they do not bow before Brahmā himself, and since the other *ṛṣis* and the heavenly gods are surprised by this offhand manner, Brahmā tells them who the *ṛṣis* are. The gods understand this so well that they immediately ask for their help in their struggle against the *asuras* (MBh 5.49): both of them are present to fulfill the function of an avatar of the supreme Puruṣa.

But their ontological identity does not create any confusion of their roles. When Nara accompanies Nārāyaṇa, Nārāyaṇa remains much closer to the Puruṣa, the perfectly immutable yogi, whereas Nara is the active character, the one who fights and whose duty it is to carry out particular tasks dealing with dharma, the cosmic order that must be preserved. This arrangement recalls the roles of Kṛṣṇa and Arjuna in the MBh. These dual roles are also expressed in the mythology peculiar to the two *ṛṣis*, notably in the story of King Dambhodbhava (MBh 5.96), which Paraśurāma tells at the court of Dhṛtarāṣṭra in order to bring the Kauravas to a better sense of reality. King Dambhodbhava, whose name indicates his extreme vanity, reigned over all the earth and deemed himself superior to all creatures. This incurred the wrath of the Brahmans (a king cannot be superior to a Brahman). They tell him cleverly that he is surely not the equal of the ascetics Nara and Nārāyaṇa and that he should measure himself against them to verify his own superiority. Dambhodbhava provokes the two *ṛṣis* in their hermitage. They try to calm him down but they do not succeed. Nara then vows to fight the king and his army alone. Total defeat ensues, and the king falls at the feet of Nara, who advises him to adopt a more dharmic attitude. Nārāyaṇa is content to be present at the scene without participating in it.

The epic also introduces the two *ṛṣis* in the story of the churning of the sea of milk, in a context where Nārāyaṇa is in fact Viṣṇu himself (MBh 1.19). Viṣṇu asks Nara to help him give the ambrosia to the gods, and the two of them then fight with the gods against the *asuras*. Nara blocks the road to heaven with rocks cut from the mountains with his arrows, thus forcing the *asuras* to retreat to the earth and the waters. The gods also give him the task of guarding the elixir of immortality, and the text gives him the title of *kirīṭin* ("diademed"), an attribute specific to Arjuna throughout the epic. In the Nara/Nārāyaṇa pair, Nara has a role that strongly evokes that of the earthly king, the keeper of dharma.

Behind the distinction between the two *ṛṣis* stands the image from the *Muṇḍaka Upaniṣad* of two birds perched on a tree, one of which eats the fruit of the tree while the other watches him but does not eat. The aim of this text is not to contrast the Puruṣa with the king but to contrast the liberated Ātman with the creature caught inside the web of earthly activities: the image is thus applicable to every man. But the ideal king can be symbolized by Nara, "Man," because, in fact, he also represents the ideal man.

M.Bi./g.h.

Matsya: The Fish and the Flood in the Work of the Mythic Imagination

Matsya, the Fish, is the name of one of the classical avatars of Viṣṇu. This myth has a Vedic prehistory in which the principal role is played by Manu, the legislator and mythical ancestor of the two great royal dynasties of the Tradition. It is the Indian version of the myth of the flood.

The *Śatapatha Brāhmaṇa* (1.8.1.1–10) gives a complete account of the Vedic myth, in which there is no mention of Viṣṇu at all. Manu is brought water for his morning ablutions. In this water is a little fish, who asks Manu to protect him, promising in return to save Manu from an imminent flood. Fearing that he will be swallowed by other fish, the little fish asks for shelter. Manu first puts the fish in a pot full of water, and then, as it continues to grow, he transfers it into a ditch and then finally into the ocean, once it is big enough to escape all danger. The fish reveals to Manu the date of the flood, and counsels him to call him when he has finished building a boat. When Manu appears in his boat, the fish draws near and allows Manu to attach his boat to his horn; then he leads him to the north slope of the mountains where he will watch over the receding waters. As the sole survivor of the flood, Manu must engender a new human race, and for that purpose he practices austerity and performs sacrifices.

This flood is thoroughly Indian, despite the universal character of the theme. Manu is a *prajāpati,* a progenitor of the human race who alone escapes the flood. His boat is not the equivalent of Noah's Ark, though it is still the symbol of salvation: it is what enables one to cross over. The Himalayas, which border India on the north, are the impassable frontier that separates ordinary mankind from the world of salvation. The land of salvation lies beyond the mountain to the north, and the fish will guide the boat there, thereby indicating that Manu is saved from the flood.

Why a fish? Clearly the flood theme calls for one, and it is risky to apply to the Vedic myth what would be true for the classical period. The text does, however, tempt us to do so, since the fish evokes the danger of being devoured by another fish: classical India indeed speaks of the "law of the fishes" to designate what we would call the "law of the jungle." The law of the fishes is set against the order imposed by a good king, an order in which the weak are protected from the strong and in which dharma rather than individual force is the organizing principle. Manu, who is in essence the legislator and the father of the traditional royal dynasties, has an obvious connection with royal power (though he cannot be reduced to this function alone). Thus it is logical that the little fish should appeal to him in order to escape the law of the fishes.

But this is not just any fish. Its horn designates it a bearer of sacrificial values, and it is undoubtedly as such that it is able to guide Manu toward the region of salvation and allow him to recreate the human race through sacrifice. Its identity, however, is not precisely defined except by the symbolic trait of its horn.

The version of the myth provided by the *Mahābhārata* (3.187) identifies the fish with Brahmā. This text's reference to the law of the fishes is even more explicit than that in the Vedic account. As for the flood, it is clearly described as the advent of the cosmic night. Manu must bring aboard with him the seven *ṛṣis* and all the known grains. Guided by the fish during the stormy flood, his boat represents "the remnant" that must survive the cosmic night to make possible the dawn of a new cosmic era. After the waters have receded, Manu recreates living beings through his acts of austerity.

It is not necessary to arrange the different versions of the myth in historical order to see how clearly the mythical imagination works in the myth of the Fish: Brahmā is close to Viṣṇu; in the Purāṇas, Viṣṇu becomes Brahmā when he awakes to create the world. But the epic does not yet make the fish into an avatar of Viṣṇu. In the *Matsya Purāṇa* 1.12ff., this step is finally taken. Manu recognizes Viṣṇu Vāsudeva in the Fish, and the Fish, speaking of the flood to come, evokes the end of a yuga, which he describes as the end of a *kalpa* complete with fire and flood. The fish avatar is always equipped with a horn of salvation. Manu no longer has to build his boat, which the gods provide for the salvation of creatures, and he must bring aboard all living creatures. A little further into the text he only has to take every species of grain with him. By spiritual concentration on the divine Fish he ties his boat to the horn, and the mooring rope is made of the snake Ananta (Śeṣa, the serpent that symbolizes the cosmic residue between two *kalpas*).

The theme of the avatar is rendered entirely banal in the *Bhāgavata Purāṇa* 8.24.7–58, when the story of Manu and the flood receives a heavenly preamble: while Brahmā is asleep, the *asura* Hayagrīva takes advantage of the situation to steal the Veda. Viṣṇu then becomes incarnate as a fish. The story takes place in a previous *kalpa,* and Manu, the son of Vivasvat (the Sun), is replaced by one of his predecessors in the role of Manu, the royal *ṛṣi* Satyavrata. This is the typical pattern of an avatar narrative, where the disappearance of dharma is provoked by an *asura* who takes what does not belong to him. Viṣṇu alone can reestablish the cosmic order, and he does this in the form of a fish. And Manu clearly has a royal function that associates him with the work of the avatar.

We thus have an exemplary myth: at the Vedic level, it can be seen as a cosmogony, as one of the many cosmogonic accounts of Revelation. But the Tradition has regarded it as secondary in comparison with the myth of Puruṣa and has used it again at the level of the avatar, where the cosmogonic theme is subordinated to the salvific function of Viṣṇu's "descents." Moreover, the story of creation per se is not told and indeed becomes unnecessary as the royal character of Manu enables him to establish dharma and not to beget Brahmans. Although there is no explicit combat with the *asura,* the martial function of the king lies just beneath the surface, and that is why Manu must be king.

M.Bi./g.h.

Narasiṃha, the Man-Lion

Narasiṃha, the avatar of the Man-Lion, is one of the "descents" of Viṣṇu that have no Vedic antecedent. His myth features two *asuras* instead of one, father and son: the first is the king of *asuras,* eager to reign in place of Indra in heaven; the second is just the opposite, a great devotee of Viṣṇu, highly respectful of dharma. There is an inherent tension between, on the one hand, the god of bhakti, dispenser of a universal salvation, the calm yogi, and, on the other hand, the avatar, who is devoted to safeguarding dharma, the socioeconomic order, and thus to the destruction of the evil *asuras* and thereby to violence. In this myth, that tension reaches its highest level.

And since in the classical myth Narasiṃha's appearance on earth is limited to the moment when he suddenly emerges in a half-human, half-leonine form to kill the *asura* Hiraṇyakaśipu, a split is also introduced between the myth and the ritual: the great temples of bhakti cannot enthrone the terrible form of a god, so they substitute for the murder scene either Lakṣmī-Narasiṃha, in which the god is seated and holds his wife (Śrī or Lakṣmī, the usual consort of Viṣṇu, though the myth doesn't say a word about her) on his left knee, or, quite often, Yoganarasiṃha, in which the half-human, half-leonine form, strangely enough, assumes a posture of yoga. This form of the descent of the god recalls that he is above all the Great Yogi and the god of bhakti, the god of all mercy. That is what the myth also says in another way, a way that has no recourse to any elements of the biography of the god.

Lakṣmī Narasiṃha. Probably from Gujarat. Private collection. Photo D. Champion.

We shall follow here the version of the *Bhāgavata Purāṇa* (7.3–8), sometimes using the variants introduced by the *Viṣṇu Purāṇa* (1.17–20), the two Purāṇas providing the two fundamental broad outlines on which the different versions are based.

Hiraṇyakaśipu is the king of the *asuras*. He is filled with hatred for Viṣṇu and with contempt for his sectarian devotees, and he seeks to escape the rhythm of the *kalpa* that the god of bhakti imposes by his yoga. He therefore devotes himself to appalling austerities (*tapas*) in order to obtain equal status with Brahmā and the possibility of substituting his own order for the dharma. The gods, made uncomfortable by the heat of his *tapas*, complain to Brahmā, who appears to Hiraṇyakaśipu to ask him what he wants. Hiraṇya asks for invulnerability (that he may not be killed either by a man or by an animal, either by one of Brahmā's creatures or by anyone who is not one of Brahmā's creatures, either by day or by night, either in the air or on the ground, etc.), equal status with Brahmā, and a *tapas* that cannot be diminished. Brahmā grants it all. Hiraṇya immediately takes advantage of this to overthrow Indra and become the sovereign of the three worlds (heaven, earth, and hell). He receives the sacrificial oblations in place of Indra. This time, the worlds and the gods complain to Viṣṇu.

The setting is precisely that of a myth of an avatar: it is classical in that Brahmā grants an *asura* a dangerous favor that the *asura* will misuse. Here the theme is stressed: if Brahmā grants favors so easily, it is because he does not really have a choice. As the personification of the ritual power of the Brahmans, he can demonstrate the efficacy of the ritual only by rewarding the *asura* for it. Here *tapas* is only an extreme variant of the ritual. This ascetic technique of producing heat is manipulated by the *asura* as a ritual designed to satisfy a desire and not as a practice of renunciation: the heat that emanates from the *tapas* is capable of setting the world on fire in a conflagration that would appear to be a "normal" (conforming to the norm) end of the world. It is like a threat of holocaust without any counterpart for the worlds. And the gods are well aware of this, since they have a direct interest in the smooth running of the "triple world" on which their lives depend.

But Brahmā is also, in classical mythology, the personification of the impersonal absolute, Brahman, the Absolute particularly of those who do not accept the gods of bhakti and instead seek deliverance outside ritual but within its extended dimension. The Brahman is the Absolute of Brahmans who might be called orthodox, who refuse salvation through bhakti, in which the privilege of birth and ritual is abolished through divine grace, and reject the gods who are its guarantors, especially Viṣṇu. This Absolute also occurs in Purāṇic literature in the form of the Brahmaloka, the "world of the Brahman" or "of Brahmā." The myth emphasizes this orthodox—but too orthodox—aspect of Hiraṇyakaśipu: he wants equal status with Brahmā (like those who have been released in the Brahmaloka); he does not want to submit to the alternating phases of emission and reabsorption of the world that characterize bhakti and that the "orthodox" refuse. The *Harivaṃśa* makes him a *brahma-bhakta,* a sectarian devotee of Brahmā or the Brahman to the exclusion of the great gods of bhakti. He does not limit himself to rejecting devotion to Viṣṇu: he lays claim to a state that the orthodox Brahmanic conception reserves only for Brahmans. In other words, he wants to add to his royal power a privilege of the Brahmans, a crime difficult to pardon.

Viṣṇu's answer to the gods is unexpected. He announces that he will "descend" to punish the wicked *asura,* according to the usual scenario of the myth of the avatar, but he subordinates this descent to the ill treatment that Hiraṇya will inflict upon his son, the devotee Prahlāda. What is unusual is the merging within one character—Prahlāda, the good *asura*—of the values of bhakti and dharma that the avatar must save. Viṣṇu's words are unambiguous: "When someone hates the gods, the Veda, cows, Brahmans, and the 'perfected ones,' when he hates the dharma and myself, he quickly perishes. When Hiraṇya hurts his own son Prahlāda, who is calm and free of hostility, strengthened though Hiraṇya may be by the favors (of Brahmā), I shall make him perish." Viṣṇu then sings the praises of Prahlāda: he is a perfect *bhakta,* and this perfection obviously includes respect for dharma, for the sociocosmic order, as well as for Viṣṇu's love. The terms that Viṣṇu listed—gods, the Veda, cows, Brahmans, etc.—form an indissoluble whole: bhakti, or the love of Viṣṇu, is incorporated within dharma, while reciprocally dharma does not exist without that which exceeds it, namely, that very bhakti. Prahlāda symbolizes the fusion of the orthodox universe with the universe of bhakti. The dharma of the Brahmans is henceforth guaranteed by Viṣṇu, but it must in return open itself to what is beyond it, by admitting, for example, that an *asura,* an inhabitant of the infernal (inferior) regions, may be a perfect devotee and may be saved. Thanks to this identification, Viṣṇu will descend to save dharma by saving his *bhakta* from the claws of his father.

In fact, Hiraṇyakaśipu fails in his effort to turn his son away from his devotion to Viṣṇu. He therefore attempts to kill him, but in vain. Here the *Viṣṇu Purāṇa* is more explicit than the *Bhāgavata*. Prahlāda's hands and feet are tied, he is thrown into the sea, and rocks are piled on him. Held prisoner at the bottom of the water, he enters into *samādhi* (the mystical state) and experiences oneness with Viṣṇu, whereupon his bonds fall away and he rises to the surface alive and well. Viṣṇu asks him what he wants. Nothing more than always to be the devotee of Viṣṇu, and the pardon of his father. When Hiraṇyakaśipu sees his son reappear, he repents, but he is quickly killed by Viṣṇu, who appears in the form of Narasiṃha.

The scene in which Prahlāda is thrown into the sea and there experiences oneness with Viṣṇu is symbolic: the devotee is released by his god from the ocean of rebirths. The chains of servitude fall, and he is united with his god. The scene is symmetrical with the one in which Hiraṇyakaśipu asks Brahmā for a parody of release. The emphasis on this aspect of the intervention of Viṣṇu results in the weakening of the central theme of the myth of the avatar: the murder of the *asura*. The narrative dismisses it in one line and implies that Hiraṇya is released.

On the other hand, the *Bhāgavata Purāṇa* does not introduce an account of Prahlāda's release but tells the well-known scene of the murder of Hiraṇyakaśipu by Narasiṃha. Hiraṇya wants to kill his son, who resists all his attempts to seduce him, and he defies him to prove that his god is ubiquitous: Can he emerge from the pillar of his palace (which he kicks)? The response is immediate: Narasiṃha (neither man nor beast) cracks open the pillar at twilight (neither by day nor by night) and kills Hiraṇya whom he suspends across his thighs (neither on earth nor in the air, but the thighs symbolize the earth, through a Sanskrit play on words). It is more than likely that the pillar of the palace of Hiraṇyakaśipu here symbolizes the sacrificial pole, transforming the scene of the murder quite appropriately into a blood sacrifice, a martial sacrifice: Hiraṇya struggles with Narasiṃha before he is killed, and he dies as a warrior. As for Viṣṇu, by assuming a leonine form he has taken on a royal appearance that makes him fit to fight against a king.

The difference between the two versions illustrates the tension that exists between the two points of view, that of bhakti and that of the avatar, despite their reconciliation in the character of Prahlāda. The god of bhakti can only be good, the giver of grace, as calm as any yogi. The avatar can only be terrible, since he comes to kill. The myth has to be scattered in complementary versions in order to say all that it has to say. Correlatively, the temples of Narasiṃha differ, ranging from rather inaccessible sanctuaries on top of a mountain to their counterparts at the foot of the same mountain. The temple above most often (perhaps always) houses a terrible form, symbolizing the protection that the avatar extends to the whole territory, while the temple below should contain a kindly and calm form of the god.

M.Bi./g.h.

Paraśurāma

The myth of the Brahman warrior known as Rāma "with the ax" resembles the myth in which Vasiṣṭha and Viśvāmitra oppose each other. This is an echo of the many historical conflicts in which Brahmans and Kṣatriyas oppose each other. Paraśurāma, also known by the name of Rāma Jāmadagnya, the son of Jamadagni, is a great destroyer of Kṣatriyas, so great that Daśaratha, the father of Rāma the hero of the *Rāmāyaṇa*, grew pale when he saw him arrive to put his son to a test. However, in the MBh and even more clearly in the Purāṇas, he is one of Viṣṇu's avatars. He has a very rich mythology, with popular extensions in all of the Deccan, thanks to his mother, Reṇukā, who plays an important though passive role in the myth. His unusual status as a Brahman warrior (of which there are some other examples in the MBh) brings fully to light the opposition between Brahmanic purity (represented by his father and even more by his four older brothers) and the impurity of the warrior, which he takes on himself. In one way or another, this opposition is always present in the avatar. For example, it is found in the same form in the myth of Kalkin, the avatar of the future. Moreover, in all the versions that have evolved, the myth involves the decapitation of his mother, Reṇukā, which pushes violence to its highest point. In general, myth tends to describe extreme situations that make meaning more apparent. In the MBh, it is parallel cousins, that is, brothers, who fight for the sovereignty of the earth. Here the mission of the avatar seems to take place through the murder of his mother—the account of which is at first sight loosely tied to the rest of the myth. But the meaning is not necessarily the same as in the MBh. In particular, we must not forget that Reṇukā, the Goddess of the Deccan, is represented sometimes only by a head, sometimes by a headless body (she can appear in both forms in the same locality, one for the pure castes, the other for the impure). She has a counterpart in the north of India, where the Tantric goddess Chinnamastā ("with her head cut off") cuts off her head to let all creatures (and her own head) drink her blood. There seems to be in this a theme of the beheaded Goddess, which theoretically appears only in very veiled and indirect forms. The myth of Paraśurāma may help us to approach this theme and to put it in the proper perspective.

We shall follow here the version given in the MBh 3.115–17 (other versions can be found in MBh 12.49, *Bhāgavata Purāṇa* 9.15–16, *Brahmāṇḍa Purāṇa*, *Reṇukā Māhātmya*, etc.). Arjuna Kārtavīrya, king of the Haihayas, received a thousand arms and a heavenly chariot from Dattātreya, who wanted to make him a protector of dharma. But Kārtavīrya (we will call him this to avoid confusing him with the Pāṇḍava Arjuna) lets his strength go to his head and oppresses the gods, the *ṛṣis*, and all creatures. He goes so far as to disturb Indra when he is intimately engaged with his wife. The gods and the *ṛṣis*, with Indra at their head, complain to Viṣṇu, who consults Indra to find a way to get rid of the abusive king.

Then King Gādhi (in some versions the incarnation of Indra) has a daughter, Satyavatī, whom he marries to the Brahman *ṛṣi* Ṛcīka, a descendant of Bhṛgu. Ṛcīka prepares two bowls of rice porridge for his wife and his mother-in-law, which they must drink in order for his wife to conceive a Brahman and his mother-in-law to conceive a Kṣatriya. But as the result of a confusion (or an intentional exchange made by the mother of Satyavatī, according to some versions), the two bowls of porridge are switched. Satyavatī, married to a Brahman, will conceive a son who will have in him the power of the Kṣatriya, while her mother, a Kṣatriyā married to a Kṣatriya, will have a son endowed with the power of a Brahman; his name will be Viśvāmitra. This is such a catastrophe for Satyavatī that she begs her husband to postpone this curse and bring it on her grandson rather than her son. In fact, she gives birth to the Brahman Jamadagni ("consuming fire"), who in turn will marry Princess Reṇukā. Reṇukā will bear five sons, four pure Brahmans (four like the Vedas) and a fifth, Rāma, who will have a talent for warfare as well as for learning the Veda. This version of the myth does not state clearly that he is the incarnation of Viṣṇu, but he proves to be the one whom Viṣṇu has destined to save dharma from Kārtavīrya's attacks.

The theme of the "mixing of the *varṇas*" (the four *varṇas* are the categories serving to classify castes) is thus strongly expressed. Whereas in "normal" society (in compliance with the norm) a Brahman man can only marry a Brahman woman, a Kṣatriya man only a Kṣatriyā woman, here the two generations present a mixture—and always in the right direction, since the husband is of a higher status than the wife. We may thus expect that the sons born of this mixture will have special characteristics: that Jamadagni ("consuming fire") is the son of a Brahman and a princess is not an accident, and this mixture surely has some repercussions on his conduct toward his wife and sons, as we shall see. But the mixture is aggravated in the next generation by the ritual error made at the moment of the conception of Jamadagni and Viśvāmitra, of which the result is visited upon the generation of the grandson. All these detours were needed to produce the warrior Brahman Rāma Jāmadagnya, whose profound ambiguity makes him an ideal figure of an avatar. He will be a violent Brahman—a contradiction in terms—but he will put all of this violence to the exclusive service of the Brahmans and thus of dharma. This is the paradox that the myth poses for the prince who is destined to protect dharma, but whose pride leads him to stray from the right path.

This is when, at least in this version, the episode of the beheading of Reṇukā takes place, a princess who had become the pious wife of an ascetic Brahman. One day as she goes to fetch water for her husband's ritual needs, she lingers behind at the river to watch a prince frolicking in the water with his women, regretting what she will undoubtedly never know with her Brahman husband. Jamadagni guesses why she is late and in a fit of fury asks his sons to cut off her head. The first four refuse, and their father strikes them dead with his powerful ascetic's glance. Paraśurāma, on the other hand, agrees; he decapitates his mother with one blow of an ax. Satisfied, Jamadagni asks him what he wants as a reward. He hastens to ask for the resurrection of his mother and his brothers. His wish is granted. The *Bhāgavata Purāṇa* even asserts that he agreed to kill his mother because he knew that his father could bring her back to life.

Here ends this episode. Then Kārtavīrya suddenly makes his entrance. He arrives at Jamadagni's hermitage while his sons are away. Though he is treated as he ought to be by Reṇukā, he is not satisfied and forcibly takes away the calf of Jamadagni's cow, Homadhenu, and breaks the trees of the hermitage. Other versions are more explicit: he is received sumptuously by Jamadagni and his wife thanks to their cow, who supplies whatever is wanted. The king is jealous of the Brahman for having such a cow and asks to have it. In the *Reṇukā Māhātmya* the cow defends herself by producing armies from her body. When Rāma finds out what has happened, he kills Kārtavīrya after cutting off his thousand arms. The sons of Kārtavīrya avenge their father by killing Jamadagni. Rāma then swears that he will rid the earth of all its Kṣatriyas, beginning with Kārtavīrya's sons and close relatives. He does it over and over again, twenty-one times. Some versions put the beheading of Reṇukā between the murder of Kārtavīrya and the slaughter of all the Kṣatriyas.

After the carnage, Rāma fills five holes with the blood of his victims and performs a ritual in honor of his ancestors. His grandfather Ṛcīka appears to him and stops him, undoubtedly disapproving of the excessive bloodshed and the bloody ritual. Rāma then offers a sacrifice to Indra and gives the land to the officiating Brahmans and a golden altar to Kaśyapa; then he retires to Mount Mahendra, where he is said to be still living today.

The versions that take the narrative further all show the catastrophic result of the disappearance of the Kṣatriyas: the earth must be quickly restored to them in order for it to survive, for the Brahmans are incapable of governing themselves without a king. Rāma's work was therefore essentially destructive, too destructive. He becomes so completely carried away by his wrath that in each version he must be stopped by the intervention of his ancestors. There has to be at least the possibility of a rebirth of the Kṣatriyas so that the earth may be assured of a fresh start. However, the myth is constructed much like the myth of an avatar, in which the destruction, which takes on the aspect of the end of the world, proves to be necessary for rebirth. Certain versions send Rāma to Rudra-Śiva in search of weapons. The *Reṇukā Māhātmya* makes Kārtavīrya an *asura* incarnate, which brings the myth closer to the prototype.

This is the framework in which one must view the beheading of Reṇukā. The *Reṇukā Māhāmya* makes her an avatar of Pārvatī, that is, the Goddess (Jamadagni becomes an avatar of Śiva). Even without this ultimate development, it is possible to perceive the Goddess in Reṇukā, in the sense that the Goddess is close to the earth and its interests. The Princess Reṇukā, tempted by the games of the prince, mother of the warrior avatar, preserves something of the king's wife that she was meant to be. And the king's wife always symbolizes the kingdom, the land over which her husband rules, and in particular its prosperity. When Rāma slaughters the Kṣatriyas, he deprives the earth of those who are literally at its head: the beheading of Reṇukā foreshadows the decapitation of the earth.

This episode is not just a somewhat redundant segment of the narrative. When we know the importance of the theme of the head or of the beheaded Goddess in the cult of the Goddess, we are led to seek the meaning of the theme of the Goddess per se. Death by decapitation is above all a sacrificial theme, closely tied to "the sacrifice of battle" of which the MBh speaks. The buffalo that is traditionally offered to the Goddess is beheaded in front of her, as warriors have their heads cut off on the battlefield. In the sacrifice of battle, as in any sacrifice, the victim is first and in reality the sacrificer himself, the one who offers the sacrifice. The victim that he offers is a substitute for himself. The same applies in battle—especially in the battle that, according to the myth, the Goddess wages with the buffalo-demon. This is even more true of battle, for the warrior (man or woman), who goes off to war makes a sacrifice of his life. He gives himself in sacrifice and will be the victim if he is killed. On the other hand, if he is victorious and kills the enemy, he offers the enemy as a victim, a substitute for himself. The Goddess who decapitates the buffalo-demon has by implication offered herself for decapitation. Her warrior's sacrifice is what saves the world. Reṇukā is first sacrificed by her son in a sacrifice that would be more monstrous than self-sacrifice. She is then replaced by substitute victims, the Kṣatriyas who proved to be dangerous to the well-being of the cosmic order, dharma. The theme of the beheaded Goddess thus explained could account for the mysterious affinities that seem to draw the Goddess close to the demon that she kills.

M.Bi./g.h.

Abbreviation

MBh *Mahābhārata* (Citrashala Press, Bombay)

Vāmana, the Dwarf

Vāmana, the dwarf, is one of the incarnations of Viṣṇu. The *Śatapatha Brāhmaṇa* (1.2.5.1–9) tells how the gods, conquered by the *asuras,* try to obtain a share of the earth that the *asuras* are apportioning among themselves. They go to see the *asuras,* placing Viṣṇu at their head, Viṣṇu who is the sacrifice. But Viṣṇu is a dwarf. When they ask the *asuras* for a share of the world, the *asuras* grant them a plot as large as Viṣṇu can cover with his body. The gods accept and with the appropriate ritual, of which Viṣṇu is the center, they obtain the entire earth. Several times elsewhere, reference is made to the three strides taken by Viṣṇu to open the space where Indra is supposed to reign. These two themes together form the classic myth of the dwarf. Curiously, the treatises on iconography retain the original duality of the myth using the name of Vāmana for the dwarf who tricks King Bali with his small size and Trivikrama ("he of the three strides") for the same dwarf when he assumes a gigantic size and measures the universe with his three steps.

The *Rāmāyaṇa* (1.31.4–20) gives a well-developed version of the classic myth: Bali, the king of the *asuras,* has made himself master of the three worlds in place of Indra. He makes a sacrifice. The gods, led by Indra, come to see Viṣṇu and ask him to take advantage of this golden opportunity, in which Bali is disposed to make gifts to all who present themselves to him. Viṣṇu becomes incarnate in the womb of Aditi (thus becoming Indra's younger brother, who will serve his older brother), and is born in the form of a dwarf who is a Brahmanical student equipped with an umbrella and a water jug. He appears before Bali, who grants him an amount of land equivalent to three strides. Viṣṇu then becomes master of the three worlds with his three strides, confines Bali to the kingdom of hell, and returns sovereign power over the three worlds to Indra.

The *Bhāgavata Purāṇa* (8.15–23) clearly states that Bali was made invincible by the Brahmans of the family of Bhṛgu, notably his tutor and chaplain Śukrācārya, who revived him after Indra had killed him. The same chaplain watches over Bali and wants to prevent him from giving in to the apparently modest request of the dwarf who presents himself to him, for he recognizes Viṣṇu in him and sees through his scheme. The pious Bali feels guilty of a grievous error: by keeping the promise he made to the dwarf, he disobeys his tutor and grants the three strides worth of land. Śukrācārya therefore curses him: he will quickly lose his prosperity. Indeed, although all the good omens increase, Viṣṇu grows and grows. In one stride he covers the earth and the atmosphere. With a second step he covers the sky, and with a third stride he steps beyond the upper spheres of the universe and finds no place to put his foot down. Bali, cursed by Śukra for wanting to keep his promise, is now reproached by Viṣṇu for not being able to keep it: Viṣṇu does not know where to take his third step and condemns Bali to rule in hell. But Bali, full of devotion, offers his head for Viṣṇu to put his foot on, a sign of complete submission. The deposed king thus receives the promise that he will be reborn as Indra in a future age of the world. For the moment, Indra resumes his celestial sovereignty.

The reuse of a Vedic theme as an avatar myth is easy. All the added details (the character of the king of the *asuras* and his tutor, the resurrection of Bali through the power of his tutor) are expected. The ambivalence of the *asura* is more interesting, especially as it appears in the *Bhāgavata Purāṇa:* of course he is guilty of dethroning Indra, but he tries to keep his word against the will of his tutor, which is a virtue peculiar to ascetics and the perfected ones, and his ultimate submission to Viṣṇu makes him a *bhakta,* a devotee who deserves to be reborn as Indra one day. This ambiguity in the myth is a live issue today: in Kerala, Bali is considered the king of the Golden Age, and each year they celebrate his brief return to earth from the netherworld in which Viṣṇu keeps him confined. Bali is also the grandson of Prahlāda, the *asura bhakta* of the myth of Narasiṃha. It is clear that he is no demon per se, for an *asura* may be a good *asura* if he submits to the will of Viṣṇu and to the order of the world to which he is guarantor, to the point where he can imagine "legally" leaving his inferior position of *asura* one day and becoming a *deva.* Bali is put in a situation such that his piety makes him commit two faults in spite of himself: disobeying his tutor and failing to keep his promise to Viṣṇu. But his attitude of perfect humility redeems him. He will expiate his faults, but he will also have his reward. The order of the world will be safe and Viṣṇu will not have failed in any way in his job of avatar.

In the myth of Narasiṃha, the abusive *asura* and the devout *asura* are two antagonistic characters, father and son. These two characters here form a single figure, who must be connected with the Kerala myth of Bali, king of the Golden Age. What surfaces in the myth is a fact peculiar to Hinduism that has been underestimated: quite often in India the names of places indicate that the land belongs to the local *asura,* whom the avatar deity brings under subjection, generally by killing him and granting him salvation at the moment of his death. This situation is explicit in an indefinite number of local myths that all resort to the theme of the avatar who kills the *asura.* What is expressed in this way is the opposition, basic to Hindu society, between the so-called pure castes, Brahman and others, and impure castes, inferior to the pure castes, which include the royal caste or the dominant local caste. Even if in certain cases the dominant caste adopts the vegetarianism of the Brahmans (it may occasionally be made up of Brahmans, but this is not the situation treated by the theory), the general schema stands. Hindu thought knows that this world cannot exist without resorting to impure violence, which is symbolized by the meat diet (Bali's name means "the strong one"). It is the duty of the king to resort to force, and the "impurity" of his position is made tolerable by subordinating it, in status, to the purity of the priestly castes of the Brahmans. The impure castes play the role of *asuras* on earth, while the Brahmans represent the *devas.* Viṣṇu is always on the side of the Brahmans and purity, even when he descends to punish the wicked and put the *asuras* back in their place. He is the model of the good king devoted to the Brahmans, who maintains the cosmic order against the wicked *asura* kings. India has never had any illusions: the strongest will always be tempted to rise out of their subordinate position and assert their strength. Hence the abundance of local myths in which the *asura* is master of the earth, but in which he is forced to bow before his superiors, the heavenly gods and their eminent master, Viṣṇu. One might almost reconstruct the actual social hierarchy from this myth.

M.Bi./g.h.

Kṛṣṇa as cowherd, avatar of Viṣṇu. Theophany of Kṛṣṇa on the mountain. Manuscript of the *Bhāgavata Purāṇa*, Pahari School, ca. 1750. New Delhi, National Museum. Photo Catherine Jarrige.

The Childhood and Adulthood of Kṛṣṇa

Paradoxical as it may seem, the superabundant classical and modern Hindu literature dealing with Kṛṣṇa is deceptive from a mythological point of view. It is as if bhakti in its most affective dimension had erased the fundamental structure of the myth in order to multiply and juxtapose occasions to wax ecstatic over the marvelous child and the untiring slayer of *asuras;* or better still, as if it had to be proved that Kṛṣṇa indeed became an avatar by accumulating superhuman exploits. At best, he is made into a kind of professional knight-errant. There are, however, an appreciable number of *asuras* whose names include a reference to Kāla, Time, the fundamental element of the myth of the avatar, or to the Earth, which the *asura* oppresses. Since the symbolism operates on the second or third level, one has the impression that there is nothing but a series of tales, and that dharma is nothing but the distant horizon of wonders wrought by this Indian Don Quixote. We may compare this to the grandiose claims made by certain apocryphal gospels of the first centuries of Christianity.

This observation is in a way connected with a problem raised by European Indology, but one that must be recognized as strictly a product of Western scholarship of the last century: in view of what the texts presented, they asked, how many different characters had contributed to the formation of the god Kṛṣṇa? Not a single Hindu would accept such atomization, even if it were only a dichotomy. Kṛṣṇa is Kṛṣṇa, and he could not be a god of pastoral tribes (to account for the fact that Kṛṣṇa was raised among the cowherds) telescoped together with a Kṣatriya hero (the Kṛṣṇa who is the friend of Arjuna in the MBh), and then enlarged somehow to the dimension of an avatar of Viṣṇu. Whatever the apparent disparity of these characters may be for us, it is necessary to keep them together and to see how they are organized from the Hindu point of view as one and the same god, the avatar of Viṣṇu. Not only is the historical amalgam of disparate characters highly unlikely, but the texts do not favor such an amalgam: Kṛṣṇa the cowherd is just as much, if not more, an avatar of Viṣṇu as is the epic Kṣatriya (see below). And meanwhile, Western scholarship (except for a few latecomers) completely rejected the historical value of the epic, which it saw as only a myth.

Rather than relating minutely all the exploits of Kṛṣṇa, which after all vary with the texts, we will attempt to discover how the two essential parts of his "biography" fit logically together: on the one hand his birth and youth, and on the other his adulthood and his participation in the adventures of the Pāṇḍavas. We will principally consider the MBh and the three great texts of nonsectarian Vaiṣṇava bhakti: the *Harivaṃśa* (section 2), regarded as an appendix of the MBh; the *Viṣṇu Purāṇa* (5); and the *Bhāgavata Purāṇa* (10). The MBh tells how Kṛṣṇa died but does not deal with his birth. The *Harivaṃśa* tells how he was born but fails to say how he died, integrating from the MBh only the axial episode of the murder of Kaṃsa and the confrontation with Jarāsandha, while the *Bhāgavata Purāṇa* follows him from his birth to his death, devoting much space in his biography to his relationship with the Pāṇḍavas. It is not a matter of reconciling these data, nor even of bringing out the fundamental structure of *one* myth of the avatar, because it is precisely the structure that happens to be blurred, albeit presupposed, by the accidents of literary history—the creation of the MBh. Rather, it is a matter of retracing the steps taken by the mythographers who seem to have used a theme of the avatar to make something else out of it. Obviously this reconstitution remains largely hypothetical; its sole merit is to introduce a little intelligibility into an otherwise confusing overall picture.

One must start from the MBh, without necessarily putting it chronologically before the HV; on the contrary, the logical necessity of a myth of Kṛṣṇa's birth and youth will visibly emerge out of the epic narration. It matters little when the myth took on a literary form if its idea belongs to the epic itself.

Unlike the *Rāmāyaṇa*, the MBh centers its narrative not on the avatar but on the character of the ideal earthly king, who must imitate the avatar and be tied to him by a devotion that goes as far as ontological identity. The plot in its quasi entirety must thus be reserved for Arjuna (and his brothers), while keeping the rank of avatar unequivocally for Kṛṣṇa. Kṛṣṇa is a Kṣatriya of the same "lunar" dynasty as the Pāṇḍavas; he even belongs to the older branch of this dynasty, which assures him of a superiority over the Pāṇḍavas; but because of a curse the older branch, going back to Yadu, the elder son of Yayāti, was condemned never to reign. This explains why Kṛṣṇa is not a king in the epic, not even in his own city of Dvārakā, where King Ugrasena owes his power to him, and why the "universal" royal functions are reserved for the Pāṇḍavas, descendants of the youngest son of Yayāti, whose father enthroned him as his successor.

None of this alters the fact that from one end of the epic to the other, Kṛṣṇa—flanked by his older brother Balarāma, the incarnation of Śeṣa—affirms that he is, and is recognized as, the avatar of Viṣṇu, as well as the incarnation of the *ṛṣi* Nārāyaṇa. Since Balarāma is the earthly incarnation of the serpent Śeṣa, his relationship to Kṛṣṇa is analogous to the relationship between Bhīma and Arjuna. Like the avatar, the king upholds (hence the relation of younger to elder) the values of this world, the values of dharma and its indispensable accessories, *artha* and *kāma,* what could be called the values of life (Bhīma is the son of Vāyu, the wind, and also the breath of life). The assertion of Kṛṣṇa as avatar is, however, set more on the level of discourse (the *Bhagavad Gītā* is the best example of this) than in the sphere of action. There is only one minor exception: during the war of extermination that the opposed cousins wage on one another, the peacetime dharma is more than once set amiss by the heroes of the camp of dharma themselves. They have to kill Bhīṣma, the common ancestor; Droṇa, their tutor, whose extreme virtue they recognize; and their parallel cousins, who, despite being demons incarnate, are no less their brothers. They will even discover after the battle that they have killed Karṇa, their half-brother. Arjuna has difficulty accepting this situation, whence his name of Bībhatsu, "he who is loath"; the *Bhagavad Gītā* is the teaching of Kṛṣṇa, who justifies the murders perpetrated on the battlefield for the triumph of dharma. In our terms this would be a case of the means justifying the end. India prefers to speak of "dharma for hard times"—*āpad-dharma.* But it is significant that all the responsibilities are thus borne by the avatar himself by virtue of his qualifications, since in the *Gītā* he offers himself explicitly as a model to follow. He is not the "ideologue" of the camp of dharma; he is its ideology incarnate and the assurance of its victory. It is because of him that the epic drama takes its form, and that one recognizes in the deeds of the Pāṇḍavas, and particularly of Arjuna, the structure of an avatar myth. In a serious crisis the extent of the royal power is laid bare, revealing what is most exorbitant about it. Hindu mythic thought could not find a better symbol of this situation than the time of the avatar. At the same time, making Kṛṣṇa Arjuna's charioteer throughout the battle is an inspired invention. There were not many ways of expressing the dual position of servant (of the good of the worlds) and leader (of the worlds), which is simultaneously the dual position of the avatar and the king.

The role of the supreme master—who is at the same time on the narrative level the one who pulls the puppet-strings—allows Kṛṣṇa a certain inactivity, or at least a certain distance from the main action. There one can see at every moment his profound nature as a yogi, the essential dimension of the avatar, since it excludes any striving for the sake of personal interest and substitutes for it the sole pursuit of the "good of the world": every time that Kṛṣṇa's presence or help is suddenly required he seems to be found asleep on his bed. Clearly, Kṛṣṇa's bed and slumber are reminders of Nārāyaṇa's yogic sleep on Śeṣa and the ocean of the cosmic flood. The dichotomy that the MBh sets up between the avatar and the king rather paradoxically makes the yogic dimension all the more evident, since Kṛṣṇa preaches a yoga of action. Nor does he disdain to act at critical moments like a deus ex machina, as the supreme god that he really is: hence the resurrection of the stillborn child of Uttarā, bearer of all the hope of the lunar dynasty.

Thus the MBh is the text that best makes it possible to situate the character in all his breadth and purity of lineage, with relative discretion as to the display of his power. It is also the only text to make systematic use of the tradition according to which Arjuna and Kṛṣṇa are incarnations of the two *ṛṣis* Nara and Nārāyaṇa and not only the descents of Indra and Viṣṇu. This invention is connected with the necessity to express the intimate link between the king and the avatar. Beyond this, the epic does not allow us to sketch a biography of Kṛṣṇa. His interventions are sporadic but situated at the critical moments of the narrative, such as the eighteen-day battle. We learn that he had a bone to pick with Śiśupāla, notably over his wife Rukminī, which allows him to kill Śiśupāla, the reincarnation of Hiraṇyakaśipu and of Rāvaṇa, who refuses to give him precedence at the time of Yudhiṣṭhira's royal consecration. Śiśupāla is, like the Pāṇḍavas, his cross-cousin, but he represents the attitude that is the complement to bhakti, perfect hatred, which wins salvation for him when Kṛṣṇa kills him. It is also known that his absence from the scene of the game of dice was motivated by his struggle against the incarnate *asura* Śālva, king of Saubha. Śālva was said to be the husband that Ambā had chosen for herself. Ambā, the eldest daughter of the king of Kāśī, refused to marry Vicitravīrya, Bhīṣma's half-brother, on whose behalf Bhīṣma had abducted her. One of the traits of the "avataric" actions of Kṛṣṇa appears here: the actions often form a counterpoint to the episodes of the epic, more or less symbolic depending on the case.

Dance of Kṛṣṇa and the Gopīs. Manuscript of the *Bhāgavata Purāṇa,* Kulu school, ca. 1794, Banaras, Bhavat Kala Bhavan. Photo Catherine Jarrige.

But it is in connection with the murder of Kaṃsa (perpetrated by Kṛṣṇa and reported by him) and the murder of Jarāsandha (which he left to Bhīma) that his role of avatar seems to be asserted in action. Kṛṣṇa killed Kaṃsa, the king of the Bhojas at Mathurā and his maternal uncle, who had been abandoned by his kinsmen. Kṛṣṇa himself tells of this murder and proposes his action as a model for the sages of the court of Dhṛtarāṣṭra, notably Bhīṣma and Droṇa, who were supposed to have sacrificed Duryodhana in order to avoid a war. When Jarāsandha, the father-in-law of Kaṃsa and the king of the Magadhas, attacked Mathurā to avenge the death of his son-in-law, Kṛṣṇa preferred to refuse to fight with him and to transfer the entire population of Mathurā, with its king Ugrasena (the father of Kaṃsa and usurper of Kaṃsa's throne), to Dvārakā, on the coast of Saurāṣṭra. This event is surely of great importance. For one thing, at that point Kṛṣṇa leaves Mathurā, situated in the middle of Madhya-deśa, the land of the Bhāratas, to transfer his residence to the outer limits of the earth, to a city whose name implies that it is an "entrance," a "gate": but a gate to what? The land of the Bhāratas that eluded the dharmic princes and needs to be reconquered? The gate of salvation? But this comes to the same thing. We must bear in mind that one never enters a place through the gate to attack it, but through "what is not the gate"—*advāra.* This supplies all the symbolic weight of the name of Kṛṣṇa's residence, which is already his own when he appears in the MBh.

On the other hand, when Yudhiṣṭhira wants to receive the royal consecration, Kṛṣṇa tells him that he must first get rid of Jarāsandha, whom he himself cannot kill. What follows is an extraordinary nocturnal expedition of three men, Kṛṣṇa, Arjuna, and Bhīma, who take the form of false Brahmans to enter through "what is not the gate," into the capital of Jarāsandha. Kṛṣṇa already emerges as the leader. He has in him the *nīti,* the art of leadership, of governing (the charioteer is the *netṛ,* from the same root), whereas he attributes victory to Arjuna and force to Bhīma. It is Bhīma who is charged with liquidating Jarāsandha, the enemy of the kings and the devotee of Rudra Paśupati. Has he not begun to collect in this prison kings whom he means to sacrifice to Paśupati when he has collected a hundred of them? The name Jarāsandha, which a myth of birth accounts for, evokes the decline of the world (*jarā* means "old age"). He is the one who has made a pact with the decline, or who has vowed the decline of the world, for the sacrifice of the one hundred kings expresses a totality that would leave the world kingless, and thus headless and destined for death. It is logical that Bhīma, the son of the breath of life, is charged with carrying out the sacrifice. In place of the hundred kings Bhīma sacrifices Jarāsandha, who is of course the incarnation of an *asura.* By murdering Jarāsandha, Bhīma gives the earth a renewal of life that makes possible the royal consecration of Yudhiṣṭhira. But when one learns that Kaṃsa is only the incarnation of the *asura* Kālanemi—a mythic variant on the well-known expression *kālacakra,* "the wheel of time"—one thinks of the way that the stage of the MBh is set at the junction of the two worst yugas, the Dvāpara and the Kali, in which two of the protagonists are the incarnations of the *asuras* Kali and Dvāpara. This new contrapuntal play in the narrative is now duplicated: Kṛṣṇa is the agent in the murder of Kaṃsa, and he fully assumes his role of avatar by allowing the world to overcome the crisis that threatened its existence (the wheel of time always has an inauspicious connotation). It is this model that he proposes to the epic heroes. In the murder of Jarāsandha, whom he voluntarily abandoned because of his concern for Bhīma and Arjuna, he transfers his responsibilities to the Pāṇḍavas.

In other words, in order for Kṛṣṇa to be able to emerge fully as an avatar, he must at some time justify the incarnation through his acts. By making earthly heroes the protagonists of the action, the epic must project back into Kṛṣṇa's past his active role of avatar, which seems to culminate in the murder of Kaṃsa. The murder of Kaṃsa and by correlation the story of Kṛṣṇa's childhood, which Kaṃsa entirely decreed, thus become logical parts of the horizon of the MBh, and it is necessary to evoke them for the credibility of the avatar. In this way, the epic is laden with the myth of Kṛṣṇa's birth and childhood, but does not deal with it except in passing. This is why the HV, which is the first text to furnish the myth, appears as the complement of the MBh.

We will not dwell on the mythical prehistory of Kṛṣṇa in the HV, but it is interesting that before his descent among men, he battled with the *asura* Kālanemi on behalf of the gods, in the combat known as the combat of Tārakā (more precisely, "made of Tārakā"—of "her who gives deliverance"). So there is a heavenly counterpart to the battle between Kaṃsa (Kālanemi) and Kṛṣṇa. Immediately after the victory of Viṣṇu over Kālanemi, which is thus a duplication, the earth comes to Brahmā and in the presence of all the gods complains of the burden crushing her; here the myth of the avatar type takes shape. Brahmā asks Viṣṇu to become incarnate, and in an innovation full of insights, Viṣṇu now asks for the collaboration of the Goddess, who, we learn, is merely his *yoga-nidrā,* his yogic sleep. Within Viṣṇu, she keeps him asleep with the world reabsorbed in him; outside of him, she becomes Devī, Māyā ("Divine Illusion"), Līlā ("Divine Play" in creation), in short all the feminine energy of the deity, which is the web of the life of the world. Viṣṇu will be content to descend into the womb of Devakī, the sister of Kaṃsa, but all the manipulations are left to the care of the Goddess, including her own "sacrifice."

Meanwhile, on earth, Nārada, the "busybody" of the gods, informs Kaṃsa that his sister's eighth child will kill him. Kaṃsa therefore decides to place Devakī and her husband Vāsudeva under close guard. As an added precaution, he himself takes charge of killing the newborn babies one by one. For the first six, the solution is simple. Viṣṇu goes to get six *asuras* who are waiting in hell in the form of six "embryos." These are the six sons of Kālanemi himself, so the father (Kaṃsa) will kill his own children by killing the six firstborn children of Devakī. They owe their unfortunate fate to the curse of Hiraṇyakaśipu, and the solution is in the end to their benefit, for they will thus be quickly delivered from the curse and will be able to enjoy in peace the protection that they have obtained from Brahmā. The case of the seventh embryo is more complicated. At the end of the seventh month of pregnancy, the Goddess is charged with transferring the embryo carried by Devakī into the womb of Rohiṇī, another wife of Vāsudeva, whom Kaṃsa does not distrust. This embryo will become Balarāma, also known as Saṅkarṣaṇa. As for the eighth, who is the incarnation of Viṣṇu, the Goddess must play an even more delicate role for him. When he descends into the womb of Devakī, she is to "descend" into the womb of Yaśodā, the wife of the cowherd Nanda, who lives at Gokula, near Mathurā, on the Yamunā River. Both of them will be born at the same time (at night), and Vāsudeva, duly warned, is to transport his newborn son immediately to Gokula and substitute him secretly for the daughter of Yaśodā, whom he will bring back to Mathurā. The next day, Kaṃsa learns the news of the birth of the eighth child and, despite its sex, seizes it and smashes it to death on a rock (*śaila:* we know that Pārvatī, "the daughter of Parvata, the mountain," is also called Śailajā, one of the synonyms of *Pārvatī*). The Goddess then escapes into the air, announcing to Kaṃsa that his murderer is already born. Kaṃsa will look for him in vain, for he cannot suspect that he is the alleged son of Nanda and Yaśodā (*yaśo-dā,* "giver of glory," is a name that echoes *śrī* or *lakṣmī,* as well as *rādhā* and *rukmiṇī*).

Balarāma, the son of Rohiṇī, will also be entrusted to Nanda to be raised with Kṛṣṇa ("the black"), and Vasudeva himself will take charge of the rites that mark the birth and childhood of his two sons; this is an important detail, for it confirms their Kṣatriya nature. But they are raised at the *vraja,* the grounds of the herdsmen, among cowherds, like the children of cowherds. Nanda and Yaśodā believe that Kṛṣṇa is their son. Of course Balarāma, but especially Kṛṣṇa, performs all sorts of marvelous feats that we will not describe in detail now, and they kill their first *asuras,* who are sent by Kaṃsa or are enemies of the cows that they bring to graze in the forest. Kṛṣṇa is the favorite of the cowherd women, the *gopīs,* who have maternal feelings for him until the child has grown sufficiently for maternal love to turn into plain love. Rādhā, the favorite *gopī,* the lover of Kṛṣṇa, will appear much later in Kṛṣṇa literature.

The importance of the theme of the *gopīs* is one of the elements that could contribute to a digression from the avatar myth if one were to forget that the avatar only forms a unity with the god of bhakti, and that he is often the preferred form in which devotees worship him. In fact, bhakti recounts a certain number of sentiments that the *bhakta* can have for his god and that assume that he has a human form. Among these, maternal love in particular shows the extraordinary development of the myth and iconography of the childhood of Kṛṣṇa: thus they speak of Bāla-Kṛṣṇa, "the child Kṛṣṇa" (the one who plays with a butterball stolen from his mother, a butterball that symbolizes the earth that has become the substance of the oblation). But this is also a theme that runs through all of Hindu bhakti: there is a Bāla-Subrahmaṇya, a Bāla-Dattātreya, a Baṭuka-Bhairava ("little Bhairava"), in which childhood also obviously implies sexual abstinence. The love between two lovers is another such sentiment, and this produces the *gopīs* of the *rāsa-līlā,* "the game made of *rasa*" (or of the *rāsa-maṇḍala,* "the circle made of *rasa*"), in which each *gopī,* in love with Kṛṣṇa, thinks that she has Kṛṣṇa all to herself: the play of god in his creation and with his creatures. But hatred is also one of the recounted sentiments, which makes possible the salvation of Śiśupāla, who is assured definitive deliverance after his decapitation by Kṛṣṇa in the MBh.

However, the major problem raised by Western critics, although it has never troubled Hindu consciousness, is the transformation of Kṛṣṇa and his brother into cowherds. It is true that this is not a simple episode of transition, since it is as cowherds that the two brothers are called to Mathurā by the suspicious Kaṃsa. After their exploits among the cowherds, he wants to match them against adversaries of his choice who can kill them. The test rebounds to embarrass him and then destroy him. Kṛṣṇa and Balarāma kill their adversaries and then Kaṃsa himself. They are recognized as the Kṣatriyas that they never stopped being, and Kṛṣṇa is offered the kingship of Mathurā, which he refuses in order to put his maternal great-uncle Ugrasena back on the throne. It is then that the two brothers become initiated as warriors and bring the son of their guru back to life after he has been killed by the sea monster Pañcajana ("the five nations"); this favor serves as their traditional tuition gift to their teacher. Kṛṣṇa, moreover, wins the famed Pāñcajanya conch shell, which he generally carries in his upper left hand (when he is represented with four arms) and which is a symbol of the group of peoples who live under the same Brahmanic dharma. A little later the threat of Jarāsandha takes form. His troops are repulsed several times, but he is invincible. The people abandon Mathurā for the first time, moving toward the south under the leadership of Paraśurama. Kṛṣṇa and Balarāma receive Viṣṇu's weapons and a mission to ensure the victory of the gods. When Jarāsandha appears he is defeated and takes flight. But after a few turns of fortune in which there is talk of Rukmiṇī and Śiśupāla—Kṛṣṇa finally carries off Rukmiṇī (an incarnation of Śrī) after he is installed in Dvārakā—Kṛṣṇa and Balarāma return to Mathurā and decide to take shelter from Jarāsandha in Dvārakā, on the seashore (note that Paraśurāma had been exiled to the end of the earth, that is, to the seashore, when his role of avatar had come to an end). The moment when Kṛṣṇa emigrates to Dvārakā marks both a farewell to the world of the cowherds of his childhood and in a way a farewell to his active role as avatar: he hands over the power to the Pāṇḍavas.

The child Kṛṣṇa. Detail of a shrine column at Akkiripalli (Andhra Pradesh). Photo M. Biardeau.

This may explain the repetitious character of the episodes that constitute the second part of Kṛṣṇa's biography in the HV. One *asura* succeeds another. Not that the episodes are without meaning; for example, the intervention of Śiva and the Goddess in the fight against Bāṇāsura is interesting in more than one respect, and one can hear echoes of the MBh in it. Similarly, the fight against Narakāsura recalls that in the epic Karṇa is regarded as an incarnation of that Naraka, and so forth. But the accumulation of motifs that brings nothing new expresses an unbridling of the mythical imagination as it pursues its relentless course. The avatar myth loses in purity of line what it gains in proliferation of motifs. It is the *bhakta*'s love that is at work rather than his intelligence.

To return to the central problem, the child Kṛṣṇa is a clandestine avatar. He must therefore wear a kind of disguise that, like the disguises of the Pāṇḍavas during their year of clandestine life with King Virāṭa, must simultaneously hide and reveal his true nature. He is disguised as a cowherd, and one may recall the disguise of a cowherd that is worn by the last of the Pāṇḍavas, Sahadeva, the expert in *nīti,* in the MBh. Is this so strange and unexpected when we know the symbolic role of the cow in the scheme of Brahmanic values? In the MBh, Arjuna would rather violate an agreement made with his brothers than ignore the call for help from a Brahman whose cow was stolen. Karṇa is cursed by a Brahman for having killed his cow entirely by accident, a sure sign that he is not worthy of royalty. When one lists all that the avatar and the good king are supposed to protect, the cow is always there next to the Brahman and dharma, to the point that there is an expression *go-brāhmaṇa* that designates either Brahmans and cows as an inseparable whole, or Brahmans who are characterized by their cows (as opposed to other castes which seek to set themselves apart from Brahmans, but claim their status). Starting with the Vedic hymns, the epithet *go-pati,* "master of cows," characterizes Indra especially and is connected with his royal status, whereas *go-pa* designates any protector and not only a cowherd. The king as master of cows is also their protector, the one who can give them to the Brahmans. If one holds that the avatar is the image of the ideal king, both of them must be protectors of cows, and their role becomes sufficiently defined by this symbol.

But why is Kṛṣṇa a clandestine avatar? Why this recourse to a disguise? Here is where the logical link with the MBh appears to be essential. For one thing, Kṛṣṇa is not supposed to be king, in order to leave this function to another, but he has to be a Kṣatriya in order to be a valid model for the king. Note that the epic reinforces the equal status of Kṛṣṇa and Arjuna through bonds of kinship. With this as a starting point, a framework must be established that will permit the avatar to prove his nature, to kill an *asura* who endangers the world. But the secrecy imposed on Kṛṣṇa in his disguise as a cowherd answers to yet another necessity, the source of which is also found in the epic: in order to accede to an incontestable kingship, the Pāṇḍavas must suffer an exile in the forest, a symbol of renunciation, and a period of living incognito, conceived as a preparatory consecration for the sacrifice of war. The childhood of Kṛṣṇa among the cowherds is the symbolic echo of this dual necessity. The cows of the *vraja* graze in the forest, and the two brothers cleanse the forest of its *asuras* for the good of the cows and their guardians, just as Bhīma kills several *rākṣasas* during his exile (among them the *asura* Baka, during the first exile, to save a family of Brahmans). The two brothers strike camp when Kṛṣṇa thinks they should, to find a forest with richer pasturage; to instigate this move, he produces wolves from his body to cause damage and create panic among the cowherds—a curious echo of a world crisis, in which one must destroy in order to start over again. Soon after this migration, Kṛṣṇa imposes his superiority upon Indra. The prodigal son is thus simultaneously hidden, humble, and close to the cowherds whose life he shares, but he is orchestrating the game. His life unfolds for the most part in the forest, the place where the cows pasture; in a parallel development, when Duryodhana wants to gloat over the sight of the Pāṇḍavas condemned to an ascetic life in the forest, he uses the pretext of checking on his father's herds nearby. Finally, since the period of childhood is connected with sexual abstinence, Kṛṣṇa lives at Gokula as a young *brahmacārin* (a Brahmanic student sworn to absolute chastity). He marries Rukmiṇī—and a few others—only at Dvārakā. In brief, the childhood of Kṛṣṇa seems to be a brilliant invention that can respond to all aspects of the problem: it paves the way for Kaṃsa's murder, which is the culmination of his active role as avatar. Although Kaṃsa was duly warned about what awaited him, this is because Kṛṣṇa must undergo both a period of ascetic life and a period in hiding, to symbolize both the dimension of renunciation and the preparatory consecration for the sacrifice that consists in the murder of Kaṃsa.

Thus the biography of Kṛṣṇa is made up of two or even three rather heterogeneous parts, of which the first two at least fit together perfectly: the child Kṛṣṇa grows up among

Kṛṣṇa and Rādhā. Manuscript of the *Gītagovinda* of Manaku, 1730. Lahore, Pakistan, Central Museum. Photo Catherine Jarrige.

the cowherds until the day when he asserts himself as avatar by killing Kaṃsa. The Kṛṣṇa of the MBh, detached from his role as savior of the world, shows the ideal king how to become a savior; he continues to pull the strings offstage, since he is still the supreme god incarnate, who gives victory to the defender of dharma. Finally, the biography of Kṛṣṇa at Dvārakā, which the HV attempts to construct in parallel to the events in the MBh but without any major connection between them, is less successful, because it is largely superfluous. From one end of his myth to the other Kṛṣṇa is indeed the avatar of Viṣṇu, one and the same person, conceived first for the role that he plays in the epic.

One can cite as an example of the profound unity of the three parts of the life of Kṛṣṇa the three episodes that describe his relationship with Indra. In the myth of childhood, Kṛṣṇa teaches the cowherds to substitute for the sacrifice to Indra the sacrifice to cows, to the mountain, and to Brahmans. He asserts that he is identical with the mountain, which accounts perfectly for his ritual role as the god who is sovereign over the territory. The unhappy Indra sends cascades of water down on Mount Govardhana ("the one that makes the cows thrive") and upon the cowherds and their herds. Kṛṣṇa then lifts up the mountain with his finger to give shelter to man and beast. Indra is forced to admit defeat and to recognize that the supremacy of Kṛṣṇa is for the good of the worlds. We know that the avatar's mission is to deliver the gods from the *asuras,* who by definition are stronger than the gods. One of the characteristics that qualifies him as an avatar is his capacity to defeat "even Indra," which makes him at least the equal of the *asuras.*

The same theme appears in the epic. This time it is actually Arjuna who, while preparing for his role as a king who in fact is another avatar, braves Indra's anger together with Kṛṣṇa to please Agni, the sacrificial fire, and to allow him to burn the Khāṇḍava forest where a few of Indra's friends live. In the epic this episode is referred to frequently to show that Arjuna can defeat Indra. But he defeated Indra only in association *with Kṛṣṇa.* And Indra, Arjuna's father, congratulates both heroes when they succeed, but the action is attributed to Arjuna rather than to the avatar. Finally, during Kṛṣṇa's stay in Dvārakā, he has his celebrated confrontation with Indra for possession of the *pārijāta,* a tree in Indra's heaven that assures him prosperity and grants him all he desires. Kṛṣṇa's favorite wife, Satyabhāmā, wants to have the tree, which is the property of Indra's wife, Śacī. Indra refuses to give it up and the two gods fight. Indra is clearly beaten, and the *pārijāta* will remain on earth for one year, according to some versions, or for as long as Kṛṣṇa lives, according to others. Underlying this episode is the rivalry between Rukmiṇī and Satyabhāmā, Kṛṣṇa's two principal wives, and Satyabhāmā's jealousy of Rukmiṇī, to whom Nārada brought a flower of the *pārijāta* from heaven. Whatever may be the symbolism associated with the two wives (Rukmiṇī is Śrī) and with the *pārijatā,* this episode cannot be said to be necessary. Kṛṣṇa has already done the work of an avatar; he no longer needs to prove his superiority over Indra, and the *pārijāta* will continue to belong to Śacī. The theme here thus seems simultaneously to undergo a kind of degradation and to become redundant.

M.Bi./g.h.

BIBLIOGRAPHY

G. DUMÉZIL, *Mythe et épopée* 1: *L'idéologie des trois fonctions dans les épopées des peuples indo-européens* (Paris 1968); *Mythe et épopée* 2: *Types épiques indo-européens—un héros, un sorcier, un roi* (Paris 1971). A. HILTEBEITEL, *The Ritual of Battle: Krishna in the Mahābhārata* (Ithaca 1976). H. H. WILSON, trans., *The Vishnu Purana: A System of Hindu Mythology and Tradition* (London 1840; reprint, Calcutta 1961). J. M. SANYAL, trans., *The Srimad-Bhagavatam,* 5 vols. (Calcutta, n.d.). M. A. LANGLOIS, trans., *Harivansa ou histoire de la famille de Hari,* 2 vols. (Paris 1834–35).

Abbreviations

MBh *Mahābhārata*
HV *Harivaṃśa*

Gaṇapati

Purāṇic mythology makes Gaṇapati the brother of Skanda, since Śiva and Pārvatī are his parents and the two gods are symmetrically arranged on each side of the sanctuary in a number of temples of Śiva or the Goddess. But their symmetry and kinship should not create an illusion: although they are two, they are not identical, but together they form a significant whole.

When Gaṇapati (also called Gaṇeśa) appears alone in one of the innumerable sanctuaries that are consecrated to him throughout India, he is not worshiped on the same level as Skanda-Subrahmanya in the South. He is only *gaṇa-pati* (or *gaṇa-īśa*), commander of Śiva's *gaṇas,* while his brother is *devasenā-pati,* commander of the armies of the gods, which is unquestionably a nobler, more royal status. On the other hand, Gaṇapati may be compared with Hanumān, the god who covers all of North India and much of the Deccan with his sanctuaries. Both of them are often represented very crudely, on a prominent rock in which the figure is barely outlined and invariably smeared with a layer of red lead: this last detail always seems to symbolize the function of a guardian in the service of a superior and royal deity or of a transcendent order, dharma. This is also what the myths of the birth of Gaṇapati indicate, myths essentially Purāṇic and relatively late.

So popular a god must have an abundant mythology, the essential point of which concerns his birth and his elephant head. This will be presented here only synthetically, since an abundance of narrative is not necessarily the sign of a richer mythology. The most significant versions of his birth can be roughly divided into two groups: those in which he is born from Śiva and those in which he is born from Pārvatī, for his birth is no more "normal" than Skanda's. The versions in which he has both Śiva as father and Pārvatī as mother are the least interesting, for they give a poorer account of the god's peculiarities.

When Śiva creates Gaṇapati, it is always at the request of the gods and *ṛṣis* who want a distinction to be made between good and evil; not only must the success of auspicious enterprises and the failure of evil ones be assured, but the wicked must be prevented from performing meritorious actions and the good must be protected and guided in pious actions, a challenge in which the *asuras* and the *devas* and the cause of dharma loom large. This is why Gaṇapati is also called Vināyaka, "the one who removes (obstacles)," and Vighneśvara, "lord of obstacles." The obstacles may be the work of those malicious and alarming *gaṇas* of Śiva's that Gaṇapati is responsible for controlling.

The son that Śiva emits from himself is handsome, like another self. He seduces all the women around him, which offends the ascetic disposition of Pārvatī: So she condemns him to have the head of an elephant and a large belly, in other words, to be ugly. There are other examples in Hindu myths of ugliness signifying "terrible." The fatherhood of Śiva, the ugliness inflicted by Pārvatī associates the god thus formed with the terrible *gaṇas* that he controls. These factors also seem to commit him to celibacy, but his own qualities are sometimes cast in the form of two wives—two abstractions without myth but significant in themselves: Buddhi: Wisdom, and Siddhi: Success. His vehicle, the rat, is associated with the same qualities.

In the versions in which Gaṇapati is born from Pārvatī, the Goddess sometimes wants to procure an absolutely trustworthy guardian for her door, and sometimes the gods and *ṛṣis* whom Śiva sends to her petition her to prevent the success of the wicked and to guarantee success for the good. In both instances, it is his function as guardian—of the Goddess, that is, of the Earth and the manifested Universe, or of dharma, the cosmic order: it is all one—that is imperative.

Here the versions diverge: according to the *Śiva-Purāṇa,* when Pārvatī decides to procure a reliable guardian for her door—in particular to avoid the untimely visits of her husband Śiva—she creates him from the secretions of her skin, that is, from her natural impurities. Vighneśvara (he is not yet *gaṇa-pati*) then assumes his functions and mounts guard at the door of his "mother," until the inevitable day when Śiva comes to see his wife when she is not receiving visitors—she is in her bath. Vighneśvara makes no exception: he blocks the door. Śiva wants to be received and instead receives several blows. Śiva then unleashes against him his *gaṇas,* but Vighneśvara subdues them. Viṣṇu and Subrahmaṇya try in their turn without result. Pārvatī emits two subordinate goddesses who come to the aid of her guardian. Viṣṇu finally resorts to his *māyā* (magic illusion) to create confusion on all sides, which enables Śiva to cut off Gaṇapati's head. Pārvatī, furious, sends a thousand goddesses to harass the gods and will let herself be appeased only if her son is resuscitated. Śiva sends the gods toward the north, ordering them to cut off the head of the first living being who appears, to replace Gaṇapati's head (Where had it gone?). It is an elephant that appears, with a single tusk: it is therefore an elephant's head with one tusk that is attached to the body of the Goddess's guardian, which proves satisfactory. She presents her son to Śiva: a reconciliation for the greatest triumph of cosmic order. Vighneśvara submits to Śiva, who makes him *gaṇa-pati.*

Several well-known themes appear in this account, to which so brief a summary does not do justice. First there is the "impure" origin of the god, from the secretions of the Goddess's skin, which recognizes the necessary participation of the impure in the order of the cosmos. This factor assigns Gaṇapati, at the start, to the class of inferior gods and those who are devoted to potentially polluting tasks. But the situation does not remain so simple: it is Śiva's unexpected visit that has induced the Goddess to create her guardian. The detail of the bath is revealing: there is no doubt that the

Gaṇapati. Private collection. Photo Dominique Champion.

Goddess here is the Creation, which according to an image that is well known but inverted by classical philosophy escapes from the sight of the Primordial Male, in which she risks destruction. The Goddess who does not want to be seen in her nakedness denies herself reunion with the world of release, affirms the value of this world, and desires its well-being. This suggests that Gaṇapati, as guardian of the Goddess, oversees *bhukti,* the auspicious progress of earthly affairs, rather than *mukti,* deliverance.

The battle with Śiva, its consequences, Viṣṇu's decisive intervention, and the decapitation of Vighneśvara evoke other well-known themes: first note Viṣṇu's collaboration in Śiva's enterprise by the subterfuge of his power of illusion: the same *māyā* enables him to outwit the vigilance of the *asuras* during the churning of the ocean of milk, from which the gods secure the elixir of immortality (in the same myth, Śiva consumes the poison produced by the churning in order to neutralize its effect on the world). Viṣṇu's *māyā* is in a sense also the Goddess, the Earth, the Primordial Creation, whatever one wishes to call it—the feminine form of the divine that deludes creatures and makes the world exist; but

Viṣṇu's power produces the cosmos only to allow it to achieve release. As for the decapitated Vighneśvara, he becomes in this way a sacrificial victim. His own head necessarily disappears, since it constitutes the sacrificial offering in the Hindu (and no longer Vedic) animal sacrifice. This transition through the sacrifice evokes the case of so many *asuras* whose original wickedness is obliterated at the moment of their sacrificial death and who are transformed into the guardians of superior divinities: this "sacrifice" of Vighneśvara by Śiva may be what enables this impure creature to reach the world of dharma, by placing him in the service of pure causes. The elephant's head symbolizes power, and often royal power, but this meaning is effaced here; however, it is not just any power: like Hanumān the Monkey, the elephant combines power with a vegetarian regimen. He therefore unites in himself what is required to make a good guardian and the purity that is needed for being auspicious (Bhairava, Śiva's guardian, could not play the same role). Moreover, his single tusk, unexplained in the myth, is an evocation of the sacrificial stake, while his trunk may suggest the fertile sexual organ, the tusk and trunk uniting in a double symbolism of Śiva's linga: the iconography shows the trunk poised on a dainty morsel held in his left hand, or even on the sexual organ of a goddess seated on his left thigh. The sacrificial meaning of the decapitation is confirmed by the transformation that Gaṇapati undergoes. He is thereafter submissive to Śiva: *bhukti,* without renouncing its rights, acknowledges the transcendence of *mukti.* This submission consummates his inclusion in the Hindu sacrificial system and renders him fit to control the adverse forces that may create obstacles to the success of the virtuous.

The orientation of Gaṇapati toward the world of *bhukti* also appears in a version of his myth in the *Skanda Purāṇa:* this time the initiative comes from the gods, but Śiva is the guilty party. Did he not grant salvation to all those, good and evil, who visit his temple at Somnath? Heaven is overpopulated, and not just by people of good society: by Śūdras, women, etc. The gods are nearly turned out of the gates of heaven by this excess population. They therefore go to complain to Śiva about the disastrous effects of his grace. But he cannot break his promise. The gods must appeal instead to Pārvatī. The Goddess, praised and propitiated by the gods, who invoke her in particular as Kālarātrī—the "Night of Time"—takes pity on the gods and by rubbing her skin produces a Vighneśvara with four arms and the head of an elephant. He is ordered to remove the Somnath devotees, except those who worship him.

This version of the myth, less rich than the preceding one, evokes other well-known themes: the overpopulation of heaven, and especially the fact that all beings may be found there, is an attenuated form of the theme of the occupation of heaven by the *asuras.* But this situation is created by *bhakti*: the Hindu conscience continually collides with the contradiction between the universality of salvation afforded by devotion to a great god like Viṣṇu or Śiva and the necessity of maintaining the Brahmanical order, without which the world cannot endure. One cannot accord salvation to Śūdras and women and at the same time maintain dharma, the sociocosmic order with all its hierarchies and exclusions. Gaṇapati must act as a filter: from the guardian of the Goddess he has become the guardian of the gate of heaven. This new Saint Peter has no keys, but he can place obstacles where necessary or remove them from the path for those who merit it. Since it is a matter of guaranteeing the auspicious operation of dharma, the worship of Gaṇapati that the Goddess establishes symbolizes above all obedience to dharma, the cause of success in this world and in the other (even for Śūdras and women): it is for this reason that Gaṇapati adorns the lintels of many sanctuary doors. He shares this honor with Gaja-lakṣmī, the goddess of prosperity, who is framed by two elephants who sprinkle her with their trunks. The same two divinities figure alternatively on the door lintels of traditional high-caste homes.

Thus traits that are deemed impure and have a function in the service of Brahmanical purity are again seen combined in the same divinity. We can also understand what renders this god both "popular" and the jealous property of the Brahmans who officiate for him. He is the god of every beginning: his blessing must be obtained if an enterprise is to be brought to a successful conclusion. Evidently "popular" piety retains above all the guarantee of success that he offers to his devotees and that tends to distinguish two representations: the most common one shows the trunk turned toward the left, because it is normally to the left of a god that his wife or the Earth, whom he protects, is situated, and the Earth is represented in his hand by a dainty morsel. But there is a form that is more refined, with a more elaborate ritual, that is called Siddhi-vināyaka, "the one who removes (obstacles) to success," or "the one who leads to success," or, in Tamil, Valampuri-vināyaka, "Vināyaka (with his trunk) turned toward the right." The end of his trunk is coiled from left to right, clockwise. This direction, which is also followed in circumambulating a sanctuary, is considered particularly auspicious. This form of Gaṇapati captures only his aptitude for bestowing success.

M.Bi./b.f.

BIBLIOGRAPHY

A. GETTY, *Gaṇeśa, a Monograph on the Elephant-Faced God* (2d ed., New Delhi 1971).

Skanda, a Great Sovereign God of South India

Skanda is one of the most ancient figures of pan-Indian mythology, since the MBh gives several versions of his myth, and iconography also bears witness to him at an early date. The *Chāndogya Upaniṣad* at least knows his name. But it is in South India that he has been recognized until the present as a great sovereign god—one might even say *the* great sovereign god, were it not for AiyaNār-Śastā, who has the same function. Skanda, better known in his shrines as either Subrahmaṇya or Ṣaṇmukha ("the six-headed one"), seems to hold the position that Rāma and Kṛṣṇa, the two great avatars of Viṣṇu, hold in the north. Skanda is regarded as the son of Śiva (as is AiyaNār), although the myths of his birth make the paternity rather indirect. Furthermore, the iconography of the south, at least at a certain period, insists on depicting the group known as Somaskanda, "(Śiva) with (his wife) Umā and Skanda," although Skanda was not born of Pārvatī-Umā.

To simplify an extremely rich and complex mythology, we shall limit ourselves to the evidence given by the great epic. The MBh provides two distinct myths, both of which narrate both Skanda's birth and his confrontation with an *asura,* and these two passages may be considered the reference myths of the numerous Purāṇic variants. We cannot talk about one without talking about the other, since the two shed mutual light on each other. Although the general arrangement of the avatar myths prevails here, the insistence on the myth of birth and its complexity show how formidable Rudra-Śiva's offspring was to the gods: there was thus a basic opposition between Viṣṇu's avatars, who are "descents" of the supreme god at the request of the heavenly gods, and Śiva's son, who must earn the trust of the gods and virtually imposes himself on them through his great power. He is *su-brahmaṇya,* that is, as devoted to the triumph of the gods and of the Brahmanic order as the avatars are. Skanda's relationship with the avatars of Viṣṇu is somewhat like the relationship between Rudra-Śiva and Viṣṇu. Viṣṇu is unquestionably the sovereign god in the Epic, the one whom the devotee addresses freely. Rudra-Śiva remains the terrible god to whom prayers are addressed in very specific circumstances: prayers to get weapons, to wreak vengeance on someone, to acquire a power not sanctioned by dharma; but in the last resort, all of this also serves a dharma whose total design escapes mankind. Similarly it may be possible to discern features peculiar to the *asuras* whom Skanda opposes, although *asuras* inimical to the gods seem at first sight to have very few special features.

In the third book of the MBh (223ff.) the setting is wholly classical. The gods have been defeated in a fight with the *asuras,* and Indra, worried, searches for a good "general of the army of the gods" (*devasenāpati*), that is, one who can defend the inhabitants of heaven against their hereditary enemies. He meets a young woman abducted by the *asura* Keśin, and he rescues her. Her name is Devasenā ("army of the gods"), and she asks Indra to give her a husband (*pati*) who will protect her. Indra consults with Brahmā, and both agree that a son born of Agni (the sacrificial fire) would make an ideal *devasenāpati,* simultaneously general of the army of the gods and husband of Devasenā.

Indra then goes to the place where the divine *ṛṣis* are conducting a sacrifice and have invited Agni to participate. Agni falls in love with the wives of the *ṛṣis,* and as he sits comfortably in one of the sacrificial fires, he looks at them at his leisure. However, his despair over not being able to possess the wives of the *ṛṣis* drives him to abandon his body (the concrete sacrificial fire) and take refuge in the forest. He is followed there by Svāhā (the personified invocation that accompanies any oblation to the gods as it is poured into the fire). She is in love with him, and in order to unite with Agni she takes the form of six of the seven *ṛṣis'* wives in succession. Six times Svāhā collects Agni's seed in her hand and brings it to the White Mountain that is covered with a forest of reeds. She deposits it there in a golden pot, from which a child is born—Skanda Kumāra, an infant with six heads, who reaches adult size by his sixth day of life. His sixth head is that of a goat.

He frightens everyone, and there are disputes about his birth and parentage. Only Viśvāmitra, who has secretly followed Svāhā, knows whose child he is and is the first to "take refuge" in Skanda (the fixed formula of both Hindu bhakti and Buddhist piety). The gods advise Indra to kill him, for Skanda might try to take his place, but Indra declares his impotence. He dispatches the *Mātṛ*s (mothers of the worlds) to go to see the child, but on seeing his strength, they too take refuge in him and adopt him as their son. His goat head is especially dear to them. Agni comes to see him with his goat head (the goat is the paradigm of the sacrificial victim), and then come groups of unsavory characters, the Gaṇas, who also appear around Rudra-Śiva. Indra finally visits him with all the gods. Before Skanda's obvious superiority the gods forsake Indra and take refuge in Skanda. Indra has to do the same after attempting to put up a fight. Śrī then comes to live with him. The Brahmans worship him and the *ṛṣis* propose that he become the new Indra. But Skanda refuses the kingship. He would rather be Indra's servant, so Indra asks him to be the general of the army of the gods and gives him Devasenā for his wife.

At this point the text specifies that Skanda is Rudra's son, since Agni is Rudra. He has many mothers: the *ṛṣis'* wives claim this title, as do the Mātṛs and Svāhās. Skanda gives the Mātṛs the power to inflict all sorts of pain and sorrow on children up to the age of sixteen. He has a whole court of demons and demonesses, the Kumāras and the Kumārīs, the Grahas ("kidnappers") who symbolize all the misfortunes reserved for children.

Rudra comes in his turn to see Skanda, who meets him halfway and assures Rudra that he is at his command. The *asuras* attack and the buffalo *asura* Mahiṣa charges Rudra's chariot. Rudra refrains from killing him in order to leave this task to Skanda, who splits Mahiṣa's head in half with his *śakti* (a magical or real weapon that symbolizes his power to act in the world). The falling head clears a passage in the mountain and opens up an access road to the Uttara-Kuru, the "Kuru of the North," a paradisiacal country. The *asuras* are defeated, and Rudra advises the gods to regard Skanda as another form of Rudra.

The MBh 13.84–86 narrative about Skanda is inserted in a speech glorifying gold. We should note that, for the Hindus, gold is solid fire and therefore closely connected not only with the sacrificial fire and sacrifice (sacrificial fees of gold and cows are the most highly valued) but also with Śrī.

Rudra married Rudrāṇī (a name that the Goddess takes on) and they remain in a long sexual embrace until the gods, afraid of the offspring that would result from such a union, ask Śiva to abstain from procreating; they argue that the world could not bear a son born of him. Rudra consents and henceforth practices complete sexual abstinence. The furious Goddess curses the gods and condemns them to be childless themselves. Agni (the sacrificial fire) is absent at the moment of this curse, but some of Rudra's seed has fallen to earth, into the fire.

At the very same moment, the gods are harassed by the *asura* Tāraka and seek counsel from Brahmā, who has granted invulnerability to Tāraka. Brahmā believes that only a son of Agni can oppose the demon. They set out to find Agni, who has vanished in order to sleep. Betrayed by a series of indiscretions, he keeps changing his hiding place until the gods finally find him in the *śamī* tree. The gods make their request, and Agni agrees to help them.

Agni unites with Gaṅgā and deposits within her an embryo (the seed obtained from Śiva). But Gangā is unable to bear the embryo, which carries within it all the heat of Agni. Suffering greatly and against her will she deposits it on Mount Meru. It looks like a gleaming piece of pure gold that illuminates the whole mountain. Everybody rushes to see it and is set aglow by its brightness.

After completing the task assigned him by the gods, Agni disappears with Gaṅgā. The embryo develops in a forest of reeds. The Kṛttikās (wives of the *ṛṣis,* who are identified with the Pleiades) see him and nurse him.

Procession statues of Subrahmaṇya and his two wives. Tiruttani (South India). Photo IFI.

After an interruption, the narrative resumes: the Kṛttikās give birth simultaneously to six parts of the embryo, which they reduce to one, but with six heads. The child takes refuge in a grove of reeds where the Kṛttikās nurse him.

All the creatures, headed by the Trimūrti and the celestial gods, come to see him. The gods think that the *asura* Tāraka is already doomed. They appoint Guha (one of Skanda's names) general of their armies and tell him about the trouble that Tāraka is causing them. Guha kills Tāraka with his infallible *śakti*.

The two stories begin in very different ways, but with an identical narrative process. In one case the defeated army of the gods needs a general, and the youthful Devasenā, harassed by an *asura*, asks for a husband. In the second version the gods ask Rudra not to procreate, which causes them to be cursed with sterility. The double sterility immediately becomes the demon Tāraka, who afflicts the gods and from whom they must be freed. The first part of the second story must be structured in this way, partly because of the name of the *asura* (Tāraka, "he who delivers") and also because of the subsequent corollary: Agni has vanished to go to sleep, which implies a suspension of all sacrificial activity on earth and thus a threat of cosmic death. By asking Rudra to observe perpetual continence, in fear of his offspring, the gods send the Great Yogi back to his yoga without allowing him to alternate the phases of cosmic emission and reabsorption. They thus condemn the world to final deliverance without any hope of a new beginning. So terrible a prospect must take the form of an *asura*, and the favor granted by Brahmā to the *asura* is merely another form of this inconsiderate step of the gods. The two stories open on an avatar theme, the first in a classical manner, the second with unusual details. At issue is more than a mere reversal of the normal cosmic order that needs to be reestablished. The very existence of the cosmos is at stake. It may be said that the first account is at the junction of two yugas, while the second tells of the threat of a definitive end to the world. But this threat is obviously idle, since some of Rudra's seed has escaped from him and has been collected in fire on earth. The seed is the "remnant" necessary for every new beginning of the world.

The second account immediately places Rudra in the forefront, and the seed that Agni deposits inside Gangā is Rudra's; this is not said explicitly, but as in the first account, Rudra and Agni are identified. The theme of linear descent is thus substituted for the theme of the avatar, and Rudra appears instead of Viṣṇu. There is probably a connection between this choice and the particular character of the *asura*, who is none other than the terrible aspect of Rudra, the one with which he annihilates the world, and also the one that makes him the god of deliverance for the yogi. It remains to show that the Mahiṣa of the first account (the *asura* usually seen in connection with the Goddess) is different from the *asura* who confronts the avatar. Here we can only offer some rather indirect hints, which the myth of the *Devī Māhātmya* does not corroborate. This remains an open issue.

The first account insists less on the connection between Rudra and Skanda. We are reminded almost by conspicuous silence that Agni is identical to Rudra, and that Skanda is consequently Rudra's son. Only at the end does Rudra explicitly charge Skanda with the task of slaughtering Mahiṣa, and only then does he give him his blessing. On the other hand, the gods have every reason to be frightened by the child and his extraordinary power, and their fright is much like the one that they experience in the second account at the thought of Rudra having a son. Skanda is soon surrounded by *gaṇas* ("troops") that in Śaiva mythology turn out to mean all kinds of disquieting creatures, collective or individual, including *asuras* that are devotees of Rudra, as they are of Skanda in this case. Skanda is also associated with the Mātṛs ("the mothers"). There is no reason to believe that these are identical with the *saptamātṛkās* of the *Devī-māhātmya*, but their function is made clear. In popular worship, Skanda has the reputation of being a god "who kidnaps" children, but also a god to whom people pray to have children. That is probably why he has six heads: he is associated with the goddess Ṣaṣṭhī ("sixth"), who presides over the sixth day after birth, the period regarded as crucial to the survival of a newborn child. In the epic myth, his "kidnapping" function seems to be given over to the Mātṛs, and even more characteristically to the Kumāras and the Kumārīs who surround him and who bear one of his names, Kumāra ("the young boy, the young man"). This name connotes at least mythically the state of an unmarried young man who has taken a vow of chastity, which accords with Skanda's residence in the mountain. In some parts of India women are not allowed inside his temples for that reason. The Kumāras and Kumārīs thus participate in his asceticism, and there is a connection between the divine yoga and the power that the god has to reabsorb all creatures within him.

Moreover, Skanda Kuāra is born on a mountain covered with a forest of reeds. This motif appears elsewhere. The Brahman warrior Kṛpa and his twin sister Kṛpī, the future wife of Droṇa in the MBh, are born in a clump of reeds on which the seed of their ascetic father has fallen. Kṛpa ("pity") is more expert in warfare than in the Veda, although he is a Brahman, and his brother-in-law Droṇa is also a warrior Brahman. Kṛpa is an incarnation of the Rudras (a group of lesser deities associated with Rudra), and his nephew Aśvatthāman, the son of Droṇa, is an incarnation of Rudra, Antaka (death), Krodha (wrath), and Kāma (desire). The reeds (*śara-vana*) evoke arrows (*śara*), and this theme, which all the myths of Skanda associate with birth, gives him simultaneously the character of a warrior and of an ascetic, and connects him indirectly with Rudra. Skanda thereby evokes Rudra, the terrible ascetic, and may himself presage the end of the world. Skanda, who had such difficulty being born because of his illustrious and complex parentage, is logically associated with the fate of earthly children. There is there no need to posit two Skandas or two traditions about Skanda (the problem of AiyaNār-Śāstā is posed in very similar terms): his character as a terrible ascetic connected with Rudra gives him his reputation as a kidnapper; an adapted cult is enough to transform the threat that he constitutes into a blessing. A god so dangerous and at the same time so essential to the world's salvation naturally finds Viśvāmitra an ideal devotee.

Skanda is rather far from the character of the avatar. Although in his great shrines his function is very close to that of Viṣṇu's avatars, he cannot be confused with any of these "descents," and his connection with Śiva remains essential. Closer to the demons than any avatar (including the Goddess), within the myth he fulfills a more permanent function then they do, since he is the general of the armies of the gods. The order over which he watches is the same as the dharma connected with the avatar, but he cannot be considered a model king. He consecrates or illustrates Rudra-Śiva's participation in the Brahmanic order, as well as the participation of lesser deities and demons. This ascetic receives no less than two wives, Devasenā in the MBh and Vaḻḷi, a daughter of the mountain and huntress, both of whom undergo infinite variations within Purāṇic mythology. A god interested in the order of the world cannot do without a wife any more than he can do without demons who are subordinate to him. Skanda Kumāra has the same ambiguity as Rudra-Śiva, yogi and spouse of Pārvatī, and the Goddess, virgin and spouse of Śiva. The renunciation of the world always governs the order of the world and is closely implicated in the order of the world.

M.Bi./g.h.

BIBLIOGRAPHY

P. K. AGRAWALA, *Skanda Kārttikeya: Study in the Origin and Development* (Banaras 1967). A. K. CHATTERJEE, *The Cult of Skanda-Kārttikeya in Ancient India* (Calcutta 1970). F. L'HERNAULT, *L'iconographie de Subrahmaṇya ou Tamilnad* (Pondicherry 1978).

Abbreviations

MBh *Mahābhārata* (edition: Citrashala Press, Poona)
DM *Devī-māhātmya* (edition and translation: "Les Belles Lettres")

Devī: The Goddess in India

Devī: the Goddess. She is given this name in order to encompass all the individual proper names that are given to her in the great temples and village sanctuaries of India. No matter what level her function may be situated at, it is always the same. Sometimes associated with a great god, usually a form of Śiva, sometimes independent, she cannot be mistaken: she is the Goddess who confers the favors necessary to a happy earthly existence and leads to the god of final release. She is a benevolent goddess for her devotees, but her anger is terrible. She carries off children and gives children to sterile parents, unleashes epidemics and cures diseases. By the evils that she unleashes she is close to the *asuras;* but she also kills the buffalo-*asura* for the gods and thus ensures the prosperity of the triple world. She gives victory to Kṣatriyas who pray to her. She is also sometimes called Yogeśvarī and thus participates in the function of the Great Yogi: for in order to attract the attention of Śiva, whom she wanted to marry, it was necessary for her to become an ascetic and to rival in her austerities the one whom she desired. She is often considered a virgin as well, when she is alone in her temple. In the form of Satī, she dies because of the quarrel between her father Dakṣa and her husband Rudra, and thus becomes the model for wives who commit suicide on their husband's funeral pyres.

When we pass from *bhakti* to Śāktism (the nuances of the transition from the one to the other are infinite), she becomes the preeminent divinity, the Śakti who is superior to Śiva, and this reversal of the usual hierarchy is accompanied in a few cases by a reversal of dharma: what was prohibited becomes permitted, the impure becomes pure, and mundane objects of pleasure become instruments for salvation.

In every way, even when she presides over release, she is closer to earthly values than the god is, more attentive to the prayers and needs of her devotees; but she is also more apt to make use of the violence without which the earth could not live. It is thus not surprising that one of the myths of her birth, the least developed and also the least interesting, has her born from Parvata, "the mountain," which makes her Pārvatī, the daughter of the mountain. Here the mountain evokes both the mythic support of the world that makes the world habitable and the Himalayan dwelling of Rudra-Śiva, which is inhabited by the solitary yogis.

There is a tendency to simplify the Goddess by making her into a Śaiva goddess, the wife of Śiva—even when she is alone, independent, and a virgin in her own sanctuary—in opposition to Śrī or Lakṣmī, who would be the Vaiṣṇava goddess. The two must be distinguished: Śrī is never the warrior goddess, except in certain regions of India where she is found with the name of Mahālakṣmī; but in this case she is merely the Goddess. Śrī in the strict sense is always associated with Viṣṇu, just as prosperity is associated with the sacrifice; this is another way of saying that she is always on the side of dharma. As a goddess she is also closer to worldly concerns than the god is: incarnate as Draupadī or as Sītā in the epics, she is the catalyst for the plot. It is for her and at her instigation that people fight. She is thus not as completely opposed to the Goddess as might have been thought.

The main reason we cannot set the Vaiṣṇava goddess and the Śaiva goddess in opposition is that the Goddess has a tie with Viṣṇu which is as essential as her tie with Śiva. When the myth makes her a daughter of Dakṣa, she is related to the sacrifice and thus to Viṣṇu. But the two most important myths about her origin associate her directly with Viṣṇu. In the *Harivaṃśa,* the book of the acts of Kṛṣṇa and the appendix to the *Mahābhārata* (2.2), Viṣṇu asks Nidrā, the "sleep" of Time—i.e., the sleep of the cosmic night, whose name is feminine in Sanskrit—to "descend" to the earth to undo the criminal designs of Kaṃsa. She is to descend into

Durgā, the buffalo killer. Probably from Gujarat. Note the buffalo head on the pedestal, at the right. Private collection. Photo Dominique Champion.

Durgā standing on the head of a buffalo. Bisnagar, Gwalior Museum. Photo O. Divaran.

the womb of Yaśodā, the wife of the cowherd Nanda, and he will descend into the womb of Devakī, the wife of Vasudeva and the paternal aunt of Kaṃsa, the incarnate *asura*, who kills his aunt's progeny as soon as they are born. At the time of birth, in the night, the two newborn infants are exchanged. Kaṃsa then takes her away to kill her by crushing her against a rock (an echo of the theme of birth from a mountain), from which she flies up into the sky. Viṣṇu then describes her in terms that make it easy to recognize the Goddess in her: like him, she is black, dressed in dark blue and yellow silk, and she lives in the Vindhya Mountains, where she is devoted to celibacy. This goddess Nidrā thus comes to be associated with the function of an avatar of Viṣṇu, and is elevated to the level of great Goddess. This myth is the source of the common belief that the Goddess is the sister of Viṣṇu.

The *Devīmāhātmya*, a famous poem to the glory of the Goddess which is found within the *Mārkaṇḍeya Purāṇa*, specifies who Nidrā is, and in doing so brings her even closer to Viṣṇu. It must be recalled that during the cosmic night Viṣṇu sleeps in a yogic sleep on the serpent Śeṣa, and that at the dawn of a new cosmic day a lotus bearing Brahmā emerges from his navel. The DM adds to this scenario the presence of two *asuras*, Madhu and Kaiṭabha, born from Viṣṇu's earwax, who attempt to kill Brahmā. In order to awaken the still sleeping Viṣṇu, Brahmā then sings the praises of Yoganidrā, the goddess who lives in the eyes of Viṣṇu and keeps him asleep. We recognize her as the Nidrā of Time of which the HV spoke. This Nidrā is the yogic sleep of Viṣṇu, identical with the sleep of Time, whence comes her name of Yoganidrā. Brahmā praises her as the cause of the creation and dissolution of the worlds; in other words, she is the projection of the yogic activity of the god. She is the double of the god as the supreme Puruṣa who is immutable and collected into his yoga, and as the female energy by which he comes out of his yoga to preside over the fate of the worlds by emitting and reabsorbing them in turn. Praised by Brahmā simultaneously as the Night of Time—Kālarātri—which provokes the yogic sleep of Viṣṇu and his absorption of all creatures and as Mahāmāyā, the cosmic illusion that, once outside of Viṣṇu, makes the world appear and allows it to exist by blinding it to its own nature, Yoganidrā goes out of Viṣṇu, thus making the god wake up and confront the two *asuras,* whom he finally destroys.

We have here, in mythic terms, all of the elements of the Goddess's complexity, both as a power that causes the delusion of all creatures and as an instrument for their salvation. As such, she is essentially bound to Viṣṇu before she is connected with Śiva. This reason alone would seem to constitute a very solid argument for taking the Hinduism of the *smṛti* tradition to be logically prior to the sects. It is normal that the tie with Viṣṇu should be more fundamental than the relationship with Śiva—she is or is not the wife of Śiva—to the degree that it is Viṣṇu who is the supreme god of Hinduism of the *smṛti* tradition, especially as it is presented in the epics. Furthermore, it is for the benefit of Brahmā, and thus apparently for the whole Brahmanic order, that she awakens Viṣṇu. His intervention is beneficial for the creation that has been endangered by the *asuras.*

But the *Devīmāhātmya* is mostly the account of the victory of the Goddess over the buffalo demon Mahiṣāsura. Although other demons combat her after Mahiṣa, the story is clearly centered upon Mahiṣa. The ritual iconography of this form of Durgā is immense: its popularity would be hard to explain if it were not connected with the annual sacrifice of one or more buffalos to the Goddess which took place until recent times, whenever she was the protectress of a kingdom or locality. This is far from the Vedic sacrifice, at least apparently. The victim is an *asura,* an evil being whom one must get rid of, who must be killed by an untouchable and eaten by untouchables. It is no longer an individual sacrificer who offers the sacrifice but the whole local community led by its chief, king, or local equivalent, and all the castes are associated with the event, even if they do not all participate in it physically. The ritual is extremely varied, but we may point out a particularly revealing trait found in the buffalo sacrifice as it is performed in most of the villages of Andhra Pradesh (the eastern coastal region north of Madras): the severed head of the buffalo is offered to the Goddess, whose image is a temporary one made of clay for the occasion, and is then carried, along with the clay image of the Goddess, to the outer limit of the village lands. The victim represents an evil that must be gotten rid of, and this evil seems also to be connected with the Goddess, whose image is also expelled. The buffalo sacrifice takes place, depending on the region, at the time of the annual temple festival, at the beginning of spring, or for the autumn Navarātri. But the Goddess's victory over the buffalo is itself invariably celebrated at Vijayādaśamī, the day following the nine nights of Navarātri, the "tenth" day of "the Victory."

The myth itself very much resembles a myth of an avatar which has been edited and corrected by the epic: when

Durgā, the buffalo killer. Private collection. Photo Dominque Champion.

Mahiṣa, the buffalo-*asura,* is the king of the *asuras,* the gods and the *asuras* wage a long war; the *asuras* are victorious and Mahiṣa becomes the king of heaven in Indra's place. The gods, led by Brahmā, go to the dwelling of Śiva and Viṣṇu and tell the two gods what has happened. From each of the great gods, from Brahmā and from each of the celestial gods, great rays of light shoot out and unite into one light and take a feminine form. Each then gives her a weapon. The Goddess shakes the world with her roar. A battle begins between her and Mahiṣa; it will end in the victory of the Goddess and the death of Mahiṣa. The Goddess drinks heavily during the battle. The account continues with a description of her victories over other *asuras,* Śumbha and Niśumbha, who have occupied heaven once again. This scenario is even simpler: the gods go directly to the Himalayas (where the Goddess lives under certain forms) and sing the praises of the one they call Viṣṇumāyā. This is of course still the same Goddess. They ask her to rid them of Śumbha and Niśumbha. Śumbha tries to win the Goddess for his wife (in Karnataka, she is sometimes considered the wife of the buffalo that is sacrificed to her), but she slips away from him and provokes the insolent *asura* into battle. The lion that is her vehicle, her terrible Kālī form, which she emits from her

Durgā of the Durgāpūjā in Bengal. Photo Pierre Amado.

Durgā. Shrine at Kalo. Photo Pierre Amado.

angry forehead, and the *śaktis* (female energies) of the gods Brahmā, Śiva, Skanda, Viṣṇu, and Indra, lend her strength. Viṣṇu's *śakti* in fact divides into two parts, one the female replica of Viṣṇu—Vaiṣṇavī—and the other the female replica of the sacrificial boar of Hindu cosmogony. To these are added the *śakti* of Narasiṃha—Nārasimhī—another form of Viṣṇu. These together form the group of the "Seven Mothers"—*saptamātṛkās*—who are well known in iconography. The Goddess sends Śiva as a messenger to Śumbha and Niśumbha to demand that they restore heaven to Indra. Thus it is again the whole divine community, along with the supreme gods and the celestial gods, who take part, just as on earth it is the whole local community that assembles for the sacrifice of the buffalo to the Goddess. The *asuras* refuse, which is the signal for a great battle. The Goddess devours all those who fall to earth, which puts the whole army of the *asuras* to flight. Then the *asura* Raktabīja rises up, and from every drop of his blood as it falls on the ground a new *asura* is produced. Thousands of *asuras* are thus produced, to the despair of the gods. The Goddess therefore commands Kālī to collect in her open mouth all the blood that flows from Raktabīja and to devour the new *asuras* born from his blood. The long digressions which follow add nothing to the structure of the whole, apart from a repetition of the carnage that leads to the final victory.

The Goddess—who calls the battle, as in the epic, "the sacrifice of battle"—fears neither blood nor wine; in other words, she fears neither impurity nor violence, when they are for the good of the gods and the worlds. She can support the great god in the eternal battle against the demons, and her aid is necessary because in his temple the great god is always a pure god who avoids all killing. The violence of the Goddess, however, eventually becomes transformed in her ritual into blood sacrifices and offerings of wine. This brings her very close to the demons that she kills: this is why the mythic motif of the avatar of the god—whose ideological justification lies elsewhere—must be duplicated by the Goddess who kills *asuras*. The low tasks are left to the Goddess so that the purity of the god may be maintained; and extreme Tantrism, known as Śaktism, only glorifies her role and cleanses it of any suspicion of impurity. This phenomenon is thus not a vulgar return of "mundane" appetites rebelling against renunciation, but the affirmation, carried to its furthest limits, that the world must exist in order for there to be release from the world.

M.Bi./d.w.

BIBLIOGRAPHY

Célébration de la Grande Déesse (Devī-māhātmya), Sanskrit text translated and commented upon by Jean Varenne (Paris 1975).

Abbreviations

DM *Devī-māhātmya*
HV *Harivaṃśa* (Citrashala Press, Poona)

Kāmadhenu: The Mythical Cow, Symbol of Prosperity

Kāmadhenu (or Kāmaduh) is the most common, virtually generic, name of the cow that symbolizes in India the source of all prosperity; she is the cow "from whom all that is desired is drawn." The proper names that she is given, such as Śabalā (the spotted one) and Kapilā (the red one), do not prevent her from also receiving the epithet Kāmadhenu. All the values that the Hindus attach to the cow in general are projected onto the Kāmadhenu.

The Kāmadhenu of myth is always closely associated with the Brahman, whose entire wealth she represents. The Brahman is the priest of the Vedic sacrifice, and the first prerequisite for a sacrifice is the material oblation of cow's milk and its derivatives, particularly clarified butter, which is poured on the sacrificial fire as an offering. Kāmadhenu sometimes becomes Homadhenu, the one "from whom oblations are drawn." Thus in myths it is common to find the function of the Brahman associated either with the cow or with milk. Sacrificial payments were once measured in cows, and even today it is an act of piety to give a cow to a Brahman. It is commonly said that a Brahman without a cow is not a Brahman. From all of this, one can understand how it is that the cow is associated with everything that defines the Brahmanical order: respect for the cow is a corollary to the respect that is given to Brahmans, gods, and dharma in general, that is, to the sociocosmic order.

The sociocosmic order (dharma) can be maintained only through sacrifice, which nourishes the gods of heaven, who in turn cause rain to fall on the earth at the right time; it is thus as a result of sacrifice that plants grow and that animals—notably the cow—and men can be nourished, and that they can prosper, and that they can offer sacrifices. This order is a closed circuit that should function forever if everyone respects it, and the cow occupies a preeminent place in it by virtue of its role in the sacrifice. The sociocosmic order, on which the prosperity of the world depends, since it is founded on the principle of sacrifice, would not exist without the cow. That is why the cow is the symbol both of the Brahman's power and of all wealth, since the prosperity of the world springs from the oblation of clarified butter.

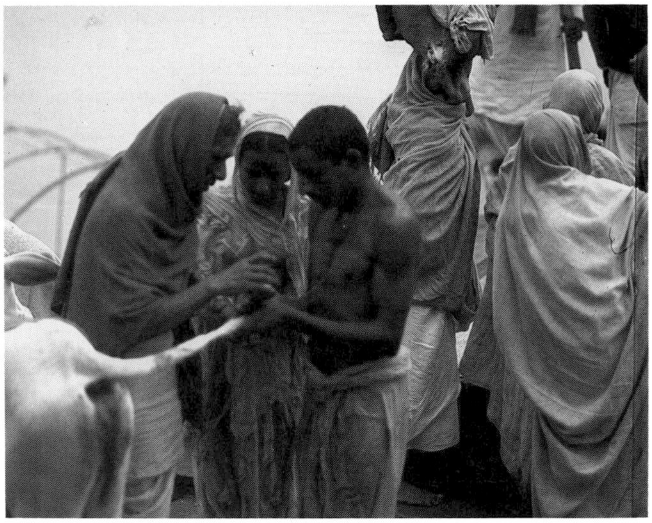

Gift of a cow at Banaras. Photo Pierre Amado.

By the same token, the mythical cow Kāmadhenu is very close to the fertile earth, and in Sanskrit, "cow" is a word frequently used for "earth." Furthermore, the cow, a feminine agent, is necessarily related to the Goddess who is also at least partially related to the earth. As a possession of the Brahman whose status forbids him to defend himself and who relies on the prince's protection, the cow becomes the Brahman's best protection in the event that he is attacked by an abusive prince seeking to deprive him of his power. As a goddess, the cow can become a warrior or at least produce the armies needed to protect herself and her owner.

M.Bi./g.h.

Symbols of the Earth in Indian Religion

Contrary to widespread ideas about Hindu spirituality and the desire for deliverance that all Hindus supposedly share, the earth, and above all the land of India, stands at the very center of all mythico-ritual speculations in India. The theoretical foundation of its perpetuity and the guarantee of its prosperity are issues of prime concern. This concern was, perhaps from the very beginning (if the notion of historical origin has a meaning in this context), compounded with the values symbolized by the renunciants. In broad outline, the earth is the world of sacrifice and transmigration, while renunciants represent what lies beyond sacrifice, which the world of sacrifice must integrate to ground itself in the absolute.

Moreover, the cosmological representations of the Hindus do not allow us to isolate a precise image of the earth. Except for their concept of seven islands surrounded by seven oceans, they are more preoccupied with situating the earth within the vertical hierarchy of the worlds, or with isolating in one of the seven islands the land of India, the land of the Middle—*madhyadeśa* (not because the Aryans actually occupied and settled the center of the plain between the Ganges and Indus rivers, but because the land of the Bhāratas, as they call themselves, must by definition be the center of the world). The land of men is located between the netherworld and the sky, and there the fate of the triple world is sealed by the joint effect of sacrifice and renunciation. But in another sense, the earth of the myths may also be this triple world, which is entirely swept away in the cosmic catastrophe at the end of an age of the world and is reborn after a cosmic night. When the earth figures symbolically in a myth, it does not matter whether it is the earth itself or the triple world, since they are interdependent. For instance, the bad government of a king on earth reveals an invasion by the inhabitants of the lower worlds and threatens the peace of the gods in heaven; the absence of sacrifices on earth causes a famine among the gods, which in turn results in a drought on earth.

Consequently the symbols used in myths to signify the earth are determined, not by physical representations of the earth, but rather by the values by which its fate is acted out.

First of all, although the primordial male, the supreme Puruṣa, soon emerges as the hypostasis of release, the one toward whom creatures freed from rebirth aspire, the Goddess at the opposite end of the spectrum is the world that emanates from the deity, the world of transmigration, the earth in the broadest sense. Since release is on the side of renunciation, while transmigration is based on sacrifice, the Goddess has to be closely associated with sacrifice. She is therefore sometimes black—Kālī, Kṛṣṇā, Nīlā, Tillotamā, Śyāmā, all names for the Goddess or related mythical individuals meaning "black"—and sometimes gold: then she is called Lakṣmī or Śrī. These two colors of the Goddess are also the colors of fire, which is *kṛṣṇavartman* (the black-traced one) and in its solid form appears as gold. The two features complement each other: Lakṣmī is prosperity, which sacrifice can bring, and gold is the best symbol for this prosperity. The thirst for gold that Hindus still have today has its roots in this concept. Of course, it is not possible to separate gold from its economic value. The young groom who brings his wife into the house also brings in Lakṣmī. The new bride must have a sari with at least one gold brocade border, and she is covered with gold jewels. These jewels are her personal property and remain in the house so long as circumstances allow her to keep them, for they are signs that Lakṣmī is present.

But prosperity is never there once and for all. It must constantly be made through sacrificial rites, in which fire also plays a destructive role: without the permanent consumption of the victims by fire—that is, their consumption by the gods—the earth could not survive. This destructive aspect of fire constantly confronts the earth with the darkness that threatens the world, but fire is in itself "dark" (*tāmasic:* since it is associated with killing; this accounts for the dark complexion of the goddess: Kālī, the name of one of her bloodiest forms, is also the Vedic name of one of the seven tongues of the sacrificial fire. There is a continuity between this meaning of the color black and a common example used by classical Indian philosophy that indicates that the earth, naturally black, turns red through the action of fire; potter's earth is not normally black.

By extension, when a text stresses the dark complexion of a mythical woman who is not identified with the Goddess, one can suspect the presence not only of the meaning "Goddess" but also of the meaning "earth" (feminine beauty implies, by contrast, a fair complexion, a sign of high caste). The same can be said about odor: since odor is the characteristic property of the earth, the property that reveals the presence of the element earth wherever it may be, when a text stresses a woman's fragrance (or bad smell), her symbolic link with the earth becomes apparent. Thus Satyavatī, who was born of a female fish, has the smell of fish but then loses that smell and receives a penetrating fragrance on the day that she conceives a Brahman, the *ṛṣi* Vyāsa (also called Kṛṣṇa, and dark in complexion like his mother), the promulgator of the Vedas (*Mahābhārata* 1.105).

But the earth also appears under less transparent symbols, whose common feature is a more or less direct association with the sacrifice or the sacrificial fire. Because the earth is above all an anisotropic space, whose cardinal points assume complementary values, a square object easily evokes it. This object can be complex in itself: when, after beheading his mother and making his father revive her, Paraśurāma destroys all the Kṣatriyas on earth and then gives the earth to the Brahmans, his gift of the earth to the Brahmans, who must set it back in motion, is symbolized by a golden altar, which he gives at the end of a great sacrifice to the principal celebrant, Kaśyapa, one of the progenitors in Hindu mythology. The sacrificial altar, the *vedī*, is not generally square, but at this highly complex level of Hindu symbolism the shape of the *vedī* probably merges with the square shape of the sacrificial fire in which the oblations are offered (each solemn Vedic sacrifice has three main fires). In the present-day ritual of the temples, the oblations are made into a square hearth next to a *vedī* that is also square. The golden altar that Paraśurāma offers is the earth purified by the sacrifice of the Kṣatriyas. The square base of the linga, which represents Brahmā and his four Vedas, in all likelihood also evokes the world organized according to the four cardinal points in the Vedas.

Since forms take on value only insofar as they are signs, there is no paradox in also seeing the earth as symbolized by all kinds of spherical objects: the ball of sweets placed in Gaṇapati's left hand is one example; others are the balls with which so many princes and princesses of the epic play, and the ball of butter that the child Kṛṣṇa steals from his foster mother. This symbolism is more complex, and the nuance that separates balls of food from balls in games should be appreciated. The guiding idea that lies behind the entire sacrificial economy and that specifically informs the concept of the cosmogonic Puruṣa is that in any sacrifice, the true victim is the one who offers the sacrifice, and the victim actually put to death is only a substitute. This idea, reworked by the epic to elaborate the notion of a sacrifice appropriate to the warrior, reappears in the mythical theme of the beheaded goddess: the warrior-goddess, victorious over the buffalo-demon, can triumph over her enemy only because she offered herself in sacrifice at the start of the combat. She would have been beheaded if she had not beheaded him. And perhaps she beheads herself by beheading her enemy, who is only a part of her since she is the mother of the universe.

The earth lives only by sacrifices. She is more or less identifiable with the Goddess, and thus constantly finds herself in the position of a sacrificial offering. But there is a difference: whereas the Goddess is often represented in her shrine as a bodiless head—or more rarely as a headless body—the earth symbolized by the myth is more often assimilated to a ball of food, since any sacrificial offering is food for the gods and since the ball of food figures explicitly in the ritual for the ancestors beginning with its Vedic forms. Kṛṣṇa's ball of butter instead evokes the melted butter that fuels the sacrificial fire. The ball of sweets is another version of this and gives its name to the episode of the Khāṇḍava forest in the *Mahābhārata* (1.222ff.); *khāṇḍava* is the name of a candy, and the forest that Agni, the sacrificial fire, devours with the help of Kṛṣṇa and Arjuna is an image of the earth consumed by the cosmic conflagration at the end of one of the ages of the world: the fire that devours the Khāṇḍava had been made ill by the excess of clarified butter and seeks a cure by a change of diet. This is thus an opposition between butter and candy. The candy, substituted for butter when the sacrificial mechanism is derailed, recalls the ball-shaped food for the ancestors, or better still, the funeral sacrifice of which the cosmic fire is a transposition.

The balls that princes and princesses play with in crucial episodes—the Kaurava princes during the arrival of Droṇa, Devayānī and Śarmiṣṭhā in the Yayāti myth, and Kuntī when her father Śūra gives her to King Kuntibhoja—recall that the fate of the earth is in the hands of the princes. The king's principal wife symbolizes his kingdom, and her attachment to the king symbolizes her attachment to his kingdom. The element of play introduced by the ball connects the king closely with the deity who plays with his creation: this is the Hindu image of gratuitous activity. Just as the deity has no need of creation but creates in a spirit of play (but also for the good of creatures), so the king must rule his kingdom without pursuing his own personal interest. At the same time, the play has a sexual connotation: the Puruṣa and the Devī, the king and his wife, the ruler and his kingdom, are all united according to a set of interrelated connections. If gratuitous activity and sexual relations are taken together, this is close to the guiding idea of *śākta* Tantrism: to control pleasure through the exercise of pleasure.

Finally, there seems to be a simple play on words at the origin of yet another image of the earth, which seems at first glance to be aberrant: *urvī,* one of the terms for the earth, means "the broad one," "the one spread out" (as does the word *pṛthvī,* or *pṛthivī*). This is the feminine form of the adjective *uru.* The word *ūru,* with a long *ū* in the first syllable, means "thigh." This may explain why Aurva is born from his mother's thigh, where he had hidden to escape the massacre of the Bhṛgu Brahmans by the descendants of the Kṣatriya Kṛtavīrya. It is also why Narasiṃha lays Hiraṇyakaśipu across his thighs to kill him, because Hiraṇyakaśipu could not be killed on the ground or in the air: Narasiṃha's thighs thus offer a perfect solution.

M.Bi./g.h.

Ganges and Yamunā, the River of Salvation and the River of Origins

Although the mythology of the Gaṅgā (the Ganges) is infinitely richer than the mythology of the Yamunā, it would be an error in perspective to treat one separated from its connection with the other. Although the Gaṅgā, the white river, is the river of salvation, the Yamunā, the black river, is the river of origins. Their confluence at Prayāga (near modern Allahabad) is one of the most sacred sites in India.

Moreover, to speak of the Gaṅgā and the Yamunā is to speak of Viṣṇu and Śiva; the relation of the two gives rise to a third term: Viṣṇu and Śiva evoke Brahmā, the necessary complement of the Trimūrti; while the Gaṅgā and the Yamunā give rise to the Sarasvatī (which is supposed to be present but visible only to yogis at the confluence at Prayāga). This similarity is no accident: Gaṅgā and Yamunā personified are also have a connected with Viṣṇu and Śiva, while Sarasvatī is one of the names of the consort of Brahmā. In the *Mahābhārata,* Gaṅgā is the mother of Bhīṣma, the hero who sets in place the protagonists of the drama that will save the world by provoking a great massacre, while the Yamunā (the unpersonified river) is the birth place of the Brahman *ṛṣi* Vyāsa, the promulgator of the Vedas (the necessary prelude to a creation of the world) and one of the incarnations of Viṣṇu in the epic. Eventually, the Sarasvatī traverses Kurukṣetra, where the great battle of eighteen days takes place. In the ancient temples of northern India, the opposition of the two rivers is found on the doorjambs of the sanctuary, where Gaṅgā, on one side, is mounted on a *makara,* while Yamunā, on the other, rests on a tortoise. The *makara,* a mythical crocodile with a constantly gaping mouth, symbolizes the time of salvation, the cosmic night when the divinity "swallows" the world, whereas the tortoise is a cosmogonic theme known from Vedic literature. Gaṅgā and Yamunā are associated in the same way as the two kinds of grace that are embodied in the god of the sanctuary: the grace that bestows salvation (*mokṣa* or *mukti*) and the grace that bestows the benefits of this world (*bhukti*). The complementarity of the two rivers is therefore necessary to symbolize the duality of the god, at once yogi and creator.

Nevertheless, the Yamunā hardly occurs in the mythology in a personified form. She preserves her character as a river, and it is necessary to pay attention to all the events that take place on the banks of the Yamunā or on her waters (such as the conception of Vyāsa and the childhood of Kṛṣṇa). But Vedic literature presents her as the sister of Yama, the god of death, identified later with Dharma. She may be seen as the female and therefore fertile complement of the god whose function is to empty the earth of its excess human beings. Yamunā is charged with assuring the renewal of the multitude of creatures, but this is barely suggested; it is inferred, rather, like her connection with the Gaṅgā, from the place that the Yamunā, as a river, has in various myths.

Gaṅgā has a broadly diffused myth, with multiple variants, which must account for her ritual role: she is the river in which the ashes of a dead person must be immersed in order to assure him salvation. All kinds of beliefs are connected with the sojourn of the ashes in the river, but all these beliefs recognize the Gaṅgā as the river of salvation. It is probable (see below), but not proved, that the river's powerful course, which terminates with a delta into a vast ocean, distinguishes it as the type of river that the Upaniṣads evoke when they compare the disappearance of individual *ātmans* into the one Brahman with the disappearance of multiple rivers into a single ocean. But salvation in India, where one always hesitates between the pleasure of favorable rebirths and absorption into the Absolute without return, is an eminently ambiguous thing. It is even more ambiquous when one passes from individual to collective salvation, for this may signify the end of the world, which no one wants. The myth of the Gaṅgā—which will be treated separately—bears the mark of this ambiguity. We will cite the narrative from the *Mahābhārata* (3.106ff.) here, but the *Rāmāyaṇa* (1.42–43) tells a similar version of the myth.

The Gaṅgā has not always flowed on the earth; her myth is the story of her descent from heaven (or from Viṣṇu's big toe, as Purāṇic tradition maintains). This story is in turn connected with the story of the sons of Sagara, the Sāgaras (*sāgara,* "ocean").

The good king Sagara had two wives, evidently too proud (*darpita*) of their beauty, for he had no descendants from them. He had to propitiate Śiva with harsh austerities in order to obtain progeny: Śiva granted him sixty thousand sons from one of his wives, arrogant (*darpita*) warriors destined to perish all together, and a single son from his other wife, who would assure the continuity of the line. The sixty thousand sons apparently could not be born in a normal manner: their mother was delivered of a kind of gourd whose seeds had to be extracted so they would grow in pots

Devprayag. The confluence, in the Himalayas, of the two rivers that form the Ganges. Photo Pierre Amado.

Kedarnath. Sanctuary to Śiva at the sources of the Ganges. Photo Pierre Amado.

filled with clarified butter (which had the effect of transforming them into oblatory material). These sixty thousand sons of Sagara soon behave in such a manner that the gods request Brahmā to rid them of these warriors: the gods need not fear, the Sāgaras will perish quickly. From his other wife, Sagara has had a better son, whom he has had to exile, but by whom he obtains a pious grandson, Aṃśumān, the continuator of his line.

Sagara offers a horse sacrifice and, in conformity with the ritual, releases the sacrificial horse, ordering his sixty thousand sons to protect it during its year of wandering (the idea being that wherever the horse might freely wander, even if at the cost of battle by his guardians, the sacrificing king is acknowledged as sovereign). But at a certain moment the horse disappears and the Sāgaras return to their father to relate their misadventure. He enjoins them to search everywhere for the horse and not to return without it. The Sāgaras scour the earth, and finally go underground to gain access to the subterranean world. In doing this, they overpower the inhabitants of the infernal regions as they have overwhelmed gods and men. In the end, they find the horse in the depths of the lower regions (assimilated eventually to the bottom of the ocean that had been drained previously by Agastya: he had consumed all its water to make it possible for the gods to kill an *asura*); the horse is grazing quietly near a *ṛṣi* resplendent in meditation: Kapila in person, a form of Viṣṇu. The Sāgaras, taking Kapila for the thief, begin to insult him. The sage, disturbed in his meditation, glances at them and reduces them to ashes on the spot. Nārada, the messenger of the gods, goes to inform Sagara of what has happened. The king sends his grandson to recover the horse in order to make it possible for him at least to finish his sacrifice and thus to save himself from the lower regions. Aṃśumān conciliates Kapila so completely that he obtains not only the return of the horse but the promise that his grandson by the grace of Śiva will succeed in causing the Gaṅgā to descend to earth to purify the ashes of his uncles and to assure their future in the beyond.

This is a theme of the avatars, although Kapila is not included in the list of the ten classical avatars. It is clearly Viṣṇu who intervenes to save Sagara and the Sāgaras. Moreover, the Gaṅgā, in descending to earth, will fill the ocean, covering the ashes of Sagara's sixty thousand sons, who will thereafter be able to partake of salvation: there is therefore an explicit link between the descent of the Gaṅgā to earth and the emptying of her waters into the ocean; and the identification of the waters of the river and of the ocean may well be one of the mythical transformations of the comparisons of salvation with the flowing of rivers into the sea.

The son of Aṃśumān will try in vain to obtain the purification of the Sāgaras, and it is his grandson Bhagīratha who accomplishes this feat: he goes to the Himalayas to practice austerities in order to propitiate Gaṅgā, who eventually appears to him and promises him what he desires. She will come to earth to purify the sons of Sagara and to fill the ocean. But the violence of her current means that the earth will not be able to withstand the shock. Bhagīratha must therefore devote himself to further austerities on Mount Kailāsa, this time to obtain Śiva's mediation: Śiva agrees to receive the Gaṅgā on his head when she descends from heaven. The river falls on his head, is split into three streams of water (the three Himalayan torrents that unite to form the Ganges), and asks Bhagīratha to show her the course she must take. Bhagīratha accompanies her to the dried-up ocean where the ashes of the Sāgaras await their purification.

The myth therefore establishes a double connection, between the Gaṅgā and the ocean, on the one hand, and between Viṣṇu(-Kapila) and Śiva on the other hand, in which structures known from other sources are encountered again. That Śiva the destroyer here plays the part of mediator is not surprising. His function as "swallower" of the worlds is apparently transferred to the Gaṅgā, which receives the ashes of the dead, but his intervention signifies the first act in the drama of salvation. There must be death, the funeral pyre, and ashes—all things connected with Śiva—in order that the second phase, salvific immersion in the waters of the deluge or of the Gaṅgā, may unfold. Moreover, it is Śiva's yogic power that makes it possible for him to receive the violent flood that has come down from heaven.

The iconographic career of this myth attests its importance: recall the immense stone relief of Mamallapuram, to the south of Madras, that illustrates the descent of the Ganges, and the representation of Śiva as the "bearer of Gaṅgā"—*gaṅgādharamūrti*. Moreover, it might be very instructive to make an exhaustive survey of all the rivers in India that have received a compound name terminating in *-gaṅgā*. In the final analysis, every river and every temple pond is Gaṅgā.

M.Bi./b.f.

BIBLIOGRAPHY

M. E. ADICÉAM, "Les images de Śiva dans l'Inde du Sud," 15: "Gaṅgādharamūrti," *Arts Asiatiques* 32 (1976). O. VIENNOT, *Les divinités fluviales Gaṅgā et Yamunā aux portes des sanctuaires de l'Inde* (Paris 1964).

Pre-Islamic Iran

During the third millennium B.C., various Indo-European tribes emigrated from their original habitat in eastern Europe and reached Central Asia, where they remained for a time. They then gradually moved south, and at the beginning of the second millennium their presence can be detected on the Iranian plateau and in the mountains of Afghanistan. Some of these tribes, starting from Kashmir and the Punjab, undertook the conquest of India, while others took over all of Iran up to the confines of the Caucasus and Mesopotamia. Around 1800 B.C., a vast Iranian domain had thus come into being, extending from Zagros to Transoxiana.

As they settled into the various provinces of this territory, the conquering tribes maintained a certain distinctiveness, especially in their dialects, but they also shared a sense of community, like the Greeks, who considered themselves Greek despite the rivalries among their cities. The Medes occupied the northwest,the Persians settled in the southwest, while the east was held by tribes of unknown name, closely related to the tribes that occupied the Punjab. In the extreme north, the Scythians led a nomadic life and spread their influence from the Ukraine to Siberia. On several occasions they attempted to penetrate Iran and India, where they managed to found a dynasty in the first century B.C. At the same time, other Iranian tribes, particularly the Parthians, appeared in Persia and in India, where from time to time powerful empires were constituted that contributed to the cultural unification of these peoples.

The Aryans

It is also significant that these tribes all called themselves Aryans (in Sanskrit: *ārya*; in ancient Iranian: *aïrya*), in contrast with the native populations who are considered "barbarians" (that is, incapable of speaking correctly) and more or less as "demoniacs" (because they worshiped false gods). The word refers both to an ethnic reality, in which men with fair skin conquered darker native peoples, and to a socioreligious community, in which people practiced similar rites and organized their social life in analogous ways. Even today the country is officially called "the domain of the Āryas" (in Persian, *īrān shahr,* a transposition of the ancient formula *aïryānām vaejo,* which has the same meaning).

Of course, there is no exception here to the rule of religion as the main piece in the cultural edifice of civilizations at this level; indeed, it is religion that gives this community of interests its reason for existing and its basic justification. Equally, it is religion that provides the ideology on which the very notion of being Aryan is based. This can be seen in the fact that the Aryans understood the conquest of territory as the sacralization of ground considered profane prior to the first lighting of the ritual fire. This remained true in Iran up to the ending of the Sassanian empire in the seventh century under the blows of Islam. Likewise, any individual introduced into the Aryan community had to be "adopted" by the fire god, to whom he was solemnly presented. Thus, the assimilation of indigenous populations could be carried out on a grand scale, because in the final analysis the decisive criterion was the adherence of the newly introduced person to the religion of the "masters."

And, in fact, this is what happened in Iran as in India: only a few centuries after the settling of Indo-Europeans in these two countries, all the inhabitants had converted; this made intercommunal marriages permissible and led to a general mixing of populations. At all levels of society, the same religion was practiced, the same language spoken, the same customs observed. When the first authentic historical evidence appears, Iran has already completed its cultural unification, even without political unity. It should be said, however, that we do not know this religion well, mostly because of the disparate nature of the sources that we can use in our attempt to understand it.

Strangely enough, it is only with Herodotus that we have the first description of Iranian religious customs. From him we learn that the Persians did not build temples but worshiped their gods in the open air, that they had no statues of the gods, that sacrifices were made in the presence of fire and included the killing of animals whose flesh was consumed, and finally that they did not bury or cremate corpses but rather exposed their dead on hills, where they were devoured by vultures. All these characteristics are truly Iranian, but as an explanation of the whole, the description falls short. About the gods themselves Herodotus is even more vague: he sees them as natural forces and elements and as what he calls "the Sky."

Less than a century before, Darius had had an inscription engraved in which the name of this god of the Sky is revealed: Ahura Mazdā. King Artaxerxes II (405–359) boasts in another inscription of being the protégé not only of Ahura Mazdā but also of Mithra and the goddess Anāhitā. From this period on, the available documentation increases considerably: thanks to the bas-reliefs we have some idea of the costumes, the ritual gestures, and the shape of the altars and of some liturgical instruments, notably the mortar that is used to pound the *haoma.* The god Ahura Mazdā appears in the form of a winged disk (perhaps symbolizing the Sun), sometimes crowned with the bust of a bearded figure, and often accompanied by imaginary animals: winged lions, bull-men, scorpion-men, etc. Many of the scenes remain a mystery, lacking as they do any explanatory inscriptions. Much later there finally appears the name of Zarathustra (the "Zoroaster" of the Greeks), whose doctrine becomes the official religion of the Iranian Empire starting from the third century A.D. (the Sassanian dynasty). We will see below what problems are raised by this belated victory of the Zoroastrian prophet, all the more since it is at about the same period that the mysteries of Mithra start to spread in the Roman Empire, along with the diffusion of the cult of this god in western India; but Mithra is only given a modest position in Zorastrianism itself!

The Avesta

It would be very difficult to piece together all these apparently contradictory factors if we did not have the Avesta, the sacred book of Zoroastrianism. In this book, the archaeology and religious history are made clearer, rites are described, formulas to be recited given in extenso, etc. At the heart of this collection is a unique section, differentiated from the rest of the work by style, the dialect in which it is written, and literary genre. It is composed of hymns of medium length (fifteen or so strophes) attributed to Zarathustra himself and called simply "Songs" (*gāthās*). Other, longer, hymns, written in a different dialect, constitute together with the Gāthās what by convention is called the Yasna ("the sacrifice," that is, texts suitable for recitation during the sacrifices). There are also about twenty liturgical poems that are different from the preceding ones and that the Avesta groups according to the "characteristic of the time" for a particular prayer (the Yasht). Finally, the section called Vidēvdāt ("against demons") concerns ritual impurities and the means of avoiding them or effacing them. Here there are directions concerning daily life and considerations about the destiny of the soul after death. Several chapters of lesser interest complete this certainly archaic collection.

Indeed, philological comparison shows that the dialect of the Gāthās is of the same linguistic stratum as that of the Veda, estimated to have been composed about 1500 B.C., if not several centuries earlier. The other dialect, that of all the Avesta (except the Gāthās), is a little more modern and resembles the Sanskrit of the year 1000 B.C. Thus with the Avesta one has arrived at an Iranian religion in the full sense of the word, a religion that took shape once the Aryans, who had been settled in the country for several centuries, finally brought about the cultural unity of their "domain" (*vaejo*). Unfortunately the precious testimony of the Avestan hymns is flawed by a twofold misadventure that befell the sacred text: on the one hand, the book that we have is truncated, representing only one-fourth of the original Avesta; on the other hand, Zarathustra, acting as a reformer, overturned the theology and contributed to the disappearance of important information about the former religion.

We must therefore realize that the Avesta took its definitive form only under the Sassanians, when Zoroastrianism had been consecrated as the "national faith." The priests of that time, by their own admission, retained from the former traditions only what seemed to them to be suitable to the practice of the reformed religion and of the rest gave us a sibylline summary, just enough to render appreciable the extent of the loss. From the third and fourth centuries on, and even more after the Islamic conquest, Zoroastrian theologians composed exegetical treatises for the priests that were designed to preserve the spirit of what they called "the Good Religion." Thanks to these works composed in old Persian and then in classical Persian, many aspects of the tradition are revealed to us, for example the domestic cult that the Avesta does not mention at all; what is more, the mythology is clarified by these encyclopedic instructions. As examples we can cite from among these books the *Dēnkart*, dating from the tenth century, the *Zartusht Nāma* (thirteenth century), which narrates the legendary life of the Prophet, and the *Rivāyāt*, letters exchanged around the seventeenth century between the Zoroastrians of Iran and their brothers who had emigrated to India.

It can be seen from this brief overview that the sources that we have at our disposal for the study of the Iranian religion are often disappointing, because they are fragmentary and reformational in intent. Modern scholarship, however, has succeeded in giving an order to these heterogeneous pieces of information, and has discovered behind their impartiality the essentials of what can be called the original theology. This work was begun at the end of the eighteenth century when the French scholar Anquetil-Duperron succeeded in having some Parsis (Iranians who had emigrated to India) transmit the Avesta to him; these Parsis, however, had only a passing knowledge of the Avesta, and Anquetil's contribution would have been negligible if the text he brought back from India had not been correctly deciphered by nineteenth-century philologists, notably Burnouf, who in 1833 constructed his first key to the Avestan language with the first translation of the Yasna.

Having recognized the relationship of the Iranian dialects to Sanskrit, Greek, Latin, Germanic, and the other Indo-European languages, the linguists of the nineteenth century kept refining the study of Avestan vocabulary and syntax until another French scholar, J. Darmestéter, managed to complete a translation of the sacred scriptures of the Zoroastrians (*L'Avesta*, 1892, republished in 1960). In this monumental work, authoritative even today, the only weakness was the interpretation of the Gāthās. The considerable progress of comparative grammar in the first half of the twentieth century made it possible for J. Duchesne-Guillemin (*Zoroastre*, 1948) and H. Humbach (*Die Gāthās des Zarathustras*, 1959) to make translations that can be considered definitive.

At the same time, the study of religion was being organized in a similar fashion by the systematic comparison of the main elements of Iranian religion with those elements that form the basis of our knowledge of Indo-European beliefs. For the most archaic period, the most important point of reference was obviously Vedic India, with which the linguistic connection was extraordinary, especially for religious vocabulary: *daeva/deva, ahura/asura, mithra/mitra, haoma/soma, daenā/dhenā, yasna/yajña*, etc.; it was easy for specialists to show that the realities expressed by the words also coincided, with some allowance being made for local distortions. For the classical and later periods, the autonomous development of Iranian religion made the comparison with India less and less meaningful, but it did make possible some connections with the beliefs of the Romans and the Greeks, as well as with the lesser-known beliefs of the Scythians and the Slavs.

The crowning achievement of this comparative effort can be seen today in the work of Georges Dumézil, who must be given credit for demonstrating the trifunctional structure of Indo-European ideology; by means of this key, the Iranian pantheon, which had once seemed chaotic, recovers its harmonious order and its coherence. Thus we can under-

Temple of fire, a structure known as the Kabba of Zarathustra. Naqshi-i Rustam, near Persepolis. Photo Lucien Hervé.

stand how the populations of this region of Asia could have remained attached to their gods for such so long (three millennia); and Henri Corbin has shown how even Islam has been affected by that pantheon, as in the Iranian version (Shiism) and particularly in the Sufism of a Sohrawardī. These diverse considerations have given rise to so many historical references that we should say something about the evolution of the Zoroastrian religion before proceeding to analyze it in detail.

Historical Background

When the Aryan tribes undertook the conquest of Iran and India, they had in common a whole collection of beliefs and rituals that had remained close to those of their Indo-European ancestors; the Veda (composed during the second millennium B.C.) gives a very complete picture of these. On both sides of the Hindu Kush, the pantheon was divided between Asura gods (in Iran, *Āhura*) and Deva gods (Iranian, *daeva*), sacrifices were offered (*yajña/yasna*), and people hoped to be admitted after death to the celestial dwelling place of the perpetual Light; to do this, one had to act according to the good (*ṛta/arta*) and reject evil (*druh/druj*), etc. The parallelism must have been even closer than we can imagine, and the evolution of both religions would probably have taken very similar paths if a major event had not totally upset the situation in Iran—the preaching of Zarathustra and the gradual conversion of the Iranians to the teachings of the Reformer. The whole thing remains something of a mystery.

Keeping to the least doubtful probabilities, the Prophet can be assumed to have lived in Chorasmia (south of the Aral sea) or in Sogdiana (the upper basin of the Amu Darya) at an indeterminate time. The later Zoroastrian tradition gives the dates 628 and 551 B.C., but seems to confuse the birth of the Reformer with the fall of the Achaemenid Empire; moreover, the language of the Gāthās is so archaic and so close to that of the Ṛg Veda (eighteen hundred B.C.) that one hesitates to ascribe such a recent date to the birth of Zarathustra. Whatever the solution may be, the man must have had a strong personality, considering the radical nature of his reform and the passion that infused the hymns that he composed. As a priest (*zaotar;* in India: *hotṛ*), he seems to have been able to impose the values of his caste at the expense of those of the warrior aristocracy: for example, he attacked the practice of blood sacrifices and the rites of the *haoma* (Sanskrit, *soma*), which were the preserve of the gods of the warriors function.

In India, their chief was called Indra, "king of the *devas*"; it is significant that in Zoroastrian theology, the *daevas* are "demons" and that Indra was the name of one of these "demons." Inversely, the deities of the priestly function were often called Asuras in the Ṛg Veda, and Zarathustra chose to name Ahura Mazdā ("the Wise Lord") the supreme God, whom he recommends as the exclusive object of worship. This last characteristic is remarkable in an ideological context such as that of ancient Iran, and we can understand why the message was badly received. Persecuted, Zarathustra had to leave his country and take refuge further south, probably in Seistan (the south of what is now Afghanistan). He is said to have converted a minor local king, the *kavi* (prince) Vishtāspa, who had given him asylum and devoted himself to the diffusion of the doctrine of the Prophet, by arms if necessary. The Prophet was nevertheless assassinated at an advanced age (seventy-seven years, according to tradition).

If we recall that Zoroastrianism became the official religion of Iran only during the third century A.D., we realize that the reformed faith was propagated very slowly; some scholars think that the Iranians never adhered to it unanimously. In proof of this they cite the fact that, at the time of the Roman Empire, it was not the cult of Ahura Mazdā that was spread in western Europe but that of Mithra, whom Zarathustra had repudiated as he had all other gods but the Wise Lord. The doctrine of the Prophet seems first of all to have won over the Medes with whom the tribes of Sogdiana were in permanent contact. From Herodotus we know that the priestly function among the Medes was in the possession of the clan of the magi (*maga*), who enjoyed great prestige throughout the entire Iranian domain. Their conversion therefore added greatly to the fame of the Reformer. At the time of Plato, the Greeks already associated magic ("the wisdom of the magi") with Zoroaster, whom they considered to be a demigod (he was called "the son of Ahura Mazdā").

In light of this special situation, it is noteworthy that the Iranians should have rejected the reformed religion for so long: that rejection indicates that polytheism was deeply rooted in people's minds, doubtless because it corresponded better to the structure of the society. It will be shown below that triumphant Zorastrianism "recovered" the essential part of the archaic religion, at the price of changing its perspective. The organization, in the third century, of a veritable Zoroastrian church with a sort of pontiff at its head was most certainly a defensive reaction against Christianity and Manichaeanism, which were also organized in churches. The Iranian religion at least managed to gain the upper hand over its two rivals and gave way only before Islam, which seized political power in two centuries starting in 635 and succeeded in converting a very great majority of the population.

Little Zoroastrian communities survived in the southeast of the country, and there are still five active temples of fire in the region of Kerman (with about twenty thousand worshipers called "Ghebers," from an Arabic word for non-Muslims). Other Zoroastrians emigrated to India, to the region of Surat (north of Bombay), where there were Iranian trading posts. They prospered there, and in the nineteenth century their community played an important role in the economic life of the British colony. It was to these Parsis (as the Indians called them) that Anquetil-Duperron went in search of the Avesta. The religion that they were practicing then had become highly formalistic, because they no longer understood the text, though they recited it scrupulously and in its entirety during their religious ceremonies. Today the situation has improved a little because, thanks to European philologists, the Avesta has been rendered intelligible and translated, its content explained by comparison with other forms of religion, etc. This is what J. Duchesne-Guillemin called "the response of the West to Zoroaster." Nevertheless, the Parsi community remains so reduced in number (less than a hundred thousand worshipers) in relation to the enormous mass of the Hindu population (more than six hundred million) that it has a tendency to remain closed in on itself and thus to accentuate the formalism of its religion. This can be especially noted in the refusal of external conversion, even in the case of marriage, an attitude obviously opposed to the teachings of the Prophet, who had hoped that the entire world would belong to the Good Religion. There is thus little to be learned from the Parsis; yet they can be admired for their faithfulness to their ancestral religion (even if they retained nothing of it but the letter).

The Rites

The study of the beliefs and practices of pre-Islamic Iran remains thus in the purview of the historian of religions, who relies essentially on philology, with some help from archaeology. Following a proper method, such a historian will differentiate rites, mythology, and theology and present them in this order, as all religion is first of all orthopraxy. As we begin to analyze the Iranian ritual we are struck by the fact that it is centered on fire: there is no religious ceremony, public or private, official or domestic, that does not require the presence of a hearth, around which the ceremony is organized.

Fire-centeredness is characteristic of Indo-European liturgies, but it is unusually well developed by the Indo- Iranians, to such an extent that the Parsis have often mistakenly been called "fire worshipers," when in fact they worship only Ahura Mazdā. It is true that a perpetual fire burns in their temple, and the priests recite their prayers in front of it, but for modern Zoroastrians the flame is only the symbol, the perceptible sign of the purity and beauty and light of the Wise Lord. Nevertheless, far in the past fire was indeed a deity and, as such, an integral part of the pantheon into which the divine society was organized, rich in individuals of both sexes. A modest god, at first sight, because he was without the mythological pomp enjoyed by the Rulers and the Warriors, he nevertheless occupied a position of the greatest strategic importance because of his special role in the ritual.

The Sacrifice

For the ancient Iranians, as for the Vedic Indians, the gods were able to keep their immortality only to the degree that mortals nourished them with oblations, just as mortals won their place in Heaven by preparing their offerings and consuming them together with their divine guests. The question arises, however, as to the contact between the world on high and this world: invisible, untouchable, radically nonhuman, how can these "absolute others" hear the invitation that we address to them to come to us and share our meal? A mediation is necessary, and Indo-Europeans all agree that this task devolves upon fire, either through force (the Promethean myth of the theft of the divine fire) or through the free choice of the deity whose external form is fire. The Indo-Iranians tend to the latter and never cease thanking the fire god for having consented to come to live among men. Moreover, only a part of the activity of this deity is thought to be exercised here below: there is a fire in the sky (which is the sun), a fire in the atmosphere (lightning), and lastly, a fire on earth (the one that glows in our hearths and on our altars).

No matter what the form of the myth, the point remains that the fire god has established his dwelling on earth among men and that he fully assumes his role as intermediary between his peers, the other gods of the pantheon, and the worshipers. Thus, when a ritual ceremony is to be celebrated, a sacred ground, rectangular in form, is marked out by a furrow on the cleared earth at some distance from the village. Herodotus noted this fact with surprise; but this was because he knew nothing about the religion of his distant ancestors: they too venerated the gods in the open air, away from their dwelling places, in clearings and glades; they too regarded the sacrifice as a cosmic drama that concretely enacted the junction of the sky (that luminous dome over their heads) with the earth (the ground lying fallow under their feet). That was the norm in the Indo-European period, and remained so in India until the demise of Vedic religion.

The Greeks and Romans, by contrast, very early assumed the habit of building temples sheltering the dedicated images of the deities. As for Iran, it moved in a different direction: the Zoroastrian reform made the spread of religious images impossible, and it was to fire itself that the honor of a special building was reserved. From the Achaemenid period on, there were fire temples (pyrea) throughout all of Iran, from Susa to Bactria, and even nowadays Zoroastrians build them; they can be seen in some areas in southeastern Iran, as well as in India among the Parsis of Bombay. The buildings all contain a square room in which the sacred fire burns in perpetuity. The worshipers can see the flame through openings, and at certain periods, notably under the Sassanians, the raised hearth was constructed on top of elevated areas from which it shone as the sign of imperial power and of the "Aryanization" of the conquered territories. It must be remembered that in Rome, in a similar manner, the temple of Vesta sheltered the national hearth that was guarded by consecrated virgins.

It is important to note that the sacrifice was celebrated, not in or in front of this hearth, but at a distance, in another spot, where a rectangular room, carefully oriented, reconstituted the sacrificial arena of ancient times: one or several fires were lit there, for ritual use only, an additional sign of the fundamental distinction between the fire as symbol, a terrestrial image of the Wise Lord (Ahura Mazdā), and the fire as eater of offerings, whose mythological function is to assure and maintain relations between the world of men and that of the gods. To the first fire personal prayers and hymns of praise are dedicated, while the second fire is asked to assemble the deities to whom the sacrifice is dedicated and to transmit to them the food specially prepared for them. The one is thus a great god, while the other seems to be only a simple messenger, almost a servant. A messenger, indeed, but also a witness and thus perhaps a judge.

This new mythological appearance of the fire god makes it possible to understand why the Indo-Iranians never really dissociated the two aspects of a deity that they knew to be singular. Here too it is the sacrificial ritual that has provided the key to the problem: if Fire can receive offerings and distribute them to those for whom they are meant, it is because Fire is capable (perhaps the only one capable?) of hearing the request made by the one who sacrifices at the beginning of the ceremony and then, as the ceremony unfolds, interpreting the words of the person making the invocation. When, for example, an offering is presented to Mithra (Vedic, Mitra) the *zaotar* (Vedic, *hotṛ*) throws it in the hearth placed before him, saying, "This is for Mithra!"; the flame is believed to understand the meaning of these words; when the oblation has been consumed, it is in fact "carried" by the fire god to his friend Mithra, to whom the Messenger bears witness to the sacrificer's correct intention and to the fact that his gestures conformed precisely to the ritual protocol. In addition, the prayers, sometimes public but often secret (that is, mental, not expressed), are transmitted at the same time to the one for whom they are meant, which implies that the fire god has the power to read the hearts of men. This shows the importance of the *zaotar*, the priest of both the oblation and the invocation, whose role is essential in the practice of the religion, as he is the one who represents humans (and notably the one who sacrifices) before the fire god, just as the latter represents the deities of the pantheon to mortals. Zarathustra was a *zaotar* by profession, which assured him of constant dealings with Fire, and this explains why he never ceases to invoke the flame as witness to the purity of his intention of reform. This is also why he has chosen Fire as the favored symbol of the majesty of Ahura Mazdā, who has been promoted to the rank of sole god in his theological system. A certain equivocation remains in the religion of Zarathustra himself, and even more so in that of his followers. In many respects the impression remains that Fire has retained something of its role of mediator in the emotions of these worshipers: the priests who are seen officiating before the flame in innumerable Iranian bas-reliefs are in all likelihood waiting for Atar ("Fire") to transmit their prayer to the Wise Lord, who can be seen in the sky in the form of a winged disk suspended above the hearth. The reverence accorded to this "angel messenger" is so great that one must bathe and change one's clothes before approaching him and address him only if a cloth has been placed in front of one's mouth, for fear of contaminating him with impure breath. In their houses today, Zoroastrians keep a sacred fire burning (often in the form of a simple oil lamp), and it is here that they recite their daily prayers, in conformity to an ancient custom.

The Domestic Cult

This presence of Fire in the very heart of the dwelling place is moreover necessary for the celebration of the domestic cult and especially of the sacraments that provide the rhythm for the life of the individual: the giving of the name, initiation, marriage, funeral. For the Indo-Europeans, religion was primately a family affair. At first there was no priest, but the head of the family presided, perhaps assisted by a liturgist, that is, by a ritual technician whose role did not go beyond that of a paid adviser. The ceremonial, even when extended to the clan, the tribe, or the "city," remains astonishingly faithful to its domestic origins, as it always includes preparing a meal, which the patron (the one who sacrifices, himself as an absolute rule the head of a family) offers to the gods and to those mortals whom he has invited to share the food that the Fire-Messenger has not consumed in the name of the divine guests.

Gradually, however, the ceremony becomes more complicated; in India and Iran, the technical experts of the sacrifice assume an increasing role and tend to form a sacerdotal caste. We know that the post-Zoroastrian religion has at its disposal a veritable clergy in the magi, whose privileges become very substantial under the Sassanians. Nevertheless, the fundamental structure of the ritual, even in this case, remains what it was in the beginning: the sacred texts (the Veda in India, the Avesta in Iran) teach categorically that the priest is merely the servant of the lay person offering the sacrifice, who is the sole patron of a rite that without him would not exist.

Thus, the *zaotar* is nothing unless he has been hired by the head of a family, and we know what an anguished search Zarathustra conducted, going the length and breadth of Iran looking for a prince who would accept him as chaplain despite his heretical positions. In fact, the Reformer was

A traditional representation of Ahura Mazdā as an eagle with wings extended. Photo Lucien Hervé.

unable to preach his doctrine until Vishtāspa had become his patron. Everything therefore leads back to the family and to its head and more particularly to the domestic hearth, where the sacred Fire burns in perpetuity. Hence, all the sacraments will appear as stages in the life of the family ("incarnated" in some sense in each of its members) and will take place in the home in front of the hearth.

One of the most important of these liturgical moments is the *naojote* ("new birth"), which marks, at the ending of childhood, around the age of twelve, the entry into the world of adults. In the beginning, the rite concerned only boys and inaugurated their professional apprenticeship, which would be completed by the marriage that was obligatory for everyone. From a theological point of view, biological birth conferred on the ancient Iranian nothing more than a bare existence inferior even to that of animals: this is because man is a being with a spiritual essence, and his passage on earth is like that of an exile. In order to regain his heavenly homeland, he must have the spiritual seed quickened in him so that he can, throughout his life, make it grow and blossom. If he is successful, he will be "delivered" and win the realm of unextinguishable light, the Dwelling of Song (*Garō Demānā*), in a word, the Paradise whose name (*pairidaēza*, the "Other Country") was borrowed by the Bible from the Avesta.

The *naojote* is thus an initiation, normally conferred by a father on his son. Stripped of his childhood clothes, the young man puts on a new tunic (*surdēh*) and girds himself with a belt (*kūsti*). He then learns his true name, which has been kept secret until then, and he is presented to the Fire, which literally "recognizes" and "adopts" him. For the first time he recites his prayers before the witness god and from then on the head of the family can die in peace, because the continuity of the family line has been assured. The girls, for their part, received their initiation from their husbands during the marriage ceremony, because their real existence (and thus their spiritual blossoming) began only at the moment when they were adopted by the Fire of their father-in-law. This must be put in the past tense, however, because, at an unknown but relatively recent time, they were admitted to the *naojote*. In any case this is the custom of Zoroastrians today, in India as in Iran. The important element is the relation to Fire, which is felt to be both a factor of spiritual development (one can reach Heaven only through sacrifice, which requires the ministry of the mediator god) and as a guarantee of the perennial duration of the succession (for the Fire adopts new members: sons born to the family, daughters from the outside who enter through marriage).

The marriage ceremony itself is conducted around the family hearth: it is in the presence of the domestic Fire that the father designates the two messengers who are to go to request the hand of the young girl that he wishes to marry to his son. It is in front of the Fire of the future family-in-law that the messengers are received and that the sacramental "yes" is pronounced by the father of the fiancée. When the actual wedding is celebrated, the Fire again is witness, receives the propitiatory offerings, and thus makes himself the guarantor of the union. It should be emphasized that only the father and his child have a role to play in the *naojote,* and likewise only the respective fathers and the others concerned are sufficient to perform the marriage ceremony. As customs evolved and religious studies fell into disuse, the liturgists were transformed from mere counselors into officiating priests: nowadays many Zoroastrians think that the *dasturs* ("priests") are necessary for the regular administration of the sacraments. However, one has only to listen to the texts that they are reciting to realize that they are nothing but spokesmen, in the literal sense of the term, for their lay patrons.

As for funerals, the Fire no longer played its mythological role of psychopomp after the Iranians, breaking with Indo-European tradition, stopped cremating their dead. This change took place fairly far in the past, since Herodotus remarks on it already in the fifth century B.C. For fear of soiling the elements that make up the universe, the bodies of Zoroastrians are neither burned, submerged in water, nor buried, but are abandoned on boulders or cliffs where beasts of prey devour them. Often (and this is the rule today) circular enclosures are built (the *dakhma,* known in the West as "towers of silence") where bodies are brought and placed out of sight to be torn to pieces by vultures. This absence of the mediator god is unusual and corresponds in all likelihood to an abandoning of the tradition. Modern theologians try to justify it by stating that death is a complete defilement, capable of contaminating even Fire; but how is it possible to believe that he who is the ultimate Purifier could be affected by the death (so necessary to the maintenance of cosmic order) of any individual? Moreover, the intimate relations between the head of the family and his hearth seem to be broken off at that most decisive moment when the deceased will have to undertake the difficult eschatological voyage: it is a great aberration for him not to receive the provisions for the journey from his regular protector.

The Zoroastrians of today are profoundly conscious of this feeling of abandonment, foresakenness, and solitude. Such a situation, combined with the prospect of what will happen to the body in the *dakhma,* overwhelms the worshipers and arouses in their consciousness a kind of despair, countering the optimism that is usually and rightly attributed to the Zoroastrian religion, which is entirely oriented toward the enhancement of life, the celebration of light and happiness, the striving after earthly prosperity, the promise of Paradise, etc. Of all this, fire—glowing, warm, crackling (which is referred to as "singing")—is the central symbol, along with the Sun. Its absence from funeral ceremonies can only be an accident and does not in any way hinder its prestige or the Zoroastrians devotion to it.

The *Haoma*

There remains, in the domain of ritual, the difficult problem of *haoma* ("juice"; in India, *soma*). It is known that in the distant past certain solemn sacrifices (that is, those outside the domestic ritual) included the preparation of a "drink of immortality," which the worshipers consumed after pouring the part that they owed to the gods into the fire. This practice is found throughout the Indo-European realm and seems to be linked to a form of esoteric cult, one reserved for certain individuals who received a special initiation that gave them access to it. The idea is that drinking the potion assures immortality and makes one an "almost god," a hero in the Greek sense of the word. It is even thought that the gods are what they are because they have drunk ambrosia, and that they retain their divine status only under the express condition of continuing to drink it. This *haoma* had been stolen from the gods and given to man (a variation of the Promethean myth): an eagle had brought it to them to enable them to become gods too. From this time on, the members of the pantheon are tributary to mortals: if mortals were to lose their faith, if they should cease to "press out the *haoma* for the gods," according to the consecrated formula, the Immortals would know death and disappear. This "twilight of the gods" would bring on the end of the world.

Such a theology has certainly never been "popular," for it undermines the foundation of devotion and impairs the respect and fear that the worshipers feel toward their gods. Nevertheless, the magical enchantments of the *haoma* must have enjoyed great prestige, above all in the aristocracy, because the sacrifice of the *haoma* tends progressively to become the norm of the "solemn" liturgy (that is, the liturgy of the king and the chiefs of the clan). In the beginning, this type of ceremony probably belonged to the special initiation of warriors and to its renewal each time a military mission was being prepared or had been achieved. Furthermore, in Iran as in India, the dominant religion became that of the prince, especially when the first empires were constituted. The other classes of society then required, and soon obtained, the right to participate in the ritual of the *haoma*. Thus during the "classical" period of the Vedic and Avestan religions (around the tenth century B.C.), every important sacrifice included the pressing out and the drinking of the *haoma/soma*.

It should be noted that the "juice" in question was no ordinary drink. Its consumption, according to the ancient texts, brought on a sort of drunkenness or ecstatic trance, which was said to be a "foretaste of the celestial delights." At the same time, it was stated that, by drinking the *haoma*, warriors acquired strength, courage, and above all that "furor" (*aēshma* in Avestan, *furor* in Latin, *hubris* in Greek) by virtue of which they could accomplish great exploits on the battlefield and impose victory even on an enemy of greater numbers. It is not known from what plant this juice was extracted, but, to judge from the effects that its absorption produces upon the minds of the worshipers, it seems likely that it was a hallucinogen. Alcohol must be excluded as a possibility, as the texts state that alcohol must be reserved for profane feasts. Hashish has been considered (*bhanga* in Iranian, *bhangā* in Sanskrit), but a passage from the Dēnkart seems to contradict this suggestion, for we read that Zarathustra's patron, King Vishtāspa, drank one day a cup of *haoma* mixed with hashish (*hōm ut bhangh;* see Widengren, p. 89); so the two ingredients could not have been the same. Recently, R. G. Wasson has put forth the intriguing hypothesis that the preparation was based on the *Amanita muscaria* (fly-killing amanita, or false orange mushroom). Approved by considerable men of learning, with Claude Lévi-Strauss in the front rank, this theory seems to take account of all the difficulties and to resolve them convincingly.

In any event, it was a toxic beverage, a drug whose use was made part of an aristocratic liturgy of a "Dionysian" character in contrast to the "Apollonian" serenity of the domestic rites. It is to be observed, however, that throughout the Indo-European domain, "mysteries" of this type aroused the hostility of the priestly circles, in the name of the morality and dignity of the religion. This explains why the secret of the "nectar of the gods" was lost during the historic period in the West, notably for the Romans and Greeks, who retained of it only a mythical memory. It did remain in the possession of very closed circles, as was the case, for example, among the Celts and the Germans until the advent of Christianity. In Iran, Zarathustra was the incarnation of this hostility, which he expressed with a violence that says much about the resistance his reform encountered. In one of the Gāthās (Yasna 48), he does not hesitate to call the *haoma* "filth" and accuses it of causing warriors to lie and to commit cruelty and gratuitous violence (strophes 10 to 12), which make them "bad princes" in his eyes. Carrying out a measure that will meet with similar success in India, the Prophet in his reprobation associates the killing of animal victims with the enchantments of the *haoma*. In doing this, he says explicitly that these two aspects of the religion of his fathers are closely united and that they must be rejected together in order to establish the Good Order (*Arta* or *Asha*) that is both religious and political, the Empire (*kshatra*) in which men will be able to dedicate themselves to the peaceful breeding of cattle while venerating the unique god Ahura Mazdā.

This last recommendation obviously implies the rejection of all the deities of the Indo-European pantheon, leveled by Zarathustra to the rank of pernicious demons. It will soon be seen that the force of popular sentiment and the dexterity of the theologians made it possible for the aforementioned deities to survive clandestinely in the Zoroastrianism, in the same way that the *haoma* was reintegrated into the body of the ritual. This could of course only be done at the cost of softening the ritual, which was reduced to a primarily verbal ceremony with little place for gestures or manipulations. Nowadays, and it has probably been thus since the time of the Arsacids (third century B.C.), the Zoroastrian ritual (*mazdā-yasna*) has excluded the killing of animal victims: it is enough to offer as an oblation a very small quantity of fat at a certain moment during a ceremony consisting essentially of the recitation of the entire Avesta.

The *haoma* has been replaced by a substance that keeps the same name but with the explicit indication that it is only a substitute (*parā-hōm*). Moreover, the priests consume only a few drops of it, as though to emphasize the henceforth symbolic character of the rite thus preserved (which "keeps in memory" the *hōm* pressed out by Yima, the first man, at the beginning of time). The plant used for this purpose by the Parsis of Bombay is the *Ephedra vulgaris;* a few sprigs of it are powdered in a mortar together with some pomegranate grains; the whole is "drowned" in a proportionately much greater quantity of holy water. It goes without saying that such a drink has no toxic effect at all; yet for this harmless substitute for the former ambrosia the Zoroastrian priests have still chosen a plant whose essence (ephedrin) could eventually produce a kind of intoxication if it were extracted and prepared to this end and in sufficient quantity.

To permit the reintegration of *haoma* into the reformed religion, a mythological hymn had to be composed and a place found for it in the definitive compilation of the Avesta that was made just before the Islamic invasion. This hymn was the Hōm Yasht, in which the Prophet engages in a dialogue with the "genies" of *haoma* and concludes by recognizing in him a "just one . . . who keeps death away and procures long life." The form taken by this justification reminds us that during the Indo-European period every element of the sacrifice was regarded as the tangible manifestation of the power of a particular god. The pre-Zoroastrian *haoma* thus began as a deity, worthy of being the object of a cult, like the god Soma in India, whose praises the poets of the Ṛg Veda never tire of singing.

Because the reform of the Iranian religion effected by Zarathustra excluded all forms of polytheism, it was no longer possible to detect the presence of a god in the plant that gives eternal-life. But people continued to see it (and especially its sap) as a manifestation of the power and bounty of the Wise Lord, a manifestation whose guardian could be a genies or an angel. This was how the Zoroastrian theologians reasoned, and this was how they justified the retention in the liturgy of strophes such as the following (Yasna 9.17): "I ask you for wisdom, golden Haoma! I ask you for vigor, for victory in battle, for physical health and prosperity, for power and glory, for learning! I ask you for the power that will let me reign over the earth, to make order reign there, to keep Evil away from it." Such passages, which closely resemble parts of the Veda, surely had their origin in the hymns that the first Iranians recited in order to propitiate the *haoma* in its aspect as divine person; but they carry little weight, for the theologians cleverly succeeded in making such invocations "inoffensive," so to speak, by interpolating "modern" notations into them whose presence alone was sufficient to demote the *haoma* to the rank of creature (and servant) of the one God. Thus the sixteenth verse of Yasna 9 says: "The Haoma is good because it has been created good [*hudhātō*]"; and elsewhere (Yasna 10, verse 10): "Haoma, it is the good God who has made you [*tatakhshat*]." Many more examples could be given; all imply that Ahura Mazdā has made the plant, given it special virtues, and used the Power (which he has given it) to make his goodness shine out for those men who merit it.

The Myths

The recognition of this state of affairs makes it possible to appreciate the breadth and complexity of the problem (for it is one) posed by Iranian mythology. Strictly speaking, Zoroastrian orthodoxy permits of no mythology, in the proper sense of the term, within the framework of the religion, anymore than there can be a mythology, theoretically, in the Judaism of the prophets, for example. Nevertheless, the Indo-European traditions were sufficiently lively in Iran (as has been seen for the ritual) for the concept of the world to remain the same even after the preaching of the Reformer. Moreover, we must not forget that Zarathustra never ceased to affirm his fidelity to *ārya* ideas: he had come, he said, to reestablish the "Good Religion," which he judged to have become decadent, and not to abolish it. Bearing this affirmation in mind, Western observers, from Eugène Burnouf (*Commentaire sur le Yasna,* 1832) to Jacques Duchesne-Guillemin (*La religion de l'Iran ancien,* 1962) have detected and brought to light the survival of former patterns in the new construction erected by the Prophet of Ahura Mazdā.

To date, the most convincing work of synthesis is that of Georges Dumézil (*Naissance d'archanges,* 1945). Using the facts furnished by specialists in Iranian culture and comparing them systematically with those collected by specialists of other Indo-European religions, Dumézil has shown how Zarathustra, as a skilled theologian, was able voluntarily and consciously to rearrange the cultural patrimony that he had inherited. The mysterious Destiny (Latin, *fatum;* Greek, *anankē;* Sanskrit, *daivam*) was something to which the gods submitted, just as did all living things, as well as the universe itself; it was sufficient to see it as a conscious will, a Wisdom, in order to transform it from an archaic polytheism into a monotheism: this Will, this Wisdom, could be nothing other than the "essential" attribute of a divine personality (necessarily unique) to which the Prophet gave the name of Wise Lord, that is, "the God in whom Wisdom is incarnated," or, if you like, "Wisdom in the form of Power." This Will manifests itself in the world in various ways, according to circumstances and need: here it will be creative, there destructive, elsewhere it will preside over the germination of plants and the growth of animals; it will grant victory to one army over another, make the sun rise, inspire ideas in respectable men; it is through this Will that fire heats, water quenches thirst, cows give milk, and so on, ad infinitum. Since his contemporaries believed that an agent was necessary for each of the cosmic functions, Zarathustra explained to his disciples that these so-called deities were in fact only genies ("angels") created by Ahura Mazdā to play the role of responsible guardians.

This is what happened, as has been seen above, to the genie of the Haoma, even though its integration into the mythical edifice of Zoroastrianism certainly came long after the preaching of the Prophet. In this way, a good number of deities who had enjoyed a most prestigious status of personal autonomy (with a name, a function, and a special resting place) in the archaic religion, henceforth saw themselves limited to the subaltern position of zealous (and therefore "adorable": *yazatas*) servants of the Wise Lord.

Daevas and Ahura

This "recovery" affected only a part of the divine personnel of the ancient mythology. Another group of gods, however, was put into the camp of the adversaries—necessarily demonic—of the Good Religion. To understand this surprising discrimination, it must be remembered that the Indo-Iranians of the second millennium B.C. had inherited from their Indo-European forefathers a concept of divine society whose principal characteristic was its complexity. Far from conceiving of the pantheon as a serene and pacific world, they took pleasure in telling of its intrigues, rivalries, and combats, whether singular or collective. Even though many aspects of this situation are closed to us for lack of documentation, the general outline is clear.

This situation is essentially a struggle for universal power, in the most concrete sense of the term: who will be consecrated "king of the gods"? In Greece, Zeus wins this title by assassinating his own father; in India, Indra obtains it after eliminating Vṛtra, who had been keeping back the waters necessary to life, etc. Behind such incidents (which have something of the "duel" about them) are confrontations between definite groups: the Titans against the gods, according to the Greek terminology; the Asuras against the Devas, according to that of the Indo-Iranians. The battle is indecisive and terrible; in Greece it is the gods who gain the upper hand, in India the Devas. Or at least they gain an advantage that is always contested and always in peril. Classical Indian mythology is filled with the continuously renewed tumult of battle between Asuras and Devas. Later Hinduism, although unfaithful in many respects to Vedic religion, still maintains this outline: Kṛṣṇa can play his role of avatar only after having eliminated several Asuras; Durgā accedes to the rank of sovereign goddess only when she has killed the Asura Mahiṣa, etc.

But it is remarkable that these adversaries of the established gods are never confused with demons as such. They are clearly recognized as also belonging to the world on high by their nature; it is remembered that in the beginning they were "above" the gods, but that, when the occasion arose, they made unfortunate choices. Deprived of their celestial nobility, they attempt in vain to reconquer it. Condemned to err, they never stop making mistakes and instinctively, one could say, form their ranks behind the banner of Falsehood, Lies, Disorder, Darkness, and thus of Evil. Inversely, the gods struggle to inaugurate (or to safeguard) Good Order, Truth, Light, and thus the Good.

What counts in the final analysis are not the "virtues" specific to one side or the other but rather the free choice that they make between the eternally existing Good and Evil. It is a necessary choice, because this coexistence cannot be peaceful: the universe is a battlefield, and the destiny of each being, mortal or immortal, is sealed by the place he takes in the struggle. Moreover and above all, the universe survives only insofar as Order wins out over Disorder thanks to the valiant efforts of those engaged on the right side. The Indo-Europeans conceived of the world as formed of a multitude of parts combined to form a whole; the Good was thus the right adjustment (*arta* in Iranian, *ṛta* in Sanskrit) of these constituent elements; Evil was their dissociation (*anṛta* in Sanskrit). On the ethical level, always emphasized by the Iranians, the *arta* (also called *asha*) is the true Reality of things, their Truth, to which is opposed the *druj* (in Sanskrit: *druh*), "deceit, lies, falseness, unreality."

However, in contrast to what can be seen throughout the Indo-European domain, and especially in India, Zarathustra professed that the Daevas (the gods; in Sanskrit, Devas) had opted for the *druj*, while the Ahura par excellence, promoted to the rank of supreme deity, Ahura Mazdā, the Wise Lord, made himself the champion of the *arta*. The magnitude of the Reform can be seen: not only has the perspective been inverted (one must curse the Daevas rather than offer them veneration and sacrifices), but in addition even the mythology has been literally "erased," since the whole camp of the ancient Indo-Iranian Asuras has been absorbed into the one, solitary, all-powerful person of the Ahura, who represents Perfect Wisdom. Far from the dualism which it is often thought to be, Zoroastrianism is a pure monism, for what can the obscure forces do when faced with the radiant majesty of the Creator?

The unhappy Daevas, leveled to the rank of inferior demons, must content themselves with tormenting men, tempting them, and deceiving them with lies, in order to bring them to act against the Good Religion, etc. But simple exorcisms are enough to keep them away: moreover, the Avesta includes a particular section called Vidēvdāt (or Vendidād, "Law against the Demons"), in which there is a list of the gestures to be made and the formulas to be recited on the various occasions when the demons might appear. Thus armed, the worshiper has nothing to fear from the agents of the *druj*, if only, of course, he does not let himself be tricked by them, and always makes the "Good Choice," that is, follows the precepts of the Law scrupulously and always labors on behalf of justice (another meaning of the word *arta*), as Zarathustra himself says (Yasna 30, verse 11):

> If you men understand the instructions that the Wise One [that is, Ahura Mazdā] gave: well-being and punishment, long torture for the wicked and health for the just, all will be henceforward for the best!

Angra Manyu

This famous text, which greatly exalts the necessity of the Right Choice, nevertheless poses an additional problem: the Prophet here makes reference to a Spirit of Evil who is no longer only the *druj* (an abstract entity, a negative value) but a divine personage, an antagonist of his homologue the Holy Spirit.

> In the beginning (explains Zarathustra in the third strophe of this same Yasna 30), the two Spirits are twins, one the Good, the other the Evil, in thought, word, and deed. Of these two, the wise choose the right one, but not the fools.

What is new here is the affirmation of the existence of two Spirits (*Manyu*), placed on the same level of existence, and what is more, twins. Are they from the same mother? Do they become enemy brothers in a rivalry for the inheritance of the sovereignty over the universe? Or do they coexist for all eternity? It can be said, without fear of exaggeration, that all of Zoroastrian theology is one long dispute over these questions. For some, Spenta Manyu (the Holy Spirit) is another name of Ahura Mazdā (also called, in the Avesta, Vohu Manyu, "the Good Thought, the Spirit of Good"); from this, Angra Manyu, "the Spirit of Evil," appears as a rival of equal rank, since he is the twin brother of the Wise Lord.

In this perspective, the existence of dualism seems impossible to refute: there is neither one god, nor several, but two, and only two. It is thus neither polytheism nor monotheism but an original system, one perhaps unique in the history of religions and moreover without a name. Foreign observers (Greeks especially) believed that the opposition between Ohrmazd (a late form of the name of Ahura Mazdā) and Ahriman (for Angra Manyu) were fundamental to Iranian religion and that the worshipers considered them equal in power. The Gnostics and the Manichaeans inherited this vision and combined it with the Christian idea of Satan as "Prince of this World." Nevertheless, it does not seem that the Zoroastrians had ever professed a radical dualism. For the orthodox, Ahura Mazdā is the only sovereign god: the two Spirits are a projection of his omnipotence into two opposed but complementary forces. Just as there cannot be heat without cold (or dry without wet, light without darkness, etc.), so also one cannot imagine the Good without its contrary, Evil. At least not in this "lower world" that is by nature subject to the tensions of duality (whereas the world on high where the just go after their death is the world of unity).

Such a view involves the idea of conflict (*druj/arta*) and choice. There may even be here too the division of the divine community (Daevas/Ahura), which would entail the following sequence of events: Angra Manyu fighting with the Daevas for the triumph of the *druj*, against Spenta Manyu fighting with the angels of Ahura Mazdā for the safety of the *arta*. But we can see the imbalance of a system that cannot integrate the Ahura par excellence (the sole Ahura: Mazdā) in opposition to the Daevas, on pain of falling back into the "sin" of dualism.

An original solution to the problem of the "paternity" of these twin Spirits is said to have been proposed by certain Iranian theologians, at least if Greek evidence can be believed on this subject (Eudemus of Rhodes, cited by the neo-Platonist Damascius). In the beginning, said these priests, there was nothing but infinite Time (*Zurvān akarana*), from which came Light and Darkness, Ohrmazd and Ahriman, and, eventually, all living beings. An odd doctrine, at first view, but one that recalls Greek traditions about Kronos and Vedic traditions that exalt Kāla (time) and Prajāpati, the first god, in whom the Great Year becomes incarnate. There is, however, no formal proof that the cult of Zurvān ever had a significant existence in Iran; still it is troubling to note that Mani chose to call by this name the great god of the religion that he founded in the third century A.D.

The Ameshas Spentas

However these problems are to be solved, Zoroastrianism remains a religion marked more than many others by the belief that Evil is powerful, that it is a Spirit (that is, a cosmic energy, a divine power), and that the dynamism of his actions makes necessary a constant struggle to contain him. And there is the corollary idea that things do not always work out for the best in this battle: the order of things has a tendency to degenerate because the ranks of the just diminish. Evil, however, will not triumph, because at the end of time, just when Evil will think himself victorious, Renewal will break forth, a kind of Parousia or, better, a restoration of the golden age. This is an old Indo-European theme that Zarathustra took up for his own purposes and to which he gave a prophetic form of expression, one useful for his moral preaching. In addition, the Prophet explains that men are guided, inspired, and upheld in their salutary choice by semidivine entities (a species of angels) raised up by the Wise Lord to this end. These "Immortal Saints" (*Ameshas Spentas*) are seven in number, and the Avesta lists them explicitly in a hierarchy: at the head, Spenta Manyu (the Holy Spirit), then Arta (or Asha, Justice, Good Order, etc.), and Vohu Manyu (Good Thought, Right Inspiration); in fourth position, Kshatra (Empire), then Sarvatāt (Corporal Integrity, Good Health, Prosperity, etc.); in sixth position, Amretāt (Immortality, Eternal Life); in seventh and final place, Armaïti (Devotion).

The very names of these Immortal Saints show that they are not at all personal gods, but rather "values" that are so many "forces" or, if one prefers, "aspects" of divine Wisdom. Moreover, their respective places in the hierarchy constitute in themselves a veritable theology lesson, since it is obvious that the holy spirit, the cosmic order, and right inspiration are factors in the establishment of a kingdom in which the just will know a life without end dedicated to the service of the Lord; inversely, it is by starting with devotion that the faithful person will gain life everlasting, physical integrity, the realm, and the harmonious cohabitation with the Spirit of God. Yet other combinations are possible (and, for example, the central position of the Empire indicates the importance that Zarathustra attaches to the establishment of a "Zoroastrian state"), but it is evident that no real mythology is possible with such angels. From this, some historians of religion have concluded that Zarathustra was a kind of Calvinist before his time.

Zurvān and the two spirits: the evil spirit and the good spirit. Portion of the head of a pin in the shape of a disk. Bronze. Louristan. New York, Harramaneek collection. Photo Giraudon.

But one can avoid this anachronism by examining the list of the Ameshas Spentas in the light of the works of Georges Dumézil. The reference to the tripartite ideology common to all Indo-European peoples then appears very clearly; the three first powers obviously come from the first function (magicoreligious sovereignty), the Empire belongs no less clearly to the second (the war function, the exercise of temporal power), while the last three evoke the notions of prosperity, happiness, and health, which are typical of the third function. In fact, this analysis can be narrowed down further by taking into consideration the fact that the first and the third functions are usually "two-headed" (in India, Mitra and Varuṇa for the first, the Nāsatya twins for the third), while the second is represented by a single personage (in India, Indra). Elsewhere, the list of major gods thus hierarchized includes in the first rank a "god of beginnings," often ambivalent (in Rome, Janus of the two foreheads), and, at the end, an "all-purpose" goddess whose influence is felt on all levels.

From this we would have, at the very beginning, Spenta Manyu (a veiled designation of the Twin Spirits Spenta and Angra, as two faces of the same power, which is simultaneously good and bad), and then, to represent the first function, Arta (in India, Varuṇa, foremost guardian of the Ṛta) and Vohu Manah (in India, Mitra, the juridical sovereignty, legislative rectitude); the second function offers no problem (Kshatra replaces the god of war, in India, Indra); on the third level: physical integrity and immortality (in India, the wonder-working Nāsatya twins); and at the end of the list, the goddess Armaïti, whose devout spirit should, according to Zarathustra, inspire all actions, no matter what the level on which they are situated.

This view of things is all the more likely to be correct, since it happens that the Avesta sometimes substitutes the name of Anāhitā, a river goddess and female genie of fecundity, for that of Armaïti, thus betraying the mythological origin of

Armaïti. One can only admire the work of transposition undertaken by the Prophet and his theologians to safeguard the purity of Zoroastrian doctrine (Ahura Mazdā the only Lord) even while adjusting to the profound feelings of the worshipers of the time, steeped as they were in the polytheistic ideology of their fathers. It is, moreover, significant that a good number of the gods of the ancient religion had to be integrated into the main part of the religious source in the form of "adorable" genies (*yazatas*) who were attendants of Ahura Mazdā.

If we consult the list of Yashts, those liturgical hymns that appear in the Avesta, we notice a whole series of names that directly evoke the archaic Indo-Iranian divinities. Besides Haoma, already cited, we find the Sun, the Moon, the goddess of horses, Anāhitā, Mithra, Vāyu, Verethraghna, Fortune, the Daenā, the Fravashis, then several "moral" powers comparable to the Ameshas Spentas: Rectitude (Arshtāt), the Light of Holiness (Khvarenah), Conscience (Chistāt). It is interesting that this section of the Avesta contains the names of Indo-European deities that seem to do double duty with those of the homologous entities: what is the use of making Mithra an autonomous *yazata* when the worshiper is invited elsewhere to venerate Vohu Manah? What is the function of Verethraghna (a former god of war, homonym of the Vedic Vṛtrahan, one of the divine names of Indra) when one already has Kshatra? What is the use of Vayu and Anāhitā, when one already has Manyu and Armaïti?

The Zoroastrians have no answer to these questions, on the one hand because they see no clear correspondence between the Ameshas Spentas and the other *yazatas,* and, on the other, because the multiple "angels of the Lord" seem natural to them. But to the outside observer it is clear that this is a late "recovery," designed to make it possible to rally to the Zoroastrian reform those people who had remained faithful to the gods of their ancestors. Indeed, hardly any of these *yazatas* appears in the text of the liturgical songs (Gāthās) attributed to Zarathustra himself. Impossible to date, this "recovery" may have been carried out in the last centuries B.C.; in any case, it took its definitive form during the definitive compilation of the Avesta, under the Sassanians (around the third century A.D.).

Something of the ancient hymns has been preserved in the Yashts, but this has been done by placing it in a new framework: the Prophet is imagined questioning the Lord in order to know, for example, who Vāyu is (or Mithra, Haoma) and the answer is given in the form of a litany of divine names just like those in the Veda:

> I am called Vāyu, O holy Zarathustra! . . . I am called He-who-controls-everything . . . I am called He-who-does-good . . . I have the name He-who-goes-forward; I have the name He-who-goes-backward.

Dozens of "names" are thus cited in an uninterrupted series, until the point where Vayu explains to the Prophet that their recitation will protect him in all circumstances (and notably in battle). Zarathustra then asks:

> What sacrifice shall I offer you? What sacrifice shall I have offered to you? By what sacrifice shall your worship be accomplished?

At the end of this Yasht, Vayu promises:

> If you honor me with a sacrifice, I will tell you Words: created by Mazdā, they are Glorious and Healing! So that neither Angra Manyu nor the sorcerers (*yātus*) will be able to harm you, nor their agents, be they men or Daevas!

It is evident from this example that the Avesta does not hesitate to celebrate the virtues of sacrifice to the ancient Indo-Iranian gods, if it is conceded that these liturgical gestures will have, in addition to their intrinsic worth (for example, safety in battle, normal when dealing with a "violent" god like Vayu), the advantage of procuring for the worshiper a deepening of his intimate knowledge of the Wise Lord (here, for example, Vayu will reveal formulas of exorcism against the agents of the Evil One). But all of this is true only according to the perspective of strict Zoroastrian orthodoxy; outside this group, the *yazatas* behave like real gods: this was the extraordinary destiny of Mithra, in the first centuries A.D., throughout the entire Roman Empire.

Eschatological Myths

Nevertheless, no religion can do entirely without mythology, and whatever may have been the efforts of Zoroastrian theologians to purge their religion of it, the Avesta preserves at least the memory of certain myths. Almost all of these belong to the domain of eschatology, which is hardly surprising if we recall that every religious undertaking must regard itself as salvational. Man, in all latitudes and in all eras, asks first of "those who know" what will be his fate after death, for he believes that what he does today has meaning only in relation to his destiny in the other world. But of course this implies the belief in a hereafter and the certitude that the being that dies does not completely disappear. Gradually, a view of the world is organized in which the evolution of the universe must be taken into account: cosmogonies and apocalypses cannot be dissociated from thoughts of death and the hereafter. It would therefore be necessary to have at our disposal a great number of mythical narratives in order to reconstitute with some coherence the eschatological system of the Iranians. But we have already said that this is not the case, and we must resign ourselves to having only a partial and unsatisfactory view of this system.

This situation arises as soon as one examines, for example, the Zoroastrian concept of the human being. The human being was composed of three parts: body, spirit, and soul. This first part was strongly emphasized: as a divine creation, the body was entitled to every care, and its physical integrity was, along with its beauty, the sign of special protection by the powers on high (one of the Ameshas Spentas was named Sarvatāt and presided over the full development of the physical personality). From numerous indications it can be surmised that the ancient Zoroastrians regarded sickness as a punishment (or a trial) that employed the malevolent services of the agents of the *druj*. As a corollary, the image of the decomposition of the corpse appeared as absolute Evil, the work of a particular demon named Druj-i-Nasush. Thus it seems that death was the manifestation of a triumph of the Evil One, determined, by nature, to destroy the Good Creation, the work of the Wise Lord. This is a scandalous situation which can only be accepted if it is held to be provisional. From this comes the belief in the resurrection of bodies that many historians regard as the fundamental characteristic of the Zoroastrian religion—often adding that this belief was probably inherited by Christianity from this source. This resurrection was, moreover, supposed to take place not immediately after death, in a Paradise similar to our world, but at the end of time at the Great Renewal awaited by the Zoroastrians.

The second element of the human being is the Manah (or Manyu; in Sanskrit, *manas* or *manyu*). More than "thought," this Manah is a force of life, a quasi-divine Power through which man is radically separated from the animals and recognizes himself as a member of the Community of the Just (*artāvan:* "those who belong to the *arta,*" the Sovereign Good). This is thus the Spirit in the full sense of the word; a Spirit capable of doing Evil to others as much as Good, like the two divine Manyus who act either for the *arta* (this being Spenta Manyu, the Holy Spirit) or for the *druj* (this is Angra Manyu, the Evil Spirit). Man is thus responsible for his acts by virtue of the Manah with which he is provided, and these acts determine the fate of the third human element in the world beyond, at least for the period which precedes the Great Renewal.

This third element bears the name of Fravarti (or Fravashi) and corresponds more or less to the notion of "soul" in the Christian sense of the term. Like the Christian soul, the Fravarti is created by the Lord, is immortal, and is destined either to suffer in Hell or to rejoice in Paradise according to a particular judgment that it must undergo immediately after the death of the individual it inhabits. It seems, nevertheless, that Zoroastrians also believed that the soul, during life, played the role of guardian angel. As a witness of the actions inspired by the Manah, the Fravarti blames or approves, suffers or rejoices, like the conscience in certain forms of popular Christianity. Moreover, the ancient texts leave us to understand that the "souls of those of the dead who are just" watch over the interests of the living. One can thus pray to them and even worship them, as is indicated by a Yasht that is dedicated to them, in which these Fravartis are said to assist the Wise Lord in his role as guardian of the universe:

> If I had not given assistance to the powerful Fravartis of the just, I would not have the herds and the men that are here. . . But power would belong to the *druj,* and so would the empire, and so would the corporeal world. (Yasht 13, verse 12)

Thus the soul of a given individual becomes, after death and according to the acts accomplished on this earth, either a demon agent of the *druj* or an angel of the Lord. And so the more of the just there are, the more help and assistance the Lord will have. The reason the universal order is constantly degenerating, according to the Zoroastrians, is that the worshipers of the Good Religion are becoming less and less numerous. The hope nevertheless remains that the situation will be radically modified because the worst will be succeeded by the best at the final Renewal.

At the time of death the soul undertakes a difficult journey: a path leads it to a precipice spanned by a bridge. If the soul manages to cross over, the way will be opened toward the "House of Songs" where the just reside; if it cannot, it falls to the bottom of a ravine into the dark and icy dwelling place of the souls of the wicked. But at the beginning of the bridge the soul sees a young girl in whom it recognizes its "double," the Daenā (Sanskrit, *dhenā*). A mysterious entity, this Daenā is, in essence, the moral value of the existence lived by a given individual: if his actions were mostly good, the Daenā will be young, pretty, well dressed, perfumed, etc.; if, on the contrary, the life was bad, the Daenā will resemble a sinister witch, stinking and dressed in rags. Moreover, the Daenā seizes "the hand" of the Fravarti and leads him onto the bridge: naturally, the pretty young girl helps the soul to cross it without difficulty, while the old witch throws it into the infernal hole. According to one variation, it is the bridge itself that makes the selection (it is called Chinvat, the bridge of the Selector); it widens itself for the just and narrows for the wicked, to the point of being no more than a razor's edge! Finally, according to a third form of the mythical story, the decisive trial consists of an actual act of judgment: the soul must plead its cause before a tribunal presided over by Mithra assisted by two assessors: Sraosha and Rashnu. Yet elsewhere it is said that it is Ahura Mazdā alone who decides, after weighing the merits and demerits of the dead person.

Comparison with other sectors of the Indo-European domain demonstrates that these diverse conceptions were able to coexist without difficulty. In Greece, too, the soul was to make a dangerous crossing (the river Acheron) and to confront the judgment of Minos, Eachus, and Rhadamanthe. In India, too, there was a reception of souls by young girls, the crossing of a bridge, and the judgment (given by Yama, the first of mortals), as there was among the ancient Germans and the Scandinavians. In fact, beyond the picturesque quality of certain details (everywhere one finds the theme of the guard dogs: Cerberus, Saramā), what remains is the idea of the responsibility of the soul and the clairvoyance of the soul's judges. Zoroastrianism, because of its own special character, was obliged to insist on this aspect: did it not place Right Choice at the very center of its ideology?

Paradise (*parādesha,* or *païrideza*—the Bible borrowed this word from the Indo-Iranian) is celestial and luminous: the soul of the just person "rises to the sky," where a perpetual light (*lux perpetua*) shines, where "no shadow is made," it is said. There on high the soul tastes delicious foods and sings the praises of the Lord before the throne of gold in which he is seated (this is the source of the name of "House of Songs" frequently given to the Zoroastrian paradise). Furthermore, the Avesta has foreseen the fate of souls which are neither good nor evil: such mediocre souls await the final Renewal "in neutral ground"; like those in the Greek Limbo, they neither suffer nor rejoice but live like larvae in a gray and indistinct world. The idea of Renewal, so important in the "cosmic" eschatology of Zoroastrianism, is evidently linked to the notion of cyclical time. Like the Greeks and Indians, the Iranians believed that in the beginning, the world was perfect (the age of gold, according to Hesiod; the perfect age, according to the Veda), but that a slow process of involution made it travel the successive stages of a route leading to final decrepitude (according to Hesiod, the age of gold, then silver, then bronze, then iron). When this last age is reached, the Wise Lord brusquely reestablishes the initial situation: this return to the age of gold constitutes the Renewal that the Zoroastrians of today are awaiting impatiently.

Of course, a mutation of this dimension is bound to be accompanied by cataclysms: that which is bad must first be destroyed so that the good may unfold and blossom. Fire usually presides over this labor: it is said, for example, that a river of fire will flow over the universe, purifying everything in its path, Hell itself will then be abolished and the worst demons will become angels (again) "in three days." Over the course of time, Zoroastrians developed a tendency to regard this Renewal as definitive, whereas the Avesta sees in it the reestablishing of an age of gold that will be ineluctably succeeded by a new age of silver, etc. But "modern" theologians (those of the last ten centuries) believed that this would be a limitation of the omnipotence of Ahura Mazdā. In our day, it seems that the majority of Parsis (contemporary

Zoroastrians) conceive of the Renewal as a definitive Parousia.

But "travel accidents" could occur in the course of the ages. The best known of these events concerns Yima, the father of the first humanity. In the beginning, it is taught, the sun god Vivahvant (in India, Vivasvant), who is, in the Zoroastrian perspective, one of the privileged servants of the Wise Lord, engendered (or created from many elements) the first man, to whom the name of Yima is given (Yama in the Veda). Now the word *yama* means "twin," which implies that what was created was in fact two personages, a male and a female (in India, Yama and Yamī), who coupled and engendered in their turn innumerable human beings. Zoroastrians see in this initial incest the justification of consanguine marriages, which they advocate within the Community of the Just (the Zoroastrian church).

Yama was thus the king of the age of gold and became on his death a God (or an archangel); during his reign, says the Avesta (Yasna 9, verses 4 and 5):

> There was neither excessive cold nor heat, nor old age, nor death, nor envy created by the demons. The fathers, like the sons, had the appearance of young men of fifteen, as long as Yima, son of Vivahvant, reigned, he of the beautiful flocks!

Nevertheless, the multiplication of beings is such (because there is no death) that Ahura Mazdā must enlarge the earth three times. Finally, the situation degenerates to such an extent that the Lord warns the faithful Yima that a Great Winter is about to occur:

> First the cloud will snow from the highest mountains to the deepest valleys . . . water will flow in great waves and it will be impossible to cross over those places where now the tracks of sheep may be seen! (Vidēvdāt, chapter 2)

Little by little everything will be submerged, and all beings will perish except for a pair from each species, which Yima is invited to hide in a fort that he is to build on the highest mountain. In this enclosure, as a reserve from the age of gold, the seeds of the future will subsist along with Yima until the anger of the Wise Lord will have been calmed. At the end of the Flood, Yima will open the doors of the enclosure and the earth will be repopulated anew. According to certain traditions, the Fort of Yima still stands: it constitutes what is called Paradise; the souls of the just will await the end of time there. When this world has become irremediably evil and is destroyed, the Enclosure of Yima will be enlarged to cover the dimensions of the entire earth and a new age of gold will be installed as a Great Renewal. This notion of a remainder from which a new world is constructed is found throughout the Indo-European domain and notably in India.

Conclusion

Zoroastrian religion clearly presents a dual character: on the one hand, it has remained intrinsically faithful to the ideology of the *āryas* (and remains so even to our day, when Iranians, even though converted to Islam, constantly give prominence to their national identity), and on the other hand, because of the preaching of Zarathustra, the Zoroastrian religion is distinguished from this Aryan ideology in many aspects. The rejection of mythology is surely the most striking of these fixed "reformist" positions, but it is not the only one. There is also the repudiation of blood sacrifices and the correlative repudiation of the enchantments of the Haoma. There is, finally, the constant reference to the merciless struggle that will be waged in this world by the two Spirits for the triumph of Good (or Evil). Asked to take sides in the battle, warned that his fate in the other world depends on the choice he will make, the worshiper is led to reduce his religion to simple moralism. And in fact, many Zoroastrians today are content to recommend to their children the exercise of three virtues—"good thoughts, good words, good acts" symbolized by the three red candles lighted on feast days. One of the eleven verses of the Zoroastrian Credo (the prayer called Fravarāne, after its first word) says, in its own terms:

> I proclaim myself the adorer of Mazdā, disciple of Zarathustra, pious and believing! I praise Good Thought; I praise the Good Word; I praise Good Action; I praise the Good Religion of Mazdā . . . who is the greatest, the most beautiful of creatures, past, present, and to come; she is the follower of Ahura, the follower of Zarathustra!

But the same ambiguity that has already been noted so often above can be seen again here: if the Good Religion is a "creature," should we not see in her a female angel, an "almost goddess"? Thus the polytheism so ferociously exorcised by the Reformer makes a clandestine reentry. Mithra, Anāhitā, Verethraghna, the Fravartis, Yima are an integral part of the mental universe of the Parsis, who, it must be said, are not terribly interested in knowing the theological status of these divine beings; they are content to know that these beings are beneficent, that one can ask for their help, and that the just will meet them, up there in Paradise, after their death.

Moreover, the modern Zoroastrian, in this respect following his ancestors, is a happy worshiper: unless he shows some excess of cruelty and a deliberate will to act in an evil way, he considers himself to be assured of salvation. The ceremony of the *naojote* has introduced him into the Community of the Just, that is, into that cosmic "reserve" whose place is by right in the Enclosure of Yima. He can be excluded from it only by some abominable crime of which he would refuse to repent. Beyond this, the priests teach him that creation is intrinsically good, because it is the work of Ahura Mazdā: his duty is thus to integrate himself into it with gratitude and joy and to do his part in making it prosper. The souls of the just are invited after the death of the individuals to help the Lord in his cosmic tasks; in the same way, the believer has the duty of working, here below, toward the prosperity of everyone, beginning with himself. Thus the Parsis consider it legitimate to accumulate riches, when this is possible; we know that in the nineteenth century, in India, the community engaged thoroughly in industrialization and became in this way one of the richest and most powerful social groups of the British Empire. By acting in this way, it was following in every detail the teaching of the Prophet, and beyond this in the spirit of Indo-Iranian religion, which also invited its followers to work with confidence towards the collective prosperity.

Nor is this in contradiction with the belief in the ineluctible end of the world in which we live, because work is above all an endeavor of personal salvation. Ignoring monasticism and asceticism, Zoroastrian religion is essentially a doctrine of action; it was thus before Zarathustra, and remained so after the Reform, because that reform, like so many others, was more of a restoration than a revolution. This emphasis on action gives Zoroastrianism a modern aspect that is prized by the Parsis and compensates in their eyes for the small number of followers of the Good Religion.

J.V./t.l.f.

BIBLIOGRAPHY

Iran before Islam

R. GHIRSHMAN, *Iran, from the Earliest Times to the Islamic Conquest* (New York 1954), originally in French. HUART and DELAPORTE, *L'Iran antique* (Paris 1953). R. GHIRSHMAN, *Perses, Parthes et Sassanides,* 2 vols. (Paris 1962).

Zoroastrian Texts

ANQUETIL-DUPERRON, *Le Zend-Avesta* (1771), first edition of the sacred text, now obsolete. J. DARMESTETER, *Le Zend-Avesta* (1892), reedited in three volumes under the corrected title *Avesta* (Paris 1960); English translation in *Sacred Books of the East* series. J. DUCHESNE-GUILLEMIN, *Zoroastre* (Paris 1948), the authoritative French translation of the *Gâthâs.* H. HUMBACH, *Die Gâthâs des Zarathushtras,* 2 vols. (Heidelberg 1959). H. LOMMEL, *Die Yashts des Avestas* (Göttingen 1927). J. DE MENASCE, *Une encyclopédie mazdéenne, le Dênkart* (Paris 1928). I. GERSHEVITCH, *The Avestan Hymn to Mithra* (Cambridge 1959).

Zoroastrian Religion in General

J. DUCHESNE-GUILLEMIN, *La religion de l'Iran ancien* (Paris 1962). G. WIDENGREN, *Les religions de l'Iran* (Paris 1968). H. S. NYBERG, *Die Religionen des alten Irans* (Leipzig 1938). J. H. MOULTON, *Early Zoroastrianism* (London 1913). R. C. ZAEHNER, *The Dawn and Twilight of Zoroastrianism* (London 1961). M. MOLE, *Culte, mythe et cosmologie dans l'Iran ancien* (Paris 1964).

Zarathustra

ZARATHUSTRA (Darmstadt 1970), a collection of studies and articles. J. VARENNE, *Zarathushtra et la tradition mazdéenne* (Paris 1966; 2d ed., 1977). P. DU BREUIL, *Zarathoustra et la transfiguration du monde* (Paris 1978). W. B. HENNING, *Zoroaster* (Oxford 1951). A. V. W. JACKSON, *Zoroaster, the Prophet of Ancient Iran* (New York 1899).

Specific Studies

E. BENVENISTE, *The Persian Religion according to the Chief Greek Texts* (Paris 1929). BIDEZ and CUMONT, *Les mages hellénisés,* 2 vols. (Paris 1938; reprinted 1975). F. CUMONT, *Textes et monuments relatifs aux mystères de Mithra,* 2 vols. (Brussels 1899). G. DUMÉZIL, *Naissances d'Archanges* (Paris 1945). J. DUCHESNE-GUILLEMIN, *Ormazd et Ahriman* (Paris 1953). R. C. ZAEHNER, *Zurvan, a Zoroastrian Dilemma* (Oxford 1955). S. WIKANDER, *Vayu* (Lund 1942). H. W. BAILEY, *Zoroastrian Problems in the Ninth-Century Books* (Oxford 1943).

The Parsis

H. HAUG, *Essays on the Language, Writings and Religion of the Parsis* (London 1907; reprinted Amsterdam 1971). D. MENANT, *Les Parsis* (Paris 1898; reprinted Paris 1972). D. K. KARAKA, *History of the Parsis,* 2 vols. (London 1884). J. J. MODI, *The Religious Ceremonies and Customs of the Parsees* (Bombay 1937; reprinted 1951).

Influences on Iranian Islam

BAUSANI, *La Persa religiosa* (Turin 1959). H. CORBIN, *Terre céleste et corps de résurrection* (Paris 1960); *En Islam iranien,* 4 vols. (Paris 1977).

AHURA MAZDĀ (OR OROMAZDES, OHRMAZD)

The Indo-Iranians inherited from their Indo-European ancestors a theological system in which the divine powers were divided into three vast, hierarchically arranged realms: magicoreligious sovereignty, the exercise of physical forces, and the production of riches. The gods, who were very numerous, acted for the good of the world—that is, for the protection of the Cosmic Order—in one or the other of these sacred areas. The first function, for example, was taken care of by two great deities (aided by several others): Mitra and Varuṇa. Mitra inspired and secured ventures which brought peace (treaties, alliances) and goodwill (administration of the law). Varuṇa watched over the people, scrutinizing their behavior with his innumerable eyes and intervening in combat so that right would triumph; to do this he struck evil people with paralysis or madness; and all magic powers *(māyā)* belonged to him. In Varuṇa's presence, one was struck with sacred terror, but the just man could turn to him, as well as the repentant sinner, whom he readily forgave. Mitra presided over the day (and thus directed the course of the sun), while Varuṇa reigned over the night and the secret world of the stars.

At some point—we do not know precisely when—this order was somewhat abused by certain Iranians, who replaced the duality of powers with the idea of a single sovereign at once both majestic and terrible, following a pattern reminiscent of that followed by both the Greeks and the Romans, for whom Jupiter-Zeus alone assumed the function of the king of the gods and of the world. As Mitra and Varuṇa belonged to the class of Asuras (in Iranian,

Ahura Mazdā. Cast of a Sassanian intaglio. Paris, Bibliothèque nationale, Cabinet des Médailles. Photo BN.

Ahuras), the Supreme God became the Ahura par excellence, the Single Ahura, the Wise Lord: Ahura Mazdā. Somewhat later, perhaps towards the eighth century B.C., Zarathustra preached a veritable monotheism, which relegated all the other gods to a subordinate role as the assistants of the Lord. Ahura Mazdā was the only eternal god, said Zarathustra, the others having been created by him at the same time as other living creatures: "in the beginning." Thus these *yazatas* ("worthy of being adored") were, in his eyes, only "angels," beneficent genies, and Ameshas Spentas ("Immortal Saints"). Zarathustra also attributed to Ahura the beneficent, serene, and luminous traits of sovereignty: the Lord created a perfect Order (*arta*), just and peaceful, in which all creatures were promised a prosperous life on earth and happiness after death in a Paradise filled with light, joy, and song. The only requirement was to remain faithful to the Good Religion, to stay an *artāvan* (one of the "just"). This apparently led to the problem of Evil: how could it be that any creature would not follow the paths of the Lord? Zarathustra was satisfied by the existence of a genie of Evil, the Druj, whose role was to "trick" men. But, faithful to his original position (radical monotheism), the Prophet did not develop any mythology of antagonism between *arta/druj*. He taught that these two entities waged a constant battle under the influence of the two Spirits (*manyus*), the Wicked (Angra Manyu, or Ahriman) and the Holy (Spenta Manyu), and that men must rally under the banner of the Holy Spirit. The Good Choice is the condition of salvation, since the Wise Lord does not abandon those who are faithful to Justice (*arta*).

It must be added that the religious sensibility of the Iranians was for a long time loath to embrace such a system entirely: Zoroastrianism did not become the national religion of Iran until the third century A.D. The "Varuṇian" aspect of the sovereign function came to be attributed to Mithra, who remained extremely popular, probably because his mythology was filled out with elements taken from that of Mazdā. It is certainly not an accident that there were mysteries of Mithra (whose success outside Iran is well known) and not of Ahura Mazdā. Cleverly, the compilers of the Avesta retained certain hymns dedicated to gods such as Mithra, Vayu, Haoma, and Anāhitā and represented them as acolytes of the Wise Lord. It was in this way, surely, that they could triumph over and (much later) convert all of Iran. Today, for the Parsis, Ahura Mazdā is a figure as mythologically colorless as God the Father for Christians, majestic, sovereign, creative, intrinsically good, but distant and "without a story."

J.V./d.b.

Anāhitā (or Anahid)

Zoroastrianism gives only a very small place to female deities. In this it resembles Vedic religion (and in general, all Indo-European religions). After one has mentioned the Fravartis (or Fravashis), that is, the "souls of the just," and the Daenā (the personification of the conscience), the topic is almost exhausted; a "goddess of the horses," Drvāspā, could be included (but this may be only the name of the "power" of the god Gāush) and Vanuhi Dāītyā (or Veh Dātīg), the female spirit of the river Araxe. The Druj (Evil, Disorder, Trickery), does not seem to have ever been personified. Thus the only Iranian goddess in the full sense of the term appears to have been Anāhitā (called Anaïtis by the Greeks) or, more precisely, Ardvā Sūrā Anāhitā ("the High, the Powerful, the Immaculate"). Her anthropomorphic traits are clearly indicated in the Avestan hymn that honors her (Yasht 5): we learn (verses 126 on) that she looks like a young girl with swollen breasts; and, we are told, "she has cinched in her waist to give more charm and fullness to her bosom." Clothed in a gold brocade coat, crowned with stars and beams of light, she also wears otter furs and splendid jewels: dangling earrings, necklaces, belt. The many statuettes found at Susa confirm the accuracy of this description. Upon seeing her heavy breasts and the richness of her apparel, some Greeks were reminded of Aphrodite; others, because of her name and her priestly bearing, supposed that Anāhitā was the Iranian Artemis. In fact, it was Athena they should have thought of; as various modern scholars (notably Georges Dumézil) have shown, the goddess was known for her wisdom (she gave advice to Zarathustra and taught him a certain type of sacrifice) and for her participation in the fight for justice.

Anāhitā first appears, however, in the Avesta as a goddess of the waters: the very first verse of the Yasht that is dedicated to her formally assimilates her to the liquid element in general: purifying and life-giving water in the form of rivers, lakes, and seas, and among living creatures in the form of sperm, vaginal secretions, and milk. Rain, on the other hand, is not mentioned, as it is a natural attribute of the storm god. From this starting point, Anāhitā became a spirit (female) of prosperity in Zoroastrianism, lending her effective aid to the Wise Lord's work of creation and to the maintaining of Cosmic Order. If we add to this task Anāhitā's responsibility to fight for justice and to give liturgical lessons, we can see that she was a "tri-functional" goddess, inspiring the three major classes of activity that correspond to the three divisions of Iranian society, according to the Dumézilian interpretation of the basic Indo-European ideology. This may be why Zoroastrian theologians were unable to avoid incorporating Anāhitā into their religious system, even into the strictly monotheistic framework of the Zoroastrian reform. Anāhitā was furthermore the planet Venus, the morning star, the brightest in the sky. There are many indications that the worship of the goddess was constant throughout the vast Iranian realm and remained so until the establishment of Islam.

J.V./d.b.

Mithra (or Mihr, Mihir, Meher)

Homologous to the Vedic god Mitra, the Iranian Mithra is a person of the utmost importance, a sovereign whose majesty may well have equaled that of Ahura Mazdā and may even have surpassed it at various times in certain regions of Iran (notably in the extreme west). Furthermore, one can read in the Avesta (Yasht 10, stanza 1): "I created him to be as worthy of sacrifice, as worthy of prayer, as myself, Ahura Mazdā." Moreover, it is the cult of Mithra and not that of the Wise Lord that spread throughout the Roman Empire and northwest India during the third century A.D.

Etymologically Mithra's name evokes contractual alliance, so that he is the guardian of loyalty, the guarantor of sincere friendship, and the preeminent witness. The same *Yasht* in stanza 2 says: "Never break a contract, no more the one that you seal with a wicked man than the one that you seal with a just man, for the contract is binding on both parties!" Those who violate this rule are called *mithro-druj,* meaning both "cheats" and "enemies of Mithra." The God who sees all ("He has ten thousand spies," one reads in stanza 24) strikes them with a stupor ("You deprive their arms of strength, their feet of agility, their eyes of sight, and their ears of hearing": ibid., stanza 23), though the just come through without difficulty to the end. Conversely, the truthful, the loyal, the "true friends" (another meaning for the word *mithra*) are assured of gaining prosperity: "You enlarge their houses, you give beautiful women, beautiful chariots . . . to the just who offer sacrifice to you by calling you by your name with the appropriate words" (stanza 30).

Such promises explain the adjective that is frequently coupled with his name: *vourugauyaoiti,* "possessing vast pastures." Not that Mithra is an agrarian deity to whom one should pray so that crops may grow, but rather that he is a fighting god who brings the victory that makes it possible for the *āryas* to get control of new territories. As the same hymn (stanza 4) says: "We sacrifice to Mithra-of-vast-pastures, thanks to whom the Aryan nations receive stable and happy establishments." It is therefore a matter of placing oneself under the protection of Mithra or better still of placing oneself under his banner in order to obtain (or to maintain) through violence those material goods that Zoroastrianism considers "desirable" (stanza 33: "Grant us the favor that we implore of you . . . wealth, might, and victory!"). The vocabulary is consistently military, with references to the god's chariot, to his white hair, and to his weapon (a mass of steel as resplendent as gold and covered with sharply pointed studs). This weapon bears the name of *vazra* (stanza 96), the exact equivalent of the *vajra* with which Indra, the Vedic god of war, is equipped.

This raises the problem of the exact role of Mithra in the Zoroastrian theological system. Georges Dumézil has shown that among the Indo-Europeans (and especially among the Indo-Iranians) the administration of the sacred in its highest form, magico-religious sovereignty, was assigned to two deities (assisted by a third deity and by a few others) named Mitra and Varuṇa in the Veda. Preeminent *asuras,* these two share the task between them: one (Mitra) has shining benevolence, "solar" peace, and mercy; the other (Varuṇa) has the punishment of the wicked, "nocturnal" violence, and magic. It happens, however, that the Iranian Mithra (like Týr, to a lesser extent, his counterpart among the ancient Germans and Norsemen) has taken on numerous elements that normally belong to the second function, the one that governs the force of war. To preserve a just alliance one must sometimes wield a sword, and Mithra does not hesitate to do so. One must also fight if one wishes to give the just, in this case the Aryans, "vast pastures."

Thus progressively Mithra became a violent god, while remaining a solar god, a personification of the sun. An archer like Apollo, impossible to conquer (*Sol invictus*), he was worthy of trust, since his faithful followers knew that he would help them effectively. Simultaneously, the other Ahura was becoming the supreme (and only) god of Zoroaster, which probably allowed Mithra to inherit certain other roles of Varuṇa, starting with magic. In combat Mithra is the one who paralyzes the army of the wicked, a function which the Veda assigns, with more likelihood, to Varuṇa. Some have maintained that Mazdā was promoted in opposition to Mithra—the rivalry of functions evolving into a true conflict. When, for example, Zoroaster forbids the sacrifice of bovines and the consumption of the *haoma,* he probably points to (without actually naming it) the cult of Mithra, who requires the slaughter of animal victims and the drinking of *haoma.* Though this is altogether possible, it must be noted that the Prophet blames the *daevas* exclusively, and Mithra could not be taken for one of them. Moreover, the constant identification of this god with light (and most especially with the light of the sun) had to make him a priori a sympathetic figure to the Zoroastrians, for whom light was the most important symbol of the "Sovereign Good."

This is undoubtedly why the worship of Mithra was "recovered" by the Zoroastrians, who succeeded in separating it from the mythical elements that were too overtly connected with warfare by bringing them back to the god's coadjutors: Rashnu, Sraosha, and especially Verethraghna. Since he had become a simple servant of the Wise Lord (within the framework of orthodox Zoroastrianism), notably charged with the judgment of the souls of the dead, Mithra had to keep on some of the faithful who were more or less heretical. It is through them that we know such other aspects of the mythology of Mithra as the slaughter of the bull, the visit in the cave where water runs and magical plants grow, etc. These traits are not easy to interpret from the Iranian point of view because we lack explicit documents. Through comparison we may be able to think of the cave as the dwelling place of the sun, since in the Veda it is said that the killing of Vṛtra by Indra (known henceforth as Vṛtrahan, equivalent to Verethraghna in Iranian) allowed the waters to run, the plants to grow, and (especially) the sun to shine for the first time. They were all enclosed in a rock which the god split open to "let there be light." The killing of the bull brings to mind the elimination of the dragon Vṛtra by Indra. The comparison is not misleading if one bears in mind that in post-Vedic Hinduism the adversary dragon becomes a bull (*mahiṣa*), which the goddess Durgā must kill in the name of the gods. Nor should we forget that Mithra inspired a brotherhood of young warriors organized into an initiation society (*haênâ*). Perhaps the sprinkling of blood in the mysteries of Mithra was a reminder of the trials endured by the candidates.

J.V./g.h.

VAYU (OR VAY, VAI)

In an important hymn (Yasht 15), the Avesta celebrates a homologue of the Vedic god Vayu. Both gods preside over atmospheric movements: the wind (the first meaning of the word *vayu*) is the outward sign of their power. In a broader sense, all that is "breath" belongs to them, notably the breath of life that animates creatures and the world itself conceived as a living organism. Such a function was bound to ensure for Vayu a choice place within the religious system born of the Zoroastrian reform. In fact, the second stanza of the hymn says that Ahura Mazdā himself offered a sacrifice to Vayu, asking if "he would be so kind as to destroy the creatures of the spirit of evil and protect those of the holy spirit," a surprising formulation within the monotheistic perspective of the Avesta and one that seems to be a vestige of a time (or of theological circles) in which Vayu the Soul of the World occupied the place of supreme deity.

But a closer examination of the Avestan hymn indicates that Vayu's military role is what is most important here: he is invincible, armed with a spear, a golden helmet, a belt, boots, etc. (stanza 57); and he fights from a chariot, spreading terror among the enemies of the Aryans. Various acolytes assist him, among them Yima and Thraētaona (the dragon-slaying god). He himself bears the epithet of Rāma-Hvāstra (the name of one of Mithra's lieutenants), because he brings "pleasure" (*rām*) to the Zoroastrians by ensuring them "good (*hu*) establishments (*vāstra*)," i.e., vast pastures. This is the essential point of the praise of Mithra, and it is certain that Vayu has more or less melted into the mythical image of this deity. If he has not done so entirely, it is probably because Vayu retains a certain ambiguity. The hymn must recognize that there are indeed two contradictory sides to this character, "a good and an evil Vayu," or more exactly, "one part that belongs to the holy spirit and one part that belongs to the spirit of evil." All indications are that Vayu as the breath of the Universe was originally identified with the spirit (*manyu*).

Responsible for all thoughts, all inspirations, and all passions, the god impelled all creatures both toward the Good (the cosmic order or *arta*) and toward Evil (actually disorder). But before the time of Zarathushtra's preaching and even more after that, worshipers obviously were accustomed to distinguishing between two spirits (Spenta Manyu and Angra Manyu) in keeping with a tendency toward dualism that remains one of the basic characteristics of Iranian religion. In the end, formally distinguished from the two Manyus and reduced to his originally secondary role of fighter, Vayu survives in the Avesta only as an effective and fierce lieutenant of the Wise Lord, ensuring his victory over the henchmen of the Druj (Evil). We should note that certain later texts attribute to this *yazata* (deity worthy of worship) the role of a psychopomp. Depending on the works accomplished by the deceased during his life, Vayu leads him to the House of Songs (the Zoroastrian paradise) or casts him into hell.

J.V./g.h.

Verethraghna (or Varahran, Bahram)

The Avesta has preserved a liturgical hymn (Yasht 14) dedicated to the fighting god Verethraghna, a homologue of the Vedic god Indra Vṛtrahan, who in turn owes his name to the fact that he put to death (*han*) the demon Vṛtra, a kind of dragon (or serpent) who guarded the access to an enclosure (a hollow mountain or a cave) in which the waters, the plants, and the sun were being kept prisoners. After his victory, Indra splits the rock and frees the vital elements, thus allowing the universe to come into existence. Such a cosmogonic myth could not survive within Zoroastrian religion, since it was essential to Zarathushtra's preaching to give Ahura Mazdā alone all the credit for a creation deemed to be perfect. Given that circumstance, Verethraghna is but a "fighter for justice," i.e., for the preservation of the Good Order (*arta*) that was put in place in the beginning by the Wise Lord. In such a perspective, it is not surprising that the killing of the dragon was attributed to Thraētaona (an acolyte of Vayu): the objective was evidently to remove from Verethraghna any connection with the cosmogonic enterprise. The prestige of this god did, however, remain great within the aristocratic caste, as is witnessed by the many Iranian princes who took names in which his name occurs (for instance Varhrān I, who had Mani executed in the third century).

The Avestan hymn presents a further anomaly, unique in all the of Zoroastrianism: the god manifests himself in ten different forms. These avatars are, in order, the Wind (stanza 2), the Bull (stanza 7), the Horse (stanza 9), the Camel (stanza 11), the Boar (stanza 15), the Young Warrior (stanza 17), the Raven (stanza 19), the Ram (stanza 23), the Buck (stanza 25), and the Man in the Prime of Life (stanza 27). All is not clear in this list. For instance, the Raven of stanza 19 could be a kite; stanza 39 may refer to an eleventh incarnation, the River. In each case, however, it seems as if the authors sought to present a symbol of virile strength. We are also reminded of the labors of Hercules, the metamorphoses of Jupiter, and of course the successive incarnations of Viṣṇu (several are identical, such as the Boar and the two warriors). With regard to the Ram, we may also think of the "dreaded" fire (savanna fire used to flush out the enemy) extolled in the Veda. But since we have no mythical narratives, it remains very difficult to account for these forms of Verethraghna. We should add that the cult of the god enjoyed a great vogue in the second and third century A.D., along with the cult of Mithra in the western part of the Iranian domain, particularly among the Parthians and as far away as Armenia.

J.V./g.h.

Buddhist Mythology

I. General Remarks

Although it was first a philosophy and a physical, spiritual, and mental technique for salvation, Buddhism received a pantheon and mythical narratives that increased in number and importance in proportion as ritual played a greater and greater role. These gods and narratives were in large part borrowed from various currents of Hinduism. In Hīnayāna Buddhism, the great Brahmanical gods accompany the Buddha, serve him or guard him, and various kinds of minor divinities populate space and involve both the communities of monks and the laity. In Mahāyāna Buddhism (from about the first or second century A.D.) metaphysical Buddhas and Bodhisattvas appear who look a lot like great divinities. Their bearing owes much to the non-Buddhist models. At the same time, Hindu gods and goddesses increase in number and play a more important role now as acolytes of the Buddhas and the Bodhisattvas. But it is especially in Tantrism (*gsan-snags* in Tibetan, *mizhong* in Chinese, *mikkyō* in Japanese), from the sixth or seventh century on, that the pantheon includes a considerable number of divinities and that the narratives are more numerous. Moreover, the borrowings were made above all from Śaivism, and violent, terrible, and excessive aspects became particularly apparent.

Born in India, Buddhism developed there for some fifteen hundred years (from Hīnayāna to Mahāyāna, then to Vajrayana or Tantrism), in multiple currents according to regions (from Kashmir and Assam in the north, to Ceylon in the south), thus offering a great variety and absorbing into itself, notably in the mythology and the pantheon, many Hindu elements (Brahmanical, Śaiva, Vaiṣṇava, etc.). At the same time, it spread into many foreign countries, northern Central Asia, China, Korea, and Japan in the east, Indochina and Indonesia in the southeast. According to the historical circumstances of each particular time and region, Buddhism assumed different forms. These forms derived not only from exported materials, which differed according to the school, the date, and the region of Indian origin and were subject to the contingencies of the means of communication, the rarity of manuscripts, etc., but, even more, from the inevitable fusion with indigenous elements native to the country that received them and assimilated them over centuries. As a result, in India and even more in the foreign countries where Buddhism was implanted, there arose a series of variations of forms, inversions, and mutations.

II. Method

These transformations pose a problem. The simplest, most widespread method has the merit of bringing a certain order to the mass of forms: they are classed chronologically (by epochs), geographically (by countries), or sociologically (by environments, schools, etc.). This historic view can only record the transformations, however; it cannot explain them.

In this connection, there is generally talk of evolution, and a number of monographs have been devoted to certain divinities, narratives, and rituals. But the word "evolution" is inappropriate: it implies that the form that is passed on is effaced and surpassed in the course of ages or migrations. The resulting transformation would be a distortion, a deformation—in short, the original would have been left far behind. The new form resulting from a syncretism, from an amalgam of the original element with elements from the foreign country, would be some sort of bastard form, especially if it belonged to the "popular" milieu of the lay believers, a milieu more or less distanced from the orthodoxy of a church or the authority of canonical texts.

A number of authors have tried to explain certain transformations simply as the result of historical circumstances or various contingencies. Or else they have blithely cited exterior influences, or confusions due to bad readings of texts, misunderstood words, etc. This purely historical and philological point of view often neglects the problem of understanding why such a new form has appeared, while arguing for its late or popular character (which generally implies a deformation lacking any value or interest). It is true that one cannot always explain all the details, nor should one deny the contingent factors that could have contributed to the transformation. But the attitude just referred to is simplistic and a bit lazy; it evades deeper analysis and abandons research.

One could postulate and demonstrate, with the help of some examples, a network of relations, a coherent group with connections not only between elements of the same period and milieu but even between prior and later forms, between the aspect peculiar to the country of origin and the one it took from its neighbors. The least one could say is that such a grouping becomes apparent to the observer who is considering a more or less recent culmination of the process in such and such a country of adoption. The situation is self-explanatory: the individuals, generally anonymous but often known, who elaborated recently transmuted forms, had in their memory, consciously or unconsciously, the sum of all the previous elements, of different dates and origins, that they could know (either orally or in writing) and that we rediscover simply by looking into all the available sources.

The later aspects of the divinities of the pantheon and the new groups that they form in a particular country are not the result of random selection, irregular deformation, or an interpretation that would be rated as "false" in comparison with the orthodox and older model. One would hardly dare say (to use a common but rather unscientific phrase) that "it's as if" the developments or the later transformations were programmed in advance or logically in embryo in the earlier forms (any more than a later event can be predicted in history). But one can say, a posteriori, that a more recent transformation maintains a certain connection with the earlier forms and is integrated into a group that is subject to a kind of internal "logic"[1] of forms that are bound to certain functions and structures. Despite important changes throughout history and across different countries, there is often a great stability and even a perpetuation of old representations and their connections. Often, instead of being distanced from the point of departure by a kind of irreversible evolution, recent forms recover former models that have fallen into disuse. We may know the reasons for such a renewal or at least may locate the source that has been used, but often we have no idea how later authors, distant from the ancient model, could have been familiar with it.

This stability is certainly due in part to ecclesiastics' care in maintaining a tradition while conforming to the orthodox prescriptions that they knew. But, in spite of the desire of Buddhists in different countries to keep the adopted religion pure and authentic, they could not entirely resist the tendency of all representation and all oral or written "discourse" to undergo conscious or unconscious transformations while passing from one person to another, from an earlier to a more recent period, from one country or environment to its neighbor. The priests or the worshipers reflected upon the available texts and the visual representations. Certainly they could misunderstand and reinterpret a particular form that had become incomprehensible. But they could also sense, or clearly discover, the connections between diverse characters of the pantheon after an analysis analogous to the one we are able to remake. In following the meanderings of these connections, they could take up again characteristics or characters that had fallen out of use. They could also innovate by originating substitutions, superimpositions, identifications, amalgams, or reassemblances. Having done this, they could hardly keep in mind the historical identity of the characters or their provenance. What interested them were types; what they retained for their combinations were sometimes names or formal characteristics, motifs, or themes, connections or functions in isolation, sometimes several of these elements at once. They proceeded by analogy or by taking account of their categories of classification. But although the various elements that were combined may have had different origins or belonged to varied contexts, the choice the worshipers made implies that they recognized a connection between forms and contents.

III. Buddhist Concepts of the Pantheon

In research on the relationship between the diverse individuals of the pantheon, the contemporary scholar can and should bear in mind certain general principles of classification that the Buddhist authors were perfectly conscious of. Certainly, the classifications made in the course of centuries in various schools often complied with doctrinal preoccupations that involved a certain degree of arbitrariness, but they can be a useful indicator of the role assigned to characters, their place in the group, and their interrelationships.

The most universally applied principle is that of "incarnations" (corresponding to the "avatars"—the word signified "descent to earth"—of Hinduism). The word "incarnation" chosen by the European translators is inadequate because it designates not only the flesh-and-blood characters who live in our world but also the divinities in their apparitional form. Three Bodies for each Buddha are generally distinguished: the Dharma Body (*dharmakāya*), a kind of "form" of the Absolute; the Enjoyment Body (*sambhogakaya*), an intermediary stage permitting manifestation through acts; and the Artificial Body (*nirmāṇakāya;* Tibetan *sprul-sku,* commonly called *tulku;* Chinese *huashen*), which is the "incarnation" in an apparently material form. Indo-Tibetan Tantrism adds to these the Supreme Body, said to be of Nature itself or of Bliss (at the top of the hierarchy), and distinguishes between a peaceful, pure form and a terrible form (*krodha*). Sino-Japanese Tantrism takes a further step downwards with a Body of Assimilation (Chinese *tongliu;* Japanese *tōru*), which represents the terrible and "demonic" form that a Buddha can take to subjugate demons or bloodthirsty non-Buddhist divinities by assuming their form and acting against them. In India and Tibet, the connections between diverse figures of the pantheon are multiplied since each Buddha is believed capable of having emanations or Artificial Bodies according to the three modes of existence (Body, Speech, and Thought). Further, the notion that each primordial Buddha has his Bodhisattva who corresponds to the Enjoyment Body (for example, Buddha Amitābha → Bodhisattva Avalokiteśvara) is added to the classification according to the Three Bodies. Moreover, the peaceful Bodhisattvas have a terrible form that appears as the Body of Assimilation (for example, Avalokiteśvara → the terrible form: Hayagrīva). Finally, especially in Japan, a Buddha or a Bodhisattva, a Buddhist character, is regarded as the original Form (Japanese *honji*), whereas an indigenous divinity or one whose origin is known to be Hindu is the descended "trace" (avatar: Japanese *suijaku*).

An iconographic characteristic often marks the connection. Avalokiteśvara carries in his headdress an image of Amitābha. In China and Japan, Hayagrīva ("horse's neck") is marked by a horse's head above Avalokiteśvara (Guanyin, Kan-non). He was identified in this form with the Goddess of Silkworms (a young girl who was enveloped by the skin of the horse that she had killed and skinned). In this function, he took the form of the Bodhisattva Aśvaghoṣa (a famous theologian) because of his name ("horse's voice," Ma-Ming). Dressed in white like a female form of Avalokiteśvara (Baiyi, Guanyin), Aśvaghoṣa sits on a white lotus placed on a white horse.

A second principle allows us to spot some of the connections between certain characters of the pantheon. Consciously formulated in Indo-Tibetan Tantrism, it corresponds in fact to the Body of Assimilation of Sino-Japanese Tantrism, whose origin is unknown. According to this principle, the subduer takes the form of the subdued, and according to the ancient commentaries of Indo-Tibetan Tantrism (eighth to tenth centuries), "The name of the subdued becomes that of the subduer," or: "The subduers, heroes, or heroines, take the same aspect and the same name as the 'terrible ones' (the subdued) and trample on them." Thus Yama, the god of Death, has a buffalo's head or a bull's head. Yamāntaka ("Killer of Yama"), his subduer, has the same head. The divinities who subdue the demon Rudra have the same accoutrements as the subdued demon. The subduers of Śiva and Umā, whom they trample under foot, carry in their hands the same weapons and insignia as the subdued.

To follow all the forms of the numerous divinities of this pantheon across the ages and the lands is out of the question. We therefore offer only a few examples illustrating what has been noted above. We proceed in the order of logical priority, since chronological priority is not relevant in all cases; for the Hindu data, for example, we have used iconographic characteristics and narratives of diverse dates. Thus we begin with India and Hinduism, which provided the models—the choice of characters that we have selected as a result of our understanding of the role they played later and elsewhere.

R.A.S./d.f.

NOTE

1. This term may appear to be wrong. By employing it, we would not want to imply precision in reasoning, or rationality. It is employed here as in common parlance to designate a "coherent series," a "coherent, regular, and necessary sequence" (*Dictionnaire Robert*). It is in this way that Jean-Pierre Vernant speaks of "the logic that presides over the organization of a pantheon" (*Mythe et pensée chez les Grecs,* 1:128).

BIBLIOGRAPHY

P. DEMIÉVILLE and J. FILLIOZAT, *Le Bouddhisme,* in L. Renou and J. Filliozat, *L'Inde classique,* vol. 2 (Hanoi 1953). H. DORÉ, *Recherches sur les superstitions en Chine* (Shanghai 1929). R. LINOSSIER, "Mythologie du bouddhisme dans l'Inde," in Hackin, ed., *Mythologie asiatique illustrée* (Paris 1928). J. HACKIN, "Mythologie du lamaïsme," in ibid.; "Mythologie du bouddhisme en Asie centrale," in ibid. A. GETTY, *The Gods of Northern Buddhism* (Oxford 1928). B. BHATTACHARYA, *The Indian Buddhist Iconography* (Calcutta 1958); *An Introduction to Buddhist Esoterism* (Varanasi 1964). S. B. DASGUPTA, *An Introduction to Tantric Buddhism* (Calcutta 1958). E. SENART, *Essai sur la légende du Buddha, son caractère et ses origines* (Paris 1882).

The Guardian of the Gate: An Example of Buddhist Mythology, from India to Japan

The following article presents, as an example and in some detail, one feature of Buddhist mythology in its development and ramifications through various countries and times, beginning with India and Hinduism, which provided the model. We should emphasize at the outset that as far as the Hindu point of view goes, the choice of documents we have made does not pinpoint the precise models that might have been borrowed at a given date by Buddhists from other countries. Rather it aims to reveal the connections among the characters of the myth within the coherent framework of Hinduism alone.

I. Hinduism

Śiva, his wife, and their two sons are the heroes of a highly complex mythology and of a great number of stories. It is impossible for us to include here all of the details and variants of this mythology. Wendy Doniger O'Flaherty has devoted an exhaustive work to them, which shows the principal theme that underlies them: the ambivalence and alternation of asceticism and sexuality in the life of the yogi and in married life, as well as the resulting ambiguity in the attitudes of both the god and the goddess.

Two brothers, Skanda (the younger) and Gaṇeśa (the elder), are the children of Śiva (also called Rudra or Mahādeva or Maheśvara) and his wife Pārvatī (Umā). In most accounts, however, they are created separately, on the sole initiative of the father-god or mother-goddess. They form a pair of opposites. This bipartite structure is evident from their iconographical forms. Skanda is a handsome and chaste young man, while Gaṇeśa is fat and gluttonous. But they are inseparable, each being the inversion of the other; they draw upon the very same sexual theme and have parallel and similar functions. They appear as the mirror image of their parents' relationships, both antagonistic and complementary. The parental couple may be replaced by the one character of Śiva in a bipartite form called Ardhanārīśvara, "the lord who is half-woman" (hermaphrodite). Śiva alone also represents the ambiguity of sexual power: unbridled passion versus abstinence (asceticism). Skanda is called Kumāra (young man), Subrahmaṇya (the pure conduct of a young Brahman) and Kārttikeya (because of the women who intervene in the process of his birth). The legend goes as follows. The gods (*devas*) are in need of a general or warrior to defeat the demons (*asuras*). They persuade Śiva to give up the asceticism to which he has devoted his life and to marry Pārvatī or Umā in order to beget this general. But Śiva, good ascetic that he is, remains in sexual union for one thousand years without ejaculating. The gods, fearing that a child born of such a union would be too powerful and harsh, interrupt the coitus (notably through Agni, the god of fire). Umā remains childless and calls down the curse of sterility on the wives of the gods. Śiva is momentarily distracted and ejaculates in spite of himself. His sperm is entrusted to fire (the god Agni). Agni cannot consume it and throws it into the water (the River Gaṅgā). Or else the sperm falls directly into the water. It is finally entrusted to the reeds on a white mountain (Śveta). In some accounts the sperm is Agni's; and one or six women (the Kṛttikas, or Pleiades, bathing in the Ganges) receive it and deposit it, and a child with six heads and twelve arms is born from it. In other accounts the sperm or the embryo (received six times) remains for six days in an urn (hence his epithet of *guha,* meaning "secret") or in a reed (on a white mountain). One pseudoscientific etymology explains Skanda as meaning "gush of semen," but in yoga, Skanda is the power of sexual abstinence. According to a treatise by a Brahman converted to Buddhism (translated into Tibetan, ca. 1000), Skanda is called *brahmacārya* (pure conduct) because, like his father, Śiva, he is capable of having a wife and playing with her without getting excited. This is said to be the asceticism known as "the sword (of the *makara*)." Now this sea creature (who has an elephant's trunk) is the emblem of the god of love (Kāma; the same emblem was adopted in Tantric Buddhism for the god Rāga, "passion-desire"). It was in fact Kāma who on Brahmā's orders incited Śiva the ascetic to desire his wife and to lose his sperm. To punish him, Śiva reduced him to ashes with the burning gaze of his third eye.

In contrast to Skanda (Śiva's double), Gaṇeśa is the representative of Pārvatī, although some stories at the same time show the affinity of the two brothers. According to one of these accounts, the gods are in need of a general to fight the *asuras.* Since Śiva is engaged in asceticism and Umā has made their wives sterile, they beget Skanda-Kārttikeya by the mating of Agni (fire) with Gaṅgā (water). It is also for the purpose of conquering the *asuras,* who are at first victorious, that the gods (*devas*) receive from Śiva a part of his power in the form of a handsome creature (delivered from Pārvatī's womb). This is Gaṇeśa, also known as Gaṇapati (lord of the "troops" or *gaṇas,* obese and dwarflike creatures) or Vighneśvara or Vināyaka (lord of obstacles; he creates them and dispels them). But elsewhere it is clear that this perfect son was made by Śiva merely by glancing at Pārvatī (and without her participation). He is at first a dashing, good-looking young man who seduces all the women. But Umā becomes vexed with him and curses him, giving him an elephant's head and a fat belly. In another narrative, Pārvatī is disturbed by her husband while she is bathing. Displeased, she decides she needs a faithful doorkeeper (*dvārapāla*). With the "impurities" from her ablutions, she creates a handsome young man, who is to allow no one to enter. Śiva tries to force his way in, but Gaṇeśa stops him. Śiva calls in the troops, Viṣṇu (and Skanda) are repelled, but by means of a trick, the creation of a beautiful woman named Māyā who momentarily distracts the guard, the assailants cut off Gaṇeśa's head. Pārvatī is furious and creates goddesses who attack the gods. She finally agrees to make peace on condition that her "son" be brought back to life. Śiva cuts off the head of an elephant that *has only one tusk* and puts it in place of Gaṇeśa's severed head. He entrusts him with the command of the armies (his own "troops" or *gaṇas*). According to another Indian version, Parvatī disposes of her impurities in the River Gaṅgā. A she-demon with the head of an elephant (probably a *makara,* a sea monster with an elephant's trunk) swallows them and gives birth to a child with five elephant heads. Pārvatī takes him and Śiva accepts him as his child. The variant referred to above, told by a Brahman who converted to Buddhism, stresses the sexual theme as it is connected with the elephant god. Having severed the fifth head of Brahmā, who was guilty of incest with his daughter, Maheśvara devotes himself to an asceticism that consists of carrying skulls, to cleanse himself of his sin. Later, however, he wants to arouse the desire of the wives of the hermits (*ṛṣis*). While the hermits are away, he pays the wives a visit and exposes his erect penis. The women are aroused. Upon

Tibetan Mahākāla mbon-po Ben. Fifteenth to sixteenth century. Boston, Museum of Fine Arts (Bigelan). Museum photo.

Daikoku. Japan. Paris, Musée Guimet. Photo Musées nationaux.

their return, the *ṛṣi* curse him: his penis drops off, and he turns into an elephant living in the forest. A god appeases the *ṛṣis* with gifts, picks up the penis, and returns it to Śiva; we are not told whether or not he remains an elephant. Śiva then has intercourse with his wife Umā, but as a result of an "obstacle" (*vighna*) his sperm falls to the ground. Umā puts the head of the elephant (or of "an" elephant) into the sperm (we are not told whose head was severed), and from this is born Vināyaka (that is, Gaṇeśa, the creator and vanquisher of "obstacles").

The single tusk forms the subject of other stories. One day when Gaṇeśa has eaten too many offering cakes (*modaka*), he goes riding on his mount, which happens to be a rat. A large snake blocks the road. The rat rears up in fear, Gaṇeśa falls, his big stomach bursts open, and the cakes are scattered about. Gaṇeśa puts them back into his stomach and to prevent them from falling out again through a remaining slit in his stomach, he uses the snake as a belt. This spectacle provokes the laughter of the Moon and his wives, the twenty-seven constellations. Gaṇeśa is furious. He cuts off one of his tusks and throws it with a curse. The Moon is struck and goes dark. The gods appease Gaṇeśa, who forgives the Moon, but only halfway: he is forced to disappear periodically. According to another account, Kṛṣṇa wants to return Śiva's battle-ax to him. But Śiva is making love with Pārvatī, and the closed door to their room is guarded by Gaṇeśa. Kṛṣṇa throws the ax at him, and Gaṇeśa consents to receive the blow on one of his tusks, which breaks.

Gaṇeśa is worshiped (like Śiva) in the form of a shapeless stone, painted red, placed along thoroughfares (roads, rivers), but at an early date he became a guardian of the gate at the entrance of temples.

Another aspect of Gaṇeśa is his function as god of intelligence. In one story, when the author of the *Mahābhārata* epic dictates his poem to Gaṇeśa, the latter *pulls out a tusk* and uses it as a pen to write the poem down with superhuman speed. (In a Tantric variant, he writes down the Tantras dictated by Śiva.) In another story, Gaṇeśa is in competition with his brother Skanda to take a wife. Śiva and Pārvatī decide that whoever goes around the world faster will marry first. Subrahmaṇya (Skanda) takes off at great speed, but Gaṇeśa first salutes his parents with seven circumambulations because, according to the Vedas, the merit of this ritual is equivalent to going around the world seven times (the theme of cunning). Gaṇeśa thus gets two wives, Buddhi (intelligence) and Siddhi (success). Finally, whereas Skanda has six mothers (the Pleiades, who gathered up Śiva's sperm),

Gaṇeśa is identified with the seven mothers in the temples of Śiva, while elsewhere these seven mothers are preceded by Tumburu (Śiva) and followed by Vināyaka (Gaṇeśa).

Without claiming to list all aspects and all variations, the following table summarizes the oppositions or inversions and the connections between the two brothers:

Skanda	Gaṇeśa
represents the father (Śiva, the ascetic: sexual power/abstinence)	represents the mother (Umā, Pārvatī, wife: chastity/sterility)
born of sperm (→fire [Agni]) →water [Ganges]→six mothers	born of intimate ablutions (water, menstrual blood, impurities→water [Ganges]) associated with the seven mothers
six heads, one body	six elephant heads, one body
handsome	(handsome >) ugly (dwarf, pot-belly, elephant head, single tusk)
pure young man (sexual abstinence)	glutton (pleasure of eating)
general of the *devas* (in the fight against the *asuras*): red standard	general of the Gaṇas, Śiva's troops, red
called Guha (secret)	guardian of the door (secret of the alcove or of intimate toilet)
swift (in reality)	swift (metaphorically: knowledge and inspiration)

The sexual theme is clearly indicated (psychoanalysts will undoubtedly see castration in the loss of a tusk connected with the son's opposition to his father in defense of his mother). In Hindu Tantrism, sexual rites (*kaula*) are secret to the point that they must not even be mentioned in the presence of Skanda and Gaṇeśa. Two Purāṇas show a transformation of the myth of the guardian of the sexual secret. When the gods interrupt the union of Śiva and Pārvatī, *two* sons are born of the lost drops of sperm. They must guard the door against any further interruption, but due to an oversight by Pārvatī, it is they who see her scantily clad and are condemned to be reborn as men with the faces of monkeys. In any event, the mythology of Śiva is largely characterized by themes of incest (of which Brahmā, his "father," was guilty), by themes of opposition between father and son, and by themes of castration (Brahmā's severed head and Śiva's loss of his sexual organ).

Conversely, the woman's role is ambiguous. Her particular connection with Gaṇeśa is sometimes transferred to Śiva. According to the legend of one Purāṇa, Pārvatī must choose a spouse from among an assembly of gods. Śiva is transformed into a baby and hides in her lap, but she recognizes him and carries him off. In a fertility rite in which Parvatī is associated with Gaṇeśa, we are told that Śiva hides under her skirt. Sometimes Pārvatī holds Skanda on her lap while Gaṇeśa plays by her side. Sometimes Umā holds a little Gaṇeśa in one hand and a *linga* (phallus, that is, Śiva) in the other. In other cases, it is Gaṇeśa who replaces the *linga*. According to one account noted by a Dutchman in 1672, Gaṇeśa had sexual relations with Parvatī and was punished by the jealous Śiva. Conversely, according to one Purāṇa, Skanda's purity is explained in a curious manner. His mother, Pārvatī, at first advises him to play at his leisure. Skanda then seduces the gods' wives. To stop these misdeeds, Pārvatī sees to it that each woman with whom he wants to have intercourse will take the form of his own mother. Overcome by shame (or retreating before inevitable incest), Skanda becomes "without passion." The male sexual theme is thus duplicated on the female side. The goddess is shown to be simultaneously the mother and the wife of the same man.

II. Buddhism

Keeping a secret (*guha*) is characteristic of other individuals who share some of the traits of Gaṇeśa: the *gaṇas* (dwarfs) and the *yakṣas* (pot-bellied dwarfs, guardians of treasures and secrets, who live in caves and hence are called *guhyakas*). In Buddhism, the best known among these *yakṣas* is Vajrapāṇi, guardian of the Buddha (see below). On the other hand, the type of pot-bellied dwarf that is portrayed by Gaṇeśa is essentially a god of wealth. But he also includes the second of the three Indo-European functions described by Georges Dumézil, that of the warrior. Skanda is considered to be Śiva's youngest son. Elsewhere, this lastborn is Mahākāla (sometimes a pot-bellied type associated with wealth and food; sometimes, as in Tantric Buddhism, a fierce warrior, though still pot-bellied). The Chinese Buddhist form of Skanda is characterized by a stick or a studded sword resting *horizontally* on his arms with his hands joined in prayer; a Tibetan Buddhist form of Mahākāla (mGon-po Beṅ) has the same distinctive trait. There are other common features, especially if one takes into account forms specific to Buddhism, which accepted both brothers separately into its pantheon. The "young man" (Kumāra) type of Skanda served as a model for Mañjuśrī (raised sword held in his right hand, book of Prajñāpāramitā [the mother] in his left hand), a Bodhisattva of wisdom and intelligence, which are the traits of Gaṇeśa.

The son or double of Śiva, Mahākāla has the same features as Gaṇeśa. In the Hindu Tantras he is fierce, and he holds a stick, a club, or the trident of Śiva and of the yogi; but he is also a pot-bellied child, dressed in red. Tantric Buddhism retained all these features. His identification with Śiva is known among the Tibetans: he is for them the warrior-god (*dgralha*) of the gods, needed for the battle of the *devas* against the *asuras*. He clothes himself in many forms: red (fierce, warrior), white (peaceable, wisdom, with Gaṇeśa's elephantine features), brother-sister (lČam-dral, lČam-sriṅ, warrior). The Chinese Buddhists also recognized his identity with Śiva (Maheśvara). He is sometimes surrounded by the Seven Mothers (Gaṇeśa is associated with them too). In Nepal, both Gaṇeśa (on the left) and Mahākāla (on the right) appear as guardians of the gate of Buddhist monasteries, whereas in northern India and in Turkestan this function is guaranteed by the couple Mahākāla (on the right) and the goddess Hārītī (on the left). Among numerous aspects that we cannot possibly broach here, Mahākāla's role as god of the kitchen is particularly significant.

In Tibet, China, and Japan, the name Mahākāla has been understood to mean Great Black (it could also mean Great Time). In China and Tibet, he is the fierce deity we have just mentioned. But in Japan he has become a popular god of wealth and happiness. He is known as Daikoku, a little man standing on two bags of rice and carrying a mallet and a bag on his shoulders. The same term also designates the main pillar of the kitchen, of which he is the deity. This god, popular and authentically Japanese in appearance as he is, was nevertheless imported from India as early as the beginning of the ninth century by the founders of Japanese Tantrism (which does not exclude the possibility that this foreign model may have been superimposed on a native deity of the same type, although the existence of the latter has never been attested). For once, in this particular case, we need not imagine obscure resurgences. A written Chinese source, well known among all educated Japanese Buddhists, gives us the model: the Chinese pilgrim Yijing, who lived in northern India in the seventh century, reports in his travelogue that in Indian monasteries it was the custom to place a small statue of Mahākāla carrying a golden bag next to the pillar in the kitchen or in front of the pantry door. The name of the god probably derives from the fact that the statue was regularly anointed with oil, which turned it black. He was worshiped before every meal. The leftovers from the meal, however, were given to the goddess Hārītī, who also stood near the monastery kitchen (or refectory) or by the main entrance. She was a child-eating ogress whom the Buddha converted by taking away one of her five hundred children. He returned the child to her at the moment of her conversion. She holds a child in her arms, and three or five more play at her feet.

The feature of nourishment (abundance and wealth) and the feature of guarding the door revert back to the figure of Gaṇeśa. But instead of the male couple of two brothers, we find here a couple made up of both sexes.[1]

The goddess Hārītī (devourer and giver of children) has enjoyed great success in Buddhism from India through central Asia to the Far East. In China, she was identified with a native figure, the "Mother of Demon-Children" (Guizi mu) or the "Mother of the Nine Children" (Jiuzi mu). But like Skanda and Gaṇeśa, she has been treated as an independent and isolated individual. For all these deities, the couple has been dislocated, but, as we shall see, it has reemerged in different forms. In India, Hārītī is the wife of Pañcika (also called Kuvēra). We shall encounter her again in Chinese Buddhism. Let us first consider the husband, Pañcika, who appears here as a variant of Mahākāla in the couple placed by the door or in the kitchen.

Pañcika fits perfectly into the war/wealth or handsome young man / pot-bellied dwarf binary system. Sometimes he is the general of Kuvēra (Kubera), the lord of the north; sometimes he is identified with him (he carries a spear and a purse). Both are of the type of the dwarf, *yakṣa,* the guardian of wealth (notably of the monastery). In the art of Gandhāra he reminds one of a Greek Silenus.

Kuvēra resembles the kitchen Mahākāla: he is naked, obese, and obscene, and he carries a purse or a bag made of mongoose skin, overflowing with treasures. His double in this same aspect is Jambhala (a god of wealth, although he also has a fierce form): the purse is often replaced by a rat (Gaṇeśa's mount), or by a mongoose or ichneumon spitting out treasures. Kuvēra means "ugly body" (he has three legs, only eight teeth, a cast in one eye, and a big belly). He is one of the great *guhyakas* (guardians of secrets or of caves). But this side of him always calls to mind his other side. Kuvēra is identified with Vaiśravaṇa, whether (as in India) of the pot-bellied type or (as in central Asia and Japan) as the great warrior of the Iranian type, standing and holding a spear in his right hand and a stupa in his left, appearing as a young man, guardian of the north, god of war and wealth. According to Foucher, Kubera and Gaṇeśa often make a pair at the entrance to temples.

A site at the bottom of a lake surrounded by mountains was made habitable by boring a large hole through which the water drained out (the legend of Khotan and the valley of Kathmandu). The author of this deed is sometimes Kuvēra, sometimes Vaiśravaṇa (with their spears), but often Mañjuśrī (with his sword), all three of them types of the handsome young man. Mañjuśrī is sometimes referred to as Pañcaśikha or Five Tufts of Hair, and he is the protector (the tutelary deity) of the Mahā Cīna country (upper Asia, but not China; later, however, Mañjuśrī became the patron of China, known at that time as Mahācīna, and lives there on the Wutai shan, the "Five-Peak Mountain").

It is said with good reason that he looks like the Brahmanic Skanda-Kārttikeya or is modeled after him (Lamotte). Pañcika also means something like Five Peaks, and he is the *yakṣa* protector of China. He is connected with the rooster, which is Skanda's emblem. He has been seen as a doublet of Vajrapāṇi (Lamotte). The Chinese have in fact identified Weituo (< Skanda) with Vajrapāṇi (see below). Mañjuśrī too has been assimilated to Skanda and associated with Vajrapāṇi.

All of these are familiar members of the Buddhist pantheon from northwestern India and central Asia to the outer reaches of the Far East. Because it is so widespread, the type of the pot-bellied dwarf has caught the attention of archaeologists and art historians. A monograph on this subject by Scherman and Foucher reviews all the specimens from the Greek Silenus to the laughing, pot-bellied Buddha of the Chinese and Japanese (Miluo, see below). But most works, like N. Péri's monograph on Weituo, *isolate* these characters and merely trace the evolution of the forms, ignoring the system or the binary structure that alone can explain the various rearrangements effected in the course of time in different countries.

III. Sino-Japanese and Tibetan Buddhism

We have already named some of the individuals in this group to underscore certain relationships. But before moving on toward purely Chinese and Japanese forms (more or less popular), it would be useful to group some of them together, namely, those who appear to be transformations of the couple, which we have rather arbitrarily left behind. We hasten to add that this does not mean that the deities treated here belong exclusively to Chinese and Japanese Buddhism. They are also attested in Indian and Tibetan Buddhist texts, notably in the *sādhanas* and the Tantras, some of which have been translated into Chinese.

The two brothers, Skanda and Gaṇeśa, both sons of Maheśvara (Śiva), were known to Buddhists as Hindu deities (an example from the sixth century can be seen on the frescoes of Dunhuang). But, as we have already stated, this couple has been split up, and each of the partners has been treated individually, taking on a Buddhist aspect before entering into new binary combinations of various forms.

In Tibet and in China, Skanda does not play a major role as such. In Chinese sutras (starting in the fifth century), he appears in lists of deities next to Guhyaka, alias Vajrapāṇi (in Chinese Miji jingang, Vajra of the Secret Traces), or to Sarasvatī, or else as one of the many *yakṣas.* But for some reason the correct transcription of his name, Jian tuo, disappears in China under the Tang (seventh through ninth centuries) through a scribal error that turns it into Weituo (the characters "jian" and "wei" look alike).

The Chinese monk Daoxuan made this figure known in this specific form of Weituo or a certain General Wei, a form that philologically obscures the Hindu model of Skanda.

Skanda and Gaṇeśa below their father Maheśvara. Detail of Dunhuang, China. Paris, Musée Guimet. Photo Musées nationaux.

According to Daoxuan himself, it was during a series of visions in 667 that, in response to certain questions he put to a deity, he came to know him. Rejecting the gods' desires and adopting a chaste way of life (*brahmacārya*), this young man (*kumāra*) is a general who protects Buddhism. His protection, however, covers only three parts of the world, excluding the north (where, according to him, Buddhism is not widespread) but including, especially, the south.[2] During the same period, Weituo is identified with Vajrapāṇi (Guhyapada) and with the future Buddha Rucika.

In a sixth-century sutra translated into Chinese (and later into Tibetan), two women are contrasted to each other: one has a thousand sons who all become Buddhas (the thousandth being Rucika), while the other has only two, of whom the second becomes Miji jingang (Vajrapāṇi), who protects those thousand Buddhas. Quite early, this second protector was assigned to the post of guardian of the gate, and he was immediately split into two guardians posted at either side of the gate, each simply bearing half the name: Jingang (Vajra) and Lishi ("athlete," an epithet of Miji jingang = Jingang lishi). This reminder of bipartition connected with the door (Skanda-Gaṇeśa) may have been encouraged or reinforced by the existence of an ancient and purely Chinese god of the door, sometimes regarded as a single figure, Yulei, at other times as two, Yu and Lei. Bipartition is so persistent that the couple soon splits into two separate and isolated members, each of whom has his own double. There is a double form for Vaiśravaṇa, the handsome warrior, as well as for Gaṇeśa or Gaṇapati, the round-bellied elephant. The first forms a pair of back-to-back warriors, the second (Huan-hsï t'ien, god of pleasure) a couple consisting of a man and a woman, each with the head of an elephant, embracing face to face. We shall have more to say about these new forms of regrouping and these tendencies toward doubling. But to return to Weituo (< Skanda): not only did he become guardian of the monastery gate in China from the seventh century on (not alone, but associated with a pot-bellied type, as we shall see later), but in Chan monasteries his statue was also placed in the kitchen to ensure food for the community. Thus he fulfills the same function as his pot-bellied double, Mahākāla (> Japanese Daikoku). This role does not occur accidentally. Mañjuśrī, another figure of the type of the young man (though distanced from this role, as an important Bodhisattva of wisdom), was also placed in the refectory. And, as might be expected, in this role he was soon associated with a type of old glutton, the famous *arhat* (saint) Piṇḍola, whom we shall discuss later.[3]

Let us return to the Buddhist Weituo of China and Japan. While becoming independent of his model Skanda, he retains one of the latter's characteristic features and receives a transferred feature vaguely allusive to his brother Gaṇeśa, from whom he has been disssociated. He is famous for being a fast runner (which is in keeping with the Hindu legend of Skanda). But the Buddhist legend finds a new motivation for him. In an early version, probably dating back to the seventh century, the dying Buddha promises Indra one of his teeth as a relic. The god takes two (a "couple" of teeth), but two very swift demons steal them from him (the word "swift" is used here to translate the term *yakṣas,* creatures dependent on Vaiśravaṇa, with Vajrapāṇi as their chief). Whereas Weituo was identified with Vajrapāṇi in China, in thirteenth-century Japan he was the son of Vaiśravaṇa. A hundred years later, a Japanese legend tells that on the death of the Buddha, a demon named Swift stole *one* of his teeth and sped away. But Weituo (Japanese Idaten) pursued him and retrieved the tooth (he was even swifter). This strange apparition of the feature of the single tooth or two teeth obtained by the swift Weituo (< Skanda) appears to be a recollection of the broken tooth of his brother Gaṇeśa.

We now turn to the place and role of female characters. In the Hindu couple of Skanda/Gaṇeśa, the first is linked to the father (sperm retained through asceticism, but released involuntarily); the second to the mother (intimate ablutions). In the Indian Buddhist couple of the guardians of the gate, the refectory, or the kitchen, Mahākāla (borrowing the formal features of Gaṇeśa), guarantor of abundant food, is associated with Hārītī (the devourer and then giver of children, fertility). This Hārītī is also the wife of Pañcika (the double of Kuvēra, himself the replica of Mahākāla). For Foucher, the role of Hārītī was taken up in China and Japan by the goddess Guanyin, giver of children. So much for the potbelly type. The other type, that of the young warrior, in the form of Vaiśravaṇa, also has a wife: her name is Sarasvatī, the goddess of eloquence and intelligence (Benzaiten in Japanese), associated with water, or sometimes Śrī (Kijoten in Japanese). Although he looks like a warrior and sometimes functions as one, Vaiśravaṇa is a god of wealth. Śrī (fortune) is also Kubera's wife. The personality of these two characters is brought out by a Tibetan Buddhist ritual that associates the two. In it, Vaiśravaṇa is called *brahmā-kumāra*, an epithet that marks his status as a chaste young man (like Skanda). Kuvēra is called Maheśvara (Śiva).

Another representative of the type of the young man, Mañjuśrī (related to Pañcika through certain formal features), is generally alone (wisdom, speech), but despite his appearance as a young man, he is regarded as the mother of all the Buddhas (Prajñāpāramitā), symbolized by the book in his left hand, while his right hand holds the sword of wisdom.[4] We have seen how this young man (connected with his mother as was, inversely, his pot-bellied counterpart Gaṇeśa) became the keeper of the refectory (in place of the pot-bellied Mahākāla) and was then associated with Piṇḍola.

The ambiguous connection, often hard to perceive, between the two types of gods and a goddess is expressed in a few stories and in various regroupings of the characters. Archaeologists and historians of iconography have surmised that by withdrawing from the scene the goddess Hārītī, giver of children, served as a model for the Chinese goddess Guanyin, who has the same function. It is possible that this prototype played a role, but not directly. In this particular function, Guanyin is depicted as dressed in white and holding a single child in her arms, while Hārītī's formal characteristic of numerous children was transferred to a god depicted as a jolly pot-bellied monk (Miluo, see below). Above all, the goddess Guanyin (in Japan, Kan-non) is the transformation of the male Avalokiteśvara (Guanyin), and the highly complex question of the date of and motivation behind this transformation has yet to be resolved.

The role, place, and nature of the goddess help us understand new transformations of the group under consideration here. The goddess serves as a signifier for both the sexual theme and the nourishment theme, and she appears in both cases with the chaste young warrior and with the pot-bellied glutton.

A Chinese story that was taken up relatively late on the "popular" level (which is to say that its possible literary source—if it had one—is unknown, as is its historical time span) associates the goddess Guanyin with the guardian of monasteries, Weituo, in connection with a temple (Jietai si, near Peking), whose main chapel (at the northern end) is occupied by Guanyin with a Thousand Arms (and a thousand eyes), while the sides are adorned with five hundred *arhats* (a group of saints, usually sixteen or eighteen in number).[5] An abbot of this temple once had an empress as his faithful donor. One day, he places his alms bowl in front of the statue of Weituo so that it may be filled miraculously. By the power of this guardian god (guarantor of nourishment and wealth, the heir to Skanda, renowned for his great speed), the bowl flies off to the empress and returns filled with jewels by courtesy of this lady. The miracle is repeated daily. But one day the bowl arrives when the lady is still in bed (intimacy). Annoyed, she cries out, "Maybe you would like me to give you five hundred virgins for your five hundred monks?" Henceforth, the bowl never returns. The abbot explains that Weituo (< Skanda, chaste young man) is vexed, but that—since lying is the worst of sins—the empress had to keep her word. She therefore proceeds to send the five hundred most beautiful girls. The abbot enjoins the monks to resist their charms, but they all succumb. The abbot condemns the monks and the girls to be burned. But when the flames reach the couples, Guanyin (of whom there are forms associated with carnal love in China, as there are for Tārā in Tibet) saves the five hundred girls and five hundred monks with her thousand arms (as many as there are *arhats* flanking the goddess [Rousselle]). We lack sufficient documents to trace back the chain of transformations that have evolved into this story. But it obviously combines some features of the legends of Skanda and Gaṇeśa: the woman annoyed at being disturbed during sexual intimacy, the guardian's chastity offended and opposed to sexual license.[6] The Buddhist adaptation takes into account the functions of the guardian of the gate and kitchen that are assumed by the equivalent figures of Mahākāla/Hārītī or Pañcika (Kuvēra)/Hārītī. But the feature of abundance (wealth and fertility) is transferred from the pot-bellied type to the young man type. The assimilation of Skanda and Mañjuśrī, due to their common features, takes place in the *Mañjuśrīmūlakalpa*, a text of Indo-Tibetan Tantrism; in it, the god Kārttikeya-Mañjuśrī is placed by the second gate of a *maṇḍala* (but this god is merely a doublet of Skanda, and the Chinese translation speaks of "Kumāra *and* Mañjuśrī").

The story of Weituo becomes clearer when set against a rare ritual of the end of the seventh century that did not survive beyond the tenth century. It concerns a Mañjuśrī with a thousand arms and a thousand bowls (one in each hand). These thousand bowls contain a thousand Śākyamuni Buddhas, who multiply into millions. In another ritual, Śākyamuni performs a miracle: he makes the bowls fly in order to save creatures from their sufferings. These features must be connected with the function of Mañjuśrī, the guardian of refectories.[7] We have seen that in this function he is associated with one of the sixteen *arhats*, Piṇḍola. Now, Piṇḍola represents the second type of guardian: the glutton. The young man type does not include the feature of the bowl. Conversely, the pot-bellied type (otherwise in opposition to the young man type, as, for instance, Piṇḍola as an old man) is characterized by a receptacle or some symbol of food. The Tantric Gaṇeśa, pot-bellied and stocky, holds a skull rather than a bowl in his left hand, and pokes his trunk into it. The rare form of Mañjuśrī with a thousand arms and a thousand bowls is obviously a doublet of Guanyin with a thousand hands and a thousand eyes. These two figures face each other on the right and the left of a Dunhuang painting representing a paradise of the Buddha of Medicine. The connection between these two characters may explain the story of Weituo, since Guanyin with a thousand hands and a thousand eyes includes in the background a sexual theme (although worshipers may not have been conscious of it).

Just as we have been able to find a few isolated landmarks of the sexual type between the goddess and a god of the chaste young man type, the same sexual theme reappears as if by a necessary complementarity in a story and a ritual from the beginning of the eighth century which identify Guanyin, the goddess, not with Weituo (< Skanda) or with Mañjuśrī, but with the pot-bellied type Gaṇeśa.

Maheśvara (Śiva) has three thousand sons by his wife Umā. Fifteen hundred of them (whose leader is Vināyaka, the creator of obstacles and of ritual faults, but who can also remove them) do evil. The others (whose leader is Senāyaka, a name formed in contrast to the first) do good. This second leader is an incarnation of Guanyin (Avalokiteśvara with Eleven Faces). To overcome the wicked Vināyaka, he (or rather she) takes on the same wicked aspect as his and vanquishes him by uniting with him to form a couple called "Older Brother–Younger Brother, Husband-Wife." Their statue shows them embracing. It was placed in the bedrooms of the laity, and it was not allowed to be placed in a Buddhist temple. Translators point out that the story of this submission by coupling was based on an unidentified sutra, but that both ancient and modern masters had preserved only its mantra.

Statues of this kind, depicting two deities, male and female, with elephant heads, embracing, are attested from the middle of the seventh century. This double form of Gaṇeśa is called Nandikeśvara, "lord of pleasure" (in Chinese, Huanxitian; in Japanese, Kangiten). It was kept secret because of its sexual character, but it still serves today in Japanese Tantrism as the guardian of the entrance gate to the most secret rite, that is, to the room in which monks receive the supreme consecration (*abhiṣeka*). The secret statue is generally accompanied by the statue of Guanyin (in Japanese, Kan-non).[8] Each of the two spouses has an intact left tusk, but the right one is broken (like that of the Hindu Gaṇeśa, a reminder of the theme of the defense of woman's intimacy), but the two are distinguished by opposite characteristics: the woman is on the left, the man on the right, and there are, according to Getty, other oppositions: mouth open/closed, like the two Vajrapāṇi guardians of the gate; crowned/uncrowned; short tusks and trunk / long tusks and trunk; eye small/big. The epithet of "pleasure" also designates the round cake (a ball of rice) that Gaṇeśa Gaṇapati (Vanāyaka) holds (in his left hand, a female symbol) at the same time as he holds a turnip and a radish (in his right hand, a male symbol), a doublet of the broken tusk. The cake recalls the gluttony of the Hindu Gaṇeśa, whose large stomach bursts open and is tied together with a snake. A late Japanese account takes up this theme and tells of a king who ate so much meat that he exhausted all supplies (first all the oxen, then dead humans, and finally live humans). The title of Dasheng (Great Saint) given to the figure of Gaṇeśa, who has split into a sexual couple, is also attributed to Vaiśravaṇa (the young warrior). Protector of the north, he is the only one of the guardians of the four regions to bear this title. A third "Great Saint" also becomes part of this group. He is known as the "Monk of the Community" (*saṃgha*, Sengjia heshang). Another monk, Wanhuei (who runs fast like Skanda), learns that he is a reincarnation of Guanyin. He vanquished a "mother of the water," a "holy mother." In a temple of popular Taoism, the guardian god (Wang lingguan) is flanked by the "Great Saint" (on the left) and Guanyin (on his right).

Thus we see the goddess (in this case, Guanyin, the female form of Avalokiteśvara, himself a transformation of Śiva) associated now with one, now with the other of the two guardians, and associated simultaneously with the two themes of sex and food. In the case of Huanxitian (Nandikeśvara), she combines the two Indian pairs: the older and younger brothers and the husband and wife.

Whether we are dealing with affirmed sexuality or refuted sexuality (chastity), the relationship between Guanyin and the chaste young man Weituo is well attested in modern China. The statues of Weituo and Guanyin are often found together, along with a third pot-bellied individual, at the entrance of temples. On the road to Kangding, in the outlying Sino-Tibetan regions, the bridge crossing the Tadu River connects a temple of Guanyin with the mountain of Weituo on the opposite bank. They have a cult of two stones there, one elongated, the other one round, which are regarded as the sexual organs of the two deities.[9] According to one tradition (Lessing), a formal feature of Weituo can be explained by the relationship between the goddess and the god. In most cases, but particularly when in front of Guanyin, the young warrior joins both hands in prayer, holding horizontally across his arms a studded stick (a kind of mace or a doublet of the *vajra*). In other cases, his stick stands upright on his right palm or is pointed toward the ground, while his left hand (when he is standing) or his right hand (when he is sitting) rests effortlessly on the pommel (which represents a ball or a jewel). In the absence of precise and complete evidence, nothing can be confirmed. It is, however, possible that the horizontal position of Weituo's stick is a relevant feature indicating a relationship with the goddess characterized by respect and chastity.

We shall now return to the elephant-god, one of the partners of the couple whose transformations we are tracing. He has his own existence in Buddhist Tantrism (India, Tibet, China, Japan), sometimes as the vanquisher of and protector against obstacles (Vināyaka or Vighnāntaka, a god), at other times as the vanquished creator of obstacles (Vināyaka, a demon trampled under the feet of his vanquisher). It is not our purpose here to examine the multiple forms and functions of this elephant-god. But we do have to present the collection of features that becomes part of the bipartite system we are dealing with and shows further transformations.

When Vināyaka is the vanquished demon, the vanquisher is sometimes Tārā, but according to a Chinese account at the end of the seventh century, based on the statements of an Indian monk, it is Avalokiteśvara with a thousand arms and a thousand eyes, the same who vanquished Vināyaka (Gaṇeśa) by becoming his wife; sometimes it is Amṛtakuṇḍali ("Production of *amṛta*"), or Ucchuṣma. His Tibetan and Chinese name means "accumulated filth." In Chinese, a homophonic variant turns the name into "filthy traces" (Huei-chi). In both cases, his epithet is Vajra. He is also called Vajra with a Head of Fire, and he is identified with Vajra-yakṣa. According to one legend, he was once a man full of sexual passion, which manifested itself as a fire throughout his whole body. He became a Buddha by transforming this fire of passion into a fire of wisdom. He then took on the form of an athlete (*lishi*) and is known as Mahābala ("Great Force"). We have already seen that one of the guardians of the gate, Vajrapāṇi, split into two in China in the form of Jingang (Vajra) and Lishi (athlete). Ucchuṣma, a great athlete, thus appears as a doublet of Vajrapāṇi (who is also known as "Secret Traces" in Chinese). A Tibetan ritual of lustration has preserved a tradition that regarded Ucchuṣma as an incarnation of Vajrapāṇi Guhyapati ("Lord of Secrets"), a son of Maheśvara and Umā. Thus we find

Kangiten, Japan. Paris, Musée Guimet. Photo Musées nationaux.

again the characteristic feature of the Hindu Gaṇeśa (filth and the guarded secret). In modern Nepal, the entrance to Hindu and Buddhist temples is guarded by Gaṇeśa and Mahākāla (Snellgrove). According to a Tibetan historian of the seventeenth century, in the reign of the first king (ca. 650) the gate to the temple of Lhasa was protected by two guards, Vajrapāṇi on the right and Ucchuṣma on the left. Ucchuṣma is also regarded as the fierce form of Jambhala, a god of wealth of the pot-bellied type (like Mahākāla). In this case, he tramples on Kuvēra, king of wealth (vanquisher over vanquished). Instead of spitting out jewels, his mongoose expels them through its anus. In a cycle of Tibetan stories too lengthy to analyze here, Ucchuṣma is the transformation of excrements and other filth resulting from the submission of the demon-god Rudra-Maheśvara (through impalement) and of his wife (through coitus): his name is then Vajra-Kumāra (Young Man). He either transforms the filth that he represents into *amṛta*, or he eliminates it by means of his fire. In this last capacity, he plays the same role as another terrible warrior full of fire, Acala ("Immobile," Fudō in Japanese). Appropriately, Ucchuṣma is employed as a guardian of latrines and bathrooms, thus returning to the theme of Gaṇeśa born of the impurities from his mother's intimate bath.

Associated with Vajrapāṇi (who was identified with Weituo < Skanda) and represented as a young warrior, Ucchuṣma is also classified in the north as the other two types of gods of wealth, Vaiśravaṇa (warrior) and Kuvēra (ugly, fat). But the motif of filth relates him, instead, to the pot-bellied type of Gaṇeśa, who, under the name of Vināyaka, is depicted as vanquished by him both in the paintings of Dunhuang and in Sino-Japanese Tantrism.

In the Dunhuang paintings, two of which are clearly dated by inscriptions (A.D. 943 and 981), the vanquisher and the vanquished are depicted doubled on the right and on the left by Avalokiteśvara with a thousand hands and eleven heads (the one who vanquished Vināyaka by becoming his wife). The vanquisher is doubled by yet another related form, itself doubled on the left and on the right. Except for some cases in which the places are inverted (inversions that can be noted in other elements of this scene, without any regularity or discernible reason), they appear as follows: On the left, a form of Vajrapāṇi, whose throat is blue as a result of having swallowed poison, but whose body is red. He is called Blue Poison Vajra (homophonic variant: Vajra who dispels poison, Bidu jingang) or Blue-faced Vajra (Qingmian jingang). He may be identified with Kuṇḍali Yakṣa (Waley) or rather Amṛtakuṇḍali ("producer of *amṛta*"). He is accompanied by another form of Vajrapāṇi, "Secret Traces" (Miji jingang), whose body is blue. Facing him on the right is a form of Ucchuṣma known as Vajra with a Head of Fire (Huotou jingang) or Red-faced Vajra. He is accompanied by another fierce vanquisher with a red skin, Vajra Great God (Mahādeva) or Trailokyavijaya (vanquisher of the three worlds). The main vanquishers are seen at his feet, on the left a demon with the head of a pig, called Vinākaya, "Demon-Mother," and on the right a demon with the head of an elephant, called Vināyaka, "demon-father." We have here a form of Gaṇeśa. The variant of the head of the pig, brought in for the sake of symmetry (left/right; mother/father), may be explained both by the form (his extended snout replacing the trunk) and by the content (in China, pigs feed on excrement). Later, a double of Vajrapāṇi characterized by these inverted forms may be found. It should again be noted here that these representations go back to well before the tenth century.

A ritual translated into Chinese in the middle of the seventh century is devoted to Vajragarbha, a doublet of Vajrapāṇi (here he is the Lord of Secrets, and by the sixth century he sometimes replaces Vajrapāṇi, opposite Avalokiteśvara, on either side of the Buddha). He is surrounded by fourteen Śaiva deities, among whom we find Ucchuṣma, Amṛtakuṇḍali, and Śankara (generally, it is Śiva, but here it is a woman, the elder daughter of Vajragarbha). Amṛtakuṇḍali dispels obstacles (Vināyaka). He is blue, but has fiery red hair. He tramples on an elephant-headed demon, holding a turnip in his right hand and a "cake of joy" (*huanxi tan, modaka*) in his left hand (Gaṇeśa). Ucchuṣma too is blue with hair red as fire. He seems to be distinct from the two related characters, Vajra with a Head of Fire, who vanquishes demons, and Blue-faced Vajra, who is represented as a *yakṣa* with a blue body, trampling on a demon and surrounded by four *vajrayakṣas*. We can see that the filth of Ucchuṣma forms a counterpart to the poison of Vajrapāṇi, which, once digested and neutralized, becomes *amṛta* in his doublet Amṛtakuṇḍali.

The characteristic of gluttony of the Hindu Gaṇeśa and its connection with filth (through his mother) thus reappear in Buddhism among its gods who are vanquishers. They are particularly well illustrated by an altogether different figure known only in Tibetan Tantrism. This is a ritual object, either a mask that serves as a receptacle to light a fire, or a hollow statuette that is used to get medicine into the mouth of a sick patient: the medicine is placed in the mouth of the god, travels through his stomach, and comes out through his anus. This object does not, therefore, come under the general rubric of the guardian-gods that we are discussing. But it is appropriate to mention it because this particular form highlights the connections between the two guardians, Vajrapāṇi and Ucchuṣma.

The bodiless mask shows only one face of the fierce deity, a wide open mouth (though a rare variant at the Leiden Museum transforms the mouth into the trunk and tusks of an elephant, reminiscent of Gaṇeśa or Gaṇapati). The statuette is more pertinent. The god is of the dwarf type, with short legs and pot-belly (like a *gaṇa* or *yakṣa*). The identity of this god varies according to the source. He is a form of Vajrapāṇi called Vajraḍāka ("Walking Vajra," probably swift like Skanda) or, in Tibetan, Za-byed ("Eater," also an epithet of fire). This god helps the worshipers to cleanse themselves of their sins, which he swallows and digests with his fire (digestion being conceived of as a kind of combustion). When he is not the object of a ritual, but a member of the pantheon, he tramples on (vanquishes) a prostrate Gaṇeśa. He thus plays the same role as Ucchuṣma (the Lama Kazi Dawa Samdup in fact identified him with this god, but his source remains unknown). Be that as it may, we can see here another example of the transfer of characteristics: the warrior-guardian takes on features of the glutton (Vajrapāṇi = Vajraḍāka), while the warrior Ucchuṣma has retained the features of the bath and filth that were characteristic of the gluttonous Gaṇeśa. In Sino-Japanese Tantrism, Ucchuṣma is assimilated into another form, Vajrayakṣa (whereas in Tibet Vajrapāṇi reappears in the form of a *yakṣa*). Both vowed to eat filth. In both cases, we find in the background the theme of *amṛta* in opposition to the poison swallowed and transformed, a theme that is connected with Śiva > Avalokiteśvara as well as with Indra > Vajrapāṇi.[10] Two legends (poorly attested, to be sure—oral versions of unknown origins brought by European travelers) illustrate this theme. Whereas generally it is Śiva who swallowed the poison that appeared at the same time as the *amṛta* (hence his blue neck and his name Nīlakaṇṭha), according to one of the legends of Tibetan origin it is Vajrapāṇi (whom Buddhists identify with Indra) who has a blue neck because he had to drink the urine of Rāhu, who had stolen the *amṛta* (and then threatened to swallow the sun and the moon). Finally, according to another legend of Mongolian origin, Indra pursued Rāhu as he was swallowing the sun and the moon and slit open his belly so that he had to let them pass "through his bottom." This legend intends to explain the figure of Vajrapāṇi-Vajraḍāka, who swallows a pill and gives it back through his anus.

We now turn to the other pot-bellied types who have taken the place of Gaṇeśa among the guardian couples. First among them is Piṇḍola, who was associated (in the eighth century; see above) with the young Mañjuśrī to the left of the refectory. This function was attributed to him by the fourth-century Chinese monk Daoan, who also launched the cult of the future Buddha Maitreya. He saw the saint in a dream in the form of an old man with white hair and long eyebrows, who asked him for a meal (or in the form of a small boy who asked him for a bath). In India, his function as a guardian of the refectory is attested in the eighth century at the latest and his cult by the seventh century. On the occasion of religious meals, he would be offered a meal and a bath, while the leftovers from the meal were given to the goddess Hārītī. Piṇḍola is one of the sixteen or eighteen saints (*arhats*) and one of the four principal ones among them. These saints await Maitreya's coming on earth. They must protect Buddhism, each living on his own mountain and protecting a different country (we saw them earlier, surrounding Weituo and Guanyin).

The Tibetans translated the name of Piṇḍola as "seeker of alms" (beggar, *piṇḍāra*), and the Chinese as "immobile" (*acala*). According to S. Lévi, it means "food leftovers" (*piṇḍoli*). Indeed, *piṇḍa* designates a round mass, a ball, notably of food (rice, meat), hence: alms, quantity.[11] Various accounts illustrate his connection with abundant food, but there is also reference to his intelligence and knowledge. He learns the three Vedas and excels in triumphing over heretics in controversies, which is why his statue is also placed in the preaching room.

As a result of a sin committed in a previous life (according to a Japanese version, he broke his vow of chastity in his youth), he is always hungry and gluttonous to the point of eating tiles and bricks. In another story, he was a Brahman and had an unbearable wife. His seven daughters and their husbands demanded that he feed them. Unable to do so, he was disgusted and became a disciple of the Buddha. Or else, when the Buddha is invited to a sermon by the daughter of his patron, Piṇḍola remains sitting on his mountain, busily sewing his robe. Remembering his duty, he sticks the needle into the ground and takes flight to join the Buddha, but the mountain is dragged along with him by the thread of the needle, and a pregnant woman dies of fright at the spectacle. For this mistake, the Buddha expels Piṇḍola from the community. He must wander throughout the world and may no longer eat with the other monks. The commonest account (in several versions) attributes this punishment to the fact that he exhibited his power to perform miracles (something a saint must not do without a good reason) in order to respond to a challenge from a heretic: to catch, without touching it, a bowl made of precious sandalwood, suspended out of reach. In one of the versions, the bowl is filled with sugar and "pills of joy" (S. Lévi, *modakas*, "pellets of pleasure"), which the Buddha accepts while refusing the bowl. These pellets (*huanxu* in Chinese) are the very ones that characterize Gaṇeśa, especially in his dual form of a sexual couple (Huanxitian). According to another version, Piṇḍola performs miracles to convert a woman who refuses to believe in the Buddha or to give the monks anything to eat. Overcome by his magic, she first gives a small ball of rice, which grows bigger and bigger. She then consents to give him one small ball of rice from her own supply, but all the others follow behind the first. Piṇḍola orders the woman to bring them all to the Buddha. They are sufficient to feed all 1,250 monks of the community, and there are still some leftovers.

Whereas the bowl, the gluttony, and the abundance of cakes or balls of rice are features characteristic of Gaṇeśa, the bowl also refers us back to the forms of the young man (Weituo, Mañjuśrī). A woman plays only an obscure role in their adventures. Gaṇeśa, having doubled into a sexual couple (with Guanyin), is called "Great Saint" (*dasheng* in Chinese), and Piṇḍola "Saint-Monk" (*shengseng*). According to a Chinese Buddhist work of the early eleventh century, Chinese monasteries included three chapels (of guardian deities), one for demons (Kuei or, in one commentary, Guizi mu, "Mother of Demons," a variant of Hārītī), another for the god of the community (Chinese Qielan, Sanskrit *saṃgharama*, a variant of the "Great Saint," the *saṃgha* monk), and yet another for Piṇḍola. The latter's association with Hārītī shows once again his link with the pot-bellied type (he replaces Mahākāla > Daikoku, stocky and carrying a bag; associated with Hārītī, who receives the leftovers of food). In a little Kyoto temple dedicated to Guanyin with Eleven Faces, to whom one prays for successful childbirth, Piṇḍola is seated outside, to the right of the door, carrying a little ball of rice in his hand. In another temple of Guanyin (Tokyo, Ueno, Kiyomizu Kan-non), Kan-non (with naked stomach and breasts, giver of children, like Hārītī), on the right, is flanked by Piṇḍola (Japanese Binzuru) on the left. We have already seen the (five hundred or sixteen) *arhats* associated with a story of Weituo (< Skanda) and Guanyin. Whereas Piṇḍola was assigned to guard the refectory or the preaching room, another of the sixteen *arhats*, Bhadrapāla, was chosen to be the guardian of the bathroom (while Piṇḍola when invited for a ritual leaves behind traces on the ground, on the bed, and in the bathroom).

Another *arhat* takes on the features of Piṇḍola and brings us back to the prototype of Gaṇeśa/Gaṇapati. This is Gavampati, "chief or king of the bulls," a name that the Chinese also translated as "trace of the bull" or "look of the bull." He has the hoof of a bull and he chews the cud after eating, rechewing what he has eaten in excess. For five hundred lives preceding this one, he was a bull. Such was the retribution for a sin committed long ago that may appear rather insignificant: while picking a stalk of wheat, he dropped a few grains on the ground. Like other *arhats*, he lived in heaven so long that he was not aware that the Buddha had already entered into Nirvana, and he performed miracles.

His connection with Gaṇeśa was made specific in Burma and Thailand, where both characters are depicted back to back, their hands over their eyes. His name connects him to Śiva, whose mount is the bull Nandin and who is called Paśupati, "lord of cattle." Nandin and Gaṇeśa figure among the twelve gods in Śiva's retinue. And, most significantly, if Gaṇeśa is the guardian of the intimacy of his mother Pārvatī, Nandin (and not Skanda) often plays the role of guardian of the door of Śiva when Śiva has intercourse with Pārvatī.

Gavampati was not kept as a guardian, but he is said to have sat in the preaching room of the gods (like Piṇḍola). Like Piṇḍola, he is characterized by the theme of excessive

Weituo with a mace carried horizontally. Japan. Paris, Musée Guimet. Photo Musées nationaux.

food. The Gaṇeśa type whom we compared with Piṇḍola is thus effectively realized for Gavaṃpati; this formulation also hints of the link with Śiva (and perhaps the sexual code).

The gluttonous characteristics have been rearranged in another way in two new transformations. One is Tibetan: Ha-shaṅ, the monk of the masked dances; the other is Chinese: Budai heshang, the "Monk with the Canvas Bag," and Miluo, the fat, laughing Buddha. The choice of the name Miluo (= Maitreya) is not accidental. We have just seen how by the fourth century the cult of this future Buddha spread at the same time as that of Piṇḍola. The *arhats* (saints) have been awaiting this future Buddha by remaining in our world ever since the time of our own Buddha, Śākyamuni. They are therefore very old. Thus the formal opposition of the handsome young man and the pot-bellied gluttonous dwarf gives way to a variant: the handsome young man in opposition to the grotesque old man. Appropriately, the fat, laughing monk (Heshang, Tibetan Ha-shaṅ) was added to the series of sixteen *arhats* next to a certain Dharmatala (an old man carrying a broom, with a tiger coming out of his knee), who seems to be a variant on Bodhidharma (who in Japan became a comic and grotesque figure). The question of this list of sixteen *arhats* and the individuals who constitute it is too complicated to be broached here.

The Monk with the Canvas Bag and the pot-bellied Buddha are related characters. We do not know which one is the transformation or variant of the other (nor do we know the chronology of these forms, although they are attested by the ninth or tenth centuries at the very least). Among the stucco figurines that came from central Asia (and are dated from the sixth to the tenth centuries according to the Delhi Museum), we can see pot-bellied individuals, naked, laughing, holding their belly with their right hand, their left hand resting on a canvas bag. According to a Chinese catalog of the eighth century, there appeared as early as the first century a translation of a sutra called "The transformation of Miluo (Maitreya) into a Woman's Body." In A.D. 690, a woman, the empress Wu zetian, was declared to be the incarnation of Miluo, and already in 602 another empress was considered to be an incarnation of Avalokiteśvara.

In a remarkable spirit of inference or in a more or less conscious response to the connections inherent in the features of this coherent whole, the fat Buddha Miluo and the fat monk (Heshang, Ha-shaṅ) are both depicted surrounded by little children who climb all over them and play with them. This feature is illogical at first glance and incomprehensible in such characters as the comical, pot-bellied old men, but it is perfectly justified for the role of the woman who is the giver of children and for the iconographic prototype of Hārītī surrounded by five hundred children (associated as a guardian with Mahākāla > Daikoku, pot-bellied and holding the bag that means abundance). The ambiguous, obscure place of the goddess and the transfer of her features to the pot-bellied type respond both to the variation between the brother couple and the husband-wife couple and to the particular connection between the pot-bellied guardian (Gaṇeśa) and his mother.

The Monk with the Canvas Bag (Budai, Hotei in Japanese) was not kept as a guardian of the gate (unless he is to be identified with Miluo). But the Japanese clearly felt that he belonged to the group of deities we have been studying. Toward the fifteenth and sixteenth centuries, they formed a group of Seven Deities of Happiness that included only one woman, Benzaiten (Sarasvatī, wife of Vaiśravaṇa, a young warrior type), Bishamon (Vaiśravaṇa), two very long-lived old men (of Chinese origin), Hotei, Daikoku (Mahākāla with his bag of rice), and Ebisu (a Japanese god associated with fish).[12]

Chinese authors tried to identify Budai with a historical character (Tang, Song, or Yuan). It matters little which, for we are dealing with a *type* of saint. One art historian (Scherman) recognized in him the type of the dwarfish and obese *yakṣa* and even the popular figure of Silenus, the friend of children (Buddhists knew him from the art of Gandhāra, in which Greek models were used to represent Buddhist characters). Another author (Lessing) thought of Diogenes and his bag. But the laughter, clowning, and grotesque and paradoxical attitudes of the saint are characteristic of Chan (Zen) and Tantrism. The Chinese *arhats* are all represented as grotesque characters of the caricatured Indian type (large nose, dark complexion, and so forth). Similarly, the Tibetans made the Indian saint (*ācārya*) into a clown mask used in masked dances (the *acaras*).

Certain specific features of "Gaṇeśa" figures (sometimes taken up by his young man counterpart) can be found in the figure of the pot-bellied old saint. The Monk (Budai heshang) stuffs everything into his canvas bag; for this bag is inexhaustible and contains the three worlds. He tastes everything he receives and puts the leftovers in his bag (Hārītī gets the food leftovers), even wastes, even stones and bricks (the "foods" of the eternally famished and gluttonous Piṇḍola). In so doing, he is said to be "full of pleasure and supremely at ease" (*huanxi zicai*), an expression that echoes Gaṇeśa's double (Huanxitian) with his cakes (*huanxi*). Curiously enough, the same features can be found in India. For the sect of Gāṇapatyas (worshipers of Gaṇeśa), the elephant-god's cake is the "seed of life," and his pot-belly is a vast space containing millions of cakes, which are all the human seeds of the universe. In China, the bag of Miluo or Budai is called "the mother of breaths" (*qimu*) because it contains the primordial breath of life, the seed of all past worlds.

As interesting and amusing as these new forms of pot-bellied types may be, both of them are, like their Indian model, charged with the function of wealth, abundance, and fertility. But their existence as separate individuals is not really surprising. These characters have been used in Japan for a group of gods of happiness (wealth, ripe old age, abundance of food and children). In Tibet, in the masked dances, the Monk (*Heshang* > Ha-shan in Tibetan) plays the role of a clown and is believed to recall the famous Monk (the Mahāyāna *ha-shaṅ*) who sustained a theological debate with the Indian masters.

Interestingly, in modern China the fat and laughing Miluo is placed at the entrance of temples. A great Sinologist (Maspero) found this surprising: "We do not know why or when this particularly ugly type was chosen to welcome visitors at the entrance of Buddhist temples." The choice does not seem so arbitrary to us. We have seen that the fat Mahākāla and his counterpart Ucchuṣma (filth) were placed as guardians in the same place. Better still, their Hindu prototype Gaṇeśa is placed at the southern end of the temple, right by the entrance, looking southward, whereas his mount, the rat, looks northward. We can see immediately that this is what characterizes the position of the fat Miluo.

What Maspero does not say is that at this place and in this function, Miluo is never alone. He is always associated with a second guardian, and in most cases that second guardian is Weituo, the young warrior. Despite the dissociation of the Hindu couple of Skanda/Gaṇeśa and despite the transformations and new regroupings of each of these two characters separately in the course of history and in various countries, it was nevertheless possible—amazingly—very late and only in China, to reconstitute the couple of the young warrior and fat glutton in this new form as guardians of the gate leading to the holy of holies, to the "secret." Did the authors of this innovation somehow sense or stumble upon the system, or did they proceed lucidly through a deliberate analysis analogous to ours and based on extensive reading? It would be hard to say. But now let us examine in some detail the way the guardian couple of the temple gates has been depicted in "modern" China (for four centuries, and sometimes even for as many as eight or nine centuries).[13]

Of course, in so vast a country we are bound to encounter a great many variants. The Miluo/Weituo couple is not the only couple to act as guardians. Historical reasons, contingencies of all kinds, associations of different ideas have all resulted in other combinations. We shall give only a few examples.

In the most pertinent and undoubtedly the most widespread case, Miluo, the Buddha with the pot-belly, squatting and laughing, and Weituo, the young warrior standing, are placed back to back at the entrance of temples. Given the normal orientation of Chinese temples, where the principal deity is seated at the north end looking southward (like the emperor), and where the entrance gate opens to the south, Miluo looks southward, that is, to the outside, and Weituo northward, to the inside. It will be recalled that Weituo rules over the three points of the compass other than the north, and especially over the south, while the north is guarded by Vaiśravaṇa (sometimes with a double, the two warriors seated back to back, whereas the two Gaṇeśas, Huanxi tian, the male/female couple, embrace face to face). Sometimes Weituo (on the left) and Vaiśravaṇa (on the right) flank the main deity. As we have said, Weituo (< Skanda) was regarded as a form of the athletic guardian Vajrapāṇi (whom we will see, *doubled*, at the entrance gate). As early as the sixth century, and especially in the Tantrism of the eighth and ninth centuries, Vajrapāṇi is contrasted to and associated with Guanyin (in his male aspect, Avalokiteśvara). But what distinguishes him from Weituo (at least in the iconography of modern China) is that Vajrapāṇi brandishes his weapon while Weituo keeps his "in repose" (especially, perhaps, when he is associated with Guanyin). In modern China, the female Guanyin is found either alone looking northward, or back to back with Weituo (looking northward); or else Guanyin (with children) is at the north end, and Weituo, with his back to her, looks toward the south, where he is preceded by Miluo. Or, again, at the entrance we may find the Miluo/Weituo couple back to back, and, farther, in another couple, this time Guanyin/Weituo, also back to back.

In a pagoda devoted to Guanyin, the entrance is guarded by Qielan (the guardian of the monastery, see below) looking southward and, back to back, Weituo looking northward, but the scene is repeated in the holy of holies (at the northernmost end of temples) where Guanyin is seated, wearing the crown of Vairocana (the Buddha of the Center), with Miluo. In the preceding room, we can see Vairocana at the far end, then the young Buddha, and in front of him the couple called Huo and He, of whom we shall speak later. In another temple, we can see the same group (Vairocana, the young Buddha, and Huo and He), all facing south, but Guanyin has her back to them and faces north.

We also find, back to back, Guanyin (facing north) and Vairocana; Guanyin (facing north) and the Buddha; Guanyin and Amitābha; Weituo and Samantabhadra; and Weituo (facing north) and Dipamkara. Despite variations in which certain theological speculations intervene, there is a persistent individual link between Weituo and Guanyin and between the features connected with the back-to-back position and the northward position.

A particularly interesting case is that of the Guanyin temple on the island of Putuo, which is her most important holy place (Potalaka). Behind the entrance hall, we can see Weituo looking northward, facing Guanyin. But there is a second Weituo with his back to her, looking toward the main room devoted to Guanyin.

This doubling or splitting in two is a common way of achieving a necessary bipartite structure. In the case of Guanyin, in addition to recalling the ambiguous place occupied by a goddess who is associated sometimes with one and sometimes with another of the two members of the couple, the Chinese succeeded in finding a historical precedent for her function as a guardian. In his account of his travels in India, Xuanzang (mid-seventh century) describes the site of the Bodhi tree of enlightenment in Bodhgaya, the (immobile) "Vajra seat" on which Śākyamuni became the Buddha. The northern and southern limits of this site are marked by two statues of Avalokiteśvara (male, Guanzizai) sitting and looking eastward. It was believed that the end of the Buddha's religion would be signaled when these two statues had sunk into the ground, and at that time the one at the south is said to have already disappeared down to its navel.

For certain figures who were put in the place of the fat Miluo, the reason for assigning them the role of guardian of the gate is clear. The most frequent doublet is the god Qielan (Saṃgharama, "community" or "monastery"). We saw above that by the eleventh century, three guardian deities were needed in a monastery: Hārītī, Qielan, and Piṇḍola. It is significant that this model was not followed. Hārītī with her children gave her features both to Guanyin and to Miluo. An important pair of opposites was reconfigured by reintroducing the type of the young warrior. In the late legend of Guanyin of the South Seas (Miaoshan), Qielan sweeps the house clean for Guanyin (the theme of filth). In the iconography of modern China, he holds a purse in his left hand; the purse is also a feature of the god of wealth (Chinese), of another Chinese guardian of the gate (Jiantan), and sometimes of Miluo (or Budai heshang), who holds it instead of his usual bag. It may be recalled that this purse appears as a feature of Kuvēra-Vaiśravaṇa (variant: a rodent spitting or defecating jewels), and of Jambhala (whose fierce form is Ucchuṣma, filth), while the bag (of Budai) appears as a feature of Mahākāla, guardian of the refectory and the gate, who became the Japanese Daikoku (god of wealth and of the kitchen, but not of the gate). The gate god Qielan (Saṃgharama) has a doublet in the Monk Saṃgha (community), of whom we have already spoken, who bears the title of "Great Saint" (*dasheng*), like Gaṇeśa (doubled into a male/female couple, an elephant and Guanyin) and Vaiśravaṇa (doubled into two back-to-back warriors). According to the legend of the Great Saint (attested in the beginning of the twelfth century), he was a monk who discovered a statue of the Buddha Dipaṃkara at the site of an ancient monastery called Accumulated Fragrances (a euphemism for the kitchen and the supplies of the monks, but also the name of the Gandhamādana mountain connected with Mañjuśrī, who played the role of guardian of the gate beside Piṇḍola). He had a hole in the top of his head, which he plugged with cotton. At night when he removed the plug, fragrances would come out. The water in which he bathed his feet cured the sick. At his death, the monk Wanhuei ("Swift") stated that this saint was an incarnation of Guanyin. Speed is a characteristic feature of Weituo (and of his model Skanda), whom modern Chinese tradition regards as a disciple of Dipaṃkara (the Buddha of the past, Maitreya > Miluo being the Buddha of the future). We surmise that the Weituo/Miluo couple may have been replaced by the Weituo/Dipaṃkara couple. The swift runner Wanhuei does not appear by accident. According to the modern legend, Weituo is responsible for introducing the Buddhas invited to a great feast given by the Buddha, while Wanhuei is one of the guests invited to the feast of the Chinese goddess Xiwang mu (who gives the peach of immortality). Around the twelfth century, he is represented with disheveled hair and a smiling face, like one of those grotesque monks of the Budai heshang type, and he is identified with a popular Chinese god named Huohe ("Harmonious Union," a god of happiness), unless this god is split into two as the pair of brothers Huo and He (much like Skanda and Gaṇeśa).

According to an old Chinese custom, a god who has a double form or a double function is commonly represented as a couple. His name is then divided into two parts: we have already come across Yulei = Yu and Lei, god of the gate; another one is Xihe = Xi and He, the time-keeping god. This is also what happened to Huohe: he is either a couple of young children referred to by the formula *huantian xidi* (joy-pleasure heaven-earth, Huantian like the double Gaṇeśa), or a couple of elderly men of the *arhat* type, or a couple of fat, almost naked monks (like Miluo). Huohe is the technical term designating the harmony of the community of monks (*saṃgha-samarga*). The Huo and He couple has been identified with two famous monks, "buffoons" of the *zhan (zen)* type, known as Hanshan and Shide (regarded as incarnations of Mañjuśrī and of Samantabhadra), the former always laughing, the latter characterized by the food leftovers that he collects and the other carries away. We shall not follow their fate any farther, nor that of Huohe, because they were not kept as Buddhist characters in charge of guarding the gate, the kitchen, or the bath. Suffice it to point out their formal connections with the deities with whom we are concerned.

Let us now return to the Great Saint, the Monk "Community" or "Monastery" (Qielan), and quickly sketch his character as god of the soil, guardian of the dwelling place and of the group that dwells there. It is this quality of his that is operative when his statue, made up of himself coupled with Weituo, is replaced by that of the purely Chinese and popular god of the soil (Tudi).[14] His most common form (a dignified old Mandarin with his wife) is not pertinent for our purposes. He does, however, also have a form analogous to characters of the Buddhist milieu: an old man with thick eyebrows, white face and beard, holding a studded stick (the form is attested as far back as the twelfth century). It is the same form as Piṇḍola, and it emphasizes his function of guardian of the dwelling place. It is also typical of the saints (*arhats*) who stay here on earth and get to be very old, and as such it is widespread in Tibet and Mongolia in the person of the Old White Man (in Tibetan sGam-po dkar-po, in Mongolian Čaghan ebügen). Sometimes identified with a form of Mahākāla (White Protector) and often confused with the Chinese god of longevity (Shouxing, in Tibetan Mi che-rin), he was introduced into the masked dances beside the jolly "Monk" (Hashaṅ) surrounded by children. The variant of the Tudi/Weituo couple, which seems at first glance to be wholly contingent, may be explained in a fashion that is admittedly rather allusive and obscure if one bears in mind the associations of ideas and the formal features of the entire spectrum of characters we are dealing with here.

One final representation of the guardian of the gate remains to be looked at. In China, in addition to the couple Miluo/Weituo and its variants, or sometimes in its absence, one can always find on either side of the temple gates the Vajrapāṇi in two parts, of whom we have had occasion to speak earlier—Jingang (Vajra) and Lishi (athlete). He is, as it were, an echo of Weituo, with whom he has been identified. In Tibet, we saw Vajrapāṇi (in Chinese, "secret traces") and Ucchuṣma (in Chinese, "filthy traces") at the gate. We have already stated that Vajrapāṇi was at first a *yakṣa* standing

Avalokiteśvara. Painting from Dunhuang. Paris, Musée Guimet. Photo Musées nationaux.

next to the Buddha to protect him. According to Indian monastic rules (translated into Chinese in the seventh century), the two sides of the gate were supposed to be guarded by two *yakṣas* carrying sticks. In Indo-Tibetan and Sino-Japanese Tantrism, Vajrapāṇi became the "lord of secrets" (receiving and keeping the secret teachings). He is said to be a *yakṣa* called Secret. He is swift (like Skanda > Weituo). In certain sutras translated as far back as the sixth century, he listens to and understands the secrets of the Buddhas, or he writes down the words and acts of the Buddha (motifs characteristic of the Hindu Gaṇeśa, as we pointed out earlier). In China, starting at the end of the tenth century, two Vajrapāṇis appear at the gate of the monastery. But as ornaments or in famous caves, a variant of two athletes (the two kings, in Japanese Ni-Ō) appears as early as the sixth century.

We saw earlier that in Dunhuang paintings (tenth century), a Vajrapāṇi with a blue head is coupled with a Ucchuṣma with a red head, on the left and on the right of Avalokiteśvara, and that this symmetry is extended to the Gaṇeśas whom they vanquish. Other formal features underscore this bipartition. The two doublets of Vajrapāṇi also show symmetrical and inverted configurations. The first, on the left, Secret Traces (Guhyapada), raises his right arm and lowers his left arm (left leg bent, right leg stretched); the second, on the right, Great-God, does the opposite, but, in both, the hand on the raised arm is open and the hand on the lowered arm is closed into a fist.

In China and in Japan, these two athletes are often though not always shown with an additional formal feature that underscores their bipolarity: open mouth / closed mouth (in Japan, they are the guardians of the two opposite and complementary *maṇḍalas,* placed to the east and to the west). This feature has been interpreted as symbolic of the two monosyllabic mantras, A (open mouth) and Hūṃ (closed mouth), or else A and Vam, the mantras of the two *maṇḍalas.* Generally speaking, we may see Vajra (open mouth) and Athlete (closed mouth). But while they are always opposites, their respective places on the left and right are not fixed and may be inverted. In addition, while these two athletes are surely transformations of the doubled Vajrapāṇi or of the two *yakṣas* who guard the gate, they more precisely represent two rare guardians referred to in the *Mahāvairocanasūtra* (translated at the beginning of the seventh century); they are distinguished by the feature of the left hand open/closed. They are best known in Japan under the name of Fukaotsu ("Unsurpassable") and Sōkō ("Facing"), names taken from the Chinese sutra. In Japan, a further step was taken (in the Shūgendō tradition), making them into two demons who were vanquished by the holy founder (En-no gyōja, a yogi or Tantrist) and became his acolytes or servants. They are then put in opposition as a male (holding an ax = war) and a female (holding a vase = wealth), mouth open (A) and closed (Hūṃ), red eye and yellow mouth. In China, the two warriors took on the modern popular form of Heng (< Hūṃ) and Ha (< A) explained as the exhalation ("blower") and inhalation ("sniffer") of breath. The meaning varies depending on the doctrine. The formal features serve mainly to underscore the bipartition or polarity (opposition and complementarity). With the doubling of Vajrapāṇi, we return to the procession of couples we have seen marching past.

We have reached the end of a long voyage through time and space, from India to Japan and from Hinduism to Buddhism, in the context of a particularly significant group that is easy to discover. We venture to summarize what we can learn from this play of the imagination as it proceeds through constant transformations.

First there is the known history, the written documents and conscious interventions, dated and localized, of priests who were simultaneously traditionalist and innovative. Judging by the few available documents, the known prescriptions of the learned priests have been followed only partially or temporarily.

The Indian model indicated by Yizing (seventh century), Mahākāla (pillar, black) and Hārītī (kitchens, storehouses, entrance gates), is unknown in Tibet (Vajrapāṇi and Ucchuṣma), and partially followed in Nepal (Mahākāla and Gaṇeśa). By contrast, it used to be well known in China and Japan but has not been retained in those countries. In China neither the god nor the goddess played any role, even separately; in Japan, Mahākāla alone became important. First selected by a priest to be a protector of the temples of Tantrism (but not to stand at the gate nor in the kitchen), and then forming a triad with Vaiśravaṇa and Sarasvatī in the same setting, he finally became a popular god of the kitchen even outside Buddhism. The second Indian model known to the Chinese and Japanese through written documents (Piṇḍola and Mañjuśrī in refectories) was imposed in China by an imperial decree in 769, but did not last beyond the ninth or tenth century, whereas the cult of Piṇḍola in the refectory was already common in the fifth century. These two saints were replaced by Weituo (< Skanda) and Miluo (or variants), despite another written source (ca. A.D. 1000), which was read everywhere, that said monasteries should have three chapels, one each for Hārītī, Saṃgharama, and Piṇḍola (thus reverting back to the goddess hinted at in the seventh century, but replacing Mahākāla with Piṇḍola). Here again, only Piṇḍola was retained in Japan (but he was placed outside the preaching room), while in China it was Saṃgharama, god of the soil, who survived. Conversely, Vajrapāṇi—clearly attested in Indian Buddhism as the personal guardian of the Buddha—was doubled in China into Lishi (athlete) and Jingang (Vajra), starting in the sixth century (he appears in a festival of the end of the year), and was maintained in China and in Japan in this form or in its variants of Two Kings or of Heng and Ha at the entrance gate to temples. The Indian model only called for two *yakṣas* at this place, but Vajrapāṇi was known to have been at first a *yakṣa*.

None of the known models called for the couple of guardians at the gate that was conceived only in China (Weituo/Miluo, the chaste young warrior and the fat and smiling saint). This innovation corresponds to the Hindu couple Skanda/Gaṇeśa not only in its form, but also in its content (purity/gluttony; abstinence/abundance, and so forth) and in its function (guarding the gate or the secret). Various Buddhist characters (Pañcika, Kuvēra, Vaiśravaṇa, Hārītī, and so forth) had the same forms and functions, but not always the same content and certainly not at the same time. The most recent and the most remote innovation seems to be explained only through a kind of return to the prototype that is least consciously acknowledged. Not only is this prototype Indian, which is quite normal; it is Hindu rather than Buddhist.

Is the reference to Hindu representations justified? Chinese, Indian, and Tibetan Buddhists may well have known them. Aside from oral transmission (possible but not provable) by Indian travelers and residents in China and Tibet, and vice versa, learned priests knew a good many Hindu traditions through Buddhist works that mentioned them critically. They sometimes adopted them and gave them a Buddhist form. They could also see images. Working in China between 693 and ca. 706, an Indian monk, the translator of a Buddhist ritual, founded a Hindu temple in his host country. Between 1200 and 1400, the Indian community of Zhenjiang (Zayton) left behind Śaiva and Vaiṣṇava sculptures.

The function of guardian of the gate is all the more readily granted to a couple in that the very character of a gate implies a leaning toward bipartition (by the symmetry of right and left). This couple may be obtained either by doubling a single character (with opposite and symmetrical features) such as the warrior (*yakṣa*, Vajrapāṇi), or by the association of two characters of opposite features (thin and fat, man and woman). But the fundamental idea of a door is not in and of itself the only condition necessary for doubling. This process also applies to seemingly isolated individuals who have other functions (Gaṇeśa, Vaiśravaṇa). Their bipartition is both formal and functional. Each of them is simultaneously a god of war and a god of wealth, thin and fat.

Instead of being distinct as they are in Dumézil's Indo-European schema of the three functions, these functions are interchangeable and simultaneous. The third function, the priesthood, appears to be absent. It may have been transformed into the function of the secret (revealed and to be guarded), of inspiration, and of intellectual keenness.

Bipartition sometimes gives way to a tripartition obtained through the figure of a woman. Her status is ambiguous. By associating now with one and now with the other of two opposite and complementary characters, she may serve to bring about a new transformation and a return to bipartition, to a sexual couple.

R.A.S./g.h.

NOTES

1. As has been said, in Tibet there is a particular form of Mahākāla, called Brother-Sister (lČam-dral, lČam-sriṅ), who is a single warrior god. However, in the school of Sa-skya-pa, this single god became a goddess named dKar-mo ñi-zla, White Sun-Moon (necklace of a thousand suns and moons; diadem of skulls, surmounted by sun and moon).

2. It will be recalled that the protector of the north is either Vaiśravaṇa, of whom the type is the same as that of Skanda, or Kubera, who is pot-bellied like Gaṇeśa. Curiously, a Tamil legend (twelfth century) makes Skanda a kind of violent rogue who turns the universe upside down with his tricks and usurps the throne of the Supreme Deity. In Buddhism, Vaiśravaṇa had a son, Nuocha (Naṭa), who became the same type of turbulent god in popular Chinese legends. As for the pot-bellied type, it should be noted that Maitreya, the Buddha placed in the north, became in China the smiling Miluo with the big belly.

3. We are dealing here with an innovation, apparently arbitrary, which emphasizes the historic intervention of an individual at a definite date. But this unique and contingent event has only unleashed a process of transformation that is inherent in the system. It was in 769, at the request of the great translator and propagator of Tantrism in China, the Indian Amoghavajra, that the emperor gave the order to worship Mañjuśrī as a divinity of refectories and to place him above Piṇḍola. The author of the request based it on an Indian model and on classic texts in which the great Bodhisattvas are seen at the side of the Buddha, feather-duster in hand, while the saints of the Hīnayāna stand behind him, broom in hand. The goal was clearly political. According to another seventh-century monk, in India Mañjuśrī was placed in the refectories of Mahāyāna monasteries, and Piṇḍola in those of Hīnayāna (no examples of this are known). This seems primarily to mean that Amoghavajra affirmed the superiority of the Mahāyāna. The plan failed. In China, the cult of Piṇḍola dates from the fourth century, and his presence in the refectory is attested at the latest in the seventh century. It is maintained there until the tenth, while that of Mañjuśrī seems not to go beyond the ninth century.

4. In other cases, Prajñā is also the consort of Mañjuśrī.

5. In a fourteenth-century temple (at Hebei) devoted to Guanyin with Eleven Heads, this individual (who is not specified as male or female) is flanked by sixteen *arhats;* there are more than two guardian warriors (Vajrapāṇi) at the temple door.

6. The tale alludes, in the form of a joke, to doctrinal controversies on the nature of the saint (in the Mahāyāna and Tantrism): the necessity of asceticism opposed to the total freedom of the one who has realized the Absolute. A famous tale in the Mahāyāna depicts one monk who strictly observes the vows (repression of desires) and another (named "Sense of Pleasure," Hi-ken) who acts spontaneously and freely without rejecting the world (freedom to act even in the passions). The first falls into hell, the second becomes a Buddha in a paradise. In Hinduism, the same opposition is inherent in the ambiguous nature of the yogi Śiva: sexual power and asceticism. An Indonesian tale illustrates this opposition by representing the traits of a pair of brothers. One of these brothers is named Glutton, is the type of yogi free to do anything, lives in the east, and attains the supreme heaven of Śiva. The other is named Withered Trunk, is of the ascetic type (lean, emaciated), lives in the west, and receives only a small part of the celestial joys (Bosch).

7. In an isolated ritual, translated into Chinese in the eighth century, the Buddha Śākyamuni is flanked by Mañjuśrī, seated and offering him a bowl with both hands (to the left), and by the terrible Vajrapāṇi, standing, twirling his *vajra* (to the right).

8. The conscious explanation bespeaks rather another function of this elephant-god: to dispel the obstacle-demons (*vighnas*) who might disturb the rite. But there are forms of this god in which he is alone (trampling on Gaṇeśa; this is Vighnāntaka). The choice of the form of the sexual couple seems to imply the motif of marital intimacies. Elsewhere, in Hinduism, Nandikeśvara is the name of one of Śiva's guardians, Nandin, the bull. It will be seen that Nandin is associated with Gaṇeśa.

9. This popular interpretation, which inverts the negative sign of sexuality (chastity) into a positive one, though it initially appears incorrect or distorting, is not isolated or contingent. The other type of pure young man (*kumāra*), Mañjuśrī, has also taken an aspect of this genre. A red Mañjuśrī of Indo-Tibetan Tantrism is a doublet of the Indian god of love, Kāma (he has his bow and arrows). Another form of Mañjuśrī (as Vajrasattva) alone (*ekavīra*) is characterized by his erect, but concealed, penis. Despite the sublime status of Prajñā or Prajñāpāramitā, to whom Mañjuśrī is doubly connected (at once mother and wife), this goddess also receives in late Indo-Tibetan Tantrism (twelfth century?) a sexual coloration: a beautiful young maid of sixteen years, she holds with both hands a lotus on which the manual of eroticism, the *Kāmaśāstra*, reposes. Similarly, in the popular culture of "modern" China and Japan (i.e., for many centuries), Guanyin (Kan-non), a goddess, has had expressly sexual traits and functions. Two other forms of Mañjuśrī, proper to Indo-Tibetan Tantrism, have a marked sexual character. These are Dharmadhātu Vāgīśvara (Master of Speech) and Mahārāga or Vajrarāga Mañjuśrī (Great Passion). Each has his female consort on his left knee. Their principal hands hold the sword of wisdom and the book *Prajñāpāramitā*. The other hands hold a bow and arrows (symbolic of the god of love, Kāma, Rāga), a *vajra*, and a bell (sexual symbolism).

10. In Tantrism, the five *amṛtas* are excrement, urine, sperm, blood (especially menstrual), and human flesh.

11. The Chinese translation of his name, "Immobile" (*acala*), remains unexplained. This epithet is normally the name of a warrior god, Acala (Japanese Fudō), who destroys impurities with fire (like Ucchuṣma) and eats food leftovers. He is sometimes a form of Vajrapāṇi (Tibet, Japan). Wild in appearance, he is depicted as a young man, fat and stocky. The same form (as fierce as fire, pot-bellied youth, red) characterizes Mahākāla in Hindu Tantra.

12. In this group, the most pertinent triad had been created previously by the priests of Japanese Tantrism in the form of a Daikoku with three faces, representing Daikoku in the center, Benzaiten to the left, and Bishamon to the right. This triad recalls the opposition of the young warrior—doubled by his wife--and the fat man (see above).

13. The persons in question here are represented in high relief on two great stupas at Zhenjiang (the Zayton of European travelers) reconstructed in 1228–38, but constructed previously in 1145, according to a preserved inscription, and taking as its model the bronze stupas of the tenth century. Depicted there are the two Vajras, guardians of the gate, Weituo, Piṇḍola, Gavampati, Budai hezhang, Hanzhan, and Che-tö. But other individuals may have been added during restoration (sixteenth century) so that no certain date may be assigned to a particular representation.

14. Another case of replacement by a purely Chinese god is Guandi (face to the south), back to back with Weituo. Guandi is a warrior like Weituo. He is at the same time the god of war and god of wealth, like Vaiśravaṇa (back to back), and this from two points of view: formal and functional. Guandi, for his part, often forms a couple with the goddess Guanyin.

BIBLIOGRAPHY

H. DORÉ, *Recherches sur les superstitions en Chine* (Shanghai 1929). A. FOUCHER, *L'art gréco-bouddhique du Gandhāra,* École française d'Extrême-Orient, vol. 5 (Paris 1905). A. GETTY, *Gaṇeśa* (Oxford 1936). W. A. GROOTAERS, "Temples and History of Wanchuan," *Monuments serica* 13 (1948); "Rural Temples around Hsuan-hua (South Chahar)," *Folklore Studies* 10, 1 (1951). J. HACKIN, *Mythologie asiatique illustrée* (Paris 1928). W. KIRFEL, "Der Mythus von der Tārā und der Geburt des Buddha," *Zeitschrift der Morgenländischen Gesellschaft* 102, 1 (1952): 46–50. M. LALOU, "Mythologie indienne et peintures de Haute-Asie," 1: "Le Dieu bouddhique de la fortune," *Artibus Asiae* 9 (1946). E. LAMOTTE, "Mañjuśrī," *Toung Pao* 48, 1–3 (1961); "Vajrapāṇi en Inde," in *Mélanges de sinologie offerts à Monsieur Paul Demiéville,* vol. 1 (Paris 1966). L. DE LA VALLÉE POUSSIN, "Avalokiteśvara," in Hastings, *Encyclopedia of Religion and Ethics,* vol. 2 (1909). S. LÉVI and E. CHAVANNES, "Les 16 arhat protecteurs de la loi," *Journal asiatique,* 2d series, 8 (1916). H. MASPERO, "Mythologie de la Chine moderne," in Hackin, ed., *Mythologie asiatique illustrée.* WENDY DONIGER O'FLAHERTY, *Asceticism and Eroticism in the Mythology of Śiva* (New York 1973). N. PÉRI, "Le Dieu Wei-t'o," *Bulletin de l'École française d'Extrême-Orient* 16, 3 (1916). J. PRIP-MOLLER, *Chinese Buddhist Monasteries* (2d ed., Hong Kong 1967). G. T. A. RAO, *Elements of Hindu Iconography* (New York 1968). E. ROUSSELLE, "Die typischen Bildwerke des buddhistischen Tempels in China," *Sinica* 8, 2 (1933). L. SCHERMAN, "Die beiden Dvārapāla Figuren im Museum Rietberg," *Artibus Asia* 25, 1 (1962).

PART

8

Southeast Asia

Austroasiatic, Vedic, and Brahmanic Myths of Southeast Asia 913
Southeast Asian Origin Myths and Founding Myths 916
Earth Spirits in Southeast Asia 918
Southeast Asian Myths and Rituals of the Moon 924
The Acculturation of the Divinities of Hinduism in Southeast Asia 926
The Mythic Themes of Theravāda Buddhism in Southeast Asia 929
The Religions and Myths of Insular Southeast Asia 931
Divine Totality and Its Components: The Supreme Deity, the Divine Couple, and the Trinity in Indonesian Religions 937
The Origin of Humanity and the Descent to Earth of the First Human Beings in the Myths of Indonesia 940
Culture Heroes of Insular Southeast Asia 941
Communal Festivals in Insular Southeast Asia 947
Indonesian Rites of Passage 949
A Myth of the Origin of Grains: Hainuwele in Ceram, Indonesia 952
The *Wayang* (Ritual Theater) and Its Myths in Java and Bali 953
The *Rāmāyaṇa* in Indonesia 957
Recent Forms of Eschatology and Messianism in Insular Southeast Asia 958
Desacralization from Myths to Tales in Java 959
The Mythology of the Highlands of Madagascar and the Political Cycle of the Andriambahoaka 961
The Mythology and Ritual of the Indigenous Populations of the Southern Part of the Indo-Chinese Peninsula: Orientation of Research 976
The History and Function of Indo-Chinese Myth: Change and Permanence 979
Indigenous Indo-Chinese Cosmogony 981
The Functions and Methods of Mediators and Intermediaries among the Indigenous Indo-Chinese 985
The Number Seven, Even and Odd, among the Indigenous Indo-Chinese 988
The Ambiguous Notion of Power among Austroasiatic and Austronesian Peoples: The *Potao* of the Jarai 990
Yang: The Sacred Connection, Sacrifice, and the Ritual of Counting among the Austroasiatic and Austronesian Ethnic Groups 992
Vietnamese Mythology 995
The Origins and the First Ages in the Major Structures of Vietnamese Mythology 996
Civilizing Heroes and the Organization of the First Vietnamese Kingdom 1001

Austroasiatic, Vedic, and Brahmanic Myths of Southeast Asia

The definition of the mythologies of Southeast Asia presupposes an investigation of great complexity. Such an inquiry is dependent on a socioreligious context that, from Burma to Vietnam, presents elements that are specific from the point of view not only of their geographic and ethnic localization but also of their historical development.

It is known, in a general way, that the countries of southern Asia between India and China are set in the framework of a cultural substratum which has been given the names Austroasiatic, Austric, or Austronesian, and that the features of this basic civilization, which existed before the historical contributions of India and China, have been brought to light by the joint researches of specialists in human geography, paleontology, prehistoric archaeology, linguistics, and ethnology.

Dazzled at first by the richness of the documents from India, by the architectural beauty of the temples, by the sculpture, and to a lesser extent by the graphic art of Brahmanic and Buddhist inspiration, European Orientalists of the end of the nineteenth and beginning of the twentieth century applied themselves essentially to the study of philosophico-religious thought, to the study of artistic forms that resulted from that vision of the world and of the texts that expounded it.

Thus oriented toward India, researchers saw the mythology as overlaying and bringing together every problem posed to man: the explanation of the world, the definition of cosmic and ritual order, the birth of the gods, the themes of their abundant iconography, the exploits of each god, and the profound meaning of the sacrifice that binds the gods to human society. All was mythology in that sum of knowledge that India conceived as revealed truths, "seen" by the *ṛṣis*, the great sages of Vedic tradition.

But Southeast Asia did not remain on the outside of this long and complex tradition. She integrated it partially, made selections and transpositions, here and there culled scraps of the mythological thought, adapted divine or epic characters to the point of rendering them indigenous, or was content to use Brahmanic names for local spirits.

There is no question here of analyzing what the peoples to the east of India were able to receive and recreate, from the time when Indian civilization began to be propagated and implanted abroad, according to the diverse modalities of Indianization.

Around the beginning of the Christian era, contacts by maritime and land routes between the peoples of the Indian subcontinent and those of Southeast Asia had brought about a confrontation of two great orders of civilizations: on the one hand, an "Indianness" entering into history, attested by writing and art; and on the other hand, a civilization "of the South Seas" or of the monsoons, a veritable mosaic of peoples without writing, peoples of the plains and deltas, peoples of the forests and mountains, who all, in their way, had to different degrees acquired the mastery, or more exactly the technology, of harmony with the natural environment. Rice growers with dry, flooded, or irrigated rice fields, seafarers, gatherers, peddlers, makers of implements of stone, metal, and wood, potters, weavers, people who originally gathered and burned weeds, seminomads who gradually settled in densely or sparsely populated habitats, closed in on themselves or, on the contrary, open to the outside—these people were, from the first centuries A.D., at a period roughly corresponding to the Kushana and then to the Gupta dynasty in India, and to the Han dynasty in China, engaged in a process of development at once technological, political, economic, and religious, that is, cultural in the largest sense.

It is known that China made its mark mainly in the north of the Indo-Chinese peninsula, in particular on the civilization of the Dai-Viet in the delta of the Red River. It was obviously at the height of Hue that China directly confronted the civilization called Indianized, at a time when the Chinese command of Je-nan, recovering the lands of the Viet, had an uncertain frontier, continually challenged by Lin-yi, the country of the Cham, an Austronesian people from the coast of Annam. Until the end of the fifteenth century, the kingdom of Champa, the builder of the temples of My-Son, represented the outpost of Indianized Southeast Asia, facing a Sinicized Indochina.

If we begin with a schema a little too rigid to correspond to reality, it is to the period from the first to the thirteenth through fifteenth centuries that the first great phase should be assigned, the phase of the formation of the ancient

The goddess Umā Bhagavati in the ruins at Angkor. Photo Leclère.

The *Phnom* of Phnom Penh (mountain shrine). Includes a Buddhist pagoda as well as figures from Brahmanic mythology and earth spirits.

Head of a dragon-naga with crested head and wings at the base of its neck, mounted on the head of a crocodile. Wood, painted red and green. Laos, Sithadone province, Khong region.

kingdoms and of their evolution in the framework of institutions marked by India: the Mon kingdoms of Burma, of the north of the Malay peninsula, and of Dvāravati and Haripuñjaya in Thailand; the kingdom of Funan, so named by Chinese travelers as early as the second century, in the delta of the Mekong, along the length of the Gulf of Thailand, and in the territory of present-day Cambodia; the Cham kingdom of Champa, from the north of Hue as far as the present area of Phan-Rang and Phan-Thiet. Then the Pyu kingdom of Burma, or Srikshetra; the Khmer kingdom of the Kambujas, called Chen-La by the Chinese, the Angkorian kingdom from the ninth century; the great kingdom of Srivijaya in Indonesia and in the south of the Malay peninsula.

What had taken place, from the point of view that concerns us here? Each of the peoples settled in the area of Southeast Asia at that time had its own socioreligious structures. Each belonged to one of the linguistic families called Mon-Khmer, Tibeto-Burman, Tai-Kadai, Miao-Yao, or Austronesian. Each transmitted orally its myths, its accounts of the beginnings, the names of its tutelary powers, and its own system of the invisible. But the constitution of kingdoms and principalities, the appearance of certain forms of urbanization, the adoption of writing, the establishment of dynastic rituals where various types of chiefdoms or clan societies existed, that is, the entry of these societies into a new framework, half-imposed, half-developed in a long symbiosis, modified the style of these peoples very profoundly. There was then what might be called a "borrowed culture": the theocratic monarchies came from India, the Brahmanic gods in whom the kings of Angkor and Champa placed their trust came from India, iconographic models came from India, the Sanskrit of epigraphical texts came from India, and the alphabet, from various writing systems and multiple relays, came from India.

Nevertheless, each new kingdom was composed of ethnic groups that did not abandon their local organization and their fundamental beliefs. And there was the beginning of a profound brew, with innumerable motifs, where the indigenous and the foreign intermingled and fertilized one another.

From the twelfth to thirteenth centuries, the Tai peoples reestablished in Southeast Asia the Khmer grandeur of Angkor. The Tai kingdom of Sukhothai, then the kingdom of Ayutthaya, and the Lao kingdoms of Luang Prabang and Vientiane entered the cultural scene in turn. Buddhists from south China, the Tai assimilated the contributions of the Mon and the Khmer. In Burma, Burman unity took on a bloody character as the Mon and Shan played their own game, but Burman culture was finally elaborated; Burman culture was also Indianized by means of a Buddhism accepting of the *nats*, the local spirits.

When the West intervened in the destiny of Southeast Asia, first in the sixteenth century through Portuguese and Spanish activities, it did not understand the great cultures there: India, China, Khmer, Mon, Tai, Brahmanism, Buddhism—and such Buddhism—spirits of the earth, ogres, demons, ghosts, oral myths, written myths, local legends, legends from the great Sanskrit epics, etc. How can one find one's bearings, and above all how can one distinguish what comes from the Vedism of archaic Aryan India, from the Brahmanism of preclassical and classical India, from Mahāyāna Buddhism, and from Hīnayāna or Theravāda Buddhism, and how can one separate this from what constitutes the native ground, that is, the complex of particular forms of animism emerging from the "culture of vegetation" to which south Asia bears witness?

Thus, in approaching the mythology of this part of the world, the principal insight is that it is not a question of creating an arbitrary, arid, and lifeless division between the contribution of the religions of India and the local supernaturalism, but of perceiving the whole, deeply implicated in collective representations.

In the course of centuries, beginning with the Austroasiatic substratum, a system of relationships between man and the invisible was formed that integrated Buddhism but was not dependent on it alone. The old Mon, Khmer, and Cham peoples, and then the Burmans, Tai, Lao, were as if inseminated by the enormous germination of myths and epics from India. They acquired its gods and chose among them. They followed the teaching of the Buddha, adapting it to their own inclinations: accumulated merit leads to a happy rebirth rather than to extinction; the Buddha fulfills our desires by accepting our offerings rather than teaching us to desire nothing! His footprints are stamped here and there in the ground, in Burma and in Thailand. His statues emit light, leave their places, and perform miracles. The mythology of Buddhism, whether Mahāyāna or Theravāda, was born, paradoxically, not from speculation but from collective practice at the level of the village community.

And it is also in the village community that syncretism takes place and is lived. It is there that the god Indra intervenes at the time of ordination of a monk, and that a spirit of the earth must be propitiated in the precincts of a monastery. It is there that the acquired patrimony dissolves into an amalgam in which nothing is felt to be contradictory or incompatible. Certainly a few kings of Siam and Laos have thought it expedient, in order to preserve Buddhist orthodoxy, to promulgate edicts against the *phi*, genie or spirits in the Tai domain, particularly King Pothisarath in 1527. This was an admission of the intensity of their active presence at the heart of the official religion.

In order to introduce a little order and clarity into an account devoted to the mythology of Indianized Southeast Asia, we will single out a few striking themes, significant on some level, without isolating them from their context. It is within this perspective that we will first consider some myths of nature and of the gods. A second development gives us access to the domain of earth spirits, the *neak-tā* of Cambodia, the *nats* of Burma, and the *phi* of Laos and Thailand. Finally, a third panel of the triptych evokes the image of a Buddhism in which myth flourishes even today, of heroes, saints, living persons with supernatural powers whose legends and cult continue after their death and who are in the process of forming a kind of new Buddhist pantheon, the *luang pho* of Thailand.

The mythological material of Southeast Asia will not be exhausted, and the three groups of accounts and facts that are considered here serve only to highlight the three orders that go beyond them: the myths of Vedism and Brahmanism, the Austroasiatic myths, and the Buddhism of the Great and of the Little Vehicle. It is the selection, the integration, and the interpretation that Southeast Asia has given to these that comprise its originality in this domain and its special contribution to the religious vision of the world.

S.T./b.f.

Altar decorated with bamboo poles, erected in the fields at the time of the feast of the spirits who protect the paddy. Paris, Musée de l'Homme collection. Photo Matras.

BIBLIOGRAPHY

C. ARCHAIMBAULT, "Une cérémonie en l'honneur des génies de la mine de sel de Ban Bo (Moyen Laos): Contribution à l'étude du jeu de Ti-K'i," *BEFEO* 48, no. 1 (1956); *Structures religieuses lao: Rites et mythes* (Vientiane 1973). D. BERNOT, "Les Nats de Birmanie," in *Génies, anges et démons* (Paris 1971), 297–341. J. BOISSELIER, *Le Cambodge: Asie du Sud-Est* (Paris 1966). *Cérémonies des douze mois: Fêtes annuelles cambodgiennes* (Phnom Penh). G. COEDÉS, "La légende de la Nāgī: Études cambodgiennes," 1, *BEFEO* 11, nos. 3–4. G. COEDÉS and C. ARCHAIMBAULT, *Les trois mondes: Traibhūmi Braḥ Rvaṅ* (Paris 1973). G. CONDOMINAS, "Notes sur le bouddhisme populaire en milieu rural lao," *Archives de sociologie des religions* 25–26 (1968): 81–150. J. DE FELS,

Somdet Phra Chao Tak Sin Maharat, le roi de Thonburi, 2 vols. (diss., Paris 1976). M. GITEAU, "Le Barattage de l'océan au Cambodge," *Bull. de la Société des Études indochinoises,* n.s., 26. P. LÉVY, "Ti-Khi: Un jeu de mail rituel au Laos," *Annuaire de l'EPHE, Sciences religieuses,* 1952–53, 3–15. P. MUS, "Barabudur: Les origines du stūpa et la transmigration," *BEFEO* (1932–34; reprinted New York 1978). A. R. PELTIER, *Introduction à la connaissance des hlvṅ ba de Thaïlande* (diss., Paris 1976). PHOUVONG PHIMMASONE, "Cours de littérature lao," *Bull. des Amis du royaume lao,* nos. 4–5 (1971), 5–70. E. PORÉE-MASPERO, "Kroṅ Pali et rites de la maison," *Anthropos* 56 (1961): 179–929; *Étude sur les rites agraires des Cambodgiens,* 3 vols. (Paris 1962–69). E. PORÉE-MASPERO and S. BERNARD-THIERRY, *La lune: Croyance et rites du Cambodge,* 264–65; *La lune: Mythes et rites* (Paris 1962), 263–87. P. A. RAJADHON, "The Phi," *Journal of the Siam Society* 61, no. 2: 153–78; "The Kwan and Its Ceremonies," ibid. 50, no. 2. A. SOUYRIS-ROLLAND, "Contribution à l'étude du culte des Génies tutélaires ou 'Neak-Ta' chez les Cambodgiens du Sud," *Bull. de la Société des Études indochinoises,* n.s., 26, no. 2 (1951): 160–73. J. S. TAMBIAH, *Buddhism and the Spirit Cults in North-East Thailand* (Cambridge 1970). R. C. TEMPLE, *The Thirty Seven Nats: A Phase of Spirit-Worship Prevailing in Burma* (London 1906). M. ZAGO, *Rites et cérémonies en milieu bouddhiste lao* (Rome 1972).

Southeast Asian Origin Myths and Founding Myths

The origin myths among the majority groups of Southeast Asia are no longer "pure" in the ethnologists' sense of the term. Only the minorities have preserved intact (as far as we can tell) oral narratives of their birth and settlement, which are inextricably connected with the birth of mankind and the organization of society, and these myths have been preserved only to the extent that they succeed in transmitting fully their explanation of the world.

I. The Flood

An echo of the flood type of Genesis can be heard in the *Nithan Khun Borom* (or the *Nidāna Khun Parama,* according to the transliteration from the Pali), a great text that is simultaneously mythical, cosmogonic, historical, and gnomic; it tells of the origins of the Lao.

This long narrative includes the story of the flood, which was caused by an argument among the gods that put an end to an early phase of humanity. Following this cataclysm, three giant gourds (only two according to some versions) started growing to enormous size from a creeper growing out of the nostrils of a buffalo. The noise heard coming from inside was so great that the gods, the *khun* "lords of heaven," opened them up: one of the *khun* stabbed the gourds with a chisel and a branding iron. A multitude of men sprang out of the gourds: those who came out through the cuts made by the branding iron were black and wore their hair tied up: they were the Kha; those who came out through the cuts made by the chisel were fair-skinned and wore their hair short: they were the Tai Lao. Animals also jumped out of the gourds, and the whole crowd spread and soon multiplied and proliferated.

The *khun* taught the Sons of the Gourd how to till the land and build houses. They taught them the marriage and funeral rituals and the duties of respect for parents and ancestors. But soon men became ungovernable, and the *khun* could not manage them. They complained to the Phaya Then, Indra, the king of the heavenly realm, who sent them reinforcements in the persons of two other *khun.* But these *khun* turned out to be unable to handle men, and the god recalled them to heaven.

Then a new phase of this extraordinary story began: the god of heaven sent men his own son, Khun Borom, or Parāma, the "supreme lord." Khun Borom's descent to earth, in which he landed on a "small, flat paddy field," is undoubtedly one of the most striking mythological texts of Southeast Asia. Heaven and earth were able to communicate without difficulty at that time: some versions state that the two realms were contiguous, and others claim that they were tied together by rattan cords. Later, Indra had the rattan bridge that joined the two realms cut, "and since then, gods and men no longer communicate with one another."[1]

A gigantic creeper started growing as Khun Borom was organizing the earth. It obscured the sky and cold settled in. An elderly couple who had descended with the demiurge hero whom Laotians call the Pu Yoe Ya Yoe (also known as Pu Thao Yoe and Mē Ya Ngam) came forward spontaneously and offered to cut down the enormous creeper, which crushed them as it fell. The sun began to shine upon the world again. The two ancestors, benefactors of creation, became objects of a cult: in the festivals and processions that mark the new year in Laos, they appear in the form of monstrous masks with enormous jaws and bulging eyes. The dance of the old man and the old woman kneaded the earth and renewed the original cultivation. What we loosely call land management, or, better, the organization of space, is on the mythical level the separation of heaven and earth and the progressive creation of the earth to meet the needs of mankind.

The myth does not stop there but continues with the description of the partitioning of the new territory among the seven sons of Khun Borom. Here we enter into a very particular category of texts, characteristic of the countries in question, in which historical data are quite naturally connected with legendary origins.

In fact, the designations of the seven provinces each granted to one of the princes are geographically very precise and by and large correspond to later Laotian principalities, at least in part. For the carving out of *Nithan* out of frontier history goes beyond the historical boundaries of the country of Lan Xang (Laos) and encompasses the neighboring lands of southern China, Vietnam, Thailand, and lower Burma, as though the natural extension of the great story of the origins, conceived as the origin of men on earth, inevitably resulted in the hegemony of the Tai groups on the Indo-Chinese peninsula, uniting all the sons of the mother-gourd under the same essentially divine power.

II. Accounts of the Founding of Angkor

Many other examples of this genre of text can be found in the Annals, dealing with the founding of kingdoms and cities, whether in Khmer, Tai, or Burman territory. The numerous toponymic legends sometimes have mythological overtones. This is notably the case with the accounts of the founding of Angkor, which began with the evocation of five *devis,* or goddesses that live in Indra's paradise. They took

One of the ancestors' masks, here representing the Pu Ngoe Nga Ngoe of Laos, mythic first couple. Laos, Luang Prabang. Paris, Musée de l'Homme collection.

flight and came down to frolic on earth. One of them stole a flower and was sentenced by Indra to live a human life for six years and became the wife of a poor gardener. A remarkably talented weaver, she made marvelous silk fabrics and thus made her husband rich. Soon they had a son, who also had exceptional talents: he could dig, build, and draw all sorts of pictures on the ground. When the six years were up, his mother ascended to Indra's heaven again as the god had prescribed.

The son, however, came to be known as a semidivine person, the heavenly architect. His name in Sanskrit was Viśvakarman, "the one who makes everything, who creates everything." But in Southeast Asia, this name underwent a number of transformations and was apparently assimilated to the name of the god Viṣṇu, since in Cambodia he became Braḥ Bisnukar, which is transcribed Viṣṇukarman.

The story of the founding of Angkor tells that the son of the *devi* sets out to seek his mother. He finds her, is carried away by her into heaven, and is introduced to the god Indra. "My son," says the goddess, "is particularly ingenious at tracing figures, at sculpting, and at building temples or fortresses that are the envy of men."[2] Indra then orders the boy to join the *devaputras*, or sons of god, in his heavenly workshops. "He learned to draw, to sculpt, to make music; he learned to build ships that sail on the solid earth. He engraved gold and silver, and he learned the blacksmith's trade; he discovered the solutions to pour on clay to turn it into stone."

Satisfied with this knowledge, Indra decided that from then on Viśvakarman or Bisnukar would be the master of artisans, artists, and master craftsmen. "Every human builder will be expected to make an offering to Popusnokar. . . . If a man undertakes a work of some importance and does not make the offering to Popusnokar, may his eyes close to the light of day."[3]

A second development of the story involves Indra's own son, Braḥ Khet Mālā, whom he makes invulnerable and endows with long life by immersing him in a pool seven times a day for a week, while Brahma recites incantations over the prince and sprinkles him "to give him a life of four hundred years."

This prince inherits the kingdom of Cambodia. Indra gives it to him and suggests that he have a monument built to his liking that will remind him of the celestial palaces of his father. The prince replies that he could do nothing in his new kingdom that could equal in beauty the dwelling place of Indra, and that he would be content with an edifice as splendid as his cattleshed.

Viśvakarman is then dispatched to earth in a chariot to build the monument of the son of Indra in the kingdom of Cambodia. The legend describes him at work, embarking on a junk to search for shells with which to make lime to coat the stones; this episode is the occasion for a mythical explanation for the existence of the piles of shells found on the site of Samong Sen.

He then goes to find sesame seeds and makes from them a magical preparation to cover the earthen model that he has built. The monument turns to stone, "without beams or rafters," without joints, and finally he decorates it with marvelous sculptures.

The end of the story shows the heavenly architect still smelting iron and forging a sword with a blade as thin as a rice leaf. Until quite recently, no blacksmith in Cambodia—least of all the Kuy of the Phnom Dek region—would begin his work without first paying homage to Braḥ Bisnukar and making offerings to him.

Thus the gods and demigods, or the sons of the gods, play a part in the daily life of the people of Southeast Asia, even though they are Buddhists and even though the monastery coordinates religious activities in each village. The myths, even when they are incomplete or forgotten, prolong their existence through precise rituals or diffuse beliefs. Some now have the flavor of tales, the tales of "whys and wherefores," in which explanations are given of the origins of animals, plants, and natural phenomena.

The corpus of myths about the birth of the serpents, for instance, has never been explored; nor has the entire corpus of legends about rice and betel. The origins of tigers, cats, and mosquitoes, which are narrated in the light of popular tales designed more to entertain than to teach, are nonetheless based on a mythology of nature and the gods. We shall see that some of these gods of Brahmanism, such as Gaṇeśa with his elephant head, have become "earth spirits."[4]

This initial overview of the myths of nature and the gods may give an idea of the richness of such a long tradition. The boundaries between what came from India and "what came from the ancestors" are nonexistent in the view of the villagers. Even those who are literate, although they know that an ancient culture came to them through Sanskrit and Pali texts, tend to integrate, assimilate, and supply local exegeses. And it is evident that the moon and the sun, the *devatās* of the sky and the sea, the animals and plants, the "lords" Śiva, Viṣṇu, Brahmā, and Indra, and many others are here the deities of the Khmer, Burmans, and Tai. Demiurges like Khun Borom and divine builders like Viṣṇukarman belong to the country where they have worked.

But even more native to the locality and children of the country are the earth spirits, the *nats* of Burma, the *phi* of the Tai, and the *neak-tā* of Cambodia.

S.T./g.h.

BIBLIOGRAPHY AND NOTES

1. PHOUVONG PHIMMASONE, "Cours de littérature lao," *Bulletin des Amis du royaume lao*, nos. 4 and 5 (1971), 49.
2. G. H. MONOD, *Légendes cambodgiennes que m'a contées le Gouverneur Khieu* (Paris 1922), 140–41.
3. Ibid., 141.
4. For origin legends, see the *Recueil d'histoires khmères anciennes, Prajum ryoen bren khmêr* (Phnom Penh 1967–72). In particular, see vols. 7 and 8.

Earth Spirits in Southeast Asia

1. The *Nats* of Burma

"The mountain, by definition, is a place that the *nats* enjoy."[1] This idea of the favorite dwelling place of the local spirits is consistent with one of the defining characteristics of Austroasiatic culture: everywhere the mountain is considered a sacred place. The mountain is inhabited by invisible beings. In Burma, the famous Mount Poppa is peopled by *nats*. But spirits also abound in the forest, the world of wonders.

If we try to classify the earth spirits of Burma, or *nats*, according to their habitat, we find that our classification corresponds both to the elements of nature—the aquatic, terrestrial, and heavenly worlds—and to the parts of the house. In other words, although the *nats* appear to be first the primal inhabitants of the land, they are also inside dwellings built by men. They are, moreover, sometimes inside the bodies of men.

The legal oath[2] enumerates all the possible habitats of *nats:* "rivers, streams, and brooks, lakes and torrents, waterfalls and whirlpools, forests and trees; the sun and the moon, stars and meteors, clouds, wind, fog, and mist." There seems to be a difference between the idea of the spirits of distant and imaginary heavenly worlds or the guardians of the cardinal points, and the very vital notion of the spirits of rivers and trees frequented by men, which are experienced as a living presence. Thus, the Burmans distinguish the "lords of the river," *khyong shang*, from the "lords of the mountain," *tong shang*.[3] Yet despite this distinction, it is maintained that some *nats* have multiple habitats. A *nat* may, for example, have its seat on a mountain, like Lady Min Mahagiri, and also be found in a house, hidden high on an interior post, with its name changed. Denise Bernot, citing U Hting Aung, offers historical reasons for the double habitat. "The ritual in the home has evolved as a successor to the ritual to the *nat* on the mountain (Min Mahagiri); on the mountain, it was the object of a popular cult from before the time of Anorahta (Aniruddha); under Kyanzittha (Cançitça), 1084–1112, the cult took on an official character and continued to flourish for five centuries. In our day, the Lord of the Great Mountain has become the Lord of the Great Mountain within the Home: *eindwing min Mahagiri.*"[4]

This fact certainly reinforces the impression of the omnipresence of *nats* among men. The earth spirits are essentially guardians of a god, and they appear as simultaneously good and evil, depending on the way in which they are—or are not—worshiped. However, some *nats* seem to be rather bad and dreadful, inclined to play tricks, and others are naturally good and "respectful of the law."

One belief, which seems to belong to another order and to evoke evil spirits rather than earth spirits, concerns the "sixty-six classes of *song*." The *song* are invisible beings, sometimes taking human form or revealing themselves in a gust of wind, who are by nature dangerous, capable of tormenting, devouring, and causing sickness and death.

Nats are protectors of the village, field, and home; they are "guardians of the sea," "guardians of the forest," and "guardians of the mountain." They also exercise their protective role over ancient temples and present-day monasteries.

It is when one learns about the "history" of each *nat* that their composite origin is seen. Indeed, some are men and women who lived in the past and died a violent death at the king's command. We know, for example, that king Kyanzittha had the architect of Pagan's Ananda Temple buried alive. He then became the *nat* guardian of the monument, "and this took place as late as the middle of the nineteenth century, during the construction of Mandalay, where the guardian spirit was represented by four stone statues, armed with clubs, one at each corner of the building."[5]

The blacksmith and his sister, who figure in the official enumeration of the Thirty-seven *Nats*, had a similar origin: they were burned alive on the order of the king, who feared the power of the blacksmith. And many examples can be found of nobles and generals promoted to the status of *nat* after being sent to a brutal and unjust death by their sovereign or after suffering unjust treatment.

Other *nats* have a totally different origin and derive from the Indian pantheon, like Kuvera, who is Kubera of India, the god of wealth, and the *nats* Wirupakkha, Wirulaka, Dattaratha, and Manimekhala, whose names, more or less transformed from Sanskrit, are found throughout all of Indianized Southeast Asia.

Finally, the very nature of the *nats* has been influenced by Theravada Buddhism, for some of them have become spirits as a result of accumulating exceptional merit while alive. The mythology of these *nats* also takes on the appearance of history: one of the *nats*, the protector of the city of Thaton, long ago received orders from two Buddhist missionaries to drive away evil spirits from the city. Another is called Shin Upago, a Burmese adaptation of the name of the celebrated disciple Upagupta. Having become a *nat*, or "little Buddha," he is believed to have vanquished and converted the demon

Māra. Still others are guardians of the relics of the Buddha.

In other words, the confusion or assimilation of the heroes of Buddhist legend with the *nats* vividly shows that the boundary between the Indian contribution and native beliefs is no more precise than the line between the gods and the divinities of nature.

The multiplicity of the *nats* can be surprising when it is learned that the Burmese speak freely of the "Thirty-seven," whom they name and consider historical beings. But the *nats* who figure in different lists are not always the same thirty-seven; thirty-seven is important as a mythic, theoretical number. Indra is the foremost of the Thirty-seven that gradually became established between the beginnings of the kingdom of Pagan and the seventeenth century, receiving their official and definitive consecration from the minister Myawadi at the end of the eighteenth century. But it was then no longer Indra who was recognized as their supreme chief but a Buddhist devotee named Çeja. The battle of King Anorahta in the eleventh century to maintain Buddhist orthodoxy, particularly through the destruction of *nat* shrines, remained inconclusive. For the sovereign himself finally decided to regroup the *nats* and entrust them to a patron subject to the law of the Dhamma, thus subjecting them to the Buddha all at once.

There is much to be said about the Burman and Mon earth spirits, some deriving from ancestral localities and some drawn from Brahmanic sources or integrated with Buddhism. The ideal number of thirty-seven schematizes an increasing multitude and seems to be an attempt to delimit and define it better. It seems that these hordes are sometimes arranged in a hierarchy in the image of Burmese or Thai society, according to their power and the size of the territory that they protect. But the hierarchy is also consistent with cosmogonic themes in which the levels of the heavens correspond to categories of supernatural beings superior or inferior to one another.

Whatever their origins, habitats, and names may be, how do these omnipresent *nats* intervene in human life? This is no longer a matter of mythology in the narrow sense, but of ritualized relationships. Yet there is a constant dialogue between men and *nats*, for men know that *nats* have the power to procure for them immediate happiness, health, wealth, and luck and to preserve them from dangers. The *nats* present both a higher organization of protection and the fearsome apparatus of a power that bestows favors and refuses them. Men depend partly on the attitudes of *nats*, who can be persuaded by invocations, prayers, offerings, dances, and feasts given in their honor. Mediums address themselves to *nats* by means of the trance, which marks the entrance into a relationship with an invisible being who is invited and questioned. During certain collective ceremonies, the villagers sacrifice animals and then gather in haunted places—the confluence of two rivers, for example—while singing piously of their desires: good rice crops, good health for the family, vows to "the Lady of the River" and the "Noble Lord of the Forest."

The modalities of these relationships are numerous, varying according to the place and the particular personalities of the different spirits. But it is clear that there is a system of close bonds, a familiar cooperation among occupants of the same territory, the prosperity of some dependent on the goodwill of others. Buddhism "dresses" the whole without contradicting it, *nats* involved in the same universe as men, men in turn able to become *nats* through the effect of their efforts or their merits.

2. The *Phi* of Thailand and Laos

Like their neighbors the Burmese *nats*, the *phi* of Thailand are innumerable and populate nature. In Laos, the *phi* intervene constantly in everyday life, to such an extent that few acts, individual or collective, are accomplished without them: they are feared, they are invoked, they are consulted.

Altars called *Ho Phi* are erected to them, either in the village or within the home. According to Nithan Khun Borom, "formerly each village had for all of its inhabitants a great *Ho Phi* dedicated to its tutelary spirit, and each villager had a little *Ho Phi* inside his house where he made offerings to the *phi* of his ancestors, to the *phi* who protected the house, and even to the evil spirits like the *phi mot* and the *phi pop*."[6]

For the Laotian author cited here, Vongkot Rattana, the term *phi* includes the spirits of the land, manes of the ancestors, and "spirits" in general, good and bad. Indeed, this term seems to encapsulate for him all nondivine supernatural beings, all beings that do not derive from the essence of Indra or Buddha. But though these beings do not share the nature of those divinities, they surpass them in strength and in "magic powers," and, at a level superior to men, direct the affairs of the territory.

It is striking how the commentators on Tai and Lao religion need to show the *phi* entering into the course of history. "Generation upon generation, this cult has been practiced from remote times, probably since the reign of Khoun Kan Hang, one of the first kings of Xieng Dong-Xieng Thong."[7] And in 1359 King Fa Ngum, the founder of the kingdom of Lan Xang, dismantled the cult of the *phi* and established Theravāda Buddhism as the official religion. But actually, "the majority put shrines in their homes to venerate the Buddha, while saving the *Ho Phi* to honor the spirits."[8]

Two hundred years later, in 1527, King Photisarath faced a religious situation in which the cult of the *phi* had assumed such importance that he felt obliged to interfere: by royal ordinance he transformed the shrines, the *ho*, into dwellings for *uposat*, that is, for those who lived according to the precepts and intended to become monks.

But no steps taken have ever prevailed against the *phi*. They have continued to be present and to manifest themselves not only in the country and the villages but also among princes, at the court, and within monastery walls. *Ho* were constructed in gardens, notably in the palace park of the crown prince at Luang Prabang, in the mountains, at the confluence of rivers, in certain forested areas, at the borders of the country, and finally on land belonging to Buddhist monasteries.

Far from having disappeared or weakened after the royal ordinance of the sixteenth century, the cult of the *phi* was made official, since the governor of every province received each year a sum of silver from the royal treasury, silver that he was to distribute to the keepers of the altars to organize a great annual offering ceremony on the eighth day of the waxing moon of the seventh month. Once every three years a buffalo was offered to the spirits, probably a replacement for human sacrifice.

Thus, according to Georges Condominas, "in the cult of the *phi* one is dealing with an ancient Tai animist base enriched with the cults of the first proto-Indo-Chinese inhabitants and assimilated by their conquerors."[9]

The principal characteristic of the *phi* is that they are the masters and guardians of the soil. Or more precisely, this significance of the term shows most clearly their specific role and how they are connected to the animist religion that existed before Buddhism. The *phi muang* is the one who watches over the collectivity and is its ageless master. The *phi ban* is the village *phi*, also called *phi laksa ban*, that is, "the one who guards the village," or *phi hak ban*, "the one who loves the village." In these invisible characters, materialized through their *ho*, the sacred is concentrated in its chthonic aspect.

In Tai country the spirits of the land seem never to have been the object of systematization; nor were they reduced to an enumeration that ideally limited their number and let them be represented as historical persons. But each of them has his own mythology, involving pseudohistorical facts, or "historical legends," and most of the time a hierarchy can be discerned among them. Given the abundance of variants, we must limit ourselves to two examples, one from Laos and the other from Thailand.

The first example is the "spirits of salt" studied by Charles Archaimbault.[10] The author takes us to Ban Bo, about sixty miles north of Vientiane, where there are salt pits that the villagers exploit. The layer of salt water that feeds them is pumped out and put into great heating vats where it is brought to a boil. After the water has evaporated, the salt is collected and packed. In the village of Ban Bo there is a *ho* perched on piles above the pits: this is the *Ho Bo*, the dwelling of the guardian spirits and protectors of the salt works.

As in all places thus guarded by invisible masters, a series of taboos governs comings and goings, indeed, the very behavior of the men who settle there. The transgression of these taboos entails punishment by the *phi* and always necessitates rites of propitiation—offerings performed through the *cam*, the guardian and servant of the spirits.

Charles Archaimbault stresses the fact that the *phi* of the salt are strongly hierarchized, and that they form a society whose structure, though schematic, faithfully reflects that of the ancient royal administration: at its head presides Cao P'a Satt'ong, the monarch of the spirits of the salt. Serving directly under him are the viceroy P'ia Ong and his assistant P'ia O. These dignitaries transmit the orders of the king to the two "chiefs of the march," Ai Dan S'ai and Ai Dan K'ua. "Important works" are finally entrusted to the executioners Bak Ham and Bak K'am.[11]

We thus see an organization of the invisible, a supernatural administration of a territory exploited by men with the permission of its real masters, the *phi*. All the relationships between the spirits and the villagers illuminate both this subordination of men to a powerful order beyond them and the terms of a contract continually renewed by rituals and festivals, especially the festival called Boun Teto Ti-K'i. During this festival, where formerly a ball game known as *ti k'i*[12] was played, the important people of the village invited the spirits to be present at the rite and prepared resting places, water jugs, and betel for them. The people made offerings to the *phi* while beseeching them to protect the community: "We ask you to keep us in good health! Protect all the residents, all the traders!" The days that followed saw individual offerings accompanied by vows, then the final confrontation of two ball teams, the villagers' team and the spirits' team, the latter always emerging victorious: "Through the victory of the priestly clan, the Ti K'i confirms a previous right. It ratifies the property rights of the spirit, who long before the exploitation of the pits had already been in possession of them; the villagers' rights on the land were only rights acquired later and maintained through the benevolence of the spirit."[13]

A second type of Tai spirit is modeled on the mythic person of a king who has become a *phi:* an actual king, because we are speaking of Somdet Phra Chao Taksin, king of Thonburi after the fall of Ayutthaya to Siam in 1767, before the foundation of Bangkok in 1782. Nothing is more normal than that this sovereign should be considered a hero of spiritual renewal after the destruction of the prestigious capital by the Burmans. But King Taksin has entered into the mythology, as Jacqueline de Fels has ably shown in a recent thesis.[14] On the day that his memorial was inaugurated in Thonburi in April 1954, the Brahmans of the court performed the ceremony "inviting the soul" of the king to be present. Everywhere sanctuaries were set up and offerings of flowers were piled up at the foot of his image. Whatever the historical accounts of his death—madness, assassination, plots—King Taksin plays a part in the religious life of the Thai: "Even though the image before which they prostrate themselves most often represents the king of Thonburi in his martial aspect, it is not so much the defender of the fatherland that they now invoke as a protector who is their own, whose power can help them in their everyday life."[15]

The notion of the lord of a temporal realm has given way to that of a *phi muang*, the tutelary spirit of the kingdom: "the guardian of a land of which he is still the sovereign, he always insures its defense. He can bring good fortune and long life to everything living there—men, animals, and plants—while remaining the stern master who punishes offenses. And many residents of Thailand today place themselves under the protection of this *phi muang*."[16] In this respect they differ little from the residents of the thirteenth-century capital city of Sukhothai. In his celebrated inscription, King Rama Kamheng, while placing all the inhabitants of his kingdom "under the law of the Buddha," did not hesitate to evoke the tutelary spirit of the *muang*, "superior to all the spirits of the country. If the prince who is sovereign over the Muong Sukhot'ai offers him proper worship and presents ritual offerings to him, then the land is stable and prospers; but if he does not offer him the prescribed worship and does not present him with ritual offerings, then the spirit of the hill will no longer protect or respect the country that is falling into decay."[17] Georges Coedès, who cites this passage, makes it clear that it refers to the spirit "P'ra Khap'ung," Lord of the Summit: "This name also evokes that of the Nat or Burman spirit Mahāgiri, who lives on Mount Poppa, the holy mountain located to the southeast of Pagan."[18]

We will see comparable phenomena illustrated as we move into the Khmer domain.

3. The Cambodian *Neak-tā*

The belief in the existence of "earth spirits" or "spirits of the soil" is common to all the people of Cambodia, whether they are from towns, villages, or the countryside. Everywhere, the presence of a *neak-tā* is marked by a mixture of respectful fear and familiarity.

When we try to define the characteristic traits of the many spirits, we find a number of apparently incoherent, indeed contradictory, facts. The term *neak-tā*, sometimes written *ana'k-tā*, is recognized and understood all over the country, and means "someone, a certain individual" (*neak* or *ana'k*), "old" (*tā*). The term *tā*, moreover, is more a term of address than an epithet, and connotes familiarity, as when we say "Uncle."

But this common usage denotes individuals who can appear very different from one another. Some have a per-

Guardian *nats* in the precincts of the pagoda of Schwezigon. Burma, valley of the Irrawaddy-Nyaung-U. Paris, Musée de l'Homme collection. Photo S. Karpelès.

(Above right) Statues of *nats* in the precincts of the *Shwe Dagon*. Burma, Rangoon. Paris, Musée de l'Homme collection. Photo S. Karpelès.

sonal name, a name of their own, while others are referred to only as *neak-tā* or *lok cā's*, "old gentlemen"; some are unique, while others appear in a group; some seem to "govern" a territory and so are found in an organized, hierarchical system, while others, who live in a tree or an abandoned place, seem to have ill-defined relationships with the inhabitants of the region. Finally, some spirits are materialized in an object that is somehow permanent—a rock, a statue, or a piece of a statue—while others, more numerous, are content to be present invisibly, "dwelling" in a tree, on a hillock, in a termite hill, in a body of water or a confluence of waters—marked only by the offerings placed near their supposed habitat.

One major fact, however, remains constant: the essentially tutelary role of the spirit. Whether he is territorial or merely local, the spirit watches over, guards, and protects—as long as he is offered the appropriate worship. Here again there is an invisible tutelary organization that must be conciliated by honoring it with the customary ritual.

We have already noted that certain spirits of the land have their own names. Most of the time the name is borrowed from the place where they live, a mountain, for example, a rice field, a pond, or a particular tree: *neak-tā* of Angkor Borei (Nagara Puri), *neak-tā* of Phnom Chisor, *neak-tā* Ben of Kompon Cham, *neak-tā* of Phnom, a sacred hill in Phnom Penh. Other *neak-tā*, in addition to the term that identifies their locality, carry another designation: such is the case with the protecting *neak-tā* of the city of Pursat, south of the Great Lake, who is characterized as *neak-tā khlang muang Bodhisat*, that is, "spirit center of the province of Pursat." In other places too, the Thai word for "territory," or "province," *muang*, replaces the corresponding Khmer term, *sruk*. It is interesting that the tutelary spirit is regarded as the "center" of the territory that it protects and "governs." It is situated there within an order of cosmogonic thought well attested in

Nats at the east entrance to the temple of Thatbyinnyu. Burma, valley of the Irrawaddy. Paris, Musée de l'Homme collection. Photo S. Karpelès.

India and in the Indianized domain: the mountain is the center and the axis of the world, the seat of the divinity. We know that in Cambodia, during the centuries of Angkorian power—the ninth to the thirteenth centuries A.D.—the idea of the temple-mountain developed, simultaneously the seat of the "patron" god of the reigning king and the center of the capital. Similarly, the *neak-tā* "center of the province," *khlang muang,* makes use of the notion (unless he was the one who originated it) of a power fixed at the center, at the very axis of a particular territory, a province, a city, a hamlet—or the world.

A second notion appears in the names given to spirits: the notion of age and antiquity, already included in the word *tā*. Some spirits are called *cā's sruk,* "the old one of the country," a name that suggests two orders of questions: Are local spirits regarded as the former inhabitants of the Khmer country, the first to have governed it, in prehistory? And what are the relations that unite the *neak-tā* with the dead? The answers to these two questions are far from being settled.

Indeed, although certain spirits seem to have been established at a particular place since time immemorial, many others, by contrast, have a history that places them in a temporal context and makes them a type of "ancient dead." This is true for the *neak-tā khlang muang* of Pursat, who is certainly the most universally known to Cambodians: "Toward the end of the sixteenth century, King Cei Cedsda'r found himself in Bantay Cei, the Citadel of Victory, several miles from the present-day city of Pursat. The war against the Siamese was raging, and with the rout of the Cambodian troops the king had been placed in great danger. It was then that the governor of Pursat decided to sacrifice himself. He had a pit dug, in which he placed all sorts of weapons. Then, after saying his prayers, he jumped into it; he was followed by his wife, who did not want to survive him. The pit was then immediately filled in. A few days later, the Siamese laid siege to the citadel. But a great noise filled the night, and the Siamese fell like flies, killed by a disease: this was the work of troops of ghosts that the governor had gone to search for in the kingdom of the shades in order to save Cambodia."[19] Since then, every year people commemorate the sacrifice of the former governor who became the tutelary spirit of Pursat.

Some *neak-tā* are said to be dead children; others, men who died a violent death, like the *neak-tā* of Khone islet.

In another category—if indeed it is right, as it is convenient, to speak here of categories—are the *neak-tā* who have the names of Brahmanic divinities. The most striking of these is the *neak-tā* Gaṇeśa, the protector of diverse *sruk* of Cambodia. In the Brahmanic mythology of India, Gaṇeśa is the son of the god Śiva and the goddess Pārvatī. We know that he has the head of an elephant, that he is frequently represented together with a rat, and that he holds a pot of honey into which he dips his trunk. In India, Nepal, and Sri Lanka, he is the god of skill, intelligence, cleverness, and knowledge. In Cambodia he has become a tutelary *neak-tā,* assimilated to the land, born of the Khmer patrimony. Here is an example of the integration of a Brahmanic divinity into the mythological pantheon of the country. This example is by no means isolated. But instead of bearing a recognizably Indian name, the spirit is called by an epithet that makes it possible

(Right) *Phi* tree (a sacred tree covered by *ex-votos* and offerings) on a village street. Thailand, Krung Thep (Bangkok). Paris, Musée de l'Homme collection. Photo G. Fouquet.

Two spirits of the *nā'k-tā*. A village altar. Cambodia, near Angkor, on the Banteay Shrérï trail.

to identify him with one or another Indian divinity. Thus the *neak-tā kraham ga,* the "rednecked" spirit, to cite only one, seems to be Śiva himself, often evoked in Indian hymns by the deep color of his neck. In other cases, the original name is masked by a distortion, on which a popular etymology has been superimposed: the spirit Me Sar of Ba Phnom is known as the "white chief" or the "white mother," but it is more likely that its name results from the contraction of one of the names of the goddess Durgā, the wife of Śiva: that is, the destroyer of the buffalo demon, Mahiṣāsura.

These names, of forgotten Brahmanic origin, do not imply that the spirits in question correspond in their personalities, actions, or final appearance to the divinities whose patronymics they have received. But we have good reason to believe that "where they are found there were once temples at which these divinities were honored. Very often, moreover, we see in the hut of a *neak-tā* fragments of ancient statues that prove the existence of temples that have disappeared."[20]

Popular stories depict spirits who have no name but "the *neak-tā* of the village," usually described as "very powerful." Often their dwelling places—huts, "pagodas," or trees—are alluded to, and sometimes also their animal familiar, like the crocodile of the story of Suk the Sweet and Suk the Wicked,[21] a creature who lived nestled under his master's house, next to the river. The story of the man who dug up crabs presents a picture of a special place: the earth under the timbers of the foundation of the pagoda of the *neak-tā,* where the hero of the story, "marked" from the beginning by good luck deriving from his past merits, each day dug up crabs that he sold to make his living.[22]

Finally, still other spirits demand attention: those called by nicknames that are often crude, like *ā'c chkē,* "dog excrement," or *prahok,* "fish sauce." A termite hill that grows on top of the uncremated corpse of someone who died a violent death is often both the origin of these spirits and their place of residence.

Whatever they are named, it is clear that the *neak-tā* are everywhere intensely alive: they live together with men in a way that is simultaneously ancestral and immediate, since one event or another can lead to the birth of a new *neak-tā.* It is enough to find some material support—a rock, a newly discovered statue, a termite hill—to invite a wandering spirit to settle there permanently and thus to become the guardian and protector of the place. And the tutelary function, though constantly attested, shows a number of variants.

Some *neak-tā* are thought to be givers of rain, like the Traṅol spirit of Prei Kra-bas. Others are used to find lost livestock. They are invoked in case there are animal diseases, epidemics, and collective calamities. According to oral traditions, the rites performed in their honor once used to include blood sacrifices, in certain cases human sacrifices, often replaced by sacrifices of buffaloes. The *neak-tā* Krol of Kompong Thom seems to have received human victims until about 1904. In other cases the presence of the spirit is celebrated with dances regarded as "fertility dances": songs and dances for children, livestock, rain, health, abundance, and prosperity. The women of the village sometimes mime a sexual union with the stone that represents the *neak-tā.* Firecrackers, the shooting of guns, and offerings of vegetables, cloth, and money accompany these cults, which vary from place to place. Everywhere, however, the monks of the Buddhist monastery of the place participate, to "Buddhicize" the ceremony and because the coexistence of the earth spirits with Buddhism is always accepted and experienced without friction. Similarly, the head of the province, representing

The *nā'k-tā* (temple of the earth spirit; a small straw hut); in the foreground, a pile of ritual stones. Cambodia, province of Kratie, Sambok. Paris, Musée de l'Homme collection. Photo J. Dournes.

political authority, formerly royal authority and divine right, is present at the rite in honor of the *neak-tā.* Integrated into the temporal administrative system, he comes to give his supernatural homologue the homage that consecrates the harmony between the two orders of power.

Finally, the *neak-tā* sometimes speak, to give oracles through the mouths of *rūp,* "possessed persons," generally women, who temporarily receive the *neak-tā* into themselves. The word *rūp,* from the Sanskrit *rūpa,* "form," denotes the medium as well as an apparition or concrete image of the spirit.

The fact that all Cambodia is inhabited by *neak-tā* only confirms the permanence of the Austroasiatic Mon-Khmer substratum, as much among the Khmer majority as among the minority groups of the forests and mountains. But the two most striking characteristics of this "organization of protection" are, first, its coexistence with Buddhism—the pagodas of the *neak-tā* within the walls of monasteries, the monks reciting prayers at festivals of the *nā'k-tā*—and, second, its hierarchical aspect.

A spirit is more or less powerful according to the importance of its territory. A city, for example, may have other spirits subordinate to the protecting spirit, who are thought of as "ministers" or are given the military title of *sena.* One might ask if the tutelary *neak-tā* of the city or province are not sometimes somehow assimilated to the guardian spirits of doors, or to the guardians of the directions of space, which derive from Indianized mythology. But the *neak-tā* are not satisfied with those places: the bonds that unite them with human society are ceaselessly put into question, tightened or relaxed, according to events and to how men honor them. A system of gift and countergift is evident here, and the contract between the invisible society and the country's inhabitants—the one as real as the other—is constantly renewed, according to the norms and requirements of territorial and collective life.

At the end of this general review of the earth spirits of Burma, Thailand, and the Mon-Khmer country, it is easy to note the repetitions and parallelisms, as well as the identical character of the fundamental schemata of the myths and the rituals that concern them. All the spirits—masters of the earth, ancestral guardians, the undisputed owners of the land—dispense wealth on condition of being served. They speak and heal through mediums, or punish and torment. They represent a hierarchy superimposed upon the human hierarchy. But all of them are also subject to Buddhist law, and whether they have Indra or Çeja for their mythic sovereign does not change the fact that they constitute part of an environment profoundly marked by Theravada Buddhism. The "syncretism" that joins their cult to the practice of Buddhist observances—often to the point of making them inseparable—should not be interpreted exclusively as a one-way influence of Buddhism on the ancient religion. For in its conception of the world and in its vision of creatures, Buddhism itself gives the spirits and supernatural beings a place. This is a constant theme of Buddhist cosmogonies—especially of the Traibhūmi or Trai Phum, one of the most celebrated texts of the "explication of the world" in Southeast Asia.

S.T./d.g.

BIBLIOGRAPHY AND NOTES

1. D. BERNOT, "Les Nat de Birmanie," p. 309 in *Génies, anges et démons* (Paris 1971), 297–341.

2. Cited by D. BERNOT, "Les Nat de Birmanie," 307–8; see R. C. TEMPLE, *The Thirty Seven Nats: A Phase of Spirit-Worship Prevailing in Burma* (London 1906).

3. D. BERNOT, "Les Nat de Birmanie," 309, note 10.

4. Ibid., 309–10.

5. Ibid., 311.

6. R. VONGKOT, "Les rites du culte des Phi, au Ho Vang-Na à Luang-Prabang," *Bulletin des Amis du royaume lao* 6, 2 (1971): 95.

7. Ibid., 95.

8. Ibid.

9. G. CONDOMINAS, "Notes sur le bouddhisme populaire en milieu rural lao," *Archives de sociologie des religions* 25, 1 (1968): 85.

10. CH. ARCHAIMBAULT, "Une cérémonie en l'honneur des génies de la mine de sel de Ban Bo (Moyen Laos) (Contribution à l'étude du jeu de Ti-K'i)," *BEFEO* 48, 1 (1956); cited here from the same article reprinted in *Structures religieuses lao (rites et mythes)*, Documents pour le Laos (Vientiane 1973), 2:1–16, plates 6–9.

11. Op. cit., 3.

12. See P. DE LÉVY, "Ti-khi: Un jeu de mail rituel au Laos," *Annuaire de l'École pratique des Hautes Études, Sciences religieuses* (1952–53), 3–15.

13. ARCHAIMBAULT, "Une cérémonie en l'honneur des génies de la mine de sel de Ban Bo," 78.

14. J. DE FELS, *Somdet Phra Chao Tak Sin Maharat, le roi de Thonburi*, 2 vols. (diss., Paris 1976).

15. Ibid., 2:360.

16. Ibid., 2:361.

17. G. COEDÈS, *Les États hindouisés d'Indochine et d'Indonésie* (Paris 1964), 377–78.

18. Ibid., 377, note 2.

19. *Cérémonies des Douze Mois, fêtes annuelles cambodgiennes*, Commission des moeurs et coutumes du Cambodge (Phnom Penh n.d.), 29.

20. Ibid., 27.

21. F. MARTINI and S. BERNARD, *Contes populaires inédits du Cambodge* (Paris 1946), 138.

22. Ibid., 106.

Southeast Asian Myths and Rituals of the Moon

From the very first studies of lunar myths in Southeast Asia, it was evident that local ideas were interwoven with legends that came from India and China. In the context of this theme, the deeply composite character of the tradition, as it is received, transmitted, and lived, appeared with sudden brilliance.

In India, the moon is generally a male deity. The Vedic hymns occasionally give the moon the name of Soma, which is otherwise usually the name of the sacred plant that allows communication with the divine. The Brahmanic legends refer to the marriage of this moon god with a daughter of the sun. In China, myths evoke the moon as a female being. But in a country like Cambodia, it seems that both sexes are attributed to the moon, prevailing alternately. Thus, sometimes male, sometimes female, it is Lord Moon (Braḥ Chan), Lord Month (Braḥ Khê), or the deified month of the lunar calendar, with whom an earthly girl may fall in love; or it may be Somā, in the feminine, identified with the Nāgī, the serpent-woman, daughter of the wet and the cold, the ophidian wife of the Brahman Kaundinya, according to the Sanskrit tradition of the founding of the kingdom of Funan, or the wife of Prince Braḥ Thoṅ, the sun king and founder of the first Khmer dynasty, according to the oral tradition.

The union of lunar princesses and solar princes is the favorite theme of the dynastic legends of ancient Cambodia. The legend of the Nāgī Somā was told countless times, inscribed on stone, and narrated in the Annals. Whether it is the Brahman Kaundinya who came from India or Prince Braḥ Thoṅ, one of them meets at the seashore the daughter of the king of the Nāgas, the sovereign of the country and the lord of the land. He marries her and "founds a royal race." It is likely that the salutations to the moon that used to be celebrated at the royal palace in Phnom Penh symbolized a mystical marriage between the solar prince and the stars of the night. Each year, according to the thirteenth-century Chinese chronicler Chou Ta-kuan, the king of Angkor united with a symbolic Nāgī, thus reviving the alliance of the origins.

It is thus evident that the lunar myth, included here in the dynastic legends, is complex, since it comes to be associated with the myth of the serpent-woman, and thus with the myth of the Nāgas, half-human, half-snake, who own the land. The lunar myth is also integrated into the dualist system which opposes sun and moon, dry and damp, bird and snake, and which can be traced throughout the mythico-social universe of ancient Cambodia in conjunction with other complementary oppositions.

But the moon has been given other names. The name of Somā, made feminine by the lengthening of the final vowel of the original Indian noun Soma, may represent a scholarly and royal tradition, probably introduced by the Brahmans. In orally transmitted legends one almost always finds the name Chan, which comes from the Sanskrit *candra,* "moon." The Lord Braḥ Chan sits on his throne in heaven, where he forms a couple with the sun. A legend widespread in Cambodia tells the story of Bimān Chan, whose name means "sojourn of the moon." The story refers to the love that unites the Lord Braḥ Chan of the sky with a young girl from earth, Bimān Chan, whom he takes with him to the firmament.

The sequel to the story shows the interweaving of other themes, notably that of beheading. Badly advised by the other two wives of the Lord Moon, Bimān Chan asks her husband to carry her away higher and higher into the sky. But the wind blows hard in the high altitude and tears off the young woman's head, which falls into the pond of a monastery, while the body continues to live in the sky. Soon the head is picked up and placed before the Buddha of the pagoda. Then, after many episodes, notably the restoration of the body, the young woman becomes Bimān Chan again and marries an earthly prince, Suryavaṅ, whose name means "of the race of the sun."

These variations on the luminous couples, mixing the divine, the astral, and the royal, evoke the distant echo of the Vedic hymns to the moon and the sun, even while the Buddha appears in them. The rural tradition first emphasizes the beneficent role of the moon, male or female, depending on the story. The moon scatters the rain, which in turn fertilizes the rice fields. It marks the passing of time, dividing the month into the "bright fortnight" and the "dark fortnight." Between the two, the full moon marks the high point of good fortune, when the fates are in balance. The observation of the moon develops into a science of prediction, into the reading of the mysteries of germination, prosperity, and calamities. Treatises on divination copy this language throughout all the countries of Southeast Asia.

The moon is light and movement, as the Khmer represent it: "The moon takes upon herself the task of lighting the world during the night and of safeguarding human lives as best she can. She mounts a chariot of precious stones, covered on the outside with a layer of silver. The chariot is forty-nine *yojanas*[1] in length. The moon lights the three worlds. From any one of the four cardinal points, the moon projects her light for a distance of at least nine hundred thousand *yojanas.* The moon moves around the three worlds ceaselessly, all through the night. Together with the sun, she revolves around Mount Somer;[2] she performs the *pradakshina.* Her journey is less rapid than the sun's. From time to time, one overtakes the other, and then the sun passes his companion. When the moon disappears, the sun comes out, and when the sun disappears, the moon comes out. The two of them sustain the life of humanity."[3]

Throughout the oral narratives, it appears that most of the time the moon and the sun had human forms before becoming the heavenly bodies of the day and the night. One legend specifically states that the sun, fire, thunder, wind, rain, the star Rāhu, and the moon were seven brothers, the moon being the youngest of them all. Another legend depicts the sun, the moon, and Rāhu as three brothers; Rāhu became the monster of eclipses, the one who swallows the sun or the moon.

The myths of eclipses, in Thailand as well as in Laos and Cambodia, always show Rāhu swallowing the moon in his enormous mouth, which has only an upper jaw, from either unquenchable anger or brotherly affection. In any case, eclipses are terrifying and inspire taboos and propitiations.

The god Surya, the sun, on a ceremonial fan from Thailand. Paris, Musée de l'Homme collection. Photo Destable.

Finally, it is essential to note similar myths that are inseparable from royal or rural rituals. The ceremonies at Angkor are never described in detail. But the festivals of greeting the moon, synchronized with the agrarian cycle, continue to thrive even today. In about 1850, King Ang Duang lent all his prestige to the great ritual that followed immediately after the Festival of the Waters, in October-November, that is, during the eighth month of an ordinary year or the ninth month of an intercalary year. The king would greet the stars at the royal palace to the sound of marine shells. Installed in his floating house connected to the bank by a pontoon, he could contemplate the reflection of the rays on the surface of the waters of Four Arms at Phnom Penh. A *baku,* that is, a descendant of Brahmanic priests of older times, would come to present him with lustral water in a shell inlaid with gold, enameled in various colors, and set in a golden bowl. The king would wet his palms, lift his hands to the moon, moisten his face, contemplate, pay homage, and then sprinkle the royal children, using a leaf from the *bilva* tree (*Aegle marmelos*). The Buddhist monks were invited to dine in the throne room, thus marking the presence of Buddhism at the very heart of these rituals, which are a part of both the Brahmanic tradition and the agrarian cycle.

In the countryside, on the village squares or more often in the courtyards of monasteries, the festival included the offering of new rice that was lightly roasted and crushed with a pestle, the construction of temporary pavilions, and the burning of candles and incense when the moon was at its zenith. From the drops of wax that fell onto the banana leaves that were arranged below, one could predict the abundance or shortage of rainfall, and from the shapes of the spots formed by the wax, one could see revelations of the health of men and animals and the prosperity of the country: "O Braḥ Chan, great, magnificent, proud, and splendid, more beautiful than a diamond, clearer than crystal, O Braḥ Chan, I salute you!" Variants from village to village would have one constant: the presence of Buddhist priests, who would chant the Chanda Parittam, a prayer in Pali to the glory of the moon. It is not uncommon in some places to see them sprinkle the soil of the monastery, thus symbolizing the fertilizing rain.

Whether the king sprinkles his children, the monks sprinkle the ground, or country people offer or scatter rice or drip candle wax, the essential meaning of these rituals is clearly to perform a fertility rite, in which the moon and water are closely associated.

Finally, another cycle is worth noting. Buddhist Southeast Asia has explained the festival of greeting the moon by reference to the Jātakas, the tales of the Buddha's former lives. According to the *Sasa-jātaka*, in one of his former lives the Buddha was reincarnated in the form of a hare and from compassion and "extreme charity," he gave his flesh to a famished traveler. Since then, the image of the hare, often called the "rabbit of the moon" in popular stories and traditions, seems to be imprinted on the lunar disk, where he can be distinguished on clear nights.

Thus, from dynastic legends to village rites and Buddhist tales, the myth of the moon unfolds its rich and complex motifs, through which we can read a whole religious history that is closely tied to social behavior.

S.T./g.h.

BIBLIOGRAPHY AND NOTES

1. The measurement of the itinerary, corresponding to about two geographical miles, would be a little less than three kilometers.
2. Mount Meru of Indian cosmogony, center of the universe, became Sumeru, Somer, or Men, in Southeast Asia.

3. E. PORÉE-MASPERO and S. BERNARD-THIERRY, "La lune, croyances et rites du Cambodge," 264–65, in *La lune, mythes et rites* (Paris 1962), 263–87 *(coll. Sources Orientales, 6).*

The Acculturation of the Divinities of Hinduism in Southeast Asia

I. The Earth

We have studied several nature myths. But the Southeast Asian mythology of nature involves many other characters as well. A particularly important one is the Earth, who, under the name of Dharaṇī or Braḥ Dhar(a)ni (pronounced Thorani), appears as a young woman kneeling, twisting her long hair in both hands. We know that the goddess Earth is a figure in the Indian epics. The great Vedic hymns celebrate her under the name of Aditi, bearer of all plants and animals, mother of all beings. At the end of the Sanskrit *Rāmāyaṇa*, the Earth comes to find Sītā, the wife of Rāma, who was born from a furrow, and swallows Sītā up in her depths while Rāma rises to heaven. In Buddhist legend, the Earth rises up to engulf the armies of Māra the tempter, who is trying to turn the Buddha away from his meditations. And this is the aspect under which Southeast Asia has adopted this essentially benevolent goddess: from the coil of hair she twists an abundant river flows. Her name of Dharaṇī, "she who bears," or who supports, comes from the Sanskrit, but in Southeast Asia her legend makes her an accomplice of the Buddha in his search for supreme Enlightenment. The bronze casters, the image makers of Thailand, Burma, Laos, and Cambodia, have everywhere represented her as a lithe and smiling young woman, helpful and auspicious.

II. The Devatās

In a general way, nature is populated with divinities, *devatās*, a word whose pronunciation varies from country to country, *thēvoda, debta,* etc. These supernatural beings must not be confused with the earth spirits who have been discussed already. They constitute a pantheon originally from India, but in some sense "domesticated" or acculturated.

From the great god Brahma, ordinarily considered a single being, there arose in Southeast Asia a multitude of *brahmas* or *prohms*, immaterial beings inhabiting the various celestial levels. They are not inaccessible, in the sense that they are included in the system of transmigration and are part of the "wheel of existence." In other words, the *prohms* are not reincarnations, since they are disembodied, but the new condition of beings who, in an earlier life, were men or animals.

The *devatās* of the sky, the clouds, the sea, and the trees are usually anonymous, with the exception of certain goddesses, fairies, or nymphs such as, for example, Manimekhala, associated with the myths of the sea and lightning, and Deb Pranam, a divinity portrayed in a praying position, hands joined to make the *añjali* greeting in homage to Buddha. We could also cite Mera, called an *apsara*, a celestial dancer, who in one of the dynastic traditions of Cambodia is supposed to have married the ascetic Kambu to found the kingdom of the Kambuja.

In fact, nearly all the mythological characters of Indian legend have passed into Southeast Asia: *kinnaris*, bird-women who come to frolic on earth, on the edges of lakes, in forest clearings, and who sometimes marry ordinary humans; *gandharvas*, celestial musicians; *yakṣas*, ogre-like beings endowed with remarkable powers like flying or walking on the sea; above all, the *nāgas* and *nāgīs*, ophidian beings, half-human, half-serpent, who range over almost all of southern Asia, and who belong both to the Indian heritage and to indigenous belief. The *nāgas* are regarded as the owners of the land, and their kings have different names depending on the text and the place: Bhuvajan, Bhujon, dwelling in the deep lakes of the kingdom of Patala; or Krun Bāli, the great serpent living underground, who must be propitiated whenever a house is built.

Bird-woman, or *kinnari*, from the shadow theater of Thailand. Paris, Musée de l'Homme collection.

Two half-woman–half-bird creatures, or *kinnari*. Temple of the dawn, or "Vatarun." Thailand, Krung Thep (Bangkok). Paris, Musée de l'Homme collection. Photo Pourcher.

Besides this divine multitude, who, according to the tales and legends, are very familiar and very close to humans, some of the great gods of Brahmanism have also had remarkable careers in Southeast Asia.

III. The Great Gods of Brahmanism: Śiva, Viṣṇu, and Indra

We know that the ancient kingdoms of Angkor, Champa, and Śrivijaya consecrated most of their major sanctuaries to the gods Śiva and Viṣṇu. Śiva the creator, the powerful god, was represented both inside and outside the temples in the form of a linga, a more or less realistic or ornamented phallic symbol. The kings who built the temples were fused with him after their deaths in a ritual of apotheosis, and during their lives were identified with his power, both divine and royal, as king of the gods, *devarāja,* interpreted as "god-king."

Śiva survived after the Hinduized monarchies ended. Today one can still see the linga, decorated with garlands of flowers, on the edges of the Buddhist stupas of certain pagodas in Thailand. In Cambodian tales he is called "the Lord," Braḥ Iśvara, Braḥ Isūr, and he figures in the origin myths of the creation of animals. He also appears, but in the aspect of his wife Umā, on the ritual candlesticks of Cambodia, small bronze leaves called *babil,* "popil," used especially in marriage rites. The popil with its lighted candle is supposed to originate in the vulva of Umā and the phallus of Śiva, and thus continues the great Indian mythological theme of the linga and the yoni, the myth of fertilizing creation and of the alliance that generates prosperity.

As for the god Viṣṇu, to whom the temple of Angkor Wat is dedicated and whose name of glory was taken by the king Sūryavarman II, he is associated with epic themes drawn from the *Viṣṇupurāṇa* and the *Bhāgavatapurāṇa.* One of these themes is illustrated in one of the famous bas-reliefs of Angkor Wat, that of the Churning of the Ocean. "It is probably the Vaiṣṇava character of the myth that made it one of the favorite motifs of the Khmers, among whom the cult of Viṣṇu seems always to have been extremely popular, even during periods when Śaivism was preponderant" (Madeleine Giteau, 1951).

Viṣṇu, the god of order, permanence, and stability, who in India inspired particular movements of devotion and whose cult has spread throughout continental and insular Southeast Asia, is assimilated to the protecting king, the guardian of order. The work of the sovereign is set in parallel with the churning of the ocean of milk. Let us here briefly summarize the main myth. Exhausted by their constant battle against the *asura* demons, the gods, *devas,* come to ask Viṣṇu, also

Public reading of the Koran in Parit Mukuasang, Johore state, Malaysia. Photo Christian Pelras.

The cover of a modern Javanese work on the history of Rama with a representation of a *kayon* or *ganungan.* This accessory from the shadow theater is sometimes considered a symbol of both the "cosmic mountain" and the "tree of life."

are then supposed (or whose children are supposed) to descend to the intermediate world. The descent sometimes corresponds to the establishment of the world as an inhabitable territory, which is often shown as emerging from the primordial waters or as floating on them; this is followed more or less directly by an episode which accounts for the break in physical relations between the human world and spiritual worlds.

b. It is usually soon after the descent of the first men onto the earth that the myths recount the appearance of death and the origin of food plants.

Toichi Mabuchi gave evidence of the existence in insular Southeast Asia of three types of myths, of which two are particularly well represented in Malaysia:

—Myths of the first type tell of the celestial origin of food plants that may either have been produced at the same time as men (Batak, Toraja) or received as a gift (Ifugao, western Toraja, Ceram, Sumba, Tetun, Bali), or stolen (western Toraja, Minahasa, Ngaju).

—The second type is the one according to which food plants come from the body of a hero, and especially that of a heroine, whose death is often the first death in this world, whether the person dies naturally (Bugis, Sumba), or is killed (Banggai, Tempasuk, Ceram, Adonara), or has voluntarily sacrificed himself (Java, Sunda) or has been allowed to sacrifice (western Toraja, Tetun, Atoni, Sika, Lamaholat, Adonara, Alor).

—The third type, according to which the cultivated plants were taken or received from the lower world, is rarely found in Malaysia. Mabuchi gives only one example of this, from Kei. In fact, this type only appears in the area in which myths of the second type are more strongly represented, i.e., in eastern Indonesia and Java, where the sacrificed individual is always connected with the lower, female half of the cosmos. On the other hand, rituals of human sacrifice and headhunting, connected with the cultivation of rice, were reserved, as van Wouden has shown, for the male half.

So we note, in spite of some overlap, a definite contrast between eastern insular Southeast Asia (the Moluccas, the Lesser Sunda Islands, and Java), in which myths that assert the chthonic aspect of rice predominate, and western insular Southeast Asia (Sumatra, Kalimantan, Celebes, Philippines), in which, by contrast, myths that affirm the celestial origin of rice predominate.

An analysis of the relations between the two systems and of their distribution among the various ethnic groups still remains to be done.

Often grafted upon the diverse origin myths are the adventures of certain culture heroes (such as Mau Ipi Guloq for the Bunaq of Timor, Sawerigading for the Bugis of

Celebes, Sese nTaola for the Bare'e Toraja, also of Celebes, or of Borneo, Seraguntung for the Iban, and Silai for the Ngaju), which furnish the societies in question with a kind of archetype of the ideal hero, but which serve just as often as foundations for ritual and for the rules of social organization (particularly for marriage rules).

3. *Myths of social and political organization.* Throughout Malaysia, there are myths that connect the traditional forms of social and political organization with the events that befell the first ancestors.

For eastern Indonesia, these myths (at least those published before 1935) were analyzed by van Wouden in his study of the social structures of the region. They account for the origins of clans, their hierarchy, and their political functions, which correspond, according to van Wouden, to a double dualism: a functional dualism, founded on the opposition between a male moiety, connected with the earth and with warlike activities, and a female moiety, connected with the lower world and with agriculture; and a cosmic dualism that set in opposition a celestial moiety, devoted to spiritual matters, and a terrestrial moiety, devoted to profane matters.

When the two dualisms are superimposed, this is translated into the political sphere through the existence of a double rule: one chief, qualified as "feminine" (even though the chief is a man), who is either the master or the superintendent of the soil, is charged with the relations with the divine world and with certain agrarian rites and is considered the elder; and a "masculine" chief, who is the real holder of direct power, is charged with political matters and is responsible for the conduct of war; he is considered the younger (Sumba).

When the two dualist systems intersect instead of being superimposed, one finds more complex political systems. For example, to an (elder) spiritual chief two (younger) profane chiefs may be set in opposition, one feminine and connected with agriculture and the other masculine and connected with war.

For the other regions, there are no overall studies. It nevertheless appears that there is quite a broad variety of types of myths in this sphere, as a function of each society's type of organization.

In the unilinear societies of western Indonesia, the existence of different clans may be connected with the appearance of a certain number of ancestors, generally brothers, who were born on earth of the first parents of celestial origin (Batak), or who descended simultaneously from the sky onto different points in the region (Nias). The clans that result from them each have their own mythic histories, but they are not basically hierarchical, and their dualism is not as clear as in eastern Indonesia.

In the bilateral societies that are found in most cases (Java, part of Sumatra, Malaysia, Borneo, Celebes, the Philippines), it is mainly a matter of accounting for the boundaries of territorial units and, in extreme cases, of justifying the existence of a social hierarchy and of a certain type of political organization.

Among the Ngaju of Borneo, the nobles (*utus gantong*) are connected with Mahatala and the upper world, and the common people with Jata and the lower world. Among the Bugis, by contrast, all of humanity has its origin in the spiritual world (as much higher as lower); but the nobility comes from "white-blooded beings," *tomanurung* (descended from the sky) or *totompo'* (arisen from the depths), while the common people descend from the servants who accompanied the first *tomanurung,* Batara Guru, to earth. The *toma-*

Statue of Durga, called *Loro Jonggrang,* "the slender young woman," in the temple of Prambanan (Central Java). An offering left at the base of the statue can be seen in the photo, though the inhabitants of the area are officially adherents of Islam. Photo Christian Pelras.

A Javanese family on pilgrimage at a consecrated burial place. Kramat. Note the incense burner and the flower petals scattered on the tomb. Photo Marcel Bonneff.

nurung and *totompo'* are also the source of the principal estates, of which they were the first lords, and of which the continuity is marked by the *regalia* which are supposed to have descended from the sky with them and which are the hereditary wealth of the collective group and the guarantor of its continuity and prosperity (*arajang*): swords, banners, cloth, plows, etc.

III. The Impact of the Great Religions

Since the fifth century, but especially from the seventh century to the fifteenth, the Malay archipelago experienced a penetration which historians have called an Indianization. Perhaps following the closing of the Central Asian route (in the period of the great invasions), certain elements of Indian society (Brahmans, Kṣatriyas, and merchants) sailed in the direction of the Southeast Asian shores and contributed to the development of Indianized kingdoms, which were generally based on the cultivation of irrigated rice and which were strongly influenced by the great religions of Indian origin: Hinduism and Buddhism. The kingdoms are known to us now especially through the great temples that they left and through a rich epigraphy, sometimes in Sanskrit and always in scripts derived from Indian models.

This was a phenomenon of particularly long duration (nearly a millennium) and great complexity, which looked very different in different periods and which should in no case be considered a colonization of the region by India (which never had political control there). It should also be pointed out that although the Indianization also touched several regions of the Indo-Chinese peninsula (especially Cambodia, where the kingdom of Angkor flourished from the ninth century to the fourteenth), it took in only a few islands of the archipelago, essentially Bali and Java, as well as certain regions of Sumatra. Elsewhere Indian civilization echoed, in a more and more muted way, through the intermediary of Java. Although it is attenuated, the echo is sometimes encountered far away and in unexpected places. In 1971 in the southern Philippines a completely isolated people was discovered who had a very primitive technology: the Tasaday. People were all ready to congratulate themselves for having found a veritable "isolate," a witness to prehistoric times, until it was discovered that they designated some supernatural force by the term *dewata,* which is derived from the well-known Sanskrit term for "divinity."

The effect of the arrival of the great Indian religions was to change earlier mythologies; the pantheons were restructured as the Indian heroes—especially those of the great epics—gained a footing on the islands. On the one hand, the *wayang* ("shadow theater"), which must originally have been a ritual to evoke the ancestors, was enriched by the entire mythology of the *Rāmāyaṇa* and especially of the *Mahābhārata;* on the other hand, a written literature appeared which sought to adapt into the vernaculars (Javanese and Balinese) the great legendary themes of the Indian subcontinent. Thus there was a *Rāmāyaṇa* in Old Javanese from the ninth century, and an adaptation, also in Old Javanese, with the title of *Bharatayuddha,* of the story of the fratricidal war between the Pandawas and Kuruwas, from the twelfth century. A quite complex ritual syncretism developed in a parallel fashion.

In no case is this a simple importation of Indian mythologies; the indigenous element remained very much present under the new facade. So it is that the fourteenth and fifteenth centuries saw a development of the cult of Bima, regarded as a savior hero, of whom only a few characteristics were borrowed from India. Parallel to this, it seems that Sadewa (the twin brother of Nakula, who in the *Mahābhārata* plays quite a self-effacing role) also enjoyed a great popularity in this period. In a general sense, at the end of Majapahit there is a renaissance of mythologies from the indigenous substratum, and it is probably around this date that the famous myth of Pañji—which may be a resurgence of an ancient myth of social organization common to the whole eastern part of the archipelago—takes shape and spreads as far as Cambodia and Siam. Far from abolishing the substratum, the greatest effect of Indianization was to dress it up and brighten it with sumptuous colors. Many of the gods of ancient Java, such as Semar and even Ratu Kidul, survived without damage and even benefited from the prestigious transposition.

What complicates the matter somewhat is the fact that this Indianized stratum is no longer directly accessible today, except perhaps on the little island of Bali, on which Hinduism has continued to develop by itself, thus revealing amalgams in a discourse of Indian tonality, with certain chunks torn out in prehistory. Elsewhere a new layer came to cover the Hindu layer in a general way; starting in the thirteenth century (in northern Sumatra), and especially from the fourteenth century onward, Islam moved silently onto all of the shores of the archipelago and from there spread widely into the interior. On Java, the very old Indianized kingdoms were remodeled, even as they preserved a large part of their ancient mythology; the *wayang* was largely preserved intact, and certain collective rites of the preceding period were conserved until now, with, as in the case of the *garebeg,* for example, very few modifications. Elsewhere Islam took root directly in the substratum and, as in many other regions of the Muslim world, was able to adapt very well in assimilating many of the pagan rituals. The *kramat,* or sacred, i.e., miraculous, tombs, the objects of numerous pilgrimages, recall the cult of the saints or Maraboutism, well known elsewhere; here it represents a considerable concession to the cult of the ancestors, immanent throughout the archipelago and always near. The Islamic fast overlays a notion that already existed and is called *puasa,* which is nothing but a variant of the Sanskrit term *upavasa;* circumcision (*sunat*) also existed in more than one region at an earlier time. As for ritual prayer, in Indonesia this is often called *sembahyang,* "to place one's hands together before the *yang,*" i.e., before the paranatural force that the *wayang* already intended to evoke. Here too there was syncretism and often conservatism. It was only in the beginning of the twentieth century that an orthodox tendency, stimulated by pan-Islamicism, sought to purify Indonesian Islam by removing all of the "dross" from it.

Christianity played only a minor role in Indonesia. The Dutch prohibited the "Papists" from proselytizing and were not interested in converting those under their jurisdiction. Things changed slightly toward the end of the nineteenth century, and a few Catholic and Protestant missionaries were able to convert to their religion certain regions that had generally remained outside of Islam. Here too there was often syncretism; in Java sacred history was portrayed in the form of the *wayang;* in Toraja country, a paper cross was put between the horns of the buffalo sacrificed to the ancestors.

Also to be noted is a complete messianic mythology, still alive now, and, since the time of independence (1945), the setting up of a "national" mythology that brings together a collective pantheon and, through the intermediary of an ad hoc committee, all the "national heroes" (*pahlawan nasional*) who worked in various provinces in the anticolonial struggle and to bring modern Indonesia into existence.

D.L. and C.P./d.w.

BIBLIOGRAPHY

W. STÖHR and P. ZOETMULDER, *Les religions d'Indonésie* (Paris 1968).

1. The Traditional Systems

P. ARNDT, Mythologie, Religion und Magie im Sikagebiet. östl. Mittelflores (Endeh, Indonesia, 1932). R. F. BARTON, *The Mythology of the Ifugaos* (Philadelphia 1955). L. BERTHE, *Bei Gua, Itinéraire des Ancêtres, Mythes des Bunaq de Timor* (Paris 1972). J. DERAEDT, "Religious Representations in Northern Luzon," *St. Louis Quarterly* 2, 3 (1964). E. JENSEN, *The Iban and Their Religion* (Oxford 1974). A. E. JENSEN, *Die drei ströme: Züge aus dem geistigen und religiösen Leben der Wemale* (Leipzig 1948). P. E. DE JOSSELIN DE JONG, ed., *Structural Anthropology in the Netherlands: A Reader* (The Hague 1977). T. MABUCHI, "Tales concerning the Origins of Grains in the Insular Area of Eastern and South Eastern Asia," *Asian Folklore Studies* 23, 1 (1964). CH. MACDONALD, "Mythe de création Palawan," *Archipel* 8 (1974): 91–118. W. MÜNSTERBERGER, *Ethnologische Studien an Indonesischen Schöpfungsmythen* (The Hague 1939). C. H. M. NOOY-PALM, "Introduction to the Sa'dan Toraja People and Their Country," *Archipel* 10 (1975): 53–92. H. SCHÄRER, *Ngaju Religion: The Conception of God among a South Borneo People* (The Hague 1963). P. SUZUKI, *The Religious System and Culture of Nias* (The Hague 1959). PH. L. TOBING, *The Structure of the Toba-Batak Belief in the High God* (Amsterdam 1956). J. A. J. VERHEIJEN, *Het Hoogste wezen bij de Manggareijers* (Vienna 1951). F. A. E. VAN WOUDEN, *Types of Social Structure in Eastern Indonesia* (The Hague 1968).

2. The Impact of the Major Religions

B. R. O'G. ANDERSON, *Mythology and the Tolerance of the Javanese* (Ithaca, NY, 1965). M. BONNEFF, "Le renouveau d'un rituel royal: Les Garebeg à Yogyakarta," *Archipel* 8 (1974): 119–46. M. COVARRUBIAS, *Island of Bali* (New York 1938) (numerous editions). G. W. J. DREWES, *Drie Javaansche Goeroes; hun leven, onderricht en messiasprediking* (Leiden 1925). C. GEERTZ, *The Religion of Java* (Glencoe, IL, 1960). R. GORIS, *Bijdrage tot de kennis der Oud-Javaansche en Balinesche theologie* (Leiden 1926). K. G. P. H. HADIWIDJOJO, "Danse sacrée à Surakarta: La signification du Bedojo ketawang," *Archipel* 3 (1972): 117–30. HARDJOWIROGO, *Sedjarah Wajang Purwa* (Jakarta 1965). K. A. H. HIDDING, *Gebruiken en godsdienst der Soendaneezen* (Batavia 1935). C. HOOYKAAS, *Āgama-Tīrtha: Five Studies in Hindu-Balinese Religion* (Amsterdam 1964). J. KATS, *Het Javaansche toneel* (Weltevreden 1923). CL. LOMBARD-SALMON, "A propos de quelques cultes chinois particuliers à Java," *Arts asiatiques* 26 (1973): 244–48. MANGKUNEGORO VII, *On the Wayang Kulit (Purwa) and Its Symbolic and Mystical Elements* (Ithaca, NY, 1957). TH. PIGEAUD, *Javaansche Volksvertoningen* (Batavia 1938). R. M. NG. POERBATJARAKA, *9 Pandjiverhalen onderling vergeleken* (Bandung 1940). J. J. RAS, "The Panji Romance and W. H. Rassers' Analysis of Its Theme," *BKI* 129 (1973): 411–56. W. H. RASSERS, *De Pandji-Roman* (Antwerp 1922); *Pañji, the Culture Hero* (The Hague 1959). D. A. RINKES, "De heiligen van Java," six articles in *TBG* 53–55 (1911–13). SENO SASTROAMIDJOJO, *Renungan tentang Pertunjukan Wajang Kulit* (Jakarta 1964). P. J. VAN LEEUWEN, *De Maleise Alexander Roman* (Utrecht 1937). P. WIRZ, *Der Totenkult auf Bali* (Stuttgart 1928). R. WINSTEDT, *A History of Classical Malay Literature* (2d ed., Oxford 1969). P. ZOETMULDER, *Kalangwan: A Survey of Old Javanese Literature* (The Hague 1974).

Divine Totality and Its Components: The Supreme Deity, the Divine Couple, and the Trinity in Indonesian Religions

Although the traditional religions of insular Southeast Asia have highly diverse pantheons, and although each has an original character that should not be underestimated, it is nonetheless possible to highlight certain constants and in particular to distinguish several types of deities.

Some deities probably represent totality, both divine and cosmic, while others represent the components of that totality, in the form of a divine couple in systems that are fundamentally dualistic, or of a trinity where the tripartite system prevails.

I. Various Examples

Among the Toba Batak of Sumatra, for example, the primordial deity, Mula Jadi na Bolon, was interpreted by P. L. Tobing as the expression of totality, encompassing the upper world, the middle world, and the lower world, in which it is manifested in the persons of three deities: Ompunta Tuan Bubi na Bolon, Raja Pinangkabo, and Naga Padoha (the serpent of the lower world). Its symbol is the cosmic tree that links the three worlds together. Out of the eggs of a bird created by the totality emerges a second trinity that is entrusted with the responsibility of governing the world. It consists of Batara Guru (the deity attached to the upper world), Soripada (the deity attached to the middle world), and Mangalabulan (the deity attached to the lower world). A fourth deity, Debata Asi-Asi (the "compassionate god"), is said to incarnate the totality of the triad. For Tobing, this triad also symbolizes the three basic clans of the marriage system of generalized exchange: Soripada represents a man's clan of reference (*dongan sabutuha*), Batara Guru represents the clan from which he receives his women (*hula-hula*), and Mangalabulan, the one to which he gives his women (*boru*). In this interpretation, Debata Asi-Asi represents society in its totality, a world parallel to the cosmos.

On Nias, a primordial divine couple is made up of Lature Danö and Lowalangi. Lature Danö, the deity of the lower world, is associated with the negative aspects of the cosmos—evil, darkness, death—with the color black and the moon, and is symbolized by the snake. Lowangali, the deity of the upper world, is associated with the positive aspects of the cosmos—good, light, life—with gold and the sun, and is symbolized by the cock or the hornbill. These two deities are considered brothers, but the myths about their origins differ widely. In northern Nias, they are said to have been born from the cosmic tree (*toro'a*), from which seven other spirits also came. In southern Nias, their mother is said to be Inada Samadulo Hosi (they have no father), who came out of a rock which was the body of the first entity, Inada Samihara Luwo. In a third story, however, where they have the names of Bauwa Danö and Luo Mewöna, they are the sons of the primordial god Sirao. Lature Danö and Lowalangi are simultaneously opposed and closely linked. According to P. Suzuki, this unity within duality is symbolized by the ambiguous character of Silewe Nazarata, simultaneously the sister and the wife of Lowalangi, but also allied with Lature Danö, simultaneously benevolent and disturbing and sometimes represented by a two-faced and bisexual statue. The priests and priestesses are her disciples, and it is she who taught men the rituals of war and introduced the use of statues (*adu*).

Among the Ngaju of Borneo, the primordial divine couple is formed by Jata and Mahatala. Jata (whose complete name is Bawim Jata Balawang Bulan) is the female deity of the

In the main enclosure of Balinese temples, in the most prestigious corner, oriented in relation to the mountain toward kaja-kangin (generally northeast), it is increasingly common to find an oratory in the shape of an empty throne, as above. This oratory, formerly dedicated to Surya, the solar deity, is now usually designated as Sang Hyang Widi Wasa, the undifferentiated Divine Totality. Photo Christian Pelras.

lower world, symbolized by the water snake (hence her former name, Tambon), the moon, or the sacred cloth. Mahatala, the male deity of the upper world, appears in the form of the hornbill (Tingan), the sun, or the sacred spear. She reigns at the bottom of the primordial waters, he on top of the sacred mountain (or else she is on top of the Mountain of Gold and he on top of the Mountain of Diamonds). The union of Jata and Mahatala corresponds to the supreme deity Tambon Haruei Bungai, "the water snake which is one with the hornbill," represented by the mystical boat shaped like the body of a snake, with its prow and stern shaped like the head and tail of a bird. This deity is also symbolized by the red and white banner, the union of the sacred spear and the sacred cloth; by the *sanggaran* or the *keramen*, poles erected during funerary festivals and head-hunting rituals, poles that stand next to the representations of the hornbill and the snake; and, finally, by the three-branched tree of life or cosmic tree. In the cosmic tree at the beginning of time there was a bitter struggle between a male and female hornbill, the emanation of the double deity, out of which the first human couple was born.

The mythology of the southeastern Moluccas is dominated by the divine couple Upu Lero and Upu Nusa. Upu Lero ("grandfather sun") corresponds to the male principle, Upu Nusa ("grandmother earth") to the female principle, and the world was engendered by their union, commemorated each year by the great communal feast of *porka*. The supreme deity, It Matromna, much more remote and never addressed directly, must surely be seen as representing divine totality, and the fig tree by which the rites and sacrifices of the *porka* used to take place, as well as the banner raised on that occasion, must be symbols of that totality.

Among the Lamaholot of the islands of eastern Flores, Adonara and Solor, the relationship between duality and unity is less clearly defined. Their principal deity is Lera Wulan, whose name means "Sun-Moon," but it is not clear whether this double name expresses an original duality. This is a male celestial deity whose female counterpart is Tana Ekan, Mother Earth, born of the primordial waters, whose union with Lera Wulan was at the origin of the world.

Among the Iban of Borneo, we can again clearly see the existence of a dialectical relation between a deity of totality that differentiates itself and acts in the form of a divine couple. One version of the Iban myth states that the primordial deity Entala, sometimes called Gantallah, is a spirit "without limbs" which of its own will created two birds, one male and one female, sometimes called Ara and Irik, who fly over the primordial waters. One created the earth, the other the sky. But the earth was a little too big, and as Ara and Irik compressed it to make it fit into the sky, they made mountains burst out. Plants grew, and Ara and Irik created the first human couple. Another version says that they were created by Entala himself, but in both cases, after men appear on earth, Entala no longer participates in the subsequent acts of creation, which are then entrusted to the two Petaras, who may be another expression of the divine couple of the cosmology.

The kinship between this Iban myth and certain myths of the Philippines is rather striking, since several northern Luzon groups also know a primordial deity named Batala or Lumawig and express the idea of the creation of the world by the intercession of two birds. Nevertheless, the overall data from this region give the impression of much less clearly structured systems. In particular, while it is possible to recognize the existence of primordial deities similar to the Entala of the Iban retired into inactivity, we see no sign of deities that reflect a dualist or tripartite system.

For instance, the inhabitants of Palawan (another island of the Philippines) have a supreme deity called Ampuq, lord of the world, who has not intervened in the world since creation. At the request of the "Man of Dust," and with the help of his golden scarf, Ampuq created the earth and the sky, light, water, stars, the sea, air, and wind, and with the help of his betel quid he created man and all living creatures, whom he entrusted to the Man of Dust. In another version, he uses some earth and animates with his breath first the intercessor Diwata and then the first human couple. In yet a third version, he entrusts to the Man of Dust the task of creating Diwata, who is the protector of humanity; it is from him that the shamans draw their power and with him that they establish contact.

II. Tutelary Deities

This brings us to a third type of deity, the tutelary deities, who are often thought to be at the origin of the first humans, or at least linked to men from the very start, and with whom men have a much closer relationship than with the primordial deities. As we have seen, this is true of the Diwata of Palawan. Among some other groups in the Philippines, a similar role is attributed to Kabunian.

In fact, for some of the peoples of northern Luzon (Philippines), among them the Kalinga and the Nabaloi of Kabayan, Kabunian is the name of the principal deity, who is male, the initiator of rituals and of culture, and the guarantor of ethical laws. Among the Nabaloi he is often associated with, but never confused with, Akou, the solar deity connected with the funeral rites, and he stands in opposition and complementarity to Kabigat, another male deity, who dispenses wealth and is connected with agrarian cults and head-hunting. Kabunian, by contrast, is credited with putting an end to this practice. For the Tinguian, Kabunian is a tutelary deity, distinct from god the creator, Kadaklan, and subordinate to him. On the other hand, among the western Nabaloi and the Kankanay, *kabuniyan* is only a general term for "deity," while the Ifugao use it to designate the celestial world as a whole.

Similarly, for the Toraja of the south Celebes (Indonesia), Puang Matua, the "Old Master," "god of the center of the firmament, lord of the rising sun," is not the first god. He is the son of the goddess Simbolon Manik and the god Usuk Sangbamban, who was born of a rib of Gauntikembong, lord of the celestial world. According to another version, his mother's name was Puang Tudang, and his father, Puang Basi-Basian, was born of the union between the sky and the earth, for originally sky and earth touched one another. He is nevertheless the most important deity for humans, and myths tell how his wife, Arrang Dibatu, who was born from a rock, sent him west to look for the gold which was used to make a pair of bellows for a piston-operated forge (*sauan sibarrung*) that he used to make his own creation: by putting a fistful of pebbles in the bellows, he made the sun, the moon, and the stars; then, using flakes of gold in the same way, he created animals, plants, water, iron, rice, and finally Datu Laukku, the celestial ancestor of man. One of his children, Pong Mula Tau, was the first man to descend to earth, and he brought with him the original ritual (*aluk*).

Finally, certain deities are felt to be even closer to men because they lived among them during a certain time in their history. This is particularly true of the female deities at the time of the origin of food plants, which in a way are the earthly aspect of the primordial female deity.

We can judge the importance accorded to such deities by the survival of the cult of Roro Kidul or Ratu Kidul in Java, despite Islam. She is the "queen of the south" (*ratu*, "queen"; *roro*, or *loro*, "young woman"; *kidul*, "south"), the pre-Indian female deity who is reputed to have ruled over the southern coast of Java, where the currents and shifting sands are extremely dangerous and harbors are rare. Like another Lorelei, she lures imprudent sailors to her and is worshiped by fishermen, as well as by collectors of swallow nests, who risk their lives climbing down a rope alongside a cliff to gather the precious product. She has such a cult at Karang Bolong (fifty kilometers east of Cilacap), where offerings are placed in front of her "bed" before each new harvest. One carefully avoids wearing green garments near the coast because they would offend the queen.

But the influence of Roro Kidul is not felt only at this popular level. According to a well-established tradition, confirmed by chronicles dating back to the seventeenth century, the founder of the current Mataram dynasty, the famous Senapati (1575–1601), deliberately sought an alliance with the queen and with all the evil spirits that obey her. One night as he was meditating near the sea at a place called Parang Tritis, south of Yogyakarta, she appeared to him and they coupled. Since then, Roro Kidul continues to lend her unfailing support to Senapati's descendants, who alone have the privilege of seeing her. Several particularly sacred rituals are observed in the courts of central Java to this day to

Rite of *labuhan* celebrated in 1972 at Parang Kusuma, near Parangtritis, southern coast of Java. Immersion of offerings to Roro Kidul, a female spirit who rules over the "South Sea." Photo Marcel Bonneff.

commemorate this hierogamy. On the anniversary of his accession to the throne, the king attends a sacred dance called *bedoyo ketawang*, with nine female dancers and Roro Kidul, whom he alone sees. On the king's birthday, one of his garments is solemnly carried to Parang Tritis and cast into the water (*nglabuh*). Finally, the queen comes to visit humans with all her retinue, and her passage is manifested by a particularly violent storm (*lampor*).

D.L. and C.P./g.h.

The Origin of Humanity and the Descent to Earth of the First Human Beings in the Myths of Indonesia

One of the important episodes in the "geneses" of insular Southeast Asia is the one that tells of the first settlement of the ancestors of mankind on earth. Whether the first human beings were created inadvertently or were begotten by a primordial couple, many myths tenaciously affirm their divine descent.

This is evident, for example, in the Batak myth that ascribes the origin of humanity to the goddess Si Boru Deak Parujar, the daughter of the deity of the upper world, Batara Guru. Her older sister, Sorbayati, was supposed to marry Raja Odap-Odap, the son of Mangalabulan, the brother of Batara Guru and the god of the lower world. But Odap-Odap preferred the younger sister, Si Boru Deak Parujar, and out of shame, Sorbayati threw herself off the roof of Batara Guru's house during a dance. From her body, bamboo and rattan were born. Eager to escape from Raja Odap-Odap, who looked like a lizard, Si Boru Deak Parujar descended into the middle world among the primordial waters, and with the help of the supreme deity, Mula Jadi na Bolon, she arranged the first earth, fixing it solidly onto the back of the snake of the depths, Naga Padoha. Then she agreed to marry Raja Odap-Odap, who had finally taken on a human form. From their union (although other traditions claim that it was "from a mushroom born of the tears of Si Boru Deak Parujar," or "from a bird's egg from which the principal deities emerged") was born the first human couple, the twins Si Raja Ihat Manisia and Si Boru Ihat Manisia. When these two grew up they married, their parents returned to heaven, and the link that once united the middle and upper worlds was broken. The first human couple settled in the village of Si Anjur Mula-Mula at the foot of Mount Pusuk Buhit, to the west of Lake Samosir, and founded a family. One of their children, Si Raja Batak, was the ancestor of all the Batak. He received the first *tunggal panaluan*, the magic wand of the Batak diviner, which symbolizes the unity of the three cosmic principles and of the three primary colors. He had two sons, Guru Tatea Bulan and Raja Isumbaon, the ancestors of the two phratries into which Batak society is ideally divided; both were specialists, one in sacred matters and the other in profane matters. They were associated with the moon and the sun, respectively. From them came the eight fundamental Batak clans (five from the first and three from the second), on which the total of approximately three hundred present-day *margas* (subclans) is based.

On Nias, the mythical ancestors of the inhabitants of the island, to whom one can trace back all genealogies, are Daeli, Gözo, Hia, and Hulu. The points where they descended from heaven are marked by a temple and a sacred tree, where their descendants gather together periodically to celebrate the community festival of Börö N'adu. Hia was the first to come down, and he landed in the south, which made the earth tilt; then Gözo landed in the north, and this area also sank under the primordial waters, while the middle of the island was raised. Hulu and Daeli then came down, and the earth finally flattened out. As for their origin, one tradition claims that they were the children of the god Sirao and the half brothers of Bauwa Danö (Lature Danö) and Luo Mewöna (Lowalangi). However, according to other traditions mankind came either from the goddess Inada Dao or from a first couple that were born from the division of a child without limbs, who had been born to Lowalangi and a daughter of Lature Danö. In fact, these contradictory versions probably express the same idea: that mankind participates in divine and cosmic totality, and that it harbors within itself simultaneously the contradictory aspects of a basic dualism.

A similar interpretation may also be given to the myth of the Ngaju, where the battle fought by a male and a female hornbill (a symbol of duality) in the cosmic tree (a symbol of totality) triggers the birth of the first woman (born of fragments from the tree felled by the female) and the first man (who arose from the foam vomited by the male). The village where they settled, Batu Nindan Tarong, in the middle of the primordial waters, was naturally not yet of our world, but was rather a prototype of villages to come. The real first man was the couple's last child, Maharaja Buno. He came down to earth and became the ancestor of human beings after he created a wife out of clay. The fact that he was the brother of the ancestors of pigs, dogs, chickens, and spirits shows to what extent mankind is felt to be in close communication with nature as well as with the supernatural.

In these myths, the first earth upon which the first human beings settled seems to spring up from the middle of the primordial waters. The aquatic theme is sometimes replaced by the theme of the flood, in which one should not be too quick to see any Western influence.

Thus, in the story of Bugan and Wigan, the first couple and the ancestors of the Ifugao of northern Luzon in the Philippines, one version claims that they are the children of Kabigat and Bugan, two deities of the upper world (*kabunian*). Eager to populate the middle world (*pugao*), they sent their two children into the forest to pick tubers and then unleashed a flood that took them upstream (*daiya*) into this world. In order to ensure their survival, they sent after them a house with a granary of rice, pigs, chickens, cats, dogs, and full jars. At the start, the couple respected the prohibition against incest, but one day Bigan had sexual relations with his sister while she was asleep. At first their heavenly parents were angry, but then they consented to the marriage, from which four daughters and five sons were born. In order to lead them to perpetuate the line of descendants, the sons and daughters were brought up in separate villages. When they reached adulthood, they married, but after that marriages between brothers and sisters were forbidden. In another version, Kabigat and Bugan are the first couple, born of the supreme deity known as the celestial Wigan. Their progeny became so numerous that the earth was overpopulated, whereupon the celestial Wigan unleashed a flood, of which the only survivors were two of the children of Kabigat and Bugan, here named Balitok and Bugan.

Among the Iban of Borneo, we also find the story of Dayang Raca, the sole survivor of a flood that drowned all the rest of the original humans. Impregnated by the flame of

Shrine in the shape of a tomb, known as Puang Sanro, South Celebes. Here worshipers commemorate the reascent to heaven of Batara Guru, who rose again from this spot and was the first man, son of the prince of gods, in Bugis mythology. Photo Christian Pelras.

a fire that she had lit (which was nothing but a manifestation of Kucok, the spirit of fire), she gave birth to a child that had only half a body, and she named it Simpang Impang ("Half-gone"). When he grew up and despaired of his infirmity, Simpang Impang tried to drown himself but was pulled out of the water by a strange creature, Indai Jebua, who turned out to be the spirit of vermin. When he had lived with her for a while, he left her; she gave him a present of three enormous grains of rice, but the wind made them fall, and they broke into small pieces the size of actual grains of rice.

The myth of origin of the Bugis of the Celebes, at least as it has come down to us, contains far fewer elements susceptible to a "cosmic" interpretation (although it refers to a union between the upper world and the lower world). According to the Bugis texts, the first man to come down from heaven was not the ancestor of all of humanity but only the ancestor of the princely families. The myth describes how the deities of the upper and lower worlds decided one day to people the middle world (the earth), so that there might be human beings to recognize their divinity and serve them. The principal deity of the upper world, Patoto'e ("he who fixes destinies"), designated for this mission his oldest son, La Toge 'langi', who has the title of Batara Guru. Placed inside the hollow part of a bamboo tube, Batara Guru, during his descent and in accordance with his father's instructions, gave form to the earth and disseminated plant and animal species. After landing on earth at Luwu' on the Gulf of Bone, he first submitted to two weeks of asceticism and fasting, and then servants who came from heaven helped him to break the soil and plant the first crops. After three months, his wives descended to earth, together with his palace and the mass of his commoner subjects, who constituted the first generation of humans (thus also of heavenly origin, but from the very beginning of lower rank). Then, as he had been promised, out of the waters of the sea emerged his first cousin We Nyili' Timo, the daughter of the principal deity of the lower world, who became his principal wife.

The first child of Batara Guru, born of one of his secondary wives, was a daughter who died within seven days. From her body rice was born, whose spirit was from then on revered under the name of Sangiang Serri. Other children were born of his other wives, and finally We Nyili' Timo gave birth to the one who would inherit the kingdom of Luwu', Batara Lattu. When he reached adulthood, Batara Lattu married his cousin We Opu Sengngeng, the princess of Tompo' Tikka' (the land of the rising sun), whose father and mother, just like his own, had come down from the upper world and up from the lower world, respectively. From this marriage was born a set of twins: a boy, Sawerigading, who was the future culture hero of the Bugis, and a girl, We Tenriabeng. On the day when the two children were solemnly placed in their suspended cradle (the ceremony that marks the entrance of all Bugis children into society), Batara Guru's reign on earth ended. He returned to the upper world, followed by his wives, and Batara Lattu took his place as king of Luwu'.

D.L. and C.P./g.h.

Culture Heroes of Insular Southeast Asia

Throughout the entire world of insular Southeast Asia, every single ethnic or social group identifies itself with a particular culture hero. The exemplary adventures of these figures are first told in connection with the basic myths of each group, to whom they represent in some way an ideal personification transported back to a period when the divine world and the human world still maintained a special relationship.

The disappearance or the replacement of old religious or cultural systems by new ways of thinking does not necessarily presuppose their dismissal. They can survive and even maintain a surprising vitality under the convenient cover of tales of a national character (such as Sawerigading among the Islamized Bugis for three and a half centuries), or a popular character (like Pañji among the Javanese). But new culture heroes can also be born and can incarnate, next to the old, new values or ideals. Such is the case, in Indonesia and in Malaysia, with certain Islamic heroes, images of the ideal Muslim, but also introducers and guarantors of a new order, just as the ancient culture heroes had introduced fundamental rituals guaranteeing the fertility of men and crops. And one may wonder whether the new *pahlawan nasional* ("national heroes") are not, in their own way, additional culture heroes. Let us therefore distinguish between four types of heroes.

I. Heroes of Oral Myths

The first, dearest to anthropologists, is the hero of oral myths—of whom we will not, in such a restricted space, present a detailed analysis; rather it will suffice to evoke a few representative examples.

One such example is Mau Ipi Guloq. He is the culture hero of the Bunaq of Timor, the first man to domesticate the buffalo. He and his brother Asan Paran had trapped two wild sows, who then transformed themselves into women. But his brother kept them for himself, and in anger Mau Ipi Guloq went his separate way. One day, using the golden blowpipe that Asan Paran had lent him, Mau Ipi Guloq was hunting a crow that had been bothering his buffalo. He wounded the bird, and it flew away with a golden arrow in its body. Setting out to look for it, Mau Ipi Guloq descended into the lower world, whose ruler was ailing. Offering to take care of him, Mau Ipi Guloq noticed that his arrow was the cause of the illness. He succeeded in retrieving the arrow and replacing it with a bamboo arrow soaked in his betel pouch. As payment, he was given two oranges from a tree of the lower world, which changed into princesses.

Asan Paran proposed exchanging one of his wives for one of the princesses; when his brother refused, he plotted his murder and finally succeeded in killing him by making him fall to the bottom of a ravine. Mau Ipi Guloq's wives found him and were able to resuscitate him by using oil brought from the lower world. He went home refreshed and rejuvenated. Asan Paran asked that a bath also be prepared for him that would make him look like his brother; pretending to do what he asked, Mau Ipi Guloq's wives scalded him to death. Mau Ipi Guloq then married his sisters-in-law. He became one of the principal ancesters of the Bunaq.

Adventures which are similar, though inverted because they concern the upper world, are attributed to Sese nTaola, the culture hero of the Bare'e Toraja of central Celebes. As a child he has such a voracious appetite that his horrified parents consider killing him. So he leaves home and after various adventures arrives at the seashore with some companions acquired on his journey. After several months of swimming across the sea, and after killing the monster that barred their passage, they reach the other side (which probably represents the upper world). In the first village lives a cannibal couple whom they succeed in overcoming. Later they encounter other villages where Sese nTaola's companions one after another find wives for themselves. In the last village there rages a *guruda,* a gigantic bird who devours all the inhabitants. Here, Sese nTaola discovers a young girl hidden in a drum; she is Lemo nTonda, the sister of Datu of the Wind, who had followed him all the way from the cannibals' village. Despite her warnings, Sese nTaola attacks Guruda and his six children. He succeeds in killing all of them, but at the end of his last battle with Guruda himself, he is killed. Lemo nTonda revives him but he immediately falls asleep, and during his sleep, which lasts a month, Lemo

Illustration from a Javanese manuscript recounting the story of Pañji: the hero is received at the palace of Daha. Document Marcel Bonneff.

Bugis manuscript of the *La Galigo* cycle: drawing the ship of Sawerigading. Photo Christian Pelras.

nTonda is taken away by Datu nTo Wawo Yangi (the "Prince of the Sky"). When he awakens, Sese nTaola challenges the Datu to single combat, kills him, takes Lemo nTonda back, but again falls asleep for a month, and his companion is again taken away by Datu nTo Mato Eo (the "Prince of the Rising Sun"). This same sequence is repeated six more times, the subsequent kidnappers being Datu nTo Kasoyao (the "Prince of the North"), Datu nPayompo Yangi Sambiranya (the "Prince of the South"), Torokuku mBetu'e (the "Bird of the Stars"), and finally Momata Tibu (the "Cross-eyed"). While killing the latter, he again loses his life, and Lemo nTonda revives him again, as well as the villagers whom Guruda had killed. Then the two of them make their way back to Sese nTaola's country aboard a copper vessel that his double (*tanoana*) had constructed while Sese nTaola was asleep, during his visits to his grandfather, Toranda Ue ("he who lives in the water"). In the course of their crossing, Sese nTaola must again fight six battles, is killed in the last one, and is revived by Lemo nTonda. When he arrives in his village, he finds that his parents have died. They are resuscitated, but they must pay a fine for the hardships endured by their son.

More fundamental to the Iban of Borneo, perhaps because they are explicitly linked to the origins of rituals, are the adventures of Seragunting. Sometimes also called Surong Gunting, he is the son of the warrior Menggin (or Siu) and the celestial nymph Endu Dara Tincin Temaga (or Endu Sudan Galiggan Tincin Mas), the daughter of the god Singalang Burong.

Tincin Temaga married Menggin, who in the course of a hunt had taken possession of her feathered robe, on condition that he would never touch another bird. Soon after the birth of Seragunting, he involuntarily breaks the interdiction, and Tincin Temaga leaves him. In the company of his son, Menggin goes to look for her. He crosses the sea and reaches the land of Calaos (Tansang Kenyalang) where he finds Tincin Temaga in the stream where she bathes. She describes the path to Singalang Burong's house and explains how to avoid the traps awaiting him. Flies will show him where to put his feet so as to avoid the daggers planted in the path; another fly will settle on the dish that he should eat; a glowworm will show him under which mosquito net he should sleep, etc.

Thus Menggin stays on the veranda of the house where his father-in-law lives until his son becomes old enough to walk and talk. When this time comes, Seragunting goes to take his place at the side of Singalang Burong, who is furious and refuses to recognize him as his grandson if he does not succeed (which he does) in a series of trials: top contests, wrestling, hunting; collecting a large quantity of pearls scattered under the house; retrieving oil spread on the surrounding terrain; and finally, going to look for honey in a hive in the forest. Seragunting sends the bees from the hive after Singalang Burong, who has to seek shelter in the granary. He will not come down until he has recognized his grandson. Seragunting and his father then return to life among human beings in order to avoid meeting the celestial husband of Tincin Temaga, whose return from headhunting is announced.

Later, Seragunting returns to his grandfather's house to ask him how to succeed in farming and headhunting. On the way, he encounters the Pleiades and Orion's Belt, who show him how to use the stars in agriculture. Then Singalang Burong teaches him the art of reading omens from the flight of birds, as well as the rituals of the principal ceremonies. During his stay, Seragunting impregnates his young aunt Dara Cempaka Tempurong Alang, a crime which should be punished by death, but for which the sacrifice of a pig is sufficient. This will be the occasion to teach human beings the degrees of relationship prohibited for marriage.

II. Heroes of Written Accounts

Although Iban culture may appear to be reserved for ethnological study, Javanese civilization has long been of interest to Orientalists. The difference in cultural climate between the two types of society and between the scholarly approaches to them should not mask the existence of deep affinities between the great civilizations of insular Southeast Asia and seemingly more primitive cultures. This is what is shown by the study of a second type of culture hero, who appears this time in written narratives, apparently more profane, and who is sometimes composed of borrowed elements. One such hero is Pañji, the hero of a cycle of Javanese origin, who seems to have been important in the fourteenth and fifteenth centuries. He was also known in other areas of the archipelago (there are versions in Malay and in the languages of Sumatra, Celebes, and Lombok) as well as on the Indo-Chinese peninsula (Thailand, Cambodia). Western mythologists have been particularly interested in him and have given him an unusual fate; it is surely not paradoxical to say that he is better known today among anthropologists and other specialists than in Java, where other figures are popular. But there was a time when stories of Pañji inspired a particular genre of shadow theater (*wayang gedog*) as well as masked dances.

The interpretation of the "myth of Pañji" is difficult first because of the large number of accessible versions, which require laborious philological discussion. Aside from the Javanese and Balinese (*Malat*) versions, there are at least three Malayan versions designated by the names under which Pañji appears in each one of them: *Hikayat Cekel Wanengpati, Hikayat Pañji Kuda Semirang,* and *Hikayat Pañji Semirang*. The Javanese scholar R. M. Ng Poerbatjaraka devoted himself to a painstaking study of the texts and believes that they date from the end of the Majapahit period (as opposed to C. C. Berg, who believes them to be older).

The story tells of the quest of Pañji, a hero of divine origin, incarnated as the Prince of Koripan under the name of Raden Inu Kertapati, searching for his true love (his own sister, in fact), incarnated as the Princess of Daha, under the name of Candra Kirana. After a series of mishaps and adventures which take both of them all over Java, they succeed in finding each other and celebrate their wedding with much ceremony; Pañji, who meanwhile has triumphed over all his enemies, is declared the one and only king of the whole island.

In 1922, W. H. Rassers presented a paper in Leiden which was to cause a great stir, entitled *De Pandji-roman.* According to Rassers, the story was actually an adaptation of a much older myth which was found in the east of the archipelago; Pañji and Candra Kirana were transpositions of the sun and the moon; and in the Koripan/Daha contrast were found the representation of two totemic and exogamous moities. Pañji's quest was the representation of an ancient initiation, and the solemn wedding that ends the story was the transposition of the ceremony that concluded the initiation. All of this without putting into question certain Indian influences evident elsewhere (Pañji clearly appeared as a reincarnation of Wisnu, and Candra Kirana as a reincarnation of Dewi Sri). The more recent works of S. O. Robson, and especially of J. J. Ras (who connects the myth of Pañji with a myth of creation highly esteemed among the Ngaju of Kalimantan), seem to confirm certain proposals of Rassers. This shows in any case the importance of not separating the Javanese domain from the rest of the archipelago.

One can say as much about the Bugis domain; open to external influences, Islamized since the beginning of the seventeenth century, and even taxed by certain of the "fanatic Muslims," very actively involved in agriculture, navigation, and trade, characterized by the existence of a most elaborate political system, proud of a rich written literature, the Bugis at first seem far removed from the world of primitive Indonesia. But their monumental national epic, the cycle of *La Galigo,* harbors, under many epic or romantic episodes, an undeniably mythical base, above all in its key figure, Sawerigading, whose character remains essential for the Bugis of today.

Sawerigading is the son of the king of Luwu, Batara Lattu, and the grandson of Batara Guru, the first man descended from the sky. His adolescent adventures are related to a series of journeys which lead him all around Celebes, to the Moluccas, and to Sumbawa, as well as to countries with unidentifiable names, which could be either real or mythical places. He visits, among other places, the island where the cosmic tree (Pao Jengki, the "mango of Zanj") grows, whose branches rise up into the sky and whose roots go down as far as the lower world; he sees in the middle of the ocean the whirlpool by which the waters of the sea connect with that world. He also penetrates twice into the Land of the Dead, but must decide on the first visit not to marry We Pinrakati, a young princess who had just died, and on the second to bring back among the living Welle ri Lino, to whom he was engaged.

Upon returning to Luwu, Sawerigading meets his twin sister, We Tenriabeng, from whom he had been separated at birth. He falls in love with her and decides to marry her. All of the remonstrances of his entourage as well as of We Tenriabeng herself are in vain. Finally, his twin sister tells him of the existence, in the land of Cina, of one of their cousins, We Cudai, who resembles her exactly. And she gives him a strand of her hair, one of her bracelets, and one of her rings which will make him sure of her. Sawerigading embarks once again on a vessel carved out of the trunk of a gigantic tree, the Welenreng, which grew in the land of Luwu. After engaging in numerous battles at sea and after numerous mishaps, he succeeds in marrying We Cudai, who would give birth to, among others, a son, La Galigo (whose name was given to the cycle), and a daughter, We Tenridio, who was to become a *bissu* (shaman or medium).

After the marriage of his grandson, La Tenritatta, Sawerigading, who had broken his promise never to return to Luwu, is engulfed by the waves along with We Cudai. They replace Guri ri Selleng and his wife as rulers of the lower world, while We Tenriabeng and her husband Remmang ri Langi' inherit the throne of the upper world. All the princes of divine origin then disappear from the earth, with the exception of a daughter of Sawerigading and a son of We Tenriabeng who get married and rule over Luwu. As soon as they have a son, communications between the earth and the supernatural worlds are broken; after that, mankind is on its own.

But not entirely. For a Bugis saying now proclaims: "The Orient swallowed him; the West makes him rise again." The West is Mecca; and the mysterious Sun which had disappeared into the eastern seas in the form of Sawerigading suddenly rose once again on the western horizon, but this time in the name of the prophet Muhammad.

Thus do the Bugis affirm their dual attachment both to their ancestral personality and to their new faith.

III. Heroes Linked to Successive Acculturations (India, China, Islam)

This leads us to culture heroes of a third type, heroes whose backgrounds—if not their basic functions—are very different. They are heroes connected with the different acculturations that occurred in the historical period, most importantly Indianization, Sinicization, and Islamization. Here are a few notable figures for each:

1. *Aji Saka* is the Javanese culture hero to whom are attributed the innovations brought about by Indianization. King Saka (*aji,* "king") is said to have landed on Java with two loyal companions, Dora and Sembodra. The country was at that time under the authority of a terrible ogre who regularly demanded a tribute of human flesh (an allusion to the cannibalism of the first inhabitants?). Aji Saka offers himself as a sacrifice, but on condition that the ogre first grant him a plot of land the size of his handkerchief. The monster willingly agrees, but soon the magic handkerchief takes on an enormous size and covers the entire island. Out of vexation, the ogre jumps into the sea and turns himself into a giant tortoise. Aji Saka then opens up the forest and creates the first kingdom of Mendangkamulan, with the first cultivation of the land and the first villages. One day he wanted to get back his *keris* (kris), which he had entrusted to Dora with orders not to give it to anyone else, and sent Sembodra to retrieve it. Dora pretended to know nothing about it and the two loyal servants ended up by killing one another. To commemorate the sad event, Aji Saka carved into a tree twenty symbols corresponding to the following twenty syllables: *ha-na-ca-ra-ka da-ta-sa-wa-la pa-da-ja-ya-nya ma-ga-ba-ta-nga,* which in Javanese means: "There were two messengers, a dispute arose, equal were their merits, they both perished." He thus created the Javanese syllabary which, adapted from Indian models and transformed several times, has been maintained up to the present. According to the same tradition, he established on the same occasion "the Saka era," according to which the entire epigraphy of the Indianized period is dated (the Saka era whose beginnings correspond to 78 A.D. is known elsewhere, in India and in most of the Indianized world).

2. *Sampo.* The famous maritime expeditions across the "Southern Seas" (*Nanyang*) and the Indian Ocean, all the way to Mecca and the African coast, launched at the beginning of the Ming Dynasty by the emperor Yong Luo and under the direction of the admiral Zheng He from 1405 to 1433, are well known to us from Chinese sources, and correspond to an important moment in the commercial politics of the Chinese empire. In the Chinese communities of Southeast Asia, particularly in Java, their memory has been considerably embellished, giving rise to a whole series of local traditions centering around the character of Sampo (Zheng He was also called San Bao) or his "pilots," who are said to have landed and founded a family line on Java. Although the first Chinese communities settled on Java before the fifteenth century, and it is improbable that Zheng He himself ever actually set foot on the northern coast of Java, Sampo thus became a kind of culture hero, the initiator of the whole Chinese presence on the island.

Today remembrances of him are maintained primarily in

three places: In Djakarta a shrine is dedicated to him in the temple in Ancol, near the coast. In the beautiful Chinese temple of Cirebon, which in its present state dates from the end of the eighteenth century, a huge iron anvil is preserved which is said to come from one of the great Captain's junks. And finally, in Semarang, a little west of the city, are a cave and a temple where Sampo's memory is preserved. In Ancol, as in Semarang, a Muslim tomb is shown which is thought to be that of one of Sampo's pilots who was married to a woman of the region and who died on Java. In Semarang a big commemorative procession still takes place annually during which Sampo's statue is carried, and "his" horse is led by its bridle. On Bali, several traditions dealing with a certain Dampu Awang evoke Sampo, and in the Philippines, on Jolo, they honor a certain Pen Dao Gong, who is also thought to have belonged to Zheng He's crew.

3. Islam was introduced into Java progressively and peacefully largely by way of the ports of the northern coast (the Pasisir) from the beginning of the fifteenth century until the end of the sixteenth century. Popular beliefs hold that the conversion was essentially due to "nine messengers," or Wali Sanga (pronounced *songo*), who had come from across the sea and by their force of persuasion and their miracles were able to win over the people, who had until then been followers of *agama Boda* (a kind of mixture of Buddhism and Hinduism). The term *wali* is found in old Javanese where it denotes a certain category of dignitary; the word has undoubtedly been confused with the Arab *wali* which denotes the "representative." The number of *wali* is regularly fixed at nine (Javanese *sanga*), but the lists vary noticeably according to the region. The graves of these illustrious men—whose historical reality is certainly not always evident—are scattered from the east to the west along the Pasisir and are the goals of very frequent pilgrimages (*kramat*). There is a series of legends about these *wali* which form an integral part of the folklore.

The first *wali* are remembered in the region of Surabaya, where Islam was first introduced. The oldest is Malik Ibrahim, who is also the most historical, for he was a merchant from Gujurat whose tomb, dated from A.H. 822 (A.D. 1419), has been discovered. In the Ampel Denta quarter, in the heart of the Arab quarter in Surabaya, is the tomb of Raden Rahmat, also known as Sunan Ampel; he was thought to be the nephew of a princess of Campa, the wife of one of the last kings of Majapahit, and had gathered around him a great many disciples. Two of his sons, Sunan Drajat and Sunan Bonang (who could walk on water), are considered to be *wali*, as was one of his best pupils, Sunan Giri, who one day threw his *kalam* at some infidels who were attacking him, and the *kalam* immediately turned into krises. The prestige of these heroes spread quite rapidly among merchants, and the descendants of Sunan de Giri, who settled on a promontory (*giri*, "mountain") near Surabaya, exercised great influence all the way to the Moluccas and maintained their authority until the seventeenth century.

The figure of Sunan Kali Jaga is inseparable from the implantation of Islam into the region of Demak (the central region of the Pasisir, just to the east of what is now the city of Semarang). He had summoned all the other *wali* in order to construct a great mosque in Demak in only one night and had also assembled the "council" in charge of condemning to the pyre the impudent Siti Jenar, one of the *wali* who had committed the error of revealing the esoteric part of the doctrine. And it was Sunan Kali Jaga who managed to convert Kyai Ageng Podanarang, the regent of Semarang. By

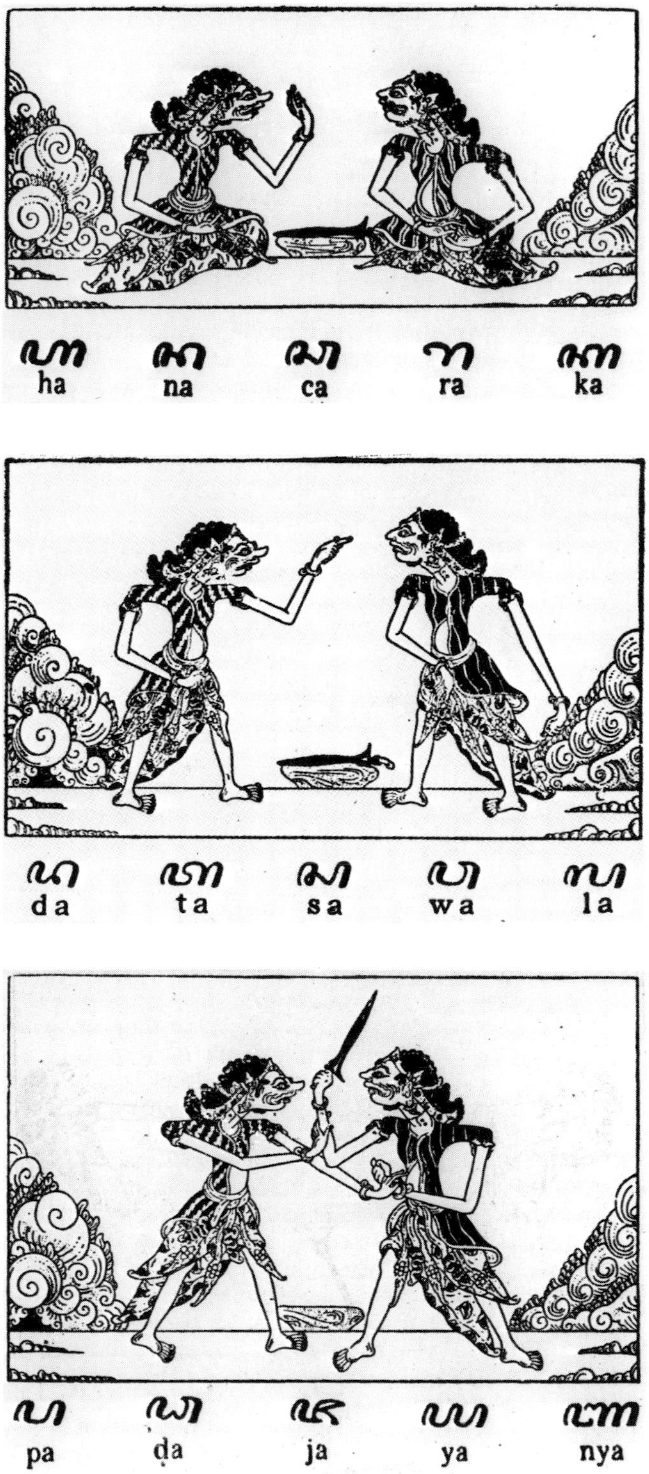

Javanese alphabet book in which the signs for the various syllables are illustrated by the dispute between the two envoys of Agi Saka.

Tomb, in Gresik (East Java), of Malik Ibrahim, one of the nine *wali*, the earliest propagators of Islam in Java. Photo Marcel Bonneff.

transforming gold into earth, and vice versa, in front of his eyes, he was able to convince Kyai Ageng of the vanity of earthly things; the regent abandoned his wealth and went off to preach the new religion in central Java. Like the other *wali*, he convinced the pagans through his miracles—putting his hand in fire without getting burned, causing a spring to arise, etc. He finally settled on a hill near Yogya, in the place called Tembayat; he was buried there and has remained famous under the name of Sunan Bayat.

Continuing further west, on the north coast of Java one finds the tomb of Sunan Panggung (in Tegal) and, most importantly, the great necropolis of Gunung Jati, to the north of Cirebon, where on the uppermost level is found the tomb of Sunan Gunung Jati (d. ca. 1570)—the most important *wali* of west Java.

Outside of Java a legend comparable to Ulakan is encountered in Minangkabau country (western Sumatra), where the tomb of Syaikh Burhanuddin—who was also believed to have introduced Islam into the region—is the object of a very important pilgrimage (especially during the month of Safar).

The introduction of Islam also had the effect of disseminating in the archipelago a completely new cycle of wonders borrowed from the myths and legends of the Arab and Persian worlds and from the Orient in general. Some of the legendary heroes were not received simply as common fictional heroes, but became totally naturalized to the point of taking a place among the local cultural heroes. We will give three such examples here: Alexander, the Macedonian hero; Amir Hamzah, the uncle of the Prophet Mohammad; and Muhammad Hanafiah, the half brother of the Shiite martyrs Hasan and Husayn.

Iskandar Zulkarnain. Known as "Alexander the Two-Horned," the conquerer of the world whose legend spread all the way to the far west in the Middle Ages is found in most of the Muslim world, where he was "recovered" as a culture hero, bringing the light of the true religion to every continent. Thus one finds "Stories of Alexander" in Arabic, Turkish, Persian, Hindi, Malay, Javanese, and Bugis. The Malay version, which has been studied by van Leeuwen, first tells in epic style about Alexander's conquests (Andalus here is notably assimilated to Andalas, another name for Sumatra), then recounts the stages of a more philosophic quest during which the hero seeks the fountain from which the water of eternity is drawn (somewhat like Bima); this search even leads him to dive to the bottom of the oceans in a sort of bathyscaphe to explore the lower worlds.

Elsewhere Iskandar was introduced into the myth of the origins of Malay rulers and he is notably linked to the region of Palembang (where his tomb can be seen at the foot of Mount Siguntang).

Amir Hamzah. In the history of the beginnings of Islam, Amir Hamzah is the uncle and one of the staunchest partisans of the prophet Muhammad. But in the Malay archipelago he is a marvelous hero at the center of an extremely rich cycle whose episodes are told not only in Malay, but also in the principal regional languages: Javanese, Balinese, Sundanese, and Bugis. The first Malay versions certainly date from before the beginning of the sixteenth century; a very famous Javanese version called *Menak,* "The Knight" (an epithet given to the hero), was recorded in central Java toward the end of the eighteenth century. Van Ronkel has shown that at the origin of the *Hikayat Amir Hamzah,* "The Story of Amir Hamzah," there was a Persian text that borrowed certain themes from the *Shah Nameh,* but the Indonesian versions were considerably amplified, using indigenous motifs.

The story, which is very long (a Malay version has 1,845 pages), recounts the entire life of the hero, from his birth in Mecca (where he miraculously escapes from a massacre of the innocents) to his apotheosis in the paradise of Allah. Just like Iskandar Zulkarnain, Amir Hamzah is presented as a champion of Islam who converted his enemies to the true religion, but this theme is not essential; somewhat like Pañji, who tried to find his fiancée Candra Kirana, Amir Hamzah tries to win the hand of the beautiful Mihrnigar, the daughter of King Nusyirwan, of whom he immediately becomes enamoured. This "quest" serves as a framework for a series of episodes, of war or of gallantry, for while he is waiting the hero has other amorous adventures and ends up with a large number of descendants. He often comes up against the jealousy and the hostility of unscrupulous rivals such as Gustehem or Bekhtek, who try to get rid of him, but he can count on the loyalty of certain companions, such as his namesake Amir, the son of Omayya (a servant of his father) born the same day as he, or, in the Javanese version, two clownish servants who recall the *punakawan* of the *wayang,* Marmaya and Marmadi.

On Java, the episodes of the *Menak* were taken up again by the *wayang golek.*

Muhammad Hanafiah. A hero of the Shiite Muslim tradition, Muhammad Hanafiah's exploits are recounted in an important Malay text, the *Hikayat Muhammad Hanafiyyah,* which was probably adapted from the Persian during the fifteenth century. The text is known through at least thirty manuscripts and a lithographed edition in Singapore. The story is no longer popular today, but it is extremely interesting in that it attests to a Shiite presence in the Malay world at the very beginning of Islamization.

The half brother of the "martyrs" of Shiism, Hasan and Husayn, Muhammad Hanafiah appears here as a brave warrior who seeks to avenge them. After the death of Husayn on the battlefield of Karbala, Yazid prepares to put his prisoners to death. But Muhammad Hanafiah gathers together the partisans of Ali and takes up the battle again. Yazid is forced to seek help from the four Oriental kings (Frankish, Chinese, Abyssinian, and Zanj); Muhammad Hanafiah is captured, and is going to be burned alive, but he is saved at the last minute and his severed arm is miraculously rejoined. Yazid tries to escape but is killed in the flames. All the prisoners are liberated, and Muhammad Hanafiah restores Zainal Abidin, the son of Husayn, to the throne. Muhammad Hanafiah then learns that Yazid's followers have gathered in a cave to prepare their revenge, and he goes there and massacres a large number of them. But a mysterious voice orders him to stop, and the door to the cave quickly closes on him. His companions mourn him for three days and three nights.

Traces of Shiism are evident elsewhere in Sumatra and in Java, where the date of the battle of Karbala, the tenth day of the month of Muharram (Asyura), was commemorated by the preparation of a special kind of pulp (*bubur suren*). Even today in Priaman, on the west coast of Sumatra, Asyura is still celebrated by throwing into the sea a cenotaph (*tabut*) which is thought to be that of the martyr Husayn, but it is possible that this ritual was introduced more recently (in the eighteenth century).

Portrait of Prince Diponegoro, leader of a revolt against the Dutch in the nineteenth century, who has been accorded the rank of "national hero" in independent Indonesia. Photo Marcel Bonneff.

IV. Modern Heroes

A last type of culture hero, which will merely be mentioned here, is perhaps not as far removed from the preceding heroes as one might think; these are the national heroes that the independent states of insular Southeast Asia have chosen to symbolize the birth of a new society: Rizal and Aguinaldo for the Philippines, and Hasanuddin, Kartini, and Imam Bonjol for Indonesia. Although they are historical, each of these figures has his myth—simplified official biographies, widely disseminated, particularly through schools—his commemorative ritual, his stereotyped iconography, etc.

The frequency with which they are mentioned shows how much modern societies, from that point of view, have traits in common with so-called primitive societies.

D.L. and C.P./t.l.f.

BIBLIOGRAPHY

W. H. RASSERS, *De Pandji-Roman* (Antwerp 1922); summarized in English in the article by J. J. Ras cited below. *Pañji the Culture Hero* (The Hague 1959); translation of articles only loosely connected with the myth of Pañji. R. M. NG. POERBATJARAKA, *Pandji-verhalen onderling vergeleken* (Bandung 1940); Indonesian translation by Zuber Usman and H. B. Jassin (Jakarta 1968). R. O. WINSTEDT, "The Panji Tales," *JMBRAS* 19, 2 (1941): 234–37. C. C. BERG, "Bijdragen tot de kennis der Pandji verhalen," *BKI* 110, 3–4 (1954). TJAN TJOE SIEM, "Masques javanais," *Arts Asiatiques* 20 (1969): 185–208. S. O. ROBSON, *Wangbang Wideya* (The Hague 1971). J. J. RAS, "The Panji Romance and W. H. Rassers' Analysis of Its Theme," *BKI* 129, 4 (1972): 411–56. P. J. VAN LEEUWEN, *De Maleise Alexander Roman* (Utrecht 1937). L. F. BRAKEL, *The Hikayat Muhammad Hanafiyyah: A Medieval Muslim Malay Romance* (The Hague 1975).

Communal Festivals in Insular Southeast Asia

Communal festivals in insular Southeast Asia are generally annual. They plunge society back into the mythical time of origins by recreating the unity of the cosmos in order to purify it from all evil influences and to ensure its vitality and fertility through the ensuing period.

At Kalimantan, among the Ngaju, groups of villages celebrate the *tiwah* in this way, in the name of the entire Ngaju people, on the occasion of lesser funerals which are generally collective, sometimes for as many as sixty dead. The public ceremonies last seven days. The first four days, which are marked by strict prohibitions, center on funerary rituals and involve two ceremonies whose purpose is to make the spiritual soul (*liau*) and the corporeal soul (*liau karaban*) of the dead pass, under the guidance of Tempon Telon, the psychopomp spirit, to the land of the dead (*lewu liau*), where they are reunited and reawakened to a new life. Parallel to this, their remains, which had been brought to the village and cremated to begin the festival, are now brought in vessels (*sandong*) intended for them. On the principal day, the fifth, which is marked by many delegations from neighboring villages bearing offerings, the prohibitions are lifted. On this day the ancestors visit the living, and the people return to the time of origins through the ritual. The final two days are set aside for the purification of the participants.

The great festival of the Iban, which is related to headhunting, is the *gawai kenyalang* or *gawai burong;* it concerns all the inhabitants of the village (which may merely correspond to a longhouse). A great number of participants are invited from outside, and much rice beer (*tuak*) is drunk. As with other Iban ceremonies (*gawai batu,* the ceremony before the clearing of the land; *gawai benih,* before sowing; and *gawai antu,* festivals of the dead among the Saribas Krian Iban), it includes among its rites augury (*beburong*), propitiary sacrifices of chickens or pigs (*ginselan*), cockfights (*sabong*), offerings (*piring*), and incantations (*pengap*).

In Sumatra, every Batak territorial unit had an annual festival of purification, called *bius.* It centered on a buffalo sacrifice and involved many mock battles.

In Nias, the *börö n'adu* was celebrated every seven or fourteen years in the various parts of the island in which the first ancestors descended from the sky; each of the places was marked by a temple (*osali*) and a sacred tree (*fösi*). It brought together many villages which were themselves grouped into cultural communities (*öri*); it lasted five days and included songs, dances, and offerings. According to P. Suzuki, the festival carried with it the idea of a periodic renewal of the cosmos, whose annihilation is first symbolized by simulated battles and by throwing into deep water the statues that each *öri* has brought. It also symbolizes rebirth through the offering of food to a sacred pig which is to remain intact for the following seven years. Through this periodic return to the time of origins, the union of men with the divine world is also clearly celebrated.

In spite of great differences in details, all of the festivals—as well as the *bua' kasalle* of the Toraja of South Celebes, the *reba* of the Ngada of Flores, the *porka* of the Southwest Moluccas, etc.—are concerned with well-defined territorial and even political units, whose integrity they attempt to ensure when they appeal for fertility and prosperity for their populations, their harvests, and their herds.

The introduction of the great religions in places where the local religion was already old did not make the latter disappear completely. One can regard the *galungan* festival of the Hinduized Balinese, and perhaps even the Muslim Javanese *garebeg,* as continuations of these.

Galungan is one of the most important Balinese festivals. As it has no direct correspondence with original Hinduism, it should probably be related to a pre-Hindu tradition. According to tradition, it was instituted to commemorate the victory that the people of Bali gained over the magician king Maya Danawa with the help of the army of the gods led by Indra. It is celebrated on the Wednesday of the eleventh week of the liturgical year of 210 days. This is a case of a true "national" festival in the strongest sense, in which the alliance of the gods with men is renewed by making the latter depositaries and life tenants of the earth, of which the former are the true lords.

A few days before the festival, temples and family sanctuaries are first purified, and some rituals take place to appease the Galungan "demon" (*buta*), the incarnation of Batara Kala, who is supposed to descend to earth on this occasion.

Yogyakarta (central Java): the royal ritual of the *garebeg.* Symbolic offerings of food in the form of mountains (*gunungan*), indications of harmony between the ruler and the people, are carried in a huge procession from the palace to the great mosque. The ceremony is made up of a number of elements of pre-Indian origin, yet today it takes place three times a year on the principal Muslim feasts. In the foreground, the female *gunungan,* and in the background, the male *gunungan.* Photo Marcel Bonneff.

Ceremonies are organized on the day of Galungan. These take place in every temple of the village: the temple of origin (*pura puseh*), the principal temple (*pura desa* or *pura agung*), the temple of the dead (*pura dalem*); in every temple of the kingdom: the mountain temple (*pura panataran*) and the marine temple (*pura segara*); in every family sanctuary (*sanggah*); and in every site considered important to the house and the territory: beds, hearths, granaries, courtyards, stables, entryways, streets, intersections, gardens, canals, lakes, rivers, springs; and, finally, in all the cemeteries where the dead await cremation. After this, everyone visits family and friends to offer their good wishes. Ten days of festivities follow, which are marked by an atmosphere of rejoicing, with dancing and theatrical presentations, ending with the day of Kuningan. This is a day of introspection that is dedicated principally to honoring divinized ancestors who are supposed to descend to earth on this day to receive homage and the offerings of men and to reciprocate with their blessing on the world of the living.

R. Goris showed very convincingly that in earlier times the

liturgical cycle must have begun on the day following Kuningan. Moreover, the name *galungan* seems to be related to the root *guling,* "turn," "make a revolution." This thus seems to be an ancient rite of the "regeneration of time," representing the death and rebirth of a universe that is conceived as fundamentally dualistic.

As for the *garebeg,* this is a great Javanese collective ritual which makes it possible for the ruler (the sultan of Yogyakarta, sunan of Surakarta, or sultans of Cirebon) to assert his power in renewing the bond that ties him to his people. The festival has been attested since the time of Majapahit, but has been greatly Islamized. Today there are three *garebegs,* fixed according to the Islamic calendar (*G. Mulud, G. Sawal,* and *G. Besar,* the last corresponding to Idul Adha); the most important is the first, which falls on the anniversary of the birth of the Prophet (*Mulud*). The people from the countryside converge upon the capital at this time, and a great fair takes place; this is also the time when taxes are paid, generally in the form of rice. The rice is then partially cooked and prepared in the form of "mountains" (*gunungan*). On the appointed day, the ruler appears in all his majesty before his functionaries and his subjects, and the *gunungan* (one considered male and the other female) are brought out with great pomp (the primary meaning of *garebeg* is "procession"). After a short trip to the mosque (to receive the blessing of the *pangulu*), the *gunungan* are given to the crowd, which falls on them to get a piece.

D.L. and C.P./d.w.

Indonesian Rites of Passage

Despite the diversity of rituals in insular Southeast Asia, the cycle of rites of passage is remarkably similar from one ethnic group to another.

Before birth, most often in the seventh month, but sometimes as early as the third or fifth month, there is a ceremony that the Malays call *lenggang perut:* a ceremonial massage of the future mother's belly, with or without propitiatory offerings. After birth, for several days, it is customary for the mother of the newborn to stay close to the fire all the time, and everywhere this time is marked by a period of taboos that ends only with the ritual purification of mother and child.

A whole series of ceremonies marks the recognition of the infant as a new member of the community and his progression to adult status: naming, cutting a lock of hair, piercing the ears (for girls), and first contact with the earth, all of which occur in the course of the first months. Then, at adolescence, circumcision (not only for Muslims), filing the teeth, and in some regions tattooing (though this has often fallen into disuse).

The filing of the teeth—a rite of passage once found among most ethnic groups in insular Southeast Asia, and performed on marriageable young men and women—involved filing down the ends (and sometimes even the whole) of the incisors and/or the canines of the upper jaw. On Bali, the ceremony is supposed to rid people of the *sadripu*—the "six enemies," or six evil spirits that personify the fundamental faults of human nature. It constitutes a step on the road that leads humans from the world below to the world above, the last step of which will be cremation. It must therefore normally take place before marriage; and if people die before they undergo this ritual, a surrogate rite precedes cremation.

Marriage rites are often highly elaborate and present many local differences; the differences depend especially on the role played by marriage alliance in the society and also on the extent to which the rites include Muslim or Christian rites. The rites also have elements common to many ethnic groups. The union of the couple is above all manifested by the public performance of an act done together: eating together, sitting solemnly together, etc. To this are added the ritual acts that mark the establishment or confirmation of an alliance between the families, which consist essentially in an exchange of customary gifts. In societies in which the alliances follow a system of generalized exchange, the goods offered by those who give the bride often include fabrics, and those coming from the groom's side include weapons. Among the Batak, the two groups even have the names of *ulos* (fabrics) and *piso* (knives), respectively; these two elements apparently represent the female and the male aspects of totality.

As for funeral practices, all techniques are or have been represented in Indonesia: besides inhumation, which is the most widespread because of Muslim and Christian influences (but which already existed almost everywhere even before), the dead are put in man-made or natural caves (southern Toraja), lie in state (Bali Aga), or are abandoned (forest nomads of Punan), inserted into a crack of a tree that will close up again over the body (Ot Kayam, Toraja), put in a coffin in the branches of a tree or on top of a post (Nias, Ngaju), buried in rock containers (north Celebes), temporarily buried with subsequent retrieval of the bones (Ngaju, north Nias), or cremated (Bali, Ngaju, Maajan); there may even be some endocannibalism (Batak, Ot Pari). But of all these funeral rites, cremation is undoubtedly one of the most spectacular.

In insular Southeast Asia, it is above all the Balinese Hindus who are known for practicing cremation, but in reality this ritual is performed by several other non-Hindu ethnic groups in Sumatra (Batak Karo), in Borneo (Ngaju), and formerly in Celebes (Bugis); in Bali itself, numerous pre-Hindu elements are apparent and indicate that we are dealing here as elsewhere in insular Southeast Asia with a double funeral ritual.

In most cases the dead are first buried and only their bones (which are sometimes even cleaned) are burned. It even happens that burial may have taken place so long ago that they must be satisfied with collecting a little earth from the tomb and burn only an effigy (*adegan*) of the dead person. Usually the ashes are scattered in a river, after they have been honored, but they may also be preserved in special urns. The general schema behind the ritual is therefore parallel to the one found among the Ngaju of Kalimantan and the one that the Batak used to practice. In all cases, the second funerals are intended to raise the dead person to the rank of ancestor (*pitra,* in Bali).

In Bali, dead princes are not buried; their bodies are preserved, as in the Toraja region, in many layers of fabrics. However, twelve days after cremation, a second ceremony takes place (*ngerorasin* or *mitra yadnya*) during which the recalled and symbolically fed soul lives in an effigy (*puspa*). The effigy will be burned after the soul has been sent back

In the Sundanese region (western Java) the circumcised child, dressed like a hero in the traditional theater, is paraded through the village. Photo Marcel Bonneff.

(Right) In the state of Johoe, young Malay newlyweds enthroned (*bersanding*) like "regents for a day," before gathered guests. Photo Christian Pelras.

Bali: for cremation, the remains of the deceased are placed in the replica of a psychopomp animal, which varies according to the caste. This bull—for a nobleman—is carried to the site of the pyre by a group of men spinning around to chase away the evil spirits. Photo X.

(*merelina*) to join the ancestors. In this particular case (which has a parallel among certain non-Islamic peoples of eastern Java), we can also speak of double funerals.

Beyond the diversity of particular cases, the double funerals are the most characteristic and constant feature of insular Southeast Asia; second funerals, often more modest than first funerals, are designed to cut definitively the ties that bind the dead to the world of the living and to make him a part of the world of ancestors; the second funerals have been perpetuated in Java in the form of the *kenduri arwah,* a votive meal that takes place forty days after burial (and double funerals remain very important in Madagascar).

The community festivals that used to take place in many ethnic groups were closely connected to ancestor worship and sometimes to funeral rites. But in many areas, they have fallen into disuse, either because of recent Islamization or Christianization, or simply because they were very costly and the local administration discouraged the practice.

On the other hand, simple agrarian rites performed within the home have survived very well until now, even in regions that have long been Islamized; the principal ones are associated with planting and harvesting the staple food (generally rice). This is also true of fishing rites in the coastal regions and of construction rites everywhere. Elements of the various rites can be found in virtually all areas. Let us cite among others the communal meals, food offerings, and sacrifices.

In Java, the communal meal is called a *slametan* and is very much in use among those known as *abagan* ("the red ones"), that is, among those for whom Islam has not eliminated many old beliefs and practices. The *slametan,* whose purpose

A Toraja funeral, in South Celebes, involves the sacrifice of many water buffalo. At the end of a cycle of ceremonies that may last for several years, the coffins are placed in cavities dug out of cliff faces. Photo Gilbert Hamonic and Christian Pelras.

is to obtain general welfare (*slamet*) for the participants, takes place before any important collective act, or sometimes after it, in order to give thanks. The meal is eaten in the traditional way, on the ground on a mat; it is preceded by a prayer or the recitation of a formula by a pious man invited for the occasion; the food, generally "yellow rice" (*nasi kuning*), rice colored with turmeric, is eaten with the fingers. In areas where Malay is spoken, they speak rather of *kenduri*. These meals, often accompanied by offerings of food to the ancestors or guardian spirits, also have a clearly sacrificial aspect; the sacrificed animals are chickens, goats (pigs for non-Muslims), or water buffaloes, depending on the importance of the occasion.

Particular cases of blood sacrifices are the cockfights (the meaning is quite clear in Bali; it is less clear elsewhere, where the sporting aspect has become dominant) and headhunting. According to Stöhr, headhunting probably represented the original murder by which food plants were introduced into the world; and it appears certain that it had something to do with fertility rites.

In many traditional religions in insular Southeast Asia, headhunting is a ritual of great importance, and it was apparently once practiced by all the peoples of the archipelago, for whom it represented the highest form of blood sacrifice, next to animal sacrifice (in ascending order of value: chickens, dogs, hogs, and water buffaloes). It was of course suppressed as soon as the colonial administration established its authority over the regions where it was still practiced. The heads that the community needed for certain rites were obtained by surprise attacks, most often on isolated and defenseless individuals (women and children) of neighboring and unfriendly communities. The heads were welcomed in the village by shouts of rejoicing.

Although there was great diversity, it seems that the heads were primarily necessary for the performance of the funeral rites that enabled the dead to reach the status of ancestors and enabled the community to be completely purified. The proper performance was a precondition for the celebration of the agrarian rites of the community and a guarantee of fertility. There is probably a connection with the numerous myths of the origin of rice and other cultivated plants, linking their appearance with the death of an original semi-divine person.

The way that headhunting was practiced limited it in practice to peoples who lived in small autonomous communities (the interior of Kalimantan and of Celebes, Ceram, Timor, etc.). Wherever there was a form of supraterritorial political unity, it tended to be replaced by sacrifices either of slaves or of water buffaloes; but although the warriors were no longer head-hunters, they remained "beheaders" for a long time.

D.L. and C.P./g.h.

A Myth of the Origin of Grains: Hainuwele in Ceram, Indonesia

W. Stöhr proposes to group under the heading of the myth of Hainuwele a series of beliefs, frequent in the Malay archipelago, which connect the appearance in the world of the first food plants (very often rice) with the death of a hero or, more frequently, of a heroine.

Hainuwele, whose name has been used to characterize this theme, is the central character of an origin myth of the Wemale (Ceram, Indonesia).

In the olden days, when the nine clans of the first humans still live on the sacred mountain of Nunusaku, the hero Ameta discovers, while chasing a boar, a fruit then unknown to him, the coconut. Soon after it has been planted, the coconut becomes a mature tree. Ameta wants to cut short its inflorescence in order to collect the sap from which palm wine is made, and he cuts his finger. From the mixture of his blood with the sap a baby girl is born whom he names Hainuwele ("palm frond"). After three days, Hainuwele, already nubile, is invited to participate in the great *maro* dance: the men of the nine original human families form a spiral, and the women sitting in the center offer them betel. But things are different with Hainuwele, as on the second night she offers them corals; on the third, Chinese porcelains; on the fourth, large porcelain dishes; on the fifth, machetes; on the sixth, a copper betel service; on the seventh, gold earrings; and on the eighth, magnificent gongs. These goods of increasing value come from the metamorphosis of her excrement. Moved by jealousy, the first men dig a hole in the middle of the dancing area and on the ninth night make Hainuwele fall into it and bury her alive. Surprised that his daughter has not come home, Ameta goes out to search for her and finally digs her up, dead: this is the first death in this world. Ameta then cuts the body of Hainuwele into pieces and buries them: these produce the tubers (yams, taro), which are staples of the Wemale diet. Furthermore, in her wrath at the murder, Mulua Satene, the woman who ruled over the first men, strikes them with one of Hainuwele's arms. Some are transformed into pigs, deer, birds, or fish; others remain human, but become mortal. Then Mulua Satene goes to live on Mount Saluhua, one of the two sacred mountains of Ceram, where she will reign over the souls of the dead.

There is general agreement that Mulua Hainuwele and Mulua Satene are two aspects of the female divinity, of which the other manifestations are Mulua Dapie Bulane (the Moon) and Tapele (the Earth). The male counterpart of the female aspect is Tuwala Lia Matai (the Sun), Lanite (the Sky), Mabitu (the Creator), who has as his home the sacred mountain of Nunusaku. As is the case elsewhere in Southeast Asia, these two entities represent the two opposite and complementary aspects upon which the cosmic whole rests. This assimilation is all the more plausible in that one finds many parallels to it throughout the rest of the archipelago.

According to one interpretation, the Dewi Sri of the Balinese corresponds only superficially to the Śrī of Hinduism, the former being a personification of the primordial chthonic and lunar female divinity, in whom are reunited the contradictory and indissolubly linked forces of death and fertility, and who is also known as Dewi Danuh, the divinity of the waters. Under the name of Sri, she becomes the goddess of ripening rice and of the monsoon; under the name of Uma, she is the divinity of germination; under the name of Durga, she is the goddess of the dead and the mistress of the *butukala* who threaten future harvests with diseases and pests; under the name of Ibu Pertiwi, she is the goddess of terrestrial fertility; finally, under the name of

Two views of the cult of Sri, the rice goddess in Indonesia. *Left:* in Celebes, in the Bugis region, an offering of popcorn (the food of the gods) from the first sheaves of the harvest, the embodiment of Sangian Serri. Photo Christian Pelras. *Right:* in Bali, a symbol of Dewi Sri, hanging in a rice field as protection. Photo Marcel Bonneff.

Giriputri, she is the goddess of the sacred mountain of Gunung Agung, from which comes the holy water that blesses the harvest, while the masculine deity of Gunung Agung is Mahādeva, a name which designates the male, heavenly, and solar god who is also hidden behind the names of Surya and Siwa.

But a Javanese account allows us to establish an even more striking parallel between Dewi Sri and Hainuwele. This account relates that from a jewel brought from the netherworld by the serpent Antaboga, a young girl named Tisnawati was born. The heavenly god Batara Guru wants to marry her. She resists his advances and dies. From her body, buried in the earthly kingdom of Mendang Kamulan, various plants come into being: the coconut palm from her head; rice from her sex organ; the banana tree from the palms of her hands; corn from her teeth. The king of Mendang Kamulan, while visiting his rice fields, sees a great serpent, which at his approach turns into a young girl who tells him she is a metamorphosis of Dewi Sri, the wife of Wisnu, who will become incarnate as his own wife.

For the Sundanese, the neighbors of the Javanese, the rice divinity Nyi Pohaci (also known as Sanghyang Sri) was hatched from an egg produced from the tears of the serpent of the netherworld, Dewa Anta or Antaboga. Dewa Wenang, fearing that the sky god Batara Guru may marry her, has her eat the fruit of the tree of paradise. Unable to tolerate other food any longer, she ends up dying of hunger. Various useful plants appear on her tomb: the coconut palm, born from her head; rice from her eyes; bamboo from her thighs, etc. The plants are brought to King Siliwangi, who instructs one of his wives, the celestial (lunar) nymph Dewi Nawang Sasih, to take care of the rice, and she teaches the people how to cook it. In those days, one spike of rice was sufficient, when cooked, to feed a hundred people. But Siliwangi broke the taboo against touching the kitchen utensils, and since then rice no longer multiplies with cooking, because Dewi Nawang Sasih has returned to the sky.

In these two accounts, there is an implicit equivalence—noted by Rassers with respect to the Javanese myth—between Dewi Sri and the semidivine female character who becomes the wife of the king. Both appear as personifications of this female lunar goddess from the netherworld, an idea found in Ceram as well as Bali.

In other regions, where outside influences were less important, the character of Sri has a more secondary place in the myth, although there are many resemblances to the preceding accounts.

Thus, for the Bugis, rice arose, in the time of origins, on the tomb of the daughter of the first being who descended from the sky. This being, La Toge' langi' Batara Guru, is the son of the principal god of the upper world, whose wife comes from the netherworld. He descends to earth to populate it, and he fathers a little girl named We O'dangriu, who dies after seven days. He ascends to the sky to share his sorrow with his father, who tells him that his child has become rice, in order that the subsistence of man may be made secure. Since then, she has been known as Sangiang Serri.

In Flores, too, it is the children of the original couple whose bodies, cut into pieces, become transformed into food plants.

D.L. and C.P./d.w.

The *Wayang* (Ritual Theater) and Its Myths in Java and Bali

The *wayang* is a very important ritual in Java and Bali, which became a performance (shadow play) only recently and under the influence of Westernization. It is also performed in certain regions influenced by Indo-Javanese culture, such as the Banjar region (southern Kalimantan), Palembang, and the state of Kelantan (on the Malay peninsula).

first *walis;* he did not die until after he had understood the true meaning of their secret and was buried behind the great mosque of Demak, where there is still a tomb said to be his.

2. Bima

Second among the Pandawas, Bima is the son of Prabu Pandu and Dewi Kunti. In the *wayang,* and more generally in Javanese mythology, he appears as a major hero, a symbol of strength, courage, and righteousness. He is also named Bratasena or Bayusuta (in his youth) and Werkudara (when he is older).

One of the oldest *lakons* that we have evidence of, the tenth-century *lakon* known as *Bima bungkus*, mainly tells of his marvelous birth: Bima is imprisoned by a particularly resistant and constricting placenta until he is set free by an elephant called Sena.

Here too, the hero of the Indian epic has taken on several characteristics that belong to much older figures. R. Goris has shown how wind, lightning, and other forces of nature become incarnate. Bima is presented as the adopted son of Sang Hyang Bayu (the wind), and as the brother of Hanuman, Begawan Maenaka, and Liman Sena, who are like his emanations. All five are represented wearing loincloths decorated with the *poleng* motif (black and white checks), which attests both to their bonds of kinship and, for our purposes, to their membership in the substratum. W. F. Stutterheim also claims to have found in the fourteenth and fifteenth century elements of what he would call a "cult of Bima"; certain iconographic details in the temple of Sukuh (near the modern city of Yogyakarta) indicate this, notably a large statue representing the hero (now in a private collection in Surakarta). This piece of evidence, together with certain popular traditions, leads us to think that Bima was honored as a benevolent deity during the waning days of the Indianized period, shortly before the people converted to Islam.

His righteousness and courage notwithstanding, Bima has something of the demoniac in him by virtue of his stature. His weapon is the *pancanaka,* a single extremely blunt nail with which he stabs all his enemies. Through his unions he also participates in the parallel world of monsters. His first wife is Dewi Nagagini, daughter of the snake Antaboga. (The five Pandawas encounter her when they flee the palace fire set by the Kurawas and take refuge deep in the seventh underground world.) She bears Bima his first son, the divine Antasena. His second wife is Dewi Arimbi, sister of the ogre Prabu Arimba, herself an ogress, who bears him a second son, the valiant Gatotkaca.

Bima also appears in *lakons* whose philosophical content reveals his extraordinary power. One of the most famous is the *lakon* called *Dewa Ruci* (or *Bima suci*), which tells of his quest for perfect knowledge. Durna, the counselor of the Kurawas, orders him to search for the water of immortality (*Toyamarta*) in the hope that he will lose his life during the search. Bima sets out courageously and heads toward Mount Candramuka, where he triumphs over the two monsters Rukmuka and Rukmakala, but finds nothing. Durna then advises him to search in the middle of the ocean. Bima goes off again, triumphs over the serpent Nemburnyawa, and finally meets his master, the dwarf Dewa Ruci, who looks just like him and who advises him to enter into him to find supreme wisdom. "I look smaller than you," he tells him, "but in fact the whole world is within me." In another *lakon* called *Sena Rodra* (Angry Bima), Bima boasts of a supernatural knowledge that comes from the countries of the West (*saking tanah brang kilen*). The gods are very uneasy when they see that he possesses and distributes the kind of knowledge, here called *Sastra Jendra,* of which they alone had previously had the secret. Bima and his family are arrested and detained for a time in a corner of paradise, but the gods are attacked by giants and must call on him. Then he is freed and returns to reign in Java.

In popular imagery there is often an image of Bima, notably a depiction of the scene where he fights with the serpent Nemburnyawa in the middle of the sea. There are even some paintings on glass depicting the same episode. Popular belief also recognizes the silhouette of Bima in the southern part of the Milky Way (*lintang Bima sekti*).

The memory of Bima remains even in modern life. The fast train that runs daily between Djakarta and Surabaya was christened "Bima" (an allusion to the swiftness of the hero who flies "like the wind"), and the three-masted boat used by the Indonesian navy as a teaching vessel was christened "Dewa ruci."

The myth of Bima can also be found in eastern Sumbawa island, where a small Sultanate used to have that name.

3. Arjuna

Arjuna is the third of the Pandawas and one of the main heroes of the Indian *Mahābhārata* and the Javanese *wayang.* Like Bima, he is a brave warrior, but with a much more

Illustration of a libretto in Indonesian telling the story of Arjuna. He is represented here as a *wayang* puppet, surrounded by the seven *bidadari* temptresses.

delicate complexion than his older brother. He is as handsome as a god, and his amorous conquests are countless. He has been called the Javanese Don Juan, but in fact it is often the women who, seduced by his charms, pursue him. He also goes by other names: Parta, Margana, Panduputra, Kuntadi, Palguna, Danajaya, and especially Janaka and Pamade.

Arjuna has a slight defect, an extra finger on his right hand, an index finger that once belonged to King Prabu Palgundi, but which Druna gave him with the talisman it was wearing, the Ampal ring, whose power is without equal. Arjuna also has other extraordinary magical weapons: the Pulanggeni kris and the Sarotama arrow. All of this makes it possible for him to gain the victory during the single combats he engages in on the occasion of the Bharatayuddha; and notably it allows him to triumph over his half brother Adipati Karna, whom he loves but who has joined the ranks of the Kurawas.

His character is, as it were, inseparable from his many wives. The two most famous are Dewi Sumbadra and Dewi Srikandi. The first is the archetype of the modest and faithful wife. She resists Burisrawa's advances and prefers to kill herself (she is later revived). She is the mother of Angkawijaya (or Abimayu), whose son, Parikesit, is to be the only survivor of the terrible fratricidal war. She triumphs over Resi Bisma, one of the champions of the Kurawas. Among the wives of the second rank, we should also mention Dewi Srimendang, a princess; Rarasati, a simple attendant, the daughter of a shepherd; and Dewi Ulupi, the daughter of a hermit. But we must not forget the beautiful Banowati, the legal wife of Suyudana, king of the Kurawas and the adversary of the Pandawas. After her husband's death, Banowati takes refuge with Arjuna.

Arjuna has one final feature that complements the others. He can control his passions and impulses perfectly, and he knows how to intensify his power and strength through asceticism. This is one of the fundamental features of Javanese philosophy: a retreat into the forest allows one to commune from time to time with supernatural forces and to "recharge" one's own energy. A famous eleventh-century poem in Old Javanese, the *Arjunawiwaha,* tells the story of Arjuna's retreat on Mount Indrakila. He takes the name of Bengawan Mintaraga and suffers the assaults of seven celestial creatures (the *bidadaris*) sent by the gods to tempt him and distract him from his meditation. The gods are in fact threatened by the giant Niwatakawaca and want to ask Arjuna's help. The hero finally overcomes the monster and receives a part of the celestial kingdom as a reward.

4. Nakula and Sadewa

In Java as in India, the twins who complete the team of Pandawas play a secondary role. We should, however, note that, like Bima, Sadewa must at one time have enjoyed the privilege of being considered a benevolent hero. Several fourteenth- and fifteenth-century bas-reliefs depict him battling the entire army of evil spirits that the dreadful Durga commands.

D.L. and C.P./g.h.

BIBLIOGRAPHY

J. KATS, *Het javaansche toneel* (Weltevreden 1923). HARDJOWIROGO, *Sedjarah Wajang Purwa* (Djakarta 1965); in Indonesian, catalog of the characters of the *wayang.* J. R. BRANDON, *On Thrones of Gold: Three Javanese Shadow Plays* (Cambridge, MA, 1970).

Concerning the *kayon:* W. F. STUTTERHEIM, "Oost-Java en de Hemelberg," *Djåwå,* 1926, pp. 333ff. W. AICHELE, "Bijdrage tot de Geschiedenis van de Wenschboom," *Djåwå,* 1928, pp. 18ff. K. A. H. HIDDING, "De Betekenis van de Kakajon," *TBG* 71 (1931): 623–62.

Concerning the character of Bima: R. GORIS, "Storm-kind en geestes zoon," *Djåwå* 7 (1927): 110–13. W. F. STUTTERHEIM, "Een oud-Javaansche Bhima-Cultus," *Djåwå* 15 (1935): 37ff. H. OVERBECK, "Bima als goeroe," *Djåwå* 19 (1939): 12–21. A. PANNEKOEK, "Een merkwaardig Javaansch sterrebeld," *TBG* 69 (1929): 51ff.

THE *RĀMĀYAṆA* IN INDONESIA

The story of Rāma reached insular Southeast Asia relatively early. There is a ninth-century Javanese version, and the main episodes can be found depicted on the bas-reliefs of the Hindu temple of Prambanan (ninth century, near Yogyakarta), and later in Panataran (fourteenth century, east Java). As in Thailand and Cambodia, certain Javanese court dances are directly inspired by the *Rāmāyaṇa.* But side by side with this tradition, which is rather close to the classical model, is another, substantially different one, which takes up several themes that have nothing to do with Vālmīki's *Rāmāyaṇa.*

The *Hikayat Sri Rama* ("History of the divine Rāma") is an old Malay text that illustrates the parallel tradition well. From Mandudari, whom he found in a bamboo, King Dasarata had two sons: Rāma and Lakṣamaṇa. The giant Rāvaṇa, king of Langka, heard of Mandudari's beauty and came to ask Dasarata for her. From the secretion from her skin (Malay *daki*), Mandudari made a frog that transformed itself into a beautiful woman in her likeness. This double, called Mandu-daki, was given to Rawana. Dasarata, however, managed to sleep with Mandu-daki first; she later gave birth to a daughter, named Sita Dewi. Following a prediction that Sita would marry Rawana's victorious opponent, Rawana got rid of the infant by abandoning it in a chest drifting downstream. Sita was saved, was raised by an ascetic, and later married Rāma. Rāma and Sita swam in a magic lake and found themselves transformed into monkeys; this is how they conceived Hanuman, who was "transferred" into the womb of Dewi Anjani, who carried him and gave birth to him. Rawana abducted Sita, but Rāma retrieved her with the help of Hanuman.

D.L. and C.P./g.h.

BIBLIOGRAPHY

W. STUTTERHEIM, *Rāma Legenden und Rāma-Reliefs in Indonesien,* 2 vols. (Munich 1925). A. ZIESENISS, *Die Rāma Sage bei den Malaien, Ihre Herkunft und Gestaltung* (Hamburg 1928). P. L. AMIN SWEENEY, *The Ramayana and the Malay Shadow-play* (Kuala Lumpur 1972).

Two Javanese views of Rāma: on a bas-relief of the temple of Prambanan (expedition against Lanka, with the help of Hanumān and his army of monkeys); and as performed by a dancer at the court of Yogyakarta.

Recent Forms of Eschatology and Messianism in Insular Southeast Asia

If it is the case that the mythologies of insular Southeast Asia are particularly rich in myths about origins—the origin of the world, of men, of cultivated plants—then it may be asked whether a mythology also developed about the future and the last things. This phenomenon is well-attested in some places: Kalimantan and Nias, and especially Java, where numerous popular movements have been colored by millenarianism. Some recent studies, notably those of Professor Sartono Kartodirdjo of Yogyakarta, have drawn attention to precisely these marginal ideologies, which are perhaps influenced by time-oriented religions (the "end of the world" of Christianity, the *kiamat* of Islam) and exacerbated by social and colonial oppression.

At present, a great number of predictions (*ramalan, pralambang*) are attributed to a certain Jayabaya (pronounced Joyoboyo), who is a sort of Javanese Nostradamus. Collections of his predictions circulate among the people from time to time, especially when the political situation deteriorates and social tensions increase. This mythical figure, of ill-defined appearance, is sometimes assimilated to King Jayabhaya of Kediri, whose existence is certified by inscriptions dating from 1135 and 1141 and whose name figures in a colophon of the *Bharatayuddha,* a sacred text which told of the fratricidal battle between the Pandawas and the Kurawas, and which has inspired a great many *lakons* of the *wayang*.

In fact, Jayabaya's reputation may not be very old. It is said that his predictions were cast into a definite form by the famous poet Ranggawarsita who flourished in the nineteenth century (d. 1873), but his success was assured especially after the beginning of the twentieth century. Following the war in the Pacific, there was much commentary on the

Cover of a work about the predictions of Jayabaya.

prediction according to which "Java would be occupied by dwarfs who came from another island for a time equal to the life of a corn plant" (an allusion to the Japanese occupation); and the work of a certain Tjantrik Mataram, who attempted to connect the *ramalan* of the diviner with the phases of the Indonesian revolution, was immensely successful.

Although the figure of Jayabaya is definitely quite recent, the Javanese people's taste for the *pralambang* is certainly older. Brandes published a text of this genre which is certainly from before 1715, and since the eighteenth century there have been numerous testimonies to a latent messianism. The predictions generally announce that after a particularly troubled period (*zaman edan,* "period of madness") would come a new golden age marked by the coming of a *Ratu adil,* "King of Justice." This "Ratuadilism," as historians who have studied it name it, underlaid many of the peasant uprisings and other popular movements that erupted in Java throughout the nineteenth century.

D.L. and C.P./d.w.

BIBLIOGRAPHY

J. L. A. BRANDES, "Iets over een oudere Dipanegara in verband met een prototype van de voorspellingen van Jayabaya," *TBG* 32 (1889): 368–430. TJANTRIK MATARAM, *Peranan Ramalan Djojobojo dalam Revolusi kita* (3d ed., Bandung 1948). SARTONO KARTODIRDJO, *Protest Movements in Rural Java* (Singapore 1973). IDWAR SALEH, "Agrarian Radicalism and Movements of Native Insurrection in South Kalimantan (1858–1865)," *Archipel* 9 (1975): 135–54.

Desacralization from Myths to Tales in Java

What is probably the most interesting aspect of insular Southeast Asia from the standpoint of the study of myths is that in many cases the myths remain alive and continue to sustain social organization and daily ritual. We must, however, hasten to add that in several places in the archipelago, Islam and Western thought have also made their presence felt, encouraging the development of critical thinking and true rationalism. In Java and especially in the Sundanese region in western Java, everything that has not been recovered at one time or another in the hallowed conservatory of the *wayang* has necessarily fallen prey to this criticism. People have stopped believing in it, while continuing to appreciate its "charm." One can compare this process to the literary recovery of our own tales and legends. In the twentieth century, certain talented authors, such as the Sundanese writer Ajip Rosidi, have rewritten ancient legends, and collections have appeared in scholarly editions for young students. Echoes of Mme d'Aulnoy and Charles Perrault!

We shall give four examples of this literature of folk tales (*dongeng* or *cerita rakyat*), two borrowed from Javanese legends and two others borrowed from Sundanese legends. Mythologists will find here what he is looking for, since the structures of these stories come from far away, but the ethnologist would be wrong to compare them indiscriminately with the myths of the Far East, for example, for their social function has nothing in common with them.

I. Jaka Tarub

The story of Jaka Tarub (pronounced *Joko*) takes place in Java, but closely related versions can be found in other regions of the archipelago (Madura, central and northern Celebes), and even outside insular Southeast Asia, in Japan, for example. In a way, the legend bears a kind of resemblance to the French legend of Mélusine.

Jaka Tarub (in Madura, the hero's name is Aryo Menak) is strolling one night in the forest and discovers several maidens bathing in a pond. They are *bidadari,* or celestial creatures, who have left their winged garments on the bank. Jaka Tarub makes away with one of the garments, and he marries the *bidadari,* who is unable to fly away with her female companions; this spirit's name is Nawangwulan, and she bears him a daughter named Nawangsih. Nawangwulan is extraordinary in that she is able to feed her family with a single grain of rice at each meal, but she does this only on condition that Jaka Tarub will not come near the cooking pot. One day when she is away her husband wants to get to the bottom of the matter; he lifts the cover and sees only a single grain of rice. When she returns, Nawangwulan realizes what has happened, for there is still only one grain of rice and the spell is broken. She thus starts to hull the rice each time she prepares it, just like the other women, and the reserves are quickly used up. One day she discovers in the bottom of the

Javanese naive painting illustrating an episode from the tale of Jaka Tarub. The *bidadari* Nawangwulan, after returning to the heavenly world, comes back to visit and suckle her child. Marcel Bonnoff document. Photo Flammarion.

Cover of a comic book in Indonesian, telling the story of Sang Kuriang, the Sundanese Oedipus.

granary the winged garment that Jaka Tarub had hidden away. She puts it on and disappears.

Modern Indonesian painting has also appropriated this theme, and one often sees representations of the scene of Jaka Tarub surprising the *bidadari.*

II. Damar Wulan

Dama Wulan is a Javanese hero whose story takes place toward the end of the time of the kingdom of Majapahit, at a time when its power is tottering and the crown is worn by a princess. Originating in eastern Java, the story was probably introduced into central Java toward the end of the seventeenth century. It is never represented in Javanese shadow plays, but it is sometimes presented with flat wooden marionettes (*wayang kelitik*) or with actors (*ketoprak,* a kind of theater quite widespread in eastern and central Java). The plot goes as follows:

The kingdom of Majapahit is once again threatened, this time by the armies of Menak Jingga ("Red Knight"), who rules over the region of Balambangan (the easternmost part of the island of Java). The generals are powerless and the queen grieves; finally she promises her hand (and the crown) to whoever will save the situation. Damar Wulan, a modest gardener, offers to try his luck. He sets out toward the Menak Jingga's capital city and slips into his harem. Because of his noble bearing, he quickly manages to seduce the many wives of the old man. Two of them in particular have managed to steal from their husband his secret weapon, the famous *Wesi Kuning,* a mace made of "yellow iron." The next day, Damar Wulan has no trouble conquering his adversary. He cuts off Menak Jingga's head and returns to Majapahit triumphant. In order to attenuate whatever excessively "social" dimension the story may have (the unstoppable rise of a young commoner), certain versions point out that even though Damar Wulan was actually reduced to cutting grass in the gardens of Majapahit, he was really the son of a minister, but, because he had been abandoned, he had forgotten his noble birth.

III. Sang Kuriang

The legend of Sang Kuriang is associated with the center of the Sundanese region (western Java), and more particularly with the region of Bandung. It has caught the attention of comparativists who have made Sang Kuriang the Oedipus of insular Southeast Asia.

Princess Dayang Sumbi hit her young son, Sang Kuriang, on the head with a spoon and left him with a scar. Sang Kuriang leaves the village, wanders for many years, and one day returns by accident. He has become an adult and falls madly in love with Dayang Sumbi, whom he does not recognize and who has retained her youth. Dayang Sumbi is about to agree to the marriage when she recognizes the scar. To avoid incest, she asks Sang Kuriang first to meet a condition which she believes to be impossible: she asks him to transform the region into a lake overnight and to build a boat that will allow her to ride around in it. Sang Kuriang agrees to the condition and begins to work as soon as the sun has set. With the help of the spirits, he succeeds in damming the river Ci Tarum and creating a lake, and then he begins to build the boat. The worried Dayang Sumbi resorts to a stratagem to make the sun rise sooner. She unfurls a magic fabric (called *boéh larang*) and causes a rain of marvelous leaves to fall (*daun kingkilaban*). The cocks crow, day breaks, and the frustrated Sang Kuriang overturns the unfinished boat; this is said to be the origin of the name of the nearby volcano near Bandung: Tangkubanperahu, "overturned boat."

IV. Lutung Kasarung

This is a myth known in the western region of Java (Sunda and the area around Banuymas). The king of Pasir Batang has seven daughters; the oldest, Purbararang, vows an undying hatred for her youngest sister, Purbasari, whose charm and beauty inspire her jealousy; finally she gets rid of her by exiling her in the forest. The poor little girl soon finds a companion, a big monkey called Lutung Kasarung (*lutung,* "monkey"), who is in fact a temporary metamorphosis of the god Guriang Tunggal (or Sang Hiang Tunggal). He has dreamed of a bride who resembles his mother, and his mother, the venerable Sunan Ambu, has sent him into the middle world, promising him that he will find there what he is looking for. Lutung Kasarung begins by building a magic palace for Purbasari, and then he helps the unhappy young girl with the trials that Purbararang continues to impose on her. Purbasari thus manages to fill a pit and triumphs over her sister by quickly cultivating a *huma,* or dry field. The frustrated Purbararang then proposes a beauty contest between Lutung Kasarung and Indrajaya, her own fiancé. Lutung Kasarung resumes his divine bearing, and Purbararang is forced to admit defeat. Purbasari returns to the kingdom and succeeds her sister on the throne; a great feast is held, and Purbararang becomes the guardian of the poultry yard. This legend has been the object of a celebrated Sundanese *pantun* that has been studied by C. M. Pleyte (*VBG* 58, Batavia [Djakarta], 1910), and by the Sundanese author Ajip Rosidi.

D.L. and C.P./g.h.

THA MYTHOLOGY OF THE HIGHLANDS OF MADAGASCAR AND THE POLITICAL CYCLE OF THE ANDRIAMBAHOAKA

I call, I call
The male gods and the female gods
God who made man smell sweet
God who made hands and feet
The twelve mountains,
The four cardinal points and the fifth middle point
Halfway between heaven and earth,
The south and the north,
The east and the west,
The earth and the sky support each other so that
What is on high may come down and what is down below may rise.
. . .
We are calling you, O gods who reside on high
and all those who are here below.

—Decary, 124–25

Although the existence of Malagasy mythology has sometimes been denied, it appears to be a highly promising field of research, however complicated it may be by virtue of its being inseparable from the great mythologies of the Indian Ocean. This factor cannot be ignored, but given the present state of our knowledge of the subject, this article discusses only the most obvious comparisons; others that are no less interesting have merely been indicated in the few notes at the end of the chapter.

Throughout the Middle Ages of the Indian Ocean—extending, for our purposes, from the eighth or ninth century to the beginning of the sixteenth century, which was marked by the arrival of the Portuguese—men who had come directly or indirectly from southern Arabia, from the Persian Gulf, and from India and Indonesia, using already well-known sea routes, forged ahead beyond the coast of East Africa and, by way of the Comorian archipelago, reached Madagascar. Given this complexity, I cannot present a general Malagasy mythology. Such a mythology, following the religions, would necessarily reflect distinct facets of different heritages. A preliterate "Creole" civilization, the civilization of Madagascar is doubly syncretic in that the syncretisms that were elaborated there had already been largely primed on the distant shores of Southeast Asia, or closer, on the coast of East Africa, even before those who were destined to become the Malagasy landed on Madagascar.

The conditions of the settlement probably account for the absence of a pantheon or even a unified religion. In the different regions of the island, religion reveals elements of the cults of East African or Indonesian ancestors, combined with the one God of Islam or even with Indo-European gods.

Since I am not trying to draw up an inventory of so rich and varied a folklore (and one that reflects the great Semitic, Indian, and Indonesian mythologies of the Indian Ocean), I have chosen to limit my essay to certain established systems. Thus, the new problem will rely on a mythology that is both widespread enough to be representative of the whole island and at the same time sufficiently restricted to remain "typically" Malagasy, without going beyond any boundary of Madagascar.

A good example of this transregional type is offered by the settlement traditions of the "Arab-Persian" Antalaotra, already strongly Africanized and accompanied by their African allies. Whether Malagasy or Comorian, these traditions are inseparable from their Shirazi counterparts on the east coast of Africa and are merely the historicized version (for a period between the tenth and the early sixteenth centuries) of a myth from southern Arabia and the Persian Gulf: the myth "of the seven brothers," about the legendary destruction of the kingdom of Sheba in Yemen.[1]

The myth of I/bonia/masi/bonia/manoro, Ibonia for short, appears, on the other hand, to be unquestionably and fundamentally Malagasy.[2] Known throughout Madagascar in many different versions, it has been integrated into a cycle in the highlands that could be called the "cycle of the Andriam/bahoaka," "the princes of the people," or, with greater precision (if R. P. Webber's hypothesis is correct), "the princes of the universe" (Webber 739), for in the Indian or Indianized tradition of sacred kingship they are universal sovereigns.

There is little doubt that the Andriambahoaka cycle is connected with the first Malagasy dynasty, that of the Andriambahoaka Raminia, who, according to their traditions, came "from Mekke and Mangalore" and landed on the northern coast of Madagascar at the end of the twelfth century or the beginning of the thirteenth century (COAM 8: 12–14; Leitão 201–2). The newcomers colonized the eastern coast and, penetrating into the interior early on, introduced in most of the island new political concepts that consisted essentially of the concept and the prestigious title of Andriambahoaka, the universal sovereign, a god-king in the best Indian (or Indianized) tradition. At the beginning of the seventeenth century, the title of Andriambahoaka of the Raminia sovereigns of the eastern side is attested in the kingdom of Imamo (*Firaketana* 45–47) close to the kingdom of Imerina in the heart of the highlands. Even today those who are possessed in the royal cults of the southwest invoke this title in their trances. Clearly the concept of *Andriana* in itself conveys the whole hierarchical conception of the world and society insofar as the *andriana* claim a divine origin in order to set themselves apart from all other mortals.

One of the first functions of the Andriambahoaka cycle consists in explaining within the myth a claim to hegemony that has its origin in an unusual marriage of Heaven and Earth. Later, on the basis of this prior claim, princes belonging to different dynasties were drawn into the politics of expansion that were logically meant to result in the political unification of Madagascar. In three centuries of relentless effort, from the sixteenth century through the eighteenth, the Maroserana rulers in the south and west came very close to achieving this result, but it was the rulers of Imerina, the heirs of the Vazimba princes, who finally completed this task. In the process, they managed to convert the myth into history, even while they were slaughtering their eastern cousins.

This political saga calls attention to what may be called the "utilitarianism" of the Malagasy rulers, who literally bring Heaven to Earth, and in the absence of this impossible pantheon, simply clothe their mythology in history.

The myth of Ibonia and the cycle of the Andriambahoaka thus follow the fortunes of the Malagasy dynasties. Both of them seem to come directly or indirectly from the fortunes of the Raminias and become differentiated from one another step by step as the princes come to take into account the institutions, customs, and fundamental beliefs in different regions and among dissimilar populations: the Africans, Malays, and Africanized Arab-Persians on whom the princes impose their domination. However, just as the new dynasties that developed in the south, the center, and the west do not repudiate any of their essential heritage, so too these same myths, which are nothing but the political ideology of the rulers, preserve under the guise of an apparent surface diversity the essentials of the original framework and the original message. The Zatovo princes from the south and west "whose hands and feet were not created by God" are undeniably marked by African cultural traditions. But at the same time, like their Indianized Indonesian cousins from the highlands, they are no less Andriambahoaka.[3]

Thus it is strictly for the sake of brevity at this quite preliminary stage of the study of Malagasy mythology that I limit myself to the historical and cultural milieu of the highlands during a period approximately from the beginning of the fourteenth century to the end of the sixteenth century. Historically, we are dealing with the Vazimba period and the beginning of the Merina period (for the Imerina).

With the supernatural tales that, like Andrianoro, deal with the conditions that preceded sovereignty on earth, Ibonia constitutes a kind of crowning point within the cycle of the Andriambahoaka. Building on earlier tales, it introduces a real theory of power and sovereignty. With the marriage between a human and a princess of Heaven, Andrianoro illustrates the theme that the "sovereign has no family," in the sense of blood relatives, and that in the relentless struggle for power (as attested by bloody interregnums until well into the nineteenth century) he finds his support in his wife, who is a sign of the continuity of his lineage, and in his people. The Princesses of Heaven, strange Green Princesses whose strangeness could not be diminished by Gérard de Nerval's *Voyage en Orient*, play a central role. By contrast, the people remain significantly in the background but nonetheless always present. Such a scheme ties the cosmic and social balance to the person of the sovereign, so that he must benefit from so unusual a union. Combined, the two genealogies are ordered as follows:

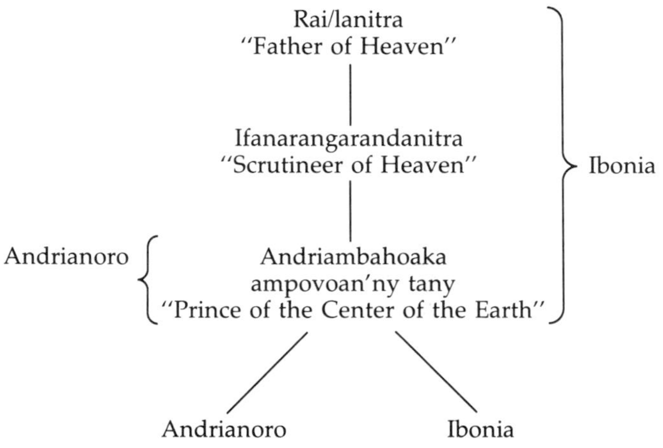

The Arabic root *nūr* (Malagasy *noro*) may explain Andrianoro, "the prince of Light," but it is no longer understood in this sense; it evokes the idea of happiness and joy, but a particular happiness, always associated with circumcision, an institution fundamentally royal in origin. Like Andrianoro, Ibonia is rendered as "son" of the Prince of the Center (from the Arabic *'ibun*, "son"?). Of the five Andriambahoaka, the one in the center and those in the four cardinal points, only the Prince of the Center has a vocation to become a universal prince. In the historical period under discussion here, it is only a matter of vocation. Several times Ibonia, after the unconditional surrender of his cousins, the four Andriambahoaka of the cardinal points, refuses the sovereignty that they offer him, content to accumulate the merits of a considerable ancestry. The historical sovereigns of the Merina dynasties make the most of this moral asset, not just within the myth but actually within history, the history of the gradual unification of the greater part of Madagascar.

Let us begin with the myth of Andrianoro, first because it logically precedes that of Ibonia, and second because its themes (some treated thoroughly, others merely skimmed over) reappear in most of the supernatural tales of the cycle of Andriambahoaka.

Andrianoro, the son of the Prince of the Center, refuses the marriages that he is offered until finally, with the help of Ranakombe the soothsayer and through trickery and magic, he secures for himself a heavenly nymph who had come to a lake to bathe. She warns him that "as a man of earth," he will not be able to live in Heaven where the words of her father are as thunderbolts, and that if her lips should touch even a drop of alcohol, she will instantly die.

The nymph imposes dangerous trials on her husband, the implications of which her in-laws do not grasp. Taking

King Merina Radama I. Tananarive, Queen's Palace Museum. Paris, Musée de l'Homme collection.

advantage of their son's absence, they break through the sevenfold wall that protects their village and force their hated daughter-in-law to drink the fatal alcohol.

Alerted by premonitory dreams, Andrianoro returns in haste, and in his grief can only arrange for a second, proper funeral. The tomb is opened, the shroud enveloping the body is unrolled, and to the astonishment of those who are present, the Princess of Heaven appears alive but with a strange diaphanous green color. Full of wrath, Andrianoro banishes his parents and warns that if they do not disappear immediately he will have them put to death by the people, "who henceforth hate them."

But the story does not end there. Grieved to hear the endless rumbling of Heaven that bears witness to the pain of her parents, the celestial wife insists on paying them a visit. Despite the tears of his younger sister and his affection for her, Andrianoro foolishly decides to accompany his wife, though he is fully aware of the terrible trials that await him.

Against all odds, he triumphs, with the complicity of his wife and the assistance of animal allies. After that, the Celestial Father recognizes the union that he had denied. The happy couple returns to earth, but in the interim, the beloved sister has died of sorrow (*Anganon'ny Ntaolo A. N.* 79–84).

Andrianoro and the Green Princesses

Andrianoro foretells most of the themes that occur in the rest of the corpus and that generally revolve around the trials undergone by heroes bold enough to disavow blood ties and endogamous marriage in favor of an infinitely more hazardous union with a princess who belongs, in every sense of the word, to another world.

When Andrianoro's beloved younger sister dies of grief, her death, by breaking away the affective register of a structural reality that turns the marriage bond into a strong link, finally severs the last bond that connects the hero to what sociologists call his family of orientation. In the masculine mode with Andrianoro and the lastborn heroes and in the feminine mode with the Green Princesses, a whole subset of marvelous tales deal with the same theme that we have already mentioned: "The sovereign has no family." In the fierce competition for political power, the closest relatives, generally brothers or father's brothers, are the most formidable opponents. The wife, in the cycle of the Andriambahoaka, always a single wife of superior essence, is both the pledge and the assurance of the continuity of the line. One can understand that the aggression of the brother, even of the father, against the Prince, which is motivated in the first place by jealousy, complies in fact with more deeply rooted motives. What is at stake is the breaking of the line through the assassination of the sovereign or his wife, and thus the dishonored rival kingdom is doomed "to a heritage of dogs and boars"—that is, the escheated property is left for anyone to claim. All of this explains the harshness of the punishment that Andrianoro does not hesitate to inflict on his parents, a punishment worse than death, since as a result of the banishment that condemns them to wander in misery, their remains are scattered far from the family tomb.

At the start, the wicked deeds that overtake heroes or heroines either directly or through the lives of their spouses are motivated by the resentment inspired by certain qualities that are inherent in heroes, that is, that belong to their very nature. It is never a matter of unimportant qualities but of the real qualifications for the exercise of sovereignty. The older relatives of Imbahitrila do not forgive him for the goodness and compassion that induce him to redeem and free trapped animals (making an implicit pact that all the kites and rats will remember; *A.N.* 104). Ramanongavato and the young prince of *Ny niandohan'ny vonoan'olona* (the origin of executions) show qualities of boldness and courage that explain both their popularity among the people and their elder brothers' resentment (Renel 1.1–8; *A.N.* 69–74). For heroines the image is different, and the attribute that is by far the most detested is the primary characteristic of these Mélusines: fertility. [Mélusine, in French folklore, was cursed to become a serpent from the hips down every Saturday. When her husband broke his promise never to look at her on a Saturday, she disappeared forever.—Ed.] This fertility is often outrageously excessive, such as that of the last and favorite wife of the Andriambahoaka, who boasts of having given birth "in one fell swoop" to two boys and a girl. This maternity occurred, unfortunately for her, during the absence of the Prince (*Haitraitra an'olombelona, Zaka an'nanahary:* "Man proposes but God disposes"; *A.N.* 64–69).

The ill-advised bragging in front of co-wives who suffer from barrenness (the worst of curses)[4] gives evidence that these Princes and Green Princesses, somewhat in the style of the Zatovos in the south and the west, "seek out misfortune," if only through the hatred that their mere presence is able to provoke. Between them and their rivals there is a

It is sometimes an explicit or implicit question of the worlds above and below, such as the explanation of eclipses given in 1616–17 by the Raminia princes to an incredulous Portuguese missionary (COAM 2.163)[11] or better yet the explanation for the god of the kingdom of the dead (though what we have here is an abridgment by Renel: Renel lexicon 2, 323–24). In practice, the three-way opposition, earth/lower world/upper world (heaven), can be reduced to a simple dual opposition (right/left, God/human, masculine/feminine) that reinforces the opposition between heaven and earth.

The world of heaven as it is represented in Malagasy mythology and folklore is difficult to define. But it seems to be conceived on the model of the worlds of Indonesian spirits (for example, Alkema and Bezemer 203; Jensen 93, 105, 109, etc.), characterized from the start by systematic inversions. For example, thin cows graze in rich pastures, and fat cows feed on sterile laterite. Men of the earth who visit heaven must also conform to the inversions. They must eat green bananas, drink muddy water, cross waterfalls without going around them. Besorongola's brothers, who are not aware of these prescriptions, are changed into dogs. Another imperative is not to be surprised by or to laugh at such unexpected sights as the inhabitants of heaven removing their lips or their skin, ridding themselves of their bones (so as not to break them), legs without bodies; that is, to guard against any unseemly and noisy reaction that might deny the "normality" of the situations they witness (*A.N. Imbahitrila* 112–13; Renel 1, *Besorongola* 58–64; *Faralahy* 71–74).

On the instructions of his wife, Andrianoro counteracts the treacherous invitations of his father-in-law. In an effort to outbid the latter, who has invited him not only to take the place of honor at the north end of the house, but indeed to sit on his own throne of gold, Andrianoro accentuates his humiliation in reverse by assuming the status of a servant, choosing to squat in the southeast corner of the house, which is reserved for fowls and servants. In another story, the hero, who has been ordered to go west to cut wood or to pick bananas, goes east, thus avoiding the thunderbolt that strikes in order to destroy him (*A.N.* 122–23).

In the case of Andrianoro, this inversion of behavior, dictated by his refusal to accept a false and deceitful reciprocity, is justified on two counts. He is a man of earth in the kingdom of heaven, but he is also the son-in-law in the presence of his unwelcoming father-in-law. In other words, in the Malagasy tradition of the highlands (consistent with the Indonesian tradition on every point in this matter), he is a debtor and forever beholden to his father-in-law, who in his capacity as a wife giver (however reluctant) is superior to the wife takers.[12]

In the eyes of God, this de facto marriage which results from a rape is no marriage at all, having been made without the indispensable consent that in any event would not have been given, since in Malagasy tradition the marriage of a high-ranking Princess with an inferior always remains unthinkable. This indicates the nature of the emotions that one should feel toward the impudent young man whose scandalous marriage will not be recognized de jure until after he has passed certain tests that would normally prove fatal to him.

The God of Ibonia compels respect in the image of that great beyond where "all love one another like brother and

The royal palace and house of noblemen. Tananarive, Queen's Palace Museum. Paris, Musée de l'Homme collection.

sister," in contrast with the cheating that is widespread on earth (Becker 42). The God of Andrianoro is different: starting with the traps he sets; the celestial father of his wife is a cheat. Tied all the same to heaven, to light, he reveals himself through lightning, the most dazzling expression of this same light, through thunder, and also through his insidiously treacherous maneuvers, to be a dangerous and frightening god. His word is effectively lightning and thunder, which, though they constitute his normal mode of expression, such as the rumblings that express his grief at being separated from his daughter, nonetheless each time cause the hero to faint.

Formidable as he is, this Rai/lanitra, "Father of Heaven," is also known as Zanahary, the creator god, "he who molds feet and hands," and also as Andria/manitra, "the sweet-smelling Prince," a quality that he transmitted to humans, if we are to believe the invocation text reported by Decary (ibid.). Yet the Trimos and other monsters (who thereby establish themselves as Trimos, i.e., ogres) shout *maimbo olombelona* ("This reeks of human!") when they suspect the presence of humans. The Webber dictionary gives the following definition for the root *imbo:* a strong and unpleasant odor such as tar, resin, *smoke, onions* (italics mine). That onions are abhorred by idols is one of the most common taboos. As for smoke, it is one of the elements that most annoys God, and incorrigible humans, aware of this, do not fail to smoke him out (Renel 3.69–74 and 119–21).

Nevertheless, God's attitude is not systematic, and whatever his wrath is, as soon as the trials are overcome, his attitude changes radically, and the couple is showered with gifts. Since that time, by matrilineal descent, the basic traits and attributes of his own nature pass on to members of his half-divine, half-human line of descendants, i.e., the Andriana, who will be demigods before they are worshiped as the *Andriamanitra hita maso* ("gods that one sees with one's own eyes") or, as Ibonia proclaims, the "gods on earth."

This brings us to the crux of the matter: the intrinsic nature, the essence of these inhabitants of heaven, namely, "brilliance" and what might be called their permanent and complete identity.

The creatures of heaven are creatures of light whose beauty, especially that of the women, is always described as dazzling, in the strict sense of the term. Their marvelous beauty unsettles the mind of humans, who are incredulous in the face of such apparitions, the likes of which do not exist on earth. Their complexions are luminous and white unless they appear to be that strange diaphanous green; their eyes are like mirrors; their long black hair, sometimes green for certain girls of the water, flows down over their shoulders; they are as beautiful as the rising sun. The literature is very rich in expressions of the ineffable feelings that they inspire. Although less is said about the beauty of the Princes, the Andrianoro and Iboniamasiboniamanoro bear within their names the mark of this light.

I have now come to the other fundamental characteristic that permeates all the physical and psychological aspects of the creatures of heaven: their complete identity, what may be called their continuity, their transitivity in space and time. They are immutable and permanent in every sense of the terms.

Their identity is first understood as a physical identity that makes them completely indistinguishable from one another if they are of the same sex. This is the source of the previously mentioned theme of the tests of recognition: to know how to identify the daughter as distinct from the mother is obviously impossible, since the Princesses are called Ra/manaha/dreny or Ra/mitovi/aman/dreniny, meaning "the equal or likeness of her mother" (*A.N.* 84; Ferrand 103). The same test can also be applied to the herds, which indicates that in the kingdom of heaven, identity extends to all beings.[13]

The psychology of gods as well as of all supernatural beings (including monsters) is marked by the same permanence and stability, which as a result makes all their behavior entirely predictable, allowing humans to practice all the tricks that they will not fail to indulge in. This is fairly clear as far as dealings with the gods are concerned; but, it should be pointed out, if humans have to trick the gods, they generally trick them with deference, never ridiculing them as they do monsters. As a matter of course, monsters are represented as stupid and their behavior as perfectly mechanical. When the Green Princesses flee with their lovers, they gain time by scattering on their path such goods as seeds, which their fierce adoptive mothers never fail to pick up and invariably bring home before resuming their pursuit (*A.N.* 76–77; Renel 1.38–41). The monsters provoke laughter as a result of their imbecility and their candor, like the ogresses who, at Isilakolona's demand, persist in fetching water in fishing nets (*A.N.* 119).

There is yet another difference. Directly grappling with the monsters, the heroes deceive them without showing them any kindness and kill them as soon as they can. With God, by contrast, they use trickery only through the mediation of interposed helpers: the soothsayer Ranakombe or more frequently the wife or the son of God. There is constant recourse to animal allies, acquired at the very start of the narratives through a sympathetic attitude. It also happens, and Andrianoro is an example of this, that the help of animals is directly solicited and that cattle are sacrificed to seal the contract. In all cases, the most decisive help comes from the daughters or sons of God who reveal the fundamental rules to which humans will have to conform.

Identity and permanence persist in time. Unlike humans, the creatures of heaven are exempt from the pains of birth, life, and death. The beauty of mothers is entirely equal to that of their daughters, since no distinction is possible.

This whole set of characteristics, the distinctive attributes of the creatures of heaven, tends to contrast them with humans, who live in a state of discontinuity and who, like "all those whose gates face west," are aware of the cycle of life and death. Several tales represent death as the result of a choice proposed to men by God: instead of the death of the moon which is reborn, men apparently preferred the death of the banana tree, which does not disappear until it has perpetuated itself with its shoots (Renel 3.54–55, 75–76).

Although the gods are "identical," humans are above all dissimilar in their appearance, their clothing, and their social statuses, i.e., in their nature and their psychology, these two aspects being inseparable. But although they act according to their nature and in this context, it is possible to distinguish differential psychologies that correspond to the sexes, or even more, to social groups. There is always something unpredictable about them, an unpredictability well expressed by the proverb that compares the vagaries of human beings to the zigzags that eels trace in water (Houlder 1). In the Andriambahoaka cycle, this mobility and lack of attachment to a firm base makes possible the victory of human heroes, laughable in their weakness, over infinitely more powerful beings. Their victory is consecrated by the successful marriage with a princess from the other world, who thereafter will give birth to a new category between gods and men, the category of the Andriana.

Portrait of King Merina Andrainampoinimerina. Tananarive, Queen's Palace Museum. Paris, Musée de l'Homme collection.

island, the symbolism of the special royal vocabularies is unequivocal. Take Imerina, for example: the sovereign does not die, he "turns his back"; "to hide" means to bury: "the sun is hidden" (Cousins 77). Elsewhere, in the west (the direction of death), the expression "the sky is broken" announces the sovereign's death. They also speak of a "hole in the sky" which refers to the Betsileo legend of the dead Prince who is seized by a waterspout and sucked straight up to the sky, which gapes wide open to receive him (*A.N.* 177). The waterspout and thunder, lightning, meteorites, and the rainbow are attributes of the deity.

Yet Ibonia, as he himself asserts, will experience death; he will follow "the road of all those whose door faces west" (Becker 131), but he immediately adds "his body is not one of those that are buried to rot, but one of those that are planted to grow" (ibid.).

This recalls a previous theme: even when they die, the sovereigns supposedly keep the attributes of the divine; they "die with the odor of sanctity"; their bodies do not decompose. In a supernatural tale, the young princess discovers the bodies of her two brothers, lifeless but not decomposing; "they do not smell bad, and their faces have not changed at all" (*A.N.* 69).[20]

Ranoro and Imaitsoanola: The Malagasy Mélusines

There are two reasons why the Green Princesses occupy a central place in Malagasy mythology. First, they tie together themes that otherwise appear to be distinct. Second, they allow comparisons outside of Madagascar (if only by formulating new hypotheses) that can shed light on the cultural history of this part of the Indian Ocean. This raises several points relating to the Malagasy tales and the comparative folklore of the Mélusines.

The tale of "A Thousand and One Nights," the story of Beder, the prince of Persia, and Giauhare, the princess of the kingdom of Samandal (ed. Galland, vol. 2, pp. 311–75), tells the story of the marriage of a prince with a Mélusine princess of the sea. After an initial period of time during which she maintains an obstinate silence, the princess succeeds in subjugating her husband to the point where he dismisses all the women of the harem, keeping her as his only wife. This plot occurs in a number of Malagasy tales (*A.N.*, 60–64; Renel 1.187–90; Ferrand 1893.91–92). However, four supernatural tales—"Imaitsoanala" (the green woman in the forest) and "The Hornless Cow" (Renel 1.35–45), on the one hand, and "Ifaranomby" and the already-mentioned tale of "Haitraitra . . . " (Man proposes, and God disposes: *A.N.* 90–93, 64–69), on the other—use the well-known theme of "the sovereign who has no family . . . and has only one wife," to develop the transition from polygynous marriage to monogamous marriage that Ibonia exalted. Monogamous marriage, which is characteristic of the Princes of the Center (at least from the point of view of royal succession), could be posthumous, as in the case of Ifaranomby, the assassinated wife who—in this version—does not come back to life.

"Imaitsoanala" and "The Hornless Cow," natural or adopted daughters of a monstrous mother, share the pattern of an extraordinary birth from an egg that, in one case, will take years to hatch (cf. Ibonia). The sympathetic attitude of the mothers is repaid by ingratitude when the daughters, without even asking their mothers' consent, agree to follow the Andriambahoaka princes. Quite understandably, this action provokes the mothers to anger, which leads to the pursuit of the fugitive couple and the terrible penalty with which we are familiar: flaying the bodies and gouging out the eyes of the victims. However, at the moment when the green daughters are overwhelmed with pain, just as the Andriambahoaka princes despair of accomplishing their obviously impossible tasks, the mothers—once again sympathetic—intervene, complete the prescribed tasks, and on the day of the contest, at the public appearance of all the women in the Andriambahoaka, display their daughters at the height of their beauty, dressed in the richest clothing and even, in one case, furnished with a golden throne. We know the end of "Imaitsoanala"; the plot of the hornless cow does not stop at this point but surges ahead. Feigning an illness, the rivals demand as a remedy the sacrifice of the hornless cow, who surrenders. But following the cow's instructions, her adopted daughter must gather up her bones and bury them on the site of the sacrifice, where a supernatural tree soon sprouts. Trying to get the tree's flowers and fruits of pearl and silver, just as the adopted daughter did, the rivals become leprous when they touch the tree. Still alive, they are exiled in a miserable shanty that will serve as their tomb when they die.

"Ifaranomby" and "Haitraitra" start with the jealousy of two sterile co-wives on whom the prince imposes a young rival. In "Ifaranomby" (which contains the root *omby,* "ox, cow"), taking advantage of the prince's absence, the elder daughters assassinate the lastborn daughter, who has just given birth to an only son. In order to disguise their heinous crime, they pretend that their younger sister died of shame after having delivered "objects of misfortune": an old worn-out broom and a chisel. They treat the child like a slave that they pretend to have bought. The years go by; the child plants on his mother's tomb a seedling that becomes a marvelous tree. The prince returns. Attracted from the beginning by the child, he asks him to pick the flowers of gold, silver, and coral. The failure of the first wives proves their guilt. They are driven out, and the prince stays with his son. "Haitraitra" does not contain the episode of the marvelous tree but tells of the substitution of the same objects and a burnisher for the two newborn boys and the newborn girl (*A.N.* 64–65). The children are abandoned in a box that floats down the river. Providentially, the box is picked up by Ranakombe; the rest is predictable: the two elder co-wives are put to death for their crime.

The theme of the children abandoned in the river is taken up again in the legend of the founding of Majunga, in which the Sakalava sovereign named Andriamandisoarivo, the founder of the kingdom of Boina (at the beginning of the eighteenth century), abandons one of his granddaughters in the waters of the Betsiboka River. The Antalaotra discover the box containing the young princess and proclaim her their queen (Guillain 21–22).[21] In India, the legend of Goriyā is built on the same theme: the marriage of a king to a goddess (Kālī) who soon becomes pregnant by him. His first seven wives become intensely jealous, and when she gives birth, they substitute a stone for the newborn child, whom they abandon in a box and leave to drift downstream. The box is picked up by fisherman (Gaborieau 152).

Narrated during sessions of possession, this legend is supposed to provoke trances, and if one recalls the sessions of possession that are inseparable from the previously mentioned royal rituals, this indirect connection makes possible a clearer understanding of the significance of the Malagasy supernatural tales, as well as of the mysterious propitiatory formulas that accompany their recital. The word "tale" is a very poor equivalent for the Malagasy *angano* (our corpus is referred to as the *Anganon'ny Ntaolo*, "the *angano* of the forefathers"), a word which, apparently borrowed from Swahili, expresses along with the idea of the extraordinary, that of misfortune and of calamity, which may be the reason for the awe-inspiring atmosphere that prevails in Madagascar during the recounting of these supernatural tales.

The *Tantara Ny Andriana* "The history of the kings of the Imerina" tells the legend of Andriam/Bavi/Rano, "the Princess of the Water," who fell from heaven in the form of a fragrant leaf into a lake located on the top of Mount Angavo, about twenty kilometers east of Antananarivo. The Vazimba prince, Andriamanjavona, who appears in a genealogy as the first cousin of another son of Andrianerinerina (the fallen son of God, who becomes the first Vazimba sovereign), tries to seize her and succeeds only after pronouncing the sacred phrase from tales and stories: "If, by my father and by my mother, I am *andriana* . . ." He locks the leaf in a box; it is transformed again into a goddess, according to the text, and the prince marries her.

Then we come upon the familiar plot: Andriambavirano is the victim of the hostility of the first wife, who, after bearing him two sons and a daughter, substitutes for them the same unusual objects (a used broom, a burnisher, and a polished stone). The children abandoned in a box set adrift in the water are rescued (Callet note pages 17–18).

The History of the Kings of the Imerina reproduces this legend, to which the translators add a second legend, collected in central southeastern Madagascar, that belongs to the clan of the Zaza rano, "children of the waters" (see the tale cited by Ferrand 1893: 91–92):

> The members of this clan believe that their common ancestor must have been the eldest of triplets [*sic*] born of Andriambavirano, *who was known under the name of Fatima*. . . . According to the version we have been given, *Fatima supposedly left her husband Andriambahoaka* after a marital quarrel, when he had broken the promise . . . that he made to his wife when she was dragged out of the waters of the river . . . in a fisherman's net . . . never to refer to her . . . origin. (Callet, Chapus, Ratsimba, note 15, 16–17; italics mine)

One can understand the significance of this legendary tradition of a clan known for having been originally converted to Islam and for its close ties to the Raminia dynasty. One can also understand the great advantage in this identification of the Green Princess—the Mélusine, Andriambavirano, herself considered a goddess—with Fatima.

Of course, Shiite Islam regards Fatima, the daughter of the Prophet and the wife of the fourth caliph 'Alī (whose assassination marks the origin of the Shiite sect), as the mistress of the waters, so that in their esoteric version of the Koran, most Shiites believe that verse 31 of chapter 21—"Water is the source of all life"—refers to her. As a further example, the *ta'ziye* of the Persian theater, which are dramatic enactments and commemorations of the passion of the Imam Hussayn at Karbala, follow this tradition (Calmard 73–126), according to which Fatima is said to have received from God himself authority over all the waters of the world (Virolleaud 33, 41). Mistress of the water, Fatima is also the mistress of salt (see Ranoro) (Masse 225) and her day is Friday, the Great Day, the day of sovereignty in Madagascar; all over the island the expression "wait for Friday" is endlessly repeated both in tales and in historical traditions. When Ibonia's archrival wants to put him to death, his own father forbids him with these words: "Wait . . . for Friday, Thursday is still mine" (Becker 119–20). In the same way, the last Vazimba princess, eager to set up an "arranged" succession (*fanjakana arindra*), foresees that Thursday will be for Andriamanelo—the first sovereign of the Merina dynasty—and Friday for his younger brother.

When she is dying, Fatima orders that a small box be placed on her chest and that a sealed paper should be enclosed in it on which is to be inscribed in *green ink* (italics mine) the contract stipulating the price for the blood of Hussayn, whose martyrdom is destined to redeem all Shiites (Virolleaud 40–41). Green, which in Islam is the color of paradise, has become, in opposition to the black of the Abbasids, the emblem of the descendants and partisans of 'Alī, in other words, the Shiites (Laoust 98).

We will return to Fatima, to the Green Princesses, to 'Alī, to Andrianoro, and to Shiism. For the moment, the comparative folklore of the Mélusines will allow us to shed light on other points, all of which revolve around the aforementioned fertility of the Mélusines. This fertility, which is the best guarantee of the continuity of their lineage, quite naturally connects them with agriculture, and in Madagascar particularly with rice, the grain that symbolizes agriculture most completely.

In Java, in very ancient times, a civilizing hero hunting wild birds (like certain Andriambahoaka) discovers in the middle of a dense forest a pond where celestial nymphs who have come to bathe are taking off their clothes. He approaches, steals the clothing of one of them, and takes her for his wife. Thereafter there is no shortage of rice, although the nymph from heaven never seems to refill the storehouse. On one occasion, she asks him to keep an eye on the rice that is cooking but not to lift the cover, a prohibition that the curious hero ignores. Since the Mélusine condition has been violated, the celestial nymph returns to heaven (Rassers 266–67).

The couple are regarded as the founders of the Javanese people, the woman being connected to heaven, rice, and agriculture, and the man to earth and hunting (ibid. 270–73). In the same way, the Malagasy Mélusines, notably the daughters of God, are connected to agriculture, to cultivated plants and especially to rice. Of divine origin, rice is presented (rarely) as a voluntary gift or (more often) as an involuntary gift of God, from whom it is stolen by one of his daughters, who brings it as a dowry for her human husband. A historical legend explains how rice was supposedly introduced into the Ankaratra region (the center of the island) by a daughter of God, who, as she leaves heaven, asks her father to give her the gift of a rooster and a hen. When she arrives on earth, she quickly sacrifices the rooster in order to plant the paddy contained in his gizzard. This takes place in *Am/bari/andramanitra* ("In the place of the rice of God") (Callet, Chapus, Ratsimba, note 2, 20).

In his collections, Renel has several versions, all of which emphasize the trick involved in the theft. In one case, the daughter of God hides the grains of rice in the curls of her hair (Renel 3.19–21), but two other versions repeat the sacrifice of the fowl (ibid. 29–31 and 32–36). The second one holds an even greater interest for us, since it is an exact reprise of the first part of the Andrianoro plot in which the hero, here called "the one not created by God," with the help of Ranakombe's magic and his transformations manages to seize one of the three celestial nymphs who had come to bathe in the lake. The trial in heaven is less difficult; the hero has to identify the throne of the daughter of God, which is quite obviously green. The rest of the story repeats the stratagem of the sacrificed fowl.

In all of these tales, the heroine is expressly referred to as a daughter of God. The connection between heaven and rice is evident in all Malagasy folklore. In another tale about the origin of rice, it is lightning that comes to fertilize a few grains that have accidentally fallen in a swamp (ibid. 109–10).

A text from the *Tantara ny Andriana* on the origin of the fate of men and rice (Callet, Chapus, Ratsimba, vol. 1, 30–31, note 40) verifies in its own way a "fable" reported by Flacourt on the origin of the social orders (COAM 8.14);[22] it stresses that whatever they may do, the men who belong to different social orders can think and act only in accordance with the nature of the orders to which they belong *by virtue of their line of descent*. This is a constant of thought, at least of ancient Malagasy thought as it appears in its products.

The problem is the following: Is it possible to establish correlations that will explain within this order of thinking the essential characteristics and features of the heroes of the Andriambahoaka cycle, and particularly of the Andriana, or assimilated heroes?

To the extent that we accept this determination of marriage by line of descent and by nature—always clearly spelled out—we can first note that all Andriana marriages result sometimes from a rape (more or less consented to *afterwards*), sometimes from a contest, and sometimes, as in the case of Imaitsoanala and other heroines who are the daughters of monsters, from a marriage of free will or by mutual consent. The three elements may be more or less related to one another. In India, however, these three types of marriage, among them *svayaṃvara-*, or marriage by contest, are given as characteristic of the noble class of warrior princes (Kṣatriya). No mention is made of the solemn Brahman marriage in which the father gives his daughter to the suitor, since, as we have seen, the reverse is the case here: the union has no authorization from those on whom the Princesses depend.

Although these marriages are permissible for the Kṣatriya class, the *Mānava Dharmáśāstra*, or *Laws of Manu*, nonetheless generally looks askance at them and says that the products of these unions will be "cruel and deceitful . . . hating the Vedas and the sacred law" (3.41). Among these marriages, the one by mutual consent "stems from desire and has sexual relations as its purpose" (3.32), and, what is enlightening, it is referred to as a "Gandharva marriage." The Gandharvas are aerial spirits, the husbands of the *apsarases*, or celestial nymphs (Renou 1963, 208) and nymphs of the waters (Auboyer 218–19), "whose beauty, created for the pleasure of the gods, inspired passion in men" (ibid.). Renou adds that these nymphs, inhabitants of heaven, would visit earth, where various amorous adventures would await them (Renou 1963, ibid.), and Auboyer goes on to say: "It was thought that they would be an easy catch. All one had to do was surprise them while they were bathing in a river and sneak away with their clothes for them to be at the mercy of men" (Auboyer ibid.; also Renou 97–109).

The price for the marriage by rape or mutual attraction is familiar: a moral blemish that may well be that of all the Princes whom the harsh laws of sovereignty force "not to have a family" but that in the supernatural tales often appears not as a moral blemish but as a physical defect or abnormality. European medieval folklore explains this: from the marriages of the Mélusines and human beings are born exceptional children, endowed with physical gifts (beauty for girls, strength and intelligence for boys) but blemished and unlucky (Le Goff and Le Roy Ladurie 598–99). The physical defect may appear on the face or may manifest itself in other ways, for example, by paralysis or palsy (ibid. 589).

It is useless to go any further, since Malagasy folklore does not indicate (given the current level of knowledge) a line of descent so direct that it can come full circle and make the lastborn sons, always reputed for their courage and superior intelligence, the sons of the Green Princesses and the Princes of the Center.

The Position of the Andriambahoaka Cycle

Like Andriambavirano, who is both a Princess of the Water and a Green Princess, Fatima is connected with the water that she received from God, with salt, and finally with light, which, "when she was born, emanated from her body so much that all the earth was illuminated by it" (Virolleaud 14, note 1). I have long insisted on the identity in nature and essence of the creatures of Heaven and the Andriana. This same identity makes it possible to ask whether, just as Fatima is related to the Green Princesses, their husbands, the Andriambahoaka, and particularly their sons, the Princes of Light, could not be related to 'Alī.

The two main schools of Shiism, the duodecimal and the Ismaelian, agree in seeing in 'Alī "the friend of God" and in the Imams his successors, "those who bear within themselves the light of the Prophet" (*al-nūr al-muhammadī*). This light alone bestows on them the necessary infallibility that allows them to understand the hidden, esoteric aspects of the Koran and to relate them to its explicit aspects. As descendants of the Prophet by his daughter Fatima and by 'Alī, the Imams share in the purity of the Prophet and of Fatima, who is herself the source of this light, *nūr* (for example, Nasr 199–200; Ṭabāṭab'ī 173–217).

The links with Malagasy mythology are clearest in the Persian theater, in the *ta'ziye*, the stagings of the drama of Karbala and the Passion of the Imam Hussayn, the son of Fatima and 'Alī (and thus through his mother the Prophet's grandson). The "King of lights" for all of Shiite Islam (Massé 16), 'Alī, the "light of lights," is said to have "created Muhammad with his own light," according to some extremist sects (Virolleaud 14, note 1).[23] At the same time, not to be outdone by his wife, Fatima, who had received from God as a dowry "all of the waters of the universe" (ibid. 33–39), 'Alī is presented as the "master of the waters," who distributes the waters of paradise and on earth gives the waves of the sea their thrust, just as Andrianoro's mother did. These two attributes, light and water, can be joined together: hence, the representation of 'Alī emerging from the sun while water gushes forth at his feet (ibid. 14, note 1).

There is little doubt that the Shiite conceptions that are so apparent in Malagasy mythology were brought by the Raminias. At the beginning of the seventeenth century, the Portuguese, familiar with the Sunni mode of Islam, were disconcerted by the beliefs of the Raminias and did not know whether what they saw was religion or idolatry (COAM 2.193–94). However, a century earlier, those newcomers who, Flacourt says, were despite all appearances sent "by the caliph of Mecca," made no mistake, and being zealous Sunnis, they waged a war of extermination upon the Raminias on the shores of Matitana (COAM 8.39–40). This war was, in my view, symbolized by another myth, the myth of the giant Darafify or Darafely.

Ramini, the eponymous ancestor, himself a "great prophet," marries Fatima, the daughter of Muhammad, whom a tale that we have already cited presents as the wife of an Andriambahoaka who thus establishes his identification (Callet 16–17, note 15). The exceptional nature of Ramini stems from the fact that God did not make him as a descendant of Adam like all other men, but rather "created . . . [him] on the sea, either making him come down from the sky and the stars or creating him out of the foam of the sea" (COAM 8.82), a version confirmed by Léguevel de Lacombe, who in turn shows that Ramini was said to be created "from the purest portion of the foam of the ocean . . . activated by a spark of celestial fire" (Léguevel de Lacombe 1.180).[24]

In these versions, fire is closely connected with light. Recall the miraculous birth of Ibonia and his bath in a blazing fire that similarly failed to consume the grasshopper talisman out of which he had emerged. This theme is taken up again to a large degree in the supernatural tales in which the Princesses who have come from elsewhere do not hesitate to dive into the devouring fires, while these same fires immediately consume their rivals, who are foolhardy enough to dare to imitate them (Renel 2.257).

In historical terms, the dynasties of the Andriambahoaka Raminia reigned over the east coast from the end of the twelfth century or the beginning of the thirteenth century until the beginning of the sixteenth century, after which they were confined to the southeasternmost corner of the island. Délivré believes that the first Andriana appeared on the eastern side of the forest-covered cliff in the highlands during the first third of the fourteenth century (Délivré 233–34). There is little doubt that there was a connection between the Raminia Andriambahoaka and the highlands Andriambahoaka of the Vazimba dynasty, which preceded the Merina dynasty. The Raminia genealogy indicates that the younger brother, Rakoube, fleeing from his elder brother by going up the Mananjary River, reached the highlands (COAM 8.82–89) or, according to the version found in an Arabic-Malagasy manuscript, Alasora, the cradle of the Merina dynasty (Ferrand 1910).

In mythological terms, this identity is attested by the identification of Andrianoro, Ibonia, and Imaitsoanala with the first legendary Vazimba sovereigns, for example, with the Green Princess of the Water named Andriambavirano, the wife of Andriamanjavona, the son of Andrianerinerina. This Andrianerinerina, the first sovereign of the Vazimba dynasty, was a son of God who fell because the Vazimba knowingly made him eat defiled food, for which they were condemned to serve him (Callet, Chapus, Ratsimba 13, note 7). Here the legend appears as the inverse of the myths and supernatural tales in which, by contrast, the sovereigns are "promoted" human beings. The advent of the Merina dynasty with Andriamanelo, the son of a Vazimba princess from the same village of Alasora that Rakoube reached, does not put an end to these exceptional marriages, since Andriamanelo himself marries Imaitsoanola, "the green woman of the forest," who gives birth to Ralambo. However, when it comes to circumcision, which was introduced as a fundamental innovation by Andriamanelo, it is not a matter of *the only son*, but of two other sons, who are undoubtedly legendary, if we consider their names: Ra/masy and Ra/noro, the two qualifying terms essentially connected with circumcision (ibid. 135). These points of reference, together with ethnographic fragments and what can be learned from a natural environment still covered with vast unknown and virtually unexplored forests, lead one to believe that these myths, historical legends, and the whole oral tradition that comes with them deal with the remote period of the end of the Vazimba dynasty and the beginning of the Merina dynasty which, as we have said, probably extended from the beginning of the fourteenth century to the end of the first half of the sixteenth century.

During this period, the cycle of the Andriambahoaka and the myth of Ibonia are still no more than a developing ideology that lays the groundwork for a theory of sovereignty and social stratification. This theory guarantees the incontestable superiority of the Princes of the Vazimba line and later of the Merina line, both of whom are regarded as having a divine essence. Subsequently, and starting particularly with Andriamasinavalona, the Imerina sovereigns lean on this doctrine to support their claim to hegemony. After this, the structure of the center and the cardinal points, which dancers move through successively on the occasion of royal circumcisions,[25] becomes effectively the territorial structure of the *Imerina efa-toko*, the fourfold Imerina, whose center (the heart) symbolizes both unity and totality.

This structure is repeatedly reproduced, beginning with the architectural arrangement of the *rova*, or royal residences, with their highest point occupied by the sovereign's quarters, all the way down to the construction and interior arrangements of the most humble houses. Even in the six-section Imerina of Andrianampoinimerina (the Prince in the heart of the Imerina), the military camps of the sovereign physically reproduce on the ground the structure of the center and the four parts. Indeed, the history of the Imerina is nothing but a dialectic of the center and the cardinal points with centrifugal moments of expansion and centripetal moments of coiling. At the beginning of the eighteenth century, the four sons of Andriamasinavalona, betraying the will of

On the Problems of Relationships (essentially the Indian Ocean, Arabo-Persian front, India, and Indonesia)

B. ALKEMA and T. J. BEZEMER, *Concise Handbook of the Ethnology of the Netherlands East Indies* (1961). J. AUBOYER, *La vie quotidienne dans l'Inde jusqu'au VIIIe siècle* (Paris 1961). G. BUHLER, ed., *The Laws of Manu* (New York 1969). J. CALMARD, "Le mécénat des représentations de Ta'ziye," in *Le monde iranien et l'Islam*, vol. 2 (Geneva 1974). M. DEVIC, *Légendes et traditions historiques de l'archipel indien: Sedjarat Malayou* (Paris 1878). G. DUMÉZIL, *Mythe et épopée* 2: *Types épiques indo-européens: Un héros, un sorcier, un roi* (Paris 1971). M. GABORIEAU, "La transe rituelle dans l'Himalaya central: Folie, avatar, méditation," *Puruṣ ārtha*, part 2 (1975). R. HEINE-GELDERN, "Conceptions of State and Kingship in Southeast Asia," paper no. 18, Cornell University (Ithaca 1956). E. JENSEN, *The Iban and Their Religion* (Oxford 1974). P. E. JOSSELIN DE JONG, "Marcel Mauss et les origines de l'anthropologie structurale hollandaise," *L'homme* 12, 4 (1972): 62–84. J. LE GOFF and E. LE ROY LADURIE, "Mélusine maternelle et défricheuse," in *Annales*, 1971, special issue *Histoire et structure* nos. 3 and 4. H. LAOUST, *Les schismes dans l'Islam: Introduction à une étude de la religion musulmane* (Paris 1968). H. MASSE, *Croyances et coutumes persanes*, 1 (Paris 1938). MAS'ŪDI, *Les Prairies d'Or*, 2 (Paris 1965). A. GALLAND, trans., "Les mille et une nuits," in *Contes arabes* (Paris 1965), 2:311–75. S. H. NASR, *Islam, perspectives et réalités* (Paris 1975). W. H. RASSERS, *Pāñji, the Culture Hero: A Structural Study of Religion in Java* (The Hague 1959). L. RENOU, *Anthologie sanskrite* (Paris 1961); *Contes du Vampire: Vetālapañcaviṃśatikā* (Paris 1963). H. TABĀṬABĀ'I, *Shi'ite Islam* (London 1975). CH. VIROLLEAUD, *Le théâtre persan ou le Drame de Kerbela* (Paris 1950).

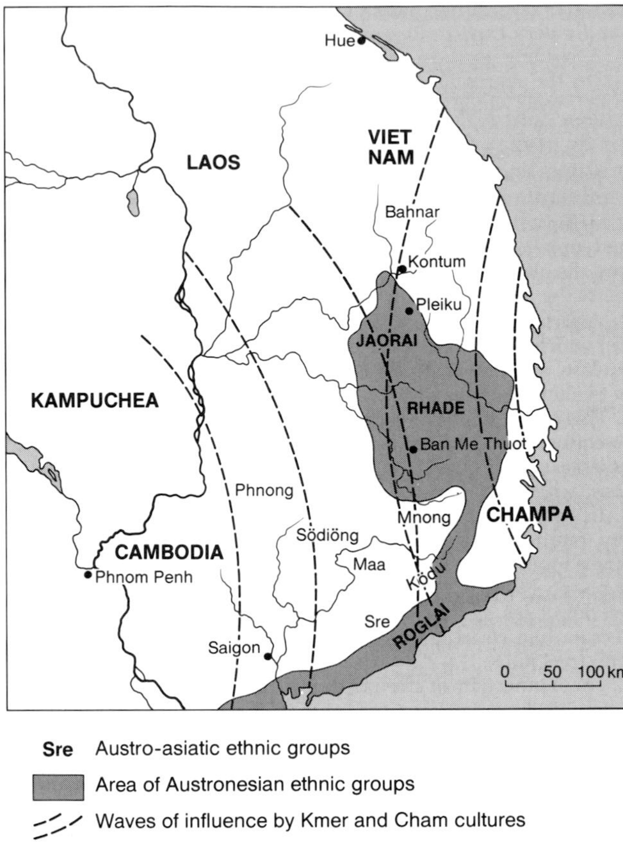

Indigenous population of southern Indochina.

The Mythology and Ritual of the Indigenous Populations of the Southern Part of the Indo-Chinese Peninsula: Orientation of Research

I. The Indigenous Indo-Chinese

The indigenous populations of the southern part of the Indo-Chinese peninsula are, by definition, neither Cambodian, nor Laotian, nor Vietnamese—or, to be more precise, they are neither Khmer, nor Lao, nor Viet, since they are all subject to one of the nations which these three peoples have constituted. Most are Vietnamese in nationality, but not at all Viet in language or culture. They are too little known for us not to present them here; they deserve a place in this work that is out of proportion with their population or their historical and political role, because they are cultures in which myth has remained alive, infusing all of existence.

The eastern part of the mountainous range between India and China is like a hand whose fingers are the ranges, valleys, and rivers (the Brahmaputra in India, the Irrawaddy in Burma, the Menam in Thailand, the Mekong in Laos and Cambodia, the Red River in Vietnam), which generally flow northwest-southeast. This seems to have been the main direction of the ancient migrations which, following these arteries, peopled the Indo-Chinese peninsula and the Pacific islands beyond. This arterial movement does not exclude certain reverse movements, like that of venous blood. Belonging to this substratum of the population, the "indigenous Indo-Chinese peoples" have been inhabitants of the peninsula the longest. They make up several ethnic groups, whose main relations were established in an east-west direction, between themselves and, farther away, with Champa (a former empire on the eastern coast) and Kampuchea (Cambodia), both Indianized states.

These groups have never formed a unit and have no common term to designate themselves. Called Phnong ("wild," the name of an ethnic group) by the Cambodians (in Khmer, *phnom* means "mountain"), Moï ("wild") by the Vietnamese, Kha ("slave") by the Laotians, they were called Montagnards ("mountaineers") by the French (hardly an appropriate name, since most of them are settled in valleys or on plateaus at 300 to 600 meters), a term picked up by the Vietnamese under the form Th'u'ong (since Moï was overly pejorative). Georges Condominas has proposed "Proto-Indochinese." Each group has its own ethnic name (for example: Mnong, Eddé, Jarai, Bahnar . . .), not to mention the distorted or entirely different names which their neighbors give them (Eddé becoming Rhadé, for instance, or Kreng). The groups together amount to about one million people, and so form an ethnic minority but one which has played a role in the demographic formation of the peninsula and the history of the nations that make it up.

Until the seventeenth century, the southern part of the peninsula was divided between two great empires: Kampuchea in the west, Champa in the east. The ethnic minorities in between were autonomous if not totally independent. They were not entirely foreign to these kingdoms, to the extent that the "Khmer are Hinduized Phnong" (Cœdès, 1948) and the Cham are Hinduized Jarai. The network of (east-west) relations among all these peoples was such that cultural influences went in both directions; it is difficult to distinguish, for example, what Jarai mythology owes to that of Champa, or vice versa, or whether there was a foundation common to the ancient Jarai and the proto-Cham. If there was some Indianization of the indigenous minorities on the western and eastern fringes of the two empires, it happened through cultural osmosis, in a muted echo of the peaceful Indianization of the Khmer and the Cham (the latter having then been partly Islamicized, something of which the culture of the Chamized ethnic groups bears no trace).

On the north-south axis things happened in a completely different way. The Vietnamese (Sinicized Austroasiatic peoples), after occupying the Red River delta, slipped between the coast and the cordillera as far as the Mekong delta without ever penetrating the central range, difficult of access from the east except through a few rare valley passes. They annihilated the Cham empire—Vietnamization, the daughter of Sinicization, took place through military conquest and systematic occupation. It was from the west that French colonial expansion won the back country and annexed the ethnic minorities—the last step in the occupation—without, however, entirely subjugating them. Here the only Frenchification we observe is in the form of lasting influences: political among the Rhadé, where the civil administration favored an autonomist program, cultural among the Bahnar, where the Catholic mission attacked the mythology. When they left, the French ceded the territory of the indigenous peoples to the Vietnamese who settled there, coming from the east, the south, and finally the north; assimilation to Vietnamese culture had begun.

The mythology of the ethnic groups of the interior gives evidence (at least by allusions, brief references) of relations with neighboring peoples: Khmer, Lao, or Cham, rarely Viet; if the French are ever named, it is in what are clearly very recent additions, and the tone tends to be one of mockery. The myth of the origin of writing belongs to the following schema, common to a number of groups: a celestial divinity inscribes instructions on skins (of buffalo or deer); these are meant to communicate knowledge to men. The Khmer, Lao, and Viet have carefully kept these skins; "we, too busy drinking our rice beer, we let a dog tear up that skin, that's why we don't know how to write." The Jarai variant on this theme: "The French wrote down on paper what the Master of Heaven dictated to them, the Lao wrote it down on wood, the Jarai on a skin" (then the dog comes along). The Sré make up for this by adding that it was they who brought the techniques to the French.

Within a large and entirely oral literature, this myth and several others are found among several ethnic groups. And yet the indigenous peoples of Indochina are divided into two great ethnolinguistic families: the Austroasiastic peoples (or Mon-Khmer), generally on the higher and less fertile lands, separated into northern and southern groups by the continuous mass of the Austronesian peoples (or Malayo-Polynesians). The Austronesian peoples penetrate them like a wedge, occupying the valleys and the richer lands—which suggests that their arrival was later and of eastern origin; but this is only a hypothesis, since we know nothing of the early history of these populations without documents, everything in their culture being perishable, except for speech. In the myths, every ethnic group claims to originate in the territory it now inhabits, after coming out of the netherworld. We find this among the Austroasiatic peoples as much as among the Austronesian peoples, although their languages are unrelated and there is no mutual comprehension between the two families.

Related linguistically to the Malayans and Indonesians (particularly to the Minangkabau of Sumatra and the Dayak of Borneo), the Austronesian people constitute groups that are strong (especially the Rhadé and Jarai) and solidly structured, in a position of superiority relative to the Austroasiatic people, whom they have sometimes mistreated (Jarai against Bahnar, for example). Yet in their material culture, their mode of life, their way of thinking and its literary expression, they are closer to the continental Austroasiatic peoples than to the insular Austronesian peoples—which permits a comparative study of the two mythologies.

The forest is the common context of their existence. It occupies a large place in the myths and provides the materials for houses (wood, bamboo, and thatch) and part of the subsistence of these peoples, hunters and gatherers, who also grow rice, maize, and some vegetables. The most remarkable productions of their material culture are weaving (cotton) and basketwork (bamboo and rattan), everyday masterpieces. The family may be matrilineal, with matrilocal residence, as among the Sré and the Jarai, or patrilineal, as among the Maa and certain Mnong groups; everywhere the mother's brother plays a privileged role. The household rather than the village constitutes a unit. The only real power is that of tradition; everyone knows what he must do to follow the path of the ancestors.

Rather than speaking of their religion as something distinct from everyday activities, it would be more correct to say that everything in their life (and all of their life) has a

Pnong warriors in a bas-relief from Angkor. Paris, Musée de l'Homme collection. Photo J. Dournes.

A Jarai in warrior's dress. Paris, Musée de l'Homme collection. Photo J. Dournes.

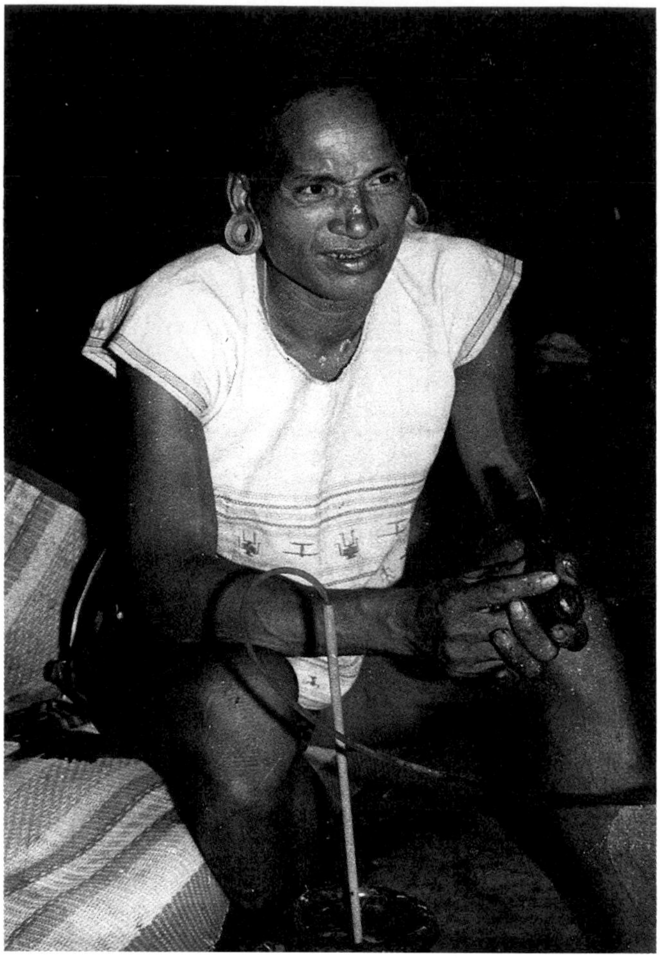

Socializing around a jar of rice beer (Mnong.) Paris, Musée de l'Homme collection. Photo J. Dournes.

religious—or, better, mythological—aspect to it, and this is true of all of the ethnic groups. Mythology is not something separate, which makes it very difficult to isolate it in cultures where everything holds together and is explained by a global world view, a unified conception of man and his place in the universe. Mythology is not limited to stories and to story time; it is also silence and the inner life. Myths are memorized by everyone (to different degrees); they bring together (and explain) the dreams and the behavior of men who never cease to live in the world that they imagine.

II. Method and Orientation of Research

The indigenous peoples of Indochina have been studied from the beginnings of colonization, chiefly by the French: explorers, military men, missionaries, then by administrative and educational functionaries, finally by ethnographers; most of their studies are limited to the ethnic group known to the writers. The mythology of these populations is scarcely known. This is easy to understand: collecting myths, understanding them to some degree, collecting commentaries, recognizing the myth's place in life and how it informs thought—all this requires long-suffering patience, great intimacy with the population studied, its confidence and its collaboration, and thus a very long stay, regular participation in daily life, an immersion in the culture that allows one to "think like them" and dream with them.

A failure to achieve this kind of knowledge of the ethnic minorities leaves the researcher with only an outside view, a view of the least essential part of their culture. The mythology of these peoples is not only the most beautiful and original of their productions, it is above all their inner life; it is the genius of these peoples, and should allow us—this is a personal opinion—to account for any trait of their culture by situating it in a totality of thought that gives it its meaning and marks it as its own. Mythology understood in this sense cannot be reduced to a collection of myths: the stories that we hear are only points of orientation, the whole set of texts collected forming a sort of map of the imaginary, a projection (into the time of recitation and the linearity of its unfolding) of the totalizing world view common to the Indo-Chinese peoples.

Their life is far from being a paradise. They have the wisdom not to make work into a value or man into a master of creation. Located in their own proper place, among other living things, they know that anything can be dangerous: the forest and its tigers, the sky and its lightning; a neighbor may be an enemy. A great pleasure is to gather around a pot of beer, to drink, smoke, and chat. It is especially in the evening that they reveal themselves: tale-tellers and orators, transmitting from generation to generation a prodigious oral literature (maxims, invocations, songs, proverbs), of which mythology is only a part. When one is lucky enough to live with populations who are not content merely to tell myths (which is itself no longer so frequent in the world), but who live them and mythicize every day, one has only to collect, transcribe, translate, interpret, and live them oneself.

Note that we are dealing with languages that are without traditional writing systems; terms borrowed from these languages are transcribed here according to the usual system used in various publications.

"Myth" is taken here in the sense of the Sré *yalyau*, or the Jarai *akhan*, that is, a traditional story, orally transmitted, without distinguishing between what we call "myth," "folktale," and "legend," and without limiting mythology, as is too often done, to "origin myths," or to stories about gods, especially since any traditional story implies the literature as a whole and reflects the global vision of the imaginary, a whole conception of the world.

Myth is also an art, the art of beautiful language, the art of telling tales, which, even more than music, has its times (preferably at night) and its conditions (some stories cannot be told completely without a sacrificial ritual, as if to "excuse" oneself for revealing hidden things, serious events).

But can we speak of *a* mythology for different ethnic groups speaking different languages? This is the orientation of our ongoing research: to bring together what remains (relatively) separate in the field and then to study the reasons for similarities and the meanings of the differences. Examples will be taken primarily from two ethnic groups: the Sré, who speak an Austroasiatic language, and the Jarai, who speak an Austronesian language, with some references to other ethnic groups of the two language families. It is thus not (yet) a matter of a synthesis but of the current results of research that tend to support the hypothesis of a common culture, and to highlight the links between this southern Indo-Chinese mythology and those of other Austroasiatic and Austronesian populations (that of the Cham, in particular), which are also too little known on this level. Without disdaining the use of Western methods of formal analysis, the research is carried out mainly from inside: at the heart of a mass of texts, memorized so that they can be brought together easily, with the knowledge of what men do and think about them—a knowledge that is also a complicity.

More than one hundred texts have been collected in this way among the Sré, and more among the Jarai; whenever one or the other of these is evoked in an article, it will be given with its number in the corpus (Ms. *n* for the former; Mj. *n* for the latter), to facilitate reference to the works and articles in which they are cited, translated, or analyzed; this allows us to avoid weighing down the articles with material that is published elsewhere.

J.D./j.l.

BIBLIOGRAPHY

1. General Bibliography

J. BOULBET, *Pays des Maa', Domaine des Génies* (Paris 1967); *Dialogue lyrique des Cau Maa'* (Paris 1972). G. COEDES, *Les États hindouisés d'Indochine et d'Indonésie* (Paris 1948). G. CONDOMINAS, "Les tribus proto-indochinoises," in *Ethnologie de l'Union française*, by A. Leroi-Gourhan and J. Poirier (1953), 2:658–78; *Nous avons mangé la forêt de la pierre-génie Gôo* (Paris 1957); *L'exotique est quotidien* (Paris 1965). DAM BO (J. DOURNES), *Les populations montagnardes du Sud indochinois* (Saigon and Lyons 1950). J. DOURNES, *En suivant la piste des hommes sur les hauts plateaux du Viêtnam* (Paris 1955); *Coordonnées, structures jörai familiales et sociales* (Paris 1972); *La culture jörai*, catalogs of the Musée de l'Homme (1972). P. GUILLEMINET, "La tribu Bahnar du Kontum," *Bull. EFEO* 45, 2 (1952): 393–561. H. MAITRE, *Les régions moï du Sud indochinois* (Paris 1909); *Les jungles Moï* (Paris 1912). A. PAVIE, *Mission Pavie Indo-Chine*, 11 vols. (Paris 1901–19).

2. On Myths and Rituals

J. DOURNES, "Chants antiques de la montagnes," *Bull. Soc. Études Indoch.*, 24 (1948); "Le maître des eaux (conte sré)," *France-Asie* 91 (1953): 25–29; "Fêtes saisonnières des Sré," *Bull. EFEO* 46, 2 (1954): 599–610; *L'homme et son mythe* (Paris 1968); "L'inceste préférentiel," *L'homme* 11, 4 (1971): 5–19; "Orphelin transformé," *Archipel* 2 (1971): 168–96; "Sous couvert des Maîtres," *Arch. europ. de sociol.* 14 (1973): 185–209; "La toupie incestueuse," *L'homme* 15, 3–4 (1975): 31–53; "La fée du figuier," *L'ethnographie* 68 (1974): 79–92; 69 (1975): 81–114; "Deux versions d'un mythe," *ASEMI* 6, 4 (1975): 97–124; *Akhan, contes oraux de la forêt indochinoise* (Paris 1976); *Le parler des Jörai et le style oral de leur expression* (Paris 1976); *Trois mythes sré* (Paris 1978); *Pötao, une théorie du pouvoir chez les indochinois Jörai* (Paris 1977; *Forêt Femme Folie, une traversée de l'imaginaire jörai* (Paris 1978).

Note: Jarai myths have been published for the most part; Sré myths are being published; for the Bahnar, thousands of pages, collected by P. Guilleminet, await publication.

THE HISTORY AND FUNCTION OF INDO-CHINESE MYTH: CHANGE AND PERMANENCE

The indigenous Indo-Chinese are not a vanished society, nor are they a primitive society frozen in some deadly archaism. Throughout the ups and downs of history, after wars and colonizations, they have managed to do more than simply survive; they live and continue to make myths. Their culture remains alive, for, while it has not ceased to change in its manifestations, this does not alter or destroy the originality of its conception. Under these conditions, a study of myths would be incomplete if it did not take into account the dynamic factor and if it did not follow the changes diachronically. Mythology is not necessarily a science of antiquity; fortunately for us (at least if the poets give it their attention), it still lives (for how long?) among people who think in myths.

The factors of change are of two kinds: the internal dynamics of the productivity of an ethnic group and contacts with other peoples and cultures. These two categories interact: the inner dynamics select what will be brought in, while outside contacts influence choices: some culture elements are retained and others abandoned, a process which can be demonstrated better in ritual than in mythology.

It is difficult to determine what the reciprocal influences were between the Austronesian peoples and the Austroasiatic peoples in prehistory. We know, for instance, that the Jarai of the north temporarily colonized the Bahnar of the south, and it is possible that they were heirs to them in somewhat the same way as the Romans were heirs to the Greeks. As for the less distant period, it may be possible, once Cham literature has been uncovered and analyzed, to recognize exchanges between it and the literatures of the eastern Indo-Chinese—a process which has already been pointed out in several studies devoted to them. Two factors should be taken into consideration: the Austronesian peoples (and their close neighbors) were "Chamized," and the Chams were Austronesian; just as the Chams assimilated Hindu cults (a statue of Śiva became the figure of the Cham king Pô-Klong-Garai; Bhagavati was adapted as Yang-Pō-Nagar, "Mistress of the country"; Indra was interpreted as Yang-In—see Mus, 1933, p. 371), the Jarai have recovered Cham deities (a Cham statue became for the Jarai a figure of Damsel Pe—see Dournes, 1970, p. 154). One can observe similar reciprocal interactions between the western Indo-Chinese and the Khmer or Laotians (Khmer is an Austroasiatic language). Before the French intervention, Sino-Vietnamese culture apparently had no impact on that of the indigenous inland peoples, although there may have been trade between them. In recent times, colonization in the Western style effected a brutal contact between the so-called modern world (because it thinks that it alone evolved) and the world of those who were called primitive. As a historical consequence of this colonization, Vietnamization became more efficient. Let us look at some examples of the effects of these changes, though it will not be possible to distinguish internal dynamics from acculturation, so closely are the two intertwined today.

Among the Jarai, who have been the most studied, myth and ritual undergoes modification in one generation. The same myth told over a period of ten or fifteen years by the same speaker or by another speaker (by an elderly woman and then by her grandson, for example) undergoes changes; passages are skipped (especially those that allude to the whole mythological corpus), elements are added (a reference to the French, to the Vietnamese), but the narrative remains recognizably Jarai and has kept its original color. The ritual changes and tends to be simplified; the great costly rituals dedicated to terrible deities give way to domestic and funeral rituals; we should also note a tendency toward rationalism: "The *Yang* always ask for sacrifices; they favor only the rich, who have all the resources and get richer and richer. We, the poor, need not offer them anything whatsoever." And in an extreme case, a simulacrum replaces the traditional ritual (a simulacrum that has nothing to do with the one that is customarily expected to be offered to possessed sorcerers).

The Catholic missions naturally encouraged this attitude, not among the Jarai (where they were not admitted) but among the Bahnar (where they settled); strange and alien rituals replaced others, and the myths disappeared from the memories of Christians who had learned that they were devilries to be destroyed along with their remarkable ritual paintings. In their attempts to remove the *Yang*, the fathers destroyed the sacred and all resistance at the heart of the ethnic group. The effects of missions and colonization were very different depending on the populations; the Austronesian peoples, who had strong social systems, resisted on the whole.

Another phenomenon that attacks the culture of minorities from the outside is recuperation. That is, missionaries borrow those elements that appear to them to be the least pagan and convert them (that is to say, denature them) in order to integrate them into an aseptic pagan Christianity. An administrator writes a literary work by joining bits and pieces of myths whose meaning is perverted; or he may traffic in the unwritten customary law in order to reinforce colonial power. Vietnamese publications cite the epics of the minorities and twist the meaning so as to find there the naturally "revolutionary" (we used to say "Christian") soul of people thus "prepared" to join their brothers in the struggle. A myth of the Rhadé tribe thus appeared in a comic strip: the hero, who has Western features, wears a feather headdress like an American Indian chief and rebels against heaven! By working on their minorities, nations foster their naïveté, deceiving especially those who would not recognize popular local cultures in any other form.

On the other hand, there is a new and highly localized tendency among some Jarai to acquire a taste for their oral literature, to collect and transcribe their ancient myths faithfully and without attempting to modernize, politicize, or moralize them.

The literature of the indigenous Indo-Chinese is of the people and for the people; it is not limited to an elite but is merely better known by cultivated people who are not materially the most comfortable; quite the contrary. Myths are profoundly embedded within each person; mythical behavior, ritual activity, and social life are not images of one another, but the man who lives by myth, the man who performs a ritual, and the man who lives with his family are one and the same man. The mythic dimension is lived in daily life, from within. The link established between myth, ritual, and behavior is a function of what we might call "the mythological mentality," which can be seen notably in the following:

—A latent desire that "everything take care of itself," by counting more on the intervention of the *Yang* than on individual responsibility, preferring the direct result "fallen from heaven" to any human effort to produce it, waiting for the "ready-made," the gift, without active participation—which is not without political consequences, especially when one sees how "aid to the Third World" functions in this way.

—A disposition to admit what is strange and unusual (which results in great tolerance for the ways of other people), to await the marvelous and to see in it a sign of the *Yang* powers, a sign rather than a miracle or magic force (as some Westerners might be tempted to interpret it).

—An aspiration, repressed by the constraints of existence, to transgress the human condition in such things as social laws; an aspiration to be in an imaginary, distant place; the temptation of the forbidden: the woman and the forest, the sister and the fairy.

—The feeling that a certain communication is possible between domains, places, and times; more than that, a feeling that there is a kind of continuum within which man is situated. The two arts that are most practiced by the Jarai and other Indo-Chinese are the recitation of myths and music, which unfold in time and are perceived by the ear, the organ of hearing and the seat of the intelligence (whereas sculpture, painting, and weaving are blocked out in space), but only in order to go beyond the passage of time. As Lévi-Strauss has stated: "Like a musical work, myth functions on the basis of a double continuum" (1964: 24). Mythological thought establishes a particular type of relationship with the universe: man is coextensive with space (one species among others, he speaks with animals and plants), and by virtue of the timelessness of myth he is contemporary with the "paradise" of his dreams and with the stories of Drit. Myth suppresses ruptures between societies (Dournes, 1955, p. 91) and between persons (the "I" and the "you"—and is that not love?)

This leads us to emphasize what seems to be the essential function of myth: to recover, to reinvent the continuum by going beyond ambiguity (which is different from continuity but is a means of attaining it) and by opposing confusion (such as the one produced by rice beer, a mixed drug, which is said to bring about oblivion in which "husband and wife no longer recognize each other and all become confused"—but the one reciting the myth, he does not drink, at least until he has finished his story).

This continuum is signified in the ritual, which through repetition and redundancy tries to plug the holes, to do all that is possible (that is, imaginable), whether through divination in which man is on an equal footing with the *Yang*, energies that we might call supernatural, or through omens in which man is carried back to the time when he understood the language of the birds.

This continuum is represented in the myth, whose hero travels through the air and the underworld, changes himself into animals, and speaks with forest creatures and domestic objects. He leaps over mountain ranges in a single bound, stops time in its course. The theme of the day that never ends because the sun suspended its course at the hero's whim (explicit or otherwise) is a classical image of Jarai mythology (Mj. 44, 47, 110, 118); this is always for the sake of prolonging the pleasures of lovers, situated outside the bounds of time. This theme reverses that of the Mang-ling Darkness, a catastrophic period during which the sun did not show its face, which makes the sun a figure of life and happiness and, more exactly, a sign of love: beyond the oppositions and successions of life and death, day and night, lovers are freed from their limitations (both as living beings and as persons), and, no longer in need of the mediation of a third term, they attain the mythological goal of a recovered unity. Perhaps they do more. Through the imaginary, these people—so distant and yet so close to us—join and link all those on earth who know that in order to escape from the life that divides and severs, one need not die or sleep; one can also dream.

J.D./g.h.

BIBLIOGRAPHY

1. For the history: J. DOURNES, "Recherches sur le Haut Champa," *France-Asie* 201 (1970): 143–62. P. MUS, "Cultes indiens et indigènes au Champa," *Bulletin de l'École Française d'Extrême Orient,* 1933, 367–410.

2. For the evolution of the literature (modifications and variants): J. DOURNES, *Le parler des Jörai et le style oral de leur expression* (Paris 1976).

3. On the utilization of the literature: L. SABATIER, *La chanson de Damsan, légende radé du XVIe siècle* (Paris); "La chanson de Damsan," *Bulletin de l'École Française d'Extrême Orient* 33 (1934): 143–302; *Recueil des coutumes rhadées du Darlac* (Hanoi 1940); and the Vietnamese publications below.

4. On the continuum: J. DOURNES, *En suivant la piste des hommes sur les hauts plateaux du Vietnam* (Paris 1955); "Le discret et le continu," *JATBA* 18, 7–8 (1971): 274–87. C. LEVI-STRAUSS, *The Raw and the Cooked* (New York 1969); originally in French.

5. Vietnamese publications (in French): *Viêtnam* (Hanoi), November 1974, p. 11. *Giai Phong* (South Vietnam), no. 6 (1975): 14–15.

Indigenous Indo-Chinese Cosmogony

I. Ndu/Adei: The Celestial Divinity

Like most of the Austroasiatic peoples of the south (Katu, Maa, Mnong), the Sré, in their myths and rituals, invoke ōng Ndu. Ōng is the general term used to designate men of one's grandfather's generation and those who are assimilated into that group (such as notables and elderly men whom one does not know); according to context, the term may be translated as "grandfather," "sir," or "my lord." Ndu functions as a proper name. Although he is anthropomorphized by the name and by mythic scenes that describe his appearance on earth, Ndu has no perceptible form or representation, apart from the wavy lines on top of the ritual festival pole among certain of the Roglai and Maa. He lives nowhere; he can be everywhere. He is unanimously said to be superior to all of the *yang* and is manifestly apart from all others—even if, thanks to a slip on the part of a bard who pronounced Ndu in place of Kö-Du (Ms. 123), it is conceivable that he may be connected with the deified mythic ancestor Kö-Du (*kö* is the particle which precedes all proper names of people among the Sré, but not the name of Ndu, who is thus not "personified" in this sense). He appears to be some kind of foster father, or providence: "Milk comes from Ndu; thus he fed men in the beginning. But when they grew up, milk was not sufficient, so Ndu created rice." Ndu is invoked with the paddy *yang* (if not on the same plane) or in the form of Ndu *yang* (which, like banyan *yang*, expresses the sacred relation between Ndu and human beings), or still in the form of (*yang*) Ndu-Ndai—a classical rhyme word of the oral style, simply echoed for the rhythm. "We ask for rice from *yang*, and *yang* seeks it for us from Ndu." There is thus no higher order, no world beyond, except, perhaps, Sun (a heavenly divinity, and female), who, according to certain Sré, entrusted Ndu with the task of feeding humans.

Among the Austronesian groups, along with the Rhadé, the Jarai use the name *öi Adei*. The term *öi* is the exact equivalent of the Sré *ōng*, and has the same uses. Adei is located above the vault of the heavens, the underside of the vault being *röngit*, the visible sky. This name is also pronounced Dei, Dai, or Diē: the reduplication ("to make an assonant balance, *pötüh*, but there is only one öi Adei") takes the form of öi Du-öi Dei (or Ködu-Ködē) in which it is easy to recognize Ndu-Ndai. It is in effect the same name, as H. Maitre once stated: "At the festival of the seed grains, all of the Mnong of diverse families offer a pot to Ndu, the supreme Spirit, the Aï Dē of the Rhadé" (Edde) (1912: 187). "He created everything," say the Jarai, "all things come from him, and without him there would be nothing." He has power over the life of everyone and stands above all; he is also invoked under the form of *yang dlong*, "on high" (as one says Elohim so as not to pronounce Yahweh), or in a parallel with *yang*: "If *yang* agrees to it, if Adei concedes it," has the sense of our "if God wills it." He has no connection with Sun, who, in Jarai thought, is *yang* manifest. Thus Adei = Ndu; it is the same word and the definition is close, but he is conceived and seen differently. To the extent that *yang* is an abstraction common to all the ethnic groups, Ndu/Adei is a variously colored mythic image: *yang* is conceived as a relationship; Ndu/Adei is perceived as a term.

In Sré mythology, Ndu intervenes in a very precise sense. "Seeing a butterfly flutter up over his house, a man recognized a manifestation of Ndu. In the night, in a dream he heard Ndu promise him assured riches. After that, he lacked nothing" (Ms. 116). "A poor man went out of a wealthy house where no one had offered him anything. A bat got caught in his hair, and wherever he went, people invited him to drink and eat; it was Ndu who accompanied him" (Ms. 117). The following account is of primary importance: "A very poor young man, Ddöi ("orphan"), goes to his mother's brother to borrow some rice. His uncle gives him nothing. On the road, he meets Ndu in the form of an old man and tells him of his troubles. Ndu then takes the form of Ddöi and brings a handful of straw to the uncle to obtain rice in exchange; the uncle chases him away. Ndu returns to Ddöi and promises to help him. Ndu gives a few seed grains to Ddöi; from this, Ddöi gets more rice than anyone in the world. The uncle wants to see the prodigious harvest; he climbs up into the rice granary, falls out of it, and breaks his bones. Then Ndu goes to look for a poor young girl who also lives alone. He brings her to Ddöi and marries them. Ndu disappears, never to be seen again. Ddöi and his wife live happily together" (Ms. 22—these texts are obviously much abridged here—cf. Dournes 1963: 52; 1971: 188). Another account, less widespread, is unique in depicting the poor man as coming to Ndu "on the border between heaven and earth"—the only case in which the man takes the initiative in the affair. The principal agrarian ritual of the Sré makes use of an element of this myth: handfuls of straw, soaked in the blood of the sacrificed she-goat, are placed at the four corners of the rice field, "the roads by which Ndu comes"; between the rice fields and the village, at the base of the ritual pole, they erect a "spirit house," *kut Ndu,* of bamboo and thatch, to receive Ndu at the time of his visit. Ndu is called first with whistles, then by a long invocation: "May the rice leave the other people and pile up here for us, and may we become very rich!" This is not in the spirit of the myth; here the man demands and sets his sights on wealth as if it ought to fall to him from the sky. At the time of the Sré new year festival, it is said, "Let us borrow rice from Ddöi, let us borrow paddy from Ndu"—and both are called *ōng* in this case.

A Sré spirit house, *kut Ndu*. Musée de l'Homme collection. Photo J. Dournes.

What about the people who call the kindly Ndu "Adei"? The Jarai myths introduce a son (more often the youngest of seven than the younger of two) of öi Adei (but never Adei himself) who descends to earth at the request of their father, who is moved by human misery, in order to transform the condition of a poor naked girl. In the form of a young man (sometimes deformed, to put her to the test), he asks permission to marry the poor girl, who has been raised by her grandmother Bush. He procures the means for her subsistence and gives her a child, then returns for good to the heavenly domain (Mg. 11, 13, 14, 66, 94). The reverse movement (of humans toward Adei) may be seen in several cases: (1) the type of "the child who did not want to die," who goes from village to village until he comes to the house of öi Adei, where he learns that one must die there too, but that on the border between heaven and earth one would not die, and yet one would not eat either (Mj. 70); (2) the type of the young boy who wants to avenge his uncle who has been killed by a powerful lord; he climbs to the house of öi Adei, who refashions his body so that it is ready for anything (exactly as the old woman Bush does for her protégés [Mj. 8, 20], but Adei [male] does so by forging, whereas Bush [female] does her work as a potter) and takes his own heart to put it in the body of the boy who, not surprisingly, kills the lord and takes his aunt back to him (Mj. 49); (3) the case of the epic heroes: the din of their battles disturbs öi Adei, who sends his servant girl Whirlpool (H'Kroah, the divinity of ascending whirlpools) to seize the hero, bring him up to heaven, and restore his strength (Mj. 24 and parallels); (4) Dier, the hero of a long epic: he climbs up to the house of Adei to marry his daughter and bring her back to earth with him (Mj. 109). In this text and in some others, Adei is a somewhat grotesque character, whom his wife awakens by pouring a bucketful of molten lead in his ear, something which would be unthinkable for the Sré if it were done to Ndu, but which would be quite appropriate for their demiurge, the good-natured giant Nyut.

The Jarai homologue for the Sré Ddöi would seem to be Drit (or Rit), which has the same meaning, "orphan." A whole cycle of Jarai mythology has Drit as its hero—he is, if not the national hero, at least a model for the argumentative and unpredictable Jarai. If we must reduce all these accounts to a single schema (which is painful since they are so beautiful), it might well be the following: the poor Drit lives with a grandmother Bush (who may be called Ya'-Pum) between the village and the forest (they are marginal people). An accident of the hunt puts him in contact with a beautiful fairy girl who has connections with the worlds of animals, flowers, and heavenly bodies, and who brings him a life of ease in the form of food and clothing (as though she were the initiator and introducer of technical knowledge). A local lord, *potao,* is jealous and takes her away from him. A series of trials, in which he is successful, allows Drit, who defeats the lord, to take back his beloved. In some accounts, the lord offers his own daughter in marriage to Drit, who does not want her and leaves her for the fairy of his dream;

in this case the lord functions as a father-in-law, that is, as a mother's brother who claims his right to the bride, and who thus corresponds to the evil uncle of Ddöi. Öi Adei apparently does not enter into the picture in any of this. Drit and his grandmother Bush are invoked ritually, notably in a long prayer addressed to the powerful divinities of the sources of rivers, Diö-Diung-Yung-Hmeng, who are legendary warriors charged by öi Adei with watching over the ritual activities of humans. As for öi Adei, he is invoked by the Jarai in a very different tone from that of the myths, and on the most important occasions: at fertility rites (before sowing) and during catastrophes (drought, incest—which are connected); the celebrants remain naked, in the manner of servants, to call respectfully to öi Du-öi Dei, parallel to ya'Dung-Dai (*ya'* is the feminine of *öi*).

This grandmother Dung-Dai, whose name is so similar to Du-Dei, is often explicitly said to be the wife of öi Adei. The study of many texts shows that she is interchangeable with grandmother Pum (Bush), the grandmother of Drit, who is in complicity with the fairies of the forest. This leads to the understanding that the Jarai Providence may well be female—öi Adei being no more than a very distant *deus otiosus*—and that the Jarai equivalent of the venerable Ndu of the Sré could be a pair of women, or rather a woman with two aspects: the old woman of the woods and the young fairy girl, a single female principle of fertility. This is in keeping with Jarai culture, where woman is everything and does everything. She is now visible in the moon, whose full face shows the old Bush under her banyan tree (cf. Sauer 1972: 88).

The Jarai Drit and the Sré Ddöi have the same character of "orphan"—that is, a loner, without parents or family, outside of all classifications, like Ndu/Adei—but they are not the same person: the Jarai seems more typed, with more character; the passive Ddöi resembles an ordinary Sré. Drit has more "liver"—as they say where he comes from—yet his victory and the goods he acquires come to him only through a woman—which is very Jarai. One may note another difference, which is connected with the character of the men of each ethnic group: the connections between heaven and earth are clearly sexualized among the Jarai (a son of god marries a daughter of men, or a son of men loves a daughter of a god), while they are not sexualized among the Sré—except when a son of men falls in love with a daughter of Sun (Ms. 13), and then we obtain the equation (Sré daughter of Sun = Jarai son of Sky) which makes the female Sun analogous to the male Adei in a chiasmic figure with the homology noted above (Ya' Dung-Dai corresponding to Ndu):

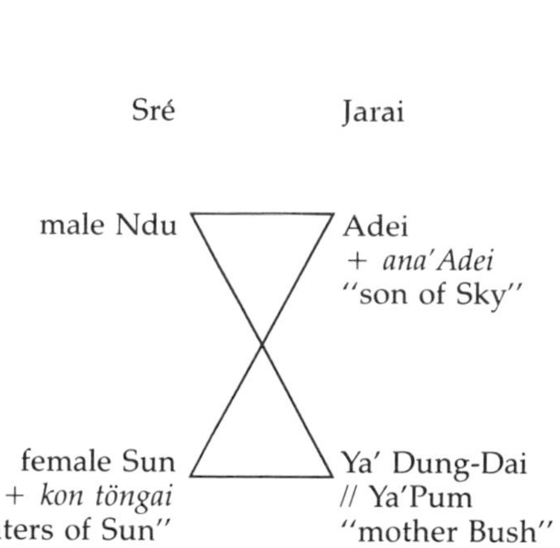

By means of cross-checking, interconnections, and intermediate figures (*mediators*), the Jarai, even more than the Sré, seem to be searching for a continuity; it appears as if the mythological figures of the two ethnic groups were weaving the same sorts of threads between them.

Ndu/Adei being a term, a separation between the distant god and the lower world would be logical; hence the *yang* relationship (abstraction) and the intermediate heroes (images) which serve to connect, to retrieve the lost unity. Such a vision nevertheless depends more on what is dreamed than on what is lived (in daily and ritual life), for only the dream voyager has no fear of straddling those distinctions which society loves so well (cf. Dournes 1975).

II. The Cosmic Ruptures

As far as origin myths are concerned, the indigenous Indo-Chinese have very little to say—although we know that this is not all there is to their mythology—apart from disconnected elements, which are nevertheless important for their representation of the universe, imagined in space and time as being marked, if not cut up, by ruptures in the initial and ideal continuum. On the occasion of traditional narrations and spontaneous conversations, it is still possible to glean diverse bits of information—a delicate operation which is worth the trouble—but more successfully among the Austroasiatic peoples than among the Austronesian peoples. The elements that follow do not reflect a rigorous chronological order.

1. The Sré Creation and the Departure from Hell

The Sré conceive the world as having seven levels, of which three are celestial and three infernal, with the earth in between. All was created in the heavens and then transported to the hells, where the demiurge Bung intervened on the side of Ndu; this creation is viewed as a work of the forge—a specifically masculine work. Bung brought plants, animals, man, and fire to earth out of the subterranean world, through the hole situated at Nkany. Then the giant Nyut thrust heaven still higher; since that time, it has been impossible to pass between the upper and lower worlds, which are inverse images of one another (in the hell called Brah-Ting, everything is done opposite to the way it is done on earth). "We, the sons of men, we are the sons of the seven" (the seventh world, in the middle).

2. The Jarai Universe and the Emergence from Earth

The Jarai believe the earth is like a round winnowing basket and the sky like another concave winnowing basket turned down on the earth; since they separated from one another, it is impossible to pass from one to the other. The sky is called the "model," *gru,* and the earth is its mirror image. Above the sky is the province of Adei; below is the world of the dead where everything is reversed. Humanity (that is, the seven Jarai clans) emerged from the earth through the hole of Dreny. Once every seven years a white buffalo is sacrificed there and its blood is poured into the hole. Only one young girl was unable to pass through because she was leading a buffalo whose horns were too wide (this detail is also found among the Sré): this is the girl of dreams whom only mythical heroes are able to join, under the earth or at the bottom of the waters. *'Mang* means at once "hole," "door," and "narrow pass"; the "hole" of Dreny, imagined as such by the Jarai and the Rhadē, may actually be a narrow pass (that of Mdrak or another one) by which the ancestors of the Austronesian people entered the central Indo-Chinese plateau.

Thirteenth-century heads of statues from Champa known as H'Bia Pē and his brother. The Jarai perform a ritual in their honor. Musée de l'Homme collection. Photo J. Dournes.

3. The Primitive Conditions of Existence

According to the Jarai, the first man flew like a bird, did not die, and spoke with plants and animals; animals were like men and men were like *yang* (the iris filled the whole outer eye, which gave them another view of things, the *yang* view: for example, what we see as buffalo is man; what we see as spider is soul, the double of a human, according to a code of equivalences which is analogous to the code that allows for the interpretation of visions seen in dreams). And öi Adei lived with them. Hoes hoed by themselves, and man only had to feed them; and wicker carrying baskets grew on trees like fruit. This continued until ruptures in space and time interrupted the harmony. This was partly the fault of men, who got drunk and forgot to feed their axes and hoes, who revolted: "In the future, if you want the earth to produce, you will have to hew and hoe!" (and see below).

According to the Sré, primitive man lived in a state of paradise: he did not have to work, and Ndu offered him immortality. Ndu dug a shallow well and asked a couple to jump into it. But the water was freezing. The man and the woman limited themselves to soaking their hands, sprinkling water on their heads, and drinking a little: this is why the nails and hair never stop growing and there are two sets of teeth. But for having refused the water of youth, men experienced suffering, old age, and death. A serpent dove into the well; he shed his skin and reemerged completely new: this is why snakes always remain young (Ms. 114).

4. The Destructive Flood

In Sré, *da' ling* is the sea, the ocean: *da' ling kwo da'ling kwa* was a flood of maritime origins, which covered all of the earth. Everything was destroyed. The *yang* entered rocks and mountains; Ndu alone did not have to flee, since he lives neither here nor there. Of all mankind, only a young man and his sister, who took shelter in a drum, survived. When the water receded, the drum landed on Mount Yang-La; out of it emerged the brother and sister and all future mankind (Ms. 7—an identical tradition is found among the Austroasiatic Katu).

In Jarai, *ling* means "flood," but the legendary catastrophe is more often designated "the boiling sea." The waters inundate everything: those who cling to rocks become *yang*, and those who cling to the pods of the cottonwood tree become stars. A pregnant woman (in one variant, it is a woman with a person called Black Dog, by whom she will have a son) enters a drum. When the waters subside and leave the drum behind, she comes out, splitting open the skin of the drum. With her son, she engenders the new humanity (Mj. 73). Thus humanity is the product of incest, between brother and sister among the Austroasiatic people and between mother and son among the Austronesian peoples; this is rare among the latter, who prefer to celebrate the mythical love of a young man for his sister (and such cases occur in reality). The famous story of H'Bia Pē and her incestuous brother (Mj. 45; Dournes 1970: 154; 1971: 13), and the ritual connected with it—drought, which is catastrophic in dry tropical countries, is conceived as the consequence of incest—are explained in the context of the account of the flood.

Another famous case of incest, again among the Jarai, brought about a tragic rupture: under the effects of a philter meant for another man, Röyot's brother falls in love with her, and she dies in childbirth. Seeing this overwhelmingly sad sight, öi Adei can no longer bear to remain among men, and he returns to the heights forever. Since then, animals do not speak to men, birds sing their dirge for öi Adei, and the *Pterocarpus* (a leguminous plant) secretes blood. The heroine and her brother became rocks (the mass of stone called "mother and child" in all the languages of the region) (Mj. 55; Dournes 1971: 12). The death of Röyot rendered the earth *cölom*, "impure," which connotes rupture (from order, from the norm, from the acceptable). Every act which is *cölom*—for example, the violation, even unconscious, of a prohibition—even today necessitates a purifying sacrifice to rid oneself of impurity and to reestablish normal relationships, to renew ties with tradition (the correct succession of actions) and with every being, because *cölom* has repercussions in the universe like a stone thrown into still water.

5. The Cold Darkness

The theme of cold darkness, like that of the flood, is common to nearly every ethnic group. Moreover, the terms used to designate this darkness are all connected, even in unrelated languages.

In Sré, the noun *börling-börlang* designates a universal upheaval described as follows: "Tired of the battles fought by men, Sun decides not to rise. It is dark and cold, and frozen water comes out of the earth. Because they soaked their heads in this water, the *börling* birds (Drongo) and *börlang* birds (Garrulax), so named after this catastrophe, are white on the tops of their heads. In the future there will be another *börling-börlang* day, which will be the end of this world and the beginning of a new one" (Ms. 132). This myth should be compared with that of Ms. 9 for the story of the warrior hero who was able to reach the Sun by means of a ladder (Dournes 1948: 25); and with the Jarai myths in which it is öi Adei who interrupts battles. The expression *börlang-kang* (*kang*, "obstruct") designates the rainbow (see below). A Sré woman announced the golden age of the new *börling-börlang* and ordered the sacrifice of all white animals.

The Bahnar equivalent of this is *mang-ling*. "According to a confused tradition, the Bahnar claim to have known an endless night that followed a disappearance of the sun. Another endless night will precede the end of the world" (Guilleminet 1963: 534). The *börlang* bird (Garrulax) seems to have no connection with this phenomenon but is used for omens. The Mnong also call this catastrophe *mang-ling* (confused with the Flood in Condominas 1953: 655 and 1957: 454). This tradition is still alive among the Katu, who connect the *mang-ling mang-ta* with the *pörleng pörlang* birds (the same as *börling-börlang*).

In Jarai, the *ling-mang* cataclysm is described as follows: "During seven days and seven nights, the sun did not rise, the wind blew, and it was cold." This does not seem to be directly connected with the *bling* and *blang* birds (names designating the same species, here the bird-judges of tradition), but, as with the Sré, a new upheaval is awaited: the "prophet" Dam Bam announced the golden age, connected with the revolt for self-government—as is frequent in the messianism of populations subjected to outside rule—as well as with mythical representations (the rice fields planted with a single grain of rice at each corner).

6. *The Secondary Ruptures*

Under the heading of secondary ruptures are grouped those phenomena that indigenous thought associates, on the level of signs, with "unique" ruptures in history.

The eclipse of the sun, whose "cause" is different from one ethnic group to another, is always frightening, especially because it is a reminder of the "Cold Darkness."

Lightning is everywhere considered to be a punishment for a fault (in general, for having put together things which should have been kept separate—and especially for incest). It is the spark of the short-circuit, which cuts off the current; it is always associated with thunderstones (prehistoric stone axes) gathered as protective talismans.

The lunar halo is interpreted as follows by the Sré: if the circle does not constitute a continuous line but is broken, for example, on the western side, then death will come from that direction.

The rainbow is, for the Sré, the manifestation of *Briang* (another form of *börlang*), a pair of celestial beings who drink blood. The upper arc is man and the lower arc woman; the colors are those of the blood that is sucked in (the red band is human blood) (Ms. 72). In Jarai it is the manifestation of tragic death, Driang, the source of ritual impurity; it causes a short-circuit by joining heaven and earth, which should be separated. Mythology endows it with an extraordinary capacity to absorb (Mj. 99). In Mnong, it is Brieng, the "eater of souls" (Condominas 1957: 128). In Bahnar, *Bödreng* comes to drink on earth, which is an omen of tragic death. The problem of cultural contacts, or of a common origin, is once again posed by these similarities, not only between words, but even more between concepts, with the ambiguity of an arc that connotes a rupture of the norm.

J.D./d.w.

BIBLIOGRAPHY

I. The Celestial Divinity

J. BOULBET, *Pays des Maa', domaine des Génies* (Paris 1967). G. CONDOMINAS, *Nous avons mangé la forêt de la pierre-génie Gôo* (Paris 1957), indes, 450, 451, 473. J. DOURNES, "Fêtes saisonnières des Sré," *Bull. EFEO* 40 (1954): 599–609, ill.; *Dieu aime les païens* (Paris 1963); "Orphelin transformé, jalons mythologiques," *Archipel*, no. 2 (1971), 168–96, bibliography; "La toupie incestueuse, ou de la distinction nécessaire," *L'homme* 15, nos. 3–4 (1975): 31–53. H. MAITRE, *Les jungles moï* (Paris 1912). C. O. SAUER, *Seeds, Spades, Hearths, and Herds: The Domestication of Animals and Foodstuffs* (Cambridge, MA, 1972).

II. Cosmic Ruptures (Bibliography by Ethnic Groups)

1. Austroasiatic Peoples

Bahnar: P. GUILLEMINET, *Dictionnaire bahnar-français* (Paris 1963).

Katu: A. FERREIROS and J. DOURNES, "Deux versions d'un mythe," *ASEMI* 6, no. 4 (1975): 97–124.

Maa: J. BOULBET, *Pays des Maa', domaine des génies* (Paris 1967), 57–59.

Mnong: G. CONDOMINAS, "Les tribus proto-indochinoises," in *Ethnologie de l'Union française* (Paris 1953), 2:658–78; *Nous avons mangé la forêt de la pierre-génie Gôo* (Paris 1957).

Sré: DAM BO, *Les populations montagnardes du Sud indochinois* (Lyons 1950). J. DOURNES, "Chants antiques de la montagne," *B.S.E.I.* (1948), 4:11–111; *En suivant la piste des hommes sur les hauts-plateaux du Viêtnam* (Paris 1955).

2. Austronesian Peoples

Jarai: J. DOURNES, "Recherches sur le haut Champa," *France-Asie*, no. 201 (1970), 143–62; "L'inceste préférentiel," *L'homme* 11, no. 4 (1971): 5–19; *Coordonnées, structures jörai familiales et sociales* (Paris 1972); "La toupie incestueuse," *L'homme* 15, nos. 3–4 (1975): 31–53; "Sam Bam, le Mage et le Blanc dans l'Indochine des années trente," *L'ethnographie* 1 (1978): 85–108.

On prophecy, see also J. MIDDLETON, "Political System of the Lugbara," in *Tribes without Rulers*, Middleton and Tait, eds. (3d ed., London 1967), 225.

The Functions and Methods of Mediators and Intermediaries among the Indigenous Indo-Chinese

I. Mediators and Intermediaries—Mending Ruptures and Seeking the Continuum

As if they were traumatized by cosmic ruptures, the indigenous Indo-Chinese, in their passion for continuity and their memory of the original harmony, imagine mediations that reestablish the unity that disappeared from existence and is recovered in myth. Creatures whose condition is ambiguous, such as those who are between two realms or between two levels of the universe, are all designated for this function; among them are the birds, between heaven and earth, who have an important place, especially among the Sré.

Yai-dam-du, the son of the stars, has come down to earth and is in trouble. He asks his sister, who has remained up above, to send him food; she entrusts it to the birds: rice to the crow, vegetables to the titmouse, and water to the drongo (*Dissemurus paradiseus*) (Ms. 14). This is only one example among many. For the Jarai, this mode of mediation is realized largely on a horizontal plane, notably between the world of the forest and that of the village: thus the woodpecker and the blackbird were sent on a mission by the old woman of the woods (Mj. 30; Dournes 1975).

Mac-mai goes to join her fiancé; they are tricked by monkey people who pass themselves off as one or the other of the lovers. Ndu sends a turtledove to reveal the truth to the two heroes (Ms. 93). Sometimes this is a young girl who transforms herself into a turtledove in order to test the feelings of the man she loves (Ms. 13). In a Jarai myth, a young man is transformed into a bird so that he can tell his father about a misfortune that has befallen the father's wife (Mj. 115); in a story of the same type, a turtledove tells the boy about the place where his mother is held prisoner (Mj. 109). The bird sees, knows, and tells all; this concept is probably linked to the practice of augury based on the direction of flight and the songs of birds.

In Jarai antiquity, the drongo was the judge charged by heaven with settling disagreements among human beings (notably the incest between Pé and her brother). The strong authoritative voice of this bird with its long tail (its "loincloth") has its echo today in the elocution of Jarai judges (or rather mediators) who recite the "words of justice." In Sré antiquity, the crow and the vulture were kings on earth and demanded human sacrifices. The hero Trong son of Tre overthrew them: he struck them, they grew wings, and they fled (Ms. 27). Man became master in place of the birds, and the buffalo replaced man as the object of sacrifice.

Today there is a particular veneration for a very small primate, the *Nycticebus kukang,* the slow loris (in Jarai *kra alé,* "bamboo monkey"; in Sré *dô glé* has the same meaning and refers to the same animal, like the Bahnar *dok glé*). This primate lives in trees, between heaven and earth; it is active only at night, but it is consulted during the day: the animal is given a little stick, which it accepts or not, thus responding to the question that it is asked; this is a form of divination. The tradition of several ethnic groups makes this primate the king (*bötaw, potao*) of animals; Jarai myths in particular (Mj. 4, 107) develop this notion: he emerges victorious from battles with elephants or rhinoceroses; he is the friend of old mother Bush, and as such is associated with Drit, the shabby little victor over all trials, and therefore, like him, is a mediator (between the animal world and the human world, and between the forest and the village). Moreover, according to Jarai evolutionism, he is regarded as the link between the animal kingdom and that of humans, and his name is invoked in a series along with the names of the ancestors.

The mythology does not lack the resources to establish bridges between the kingdoms; among the Sré as well as among the Jarai, there are many double characters: all of the *sömri* (Sré) or *rökai* (Sré and Jarai), tiger-men or ogres, are ambiguous in nature and function, usually terrifying, sometimes terrified by a small child. A man reveals himself in turn as a buffalo, a deer, and then a tiger (Ms. 80); a parallel Jarai figure makes him an elephant man (Mj. 30). These characters, who really have two natures, are to be distinguished from mythological characters (especially those of Jarai origin) who appear in the form of toads, civet cats, or pythons, but in reality are young men who test their companions and then reveal that they are accomplished and courteous men. On the other hand, they may be compared with what the Jarai call "two men:" in daylight they are like everybody else, but during the night they become vampires, reduced to nothing but a head that trails its entrails behind it like the tail of a comet; they come to suck the blood (the life) of human beings, and are associated with fruit bats—which, however, are not vampires (Desmodontidae, a native American family). In any event, all of these imaginary creatures bear witness to a taste, if not a need, to go beyond distinctions, to make categories overlap, to retrieve a continuum that was dreamed of but is disquieting (people make classifications to reassure themselves), at the same time revealing what indigenous thought associates within its own zoology, where human beings are not the privileged creatures that we make of them.

On another level, the level of practical life, man can establish rituals of alliance with animals (the tiger in particular, the slow loris among the Bahnar-*röngao*—cf. Kemlin 1917) and even with plants, to indicate a continuum (indeed a complicity, notably in the case of the hunter who makes a kind of pact of mutual nonaggression with the tiger, his rival) while maintaining a distinction. These alliances are analogous to those that are made in social life, either by a marriage, which joins two families (and a young man calls his allied father-in-law "uncle," which is what the hunter calls his allies in the forest), or, especially, by those treaties that make two strangers sworn friends or even relations (with the relationship of brothers or the relationship between a mother and son). This ritual plane cuts across the mythical plane—our distinctions do not make much sense in a homogenous system—and it does so in two types of situations: (1) the case of the hero Drit, a hunter living on the margins, who makes alliances with the animals of the forest, releasing his catch so that the animals will later come to his rescue; (2) the case of real people who are driven by their phantasms to make alliances, as in marriage, with tiger women or fairies of the woods to the point where they become possessed. In an attempt to free them, the family pronounces a ritual formula of divorce—Drit may marry a dryad, and everyone can dream about it, but it is dangerous (a sign of mental confusion) to view it as though it had really happened.

More rare are ritual alliances made with deities, in a vertical rather than a horizontal direction (living beings are not arranged in a hierarchy). These alliances result from predictive dreams, and it is by means of the dream that they join together with myth, where this type of liaison is not infrequent. It is represented by a ladder among the Sré and by a thread among the Jarai: the Sun makes a beautiful woman come down a ladder to attract a hero and to make him climb up after her (Ms. 130; cf. Ms. 10, 16, 124); Heaven sends the god of whirlwinds to seize a boisterous warrior and raise him into a small boat at the end of a cord (Mj. 24). This last detail brings us back to the hero Drit, who, going the other way, descends into the netherworld inside a small tethered boat (Mj. 15). Furthermore, among the Jarai the unwound thread of a spindle is used either to reascend toward a protecting fairy (Mj. 30) or to descend to earth to join a desired beautiful woman and to bring her back up (Mj. 36, 125). One must connect the realms and the worlds by all available means (mediations), and the mythic imagination does not lack such means.

II. The Flight and the Voyage

The dream of flying is not unique to the Indo-Chinese. When dealing with such universal themes, any attempt at comparison would be futile unless the analysis drew upon the particular coloration that a culture gives such themes through an original vision.

The myths of several ethnic groups have developed the image of flying while tied to a kite, which is already less banal; but the kite originated in East Asia, from China to Malaysia. In various Austroasiatic and Austronesian languages, it is called *klang* (or *kling* in Sré), from the same noun that serves as a generic term for hawks and falcons (like the English *kite*). The sons of Lady Kling (the name is probably not gratuitous) launch a kite, attach themselves to the cord, cut off the cord beneath them, and fly off in this way to fight their enemies, who are also suspended from a kite, but one

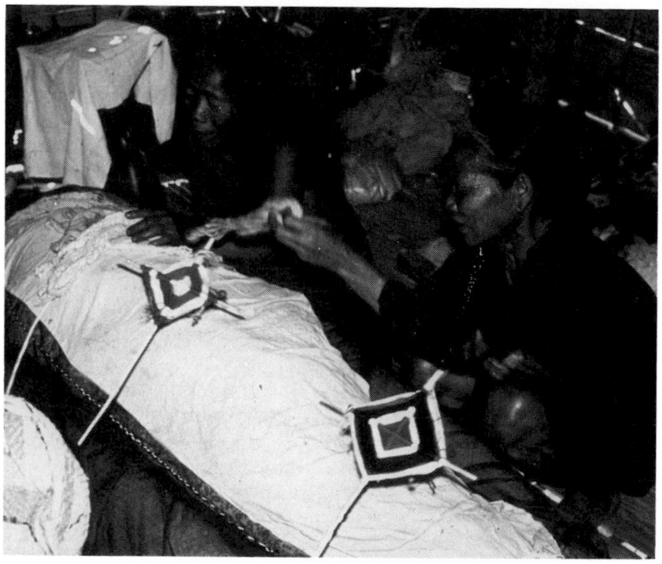

Jarai wailers around the body of a dead person in his shroud, on which flyswatters threaded with crosses have been placed (Vietnam). Paris, Musée de l'Homme collection. Photo J. Dournes.

that is tied up, which causes their downfall (Ms. 23). Drit ties himself to a loose kite to ascend from the netherworld, to which he had descended in a small tethered boat in order to win the beautiful woman whom the lord desired (Mj. 15). Another time, Drit is attached to a kite by the lord who wants to get rid of him; Drit rises through the air and flies to a marvelous country from which he brings back a talisman that allows him to overcome all difficulties (Mj. 117).

Another means of aerial transportation is the "flying horse," *aseh por* in Sré as well as in Jarai (which again underscores the probability that their myths have a common origin). It is always explicitly stated that the horse has a white coat (perhaps because such horses are rare in these regions), and it must not be too hastily assimilated to Pegasus. When Lang, the daughter of the Sun, entrusts her husband with a mission to her mother, he mounts the "flying white horse," which transports him to the Sun (Ms. 13). When a celestial girl sends her flying white horse down to earth, Drit succeeds in taming it, mounts it, and joins the beautiful girl on high (Mj. 1).

The simplest means of flying, however, is making wings for oneself, which is what the hero does, notably when the girl has the qualities of a bird. A girl of the air has come to earth to bathe in a lake; she lays her feather mantle on the ground and goes into the water. Drit suddenly appears and takes the mantle; the beautiful girl follows him back to his home, finds her hidden mantle, puts it back on, takes flight, and disappears. Drit has wings made for himself, tries to fly, arrives at the heights of the sky, and—luckier than Icarus—is reunited with the woman he loves (Mj. 16; cf. also Mj. 22, 89).

The image of flight is taken up again in a Jarai funeral rite. A flyswatter made of cross-threads, shaped in a square, is broken diagonally according to custom. The two triangular halves are placed in the coffin on either side of the corpse: "They are the body's wings," which will allow it to reach the world of the dead. Furthermore, in the course of his successive transformations, the dead person will take on the appearance of a hawk, *klang*.

To move through the air is as "natural" as to swim in the water, at least for the war heroes of the Jarai epics. Most of the single combats take place somewhere between heaven and earth, in the zone of the clouds. The two fighters step on their round shields, which transport them into the heights, when it is not the shields themselves that confront one another, as one might imagine a battle of flying saucers.

Like the shield, which is efficacious only in movement, the characters in the mythology, mainly of the epic type, cannot stand still. They engage in prodigious voyages: on earth (such as Sing-kônga's tour of Jarai country); on the sea, riding on the back of a whale (as do Drit and his Sré counterpart Trong); to the realm of the river snakes in the depths of the waters; in the air to the ends of the earth and the sky; and finally even to the world of the dead, located somewhere in the west—as though everything had to be explored and nothing left out, in order to gather everything together within the global vision of the mythology taken as a whole.

To speak of a journey is to evoke a dream, and in indigenous thought, this association leads to the particular form of shamanism practiced by the indigenous Indo-Chinese.

The mythical hero transcends taboos and categories; he crosses over intervals and frontiers—in other words, he goes too far, which one might say is what myth is made for. But this game is far too dangerous for common mortals in everyday life. During sleep, the body or "appearance" (*rup* in Sré and Jarai, *rūpa* in Sanskrit) remains visible on its bed. The permanent ego, rather than the "double" (*böngat* in Jarai, *semăngat* in Malay), can go out temporarily and leave on a journey; this is the dream. Everything that the *böngat* sees and does during its outing is the subject matter of the dream. It is essential not to go too far nor to venture where one must not go. It sometimes happens that the *böngat* returns late, because he is temporarily detained by a captivating vision or by a *yang* that stops it; this is illness. The relatives of the sick person try to determine by divination or through a shaman what sacrifice should be offered to what *yang* in order to free the *böngat* of the sick person and reintroduce it into his body.

This mythic voyage and this notion of the dream make it possible to explain how the indigenous Indo-Chinese see the function of the shaman, the *pöjau* (or *böjau, njau*) in all the languages of these ethnic groups. The *pöjau* is a man or woman who has experienced the "too-distant," like the Jarai hero Drit, who shares with impunity the intimacy of the sylvan deities, but not like the possessed person, who has surrendered to the charms of these deities and has become a wild creature. The *pöjau* is a marginal and hypersensitive person who has overcome his problems and the spirits that might otherwise lead him astray; he has made his voyage and has returned from it. Either after a flight into the forest, from which he has emerged unscathed, or after a premonitory dream entreating him to become a *pöjau*, in any case on recovering from a psychosomatic illness, the subject about to undertake the voyage takes up his duties, initiated by another *pöjau* or by his *yang*, also known as *gru* (Sanskrit *guru*), in the sense of "a model to reproduce" (just as heaven is the model for earth), and in the sense of "initiator."

The modes of action of the *pöjau* are multiple, the two principal ones being the dream and the voyage. If he is a specialist in the dream technique, it suffices for him to lie down with an object belonging to the sick person for whom his services are required. The symbolic contact of his body with the object will orient his dream. The shaman falls asleep and dreams, that is, his *böngat* goes out and has an adventure. In this case, he goes to meet the *böngat* of the sick person. He will then see what has happened to him and what *yang* holds him captive. When he wakes up, he will reveal the cause of the illness, and the family will know to what *yang* it should sacrifice.

The traveling shaman works in the same way, but in an altered state that is not sleep. Seated or standing and making some movements with his arms, swaying his torso and often accompanied by a musical instrument played by an assistant, he begins to invoke his *yang gru,* and then he enters into a kind of drunkenness without using alcohol or drugs. His *böngat,* that is, his self, has left. In his hut, the sick person and his relatives can only see a semblance of him and hear a voice, for "his mouth speaks." He gradually recounts all the adventures of his trip, the dangerous passage across a forest—the wild world, beyond the human world—where he meets tigers and malevolent deities. Almost exhausted, he reaches the spot where the sick person's *böngat* had ventured and is held captive by a *yang.* By virtue of his *gru* and the charm that he uses, he recaptures the lost *böngat,* makes the return trip with him, comes back victorious into the hut (which his body has never left), and finally reintroduces into the head of the sick person his *böngat,* which is occasionally materialized as an insect that the shaman holds in his hand (or pretends to hold—it matters little, it is a figurative language). Among the Jarai, especially, the quest for the distant captive is sexualized. The shaman courts forest girls and sees in the *böngat* that is to be saved a female figure (with the sexes reversed in the case of a woman *pöjau*). The scenario is analogous to the one in a series of myths in which the hero sets off on a dangerous mission to free a beautiful captive woman who is being kept prisoner by a monster or a wicked lord.

In a certain sense, the shaman's voyage reintegrates myth and dream into daily life. The character of the *pöjau* is ambiguous. Not only does he see what is on the "other side of the mirror," but he in fact stands on both sides of the mirror at the same time. He reconciles distinct realms without any confusion for himself, which is the most successful retort (both conceived and experienced) to the traumatizing ruptures that the shaman has personally overcome.

J.D./g.h.

BIBLIOGRAPHY

Mediators and Intermediaries

Bahnar-Röngao: J. KEMLIN, "Les alliances chez les Röngao," *Bull. EFEO* 17 (1917).

Jarai: J. DOURNES, "La fée du figuier," *L'ethnographie,* no. 68 (1974), pp. 79–92; no. 69, pp. 81–114; *Akhan, contes oraux de la forêt indochinoise* (Paris 1976); *Forêt Femme Folie* (Paris 1978).

Sré: J. DOURNES, "Chants antiques de la montagne," *B.S.E.I.,* 1948, 11–111; *Trois mythes sré* (Paris 1978).

The Flight and the Voyage

For the myths, see the bibliography for the article "The Mythology and Ritual of the Indigenous Populations of the Southern Part of the Indo-Chinese Peninsula."

On shamanism: G. CONDOMINAS, *Nous avons mangé la forêt de la pierre-génie Gôo* (Paris 1957), index pp. 439–40; shamanic voyage: pp. 147–55. J. DOURNES, *En suivant la piste des hommes sur les hauts-plateaux du Viêtnam* (Paris 1955), 25–26, 165–68; "Chamanisme à Mujat (Sarawak, Borneo)," *Objets et mondes,* 12, 1 (1972): 23–44; "Le chamane, le fou et le psychanalyste (introduction à une typologie des *pöjau* jörai)," *ASEMI,* 4, 3 (1973): 19–30 (the whole issue is devoted to shamanism; biblio.). P. GUILLEMINET, "Recherches sur les croyances des tribus du Haut-Pays d'Annam, les Bahnar du Kontum et leurs voisins; les magiciens," *Institut Indochinois pour l'étude de l'homme* 4 (1941): 9–33. G. MORECHAND, "Le chamanisme des Hmong," *Bull. EFEO* 54 (1968): 53–294.

The Number Seven, Even and Odd, among the Indigenous Indo-Chinese

Once there was a couple who had seven daughters. Unable to feed them, they put them in a basket and abandoned them in a river. The seven young women invoked the *yang,* who landed them on a beach. They met Drit and worked for him. One day, Drit's spear trap accidentally struck one of them, and she died of her wound. Only six remained. Subsequently, when the sky was inverted and moved away from the earth, they became the stars of the constellation known as "Seven Maidens" (Mj. 62). They are the Pleiades, and Drit's trap is what we call Orion's Belt. The two neighboring constellations are closely connected with the cultivation of rice among the Jarai and also among the Sré, who emphasize Orion's Belt, where they see seven stars (Dournes 1973, p. 122), and among many of the peoples of Southeast Asia, notably the Malays (Winstedt 1951, p. 44) and the Dayaks of Borneo ("the beautiful country of the seven stars that point to the work to be done"; Ling-Roth 1896, vol. 1, p. 307). According to a Malay legend, one of the seven Pleiades fell to earth in the region of Majapahit (Hamilton 1944, p.122). The "inversion" to which the Jarai myth refers is suggestive: the figure of the stars is presented as inverting reality, and that reality would be the myth itself; from the Jarai viewpoint, what we see is merely the inverse of a reality that escapes us; it is not the myth that is inverting, but reality that is inverted.

There are no fewer than eight Jarai myths in which there are seven heroes (Mj. 11, 24, 42, 43, 51, 58, 62, 69), and we find a similar situation among the Sré (Ms. 10, 20, 81). They may be the seven sons of the sky (Jarai), or the seven sons of the giant Nyut (Sré), or the six sons and a daughter, the youngest (Mj. 42, Ms. 10). Whether they are the sons of the sky or warrior heroes, among the Jarai they have the same assonanced names, which suggests that there may be a system. In the series of seven, it is always the youngest who comes out on top, for seven perfects and concludes. Journeys and battles last seven days and seven nights, as does the legendary flood. The Sré universe has seven levels and a dragon with seven heads. There are seven Jarai clans. The same applies to ritual: seven is sacred and indicates abundance. In rites of exorcism, in particular, a Jarai counts to seven and then cries: "Finished!" In the most important rituals there are seven jars of beer. This character of the number is widely attested in Southeast Asia (Jaspan 1964, p. 100; Loeb 1935, p. 96; Schärer 1963, p. 26; Skeat and Blagden 1906, vol. 1, p. 349; Staal 1940, p. 61).

Next to the ubiquitous seven, mythical *pairs* can pose a problem, but a distinction needs to be made. First of all, there are onomastic doublets of the type of Adu-Adei, the celestial divinity, designating a single individual with a kind of echo for the sake of rhythm. For both Austroasiatic and Austronesian peoples, mythology abounds with heroes who are "doubled" in this way but are in fact only one. The oral style of expression, with its play of balancing, easily accounts for this. On the other hand, there are heroes who come in couples, generally presented as elder and younger brothers, who oppose each other for no reason and with no outcome unless there is a third party. Such couples include Set/Rok (northern Austroasiatic groups) and But/Tang (their counterparts among the southern Austroasiatic groups), who have no known ancestors and are sometimes said to be the "sons of the sky." Indeed, they are imagined as civilizing heroes, if they are not fantastic enemy brothers. Finally, a third possibility, two individuals "make up a pair," "like earrings or the tusks of an elephant." They are complementary and necessary to one another, to the point of being actually only one. This is explicitly described in the story of the blind man and the lame man; the lame man rides on the shoulders of the blind man and guides him, and they form a composite figure that frightens a dragon (Mj. 43; note that the blind man is the youngest and the only survivor of seven brothers). At that moment the two are reduced to one (see Lévi-Strauss 1968, p. 275ff.); composed of two elements, a pair is singular, in Jarai too.

A glance at taxonomy clarifies the arithmetic of the myth. This is not a digression, since everything in such cultures is part of the system. In Jarai, for instance, realms are designated by binomial formulas, such as wood-stone for the plant-mineral realm, next to the animal group and the human group, all of which add up to three. Plants are usually named by two terms, comparable to our genus and species, but the complete formula has three terms; the first is the category, of which there are three: tree, creeper, grass; furthermore, these series of threes intersect and overlap through intermediate species, as if to constitute a sequence without any break in continuity (Dournes 1971, p. 277ff.). Two is perfected in three in order to approach unity. We can already see a certain opposition emerging between even and odd: an even number engenders only repetition, whereas the odd number promotes concatenation. The playing of gongs provides a useful image of this: a piece will begin with two (or four) gongs playing in binary rhythms (1, 2-1, 2); a third gong joins in and then brings along the following four (or eight) gongs, and the melody is created (1, 2, 3-1, 2-1, 2); the concerts are played by seven or thirteen (sometimes twelve) gongs.

The fact that all human beings have ten fingers does not make the decimal system universal. The Jarai count on their fingers by pressing the thumb on the index finger for one, on the middle finger for two, on the ring finger, the little finger, back to the ring finger, then the middle finger, and finally the index finger, for a total of seven. The Jarai system is septimal, and their language attests to this, as do many other languages related to Malay. There is a name for each number from one to seven; eight and nine are compound words added later (Blagden 1894, p. 40; Collings 1949, p. 85). Fourteen is "two (times) seven." The Bahnar count on their fingers, pressing the thumb on each phalanx of the other four fingers, which adds up to twelve—one of the bases of their system. These two kinds of counting are connected with the solar-lunar calendar of these people: the month is lunar (based on seven); the year is solar (twelve months).

Among the indigenous Indo-Chinese who hold seven in very high esteem (almost all of them), it is fascinating to hear the Jarai express (outside of the mythic formulation) their preference for odd numbers: "*Grop*, 'even,' is heavy, closed [like the syllable itself], full without being complete; it can no longer move nor be inventive. It is a stick-in-the-mud, like a man who has one woman and doesn't seek another. *Lé*, 'odd,' is light and open [like the syllable itself]; it calls for something else. It awaits a liaison; it is a sign of luck. If I want to know whether I will have good luck, I pick up a handful of small sticks at random. I hold them behind my back, and I count them. If the number is odd, I will have good luck; if not, I'll lose everything." Two, four, and six are bad luck, because they are closed into themselves; if unity is added to them, they open out to a liaison. Three connotes balance, five is the number of the higher deities and of the sky. Seven is plenitude, because it is the "last word" among odd numbers. Thus, these people, among whom the Jarai are no exception, cannot rest on binary oppositions (a sign of bad luck) and therefore tend to complete them with a third term, the lucky intermediate which reestablishes the continuum. This is one of the keys to the system formed by their mythology.

The mythical and mystical meaning of odd and even—and of seven in the first place—may have virtually universal correspondences (following Virgil, *numero deus impari gaudet*, Verlaine also "preferred the odd number"), but it does not have the same significance in all cultures. Here the odd number is conceived as able to connect, but it connects only if it has a mediating character, a strong third term; otherwise it remains up in the air like an "extra man," *mönuih röbeh*, a Jarai expression meaning useless, unclassifiable. There is the ambiguity of the odd number and of the hero Drit who appears as a marginal creature and whom society neglects, but who turns out to be the strong link that holds all things together and reunites the worlds.

J.D./g.h.

BIBLIOGRAPHY

C. O. BLAGDEN, "Early Indochinese Influence in the Malay Peninsula," *Journal of the Royal Asiatic Society, Straits Branch,* 1894, 21–56. H. D. COLLINGS, "A Temoq Word List and Notes," *Bull. of the Raffles Museum,* Singapore (December 1949), p. 85. J. DOURNES, "Le discret et le continu, notes complémentaires d'ethnobotanique jörai," *JATBA* 18, 7–8 (1971): 274–87; "Chi-Ché, la botanique des Sré," *JATBA* 20, 1–12 (1973): 1–189. A. W. HAMILTON, *Malay Pantuns* (Sydney 1944). M. JASPAN, *From Patriliny to Matriliny* (Canberra 1964). C. LÉVI-STRAUSS, *The Origin of Table Manners* (New York 1978), trans. from French. H. LING-ROTH, *The Natives of Sarawak and British North Borneo* (Singapore 1896). E. M. LOEB, *Sumatra: Its History and People* (Vienna 1935). H. SHÄRER, *Ngaju Religion, the Conception of God among a South Borneo People* (The Hague 1963). W. W. SKEAT and C. O. BLAGDEN, *Pagan Races of the Malay Peninsula* (London 1906). F. J. STAAL, "Folklore of Sadong Dayaks," *Journal of the Royal Asiatic Society, Malayan Branch* 18, 11 (1940). R. O. WINSTEDT, *The Malay Magician* (London 1951).

THE AMBIGUOUS NOTION OF POWER AMONG AUSTROASIATIC AND AUSTRONESIAN PEOPLES: THE *POTAO* OF THE JARAI

Potao is power among Austroasiatic and Austronesian peoples, in the form of *bötau* among the Sré, for example, or in the form of *potao* among the Jarai. But this notion of power is ambiguous.

Sré mythology conceives of power as originally exercised by cruel, carrion-eating birds. A young man stole the power from them. Since then, when one speaks of *bötau* in myths, one refers to a Cham lord (the head of a Cham principality, not necessarily the emperor of Champa) regarded as the ruler of minor indigenous chiefs and later as the intermediary between Vietnamese authority and the minorities who used to be more or less subjects of Champa. In today's common parlance, unless one refers to ancient times, the word no longer designates a person, but power or authority. It is an abstraction. The people know no lord. They deal only with an impersonal and irresponsible administration. Nothing remains now of the mythico-historical *bötau*, not even a trace in the ritual.

For the Jarai, things went very differently. The development of the notion took another direction, and the notion was completely transformed. In this respect, the Jarai are unique among the indigenous Indo-Chinese; moreover, they made *Potao* an essential element of their concept of the universe, a bridge uniting myth, ritual, and history. The *Potao* of myth is formidable but is ridiculed; the *Potao* of ritual has an awesome power but is venerated; the *Potao* of history has a different meaning depending on who speaks of it. The interplay of these meanings and transformations is difficult to grasp and requires extensive analysis (Dournes 1977); the following is the result of long research.

To this day, the entire Jarai ethnic group recognizes *Potao* masters. There are three of them, and they are metaphorically classified as Fire, Water, and Air; the neighboring ethnic groups, the Rhadé to the south and the Bahnar to the north, are not unaware of them and indeed fear them. The written literature of foreign people indicates that at least two of the *Potao* were considered kings and chiefs of state by neighboring nations, who maintained diplomatic relations with them. For the Cambodians to the west, the Jarai rulers were *samdach*, the same title that Sihanouk used; for the Vietnamese, to the east, they were *Vua*, the same title that the emperors Gia Lông and Minh Mang used. When the French first wanted to approach the Jarai country, they understood their Laotian guides to be saying that they would have to deal with its *Somdet* (the Lao form of *samdach*), which the French changed to *Sadètes* (or *Sadet*). The *Potao* agreed to be called *Samdach* and *Vua*, because this would promote autonomy for Jarai territory, viewed by neighboring states as a nation with kings. This move was useful to the Jarai, the only natives for whom outside powers had any consideration. But for the internal purposes of the Jarai, none of this applied: they didn't have those "kings of fire" that were embroidered in the imagination of foreigners.

Three types of myth connected with what might be called the "*Potao* system" show how it is conceived.

1. In stories about the *kötang*, the "hard ones" or powerful ones, the hero, who was born with a sword and shield, goes to war against a local lord, sometimes called *potao*, to rob him of his wife, his people, and his wealth. This type of epic may have been based on historical facts, notably on the struggles among Chamized principalities; certain names of Jarai warriors are akin to the names of Cham persons known through inscriptions. Through the Cham, signs of Indian influence allow us to make comparisons with epics such as the *Mahābhārata*.

2. In the cycle of Drit, the hero is exploited by a local tyrant, a *potao*, who claims the right to appropriate for himself whatever the poor Drit obtains supernaturally with the help of the inhabitants of the forest. In particular, he claims Drit's dryad fairy, who is a symbol of woman and also of all of Jarai culture. Victorious in all of the trials imposed on him by the *potao*, Drit finally overthrows him, but, unlike the *kötang*, he does not do this in order to seize power. Rather, he remains the poor little man, but free of coercion. In these first two types, the *potao* have only material power, as did the lords in the old days, and they are more or less ridiculed, like the celestial ruler in the myths but unlike the *Adei* in the rituals.

3. In the stories in which the central figure is *ddau* (a "sabre" blade), either Drit or a *kötang* discovers a marvelous sword; made red-hot, it can cool only by absorbing a human being. It controls the states of matter (fire, water, air) which it subsumes in itself. It arouses the desire of nations, which fight to possess it. It finally remains with the Jarai and safeguards their peace when it is laid down and hidden. It is thus an image of power that must no longer be exercised and is preserved by the *Potao* of today who bear the same title as those who once possessed the power. (The capital *P* here indicates the sacred character of these *Potao*, which distinguishes them from the lords of battle.) In addition, fragments of origin myths associate them with the forge (which brings iron, fire, and water into the story and has a masculine connotation) and with pottery (which brings in earth, water, and fire and has a feminine connotation). When one realizes that the Jarai "states" are concerned rather with elements of matter, matter ignited, liquified, made into a gas, one can more easily understand the confusion wrought by foreigners.

The Jarai *Potao*, sacred masters, are said to be Fire, Water, and Air, that is, they are "like fire, like water"; Lord Fire is to Lord Water as fire is to water. Symbolic guardians of rain, they are, as a group and without hierarchy, regulators of the weather in its relation to humans. Fire, Water, and Air form a system of reference to classify the three rulers into a coherent series and to situate them as mediators between the people and the states of matter, which in turn are connected with the cosmic forces. The triad Fire-Water-Air is congruent with the climatic states of heat-humidity-wind and has a mythological equivalent in the triad of thunder-lightning-typhoon.

The homes of Lord Fire and Lord Water are not very distant and are located on either side of the north/south line separating the waters of the east and west, respectively, where they each perform their ritual rounds; Lord Air lives slightly to the south of Lord Fire. This allocation between east (congruent with man) and west (congruent with woman) is very important to the Jarai because of the place that this axis of the compass points occupies in their conceptual system. Lord Fire is called "father" *Potao*, Lord Water is "mother," and Lord Air is "son" (the term is also used to designate a nephew or a son-in-law). The three *Potao* function as a representation of the geographic and social structures of the Jarai universe at its top. It is the roof under which the people live. In the house, which is oriented from north to

A view of the annual ritual of the visit to villages by the Potao (Jarai). Paris, Musée de l'Homme collection. Photo J. Dournes.

south, the east is the place for men, the west is the place for women, and the south (where one enters) is associated with descendants, in opposition to the north, the direction of the cemetery and the ancestors.

The *Potao* who belong to myth and to dated recorded history (as a result of diplomatic exchanges with neighboring courts) are simultaneously "kings" assuring autonomy for the populations that invoke them and "priests" officiating at rituals for internal use (within ethnic groups). The official activities of the *Potao*—who are ordinary peasants when they do not exercise their functions, rather like shamans, although the resemblance ends there—are divided into three types of rituals:

1. The annual rounds made by each *Potao* at the beginning of the rainy season, on his side of the dividing line of the waters. Surrounded by his assistants, whose names represent a microcosm of society, the *Potao* visits his villages, stopping in the main ones, where he presides over an impressive ceremony and recites, in the course of a sacrifice, a long invocation asking for rain, fertility, and good health. This is to assure the order of succession of the seasons and to give it meaning for fixed periods.

2. The sacrifice on the mountain, offered during catastrophic circumstances (such as abnormal drought), more solemn but closed to the common people, celebrated solely by Lord Fire and his retinue before the sacred sword and other objects of the treasury. These are usually hidden but are taken out for this occasion and venerated according to the rite that Jarai thought associates with the sacrificial festivals performed at tombs.

3. The rites of election, confirmation, and burial, punctuating the existence of a *Potao*. The periodicity of these rituals is irregular, as is that of the second type, but they are not motivated by an anomaly and are even more public than the first type, since the entire ethnic group is directly involved in them.

A more probing analysis allows us to distinguish three types of functions represented by the *potao* system:

1. Father-Fire essentially guards the sacred sword, the symbol of power, a power no longer warlike but cosmic, associated with the forge and thus with an aspect of creation, a male function connected with the heavenly deity Adei who intervenes only in the case of very serious disorders.

2. Mother-Water subsumes in the *Potao* of the west the female functions in society: the reproduction of food products and of the Jarai people, connected with the *yang* of the sources of rivers.

3. Son-Air watches over the sacred pebbles and potsherds that represent troops of warriors; his warrior function connects him with the "powerful ones" of long ago who are now more or less equated with the dangerous *yang,* with whom one must avoid contact.

This distribution has some analogy with the three functions identified by Georges Dumézil in the ancient Indo-European traditions.

By taking the *Potao* system as a whole, no longer conceived according to its titles and the individuals who incarnate them, but by considering a different level, more abstract than symbolic, we discover another interplay of functions (which do not overlap with the first set):

1. The political function, as an aspect of existence in which *Potao* joins together what myth and reality separate: the effective exercise of power (the lords of ancient history) and the tendency to give up all power (from the Drit to modern man), in the natural ambiguity of the mastery of the *Potao* and in the uncertainty of the political situation, where the rise of a powerful man is a permanent danger.

2. The familial function, with a disjunction between love and marriage in myth and in reality, in which three *Potao* men play the role of male procreator, female procreator, and the procreated, but transmit the power of these three to their son-in-law, which makes it possible for the woman to recover her place.

3. The religious function, which colors all of existence and appears in ritual, overlays the distinctions between the political and familial functions, the mythical and the real, as a third term that causes these couples to interpenetrate within the experience of the *Potao* who are everything simultaneously.

We find here again the threefold organization of the universe, and we understand the necessity within this system for a third *Potao,* Lord Air, the most "fluid" and elusive, thanks to whom two changes into three to constitute one totality, which is not only conceived as a recovered continuum but is experienced by a people with strong structures, reconciling myth and history by transcending the oppositions.

J.D./g.h.

BIBLIOGRAPHY

J. BOULBET, *Pays des Maa', domaine des génies,* Pub. EFEO, 1967, pp. 70, 133. J. DOURNES, "Pötao, les maîtres des états, position de thèse," *ASEMI,* 4, 3 (1973): xix–xxvi; "Sous couvert des maîtres, aperçu sur la pensé politique d'une ethnie indochinoise," *Arch. Europ. de Sociol.,* 1973, 185–209; *Pötao, une théorie du pouvoir chez les indochinois Jörai* (Paris 1977).

Yang: The Sacred Connection, Sacrifice, and the Ritual of Counting among the Austroasiatic and Austronesian Ethnic Groups

I. Yang, the Sacred Connection

The term *yang* is common to almost all Indo-Chinese ethnic groups (natives of the south), both Austroasiatic and Austronesian. It is a key notion in these cultures, heard in conversation, in invocations, and in mythical stories. Like many of the most current and typical words, it is very difficult to translate. Depending on the author, it means "spirits," "genies," "angels," "deities," "the Sacred." It cannot be translated by the same word in all contexts; thus "to make *yang*" is not "to make spirit" but "to make sacred," to sacrifice or to "make a connection"; it is the religious act. But *yang* has the same meaning in all languages of the area (*löh yang* in Sré is the exact equivalent of *nga' yang* in Jarai, that is, to sacrifice). The notion of *yang* can only be understood as the basis of the whole myth-making process, and this article should be read along with the other articles on the Indo-Chinese world.

In Old Cham, *yaṅ* means "god, lord" (Boisselier 1963, p. 248); in Old Malay, *hiyan* means "god, deity" (Ferrand 1919, p. 254); "*jang* is a Javanese root meaning 'spirit'" (Geertz 1960, p. 26). "In Nousantarian, the stem *iang* designates all manifestations of the deity" (Lombard 1968, p. 168), which is closest to the Indo-Chinese meaning. In Vietnamese, *dàng* means "spirit" (especially in conjunction with *thần*). In modern Malay, *yang* is a relative pronoun; another meaning is "deity." "The word *hyaṅ* belongs to the Indonesian vocabulary and designates approximately all that is sacred" (Dupont 1952, p. 152). It corresponds to the Khmer *prah/bah* and is found in this last form in several Austroasiatic languages, either instead of *yang*, among the Sedang and Stieng, or in combination with *yang*, among the Mnong, or else in the combination *brah-yang*, among the Sré. In Khmer, *preah/prah* means "divine, sacred." This list covers all of Southeast Asia and places the Indo-Chinese ethnic minorities in relation with millions of other people who think *yang*, a notion with a profound resonance in this part of the world. Comparison enhances the meaning and informs us of cultural contacts.

The *yang* have no independent existence; they have no history—with the exception of some heroes of mythology and some famous ancestors (all interrelated) who are assimilated to *yang* deities. They are abstractions that intervene only as a relation between man and nature (see Mus 1934, p. 8; Sebag 1971, p. 141). When one wants to say that a certain rock, or river, or plant "has *yang*" (i.e., that it has "a sacred character" and not a little spirit hidden within), it means that man has noticed through a sign that this object, now charged with the sacred, maintains a certain connection with him that is potentially dangerous. This connection may be temporary: we cannot say that such and such a tree is inhabited by a deity, which makes it difficult to speak of animism, a Western creation that is diametrically opposed to their reism. The universe is a continuum: minerals, plants, animals, and humans are constantly interconnected. The ambiguity of this mythological thought stems from the necessity for everything to hold together (maintain cohesion) and at the same time for everyone to keep his own place (avoid short-circuits), so that the ordered ritual may either establish beneficial connections or break harmful ones. Is this not the definition of religion itself, if we accept the etymology *religare?*

To break malevolent bonds, this bow is ready to pierce the *Yang* threatening the village (Jarai). Paris, Musée de l'Homme collection. Photo J. Dournes.

Inside a Sru cemetery, vats of beer are opened on the occasion of the sculpting of a top of a tomb (foreground). Paris, Musée de l'Homme collection. Photo J. Dournes.

Yang is legion, but *yang* is uncountable, for in all the languages, a classifier must be inserted between the numeral and the numbered object, and there are appropriate classifiers for all things, from minerals to humans. A language is thus revealing, not only through its idioms but also through its silences. It is impossible to say "two, three *yang*"; like cosmic elements and abstractions, *yang* is outside all categories. *Yang* has no classifier because it is itself a classifier, not of objects but of their connections, at a sacred level (or in their sacred aspect). There are as many connections as there are individuals. Thus my forest *yang* is not necessarily that of my neighbor. *Yang* cannot be represented concretely. When a Jarai or a Sré shouts: "Oh Yang!" he no more thinks of a personified or figurative being than we think of interstellar space when we say "Heavens!" Although *yang* does not take a classifier, it does tolerate being prefixed like verbs and adjectives, particularly in Jarai: *möyang* expresses an extraordinary mode, to "make *möyang*" is to do something very unusual—a word freely combined with *mösih,* the supernatural. The expression often occurs in mythological texts when the hero gets ready to perform a supernatural feat. "May my mouth utter *möyang,* may a rich dwelling rise up in this very place!"

Yang are signs. Everything in the universe of these people can be a sign, and this is a fundamental principle of their symbolism, which diviners and shamans are very expert in interpreting. "If we get sick after cutting down a tree, we know that the tree 'has *yang*'; it has it because it has hurt us. We must then offer sacrifice to get rid of it" (the *yang* and the hurt). "If we come down with a fever after going somewhere, it is because we have come face to face with (or gone through) a *yang* aura (*höpô' yang*); divination tells us what sacrifice we must perform to get well again." A *yang* manifestation, a hierophany, is always a sign of a sacred connection that may have been injured by some excessive promiscuity. The continuum is not a confusion.

Everything may not "be *yang,*" but everything can "have *yang.*" There is therefore no need to draw up a list. It is possible, however, to identify a few notions that are widespread among the various ethnic groups and that are, at the same time, particularly striking. *Yang* are not in a hierarchy; they are not subject to comparison, since they are not individuated. Some, however, do stand out, notably, the paddy *yang* (rice in the field), which is invoked everywhere, often together with the superior deity Ndu/Adei. Paddy *yang* is the energy of vegetation of the principal grain food; it is a power, a virtue in the old sense of the term, distinct from the principle of life, or "soul," that rice has like any other living form. Among the Jarai, quite exceptionally, this *yang* is called *hri-yang,* as if it referred to a proper name—*hri* has no other use and does not mean paddy; similarly, among the Bahnar, it is called *sri* or *hri.* This is probably the same word as *sré,* "rice field," which gave its name to an ethnic group. In Malay, Seri is the goddess of fertility, principally of rice. This Indo-Asian word comes from Sanskrit and occurs in Indo-European languages in the name of the goddess Ceres. This might explain the exceptional personification of this *yang;* we can guess that it is the product of some "Chamization," since the Hinduized culture of the Cham tended to personify as deities the notion of *yang,* which is far more abstract among the Proto-Indo-Chinese.

Water *yang* (principally in the sense of river) has in almost all ethnic groups the distinction of being imagined as a snake or a dragon (in mental representations that are not concretized in plastic art). The Sré give a reason for this: the bends of a river are the marks left by the movements of a mythical snake. Sré and notably Jarai mythologies (Ms. 24, 44, 62, 71, 99; Mj. 4, 43, 111) are rich in texts that show a dragon/serpent as master of the waters, who dwells in a rich house in the depths below, appears as a handsome adolescent, and marries a daughter of man. The connection with the Hindu *nāga* is not accidental: the word for dragon is *löngrai* in Sré, *cögrai* in Jarai, and *nögarai* in Cham, from the Sanskrit *nāga-rāja.* Here again it would appear that Hinduization (mediated through Cham) modified the entirely mental, nonfigured *yang* of the ancient natives.

The forest *yang* (of the brush, of the woods, or wild) is ambiguous, a power of attraction and repulsion for the other world (otherness connotes hostility but is also a component of love), a place where one may meet the tigers, tiger men, and ogres of mythology, but also young girls comparable to naiads and dryads, shimmering fairies who draw into the unreal all those who fall under their spell. The hunter who habitually frequents this realm has concluded some pact with this type of *yang;* the shaman who crosses it comes into contact with these *yang;* the possessed man, charmed by the forest girl, leaves his own people and lives naked in the woods; the marginal man, situated between village and forest, like Drit, a hero in the Jarai myths, can by his very nature make the link between animal girls (or plant girls), who are manifestations of *yang,* and the world of culture, through the mediation of his grandmother, who is also a tree or bird and now lives on the moon. This is the dream of recovered continuity.

Sharing meat in a Jarai cemetery. Paris, Musée de l'Homme collection. Photo J. Dournes.

Jarai tomb. Paris, Musée de l'Homme collection. Photo J. Dournes.

II. The Ritual of Counting

"Paddy from the Cham, paddy from the Katu, paddy from among the Roglai . . . I call you, I summon you, I gather you." This sequence of ritual invocations by the Austroasiatic Katu (indigenous Indo-Chinese) is one example among many of what may appear to be a gratuitous redundancy but is in fact a necessary enumeration. All the ethnic groups have this ritual reciting of a series of names of places, rivers, mountains, localities, and among the Jarai, where funeral rites are more important than agrarian rites, characters from mythology who are connected with the ancestors—a sequence of names that constitute genealogies and reveal classifications. This need to omit nothing could be illustrated by countless quotations (see the bibliographical references). Our purpose here, in connection with the other articles on the indigenous Indo-Chinese, is rather to account for the need, to indicate its general meaning in current scholarship, and to express that meaning here in the form of a sketch rather than a synthesis (which would be premature).

After a Jarai, in the course of a ritual to promote healing, has invoked all the imaginable *yang* in a series, rivers and woods, hills and clouds, he concludes with "and all the *yang* I do not know." In this way he manifests his almost maniacal taste for an organized totality, with a bit of trickery that allows him to cover all bets rather than a sacred awe of scrupulous worry; too much has been said about the "terror" in which "primitive" people are said to live.

The ritual invocations are traditional recitations in which there is little room for improvisation, as assonances provide the linkage between one formula and the next. As such they are pieces of eloquence and proofs of knowledge of the oral literature and of the correct thing to do. The same applies to the gestures that accompany the words, gestures that have been meticulously described in all their multiplicity and minutiae by G. Condominas (1957). One has to hedge all of one's bets, plug all the holes, show one's expertise; one must impress the people present at the ritual at least as much as the spiritual powers, of whom little is known. The need to tie everything together, as if in a continuous web, is seen in the sacrifice of the buffalo; the buffalo, which is offered as food for the *yang* and is eaten by the human participants, replaces a man, as is evidenced in the Sré myth of K'Du kon Bo (Ms. 11), the sacrificed hero, and is viewed as a man by the *yang*. On the subject of the food offered to the *yang* (who are no more cannibalistic than carnivorous), let us note the popular interpretation: when the head and giblets of a chicken have been left behind on the ground for *yang* and they are gone the next day, it is a *sign* that *yang* has accepted the sacrifice—even if a dog or a vulture has been seen taking it away; that doesn't stop people from saying, "*Yang* has eaten . . ."

During sacrificial rites, especially among Austroasiatic peoples, long boards and high festive poles are brightly decorated with painted and stylized motifs, depicting the sun, moon, stars, tiger cheeks, buffalo teeth, flowers, seeds, etc., juxtaposing and linking a large sampling of categories of beings in the same encyclopedic spirit that presides over the enumerations in the oral style. This tendency toward exhaustive signification is also found (among both Austroasiatic and Austronesian peoples) in woven bands on the borders of blankets, depicting plants, animals, and humans (and nowadays even airplanes). These productions are not strictly ritual, insofar as one can distinguish what is "ritual" from what is not. They are above all cultural manifestations of a well-organized knowledge, a mode of self-expression and perhaps also of reassurance: "everything is connected" (*ratio stat!*).

Festival pole. In the background, decorated ritual boards (Halang). Paris, Musée de l'Homme collection. Photo J. Dournes.

In a litany of invocations, when banyan *yang b* (*Ficus rumphii*) is followed by banyan *yang b'* (*Ficus glomerata*) during a plant series, the link is established not so much between *yang* and banyan as between the two species of *Ficus* (and other plants), on the one hand, and between this series and the series of humans who are making the invocation, on the other hand. *Yang* thus serves as a classifier, which is very important for the study of indigenous taxonomies, but at a level "higher" than that of the signs. The banyan tree is taken here to indicate the strength, fertility, and abundance that the invokers hope for. Between the chain of plants and the chain of humans, the collective *yang* weaves a web of connections that are both real (a symbiosis with the environment, which must be experienced in a proper equilibrium) and symbolic (the strength of some must also be the strength of the others, by means of the *yang* energy). This distinction is not explicit for the interested parties. The same applies more or less to litanies of the names of ancestors (in part mythical): the sacred character (*yang*) of the invocation establishes the continuity (in this instance a continuity in time) between the living and the creatures of the past.

It has been said even by indigenous Indo-Chinese that the ritual came from the myth and reenacted it. In the first place, it is not enough to say it, especially if it is in response to a question, for this to take place in just this way. Furthermore, one must distinguish between ethnic groups. Among the Sré, the principal agrarian ritual (Ndu) seems to come directly from the myth that explains it; among the Jarai, such a link is rarely perceptible. In any event, we do not know what happened diachronically. But we propose with more confidence, on the basis of current observations, that myth and ritual are projections of the same "calculating" thought, on various levels of expression and, moreover, most often on different occasions.

The Sré *hoé yang* is the exact equivalent of the Jarai *iau yang* (*hoé* = *iau*, "to call") and has the same meaning of ritual or sacred invocation, but the experience is different. Among the Sré, the ritual, both gestures and words, is prescribed to establish contact with the *yang*, who are expressly invited to live among humans and partake of their offerings. Among the Jarai, most of the rituals aim to get free of a bond that has become dangerous and needs to be dissolved, untied, loosened (the vocabulary is quite rich in this regard), rather than tied tightly. The *yang* are called and asked to take their share and to leave us in peace. A common saying goes, "*Yang* among themselves, the dead among themselves, the living among themselves." The Jarai are at ease when they feel that everything is connected, but since they are fiercely independent and have a great sense of humor, they avoid domination, like the weaver woman who takes care that the threads of the warp do not become tangled between any two movements of the shuttle that connects them. Their common culture ensures that both of these peoples are Southeast Asians, but the particular way of life of each group ensures that some think of themselves as Sré, others as Jarai.

J.D./g.h.

BIBLIOGRAPHY

1. Yang

C. O. BLAGDEN, "A Malayan Element in Some of the Languages of Southern Indochina," *Journal of the Royal Asiatic Society*, 1902, 2. J. BOISSELIER, *La statuaire du Champa*, Publ. *EFEO*, 1963. L. CADIÈRE, "Monuments et souvenirs Chams," *Bull. EFEO*, 1905, 194–95. P. DUPONT, "Études sur l'Indochine ancienne," *Bull EFEO*, 1952, 119–76. G. FERRAND, "Le Kouen Louen," *Journal Asiatique*, 1919, 254. C. GEERTZ, *The Religion of Java* (New York 1960). D. LOMBARD, *Histoires courtes d'Indonésie*, Publ. *EFEO*, 1968. P. MUS, "L'Inde vue de l'Est, cultes indiens et indigènes au Champa," *Bull. EFEO*, 1934, 1–44. L. SEBAG, *L'invention du monde chez les Indiens Pueblos* (Paris 1971).

2. The Ritual of Counting

J. BOULBET, "Börde au rendez-vous des Génies," *B.S.E.I.* 35, 4 (1960): 627–50. G. CONDOMINAS, *Nous avons mangé la forêt de la pierre-génie Gôo* (Paris 1957). J. DOURNES, "La religion des Montagnards du Haut-Donnaï," *B.S.E.I.* 24 (1949): 29–49; "Fêtes saisonnières des Sré," *Bull. EFEO* 46, 2 (1954): 599–610; "Le mort c'est l'autre, la geste funéraire jörai," *Objets et mondes*, 1975, 351–84. A. FERREIROS, *Les Kon-Cau de la Daa'-Nying* (microéd. univers., Paris 1973), 73-30-32. P. GUILLEMINET, "Le sacrifice du buffle chez les Bahnar de la province de Kontum," *B.A.V.H.* 2 (1942): 147–51. B. Y. JOUIN, *La mort et la tombe* (Paris 1949). JOUIN and BOTREAU-ROUSSEL, "Un sacrifice au génie des éléphants à Bandon chez l'héritière de Kundjonob," *Inst. Indoch. pour l'Étude de l'Homme* 6 (1943): 375–86. J. KEMLIN, "Les rites agraires chez les Röngao," *Bull. EFEO* 9 (1910): 493–522; 10 (1910): 131–58. MAURICE, "Trois fêtes agraires rhadé," *Bull. EFEO* 15, 1 (1952): 202–7; "L'âme du riz," *B.S.E.I.* 29, 2–3 (1954): 1–258. For the ritual role of plants, see: J. DOURNES, "Bois-Bambou, aspect végétal de l'univers jörai," *JATBA*, 1968, 89–156, 369–498; "Chi-Ché, la botanique des Sré," *JATBA*, 1973, 1–189.

VIETNAMESE MYTHOLOGY

The documents that allow us access to Vietnamese mythology come from two sources different in nature and time. The first and older of the two sources comprises accounts written mainly in Chinese by Vietnamese scholars. The second source, essentially oral, is more diversified and comes mostly from rural areas. It can, however, be said that there is little in either source on the subject of the creation of the universe and of natural phenomena. A few reasons may be advanced to explain this shortage.

Vietnamese scholars, imbued with Confucian biases, exercised great selectivity, like their Chinese colleagues whose models they imitated. They are not interested in creationist theories, avoid the question of the origins of mankind as a species, and are not awestruck by the configuration of the universe. Loath to explain the creation of the universe, they pay particular attention to extraordinary men who were deified at the time of their deaths because of their great deeds. They do, however, include the miraculous birth of the Vietnamese people, descended from a sovereign couple of mythical origin, and they thus euhemerize mythic themes. Although certain etiological themes that explain the causes of things are sometimes found in these collections, they deal with the plant kingdom but never with the creation of the first men or of the first animals.

In modern oral stories, there are some passages that deal with the early times of humanity. These are scattered scraps with no coherent system. Regarded by the lay reader as simple popular tales, they in fact contain mythological elements that show how the universe was given its shape, and how, after the sky and earth were formed, man passed from the Golden Age to life as it is now. Nevertheless, basic themes such as the birth of the human race and the creation of the universe are missing, and one gets the impression not only that the elite of the country rejected the creationist theory, but that the people in general had relatively little interest in it.

Finally, the history of Vietnam is itself partly responsible for this apparent indifference: the incessant invasions by Chinese armies, followed by lengthy occupations, led at least to the partial destruction of the Vietnamese cults and the substitution of Chinese deities. There are numerous traces of these newer Chinese cults throughout the country. For example, there is the temple of the war god Chen-Wu and the temple of General Ma Yän, Subduer of the Seas, who conquered Vietnam in the first century A.D. In the ninth century A.D., a Chinese general named Kao Pien was known for his gifts as a magician and geomancer. He tried unsuccessfully to eliminate the sacred powers of the great local deities by ceremonies of exorcism and magic.

But the desire for self-identity and the need to discover the origin of the first founder made it possible to preserve a few legendary features of the birth of the Vietnamese people. It is not the origin of the human species that is treated here but that of the Vietnamese people. This is a semimythical genealogy rather than a cosmogony.

In our article entitled "The Origins and the First Ages in the Major Structures of Vietnamese Mythology" (see below), a new subject emerges: the gods of nature. In discussing the sky, we thought it useful to add the names of a few deities that assist in the task of governing. The choice is certainly arbitrary, for we omitted several among them that play important parts in the Chinese Taoist pantheon: the two acolytes of the heavenly emperor, Nam Tao and Bac Dau, who record births and deaths; the god of the hearth, who is responsible for reporting annually to heaven on the conduct of men; and so forth. But the fact that their images are all too faithful copies of Chinese models justifies such omissions.

L.O.M./g.h.

BIBLIOGRAPHY

R. P. CADIÈRE and LÉOPOLD, *Croyances et pratiques religieuses des Viêtnamiens,* 3 vols. (Hanoi, Saigon, Paris, 1944, 1955, 1957). CAO HUY DINH, *Hinh tuong không lô va tâp thê Anh hung dung nuoc, giu nuoc trong truyên cô dân gian Viet-Nam* (On the giant and the enculturating heroes in popular Vietnamese stories), in *Truyên thông anh hung dân tôc* (Hanoi 1971). DAO DUY ANH, *Cô su Viêt Nam* (Ancient history of Vietnam) (Hanoi 1956). DINH GIA KHANH-CHU XUAN DIEN, *Van hoc dân gian* (Folklore studies), 3 vols. (Hanoi 1962, 1972, 1973). DOAN THI DIÊM, *Truyên ky tân pha* (Marvelous legends), Vietnamese trans. (Hanoi 1962). G. DUMOUTIER, *Les cultes annamites* (Hanoi 1907), extract from the *Revue Indo-Chinoise,* 1906; a good overview of Sino-Vietnamese and Vietnamese deities. M. DURAND, *Technique et Panthéon des médiums viêtnamiens (dông)* (Paris 1959); *Imagerie populaire viêtnamienne* (Paris 1960), "Viêtnam," in *Le monde du sorcier* (Paris 1966), 331–51. M. DURAND and NGUYÊN TRÂN HUÂN, *Introduction à la littérature viêtnamienne* (Paris 1969). P. GIRAN, *Magie et religion annamites* (Paris 1962), *Hung vuong dung nuoc* (The Hung kings, founders of the kingdom), 4 vols., vols. 2 and 4 (Hanoi 1972 and 1974). A. LANDES, *Contes et légendes annamites* (Saigon 1886); this is the richest collection of legends in French translation. ÂLVAN HAO, "Les fêtes saisonnières au Viêtnam," in *Revue du Sud-Est asiatique* (1962), no. 4. LÊ VAN PHAT, "La vie d'un Annamite: Croyances diverses," *Bull. de la Société des Études Indochinoises,* no. 54 (1908). LY TÊ XUYÊN, *Viêt diên u linh tâp,* Vietnamese trans. of Lê Huu Muc (Saigon 1961). P. MUS, *La religion des Annamites,* in *Indochine,* work published by Sylvain Lévy (Paris 1931). NGÔ SI LIÊN, *Dai Viêt su ky toan thu,* Vietnamese trans. of Cao Huy giu, vol. 1 (Hanoi 1967). NGUYÊN DÙ, *Truyên ky man luc,* French trans. of Nguyên Trân Huân (Paris 1962), Vietnamese trans. of Truc Khê et Ngô van Triên (2d ed., Hanoi 1971). NGUYÊN DÔNG CHI, *Luoc khao vê Thân thoai Viet Nam* (Hanoi 1956); this was the first published collection of documents on Vietnamese mythology. NGUYÊN KHAC XUONG, *Truyên thuyêt Hung vuong* (Legends of Hung kings) (Vinh Phu 1971). NGUYÊN VAN HUYÊN, *Le culte des immortels en Annam* (Hanoi 1944). NGUYÊN VAN KHOAN, "Essai sur le Dinh et le Culte du Génie tutélaire des villages au Tonkin," *Bull. de l'École française d'Extrême-Orient* 30 (1930): 1–33. PHAN KÊ BINH, *Nam-hai di nhân liêt truyên* (new ed., Saigon 1968). P. PRZYLUSKI, "L'or et ses pouvoirs magiques," *Bull. de l'École française d'Extrême-Orient* 14 (1914). R. A. STEIN, "La légende du foyer dans le monde chinois," in *Échanges et Communications, mélanges offerts à Claude Lévi-Strauss,* 2 vols. (The Hague 1970), 1280–1305. TÔ NGUYÊT DINH, *Chuyên coô tich* (Saigon 1969). TRAN THÊ PHAP, *Linh-nam chich quai,* Vietnamese trans. of Le Huu Muc (Saigon 1961). VAN TAN-NGUYEN LINH, *Thoi dai Hung vuong* (Hanoi 1976).

The Origins and the First Ages in the Major Structures of Vietnamese Mythology

I. The Configuration of the Universe

No one knows where the sky and the earth came from. When they first appeared, they were nothing but a mass of shapeless and chaotic matter. Everything was immersed in total darkness. At that moment a giant began to detach the sky from the earth. This colossus has the name of Không Lo, borrowed from the Chinese. He also goes by other names that generally illustrate his prodigious exploits: Sir Ocean-Scooper, Sir River-Hollower, Sir Forest-Grower, and so forth. His stride is tremendous; his breath makes gusts of wind; and his cries are the rolls of thunder. First he raised the sky with his head. Then he cleared the earth in order to build a gigantic pillar to support the full weight of the sky. Thus separated from the earth by a great distance, the sky took the form of an inverted bowl and the earth that of a square plateau. This representation of the original world was undoubtedly taken from a Chinese mythological concept. It is still given expression in the etiological legend about a kind of bread made of sticky rice that the Vietnamese now eat only at the festival of the New Year: Chung bread. In this story, which is set during the mythical dynasty of the first Vietnamese sovereigns, the Hung, the throne was to revert to the prince whose offering was most highly prized. One young prince found himself at a disadvantage, since his poverty would not allow him to compete with his older brothers. But on the advice of a deity, he began to make two kinds of breads never seen before: the one that symbolized the sky was a round cake; the other was square and represented the earth.

The same giant pulled down the supporting pillar when he noticed that the sky and the earth had become solid and dry. He broke it up into pieces and violently threw the blocks of stone around him: thus the mountains and the islands were born. The huge ditches that the giant had dug in order to build the pillar received water and became the oceans. The ebb and flow of the sea were connected to the breathing of a turtle of immeasurable size that remained motionless most of the time.

In the course of arranging the universe, a new character, a female, appeared. The two of them formed a giant couple whose relationship was amorous but also full of conflicts, the outcome of which was always in favor of the woman. To begin with, she dominated her companion by her size: her sex organ was twice as big as her partner's, if we accept the terms with which people compare their genitals; their size was measured in terms of surface area. She also had greater physical strength. Since the male giant wanted to marry her, she challenged him to a contest: each of them would erect a mountain within three days. If his should surpass hers in height, she would consent to marry him. But she was the one who won, because from the summit of her mountain one could turn one's gaze to the horizon. She kicked down the mountain that her suitor had built. She also imposed another difficult task that consisted of filling a riverbed overnight.

When the male giant's labors were almost over, she imitated the cock's crow to herald daybreak and forced the giant to stop. Other tests followed, consisting now not in creating new peaks but in moving certain already existing mountains to other regions or in lining them up straight, as happened to the Annamite mountain range in central Vietnam, which was initially made up of mountains arranged haphazardly.

Gradually, the giant's creations lost their global character; for instance, when he had erected the support pillar, he then built some mountain, identified by name. He transported from the upper region toward the plain two mountains known today by the names of Ba-vi and Tam-dao. Like all peasants, he moved earth by means of a flail. According to one current theme, the straps of his baskets broke in mid-journey. Clods of earth were cast in all directions: this is how hills were first formed on earth. In certain localities stretching toward the south of central Vietnam, in order to erect some mound, the giant had to scoop out earth from the bottom of the sea and bring it back ashore. These works were intended to allow the population to take refuge there when the rivers were in spate.

Finally, he won the hand of his female companion. On the day of the wedding, he set out for her house, accompanied by one hundred people. But as night fell, they were blocked by a river. The giant stretched out his penis to form a bridge. As his men were crossing, one of them accidentally dropped hot ashes on the giant's penis and made him jump. The men lost their balance and half of them fell into the water. The woman rescued them and hid them under her dress to warm them up again. The allusion to the sex organ does not seem fortuitous. It brings to mind a ritual now performed in secret in certain villages where the inhabitants fashion a phallus from wood and a woman's sex organ from the spathe of the areca nut, and the women and girls fight over them. The performance of this ritual is thought to be indispensable to the security of the village, and the sex of the first child born after it will correspond to that of the symbol that was won.

II. Men and Animals

This is the point where the Sky might be discussed. But we shall see that its role is so closely tied to earthly events that it has no particular autonomy of its own. Besides, many legends that concern it are closely related to historical periods that are very distant from the cosmogony. We would therefore rather deal first of all with elements that seem to have a more direct relationship with the most remote times of creation. Nevertheless, we should mention that the Sky, called the Jade Emperor, has presided over a certain number of creative acts.

Once the separation of the sky and the earth was accomplished, human beings appeared. Their creation is attributed to a supreme deity, Ngoc Hoang or the Jade Emperor, a name borrowed from the Chinese. This "creator of all beings" fashioned the first men with the finest material available in the chaotic mass. On the other hand, to make the animals, he settled for rougher materials from among the remains of the sky and the earth. He took greater care in making men; that is why their intelligence is so highly developed. The twelve "Heavenly Midwives" were responsible for modeling faces. Each shaped a certain number of organs. Physical blemishes were the results of their oversights. The twelve Heavenly Midwives also presided over the birth of babies. It was their task to teach children how to talk and walk.

III. Sun and Moon

The relationships between men and the sun and the moon were far from neighborly; a number of legends about them will be found below in the discussion of the Golden Age or Lost Happiness.

Sun and Moon were both daughters of the Jade Emperor. They were commanded to light the world; they warmed the surface of the earth, but their heat was so intense that the soil dried up to the way the earth is today. Many legends attempt to explain the appearance of the moon and the marks on it. Sometimes the explanation involves a tree, the banyan, a kind of sacred fig tree that can still be seen growing near pagodas. Sometimes it involves a fistful of sand thrown to its surface in an attempt to chase the moon away, when its heat was unbearable. For long ago, the moon did not cast a light as soft as moonlight is today. On the contrary, it emitted a burning heat which brought much suffering to mankind. Every time it appeared, it created panic among human beings, who would hurl insults at it and vow to drive it away. Quai, a young man of prodigious size and strength, climbed to the top of a mountain to await the arrival of the Moon. As soon as he saw it, he threw a fistful of sand at its face. The Moon retreated far away and since then has stayed at a safe distance from the earth.

The markings that one can see on the surface of the lunar disc come from the projectiles cast by Quai. The grains of sand have greatly reduced the moon's brightness and have destroyed its burning heat. There is another explanation for these facts: in order to relieve the sufferings of mankind, the Moon's mother had to smear ashes on the face of her daughter.

It is also said that the man in the moon was Cuôi. A compulsive liar, he was exiled there and condemned to stand forever with his arms around the trunk of the lunar banyan tree. But he continued to play his tricks. The elder son of the family joined him by means of the power of a younger brother who could make his wishes come true. On the moon, Cuôi the liar handed the elder son his stone ax and advised him to chop down the lunar tree in order to find rice. But after a full day's hard labor, he discovered that his efforts were in vain. Cuôi also advised him to crush a stone to get flour to abate his hunger.

IV. The Length of the Day

To explain the greater or shorter length of days according to the seasons, two different kinds of rotation of the sun around the earth are visualized. In the first instance, "Sister Sun" is carried in her palanquin by a group of youths; as they linger on the way, the sun leaves the earth late and the day grows long. On the other hand, when she is carried by a group of old men, she returns home quickly, because these bearers take their job to heart and perform their assigned duties conscientiously, and thus the day is short.

V. Eclipses

The husband of the two sisters, the Sun and the Moon, is a bear. The eclipses of the Sun and of the Moon are interpreted in terms of the sexual relations between the bear and his wives. The eclipse constitutes a bad omen: scarcity and destruction of crops. People try to separate the bear from his wives by sounding gongs, beating drums, and striking rice mortars with pestles. The lunar eclipse is called "the bear eating the moon."

These few fragments of lunar and solar mythology do not seem to be known by the Vietnamese people as a whole, for they have been drawn from legends of different localities and collected in recent years.

On the other hand, the festival of midautumn is quite widespread. It is dedicated to the moon and takes place every year on the fifteenth day of the eighth lunar month. It has come down to us from China, and it is easy to recognize all the elements of Chinese myth. The white round cakes especially prepared for the occasion are decorated with the jade hare, the three-legged toad, and the tree of immortality. In the course of this festival, which is primarily for children, they run around the town carrying lanterns shaped like fish and crabs. They sing a round to the beat of the Ho Khoan ("Oh hoist") and perform the dance of the lion. At nightfall, groups of young men on one side and young girls on another sing the alternating verses of a long love song, a literary contest in which each seeks to outdo the other in imagination or spirit. In certain places, this festival is the occasion for worshiping the ancestors.

The appearance of the lunar disc makes possible predictions of good or bad omens: if the moon is clear, the harvest of rice of the tenth month will be good; if it is misty, the harvest of the fifth month will be abundant. If the moon is not visible, all the crops will be lost. Women and young girls especially worship the moon; by interpreting the "shadows of the face of the moon" they are able to choose the time for betrothal and marriage.

VI. The Creation of Rice and Cotton

The appearance of men and other beings was soon followed by that of rice and cotton. This was the work of the Jade Emperor: he wanted to provide human beings with food and clothing. However, the supreme deity hesitated about the actual size that he would give to the two seedlings. He called a meeting of all the animals on earth and asked their advice. Two dominant opinions emerged from the debate. One came from the large animals, who wanted the rice grain to be the length of the elephant's tail and the ear of the cotton plant to be as bulky as the head of the pachyderm. The other opinion came from the small animals, who proposed that the grain of rice and the ear of cotton plant be the size of the tail and head of the lizard, respectively. In this way there would be no waste on the part of the small animals. The Jade Emperor favored the lizard's side—and that is why the plants are the size they are.

Parallel to this legend is another one about the size of the grain of rice which is part of the etiological myths of the Golden Age.

VII. The Golden Age

It is not usually possible to dissociate the myths of the creation of the elements and natural phenomena (plants and food) from the theme of Lost Happiness, of Death, and of the search for Immortality. Every initial creation is either prevented from reaching its goal, diverted from its purpose, or destroyed once it has been achieved. The same applies to the Sun and the Moon, which were once close to human beings but were chased away or forced to distance themselves, and to the grain of rice, which was originally abundant and obtained without difficulty but which became hard to get as a result of man's negligence. The gift of immortality was stolen from man.

Once upon a time the Sun came down to the top of the trees. Similarly, the Moon liked to come close to the world of the living to see them go about their business. But people failed to take advantage of this arrangement. Out of laziness, they would expose any object to the sun and would go as far as to dry decomposed bodies and rubbish. The Sky, who is here called the Jade Emperor, withdrew the Sun to a distance of one hundred million kilometers from the earth to punish men for their negligence. The removal of the Sun plunged mankind into a total darkness that threatened its survival. The rooster, aided by the duck that carried it on its back, set out in search of the light. The rooster crossed the eastern sea and reached the Sun in his refuge. He asked the Sun to return to earth; but the request was granted only in part: the Sun appears only when men need it. To make it come up, the rooster starts to crow—and that is why the rooster's crow announces the new day.

Once upon a time a grain of rice was enormous, like a bowl (according to some), or like a dugout canoe (according to others). Moreover, it grew by itself, without needing to be cultivated. When it was ripe, the rice rolled by itself into the granary of each household. People could just help themselves to the amount they needed, and the grain immediately swelled back to its original size. Only one condition was imposed: every housewife had to keep the pathway of the grain of rice clean. But one woman out of laziness failed to sweep her yard in time. The grain refused to come in, for it could not stand to roll over filth. The furious housewife struck the grain of rice and it broke into small pieces. Then it flew into a rage and told her: "From now on, I shall return only when I am cut with a wooden handle and an iron blade, that is, with a sickle." That is how farm work first appeared in mythology and why a grain of rice is so small today.

We should note that at the turn of the century, during his ethnographic fieldwork, Father Cadière discovered vestiges of the worship of a giant rice grain. This worship took place in a "pagoda" erected in honor of the Rice Couple, whom the villagers respectfully called "Sir Rice" and "Lady Rice." They worshiped a ball of rice the size of a coconut that tradition claimed was of ancient origin. The large grain of rice had a virtually unlimited power of nutrition, for a small fragment would swell enough when it was cooked to feed an entire family.

VIII. Immortality and Death

At the beginning of time, the Celestial Emperor wanted to let men live forever. So that his wish would be fulfilled, he sent one of his messengers to earth solemnly to proclaim that when men reached old age they would shed their skins and become young again, whereas snakes, instead of shedding them, would die. But the heavenly messenger accidentally stumbled on a brood of snakes. Threatened by the snakes, he was forced to proclaim the opposite of what he had been ordered to say, that is, that men would have to die when they got old, whereas snakes would enjoy immortality by changing their skin. The agent of this counterorder was punished severely: he was excluded from the heavenly realm and exiled to earth in the shape of a dung beetle in order to compensate for the damages inflicted on the human species. The dung beetle lives in human excrement.

The themes related to the quest for immortality may be interpreted as attempts by the popular imagination to rediscover one of the primordial conditions that were so favorable to man. These are not properly myths, since they only concern a small number of people and their efficacy was fleeting. But in the course of these adventures, for a limited time, man resumes certain special contacts with the supernatural world. Such is the story of the Man in the Moon.

Cuôi, a woodcutter, accidentally witnessed a scene during which a tigress revived her cub with the help of leaves from the banyan tree. He got this power and revived a young woman, whom he later married; he also revived his dog. He planted the magic tree in his garden. One day, as he prepared to go away, he told his wife not to urinate at the foot of the tree. But she disobeyed his order, and the tree rose up toward the sky. The woodcutter arrived just then and tried to hold it back with his ax, but the tree carried him away with it to the moon. Since then, the tree can be seen on the moon, with the wretched woodcutter at its foot.

We shall cite one more example: The future god of the mountain, Tan Viên, was also a woodcutter. While he was cutting down a tree, he came in contact with a deity who handed him a magic cane that cured the sick and revived the dead. He used the power often and thus saved the son of the king of the Waters. But soon no one heard of the magic cane any more.

IX. The Sky

In the popular consciousness, the Sky represents a supreme deity who governs the whole universe. He is notably the chief of the gods of nature and the one in complete charge of human destiny. The name he bears varies according to what position a group or a personality at the heart of Vietnamese society occupies. He is commonly called Ong Troi, Sir Sky; but in a more religious and folkloric context his name is the Jade Emperor, Ngoc Hoang. The king, his civil servants, and scholars call him the Emperor from on High, Thuong-dê.

In principle, individuals do not worship him directly; this is a concern of the earthly emperor, since the latter is his agent on earth, according to Chinese concepts of kingship. Like the Chinese emperor, the Vietnamese emperor presides every three years over a ceremony of offerings in honor of the Sky and the Earth. This is the sacrifice offered in the southern outskirts of the capital, the Nam-giao, which seem to be a faithful replica of the Chinese model.

Along with a host of other deities, the Jade Emperor belongs to the Chinese Taoist pantheon. The heavenly ruler lives surrounded by his wife and children. He governs with the help of his celestial assistants, whom he convenes in council at his court. A few human beings have been able to visit his residence by the path of dreams: first, one makes a voyage through the atmosphere, crossing nine aerial levels before reaching one's destination. This is a grandiose palace with jade doors and golden walls. To reach the court one has to pass through nine gates. The inside of the palace is adorned with the peaches of immortality, with precious pearls taken from under the jaw of the black dragon, and with magic trees offered by the kings of the netherworld.

There are no longer any direct communications between heaven and earth. Nevertheless, a few hints in the folklore suggest that they once existed: someone set up a ladder to climb to heaven to ask about his fate (in a popular song); an immortal woman would send her husband and son down from the sky by means of a cord (in the legend of the morning and evening stars); another example speaks of two celestial gods who came down onto the top of a mountain.

The role played by the wife of the Jade Emperor is not known, but we know more about his sons and daughters. Some of them were sent to earth where some became rulers, others heroes or famous persons; still others spent time there in exile. It is said that the mother of the future founder of the Early Lê dynasty (tenth century) dreamed, before giving birth, that the Emperor from on High had entrusted a Golden Boy (the name given to the sons of heaven) with the mission of ruling over Vietnam. As the Golden Boy hesitated, the Emperor took a piece of jade and hit him on the forehead. The child was born with a scar on his forehead.

The goddess Liêu Hanh, whom the practitioners of the cult of mediums recognize as the most illustrious of the Holy Mothers, is the incarnation of a daughter of the Jade Emperor. She was sent into exile on earth for having indelicately broken a jade wine cup that she was supposed to serve to guests. She was married to a human, and she bore him a son. She died when her earthly exile came to an end. But memories of the human world haunted her spirit, and she returned to earth in the form of a beautiful flutist. Men who teased her knew unhappiness and pain. She was particularly fond of beautiful secluded places. Constantly traveling, she was sometimes seen in the north of the country and sometimes in the capital, where she ran a teahouse frequented by scholars. She left without a trace at each departure, and her house would miraculously disappear. Meanwhile, her husband died and was reincarnated as a great scholar. She found him again, and they lived together until the end of her second exile. She ascended to the sky and then came down to earth again, this time with her father's consent, to become the goddess of a village in Thanh-hoa. In the seventeenth century, the imperial court regarded her as a demoness and called on sorcerers and warriors to destroy her temple. But she unleashed epidemics that killed off men and decimated herds throughout the region. The imperial court was forced to rebuild her temple and to confer a royal license on her.

In popular stories, the Jade Emperor intervenes repeatedly in the organization of the primordial world of humans. In particular, he created animals, some useful and others harmful. It is not surprising that the buffalo occupies an essential place in agricultural activities since it is a celestial deity that was sent into exile on earth as a punishment for disobedience. The buffalo was ordered by the Jade Emperor to plant a handful of rice and a handful of grass, for the benefit of man. He first threw the grass and second only half of the rice; that is why grass grows in abundance but rice is scarce. The Jade Emperor became angry and turned his assistant into a buffalo. He sent him to earth to eat grass and help men in their labors.

The mouse is also of celestial origin, as is the cat. The mouse was once an officer of the Jade Emperor, in charge of watching over the granary of heaven, but he stole the grain in order to sell it or to give it to his friends. To punish him, the supreme deity sent him into exile on earth in the form of a mouse. He continued to nibble at men's rice, and they complained to the god of the hearth. In order to give them satisfaction, the Jade Emperor sent them another metamorphosed celestial officer to chase after the mouse—the cat.

Since the Jade Emperor presided over atmospheric phenomena, he sent to earth several assistants, such as the rain god, the thunder god, and so forth. These representatives discharged their duties poorly, so that men and animals suffered disastrous consequences, as the following legend shows:

The rain god left the earth and thus caused a great drought. Men and animals died in great numbers. The toad, accompanied by the fox, the bear, and the tiger, ascended to the sky to ask for rain. The toad arrogantly beat a drum at the gate of the palace. The Jade Emperor, wearied by this insolence, sent his troops against him. But his own animals were defeated, and he had to bow down before the might of his visitor. He agreed to receive him. The toad presented him with his grievances and demanded that the rains be sent down immediately. He won his case. Since then, he has been charged by the Jade Emperor with announcing rain: all he has to do is to cry out. A maxim makes him the "mother's brother" of the Sky and asks people not to mistreat him or penalties will be inflicted on them by the Sky.

It is to the thunder god, Thien Lôi, that the Jade Emperor gave the mission of chastising criminals, blasphemous sons, and all who commit serious moral faults, or who are predestined to be struck by lightning, including animals. He even killed certain animals that had become evil spirits because of their exceptional longevity. As the divine judge, he threw an ax at the head of his victims to accomplish his task. At the same time, he hit with a hammer the drums suspended from his body, thus producing rolls of thunder. People represented him as an extremely ugly creature, with the head and feet of a rooster. That is because he had originally been punished by being transformed into a piece of meat that a celestial rooster came to pick at with terrible and painful pecks. After this incarnation, he took the partial form of a rooster and experienced great fear of this animal. For this reason, people who want thunder to go away clack their lips and suck in as if they are calling fowl. They also believe that Neolithic polished stone tools are the god's instruments, of which there are two kinds: those made of bronze kill human beings; those made of stone are used to kill animals and demons. These tools of the age of polished stone and bronze constituted talismans that sorcerers used to fight against devils and sicknesses. They could be found in places where lightning had struck after three months and ten days, for at this date they rose to the surface of the ground.

We have seen the thunder god in his terrible aspect. There are a few themes in the folklore that show him as vulnerable and unintelligent, a belief that functions as a kind of collective reaction against this heavenly executioner that everyone fears. Thus, when it is discovered that a child is destined to be struck by lightning, he is made to wear one of the ax talismans. The child will escape being struck by lightning, for he is considered to have already been struck. Similarly, the thunder god is known to execute his powers within strict limits, for he strikes without discernment wherever he is told to strike. His clumsiness is such that a young girl will escape unscathed simply by squatting with her buttocks facing the sky.

The god is made the object of derision in the following legend, in which the hero defeats him by disarming him. Cuong Bao, "the violent one," refused to perform the ritual for his dead mother. Instead, he made offerings to the hearth god. To punish him for his filial impiety, the Jade Emperor sent the thunder god to him. But "the violent one," who was warned and advised by the hearth god, covered the roof of his house with "Indian spinach" and oil. The thunder god slipped on the roof and fell, dropping his ax. "The violent one" immediately picked it up. Disarmed, the thunder god had to return to the sky and announce his defeat. He ordered the rain god to send a flood to drown "the violent one." Aided again by the hearth god, the hero built a raft on which he took refuge. The waters swelled and lifted him up to the gate of heaven. The emperor felt compelled to make the waters recede, out of fear that all the people might drown. "The violent one" was once again the victor. But when he subsequently neglected the hearth god, the protection was withdrawn from him and he was struck by lightning while crossing a field.

X. The Dragon King

The Dragon King, Long-vuong or Thuy-tê, rules the world of the waters by the order of the Jade Emperor. But he apparently deals only with matters concerning the seas; he delegates his powers to his subordinates and puts them in charge of the other waterways. He thus remains far from the world of living creatures; he has only episodic contacts with them and only through the mediation of his messengers. Much like the Jade Emperor or like an earthly king, he lives at the center of his court, surrounded by his wife and children and by an army of aquatic animals. His residence is a magnificent palace that rises from the bottom of a deep pit. Sometimes the Dragon King entrusts the building of his home to a human being. On this occasion, he chooses a human carpenter of great talent and sends two messengers to invite him to his aquatic realm. When the work is completed, the King offers him precious pearls in payment. When the Dragon King invites guests, they come to him in two ways: either the king's messengers escort them and open a way for them by miraculously parting the waters, or else they move around in the water by using a rhinoceros's horn. Both King An-duong and the future god Tan Viên made use of this powerful talisman. A human being happened to reach the palace of the Dragon King. He was a fisherman, an experienced and strong diver. He met some turtles who offered him the boon of understanding the language of the animals in exchange for his promise never to reveal to living creatures what he had seen. But when he returned home, he disclosed to his wife the mysteries of the kingdom of the waters. He died immediately, vomiting blood. The reason why the world of the waters must remain unknown is that it is *âm (yin)* and is opposed to the world of living creatures, *duong (yang);* that is also why there is a certain confusion between it and hell, one of whose names is *âm-phu.*

In popular stories, the Dragon King is presented as a being of extreme kindness. He always knows how to express his gratitude toward a human being who has saved one of his children. His sons and daughters often wander around in waterways in the form of fish or other aquatic animals, and they often get caught by fishermen. When they are released, they beg the king, their father, to invite these benefactors and to reward them. The Dragon King offers his guests gifts of magical objects or objects of great value: a book that makes wishes come true, magical claws, precious pearls, and so forth.

There are marriages between water spirits and human beings, such as Giap-Hai, who bought a turtle from a pair of boatmen and thus saved its life. Every time he goes away, a beautiful young girl comes out of the turtle's shell to prepare his dinner for him. Giap-Hai discovers the secret. He waylays the young girl and steals her shell. She is forced to admit that she is the daughter of the Dragon King. She offers to marry him in order to repay him. They get married in the kingdom of the waters. Thanks to the Dragon King, Giap-Hai receives instruction from a good master and comes in first in an examination for scholars. In another account, the daughter of the Dragon King marries a fisherman for love. She cannot return alive to her father's kingdom, for she would miss her husband and prefers to stay with him.

Another favorite theme tells the adventures of the foster parents of a sea serpent. An old childless couple found two eggs from which two serpents hatched. They brought up the serpents as though they were their own children. But when they had grown up, the serpents returned to live under water. To compensate the old couple, the real father of the serpents miraculously procured for them as much money as they desired. The two serpents became the benevolent spirits of two villages.

But not all associations with water spirits are so good. They are responsible for much misery and many catastrophes. These local "administrators," and not the sons of the Dragon King, cause calamities. They make the waters rise in order to steal wood to construct the palace. The *giai*, a kind of freshwater turtle of giant size (which must not be confused with the real turtle, who is kind), can demolish dikes. People sometimes manage to kill them by throwing rubbish at them. But the most efficacious way is to bury a metal rhinoceros under the dikes. This has the magical property of stabilizing waterways.

Even more to be feared is the *thuông-luông*, a sea serpent one hundred feet long, covered with scales and endowed with a red crest. This creature has been identified as the Chiao dragon of the Chinese, which is also known to the Vietnamese: the misdeeds of the Chiao dragon resulted in the ancient custom of tattooing. Sometimes he is encountered in a female aspect: a Chiao dragon takes the form of an old woman to probe the hearts of people, and then she makes the waters rise to drown the wicked and to save those who have treated her well. As for the *thuông-luông* we mentioned earlier, he always appears as a male and has a particular inclination for sexuality. Since he is a ferocious monster, he raises the waves to sink junks and to carry women away to his kingdom, to rape them or to force them to become his wives. One legend tells of a *thuông-luông* who devoured the people that he had shipwrecked by overturning their boats. Every year the people had to bring him a human victim. One man volunteered. He let the monster swallow him, and then he cut the monster up with a dagger and killed him.

Traces of human sacrifices to sea serpents can be found in the two following accounts. One of the emperors of the Ly dynasty (eleventh through thirteenth centuries) suffered from an eye ailment, which was connected with the overflowing of a river, according to one diviner's interpretation. To get cured, he cast a couple of oil merchants into the river as sacrificial offerings. Another emperor of the Trân dynasty (thirteenth through sixteenth centuries) had to let his favorite woman jump into the river as an offering to a Chiao dragon: the dragon, who threatened to sink the imperial junks, had demanded a human wife. Finally, King Lê Thanh-tông (fifteenth century) lodged a complaint with the chief of the kingdom of waters. The chief sent a herd of aquatic animals to punish the guilty party and to demand that he return the woman. In fact, they recovered the body of the young girl.

But the best known of all mythical animals is without any doubt the dragon. Distinct from the ferocious and sensual Chiao dragon and from the Dragon King who is the chief of the aquatic realm, the dragon represents a beneficent being, dispenser of rains, of which he became the god. His role can be compared to that of the toad during the Bronze Age of Dongson. Like the Chinese dragon, he buries himself in the earth during the off-season and arises to fly through the air in the spring; then he uses his mouth to pulverize the rains that the farmers have been awaiting. A noble animal, classed in the highest rank of the "four sacred animals," he is the emblem of royal power. He is represented on court costumes, on the throne, and on imperial junks. In 549, Triên Quang Phuc received from the Immortal Chu Dông-tu, who rode on a dragon, a claw from that animal, which made it possible for him to defeat an enemy army. The future king, Dinh Tiên-hoang, is seen as having been carried across a river by two yellow dragons when he was pursued by his uncle. Finally, the capital city Thang-long, "the Ascent of the Dragon" (Hanoi), was thus christened by the founders of the Ly dynasty (eleventh century) because a yellow dragon had risen to the sky to indicate to the king an era of prosperity.

In conclusion, with the exception of the religious representations of the deities of nature, the themes that deal with the primordial world seem at first glance to have lost their religious tenor. They are no longer stories deemed to be true so that they may be believed and actualized through rituals. Gathered indiscriminately among other folkloric documents, they appear as etiological legends rather than cosmogonic myths.

Nevertheless, if we isolate a certain number of motifs and set them next to certain elements of the mythology of neighboring peoples, particularly the mythology of the non-Vietnamese mountain tribes, we see that they are part of a more complex network of myths. Thus, the Vietnamese hunter of the Moon, Quai, evokes the Tay marksman of the twelve suns and the Chinese archer Yi, who conquered the surplus suns. The return of the sun into the world of humans took place in the same way among the Vietnamese and the same Tay: in both cases the rooster and the duck went out into the open sea to reclaim it. The theme of the giant rice grain fits into a more coherent set of myths of the first creations of the universe among the Black Tai. An analogous version of the tree of immortality that rises into the sky can be found among the Muong: it is the story of Ta Keo Rênh. As for the universal flood, no trace of it can be found among the Vietnamese, unless we see a few allusions to it in the story of "the violent one" whom the waters carried up to the sky, which implies that all of mankind was left under the waters.

These few examples lead us to believe that Vietnamese mythology did indeed exist, but that it was effaced by an imported Confucianism, and that only popular and oral traditions have been able to preserve some reminiscences of it.

L.O.M./g.h.

Civilizing Heroes and the Organization of the First Vietnamese Kingdom

1. The Mythic Origin of the Vietnamese

Ancient and modern historians have attributed the foundation of Van-lang, the first Vietnamese kingdom, to the Hung King. The documents that they cite are fragmentary and derive more from legend than from historical fact. Thus in Vietnam the mythic history of the world is identified with the setting up of the kingdom and the origins of its people. All Vietnamese readily call themselves "sons of the Dragon and grandsons of the Immortal (female)." The origin of this phrase derives from the following legend.

Lac Long-Quān, Lord Dragon of the tribe of the Lacs and the future father of the first Hung King, was a descendant of the aquatic animal of the same name. He married an Immortal of the mountain, Lady Au-Co, of marvelous beauty. After three years and ten days she miraculously gave birth to a membranous pouch, from which, seven days later, one hundred eggs emerged. From these hundred eggs were born a hundred boys. All grew up without needing to be nursed. But their mother and father could no longer live together. Lord Dragon reminded his wife that he was of the race of Dragons and lord of the aquatic element, while she was of the race of the Immortals and thus belonged to the earthly element. But the two elements water and earth (or fire) are opposed to one another. They cannot remain together. They divided their sons and each of them led away fifty boys. Lord Dragon took his sons to his kingdom of water, while Lady Au-Co went with hers to the high country.

This separation into two groups, one going toward the mountain, that is, to the northwest, and the other settling in the maritime region of the southeast, is probably an allusion to the ethnic minorities of North Vietnam, on the one hand, and to the installation of the Vietnamese themselves in the plains and coastal regions, on the other. According to this myth, the two groups have a common source.

The simultaneous birth of a hundred males not only evokes an image of fertility but also recalls the renewal of humanity described in the myths of certain neighboring peoples. Instead of a membranous pouch, we find in these myths either a piece of flesh or a gourd out of which, after the universal flood, a brother and sister come who give birth to the Vietnamese and non-Vietnamese peoples. The separation of the spouses in this legend rests on the opposition of earth and water. Moreover, the Vietnamese term for "the country," "the kingdom," is precisely "earth-water" (*dât-nouc*). It can thus be said that the union of the mythic couple already reinforces the idea of the nation.

2. The Civilizing Heroes: The Hung Vuong

The eldest of the fifty sons who followed their mother was chosen by his brothers as the first king of the Van-lang kingdom. He reigned under the title of Hung Vuong, and his dynasty included eighteen Hung kings. Recently collected legends about them reveal that they were civilizing heroes. These kings lived in close contact with their people; they taught them new techniques, discovered new food plants for their benefit and also originated new customs. Moreover, the mastery of water was and remains one of the most indispensable secrets of rice cultivation. Thus, the Hung had to battle against water monsters who started floods, destroying harvests and carrying people away.

More than twenty centuries have passed, and the Vietnamese still worship the Hung. Their temples are found especially in the province of Phu-tho (north Vietnam). In one of these temples, located on a mountain summit, a tablet can be found with the following inscription: "The tablet of the eighteen generations of holy sovereigns of the Hung family." During their annual festival, the tablets of these kings are taken out and carried in a procession, and various games are organized in their honor.

The first Hung founded his capital. He made a grand tour of the country to choose the future location of the capital. When he had found a vast, flat site, he commissioned an eagle to construct a hundred mounds and demanded that the construction work be completed in one night. When ninety-nine mounds had been finished, a cock began to crow. The eagle thought that it was already day and abandoned his work. The Hung King left this site to search for another place. He was attracted by a new site in the mountains. But a blow of his horse's hoof made a piece of a peak give way. The king judged that the site was not stable and abandoned it. He left a third site as well, for he saw a serpent there, which he considered a bad omen. Then he came upon a golden tortoise coming out of the water to greet him; the tortoise carried him on its back throughout its domain. But he found this site too narrow and decided not to choose it as a capital. Finally, one day he came upon an exceptional place and decided to settle there; he called his capital Phong-chau.

The Hung kings explored the jungle and the mountain. Myths about the Hung often suggest a mastery of the mountain and an exploration of the jungle. From there it is but one step to the idea of setting up a territory. Every time the king took part in the hunt he was accompanied by a considerable following. He took with him his sons and his daughters. The hunting party lasted several days and was interrupted by pauses for refreshments. Meals were prepared in the manner of non-Vietnamese mountain tribes.

One day the Hung King halted at the foot of a mountain. His daughters discovered some fragrant plants and brought them to their father. The king had some game covered with these fine herbs before it was roasted. He tasted it and found it much better than before. He took the herb away to plant it at his residence. Until now, people in certain places preserve a ritual that consists in offering a sacrifice to the king, a plate of chicken cooked with this herb.

The first Hung King taught the techniques of agriculture to his people. There was a time, they say, when people did not know about the plow and rice cultivation. They ate only game, roots and plants, and wild fruit. But at each flood the rivers brought new layers of fertile alluvium. The Hung King dammed up the flooded lands. With rice growing wild, he showed his people how to save its seeds and plant them. Then he went in person to pull up the young rice plants and replant them. All his subjects tried to imitate him.

This legend is accompanied by a ritual meant to reactualize the king's exploit. The ritual was preserved until very recent times in the village where the exploit is said to have occurred—Minh-nong, in the Viet-tri province in north Vietnam. The people of this village had the custom of offering a sacrifice to the Hung King. The ceremony took place under a banyan, as before. An old man was chosen to descend into a flooded rice field to repick some young rice plants symbolically. The ritual is the same as that performed during the festival to honor Than-nong, a god of agriculture among the Chinese and Vietnamese. In this substitution, then, there is an attempt to regard the ritual as being of Vietnamese origin.

The mastery of the waters took place during this protohistorical period, when the problem of water already constituted a major preoccupation. The battle against the surging floods of the water courses has been translated into mythology. The adversary was formidable and was identified with an aquatic animal. Only Lord Dragon was able to conquer it; even the Immortals failed. This fabulous beast—half-fish, half-serpent—lived in the eastern sea. It stirred up storms as it moved on its multiple paws. It sought to devour human beings. One day it changed into a white rooster and, announcing dawn, drove off the Immortals who were trying to destroy its lair. Lord Dragon, disguised as a fisherman, pretended to offer it a human victim. But instead he threw a white-hot lump of metal down its gaping beak. The beast fell, and the sovereign cut off its head and tail.

The ferocious dragon Kiao also represented hostile nature.

It devoured the inhabitants of the mountain. The Hung King understood that this fabulous animal considered the essence of people to be contrary to its own. On the advice of the king, the people tattooed themselves with figures of the monster so as to resemble him and escape his attacks. This was a way to become familiar with nature. The custom continued in all levels of society, popular as well as aristocratic, until the fourteenth century.

But the most significant example of the mastery of water is found in the legend of Son-Tinh, the Spirit of the Mountain, and Thuy-Tinh, the Spirit of Water. These two spirits struggled to obtain the hand of the daughter of the Hung King; the king did not know to which of the two he should marry the princess, for they were equal in magical power. He asked them to come back with wedding gifts; the one who brought them first would marry her. The Spirit of the Mountain brought them first and took the princess away. The Spirit of Water came late and grew furious. He led his army of aquatic animals in pursuit of his happy adversary to try to snatch the young bride away. When he came to Mount Tan-Vien, the residence of the Spirit of the Mountain, he rushed into an assault, provoking great storms. The Spirit of the Mountain stretched metal nets across the rivers in order to check their progress. The people gave him their cooperation. They built a barrier all around Mount Tan-Vien and encouraged the god with the noises of drums and rice mortars. They shot arrows in the direction of the water: the lifeless bodies of aquatic animals came floating up to the surface. This battle is taken up again every year and the floods of the seventh month are witness to it.

Tan-Vien is the beneficent god of the mountain. In the preceding legend, this god has the attributes of a divinity of nature. Later, he takes on the aspect of a divinized human being. There is a story about his miraculous conception. His mother, poor and ugly, had no husband; she became pregnant after putting her foot down on the footprint of a giant. Chased into the forest by the inhabitants of her village on account of her pregnancy, she was fed by tigers who brought her meat every day. Her son became a woodcutter and worked to help his mother. Then, one day, he received a magic wand from the hands of a god; this instrument enabled him to resuscitate the dead or kill people, depending on which end he pointed at the subject in question. In addition, this divinity charged him with guarding the mountain Tan-Vien. After this the boy brought many dead people back to life. He became a doctor as well, tending to the diseases of simple people whom he sought out himself. The people expressed their admiration for him and gave him the title of god of the mountain.

His good deeds did not stop there. A civilizing hero in the same way as the Hung kings, he brought many new techniques to the people. In one village where the inhabitants did not know how to net fish, the god taught them this technique. In another situtation, he showed his hunting companions a new way of preserving game meat. In this way the god of the mountain became the patron god of hunters. In the region of Vinh-phu where, according to a recent count, there are more than five hundred temples dedicated to the Hung family and their generals, including Tan-Vien, people offer him a sacrifice every time they return from the hunt. During these ceremonies, the hunters reenact a scene from Tan-Vien's hunt. Pigs replace game and are carried in a procession to the sound of drums and cheers; a feast is prepared in the open air. Then the participants vie with one another in tearing off pieces of red paper previously pasted onto poles stuck beside the pigs. These pieces of paper are then pasted on crossbows so that the final hunt may be more fruitful. Sacrifices are also performed to request the opening of the hunt and entrance into the forest. No one dares to go there to collect wood before this festival. It should be added that the divinity has Lord Tiger for an acolyte.

On the national level, Tan-Vien is regarded by the population as the first of the divinities of the kingdom through his great power of regulating rains and drought. His place of worship is on the peak of Mount Tan-Vien ("roundness of the parasol"), so named because it has the form of a dome. Formerly, every three years the emperor of Vietnam sent his high officials there to offer sacrifice. On this occasion, neighboring villagers would offer the divinity axes of polished stone and bronze, which they believe to be thunderstones and to which they attribute magic virtues. We are also told that during the battle against the Spirit of Water, the god Tan-Vien made these thunderstones rain down to control the floods raised by his enemy. The people sacrifice to him on the first and the fifteenth of the month. On these days, tigers, rhinoceroses, and elephants leave the jungle to come to make an act of submission to the god.

In brief, this period is marked by setting the kingdom in order. The chiefs who arranged it knew how to provide exemplary models and to furnish the qualities that characterize a civilization. The hostile natural forces were immense; they are represented by monsters. If the Hung kings were able to exterminate them, it is because they were of supernatural origin, like the multitude of generals who helped them in their task. Once the watercourses were dammed up, the land became arable and people could live in security. The rituals now observed by the Vietnamese have for their object the reactualization of the exemplary acts of the civilizing heroes of the earliest times.

L.O.M./d.g.

PART

9

East Asia and Inner Asia

Chinese Mythology 1007
Chinese Cosmogony 1008
Sky and Earth, Sun and Moon, Stars, Mountains and Rivers, and the Cardinal Points in Ancient China 1010
Ancient Chinese Goddesses and Grandmothers 1015
Mythical Rulers in China: The Three Huang and the Five Di 1018
The Great Flood in Chinese Mythology 1024
Myths and Legends about the Barbarians on the Periphery of China and in the Land of Chu 1026
Chinese Demons 1028
The Mythology of Smelters and Potters in China 1032
Caves and Labyrinths in Ancient China 1033
Some Legends about Laozi and the Immortals in Daoist Mythology 1034
Remarks on Japanese Religions and Mythological Beliefs 1037
The Vital Spirit and the Soul in Japan 1041
Japanese Conceptions of the Afterlife 1044
Buddhism and Archaic Beliefs in the Shinto-Buddhist Syncretism of Japan 1049
Mountains in Japan 1051
Magic in Japan 1053
Japanese Divination 1055
The *Yamabushi*, Mountain Ascetics of Japan 1056
The *Tengu* Demons of Japan 1059
Japanese Shamanism 1062
Japanese Festivals and Seasonal Rites: *Matsuri* and *Nenchū Gyōji* 1063
Korean Mythology 1070
Introduction to Tibetan Mythology 1075
The Importance of Origins in Tibetan Mythology 1077
Cosmogonic Myths of Tibet 1079
Anthropogonic Myths of Tibet 1082
Divine Sovereignty in Tibet 1086
The Religion and Myths of the Turksand Mongols 1089
Turkish and Mongolian Cosmogony and Cosmography 1095
Turkish and Mongolian Demons 1096
The Turkish and Mongolian Ancestor Cult 1097
The Importance of Animals in the Religion of the Turks and Mongols: Tribal Myths and Hunting Rituals 1097
The Tree of Life and the Cosmic Axis among the Turks and Mongols 1101
The Mountain as Cosmic Axis among the Turks and Mongols 1102
Turkish and Mongolian Shamanism 1103
The Sky God and the Stars among the Turks and Mongols 1105
Water among the Turks and Mongols 1107
Turkish and Mongolian Eschatology: The End of the World and the Fate of Man after Death 1107
Turkish and Mongolian Master Spirits (Ejen and Izik) 1108
The Cult of Fire among the Turks and Mongols 1109
Turkish and Mongolian Funerary Customs 1109
Heroes of the Turks and Mongols 1111
The Turkish and Mongolian Ritual of the Blood Oath 1112
The Earth among the Turks and Mongols 1112
The Personification of Thunder among the Turks and Mongols 1113

(*Continued on next page*)

Gods and Myths of the Abkhaz, the Cherkess, and the Ubykh of the Northern Caucasus 1113
Souls and Their Avatars in Siberia 1116
The Sky, the Great Celestial Divinity of Siberia 1119
Siberian Master Spirits and Shamanism 1120
Siberian Religion and Myths: The Example of the Tungus 1128
Finno-Ugrian Myths and Rituals 1132

Chinese Mythology

Ancient Chinese mythology has been very poorly transmitted to us, and it suffices to leaf through the ancient Chinese books to be convinced of this. Only with difficulty can we recognize in the Confucian classics the old myths, camouflaged as history: at their origins we find only sovereigns or sages who founded the civilization. In the writings of various philosophical schools, such allusions to legend as we find are always very fragmentary. In a general sense, mythology was transformed into history by scholars whose main concern was to teach an ethics and an art of government and who did so by referring to models that they sought in early antiquity. Nevertheless, there is enough ancient Chinese to offer fairly plentiful, if sporadic, data; and by drawing these together and comparing them, it is possible to recover the broad outlines of a mythology which turns out to be richer than would at first have appeared. But we have only a fragmentary and very incomplete knowledge of it, so that many of the visual representations unearthed by archaeology remain unexplained. M. Hentze is certainly correct in thinking that the motifs that decorated the ancient Yin and Zhou bronzes are not merely designs but have a religious significance even when they appear to be no more than geometric fillers. But the texts give us no explanation for this decoration of the ancient bronzes; by the same token, much later, many of the scenes represented on Han funerary sculptures remain enigmatic. On the other hand, the sculptures sometimes confirm what is related in the texts; thus the thunder god appears as he is described by Wang Chong in the *Lunheng,* with drums threaded together on a single strut. Archaeology thus remains a precious resource which may continue to offer much new information, the further study of which will enrich our knowledge of the ancient religions: witness the recent discovery, in tombs near Chang Sha, of two beautiful banners of painted silk, covered with mythological subjects (the sun, moon, fusang trees, the door of heaven, etc.).

As for written sources, the one with the most mythological data is incontestably the *Shanhai Jing* (Book of mountains and seas): this is a mythic geography whose eighteen chapters were written over different periods of time, all B.C. Tradition attributes its redaction to Yu the Great. He had nine sacred cauldrons (*ding*) made, upon which were represented the gods and demons in order that his subjects could distinguish the good and evil spirits that they risked encountering in their travels over mountains and valleys. The *Shanhai Jing,* an illustrated book, was probably composed for the same purpose, since it gives a great deal of information on the gods and demons of mountains and waterfalls, not only "within the boundaries of the seas," that is, within the empire, but also beyond, in the regions situated on the periphery of the civilized world.

Apart from the *Shanhai Jing,* it is the poems of Qiu Yuan (end of the fourth century B.C.), in the *Chuci* (Elegies of the land of the Chu), which are the richest in ancient mythological data, especially the *Lisao,* the *Jiu Ge* (Nine songs), and above all the *Tianwen* (Celestial questions). This last poem is composed of questions about mythology, but we are unfortunately not always provided with the answers to the enigmas, even with the aid of the commentaries.

Among the philosophical works, the *Huainanzi,* a text inspired by Daoism and written by the scholarly seers of the court of a king of Huainan in the second century B.C., contains fragments of myths that are not found elsewhere.

In the time of the Six Dynasties, a period of division in which the ascendancy of Confucianism was somewhat weak-

Han funerary ledger. Paris, Musée Guimet. Photo Arch. Phot. Paris/SPADEM.

ened, some collections appeared containing some fairly well preserved legends: the *Shiyiji* of Wang Jia (fourth century A.D.), the *Bowuzhi* of Jhang Hua (A.D. 232–300), the Shoushenji of Gan Bao (fourth century A.D.), the *Shu chi* of Jen Fang (A.D. 460–508) and the *Shen yi ching,* attributed to the Tung fang Sho of the Han dynasty, but in fact anonymous. All of these works make it possible to flesh out the most ancient information, though we have to reckon with the literary fables and morals that their authors often inserted into their accounts.

M.K./d.w.

BIBLIOGRAPHY

M. GRANET, *Danses et légendes de la Chine ancienne* (Paris 1926); *Fêtes et chansons anciennes de la Chine* (Paris 1929); *La pensée chinoise* (Paris 1934; 2d ed., 1968); *Études sociologiques sur la Chine* (Paris 1953). H. MASPERO, "Les légendes mythologiques dans le Chou king," *Journal asiatique,* 1924; *Mythologie de la Chine moderne,* in *Mythologie asiatique illustrée* (1928), reprinted in *Le Taoïsme et les religions chinoises* (1971); *Mélanges posthumes,* vol. 1: *Les religions chinoises* (Paris 1967). W. EBERHARD, *Lokalkulturen im alten China,* 1–2 (1942); *Typen chinesischer Volksmärchen,* FF Communications 120. C. HENTZE, *Funde in Alt-China* (Göttingen 1967). K. FINSTER-BUSCH, *Das Verhältnis des Shan-hai djing zur Bildenden Kunst* (Berlin 1952). W. EICHHORN, *Die Alte Chinesische Religion und das Stattkultwesen* (Leiden and Cologne 1976). WERNER, *A Dictionary of Chinese Mythology* (1931; 2d ed., 1961). IZUSHI YOSHIHIKO, *Shina shinwa densetsu no kenkyû* (Tokyo 1943). MORI MIKISABURO, *Chûgoku kodai shinwa* (Tokyo 1969). YUAN K'E, *Zhong guo gudai Shenhua* (1957). YANG KUAN, *Zhong guo shangqushi daolun,* in *Gushi Pian* 7, 1.

Chinese Cosmogony

Ancient Chinese literature has almost no cosmogonic myths. The Confucian authors, who are little given to metaphysics, are in principle hostile to the marvelous. The Daoist philosophers, more inclined to make use of legendary traditions to illustrate their theses, also have little to say on the subject. For example, we could hardly qualify as mythological what Laozi, the *Liezi,* or the *Huainanzi* say about the beginning of the world:

> The Dao gave birth to the One,
> One gave birth to Two,
> Two gave birth to Three,
> Three gave birth to ten thousand beings;
> The ten thousand beings carry the Yin on their backs and embrace the Yang. (Laozi, 42)

The commentary of Heshang Gong on this text shows a somewhat more mythic concept of origins:

> That to which the Dao first gave birth was the Unity from which proceeded the Yin and the Yang. The Yin and the Yang produced the Three Energy Breaths: the Pure, the Impure, and the Mixed, which in turn constituted, respectively, the Sky, the Earth, and Man. Together, the Sky and Earth gave birth to ten thousand beings: the Sky furnished the seedlings, the Earth transformed them, and Man raised and nourished them.

Here, the Sky and the Earth are the Father and Mother of the creatures, and the One or the Unity is a way of designating Chaos, the original state of nondifferentiation. The *Liezi* also develops a formation of the world through stages, the starting point being the *Taiyi* (here *yi* is not the Unity, but the principle of mutations of the *Yi Jing*). But it is this *Yi* mutation that becomes the *Yi* Unity.

> By mutation, the One becomes Seven; Seven, by mutation, becomes Nine. With this ninth mutation, one returns to One. One is the beginning of the mutations of forms. That which was pure and light rose and became the Sky; that which was gross and heavy became the Earth; the intermediate breaths became man. Thanks to the seeds received by Earth from Sky, the ten thousand beings appeared through transformation. (*Liezi,* 1)

The formation of the world is the end result of a cyclic evolution, which is completely in agreement with one of the fundamental ideas of Chinese thought, for which the alternations between the Yin and the Yang and the five elemental Virtues order the life of the cosmos and of man, as well as the unfolding of history.

The *Huainanzi* (chapter 3) describes the formation of the world as follows:

> At the time when the Sky and Earth had not yet taken shape, the world was nothing more than a confused, undefinable mass, which is called the Great Beginning (*Taishi*). The Great Beginning produced the Void; this produced the Space-Time-Universe which produced the original Breath (*Yuanqi*). The original Breath was a thing without limits. Its clear and pure elements rose lightly to form the Sky; its heavy and gross elements coagulated to form the Earth. Since it is easier for clear and pure elements to become concentrated than for heavy and gross elements to coagulate, the Sky took shape before the Earth became stable. The complementary essences of Sky and Earth were the Yin and the Yang; the concentrated essences of the Yin and the Yang formed the seasons; and when the essences of the seasons diversified, they formed the ten thousand beings. The warm breath of the Yang, accumulated, came to produce fire, whose most subtle elements became the sun. The cold breath of the Yin, accumulated, came to produce water, whose most subtle elements became the moon. The most subtle of the superabundant solar and lunar elements became the stars. The Sky received the sun, moon, and stars; the Earth received the waters, rivers, ground, and dust.

In the same work, we also encounter the following text (chapter 7):

> Long ago, at a time when the Sky and the Earth did not exist, there reigned a great formless mist: such darkness, such an unmoving and silent immensity whose origins cannot be known! Two divinities were thus born out of this confusion, one regulating the movement of the Sky, the other organizing the Earth. They brought about the separation of the Yin and the Yang and established far off the eight poles of the world. The hard and the soft (the Yang and the Yin) completed each other mutually and the ten thousand beings took shape. The most gross of the fluids became the reptiles, and the most subtle of the fluids became man.

Exegetes hesitate to identify the two divinities to which the *Huainanzi* refers. Most of them contend that they are Fuxi and Nüwa. These two divinities with the bodies of serpents were nevertheless popular in the time of the Hans: they wonderfully symbolize the Yin and the Yang, and their attributes, the compass and the square, well designate them as the artisans of the round and the square, of the Sky and the Earth.

Through these Daoist texts we can see how these thinkers understood the origins of the world. But we do not know what the popular beliefs on this subject were. There seems to have been a myth of Chaos that Zhuangzi used by transposing it into a fable intended to illustrate the evil deeds of overzealous bearers of civilization:

> The lord of the southern Ocean was Shu; the lord of the northern Ocean was Hu. The lord of the Center was Chaos. Shu and Hu sometimes met in the province of Chaos, who treated them with great courtesy. They thought about the best way to repay him for his good deeds: "Everyone has seven openings for seeing, hearing, eating, and breathing. He is without these. Let us try to make these openings in him." Each day they undertook to pierce an opening in him. On the seventh day, Chaos died. (Chapter 7)

In classical literature, Hundun, Chaos, is one of the ones who are banished from Zhuen. In the *Shanhai Jing,* he is a monster who resembles a sack; and he has certain points in common with the Hundun of Zhuangzi, but he is no longer the primordial Chaos. It is not until a work of the third century A.D., the *Sanwu Liji,* that the celebrated myth of Pangu appears:

> In the time when the Sky and the Earth were a chaos resembling an egg, Pangu was born in this and lived inside it for eighteen thousand years. And when the Sky and Earth constituted themselves, the pure Yang elements formed the Sky and the gross Yin elements formed the Earth. And Pangu, who was in the midst of this, transformed himself nine times each day, sometimes into a god in the Sky, sometimes into a saint on Earth. Each day the Sky rose by one *Zhang* (ten feet), each day the Earth thickened by one *Zhang,* and each day Pangu grew by one *Zhang.* This continued for eighteen thousand years, and then the Sky reached its highest point, the Earth its lowest depth, and Pangu his greatest size.

Part of this narrative is inspired by the texts of the *Huainanzi* and *Liezi* cited above, but suddenly Pangu, who is completely unknown to earlier literature, appears on the scene. This may be explained by the southern origin of this myth, which did not become known to the Chinese until quite late. The *Shuyi Ji,* a sixth-century collection of *mirabilia,* tells another version:

> Living beings began with Pangu, who is the ancestor of the ten thousand beings of the universe. When Pangu died, his head became a sacred peak, his eyes became the sun and the moon, his fat the rivers and seas, and the hair of his head and body became trees and other plants. The ancient scholars affirm that the tears of Pangu gave rise to the Blue and Yellow rivers, that his breath was the wind, his voice thunder; the pupils of his eyes made the lightning flash, and the sky was clear when he was content and somber when he was angry. According to a belief of the Qin and Han periods, Pangu's head became the sacred peak of the East, his belly the peak of the Center, his left arm the peak of the South, his right arm the peak of the North, and his feet the peak of the West. In the (southern) lands of Wu and Chu, it is said that Pangu and his wife are the origin of the Yin and the Yang.

It is impossible to know what the author intended by "the ancient scholars," and as for his assertion that there was a belief about Pangu in the time of the Qin and the Han, this is very unlikely. The *Shuyi Ji* adds that tombs of Pangu were found in the Nanha, and temples of Pangu at Guilin. Nanha (the Southern Seas) is taken to mean the coastal regions of southern China and the lands across the sea; Guilin was in the north of Guangxi, a region completely inhabited by the Miao, Yao, and other aboriginal peoples. It is certain that these texts about Pangu do not offer us the original form of the myth: they were collected through hearsay and were for the northern Chinese nothing more than strange tales. Nevertheless, this legend must have retained enough local prestige for the Daoists to take interest in it and to take it over by replacing Pangu with a deified Laozi: "Laozi transformed himself: his left eye became the sun, his right eye became the moon, his head became Mount Kunlun, his hairs were the stars, his bones were dragons, his flesh the quadrupeds, his intestines serpents, his stomach the seas, his fingers the five sacred peaks, his body hair the plants, and his heart Mount Huagai" (*Xiaodao Lun,* sixth century A.D.).

Among the rare cosmogonic myths which came from China proper, the one about the break in communications between the Sky and the Earth must be mentioned. It was almost forgotten very early, and there remain only a few very short or distorted references to it. In the *Shu Jing* (*Lüxing*) we read: "The August Lord charged Chongli with breaking the communication between Sky and Earth, in order to halt the descents of the gods." According to the exegetes, the August Lord is Zhuanxu (regarded as a historical emperor), who is said to have introduced a religious reform. He is said to have done this in order to keep the people from giving themselves up to irregular cults in the course of which sorcerers and sorceresses invoked the spirits and caused them to "descend," i.e., caused themselves to be possessed by them. In fact, this is an old myth according to which the Sky and the Earth, too close to one another, communicated in such a way that gods were able to descend to be among men.

Although the ancient Chinese did not preserve their old cosmogonic myths, they did nevertheless have legends about heroes who repaired the damage done to the world by a rebellious monster or by a flood, the latter being the Chinese version of the Flood myth. They also have a myth about the creation of mankind:

"According to popular legend, at the time when the Sky and the Earth were created, mankind did not yet exist. Nüwa began to fashion men out of yellow earth. But she found this task to be too much for her powers; therefore she went to draw some mud, which she used to make men. It is thus that the nobles were the men fashioned from yellow earth; poor people, who live in vile and servile conditions, are the men who were drawn out of the mud" (*Fengsu Tongyi,* second century A.D.).

Nüwa appears here as the divinity who created men. It is surprising that this myth is found in only one single work, to which it is incidental, at that; perhaps this was a little-known local tradition. In a more widespread myth, Nüwa intervenes to repair the damage done when the monster Gonggong made a hole in one of the pillars of the world with a thrust of his horns. The pillar swayed, and it is for this reason that the heavenly bodies flow toward the west while on earth rivers flow toward the east. As for the Sky, "Nüwa melted the rocks of five colors in order to repair it; she cut off the legs of a great turtle to erect four pillars at the four poles, killed the black Dragon (Gonggong) to save the world, and piled up the ashes of reeds to stop the overflowing waters" (*Huainanzi*). Nüwa is one of the two mythic characters who fight against the Flood. The other is Yu the Great, a renowned hero who, though presented by historians as a sort of hydraulic engineer, was surely a demiurge who organized the world with its mountains and its sacred rivers of which he became the principal god. Nüwa and Yu, moreover, have such close mythic ties that the goddess has been assimilated to the wife of Yu, the daughter of Tushan.

M.K./d.w.

Sky and Earth, Sun and Moon, Stars, Mountains and Rivers, and the Cardinal Points in Ancient China

I. Sky and Earth

Under the Han there were at least two ways of representing the world (Sky-Earth, *Tiandi*). According to the first, the universe is a chariot covered by a canopy: the canopy is round and is the Sky; the Earth is represented by the square frame of the chariot. The Sky is supported by columns, four or eight in number. There are also eight moorings (*wei*). One of these pillars, Mount Buzou, situated to the northwest of the world, was shaken by Gonggong. According to another theory, the Sky resembles an egg and the Earth is the yolk in the center of the egg. To explain how the Earth is kept in equilibrium in this position, one *weishu* ("apocryphon") said that under the Earth there are eight columns (*Hetu Juodixiang*). But in general the eight columns were erected between the Sky and the Earth.

The Earth, a great square in whose interior there were nine provinces, was surrounded on four sides by the "Four Seas." The Four Seas were not oceans, but regions peopled by barbarians: nine kinds of Yi barbarians to the east, six kinds of Man barbarians to the south, seven kinds of Rong to the west, and eight kinds of Di to the north. All these peoples were beyond the domain of civilization, but if the Virtue (*De*) of China's sovereign was powerful enough, they were submissive and came even to the capital to bring tribute. The *Shanhai Jing* and the *Huainanzi* further enlarge the vision of the world by situating "beyond the seas" (*Haiwai*) populations which are more or less fantastic, such as the Country of Women situated beyond the western sea: all the inhabitants of this country are women (they become pregnant by washing themselves in a certain pond); the Country of the People with One Head and Three Bodies; to the south is the Country of Naked Men, the Country of Men with Feathers (who can fly, but not far), the Country of Stabbed Breasts (descendants of Fangfeng, who was stabbed in the breast while fleeing Yu), etc.

The square Earth had a center: the royal capital. The capital was also square with four gates, in the image of the world. Its principal sanctuaries were also round or square according to whether they corresponded to the Sky or the Earth. The altar of the Sky was round, that of the Earth square. The Mingtang, the Temple of Light in which the sovereign revolved like a sun to conform to the seasonal rhythms, had a square base and a round roof.

Just as the Earth, inside of the Four Seas, was divided into nine provinces, the Sky comprised nine plains. But soon the Sky was imagined as nine levels high, while the Earth was nine levels deep: at the bottom were the Ninth Springs or Yellow Springs where the land of the dead was situated. But in earlier times the Yellow Springs do not seem to have been imagined as very deep underground: libations there made their way to the surface and spirits of the dead might easily escape from it in the winter, when the ground was cracked. But when the vision of the world became larger, during the period of the Warring Kingdoms, the land of the dead was situated in the far north, in an abyss from which the waters issued from the interior of the earth.

II. The Sun and the Moon

In the myth of Pangu, the eyes of the cosmic man become the Sun and Moon. The connection of the eyes with these two luminaries is very frequent. It is found in the Daoist representation of the human body conceived as a microcosm. It is also found in other myths, such as the myth recalled by the *Xuanzonggi:* "To the north on the Mountain of the Bell, there is a stone with a head like a human head; the left eye is the Sun, the right eye the Moon; when the left eye is open, it is day; when the right eye is open, it is night." In the *Shanhai Jing,* "The spirit of the Mountain of the Bell is the Fiery Dragon who has a human face and the body of a great dragon of a thousand *li;* he stands erect, very angry, his eyes fixed. If he opens his eyes, it is day, if he closes them, it is night; if he exhales, it is winter; if he inhales, it is summer." In this variant of the myth, the eyes of the cosmic dragon are luminaries that play the role of the sun.

But according to the most widespread myth, there were ten suns and twelve moons. And each of these luminaries was inhabited by animals: crows for the sun, a toad and a hart for the moon (or moons, but the lunar animals seem to relate only to a single moon). Already in the representations of the Han period, these animals were depicted in disks of the sun and the moon; the crow was often represented with three feet.

It was therefore a time when there were ten suns. They perched on the solar Mulberry Tree, the Fusang, and appeared in turn: in fact nine suns remained on the lower branches of the tree, and one perched on the upper branch (*Shanhai Jing*). But it happened that one day they all appeared at the same time, so that creatures were in danger of being scorched. Yi the archer saved the world by destroying nine of the ten suns. Yi the archer belongs to the mythology of the ancient eastern populations of China, whose ancestor was a solar being, an expert archer and fowler. According to the *Huainanzi,* Yao ordered Yi to destroy the nine undesirable suns, as well as other monsters who were ravaging the world.

After Yi's exploit, only one sun remained. The sun travels in a chariot. The *Huainanzi* enumerates the stages of his daily voyage from the Valley of the Boiling Waters (Tangqu), where the Fusang tree is located, to the Sad Springs. It is not the Sun himself who drives his chariot, but a woman who is his mother, Xihe. Xihe is the wife of the mythical emperor Di Xun (who is identified with Shun and Di Ku); the *Shanhai Jing* speaks of a country of the Xihe, descendants of the mother of the ten suns, and says that the mother washed her children in the "Abyss of the Sweet River."

The myth of the ten suns is certainly connected with the denary cycle (the ten cyclical characters called "trunks"), which, from the period of the Yin, served to designate the days: one might think that a new sun appeared on each of these ten days. As for the twelve moons, they were the twelve lunations of the year and also the twelve branches of the duodenary series of cyclical characters.

Moon goddess. Bronze. Paris, Musée Guimet. Photo Musées nationaux.

Like the ten suns, the twelve moons have a mother who bathes them in a lake situated to the west of the world. This mother of the moons is called Changxi or Changyi or Hengnge: she is, like Xihe, a wife of Di Xun, which would make the Sun and the Moon half brother and half sister, but the mythology is very uncertain, especially since the names of the deities are rendered with orthographic variants that make it difficult to find one's bearings.

The archer Yi who destroys the solar crows appears again in a legend that explains the presence of a toad in the moon. Yi had obtained the drug of immortality from the Xiwangmu; his wife Henge stole it from him and fled to the moon; there she became the lunar toad. That is why the drug of immortality is found in the moon: the imagery generally represents the hare in the act of pounding the medicine in a mortar. The moon surely designated perenniality, because its light dies and comes to life again perpetually. This idea is found again in another popular legend, apparently later, according to which there is a great tree in the moon, a cinnamon tree. A man tries to cut it down with an ax, but the injured trunk heals after each blow. The cinnamon tree furnished the Daoists with a food that promoted long life.

Like other ancient peoples, the Chinese feared eclipses, which were baneful omens. Moralists asserted that eclipses were brought on by the irregular conduct of the sovereigns and their wives. In this case, the king had to reestablish order through a warlike commotion: "While the feudal princes are all present, if the sun happens to become eclipsed, they will come to its aid behind the Son of Heaven, each of them taking up the color and weapon appropriate to his region (in other words to the cardinal direction of his fief)" (*Li Ji*, trans. Couvreur, 1, p. 439). Eclipses were the occasion for ceremonies of exorcism in which drums were beaten and arrows were shot toward the endangered sun or moon. Eclipses were brought on by a monster that devoured the luminary concerned. In the case of the sun, it was a celestial dog or wolf; in the case of the moon, it was said to be a toad, which is not very consistent with the idea of a toad present in the moon.

To this mythological data must be added the fact that the sun and the moon are the preeminent representatives of the Yang and the Yin, whose oppositions and interactions constitute the life of the universe. The sun is the perfect Yang (*Taiyang*), and the moon the very essence of the Yin. The sun is composed of fire, and the moon of water. The fire of the sun could be collected by means of an instrument called *Yangsui,* a kind of bronze mirror; similarly, the lunar dew, also called "luminous water," was collected by means of another mirror called *Fangzhu,* which was square (whereas the *Yangsui* was, appropriately, round): the solar fire and lunar water were used in religious ceremonies.

If the sun is Yang and the moon Yin, one might wonder about the nature of the animals that inhabit them. The black crow is certainly Yin: thus the Yin is in the Yang, according to a fundamental idea that requires that each of the great cosmic principles contains a portion of the opposite principle. For the moon, the question is more subtle. Liu Xiang, in the *Wujing tongyi,* spoke of two animals in the moon and added that the hare is Yin and the toad Yang. Although this last point creates a difficulty (the toad has an affinity with water and with the night; moreover, it is a metamorphosis of Yi's wife), it is interesting that the moon is found to contain the Yin and the Yang, surely because of the alternations of its light and dark phases.

III. The Stars

Ancient China had a highly developed astrology, as can be seen, for instance, in the chapter of the "Governors of the Sky" that Sima Qian devoted to it in *The Historical Accounts* (*Shi Ji,* chap. 27, trans. Chavannes, vol. 3). There were many beliefs about the stars and their connections with human events, but relatively few myths. Among the latter, the most popular was the myth of the weaver woman and the cowherd. According to the legend, the weaver woman descended from the sky on the seventh day of the seventh month; a cowherd saw the woman and took her clothes away from her, which made it possible for him to marry her. But one day she succeeded in recovering her clothes and reascended to the sky. The cowherd pursued her, but the God of the Sky separated them with the help of the Milky Way; they can be reunited only once a year, on the seventh day of the seventh lunar month (Eberhard, *Typen,* no. 34: *Schwanenjungfrau,* following various sources). This version is late, for the ancient texts speak only of two lovers who are two stars separated by the Milky Way, which they can surmount only at the time of the festival of the seventh month; they succeed with the assistance of magpies who assemble to form a bridge (this motif already figured in the *Huainanzi,* if a citation from the *Baishe liu ti* is to be believed). The Milky Way was a celestial river and still bears the name of the Han (*Tian Han*).

The festival of the seventh day of the seventh month was a women's festival connected with fertility. In that festival, women moved wax dolls down a stream of water in order to obtain children. It was also a festival in which girls "asked for skill" in their labors and resorted to various methods of divination to find out which among them would be the most skillful. Granet connected the myth of the Weaver Woman with ancient Chinese festivals of youth, festivals in the course of which young peasant men and women met at the edge of the water and exchanged songs before coupling (*Festivals and Songs*, pp. 257–58).

IV. Mountains and Rivers

From earliest antiquity, mountains and streams of water were sacred powers to which sacrifices were offered. In the Yin period (second millennium B.C.), people sacrificed to a mountain (called Yue) and to a river (the Huanghe), both of which had the power to give rain and promote the harvest. Under the Zhou, the Son of Heaven was responsible for sacrifices to the "illustrious mountains and the great rivers," that is, to the five sacred peaks (the Wu Yue) and the four great watercourses, the Huanghe, the Yangzi, the Huai, and the Ji. The feudal lords had the right to sacrifice only to the mountains and waterways of their own territory, and they were also the only ones with the power to do so, for it was dangerous to annex a sacred mountain; the mountain might refuse the offerings of the usurper and bring on a drought instead of the rains that it normally produced. A mountain was the source of fertility for the territory that it ruled and stabilized; it protected the inhabitants of that territory and watched over the destiny of the lord of the place. For the empire as a whole, the Five Sacred Peaks had the same functions; laid out (theoretically) at the four corners of space and at the center, they were obligatory stations where the Son of Heaven had to stop to perform sacrifices when he undertook his ritual rounds. The most renowned of these mountains was Taishan, the sacred mountain of Shandong, where the principalities of Qi and Lu were situated. Lying to the east, associated with the Green Emperor, the divinity of the east who presided in the spring, this mountain, more than any other, was a source of life not only for the principalities of Qi and Lu, but for the whole of China. It was on Taishan, we believe, that seventy-two sovereigns since Fuxi performed the *feng* sacrifice, by which they announced to Heaven the complete success of their government. But on a more popular level, the god of Taishan presided over human destinies; he maintained an account of the years of life of each man in a kind of ledger. From the first century A.D., since the later Han, it was believed that the dead went to reside on Taishan, but it is not certain that the god of that mountain was already the infernal judge that he was generally acknowledged to be later.

In the *Baopuzi,* Ge Hong (283–343) said that the great mountains possessed a great divinity, the small mountains a small divinity. This was certainly already true for more ancient times. The *Shanhai Jing,* whose mythical author was Yu the Great, was an illustrated book intended to show the mountains and waterways, first of China proper, then of the regions situated in the Four Seas and beyond; it also described the minerals, plants, more or less strange animals, spirits, and deities that one might encounter there. Some chapters conclude with a recapitulation indicating, for each direction, the deities of the mountains and their half-human, half-animal aspects, as well as the offerings that should be made. But this "practical" information hardly appears to correspond to a reality; it answers rather to religious fiction.

Besides real mountains like Taishan and other sacred peaks, fabulous mountains situated to the far east and far west of ancient China captured the imagination of people in search of immortality. To the east, in the sea, off the shores of Shandong, were the "three holy mountains," which were three islands inhabited by Immortals. Magicians described their wonders to Qinshi Huangdi in these terms:

> It is said of the three holy mountains, Penglai, Fanzhang, and Yingzhou, that they are found in the middle of the Bohai; they are not remote from men, but, unfortunately, when one is on the point of getting there, the boat is pushed back by the wind and turned aside. In former times, people could get there; it is there that the Immortals are found, as well as the drug that prevents death; there all creatures, birds and quadrupeds, are white; the palaces and gates are made of gold and silver there; when these people were not yet there, they saw the mountains from a distance like a cloud; when they arrived, the three holy mountains were turned upside down under the water; when the people were very close to them, a wind suddenly brought their boat back to the open sea.

The emperor Qinshi Huangdi sent a man with a band of children, boys and girls, to search for these islands, but they found "a calm and fertile place" and did not return (see *Historical Accounts* of Sima Qian, trans. Chavannes, vol. 3, chap. 28).

The *Liezi* (chap. 5) relates the story of the islands of the blessed: there were formerly five, inhabited by Immortals who flew from one to the other. The islands drifted at the mercy of the waves and the tides. The celestial emperor commanded a spirit called Yugiang to find fifteen giant tortoises to carry the five mountains on their heads, each in turn, for sixty thousand years. But a giant arrived unexpectedly and fished for six of these tortoises and carried them off, so that two of the islands drifted away and disappeared, and only three islands remained. It is likely that the author of the *Liezi* somewhat embroidered the ancient myth.

The mythical mountain of the west is Kunlun (which has nothing to do with the mountain known by geographers). It is a purely legendary mountain, whose name (with no other information) figures first in the chapter called *Yugong* ("the tribute of Yu") of the *Shu Jing*. The *Tianwen* alludes to the "Hanging Gardens," to the nine tiers of a walled city, to gates that open on the four sides of Kunlun. The *Shanhai Jing* (chap. 11) speaks of Mount Kunlun situated to the west of the Country of Tapirs; it covers an area of eight hundred square *li;* it rises to an altitude of seven or eight thousand feet; an arborescent grain forty feet in height grows there; there are nine wells with jade balustrades, and nine gates, of which the Gate of the Dawn (Kaiming: "Opening of Light") is guarded by a tiger with nine human faces. This mountain is the earthly residence of the Celestial Sovereign and the abode of one hundred deities. Five watercourses have their source there: the Red River, the Yellow River, the Xiang River, the Black River, and finally the Ruo River (whose waters are so feeble that they cannot support even a feather). In another chapter (chap. 16), the *Shanhai Jing* has a slightly different text: Kunlun is a great mountain situated to the south of the Western Sea, at the edge of the Flowing Sands (Liusha) on the other side of the Black River: it is ruled by a spirit with a human face and a tiger's body, with nine white tails; the mountain is surrounded by the waters of the Abyss of the Ruo River; all species of creatures are found there.

In the *Huainanzi* (chap. 4), Kunlun is described in considerable detail, and its size is amplified; chiefly, it is said that plants of immortality grow on this mountain and that it is there that is found the Cinnabar River (Dan Shui), whose water prevents death if it is drunk. Kunlun comprises tiers that one must climb to mount the hierarchy of sanctity: one successively acquires immortality, spiritual power, and finally the divine condition at the moment of reaching the residence of the Supreme Emperor (Tai Di). The latter might be the Yellow Emperor, since the *Mu tianzi zhuan* relates that Mu the Son of Heaven climbed Kunlun to see the palace of Huangdi. But soon it was made the residence of the Xiwang Mu, the Queen Mother of the West who had become queen of the Immortals. Hereafter, Kunlun was a paradise of immortality. "Mount Kunlun . . . is so large that it rises higher than the Sun and the Moon. It has nine tiers separated from each other by ten thousand *li*. It is covered by irridescent clouds and when one looks at it from below, one seems to see the walls of a city with porticos. . . . Crowds of Immortals mounted on dragons or cranes frolic there" (*Shiyi Ji*). Another text, drawn from the *Shanyi Jing* and cited in the *Shuijingzhu*, speaks of Kunlun and the Xiwang Mu: on Kunlun, there is a bronze column, so high that it penetrates the Sky; it is what is called the Column of the Sky; its circumference is three thousand *li*; it is perfectly round as if it had been polished. At its foot, there is a revolving room with the nine administrations of Immortals. At its summit, there is a great bird called Xiyou; it faces south; its extended left wing covers the Dongwanggong (Venerable King of the East); its right wing covers the Xiwang Mu; on its back there is a small space without feathers that measures nineteen thousand *li*; the Xiwang Mu climbs there once a year to pay a visit to the Dongwanggong.

The text of the *Shiyi Ji* cited above adds that in the western countries, Kunlun is given the name of Sumeru. Although there may be certain resemblances between these two mythical mountains, the resemblances appear only in relatively late descriptions; the earliest descriptions, those of the *Shanhai Jing*, betray no Indian influence. In the *Yuben Ji* (*Annals of Yu*), a lost work cited by Sima Qian in his final account of chapter 123 of the *Shi Ji* (*Da yuan zhuan*), it is said that Kunlun is the place where the sun and the moon hide, each in turn, and that a brilliant light emanates from there. This image could come from the myth of Sumeru, as could the image of the rivers that spring from the four sides of the mountain. But the light attributed to Kunlun is not necessarily due to a foreign influence. In the *Shanhai Jing* (chap. 2), in connection with Mount Huaijiang where the "Hanging Gardens" of the Sovereign are found (as on Kunlun), Mount Kunlun, which can be seen far to the south, sends forth a great light and effusive vapors. The light is not unexpected, since the mountain is a way of access to Heaven, a belief confirmed by the *Lunheng*, in which one reads that people who wish to reach heaven must pass through Kunlun, for it is there, to the northwest of the world, that the Gate of the Sky is found. It is also there, according to the *Shanhai Jing* (chap. 16), that the Mountain of the Sun and the Moon is found; this mountain is the axis of the Sky and seems to be identical to the Gate of the Sky mentioned immediately after, which is the place of the passage of the Sun and the Moon. (There is a strange deity there, with a human face but no arms, and with both his feet pulled up over his head.) All of these representations are simultaneously confused and in the end rather coherent in their fundamental themes. Kunlun is in the west, with the setting sun; but it is also a way of access to the sky; it is the Column of the Sky, so it is central. It is a paradise of immortality, and after having been the earthly residence of the Celestial Sovereign or the Yellow Emperor, it became, in popular belief, the place where the palace of the Xiwang Mu and of the Immortals who surround her is situated.

Among the numerous deities of the waterways that ancient China recognized (among them several female deities), the god of the Yellow River, Hebo, is by far the most important. The name signifies properly the "Count of the River," but the sense of the epithet is uncertain. It may be a simple, respectful way of naming the deity, but it may also be a true title, for according to the *Li Ji* ("Treatises on Rites," one of the Confucian classics), sacred mountains and waterways received the titles of ministers or lords.

The river god had a name: Bingyi (or Fengyi). For Daoist authors, he was a man who, having consumed an elixir and obtained the Dao, became an "Immortal of the Water." He drowned trying to cross the river, and the Celestial Sovereign bestowed on him the office of Count of the River (*Baopuzi*, cited in the commentary on the *Chuci, Jiuge*). The *Huainanzi* describes him as one who drives a chariot in the brilliance of the sun and in a kind of whirlwind, to climb to Kunlun, where he is swallowed up by the Gate of Heaven. The *Shanhai Jing* says that Bingyi inhabits a certain abyss and that he has a team of two dragons.

One ancient legend, of which only elements remain, makes Hebo and Yi the archer adversaries, perhaps because of an amorous rivalry. Hebo's wife was the goddess of the Luo River; Yi dreamed that he had relations with this divinity and the *Tianwen* seems to say that he drew his bow against the Count of the River and took the Lady of the Luo as his wife. According to another version of this event, Hebo transformed himself into a white dragon and went for a walk in this guise at the edge of the water. Yi caught sight of Hebo and shot an arrow at him that hit him in his left eye. Hebo complained to the Celestial Sovereign, who dismissed the matter (*Tianwen* and commentary).

According to the *Huainanzi*, it is because the Count of the River killed people by drowning them that Yi shot his arrows at him and hit him in the left eye. That is entirely consistent with the belief that people who have drowned are dangerous spirits (except for the female deities of the waters, like the goddess of the Luo), but it is also consistent with the fact that Hebo required human victims. At least, there was a time when sorceresses "gave maidens in marriage to the Count of the River." They chose a girl from the population and adorned her as a married woman; she was placed on a bed that was made to float on the water of the river but then drifted from the shore and sank. This practice was suppressed by Ximen Bao when he was sent by the marquess Wen of Wei (424–387) to undertake the work of canalization at Ye, a town where the cult was established. Another cult site was at Linjin at the confluence of the Yellow River and the Luo River. In 417 B.C., the duke of Qin seized the town and "then began to give princesses to the river as wives." It is probable that there was formerly a popular cult there analogous to the cult at Ye. At Qin it was practiced to secure the god's protection and also to annex an important cult in some way.

V. The Cardinal Directions

The importance of the directions in the thought and life of the Chinese cannot be exaggerated. Each of the directions of space had its specific characteristics and each was linked by a complex system of correspondences, not only to cosmic forces, to all kinds of beings and deities, but even to the weather, for each cardinal sector corresponded to a season. Therefore, it was never a matter of indifference to know how and where a town, house, temple, or tomb was to be constructed. Such was the case from the time of the Yin, who already connected the idea of death and disease with the north. As in subsequent periods, the dead were interred toward the north. Moreover, information has been obtained from the names of the winds that figure on some inscribed

The Grand Emperors of the Five Peaks accompanying the Grand Emperor of Literature and his assistants.

fragments. There were four winds (later, there were eight), each with a name. The names are found again, as are the names of the directional sectors from which the winds originate, in ancient texts such as the *Shanhai Jing* and the *Shu Jing* (*Yaodian*). It is certain that the north wind brought epidemics. Later, the spirit of the north, Boqiang or Yuqiang, was a great demon of pestilence (*Tianwen* and commentary). The *Shanhai Jing* describes him as a spirit with a human face and the body of a bird, who has a green serpent in each ear and tramples two red serpents underfoot. The same passage speaks of a mountain at the north pole of the world, but it is rather an abyss, for it is there that the waters of the sea come to be swallowed up: it is the Tiangui (celestial *gui*). The *gui* of this expression represents, according to the *Shuowen,* which provides another, more current way of writing, the waters that flow down from the four directions and into the interior of the earth. *Gui* is also a cyclical character, the last of the denary series; it is preceded by the character *ren,* which represents an embryo. *Ren* and *gui* in conjunction correspond to the north and to winter. The north was therefore simultaneously the land of unfathomable waters, of the Yin, of death, and the region from which life springs forth. The character *zi* of the duodenary series denoted the far north; but *zi* signifies "egg" or "child." Finally, in the modern language, *Tiangui* means "menses."

From the last centuries B.C., every conception relating to the directions was governed by the theories of the Yin and the Yang and of the Five Elements. It may be recalled that Yin, the feminine principle of darkness, moisture, and cold, characterizes the west and the north; Yang, the masculine principle of light, dryness, and heat, characterizes the east and the south. As for the elements (which have very little to do with the chemical elements), they are distributed in this manner: wood = east; fire = south; earth = center; metal = west; water = north. They are further associated with the seasons: the spring corresponds to the east, the summer to the south, the autumn to the west, the winter to the north, and the center is represented by a short period at the end of summer. Finally, a color is associated with each element-direction-season: east = green; south = red; west = white; north = black; center = yellow. The association with colors had a great importance in rituals and liturgy, for clothes, ornaments, and offerings had to conform to the colors. It was essential in the arrangement of the altar of the God of the Imperial Earth: the altar was square and was composed of clays of different colors oriented as stated above. To confer a fief, the sovereign took a clod of the color corresponding to the direction of the vassal and gave it to the vassal, who added it to his own mound of earth, which therefore had only one color. The system of correspondences certainly involved other domains, in particular the organs of the body, which had consequences for medical or hygienic theories and practices that sought to make the order of the body conform to the order of the universe.

Each cardinal direction was also associated with an emblematic animal. The Four Animals figure, for example, in this passage from the *Li Ji* (*Quli*): "The soldiers on the march have the Red Bird before them, the Dark Warrior behind them; to the left the Green Dragon, to the right the White Tiger." The Dark Warrior is the epithet given to the Tortoise entwined by a serpent—but, fundamentally, the animal of the north is the Tortoise. It is clear that these soldiers are thought to have the south before them and, consequently, the north behind, the Dragon to the east, and the Tiger to the west. Such was the normal, correct orientation of any authority; it was the orientation of the sovereign who "reigns facing the south." But his subjects, in his presence, faced the north, the direction of formidable powers, from which that "Dark Warrior" originates who watches over the north. To create a protected space, it sufficed to arrange around oneself the four Animals, whether represented on banners, as in the case of soldiers on the march, or mentally, as the Daoists did in the course of their meditational exercises.

All of these ideas about the directions, the elements, and colors, also deeply concerned politics and history. In 771 B.C., a duke of Qin instituted the worship of his ancestor Shaohao, who received the ritual name of White Emperor; his sanctuary was called "the holy place of the west." Later, the princes of Qin instituted cults of the Green Emperor, the Yellow Emperor (Huangdi), the Emperor of Flames (Yandi, in other words the Red Emperor). No doubt the princes of Qin wished to secure the protection of the divinities of the territories that had been conquered, or were being conquered, in the different directions. Moreover, Zou Yan (third century B.C.) devised a theory that had great reverberations; it taught that the cosmic order is governed not only by the alternation of the Yin and the Yang, but also by a cyclical alternation of the Five Virtues, that is, by the alternate influence of the Five Elements: each sovereign or dynasty governed in conformity with one of the Virtues. According to Zou Yan, the Virtues succeed one another by overcoming one another. The Sky, moreover, sends omens that announce to the people which virtue predominates: when the time of Huangdi (the Yellow Emperor) came, the Sky caused earthworms and giant crickets to appear, which made Huangdi proclaim that the energies of the Earth were triumphing; he took yellow as his emblem and, in any enterprise, accommodated himself to the element Earth (= center). Yu received omens that made him proclaim the triumph of the element Wood (east); Tang, the founder of the Yin, ruled by the element Metal (west); King Wu of Zou ruled by the element Fire (south); a red crow holding a red written document in his beak came to perch on the altar of the Earth. The *Lüshi Chunqiu* (chap. 13, § 2), which sets forth the sequence of oriented virtues, adds that the Virtue that would replace the Virtue of Fire would necessarily be that of Water, which implies that the author foresaw that Qinshi Huangdi would choose Water and Black as emblems. This question of dynastic Virtues was to occupy a great place in the speculations of historians and philosophers of the Han dynasty.

M.K./b.f.

BIBLIOGRAPHY

E. CHAVANNES, *Le T'ai-chan* (Paris 1910). M. GRANET, 1926, 1929, 1934–68, 1953. M. KALTENMARK, "La naissance du monde en Chine," in *La naissance du monde,* Sources orientales 1 (1959). H. MASPERO, 1924. MORI MIKISABURO, 1969. M. SOYMIE, "La lune dans les religions chinoises," in *La lune, mythes et rites,* Sources orientales 5 (1962).
For full citations, see "Chinese Mythology."

Ancient Chinese Goddesses and Grandmothers

Ancient Chinese mythology includes several female figures who play a more important role in its beliefs than one would have expected from such a patriarchal society. But the patriarchal structure was the culmination of an evolution that began from a form of society in which women had a much more important position. This is demonstrated by certain aspects of the familial organization, as brought to light by Marcel Granet and confirmed by mythological data.

The heroes, and especially the founders, of royal or imperial lineages are not born like mere mortals; they have always been conceived under supernatural circumstances. This is not only true of mythical characters, for the historians relate similar miracles for numerous emperors of every period, and even for some common people. Considering only legends of antiquity (which inspired those of more recent periods), we will cite the most famous cases.

I. Fubao, the Mother of Huangdi

"A great light encircled Polaris and lit up the countryside near the city; it aroused Fubao, who gave birth to Huangdi" (*Hanzhen Wu*, an "apocryphon" of the Shi Jing). As in most of these stories, the mother of the Yellow Emperor finds herself in an uncultivated countryside (*ye*) when she conceives: it is in this sort of spot, which is also a sacred place connected with the ancestor cult, that "irregular" unions of young peasants take place at the time of agricultural festivals. The very name of Fubao evokes the idea of contact with spirits and possession.

II. The Mother of Yu the Great

The mother of Yu the Great sees a shooting star, then swallows a marvelous pearl, which is a *yi-yi* (*Coix lachryma*) seed. Her chest splits open when she gives birth to Yu (commentaries on the *Shiji*). The *Wuyue Chunqiu* specifies that Yu's mother found the seed on a certain mountain, and that when she swallowed it, she had an impression of contact with a man; she became pregnant, and her side split open so she could give birth to Yu, who is here called Gaomi. Medical treatises claim medicinal virtues for *yi-yi* seeds; they are supposed to relieve and purify the body. Here, they are also pearls made of moonlight. This is why the *Weizhou* relate that Yu's mother found, in a spring at the foot of the Rock Knot mountain, a "lunar essence" (*Yuejing*) which resembled an egg; after this she became pregnant. According to another legend, Yu was born from the Rock Knot, and his own son was also born from a rock, since its mother had been petrified and Yu was obliged to split her open with a stroke of his sword in order to have the child. Yu's mother and the Rock Knot are apparently identical.

III. The Daughter of Tushan, the Wife of Yu

"Yu, in the course of his labors, met the daughter of Tushan (Mountain of Earth). Before he met her, he had inspected the southern lands. Tushan's daughter had ordered a servant girl to wait for Yu at the southern foot of Tushan, and she sang a song which said: how handsome is he for whom I wait. This was the source of the southern songs" (*Lushi Chungiu*, chap. 6). The southern songs were love songs which the Confucian orthodoxy condemned as being too licentious. This is another instance of free love, a common theme of the songs of the *Shi Jing*. In the poem entitled *Tianwen*, of the anthology of the land of Chu (*Chuci*), Yu seems to descend from the Sky to have relations with Tushan in a place called the Mulberry Trees of the Terrace. This is certainly an allusion to the celebrated Mulberry Forest, Sanglin, the sacred place of the land of Song (which inherited the Yin cults), in which gatherings of boys and girls took place which were sexual festivals. This is the source of Yu's reputation for dissolute morals (*Lushi Chunqiu*, chap. 11).

The name of Gaomi given to Yu in the *Wuyue Chunqiu* is the

equivalent of Gaomei. Gaomei is the name of a divinity whom the ritualists generally, but not always, considered to be male. According to their explanations, the name is to be translated as "Great Matchmaker." There was a royal, and later imperial, festival of Gaomei which took place in the spring, apparently for the purpose of asking for children. Actually, Gaomei was originally a female divinity whose name probably meant, rather than "Great Matchmaker," the "Great, or First, Mother." The most illustrious of these Mothers were Nüwa, Jiandi, and Jiangyuan.

IV. Nüwa

Nüwa was most worthy of being called a Mother: she created the first men. She shaped them first with yellow soil, then with mud. The men made from yellow earth became the nobles; those made from mud were people of base condition (*Feng su tong*). But her merits do not stop there: like Yu, she battled against the overflowing waters. These had been unleashed by the rebellious monster Gonggong, who had shaken the Sky and Earth when he smashed a pillar of the sky with a thrust of one of his horns. Nüwa repaired the azure sky with stones of five colors, cut the feet off of a tortoise to set up four pillars at the four directions, killed the Black Dragon (Gonggong), and piled up ashes of burnt reeds to stop the overflowing waters (*Liezi* and *Huainanzi*).

We know that Nüwa is the wife and sister of Fuxi and that the two were represented as two serpent-bodied gods with intertwined tails. They were regarded as the inventors of marriage, and it is for this reason, we are told, that Nüwa was honored as the Divine Matchmaker, Shenmei (*Lüshi*).

The "wa" character of Nüwa is defined by the *Shuowen* (a late first-century A.D. dictionary) as "the name of a holy and divine woman of ancient times who produced the ten thousand beings through metamorphosis." The mountain on which Nüwa melted the stones used to repair the Sky is called Huangmu Shan, the Mount of the August Mother (as well as Nüwa Shan). But as Gaomei she must have been a grandmother of the royal house, as were (as we shall see below) the grandmothers of the Yin and the Zhou. This is in fact the case, since she is assimilated in several texts to the daughter of Tushan, who is Yu's wife (*Shiben, Wuyue Chunqiu*). She is thus the same Gaomei as that of the Xia dynasty.

Nüwa not only creates beings by metamorphosis, but she herself constantly changes shape (commentary on the *Tianwen*). There is a rather strange text to this effect in the *Shanhai Jing* (chap. 16): in a certain "countryside" (*ye*) there lived ten genies who were the metamorphosed entrails of Nüwa; they lay across a road, blocking it. "Ten" is perhaps erroneous here, since it would be more understandable for Nüwa's entrails (she is a serpent) to be transformed into a genie, probably a reptile. This reptile blocked a road whose destination is not mentioned in the text but that was surely that sacred "countryside" prohibited to the profane. This is undoubtedly a labyrinth theme.

V. Jiandi, Mother of the Ancestors of the Yin

Jiandi is a wife of Gaoxin (Di Ku). She goes to bathe with two other women; they see a black bird drop an egg. Jiandi picks it up and swallows it. After this she finds that she is pregnant and gives birth to Xie. The *Shiyi Ji*, a fairly late (fourth century) and fantastic work, but one which has preserved many legendary themes, relates this story and ornaments it; but it specifies that Jiandi was walking at Sangye, the Country of Mulberries—this is undoubtedly the Mulberry Forest, Sanglin. The black bird is made into a swallow. The Yin family carries the name of the Zi clan because Jiandi swallowed the egg (*zi*) of a swallow.

This myth of an egg swallowed by the mother of an ancestor appears again in the case of other families, all of which are eastern, or of eastern origin. So it is with the ancestor of the Chin: Nuxiu, a female descendant of Zhuan Xu, was weaving when a black bird dropped an egg, which she ate, after which she gave birth to Daye. In the case of Zhumang, the ancestor of the Fuyu (an ancient Korean kingdom), the myth shows certain variants: the hero's mother is the daughter of the Count of the River; his father the king locks her in a room; sunbeams strike the body of the young girl; no matter where she moves, the sunbeams follow her; she becomes pregnant and gives birth to an egg; Zhumang emerges from the egg (his later adventures show that he is a solar being). There is another variant regarding King Yan of the Hiu, who is famous for having no bones. His mother gives birth to an egg, which she throws into the water. A marvelous dog finds it and brings it back; King Yan is born from the egg. The dog that intercedes here is to be connected with the dog in the myth of Panhu.

VI. Jiangyuan, the Mother of Houzi (Prince Millet), Ancestor of the Zhou

Jiangyuan is also a wife of Di Ku. She goes out to play in the "countryside," where she sees a giant's footprint; she places her foot in it, after which she becomes pregnant. The same legend is recounted of Huaxu, the mother of Fuxi, who finds the giant's footprint in the Marshes of Thunder. The god of thunder lived there with a dragon's body and a man's head: the footprint is thus that of the thunder god. But in the case of Jiangyuan, all the exegetes affirm that this is a Sovereign from On High. The *Shi Jing* has preserved several poems that sing the virtues of Jiandi and Jiangyuan. The commentators do not fail to recall that these women miraculously conceived while on the way to a sacrifice to Gaomei, but they do not explain who Gaomei was.

A poem from the *Shi Jing* is dedicated to Bigung, which was a temple of Jiangyuan or of Gaomei, according to different glosses, but the apparent contradiction is explained if Jiangyuan was Gaomei. This Bigung temple was always closed. The *Yuanmin Bao* (an apocryphon) relates that it was at Bigung, in a place called Fusang (the Solar Mulberry tree), that Jiangyuan stepped in a footprint. Here once again is the theme of the sacred mulberry, solar tree, and holy place.

An important theme that history and poetry do not fail to recall with regard to Jiangyuan and Houzi is that of the mythic ordeal that Houzi was forced to undergo. After she had given birth to him, his mother, "judging this to be a misfortune," decided to abandon him, and exposed him successively in an alley, in a deserted forest, and on a frozen pond: Houzi emerged victorious from these ordeals with the help of the animals that protected him. Granet has shown that behind this myth, which qualifies this hero as a god of the harvest, there lies a rite that prescribed depositing the newborn child on the ground (M. Granet, *Le Dépôt de l'enfant sur le sol*, in *Études sinologiques*).

VII. Xiwang Mu, the Queen of the West

Xiwang Mu is especially known as the queen of the Daoist Immortals. A very popular figure, she is represented as a beautiful lady attended by the "Daughters of Jade." She is represented on Han sculpted stones associated with symbols

The Queen of the West: Xiwang Mu (Qing dynasty). Bronze. Paris, Musée Guimet. Photo Musées nationaux.

of long life. The *Huainanzi* tells a story of the drug of immortality that Yi the Archer obtained from Xiwang Mu and that was stolen from him by his wife Henge, who escaped to the moon. But in the *Shanhai Jing* (*Xishanjing*), this Mother is a demon of plague, who dwells on the Jade Mountain (Yushan) situated far to the west, beyond the flowing sands (Liusha). She has a leopard's tail and tiger's teeth; she wears a jade ornament in her wild hair; she reigns over the stars of plagues, ruin, and punishments. She lives in a cave on the north of Mount Kunlun. Three blue birds bring her her food.

The *Shanhai Jing* is the sole text that presents Xiwang Mu as a demoness. This is probably a survival of an archaic trait that was reinforced by the classical association of the west with punishments and with the decline of the Yang, vegetation, and life in general.

A historical legend from before the Han recounts how, in the tenth century B.C., King Mu of the Zhou met Xiwang Mu while traveling in the west: "He was pleased by her company and forgot to return" (*Shi Ji,* chap. 5). This story is related in the "Novel of the Son of the Mu Sky" (*Mu tionzi zhuan*) in which Xiwang Mu, however, is only a queen of an indeterminate land to the west of China. A commentary on the *Shi Ji* cites a third-century author according to whom the common people call the spirits who preside over the east and west and over the rising and setting of the Yin and the Yang (the sun and the moon), the royal Mother and Father (*Wang fu mu*). From the time of the later Han onward, Xiwang Mu had a consort who resided in the east: this was Dongwanggong (the Venerable King of the East). There may even have been worship offered to this god of the Yang parallel to that offered to the goddess of the Yin, Xiwang Mu (*Wu Yue Chun Qiu*). A great bird on the top of the bronze Column of Kunlun shields Xiwang Mu with his right wing and Dongwanggong with his left (*Shenyi Jing*). But Dongwanggong is much less popular than Xiwang Mu. Xiwang Mu alone is portrayed in legend and in literature, and popular devotion is addressed principally to her. The *Bowuzhi* cites a remark attributed to Laozi according to which the common people place their trust in Xiwang Mu, while the Daoists of the higher levels rely on celestial male deities. The *Bowuzhi* dates from the third century, but an event from 3 B.C. indicates that faith in Xiwang Mu was already alive among the common people at that time. In that year, there was panic among part of the population of Shandtong. Crowds of people carrying "slips of Xiwang Mu," which were probably talismans, took to the road apparently with the goal of visiting the goddess at her residence on Kunlun. The pilgrims sang and danced as they offered sacrifices to the goddess. The *Shoushenji* reports this event and adds that the people had a talismanic writing that ensured immortality to those who carried it.

Since the second century B.C., at least, Xiwang Mu has been an Immortal who has recipes for long life. In a later novel of Daoist inspiration, she wants to teach the recipes to emperor Wu of the Han and offers him marvelous peaches (*Hanwudi Neizhuan*). Daoism would make her the mother of numerous Immortals, among which there reappears an ancient divinity of the land of Chu, the divinity of Wushan, the Mount of the Sorceress.

VIII. The Goddess of Wushan

The Mount of the Sorceress was a sacred place in the land of Chu. It was the abode of a divinity to whom kings offered worship, in a sanctuary, the Gaotang, situated at the summit of the mountain; this sanctuary was the subject of a poem, the *Gaotang fu,* written by a poet from Chu. Legend related that an ancient king of Chu who visited this sanctuary located in the "countryside" (*ye*) of Yunmeng (a region of sacred marshes) saw the divinity in a dream; she revealed her name, Yaoji, to him, and told him that her soul had become a plant used in love magic. The king had relations with this goddess, who was apparently a Gaomei. She figures among the daughters of Xiwang Mu, and bears the name of Blossoming Lady of the Clouds (Yunhua furen); Yu the Great visited the Mount of the Sorceress and asked her help in controlling the waters. She entrusted talismans to him and sent spirits to help him in his task. The *Yongcheng Zixian Lu* of Du Guangting (850–933), which relates this legend, states that there was a sanctuary of the goddess at the foot of the mountain and, across the river, an "altar of the divine girl, the venerable celestial of stone" (*Shitianzun Shen nü tan*). The goddess is said to have turned into a rock. This is obviously a case of conflation with the myth of Yu's wife, which is easily explained if the two heroines were both Gaomei.

IX. Water Goddesses

Among the female deities of ancient China, certain water goddesses should be cited. These are generally women who have drowned and who become associated in legend with illustrious persons. The most famous are the goddess of the Luo River and the two goddesses of the Xiang River. While the souls of drowned persons are generally dreaded demons, these female deities of the rivers are never portrayed as dangerous.

The goddess of the Luo (Luoshen), Mifei (or Fufei), was celebrated by renowned poets. Her legend may be reduced to the following: she was the daughter of Fuxi, and she drowned in the Luo River. She dwells at the confluence of the Luo and the Yi. She was, according to certain texts, the wife of the Count of the River and perhaps the wife of Yi the Archer.

The two divinities of the Xiang are the subject of two liturgical poems of the Jiuge of the *Chu Ci* entitled *Xiangjun* (the princess of the Xiang) and *Xiang furen* (The Lady of the Xiang). The *Shanhai Jing*, 5, says that they lived on an island in Lake Dongting (the Xiang runs into this lake), that they frequented a Chasm of the Lake, and that they brought together the effluvia of the three rivers: they unleash whirlpools and torrential storms. When Qin Shi Huangdi visited the "temple of the Xiang mountain," he encountered a violent tempest and learned that this was the place in which the daughters of Yao, the wives of Shun, were buried. The *Shanhai Jing* simply says that they were the daughters of the Sovereign (from On High), but Yao may very well be taken as a celestial Di. Whatever the case, the legend would have it that Shun took a voyage to the south, and that he died there; his two wives followed him and drowned in the Xiang. In the Tang period, these two divinities of the Xiang were still worshiped.

M.K./d.w.

BIBLIOGRAPHY

W. EBERHARD 1942. L. GRANET 1929. KALTENMARK, "Notes à propos du Kao-mei," *Annuaire de l'École pratique des Hautes Études*, 5th section, 1966–67. K. SCHIPPER, *L'Empereur Wou des Han dans la légende taoïste* (Paris 1965). Full citations in "Chinese Mythology."

Mythical Rulers in China: The Three Huang and the Five Di

Ancient Chinese historians, all more or less Confucian, eschewed anything bizarre and supernatural, things that Master Kong refused to talk about. But when they had to talk about the beginning of history, if not the origin of the world, they resorted to the names of certain deities, heroes, and ancestors derived from various traditions in order to integrate them into a system. The same system was based on metaphysical, moral, and religious concepts, so that ancient myths that came from different local cultures were gradually replaced by a new mythology, an invention of scholars of the last few centuries B.C. It is a genuine mythology, for the heroes that appear have nothing historical about them and fragments of real myths are retrieved by changing their meaning. The historians' task was to extract a moral teaching and to show how the order of the world gradually deteriorated. At the beginning of history, perfect rulers ruled, while recent times have been decadent and violent. Formerly, there was harmony between man and nature, and the sovereign ruler, thanks to his virtue (*De* or *Daode*), had the blessings of Heaven, for Heaven conferred the heavenly mandate (*tianming*) only on virtuous rulers and took it back from evil monarchs. The accord between the ruler and heaven was made manifest by miracles of good omen: the appearance of supernatural animals and plants and of precious objects of talismanic value that were carefully preserved in the dynastic treasury.

Those were the happy times, when the three August Ones and the Five Emperors (*Sanhuang Wudi*) ruled successively. This expression has become a stereotype designating the beginning of history. After these two periods came the Three Kings, or rather the Three Dynasties and the Five Hegemonies (*Sanwang Wupa*). There is significance in the recurrence of the numbers three and five, numbers charged with symbolic value; three is an expression of perfection and totality, and five evokes a cross with its center and is thus an expression of universality. The three royal dynasties are the Xia, the Yin (also known as Shang), and the Zhou. The Xia Dynasty is purely mythical. With the Yin and the Zhou, we enter into history, albeit a history heavily mixed with legend.

I. The Sanhuang (Three August Ones)

Since the time of Qinshih Huangdi (221–210 B.C.), the title for the emperors of China has been *huangdi*. Before that, rulers bore the title of prince (*hou*) or king (*wang*). All of these terms once had religious meaning. *Di* was the highest deity of the Yin, probably identical with their first ancestor. The same term designated the sacrifice that was offered to him. Originally (on bronze inscriptions and in the oldest texts of the Zhou), *Huang* was only an adjectival form expressing the brightness and glory of certain divine beings: Heaven, the Ruler on High, the ancestors. As the name of a god, Huang first appears in the *Lisao* and in the *Jiuge* (The Nine Songs) of *Chuci* (a famous anthology from the land of Chu). These poems attributed to Qu Yuan (332–295 B.C.) must date from the beginning of the period of the Warring States. The *Lisao* mentions a Huang from the West (Xi Huang), and the first of the *Jiuge* (liturgical chants) is dedicated to a deity called Dong Huang Taiyi (Supreme Unity, Huang from the East). In the same poem, the god is also called Shang Huang (Huang from On High): it seems as if *Huang* in this case replaced the *di* of the classical Shangdi, that is, the supreme deity of Heaven. But the Dong Huang Taiyi is certainly the Rising Sun, so it

Fuxi. Portrait album, n.d. (Smith-Lesouef collection). Paris, Bibliothèque nationale. Photo BN.

seems that the sun is identified with the celestial deity. The Xi Huang of the *Lisao* could be the setting sun. Whatever this deity may be in the land of Chu, *Huang* soon came to designate a series of human rulers, the Three Huang. The August Ones (if we keep the translation proposed by Granet) were characterized by a complete and luminous spirituality. Virtue among the succeeding rulers steadily declined. The Di had the intelligence of the *Dao,* the Wang that of the *De;* as for the Ba (The Hegemonies), all they knew was the use of military force (*Guanzi*). The *Fengsu-tongyi* (second century A.D.) celebrates the Three Huang whose action, or rather inaction, is like that of Heaven, which does not speak or move, leaving the natural and vital rhythms free to follow their own course.

When the Zheng king of Qin had completed the unification of China, the title of the emperor was deliberated. His ministers proposed the title of *Tai Huang* (the Supreme August One), and explained that "long ago, there was the Celestial August One (*Tien Huang*), the Earthly August One (*Di Huang*), and the Supreme August One, the latter being the highest in dignity." But the emperor refused this title and declared that his title would be Huangdi, adding to *Huang* the "imperial title of high antiquity" (*di*). Qinshih Huangdi felt that he embodied the virtues of the Three August Ones and the Five Di. The *Lüshi Chunqiu* composed in Qin in 239 B.C. already spoke of the San Huang without actually identifying them. As for the Di, we shall see that they were said to be historical emperors, but also celestial deities who had played a key role in the religious history of the new emperor's own family. The Chinese of those remote periods did not distinguish ancient rulers from celestial deities; they usually assimilated them without reaching agreement as to their real identities, which differed depending on the regions. There seems to have been in Qin a series of three *Huang,* one of heaven, one of earth, and one supreme *Huang.* But this concept evolved under the Han when the *Tai Huang* was replaced by the *Huang* of Man, in keeping with an idea very much in vogue at this time, whereby heaven, earth, and man constituted a sort of triad representing the three great spiritual forces of the universe. But these rather abstract entities could not fit into the overall picture if the Three August Ones were historical rulers. Therefore the three *Huang* became three individuals chosen from among prestigious mythological figures who were later transformed into important people of antiquity. We do find, however, in the *Weishu* (apocrypha completing the Confucian classics) and in other works, several lists that diverge about one of the characters but agree in making Fuxi and Shennong two of the Three August Ones. The third is sometimes Nüwa, although she is well known in other contexts (being not only Fuxi's wife, but also an independent deity); sometimes Zhurong, a god of fire; or else Suiren, an inventor of fire and of cooked food. We shall limit our remarks here to Fuxi and Shennong.

Fuxi (or Paoxi) was from the time of the Han dynasty regarded as the oldest ruler, but, curiously enough, the historian Sima Qian makes virtually no reference to him. Yet he was famous through two separate legends. He was, first, the inventor of the eight trigrams that were the basis for the hexograms of the Yi Jing. Consequently, the great appendix to this classic, the *Xici,* refers to him in the following terms, taken from the Annals of the *San Huang,* which Sima Qian added to the *Shi Ji:* "Lifting up his head, he contemplated the figures that are in the sky; lowering his head, he contemplated the forms that are on the earth. All around him, he contemplated the brightly colored birds and animals and also what belongs to the soil. Closer to him, he considered all the parts of his body; in the distance, he considered all living creatures. He was the first to trace the eight trigrams by means of which he gained access into the potency of divine spirits and separated into distinct classes the varying natures of beings. He was the first to regulate marriage between man and woman. . . . He built nets and snares and taught hunting and fishing. . . . He built a lute with thirty-five strings." According to this text, Fuxi invented the divinatory diagrams when he was inspired by heavenly and earthly phenomena and by living creatures, including his own body. He did all this at a time when writing did not exist. Divinatory symbols in fact constituted a universal symbolism far more meaningful than any other kind of writing. He is also credited with inventing a kind of notation system that operates by means of knotted ropes. In the postscript of the *Shuowen,* this invention is attributed to Shennong, but the attribution to Fuxi is quite reasonable, since he was also the inventor of nets.

According to another mythical depiction of Fuxi, certainly a very popular one, he had the body of a snake. That is how he is depicted on several sculpted stones of the Shandong, as part of a couple with his wife Nüwa, who also has the tail of a serpent: the two tails are intertwined. In these images, Fuxi holds a carpenter's square and Nüwa, a compass; in this they are visibly a pair of demiurges who hold in their hands the symbols of their creative and civilizing virtues. But according to Chinese concepts about circles and squares (associated, respectively, with heaven and earth, and with Yang and Yin), we would normally expect Fuxi to hold the compass and

Nüwa, the carpenter's square. Here, their attributes are reversed, and this reversal may be explained by a rather subtle philosophical idea: Yin and Yang are effective only through one another, by mutual collaboration. This is also shown by the illustrated representations of the sun and the moon in which the Yang star is inhabited by a Yin animal, and the Yin star is inhabited by a Yang animal. We should, however, note that Nüwa, the wife of Fuxi (and also his sister—which brings in a different theme, the theme of the primordial couple or the couple that survived the flood), was also, and principally, an independent deity about whom there were many more legends than about Fuxi (who remains a rather dim figure).

Shennong, the Divine Plowman and the second August One, is, as his name implies, a god of farming, but he also became a god of fire because he was assimilated to the god of fire, Yandi, who was really an independent deity. The assimilation nevertheless prevailed, and Shennong became a god of the fire used to clear fields: "He struck the weeds and trees with a red whip" (*Mémoires historiques,* vol. 1, p. 13). "He was the first to test the hundred species of plants and the first to find healing drugs" (ibid.). This is the second feature of Shennong: he is the patron god of doctors and apothecaries. The first *Bencao* (treatise on medicinal plants) is attributed to him, as is the invention of markets and commercial trading. As a result of his identification with Yandi, he was made the adversary in a fight with the Yellow Emperor Huangdi, though the battle between Yandi and Huangdi itself is merely a double of the battle between Huangdi and Chiyou. But there is nevertheless a trait held in common by Shennong and Chiyou: both of them have horns; but Chiyou was most probably a fighting bull, while Shennong, the god of agriculture, was a peaceful plowing buffalo.

Shennong. Portrait album, n.d. (Smith-Lesouef collection). Paris, Bibliothèque nationale. Photo BN.

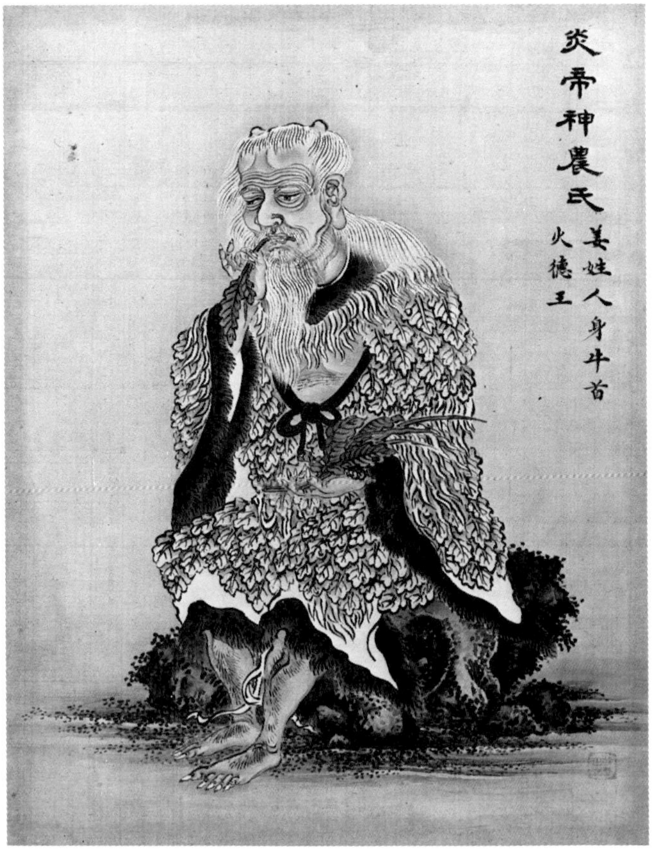

II. The Wudi (Five Emperors)

For the historian Sima Qian, the Five Emperors whose reign marks the beginning of his *History* (*Shi Ji*) were human rulers who lived in very remote times, with no particular chronology. He acknowledges that the Confucian classics, especially the *Shu Jing,* do not mention them, at least the first two, Huangdi and Zhuan Xu. For the orthodox, history begins with Yao. But Sima Qian conducted his investigation in several regions, questioning "notables and old men"; he noticed that there were other accounts besides the official versions, and that those accounts could not be neglected. He does, however, warn the reader that he has expurgated the information obtained by word of mouth or in noncanonical texts. He thus reestablishes history, free of anything supernatural and thus true to life. Fortunately, the commentaries partially compensate for this shortcoming by referring to ancient sources that sometimes betray the true character of these rulers: they were actually the divine ancestors of different clans and the heroes of many myths and legends, of which we unfortunately have only scattered fragments.

Huangdi (the Yellow Emperor). Huangdi has remained a highly popular figure to this day. He was connected with enough legends to perpetuate his memory, and he was above all the inventor of numerous crafts, so that many guilds recognized him as their patron. He was credited with treatises on medicine (among them the classic of Chinese medicine, the Huangdi Neijing), sexuality, astrology, and the martial arts. His yellow color gives him a central position with respect to the other emperors, so that, more than the others, he represents absolute sovereignty. To a great degree, he is the equivalent of the Ruler on high. In antiquity, he was the ancestor of a dozen clans.

His personal name is Xianyuan. "His mother, Fubao, went to take a walk in the country (*ye*), and saw great lightning around the Big Dipper. She was aroused, and she conceived. Twenty-four months later, she delivered Huangdi on the mound of Shou (longevity) or on the mound Xianyuan, after which he was named." This legend is built on the same model as numerous supernatural ideas that embellish the biographies of heroes or rulers. Their prototype is the mating of young peasant men and women in the "brush" (*ye,* "uncultivated fields") during spring festivals, a custom that is well described by Granet through the love songs of the *Shi Jing.* The event that marked the reign of Huangdi was the combat that he waged against a rebel, Chiyou. He is also said to have fought against Shennong, who is identified with the Emperor of Fire, but the original myth probably included only one battle. According to certain texts, Chiyou had seventy-two or eighty-one brothers. "The eighty-one brothers had the bodies of animals and human voices, brass heads, and iron foreheads. They ate sand. They invented arms" (Granet, *Danses et légendes,* p. 354, citing the *Guizang*). "The seventy-two brothers had brass heads and iron foreheads. They ate iron and stones. In the province of Ji, when one digs into the ground and finds skulls that appear to be made of brass or iron, these are the bones of Chiyou" (*Shuyi Ji*). This monstrous rebel, whose head had horns, fought with Huangdi. When he fought with his horns, no one could resist him. He was, however, defeated at Zhuolu in northern Hebei, but his tomb was thought to be in Shandong. At the

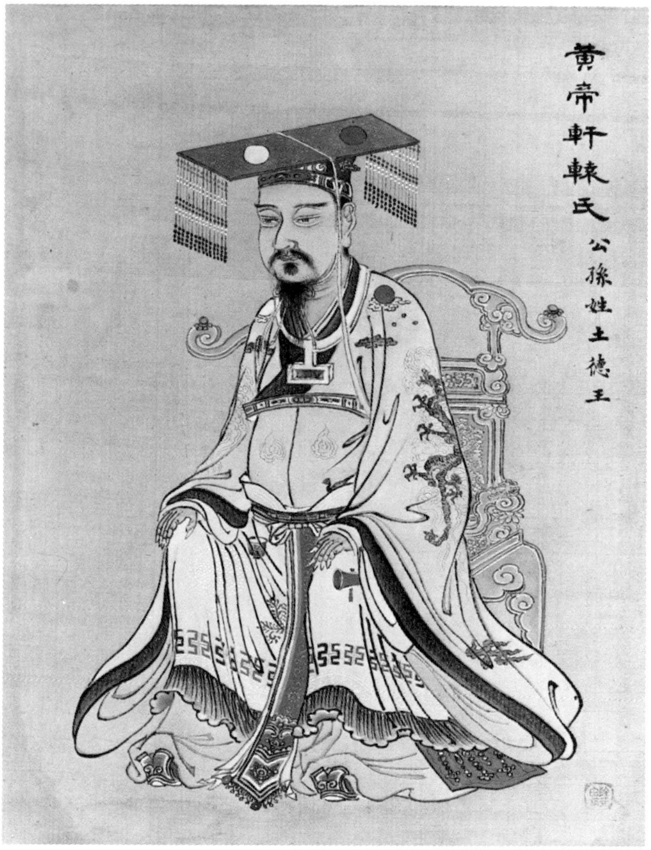

Huangdi. Portrait album, n.d. (Smith-Lesouef collection). Paris, Bibliothèque nationale. Photo BN.

battle of Zhuolu, Chiyou caused a thick fog to spread so that Huangdi and his soldiers lost their way. But Heaven sent down a "Dark Girl" (Xuannü) who taught Huangdi how to use the compass and gave him a military talisman. This was really a struggle between magic of two kinds: Chiyou called on the gods of wind and rain, but Huangdi called down a daughter of Heaven called Ba, Drought. He also enlisted the aid of a winged dragon, Yin. After the death of Chiyou, whenever trouble arose, all Huangdi had to do was draw an effigy of his defeated enemy to exact respect from the empire.

During this memorable struggle, Huangdi invented a war drum: "In the eastern sea, on Mount Liubo, there is an animal called Gui. It looks somewhat like an ox, all blue and hornless, and it has only one leg. Whenever it comes in or out, there is wind and rain. It is bright like the sun and the moon. Its roars sound like thunder. Huangdi took hold of it and used its hide to make a drum which he beat with one of the bones of the Beast of Thunder. The noise could be heard five hundred *li* away and exacted respect from the whole empire" (*Shanhai Jing* 14).

Outside of the battle of Zhuolu, the event that fired the imagination the most was the final apotheosis of Huangdi. The myth has a Daoist flavor and was in fact used by the Daoists as an exemplary story. In order to persuade Emperor Wu of the Han that he ought to follow the example of Huangdi, who was able to enter into communication with the gods and to perform the Feng sacrifice to Heaven, one of the *fangshi* (magicians) of his court tells him of this apotheosis in the following words: "Huangdi took copper from Mount Shoushan and forged it into a tripod at the foot of Mount Jing. When the tripod was finished, a dragon with a hanging dewlap beard came down to fetch Huangdi. Huangdi mounted the dragon. His ministers and his wives, numbering seventy, mounted behind him. Then the dragon rose up. The other subordinate officers, who had not been able to mount him, hung on to the dragon's beard. The strands were torn out and the officers fell; they knocked down Huangdi's bow. The crowd looked up and beheld (the apotheosis) from afar. When Huangdi reached heaven, the people below, crying out, picked up his bow and the hairs of the dewlap. This is why succeeding generations have called this place 'tripod lake' and the bow has been called 'the cry-of-the-crow'" (*Mémoires historiques,* vol. 3, p. 488). According to the *Feng su tung* and a commentary of the *Huainanzi* quoted in footnotes by Chavannes, the "cry of the crow" (*wu hao*) is the mulberry tree that is used for dye. When a crow is perched on a branch of this tree, the branch bends down to the ground; the crow does not dare to fly and cries out (*hao*); the branch is cut and an arrow is made of it; this is how the bow gets its name. This legend recalls the solar crows shot by the archer Yi. The fact that the crow is perched on a branch of the mulberry tree from which a bow is made is significant, because the mulberry tree is a solar tree. Recall, too, that during an eclipse, arrows were shot to rescue the sun. Here Huangdi reappears as a sun. Although yellow is the color of the element earth, it is also the color of gold (*huangjin,* "yellow metal"), which is a solar essence.

Zhuanxu. Zhuanxu is a less-defined individual, but he too seems to be a sun. He is called Gaoyang (the great Yang). Like the sun, he bathes in a pit. He fought against Gonggong, the rebel who threw the world into havoc and caused a great flood. He is an ancestor of the princes of Chu and of Qin. The *Pohu tong* states that he wore the *wu* sign on his head (the cyclical sign of the south). He is the ruler responsible for the separation of Heaven and Earth, because "he ordered the leader of the south, Zhong, to look after heaven and thus to have the gods under his care; he ordered the leader of the fire, Li, to look after the earth and to have the people under his care. He saw to it that [the gods and the people] observed anew the ancient rule, did not encroach on one another, and stopped being negligent" (*Mémoires historiques,* vol. 3, pp. 324–25). Zhuanxu is also known to have had three sons who became demons: one resides in the Blue River (the Yangtzi) and became a demon of fever; another became a demon of the waters and the woods; the third one dwells inside houses and frightens children. These demons were expelled in the twelfth month during the No ceremony.

Gaoxin. Gaoxin, or Emperor Gu (Di Ku), about whom the historian has virtually nothing to say, is interesting because of his wives, who are mothers of the royal races, impregnated through the action of Heaven. One of them is the mother of ten suns; another is the mother of twelve moons. Modern epigraphers assimilate this emperor to the ancestor Gui, who figures in Yin oracle inscriptions. Sometimes called Di Xun, he may have been a solar crow.

Yao. Yao is one of the principal figures of Confucianism, appearing as a model of virtue in the *Shu Jing* and other classics. With this ruler, we enter into orthodox history. The *Shu Jing* depicts him as taking pains to establish the calendar "in order to indicate the seasons carefully to the people." To this end, he made use of six individuals: Xi and He, two younger brothers of Xi, and two younger brothers of He. The first two were assigned to watch the sky and to calculate the movement of the sun and the moon. The last four were in charge of the seasons. The youngest brother of Xi lived in the east and took care of spring. The next youngest lived in the south and took care of summer. He's youngest brother lived in the west and took care of autumn; and the next youngest lived in the north and took care of winter. The youngest brother of Xi and the youngest brother of He governed "with respect" the exit and reentry of the sun (*Mémoires historiques*, vol. 1, p. 43ff.; Granet, *Danses*, vol. 1, p. 252ff.). By instituting "the offices of Xi and He," Yao "clarified the seasons and rectified measurements; as a consequence, Yin and Yang were in harmony, the wind and rain were well regulated, bounty and good influences prevailed; the people stopped suffering untimely deaths and illnesses." We have here a perfect example of the distortion of an ancient mythology in order to create a new one. The purpose is to show how a ruler worthy of this name organizes time and space, which are interdependent in Chinese thought. Originally, Xi and He were just one name, Xihe, a name borne by a goddess who was the mother of the ten suns.

In the system of basic virtues (*Wude*), according to which each ruler or dynasty reigns under the sign of one element, Yao comes under the sign of fire. His name may have some connection with fire, and the fact that he was held in fiefdom to Tao ("pottery") would associate him with the crafts of fire. But all of this remains uncertain. What is known is that the Han emperors regarded Yao as their ancestor, starting with the time when this house chose fire as the color of the dynasty.

Shun. When Yao became old, he did not transfer his power to his son but to a pious man of the people, named Shun, who is also, for Confucians, a model of virtue and especially a model of filial piety. There are many ancient legendary elements in his "biography." Before succeeding Yao, Shun underwent a certain number of trials. The first one was his own marriage: Yao gave him his two daughters as wives. He also entrusted him with his nine sons to see what kind of leader of men he was. This was a double test, good for the "inside" (*nei*), that is, private family life, and for the "outside" (*wai*), that is, public life. Shun passed both tests splendidly, and, most notably, his wives "did not insultingly boast of their nobility . . . [and] they served their parents-in-law." Unfortunately, the parents-in-law were bad. "Shun's father, Gu Sou, was blind. When Shun's mother died, the father took another wife who bore Xiang ('elephant'). Xiang was arrogant. Gu Sou loved his son by his second wife and relentlessly sought to do away with Shun." As a result, there were more trials: "Shun's parents sent him to repair the attic; they took away the ladder and Gu Sou set the attic on fire." Shun used two large hats as a parachute and escaped death. A second trial was imposed: to dig a well. When he was at the bottom, his father and brother threw in enough dirt to fill the well, but Shun escaped through a side exit that he devised. Thus he was victorious in this double test of fire and water. But he escaped these dangers with the help of his wives, the daughters of Yao, for he was able to get down from the burning attic because they had taught him "the art of the bird," and he emerged from the well because they had taught him "the art of the dragon," which made it possible for him to come out of the earth.

Shun underwent yet another trial. Yao sent him into a great forest on the mountain. "There was a violent wind, thunder, and rain; he was not troubled. Yao then recognized that Shun was worthy of being given the empire."

No sooner had Yao transferred his power to Shun than the latter proceeded to a quadruple expulsion; he eliminated four monsters or demons (depicted as rebels) that were the "harmful remnants of once Sovereign Virtues whose rule had come to an end" (Granet, after the *Tso Chuan*). This is how the *Shi Ji* summarizes the event: "When Shun went to welcome his guests at the four gates, he exiled the four criminal families and banished them to the four frontiers, so as to bring the demons under his sway. Then the four gates were opened and it was announced that there were no more criminals." The four gates are probably the gates of the capital, but they could also be the gates of the Mingtang, a kind of square temple from which the sovereign ruler regulates time-space by circling it like the sun. From his capital or his temple, Shun, the ideal sovereign, receives his vassals, who bring tribute to him, and expels to the ends of the world the agents of his predecessor, in order to subdue the demons who in this context are merely the Barbarians at the borders. But there was another version of the legend of Shun according to which he behaved quite differently toward his king and toward his father and brother: he reduced Yao to the condition of his vassal, banished his father Gu Sou, and killed his young brother (*Hanfeizi*). The old chief was thus eliminated by force, as was his elderly father, and especially his younger brother. Myths of this kind were, however, too much at variance with the Confucian ethic, and they were practically expelled from the written accounts. One would have liked to know more about the connection between Shun and elephants. His brother is an elephant; elephants plow the fields for Shun in Cangwu (in the Guangxi). Xiang the

Yao. Portrait album, n.d. (Smith-Lesouef collection). Paris, Bibliothèque nationale. Photo BN.

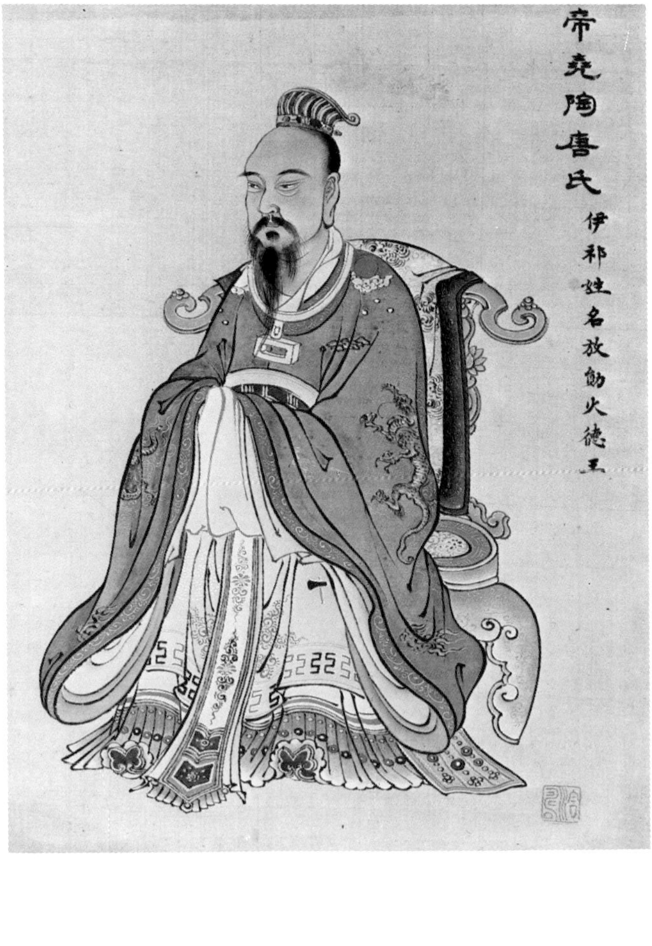

elephant, Shun's brother, received as a fiefdom a domain called Yubi hsü (domain of the nose), where there was a temple of Xiang at the foot of a mountain (*Shuijing zhu,* 38). These legends must go back to the time of the Yin dynasty, because archaeology has shown that elephants were common then, although they are not mentioned later. This would also confirm the identification of Shun with Di Ku as the ancestor of the Yin and therefore as someone from the east. Mencius recalled that Shun was a Barbarian from the east, and he tells that in his time there were still popular traditions about him in eastern Qi, in Shandong.

Yu. Yu is one of the most renowned heroes of ancient China. He succeeded Shun, who gave his throne to him just as Yao had done for Shun. But since Yu's own son succeeded him, he (Yu) became the founder of the first dynasty, that of the Xia; that is why he is called Yu of the Xia and, often, the Great Yu or Yu the Great (Da Yu), because of his great merits. He is most famous for having fought against the unleashed waters of a great flood that suddenly struck in the time of Yao and continued during the reign of Shun. Yao had first appointed the father of Yu, Gun, to stop the flood, but Gun failed and was put to death. Yu inherited his task and succeeded at the cost of heroic efforts that left him half paralyzed and crippled.

Many texts reveal the mythical character of Gun and Yu. Both were demiurges who were the first to organize the fields (*bu tu*) and stabilize the nine provinces, that is, the entire territory of the empire. But Gun rebelled, furious for not being named minister (*sangong*). Shun had him dismembered on the Mount of Feathers. He then transformed himself into a yellow animal; it is unclear whether this animal was a bear or a turtle. As this animal went into some kind of hole, chances are it was a turtle, although the reading of "bear" is not impossible, since Yu can change into a bear at any given moment. The etymology of their names, however, suggests that Gun and Yu were aquatic animals.

According to the written tradition, Gun fought the flood by using a system of dikes, while Yu dug channels: actually, he cut through mountains. But according to many texts (*Shanhai Jing, Tianwen, Huainanzi*), Yu used the same methods as Gun, diked the waters, plugged the openings, and so forth. Gun was punished not so much for his poor technique as for stealing from the Ruler on High the magic (swelling) earth he used to build the dikes and walls. Furthermore, Yu used the same swelling earth to make great mountains. Yu appears as a true architect of the world, which he surveyed from east to west and north to south, so that one encounters "traces" of him almost everywhere (a prominent theme in the ancient literature).

After he had organized the world, Yu presided over the Great Mounts and Great Rivers (*ming shanchuan:* the sacred mountains and rivers of the territory). He summoned the deities of the mountains and rivers in a great assembly on Mount Guiji, which is his sacred mountain. At this assembly, the giant Fangfeng arrived late and was killed by Yu. Fangfeng, perhaps a wind god, had a dragon head with one eye; his descendants tried to rise up against Yu but lost their nerve and stabbed themselves in the chest. Yu revived them, and ever since then there has been a people known as "stabbed chests." As chief of the divinities of the mountains and rivers, Yu was worshiped as a "god of the soil" (*she*), just as Hou Ji, the ancestor of the Zhou, a god of farming, became the "god of the harvest" (*ji*). Together they are called Yu and Ji, just as the altars of the soil and the harvest together formed a double sanctuary that in official cults symbolized dynasty and homeland.

The fact that Yu became a god of the soil must be connected with the name of his wife, the daughter of Tushan, the mountain of the earth. This daughter was one of the "licentious" girls celebrated in the *Shi Jing* and condemned by moralists. She met Yu in the "countryside" (*ye*), among the mulberry trees, an instance of the typical theme of meetings on a holy site. This theme characterizes the "irregular" but common love affairs among young peasant men and women during seasonal festivals and is also associated with miraculous conceptions by mothers of heroes. One day Yu's wife saw her husband turn into a bear at the wrong time. She was turned to stone, but since she was pregnant, Yu had to cut her open with his saber to get his son. Yu himself was born of a stone. There is surely a connection between these split stones, the labors of Yu in drilling into mountains, and the standing stones that once adorned the mounds of the soil, along with trees, and which also constituted at least one element of the shrines of Gaomei, the Great Mediator, or Great Mother. Unfortunately, the texts say almost nothing about these sites of archaic cults, but it appears that there were female deities of the soil beside, or before, the male deities of the soil who are discussed in the classics.

The Rulers of Perdition. The Xia and Yin dynasties founded by heroes worthy of the heavenly mandate were ruined by two kings who lost the mandate because of their misbehavior. The texts tirelessly attribute the most scandalous acts and the most horrible crimes to them. Jie, the last of the Xia, and

Shun. Portrait album, n.d. (Smith-Lesouef collection). Paris, Bibliothèque nationale. Photo BN.

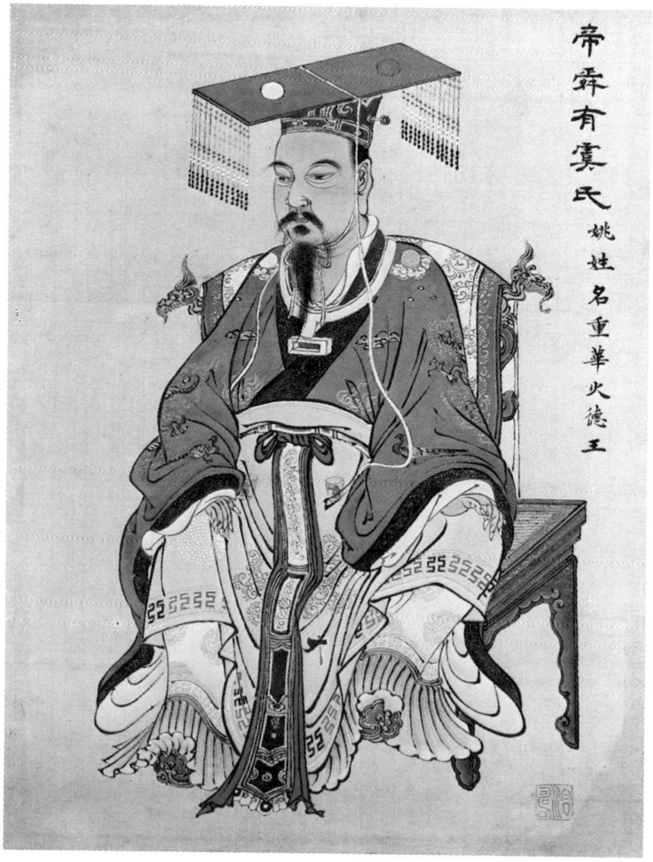

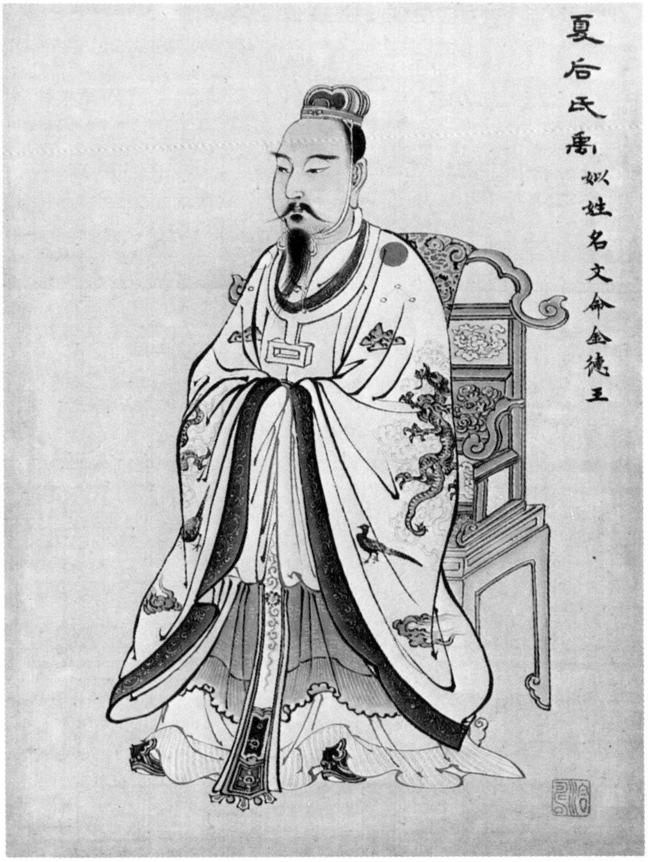

Yu the Great. Portrait album, n.d. (Smith-Lesouef collection). Paris, Bibliothèque nationale. Photo BN.

Zhouxin, the last of the Yin, were tyrants for whom historians use the same themes. Both loved luxury and debauchery. They were excessive and "had special talents for evildoing." Zhouxin had superhuman strength; he could crush wild animals with his bare hands. He invented cruel methods of punishment and torture, such as torture on a metal beam placed over a fire. These evil rulers left their principal wives and amused themselves with beautiful captive women, like Daji, who loved to attend torture sessions. They commissioned lascivious music and dances. This music was ill-fated. When Zhouxin was defeated, his music master drowned himself in the river, and at night one could hear his melodies coming from the riverbanks, but "whoever first hears them, his kingdom shall be diminished" (*Hanfeizi*). Zhouxin "gave great parties at Shaqiu (the hill of sand where the tyrant had had parks and terraces built). He created a pond of wine; he suspended great cuts of meat so as to make them look like forests; he sent naked men and women to seek one another there; he gave orgies that lasted all night." These tyrants did not heed any remonstrances and killed the sage who voiced them. Thus the sage Bigan admonished Zhouxin, who replied, "I have heard that the heart of a sage has seven openings," and he cut Bigan in two to look at his heart. The best counselors fled: "The great tutor and the second tutor of the Yin took their sacrificial utensils and their musical instruments and took shelter with Wu, king of the Zhou." Wu took charge of a group of lords to attack Zhouxin, who lost the battle: "He [Zhouxin] climbed up on the Terrace of the Deer; he put on his clothes adorned with precious jewels, threw himself into the fire, and died. Wu, king of the Zhou, then cut off Zhouxin's head and hung it from a white standard; he killed Daji."

The fall of the tyrants was announced by disorders of nature: stars falling from the sky, earthquakes, mountains collapsing, rains of earth, women turning into men, and the appearance of two suns, one setting and symbolizing the tyrant, the other rising and symbolizing the new Son of Heaven. This final theme is not a mere image, but recalls the solar character of the ancient kings. On the list of the first eight Yin kings, it is noteworthy that the names of the second, fourth, sixth, and eighth designate four moments in the day, four positions of the sun: Zhaoming, morning; Changro, noon; Ming, evening; and Wei or Hunwei, night.

M.K./g.h.

BIBLIOGRAPHY

ERKES, *Zur Sage von Shun* (T'oung-pas 1939). E. CHAVANNES, *Les mémoires historiques de Se-ma Ts'ien,* vol. 1. M. GRANET, 1926. M. KALTENMARK, "Religion et politique dans la Chine des Ts'in et des Han," *Diogène,* no. 34 (Paris 1961). KOU KIE-KANG, "San houang k'ao," *Kou-che pien,* 7. YANG K'OUAN, *Introduction.* For full citations, see "Chinese Mythology."

The Great Flood in Chinese Mythology

The *Shu Jing,* cited in the "Historical Accounts" (*Shi Ji*) of Sima Qian, relates that in the time of the emperor Yao there was a great flood; Yao commanded Gun to struggle against the waters; Gun failed in his task and was put to death. It was Gun's son, Yu the Great, who was credited with putting an end to the flood. As it is recounted in these classical texts, the flood in the time of Yao, which continued under the reign of Shun, was a simple catastrophe such as has always occurred in China and elsewhere. There is nothing to suggest that it was a mythical Flood that was supposed to have annihilated humanity. What interested the authors was to elucidate the great virtues of these sovereigns and, in particular, the virtues of Yu, who devoted himself to the public weal, which allowed him to succeed to the throne that the aging emperor Shun ceded to him. Remaining within the context of the text of the *Shu Jing,* one would be tempted to say that the ancient Chinese were not acquainted with a myth of the Flood (which Frazer affirmed in *Folklore of the Old Testament*). One must, however, bear in mind the fact that the ancient historians were, above all, moralists who zealously applied themselves to the rationalization of ancient legends. In this edifying narrative, the flood is a rather secondary element, but one gathers from certain descriptions that it might well have been, originally, a true Flood, as is suggested in particular by that often-used expression: the enormous mass of waters "rose up to the sky." But humanity was not destroyed; the text says only that "the people below lamented," and in *Mencius:* "In the time of Yao, the waters, stopped in their courses, had overflowed and flooded the empire. The land was full of serpents and dragons; men had no place to settle. In the lowlands, they made nests for themselves (on piles); in the highlands, they hollowed out caves."

One of the points that interested the Confucian authors in the story of Gun and Yu was the opposition of two techniques and also of two moral philosophies. Gun, who is the inventor of ramparts, attempted to contain the waters by constructing barrages and dikes. Yu, by contrast, constructed outlets; he is famous for having cut the channel of Lungmen. The lesson of political ethics that might be drawn from these two attitudes is not ambiguous. In fact, in an older account of the legend, it appears that Yu employed the same methods as Gun, and that he also tried to contain the waters by damming them up. The reason the sovereign (Yao, Shun, or the Shangdi, the Sovereign from On High) punished Gun is that he had acted contrary to the sovereign's will and had stolen from him the magical earth (swelling earth) that had the property of being inexhaustible.

Another version of the Flood brings into play not only Gun and Yu, but Gonggong and Nüwa. Gonggong is a monster who, vanquished in a combat for sovereignty, had, in his fury, battered in, with thrusts of his horns, a mountain that was one of the pillars of the world: Mount Buzhou ("noncircular, cracked"). This column of the Sky was therefore shattered, and the moorings of the Earth broken; the Sky inclined toward the northwest so that the sun, moon, and stars now move in that direction, while the waterways flow toward the east, where the Earth is swallowed up. Nüwa restored the Sky with stones of five colors that she had smelted, cut off the feet of a great tortoise to erect them at the four poles, killed Gonggong, and finally heaped up the ashes of reeds to arrest the overflowing waters. The waters seem to be only one of the elements of the disaster caused by Gonggong.

The version of the myth in which Nüwa intervenes may be what led some to suspect the existence of a true Flood in the background of these legends. It should be recalled that the deity with the body of a serpent (or a dragon) forms with Fuxi a married couple and also a brother-sister pair. Now, it is through the incestuous union of a brother with his sister, the only survivors of the Flood, that humanity is saved from annihilation in numerous variants of the myth among the aborigines of southern China, and the two spouses/siblings are often called Fuxi and Nüwa. It should also be remembered that the Chinese Nüwa is the creator of humanity. Moreover, Nüwa and Yu have so many points in common that the goddess figures as a kind of female counterpart to the hero. She is assimilated to the daughter of Tushan, the wife of Yu. There is a certain relationship between the two pairs of demiurges: Yu and Tushan on the one hand, Fuxi and Nüwa on the other hand. The two great floods, that of Yu and that of Nüwa, are probably only two versions of the same myth. In both cases, the flood is not localized, but extends over the whole empire, that is, the whole Earth, thus approaching a true Flood. But it is either a natural catastrophe or a disaster caused by a demon; it does not arise as the punishment for any transgression or fault. There are, however, local legends in which this theme does occur. Before examining them, let us speak of the myth of Yi Yin.

Yi Yin is a celebrated figure who aided T'ang the Victorious, the founder of the Yin dynasty. The story of his birth is recounted thus in the commentary of the *Tianwen*:

> The mother of Yi Yin, who was pregnant, dreamed that a divine woman said to her: when the mortar and the furnace produce frogs, hurry up and get away, but without turning around. Some time later, frogs were born in the mortar and the furnace. The mother ran toward the east and turned around to look at the town: the town was completely covered by a flood. The mother drowned and was transformed into a hollow mulberry tree. When the waters had subsided, there was a small child crying on the bank of the river. Some people took him in and raised him. When he was fully grown, he distinguished himself by his exceptional gifts.

The *Lüshi Chunqiu* recounts the same legend in slightly different terms; in particular, it is just a matter of water coming from a mortar. But the version cited above is notable in that the mortar is evidently a Yin symbol, and therefore aquatic, and the furnance is a Yang symbol, and igneous. But the character *chao,* which designates the furnace, is composed of two elements: "cavern," or "hollow," and "frog." Therefore, even etymologically, there was a connection between the furnace and frogs, an essentially aquatic animal. (Frogs were used to obtain rain.)

The theme of the hollow mulberry tree that occurs here must be emphasized, for the mulberry tree is a solar tree; that is why, here, the mother of Yi Yin flees toward the east. The theme is also connected with Sanglin (the forest of mulberry trees), which was the holy place of the Yin and of their heirs, the princes of Sung: this holy place is constantly linked to the theme of miraculous conceptions.

Finally, the theme of the prohibition against turning around and the sanction (here, the metamorphosis into a hollow mulberry tree, elsewhere petrifaction) is encountered in multiple versions of a well-known legend, the legend of the Inundated Town (the theme of the town of Ys).

The most famous case was that of the town of Liyang, which was a subprefecture of the kingdom of Huainan, in the present-day province of Anhui. The *Huainanzi* (chap. 2) alludes to it, which provides the commentator Zhao Yu with the opportunity to recount the legend:

> There was (in Liyang) an old woman who always did good deeds. Two young scholars happened to pass by and said to her: this land will be flooded and will become a lake. They advised her to watch the threshold of the eastern gate of the town, and when she saw blood there, she would have to flee, climb the Northern Hill, and not turn around. From that moment, the old woman constantly went and watched the threshold of the gate. The keeper of the gate asked her why, and the old woman told him what the scholars had said. That night, the keeper killed a chicken and sprinkled its blood on the threshold of the gate. The next morning, the old woman, noticing blood on the gate, climbed the Northern Hill without delay. The whole country was inundated by the waters and became a lake in the space of one night.

A variant specifies that the old woman had turned around and that she was changed into stone. The same story is recounted, with variations, for other regions. Instead of the bloody threshold, one more often encounters a stone tortoise, or sometimes a lion, whose eyes are smeared with blood.

Among the numerous local legends on this same theme, the legend of the lake of Qiong Du, in Sichuan, deserves to be cited. This region was inhabited by "barbarian" populations in the time of the Han, and it is in connection with these peoples that the commentary on the Book of the Second Han (*Xu Han Shu,* chap. 86) relates the story of this lake. In it there were many fish whose heads are peculiarly large, so large that from a distance one would believe that they were capped with iron pots. Now, there was once a very poor old woman who lived alone. But a small horned serpent came to visit her in her bed. The old woman fed the serpent and it grew. It happened that the serpent killed the horse of the prefect. The prefect, furious, demanded that the old woman hand the serpent over to him, and since the serpent was not to be found, he had the old woman put to death. The serpent warned that it would avenge its "mother." For forty days a storm was unleashed; the people discovered that they had the heads of fish. In one night, the town and its region became a lake. Only the house of the old woman remained intact; it served thereafter as a shelter for fishermen. In clear weather, the walls and houses of the submerged town can be seen.

Here there is a frequent characteristic of the legends of towns (or sometimes of a great house) that are flooded: the residents are transformed into fish. Very often, the inundation occurs after a collective fault: the killing of an extraordinary animal, a great fish or a white buffalo, which is eaten. One woman does not participate in the feast; she is forewarned, but she turns around and is petrified. She is nonetheless venerated as a patron divinity of fishermen.

M.K./b.f.

BIBLIOGRAPHY

W. EBERHARD, 1942. IZUSHI YOSHIHIKO, 1943. H. MASPERO, 1924. MORI MIKISABURO, 1969.
For full citations see "Chinese Mythology."

Myths and Legends about the Barbarians on the Periphery of China and in the Land of Chu

The "barbarians" that surrounded the central states of ancient China had myths and legends which were entirely their own. Certain of these traditions were taken up in dynastic histories and in other texts and thus became celebrated in China itself. For the Chinese, moreover, the barbarians were the objects of beliefs that assimilated them to animals. The Chinese names for them are most often represented by written characters with the classification of quadruped or insect. Furthermore, campaigns against these peoples were considered more as hunting expeditions than as military operations. Only the civilized world was truly "human": the "Four Seas" constitute an unreliable zone in which barbarians, animals, and demons are indistinguishable from one another. At the same time, Chinese civilization slowly spread on these peripheral borderlands, assimilating certain peoples and subjugating others (these were called "cooked"), with still other peoples managing to maintain their independence and putting up greater resistance (these were called "raw"). These complex and ambiguous relationships between Chinese and barbarians are reflected in legends which the Chinese collected more or less faithfully. We may add under this heading the legends of the land of Chu, even if this is not considered to be "barbarian" in the strict sense of the word.

I. Panhu, the Ancestral Dog

Several aboriginal ethnic groups of southern China have a myth concerning an ancestor who was a dog and whose name was Panhu. There are numerous versions of this legend, of which the best known is that related in the *Hou Han Shu* ("History of the Later Han"), at the beginning of the chapter about the Man (a Chinese name, unrelated to the English word), the barbarians of the South. In the time of the (mythic) emperor Gao Xin (that is, Di Ku), the Rong Dog (the Chinese name means dog) barbarians were causing trouble and it was impossible to subdue them. The sovereign made a proclamation: anyone who brought him the head of the enemy general would receive a great reward of gold and a fief comprising one thousand households, and would receive in marriage the emperor's own youngest daughter. The emperor had a dog whose coat was of five colors; it is this dog, named Panhu, who brings back the head of the enemy. The emperor is embarrassed, but the princess persuades him that he cannot break his word. The emperor therefore gives her to Panhu, who carries her on his back and goes into the mountains of the south, where he takes refuge in a "room of stone," in a place of difficult access. The emperor does his best to send emissaries in search of his daughter, but all of these fail because they run into storms that halt their advance. The couple has six sons and six daughters who, after the death of Panhu, intermarry and give birth to the Man tribes. The emperor grants them an exemption from taxes and statute labor because of the merits of Panhu and because their mother was a Chinese princess. This legend has remained very much alive among the Yao, the Miao, and the Xiamin of the southern provinces of China, Zhojiang, Guangxi, Guizhou, Yunnan, and the mountains of Tonkin. Not only is there an altar of the ancestral dog in their houses, but his memory is also evoked through certain details of clothing and in particular through women's headdresses. According to the Xiamin version, Panhu, in the face of the emperor's hesitation to give him his daughter, advises him to place him under a golden bell for seven days and seven nights, after which he will be transformed into a man. But on the sixth day, the princess lifts up the bell: Panhu's body has already been transmuted, but his head is still that of a dog. Panhu dresses in clothing and the princess adopts a headdress like a dog's head. They then marry and go into the mountains, where they have three boys and a girl.

According to a widespread version (already cited in the commentary on *Hou Han Shu*), whose aim is to explain the name of the ancestral dog, there was in the palace of Gao Xin an old woman who had an ear disorder: from her ear a sort of cocoon is extracted; this is placed in a gourd (*hu*) which is covered with a tray (*pan*); the cocoon turns into a five-colored dog, who is named Panhu.

This legend, which is widespread in this form among the southern aboriginal peoples, leaves some problems unresolved:

a) What is the relationship between Panhu and Pangu? Pangu is the cosmic man who was born inside the primordial Chaos; he then grew so much between Heaven and Earth that they moved apart from one another, until finally the different parts of his body became the heavenly bodies, the mountains, the rivers, and the other constituents of the universe. This myth is very different from that of Panhu, yet there is certainly a connection between the two names Panhu and Pangu; in addition, the two myths belong to the same regions and the same populations. It nevertheless appears, judging from ethnological investigations, that the Panhu cult is the more widespread of the two at present, but that the two names may at times be interchanged out of confusion. Numerous tribes preserve with pictures the account of the legend of Panhu: it is important to them that the text of this account contain the exemption from taxation and statute labor that the sovereign is said to have given to their ancestors.

b) In the account in the *Hou Han Shu,* the enemy who is to confront Panhu is the general of the Rong Dogs. These peoples inhabited the Shaanxi and Shanxi. Their very name indicates that they must have had close connections with the dog. The *Shanhai Jing,* on the subject of the Rong Dogs, says that there was a genie there with an animal's body and a human face, referred to as Quanrong. And elsewhere (chap. 12), this country is also called Quanfengguo, the enfeoffed Land of the Dog. The inhabitant shown in the illustration accompanying the text had the appearance of a dog; a young woman kneeling before him offered him food and drink. It is impossible to tell whether this text is referring to the legend of Panhu. The commentary of Guopu summarizes two legends, that of the *Hou Han Shu* and another according to which Quanfengguo was a Land of Dogs whose inhabitants were descended from a pair of white dogs. There are "Lands of Dogs" in the north as often as to the south and west; if the males there are dogs, their wives are always women who dress and eat like the Chinese, whereas the Dogs (sometimes with a human body and the head of a dog) have no clothing and eat raw meat. Thus, in all of these traditions, the Dog represents the state of savagery and nature, while the woman represents culture. Yet it was a woman who prevented Panhu from becoming completely human. This brings us to another theme which will allow us to bring together the two myths of Panhu and of Pangu (cf. Eberhard, *Lokalkulturen* 2, p. 80). Pangu is born in Chaos, in Hundun. This is the cosmic egg: it is also a sack. Among the descriptions and comparisons of Hundun in the ancient texts, we find one which speaks of its resemblance to a dog whose eyes cannot see and whose ears cannot hear. A Man tribe recounts that, when Panhu died, he was placed in a tree and pierced with needles. The meaning of this act is unclear in this context, but it may recall the ancient legend of a Yin king who, in an act of defiance, had a skin bottle filled with blood and suspended so as to represent Heaven and used as a target for arrows. It is nevertheless difficult to believe that Pangu is Heaven; on the other hand, if he is Hundun or Chaos, the act of piercing him could be connected with the Hundun of Zhuangzi, in which two other divinities wished to make openings, that is, sense organs.

It is thus not impossible to find a link between Pangu and Panhu, whose myths at first glance have nothing whatsoever in common. It must be added that the myths and legends about the dog are numerous and complex and are disseminated throughout the Far East; and it is not inconceivable for legends on this subject to be encountered among peoples quite distant from one another. The writings of the Chinese certainly contributed to their dissemination as well.

II. Linjun

Linjun is the ancestor of one of the clans of the Man barbarians of Ba (eastern Sichuan). All of these peoples came from Mount Chungli, which had two caverns, one red and one black: the Ba clan came from the red cavern and the others from the black. Since they had no leader, they agreed to choose the one who could reach one of the caverns by throwing his sword. Only one man of the Ba clan succeeded, and a second ordeal was agreed upon: he who could cause a boat made of earth to float would be made leader. Again the man of the Ba clan passes this test, and he thus becomes the leader of all of the clans, under the name of Linjun (the Lord of the Granary). Sailing his earthen boat, he arrives at Yanyang, where there is saltwater and a goddess of salt who wishes to keep him there. When he refuses, the goddess transforms herself into an insect surrounded by a cloud of other insects and obscures the sun. The world is plunged into darkness for over ten days. Through a trick, Linjun succeeds in killing the goddess with an arrow, at which point "Heaven opens and shines forth." Linjun continued his voyage in his earthen boat to the place where he founded a city. When he died, his soul became a white tiger to whom human victims were sacrificed.

There were other female divinities of salt in Sichuan, and these also demanded human sacrifices. At Renzhou, in the southern part of the province, there was a fountain of salt attached to the temple of a Daughter of Jade. Since she had no husband, she was offered young boys, who were thrown into the fountain to keep it from drying up. There was also, in a mountain of the same region, a great serpent called "the God of the Western Mountain." The inhabitants periodically sacrificed to him a girl who would serve as his wife. This continued until the day when a wise governor conceived the idea of marrying the serpent god to the Daughter of Jade so that the custom of human sacrifices ceased.

III. The Kings and Heroes of Shu (Sichuan)

The most ancient king of Shu was Cancong, who was succeeded by Po-huo and Yuxiao, each of whom reigned for several hundred years. The name Cancong means "grove of the silkworms," which is not without interest, since it is in Sichuan that we find a famous legend about the origin of silkworms.

A man goes off on a voyage and his wife promises their daughter in marriage to any man who will bring her husband back. His horse brings her husband back, but instead of keeping her promise, she has the horse killed and has its skin dried in the courtyard. The hide envelops the daughter, who becomes a silk cocoon.

Cancong taught his people agriculture and the art of raising silkworms. Sacrifices are offered to him under the name of "the God of the Green Robes" (Qingyi Shen).

After the three ancient sovereigns, Duyu reigned; he took the name of Wang Di after he married a girl who came from a spring and may have been a divinity of salt. After him came Bieling, a man from the state of Jing (Chu): this was a dead man whose corpse had floated upriver to Chengdu, where he returned to life. Wang Di made him a minister because he knew how to master the floodwaters. At this point, there are two versions of the account. According to the first, Wang Di seduced the wife of Bieling; according to the second, it was, on the contrary, Bieling who seduced the wife of Wang Di. The latter cedes the throne to Bieling, or is killed by Bieling and becomes a cuckoo. The bird cries until it spits up blood. Hearing the cuckoo is inauspicious, since it portends a separation. The people know that the cuckoo is the soul of an ancient king of Shu.

Bieling is a famous hero, quite similar to Yu the Great, since he also goes through mountains. It is because of his works that the land of Shu became habitable. His name designates him as "the spirit of a tortoise." Following the abdication (or the murder) of Wang Di, he became king under the name of Kaiming ("Opening of Light").

In the time of King Kaiming five giants (Wuding Lishi) were born who could move mountains. Whenever a king died, they erected a great rock upon his tomb: these came to be called the "stone bamboo shoots" (of Chengdu). According to another legend about a Mountain of the Five Wives (Wufu Shan) at Zitong, the king of Qin had offered five beautiful girls to the king of Shu. The latter sent the five giants to meet them, but on their return trip they saw near Zitong a great serpent who entered a cave. When they tried to pull it back by the tail, the mountain collapsed, crushing the five men and the five Qin women: the mountain was thus broken up into five hills which are called "the Tombs of the Five Women" or "of the Five Giants" (*Huayang Guozhi,* chap. 3). According to another version, the five girls are changed into stones. These are some of the legends about the megaliths of Sichuan.

Another renowned hero from the land of the Shu is Li Bing. A magistrate in the region in the third century B.C., he cleansed the country by digging through a mountain to make a passage for the waters of a river so that they irrigated the plain instead of flooding it. Furthermore, he tames a water monster and himself becomes a god of the waters. The god of the confluence of two rivers near Chengdu each year demanded the sacrifice of two girls whom he made his wives. Li Bing takes the place of one of the girls, and arriving at the sanctuary of the god, offers him something to drink; but the god slips away. A combat ensues: two water buffalo are seen fighting on the shore of the river; one of them is Li Bing, and he is losing the fight. He indicates to his soldiers how they may recognize the enemy buffalo, and they kill it with their arrows. Li Bing thus became the god of the waters at Kuan-hien. Before his temple stands a stone ox who protects him from the waters (it is a common practice to erect a stone or bronze ox on the shore of a river or lake). Under the Song, Li Bing was associated with another divinity who was taken to be his own son, Erlang. Legend attributes to him the merit of having slain the buffalo-dragon against which his father had fought in the river. He became a popular divinity in every province, and is represented as a young hunter accompanied by his dog.

IV. Zhuwang, the Bamboo King

The *Hou Han Shu* speaks of an ancient barbarian kingdom of the southeast named Yelang, whose first leader is the Bamboo King. A girl of this country was bathing in a river when a great bamboo stem with three nodes passed between her feet. She heard cries coming from inside the stem. When she split it open, she found a baby inside it, whom she took home and fed. When the child grew up, he proved to have great skill in warfare and became the king of Yelang. His name was Zhu (Bamboo). The bamboo stem from which Zhuwang was born became a forest in which the sanctuary of the hero is located. Although this story as it is recounted in the *Hou Han Shu* is close to the theme of Moses (cf. the birth of Yi Yin), it is possible that in the original version this was a miraculous conception. It is also very close to the theme of the mother of the dragons. This is a woman who finds in the water an egg from which dragons are born; but according to certain variants, it is the mother herself who gives birth to the dragons after she has eaten the egg, or after she has been touched by a piece of wood (see Eberhard, *Typen,* no. 58 and no. 60). This final theme is found in the origin legend of the Ailao, a people of the Yunnan. Again, it is the *Hou Han Shu* that recounts this myth: a woman fishing in the river is struck by a piece of wood floating in the water; she becomes pregnant and gives birth to ten sons. The piece of wood transforms itself into a dragon who leaves the water and comes to demand that its children be returned. Nine of these flee when they see the dragon; the youngest cannot flee, and sits on the back of the dragon, who licks him. He is named Jiulong (Nine Dragons), but this name, in the mother tongue, means "seated on the back." Jiulong would become the first king of the Ailao.

M.K./d.w.

BIBLIOGRAPHY

W. EBERHARD, *Lokalkulturen im alten China,* 1–2 (1942). H. MASPERO, "Chinois et Tai," in *Mélanges posthumes,* 1: *Les religions chinoises* (Paris 1967).

Chinese Demons

I. The Chinese Conception of Demons and Spirits

The Chinese term for demons in general is *gui.* In rituals, *gui* is the name of the inferior soul, *po,* which is connected to the blood and bones during life but becomes more or less detached from them after death. Also after death, the superior soul (*hun*) becomes a spirit (*shen*) that leaves the body and tends to roam but must be fixed to the slab by the mourning rituals. The *po* that has turned into a *gui* becomes a dangerous ghost unless it too is fixed in a sepulcher. At the time of the sacrifices of the ancestor cult, the two souls, the *hun* and the *po,* or the *shen* and the *gui,* are reunited, and the sacrificers feel that the reconstituted ancestor is present at their side. But when people speak of *gui,* they also think of all sorts of malevolent demons and not only of ghosts. There are, moreover, many other names for the demons, but they are less general.

The Chinese have always lived in a world populated by invisible beings; some are benevolent, but more often they are alarming and dangerous. To contend with the dangerous ones, there were fortunately rites of exorcism, and, more recently, Daoism provided efficacious recipes to use against the demonic armies.

The Confucians, skeptics on principle, did not speak of demons unless to scoff at "superstitions." It is in criticizing popular beliefs that Wang Chong (first century A.D.) gives us much information on this subject. But earlier, the philosopher Mozi (fourth century B.C.), an adversary of the Confucians, was a pious man who believed in the gods and demons. In a chapter entitled *Ming gui* (Proofs of the existence of demons), he refers to the evidence and cites ancient texts that prove that spirits and demons have always been seen and heard, not only by isolated individuals, but even by whole crowds. He defends his belief in spirits for chiefly moral reasons:

1. Spirits (*guei-shen*) punish those who have killed innocent people: such was the case with two persons who were assassinated by great lords and whose phantoms returned to punish the guilty ones, in both cases in the course of hunting parties in sacred parks or marshes.

2. Spirits punish priests who have been negligent in their choice of jades and offerings: Mozi gives an example in which a spirit comes to complain of such negligence (apparently through the mouth of a sorceress) and assaults the sacrificer in the act of officiating.

3. Spirits punish perjurers. The example chosen is that of two litigants sent by a duke of Qi to the hill of the God of the Earth: they must take an oath by sprinkling the altar with the blood of a ram. The ram strikes the perjurer with his horns and kills him.

In the *Lunheng* (the chapter called *Dinggui,* Reflections on the *gui*), Wang Chong sets forth various opinions, including his own, concerning demons. He is of the opinion that the apparitions of *gui* are not caused by spirits of the dead, but by the thoughts of the living when they are ill. A sick man is afraid, and then demons appear to him. He is the victim of an obsession that Wang Chong compares to a strong mental concentration. After this rationalist opinion, he cites other explanations: a man sees demons when the "light of his eyes" is disturbed. In the state of sleep, this light turns inward and is directed toward the interior of the sleeper, who sees forms (dreams). It is the same in the case of sickness or madness. In these three cases—dreams, sickness, madness—there is fatigue and the light of the eyes turns inward. A demon is the breath, the energy (*gi*) of sickness. This breath is inharmonious and manifests itself in the illness as a demon. In reality, the demon issues from the environment: in a forest, for instance, it will be the spirit of a tree (but when the breaths of man and nature are in harmony, the spirits of nature are vivifying). The *gui* are the spirits of old things that can assume a human appearance, in particular in the case of succubi and incubi. The *gui* are beings like the others, but they originate from countries outside of China; they have human or animal form. They are seen only in the case of sickness, but they are not illusions. Thus the two spirits Shentao and Yulei catch them and feed them to tigers (see below). There are people who are possessed by demonic "breaths," such as sorcerers, mediums, and other inspired people who utter words said to be prophetic. For Wang Chong, these breaths are of solar origin (for him, the Yang, when it is excessive, is injurious).

Such were some of the more or less rational or fantastic ideas that were held to explain demons. Demons, for most people, were quite real, and the world was populated with them. Certain demons were particularly famous for having played a great role in the very distant past: they are Chiyou, Gonggong, and the Four Malefic Beings expelled by Shun.

II. The Famous Demons

Chiyou is, for history, a rebel who fought Huangdi, the Yellow Emperor. He is the inventor of arms and a god of war. The battle that placed him in opposition to Huangdi was, in fact, a contest of magic in the course of which the two adversaries were aided by all sorts of spirits. Chiyou is a monster with teeth two inches long, so solid that they cannot be broken. He has the body of a man, the hooves of a bull, four eyes, and six hands. According to one text, he had the head of an ox; according to others, he and each of his brothers (seventy-two or eighty-one) had a copper head and an iron face. He ate iron and stones. Sometimes, the "bones of Chiyou," which seem to be made of copper and iron, are found in the earth. When Huangdi had defeated him, he made an image of him to inspire terror. When sacrifices are made on his tomb (situated to the west of Shandong), a red cloud, which is called "the banner of Chiyou," issues from the tomb. There were quite diverse traditions about this monster, who sometimes appears to be a serpent who is defeated by a winged dragon. But he is above all a personification of the forge, in which arms—instruments of misery, as Laozi calls them—are made.

Gonggong is another rebel who is chiefly famous for having, with a thrust of his horn, battered in Mount Buzhou, one of the pillars of the world. This exploit caused the sky and earth to swing and the waters to overflow. The goddess Nüwa restored the sky and contended with the inundation. This labor is sometimes attributed to Yu the Great, but that is another version of the myth. Gonggong is described as a serpent with a human head and red hair. A vassal of Gonggong, called Xiangliu, looked just as terrible: he had nine heads and the body of a serpent, and he was coiled around himself. With his nine heads, he ate on nine mountains. Where he vomited, foul swamps formed. By obstructing the overflowing waters, Yu succeeded in drowning him, but on the spot where his corpse lay, there was so much putrid water that one could neither cultivate nor live there. Yu purified this ground and the emperors built terraces there (*Shanha Jing,* 17).

Marcel Granet has clearly shown how a good sovereign inaugurated his new reign. He had to establish a calendar: this is what Yao did by sending the Xi and the He to regulate space and time. Moreover, he had to expel the lapsed Virtues: this is what Shun did at the moment when Yao ceded power to him. He eliminated "four evils," four monsters that the *Shu Jing* designates by their names and the *Zuo Zhuan* by their nicknames. Among these monsters are Gonggong and Gun (the father of Yu). Gonggong is also surnamed Qiongqi, the Rogue, and Gun is called Taowu, the Stake. The other two who were expelled are Huandou, surnamed Hundun (Chaos), and San Miao, surnamed Taotie (the Glutton). We know that the masks on ancient bronzes are called Taotie, but this identification is modern.

Gun, the father of Yu, is famous for having been commanded by Yao to fight the overflowing waters and for having failed after nine years of effort. "Shun then banished Gun to the Mount of the Feather (Yushan) and dispatched him with the sword of Wu (a country celebrated for its weapons)." But the legend most often states that Gun threw himself into an abyss, where he was transformed into a yellow animal, a bear, or a tortoise; he became the god of the abyss. It seems clear that Gun was a fish spirit, as is suggested by his name, which is written with the character for fish. According to an odd tradition reported by the *Tianwen* and the *Guizang,* the body of Gun remained intact for three years; when it was opened with the sword of Wu, Yu emerged from the body. But the legend generally says that Yu was born from a stone (*Huainanzi*).

San Miao (Three Miao) were assailed by Shun because they

possessed a Virtue for disorder that "was making them lose their place in the numbers of the Calendar." But it was Yu who, holding a shield and an ax in his hands, danced between two staircases (leading to the great hall of the ancestral temple), which resulted in the submission of the Three Miao. In another version, the lord of the San Miao was slain by the Sovereign, and his people (the Miao) revolted and entered the Southern Sea (Miao is the name of an aboriginal people of southern China).

Huandou is assimilated by Chinese scholars to Danzhu (Vermilion Cinnabar), who was a son of Yao but who, quite unworthy of his father, was exiled to the bank of the river Dan (Cinnabar). In the same way, Huandou was expelled to the south, among the Man barbarians. The *Shanhai Jing* speaks of the country of Huandou, whose inhabitants have human faces but the beaks and wings of birds, and who catch fish.

In spite of the uncertainty of the texts that represent various traditions about each of the four demons, classics like the *Shu Jing* and the *Zuo Zhuan* state that they were dispersed to the four ends of the world, where they became the subduers of the demons who populate the borders of the civilized world. Perhaps one can subdue demons only by being a demon oneself.

There is, in the anthology of poets of the ancient principality of Chu, the *Chun Qiu,* a poem attributed to Song Yu (third century B.C.), entitled "Recalling the Soul," *Zhaohun.* The ritual of recalling the soul occurred, in the classical religion, just after death. A priest (or priestess) of Chu in this poem performs this recalling for a sick person: he or she calls the patient's soul by pointing out the dangers that await it in each of the directions of space, in the Sky, and on Earth. Among these dangers, the most terrible are those due to monsters and demons. The soul is therefore invited to return home, for:

To the east are giants who seek to get hold of souls to devour them. Moreover, the ten suns that emerge all at the same time cause even metals and stones to melt.

To the south is a region where the Tattooed Faces and the Black Teeth live, who make sacrifices of human flesh; there are also a great many enormous reptiles there, giant foxes, and serpents with nine heads whose greatest pleasure is to swallow people.

To the west is the country of flowing sands: you are in danger of entering the lair of the Thunder there. If you escape from there, you are lost in an immense desert inhabited by ants as big as elephants and by giant black wasps.

To the north is the land of ice and snow (the poet does not say anything more about this region).

Toward the Sky, the soul will encounter tigers and leopards that guard the entrances to the nine tiers. A giant with nine heads, accompanied by terrifying wild animals, amuses himself by snatching the imprudent who come that far and hurling them into a deep abyss.

Toward the lower world, in the Earth, is the Residence of Darkness where Tubo, the Count of the Earth, lives. He is a horned monster whose sinuous body makes "nine curves." This last expression is the very one that designates a labyrinth. This demon of the Earth and Darkness is not distinguished from the sinuous path that leads to the subterranean world and that it is his function to bar. The poem continues by showing how Tubo pursues the travelers who stray into these parts and takes possession of them by marking them with the print of his bloody fingers. The text adds a few words which commentators connect with the description of Tubo, but which appear to concern another monster with the body of a bull and three eyes. "All these demons are greedy for human flesh."

Numerous *gui* figure in the ancient literature but, as is the case for divinities and heroes, the information on the subject is confused and contradictory. In Confucian works, the *gui* become historical figures, such as Kui, who is sometimes Shun's music master, sometimes a horned demon with one leg. He is identified with the Shanxiao, demons who live in the mountains and who cause fever. These demons are very small and are naked. They have only one foot and resemble a drum, which brings us back to Kui, who, according to the *Shanhai Jing,* is a one-footed animal that Huangdi captured, later making a drum out of his skin.

The emperor Zhuanxu had three sons who died in infancy and became demons. The eldest inhabits the Yangzi Jiang and is a spirit of pestilence. A second, Wangliang, is a spirit of the mountains; he mimics a human voice to lead people astray. He resembles a small three-year-old child, but has red eyes and long ears. A third son of Zhuanxu haunts the corners of houses and loves to frighten small children. He himself is a child-demon (*Lunheng,* 22). The souls of children who died in infancy were greatly feared. The most dangerous demons look like small children.

Yu the Great, to contend with the great flood, traveled the earth and thus became acquainted with the gods and demons that are encountered during travels. Tradition attributes to him the redaction of the *Shanhai Jing,* a geography that describes spirits of all kinds who haunt various sites. These spirits were also represented on the nine caldrons that Yu cast in order that men might know "the divine things and the impure things; the Chinese can therefore go on the rivers and through the marshes, in the mountains, and in the forests without ever running afoul of hostile beings and without the Chimei and the Wangliang ever harassing them" (Granet, *Dances,* p. 489, citing the *Zuozhuan*).

More than anyone, the Daoists were people who needed to frequent uninhabited places, mountains, and forests, whether to retire there in solitude or to search there for medicinal or magical plants. Therefore they needed to know the demons that they were in danger of encountering and the means of guarding against them. Ge Hong (283–343), a physician and alchemist, provides much information about this in the *Baopuzi.* But one text was particularly important for him because it recommended methods of controlling divinities and avoiding demons. This book, the *Sanhuang Jing* or *Sanhuang Wen* (Texts of the Three Majesties), is lost, but the tradition is preserved in a late treatise on it that figures in the *Dao Zang* (fasc. 575) under the title (which we abridge) *Taiqing . . . Sanhuang nei biwen.* The first chapter of the book gives lists of divinities and demons. These last are classed in two categories, the *gui* and the *jing.*

III. A Classification of the *Gui* and the *Jing*

There are forty *gui,* eight for each of the four directions and eight for the center. These demons are rather like different kinds of policemen in the orders of celestial divinities; they pursue and punish malevolent powers and sinners. They maintain armies in their own orders to aid the "correct emanations" of Sky and Earth. The Daoist who has the proper formula to do it, moreover, can also mobilize these celestial hordes. It suffices for him to draw a certain talisman with vermilion on a yellow fabric and reduce it to ashes so that he can swallow it, and he will have the power to subjugate evil spirits. Other formulas enable him to make demons appear at will and cause them to assume all sorts of appearances. All this magic must, however, serve only for good.

Unlike the celestial *gui*, the *jing* (a term that also signifies "subtle essence"), seventy in number, are independent demons; they answer neither to the Sky nor to Earth, nor to any divinity. Each of the demons is described and its name is given. The person who knows the names of demons has a hold over them and can make them disappear. The *jing* demons clearly affect daily life more than the preceding forty *gui* do. Many of them figure in story literature, but some of them belong to the oldest tradition. The Wangliang, for instance, figures in that tradition, but he is not a very dangerous demon; he is some ten feet tall; he has eyes of fire; there is a danger of meeting him at night at the edge of water or on a deserted path; he makes people sick, but not seriously. This spirit is produced by a stone, a clod of earth, or a branch of a rotted tree, in contact with moisture.

A few examples chosen rather at random will give an idea of the richness of this collection. The first demon on the list is called "Demonic Soul, Swallower of Corpses": he looks like a beautiful young girl, but he produces all sorts of malevolent prodigies in places of habitation; he is in reality the spirit of a fox that is ten thousand years old. If this demon is encountered in the mountains, he can be recognized by a violet hair that grows from his left eyebrow. To make him disappear it suffices to call him by his name. Another demon looks like a handsome young man, but he has only one leg; he sows trouble in houses, abuses daughters and wives there, and brings stolen objects there: he is the spirit of an old servant. A certain spirit assumes the form of a very ugly old woman. By night he enters the bellies of small children and steals their souls from them, which makes them cry in the night. Certain demons are inoffensive, such as the spirit of copper ore that is a tamed tiger; he wanders at night on high summits. There is also a spirit of old gold nuggets that appears as a young girl dressed in yellow with red feet and walks at night holding a flame, but without causing any harm. There is a spirit of silver nuggets that assumes the aspect of a young boy dressed in white and walks along paths during the day, playing with a fish. (For the last two spirits, there is an inversion of the boy and the girl, for gold is Yang and silver is Yin.) But the amiable demons are exceptional; most are terrible: the soul of a man assassinated in the solitude of a mountain appears as a specter with unruly red hair and green eyes; he calls people by name and beats them to death with stones. Similarly, the soul of a drowned man who has retained too much vital power will assume the appearance of a woman who is drowning: if someone comes to her rescue, she drags them into the waves. These last two are souls who are seeking a substitute in order to be liberated (and to be able to reincarnate). The demon "Red Serpent with a White Face" is also the soul of a drowned man who walks at the edge of the water: he blows his breath on anyone who happens to pass by and that person throws himself into the water against his will. The spirit of a very old tree may lurk in an altar of the Earth (*Tudi*) and jeopardize the lives of those who come to lay down offerings. The spirit of an old carp assumes the aspect of a young girl in mourning clothes who weeps at the edge of the water. Old statues of deities, in certain houses or in temples, may become dangerous demons. A white serpent three thousand years old becomes a beautiful young girl who seduces and bewitches young men who happen to walk in deserted places, near old altars, or in abandoned houses: she enchants them by reciting poems and singing songs. But she can be recognized by a green hair in her right eyebrow.

IV. Exorcism

To contend with all the demons that populate the world, there were from antiquity numerous methods of exorcism. In more recent periods, religious Daoism elaborated a rich collection of diverse recipes: magic formulas and dances, talismans, etc. Daoist priests, when they took on the function of exorcists, knew how to summon transcendent armies that hurried from the sky or that the priests drew from their own bodies. But at the origin of certain of these Daoist rites were ancient practices that should be mentioned briefly.

Yu the Great is famous for having invented a magical dance, the "step of Yu," which is still used by Daoists. It was a sort of hopping dance (Yu, after his hydraulic labors, was paralyzed on one side) that the sorcerers danced to expel demons. But it was also danced by a certain venomous bird who thereby caused stones to split in order to dislodge serpents (Yu has close ties with cleft stones).

To expel pestilence, there was in antiquity a ceremony that was celebrated on the occasion of the new year. Granet has described in detail this ceremony, called Da Nuo (*Dances and Legends*, p. 298ff.). We can do no better than to return to those important pages and give here a brief summary. The ceremony took place in the palace and required many people: one hundred and twenty young boys, ten to twelve years old, each dressed in a red cap and a black tunic and holding a tambourine. The principal figure, the Fangxiangshe, wore a mask with four eyes. His outer apparel was black, his inner garb red; he held a lance and a shield. There were also twelve dancers disguised as horned animals. The ceremony consisted principally of a dance by the Fangxiangshe and the twelve animals. At a given moment, all of them drove out the pestilences and went to throw them in a river. The expulsion concluded, figurines of men, made from the wood of a peach tree, were arranged on the gates.

The custom of renewing the images on the gates at the new year has remained very much alive even to our time. The custom dates back to antiquity. According to one legend that has several variants, two spirits called Shentao and Yulei have the function of seizing the *gui*. They inhabit the Eastern Sea, on Mount Dushuo, and cling to an immense peach tree whose sinuous branches cover thousands of *li*. Among these branches, to the northeast is the "Gate of the *gui*" (*guimen*) by which the innumerable *gui* come in and go out. With cane ropes, the two spirits bind the *gui* that they catch and give them to tigers to eat. A variant states that they drag the *gui* with a bow made of peach wood. This tree with sinuous branches, in which the Gate of the Demons is situated, appears to be a transposition of the theme of the labyrinthian passage that, in so many mythologies, leads, but dangerously, to the world of the dead. Only here the theme is inverted; it is the *gui* who encounter the obstacle.

M.K./b.f.

BIBLIOGRAPHY

DE GROOT, *The Religious System of China,* vol. 5, part 2. K. SCHIPPER, "La démonologie chinoise," *Sources orientales* 8 (Paris 1971). KIANG CHAO-YUAN, *Le voyage dans la China ancienne* (Shanghai 1937; new ed. 1975).

See also the general bibliography for "Chinese Mythology."

THE MYTHOLOGY OF SMELTERS AND POTTERS IN CHINA

The arts of fire—smelting metals and firing ceramics—occupy an important place in ancient Chinese civilization, as may be appreciated by the magnificent ceramic and bronze objects that have been left by the Yin and the Zhou. Since bronze utensils were mainly used for cultic purposes, it is not surprising that smelters were set apart from others, and that casting was an operation that had a mystic character. The potter's art is hardly less prestigious, as the two crafts are fused in the mythology; the creation of the world is assimilated to the work of the potter and not to that of the smelter, because the potter fashions his clay on a wheel, which is not the case with the smelter. (Cf. the myth of Nüwa, who shaped men out of earth and mended the sky with the stones of five colors that she had smelted.)

The mythic sovereigns, particularly Huangdi and Yu the Great, are the smelters of sacred caldrons. When Huangdi had completed the casting of a tripod (*ding*), he rose into the sky on a dragon's back. Yu cast nine *ding* out of metals that came from the nine provinces (i.e., from the whole empire); represented on these tripods were the divinities and demons that his subjects would have wanted to know about while traveling.

It is useful to recall Huangdi's battle with Chiyou, the inventor of weapons, who was a monster with a copper head, a bronze forehead, and metal bones. Granet, starting from the fact that owls were sacrificed to Huangdi and comparing themes about this bird, came to the conclusion that the owl was the animal emblem of a royal clan of blacksmiths (*Danses et Legendes,* 2, p. 537). Eberhard refers to a tradition (drawn from a late work) according to which Chiyou's wife was an owl (*Lokalkulturen,* 1, p. 136).

Blacksmiths could distinguish the sexes of the metals they used in the manufacture of objects that went in male-female pairs. The same is the case with swords. When a magic sword is smelted, all of the gods are present: the *jiao* dragons hold up the furnace, the Red Sovereign loads it with charcoal, the Master of the Rain washes down and sweeps, and the Genie of Thunder operates the bellows of the forge. Two swords, one male and one female, were famous: Ganjiang and Moye. These two names are also those of two smiths, who were husband and wife, about whom the following legend is told: Ganjiang receives the order to forge two swords. He gathers together iron from five mountains and gold from the ten directions. He examines the Sky and the Earth, the Yin and the Yang; after three months of effort, he has not succeeded in fusing the metals. Moye recalls the principle that the transformation of metal requires a human sacrifice. Ganjiang then tells how his master had been obliged, in order to effect the fusion, to throw himself along with his wife into the furnace (according to one version, the wife alone sacrificed herself). Moye (or the two of them) sacrifices her hair and nails and orders three hundred boys and girls to operate the bellows. Moye, according to one version, jumps into the furnace alone. The smelting, following these sacrifices and sacred unions, was successful and the two swords could be completed. The male sword was named Ganjiang and the female Moye. Ganjiang hides the male sword and presents only the female sword to the king. The furious king kills Ganjiang, who had earlier told Moye, when she was pregnant, to show the son she would give birth to later the place where he had hidden the male sword.

Tripod vase. Zhou dynasty. Paris, Musée Guimet. Photo Arch. Phot. Paris/SPADEM.

The son does in fact find the sword and dreams of avenging his father. Since there is a price on the son's head, a stranger proposes to cut it off and carry it to the king, and then to kill the king. The son agrees to this, and the stranger carries his head to the king; the king tries to boil it in a caldron, but it will not cook. The stranger cuts off the head of the king, which falls into the boiling water; then the stranger kills himself, and his own head unites with the two others. At this point, the three heads cook and become indistinguishable. Three tumuli are raised and are called the tombs of the Three Kings.

Swords are not the only metal objects that are sexualized and go in pairs. The same is the case with bells, which like to fly through the air or hide in the water, as well as for bronze drums, which are sacred objects for the aboriginal populations of the south.

An apotheosis of a smelter, analogous to that of Huangdi, may be found in the *Liexian zhuan,* a Daoist hagiographic collection dating from the beginning of the first century A.D.: a person named Tao Angong was a master of the forge. One day, the flames of his forge rose up on all sides to the sky. Tao Angong prostrated himself at the foot of his forge and begged for mercy. A red bird alighted on the top of the forge and said to him, "Angong, Angong, look, your forge has entered into communication with the sky; on the seventh day of the seventh month, a red dragon will come here for you." A red dragon did come on the appointed day, and the smith climbed onto its back and flew up toward the southeast. In this story the elevation of the Daoist smith is effected through a red dragon and by following the luminous path that leads from his forge to the sky. The Daoists normally rise up on a trail of light, but in the example of Tao Angong it is the smiths who are destined to rise up into the sky in flames, especially when they sacrifice themselves in the furnace.

Ning Feng Zu, another character in the *Liexian zhuan,* was a master potter of Huangdi who had learned to produce five colors of smoke. Ning Feng Zu made a pyre and burned himself on it; he rose and fell with the puffs of smoke. It is probable that the potter was also obliged to sacrifice himself in order to succeed in firing his vases, which shows how closely the two crafts were related (*tao,* in the name of Tao Angong, means "potter").

It is not surprising that the principal god of fire, along with the Emperor of the Flames, was Zhurong. He was the "Regulator of the Fire," *Huozheng,* and his name seems to mean "Brilliance of the Forge."

M.K./d.w.

BIBLIOGRAPHY

W. EBERHARD 1942. M. GRANET 1926. L. LANCIOTTI, "Sword Casting and Related Legends in China," *East and West,* July 1955. Full citations in "Chinese Mythology."

Caves and Labyrinths in Ancient China

Numerous Chinese legends treat the theme of the labyrinth and related motifs: meander, cave, shell, pearl, and dance. Although there is no Chinese term that corresponds exactly to "labyrinth," the idea is frequently conveyed through expressions containing the character *qiu* (in the sense of "curve," "bend," "meander"), which figures in many geographical names. The course of the Yellow River traces bends that are known as the "nine curves (*jiuqu*) of the Huanghe," an expression in which "nine" is merely symbolic, or even mythic in this occurrence: the river was believed to have its source at the mountain Kunlun, a legendary mountain, which, with its nine tiers, gives access to the nine storeys of heaven. In order to attain the highest heavens the nine bends of the river had to be crossed and the nine storeys of Kunlun climbed.

Labyrinth themes are abundantly represented in Daoism. They are present in the holy places called "cave heavens" (*dong tian*). A significant and particularly celebrated example is that of Linwu dong tian, which is a cave in an island of Lake Taihu, once situated between the kingdoms of Wu and Yue. The island is called Dong ting ("salt cave") and the sacred cave is nestled in a hill named Baeshan (which can be interpreted as "mountain of the sorcerer or sorceress"). This cave is connected with a legend about some famous talismans that involves Yu the Great. A "holy man" revealed to Yu the "five talismans of the *Lingbao,*" which allowed the hero to conquer the great flood; but he commanded Yu to hide them, after he used them, in a sacred mountain. That is what Yu did: he hid the talismans in the cave of the Baeshan. Later, King Helu of Wu, a contemporary of Confucius, ordered a hermit to enter the cave. It was a real labyrinth; not until he had traversed thousands of *li* did the hermit reach a city from which a lunar light emanated. He discovered the sacred writings there and brought them back to offer them to the king. Since the talismans were enigmatic, Helu sent someone to ask Confucius what they meant.

Sacred caves, of which the cave of Linwu is a typical example, are thus labyrinths; they are, moreover, illuminated within either by a characteristic moonlight that owes nothing to the sun (*Shengao,* 2) or by an opening that allows the penetration of a ray of light coming from the sky. People go to caves containing bats—animals that know how to eat in such a way that they do not die—to search for drugs that give immortality, or even texts and talismans that offer salvation. In every case, these are principles of life that are hidden within the entrails of the earth and that must be discovered; to find them, one must undergo trials, cross difficult passages, and discover the entrances and exits of the holy places.

The theme is found again in Daoist texts about the heavens and the hells. The celestial residence (*xuandu*) comprises a terrace with nine circumvolutions (*jiuqutai*); through "ten detours and nine circumvolutions," it communicates with the eight directions of the world (*bafang*). The concise text, which describes this celestial residence and which figures in diverse works dating from the six dynasties, speaks also of communication with the world above through some sort of column or spiral emanation. In contrast, the Daoist world of the dead is the residence of the north, in the ocean of the north; a tribunal called by many names can be found there: "The Tribunal of the (Yellow River's) Sources and Windings" (*Chuanqu Zhi fu*), "The Tribunal of the Nine Shadows and the Long Night" (*Jiuyou changye zhi fu*). The theme of the Long Night is often linked with that of the orgies of the kings of hell; the orgies take place in the labyrinths. Granet has shown the meaning of the complex theme of the "long night": first in connection with the popular festivals of the winter solstice, exuberant and orgiastic, then with the legends of the "kings of hell" (those who lose their kingdom through their excesses; cf. *Civilisation chinoise,* p. 236ff.). In the background of this mythology of orgies, peasant and aristocratic, it is not difficult to find ancient rituals in which the longest night (that of the solstice) and the resurrection of life are celebrated together. The theme of the orgy in its connection with the labyrinth is perfectly illustrated by the celebrated "Pavilion of Wanderings" (*Milou*) of Emperor Yangdi of the Sui. The same themes are found earlier in the story of the platform of Gusu that King Helu had constructed to "drink the night away" (this is the same Helu who appears in the story of the labyrinth cave of Baoshan). Here there is no longer an underground cave but an elevated construction that was the scene of orgies and drinking bouts; there was no access to it, however, except through a "road with nine detours," *Jiuqu lu.* One text says that King Helu had the tower constructed in order to contemplate from afar Lake Taihu, the site of the same Baoshan with its cave where the Ling Bao talismans were discovered. But the talismans were bad luck for Helu and his kingdom. He had no right to the talismans: Yu, to whom they were revealed, is the ancestor, not of the kings of Wu, but of the kings of Yue, the rival state to Wu. Helu's desire to possess the talismans, his construction of an excessively high tower, and his ambition to reach the sky all joined together to cause the downfall of King Helu.

Thus the motifs of labyrinth, cave, and spiral tower are closely linked to the great themes of life, death, and resurrection (the theme of the orgy merely expresses the idea that all excess pushed to an extreme gives birth to a renewal). It is significant that the Daoist term denoting the male sexual organ is "nine detours," *Jiuqu*, the same expression that denotes a river's windings or Helu's labyrinthine road of Gusu.

This expression *Jiuqu* is found in a legend that strangely recalls the shell of Daedalus, when he was tested by Minos, who was pursuing him in Sicily. We hear of a pearl pierced by a winding hole and therefore called "the pearl with nine windings," *Jiuqushu*. According to one version of the legend, known only through brief allusions, Confucius knew how to pass a thread through the pearl: it was sufficient to glue the thread to an ant who would pull as it passed through the hole. In another version that figures in a late work (the *Tianzhongji* of the Ming dynasty), during a journey, Confucius meets two young girls who are gathering mulberry leaves. They warn him that he will be in danger and will have to submit to a test: he will have to pass a thread through the "pearl with nine windings." Thanks to the young girls who reveal the trick to him, Confucius got free. The story specifies that smoke is used to force the ant to penetrate the pearl.

The poet Su Dongpo makes an allusion to this pearl in a poem entitled *Xiangfusi jiuqu guandeng*, "The festival of lanterns in the labyrinth of the monastery of Xiangfu." The image of the pearl comes into the poem to describe the crowd of devotees who enliven the monastery at dawn. But this is surely also an allusion to a labyrinth game that was played in certain regions on the occasion of the festival of lanterns (the fifteenth day of the first moon). Thus, at Beijing, a labyrinth was made of Sogho mats and decorated with numerous lanterns; this was called "the lanterns of the nine windings of the Yellow River." When someone entered this construction he would get lost and wander there for a long time before getting out.

The labyrinth is associated with New Year's festivals in Sichuan, at Gui Zhou: there, the population used to go walking in a place called the "rocks of the eight cohorts" (Bazhentu). There, they say, was the famous "labyrinth of the eight cohorts" of Zhuge Liang, the celebrated hero of the Three Kingdoms: if someone entered, he would lose his way and no longer be able to get out. And women look for little rocks with holes in them which they thread and wear like amulets on their heads. The close resemblance between this fertility ritual and the *Jiuqu* pearl is obvious.

Among the numerous legends in which the themes of interest to us occur we will take up those in which Yu appears—Yu who hid the talismans at the bottom of the labyrinth cave. Other sources say that the sacred writings were revealed to him, or that he hid them in a holy mountain, Mount Guiji, or, more precisely, on one of the peaks of that mountain, the Yuanwei Shan, whose name seems to signify that it is a labyrinth. In this mountain there is a cave named after Yu. A later poet, Ai Tingtao, in a poem consecrated to a promenade in Linwu dong tian (where the five talismans were hid), in two parallel verses evokes first the "pearl with nine windings" that the ant goes through, and then Yu's Cavern, which is a labyrinth, for "he who wishes to penetrate Yu's Cavern gets lost in the east and in the west."

Another legend is told in the *Shiyi Ji* (chap. 2): Yu the Great, when he got through the Longmen pass, entered a deep cave. There was an animal there resembling a pig who had in his snout a "pearl that brightened the night," whose brilliance was like that of a torch; there was also a green dog that barked in front of the cave. Escorted by the animals, Yu finally came upon a god with a serpent's body who was none other than Fuxi; he then received the supreme initiation from this divinity. The voyage through the cave illuminated by this supernatural pearl, which is simultaneously the moon and the sun, is equivalent to climbing to the sky. This is why the sacred caves are the Caves of the Sky.

M.K./d.g.

BIBLIOGRAPHY

M. KALTENMARK, *Ling-pao: Note sur un terme du taoïsme religieux*, a collection published by the Institut des hautes études chinoises, vol. 2: *A Mythological Study on Chinese Religion. Themes of Labyrinth and Grotto* (in Japanese), Annual of the Sanko Research Institute for the Study of Buddhism, no. 2 (Tokyo 1967).

See also the general bibliography of "Chinese Mythology."

Some Legends about Laozi and the Immortals in Daoist Mythology

Religious Daoism, which must be distinguished from philosophical Daoism (Laozi, Zhuangzi, Liezi), has its own mythology, but it is not always easy to recognize the authentic legends in the midst of the theologians' artificial constructs. In this article, we shall limit ourselves to an overview of a few legends concerning Laozi and the Immortals. Speculations about the hierarchies of the heavens and the countless deities in the macrocosm and the microcosm, who are often merely names, are of only limited interest to the history of Daoism, of which we still know relatively little.

I. Laozi

The figure of the historical Laozi is so obscure that we cannot be sure that he ever really existed. The book attributed to him, the *Laozi* or *Daode Jing*, has an uncertain history, and scholars do not agree on its date. Yet it is the most famous book of ancient China, the one with the most commentaries, and it is by far the most often translated. To Daoists, it represents a particularly sacred scripture, and Laozi became a deity by the last centuries B.C.

As early as 100 B.C., Sima Qian admits in a short biography devoted to Laozi that he was able to collect only uncertain and contradictory data about him. He states that Laozi's family name was Li, that his personal name was Er, and that he was styled Dan. He was born in a village in the state of

Chu (modern Henan). As for his life, Sima Qian says that he was an archivist at the royal court of the Zhou; Confucius came to visit him; when he saw the Zhous falling into decadence, he left to go west; en route he dictated his book in two chapters (the Book of the Dao and the De) to the guardian of the Xiangu Pass; he finally vanished without a trace. But other traditions claim that Laozi had cultivated his vital forces in such a way that he lived more than two centuries. It is clear that in the time of Zima Qian, Laozi was a legendary figure.

The meeting between Laozi and Confucius is very famous; it has been told often and with many variants, and has been depicted on several sculpted funerary stones of Shandong province (second century A.D.). Confucius came to consult Laozi about rituals and was reprimanded and exhorted to adopt a Daoist attitude. He was so impressed that he compared Laozi to a dragon.

Laozi's departure for the west and his mysterious disappearance have given rise to a later legend according to which the Daoist master became the Buddha. Later still, about 300, Daoists composed an apocryphal sutra on this theme, the "Book of Laozi Who Converted the Barbarians" (*Laozi hua hu ching*). For centuries, this book has inspired violent polemics between Buddhists and Daoists.

During the Han period, the main Daoist current was called *Huang Lao Dao* ("the Dao [way, doctrine] of Huangdi and Laozi"). This school taught methods of government and techniques of longevity. The association of the Yellow Emperor with Laozi is the result of interactions between the shifting and highly complex state of the Han imperial rituals on the one hand, and on the other, popular beliefs, of which little is known, political and religious speculations of the school of Zou Yan, and beliefs about the Immortals and longevity.

The doctrine of that school revolved around both the art of governing (through "nonaction") and techniques of longevity. It is well represented by the commentary of Laozi called "of Heshang gong." In the hagiography, Laozi is expert in these techniques; it has been noted that the *Shi Ji* mentions traditions according to which he lived more than two hundred years. The *Liexian zhuan* places his date of birth under the Yin (second millennium B.C.). This ancient hagiographic collection goes on to say that he knew how to nourish his vital energies and that he attached major importance to sexual methods.

In the text of an inscription composed in 165 by order of the emperor Huan of the Han, on the occasion of a sacrifice to Laozi, there are references to exercises for mental concentration and to techniques for longevity, through which the sage was transformed into an Immortal and "shedding its skin as a cicada would, he escaped from the world." This inscription also summarizes some of the beliefs about Laozi that were current in popular circles: the sage has become a deity, a cosmic god who exists at the center of primordial chaos; his place is in the center of heaven; he transformed himself nine times in accordance with the movement of the sun and with the rhythm of the seasons; he is surrounded by the Four Emblematic Beasts (Green Dragon on the left, White Tiger on the right, Red Bird in front, and Turtle behind). He has taught the Doctrine to the Holy Sovereigns beginning with Fuxi and Shennong. In the final expression of praise in the inscription, Laozi is a radiant deity who contributes to the brilliance of the sun, moon, and stars, and who moves back and forth between heaven and earth.

It is interesting that the idea of Laozi's transformations already appears in this text, and this for two reasons. First,

Laozi leaving for the west. Qing bronze. Paris, Musée Guimet. Photo Musées nationaux.

the same theme and the same expression of "nine transformations" in connection with the sun appear in the myth of Pangu. This myth of southern origin first appears in texts from the third century A.D. We also know that the theme of the dismemberment of the cosmic man, whose body becomes the world, was transposed to Laozi. It would thus seem that this myth existed at least in the second century. But the theme of the transformations of Laozi or of a cosmic being in general is certainly Chinese, and it it hardly likely that it was borrowed (compare the myth of Nüwa, and the ideology of the *Yi Jing* as a whole). Moreover, the "nine transformations" are connected with exercises of meditation in which the practitioner used mirrors and visualized a series of nine spirits who might have been the various visible forms of Laozi. Certain texts gave detailed descriptions of him during these transformations, which were to be visualized: "Laozi has seventy-two *xiang* signs and eighty-one *hao* signs. He transforms himself nine times. During the first metamorphosis, he is six feet six inches tall, wearing the cap of the magpie and the fish and the eight-bordered clothing of the phoenix. During the second metamorphosis, he is seven feet seven inches tall, wearing a multilayered cap on his head, a white cloak with red collar and crimson sleeves . . ." (*Sandong Zhunang,* cited by A. Seidel, *La Divinisation de Lao-tseu*, p. 37). Laozi was visualized with nine names and seventy-two and eighty-one extraordinary signs marking his physical appearance. His devotee depicted him the way he was before his birth, during the period of gestation that lasted seventy-two or eighty-one years.

The second point to be made about the transformations of Laozi on the inscription of the year 165 concerns a book that has come down to us in manuscript form, the *Laozi Bianhua Jing* ("Sutra of the transformations of Laozi"). It may date from the later Han and may have originated with a popular messianic sect (see the study done on this text in A. Seidel, op. cit.). In this book, we find no exercises of meditation but rather transformations in the course of history: Laozi periodically descends into the world to teach rulers the art of governing and of becoming immortal—a theme indicated by a passing reference in the inscription. Here again, Laozi is a primordial being, "Ruler of all deities, ancestor of Yin and Yang, soul of the thousand beings, potter and founder of the void, creator-transformer." He appears in the guise of different individuals whose names are given in the text, beginning with the reigns of the three August Ones (*San Huang*), the Five Emperors (*Wu Di*), and so forth, until the end of the later Han. However, before speaking of these historical appearances, the text mentions nine transformations and gives a series of nine names: though it is not stated explicitly, these must be again the nine appearances that Laozi puts on in the course of his meditation.

There are in the legend of Laozi elements that betray the influence of Buddhism, first in the stories of his birth, particularly the fact that he was delivered from his mother's left side. On the other hand, the theme of his miraculous conception is Chinese: Laozi's mother was aroused by a shooting star, just like the mother of Yu the Great and the mothers of many other heroes. As for Laozi's appearances as the master of emperors, the resemblance to the avatars of the Buddha may lead us to suspect an Indian influence, though this need not be the case: the belief in immortality and in the condition of the *Xianren* (the Immortals) who disappear and reappear in the course of time is a very Daoist theme, and it suffices to explain the legend in question.

Laozi, deified since the Han, occupies an important place in Daoism, but he has no longer been at the summit of the pantheon since theology devised a multitude of hierarchical divine entities. Furthermore, such Daoists as Ge Hong denied his divinity and saw in him no more than an exceptional man. For others, in his aspect of Laojun (Lord Lao), he is part of a divine triad. At the top is the Yuanshi Tianzun, a kind of celestial father who reveals a doctrine of salvation to his disciple the Daojun (Lord of the Dao), who transmits it to the Laojun, who in turn spreads it all over the world, a task in keeping with his role as a savior god in close contact with mankind. These three deities are personifications of the Dao.

II. The Immortals (Xian, Xianren, Shenxian)

The Daoist ideal was to live as long as possible and even not to die. To reach this goal, they used many methods, both physical and spiritual. These methods became increasingly numerous and complicated as time went on, but many of them had been in existence since late antiquity. Physiological techniques were known to Laozi and Zhuang Zi. While Zhuang Zi taught mostly spiritual asceticism, Daoists in general did not distinguish between the two ways of conceiving the achievement of salvation. Spiritual exercises and various physical techniques went hand in hand, and both of them helped increase the power of life in such a way that the practitioner rose to a higher state, that of the *Xianren*, the Immortals. An Immortal is a quasi-divine being, for not only does he not die, but he is free from the various constraints of this lower world, his body is lightened, he becomes luminous, he frolics in space, travels on dragons and cranes, or flies on wings. Such individuals can be seen depicted on sculpted stones and on various pieces of Han bronze and lacquer ware. They are also the object of much discussion in texts. The *Lunheng* of Wang Chong explains that the Immortals are depicted in pictures with their bodies covered with down and feathers, with their arms transformed into wings, flying through the clouds. These winged Immortals are connected with the Barbarous Birds that the ancient books place somewhere in the Orient. They are discussed in the *Yu Gong* of Shu Jing, and when speaking of the land of feathered men (*Yumin Guo*) the *Shanhai Jing* states: "These men have elongated heads; feathers grow out of their bodies." About the land of men with the heads of *huan* birds (descendants of Huandiu, the minister or son of Yao, the banished ancestor of the Miao), Guopu says they are depicted as *Xianren*. In the same series of eastern peoples, the *Shanhai Jing* speaks of the "land of people who do not die," where there is a tree of immortality and a fountain of life. Also in the East were the wondrous islands accessible only to those who could fly. This entire mythology of the *Xianren* long antedates the formation of religious Daoism, but the religious movements that developed in the province of Shandong at the end of the Warring States Period and during the Han dynasty played an important role in the formation of Daoism, so that its influence on the mythology of this region is not surprising. This of course does not exclude other influences, in particular the influence of shamanistic cults of the land of Chu. The theme of the "Distant Wanderers" (*Yuanyou*), which appears in the title of a poem of the "Elegies of Chu" (*Chuci*), is already clearly Daoist: the shaman poet eats solar emanations and visits the birdmen on Cinnabar Mound: "The poet goes to find the Immortals in a brightly shining home; the Cinnabar Mound is, night and day, eternally luminous." He later adds that once a man has attained the Dao, he grows feathers on his body.

Following are some examples of biographies of *Xianren* taken from the *Liexian zhuan*, a collection of legendary biographies attributed to Liu Xiang (77 B.C.).

> Chisangzi (Red Pine Tree) was Master of the Rain in the time of Shennong. He consumed liquid jade and taught this diet to Shennong. He could walk into fire to consume himself in it. He often went to Mount Kunlun and stopped in Xiwangmu's stone chamber. Following the wind and the rain, he rose and descended. The youngest daughter of Yandi (Shennong), who ran after him, also obtained the state of an Immortal and left with him.

Chisangzi is a complex figure, a god and sorcerer of the rain, but also connected with fire. Among the procedures to make rain, those that used heat and fire were particularly effective: one could burn a mountain or a witch, or simply expose her to the heat of the sun; some Mandarins offered themselves in order to put an end to drought by being burned at the stake. This was, moreover, a way of attaining freedom from one's perishable body (*shijie*), which was surrendered to the flames. The name of Red Pine Tree is interesting because the pine, an evergreen, symbolized a great vital force. Its red color is that of the Yang, of life and vigor; it is evidently also connected with fire. One legend about the daughter of Yandi (the Emperor of the Furnaces, identified with Shennong) tells us that she was sometimes a woman and sometimes a magpie. She went to live on the top of a mulberry tree and built a nest there with twigs that she brought back in her beak. The Red Emperor (i.e., Yandi) tried to bring her back, and, failing, set her nest on fire; his daughter thereupon rose to heaven.

> Ning Feng Zi was a man who lived in the time of Huangdi. According to tradition, he was Huangdi's master potter. A spirit came to visit him and took over his fire. This genie was able to produce smoke in five colors. After some time, he taught his art to Ning Feng Zi, who built a pyre and set himself afire; following the billows of smoke, he rose and came down. When they examined his ashes, they found his bones.

The *Yunji Qiqian*, an important Daoist encyclopaedia, refers to this biography of the *Liexian zhuan* as an example of "deliverance by fire" (*huojie*), but originally it must have been about the sacrifice of the potter. As in the case of the Red Pine, it is a matter of something more than a simple *huojie*, even from the Daoist viewpoint: the column of five-colored smoke forms a road on which the Daoist climbs up and down.

> Rong Chen Gong presented himself as the teacher of Huangdi . . . He knew perfectly the technique of "repairing and leading." He used to draw up the essence in the "mysterious female." His principle was that "the living spirits that reside in the valley do not die," for this is how life and breath are sustained. His hair, once white, became black again, his teeth, which had fallen out, grew back. His techniques were identical to those of Laozi. He is also said to have been Laozi's teacher.

This mythical Daoist was famous for his sexual prescriptions for longevity. The expression "repair and lead" is one of those that designate these practices. The sentence "the living spirits that reside in the valley do not die" is taken from a famous passage in the *Daode Jing* (chapter 6) in which it refers to the universe, whereas here it refers to the microcosm with a precise physiological meaning having to do with the same sexual practices.

M.K./g.h.

BIBLIOGRAPHY

H. MASPERO, *Mélanges posthumes*, vols. 1–2; *Le taoïsme et les religions chinoises*. M. KALTENMARK, *Le Lie-sien tchouan*, translated and annotated (Beijing 1953). K. SCHIPPER, *L'empereur Wou des Han dans la légende taoïste* (Paris 1965). A. SEIDEL, *La divinisation de Lao tseu dans le taoïsme des Han* (Paris 1969).

Remarks on Japanese Religions and Mythological Beliefs

These introductory remarks will briefly summarize the major currents of Japanese religious history and provide a framework for what is treated in detail in other articles. We have identified eight major themes, which are treated in eleven articles of varying length. Here we will present some ideas and some important entities in the Japanese pantheon which in other works have often been examined too briefly or even neglected. We have not taken up questions already presented in current works, even if we could have treated them in a different or improved form. Instead, we refer the reader to the bibliography that concludes this article.

We will examine some basic concepts of the religious and mythic universe of Japan, and these in detail. The choice is necessarily subjective and includes the following: *tama* ("the vital or sensory spirit"), an idea that is certainly older than that of the *kami* ("deities"), whether these were personified or not. The *kami* will be presented in connection with the Buddhist divinities and the theory called *honji suijaku* ("state, original body" = the Buddha; and "descended trace" or "temporal manifestation" = Shinto deities, *kami*). An examination of the other world, although the subject of a separate article, is closely tied to the worship of mountains, which occupy a very important place in Japanese religious thought. The mountains, inasmuch as they represent the other world, are not only the kingdom of the dead, of the spirits of the ancestors, but are also the site of asceticism and the training of magicians. As a representative example of these shamanic magicians, if a highly complex one, we will use En no Gyōja, the semihistorical founder of mountain asceticism. But mountains are also very often associated with the world of demons; we will use as one example the concept of the *tengu*—both in general and in relation to the mountain ascetics called *yamabushi*. Finally, mountains and the mountain god play a major role in many festivals and seasonal rites; we will in particular evoke the rites of *bon* ("the festival of the dead") and of the New Year.

The bibliographies that follow each article are not exhaustive. They merely suggest certain works—in Japanese and in Western languages—which will allow readers to pursue more deeply the questions that have been raised. Under the heading of *Sources* are books which offer basic materials. *Monographs* include works entirely or principally devoted to the subject treated in the article. Finally, there are *articles* from periodicals. *Miscellaneous* brings together works which, although very useful, treat the problem addressed only in passing. At the beginning of each section are works in Western languages, but this is merely for convenience.

1. Archaeology

Many centuries before the arrival of Buddhism, the religious universe of Japan was marked by a number of notions to which the name of Shinto ("the way of the *kami*") was later given. Our knowledge of these religious notions from the earliest period of Japanese culture comes largely from archaeologists and their hypotheses. The Jōmon period (named from pottery designs made with strings) is characterized by clay statues (*dogū*) and polished stone cylinders (called *sekibō*), which have been found among piles of shells. The interpretation of the *dogū*—which often represent pregnant women—is not easy. They have often been connected with generative powers and fertility cults; other statues, whose limbs are broken, are supposed to represent wounds or diseases, which were magically transferred to the figurines. The *sekibō* are usually connected with phallic cults or interpreted as signs of authority. From the following period, the Yayoi period (named after a district in Tokyo where excavations were carried out), the famous *dōtaku*, bronze bells, have particularly captured the attention of historians, especially the bells without clappers: an enigma still far from clear. Enigmatic as well are the *magatama*, jewels in the curved shape of a comma, which date from the time of the Kofun (or the time of the "tombs"); they must have been used during outdoor prayers and ceremonies for fertility or a good crop. The presence of boats in the tombs may testify to a belief that the dead (or their souls) used a ship to reach the beyond on the other side of the sea.

2. Written Sources

The first literary sources about the life and religious concepts of the Japanese are found in the Chinese chronicles,

Sacred tree and small shrine. CERTPJ photo archive. Photo R. Stein.

notably the *Weishi* ("Chronicle of the Wei," from the end of the third century). They tell us, among other things, that divination and tattooing were once in vogue in Japan, during the reign of a queen named Himiko, who was devoted to magic and had the power to bewitch.

On the Japanese side the earliest sources date from the eighth century: the *Kojiki* (The record of ancient matters, 720), the *Nihongi* (Chronicle of Japan, 720), the *Fudoki* (Notes on the customs and provinces, middle of the eighth century), and the *Man'yōshū* (The collection of ten thousand leaves, the oldest anthology of Japanese poetry, eighth century). But these sources may go back to the sixth century for part of their contents. They are thus the foundation for all research on ancient Japanese beliefs. The order to compile the *Kojiki* was given by the Emperor Temmu (at the end of the seventh century) in the hope of assembling the oral texts and traditions of earlier epochs. Redacted from a point of view that was above all political, this work, a selection drawn from the mass of existing legends, is nevertheless a very precious source for knowledge of the customs and religious and mythic ideas of the ancient Japanese. The *Nihongi* (also called the *Nikon shoki*), completed eight years after the *Kojiki*, reveals more Chinese influence. The influence is expressed, for example, in the attempt to systematize dates on the model of Chinese chronology. Like the *Kojiki*, the *Nihongi* is based on lost works; it differs from the earlier work, however, in bringing together many more materials. From these a specific version of a myth or legend is chosen, and the others, valuable as variants, are preserved only as its "different versions." The *Fudoki* contain mainly local legends, notes on place names, and the like.

3. Mythology

In their first parts, the *Kojiki* and the *Nihongi* narrate the events of the "age of divinities" (*kamiyo*), which begins with the divine creative couple, Izanagi and Izanami. From their descendants were born Amaterasu, the sun goddess, and her brother, Susano-o. Amaterasu reigned on the high celestial plain (*Takama ga hara*), Susano-o, exiled, on the earth. From him was born the divinity Okuninushi, who ruled the land of Izumo. This *kami* finally ceded his power to Ninigi, the grandson of Amaterasu, who from then on governed the "land of the eight great islands." From Kyūshū, where Ninigi had descended, Jimmu Tennō, according to the *Kojiki* and *Nihongi*, would lead his clan toward Yamato to become the first emperor of Japan.

The sources cited above are particularly rich in information about the divinities called *kami*, forces and phenomena of nature, such as trees, animals, mountains, and the like. Strongly impregnated with magic and with animistic notions, this religion of nature did not have a well-structured pantheon; it is only when a strong clan came into power that the diverse divinities venerated by the others were grouped around Amaterasu, the sun goddess.

4. Buddhism: From Its Introduction to the Nara Period (Sixth to Eighth Centuries)

The introduction of Buddhism became the object of a controversy among several great families: on the one hand, the Mononobe and the Nakatomi, who since ancient times were in charge of the cult of the *kami;* and on the other, the Soga, who controlled the administration, finances, and so forth. A principal reason behind the receptive attitude of the Soga was a concern to assure profits and other "immediate advantages" (*genze riyaku*), which they thought this prestigious religion could give them—especially in curing illnesses. By contrast, the Mononobe, responsible for the cult of the *kami*, feared the anger and curse of their divinities.

Although the Soga eventually triumphed over their political and religious adversaries, and consequently Buddhism was favorably accepted, on the whole, and could implant itself in Japan, we should not forget the lasting opposition to the new religion, as well as to foreign influence; such a resistance was also observable in literature. Thus the first great anthology of Japanese poetry, the *Man'yōshū*, presents only very weak and sporadic traces of Buddhism (cf., for example, poems 345, 348, and 351, or even 3849 and 3850, which sing of the instability of the world). One might ask if the paucity of explicit references to Buddhism in the *Man'yōshū* is not explained by the fact that this religion was then the concern of the state, which offered it favor from above, while it was still little understood or accepted by the people. Although the nobility with the necessary financial means was charged at the beginning with the construction of sacred edifices and the organization of the rites, it was the state that, during the time of the Emperor Shomu (the first half of the eighth century), favored the expansion of the new religion into the provinces, through the construction of sanctuaries called *kokubunji.*

5. The State Buddhism of the Nara Period (Eighth Century)

The expansion of Buddhism was reinforced by the diffusion of two sutras (the *Konkō myō-kyō* and the *Ninnō-kyō*), both of which were by their very contents qualified to serve as a protection for the state. Many monks, civil servants in practice, were sent to study in China. Research on Buddhism was carried on within diverse schools, often brought together in a single monastery. Nara Buddhism thus merits the two epithets frequently attributed to it: *gokoku bukkyō* (Buddhism destined for the protection of the state) and *gakumon bukkyō* (Buddhism as an object of study). Yet for all this, Buddhism did not entirely lack popular dissemination, as is proved by the first collection of Buddhist anecdotes (*setsuwa*), the *Nihon Ryōiki* (Collection of miraculous and strange stories of Japan, from the beginning of the ninth century). In addition to its importance for the knowledge of Japanese life of the time, the *Nihon Ryōiki* is valuable for its presentation, with innumerable variants, of a concept predominant at that time—the Karmic retribution for deeds (*inga*).

Sacred tree encircled with the ritual cord, the *shimenawa.* Sumiyoshi shrine, Osaka. CERTPJ photo archive. Photo L. Frédéric.

6. Esotericism

Two new sects were transplanted to Japan at the beginning of the ninth century, Tendai and Shingon. The basic teaching of Tendai is that all beings are essentially "Buddha" (have the "Buddha nature"). From the point of view of this doctrine the most important sutra is the *Hokekyō* (the Lotus Sutra), whose teaching, for the Tendai sect, constitutes the supreme word of Shākyamuni the Buddha; everything else that he had preached was merely preparatory.

It is fitting to mention briefly here esoteric Buddhism, or *mikkyō,* a term that must be understood in opposition to *kengyō,* the "open doctrines," which are easy to understand. *Kengyō* is what the Buddha Shākyamuni has explained, but *mikkyō* was preached by the Buddha Dainichi Nyorai. The first contacts with the teachings and conceptions of *mikkyō* go back to the Nara period; it is only at the beginning of the Heian period, however, that these doctrines were presented in systematic fashion, by the Shingon sect. Shingon identified the whole world with the Buddha Dainichi Nyorai, who represents the metaphysical body (*hosshin*) of the universe. The illusory body of phenomena is purely and simply identical to the ultimate reality (*sokuji ni shin*); man may, with the help of mantras (Japanese: *shingon,* "magic formulas") and meditation, attain illumination and unite instantaneously with the Buddha (*sokushin jōbutsu*). Alongside very difficult and complex philosophical speculations, Shingon has also elaborated a detailed system of practical magic. During the Heian period, the two sects, Tendai and Shingon, rivaled one another in magical rites and exorcism at court and throughout society. Shingon elaborates the concept of the "three mysteries" (*san mitsu*), which lead to shelter from all danger and unification with the Buddha in a mysterious way—through thought, word, and acts; it has thus given birth to many rites, whose most important aspects are the formation of "seals" or gestures with the fingers (*in*) and the recitation of incantory formulas (*shingon*).

Legends soon multiplied around the Japanese founder of Shingon. According to the best-known legend, Kōbō Daishi, in a position of *samādhi* (*samai*) in his tomb in *Oko no in* on Mount Kōya, awaited the arrival of the future Buddha, Miroku (for literary traces of this belief, see songs 234 and 295 of the *Ryōjin hishō,* from the twelfth century). In the ancient traditions about mountains (*sangaku shinkō*), Mount Kōya was associated in the tenth century with the idea of *jōdo,* the "pure land." People go to this mountain on pilgrimage to purify themselves; the dead are also buried there. Beliefs and customs connected with Kōya were spread by monks called (*Kōya hijiri,* or "holy men of Mount Kōya."

7. The "Pure Land" and *Nembutsu*

Among the contributions of Buddhism to the religious thought of Japan, an important place should be given to the ideas of *gokuraku* ("paradise") and *jigoku* ("hell"). Beliefs connected with *jōdo* (the "pure land") go back to the Nara period. During the next period, the Heian, *nembutsu sanmai* was practiced on Mount Hiei; this consisted in repeating the name of Amida Buddha for ninety days in a building especially constructed for that purpose, the *jōgyō sanmai do.* Later, the *nembutsu* was interpreted as a way of achieving salvation, for Amida had once made a vow (*hongan*) to save every being who put confidence in him and invoked his name. The illustrious monk Genshin (942–1017) set forth the doctrine of *jōdo* and *ōjō* ("to become reborn in Amida's paradise") in his book *Ōjōyōshū* (The essentials for rebirth in the pure land, 984); there he depicts in full both hell and the paradise of the west, where Amida reigns. The *nembutsu* of Genshin is still rather meditative, and it is not until Hōnen (1133–1212)—after Genshin the true founder of Japanese Amidism—that the accent is put on the repetition of the name of Amida. With this type of *nembutsu*, Hōnen made access to Buddhist doctrine much easier; he opened up an "easy path" (*igyō*), a path to salvation accessible to everyone. A disciple of Hōnen, Shinran (1173–1262), the founder of the *Jōdo Shinshū* ("the true sect of pure land"), took this faith in the force of *nembutsu* a step further. If all really depends on the grace of Amida, which transcends man (*tariki*, the "force of the other"), anything else is useless for making merit. Even the repetition of the name of Amida becomes useless; it is enough to have pronounced it only once. Shinran thus rejects the final attachment to *jiriki* (or "one's own power"), a trace of which is still maintained in the concern to assure the *ōjō* in Amida's paradise securely for oneself through the effort of repetition in the *nembutsu*. These ideas of Shinran are set forth in the famous *Tannishō* (Treatise deploring heresies), compiled by one of his disciples after his death. Finally, the founder of the Jishū tradition, the monk Ippen (1239–89), propagated a form of *nembutsu* with song and dance; Ippen's thought reveals a highly syncretistic tendency.

8. The Middle Ages (Twelfth to Sixteenth Centuries)

Two notions characterize the Middle Ages, *mujō*, the instability of all things in an ephemeral world, and *mappō*, the decline of the Buddhist law. This notion of "decline," the third phase in the period since the death of the Buddha Shākyamuni, was known in China since the sixth century. It was taken up in Japan by certain Nara sects, and later by Saichō and Kūkai, the founders of the Tendai and Shingon sects. On the one hand, the concept of *mujō* inspires a need to leave the world; on the other, the concept of *mappō* facilitates access to the "easy way" propagated by Jōdo Buddhism.

9. The Edo Period (Seventeenth to Nineteenth Centuries)

The Tokugawa government, which tended to favor Buddhism as a state religion, exercised strict control over all aspects of religious life, in particular, obliging each family to belong to a temple. The sanctuaries adapted very quickly to this rule, which, among other advantages, assured them of regular revenues. Moreover, the already popular customs of *kaichō* (the exhibition of the treasures and icons of the temples) and *tomitsuki* (lotteries) guaranteed them respectable profits. But though the number of sanctuaries increased, spiritual and religious life was in decline. Buddhism and the general state of religion were severely criticized by Confucians who initiated a sort of anti-Buddhism. In the pilgrimage traditions of the medieval period, the *o-kage-mairi* to Ise answered to the religious aspirations of the people while at the same time satisfying a certain taste for travel among them. The *o-kage-mairi* helped to maintain the popular fervor for Shinto at a time when Buddhism enjoyed the protection of the state. The interest in Shinto, which from the Heian period remained alive in close connection with Buddhism, was stimulated on the one hand by the philological and literary researches of the *kokugaku* ("national studies") movement, and on the other by popular sermons, called *shintō kōshaku*.

A characteristic trait of the period is resort to magic to cure disease or to assure divine favor. *Shugendō*, Daoism, and esoteric Buddhism kept for the use of their congregation magic formulas which could banish evil and assure advantages. Tokugawa policy had particularly affected the *yamabushi*, the representatives of the Shinto-Buddhist syncretism known as *Shugendō*. And so these *yamabushi*, deprived of part of their resources, specialized even more in magical operations (*majinai*) and divination (*uranai*).

10. The Meiji Period (1868–1912)

In restoring to the emperor his ancient authority and earlier functions, the Meiji reform made him an absolute sovereign and even recognized his sanctity as a descendant of the sun goddess Amaterasu. In instigating a quasi-divine veneration of the sovereign and favoring the principle of *saisei-itchi* ("union of church and state"), the reformers were also pursuing an anti-Buddhist policy (*haibutsu kishaku*) and trying to purify Shinto, the national religion, from everything foreign, that is, Buddhist. Alongside official Shinto (the "Shinto of the sanctuaries"), which was something of an ethnocentric ideology, a religious Shinto was also tolerated. The latter was known as the "Shinto of the sects," and under this label a great number of groups and beliefs burgeoned, including the first of the "new religions" (such as Tenri-kyō, Kurozumi-kyō, and Konkō-kyō).

H.O.R./d.g.

BIBLIOGRAPHY

1. Sources

W. G. ASTON, *Nihongi: Chronicles of Japan from the Earliest Time to A.D. 697* (reprinted London 1956). B. H. CHAMBERLAIN, *Kojiki or Records of Ancient Matters*, TASJ 10, supplement 1882. K. FLORENZ, *Nihongi Zeitalter der Götter*, MOAG supplement 1901; *Die historischen Quellen der Shintō-Religion* (Göttingen 1919). D. PHILIPPI, *Kojiki* (Tokyo 1968). M. SHIBATA, *Kojiki, chronique des chose anciennes* (Paris 1969). A. R. TSUNODA, *Japan in the Chinese Dynastic Histories* (South Pasadena, CA, 1951).

Additional sources: ALLAN ANDREWS, trans., *The Teachings Essential for Rebirth: A Study of Genshin's Ojōyōshū* (Tokyo 1973). YOSHITO S. HAKEDA, trans., *Kūkai: Major Works* (New York 1972). IAN H. LEVY, trans., *The Ten Thousand Leaves: A Translation of the Man'yōshū, Japan's Premier Anthology of Classical Poetry*, vol. 1 (Princeton 1981). *The Manyōshū: The Nippon Gakujutsu Shinkōkai Translation of One Thousand Poems* (New York 1965). KYOKO MOTOMOCHI NAKAMURA, trans., *Miraculous Stories from the Japanese Buddhist Tradition: The Nihon Ryōiki of the Monk Kyōkai* (Cambridge, MA, 1973).

2. Monographs

M. ANESAKI, *History of Japanese Religions* (Tokyo 1963); *Japanese Mythology: The Mythology of All Races*, 8 (Boston 1928). W. G. ASTON, *Shintō, the Way of the Gods* (London 1905). S. ELISSEEFF, "Mythologie du Japon," in *Mythologie asiatique illustrée* (Paris 1927). W. GUNDERT, *Japanische Religionsgeschichte* (Stuttgart 1943). CH. HAGUENAUER, *Origines de la civilisation japonaise: Introduction à l'étude de la préhistoire du Japon*, part 1 (Paris 1956). G. KATŌ, *Le Shintō* (Paris 1931). J. E. KIDDER, *Japan before Buddhism* (London 1959). J. KITAGAWA, *Religion in Japanese History* (New York 1966). FR. K. NUMAZAWA, *Die Weltanfänge in der Japanischen Mythologie* (Freiburg, Switzerland, 1946). D. SAUNDERS, "Japanese Mythology," in *Mythologies of the Ancient World* (Garden City, NY, 1961). STEINILBER-OBERLIN/MATSUOKA, *Les sectes bouddhiques japonaises* (Paris 1930). R. TAJIMA, *Les deux grands mandalas et la doctrine de l'ésotérisme Shingon* (Tokyo and Paris 1959). M. W. DE VISSER, *Ancient Buddhism in Japan*, 2 vols. (Leiden 1935). S. HISAMATSU, *Kodai shiika ni okeru kami no gaisetsu* (Tokyo 1941). KANASAKI/KASAHARA, *Shūkyō-shi: Taikei Nihon shi sōsho* 18 (Tokyo 1969). T. MATSUMURA, *Nihon shinwa no kenkyū,* 4 vols. (Tokyo 1955–58). T. OBAYASHI, *Nihon shinwa no kigen* (Tokyo 1964); *Nihon shinwa no kōzō* (Tokyo 1975). S. TSUDA, *Nihon no shintō,* Tsuda Sōkichi zenshū 9 (Tokyo 1964).

Additional monographs: RICHARD M. DORSON, ed., *Studies in Japanese Folklore* (New York 1980). H. BYRON EARHART, *Japanese Religion: Unity and Diversity* (3d ed., Belmont, CA, 1982). GARY L. EBERSOLE, *Ritual Poetry and the Politics of Death in Early Japan* (Princeton 1989). ROBERT S. ELLWOOD, *The Feast of Kingship: Accession Ceremonies in Ancient Japan* (Tokyo 1973). JOSEPH M. KITAGAWA, *Understanding Japanese Religion* (Princeton 1988). MINORU KIYOTA, *Shingon Buddhism: Theory and Practice* (Los Angeles 1978). JIN'ICHI KONISHI, *A History of Japanese Literature,* vol. 1: *The Archaic and Ancient Ages* (Princeton 1986). FANNY HAGIN MAYER, *Ancient Tales in Modern Japan* (Bloomington, IN, 1985).

3. Articles

R. BEARDSLEY, "Japan before History: A Survey of the Archeological Record," *Far Eastern Quarterly* 19, 3 (1955). D. C. HOLTOM, "The Meaning of Kami," *MN* 3–4 (1940–41). J. KITAGAWA, "The Buddhist Transformation in Japan," *History of Religions* 4, 2 (1965); "Prehistoric Background of Japanese Religion," *History of Religions* 2, 2 (1963). R. PEARSON, "The Contribution of Archeology to Japanese Studies," *Journal of Japanese Studies* 2, 2 (1976). H. O. ROTERMUND, "Les croyances du Japon antique," in *Encyclopédie de la Pléiade, Histoire des Religions* 1 (Paris 1970).

Additional articles: ICHIRO HORI, "Japanese Folk-Beliefs," *American Anthropologist* 61 (June 1955): 404–24. ALAN L. MILLER, "*Ame No Miso-Ori Me* (The Heavenly Weaving Maiden): The Cosmic Weaver in Early Shinto Myth and Ritual," *History of Religions* 24, 1 (August 1984): 27–48. TARYO OBAYASHI, "The Structure of the Pantheon and the Concept of Sin in Ancient Japan," *Diogenes* 98 (Summer 1977): 117–32; "The Origins of Japanese Mythology," *Acta Asiatica* 31 (1977): 1–23.

4. Miscellany

D. SAUNDERS, *Mudra: A Study of Symbolic Gestures in Japanese Buddhist Iconography* (New York 1960). M. ANZU, *Shintō shisō ron-sō* (Tokyo 1972). R. SAWA, *Butsuzō zuten* (Tokyo 1962). SHINTŌ BUNKA KAI, ed., *Sengo shintō ronbun senshū* (Tokyo 1973). M. TAKAZAKI, *Bungaku izen* (Tokyo 1967). Y. TAKEDA, *Kami to kami wo matsuru mono to no bungaku* (Tokyo 1940).

The Vital Spirit and the Soul in Japan

Tama, which is ordinarily translated as "soul," is closer to "vital spirit": from a functional viewpoint, *tama* designates the forces that are felt behind every phenomenon, somewhat like *mana,* though the two should not be identified. Although they are attached to objects or bodies, these vital or sensory forces have the ability to distance themselves from them, to move freely, and are thus transferable. But *tama* also designated more impersonal forces, especially the *kotodama* (the power inherent in words). The conception derives from the conviction that pronouncing a name (the importance of which is stressed by the name of *zumon uta* that the *Fukuro sōshi* gives to "magical poems") enables one to obtain what one desires by virtue of the power inherent in the words. This "spirit of words" may be used for good as well as for evil, for personal gain as well as for the harm that one may inflict upon others.

The best-known example of this double character in ancient times is that of the *norito,* "the chanted prayers," which may originally have been the words of a deity, or words which were spoken to it by a man. Speaking of auspicious things, it was thought, made them become real, and the same was true of inauspicious words and things. A classical example—outside of the sphere of the *norito*—attesting to the capacity of certain words to harm, like a malediction, is the episode of the lost fishhook, as related in the *Kojiki.* The fact that certain words are placed under a taboo, and that in their place *imikotoba* are used ("taboo words," to which the earliest references are already found in the *Nihongi*), is also a result of the vast sphere encompassed by the concept of *kotodama.* The earliest examples of the term are to be found in the *Man'yōshū* (nos. 894, 2506, 3254). The phenomenon was from the start very closely associated with beliefs about the *kami,* whose words were transmitted and revealed by Shinto priests or the ruler. Over the centuries, this close—and above all religious—connection was lost, and *kotodama* came to operate without restriction and independent of the individual: anyone could invoke them, since it was in the words themselves, which were still held to be divine, that the authority of the *kami* resided. At still another stage in the history of the notion of *kotodama,* the efficacy was attributed to language in general, and its divine origin was forgotten.

Analogous to the concept of *kotodama* is that of *kotoage,* "raising the voice" (see, for example, *Man'yōshū,* nos. 3253, 4124) to speak to the deities. More precisely, it is the *kotoage* that brings the *kotodama* into play. A poorly executed *kotoage* is immediately followed by divine punishment, as, for example, in the *Kojiki* and the *Genji-monogatari.* The *Kojiki* relates that the hero Yamato-takeru (son of Emperor Keikō) met, near Mount Ibuki, the messenger of the deity of that mountain—a white boar—whom he intended to kill upon his return from the summit. At that point the deity caused it to hail so heavily that Yamato-takeru fainted, which one gloss of the *Kojiki* explains as a result of his sacrilegious *kotoage.* The *Genji-monogatari,* in the "Suma" chapter, tells how Prince Genji, exiled from the court for his carnal relations with his stepmother, observed a ritual of purification (*harae*) at Suma on the seashore, addressing himself at that time to the *kami* to tell them that he had not been conscious of having done any evil—and from this improper *kotoage* a storm arose.

We will enumerate here some examples of the act of *kotodama,* among many in the literature. The *Kojiki* contains a poem about the deity Okuninushi who is trying to appease the jealousy of his wife, Suseri-hime, at the time of his departure to the land of Izumo; the answer of Suseri-hime, which is also a poem, and especially the accounts that follow, reveal that the jealousy and anger of the goddess have in fact been dissipated. Elsewhere, a girl who had negligently given the sovereign (Yūryako Tennō) a cup of sake into which a leaf from a tree had fallen assuages his anger with a poem that eulogizes the palace and the empire (and thus the sovereign himself). Finally we cite the *Kojiki,* which contains the myth of Ame-no-waka-hiko, one of the deities sent to Japan to govern it. Upon his death, caused by an arrow fallen from the sky, a divine friend, Ajisuki-takahikone, comes to offer his condolences. When he is seen approaching, with his appearance so like that of the dead man, it is thought that the latter has been resuscitated by lamentations and by songs and dances. In his anger at having been taken for someone who was dead and also out of fear of the defilement that any association with death carries, Ajisuki-takahikone destroys the mortuary hut before departing. The poem that Taka-hime, the wife of the dead deity, then recites to calm his anger clearly brings out the importance attached to the utterance of the proper name of the god. The same magical pacification of the *tama* (*chinkon*) appears in cases of sickness and death. The *Nihongi,* in the twenty-first year of the reign of the Empress Suiko (613), describes the meeting of Prince Shōtoku (574–622, son of Emperor Yômei) with a starving mendicant. Shōtoku restores him by means of a poem and furnishes him with food and clothing (see also poems nos. 415 and 3020 of the *Man'yōshū*). When the mendicant dies, his corpse is placed in a tomb, but—is it to mark his supernatural origin?—he disappears from it shortly thereafter. A well-known poem of the poet Kakinomoto Hitomaru (late seventh century) is addressed to a dead person whom he encounters while walking (*Man'yōshū,* no. 220). The *Fukuro sōshi,* from the Heian period, mentioned a poem which protects anyone who meets a corpse. A fairly plausible explanation for these practices is that in ancient times when one accidentally came into contact with sick people or especially with the corpse of a person who had died while traveling, one performed a sort of *tamafuri* ("shaking of the *tama*") to give the sick body new *tama*—which are, as has been noted, transferable—in order to comfort and reanimate it; or to pacify the spirit of the dead which wanders without rest and is thus dangerous. The *Tsurayuki-shū* anthology presents one of the best examples of the use of a poem as an offering. The poet Ki no Tsurayuki (868?–945?) travels on horseback south of Osaka; suddenly his horse stops moving. The people explain to him that the deity Aridōshi Myōjin dwells there and is surely full of wrath against Tsurayuki for passing without making an offering to him. The poem that Tsurayuki composes at their suggestion calms the *kami,* especially through the evocation of his name. The offering of a poem is an offering of the forces of *tama* that it contains and that its recitation has liberated. An analogous idea appears in certain poems of the *Man'yōshū* (nos. 141, 1230) in which a person ensures for himself the favor of a god by evoking his name in a place name.

Related to the offering of *tama* through a recitation (which sometimes accompanies an offering) is the magical action of "knotting" (*musubi*) together grasses and branches in order to make an offering to a deity of its own *tama,* or (the distinction is a difficult one to make) to bind up a malevolent spirit. This is especially practiced by travelers, particularly upon passing through a crossroads or a mountain pass. The generally accepted etymology for the word that means pass, *tōge,* i.e., the contraction of *ta-muke* ("turning the hand"—in a movement of offering?), does not contradict this, no more than does the popular depiction of a dreaded *kami,* Sodemogisama, the "lord who tears off the sleeves." He is one of the great number of deities of passes, roads, and crossroads, who demand from those who pass before their abodes certain pieces of clothing (or the *tama* in them), failing which they are thrown to the ground and a piece of their sleeve is torn off (see also poem no. 421 of the *Kokinshū,* 905). It should be noted that the earliest offerings made to the *kami*—the *nusa*—were of cloth, which was later replaced with paper.

The *Unkin zuihitsu* (1861) tells the legend of Gyōgi *bosatsu,* who meets a merchant who has loaded his horse with mackerel for the market. When the monk finds that he has been refused even a single fish as alms, he recites a poem that makes the horse sick. When he realizes with whom he is dealing, the merchant makes amends and Gyōgi undoes the charm by modifying a word of the poem, which changes a negation into an affirmation. Numerous legends about a monk and a merchant are current in Japan. Their religious foundation seems to be the distant reflection of an ancient form of veneration of the deities of crossroads, passes, major roads, and various routes.

To return to the term *musubi,* certain poems of the *Man'yōshū* (nos. 10 and 141) attest the custom, which was alive in antiquity, of ensuring the safety of moving to a different place by the act of tying together branches or blades of grass. And many texts speak of an analogous action consisting of making a knot in the cord of one's garment (see *Man'yōshū,* no. 251). This is a case of "fixing the *tama*" (*tama musubi*), hindering them from circulating freely (see the legend of Urashima Tarō, and passages in the *Genji monogatari,* the *Ise-monogatari,* story no. 110, or poem 763 of the *Man'yōshū).* For greater security during a journey, one may fix these *tama* to something, for instance, in poem 251 of the *Man'yōshū,* to the husband's clothes when he leaves on a journey, to ensure that he returns safe and sound—since the *tama* tend to return to the vital spirits from which they depart. To undo the knot means, reciprocally, to grant leave to the *tama* and to break with their bearer (*Man'yōshū* no. 3427).

To conclude this survey of the use of *waka* (poems) as offerings, let us look at the presentation to the sovereign of *kuniburi* songs, or "songs of the provinces" (*kuni tamafuri?*), at the time of the Oname matsuri. At the time of this festival the newly enthroned ruler addresses himself for the first time to the *kami,* and the *miko* (female shamans) of various provinces offer these songs, the aim of which is to cause the *tama* of the local deities, who are captured in the different provincial toponyms, to enter the body of the emperor, whose well-being and strength one wishes to ensure, while demonstrating their submission and loyalty.

The Japanese poem is also the magical means of gaining divine assistance. Thus poem 40 of the *Kojiki* transformed, through speech, the sake that Jingū Kōgō offered to her son Ojin Tennō, on his return from Yamato, into a sake prepared by the deity Sukunabikona ("the master of medicines," who "rises like a crag in the land of the world beyond [*tokoyo*]"); into *sake,* the poem continues, that the god had sanctified and blessed and carried from the other world. Sukunabikona, coming from beyond the sea to Izumo, will aid Okuninushi to reign over Japan and to heal diseases. According to other passages in the same text, this *tama* spirit in the form of a visiting deity (*marebito*) is a kind of alter ego of Okuninushi, who comes from the other world at certain times of the year to bring good fortune and, in particular, a rich harvest. Both Okuninushi and Sukunabikona are considered to be *ishigami* ("deities of stone") and protectors against disease. The invocation of the name of the deity (see above) is supposed to bring his intercession in the presentation of sake; in the same way, certain terms, associated in the poem with the act of blessing, of sanctifying—terms interpreted as designating gestures or dances accompanying the preparation of sake (see also no. 41 in the *Kojiki*)—translate the idea of a transfer of *tama,* freed by motion and by the word, into the sake. A similar belief in the possibility of the transfer of *tama* may also be derived from the myth of the sun goddess Amaterasu in the celestial cave.

A few characteristic elements are inherent in the notion of *tamafuri* (the magical act of shaking the *tama*) already mentioned. The *tamafuri,* or *mi-tamafuri* when one is speaking of the emperor (see *Nihongi,* 24th day, 11th month, 14th year Temmu), is a magical act intended to reinforce or pacify the vital spirits, the *tama.* These dwell in objects as well as in the human body, influencing the physical condition of humans by their growth or diminution.

At one extreme, the deficiency in *tama* necessarily results in death. Thus, for the ancient Japanese, life and death were defined by a greater or lesser supply of *tama*, which was considered essentially the same in man and in nature and in certain objects (such as swords, jewels, and branches of the sacred tree called *sakaki*). Passages in both the *Kojiki* and *Nihongi* chronicles that speak of an offering of swords or jewels to the emperor may be read in the light of a magic rite consisting of offering through such objects the powers that they contain, in order to increase the sovereign's supply of *tama*. The passage of the *Nihongi* (24th day, 11th month, 14th year Temmu) cited above, that speaks—without giving details—of an act of *mi-tamafuri* performed for the benefit of the emperor, is also revealing. The two Chinese characters ("recalling of souls") in which the *Nihongi* gives this reading of *mi-tamafuri* show that, in China at least, funerary practices were at the foundation of the ritual, but this was not necessarily the case in the Japanese context; probably these rituals aimed at restoring the *tama* of the emperor (who does not die until some time thereafter).

The fact that the emperor was weakened, if not sick, and the date on which the ritual mentioned in the *Nihongi* was performed may give some information as to its probable meaning. The date is that of a festival that the imperial court would later observe under the name of *chinkonsai* ("festival of the pacification of the souls"), also called *tamashizume* ("to pacify the spirits") or *tamafuri-* ("shaking the *tama*") *matsuri*, a term that indicates the complex character of the rite. Its central element is, according to the *Ryō no gige*, the concern to comfort the *tama* (vitality) of the emperor. The performance of the *chinkonsai* coincides with the time of the winter solstice (the moment when nature is at its lowest level of strength and vitality) and seems clearly to indicate a magical ritual of consolation.

Principally undertaken by the *miko* (shamans called Sarume), the magical acts of the *chinkonsai* strikingly resemble the one that is described in the myth of the withdrawal of the sun goddess Amaterasu into the celestial cave. And since no Uzume, the shamaness of the myth, is regarded as the ancestor of the Sarume, mythologists tend to see in this story of Amaterasu and Uzume a sort of etiological myth about what would later become the *chinkonsai*, bringing together elements of magic through acts (dance) and verbal magic (songs: *chinkon-ka*).

When the goddess withdraws into the cave after the sacrilegious acts committed by her brother Susano-o, the world is plunged into darkness. The other deities, anxious to bring the wrathful goddess out, perform a divination, placing before the entrance to the cave a sacred tree (*sakaki*) to which they attach mirrors, curved jewels (*magatama*), pieces of cloth, etc.; and they recite *noritos*. The crucial element, nevertheless, is the dance executed by the goddess Ame no Uzume, which arouses the curiosity of Amaterasu to such a degree that she finally comes out of the cave. Starting from this dance, which is described as violent and lascivious, it may be possible to attempt a kind of synthesis of the different interpretations given to the myth (as an etiological myth of the *chinkonsai*, as a magical practice aimed at driving away the eclipse of the sun, as a funerary rite, etc.) by viewing it as an act with the character of a *tamafuri*, i.e., an act destined to remedy a decrease of vital forces, of nature and of man, if not to give new impulse to a declining sun. Although we are tempted to conclude that this is a myth about the eclipse of the sun, with practices analogous to those observed among numerous other peoples (dance and noise accompanying the driving out of evil spirits), the dance that we also encounter at the time of funeral ceremonies might lead us to explain the myth in connection with funerals. The funerary aspect of the myth might also be read in the allusion the text makes to the "door of the celestial cave" which scholars have associated with the stones placed at the entrance to a tomb (*kofun*). Other significant terms (*iwagakuru:* to hide in the cave of a cliff; cf. the *norito* of the "Appeasement of Fire," in the death of Izanami; or, as in poem 418 of the *Man'yōshū*, *iwatate:* to erect a stone = close the entrance to a tomb?) may indicate that as early as the seventh and eighth centuries the myth of Amaterasu was supposed to reflect an ancient funerary rite.

We have passed in review several important elements, including the extremely complex concept of *tama*, especially in its impersonal aspect, as expressed by the idea of *kotodama*. A final question should be posed in this context: what happens to the *tama*, particularly those of humans, after they have left the body, i.e., after death? We have said that the *tama* could move freely, that they were transferable, etc. It must be added that they are, depending on the situation, visible or invisible, as is evident from the story about Sukunabikona (see above). If they take a form, it is usually that of a bird (see song 35 of the *Kojiki*, which speaks of the death of the hero Yamato-takeru), or—as poem 148 of the *Man'yōshū* seems to suggest—of clouds.

The story of Prince Homutsu-wake (*Nihongi* 8th day, 10th month, 23rd year of Emperor Suinin) brings together clearly the principal characteristics of the *tama:* the possibility of increasing their mass through contact and/or addition, their transferability, and their transformation into a bird. The story of the *Nihongi* relates that at the moment when a swan—a vehicle of the *tama*—flew over the prince, although he was already thirty years old and still unable to speak, he finally gained the ability to express himself.

The story of Ōkuninushi and Sukunabikona also brings to light a final component of the concept of the *tama:* they come to men from beyond the sea, which seems to be confirmed by songs 71–73 of the *Kojiki*. These songs speak of a wild goose that laid its eggs in Japan; the emperor (Nintoku) demands an explanation for this phenomenon from the sage Takeuchi no Sukune, who explains it (in the form of *hogi-uta*, songs destined to bring happiness) as a favorable augury for a long reign by that sovereign. What is interesting is that this involves a wild goose, an aquatic bird that comes from Siberia to Japan over the sea; i.e., from beyond the sea, where the *tokoyo* world is situated. In this way the song of Takeuchi no Sukune quite clearly takes on the character of a magical act of the *tamafuri* type, based on the belief in vital and sensorial spirits and in the power inherent in words.

H.O.R./d.w.

BIBLIOGRAPHY

1. Monograph

G. EBERSOLE, *Ritual Poetry and the Politics of Death in Early Japan* (Princeton 1989).

2. Articles

CH. HAGUENAUER, "La danse rituelle dans la cérémonie du chinkon-sai," *Journal asiatique* 216 (1930). H. O. ROTERMUND, "Les croyances du Japon antique," *Encyclopédie de la Pléiade, Histoire des religions* 1 (Paris 1970). I. HORI, "Waga kuni ni okeru reikon no kannen," *Nihon minzokugadu* 3. M. NISHITSUNOI, "Chinkon kashū toshite no Man'yōshū," *Minzoku bungaku kōza* 4, "kodai bungei to minzoku" (Tokyo 1960).

Additional articles: GARY L. EBERSOLE, "The Buddhist Ritual Use of Linked Poetry in Medieval Japan," *The Eastern Buddhist* n.s. 16, 2

(Autumn 1983): 50–71. TETSUO KURE, "Mogari no miya no genkei," *Kodai bungaku* 18 (1979): 48–54. NARIMITSU MATSUDAIRA, "The Concept of 'Tamashii' in Japan," in Richard M. Dorson, ed., *Studies in Japanese Folklore* (New York 1980), pp. 181–97. ITSUHIKO OHAMA, "Chinkon no fumi: Man'yo shiron," *Bungaku* 39, 9 (September 1971): 1–11. YUTAKA TSUCHIHASNI, "'Miru' koto no tamafuri-teki ishiki," *Man'yō* 39 (April 1961).

3. Miscellany

T. NISHIMURA, "Uta to minzokugaku," *Minzoku mingei sōsho* 6 (Tokyo 1960). M. NISHITSUNOI, *Kodai saishi to bungaku* (Tokyo 1967). Z. OTA, "Kodai Nihon bungaku shichō-ron I," *Hasshō shi no kōsatsu* (Tokyo 1967). T. SOKURA, "Nihon shiika no kigen ronsō," *Kōza Nihon bungaku no sōten* 1, Jōdai-hen (Tokyo 1969). M. TAKASAKI, "Koten to minzokugaku," *Hanawa sensho* 2 (Tokyo 1964). Y. TSUCHIHASHI, *Kodai kayō to girei no kenkyū* (Tokyo 1966).

Japanese Conceptions of the Afterlife

I. Before Buddhism

It is very difficult to gain an idea of Japanese conceptions about the afterlife for the period before the first written Japanese documents.

During the period of Jōmon (4000–250 B.C.), the diversity of the modes of burial, while bearing witness to religious preoccupations, poses many problems. For instance, sepulchers have been found in which the skeleton was curled up, others in which it was stretched out, some in which stones were placed on the chest or the head. Does the fetal position, which has survived in the northwest of Japan, signify the return to the womb, or is it a precaution taken against the dead person? In addition, it might be asked if such diversity does not derive from differences in culture or social distinctions.

During the period of Yayoi (third century B.C.–third century A.D.), continental influences added another element to the preceding period's diversity of religious data. Certain archaeological discoveries indicate the existence of beliefs that are found in later periods. For example, in a tomb from the Osaka region, a wooden bird has been found which may have been attached to a baton. It may have been the image of the soul of the dead flying toward heaven, a flight comparable to the one described in the *Kojiki* in the passage on the death of the hero Yamato-takeru.

Beginning with the period of large *kofun* sepulchers (fourth to seventh century A.D.) the archaeological data may be correlated with the first written documents, which, though dating from the beginning of the eighth century, report earlier beliefs and practices.

1. The Myth of the Visit to Yomi No Kuni

Still, the problem remains complex. Although there are imposing funeral mounds such as the one attributed to Emperor Nintoku (312–399), the texts are very meager and often vague about beliefs in the afterlife or funeral practices. The only somewhat extended account in the earliest texts (*Kojiki, Nihongi*) is that of the visit paid by Izanagi to his wife Izanami in *yomi no kuni.*

In the *Kojiki* version, Izanami dies after giving birth to fire. Her husband Izanagi sets out to rejoin her in *yomi no kuni* in order to try to lead her back. But he arrives too late, for she has already eaten food cooked in the fire of *yomi no kuni.* Despite a prohibition, Izanagi lights a tooth of his comb and discovers the decomposed body of his wife. He flees, pursued by the furies, whom he holds off by throwing magical objects behind him. When he arrives at the limits of the country, *yomotsu hirasaka,* he closes the passage between the two worlds by rolling a giant stone across the entrance. Polluted by this visit, Izanagi goes to purify himself in the sea.

What does this account tell us of *yomi no kuni?* (1) It is an obscure place (the word *yomi* is formed from the same root, *yo,* as *yoru,* "night"; further, Izanagi had to light a torch in order to see his wife). (2) It is the land of impurity, symbolized by the decomposing corpse, contact with which brings pollution that requires purification. (3) There is a passage between the land of the dead and the world of the living, a passage closed by a boulder. (4) *Yomi no kuni* is inhabited by furies and thunderbolts; nevertheless it is not clearly stated who governs it: at the end of the account, Izanami is called "the great deity of *yomi,*" even though at the beginning she goes to ask the advice of other deities. (5) This land is not entirely different from our world, for there is a palace there, people eat there, and trees even grow there. (6) There is never any question of judgment of the dead or of souls. This conception of a somber and impure afterworld is presented more precisely in the *norito,* collections of prayers which were written down in 905, but certain of which are much older. In the *Ho shizume no matsuri norito,* the festival of the appeasement of fire, the subterranean character of *yomi no kuni* is well marked, while it cannot be assumed in the *Kojiki* account.

The *Michi ae no matsuri norito,* the festival of the meals offered on the roads, expresses the notion of an impure land regarded as a source of diseases. Here the term *yomi no kuni* is not used, but there are two terms that are equivalent to it: *ne no kuni* (*ne* can refer to the notions of base or origin) and *soko no kuni* (*soko* has the sense of "basis," but *soko no kuni* is sometimes compared to *tokoyo no kuni*). The prayer asks the deities who protect the roads to prevent the malevolent beings who "come from the land of *ne,* the land of *soko,*" from doing harm.

The conception of another world as a source of evils and calamities is preserved in the popular traditions revolving around the *dōsojin* (deities who protect the roads), who are related to the deities of diseases and whose prototype would be the boulder put in place by Izanagi. Still, it is difficult to believe that the *yomi no kuni* as it appears in the myth of the visit of Izanagi would be the only vision that the ancient Japanese had of the next world.

2. Yomi No Kuni, Ne No Kuni, and Soko No Kuni

In other contexts *yomi no kuni* seems much less somber and gloomy than in the myth just discussed. Thus, Susano-o (the brother of the solar goddess Amaterasu) refused the ocean which Izanagi assigned him to govern, in order to go to the land of his mother (Izanami), to *ne no kuni.* Why would he choose to visit a gloomy place? In a variant of the *Nihongi,* after he has been chased from *takama no hara,* the high celestial plain, Susano-o must go to *ne no kuni* where he outfits himself in a straw raincoat and a large sedge hat, that is, in the guise of a *mare bito,* a voyager coming from the next world to bring prosperity.

In the myth of Okuninushi, Susano-o governs *ne no kuni.* Although this land shelters snakes and wasps, it also contains various objects that assure sovereignty. This is also the dwelling place of the daughter of Susano-o, who will become

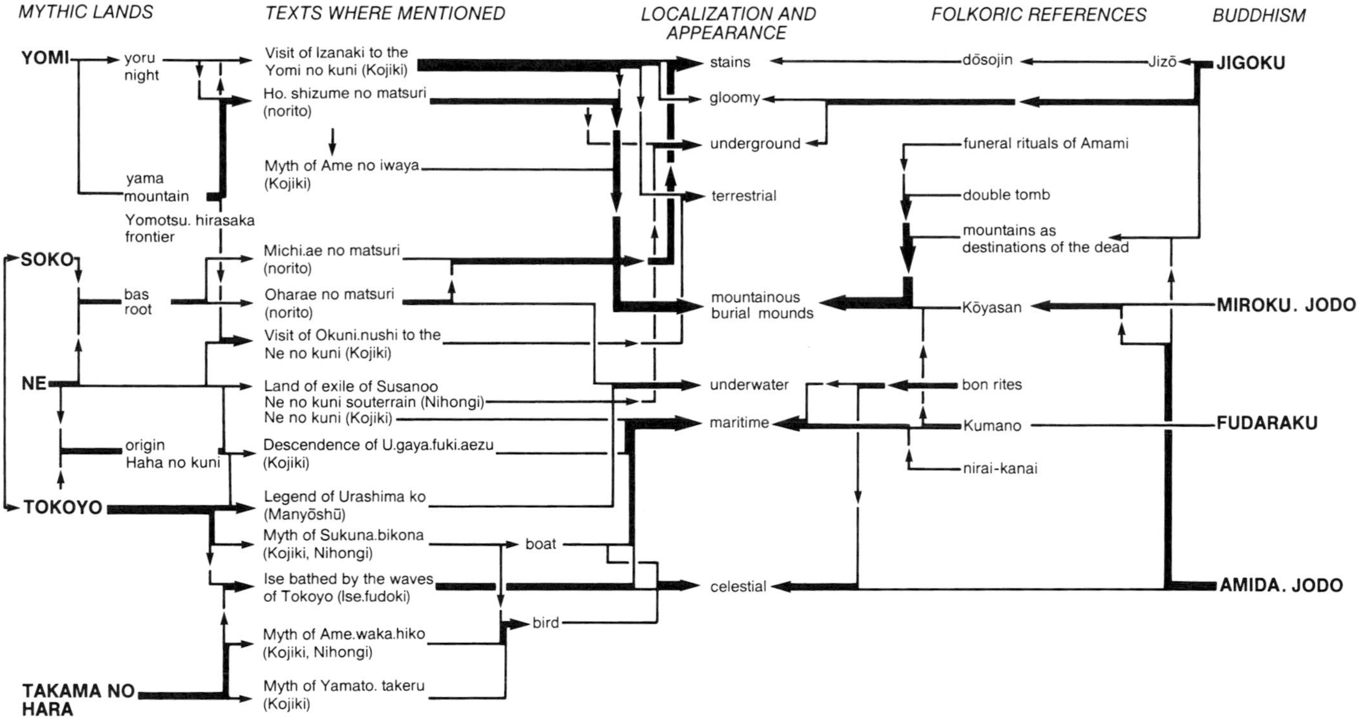

Concordance among myths, characteristics, and popular rituals concerning various forms of the afterlife. Drawing Fr. Macé.

the wife of Okuninushi. One explanation of the myth compares the trials that Okininushi undergoes to the rites of initiation, which, by a symbolic death, cause the initiate to be reborn into a new life.

In this case, death no longer brings pollution; it regenerates. The land of the dead is not only a repugnant land but the place from which the forces of life, *tama,* spring.

Ne no kuni (*yomi no kuni*), the maternal land, the land of the ancestors who come back to bring prosperity, has been compared to the *niraikanai,* the mythical world from which the inhabitants of Okinawa expect the ancestors, the heroes who bring civilization, to come. This paradisiacal land is situated beyond the seas. As we have already seen, *ne no kuni,* through the mediation of Susano-o, is also connected with the ocean. Further, in the *Ō harae no matsure norito,* the festival of the great purification, one expels pollution to the *ne no kuni* and *soko no kuni,* the land located in the oceanic plain. There the pollution disappears. This text situates *ne no kuni* in the ocean and connects it with another mythical country, also maritime, *tokoyo no kuni.*

3. Tokoyo No Kuni

The allusions to *tokoyo no kuni* in the ancient texts are brief, vague, and sometimes contradictory. One of the more illuminating is contained in the myth of Okuninushi. A female deity named Sukunabikona appears there sailing on a boat and dressed in bird feathers or butterfly wings, depending upon the version. She comes to aid Okuninushi in creating the country and then departs again for *tokoyo no kuni.* We are again dealing with a country conceived in terms rather close to that of *nirai-kanai,* the country from which civilization and prosperity come.

But *tokoyo no kuni,* in this first text, does not appear to be a place of residence for the dead, although certain indications seem to suggest this. The hypothesis has been advanced that the *tokoyo* of *tokoyo no kuni,* signifying eternity, is the same word as *tokoyo,* the eternal night.

But it seems that this comparison is after all not possible, for linguistic reasons which we will not discuss here. However, in the passage of the *Kojiki* giving the lineage of Ugaya Fuki Aezu, it is said that Mikenu sets off across the crests of the waves toward *tokoyo no kuni,* while Inai enters into the ocean, the country of his mother. These disappearances, which can be interpreted as deaths, recall those of Sukunabikona and Susano-o.

Thus there are connections between the ocean, the land of the mother, *tokoyo no kuni* and *ne no kuni* (*yomi no kuni*), which make possible the interpretation of certain archaeological remains. The famous fresco of the funeral mound of Mezurashizuka, in the province of Fukuoka, represents a boat guided by a bird, carrying a man (the dead person?): it has been suggested that this boat leads the dead person toward *tokoyo no kuni.*

4. The Mountain

But there is another difficulty. Most of the poems of the *Man'yōshū* that allude to the abodes of the dead speak of the mountains or the sky, places to which one can only cautiously attach the conceptions that have been presented concerning *yomi no kuni* or *tokoyo no kuni.* However, mountains have played an important role in the Japanese vision of the afterworld. They are the privileged locus of divine manifestations, the wild and uncultivated world in a land of rice cultivation, but also the sources of water and thus of prosperity.

For these diverse religious reasons and also because in a country as mountainous as Japan very little available space remains, the mountain was the preeminent burial place.

The first funeral mounds seem to have been gently sloping hills. Then they were designated by the term *yama,* mountain. Even during the Heian period (794–1185), when the Japanese had ceased to construct mounds for the emperors, their tombs continued to be called *yama.*

Furthermore, in the popular traditions, the mountain retained a very important place during funerals and funeral rites. In many regions of Japan, the coffin is called *yama oke,* "the box of the mountain," and the activity of digging the grave, *yama shigoto,* "mountain work." In the Amami archipelago (south of Kyushu), until recently, the body of the deceased was placed in thickets called *goshō yama,* the "mountain of the other world."

In other regions of Japan, there is or was a system of double burial: one grave in which the body is laid, which is at some distance from the village, and an empty grave near the village, which is visited on festival days. Frequently the term that denotes the first grave refers to mountains, for example, *yama no haka,* the "mountain tomb."

The mountain, the residence of the dead, is still at the center of numerous rites of the festival of *bon. Bon* originated as a Buddhist festival for the salvation of the souls of the dead, but many non-Buddhist elements have been incorporated into it. It lasts from the thirteenth to the sixteenth day of the seventh lunar month.

During this period, the ancestors are thought to return to their families. The rites of welcome vary according to the region, but a very large number are connected with the mountain: a fire lit on a summit, a path opened between the summit and the village, the gathering of flowers on the mountain (the flowers are regarded as the repositories of souls, as are dragonflies, which it is forbidden to capture during this period).

Many mountains have become the special centers of beliefs connected with death and are regarded as residences for the dead, such as the mountains Kōya, Asama, Osore, Tate, etc.

It seems therefore rather curious that the myths of the *Kojiki* and the *Nihongi* do not refer clearly to the residence of the dead in mountains.

Is it not possible that the *yomi no kuni* was situated in the mountain? (The word *yomi* might then be related to *yama,* "mountain.")

The subterranean position of *yomi no kuni* is but rarely specified, except, for example, in one of the versions of *Nihongi* that tells of the expulsion of Susano-o from *Takama no hara* and in the *Ho shizume no matsuri norito;* but these two texts are probably rather late. Furthermore, in this *norito,* another conception of the world of the dead is apparently juxtaposed to the first, for it is said there that Izanami, because her husband had looked at her, "shut herself in the rock grotto." In archaic texts this expression often signifies the death of important personnages.

It is probably in this sense that the term is used in the myth of the reclusion of Amaterasu. The practice might originate in an ancient custom of burial in caves. In particular, in the province of Izumo, the region in which the *Kojiki* places the entrance to *yomi no kuni,* a cave has been discovered that contains numerous skeletons from the Yayoi period. "To shut oneself in the rock grotto" may also refer to the stone rooms of the artificial mountains that are funerary mounds.

5. The Sky

As we have seen, certain poems of the *Man'yōshū* allude to a celestial residence of the dead. The account of the death of Yamato-takeru refers to the same residence. This account states that a white bird flew from the funerary mound and, after many stops, disappeared into the sky. The ascension recalls the term used in ancient texts for the death of emperors, *kamu agaru,* "ascend divinely."

Further, in the account of the funeral of Ame-no-waka-hiko, different birds play the roles of mourners, bearers of offerings, and members of the retinue. Might these birds not also be there to welcome the soul that will fly away in the form of a bird?

6. Conclusion

There are, on the one hand, various words—*yomi no kuni, ne no kuni, tokoyo no kuni, haba no kuni* (the land of the mother)—and, on the other hand, many places regarded as abodes of the dead: subterranean world, funerary mound, mountain, submarine world, ocean, sky. A single explanation could not clarify this diversity or the connections that unite the various terms.

First of all, the content of the terms seems to have changed with time, along with the expansion of continental influences. Thus, one cannot exclude the hypothesis that the words *ne* and *tokoyo* may refer to a single conception, that of a maritime afterworld, a land of ancestors, from which prosperity comes. Then, little by little, the terms *yomi, ne,* and *soko* may have come to be applied to the negative aspects of death, for example, death as a source of pollution. At the same time, the Japanese may have borrowed certain characteristics of the Chinese hell. On the other hand, *tokoyo no kuni* seems related to other Chinese conceptions, especially that of a land of immortals in which there is neither old age nor death. It is also the land to which the legendary Tajimamori goes in search of the fruits that give immortality, the land to which Urashim Taro goes to spend three years that last longer than a lifetime.

The ancient Japanese seem to have conceived of many abodes for the same dead person. For example, a provisional abode was situated in the surroundings of the tomb or the funerary shelter, where the body awaited a transformation that made possible the transfer to the final destination. On the other hand, as the rites of *bon* and the new year suggest, the souls of the ancestors must have been invited to visit their family at regular intervals. Finally, the funerary chambers of the mounds must have been constructed with the aim of assuring a certain survival which, nevertheless, did not have to be limited to a single subterranean abode.

The differences among the abodes in the next world may have been regarded as almost automatically dependent on the type of death, certain deaths being judged infamous, others glorious. Is it not here that one must seek an explanation for the gloomy character of *yomi no kuni* to which Izanami goes when she has died in childbirth (see above)? This kind of death, regarded as particularly abnormal, had for a long time been the occasion of a special mode of burial.

Another source of differentiation may have been the social order. The members of the aristocracy who could have large tombs constructed for themselves no doubt believed that in this way they assured themselves of another world that would be happy. Thus, the members of the imperial family must have hoped to reascend after their death to *Takama no hara,* the land of their ancestor Amaterasu. But since this destiny was probably not available to everyone, what could the hope of survival have been for those who were abandoned without burial?

The different origins of the populations of Japan might in part explain certain divergences in their conceptions of the afterworld. Thus, the horizontal conception of space which locates the other world beyond the seas (characteristic of the

Osore-san Mountain, Aomori prefecture, at the time of the festival of the dead (*o-bon*) in August. *Left:* The marker indicates the site of the inferno of the king of the *shuras*. *Right:* Pilgrims cross the lava field to offer "the great penitence" at the temple. CERTPJ photo archives. Photo Th. Lesoual'ch.

myths of the Izumo cycle) is opposed to the vertical representation of a world divided into three parts superimposed one upon the other: sky, earth, and underworld, a representation of the cycle of *takama no hara* that bears the ideology of the imperial clan.

Another explanation arises from the hypothesis that a people who came from the sea retained a nostalgia for the land of their ancestors. As this people penetrated the new regions, they would have gradually absorbed into their original beliefs other beliefs, particularly about mountains.

The present state of research precludes any synthesis of these hypotheses. Moreover, it is rather futile to speculate about an original condition, given the poverty of the sources available to us. On the other hand, it is very interesting to note the connections between the different abodes that have been examined. For instance, on the occasion of the *bon* festival, the welcome might be made in the form of flowers picked on a mountaintop, which connects the mountain and the sky. The souls are often brought back by placing rafts in the river or the sea. There is, therefore, a triple connection that the rites of *bon* deploy: sky, mountain, ocean. This triad is found in the fresco of the funerary mound of Mezurashizuka, an artificial mountain, where the association of a bird and a boat—just as in the myth of Sukunabikona—blurs the distinction between ocean and sky.

II. Buddhism

Buddhist beliefs arrived very early in Japan, even before the traditional official dates of 538 or 552.

However, the diffusion of Buddhist ideas about the next life seems to have been particularly slow, and the adoption of Buddhist funeral rites was very gradual. Empress Jitō at the beginning of the eighth century was the first sovereign to be cremated according to a Buddhist ritual. Though the aristocracy gradually followed her example, cremation encountered such resistance among the people that even now certain regions still do not practice it. Furthermore, even where it has been implanted, it seems to be regarded as a means of accelerating the process of separating the flesh from the skeleton, which is also the aim of the double interments as they have long been practiced in the Amami archipelago.

On the other hand, Buddhist terms have prevailed in almost the entire vocabulary dealing with death or the afterworld, to which they give their own connotation. The imprint has been so strong that Buddhist sects have a monopoly over funerals, whether they use cremation or not.

The new religion arrived in Japan with a doctrine that presented a coherent and elaborate vision of existence. Considering the resistance that it must have encountered, we may justly ask how the doctrine endured in Japan.

The conception of the cycle of rebirths seems to have turned away from its original significance. Since the Buddhist believer must attempt to break the cycle and the bonds that maintain it, some have committed suicide (double suicide, *shin jū;* suicide of vassals at the death of their lord, *junshi*) in order to create a bond that would assure a common future existence. In addition, from the Buddhist point of view, human life is devalued, considered as ephemeral, and characterized by suffering. Thus, though the consciousness of the impermanence of things has occupied an important place in Japanese sensibility and poetry, the deprecation of this world could only with difficulty become rooted in a society that honored its ancestors and therefore took care to guarantee that there would be descendants; in popular belief, the dead without families are *gaki,* "hungry ghosts," whose fate is similar to that of the damned. People who wished to die with the hope of being reborn in a better existence had to rely on the mercy of the Amida Buddha; but they could also count on the family, whose duty it was to improve the lot of the dead through their prayers and offerings—through the principle of the transfer of merit (*ekō*).

Finally, the various forms of rebirth which normally would have remained in an abstract state were often conceived of in a very concrete manner in the popular traditions.

1. Hell (*Jigoku*)

King Emma (Sanskrit: Yama), who, in the beginning, had ruled at the crossroads to judge the guilty and to send them back to be reborn according to their merits on one path or another, became sovereign of the eight hells, which were organized and administered according to the mode of Chinese administration. The various hells, in which the damned resided according to their crimes, are well known to us through painted scrolls and from the testimony of those who, according to tradition, have returned from them. One can indeed return from hell, since one might have been summoned there by mistake, or the Bodhisattva Jizō might intervene. Jizō, protector of roads and crossroads, advocate of the dead before King Emma, became Emma's enemy. The farces of the Middle Ages (*kyōgen*) transformed Emma into a king of demons who was deceived by every kind of trick and always lost against Jizō. Apparently *jigoku* has lost its terrifying content.

From another perspective, popular beliefs have situated *jigoku* in the mountains. The volcanic activity that was frequent in Japan must have favored such a location, as well as the role of the mountains in pre-Buddhist beliefs about the afterlife (see above). Indeed, *jigoku* is not situated in a single mountain but in the regional centers cited above as local abodes of the dead. *Jigoku* took the place, therefore, of a previous conception of the afterworld. We have confirmation of this in an account of *Nihon ryō iki*. In this account, the monk Chikō is taken to hell because of his jealousy. But the abduction is merely a warning; after he has undergone much suffering, he is sent back to earth with a final recommendation that is utterly surprising in a Buddhist text: "Do not eat the food cooked in the fire of *yomi*." Finally, the current explanation states that the ancestors arrive during the *bon* festival because the cover of the caldron of hell is ajar during this period. Taken literally, this would imply that the ancestors are among the damned.

Although they have distinct origins, the ways of the *gaki* and *ashura* (demons) have entered into the shifting development of *jigoku*.

The *gaki* are a type too close to that of the damned to be separated from them. As for the way of the *ashura*, it is reserved for those of the dead who continue to be devoured by their passion and who are transformed into demonic beings. Held back by their attachment to the world, they continue to haunt the places that were familiar to them. Their apparition would provide the material for numerous literary works, and in particular the No plays. But the success of ghost stories may also rest upon a more ancient belief that the dead remain close to the world of the living and continue to intervene in the life of their descendants.

2. The Pure Lands (*Jōdo*)

It seems that very early the possibility of reincarnation was envisaged only for young children, who, as a result, were not interred in the usual places, but near the house or even inside. The great hope was to be reborn in paradise, in the "pure land," *jōdo*.

One of the "pure lands," that of the Bodhisattva Miroku (Maitreya), is at the center of a legend about the monk Kūkai. The legend recounts that Kūkai had himself entombed alive in a meditation room and that, immobile, he awaited there the coming of Miroku, the Buddha of the Future. This legend incontestably reinforced the attraction that Mount Kōya already exercised as a burial place. Waiting for the reign of Miroku is also at the origin of certain mummifications, *miira*, at least those that are prepared in observance of the fast unto death. The belief in another pure land, that of the Bodhisattva Kannon, gave birth to specific practices. In order to arrive in the pure land situated toward the south, on a mountain beyond the seas, certain fervent believers went so far as to embark on boats that they set adrift on the open sea off Kumano. The choice of Kumano as a point of departure may be explained by the bonds with the afterworld that this great religious center had maintained since antiquity. Are not the banks of Ise, nearby, bathed in waves that are supposed to come from *tokoyo?*

But the pure land par excellence is that of Amida, and its success is linked to that of the Amida sects. Belief in the paradise of Amida spread through every layer of the population, from monks to laity, from people of the court of the Heian period to the lower classes influenced by the popular preachers of the Middle Ages. The most fervent among the believers, ready to commit suicide in order to go there and be reborn, at the last moment had the vision of a purple cloud and heard the celestial music of the cortege of Amida, come to welcome them (*raigō*). Popular beliefs also transposed the land of felicity known as *jodō* to mountains such as Mount Kōya.

F.M./m.s.

BIBLIOGRAPHY

1. Monographs

S. GORAI, *Kōya hijiri* (Tokyo 1975). CH. HAGUENAUER, *Origines de la civilisation japonaise: Introduction à l'étude de la préhistoire du Japon*, part 1 (Paris 1956). SH. INOGUCHI, *Nihon no sōshiki* (Tokyo 1965). Y. YOBAYASHI, *Kofun no hanashi* (Tokyo 1974). N. KOIKE, *Hito no shigo no hanashi* (Tokyo 1972). T. OBAYASHI, *Nihon shinwa no kigen* (Tokyo 1973); *Sōsei no kigen* (Tokyo 1965). T. SAKURAI, *Nihonjin no sei to shi* (Tokyo 1968). Y. SATO, *Sōsōgirei no minzoku* (Tokyo 1968). M. SAWADA, *Jigokuhen* (Kyoto 1976). T. TAMAMURO, *Sōshikibukkyō* (Tokyo 1976). SH. WATANABE, *Shigo no sekai* (Tokyo 1959). T. YAMAORI, *Nihonjin no Reikonkan* (Tokyo 1976). K. YANAGITA, *Senzo no hanashi* (Tokyo 1946); *Yamamiya kō* (Tokyo 1947).

Additional monographs: GARY L. EBERSOLE, *Ritual Poetry and the Politics of Death in Early Japan* (Princeton 1989). ICHIRO HORI, *Folk Religion in Japan* (Chicago 1968). KAZUO KASAHARA and JUNKO OGIRI, eds., *Iki-zama, shini-zama: Nihon minshū shinkōshi* (Tokyo 1979). YANAI KYUSAKU, *Ama no iwato shinwa no kenkyȳ* (Tokyo 1977). TAMURA YOSHIRO and MINAMOTO RUŌEN, eds., *Nihon ni okeru sei to shi no shisō* (Tokyo 1977).

2. Articles

CH. HAGUENAUER, "Du caractère de la représentation de la mort dans le Japon antique," in *T'oung pao*, no. 33 (1937): 158–83; "La danse rituelle dans le Chinkonsai," *Journal asiatique* (April–June 1930), 299ff. J. HORI, "Manyōshū ni arawareta sōsei to sekaikan, reikonkan ni tsuite," in *Nihonshūkyōshikenkyū* (Tokyo 1963), 2:49–93.

Additional articles: KEN AKAMATSU, "The Significance of the Formation and Distribution of *Kofun*," *Acta Asiatica* 31 (1977): 24–50. TOSHIO AKIMA, "Songs of the Dead: Poetry, Drama, and Ancient Death Rituals of Japan," *Journal of Asian Studies* 41, 3 (May 1982): 485–509.

GARY L. EBERSOLE, "The Religio-Aesthetic Complex in *Manyōshū Poetry* with Special Emphasis on Hitomaro's *Aki no no* Sequence," *History of Religions* 23, 1 (August 1983): 18–36. TAKESHI MATSUMAE, "The Heavenly Rock-Grotto Myth and the Chinkon Ceremony," *Asian Folklore Studies* 39, 2 (1980): 9–22; "Taiyō fune to tokoyo shinkō," *Kokugakuin zasshi* 62, 2–3 (February–March 1961): 23–43. TAKAYOSHI MOGAMI, "The Double-Grave System," in Richard M. Dorson, ed., *Studies in Japanese Folklore* (New York 1980), pp. 167–80. SUSUMU NAKANISHI, "The Spatial Structure of Japanese Myth: The Contact Point between Life and Death," in Earl Miner, ed., *Principles of Classical Japanese Literature* (Princeton 1985), pp. 106–29. NELLY NAUMANN, "*Sakahagi:* The 'Reverse Flaying' of the Heavenly Piebald Horse," *Asian Folklore Studies* 41, 1 (1982): 7–38. NOBUTSUNA SAIGO, "Yomi no kuni to ne no kuni: Chika no sekai ni tsuite," *Bungaku* 39, 11 (November 1971): 19–35. MASAO SUGANO, "Tokoyo-yuku shinwa no keisei," *Kokugakuin zasshi* 62, 10 (October 1962): 42–48. SHIGEKI WADA, "Mogari no kiso-teki kōsatsu," *Shirin* 52, 5 (September 1969): 32–90.

3. Multivolume Works

T. MATSUMURA, *Nihon shinwa no kenkhū*, 4 vols. (Tokyo 1954–58). *Nihon no kōkogaku*, 7 vols. (Tokyo 1965–67), vols. 4 and 5 on Kofun jidai. SH. ORIKUCHI, *Kodai kenkhū*, 6 vols. (Tokyo 1974). *Shinpojiumu Nihon no shinwa*, 5 vols. (Tokyo 1972–75).

Buddhism and Archaic Beliefs in the Shinto-Buddhist Syncretism of Japan

The rapprochement of Buddhism and archaic beliefs had already been initiated in the sixth and seventh centuries. Buddhism, introduced in Japan as a part of mainland culture, was actively supported by the rulers. The second article of the "Seventeen Article Constitution," promulgation of which is ordinarily attributed to Prince Shōtoku (574–622), recommends, for example, the veneration of the "three jewels" (*sanbō*). A decree dated the twenty-seventh day of the third lunar month of the fourteenth year of Emperor Temmu (686) orders the construction and veneration of Buddhist statues (cf. the *Nihongi*). This political support furthered the mixing of the two belief systems, since the emperors were also the highest functionaries of the national religion, Shinto. The fact that the Shinto religion did not have statues of deities made it even easier to accept Buddhist iconography and the ideas it expressed. The incorporation of Shinto deities within Buddhism, when Shinto did not have, in this encounter with Buddhism, clearly defined ethical and philosophical concepts, took place chiefly in Shingon esotericism, which affirmed that the entire universe was nothing but a manifestation of the Buddha Dainichi. Also, from the point of view of its rituals, Buddhism was attractive. It was rich, for example, in practices of exorcism which corresponded easily to the pre-Buddhist magic that was employed during prayers for rain (*amagoi*). As for the *kami*, people originally viewed them with respect and fear; when, with time, the respect gave way to fixed forms of veneration, people developed the idea that they could secure the supernatural forces of the *kami* for themselves. Soon it was common to read the sutras before the *kami*. More generally, the new form of Buddhism that the Tendai and Shingon sects represented gave an important place to the "magical" use of the sutras, accentuating tendencies that already existed in Buddhism during the Nara era.

But the rapprochement of Buddhism and Shinto had also been furthered by the proximity, if not the actual geographical identity, of the cult sites. In its concern to assure the economic equilibrium of the temples in the provinces, Buddhism hoped to rely on local cults. Although the new religion had been rapidly accepted by the aristocratic class, who most often lived in the capital, ancient Shinto always reigned in the provinces and among those who worked in the domains of the Buddhist temples. The better to protect these lands, where ancient beliefs were still alive, Buddhism sought the support of local deities and made them the protecting deities of their temples. In order to justify the construction of the temples, they forged legends according to which, for example, at such and such a place an old man—the local deity in his human aspect—had asked for the temple for himself. At the time of the construction of the "Great Buddha" of Nara, the deity Hachiman of Usa (at Kyushu) was "transferred" to the capital, probably to avert the disturbance or resentment of people alarmed by the diffusion of Buddhism, but also to further the alliance of the two religions.

In architecture the close bonds between Buddhism and Shinto were manifested in the construction of *jingūji*, Buddhist annexes to Shinto sanctuaries in front of which the sutras were recited and Buddhist ceremonies were carried out. The opening of Buddhism to other religions was at least partially the cause of the growing tendency to regard the recitation and the offering of the sutras before the *kami*—protectors of the Buddhist law—as an act that could bring salvation and joy to the *kami*. During the Nara period, it was already common practice to count the *kami* among those beings who—like the humans attached to this world of illusion and suffering—could find salvation through the Buddhist law. The next stage was to give the name and title of *bosatsu* to these Shinto deities, who were thought to have arrived at the state of a bodhisattva (Japanese *bosatsu*) through the power of the Buddhist law. The first example of such a promotion is Hachiman, who was called *Hachiman dai bosatsu* in 781. Endowed with the quality of future Buddhas (that is, of bodhisattvas), the *kami* were finally raised to the same level as a Buddha, but they are only avatars (*gongen*), and it is with this title that they are venerated by Buddhism; they are the "trace descended on earth" (*suijaku*) of the Buddhas, who themselves are the "original state" (*honji*) of the *kami*.

This same concept of the *honji suijaku*, which allowed the *kami* to be held as temporary manifestations of Buddhas, at the time of the propagation of Buddhism in China, served to mark the superiority of Buddhism over Confucianism and Daoism. In Japan, no religion could rival Buddhism, on either the ideological plane or the institutional. People therefore chiefly tried to find a new interpretation of the nature of Shinto deities in Buddhist terms. There was not yet a true syncretism during the Nara period, but during the Heian period the concept of *honji suijaku* took form, though it did not yet attribute to each deity a particular Buddha who would be its *honji*. *Kami* and Buddhas were simply thought to be identical, the Buddhas "softening the light of their wisdom" (*wakō*) to allow their emanations to descend in multiple forms upon the earth, where they adapted themselves to the unequal receptivity of beings (*dōjin*).

The Kamakura period (1185–1333) saw the most fully marked evolution of the *kami* toward Buddhism, through the concept of *honji-suijaku*. This is most apparent in the celebrated collection of *setsuwa* entitled *Shasekishū*. These didactic anecdotes show clearly the change that took place on the threshold of the Middle Ages in the vision of the *kami;* here they are described as animated by a profound desire to turn humans away from this lowly world, to take them away from seeking *genze riyaku* (immediate or material profit), and this concern is accompanied by a marked insistence on the future life (*gose*) as the only thing of value. In order to aid in the liberation from the cycle of samsara, the deities put at man's disposal the *hōben* (expedients) which facilitate access to the Buddhist path. The *kami* lost, then, the characteristics which distinguished them from Buddhas; they were assimilated functionally as well as existentially.

The primary cause of the different manifestations under which Buddhist and Shinto deities appear is Dainichi Nyorai in the metaphysical body (*hosshin*). To humble oneself through *hōben* (by compassion for beings) or, to put it another way, to conceal one's true nature as a Buddha in order to manifest oneself as a *kami* in the dust of this lowly world is the major concept of medieval Shinto, *wakō dōjin*. The term, which derives from a passage of Laozi (*Daodejing,* "masterpiece of the path and of the power"), passed into Buddhist texts, notably the famous *Maka shikan* (594) of Zhikai, founder of the Tendai sect in China. By the transmission of this text, as well as that of the sutras and other works, the notion of *wakō dōjin* was known at that time by the Japanese and taken up not only in the literature of the time (which had a strongly Buddhist tint—as in the *Hōgen-monogatari,* the *Gikeiki,* the *Taiheiki,* etc.), but also in the "words of the law" (*hōgo*) of certain monks (like Ippen), in the popular religious songs (*imayō*) of the *Ryōjin hishō,* in No plays (like *Aridōshi*). The idea of *wakō dōjin* and what it makes of the *kami* are well illustrated in the *Shasekishū,* already mentioned, in which certain of the anecdotes could even be regarded as the beginning of an evolution that ends by reversing the position of interdependence between the *kami* and the Buddha (still fixed in the *honji-suijaku*), to the detriment of the Buddha. This evolution had only begun in the *setsuwa*. The history of En no Gyōja presents Shākyamuni and Miroku *bosatsu* as inferior to a *gongen* (in this case, Zaō Gongen) in the difficult task of guiding and saving beings at the time of *mappō*. During the time of *mappō* many beings lack *dōshin,* that pious spirit whose absence is especially contrary to the will of the *kami* (fundamentally of the Buddhas). Eichō Sōzu, for example, who carries on a dialogue with the divinity of the sanctuary of Kasuga concerning the doctrines of the "nothing-but-thought" (*yuishiki*), is nevertheless told that he is incapable of seeing the august countenance, because of his lack of *dōshin*. There is the same insistence in the reactions of the *kami* to those who lack the "wide-awake heart" (*bodaishin*). The state of the spirit—a necessary condition for deliverance from samsara—is deemed more important than the maintenance of Buddhist temples. Defined by reference to the future life, this insistence on the value of *bodaishin* is also characteristic of the *kami* of the Middle Ages, as is the compassion mentioned above. The compassion (*jihi*) not only suffices to motivate all the intervention of the *kami* in the world of men but is held to be more important, finally, than the observance of traditional taboos (such as those of impurity). This is what the divinity of Yoshino teaches the monk Jōkan, who wrongly thinks that he is defiled by contact with death and thereby prevented from approaching the *kami*.

All the evidence indicates that it was the theory of the *honji-suijaku* that made possible the transfer of the virtue of compassion, originally characteristic of Buddhas and bodhisattvas, to their avatars. The diverse *engi* ("accounts of the origin," in particular of sanctuaries) contained in the *Shintōshū* (mid-sixteenth century) and the *otogi-zōshi* (popular tales of the epoch of Muromachi)—notably the *honji-mono*—go so far as to make the compassionate *kami* experience all the suffering of humans. Moreover, in order to mark clearly their disapproval of self-seeking demands (*genze riyaku*), the *kami* counter them with inertia and impotence; on the other hand, they abound in *hōben,* which are expedients to hasten beings on the path of Buddhism, and they predict, for example, particular hells (such as the hells beneath the sanctuaries of Kasuga and Hiyoshi) as places of spiritual reeducation.

In summary: at the beginning of the Middle Ages, the concepts of *honji-suijaku* and *wakō dōjin* had made it possible for Shinto deities to be regarded as avatars of Buddhas; then, finally, because of the affinity of character and function ascribed to them with the Buddhas of whom they are the emanation, they became "Buddhist" *kami,* tributaries, in their thought and their reactions, of traditional Buddhist values.

H.O.R./d.f.

BIBLIOGRAPHY

1. Sources

H. O. ROTERMUND, ed. and trans., *Collection de sable et de pierres, Shasekishū* (Paris 1979).

Additional source: ROBERT E. MORRELL, trans., *Sand and Pebbles (Shasekishū): The Tales of Muju Ichien, a Voice for Pluralism in Kamakura Japan* (Albany, NY, 1985).

2. Monographs

A. MATSUNAGA, *The Buddhist Philosophy of Assimilation: The Historical Development of the Honji Suijaku Theory,* MN Monograph (Tokyo 1969). T. HARADA, *Nihon shūkyō kōshō-shi ron* (Tokyo 1969). J. HORI, *Waga kuni minkan shinkō-shi no kenkyū,* 2 vols. (Tokyo 1953). SH. MURAYAMA, *Shinbutsu shūgō shichō,* Sara sōsho 6 (Kyoto 1964); *Honji suijaku,* Nihon rekishi sōsho 33 (Tokyo 1974). K. OYAMA, *Shinbutsu kōshō-shi* (Kōya-san 1944). T. SAKURAI, *Shinbutsu kōshō-shi kenkyū* (Tokyo 1968).

Additional monographs: J. H. KAMSTRA, *Encounter or Syncretism: The Initial Growth of Japanese Buddhism* (Leiden 1967). CHRISTINE GUTH KANDA, *Shinzō: Hachiman Imagery and Its Development,* Harvard East Asian Monographs 119 (Cambridge, MA, 1985). WATASE MASATADA, *Kakinomoto Hitomaro kenkyū,* 3 vols. (Tokyo 1976).

3. Articles

H. O. ROTERMUND, "La conception des kami japonais à l'époque de kamakura: Notes sur le premier chapitre du Sasekishū," *Revue de l'histoire des religions* 182–83 (1972).

Additional article: TOSHIO KURODA, "Shintō in the History of Japanese Religion," *Journal of Japanese Studies* 7, 1 (Winter 1981): 1–21.

Mountains in Japan

Among many signs of the veneration of mountains in ancient Japan are not only archaeological finds (mirrors, vases, ritual utensils) but also literary vestiges, such as the passages of the myths in the *Kojiki* and *Nihongi* that deal with obedience to the deities of the mountains. Various classifications of mountains have been advanced (cf. Kishimoto, Ikegami, Hori, etc.), the criterion being the nature and form of the mountains or the cults observed on them. Thus, by the first criterion, volcanoes are usually considered the residences of deities; other mountains are revered as sources of water or as the place of the souls of the dead (which implies a mountain burial) or as a place of passage for souls on their way to the world beyond. Depending on the form taken by the cult practiced there, a distinction is made between mountains that are climbed at a designated time, by people who wish to go into a retreat there or to devote themselves to religious practices, and mountains that are climbed as often as possible, the climbing being an exercise in and of itself. Taking the second point of view, and placing the emphasis on the principal element of the cult, Ikegami distinguishes among the following: (*a*) mountains of pilgrimage closely associated with the spirits of the dead (for instance, Mount Osore); (*b*) mountains that are revered for themselves, the mountain being the "body of the deity" (*shintai*), a typical example of which is Mount Miwa; people do not climb these mountains but worship them from below in a hall of veneration (*haiden*); (*c*) mountains that people climb with the aim of uniting with the deity on the peak (for example, Mount Ontake and Mount Fuji); (*d*) mountains more specifically associated with multiple functions in popular belief: the place where the souls of the ancestors reside, the place of the *ujigami* and/or of the *yama no kami;* and finally (*e*) mountains suitable for *shugendō,* those that are places of religious practices and asceticism.

A word about mountains as sources of water and as the dwelling places of "deities that give water" (*mi-kumari no kami*). Since popular beliefs and many seasonal customs have been closely associated with agriculture, with the dead, and with the spirits of the ancestors in Japan from the earliest times, and since wind and rain are of major importance to the farmer, it was quite natural that religious concerns would extend to the mountains, from whose peaks the water flows that is so precious for rice cultivation. In the sanctuaries known as *mikumari,* the deities of wind and rain were worshiped. The *Engishiki* (927) informs us of the existence of four of these shrines in Yamato, in particular at Yoshino and Katsuragi. The cult of Komori Myōjin, observed in such shrines, apparently developed as the result of a phonetic confusion between *kumari* and *komori.*

The function of mountains as burial sites appears clearly in poem 165 of the *Man'yōshū,* in which Princess Oku mourns the death of her brother, Prince Otsu. The particular connection between mountains and death is also manifested in numerous terms from the vocabulary of folklore (for example, *yama shigoto,* meaning both "to work in the mountains" and "to dig a grave"), and becomes eminently clear in the *banka* (elegies) of the *Man'yōshū,* which mostly indicate that the soul rests in the mountains; a few of these poems give the sky or the clouds, the rocks or the sea, as an abode of the soul, and only a very small minority speak of anything like a hell. The importance of mountains in the religious life of the Japanese is also reflected in the presence of the *yama-miya* ("shrines in the mountains") and the *sato-miya* ("shrines in the villages at the foot of a mountain"). The rituals connected with the *ujigami* ("deity of the clan") and with the *yama-miya* shrines are explained by the belief that the souls of the dead—which gradually rise to the stage of *kami*—reside in the mountains but come down to the villages at certain times of the year. That the mountain is a place of passage to the afterlife is expressed in the concept of *shide no yama* ("the mountain of the voyage beyond the tomb"), a mountain that Buddhism has made into a dangerous place, peopled with evil demons, as seems to be indicated by a reference in poem 858 of the *Shin zoku kokin wakashū* (1439). A messenger between the world below and the world beyond, the cuckoo is supposed to pass through this same *shide no yama.* This is what is said in poem 1307 of the *Shūi Wakashū* (perhaps from the beginning of the eleventh century). Of the innumerable seasonal Japanese feast days, it is *bon* that best translates, in its diverse ritual forms, the close ties between mountains and death.

Since ancient times, Japanese sacred mountains, particularly Mount Yoshino, have been the destination points for imperial voyages. It was at Yoshino that Emperor Jimmu was blessed with a revelation in a dream; and many empresses, Jitō among others, went to Yoshino. In the first Japanese anthology of poems in the Chinese style, entitled *Kaifūsō* (eighth century: see poems 48 and 73), the sacred character of Mount Yoshino is emphasized by qualifiers that refer to the spirits and the immortals (*sen*) of Daoism. One likely explanation for these mountain visits was the quest for sacred water. Called *haraegawa* or *mitarashigawa,* the streams of water situated near sacred mountains were regarded as the boundary between our world and the world beyond. Yet another aspect of mountains in Japan is that of the fertile mother who has the (magical) power to grant life and to bring about rebirth. And this leads us to the divinity of the mountain, *yama no kami.*

Among the various classes of Japanese *kami,* the *yama no kami* is especially important, and the worship of these deities is at the heart of the *sangaku shinkō.* There are different sorts of *yama no kami,* which can remain fixed in a definite region or vary according to the social nature of the worshipers. Thus woodsmen and hunters have their own *yama no kami;* for the rural community, the *yama no kami* is above all the deity that comes down from the mountains when the season requires, in order to become the *ta no kami* or "deity of the fields"—a belief that is connected with the belief in the visiting deities who come from the world beyond in order to bring good fortune. The idea of such a visiting deity coming from the world beyond the mountains—and not, as in a more remote period, from the world beyond the sea (like the deity Sukunabikona)—seems to have taken shape at the time when the ancient Japanese began to leave the seacoast to settle farther inland. It is notably during the period when the rice is transplanted that the *yama no kami* becomes the object of attention: then they welcome him to the fields and address him with prayers for a good crop. While waiting for the crop to be garnered, the deity (who has become *ta no kami*) will remain in the plain to ensure prosperity. The custom of going right up to the mountain to welcome the deity, often taking well-designated paths and observing certain practices, as well as the fact that the mountains were places for the initiation of boys when they reached maturity, have influenced the practice of the *shugendō* known as *haru-yama* ("spring mountain").

The mountain deity is difficult to characterize in terms of external appearance. Sometimes it appears in the form of a

Yudono-san Mountain, Yamagata prefecture. A group of pilgrims (*kō*), fulfilling their ascetic duties by climbing the "three summits of Dewa" (*Dewa sanzan*) before worshiping the "body of the deity" (*shintai*) of Yudono, represented by this rock, from which mineral waters spring. In front of the rock is a stone niche in which pilgrims place and light candles. CERTPJ photo archive. Photo taken in 1936 by A. Togawa.

snake; at other times it looks more like the fabulous creature called the *tengu.* Often it is female, and representations of *yama no kami* often depict ugly features (the deity is one-eyed, one-legged, etc.) and signs of a nasty temperament (for this point of view, see the provincial chronicles: *Harima Fudoki, Hitachi Fudoki.*) The female character is underscored and is confirmed by various facts. A play from the Heian period, which is referred to in the *chinkonka* songs ("for the appeasement of souls") cited in a work entitled *Nenjūgyōji hishō* (Secret notes on seasonal rituals), mentions, for example, the belief that a female deity (O-hirume or Amaterasu) would bring "a box of souls" *tama tebako* from a sacred mountain to the new emperor (see Hori). *Juni-sama* ("the lady of the twelve months") is another name for the *yama no kami,* who is supposed to give birth once a year to twelve children, that is, the twelve months of the year. Numerous ritual practices connected with birth are also more easily interpreted in the light of a female *yama no kami,* protector of childbirth.

Nowadays it is believed that these concepts originated in an ancient belief of hunters in a mother deity of the mountains. Yanagita, for example, distinguishes three categories: (*a*) the so-called Kōya type, in which the deity and her son grant permission to build temples or houses on the mountain (this type owes its name to a legend attributing to Kūkai a meeting with Nifutsuhime, the deity of Mount Kōya: following this encounter, Kūkai is said to have obtained permission to build his monastery, but he also built one in honor of the deity and her son Kariba Myōjin, who, disguised as a hunter, had met Kūkai on the mountain and had brought him to his mother); (*b*) the Nikko type, in which we see the goddess granting the right to hunt, as reward for a good deed, to a certain Banzaburo, who will later emerge, in the region of Nikko, as the ancestor of the hunters; and (*c*) the type called Shiiba (a village in Kyushu), in which the deity *yama no shinbo* ("the mother goddess of the mountain") is disguised as a young girl, testing the character of hunters, such as the two brothers Oma and Koma, one hard-hearted, the other generous.

As Hori has well demonstrated in numerous studies, beliefs about mountains have significant characteristics in common with ancient forms of shamanism. The concept of the sacred mountain as the realm of the dead, the place of passage between this world and the world beyond or the meeting place between the dead and the living, and the idea that the mountains are the domain of spirits or deities (Buddhist or Shinto), or a place where shamans practice asceticism, are the basis on which the *shugendō* was established. The existence of ties between the mountain ascetics of the *shugendō* and hunters can also be seen in certain rituals practiced by hunters.

H.O.R./g.h.

BIBLIOGRAPHY

1. Sources

Sangaku shūkyōshi kenkyū sōsho, 12 vols. (Tokyo 1975).

2. Monographs

N. NAUMANN, "Yama no kami, die japanische Berggottheit," *Folklore Studies* 22 (1963–64). K. HIGO, *Nihon ni okeru sangaku shinkō no rekishi,* Sangaku shinkō series no. 4 (Tokyo 1949). I. HORI, *Nihon ni okeru sangaku shinkō no genshi keitai,* Sangaku shinkō series no. 2 (Tokyo 1949). K. HORITA, *Yama no kami shinkō no kenkyū* (Kuwana 1966). N. MIYAJI, *Kumano sanzan no shiteki kenkyū* (Tokyo 1956); *Sangaku shinkō to jinja,* Sangaku shinkō series no. 3 (Tokyo 1949). I. OBA, *Nihon ni okeru sangaku shinkō no kōkogakuteki kōsatsu,* Sangaku shinkō series no. 1 (Tokyo 1948). SH. TAKASE, *Kodai sangaku shinkō no shiteki kenkyū* (Tokyo 1969).

Additional monographs: H. BYRON EARHART, "The Celebration of *Haru-Yama* (Spring Mountain): An Example of Folk Religious Practices in Contemporary Japan," *Asian Folklore Studies* 27, 1 (1968): 1–18. ICHIRO HORI, *Folk Religion in Japan* (Chicago 1968). YOSHIKO YAMAMOTO, *The Namahage: A Festival in the Northeast of Japan* (Philadelphia 1978).

3. Articles

H. IKEGAMI, "The Significance of Mountains in the Popular Beliefs in Japan," in *Religious Studies in Japan* (Tokyo 1959). I. HORI, "Mountains and Their Importance for the Idea of the Other World in Japanese Folk Religion," *History of Religions* 6/1 (1966). H. KISHIMOTO, "The Role of Mountains in the Religious Life of the Japanese People," *Proceedings of the Ninth International Congress for the History of Religions 1958* (Tokyo 1960). T. HARADA, "Yama no sūhai to yama no kami-toku ni yama bukkyō to no kanren ni oite," *Nihon shūkyō kōshō-shi ron* (Tokyo 1949). I. HORI, "Yama to shinkō," *Kokugakuin daigaku Nihon bunka kenkyūjo kiyō,* vol. 12 (1963). H. IKEGAMI, "Sangaku shinkō no sho keitai," *Jinrui kagaku,* vol. 12 (1960). K. KINDAICHI, "Yama no kami-kō," *Minzoku* 2/3. SH. SUZUKI, "Genshi sangaku shinkō no ikkōsatsu: Tōhoku ni okeru Hayama shinkō," *Shūkyō kenkyū,* vol. 170 (1961). A. TOGAWA, "Yama no kami to ta no kami," *Shōnai minzoku,* vol. 22 (1960). K. YANAGAWA, "Sonraku ni okeru sangaku shinkō no soshiki," *Shūkyō kenkyū,* vol. 143 (1955). K. YANAGITA, "Yama miya-kō," *Yanagita Kunio shū,* vol. 11; "Yama no kami to okoze," *Yanagita Kunio shū,* vol. 4.

Additional articles: ICHIRO HORI, "Mysterious Visitors from the Harvest to the New Year," in *Studies in Japanese Folklore,* Richard Dorson, ed. (Bloomington, IN, 1963), pp. 76–106. ITSUHIKO OHAMA, "Jitō tennō wa naze Yoshino e itta ka?" *Kokubungaku: Kaishaku to kanshō* 34, 2 (February 1969): 60–64. YOSHITAKA YOSHIDA, "Yoshino sanka to Jitō chō," *Kokubungaku: Kaishaku to kyozai no kenkyū* 28, 7 (May 1983): 122–27.

Magic in Japan

Traces of magic as a central element in popular beliefs are found in the earliest documents of Japanese literature. We know that magical action is ordinarily distinguished from verbal magic. Magical action is characterized by analogical effects (imitation, attraction between things that resemble one another), contact (action through contiguity), or sympathetic acts (those which rest on the belief in an internal relationship between things or phenomena, as is expressed, for example, by the adage *pars pro toto*). One might ask, however, if a distinction between imitative magic (for example, *amagoi:* a prayer for rain; and *taue:* the replanting of rice), magic by contact, and sympathetic magic (in the case of *hitogata:* an anthropomorphic figurine to which the blemishes and sins of men are transferred in a ritual of purification) always takes into account the complex reality of popular Japanese beliefs. One could just as well, for example, distinguish between acts of individual and collective magic, or between those acts that are executed in a clearly delineated

Kyōto. Woman with eye disease; she has touched the eye of the turtle and then her own diseased eye with the intention of healing it. CERTPJ photo archive. Photo P. Bonicel.

Daruma and *Himedaruma,* Sendai, 12 and 10 cm. Dolls of this kind, built so as always to remain upright, symbolize man's resilience in the face of difficulties. Commercially sold *darumas* have only one eye; the second eye is painted on after a wish that has been made on the doll comes true. CERTPJ photo archive, Berval collection. Photo L. Frédéric.

Shakushi or *shamoji,* rice spoons (Okayama prefecture), which are offered as ex-votos. Below a Sanskrit letter, they bear a votive formula, the name and age of the donor, and the date of the offering. CERTPJ photo archive. Photo H. O. Rotermund.

fashion and are always the same and those that vary with circumstances.

From the standpoint of the phenomenology of religions, magical behavior is based on the conviction that man has the capacity to manipulate his environment at will—objects, phenomena, evil spirits, demons, and even deities. This attitude is particularly illuminated by the verbal magic based on the belief in *kotodama.* From a functional standpoint, Japanese magic can be divided into three main categories: (*a*) to increase one's wealth or to make a profit; (*b*) to curse someone or harm him; and (*c*) to protect oneself from evil and calamities. In some of the latter practices, such as the *mushi-okuri,* which repels insects, or the *amagoi,* the prayer for rain, one can see elements of a therapeutic and prophylactic order grouped together. But it is not easy to distinguish the so-called magic attitude from the attitude that stems from a truly religious conviction, such as the *gankake* (vow) and the *kigan* (prayer, supplication), etc.

The whole life of the Japanese was formerly, and remains to a large extent today, punctuated by magical actions. This is especially true of birth and education (often imitative magic). It is also true of times of sickness, when magic is combined with therapy based on experience. Illnesses were often interpreted as the machinations of evil spirits, and efforts were made to chase them away, to transfer the evil to other objects or persons, to abandon it at crossroads, or even to "sell" it. Among magic objects or acts that could be used in this kind of healing are the saber, the knife, fishing, etc. Suspending a rice ladle (*shakush*) or garlic at the entrance of a house was a means of preventive therapy. Amulets (*o-fuda*) were used. Sacred ropes (*shimenawa*) were pulled. People used the *nembutsu* (notably in the form of the *hyakuman-ben nembutsu*) or a threatening *kigan*. They would force a deity to act, as in the case of Shibari Jizō ("bound Jizō"). Occasionally, the demons of diseases were dismissed (*ekibyōgami-okuri*) by simulating another time of year (notably by celebrating the New Year) or by some other way of disguising reality. Certain legendary events—as is obviously the case in the history of the teahouse on the Yu no O mountain pass—serve as the background for traditions that can often be summarized under the rubric of homophonic sympathy.

As far as death is concerned, magic rituals aimed above all to provide protection against impurity, to interrupt the relationship between the living and the dead, and to make sure that the dead would not return. While the "hunting of the demons" (demons of disease), referred to above, was carried out ad hoc in the event of illness, there were also other events, seasonal in character and propitious for such actions, including, most notably, the day of *setsubun* (the changing of the season). On that day, as on New Year's day, or on another two days known as the *kotoyōka* (the eighth day of the second and twelfth months), one could engage in a *mushi-okuri* or a *mushi-yoke,* otherwise performed right after the *taue.* The principles upon which the "insect hunt" is based have many points in common with the protective measures taken against the spirits of the dead, the *goryō* (angry spirits that inflict curses), a belief that goes back to the Heian period.

Numerous well-known practices take place at the beginning of the year, notably the *narikizeme,* a form of magic designed to ensure the fertility of trees. Most often the magical act is accompanied by the recitation of formulas (*jumon, tonaegoto, majinaiuta*), as the concept of *kotodama* demands.

H.O.R./g.h.

BIBLIOGRAPHY

1. Sources

SH. KARASAWA, *Shinbutsu hihō taizen* (Tokyo 1909). MEISHIN CHŌSA KYŌGI KAI, ed., *Nihon no zokushin,* 3 vols. (Tokyo 1952). K. ONO, *Kaji kitō himitsu taizen* (Tokyo 1970).

2. Monographs

B. FRANK, *Kata-imi et kata-tagae: Étude sur les interdits de direction à l'époque Heian,* Bulletin de la Maison Fr.-Jap., n.s., 5:2–4 (1958). H. O. ROTERMUND, *Majinai-uta.* Grundlagen, Inhalte und Formelemente japanischer magischer Gedichte des 17–20. Jahrhunderts. Versuch einer Interpretation, *MOAG,* vol. 59 (1975). Y. FUJIKAWA, *Meishin no kenkyū* (Tokyo 1932). T. HINO, *Meishin no kaibō* (Tokyo 1938). SH. INOGUCHI, *Nihon no zokushin* (Tokyo 1975). E. INOUE, *Yōkaigaku* (Tokyo 1930). T. KANEKO, *Kodai no juteki shinkō* (Tokyo 1968). E. KONNO, *Gendai no meishin,* Gendai kyōyō bunko (Tokyo 1969). Y. MIYANAGA, *Majinai no kenkyū* (Tokyo 1911). T. YOSHIDA, *Jujutsu* (Tokyo 1970). H. YOSHINO, *Nihon kodai jujutsu: Onmyōdō gogyō to Nihon genshi shinkō* (Tokyo 1975).

Additional monographs: GEOFFREY BOWNAS, *Japanese Rainmaking and Other Folk Practices* (London 1963). WINSTON DAVIS, *Dojo: Magic and Exorcism in Modern Japan* (Stanford 1980).

3. Articles

T. HARADA, "Zokushin," *Nihon minzokugaku taikei,* vol. 7 (1962). I. UENO, "Majinai ni tsuite," in *Minkan denshō,* 13:11.

Additional articles: U. A. CASAL, "Magical Vengeance in Old Japan," *Asiatische Studien* 10 (1956): 114–29. HAKU ITŌ, "Man'yōjin to kotodama," in *Man'yōshū kōza,* vol. 3 (Tokyo 1973), pp. 46–63. YOSHII IWAO, "Yamato-takeru no mikoto monogatari to majinai uta: Sono sōka ni tsuite no icki ksetsu," *Kokugo kokubun* 27, 10 (October 1958): 52–62. TSUNOSUKE NAKAGAWA, "Waka darani setsu," *Kokubungaku kō* 20 (1957): 20–29. EDWARD NORBECK, "Yakudoshi: A Japanese Complex of Supernatural Beliefs," *Southwestern Journal of Anthropology* 8, 1 (Spring 1952): 269–85.

4. Miscellany

N. MIYATA, "Kinsei no hayari-gami," *Nihonjin no kōdō to shisō,* 17 (1972). SH. ORIKUCHI, "Kodai kenkyū," *Orikuchi Shinobu zenshu,* 1–3. T. SAKURAI, *Minkan shinkō to gendai. Ningen to jujutsu,* Nihonjin no kōdō to shisō, 9 (1971).

JAPANESE DIVINATION

Japanese divination is, on the one hand, the passive act of interpreting omens (*kizashi, zenchō*) and, on the other, that of prophesying the future with the help of procedures called *urani* (or *bokusen*). The first of these derives from the belief that certain omens (the presence of animals, manifestations of natural phenomena, symptoms in the human body, etc.) indicate the coming of a specific event. Thus, since ancient times, falling stars (*nagareboshi*) have been regarded as harbingers of death or imminent catastrophe, as is the cry of the raven (*karasu naki*). Peasants attempted to interpret certain meteorological phenomena out of a concern for the coming harvest: for example, snow at the beginning of the year promised a good harvest. Dreams (*yume*) are given a particular place in the interpretation of omens, and their images are perceived sometimes as good omens and sometimes as bad omens. Among the dream images that are good omens are the *takara-bune* ("treasure boat"), Mount Fuji, the animal messengers of the gods, etc. Among the evil omens are monks, the *taue* (the transplanting of rice), fishing, etc. Good dreams could be bought from another person, and those that boded ill changed for the better through certain magical acts.

The practices called *urani* actively sought knowledge of the future. One of the oldest known practices of this sort in Japan is scapulomancy (*futomani*), as attested to in the *Kojiki,* the *Nihongi,* and even the early Chinese chronicle known as the *Wei Che.* Divinatory acts, either *koboku* (the burning of turtle shells) or the use of sticks, were very popular from the earliest times, in which they were overseen by two state ministries. The people who occupy themselves professionally with this (the *ekisha*), who were especially prosperous during the three centuries of the Edo period, enjoy great popularity even today. The consulting of horoscopes (*o-mikuji*) also remains very popular, and horoscopes are sold in sanctuaries, where they are in demand especially at certain times in a life (marriage, examinations, etc.), or certain times in the year (New Year's, etc.). The *kayu-ura* ("divination through the use of rice paste")—which attempts to ascertain whether the harvest will be good—and the *mame-ura* ("divination through the use of beans," a kind of meteorology) are but two examples which testify to the vitality of the ancient traditions of divination in Japan.

H.O.R./d.w.

BIBLIOGRAPHY

1. Monographs

BAN NOBUTOMO, *Seiboku-kō,* Zenshū 2 (Tokyo 1907). SH. KANEZASHI, *Hoshi-uranai, hoshi-matsuri* (Tokyo 1974).

2. Articles

M. TSUBAKI, "Nihon ni okeru bokkotsu, bokkō, bokuhō," *Shūkyō kenkyū* 210 (1972). YANAGITA KUNIO, "Ishiura no shurui," *Yanagita Kunio shū* 30; "Toshi-ura no ni-shu," *YKS* 13; "Arata naru taiyō," *YKS* 13.

Additional article: SEY NISHIMURA, "Retrospective Comprehension: Japanese Fortunetelling Songs," *Asian Folklore Studies* 45, 1 (1986): 45–66.

3. Miscellany

K. HIGO, *Nihon ni okeru genshi shinkō no kenkyū* (Tokyo 1947). T. WAKAMORI, *Nenjū gyōji* (Tokyo 1957).

Takarabune ("boat of treasures"). Meiji period. This representation was placed beneath one's pillow on New Year's Day to guarantee a lucky dream. The animals, objects, and figures in the boat are symbols of longevity and prosperity. CERTPJ photo archive. J. P. Hauchecorne collection. Photo Frédéric/Rapho.

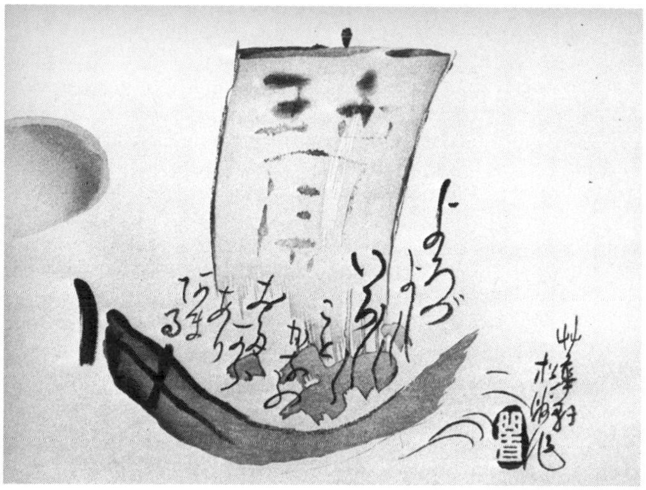

The *Yamabushi*, Mountain Ascetics of Japan

The term *yamabushi* ("those who sleep in the mountains," also called *shugenja*) designates ascetics and refers to one of the most peculiar forms of popular Japanese belief, *shugendō*. The *yamabushi* may be lay persons or monks; they practiced in the past and to a certain extent they still today practice the climbing of sacred mountains at certain times of the year; there, in the heights, they devote themselves to religious exercises of a psychophysical nature, acquiring in this way supernatural powers that qualify them as exorcists. *Shugendō* is "the path (the method, *dō*) for acquiring, by the practice of magico-religious exercises (*shu*)—in the mountains—supernatural forces assuring miraculous powers (*gen*)."

Our earliest information about the mountain ascetics and *shugendō* was furnished by missionaries of the second half of the sixteenth century (Lancelotti, Frois, Vilela, etc.). Their interpretation of *shugendō* is clearly influenced by Christian conceptions, resulting sometimes in a rather distorted representation. Analyzed with prudence, their accounts nevertheless preserve a good number of valuable elements. Two centuries later, it was Kaempfer who, in his *History of Japan*, was to contribute to our knowledge of the *yamabushi* and *shugendō*.

Nothing is known about the precise date when the term *shugen* was formed. A passage from the *Sandai jitsuroku* (True chronicle of the three reigns, 901) refers to a monk who had lived from his youth in the mountains of Yoshino and there acquired supernatural powers (*shugen*). In the *Konjaku monogatari-shū* (Tales of times now past, beginning of the twelfth century), a collection of Buddhist anecdotes, it is said of a monk that he "loved the *shugen*" and traversed numerous mountains, crossed the sea, and applied himself to harsh and difficult exercises. These passages clearly show that mountains were chosen by preference as the place for asceticism and the acquisition of magical powers. The word *dō* ("path") was probably added to the word *shugen* when, at the beginning of the Middle Ages, the *yamabushi* imposed upon themselves specific exercises, conceived religious categories distinct from those of other sects, and followed a training according to fixed rules: that is, at the time when a method and a tradition of *shugen* practices began to be made manifest as such. *Shugendō* was not, however, conceived in the Middle Ages as a true sect, as the terms *shugendō* and *yamabushi-dō* distinctly prove. It is really only at the beginning of the Tokugawa period (seventeenth to nineteenth centuries) that these beliefs were called *shugen-shū*, or just *zōshū*.

The central element, the most important of the characteristics of *shugendō* that date back to prehistory, is the veneration of nature, particularly the veneration of mountains (*sangaku shinkō*). The worship of mountains is certainly not limited to Japan, but there it has assumed a very important place in various popular beliefs, largely because of esoteric Buddhism (*mikkyō*), the second element constituting *shugendō*. In the course of its diffusion in India, Buddhism had already incorporated certain popular deities of Brahmanism in the same way as it had incorporated numerous religious conceptions; and it is particularly through these popular aspects that esoteric Buddhism was readily assimilated into the beliefs of the Japanese people. Copying a sutra, offering sutras, accompanied, for instance, prayers for rain (*amagoi*) or for curing illnesses and all other apotropaic acts. But pre-Buddhist magic and divination were not rejected or suppressed by Buddhism; it was rather a change of nuance.

Hall of Zaō Gonzen, Zaō-dō, at the Kinpusen-ji monastery on Mount Kinpu, Yoshino, Nara prefecture. In the foreground, preparations for the *saito-goma*, a ritual characteristic of *shugendō* that brings together apotropaic, expiatory, and sacrificial elements and is addressed either to Fudō myōō ("king of knowledge, the immutable," Acala) or to Aizenmyōō ("king of knowledge of attraction," Rāgavidyārāja). CERTPJ photo archive. Photo A. Stein.

Saito-goma of the *yamabushi* of Goryūson ryū-in. Kojima, Okayama prefecture. CERTPJ photo archive. Photo H. O. Rotermund.

"Free monks" (*shido-sō*), "holy men" (*hijiri*), *yamabushi*, etc., contributed through their pilgrimages to the diffusion of the rites and magical practices of popular esoteric Buddhism even in the remote provinces. They contributed to the amalgam with Shintoist elements. The way in which esoteric Buddhism and practices in the mountains were mingled in *shugendō* is made clear by the concept of *sokushin jōbutsu* ("to realize the nature of Buddha in our actual bodies"). For *shugendō*, that realization does not result, as in esoteric

Buddhism, from a mystic communion with the cosmic Buddha in word, action, or thought. In the manner of shamanism, rather, the spirits of the dead (ancestors), or Dainichi nyorai, in his concrete form of Fudō myōō (the "King of the Immutable Science"), are believed to take possession of the practitioner, endowing him with supernatural faculties: oracles, the power to cure illnesses, etc.

In the early period of Buddhism in Japan, that religion at first remained concentrated in the plain of Yamato and in its state-subsidized temples, where a privileged class of monks studied the doctrines. Contact with the population was limited to ascetics who mingled with the people, in whose service they often performed missionary activities. The most famous ascetic was Gyōgi, venerated later under the name of Gyōgi *bosatsu*. Like him, numerous ascetics in the mountains followed their own religious path; they often came into contact with shamanic practices reputed to confer extraordinary gifts. Among the most celebrated of these magicians are E no Ozunu and the monk Taichō. The principal region of the "Buddhism of the mountains" was Yamato, particularly the region of the Yoshino and Kumano mountains. Eventually, periods of asceticism on a mountain were vigorously encouraged as an essential part of a monk's spiritual training by Dengyō Daishi and Kōbō Daishi, the two founders of esoteric Buddhism in Japan; even before the Tendai and Shingon sects, esotericism may have had some place in the doctrines and studies of other sects. This suggests, too, that the custom of making pilgrimages in the mountains was propagated mainly by Japanese monks who had spent some time studying in China. But before the period of Dengyō and Kōbō Daishi, esotericism had been only one aspect of Buddhism. The new Buddhism of the mountains attempted to familiarize the Japanese people with ideas and conceptions proper to the "great vehicle" (*mahayana*), and in this task it was aided by the magico-religious elements of esotericism.

Esotericism established, with the help of mudra and mantra, a system of magical rites, utilized specially to protect against the many perils and dangers of daily life. Those who performed these rites and practices were "free monks," *ubasoku* (pious lay persons), "holy men" (*hijiri*), exorcists (*genja*), and finally *yamabushi*. Buddhism thus propagated was no longer pure Buddhism; it had become intertwined with non-Buddhist conceptions, such as the worship of mountains, the veneration of *yama no kami* ("deities of the mountain"), and numerous other popular beliefs. In close contact with shamans, often living at the foot of mountains, Buddhism won new domains of activity by absorbing preexistent ancient religious practices.

The shamanic aspect is another popular constituent element of *shugendō*. The life and activities of one such shamanic magician from the ancient period, living in the mountains and known for his miraculous powers, might constitute the foundation of the story in the *Shoku Nihongi*, which gives an account of E no Ozunu (En no Gyōja), the legendary ancestor of the *yamabushi*. Magic is another characteristic element of *shugendō*; the acquisition of magical powers was, as has been seen, the direct goal of exercises on a mountain. The importance attributed to the acquisition of these powers—which were then used in various domains of daily life—was expressed by the custom of a "competition of powers" (*gen kurabe*), one of the most spectacular forms of which, still practiced, is *hiwatari*, walking on fire. Such a successful demonstration of acquired powers was considered to be a guarantee of abilities to cure illnesses in a *kitō* (exorcism).

Another element constituting *shugendō*, still active today, is divination, a domain in which Daoist influences are clearly evident. Deciding the direction in which one must go and identifying lucky or unlucky days are classical aspects of it, as are also the practice of *kugadachi* (or trial by boiling water) and the rites of *yudate* (purification by boiling water). The last major element of *shugendō* is the concern for the elimination of sins (*metsuzai*), which is not foreign to Buddhism in general, but has taken in *shugendō* the specific form of an expiation by the sacrifice of life. Such suicide has been practiced by the *yamabushi*, in the form of *shashin-gyō* ("the practice of abandoning the body"), since the ninth century. That it may have been quite widespread is attested by the prohibition of its practice that is found in the *Sōni-ryō* (Code for monks and nuns, 701). The present form of *shashin-gyō*, as it is practiced on Mount Omine, is *nozoki* ("gazing into the valley").

When the period of exercises on a mountain became a criterion for acquired powers, there began to be a custom not only of "practicing" on a single mountain, but of climbing the most accessible of them, which favored a great diffusion of this kind of asceticism and also changed its character: more than the eremitic life, it was life in pilgrimage that was preferred and that became the most important characteristic of the *yamabushi*. The popularity of their pilgrimages coincided with the custom among nobles of going to Kumano, and for this kind of pious expedition the *yamabushi* were taken as guides. From the end of the Heian period they occupy an important place in the religious world of Japan. They begin then to distinguish themselves from other religious groups by outward dress and to become, on the threshold of the Middle Ages, the most characteristic figures of Japanese syncretism. In their aspect of monks in pilgrimage to the local centers of *shugendō*, they were called *kyakusō* ("monk visitors"). Often they traveled through the provinces by routes that they had opened and that they alone knew; at the beginning of the Muromachi period (fourteenth century) they were everywhere. In the course of a pilgrimage, a *sendatsu* accompanied them, a guide who also directed the ritual climbing of the mountains (*mine-iri*) and whose tasks were, in addition, to organize and perform rites during the period of the ascent and to point out certain taboos that, even today, affect the consumption of food and drink, as well as the use of certain words. When these itinerant ascetics encountered one another on the way—where they subsisted principally by *takuhatsu* ("the search for alms")—their custom was, in the Middle Ages, to practice *mondō*: ritualized dialogues, with stereotyped questions and answers. This is a custom that is sometimes still observed, but then it took place in the context of certain rites of the *yamabushi*. The tradition of such *mondō*, which in the Middle Ages were already ritualized in the *yamabushi-seppō* ("preaching of the *yamabushi*"), included the *saimon* ("ballads") from the end of the Middle Ages; in the Edo period these became the *uta-saimon* ("sung *saimon*"), already approaching entertainment, and, still later, the *Naniwa-bushi* ("expressions of Naniwa").

On the cultural plane, the role of the itinerant *yamabushi* was manifested in the literary domain (see the *otogi-sōshi*, popular stories, and the *gunki-mono*, epics of war) and in the domain of *geinō*, popular dramatic arts (as, for instance, the *yamabushi-kagura*). The art of Japanese syncretism is to some degree identical to the art of *shugendō*. This is suggested, for example, by the mandalas (graphic representations of the spiritual world of a Buddha, Bodhisattva, or other deity) or the statues of the *myōō* ("kings of knowledge"). A typical expression of the art of *shugendō* is the *kake-botoke* ("hanging Buddhas") chiseled on the back of a votive mirror.

What were the tasks of the itinerant *yamabushi*? The role of the *sendatsu* has already been mentioned. The most impor-

The depiction of the *tengu* has endowed these demons with the features of birds, with wings, a beak, and claws, but at other times they have a long nose and an entirely red face. The literature has many references to these features of the *tengu:* beaks and wings, for instance, in the *Konjaku monogatari shū*. The *Taiheiki* interprets the spoor of birds on mats as the sign of a gathering of *tengu.* As for dress, the *tengu* are rather like monks and *yamabushi;* but although there is no longer anything to indicate a connection with the bird, the *tengu* monk may, in certain representations, display a sign of this affinity, for example, a fan made of feathers. From numerous detailed descriptions in the literature (see *Genpei seisui-ki, Taiheiki*), one may surmise that the *tengu* look like kites, and that they wear clothes typical of the *yamabushi:* the khaki *kakigoromo* and the *tokin,* a small linen cap.

Let us now consider the nature and function of the medieval *tengu* before examining in this light their connection with the *yamabushi.* The medieval *tengu* are chiefly monks who have fallen, through the sin of pride. The *Shasekishū* (Collection of sand and pebbles, thirteenth century) distinguishes between the evil *tengu* and the good; the good ones make themselves useful to men, assist them, and sometimes transfer their supernatural abilities to them: for example, to a monk, the mantra that makes one invisible (see *Shasekishū*), while, in the *Nō Kurama Tengu,* the hero Yoshitsune learns the martial arts from the *tengu* of Mount Hurama. The *Miraiki* "ballad" (*kōwaka*) shows the *tengu* of Mount Hira as being animated by feelings of compassion toward humans. Their supernatural faculties predispose the *tengu* not only to fly and to become invisible, but also to adopt at will any appearance whatever, and to simulate, for instance, the apparition of a Buddha. But it is their evil humors and the numerous expressions of their hostility to the Buddhist law, far more than any of their positive aspects, that the texts of Japanese literature recount: they carry off children, cause objects to fall and buildings to collapse, and sow dissension. The presence of a *tengu* is often signaled—as in the *Heike monogatari*—by the sound of falling trees. Other acoustic manifestations of the presence of a *tengu,* such as the *tengu-warai* (laughter) and the *tengu-ishi* (falling stones or pebbles), also have the character of a sudden event in the solitude of the mountains or forests. The main point of the inauspicious activities of the medieval *tengu* may be described as anti-Buddhism. The *Taiheiki* and the *Kokonchomonshū* abound in stories of *tengu* who disturb the spiritual exercises of monks. These texts for the first time, as the war epics from the Muromachi period were to do later, explicitly allude to the identity of the *yamabushi* and the *tengu,* to such an extent that the terms *tengu* and *yamabushi* served equally to name those who, in these Buddhist stories, molest monks, kidnap them, or lead them away on a forced visit to their previous dwelling places. Among the narratives that have as a common theme the kidnapping of a *chigo* (a novice in a temple), see especially the *Aki no yo no naga monogatari,* a story that, the *Shasekishū* records, refers for the first time to the sufferings to which the *yamabushi-tengu* are exposed. Sometimes they are consumed by flames, sometimes demons from hell make them drink melted copper from sake cups, or put them to death, temporarily, by burning. In this context, certain sources describe a dance of the *yamabushi,* probably there a reflection of their custom of performing, after practices in the mountains (*mine-iri*), certain dances called *ennen-mai* ("dance for the prolongation of life").

Tengu from Yamagata wearing the *tokin,* the usual attribute of the *yamabushi.* The inscription on the left reads "Dewa sanzan." CERTPJ photo archive. Berval collection. Photo L. Frédéric.

Though it is easy to ascertain the close kinship between *yamabushi* and *tengu,* it is much harder to understand the reasons for it. In brief: the Heian period, strongly imbued with ideas about the existence of demons, conceived the *tengu* as a being of a terrible nature, hostile to the Buddhist Law, having the appearance of a kite. As fomenters of trouble, the *tengu* were compared to "malevolent spirits"—the *goryō*—which resulted in attributing to the *tengu* a social function analogous to the function that accrued to the *goryō.* The Kamakura period, marked by the idea of powerful forces controlling human destinies, interpreted the activities of the *tengu* as the consequences of an unforeseeable destiny.

The disorder created by warrior-monks, who moved through narrow passes to intimidate the capital, and the quarrels between temples may have appeared to be the evil work of the *tengu,* as was the haughty attitude assumed here and there by monks too sure of their power and too negligent of monastic discipline. Moreover, among the monks who fomented disorder in the Middle Ages, one must include certain *yamabushi,* who had begun in the Kamakura period (twelfth to fourteenth centuries) and the Muromachi period (fourteenth to sixteenth centuries) to organize themselves and to concentrate their forces: among the seven kinds of Japanese *tengu* enumerated in the *Tengu no sōshi* (Story of the *tengu,* thirteenth century) are the "monks of the Daigoji temple," otherwise called *yamabushi.* But the *tengu* and the *yamabushi* also shared the mountains, the *tengu* to take their kidnap victims there, to hold their meetings there, etc., and the *yamabushi* for their exercises—from which arose the suspicion that the *yamabushi* were connected with demons, were possessed by them, and in fact were one with them. The *yamabushi*—like many shamans—were often recruited among the natives of the mountains, who, as we have just seen, were sometimes confounded with the *tengu.*

But other reasons are connected with the very figure of the *yamabushi.* The mountains were, for them, the place where they strove to acquire, by various exercises and mysterious practices, supernatural gifts (among others—see the *Taiheiki*—the ability to bring the recently dead back from hell) that could not fail to hold the attention and stimulate the

Tengu in the character of a *yamabushi* at Mount Takao-san, Tokyo, Hachiōji-shi. Identifiable as attributes of the *yamabushi* are the *tokin* and the *yuigesa* stole. In his left hand the *tengu* carries a fan of feathers, symbolizing his ability to fly. CERTPJ photo archive. Photo H. O. Rotermund.

imagination. The account from the *Taiheiki* that narrates the visit of the *yamabushi* Unkei to Mount Atago, where he attended an assembly of *tengu* deliberating the fate of the world, attests, on the one hand, the *yamabushi* practice of foretelling the future and at the same time brings them closer to the *tengu,* who were thought to be able to tell the future and influence the course of the world.

Should we assume that the *yamabushi* were inclined to arrogance, conceit, and the abuse of the powers of the exorcists and diviners in contact with the supernatural world? The fate that was usually imagined for those who had committed the sin of pride was to fall among the demons. Moreover, that the *tengu-yamabushi* were, as we saw, hostile to Buddhism, that they burned down temples and molested and kidnapped monks, signifies perhaps a repugnance on the part of the *yamabushi* for other sects that, in their turn, were ready to criticize their mode of life harshly (see *Shasekishū*). With a most original point of view, Tsuda Sōkichi holds that demons, and particularly the *tengu,* were supposed to have power only over monks who were negligent in Buddhist discipline or services. It is likely that the *yamabushi* themselves—by their garb, their bizarre exercises, and their behavior—contributed to maintaining the fear that was inspired by the belief in their kinship with the terrible *tengu.* For them, this went so far as the veneration of the *tengu* (see, for example, in the *Genpei seisui-ki,* the story of the ascetic Mongaku) as patron deities of the *shugendō.*

H.O.R./b.f.

BIBLIOGRAPHY

1. Monographs

H. O. ROTERMUND, *Die Yamabushi: Aspekte ihres Glaubens, Lebens und ihrer sozialen Funktion im japanischen Mittelalter* (Hamburg 1968). M. CHIGIRI, *Tengu-kō, jōkan* (Tokyo 1974); *Tengu no kenkyū* (Tokyo 1975).

Additional monograph: CARMEN BLACKER, *The Catalpa Bow: A Study of Shamanistic Practices in Japan* (London 1975).

2. Articles

M. W. DE VISSER, "The Tengu," *TASJ* 36 (1908). E. INOUE, "Tengu-ron," *Meishin to shūkyō* (Tokyo 1916).

Additional articles: U. A. CASAL, "The Tengu," *Occasional Papers of the Kansai Asiatic Society* (Kyoto 1957); "The Goblin Fox and Badger and Other Witch Animals," *Folklore Studies* 18 (1959): 1–94. W. MICHAEL KELSEY, "The Raging Deity in Japanese Mythology," *Asian Folklore Studies* 40, 2 (1981): 213–36. TAKESHI UMEHARA, "The Genealogy of Avenging Spirits," *Diogenes* 86 (Summer 1974): 17–30.

3. Miscellany

K. YANAGITA, "Yama no jinsei," *Yanagita Kunio shū* 4 (1963).

Nebuta festival (July) in Hirosaki, Aomori prefecture: ritual of exorcism preceding the festival of the dead. The rumbling of the giant drum is supposed to drive away evil spirits. CERTPJ photo archive. Photo L. Berthier.

in these areas. The impact of rice cultivation on communal beliefs cannot be denied, but it appears to be a factor that has reinforced and perpetuated the festival rather than one that created it. The agrarian character of the deity to whom the festival is addressed seems secondary.

2. *The Gods*

The Japanese gods venerated in the sanctuaries are known, depending on the village, by three different names: *uji-gami*, *ubusuna-gami*, and *chinju-gami*. The word *chinju*, which is of Chinese origin, names the god as guardian of a place. In principle, this is not an indigenous deity, but it is often confused with *ubusuna-gami*, the local deity associated with a place and the people that live there. The idea of *uji-gami* is slightly more complex: it is either a tutelary deity of an *uji*, a family or clan, or the ancestral deity of that *uji*. In both cases, its role is to watch over the *uji-ko*, the children of the *uji*, who are regarded as the members of the community that the deity protects or as the deity's descendants. The problem is thus one of knowing whether there is a family relationship between the god venerated at the time of the annual festival—or festivals—of the sanctuary and the community of worshipers.

Japanese belief would have it that when someone dies, his spirit becomes a god after a time of varying length. In other words, at the end of a certain period, the spirit of the dead person loses its individuality and becomes fused into the ancestral spirit of the lineage to which it belongs. It is thus logical to regard the deity as the ancestor of the villagers. But this implies that all of the inhabitants of a place belong to the same clan. The growth of villages and increasing population movements entail certain modifications in this state of affairs. When individuals from outside of the clan come to settle on its lands, they sooner or later become integrated, mainly for economic reasons, into the community of worshipers—but this does not make them descendants of the ancestral spirit. The spirit loses its ancestral character and takes on a "local" coloring; then it tends to become a protector, an *ubusuna-gami*. In a third stage, the intensification of communications spreads the cult of a given prestigious god who appears to be more powerful than the local deity; the god is then simply imported, in the role of guardian of the site, and it generally supplants its predecessor. There is thus no fundamental difference between the three categories of gods, and the festivals dedicated to them are generally thought of as a group.

The ancestral deities also seem to have an agrarian character. The sanctuary festivals are essentially celebrated on the second and eleventh months of the old lunar-solar calendar (March and December), these being periods which apparently correspond to the beginning and end of agricultural work. A frequent assimilation of the ancestral god to the *ta no kami*, the god of the rice paddy, should also be noted, along with the fact that, according to popular beliefs, the *ta no kami* comes down from the mountain in the spring and returns there at the end of autumn, when it becomes the *yama no kami*, the deity of the mountain. But in Japan the mountain is the abode of the dead. Thus, agrarian characteristics are attributed to the ancestral deity in an agrarian context, which is not surprising.

3. *Organization of Worship*

Given the ancestral character of the deity, it is natural for the entire community to take part in the festival. Traditionally, participation is obligatory, and anyone who refuses runs the risk of bringing the wrath of the deity down on him and on the whole community.

Today, the Shinto priests (*kannushi*) generally celebrate the festivals in front of the worshipers, but there are still numerous examples of festivals performed by the *uji-ko* themselves. The entire community still participates in the festival in certain villages, where life is completely interrupted throughout the rites. The most celebrated example is that of the *igomori matsuri*, "the retreat festival" of the village of Hōzono, south of Kyoto. All of the villagers respect very strict prohibitions for two days; only after the purification of all of the participants does the festival of the tutelary deity take place. The inhabitants sleep all day and stay up all night, and their life is governed by the essential rule of not making any noise. In general, there are very strict rules concerning the use of a "pure fire" lighted with flint, as well as innumerable food taboos.

Nevertheless, it is clear that the prohibitions weigh very heavily on the life of the community; it would have been natural for them to attempt to lighten the load by establishing a rotating system. This is probably the source of the system of the *tōya matsuri*, festivals performed by certain members of the community in the name of everyone, following a system of rotation. The man who is assigned to direct the rites of a village, generally over the period of a year, is called the *tōya* or *tōnin*, which means "chief" or "he whose turn it is"; he is also given the name of *ichinen kannushi*, "priest for the year," or "priest for one year." The way of naming the *tōya* varies from one village to another (by the distribution of houses, a lottery, etc.). If several villages participate in the same festival, each of them has its own *tōya*.

Another sort of local organization is the *miya-za*, which was especially widespread in the Kinki era and in Kyushu. The *miya-za*, which today appear as associations for organizing the festivals, in earlier times administered the whole of economic, social, and religious life. Their composition varies considerably among villages, but originally they were associations made up of the most influential members of the village; even today, there are certain *miya-za* in which all of the members belong to a single family which is supposed to have founded the village. Economic pressures have forced the associations to become more open, and they may include men from all the important families of the village or even all of the village men. Women and children are generally excluded from them. The *tōya* is named from among the members of the *miya-za*.

The final stage of the development of the festival community was completed with the establishment of a professional clergy. This development did not, however, follow a linear trajectory, as this discussion might lead one to believe, and there are numerous intermediary stages.

4. *The Festival Site*

When the entire community participates in the festival, it is constrained to live in the vicinity of the deity, a fact that imposes on the community all sorts of interdictions and purifications that are incompatible with a normal active life. It may be for this reason alone that sanctuaries were constructed for the yearlong residence of the deity. Although this argument may appear insufficient, it is nevertheless true—with the exception of very old sanctuaries and those of great renown such as Ise or Izumo—that the *jinja,* or Shinto sanctuary, does not appear to be essential to festivals. When there is a *tōya,* the sacred palanquin which shelters the divine symbol is transported incognito to its dwelling on the eve of the festival, to be brought back in great pomp to the sanctuary only after the rites have ended. If there is no *tōya,* the festival begins with a procession that brings the sacred palanquin to the *o-tabi-sho,* the "place of travel," where the ceremonies take place. When the ritual has ended, the palanquin generally makes a ritual tour of its territory before returning to the sanctuary at the end of the rites. The *o-tabi-sho* may be identical every year—the most common procedure today—an outstanding tree, for example, being chosen as the material support for the visiting god. It may also change with each ceremony; its placement is then in principle designated by divination. The place of travel is above all a pure area into which the deity may descend without being affected by any pollution. It is brought to the attention of the deity and of men by the *shimenawa,* strings of rice grass from which paper cutouts are suspended.

5. *Preparations*

No one may approach the festival ground unless in a state of perfect purity. To attain this ideal state, two complementary methods are used. The first, which is passive, consists in respecting the prohibitions; the other requires active purifications called *misogi*—purification through the use of water (bathing in the sea or in a given river, picking up seaweed or pebbles, and sprinkling oneself with water drawn from a spot designated by tradition, etc.)—and *harai:* taking *gohei,* sticks hung with strips of paper and symbolizing the god, and shaking them over one's head. In most cases people in mourning may not participate in the festivals, because the pollution that weighs upon them, that of death, is the most terrible and may bring the wrath of the deity upon them, or even contaminate the deity. Festivals are thus always preceded by a taboo period, *mono-imi,* whose duration varies widely, from several weeks to a few hours. Finally, in order to ensure maximum safety, the purifications are increased throughout the period, in case some pollution has become attached to anyone.

6. *Welcoming the God*

When the purifications have been completed, the god is welcomed. It may manifest itself under various forms, with its spirit "clinging" to any material support, which is called a "divine body" (*shintai*). The supports are generally classified into three categories: natural, artificial, and human. Natural supports—the oldest ones—are plants, trees, stones, mounds, mountains, animals, etc. In the case of animals, one does not always know whether these are messengers of the gods or, more directly, the appearance that the gods take on. At festivals, moreover, it is rare to see any animals but horses, which, being the mounts of the nobility, were assimilated to the mounts of the gods. People may also offer horses (in stone ex-votos, for example) or regard them as beings that are sent by the deities and that participate more or less in their divine nature.

The most common artificial supports are the *gohei,* sticks from which white paper streamers are hung. The essential part of this cultic object is the wooden handle, which is a portable miniature of the tree or pillar, the most common natural representation of the deity. Alongside these ritual objects may be found a broad diversity of instruments: brooms, mortars, pestles, baskets, shoes, ladles, sickles, chopsticks, etc. In urban festivals, the symbol of the deity and the festival site are artificially brought together: these are immense chariots (called *yama, hoko, dashi,* etc.) which are richly decorated and on which the presence of the god is generally marked by an object such as a lance or a pole. The sacred palanquins, the *mikoshi,* are so widespread today that the word *matsuri* evokes their image. These sometimes enormous golden palanquins shelter a divine symbol which may be quite simply a piece of paper stuck to its ceiling or a twig, a mirror, etc.

The final sort of support of interest to us here is human. Two clearly different categories of these may be distinguished: that of mediums, generally feminine, *miko,* who in the past went into trances in order to transmit the oracles of the gods (today, they are most often female students who learn a few dance steps for the occasion in order to earn some pocket money); and that of the *yorimashi,* children in whose bodies the deity resides at the time of the festival: so it is that a baby wearing powder and makeup rides on a horse or on a man's back. It is considered to be a good omen when the baby sleeps through the whole of the ceremonies.

The coming of the god and its welcome, *kami-mukae,* constitute the primary elements of the festival. In the beginning, the welcome took place on the night preceding the ceremonies and had a secret character, but today, especially in the cities, where the theatrics are more developed, it becomes a grandiose procession that draws a crowd of spectators—for tourism and pilgrimage are becoming more and more mixed together.

7. *Offerings and Prayers*

Once the deity has been installed in the *o-tabi-sho,* offerings are made to it in order to delight it and to win its favor. The offerings are extremely varied goods of the highest quality: marine products, fish, mountain products, vegetables, dried fruits, and especially agricultural products, rice, cooked and ground rice cakes, *mochi,* and sake. The preparation of the offerings is very complex and often constitutes the essential part of the *tōya*'s duties. When the offerings are placed before the deity, one or more *norito,* prayers that announce the requests of the worshipers, are read in front of the divine symbol. Today the prayers generally consist of stereotyped texts requesting abundant harvests and asking that the community be spared any catastrophe. Then a meal follows, the *naorai,* during which offerings are consumed and sacred sake, called *miki,* is drunk. The communal meal with the deity has the function of transmitting the energy of the deity into the *uji-ko.* Inasmuch as the ancestral deity is often considered to be the rice god, and the offerings are essentially rice or derivatives of it, the worshipers are nourishing themselves with the vital strength of the ancestral spirit.

8. Closing Rites

The final phase of the festival consists in accompanying the deity back to its dwelling or, in the majority of cases, to the *jinja;* this is the *kami-okuri,* the separation from the deity. This closing rite corresponds to the welcome described above, which it closely resembles. Offerings may be made again and some dances executed again at the sanctuary before they finally leave the deity, who is not to return to the world of men until the following festival.

9. Entertainments

The rites constitute only the skeleton of the festival, which also generally includes an element of spectacle, the *kami-waza,* whose function, it is said, is to delight or appease the spirit of the god. Most often, the *kami-waza* are regarded as kinds of spectacles offered as a "bonus" to the gods and to men; there is a dissociation between the festival itself, conducted by the priest of the *tōya,* and distractions of a purely profane character dispensed to the worshipers. Yet a study of the contents of the *kami-waza* suggests that such was not always the case. Three categories of *kami-waza* may be distinguished:

—Competitions, sumo wrestling, footraces, archery, and contests to win an object which is sometimes a symbol of the deity used to have a divinatory goal. Today, it is believed that the winners will enjoy a more favorable fate than the losers during the year; but it must be noted that the sportive aspect of the rites is much more important than their religious value.

—Dance performances present the trances of a medium who formerly gave oracles. In the course of time, the oracle itself lost its importance, which devolved instead upon the atmosphere in which it was given; the *miko* gave up divination in order to dedicate themselves to *kagura* dances, whence their name of *kagura miko.* Thus, often there are *yudate kaguras,* "dances of boiling water," in which young girls in red and white priestly robes dance, a dwarf bamboo branch in their hands, sometimes in front of caldrons of boiling water. Formerly, the steam rising from the caldrons served to create an atmosphere that was propitious for giving oracles, and the *miko,* in their trances, transmitted the god's answers to the assembled worshipers. Today, in most cases, they content themselves with dipping the dwarf bamboos into the water and shaking them in the direction of the spectators.

—Theatrical presentations underwent a special development; it is difficult to recall, when one sees a No play presented by famous professionals, that the plays of the classical repertory thus presented have an origin similar to that of the *kagura.* Alongside the No theater, there are peasant dances, marionette plays, dances and music of the court, etc.

10. The Mythic Prototype of the Festival

According to tradition, the origin of the spectacles goes back to a dance performed by the goddess Ame no Uzume no mikoto before the "celestial abode of the rock grotto," in which the sun goddess Amaterasu had shut herself when she was terrified by the injuries that her brother Susano-o had caused her. Susano-o, having skinned a colt, pierced a hole in the peak of the roof of his sister's house and threw in the animal's corpse. When she saw this, one of the goddess's friends, stupefied, died with her genitalia run through by a shuttle, according to the *Kojiki* (Records of ancient matters, 712). Another version of these events, however, reported in the *Nihongi* (Chronicle of Japan, 720), declares that it was the goddess herself who died; mythologists agree that it was in a later period, when the goddess was established as the ancestor of the imperial family, that, shocked by the idea that this powerful goddess could have died in such a way, one of her friends was substituted for her. Whatever the case, once the goddess secluded herself in a cave, the world was plunged into darkness. The gods consulted with one another to find a way to bring her out of her retreat and appealed to Uzume, who turned over an empty tub in front of the door to the cave and, carrying dwarf bamboo branches in his hand, began to dance on top of it. At the height of her dance, she uncovered her breasts and lowered the belt of her garment down to her genitalia. Seeing this, the eight hundred myriads of gods burst out laughing. Amaterasu, amazed that it was possible to rejoice in her absence, partly opened the door to her cave and saw her reflection in a mirror that was held out to her; more and more intrigued, she came out of the cave, which a deity closed behind her.

Flower festival (*hana'-matsuri*), the Temple of Shin Yakushiji at Nara (month of April). The branches, which used to be gathered in the mountains, are the symbolic support of the deities. The seated figure at the right is the Buddha as healer, Yakushi nyori; at the left is Basara daishō, one of the "twelve generals" (*jūni shinshō*) in the entourage of the Buddha Yakushi. CERTPJ photo archive. Photo L. Berthier.

This myth is interpreted as the prototype for the rites of the "appeasing of the soul" (*tama-shizume*) and for popular rites executed immediately after the death of an individual in order to restore him to life. It describes the rebirth of the sun goddess, a rebirth made possible by certain rituals. This was a fertility rite consisting of the dance of Uzume, the ancestral goddess of the *miko,* who undressed herself. It is a rite whose aim is to reunite the body with the spirit that is escaping, by making a great racket to call it back: people stamp their feet in order to drive the forces of evil into the ground and to reawaken the vital forces that are hidden in the earth. This trance makes possible the revival of supernatural spirits whose strength becomes exhausted over time. Similarly, the *matsuri* functions to increase the deity's power by means of the energy generated through the ritual; and consequently to augment the strength of the entire community which, through the communal meal taken with it, participates in its power. The role of the festival seems to be more prophylactic than propitiatory, with divination playing only a very minor role.

The *matsuri* corresponds quite closely to what Malinowski called "religious activity," as opposed to "magical activity." We would say, borrowing the anthropologist's terms, that it expresses the cohesion and consciousness of the community, but that it prefigures no future event that it would bring on or forestall. In diametrical opposition to seasonal festivals, it includes its end in itself, in the energy that it generates and projects upon the community.

II. *Nenchū gyōji*

The expression *nenchū gyōji* means "things accomplished during the year" and designates the ensemble of rituals executed in Japan throughout the twelve months of the year. Although the term appears only in texts starting from the Heian period (eighth to twelfth centuries), it encompasses a much older reality. Popular language makes use of quite diverse terms that imply the idea of ruptures in time or transitions or denote taboos. These days were experienced in a particular fashion and placed outside the daily order whose normal unfolding they ensured.

Seasonal rites have various origins. Three principal currents may be distinguished: rites of the noble class inspired by ceremonies of the court, rites of warriors, and rites of agrarian origin. This classification is arbitrary, since the three sorts of rites exerted a perceptible influence on one another and were transformed and refined under the influence of customs and the Buddhist religion that came from the continent by way of the court. The agrarian rites remain the most archaic, since these are the only ones that are truly connected to the daily necessities arising from the vicissitudes of agriculture, vicissitudes made all the more serious by the fact that today this is often the monoculture of rice.

1. The Calendar

A note to a Chinese text composed in the third century, the *Wajinden,* specifies that before the introduction of the Chinese calendar, the Japanese knew only two seasons: spring, the plowing season, and autumn, the harvest season. Thus they conceived of a year whose subdivisions were founded upon the rhythm of agriculture. Furthermore, the study of ancient texts, like ethnographic research, shows that rituals generally took place in the second and eleventh months, at the beginning and end of the agricultural work. Thus the real year was spread over only ten months, with the two winter months constituting a sort of blank that corresponded to a time of rest. Nowadays the rites of *koto-yōka* (rites of the eighth day of the second and eleventh months) mark the extremities of this year; the period that separates them is a ritual period rich in prohibitions and centered upon the preparation and celebration of the New Year.

With the introduction of the Chinese calendar, the Japanese began to divide the year into four seasons. The calendar is founded upon two principles: a lunar time which gives rise to a twelve-month year and a solar time yielding a year composed of twenty-four seasonal breaths. The lunar year begins on the "initial day" of the year (*ganjitsu*), while the solar year begins on "the day of the starting point of spring" (*risshun no hi*). Since the two types of years have different lengths, the *ganjitsu* and the day of *risshun* coincide only once every nineteen years.

The introduction of the Western calendar—which is one month behind the lunar-solar calendar—only aggravated the disorder created by the superposition of the Chinese calendar upon the indigenous one, and tangled the situation inextricably.

2. Rites of the New Year

Today the New Year is set at January 1, but it seems that in the past the Japanese considered the month to have begun at the time of the full moon, i.e., the fifteenth. So there must have been two groups of rites, those of the "Great New Year," *ōshōgatsu,* around the first day of the first month, and those of the "Small New Year," *koshōgatsu,* around the fifteenth. The rites of the former are dedicated to each family's welcoming of the deity of the year (*toshi-gami*), to whom they give offerings—essentially of rice cakes, which are placed in a small alcove (*toshi-dana*) that serves as an altar. The presence of the deity in the house is marked by a few pine branches (*kado-matsu*) artistically arranged in a pot set on the threshold of the house; the branches serve as the material support for the spirit of the deity. The nature of that deity is fairly imprecise, and the oral tradition describes it as an old man with an elongated head, a one-legged god, or a god who is mounted on a headless horse and shakes a small bell. These fantastic descriptions associate him with the god of the mountain who comes down to the plains at the beginning of the plowing in order to transform himself into a rice deity. Yet, it is still too early to begin farm work; the god is also the ancestral or tutelary deity of the clan. The ancestral deities are appealed to to protect the coming year, and propitiatory rites are carried out; the master of the house, early in the morning of the first day of the first month, draws from a well the *waka-mizu* (the water of youth) which is used to prepare the first tea and to write the first words. Rites of "the beginning of the labors" (*shigoto hajime*) are executed either by striking the ground of the rice paddy three times after making an offering of a few grains of rice to the deity or by going out to sea to enact symbolically the movements of fishing. Finally, gifts are exchanged, with superiors giving more than inferiors by way of renewing the annual contract: the deities give rice to men, who offer them a few grains in exchange, while the lords offer their vassals rice cakes, *mochi,* as a means of renewing their ties of obligation.

The Small New Year seems to be more closely related to agrarian life; it consists essentially of propitiatory rites and divination. In the rice paddies or at the sanctuary, people mime the different stages of rice cultivation (*niwa ta ue*), and chase after young married couples to spank them with long sticks (*iwai-bō*) in order that they may have many children; children run around the fields hunting moles and birds to the accompaniment of ritual phrases. Finally, divination is practiced: people grill beans to deduce, from the way they brown, the sunshine, rains, winds, and storms of the twelve months of the coming year.

The rites may take place partly on the day of *setsubun*, the eve of *risshun*, which constitutes a sort of New Year. But usually people are content to throw the beans into the house while shouting, "Fortune inside, demons out."

The deity of the New Year leaves either at the end of the Great New Year, the seventh, or at the end of the Small New Year, the fifteenth. A great fire is lit, in which all of the New Year's decorations, including the *kado-matsu*, are burned; the *toshi-gami* departs, riding the smoke that rises from the fire. Numerous traditions assert that if one is exposed to the smoke or eats rice cakes cooked in the fire, this will bring long life. The fire, which is kindled at the moment when the sun sets, is a source of life for that heavenly body, to which it imparts strength, just as it does to men. Furthermore, the destructive power of the sun drives away inauspicious spirits.

3. The Rites of Spring

It is with the passing (*koto-yōka*) of the eighth day of the second month that the working year begins. On this day, a one-eyed monster visits all of the houses; to drive it out, people leave objects having many "eyes" on the threshold, especially strainers. The monster wastes its time counting the eyes until it is finally too late for it to enter. This strange visitor was formerly the "visiting god" or the "rare deity" (*marōdo-gami*) who came from afar during the period of the beginning of the agricultural work. People awaited it in their homes, without moving and with respect for the prohibitions; today, perhaps because it was necessary to portray it as dangerous so that people would not leave their houses, this powerful and fearsome god has become transformed into a monster. The *marōdo-gami*, whose mythic prototypes are Susano-o, a violent god who offered men the boon of cereals, and Omononushi, a healing god, come from the world beyond to bring civilization to men.

The beginning of spring is marked by rites of propitiatory offerings. One of the most interesting, because it has an equivalent in autumn, is that of the day of the young wild boar (*Inoko*), in the second month. The deity of the rice paddies descends from the mountains onto the plain; he is offered rice and the paddy is ritually plowed. In the countryside, this is a day off from work.

It is necessary at the same time to drive away evil powers, so there are numerous exorcisms and purifications. March 3 is known today as the day of the festival of the dolls (*hina-matsuri*), celebrated in honor of little girls. The dolls dressed in brocade that today decorate tiered platforms were formerly nothing more than rag, wood, or straw effigies that were thrown into streams or the sea as scapegoats to carry off all impurities. On the fifteenth day of the third month, the rites of purification are repeated: *mochi* are placed at the entrances of houses, hooked onto dwarf bamboo branches. These are then thrown down at crossroads with sheets of paper on which is written "May the 404 diseases go away!"

Sometimes it is not until after these rites—or even later, on April 8, the Buddha's birthday—that the deity of the rice paddies is greeted. But in the country this is the day of the deity of the mountain, whom the people go to seek on the heights where they gather branches and flowers that will serve as supports for the deity when it comes to watch over the work in the fields.

4. The Rites of Summer

The rites of the beginning of the summer concern the transplanting of the rice, which is one of the important phases of rice culture; exorcisms and fertility rites are frequent at this time. The fifth day of the fifth month, the day of little boys, is consecrated to such rites. Samurai dolls set out on decorated tiered platforms are colorful reflections of ancient scapegoats. In the countryside, children gather armfuls of irises and slap the ground with them; they wrangle on the borders of the settlements while men and women throw stones at each other or gibe at each other. This is the only day of the year on which women may assert themselves; formerly, men were obliged to leave their homes for the night, because their wives were being visited by the rice deity who came down from the mountain for the transplanting. On this occasion, the ancestral altars are cleaned out and the deity is offered three small rice plants which are left intact in a corner of the field. The work of the first day of transplanting is done in festival costume, to the sound of the flute and drum. When the transplanting has been completed, the rice deity rises back up into the sky or onto the mountain.

Preparations are then made to welcome the second half of the year. The sixth month, essentially consecrated to the water deity, is marked by numerous rites of renewal. On the first day of this month the last rice cakes of the New Year are eaten, with the idea of once more calling upon their therapeutic virtues. People purify themselves in every way possible, this being the original sense of the *Tanabata* festival. A Chinese legend recounts that two stars of the Eagle (Aquila) and the Harp (Lyra), separated by the Milky Way upon the order of the Celestial Emperor, because of the lassitude which their love had inspired, meet only once a year, on July 7, which is the day that their reunion is celebrated throughout the country. On the sixth, in the hope of becoming skillful calligraphers, children write their wishes on strips of paper which they hang on bamboo branches placed in the gardens. On the morning of the seventh, the decorations are thrown into the river, to send their messages to the deities. This involves a necessary expulsion of evil forces and a purification, both of which are done in anticipation of the second great welcome of the ancestors, which marks the renewal of the year.

5. The Rites of Bon

The period of *bon* opens with the *kamabuta-tsuitachi*, the "first (day) of the lid of the caldron": on this day, the cover of the caldron of hell is partly lifted so that the spirits of the dead may come out; people can hear their cries at this time by pressing their ears to the ground. Preparations must be made to welcome them: a path is traced from the cemetery or the mountain to the village, and the tombs are cleaned. Two sorts of spirits are awaited: the ancestors and the "spirits without ties," who have no family (the *muen-botoke*) and who, many of them having died under tragic circumstances, may return to torment men. Their coming is especially marked by the fires that are kindled on their tombs and in the hills. The people rejoice with the ancestors: this is the *bon-gama*, a meal eaten outdoors where two paths cross or in a hut, and during which children sometimes eat offerings made to the ancestors. There are also the *bon* dances (*bon-odori*), which animate cities and villages for three days, on the fourteenth, fifteenth, and sixteenth. On the sixteenth, the people part from the

Wakamiya festival (*Wakamiya [on.] matsuri*), in the sanctuary of Kasuga at Nara (month of December). The *miko* are dancing in front of the "travel place" (*o-tabisho*) of the deity. At the right is the orchestra (koto, flute, drum, and mouth organ). CERTPJ photo archive. Photo L. Bernier.

ancestors; the offerings made to them are wrapped in leaves and thrown out on the edge of the village. Straw boats are set adrift, and thousands of lanterns are set afloat in streams and seas; people may also light a fire in the cemetery or on the threshold of the house.

6. *The Rites of Autumn*

Starting on the fifteenth day of the eighth month, the people welcome a person whose nature is not well understood. This must be a "visiting god," a *marōdo-gami*, whose role is played by children who steal potatoes and rice balls. The size of their thefts guarantees the abundance of the harvests. When the harvest approaches, rites of exorcism and purification are carried out.

The harvest itself is accentuated by three festivals, the *San-ku-nichi*, "the three nines," the ninth, nineteenth, and twenty-ninth of the month, which are festivals of the rice deity, of the peasants, and of the city dwellers. Offerings are made to the grain deity, but the people in the countryside are too busy to organize any large festivals. The *ni-name* rituals, the first offerings of grains, are more important. Given the name of *Tōkan-ya*, the Night of the Ten, or *Inoko*, the Day of the Young Wild Boar, these mark the departure of the rice god for the mountains. The *Ae-no-koto* rite in the region of Nōtō (district of Ishikawa) is certainly one of the most interesting. The rice god who has come down to the rice paddy on the ninth day of the first month is welcomed into the peoples' homes on the fourth or fifth day of the eleventh month. The head of the household brings home two balls of rice, which are the divine couple of rice. As soon as it has arrived, the deity, in the person of the head of the household, takes a bath and receives numerous offerings which must be named aloud for him, since he is blind because of his long sojourn underground. The offerings particularly include two huge radishes, one straight and the other forked, which are sexual symbols. It is the grains preserved in the two balls of rice that will be sown in the rice paddy in the spring. This closes the cycle of the work of rice culture.

7. *The Rites of Winter*

Agrarian rites are sparse in the winter, the most important being that of the *Taishi-kō*, the twenty-third day of the eleventh moon. Tradition consecrates this festival to the Buddhist sage Kōbō-daishi (774–835). One evening, the sage asked for hospitality at a poor house. The woman of the house, who had nothing to give him, went to steal acorns or chestnuts from her neighbors. The holy man, filled with pity, made snow fall in order to cover her footprints, which were easy to recognize since she had a limp. An older version makes the sage himself, who has nothing left to feed his numerous children, the thief. The event is celebrated by offering Kōbō rice balls and *miso* soup, which are eaten with chopsticks of unequal length in memory of the woman with the limp. The rite is addressed to the mountain deity and marks the beginning of the gathering of mountain fruits and vegetables. Since it is now nearly the winter solstice, the people eat pumpkins, whose form evokes the sun, in honor of the "winter solstice of Kōbō."

The *Shichi go san*, a festival for children three, five, and seven years old, is also celebrated. These three ages formerly marked the child's accession into the religious community (age three), the entrance into the childhood group (age five), and the attainment of that age (seven) after which the child is an entirely independent being who has the right, in case of death, to full funeral rites. This is a kind of rite of passage of the end of the year.

8. *End-of-Year Rites*

The active year ends with the *koto-yōka* of the eleventh month. Preparations for the new year begin on the thirteenth: the necessary decorations, foods, and instruments are prepared, and a period of taboo begins, which continues until January.

All preparations must be completed before the last day of the year, the *Omisoka*. Work is prohibited on the last night of the year: men, animals, and even objects, carefully laid on their sides, lie idle. In very traditional villages, the people try to stay awake as late as possible, for failing to do so brings on an early death, and they try to keep children from sleeping. People stay indoors to await, awake, the deity of the year. There is but one task which must be done during the night: to make sure that the fire in the hearth does not go out. During this time, crowds of people rush into the great sanctuaries to gather up a piece of the new fire that the ministers of the cult have kindled and with which the first meal of the new year will be cooked.

Thus the year involves two great periods of agrarian rites which run from the second to the sixth month and from the seventh to the eleventh month. The rites are separated from one another by two periods dedicated to renewing the forces of nature which are closely associated with the ancestors—who periodically return from the world beyond to watch over men, especially at the time of *bon*, whose funerary character has been accentuated through the influence of Buddhism. The rites themselves are rather monotonous despite their apparent diversity: at each pivotal time, evil forces are expelled and those which are favorable summoned and thanked once they have fulfilled their tasks. Offerings and divination allow the worshiper to enter into a contractual relationship with the beneficent powers. These are practical, effective, and indispensable rites.

L.Be./d.w.

BIBLIOGRAPHY

1. Sources

BUREAU DES AFFAIRES CULTURELLES, *Nihon minzoku chizu* 1, 1–2, *Nenchū gyōji* (Tokyo 1969). K. YANAGITA, ed., *Saiji shūzoku goi* (Tokyo 1939).

2. Monographs

Y. HASHIURA, *Tsuki goto no matsuri* (Tokyo 1966). J. MIYAMOTO, *Minkan-goyomi* (Tokyo 1942). N. MATSUDAIRA, *Matsuri no honshitsu to shosō* (Tokyo 1943–46). MINZOKU-GAKU KENKYŪ-KAI, *Nenchū gyōji zusetsu* (Tokyo 1953). M. NISHITSUNOI, "Ujigami shinkō to sairei," in *Kyōdo kenkyū kōza*, vol. 6 (Tokyo 1957–58). U. SAKAI, *Ine no matsuri* (Tokyo 1958). Y. TAKAHARA, *Nihon katei saishi* (Tokyo 1944). H. TAKEDA, *Nōson no nenchū gyōji* (Tokyo 1943). T. WAKAMORI, *Minzoku saijiki* (Tokyo 1970); *Nenchū gyōji* (Tokyo 1958). K. YANAGITA, *Nihon no matsuri* (Tokyo 1942); *Nenchū gyōji oboe-gaki* (Tokyo 1955); *Saijitsu-kō* (Tokyo 1946).

Additional monographs: FELICIA G. BOCK, trans., *Engi-Shiki: Procedures of the Engi Era, Books I–V* (Tokyo 1970); and *Engi-Shiki: Procedures of the Engi Era, Books VI–X* (Tokyo 1972). U. A. CASAL, *The Five Sacred Festivals of Ancient Japan: Their Symbolism and Historical Development* (Tokyo and Rutland, VT, 1967). FRANK HOFF, trans., *The Genial Seed: A Japanese Song Cycle* (New York 1971). YOSHIKO YAMAMOTO, *The Namahage: A Festival in the Northeast of Japan* (Philadelphia 1978).

3. Articles

B. FRANK, "Dates des *setsubun* et des commencements de saison: Les vingt-quatre souffles de l'année solaire sino-japonaise," in *Kata-imi et kata-tagae*, appendix 3, *Bulletin de la Maison franco-japonaise*, n.s., 5, nos. 2–4 (1958); "A propos de la 'vieille année' et du printemps," in *Asien Tradition und Fortschritt*, Festschrift für Horst Hammitzsch (Bochum 1971).

Additional articles: FELICIA G. BOCK, "The Rites of Renewal at Ise," *Monumenta Nipponica* 29, 1 (1974). H. BYRON EARHART, "Four Ritual Periods of Haguro Shugendō in Northeastern Japan," *History of Religions* 5, 1 (Summer 1965): 93–113. ROBERT S. ELLWOOD, "Harvest and Renewal at the Grand Shrine of Ise," *Numen* 15, 3 (November 1968): 165–90; "The Spring Prayer (Toshigoi) Ceremony of the Heian Court," *Asian Folklore Studies* 30, 1 (1971): 1–29. FRANK HOFF, "The Taue-zoshi: A Poetry of Growth," *Literature East and West* 15, 4 and 16, 1–2, pp. 680–92.

4. Miscellany

M. NISHITSUNOI, *Kagura kenkyū* (Tokyo 1934). K. HIGO, *Miya-za no kenkyū* (Tokyo 1941); *Orikuchi Shinobu zenshū*, vols. 2, 3, 15, 16, 17 (Tokyo 1954–59). K. YANAGITA, *Senzo no hanashi* (Tokyo 1946); *Yama miya-kō* (Tokyo 1947).

KOREAN MYTHOLOGY

In Korea, there are very few myths that mention the origin of the world;[1] a few oral traditions simply say that the universe was primordially a chaos, but that a crack finally appeared so that the sky could be separated from the earth. Two suns and two moons then illuminated the world, but one sun and one moon were brought down with an arrow; man was made from earth.

Archery is of great importance in the ancient beliefs of Korea. A primary abode of the Koreans was called "land of the dawn" or "earth of the bow." Their legendary ancestor is called Tangun, "lord of the birch." He is sometimes regarded as the father of the founder of Koguyuřyo, one of the three ancient kingdoms of Korea. It is not at all surprising that this last individual, named Tongmyŏng,[2] was also known as Čumong,[3] "the good archer."

The circumstances of Čumong's birth are mysterious. The *Wei chou* (chap. C) relates that the eldest daughter of the deity of the waters was bathing in a spot called the Heart of the Bear when she was surprised by Hämosu, her future husband. The birth of Čumong resulted from this encounter.

"In the capital of Eastern Fouyu, a man appeared, it is not known from where, who said his name was Hämosu,[4] and who claimed to be the son of the Heavenly Emperor who had come to found a state." The daughter of the deity of the waters explains how she came to know the son of the god of the sky: "I saw the man. After he had lured me into a house located at the spot called the Heart of the Bear . . . he made me commit adultery with him. After that, he left and never returned."

In this way the girl conceived an egg from which Čumong emerged. The same text says:

> Ryuhwa (= the name of the girl) was shut up in a room. The light of the sun fell on her. Shielding her body, she avoided it, but the light of the sun pursued her. After that, she conceived and gave birth to an egg. The king (of Fouyu) . . . had the egg thrown to a dog, and then to a pig, but neither the dog nor the pig ate it. It was abandoned on a road; cattle and horses avoided it. Later, it was left in a field; the birds covered it with their wings. The king . . . tried to break it, but without success. He gave it back to the woman (who "gave birth"). She wrapped up the egg and put it in a warm place. A boy broke its shell and emerged from it. He had beautiful features.

The miraculous birth of a legendary hero is nearly always connected, in Korean mythology, with the light of the sun and an egg. Examples of this are cited in the *Samguk yusa:* the founder of Silla,[5] a southern kingdom of Korea that rivaled that of Koguryŏ, was born from an egg that a white horse deposited on the ground when an extraordinary blast, like a lightning bolt, touched the earth (chap. 1); the six eggs, which transformed themselves into boys, of which one was the founder of the land called Karak,[6] were deposited at a spot that was touched by a violet cord that descended from the sky (chap. 2); Alji, creator of the Kim clan, one of the royal families of Silla, is no exception: "Prince Ko noticed, one night, a light which emanated from the forest called Forest of the Cock; in the midst of the purple clouds that connected the sky with the earth, a chest hung from a tree. The king had the chest opened and found a boy inside. (This boy) later took the throne of Silla" (chap. 1).

It is clear that the egg, or the chest that symbolizes it, does not yield its "fruit" until after it has been fertilized by the light of the sun. It should be noted, however, that in these cases of "miraculous" births the maternal role is insignificant; the mother is a mere celestial messenger sent to earth and may be replaced by an animal, such as the bear who gave birth to Tangun (*Samguk sagi,* chap. 1).

The passage already cited from the *Wei chou* about the abandonment of the egg[7] merits further attention. What does it mean that neither the dog nor the pig wanted to eat it, that cattle and horses avoided it, and that birds covered it with their wings? A comparison with other texts shows that this is a case of a "divine" gesture on the part of the animals. For example, it is said in the *Luen heng* (chap. 2) that the abandoned "child" was saved in succession by the pig and the horse who breathed into its mouth; and, according to the *Heu Han chu* (chap. 85), this was how it was known that this child was a deity. According to the *Wei che* (chap. 30), the chiefs of the clans of Fouyu were designated by an animal name: the horse chief, the cattle chief, the pig chief, the dog chief, etc. Each of these animals was probably venerated as the ancestor of a clan and thus Čumong inherited all of the ancestral sacred powers before he was born. The primitive Ye, the neighbors of the men of Koguryŏ, considered the tiger their god. Čumong's relationship with animals signifies the initiatory tests that he had to undergo before penetrating the new milieu dominated by the animalized spirits. This explains why the hero was as much protected as molested before his birth.

Čumong was a good archer.[8] About this, the *Samguk sagi* (chap. 13) says, "He made his own bow and arrows at the age of seven. Every time he shot, his arrows hit their target. In the popular language of the Fouyu, the word *čumong* means good archer. It is said that it was for this reason that he was given this name. Kŭmwa (= King of the Fouyu) had seven children who always played with Čumong, but whose talent was less than his. The eldest son, whose name was Täso, said to the king that his son was not the issue of a human being at all, that he had courage, and that he feared that there would be a disaster if people did not pay attention to this. Later, when the people were hunting on the plains[9] . . . because Čumong shot well, he was given a small number of arrows, but the animals he killed were great in number. The sons of the king and the vassals plotted once more to kill him. Accompanied by his three friends . . . Čumong came to a stream. They wanted to cross, but there was no bridge. Fearing that the pursuing soldiers would follow, Čumong announced to the river that his ancestor was the Heavenly Emperor, his mother, the daughter of the deity of the waters, and that today he had been forced to flee, but he did not know how to get rid of the soldiers who were pursuing him.[10] Then the fish and shellfish came out and made a bridge, but they dispersed as soon as Čumong had crossed over them, and the pursuing horsemen were unable to cross (the stream)."

But what magical power does the bow represent in Korean mythology? The *Tongguk Li Sangguk čip* (chap. 3) provides particularly valuable information on this subject; according to this text, when Čumong was ready to leave Fouyu, his mother gave him the grains of five cereals, which he lost in the course of his flight. While resting at the foot of a great tree, he noticed a pair of pigeons who had just alighted there. Telling himself that it was surely his divine mother who had sent them there, he shot an arrow that killed the pigeons, and from their throats the cereal grains fell out. After this, he threw water over the pigeons, which resuscitated them, and they flew away.

The fertility of the soil symbolized by the grains of the five cereals is connected here, through the intermediary of the bow and arrow, with the fertility of the woman, in this case the mother of Čumong, daughter of the deity of the waters. It is also significant that Čumong finds himself at the foot of a tree: like the bow, this allows him to make a magical ascension and connects the three cosmic worlds, the sky, the earth, and the subterranean world. We also understand why Čumong had to demonstrate his talent as a good archer before King Songyang, of a neighboring country, in order to prove that he was really the successor of the celestial god; the document that we have just cited (chap. 3) says that the hero succeeded in hitting the navel of a deer from a distance of one hundred steps and in breaking a jade basin from a distance of more than a hundred steps.[11]

However, to demonstrate that one really has this royal virtue, it is not enough merely to possess the power represented by the bow. So, according to the *Tongguk Li Sangguk čip* (chap. 3), Čumong, who had just founded his kingdom, laments in these terms:

> "We still do not have the ritual of the drum and the horn. The messenger (of King Songyang) . . . is arriving, and I am unable to greet him with the ritual. He will scorn us." A vassal . . . presents himself and offers to go and take the drum and the horn (from King Songyang) . . . for the great king (= Čumong). The king says "How will you take the treasures of a foreign land?" (The vassal) answers: "These are the presents of heaven. How can one not take them? Who could have thought that the great king would arrive here when he was in trouble at Fouyu? May the great king now have the courage to confront the danger of ten thousand deaths, and may he cause his name to resound. This is a fate fixed by heaven, and it shall be realized. What is there that we cannot do?" After this, (the vassal) . . . and two others left . . . and returned with the drum and the horn.

The drum was used at Koguryŏ to accompany the dance and ceremony of funerals, which suggests that the drum was used to communicate with the world beyond by means of its magical sounds, and that this instrument might have had the special quality of being an ascensional symbol for the dead. We know nothing about the horn, but that the drum had this value is evident from the fact that, according to the *Samguk sagi* (chap. 14), a prince of Koguryŏ named Hodong seduced a daughter of the commanding officer of the Chinese commandery of Lolong so that he could finally smash the officer's magical drum. The destruction of the instrument caused the total ruin of the commandery.

Once he has thus obtained this other power represented by the drum, Čumong undertakes the conquest of the land of

Flying horse. Discovered in 1976 at Kyongju, ancient capital city of the kingdom of Silla, in the tomb known as "Č'ŏnma" ("heavenly horse").

Scene of a ritual hunt. Wall painting from Koguryu. Fourth century.

King Songyang. The *Tongguk Li Sangguk čip* (chap. 3) relates that he succeeded in destroying it by inundating it with a rain that he caused by uttering an incantation before a white deer that he had captured during his campaign:

> "If the sky does not cause the rain to fall to inundate the capital of the King (Songyang) . . . , I will never release you; if you wish to escape, entreat the sky." The deer cried out sadly and his cry reached the sky, which caused to fall, over seven days, the rain that submerged the capital of King Songyang; King Čumong crossed the water with a rope made of reeds and climbed onto the back of a duck. The inhabitants of the country all grabbed the rope. With his whip, Čumong traced a line on the water which immediately dried up. Songyang came and surrendered himself and his country to him.[12]

The hero dries up the water with his whip and thus causes a resurrection. This is not a strange phenomenon for the people of Koguryŏ, whose religious beliefs gave the whip a symbolism identical to that, for example, of the bow and arrow. The exploit by Čumong would not have been accomplished if the "father" and "mother" of Čumong had not met at the spot called "Heart of the Bear." The bear represents both death and resurrection, as is shown in the myth of the birth of Tangun, the lord of the birches. The *Sambuk yusa* (chap. 1) says that the bear had to take a tuft of artemisia and twenty garlic bulbs and to avoid the light of the sun for a hundred days, in order finally to acquire the form of a human being. The hero is regarded as the son of the lord of the birches, who is himself the son of the bear. Underlying all this is the fact that Čumong is a deity endowed with a sacred power that allows him to inhabit the sky and the subterranean world which water represents, as is suggested in a passage from the *Tongguk yŏji sŭngram* (chap. 51) according to which Čumong, while living in the sky, could often pass over to the subterranean world through a cave.

The ability to join the two worlds was also necessary so that Čumong could recognize his child as his legitimate heir. The *Samguk sagi* (chap. 13) says about this:

> When Čumong formerly found himself at Jouyu, he married a woman. She became pregnant and gave birth to a child after Čumong's flight. He was named Yuri. When he was small, the child amused himself in the street by shooting at sparrows. By accident, he smashed an earthenware object that a woman was using to draw water. She insulted him, saying that the child had no father and that was why he was so mean. He asked his mother, "Who is my father? Where is he exactly?" His mother answered, "Your father is an extraordinary man. Knowing that no one wanted to have anything to do with him in this country, he fled toward a southern land, founded a state there, and made himself king. While fleeing, he asked me, if I gave birth to a boy, to reveal to him that his father had hidden an object at the foot of a pine growing out of a heptagonal stone. If the child is able to find it (he would recognize him as) his legitimate son." After hearing his mother speak in this way, Yuri left to search for the object in the valleys of the mountains, but he returned exhausted without success. One morning, when he was in the house, he had the impression that he had heard a voice between the pillars. He went to see and noticed that the pillars had seven angles. He then searched below the pillars and saw a piece of a broken sword. With this object . . . he went to see his father and presented the broken sword to him. The king brought out the other piece of the broken sword which he possessed and reunited the two fragments, which made a single sword. The king rejoiced and named the child his crown prince.

In Korea, the tree or pillar that connects the three cosmological worlds is symbolized by a pole on whose summit one or two birds are sculpted. This tradition has continued for at least two thousand years; the *Wei che* (chap. 30) says that in the southern half of the Korean peninsula, a pole was planted in a sacred and inviolable place and on its top one or more small bells were hung.[13]

In any case, Čumong's extraordinary powers are evident from the fact that, according to the *Samguk sagi* (chap. 13), three men, who entered into the service of the hero even before he could have founded his state, wore, respectively, a hemp coat, a long robe, and a uniform made from aquatic herbs. We know that these are the costumes of shamans, who would have been so differentiated because of the functions that were assigned to them in remote antiquity. Hemp is the material that is still used today for funerary dress, which suggests that the function of the man who wore this garment was communication with the world inhabited by the dead, i.e., the sky. The second type of costume was worn, until relatively recently, by Korean Buddhist monks, and was black. This was probably a Korean shamanic tradition that the Buddhists finally adopted, for the color black was often the sign of the presence of a shaman. The pole that is set up, even now, to indicate the dwelling place of a shaman, carries a black cloth ribbon at its summit. In a village festival at Čain (in the province of Kangwŏn), the inhabitants form a procession behind a great pole, the *kamsattuk,* at the top of which black ribbons are hung. These two kinds of costume are reminiscent of the distinction that is made, among the Buryats, for example, between the two categories of shamans, the black and the white. The uniform made from aquatic herbs may be compared with the costume that the shaman continues to wear today to dance in village festivals on the east coast: a bamboo belt hung with seaweed and ribbons of different colors. This costume symbolizes a descent into the water, as do the ducks' feet, designs of diving birds, etc., that are hung from the dress of Siberian shamans.

The preceding evidence suggests that Korean mythology required three kinds of specialized shamans: black and white shamans and shamans who communicated with the world of the waters. The fact that Čumong had these three shamans as servants clearly proves that he could connect the three cosmological worlds. It is evident that he inherited this power from his father, Hämosu, the son of the Heavenly Emperor. Proof of this is to be found in a passage from the *Tongguk Li Sangguk čip* (chap. 3) which shows how the deity of the waters was able to recognize Hämosu as a true son of the god of the sky, by imposing upon him a proof of metamorphosis:

> The deity of the waters transformed himself into a carp. But the king (*Hämosu*) became an otter and caught him; the deity of the waters took the form of a deer and ran away, but the king became a wolf and pursued him; the deity of the waters turned himself into a pheasant. He was attacked by the king, who had metamorphosed into a falcon; the deity of the waters thus knew that this was really a son of the Heavenly Emperor.

Such a capacity for metamorphosis was necessary to a "chief," as is proven in the myth of Sŏk T'alhä, the fourth monarch of Silla. According to the *Samguk yusa* (chap. 1), the latter could not rival the king of Karak in this art and had to leave the country without achieving his desire to conquer it.

The mythology of Čumong is divisible into three parts: the transmission of the power to communicate with the sky and the submarine world, the protection of the ancestral animal spirits, and the specialization of the functions of the shaman. The elements that play the most important role in these are sky and water, as in other myths from northeastern Asia. The mythology of Čumong has undoubtedly degenerated and does not offer a single detail about the celestial world or about the submarine world. This is equally true of all Korean myths, of both written and oral transmission; only certain novels give a more or less detailed description of the two worlds, under the influence of Chinese literature. It is thus difficult to find the original form of the Korean myths in the mythology of Čumong. Another enigma is posed by the myth about Tangun in which there is no water at all. Is this because it is earlier than those in which water is inevitably connected with the sky? It is difficult to answer this question.

But what is noteworthy is the evolution of the process of ascension into the sky. Čumong simply flew to arrive there, but the other Korean mythic heroes climb to the summit of the mountain to come near to the celestial god and to receive the message from the sky.[14] After he has undergone the test of crossing the waters, King T'alhä climbs a mountain, builds a stone cave in which he remains for seven days, and in the end discovers an "omnipotent" dwelling place at the foot of a hill which curiously resembles the crescent moon, a sign of prosperity. The first inhabitants of the land of Karak also climb to the summit of a mountain from which the voice of an invisible being had come, and upon it they discover the six eggs that are transformed into boys, of which one is the future king of the country. After a long sea voyage, the wife of the king arrives in the country and climbs the mountain to perform a rite which consists in offering her trousers to the spirits of the mountain (*Samguk yusa,* chap. 2). This should be compared to the Japanese myth of Ame no Uzume Mikoto who, in order to draw the great goddess Amaterasu from her hiding place, must expose her breasts and her sexual organ (*Kojiki,* chap. 1).

What was the concept of the earth held by the people of Koguryŏ? The Korean myths say nothing about this. The historical texts, such as the *Wei che* (k. 30), relate that the land of Koguryŏ was divided, from the time of its foundation, into five parts, the one occupied by the royal clan and the four

Pair of birds decorating a celestial pole. Third century. South Korea.

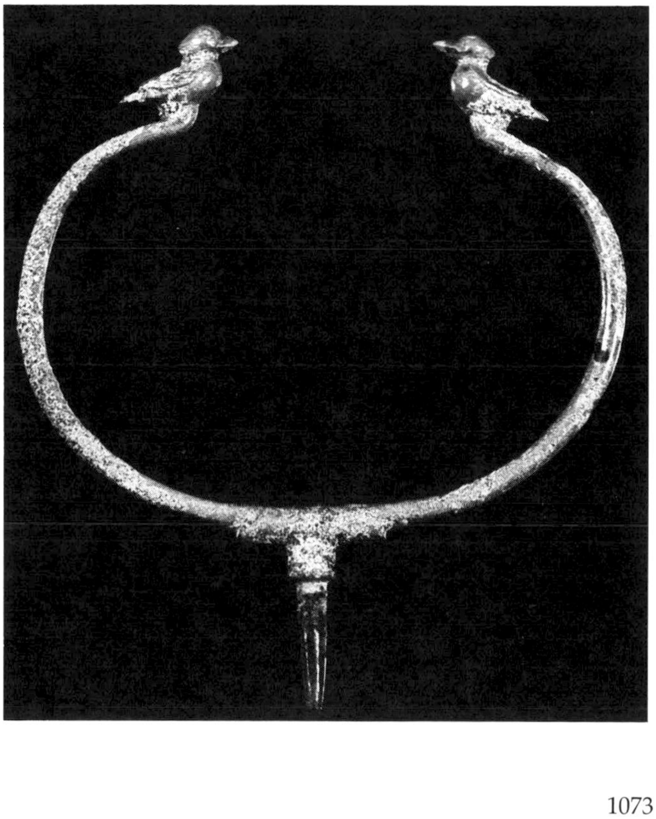

(Tucci 1949, p. 711, *Klu-'bum* fol. 117b; summary in Stein 1962a, p. 210):

> From the uncreated being a white light originated, and from the essence of that light a perfect egg came out. Outside it was luminous, it was good; it had no parts, it had no hands and no feet, but it was possessed of the power of motion; it had no wings but could fly, it had neither head nor eyes nor mouth, still a voice came out of it. After five months, this miraculous egg broke and a man came out.

His dwelling was a continent in the midst of a great ocean. He was seated upon a golden throne. The *klu* came to pay him homage and he ordered the universe, regulated the passage of time, invited the gods to protect the living, and triumphed over demons.

The basic structure here is the same as the one in the *rLangs po-ti bse-ru:* (*a*) starting from an undifferentiated beginning (*b*) an egg takes shape from which (*c*) a demiurge who has a human form—but who is also clearly conceived here as an aquatic being, a *klu*—is born. This demiurgic and beneficent being orders the universe, and is consequently known as bsKos-mkhan ("he who assigns") (Stein 1959, p. 300, n. 16; 1962a, p. 207; he translates his name as "the elect") and as Srid-pa'i mkhyen ("he who knows the visible world").

We will limit ourselves to one more example of this type of myth (Tucci 1949, p. 712, *Klu-'bum* fol. 132b): a series of transformations—from the void to a blue light, then to a rainbow, then to steam, then to a "subtle splendor"—end up producing an egg, whose different parts give birth to diverse aspects of the world: from the vapor steam and heat arise, from the skin seven golden mountains, from the creamy part space, from its heat fire, etc.; and from the inside of the egg a *klu* demiurge is born.

The egg is in fact the preeminent matrix and the place of origins. It is not only in the context of the world's coming into existence, but in many other contexts, too, that the egg symbolizes an absolute beginning. Thus the *Klu-'bum* cites the egg as the origin of the social divisions; the five classes of *klu* are born from six eggs: from a golden egg the class of kings emerges, from a turquoise egg the class of servants, from an iron egg the class of Brahmans, from a bronze egg the class of pariahs, and from a copper egg the class of animals (Tucci 1949, p. 711, *Klu-'bum* fol. 126a; summarized in Stein 1962a, p. 210). This myth clearly draws upon the Indian schema of the four social classes (Brahmans, warriors, merchants, and servants), to which are added the animals (a *klu* may have an animal form). Elsewhere, an egg may be the origin of lakes: this is the case of the four lakes that ring *Ti-se* (Kailāśa), the sacred mountain of western Tibet, lakes which are said to have come from four eggs. From a white egg came Lake Gur-rgyal lha-mo, from a turquoise egg, Ma-pham g.yu-mtsho (Mānasarovar), from a golden egg, La-ngag bsil-mo (Rākastal), and from a silver egg, Gung-chu dngul-mo (Tucci 1949, p. 712). In the Tibetan epic, the hero Ge-sar is born from an egg (Stein 1959, p. 202). Further, eggs are the source of the six primordial clans of Tibet: two birds laid eighteen eggs, divided into three groups of six: white, yellow, and blue (the colors of the sky, earth, and the underground waters). These were shattered by the smiths of the gods (*lha*), the atmospheric demons (*gnyan*), and the *klu*, respectively, while the six eggs in the middle produced the six clans (Stein 1961, pp. 21–22; cf. Hermanns 1949, p. 277). Finally, certain divinities are recognized as having been born from eggs. According to a Bonpo text, there were nine terrifying goddesses, called *byin-te,* who were born from nine eggs that were the fruit of the union of Srid-pa'i rgyal-mo ("Queen of the Visible World") and Lha-rgod thog-pa: an egg as white as a conch rose to the sky, where it was hatched by the wind of the gods (*lha*), and out of it came a white woman, gNam-gyi byin-te chen-mo ("Great *byin te* of the Sky"); a yellow egg descended into the earth, and so forth (Nebesky-Wojkowitz 1956, pp. 313–14). Likewise, another Bonpo text, the *gZi-brjid,* describes the birth of a *wer-ma* divinity from an egg (see Snellgrove 1967, pp. 61–63). An egg may also be the source of parasites, of evil omens, of diseases, etc. (Snellgrove 1967, p. 71).

II. The Birth of the World from the Body of a Cosmic Being

Another cosmogonic motif, which is structurally connected to the cosmic egg, is the birth of the world from the body of a cosmic being, which often, but not always, entails the death of that being. The *Klu-'bum* offers a good example of this type of cosmogony (Tucci 1949, p. 712; summarized in Stein 1962a, p. 210):

> A *klu-mo* (female *klu*) born from the void . . . was named Klu-rgyal-mo srid-pa gtan-la phab-pa ("the Klu Queen who set in order the visible world"). The sky arose from the top of her head, the moon from the light of her right eye, the sun from the light of her left eye, four planets from her upper teeth. When the *klu-mo* opened her eyes, it was day; when she closed them, it was night; from the other twelve lower and upper teeth were born the lunar mansions. From her voice was born thunder, from her tongue lightning, from her breath the clouds, from her tears rain, from the fat of her tongue the hailstorms, from her nostrils the winds, from her blood the five oceans, from her veins the rivers, from her flesh the earth, from her bones the mountains, etc.

There is no question of an egg in this case: the entire cosmos arises from the body of the primordial *klu-mo.* The same theme is found in different variants, which bring into play the death and cutting into pieces of an animal or a monster. The Tibetan epic relates, for example, how a divine toad was transformed into a number of elements, all of which play a role in the setting of the epic (Stein 1959, p. 463):

> The uncreated blue toad of turquoise was carried up into the sky of Brahmā, the God of the world, but falling back to earth it shattered into several pieces from which Rin-chen dar-lu (the chief of one of the families of the Gling clan, that of the hero Ge-sar) was born; his joints, falling onto the plain, gave birth to his horse, Pha-wang drel-dkar; the toad's hairs, scattered by the wind, gave birth to the thirteen sacred junipers of the divine mountain of rMa, and the blood of the toad gave rise to the thirteen lakes of turquoise, etc.

The cosmogonic animal may also be a tiger (ibid.):

> The tigress who drank milk and ate men was captured. When her head was thrown to earth, it became the sacred mountain Ger-mjo; when her skin was spread over the plain, it became the sTag-thang khra-mo ("Spotted Plain of the Tiger"); when her tail was cut off, it became the wild gorges of lCags-nag on the rMa River; her kidneys became the ten thousand men and the hundred thousand horses of the clans of sGa and 'Bru.

As in the case of the cosmic egg, the fragmentation of the body of a mythic being does not necessarily take place in connection with the coming into being of the world in its totality, but may concern only a part of the world or, more exactly, the world as conceived from the viewpoint of a particular region or locality, as in the following account from western Tibet (Francke 1905, p. 17; discussed by Stein 1959, pp. 461–62):

> A young boy named Dong-gsum mi-la sngon-mo loved to go hunting with two dogs. One of his dogs caught a nine-headed ogre on a cliff above a hermitage. The ogre begged the boy not to kill him, and promised that he would help him both in war and in sports. The boy . . . went to ask the lama what he should do, and the lama said he should kill the ogre, from whose body the land of Gling would come into being:
> From four of its heads would be born the four walls of the Gling castle,
> from four others the four corners of the Gling castle;
> from one of its heads the floor of the castle;
> from its legs the great beams,
> from its arms the smaller beams,
> its fingers would become the roof slats,
> its ribs the thatch of the roof,
> the stomach would become the Gro-ma plain
> the entrails the rGyu-ma gorge
> the bottom of the stomach would become the sPo-mtho nang-ma hunting ground,
> and the eyes the Tshang-ya spring.

The murder of a primordial being is of course a frequent cosmogonic theme in the history of religions. Even if it is difficult to say whether Tibetan mythology was affected by foreign influences, we cannot help but think of similar motifs which appear in India as well as in China.

III. Dualist Cosmogonies

Whereas the cosmogonies considered up to this point see the world as emanating from a single preexisting substance, there are others which bring into play, at least in their most significant aspects, a dualistic schema according to which the world comes into being in the course of a combat that opposes two principles which are generally defined as "light" and "darkness." A good example of a cosmogony of this sort is found in the *Klu-'bum.* The passage in question has been translated by Tucci (1949, pp. 730–31) and by Macdonald (1959, pp. 441–46); it was summarized by Stein (1972, p. 246) and discussed by Kvaerne (1987, pp. 167–70). The following outline follows the interpretation of Kvaerne, 1987, which basically agrees with Tucci, 1949, but differs from Macdonald, 1959:

There is first of all a primeval state of nonexistence in which there is neither time (the four seasons), nor space (mountains, houses), nor living beings (animals, gods, and demons). Two lights appear all by themselves; one is white and one is black. From the rays of these lights are born a black man and a white man. The black man, the lord of nonexistence, of murder and destruction, begins to create all that is noxious and destructive: among the stars and planets he creates the demons; among the birds, the falcon; among the wild animals, the wolf; among the fish, the otter; for trees he creates the ax; for the grasses, the sickle; for men, every sort of disease, etc. The white man, the "Luminous One," or "the lord who loves the visible world," creates all that is wholesome and beneficial: he gives the sun its heat and the moon its clarity, he separates night from day, he causes plants and trees to grow and procures the well-being of every living thing. He wishes birds to be without enemies and horses without diseases, etc.; he wants Buddhist stupas and Bonpo temples to be built, scriptures to be written and recited, lamas to be venerated, etc.

Even if the references to stupas, etc., are manifestly the result of Buddhist influence, the main theme of the myth is clearly non-Buddhist. The dualistic schema that appears in it implies an idea of the world that seems to be particularly well attested in Bonpo sources. It has been suggested (Tucci 1949; Karmay 1975, p. 195) that this dualism may reflect an Iranian influence upon some stage of Tibetan religion. We are reminded here of the similar creation of the elements of good and evil by Ohrmazd and Ahriman, as it is described, for example, in the *Bundahishn.* Nevertheless, similarity does not necessarily imply historical connection, and definite textual proof of Iranian influence on Tibetan mythology has so far not been brought to light (cf. Kvaerne 1987).

The same theme of opposition between "light" and "darkness" is explicitly combined with that of the cosmic egg in an elaborate cosmogony found in a Bonpo text, the *dBu-nag mi'u 'dra-chags,* "The Origin of the Dwarfs with Black Heads," that is, of the human race (summarized in Hoffmann 1966, pp. 104–5, and translated by Karmay 1986, pp. 107–8):

Out of an initial state of void, two principles manifest themselves, the one consisting of light and paternal, the other consisting of rays and maternal. From frost and dew arises a lake which is like a mirror, and from this lake an egg appears.

Two eagles are born from this egg, one named "Bright Light" and the other "Dark Rays."

From the union of these birds come three eggs, one white, one black, and one spotted. From the white egg is born the lineage of the gods, from the black egg appear two black men, and from the spotted egg is born the primeval man, King Ye-smon.

Ye-smon creates the world in the form of three pairs of mountains and valleys, and at the same time creates three classes of divine beings. These are, in succession, the Phyva, the dMu, and the gTsug.

In this case the dualistic element is clearly present, but its function is limited. Two antagonistic principles give birth to one egg, and the three birds which result from it through incubation produce three eggs, from one of which is born the demiurge, who in turn creates three classes of divine beings.

As was the case with the other cosmogonic myths, dualistic cosmogonies may also be used to explain the origin, or to justify the employment, of rituals, instruments, etc. For example, the mythic archetype of a magical ritual is discovered in a battle between the demon (*bdud*) rNgam-rje btsan-po ("the powerful lord of rNgam," rNgam being the realm of the demons), and the god of the world (*srid-pa*), King Ye-smon. rNgam-rje mounted "a black fiendish horse with long cheeks. He headed a host of many jackals." King Ye-smon "struck him with a lump of melted bronze in the shape of a vajra and hit his feet, arms, and head. Then he bound him with an iron chain and put him upside-down inside the left horn of the yak in a place where three roads meet" (Tucci 1949, p. 717; see also Tucci 1970, pp. 259–61, and Karmay 1975, pp. 203–4).

The theme of a battle between two opposing principles is also found in epic form. Of particular interest is the combat between the lord of the demons Khyab-pa lag-ring ("Penetrating long hands") and the central figure of the later Bonpo tradition: sTon-pa gShen-rab, "Teacher, the best of the *gshen* plant them in the center of the country, at rTse-sdang (rTse-thang) in the region of Yar-lung.

We know of still other variants of the same myth. Thus, in a rather complex version, six eggs result from the union of the monkey and the demoness, from each of which a being is born who represents one of the six states of existence. But beside these a son is also born, who is manifestly identical to the primordial man of the cosmogonic myths, since he bears the name of Ye-smon rgyal-po, King Ye-smon. It is from this last son that the Tibetan clans are descended (Hermanns 1949: 277–78). Finally, in an oral version collected recently, the offspring of the ogress and the monkey are said to have been "so numerous and diverse in character—beasts, birds, fishes, creeping things, and man—that in the course of time the children of men emigrated to Mount Kunlun, down whose four sides flowed four great rivers issuing from the mouths of a horse, an elephant, a lion, and a peacock; and following these several streams, they became widely separated and divergent in race" (Combe 1926: 36; 38, with the citation of a Bonpo informant). Of course, in this last example, there is no way of deciding whether it is a case of a well-established variant or simply the interpretation of a particular person.

No pre-Buddhist version of this myth has been preserved, and I believe that it is a Buddhist fabrication. But it is possible to isolate the non-Buddhist elements that were combined in it. There is first of all the fact that the "Scroll of the Words of the King" (*rGyal-po bka'i thang-yig*), a text which dates from the fourteenth century, but which certainly preserves older traditions, describes in one of its chapters a series of mythic beings of demonic nature who dominated Tibet before the first king rose to power. "First a black demon held sway, and the land was known as the land of devils. . . . As a result, sprites called *nyen-po* and *tsen-po* appeared. Next a devil and an ogress held sway, and the country was called the land of the two divine ogres. As a result, red-faced flesh-eating creatures appeared. Next the serpents (*klu*) and the powers (*btsan*) held sway, and the country was called the realm of Tibet with its many parts. As a result, grain appeared, active in the waters" (this translation follows that of Snellgrove 1957: 129–30; a somewhat different translation is in Tucci 1949: 732). Here it is the second generation of demonic beings that interests us. At a certain moment in its mythic prehistory, Tibet is dominated or characterized by two demons, one male and one female, the latter explicitly called *srin-mo*, "ogress." From these there arose "red-faced flesh-eating" creatures. But although this designation is often applied to demonic creatures in general, it is also used to describe and distinguish the Tibetans from other peoples, as is attested by Chinese texts of the Tang dynasty, which say that the Tibetans painted their faces red (Hummel 1958; Stein 1958: 6). Much may be said about the religious and magical significance of the color red, but one reason why the Tibetans painted themselves in this way was perhaps their belief that they were descended from red-faced beings.

This passage is also interesting for the fact that it can be connected with a third version of the anthropogonic myth, which is found in the *Maṇi bka'-'bum*. This time it is said of the six little monkeys that, "because they had a monkey for a father, their bodies were covered with fur, and their faces were red. Because they had an ogress of the cliffs for a mother, they were without tails and craved raw meat and blood." (For translation, see Rockhill 1891: 355–61; Hermanns 1949: 817–21; and Macdonald 1959: 435–39. The translation here follows Macdonald. For another version, that of dPa'o gtsug-lag 'phreng-ba, see Dargyay 1972: 164–65.) A fourth version is found in the "Book of the Words of the Ministers" (*Blon-po bka'i thang-yig*) in which it is said of the son, this time an *only* son, that he stood upright and had "a red flat face, and no tail. He ate red meat and drank warm blood" (Snellgrove 1957: 124–26). One may conclude from this that one of the components of this anthropogonic myth is the pre-Buddhist notion that Tibet, at a certain moment in mythic time, had been dominated by two demons, from the union of which arose these red-faced flesh-eating creatures.

The *rGyal-po bka'i thang-yig* indicates that the cultivation of grains appeared in the following generation. This corresponds to the anthropogonic myth in which grain appears in the first or second generations that followed the Bodhisattva monkey. The formula "active in the waters" could, if the translation is correct, signify that this concerns rice (pace Tucci 1949: 732). In this case, we are led to southern Tibet, the only region in which the cultivation of rice is possible. This is interesting, since the second component of the myth, the origin of men beginning with the monkey, comes from the region that lies between Tibet and China, where it is found among Tibeto-Burmese peoples of western China. These are peoples who are very close to the Tibetans in language and religion, but who have known the influence of Buddhism only to a very small degree.

The best known of these nations, the Chiang, in recent times has lived in the west and north of the Chinese province of Sichuan (cf. Tucci 1949: 713; he stresses the importance of these regions; the following summary is based on Stein 1958). Chiang mythology relates that they had previously lived elsewhere, and that, when they were forced to emigrate to their present territory, they had to fight and drive out beings called *Qa*. These *Qa* are described as strong but stupid, heavyset, with long teeth, a low forehead, and a long tail; in short, these are monkeys. They lived in caves and ate fruits, roots, and grasses. And it was only when a divinity revealed to the Chiang how they could keep the *Qa* away that they became capable of plowing the earth and developing social institutions; only then did they become fully human. Thereupon the Chiang named themselves the *rmi* or *rma*, "men," a word which can be associated with the Tibetan *mi*, "man." This is a passage between nature and culture which is wholly analogous to the change in condition that the children of the Bodhisattva monkey underwent as a result of the intervention of Avalokiteśvara. But there is an even more obvious connection between the Chiang myths and Tibetan anthropogonic myths. Chinese annals report that the Chiang claimed to be descended from the family of *mi* monkeys. According to Chinese dictionaries, this is a large monkey with a red face and a short tail; in other words, an anthropoid. It is also called *mu*. This makes it tempting to regard this name as a borrowing on the part of the Chinese, and to connect the word with the Tibeto-Burmese word for "man" (*mi* in Tibetan, *rmi* in Jyarong, *rme*, *rma* among the Chiang, etc; compare also the Tibetan clans *rMu*, *rMe*, *rMa*, etc.).

Ancient Chinese sources relate that another border people was composed of dwarfs, who had that form because they were descended from monkeys who had raped some sleeping women (Eberhard 1942: 144); this is interesting when compared with Tibetan sources which often call the first Tibetans *mi'u*, "dwarfs." In any case, the crucial role of the monkey in the present Chiang religion is remarkable. They adore a divine ancestor named Abba ("father") Mu-la ("heaven"?) Sei ("god"). This god is ritually represented by the skull of a monkey wrapped in white paper together with its lungs, liver, intestines, lips, and nails, and he is addressed as "Old Master Ancestor" (Stein 1958: 8). If we combine these notions with that of the two demons who dominated Tibet, we arrive at the anthropogonic myth of the Tibetans.

III. The Work of the Tibetan Buddhists on the Mythic Elements

The question remains: How was it possible for the Buddhists of Tibet to combine these two myths and make a Bodhisattva of this ancestral monkey? In fact, it was easy. In more than one version the monkey is named Hanumān; that is, he is identified with the brave and loyal monkey-king of the *Rāmāyaṇa*. This Indian epic was known early in Tibet, in any case before the eleventh century (de Jong 1972). Another lead may perhaps be found in the Buddhist Jātaka literature, where a wise and clever monkey who would later be reborn as the Buddha Śākyamuni is the central figure of a famous Jātaka found in the Pāli canon in the *Mahāvastu,* and in a Chinese version (van Lohuizen-de Leeuw 1947). In another Jātaka, the Bodhisattva appears, in an earlier existence, as the king of the monkeys (Cowell 1895, 1:144, Jātaka no. 58).

Another motif, although not specifically Buddhist, is of Indian origin: that of the ogress dominated by intense sexual desires. It was her insistent advances that were the direct cause of the Tibetan people. Yet the Tibetan tradition does not seem to furnish a basis for such an idea of demons, whether male or female. In the Indian tradition, by contrast, it is considered to be an established psychological truth that women have a sexual need so intense that neither reason nor morality can curb it when it has been awakened. This notion is here combined with the motif of the ascetic who during his meditation is solicited by a woman to whom he finally succumbs, which is a familiar theme of Indian religion.

Thus the myth of the origin of the Tibetans was created from diverse elements. It remains for us to show how the finishing touches were applied by the Buddhist tradition. The *Maṇi bka'-'bum* which was referred to above is particularly centered upon the cult of Avalokiteśvara. In this text, as well as in the *Blon-po bka'i thang-yig,* there is a sort of prelude to the myth, in which the Buddha Amitābha summons Avalokiteśvara and orders him to populate Tibet in such a way that the country may later be converted to Buddhism. Avalokiteśvara returns to his seat on Mount Potala, and looking over Tibet with his divine eye, causes a ray of light to shoot forth from the palm of his left hand; this ray transforms itself into a monkey. In the same way, Tārā transforms herself into an ogress, and thus it is the two gods themselves who are united in what follows. In late Buddhist tradition, for example in the chronicle of the fifth Dalai Lama, this is taken to its logical conclusion: the concupiscence of the ogress is no longer mentioned; on the contrary, the goddess "took the illusory form of a wild beast, but her heart was as immaculate as the new moon when it rises."

In the *Maṇi bka'-'bum* there is also a short epilogue in which the Buddhist propaganda is particularly transparent. But there is also a synthesis between the two versions with regard to the offspring of the monkey: on the one hand, six or four young who were monkeys first; and, on the other, a son who was semihuman but who copulated with female monkeys. This text first speaks of six baby monkeys, but also tells us that after they had received the grain which gradually rendered them human, Avalokiteśvara created once more: this time a little boy who had all the signs of a supernatural beauty. When the monkeys ask him why he is so handsome, he replies that it is because he abhors the ten sins and practices the ten virtues. At this point he instructs the monkeys in the doctrine of the Buddha, and they gradually become men (Macdonald 1959: 438–39).

One might nevertheless wonder whether the use that Buddhism made of the ancient mythic traditions for its own ends was altogether fruitful in the case of the anthropogonic myth. A Bonpo work of the fifteenth century dismisses the whole account as obviously erroneous, noting with sarcasm, "There are those who claim that the Tibetans are descended from the union of a monkey and an ogress, and that they once had tails. But this is not true, since the Tibetans do not have tails. Furthermore, it is said that there are people with tails near the border, in China, toward the east; but there is a difference between those beings and the human race" (Laufer 1901: 25). It is at least likely that the non-Buddhist elements were too conspicuous to pass unnoticed. As a consequence, this myth had to compete with another account which should perhaps be characterized rather as "legend," since it is set in a well-defined historical perspective, associating the origins of the Tibetan people with a great conflict whose historic character is beyond doubt, a conflict that appears in the *Mahābhārata.*

IV. A Rational Legend about the Origin of the Tibetans

A rational legend about the origin of the Tibetans was penned by the great Tibetan scholar Bu-ston (1290–1364) in his *History of Buddhism,* here cited in the translation of E. Obermiller (1932: 181; cf. Tucci 1949: 731; he shows that this version may be connected with a definite source, Prajñavarman's commentary on a canonical text, the *Devātiśayastotra.* Prajñavarman was an Indian translator active in Tibet in the second half of the eighth century. On Rūpati who will be mentioned here, see Haarh, 1969: 176–79. No prince of this name is mentioned in the *Mahābhārata;* cf. S. Sörensen, *An Index to the Names in the Mahābhārata,* London 1904–1925):

> As for the way in which the first men appeared in Tibet, says Bu-ston, one may read in the Commentary on the *Devātiśayastotra* that, when the five Pāṇḍavas battled with the twelve armies of the Kauravas, King Rūpati fled into the mountains of the Himālaya with a thousand warriors dressed as women. It is from these that the Tibetans are said to have descended.

Here there is no trace of the supernatural. Having provided this completely rational account, Bu-ston does nothing more than indicate without commentary the other version of the origin of the Tibetans (the tale of the monkey and the ogress), showing an attitude that is clearly nonmythological. This rationalistic attitude is carried to its logical conclusion by a Buddhist scholar of the early nineteenth century, who states that, "As for the origin of the people of the country of Tibet, it is difficult to make a decision, because they are explained by the Tibetans as having been produced from a monkey; by the Indians as having been produced by Rūpati and his army; and according to old chronicles of the Chinese as having been produced from Zan-me'o and his army." He then concludes that since there were many different clans, as well as Mongolians and Chinese, "among the kings, ministers, and translators of Tibet in former times . . . it is not certain that there was only one racial origin" (Wylie 1962: 113).

Other anthropogonic myths existed in Tibet, but were not as widely received as that of the ancestor-monkey. Thus the *rLangs po-ti bse-ru* testifies to a rather complicated genealogy that begins with the Primordial Man *Ye-smon rgyal-po* and, after numerous generations of divine beings, ends with the six original tribes of Tibet; in other words, with mankind (Macdonald 1959: 428–29). At no time in this anthropogony which is also a theogony is there any mention of a monkey, or of a monkey and an ogress, or of Avalokiteśvara. This account is, in essence at least, entirely pre-Buddhist.

P.K./d.b.

BIBLIOGRAPHY

See the general bibliography for "Introduction to Tibetan Mythology," above.

Divine Sovereignty in Tibet

According to the "Scroll of the Words of the King" (*rGyal-po bka'i thang-yig*), a fourteenth-century text, Tibet was originally governed by a succession of demoniacal beings. During each era a new element of culture was introduced—first grain, then weapons, horses, ornaments, good manners and polite conversation, and finally the first king, named sPu-rgyal btsan-po, "sPu-rgyal the Mighty" (Snellgrove 1957, pp. 129–30). Myths about the first king of Tibet and his immediate successors form a significant part of Tibetan mythology. But these are extremely complex traditions that present a confused picture, full of gaps and contradictions. We will thus introduce only the most characteristic elements of these myths, leaving aside numerous variants and secondary elements. (Detailed studies are found in Haarh 1959, notably pp. 168–288, and in Macdonald 1971.)

I. The First King: A Pre-Buddhist Version of the Myth

When the Tibetans came into contact with Buddhism in the seventh and eighth centuries, they were governed by sacred kings who constituted the focus of an elaborate cult in which priests—called *bon* and *gshen*—played a decisive role. The institution of sacred sovereignty lasted until the fall of the national dynasty in 842, that is, about a century after the effective introduction of Buddhism. Consequently, myths about the celestial origin of the first king were preserved and remembered, but as far as the later sources are concerned, only after they had passed through a reinterpretation that tended to be rationalist. We can, however, begin by studying a pre-Buddhist version of the myth, preserved in a manuscript from Tun-huang, a version in which the first king is called Nyag-khri btsan-po (which later became gNya'-khri btsan-po). (This text is found in Bacot/Thomas/Toussaint 1946, p. 81, translation pp. 85–86; cf. also Macdonald 1959, p. 426, for the first lines, and Snellgrove/Richardson 1968, pp. 24–25):

He came from the heights of the heaven of the gods,
the son of the six Lords, the ancestral gods
who dwell above the mid-heaven . . .
He came to earth as Father-of-the-Land, as Lord,
he came as the rain that impregnates the earth.
When he arrived at the divine mountain *Gyang-do,*
that great mountain bowed low again and again;
the trees came together,
the springs rippled with their blue waters,
and the rocks and boulders saluted him respectfully
in order to honor him.
He came as the lord of Tibet of six regions
and when he came for the first time to the earth
it was as lord of everything under heaven.
He came to the center of the sky,
to the center of the earth,
the heart of the world,
fenced round by snow-mountains.
And after the Son-of-the-gods had lived
as ruler in the land of men,
he returned visibly to heaven.

The central element of this myth is found extensively in central and eastern Asia, and is perhaps of Altaic origin, for other myths, which are often surprisingly similar, are found among the Mongols, Koreans, and Japanese. The basic idea is always that the first king of the people or the tribe was an atmospheric or celestial divinity who, sometimes in response to prayers, descended through the different levels of the atmosphere to the summit of a mountain (Waida 1973 for the Korean and Japanese myths). This mountain plays the role of an *axis mundi*—in this case the king is said to come to the land that is "beneath the center of the sky"—and it is often considered, at least in Tibet, to be a divinity, and worshiped accordingly. The descent of the king from heaven takes place to establish sovereignty—that is, the social order as it is known in the present time—and simultaneously to ensure fertility on earth. It is thus evident that this Tibetan myth belongs to a very widespread mythic and cultic schema. The importance of the first king in the world view of the ancient Tibetans is attested by several inscriptions that have been preserved from the eighth and ninth centuries. Each of them is preceded by a brief account of the arrival on earth of the first king, named 'O-lde Spu-rgyal (see Richardson 1985 for a study of the entire corpus of inscriptions). Only through an invocation to the first king can the reigning king affirm his own status and authority.

The "Scroll of the Words of the Ministers" (*Blon-po bka'i thang-yig*) also offers a version of the myth which is worth translating in its entirety (Hoffmann 1950, p. 347, for the text; translation, p. 248; another translation in Tucci 1949, p. 732; and in Haarh 1969, p. 235):

The Lady Gung-rgyal (Queen of Heaven) of the land of sPu
gave birth to the nine *the'u-brang* brothers;
he descended from the youngest of them, 'U-pe-ra.
It is difficult to tell the heavy task he undertook.
The son of Khri-rgyal-ba and Dri-dmu tri-btsan,
gNya'-khri btsan-po was born when the moon was full (*nya*),
so that he was also called Nya-khri btsan-po.
At that time there were only petty kings in Tibet,
and they could not stand up to the four great kings of the four cardinal points.
As three maternal uncles, the minister (they were thus four),
and two wise men of the six clans of the subjects went to find a ruler,
the lord sKar-ma yol-sde said:
"The son of the gods, who is called gNya'-khri btsan-po,
who lives above the five levels of the sky,
is the nephew of the *dmu,* so invite him then!"
But gNya'-khri btsan-po said: "There are (in Tibet) six things to fear,
theft, hatred, enemies, yaks, poison, and evil spells!"
(to which replied) sKar-ma yol-sde, the "rib-god":

"Here in Tibet we have punishments for thievery,
we oppose love to hatred, we have allies against our enemies,
and against yaks we have weapons, against poisons, medicines,
against evil spells we have means by which one can be freed."
And bringing the ten *dmu* objects, (gNya'-khri-btsan-po) came.

In other words, we learn that the king is descended from a group of divine beings, the *the'u-brang,* who at a later period ended up as demons in the popular religion. But he is also associated with the *dmu,* and when he comes to earth, he carries *dmu* objects. This word, which is derived from a Tibeto-Burman root meaning "heaven," designates a group of divinities intimately associated with the Tibetan kings (Stein 1941, pp. 211–16; Tucci 1949, pp. 714–15). It is even said in other versions that the king descended to earth by means of a *dmu* cord or a *dmu* ladder. The mountain upon which he landed can itself be qualified as "the heavenly ladder" (*mtho-ris them-skas*) (Tucci 1970, p. 242).

The theme of the celestial origin of the first king, who appears on top of a mountain, was also applied to later, local dynasties. Thus the genealogical account of the kings of Derge, a principality in eastern Tibet, tells that the ancestor of the kings was a divine youth who descended to the peak of a mountain in the east; because he had come from the sky, people called him gNam-tsha-'brug, "the Dragon who is the offspring of Heaven" (Kolmaš 1968, p. 25).

II. Buddhist Rationalization

Buddhism could accept the myths of the first kings only by subjecting them to a radical process of rationalization. The myth results, for Bu-ston, the famous scholar (1290–1364), in what follows (translated by Obermiller 1932, pp. 181–82; Macdonald 1959, p. 422; and Haarh 1969, p. 179; detailed discussion in Haarh 1969, pp. 171–212):

> Regarding the Tibetan royal dynasty, there are those who say that its ancestor was the fifth descendant of Prasenajit, king of Kosala, others who say that he was the fifth descendant of sTobs-chung, the youngest son of Bimbisāra. Still others claim that when the Tibetans were oppressed by the twelve minor kings of the demons and spirits, Udayana, king of Vatsala, had a son. The eyes of this child closed from below upwards, and his fingers were joined together by a membrane. Faced with such strange signs, the king placed him in a sealed copper vessel and threw him into the Ganges. A peasant then found him and raised him, but when he had grown up the young prince was unhappy to learn what had happened, and fled into the Himalayan mountains. He arrived at the foot of the divine mountain Lha-ri yol-ba, the "Royal Plain of Four Portals." Some *bon-po* then said to each other: "He has come by way of a *dmu* cord and a *dmu* ladder; he is therefore a god." And they asked him, "Who are you?" "A King," he replied. They asked him where he came from, and he pointed to the sky. Since they did not understand what he had said, they put him on a wooden throne which four men carried on their necks. "Let him be our king!" they said, and he was given the name gNya' (neck) khri (throne) btsan-po (king).

What is most striking in this narrative is that what referred most explicitly to the divine and to the mythical times has been systematically eliminated. It is true that the central figure of the narrative is the son of a king whose unusual physical characteristics set him apart from other men. But when the Tibetans choose him as king, it is because of a misunderstanding caused by their inability to comprehend him. Furthermore, the very widespread motif of the future hero who is at first abandoned and is raised by adoptive parents (cf. for example, the lives of Moses and Kṛṣṇa) was introduced into this story. Finally, there is an evident wish to provide an explanation for the name of the king. While these explanations manifestly are the result of either learned or popular etymological speculation, one of them at least (being carried on the necks of four men) is perhaps not entirely arbitrary, for in Iranian as well as in Byzantine civilization the divine sovereignty of the king was affirmed by his being lifted on the necks of his subjects (L'Orange 1953, pp. 87–89).

Bu-ston presents the Tibetan royal dynasty as a branch of an Indian family, and Udayana, king of Vatsala, is in fact a historical personage, the contemporary of the Buddha Śākyamuni. The myth has thus been rendered completely historical and profane, while continuing to legitimize the Tibetan kings, since they are connected to India, the land of the Buddha. It is interesting to note that Tibet was later to play a similar role vis-à-vis Mongolia, Mongolian chronicles explaining the genealogy of the Khagans by linking them to Indian dynasties through the mediation of mythical Tibetan kings (Haarh 1969, pp. 92–98). In a similar fashion a fifteenth-century Bonpo text makes the first Tibetan king a son of Pāṇḍu, the father of the heroes of the *Mahābhārata,* which connects him to a period which, according to traditional chronology, precedes the life of Śākyamuni, whom the Bonpo did not accept as being the Buddha (Laufer 1901, pp. 29–30; summarized in Tucci 1949, p. 731).

Despite all these innovations, one can see that Bu-ston has kept the chronology that was consistent with the series of demoniacal beings who are said to have governed Tibet before the arrival of the first king. He has also kept the central motif of the association of this future king with a mountain, no longer, it is true, in the form of a descent from the heights of the heavens onto the top of the mountain, but using the idea of a descent from the mountain itself. He still speaks of the invitation made to the king; and when the king comes down from the mountain, he enters a plain that has "four doors," which is thus a quadrangular, sacred area where he is encountered by *bon-po* (in whom we recognize the representatives of the pre-Buddhist religion) who were apparently awaiting a divinity coming to them by means of a celestial cord or ladder. In a later version, supplied by Sum-pa mkhan-po in the eighteenth century, it is said that the king was met by "twelve men who were worshiping the local divinity" (Snellgrove 1957, p. 127). The term used here, *yul-lha,* designates the sacred mountain of the country, the one onto which the mythical ancestor-hero descends.

But other versions are even more rationalist; the future king is welcomed by "shepherds" (Kuznetsov 1966, p. 46; translation by Hoffmann 1950, p. 297), "hunters" (*La-dvags rgyal-rabs,* cited by Hoffmann 1950, p. 312), "some fortunate Tibetans" (*dPa'o gtsug-lag 'phreng-ba,* translated by Haarh, p. 175), or, in an effort of synthesis, "twelve wise men, *bon-po* and others, who were watching over their herds" (*Chronicle of the Fifth Dalai Lama,* translated by Haarh 1969, p. 182).

Thus there have been diverse traditions about the first king. In fact, the situation must have already become confused very early on, for one of the manuscripts of Tunhuang, probably from the tenth century, gives three different versions of his origin, one being that he was one of the "twelve little kings," the second connecting him, although obscurely, to a class of demons, and the third being the account of his well-known descent from the sky "above the thirteen levels of the heavens." The passage ends with the remark that "one cannot know clearly who he was" (Macdonald 1971, pp. 214–19). The subsequent tradition preserved the idea of three different versions. The "Scroll of the Words of the Ministers" classifies them thus (Hoffmann 1950, p. 247; Haarh 1969, p. 169; Macdonald 1971, pp. 206–13; Stein 1988, pp. 1420–21):

> Concerning king gNya'-khri btsan-po, who descended from the gods,
> we are told that there are several versions; one "secret," one "public" and one "ultra-secret."
> According to the "secret" version, he is descended from kings;
> this is the version of *chos* (Buddhism).
> According to the "public" version, he is descended from gods;
> this is the version of *bon.*
> According to the "ultra-secret" version, he is descended from the *the'u-brang;*
> this is the version of the people and the ministers.

Sum-pa mkhan-po, after giving the Buddhist version in great detail, mentions the other two traditions. But he cannot help adding his own commentary, which in one stroke reveals the inability to understand the ancient myths which is so characteristic of Buddhist scholasticism:

"All these tales of a descent from the sky come from the fact that the Bonpo like the sky. It would be quite wrong to pursue these falsehoods."

III. Myths about Subsequent Kings

But if we wish to "pursue these falsehoods," we must see how Tibetan mythology describes the destiny of the subsequent kings. In this connection there is a myth of quite special interest which tells how Gri-gum btsan-po, the eighth king, was the first to leave his body behind him on earth, just like ordinary mortals. This myth explains the origin of the funerary mounds that were built for kings, one of the most striking or at least best-known aspects of the pre-Buddhist religion (Tucci 1950; Haarh 1969, pp. 327–97).

We have seen that the first Tibetan king was believed to have returned bodily to heaven. Subsequent tradition specifies that this body and those of his first six successors became rainbows that faded into the sky. They were known by the collective name of the "Seven Enthroned Ones of Heaven" (gnam-gyi khri-bdun). The seventh successor, however, was Gri-gum btsan-po. The tales about this king are particularly complex; they have been studied by Haarh (1969, pp. 142–67 and 401–6). From the oldest version, which comes from a chronicle discovered in Tun-huang, one can learn the following (translation by Bacot/Thomas/Toussaint 1946, pp. 123–28; Snellgrove 1957, pp. 131–32; and Haarh 1969, pp. 401–6):

Because of a misunderstanding for which his nurse was responsible, the king was given the ominous name of Dri-gum btsan-po ("the mighty one killed by pollution," which in later texts always becomes Gri-gum btsan-po, ". . . killed by the sword"). Since he was descended from the gods and therefore differed from other men, he had the miraculous power to disappear into the zenith. However, he challenged his nine paternal and three maternal kinsmen to fight against him. Each one in turn declined. He then asked his chief groom, Lo-ngam, to fight with him, but when he too declined the offer, the king would not let him. Lo-ngam then said that he would fight, but only on condition that he be given the treasures of the gods: the lance that throws itself; the sword that strikes by itself; and the armor that dons itself. This the king accepted. When they met at the place set for the battle, the groom asked the king to cut the celestial cord and reverse the ladder of the nine spheres, and this too the king agreed to do. Then Lo-ngam fixed two hundred spear points on the horns of one hundred oxen and loaded ashes on their backs. The oxen fought among themselves, and the ashes were scattered everywhere, so that Lo-ngam was able to prevail in the confusion. Since the king no longer had the benefit of the *dmu* cord, he perished, and his two sons built him an earthen tomb in the shape of a tent.

From that day, kings left their bodies behind them on the day of their death. In other versions of the myth, it is explicitly said that Lo-ngam first managed by means of a ruse to get the king's tutelary divinities to abandon him, and subsequently easily triumphed over him when the king at last inadvertently cut the celestial cord (Haarh 1969, pp. 142–67; Kuznetsov 1966, p. 47; Tucci 1949, p. 733).

Thus, for the Tibetan kings death is the result of a misunderstanding or an accident. Moreover, divine revelations, supernatural powers, immortality, etc., depend on the tree, the cord, or the ladder that make communication between the sky and the earth possible. To break the *dmu* rope was a disaster. To tie it together again, in the context of a ritual, signifies life, prosperity, and the reassertion of royal power. This is why the *gZer-mig,* the biography of the Buddha of the Bonpo, the Teacher gShen-rab, states that when his parents were married, and likewise when he himself married his first wife, the *dmu* cord, among other rites, was tied by the *dmu* (Hoffmann 1950, p. 141). It is a striking example of the continuity of ideas in the history of Tibetan religion that during the marriage ritual of the Bonpo of today, a cord, called the *dmu* cord, is attached to the groom's sinciput (Karmay 1975, p. 210).

In closing, let us mention a curious ceremony that was practiced in Lhasa until the first decades of the twentieth century. During this ritual, three men of the province of gTsang slid down a rope at a terrifying speed from the roofs of the Potala to an obelisk at the foot of the palace, hundreds of feet below. In theory this ceremony took place to commemorate the defeat of a king of gTsang by the Mongols in 1641. But that defeat also had the effect of making the fifth Dalai Lama the recognized head of all Tibet, and of restoring Lhasa, the capital of the ancient kings, to its political primacy. And it is thus not absurd to see in this ceremony of the recent past an expression of the continuity of royal power which links the Dalai Lama to the earliest mythical kings of Tibet (Snellgrove 1957, pp. 133–34).

P.K./t.l.f.

BIBLIOGRAPHY

See the general bibliography for "Introduction to Tibetan Mythology," above.

The Religion and Myths of the Turks and Mongols

I. Religion

The Turks and Mongols, whose languages are related (Turkic and Mongolic are subfamilies of the Altaic family), have exerted strong influences upon one another. Their religions stem from the same system.

We do not know when that religion took shape, but it surely goes back to prehistory. The oldest word in their vocabulary that has been reconstructed with certainty, namely, the word used to designate the sky god, *tengri,* comes to us from the Xiong Nu confederacy that settled on the frontiers of China in the second century B.C. It is possible that this formation had both pre-Turkic and pre-Mongolian ethnic elements. What we know of Xiong Nu religion does not seem very different from what was to become Turco-Mongolian religion, but it also greatly resembles the religion of the Scythians. Similar phenomena must have occurred throughout the Eurasiatic steppe in the course of the first millennium B.C.

The oldest proto-Mongolian peoples seem to have appeared in the first century A.D. Among them are the Wusun, though some believe that these were Indo-Europeans; more certain are the Xianbi and the Wuhuan, heirs of the Donghu; the Ruanruan (Avar?), whose dominion stretched from Korea to the high Irtysh and to Yangi; and finally the Khitan, who made their presence felt in China from the end of the seventh century and settled there later in the tenth century under the dynasty name of Liao. The proto-Turks were represented by the Toba (Tabgach), who began to come down from the Baikal region toward the Chinese borders around A.D. 260, and the Goujiu Dingling, one branch of whom would later give rise to the Tölesh and the Uighur. Even then all of these peoples seemed to have the religious concepts that would become those of their successors. But in order to form a relatively precise idea of these concepts we must begin with the Tujue (Turks), the former vassals of the Ruanruan in Altai, who settled on the upper Orkhon in the course of the sixth century, ruled over northern Mongolia, and spread westward (the Western Tujue) to begin the "Turkization" of Transoxiana. We must then consider the other peoples who were their adversaries or their subjects, namely, the Türgesh and the Qarluq, located south and east, respectively, of Lake Balkhash; the Tölesh more to the east; the Toquz Oghuz and the Basmil living in northern Mongolia; and the Kirghiz who settled along the banks of the Yenisey. Information of considerable significance may also be garnered in the west from the Oghuz, whence came the Seljuk and the Ottomans; the successors to the western Tujue who had reached the lower course of the Syr Darya, the Ural, and the Volga; the Pecheneg or Comans, who were destroyed at the end of the eleventh century by the Byzantines; the Judaized Khazar living along the Caspian Sea, and the Qipchaq, cousins of the Kimek of Siberia; and to the east the Uighur, who were allied with the Basmil and the Qarluq and who had replaced the eastern Tujue before being expelled by the Kirghiz toward eastern Gansu and the regions of Turfan, Beshbaliq, Kucha, and Yangi, where their kingdom prevailed until the fourteenth century, but not without their conversion to Buddhism, Nestorianism, and Manichaeism at around the same time.

Despite the relative wealth of documents pertaining to the Tujue, it is only from the time of the founding of the Mongol Empire by Genghis Khan in the thirteenth century that sufficient religious data are available. A comparison of the documents of the eighth and thirteenth centuries reveals strong resemblances and leads to the conclusion that in its broad outlines the religion did not change. However, those are generally official documents concerning rulers, and it is possible that there was a popular religion that largely escapes us. There are many good reasons to think that shamanism *stricto sensu* already had in the Middle Ages some of the characteristics that we associate with it today.

There is less certainty about other religious issues. The economic ruin of Central Asia after the fourteenth century, the virtually total triumph of Islam and Buddhism, and the Chinese and Roman conquests succeeded in profoundly altering the beliefs of those rare peoples who remained shamanists. In any event, one should not expect to find perfect uniformity over a span of some two thousand years and over an area stretching from the far reaches of China to the Balkans and the Slavic territories. It is true that the contributions from neighboring China and distant Iran were harmoniously blended at the center of the first empires, but it is not at all difficult to detect regional influences here and there. We must therefore speak in terms of diversity within unity.

Contrary to widespread opinion, shamanism was not the religion of the Turco-Mongols, nor did it account for more than a part of their spiritual lives. It was not even the only means of divination or the only basis of magic. Coexisting with shamanism were haruspicy perhaps, scapulimancy for sure, and astrology, as well as other secondary techniques. The *yadaji,* experts in the art of bringing rain and storms by the use of a bezoar stone, were among others able to form a corps of magicians independent of shamanism.

The religion was a monotheism with multiple gods. The great god was the sky, Tengri, who dispensed the viaticum for the journey of life (*qut*) and fortune (*ülüg*) and watched over the cosmic order and the political and social order. People prayed to him and sacrificed to him, preferably with a white horse. The ruler, who came from him and derived his authority from him, was raised on a felt saddle to meet him. Tengri issued decrees, brought pressure to bear on human beings, and enforced capital punishment, often by striking the offender with lightning. The many secondary powers—sometimes named deities, sometimes spirits or simply said to be sacred, and almost always associated with Tengri—were the Earth, the Mountain, Water, the Springs, and the Rivers; the master/possessors of all objects, particularly of the land and the waters of the nation; trees, cosmic axes, and sources of life; fire, the symbol of the family and alterego of the shaman; the stars, particularly the sun and the moon, the Pleiades, and Venus, whose image changes over time; Umay, a mother goddess who is none other than the placenta; the threshold and the doorjamb; personifications of Time, the Road, Desire, etc.; heroes and ancestors embodied in the banner, in tablets with inscriptions, and in idols; and spirits wandering or fixed in Penates or in all kinds of holy objects. These and other powers have an uneven force which increases as objects accumulate, as trees form a forest, stones form a cairn, arrows form a quiver, and drops of water form a lake.

Animals play a major role. All species have at one time or another been valorized by religious representations, but some have had a more brilliant career than others, more

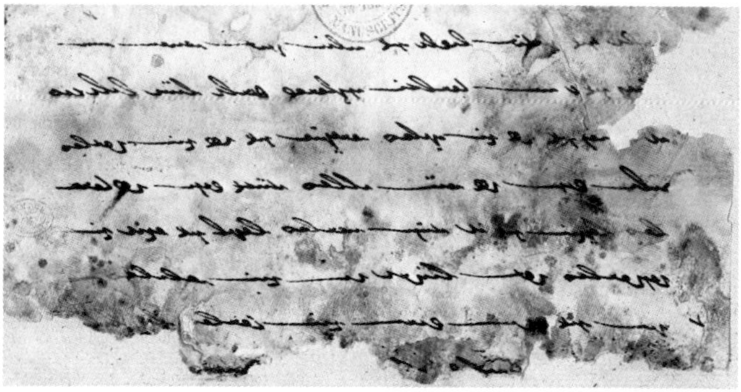

Manuscript of the Orghuz *name* (suppl. turc 1001, p. 1). Paris, Bibliothèque nationale. Photo BN.

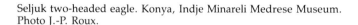

Seljuk two-headed eagle. Konya, Indje Minareli Medrese Museum. Photo J.-P. Roux.

through historical circumstances than through their own aptitude; among these are the wolf, the lion, and the eagle. They play virtually infinite roles as classifiers, allies, or adversaries of men and particularly of shamans, as envoys or agents of the sky god, as advisers about things to come, as guides and leaders, and as sacrificial victims. Their form was the essential form, the form of human souls before birth and after death, a form that a man wanted to put on whenever he could or when he was initiated. They appear principally as ancestors, either uniting among themselves to give birth to a human or uniting with humans. This primordial union was commemorated in the form of a combat that men waged among themselves or against animals when they reached puberty.

Compared with the attention that the Turco-Mongols paid to their origins, the attention they gave to cosmogony and eschatology appears scanty. Their conceptions of the formation of the world, first made up of two, then three parallel zones, and then of successive stages, is known only from a few ancient lines and a few relatively late texts. The universe may eventually come to an end but only man's death matters. Death does not, however, put an end to life. Multiple souls go on living eternally, in the sky especially (or, in the earliest texts, on the mountain of the ancestors), or else in the tomb, in the erected stone (*balbal*), or on the banner sign. Funeral ceremonies, which never were of a uniform type (burial, cremation, exposure), were celebrated solemnly and with rituals (lamentations, mutilations, declamations, sacrifice, communal meal). The fate of the dead human or animal also depended on manner of death (with or without bloodshed) and the way in which the bones were treated, since the skeleton, the skull, and the blood contained souls.

In addition to the rituals dedicated to the sky and the funerary rituals, there were ceremonies of prayers and offerings to secondary deities and to spirits, libations of milk and koumiss, processions around a central point, animal races and fights, purification sessions, and pilgrimages. Countless prohibitions intervened in every action of daily life.

Various great universal religions undertook to conquer the Turks and the Mongols during the Middle Ages, but only Buddhism and Islam were ever to enjoy significant success. The Mongols embraced Buddhism. Henceforth known by the names of Buryat, Khalkha, Kalmuk, and Ordo, under their new official religion they kept many of the features of their former beliefs. The great majority of the Turks adopted Islam. Only a few small ethnic groups of the Altai (the Tatars) and Siberia (the Yakuts especially) preserved their primitive shamanism until the Russian revolution, not without being influenced by the Russian Orthodox church.

In 960, the Qarakhanids, Turkic dynasts of Kashgar, converted to Islam. The Oghuz Turkic masses which had already made contact with the religion preached by Muhammad entered the Muslim lands in hordes in about 1031, and from 1071 they began to colonize Asia Minor, henceforth known as Turkey. The traditions of Central Asia changed even more when they made contact with Islam, but these changes were not absolute. The Kazaks, who converted as late as the eighteenth century, the Kirghiz, and the Turks of Turkey themselves even today have many characteristics that reflect traits from the eighth century. This does not mean that everything that appears to be aberrant in Turco-Islamic civilization stems from Turkic tradition. Anatolian substrata along with Greek, Christian, Iranian, and Arab contributions have often been inextricably blended together.

Very different fates awaited the religion of the Turks in Islam depending on whether the traits fit together or were incompatible and on how vigorously they were defended by those who held them.

The ancient Altaic prescription to kill an animal without shedding a drop of its blood entailed a contradiction of the Sharia, which required that meat be bled before it was consumed, and so this prescription quickly fell into disuse. On the other hand, it seems clear that Islamic funerary art, despite the Koranic prescription that the dead be buried in the desert in an unmarked grave, was born of Turkic funerary art. The rich iconography that developed in the minor arts and in Islamic architecture starting in the twelfth century reflects above all Central Asiatic beliefs. We find, for example, a prince in his majesty sitting cross-legged, holding a goblet in his right hand which rests on his chest; a double monumental representation, in painting and in sculpture, of the great myth of the struggle against the bull that was to be told shortly thereafter in the *Kitab-i Dede Qorqut;* and pairs of animal ancestors fighting, corresponding to the blue wolf and fallow doe of the Central Asiatic empires; and other such animals, which were tirelessly reproduced by coppersmiths, ceramists, miniaturists, and sculptors. The one-headed or two-headed eagle in time sat on the top of trees of life, as is still the case in the pagan Turkic world of the Siberian Yakuts. The coat of arms, which later developed especially among the Mamluks, may have been a distant memory of totemism, as was perhaps also the immoderate use of the names of animals, especially during the Seljuk era, when the Arslan (lion), Kilich Arslan (saber lion), Toghrul (falcon), Bars Bay (rich tiger), Turumlay (merlin), Tay Boga (colt-bull), and Kurt (wolf)—all abound.

Until recently, the Sunnite Turkic world, even in its loftiest circles, preserved some customs from the pre-Islamic Turkic world: strangulation of princes, organization of ritual fights, exhumation and incineration of the corpses of enemies, self-sacrifice of a healthy man to save a sick man, wearing feathers as part of a headdress, decorating flags with the tails of yaks or horses—all of these are traits that can only be explained as shamanic representations.

The Islamization of the masses in Anatolia was slow, even when the culture spread, because the true religious propagandists—the Turkoman babas, Baba Ishaq, Barak Baba, Sari Saltuq, and many others—were clearly shamans disguised in Islamic garb. At the end of the thirteenth century, the poet Sheyyad Hamza translated and commented to his audience on the *bismillah* ("In the name of God the Merciful, the Compassionate"). At the end of the fourteenth century, a commentary on the Koran in Kastamuni Turkish deemed it necessary to explain Allah with the word *tengri.* The founder of the Bektashi order, Hadji Bektash, showed in his book, the *Vilayet Name,* that he drew heavily on the pre-Islamic tradition of the Oghuz.

Very briefly, Tengri the sky god was assimilated to Allah well before he acquired all of Allah's features. His viaticum for life, the *qut,* became grace; his order, the *yarliq,* which was expressed by the imperial authority, became intercession or pardon. Islamic notions of divine mercy and clemency remained alien for a long time. Secondary deities and master possessors did not disappear immediately, since in the *Kitab-i Dede Qorqut,* under the same circumstances and in comparable terms, prayers were still addressed to God, to the mountain, water, trees, and certain animals. Sometimes they were identified with jinn or with peris, or else they kept their original meaning by virtue of the presence, real or imagined, of a saint (numerous sites where people worship a tree, a plot of ground, a body of water near a tomb). Sometimes they were transformed under the influence of mysticism (the gate, formerly a deity, became a symbol of access to knowledge). At still other times they would vanish, leaving behind only traces of almost magical practices (placental rites inherited from the ancient goddess Umay). Islamic symbols and readings from the Koran helped the Turks preserve their traditions. The anecdote of Nemrud shooting arrows at God shows how myths of struggles against evil heavenly spirits persisted. The symbol of the soul as bird allowed free use of the euphemism "he became a gyrfalcon" to mean "he died," and probably also the belief in the notion it suggests.

But interferences from Altaic religion were not all that Turkish Islam had to contend with. The Christian substrata of Anatolia and Thrace, and, beyond those, ancient Greek substrata also intervened. Where Hellenism had taken root, its resistance to Islamization promoted within the local literature the introduction and preservation of old Asiatic legends when they had points in common with Greek legends. The legend of the petrified woman weeping over her children, the one-eyed monster Tepegöz, and the struggle between man and the angel of death survived only because of Niobe, Polyphemus, and Alcestis. Symbioses occurred. When Turkish women bathed in the ancient holy fountains of the Greeks in order to ensure their fertility, were they acting in accordance with local traditions or with those of Central Asia? Did the cult that developed in the Cavern of the Seven Sleepers of Ephesus come within an Islamic-Christian perspective or a shamanic perspective? The cult whose sanctuary was Mount Ida (*Kaz Dagi*) enriched with purely Turkic representations the complex created by the marriage of ancient myths, Mariology, and alevism.

Dragon. Thirteenth century. Konya, Inje Minareli Medrese Museum. Photo J.-P. Roux.

Drawing on stone wall of Mount Pissanaja-Jora. From Appelgren-Kivalo, *Alt-Altaische Kunstdenkmäler* (Helsinki, 1931). Paris, Bibliothèque nationale. Photo Flammarion.

The situation in Turkey is, therefore, never clear, and much work remains to be done if we are to understand it better. What already seems certain is that a true mythology is not to be found, since Islam excluded it. At most we may discover mythological vestiges which will always refer us back to a previous religious system.

II. The Deities

It is practically impossible to isolate the deities of the Turco-Mongol world, in part because they can only be manifestations of the sky god, and in part because, since everything is a force, everything may conceivably obtain divine status at any moment. Two examples follow.

The great eagle that flies near the sky and is sent by the sky is a messenger of god, but it may be regarded as a divine epiphany. The ancestor, who is a guiding spirit, becomes a true god in the tradition of the Mongols after Genghis Khan.

We must therefore consider the names of deities cautiously when we first encounter them in Paleo-Turkic texts. Öd Tengri or *Öd,* whom the *Qutadgu Bilig* later named Ödlek and depicted as Time personified, rode on horseback and acted simultaneously as the moon. Was he a "god of time," a "heavenly time," or the sky god who organizes time? Yol Tengri, also on horseback, repaired what was broken, made peace, and distributed the viaticum of life (generally a gift from heaven); he may have been a "god of the road," or a "god of fortune" (depending on the meaning given to the word *yol*), or "divine luck" ("the divine way"), or, finally, the sky god as distributor of luck. A "sacred god" (*tengri iduq*) who hears prayers such as "Lead us not astray" is even more mysterious. Today, *tengri* is the name given to the multiple deities who are often the children or the messengers of the heavenly god.

We will discuss the meaning and functions of the earth, the mountain, fire, water, and trees, which in many cases represented something very particular that it would be hard to treat as divine but that became gods not only in modern times but also in the past. The earth in particular appeared as a great goddess, often connected with the sky god. But we also find a few individuals who occupy an important position during the Tujue period.

The place of the stars in the sky does not always allow us to say whether the divine role attributed to them was independent of that of the sky. Some of them, in particular the sun and the moon, seem to have been highly venerated in themselves. Venus seems to have had a special career of her own. First named Erlik (or Erklik), the "virile one," "the valiant one," a title also given to diverse powerful individuals, she was a warrior who killed the stars at dawn. Under Buddhist influence she became a god of hell and king of demons, the equivalent of Yama, attested in Turkish as early as 1202. A tendency toward dualism led her in certain cases to enter into a rivalry with the sky.

From the eighth century, Umay, the placenta, a fertility goddess, was exceptionally well known. Held in high esteem, she was named "Empress" (*Qatun*); the sovereign queen resembled her; her role was parallel with that of the sky, and she was called upon to act along with the spirits of the earth and the water. She is sometimes confounded with the earth. Kashghari says, "If she is worshiped, a child is born." At that time, as today (when she appears among the Yakuts unchanged, except that her name has become Ayisit), she protected newborn children and mares during the first three days of life. Many placental rites of the Muslim Turkish world stem from her ancient cult.

Not until the Mongol period do we begin to see the god of the gate. According to *The Secret History of the Mongols,* he resides in the frame of the gate, which "bestows happiness." In fact, he was also situated in the wood of the threshold, on which it was forbidden to walk under penalty of death, as all travelers visiting Central Asia were quick to learn.

In the thirteenth century, too, travelers unanimously mentioned the existence of numerous idols made of felt, fabric, or wood that were suspended inside houses or displayed on carts. These idols were fed and sprinkled with milk and koumiss and were said to dispense milk and promote growth; they resemble the idols that are known from excavations as well as those that ethnographers have collected. They must have represented many things—the earth, "the wife and sons" of the earth perhaps, shepherds, the dead, the ancestors. Among these objects was a sheepskin stuffed with wool and considered to be the deity of the home. Not much is known about them, but they seem to correspond to what ethnologists today call *ongon,* idols of the hunt, medicinal idols, idols of stockbreeding, etc. In the thirteenth century, however, the word *ongon* referred to something altogether different. According to Rashid ed-din, it referred to the bird, different for each Oghuz tribe, which each tribesman knew and was forbidden to hunt. Corresponding to Rashid ed-din's list are the lists, less clear and peculiarly presented as lists of deities or of paragons of virtue, that were furnished earlier by ibn Fadhlan for the Bashkir and by al-Mada'ini or the *Qutadgu Bilig* for other Turkic peoples. Perhaps these *ongon* were represented by idols, but there is no proof of this. They may be totems, but they are certainly not gods.

Ancient Turkic stelae. From Appelgren-Kivalo, *Alt-Altaische Kunstdenkmäler* (Helsinki, 1931). Paris, Bibliothèque nationale. Photo Flammarion.

The different *tengri* of the Turks and Mongols of the time are discussed in the chapter devoted to the sky god. We should note, however, that among the Mongols a few personalities were distinguished in importance: the god of fire, Genghis Khan, the "Old Man in White" (*Tsagan Ebügen*), the lords of the earth and the waters, the god of fertility, and the god of war (*Dayichin tengri*).

The treatment of the deities in the Turkish pantheon in Muslim Anatolia was marked by the idea, crucial in Central Asia, that what is called a "god" is above all a power that emanates from objects, comparable in some respects to what the Arabs call *baraka.* Nor did the trend toward monotheism and the existence of the sky god constitute an insuperable obstacle to Islamization. Consequently, deities did not quickly disappear, and when they finally did, they left traces that are visible today.

The *Kitab-i Dede Qorqut* presents a divine triad to whom one addressed prayers of the same nature and structure as those that were addressed to Allah. They include affirmations of faith; references to Islamic events, real or imagined, and to events of daily life; and requests from the supplicant. It is, however, unlikely that any reader of the book would have given the title of god to the members of this triad: the mountain, the water, and the tree. The same text also addresses and praises animals, notably, horses, camels, and sheep, and shows that their behavior or fate determined the behavior or fate of men. The same idea appears in certain old texts of Central Asia, and therein lies an essential fact.

Among the ancient deities that are still faithfully remembered in contemporary Turkey but that have at least officially lost divine status, let us mention the deity of the gate, which is quite explicit. At the popular level, people probably no longer know why they must not step on the threshold, nor why they must prostrate themselves in front of it and kiss it. But in mystical heterodox circles the words of Muhammad provide a basis: "I am the city of knowledge, and Ali is its gate." The gate is thereby taken as a symbol of entrance into the light of knowledge. The various parts of the gate represent the family of the Prophet: the lintel is Muhammad; one doorjamb is Hasan, the other Hussein; the threshold is Fatima; the hinge is Ali himself.

J.-P.R./g.h.

BIBLIOGRAPHY

I. Sources: Ancient and Medieval Periods

The religions of the Turks and Mongols may be known from the still incomplete data of archaeology and linguistics, from published texts, and from information of foreign origin.

We possess no religious texts as such. The eastern Tujue have left three great inscriptions on stelae in the Orkhon region, those of Ton Yuquq (725), Kül Tegin (732), and Bilge Kaghan (735), often designated, the first as the inscription of Baïn Tsokto, the latter two as inscriptions of Kocho-Tsaïdam. A fourth inscription, that of Ongin, is shorter, clearer, and undated. Written in "runic" characters, they were deciphered by W. Thomsen at the end of the nineteenth century and have been studied many times since:

W. THOMSEN, *Inscriptions de l'Orkhon déchiffrées* (Helsinki 1896); "Alttürkische Inschriften aus der Mongolei," *Zeitschrift der Deutschen Morgenländischen Gesellschaft*, 1924–25, 121–75. W. RADLOV, *Die Alttürkischen Inschriften der Mongolei* (Saint Petersburg 1895). H. N. ORKUN, *Eski Türk Yazitlari*, vol. 1 (Istanbul 1936). R. GIRAUD, *L'inscription de Baïn Tsokto* (Paris 1961). G. CLAUSON, "The Ongin inscription," *Journal of the Royal Asiatic Society*, 1957, 177–92.

Of the western Tujue, we have five brief stone inscriptions and an engraved staff from the region of Talas. Of the Kirghiz, a considerable number of small inscriptions, undated but after the seventh, indeed the eighth century, were found in the valley of the upper Yenisey. The Uighurs of Orkhon are probably responsible for ten small inscriptions from the Valley of the Hoytu Tamir:

W. RADLOV, *Atlas der Altertümer der Mongolei* (Saint Petersburg 1892–99); the plates have been retouched. S. E. MALOV, *Enisejskaja Pismennost' T'urkov* (Moscow and Leningrad 1952). H. N. ORKUN, *Eski Türk Yazitlari*, vols. 2–4 (Istanbul 1939–41). L. BAZIN, "L'inscription d'Uyug Tarliq (Iénissei)," *Acta Orientalia* 22 (1955): 1–7.

The runic alphabet is still employed by the author of a small book of omens, the *Irq Bitig* (end of the tenth century), written in a Manichaean monastery in the Tuen-huang region but conforming to the nomadic and shamanic traditions of the Turks:

W. THOMSEN, "Dr. M. A. Stein's Manuscripts in Turkish 'Runic' Script," *Journal of the Royal Asiatic Society*, 1912, 181–227. H. N. ORKUN, *Eski Türk Yazitlari* (Istanbul 1939), 2:71–93.

Almost all the manuscripts of the rich Uighur literature, written in a newly borrowed alphabet, belong to the world religions, but several preserve substrata:

W. BANG and A. VON GABAIN, *Türkische Turfan-Texte*, Akademie der Wissenschaften (Berlin 1928–31). Certain selected texts in A. VON GABAIN, *Alttürkische Grammatik* (Leipzig 1950).

The text of a version of the legend of Oghuz Khan in Uighur characters, at the Bibliothèque Nationale in Paris, is from after the thirteenth century but reveals an earlier state of the mythology:

W. RADLOV, *Das Kudatku Bilig* (Saint Petersburg 1891), 232–44. R. NOUR, *Oghouz-name, épopée turque* (Alexandria 1928). P. PELLIOT, "Sur la légende d'Uγuz Khan," *TP*, 1930, 247–358. BANG and RACHMATI, *Die Legende von Oghuz kagan* (Berlin 1932).

This legend, altered, reappeared in the Persian historians of the thirteenth century and in the seventeenth century in the Turkish author of Khiva, Abul Ghazi Bahadur Khan:

K. JAHN, *Die Geschichte des Oguzen des Rašid-ed-din* (Vienna 1969). DESMAISONS, *Histoire des Mongols et des Tartares*, 2 vols. (Saint Petersburg 1871–74). A. N. KONONOV, *Rodoslovnaia Turkmen* (Moscow and Leningrad 1958).

In the second half of the eleventh century, a Turk from Kashgar, Mahmud al-Kashgari, wrote, in Arabic, the most ancient dictionary of Turkish dialects, an inexhaustible source, especially for proverbs and archaic poems:

BROCKELMANN, *Mitteltürkischer Wortschatz nach Mahmud al-Kašγari Divan Luγat at-Turk* (Budapest and Leipzig 1928). B. ATALAY, *Divanü Lûgat-it Türk*, 4 vols. (Ankara 1939–43).

His compatriot and contemporary Yusuf Khass Khadjib is less interesting for our subject:

W. RADLOV, *Das Kudatku Bilig* (Saint Petersburg 1891). R. R. ARAT, *Kutadgu Bilig* (Istanbul 1947).

Although far less valuable than that of Kashgari, other dictionaries or glossaries often furnish complementary information:

A. BATTAL, *Ibnü Mühenna Lugati* (Istanbul 1934). K. GRÖNBECH, *Codex Cumanicus* (Copenhagen 1936); *Komanisches Wörterbuch* (Copenhagen 1942). A. CAFEROĞLU, *Abu Hayyan Kitab al-Idrak li lisan al-Atrak* (Istanbul 1931). M. TH. HOUTSMA, *Ein Türkisch-arabisches Glossar* (Leiden 1894).

Mongol sources are even less numerous than Turkish sources. The essential document is the *Histoire secrète des Mongols*, written in 1240, the text of which was reconstituted and partially translated (six chapters) by Pelliot on the basis of a Chinese version and was later recovered:

P. PELLIOT, *Histoire secrète des Mongols* (Paris 1949). P. POUCHA, *Die geheime Geschichte der Mongolen* (Prague 1956). E. HAENISCH, *Die geheime Geschichte der Mongolen* (Leipzig 1937–41). P. A. MOSTAERT, "Sur quelques passages de l'Histoire secrète des Mongols," *HJAS* 13–15. (1950–52). F. W. CLEAVES, *The Secret History of the Mongols*, vol. 1 (Cambridge, MA, 1957).

Some letters by rulers, edicts of tolerance, documents of chancellery, in Mongol and Chinese, complete our information for the thirteenth and fourteenth centuries:

CLEAVES, "The Sino-Mongolian Inscription of 1362," *HJAS*, 1949, 2–133. P. A. MOSTAERT, "Une phrase de la lettre de l'Ilkhan Argun à Philippe le Bel," *HJAS*, 1955, 200–220. P. PELLIOT, "Les Mongols et la papauté," *Revue de l'Orient chrétien* 19 (1924): 225–35; 27 (1931): 3–84. E. CHAVANNES, "Inscriptions et pièces de chancellerie chinoises à l'époque mongole," *TP*, 1904, 357–447; 1905, 1–42; 1908, 297–428.

Other chronicles are more recent and deal less with the original religious facts:

BAWDEN, *The Mongol Chronicle Altan Tobči* (Wiesbaden 1955). W. HEISSIG, "A Mongolian Source to the Lamaist Suppression of Shamanism in the 17th Century," *Ant.* 48 (1953): 1–29 and 493–536.

Almost all the rest of the classical Mongol literature is Buddhist.

The insufficiency of Turkish and Mongol sources is in part compensated for by the relative wealth of foreign sources. The earliest are the Chinese annals, which have been translated or studied for a long time but which have been truly exploitable only from the most recent and reliable versions. Hence one must be prudent with the older works:

DE GUIGNES, *Histoire générale des Huns, des Turcs et des Mongols*, 4 vols. (Paris 1756). S. JULIEN, *Documents historiques sur les Tou-kioue (Turcs)*

(Paris 1877). WIEGER, *Textes historiques chinois,* 3 vols. (Hien Hien 1905). J. J. DE GROOT, *Chinesische Urkunden zur Geschichte Asien,* 2 vols. (Berlin and Leipzig 1921). PARKER, "The Early Turks," *China Review,* vols. 24–25; *A Thousand Years of the Tartars* (London 1924).

One may rely upon:

E. CHAVANNES, *Documents sur les Tou-Kiue (Turcs) occidentaux* (Saint Petersburg 1903). EBERHARD, *Çin'in Şimal Komşulari* (Ankara 1942); "Kultur und Siedlung der Randvölker Chinas," *TP* 30–36 (1942). LIU MAU-TSAI, *Die chinesischen Nachrichten zur Geschichte der Ost-Türken (T'u-küe),* 2 vols. (Wiesbaden 1958).

The works devoted to the Khitan are important:

R. STEIN, "Leao tche," *TP* 25:1–154. WITTFOGEL and FENG, *History of Chinese Society: Liao, 907–1125* (New York 1949).

The Greek sources, which were already given by Chavannes (*Documents sur les Tou-Kiue (Turcs) occidentaux*), are more complete in G. MORAVCSIK, *Byzantino-turcica,* 1, 2 (2d ed., Berlin 1958).

Muslim geographers, historians, and travelers often give the essential information from the ninth century (al-Mada'ini, ca. 752–840; ibn Khurdadhbeh, † 885). In the tenth century, ibn Fadlan reported extensively on his travels among the pre-Slavic Bulgars of the Volga; the *Hudad al-Alam,* Mas'udi, ibn Rusteh, Abu Dulaf Mis'ar, Maqdisi are fairly rich. Later, Gardizi, ibn Sina, Marwazi, and Idrisi remain valuable sources on certain points. In the thirteenth century, the two great Iranian historians Juvaini and Rashid ed-din are especially interesting for data on the Mongols. Wassaf and Khondemir (fourteenth–fifteenth centuries) sometimes complement them. The chroniclers of the Crusades, Western, Armenian, and Syriac, G. de Nangis, Joinville, Guiragos, Haytton, Grigor d'Akanč, Bar Hebraeus, are often less well informed, but their contributions are not useless.

BROCKELMANN, "Alttürkische Volksweisheit," in *Festschrift für Hirth* (Berlin 1920). HOMMEL, "Zu den alttürkischen Sprichwörten," in *Hirth Anniversary Volume, Asia Major* (London 1932). M. CANARD, "La relation du voyage d'ibn Fadlan," *Annales Inst. Ét. Orientales* 16 (1958): 41–146. Z. V. TOGAN, *Ibn Fadlân' Reisebericht* (Leipzig 1939). V. MINORSKY, *Hudud al-Alam* (London 1937); *Sharaf al-Zaman Tahir Marvazi* (London 1942); "Tamim ibn Bahr's Journey to the Uyghurs," *BSOAS* 12 (1947–48): 257–306. AL-MAQDISI, *Le livre de la création et de l'histoire,* translated by Huart, 6 vols. (Paris 1899–1919). AL-MAS'UDI, *Les Prairies d'Or,* text and trans. of Barbier de Meynard and Pavet de Courteille, 2 vols. (Paris 1866–77). IBN RUSTEH, *Les Atours précieux,* translated by Wiet (Cairo 1955). IBN SINA, *Le livre des directives et des remarques,* translated by Goichon (Paris 1951). AL-IDRISI, *Kitab Rojar (Géographie d'Idrisi),* 2 vols. (Paris 1836–40). QUATREMÈRE, *Histoire des Mongols de la Perse* (Paris 1836). BLOCHET, *Introduction à l'histoire des Mongols* (Leiden and London 1910). J. A. BOYLE, *The History of the World-Conqueror,* 2 vols. (Manchester 1968); *The Successors of Gengis Khan* (New York and London 1971). K. JAHN, *Die Geschichte des Oguzen des Rašid-ed-din* (Vienna 1969). BAR HEBRAEUS, *The Chronography of Gregory Abul Faradj,* translated by E. A. Wallis Budge (London 1932). BLAKE and FRYE, "History of the Nation of the Archers (the Mongols) by Grigor of Akanč," *Harvard Journal of Asian Studies* 12 (1949): 269–399. Finally, see the collection *Recueil des historiens des Croisades* (Paris).

In the period of Mongol domination, many Western travelers visited Central Asia and made essential contributions:

L. HAMBIS, *Marco Polo: La description du monde* (Paris 1955). JEAN DE PLAN CARPIN, *Histoire des Mongols,* translated and annotated by Dom Jean Becquet and L. Hambis (Paris 1965). W. W. ROCKHILL, *The Journey of William of Rubruck* (London 1900). D. SINOR, "Un voyageur du xiiie siècle: Le dominicain Julien de Hongrie," *BSOAS* 14 (1952): 589–602.

II. Sources: Modern Period

We have much more information for the modern period. The travels in Central Asia that ceased just after the fall of the Mongol Empire resumed beginning in the seventeenth century and became more and more numerous. Among a rich literature, we cite:

OLÉARIUS, *Relation du voyage en Moscovie, Tartarie et Perse* (Paris 1666). WITSEN, *Noord en Oost Tartarye,* 2 vols. (Amsterdam 1705). STRAHLENBERG, *Der Nord- und Östliche Theil von Europa und Asien* (Stockholm 1730); *Description historique de l'empire russien,* 2 vols. (Amsterdam 1757). J. G. GEORGI, *Bemerkungen auf einer Reise in russischen Reiche* (Saint Petersburg 1755); *Beschreibung aller Nationen des russischen Reichs* (Saint Petersburg 1776). J. G. GMELIN, *Reise durch Sibirien,* 4 vols. (Göttingen 1751–52). PALLAS, *Sammlungen historischen Nachrichten über die mongolischen Völkerschaften,* 2 vols. (Saint Petersburg 1776–1801); *Reise durch verschiedene Provinzen des russischen Reichs,* 3 vols. (Saint Petersburg 1776); *Voyages en différentes provinces de l'Empire de Russie,* 5 vols. (Paris 1783–93). LEVCHINE, *Description des hordes et des steppes des Kirghiz-Kazak* (Paris 1840). HUC, *Souvenir d'un voyage dans la Tartarie, le Tibet et la Chine* (Paris 1850).

It is also interesting to read Clarke (1813), Ermann (1848), Struys (1720), Helmersen (1848), Ides-Isbrand (1699), Smith (1630), Timkowski (1827), Lebedur (1829), Middendorf (1851), Tchiahtcheff (1845), etc. From the end of the nineteenth century, the researchers collected texts and documents. Vast collections of data may be found in:

A. SCHIEFNER, *Heldensagen des Minussischen Tataren* (Saint Petersburg 1859). W. RADLOV, *Aus Sibirien,* 2 vols. (Leipzig 1884); *Proben der Volksliteratur,* 8 vols. (Saint Petersburg 1866–96). COXWELL, *Siberian and Other Folk-Tales* (London 1925). N. TH. KATANOV, *Volkskundliche Texte aus Ost-Türkistan* (Berlin 1943). P. A. MOSTAERT, *Textes oraux ordos* (Peking 1937); *Folklore ordos* (Peking 1949). RINTCHEN, *Les matériaux pour l'étude du chamanisme mongol* (Wiesbaden 1959–61).

Among others, Castagné has studied the "Survivances d'anciens cultes et rites en Asie centrale," *Revue Eth. et trad. popul.,* 1923, 245–55.

The great Kirghiz epic of Manas is an essential source on which Hatto is now working (for example: *Asia Major,* 14:2, 19:1; 18:2; CAJ, 13:3; 15:2, 4). A fragment containing the episode of Er-Töshtük has been translated into French: P. N. BORATAV, *Er Töshtük: Le géant des steppes* (Paris 1965).

III. Turkey

In the Islamic Turkish literature, which preserves rich pre-Islamic substrata, the *Book of Dede Qorqut,* known from two sixteenth-century manuscripts but edited in the fifteenth century, occupies the first place:

E. ROSSI, *Il Kitab-i Dede Qorqut* (Rome 1952). M. ERGIN, *Dede Korkut Kitabi* (Ankara 1958). J. HEIN, *Das Buch des Dede Korkut* (Zurich 1958).

Stories and epic tales from the first centuries of Islamization in Asia Minor (*Saltikname, Darabname, Kissa-i Melik Danishmend Gazi, Kissa-i Abu Muslim*) are still scarcely accessible. On the epics and epic stories, see:

P. N. BORATAV, *Köroğlu Destani* (Istanbul 1931). GÖLPINARLI and BORATAV, *Pir Sultan Abdal* (Ankara 1943). I. MELIKOFF, *Abu Muslim le Porte-Hache du Khorassan* (Paris 1962).

The work of the founder of the Bektashi order, Hadji Bektash, merits particular mention:

E. GROSS, *Das Vilâyet-nâme des Haǧǧi Bektasch* (Leipzig 1927).

It is often thought that the traditions of Central Asia were more numerous among the heterodox Alevi-Bektashi than in the Sunni majority, and they are naturally more numerous in the popular literature than in the official Ottoman literature. See:

P. N. BORATAV, *Contes turcs* (Paris 1955); *Türk Halk edebiyati* (Istanbul 1973); *Türk Folkloru* (Istanbul 1973). W. EBERHARD and P. N. BORATAV, *Typen türkischer Volksmärchen* (Wiesbaden 1953). I. BASGÖZ, *Izhali Türk Halk edebiyati Antolojisi* (Istanbul 1956).

Numerous ethnographic documents have been collected in Turkey, but chiefly in Turkish. There are numerous records in *TFA* and in *Halk Bilgisi Haberleri* (Istanbul). See also *Türkiye'de Halk ağzindan söz derleme dergisi,* 6 vols. (Istanbul 1939–52); *Türkiye'de Halk ağzindan derleme sözlüğu,* A.G., 6 vols. (Ankara 1963–72). AZRA ERHAT, *Mitoloji Sözlüğu* (Istanbul 1972). Among the monographs, we cite ALI RIZA ÖNDER, *Yaşayan Anadolu efsaneleri* (Kayseri 1955). M. ÖNDER, *Anadolu efsaneleri* (Ankara 1966). Y. Z. DEMIRCIOĞLU, *Yürük ve köylülerde hikayeler masallar* (Istanbul 1931).

For works in European languages, see the *Encyclopédie de l'Islam* (1st and 2d eds., Leiden); *Philologiae Turcicae Fundamenta,* 2 (Wiesbaden 1964). See also the monographs of J. P. ROUX, *Les traditions des nomades de la Turquie méridionale* (Paris 1970). M. NICOLAS, *Croyances et pratiques turques concernant les naissances* (Paris 1972).

IV. Studies

The religion of the Turks and Mongols (Altaic religion) is almost unknown in its ancient form. The works devoted to it are few in number, but almost all the works of history devote a chapter to the spiritual life:

VAMBERY, *Die primitive Kultur der Turko-Tatarischen Volkes* (Leipzig 1879), and *Das Türkenvolk* (Leipzig 1885) are old.

The basic work, by U. Harva, is largely outdated and full of prejudices, but it assembles many facts, generally recent:

U. HARVA, *Die Religiösen Vorstellungen der altaischen Völker* (Helsinki 1938); French trans., *Les représentations religieuses des peuples altaïques* (Paris 1959).

This author had previously published a more limited book, under the name of Holmberg:

HOLMBERG, *Siberian Mythology* (Boston 1927).

Much discussed, the works of the lamented Paulson are limited to the Arctic peoples. See his contribution in:

PAULSON, HULTKRANZ, and JETTMAR, *Die Religionen Nordeurasien und der amerikanische Arktis* (Stuttgart 1962); French trans., *Les religions arctiques et finnoises* (Paris 1965). See also the other title below.

Turkish mythology and beliefs have given birth in Turkey to two works, the second less trustworthy:

A. INAN, *Tarihte ve bugün Şamanizm* (Ankara 1954). B. ÖGEL, *Türk Mitolojisi* (Ankara 1971).

The large book edited by DIOSZEGI is a collection of articles of which some concern solely the Turks and Mongols: *Glaubenswelt und Folklore der sibirischen Völker* (Budapest 1963). There are others regrouped in a more modest volume: *Traditions religieuses et para-religieuses des peuples altaïques* (Paris 1972).

The beliefs of the ancient Turks have been studied by A. VON GABAIN, "Inhalt und magische Bedeutung der alttürkischen Inschriften," *Ant.* 48 (1953). R. GIRAUD, *Les règnes d'El-Terich, Qapghan et Bilgä, 680–734* (Paris 1960), chap. 5. J. P. ROUX, "La religion des Turcs de l'Orkhon," *RHR*, 1962, 1–24 and 199–231. Those of the Mongols, by Heissig and Pallisen especially: HEISSIG and TUCCI, *Die Religionen Tibet und der Mongolei* (Stuttgart 1970), French trans., *La religion du Tibet et de la Mongolie* (Paris 1973). N. PALLISEN, *Die alte Religion des mongolischen Volkes* (Marburg 1949). See also the reports of: J. CURTIN, *A Journey in Southern Siberia: The Mongols, Their Religion, Their Myths* (London 1909). The work of: E. DORA EARTHY, "The Religion of Gengis Khan," *Numen* 2, 3 (1955): 228–32, is bad.

Among the works that shed light on the role of the world religions among the Turks of Central Asia: P. PELLIOT, *La Haute Asie* (Paris n.d.), is brief but illuminating. A. VON GABAIN, "Die alttürkische Literatur," *Philologiae Turcicae Fundamenta,* 1964, longer, gives valuable information.

Works about the Turkish traditions of Turkey, the borrowings made by the Turks, and the contacts of the Turks of Turkey with Christianity are still insufficient. We cite: NACI KUM ATABEYLI, "Anadolu'da Oğuz destani," *Ün* 1, 5 (1934): 81–83. J. K. BIRGE, *The Bektashi Order of Dervishes* (London 1937). P. N. BORATAV, "Vestiges oghuz dans la tradition bektasi," *XXIV. Int. orient. Kongress, München 1957* (Wiesbaden 1959). C. CAHEN, *Pre-Ottoman Turkey* (London 1968). W. CROOWFOOT, "Survivals among the Kappadokian Kyzylbash," *JRAI* 30 (1900). GORDLEVSKY, *Gosudartsvo Seldzukidov Maloy Azii,* 1941. M. S. GÜNALTAY, "Selcuklarin Horasan'a indikleri zaman Islam dünyasinin siyasal, sosyal, ekonomik ve dini durumu," *Belleten* 7 (1943): 59–92. HASLUCK, *Christianity and Islam under the Sultans,* 2 vols. (Oxford 1929). M. F. KÖPRÖLÖ, *Turk edebiyatinda ilk Mutasavviflar* (Istanbul 1919; 2d ed., Ankara 1966); "Influences du chamanisme sur les ordres mystiques musulmans," *Mémoires institut turcologie Univ. Istanbul,* n.s., 1 (1920). K. E. MÜLLER, *Kulturhistorische Studien zur Genese pseudo-islamischer Sektengebilde in Vorderasien* (Wiesbaden 1967). C. S. MUNDY, "Polyphemus and Tepegöz," *BSOAS* 18, 2 (1956): 279–302. A. SOYALI, "Turks in the Middle East before the Seljuqs," *Jour. American Orient. Soc.,* 1943. O. TURAN, "Les souverains seldjoukides et leurs sujets non musulmans," *Studia islamica,* 1953. H. Z. ÜLKEN, "Infiltration des religions païennes dans les mœurs et les coutumes anatoliennes," *Traditions religieuses et para-religieuses des peuples altaïques* (Paris 1972).

On particular points, barely touched on here, see, on divination: ROUX and BORATAV, "La divination chez les Turcs," *Divination,* 2 vols. (Paris 1968), 2:279–329. A particular technique is examined by: R. ANDREA, "Scapulimantia," in *Boas Anniversary Volume* (New York 1906), 143–65. BAWDEN, "Scapulimancy among the Mongols," *CAJ* 6, 1 (1958): 1–31. On rites to produce rain, refer to BORATAV, "Istiska," *Islam Ansiklopedisi* 54:1222–24, and M. F. KÖPRÜLÜ, "Une institution magique chez les Turcs: Yat," *Actes 2e congrès Int. Histoire Relig. 1923* (Paris 1925), 440–51.

Turkish and Mongolian Cosmogony and Cosmography

We know only one ancient Turkish cosmogony, the celebrated genesis of Orkhon, of the Tujue period, which is as undidactic as can be: "When, above, the blue sky, below, the dark earth were formed, between the two appeared the sons of Kishi (= of man)." The old translations using "create" are faulty, as the verb used is the passive reflexive of *qil,* "make, form." It is the same verb that is used again later with regard to men. The problem of the origin of the universe thus little preoccupied the Turks and Mongols, who were more interested in tribal myths. The word "eternal" (*möngke*), which always accompanies the name of the sky in the period of Gengis Khan, seems opposed to the Tujue notion of a formation of the sky and the earth; this is one of the reasons why it was believed that the sky and the earth drew apart or separated.

The fact that more recent cosmogonies were influenced by foreign religions such as the Judeo-Christian tradition, as is proved by the name Ay-wa for the first woman, also tends to prove that there never was a great indigenous myth. According to an Islamic manuscript from the beginning of the fourteenth century, which was inspired by a version going back to the tenth century if not earlier, when a cave of the Kara Tag (black mountain) was flooded, a hole became filled with mud. Under the effects of heat, the mud dried up and formed the first man, Ay Ata, Father Moon. His companion was born four years later from another flood. There are some variants of this account, which demonstrate its reception. Abd al-Qadir Buda'ini relates that a Turkish sovereign of India was born during an eclipse of the moon (which is why he is named Moonbeam). A Qipchaq tradition calls the first man My Father Moon (Ay Atam). He was born from a piece of clay heated by the sun.

Unlike their ancestors, contemporary Turks and Mongols have multiple cosmogonies. The most renowned was reported by Radlov for the Altai: "Before the Earth and the Sky existed, all was water. There was no earth. There was no sky. There was no sun or moon. Then Tengere Kaira Kan, the highest of the gods, the beginning of all creation, the father and mother of the human race, created, first of all, a being resembling himself called Kishi (Man)." The Buryat say that in the beginning there existed only the gods to the west and the evil spirits to the east. The gods created men.

In Turkey, popular cosmogonies introduce certain Turkish traditions which are inserted into a strongly Islamicized context. In Istanbul, it is said that God sent the angel Gabriel to take a handful of clay to make man. The earth, knowing that man would sin and burn in hell, begged the angel to renounce his mission. A more elaborate Anatolian version says that God sent in succession the archangels Israfil, Michael, and Jebrail, who refused to take the humus. Finally Azrail, the angel of death, ignored the earth's pleas and man was created. Among the Alevi-Bektashi, it is believed that

Allah first created a green ocean out of which came a precious stone. Allah cut this in half, and one-half was the green light of Muhammad and the other the white light of Ali. Then he created an angel.

The representation of the world has undoubtedly evolved over time. It is likely that originally, since there was only the sky above and the earth below, the underworld did not yet exist and was an important later borrowing, probably from Buddhism. We do not know when the sky and, for reasons of symmetry, the underworld, sometimes called hell, came to take on seven or nine levels. The ancient texts say nothing on this subject, whereas recent texts are very prolix; but certain cave paintings may point to the existence of these levels in prehistory. The sky covers and shelters the earth which supports it. The two are connected by a central axis which is a pillar, mountain, tree, or perch, rising from the navel of the earth up to the navel of the sky. The Chinese conception of the square earth and the round sky is probably the most ancient: the disinherited peoples are not under the sky but at the four corners of the world. Later, in the western regions, the earth is a disk, which represents a radical ideological change due to Muslim influences and, beyond this, to the Ptolemaic conception. Four or five elements compose the universe. According to Theophylactus Simocattes and modern Bektashism, there are four: water, fire, earth, and air; according to Jean de Plan Carpin, if he is not mistaken, there are five: water, fire, earth, moon, and sun.

Other notions complement or embellish the essential schema; it is difficult to judge their antiquity. The sky rests upon four pillars situated at the four cardinal points; the earth is surrounded by the oceanic river—an idea which may perhaps be glimpsed in the eighth century inscription of Ton Yuquq—or by a chain of mountains; it is held up by a turtle or by the horns of a bull whose movements provoke earthquakes. The theme of the turtle who bears the world may have been borrowed from China in the first century A.D. Certain peoples have conceived of several animals, one on top of the other, beneath the earth: taking up the theme of a mythic sexual combat, they transmit a powerful cosmogonic vision. In a popular Turkish song, the majestic eagle unfurls its wings on the top of a mountain to cover the earth. This notion may be ancient, since the eagle often symbolizes the sky god.

J.-P.R./d.w.

BIBLIOGRAPHY

There is very little about cosmogony. J. P. ROUX, "La naissance du monde chez les Turcs et les Mongols," in *La naissance du monde* (Paris 1959), 283–97. P. N. BORATAV, "Le mythe turc du premier homme," in *Proceedings, 23rd Int. Congress of Orientalists* (Cambridge and London 1954), 198–99. H. ÖRDEMIR, *Die altasmanischen Chroniken als Qvelle zur türkischen Volkskunde* (Freiburg 1975). See also the manuals of HARVA and RADLOV, *Proben* (Saint Petersburg 1866), 1.

Turkish and Mongolian Demons

Evil spirits are innumerable in the Turkish and Mongolian societies of central and northern Asia, but we know little of the ancient demonology. Chinese and Western texts often mention demons that we understand poorly. Several of the demons, decidedly vague, are surely the enemies of men, occupied with leading them astray on their journeys, playing tricks on them, and stealing their souls. The shamans, the protectors of human life, struggle against these. Other spirits, from all the evidence, assist the shamans, and the term "demon" is not appropriate for them.

"Demons," "devils," "satans," according to the various meanings that the medieval glossaries give to the work *yek,* cited five times by Kashgari, seem to appear rather late. The *yek,* whose name is derived from *yemek,* "to eat," is an eater of men, perhaps the cannibal of later literature. According to an Arab-Qiptchaq vocabulary, he has the aspect of a squall accompanied by a spindrift, but he can also be any unseasonable and dangerous manifestation.

Nearly every people has a special name to designate demons, and there are few differences between them. The Yakuts apply the word *yör* to the unsatisfied and anthropophagous dead who roam the earth. The Mongols see in the *chidkür* the soul of a dead person who brings misfortune to the living. The medieval *abaji, elkin,* or *yelkin* are phantoms, specters.

Venus, under the influence of Buddhism, becomes in the eastern zones of the Turco-Mongolian world equivalent to Yama, the king of demons.

Since Islam admits the existence of various supernatural beings, angels, jinn, these beings are encountered among Muslim Turks (*jinn, peri, makir, shaytan, ifrit, dev*). The *jinn* bring on illnesses and appear chiefly in accounts that have the support of magical beliefs and operations. Specialized healers have the power of summoning them in order to attempt to win them over. The *peri,* who manifest themselves in the form of birds, often pigeons, belong rather to marvelous stories. Some demons have more personality. Al-Basti, or Al-Karisi, or Al, "the Red Woman," "the Red Mother," is a female who attacks women in childbirth and gives them puerperal fever. She rides horses during the night and abandons them in a sweat in the morning. Her prototype from Central Asia, in the thirteenth century, was equally identified by the sweat that covered the horses at dawn. It is uncertain whether she should be identified with Albiz (or Albin), a demon attested among the Ottomans from the sixteenth century and known also in Central Asia and Siberia. The Hortlak, called also by the Persian name of *jadi,* is a ghost who feeds on the flesh of the dead and digs up corpses during the night. Kara Kondjolos is a malevolent being, certainly of Greek origin (Kallikantzaros), who rages in the winter, poses questions to passersby and kills, with a comb, those who do not answer. Charshamba Karisi, "the Woman of Wednesday," is a female demon thus named because she rages only one day a week. Kara-Kura resembles a she-goat the size of a cat and pounces on men at night to suffocate them. This may be why she is identified with nightmares.

J.-P.R./b.f.

BIBLIOGRAPHY

In addition to manuals such as that of Harva, see: U. JOHANSEN, "Die Alpfrau," *ZDMG* 109 (1959). E. BENVENISTE, "Le dieu Ohrmazd et le démon Albasti," *Journal asiatique* 248 (1960). A. INAN, *Samanizm.*

The Turkish and Mongolian Ancestor Cult

The ancestor cult can to a certain extent be confused with the cult of animals, since the preeminent ancestor is an animal. We will here consider the one to whom the animal gave birth as the true founder of the tribe or family.

In the most ancient times, the ancestor cult developed in the territory of the origin myth and was therefore bound to a precise geographical site. It was performed each year by the sovereign in person or, when he was absent, by an official delegation. According to the Chinese, the Tujue sacrificed to the ancestral progenitor on the seventh day of the seventh month. This sacrifice had an importance comparable to the sacrifice offered to the sky.

In the same societies, and more generally when the burial place was not kept secret, the cult developed around the tomb, eventually in a funerary temple (Tujue, Qarluq), or at least near an inscribed stela (which the ancient Turks called the "eternal stone") and near the statue of the dead person. In the tenth century Istakhri declared that the Khazar can never pass near the royal tomb without dismounting from horseback and praying. Later, Abu'l Ghazi ascribed the origin of idolatry to the ancestor cult. The habit arose, he said, of making images of the dead, and then people began to worship them. This simplification is not devoid of sense, and several ethnographers have believed that they could prove that shamanism derived from the veneration of ancestors. At least, there have been found in dwellings statuettes of the dead which were fed, watered, and revered, or tablets upon which their name was engraved.

One of the most interesting forms of the ancestor cult is the cult of the flag. The soul of the founder of the empire, first that of the animal, then that of the man, came to dwell in the flag. According to the meaning of the word *sülde,* used in Mongolian times in the expression *tug sülde,* which designates the flag containing the good fortune of Genghis Khan, it was a "traveling companion," which guarded and protected the empire. In recognition of this, sacrifices were made to it. The incarnation of Genghis Khan in the banner gave a particular brilliance to something which was already very old: the ceremony of the deployment of flags was solemnly carried out and had such significance that it was preserved for a long time, until the Mogul Empire in India. As for the banner of the Tujue, ornamented with the head of a wolf, it seems to have been the prototype of all those which were subsequently seen in the Turkish Muslim world, the Ottomans included, and which were ornamented with yak or horse tails, embroidered with astrological and zoomorphic images.

J.-P.R./d.f.

BIBLIOGRAPHY

HEISSIG and TUCCI, *La religion du Tibet et de la Mongolie* (Paris 1973). J.-P. ROUX, *Faune et flore sacrées dans les sociétés altaïques* (Paris 1966). ZELENINE, *Le culte* (Paris 1952).

The Importance of Animals in the Religion of the Turks and Mongols: Tribal Myths and Hunting Rituals

I. Human Life and Animal Life

Animals intervene constantly in the magical and religious life of the Turks and Mongols and therefore occupy a place of primary importance in their concerns. Even though the Tujue inscriptions do not seem to reflect this, all the other documents and informants are explicit enough to allow us to be sure of this. As we move forward in time and men choose more and more often the names of animals as patronyms (this trend reached a high point during the twelfth and thirteenth centuries), we see more clearly the close relationships that were established between human and animal life. This relationship went from one of comparison to one of fusion, by way of participation and mutation, stemming from a belief in the fundamental unity of life, which was manifested in various ways, but whose ultimate reality could be seen in the animal, and whose essential form was that of the animal. Although the animal was totally other, he was also totally similar, having, as men did, a social life and an organization into clans, with their leaders and saints. With few exceptions, he was not a god, despite what certain unenlightened informants seem to say, but he is superior to man in his gifts, because he has not lost to anthropomorphism his original form, which is that of the human soul (especially in the form of birds), as is proven by the existence of the soul, before incarnation, as a small bird on a celestial tree, by its transformation into a gyrfalcon after death, or by its flight toward heaven.

Because the animal is superior to man, man utilizes the animal's power by using his organs for divination (scapulimancy, haruspicy) and for magic (bezoars for bringing rain). Alliances were made with him, so that he would agree to give his wool, milk, and meat. These alliances corresponded to conflicts regarded as tribal wars and were to be resolved by hunting rituals. The animal was considered appropriate for sacrifice to the sky, to the gods, and to the ancestors. He was thought to be the best means of classifying tribes and time; hours, days, months, and years were all determined by the Calendar of the Twelve Animals, which came from China and arrived on the Volga in about 603, but was so completely adopted by the Turks that they developed their own etiological myth around it, whereby each animal in the series entailed in his own characteristics the characteristics of the year.

Because the animal resembled man, it was thought that conversations with him were possible, that his behavior could be imitated, that certain of his physical traits could be acquired, and that he could appear in human form just as man could appear in animal form—and this was always done by the wearing of skins, feathers, wings, and horns. Feathers decorating the heads of shamans, princes, and others led to the Islamic style of decorating with feathers that is so clearly indicated on miniatures. This remarkable proximity naturally permitted matrimonial relations, which were commemorated or renewed during ritual battles and which resulted in making animals, who often came from the sky (which was identified with light), into the founders of clans, the ancestors of shamans, and then, as a result, into protectors or guides.

All of the conditions were ripe, or almost ripe, for the animal to become a totem. But totemism requires a division into phratries, while Turco-Mongolian history is a continuous attempt to establish empires at the expense of the tribal order. These empires tended to suppress the totems of vassalized clans in order to exalt their own. This explains the preponderance of certain species of animals, even though all animals, without exception, were called upon to play a role.

II. The Principal Animals

We can indicate here only the main functions of the principal animals.

The wolf, ancestor of the Tujue and the Mongols, is the most important animal figure in ancient Turco-Mongolian mythology. His role as ancestor is less frequent in modern times, but he remains the guide and protector of the Oghuz, who often have a taboo about his name. In Turkey, the traces of this cult have almost completely disappeared.

The dog is often substituted for the wolf. The dog is also the sacrificial animal of the ancient Comans and Bulgars and of certain modern-day Siberians. Held in suspicion by Islam, he lost his position bit by bit, and his untimely barking, which in the past was generally considered lucky, began to be regarded as a bad omen.

A recollection of the tiger, certainly a divinity of the ancient Siberians and in the *Irq Bitig,* is retained in the name of the Turkish hero Alp Er Tonga and in the Calendar of the Twelve Animals. During the Qarakhanid and Seljukid eras, he was replaced by the lion, whose introduction as an ancestor in the tribal myths must have come through the Uighurs and the Oghuz. Islam, which declared Ali the Lion of God, reinforced his position among the Muslim Turks.

The bear is generally considered to be a man in disguise and is often viewed as a father. His cult, very important today in Siberia (among the Yakuts), must have been found among all the Turks at one time, as vestiges are found in Turkey. In Turkey, as in Central Asia, it is believed that the bear can have sexual relations with girls. A lunar animal, he is also sometimes considered to be the master of the forest.

The stag is not always identifiable, since his name also designates game in general; but in Turkey the stag is not hunted, because he is connected with the saints and the herd leaves blessings wherever it passes. Perhaps a symbol of the earth in the ancient mythology(?), the stag maintains a relationship with the sky, which gives him the same *qut* (viaticum for the journey of life) as men. His horns are powerful talismans, which are placed in front of homes.

The horse is man's inseparable companion in life as in death and the principal animal sacrificed to the sky. In the animal calendar, the month of the horse is that of the solstice, the period when the sun is at its zenith; in Turfan, the horse is often painted blue and he is made to run in a circle about a center point. It may be concluded from this that he symbolized the Sky or the Sun. In the *Qutadgu Bilig,* he is a symbol of time. In Central Asia, as in Turkey (in the *Kitab-i Dede Qorqut* and the oral legend of Urfa), there are traditions about a horse born of the water or of an aquatic animal. Certain graves of horses are considered sacred places.

A double tradition exists regarding the camel, which must, or must not, be eaten. In the *Irq Bitig,* the spume of the camel reaches the sky and penetrates the earth; the camel wakes those who sleep. In some myths, he seems to play the role of an ancestor: camel fights, organized from prehistoric times until the present, make this hypothesis more likely. In Turkey, the skull of the camel is a talisman (*nazarlik*) that wards off evil.

The Bulgars did not kill serpents, and Bashkirs included them among the "twelve gods" who were their twelve tribal ancestors. The serpent therefore occupies a position of considerable importance, but he is especially important because of his king, the dragon. The dragon was borrowed from the Chinese under the name of *luu* and was subsequently named *ežder* or *evren;* he became acclimatized over large parts of the steppes, but certain groups (Azeri, Turkmen, Uzbek) did not accept him, replacing him on the Calendar of the Twelve Animals with the crocodile or the fish. The name *evren* refers to his basic function, which was to turn on himself (see, in the iconography, the loops of his body) and in the universe. He spends the winter underground, and he emerges in the spring to rise up to the sky. In the Bektashi traditions, Hadji Bektash flushed him from his grotto to send him into the blue. He is therefore ambivalent. This explains why he is shown on Anatolian Seljukid monuments as supporting the tree of life or as an ornament on the cornerstones of arches. His open mouth juts out, with its menacing pointed teeth, suggesting that he is a swallower of men. Later, in Turkey, he would be pictured with seven fire-breathing heads. According to a sixteenth-century tradition, still found locally today, the dragon was born of a doe. He is the protector and patron of tanners. Often in combat against men, the dragon was crushed by Hizir, the image of spring, which evokes stories about Saint George.

The boar and the pig do not appear to have received much attention except in the areas bordering on China, where they may have been regarded as ancestors. The well-known Islamic taboo canceled any possibility for their prominence in the Western world that was in contact with Islam. The same taboo affected the hare in the heterodox regions of Turkey, where this creature is held in aversion. For the Mongols, however, the hare served as a guide and was worshiped. The Qarakhanids were converted to Islam by the hare, and the Yakuts carve his image in wood, in which they see the spirit of the forest.

Birds are certainly the most numinous animals. Birds of prey, carefully distinguished by the Oghuz according to species, age, and sex, serve as emblems (*ongon*) for their twenty-four tribes. Kashgari says that their name is often carried by men, and we have innumerable historic examples of this among the Muslim Turks. Muslim Turkish texts say that falcons are "the heroes of Khorasan," and this region seems to be the area where they were most highly prized. Further east, they certainly play a role in the tribal myths of the Uighurs.

The one-headed or two-headed eagle, the latter already found on the bronzes of Ordos and placed on the headdress of Ton Yuquq, is the king of birds. He flies near the sky god, from whom he returns to earth with messages; he perches on a rock, at the top of the cosmic tree; he shades the earth. In the epic of *Er Töshtük,* he carried the hero off on a cosmic voyage. The *Kitab-i Dede Qorqut* praises individuals who have the qualities of the eagle; Seljukid iconography uses the eagle as the emblem of the king.

The goose and the swan are fused in narratives where they appear as guides and protectors and are also used as images of young girls. This metaphor may come from the ancient legend of Swan Lake (Goose Lake) known by almost all contemporary Turkish and Mongol peoples and brought to Turkey in ancient times. A man passing near a lake sees a group of naked women bathing. He steals the clothes of one

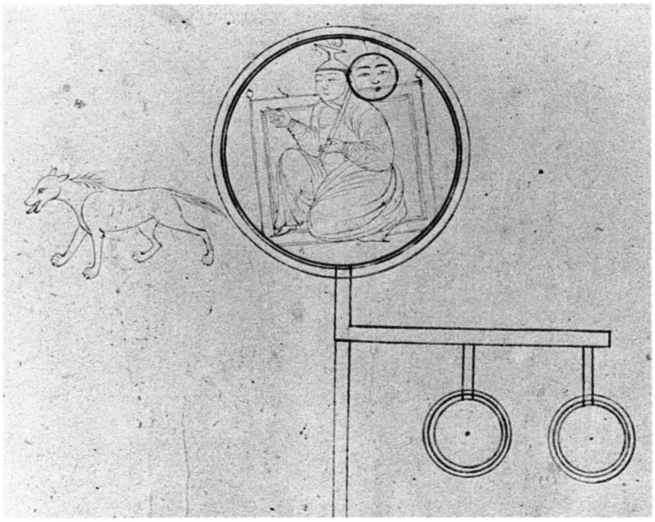

Alan Qo'a's blue wolf husband. Miniature from *Shu'b-i Panjgane.* Baysunghur album. Istanbul, Topkapi Museum. Museum photo.

of the women; the others take flight. The woman whose clothes he has taken becomes his wife and gives him children. She turns back into a swan when, through trickery, she is able to recover her clothing.

All the other birds merit our attention: the crane, worshiped by the Bashkir, the Turkish symbol of the young wife; the hen, paragon of chastity; the stork, the pilgrim father of Mecca. The rooster is notable because of the way he is represented among the heterodox peoples of Turkey: sacrificed at the tombs of saints, he is the archangel Gabriel or Selman al-Farsi, Companion of the Prophet, a friend of God, and "close to the throne" of Heaven. His morning song puts an end to the harmful activities of the jinn.

Composite or monstrous animals, such as the sphinx, the harpy, the winged lion, and the siren, are numerous and are popular subjects of Islamic art under Turkish influence. The unicorn evokes the great wild stag and destructive energy. Its horn, raised toward the sky, may serve as a symbol. Barak is a mythical dog that Kashgari says was born of a eagle and that Turkish Islam assimilated to Burak, the stallion of Muhammad's mystical ascension to heaven (*Miraj*).

III. Tribal Myths, Myths of Origin

It is likely that the primitive legend of the ancestral wolf developed in the Xiong Nu region, at an unknown date but undoubtedly very early. The legend seems to have been completely formed before the Christian era among the Wusuan of Isiq qul and Ili. The two narratives from which we know it show a female wolf nursing an abandoned child, while a crow flies above. In the fourth century A.D., the Goujiu (Dingling) take up the story, but in a slightly different form: a princess becomes the wife of a wolf. In the sixth century, the Tujue synthesized the two versions, conserving both the theme of adoption and that of the sexual union of a human with an animal: a child of a Hiong-nu tribe which was exterminated by its enemies is not put to death, but thrown into a marsh covered with grass. There he is raised by a she-wolf with whom he subsequently mates. The wolf retreats to a cave in the heart of the mountains to give birth to ten boys. From these children the Tujue descended. In memory of their origin, they decorate their standard with the head of a wolf and go each year to make sacrifices in the ancestral cave.

The breadth and duration of the Tujue empire assured the survival of this myth. It was taken up in the thirteenth century by the Mongols. According to *The Secret History,* "Gengis Khan was descended from the blue wolf (*Börte Tchino*), whose wife was the wild doe (*Qo'ai Maral*). He made his camp at the source of the river Onon, near the *Burqan Qaldun* mountain." At an undetermined date, the Kirghiz used this myth as well, but replaced the wolf with a dog who was the husband of forty young girls. There is also an echo of this myth in the Uighur legend of Oghuz Khan, where the wolf, without being specified as an ancestor, plays his role of protector and guide. A final resurgence of the myth appears in the epic of Manas (Kirghiz), during the nineteenth century, which portrays a couple made up of a wolf and an ibex, in the persons of Er Töshtük and his wife.

Other comparable myths are less frequently encountered and often come to us in an altered form. The Khitan are descended from a union between a horse and a cow who met at the junction of two rivers. The Qarakhanids may have a camel and a lion for ancestors; the Qalatch, a jackal and a woman. The Kirghiz, in addition to the dog ancestor, recognize a bull ancestor. The bull seems to have played a frequent role in the myths of origin. Oghuz Khan is himself a bull, although he may be described as having the body of a bull, a wolf, a sable, and a bear. The *Kitab-i Diyarbekriyya* (fifteenth century) reports that the ancestor of the Kara Koyunlu (eastern Turkey) was born of a woman, lost, recovered, and nursed by a cow. Themes connected with the ancestral lion are widespread in western Turkey, not without some contamination by Islam. The daughter of Qarakhanid Satuq Bughra Khan, Red Light (Ala Nur), meets a lion and faints: shortly thereafter she gives birth to a child. In the *Kitab-i Dede Qorqut* of Muslim Anatolia, Basat the child is lost, recovered, and raised by a lion; he becomes a lion and Dede Qorqut must give him a name to make him into a man. A version of this myth by Abu Bakr ben Abdallah tells that the ancestor of the Turks, the Tatars, and the Mongols is Alp Kara Arslan (Heroic Black Lion), who was born in the desert to a woman who had been raised by an eagle and carried into the mountains to the den of a lion who had him nursed by the lioness. In their most complete form (a union of two animals, of which one is often carnivorous, the other herbivorous), all of these couples resemble those depicted on the battle plaques found in the animal art of the steppe. We believe that these plaques were already illustrations of this myth.

The family of Genghis Khan, for whom we have already mentioned one myth of origin, glorified itself with a second myth, recorded in the same *Secret History.* One of the female ancestors of the emperor, Alan Qo'a, was visited every night in her tent by a shining yellow man. He came in through the smoke hole, rubbed his belly, and was engulfed by his own light; then he left, in the form of a yellow dog, by climbing the rays of the sun and the moon. From this hierophany were born three sons who were, said Alan Qo'a, "evidently the sons of Heaven."

The confusion between the animal and the ray of light is an attempt to harmonize two images completely different in appearance. According to many myths, light is responsible for the impregnation of women. We think we have found the earliest manifestation of this belief among the Tchao. Accord-

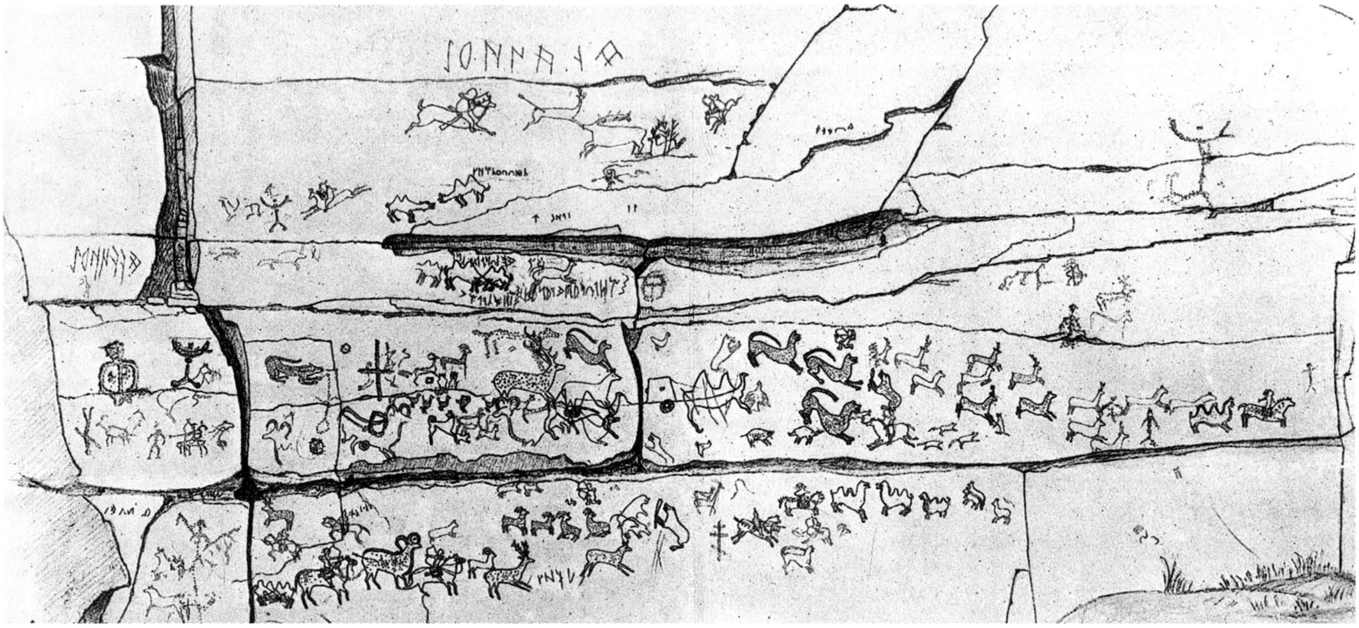

Hunting scenes. Stone from Kara Yüs. From Appelgren-Kivalo, *Alt-altaische Kunstdenkmäler* (Helsinki 1931). Paris, Bibliothèque nationale. Photo Flammarion.

ing to the Khitan, whom we have mentioned with reference to another myth, the great king A-pao-ki was conceived by the sunlight which fell into his mother's womb. Many characters from history and modern stories are named Rays of the Moon and Rays of the Sun. According to the Kalmuks, the daughter of the khan named Ray of the Sun spent the night near a tree with a minister named Moon. Elsewhere, the khan marries first a woman named Ray of the Sun and then one named Ray of the Moon. The moon impregnates women so often that the word *inal,* defined by Kashgari as "son of a prince and princess," is sometimes glossed as *Ay-nal,* Ray of the Moon.

The tree mentioned among the Kalmuks becomes a protagonist of the light in the Uighur myth of Buqu Khan. Between Tola and Selenga two trees grew. The ground rose up to form a mound on which the celestial light descended. From one day to the next, the mound increased in size, until one day it exploded and gave birth to five children. When the children were able to speak, they asked for their parents. They were shown the trees. They approached the trees and showed them the respect a child shows its parents. But the light only appears in the second part of the story. Buqu, the last of the five children, was visited by a celestial young girl, who came in through the opening in the top of his tent; he carried her off to the mountain to unite with her. The combined play of tree and light occurs again in the epic of Oghuz Khan, where one of the wives of the hero is described as a luminous girl born in a tree. In the *Book of Dede Qorqut,* the Cyclops Tepegöz is also born in a mound, but his father is the tree; according to another version, his parents are a bird-catcher woman and the son of a shepherd. In Turkish folklore, the character called Bey Börek, already known from the *Kitab-i Dede Qorqut,* marries the daughter of the white poplar.

The ingestion of various objects, generally described as coming from the sky, can cause pregnancy. Among the ancient Xianbi, a pellet of hail falls into a woman's mouth. In our day, a Siberian woman swallows an icicle cube. Quite often a solemn banquet or the chewing of an apple (Turkey) is enough to end sterility and cause the birth of a hero. In Altai and Siberia, ancestors and shamans are born from the intervention of all sorts of animals and objects. Yakut women became pregnant by eating a white worm; an old Gagauz woman, by eating lentils. One Karagasse clan is descended from a mole, another from a small fish. Among the Buryat, women united with bulls, swans, wolves, burbots, and boars. Among the Mongols, a girl who has been seduced is married to a prayer rug and her child is considered to have come from the sky.

The sexual union of the ancestors, whether both are animals, both are human, or one is human and one animal, is most often regarded as a fight between zoomorphic beings. The tribe resulting from the combat renews it in a ritual, generally at the beginning of the year. More remarkably, at the time of puberty, they organize a ritual fight against the animal, which gives the young man access to the women, allows him to make a name for himself, and makes the winner into a father almost immediately. Naturally, in Turkey and in other areas of the contemporary Muslim Turkish world, all idea of sexual and mythical union has been forgotten, but the manifestations which support it still survive. Folkloric dances make allusion to the union, and in the clans, until the beginning of the twentieth century and perhaps even today, young people are made to fight rams, bull calves, and colts.

The cult of the blue wolf is almost forgotten in Turkey, although in certain areas, sterile women call upon this beast in the hope of conceiving. On the other hand, the possibility of sexual union between bears and women is firmly believed in—a typically Siberian theme. A bear steals a young girl, marries her, and impregnates her. Her brothers come to save her, kill the animal and the children that he has given her, and take her back to their home. But the girl weeps for her lost husband.

IV. Hunting Rituals

Although innumerable hunting rituals exist today in Siberia and Central Asia, and traces remain in Turkey, Turkish and Mongol hunting rituals were little known before the eighteenth century. Yet they seem to appear on cave drawings and funeral stelae: is the game depicted there for purposes of sympathetic magic or to commemorate the hunt? In the *Irq Bitig,* we see for the first time the encirclement of the animals and the king's obligation to seize the animal with his own hand. This rite, so rich in meaning, evokes the privilege of the leader or father to hunt with dogs, the prohibition against bloodshed, and the theme of the first hunt.

The privilege of hunting with dogs arose out of the social hierarchy and the danger posed by the first kill; it was important that the one in charge be responsible for this activity. For this purpose, it was necessary for him to give the right to hunt in his name in the course of an initiation ceremony performed at puberty.

The prohibition against bloodshed, which was respected for domestic animals, was difficult to obey in the case of wild game. Efforts were made, however, to adhere to it whenever possible by hunting with falcons, putting buttons on the tips of arrows, and using traps, clubs, and stones.

The first hunt in a person's life or the first hunt of the year, since it was the most dangerous, was accompanied by many precautions, ceremonies, and rituals.

The hunter often wore the skin of the animal or imitated his cry. This was certainly a hunting trick; particularly necessary, not, as has often been written, in order to fool the animal, but in order to enter its society. In the same way, in Siberia, the fallen bear is introduced into tribal society disguised as a man: it is one of the important events of the great bear festival and an essential part of the religious life of the northern tribes. To fool the game, where that is deemed necessary, the hunter assures the animal that someone else was responsible for its death; this feature must be recent. Older perhaps is the practice of asking the animal's forgiveness for having killed it. But, in a general way, the kill is performed according to laws similar to the rules of war. The tribes do not hunt certain species that are their allies. Care is always taken not to exhaust a particular species. This involves closing the hunting season annually, as well as letting some animals escape from the closed circle of the hunting area. In contemporary societies, strict attention is paid to weapons which are only efficacious in certain conditions: the game must not be insulted, lest it refuse to allow itself to be killed; the name of the animal must not be spoken; women are generally considered dangerously impure for the hunter and his instruments. To allow the animal to come back to life, care is taken to not break any bones of his skeleton. That this is an ancient custom seems to us to be proven by Siberian and Turkish legends about the skeletons of stags that were reconstructed with ribs of wood to replace those that had been lost by accident. The ingenious hunter, killing a stag some time later, was surprised to find the rib he had made.

The custom of giving a piece of meat from the slaughtered animal to the next passerby (*pay vermek,* "to give a portion," in modern Turkish, *shirolga, sauga,* in the Middle Ages) appears widespread since ancient times.

J.-P.R./d.b.

BIBLIOGRAPHY

Rituals of the hunt are discussed in: BAWDEN, "Mongol Notes," 2: "Some 'Shamanistic' Hunting Rituals from Mongolia," *Central Asiatic Journal* 12, no. 2, 101–43. HOLMBERG, "Über die Jagdtritten der nördlichen Völker Asiens und Europas," *JSFO* 41, no. 1 (1925): 1–53. E. LOT-FALCK, *Les rites de chasse chez les peuples sibériens* (Paris 1953).

The ritual of dividing up the game is examined in: EBERHARD, "Remarks on Siralʏa," *Oriens* 1, no. 2 (1948): 220–21. PELLIOT, "Sirolʏa Širalʏa," *TP,* 1944, 102–13. J.-P. ROUX, *Faune et flore sacrées dans les sociétés altaïques* (Paris 1966), 87–118.

This article shows the importance of the animal world among the Turks and the Mongols. Miss von Gabain did this earlier in "Über die Bedeutung frühgeschichtlicher Tierdarstellungen," in *Mélanges F. Köprülü* (Istanbul 1953).

On animals one may read especially: P. N. BORATAV, *Les histoires d'ours en Anatolie* (Helsinki 1955). G. CLAUSON, "Turks and Wolves," *Studia Orientalia* 28 (1964): 1–22. R. DANKOFF, "Barak and Buraq," *Central Asiatic Journal* 15, no. 2 (1971): 102–17. DYRENKOVA, "Bear Worship among the Turkish Tribes of Siberia," *Proceedings of the 23d International Congress of Americanists,* 1928 (New York 1930). C. M. EDSMAN, *Bärenfest in den Religionen in Geschichte und Gegenwart* (3d ed., Tübingen 1957). STERNBERG, "Der Adlerkult bei den Völkern Sibiriens," *Archiv für Religionswissenschaft* 28 (1930): 125–53. Z. TEOMAN, "Bozkurt efsanenisin Anadoludaki Izleri," *TFA* 33 (1952). M. R. GAZIMIHAL has written many notes on animal worship in Turkey: see *TFA* 147 (1961); 14 (1959); 126 (1960); etc.

Altaic totemism is discussed in: CHODZIDLO, "Spuren des Totemismus bei den Jakuten?" *Ant.* 41–44 (1946–49): 359–65. HAECKEL, "Idolkult und Dualsystem bei den Ugrien," *Archiv für Völkerkunde* 1 (1946): 95–163. JUSSIPOW, "Totemistiche Relikte bei den Kazaren Tataren," in DIOSZEGI, *Glaubenswelt.* POTAPOFF, "Traces de conceptions totémiques chez les Altaïens," in "Exposition d'art iranien," by L. MORGENSTERN, *REV. ARTS ASIATIQUES* 10 (1936): 199–210. ROUX, *Faune et flore sacrées.* ZOLOTAREV, *Perezitki totemisma u Narodov Sibirri* (Leningrad 1934). And in a rather confusing way, according to the Calendar of Twelve Animals, in OSMAN TURAN, *Oniki hayvanli Türk Takvimi* (Istanbul 1961).

On sacrifice, one may read: GAHS, "Blutige und unblutige Opfer bei den altaischen Hirtenvölker," *Semaine Int. Eth. Religieuse* (Milan 1925, Paris 1926), 217–26. BOYLE, "A Form of Horse Sacrifice amongst the 13th and 14th Century Mongols," *CAJ* 10 (1965): 145–50.

On the goose (or swan) girl, see: EBERHARD, "The Girl That Became a Bird," *Semitic and Oriental Studies* (Berkeley 1951). HATTO, "The Swan Maiden," *BSOAS* 24, no. 2 (1961): 326–52.

THE TREE OF LIFE AND THE COSMIC AXIS AMONG THE TURKS AND MONGOLS

The Turks and Mongols developed many myths and beliefs about the Great Tree, the Solitary Tree, the Dry Tree, the Old or Withered Tree, and many shrubs of lesser importance, as well as groups of trees in groves or forests. Almost all of these myths and beliefs may be reduced to two basic concepts: the tree of life and the cosmic axis.

It is difficult to prove that the deification of the tree was the result of these representations. It does appear to have taken place quite often, if one is to believe the various sources reporting a cult or a religion dedicated to a tree, or the Turkish prayers to a tree, or Kashgari's statement, "The Turks give the name Tengri (god) to all that is great to the eye like a great tree."

Many ancient Uighur, Qipchaq, and Oghuz myths assign a role in the births of great men to a tree, which is their father or mother. Sometimes the kinship between tree and man is shown by the advice that a man passes on to his children. To this day, the Yakuts believe that the first man was nursed by a woman who appeared, naked to the waist, in the cosmic tree; this myth has existed in the Sogdian region since the beginning of recorded history and can be found in a slightly different form in the *Oghuz Name.* In Anatolia they still tell the story of a woodcutter who was about to chop down a tree when a girl appeared to him in the tree trunk. This notion must have given birth to the goddess of the tree, popular in Central Asia and Siberia during the nineteenth century. The Yakuts pray to this goddess, thanking her for watching over their flocks and protecting their wild game. Among the Kazak, sterile women roll on the ground at the foot of a lone apple tree in order to have children. The Turks of Turkey spend the night at the foot of a tree and dream that an old man visits them. The power of the tree to produce offspring and its influence on human life are evident in other instances. Among the Khitan, a ceremony was held periodically at the base of a forked tree: the emperor lay on the ground while an old man tapped on a quiver and cried, "A son is born!" Among the Mongols, as in contemporary Turkey, it is believed that the man who plants a tree will have a long life; in Turkey, a peasant who chops down a tree can have no more descendants. The tree has also played a role in resurrection and eternal life. The Yakuts, among others, buried their dead under a tree, while the Mongols planted a tree for the souls of the dead. More often, the body was put up among the branches of the tree for the flesh to decompose or be eaten by beasts of prey, but also in order to place the dead person in closer proximity to the sky and to allow him to become a part of the life cycle of the tree. For this same reason, they hung up the skins of sacrificed horses, impaled them on long poles, and made a rudimentary casket from a hollowed-out trunk. The Tujue in particular waited until the leaves fell or grew again before celebrating funeral rites.

The cosmic tree, briefly documented in ancient times, is very evident in our day. The Tatars of Altai say that "at the navel of the earth and the center of all things the largest of all earthly trees grows, a gigantic pine whose top branches touch the home of Bay Ülgen (the great God)." The Yakuts tell of an enormous tree at the center of the earth whose branches cross the sky and from whose roots an eternal wave gushes, spreading as a foaming yellow liquid. If a passerby stops to drink, his fatigue and hunger disappear. In the Er-Töshtük episode of the epic of Manas (nineteenth-century Kirghiz) a splendid tree inspired the belief that the vault of the heavens rested upon it. This cosmic tree, which functions like the cosmic mountain, is thought to make it possible for the two or three levels of the universe to communicate. Sometimes it holds up the sky, and it plays an important role in shamanism. Planted at the center of the yurt so that the trunk goes through the upper opening (Tatars of Altai; Buryat), often sprouting seven or nine branches (Tatars of Altai), it is used as a ladder by the magician during his celestial voyage.

Although the tree of life and the cosmic tree retain their symbolic value in Turkey, they are not necessarily of Central Asian origin in that country. However, during the first centuries of Islamization, trees were venerated and prayed to; people would say to a man, "May your large shade tree never be cut down." They invoked a "tree without top or bottom." In an ancient Oghuz version of a myth, a legendary sovereign saw three trees growing from his navel, giving shade in all quarters and reaching to the sky; this myth reappears among the Ottomans: a tree rises from the navel of Osman, the founder of the dynasty, and the shade from its branches covers the entire earth. Today it is not only in forested regions that stories of holy trees are told. Yoruk cattle breeders and many nonmigratory groups worship the birch, the pine, the myrtle, the cedar, plane trees, very old and very large trees, and small bushes called *koca,* an ancient term meaning "powerful." Such trees are called "holy" (*yatir, evliya*). People make pilgrimages to them, walk around them, build cairns at their feet, and make vows to them, often by tying or nailing on pieces of cloth to represent an illness to be cured. These trees are not cut down. Tahtaci woodcutters call them "masters" (*rabbi*). The founder of their craft, Hajib Nadjar, whom they may really invoke by this title, is the master of trees.

The forest of the Kara Koyunlu grew from the half-burned scepter of Karajaoglan, whose name is a euphemism for "bear." Surely this medieval legend reveals a belief, known elsewhere, in a bear who is the master/owner of the forest. This owner is more usually a saint who is supposed to protect the trees. A tree planted near a sanctuary is said to acquire its virtuous qualities. Jinn may also assemble around trees and bring them to life. The theme of dead wood that becomes green again, of Old Testament origin, entered the Alevi-Bektashi tradition in the fifteenth century and is still in evidence there. In the mystical theology of this same tradition, the gallows, *dar agatch,* is a reference to the torment of the famous Mansur Halladj. In religious worship, it refers to the center of the site where this torment was enacted. There are numerous sacred groves in Turkey. They recall those of Central Asia, for which the mountainous forest of Ötüken may be the prototype.

J.-P.R./d.b.

BIBLIOGRAPHY

J.-P. ROUX, *Faune et flore sacrées dans les sociétiés altaïques* (Paris 1966); *Les traditions des nomades de la Turquie meridionale* (Paris 1970). C. KUDRET, *Karagöz* (Ankara 1969). L. BARBAR, "Baumkult der Bulgaren," *Anthropos* 30 (1935). HOLMBERG, *Der Baum des Lebens* (Helsinki 1922–23).

The Mountain as Cosmic Axis among the Turks and Mongols

In the mythology of the Turks and Mongols, the mountain always played an important role. As a powerful symbol of verticality close to the sky god and sometimes holding him up, the mountain was situated at the center of the universe, where it served as a cosmic axis, the cradle of the race, its snowy woodlands inaccessible and mysterious.

Any mountain, any elevation of the terrain, however minor, could be charged with meaning, but certain summits designated by name received particular attention. Such was the case with the Red Mountain, the abode of the dead, among the Wuhuan. Among the Tujue, there was the *ötüken* (in the Khanghai), foremost among strategic spots, a sacred power (*iduq*) like earth and water, with which it was sometimes identified. There was also the mountain where the ancestral cave was found, perhaps the *Kögmen* that is cited among the divinities in the inscription of Ulan Bator, and a rather mysterious *P'o-teng-ning-li,* the Chinese transcription of *But Tengri.* Among the Khitan, the sacred mountain is the *Mu-ye,* where the founders of the race had gathered, and among the Mongols, it is the *Burqan-Qaldun,* on which Genghis Khan took refuge; since it had saved him, "He offered sacrifice to it every morning, and he invoked it every day." But there were still others, among the Chigil, the Qarluq, and probably among all the Turco-Mongolian peoples of the steppe.

The connections between the divinity of the mountain and the divinity of the earth are not very clear. The Turkish noun *ötüken* is derived from *öt,* "prayer, counsel, opinion," and seems to be the root of the words *Etüken/Itügen* (the *Itoga* and *Natigay* of Western travelers), which for the Mongols of the thirteenth century designated the earth goddess. Among the Uighur, *ötken* is the personification of the sacred homeland. As for the *P'o-teng-ning-li,* the Chinese see in it the god of the land of the Tujue.

In the course of their migration to Turkey, the Turks rebaptised a number of high places with names that they had used in Central Asia, and they established a cult there. At the same time, they regarded as holy certain summits that were sacred in native traditions: for example, Ararat, where Noah's ark landed; the Kaz Dagi (Mount of Geese); and the ancient Mount Ida, where Greek traditions about the judgment of Paris, Christian Mariolatry, and a Muslim mystical strain exalting a daughter of Fatima (herself the daughter of the Prophet), combined to form a shamanistic worship of woman. The Kaf Dagi, sometimes confused with the Kaz Dagi (which has, however, been identified with the Caucasus), was the dwelling place of the *divs* and the peris, or the wall surrounding the earth and perhaps supporting the sky. Numerous summits bear shrines dedicated to various saints, but these saints are often unknown and could be considered personifications of the mountain.

There is little doubt that the mountain kept much of its divine value during the first centuries of the Islamization of the Turks. In the *Kitab-i Dede Qorqut,* prayers were addressed to the Qazilik Tag, evoking the misfortune of its collapse and its aging. Up to our own day, especially in the Taurus mountains, natural sanctuaries are visited by pilgrims who pray or offer sacrifices there.

J.-P.R./g.h.

BIBLIOGRAPHY

See the bibliography of the article "The Earth among the Turks and Mongols." See also P. N. BORATAV, *Köroğlu destani* (Istanbul 1931). H. TANYU, *Ankara ve çevresin de adak ve adak yerleri* (Ankara 1967).

TURKISH AND MONGOLIAN SHAMANISM

In the narrow sense of the word, shamanism is a technique specific to the Altaic (Turks, Mongols, Tungus) and Siberian peoples. It involves a representation of the world as divided into levels connected by a central axis and the use of the trance as a means to accomplish the cosmic voyage, to heal the sick, and to foretell the future. Widely documented and studied in modern times, it long appeared doubtful in antiquity and the Middle Ages. There can no longer be any doubt that shamanism has existed from a very early period, if only for the reason that the Turkish name for the shaman, *qam,* is attested in the Tang Annals on the subject of the Kirghiz peoples; but it is not certain that it held as central a position then as it subsequently came to have. Old Turkic inscriptions are silent on the subject, and foreign sources say little more. The only documents at our disposal are archaeological, and they do not permit a complete analysis. In any case, it appears that up to the end of the first millennium, if not longer, the quest for magical powers, which is today its essential constituent, did not exist. We can thus only conjecture that among the Ruanruan the cosmic voyage was carried out by the rulers of the Tujue through the personal intervention of heaven. Travelers and historians often speak of magicians or sorcerers, but without giving any details. One may see in the werewolf of pre-Slavic Bulgaria a shamanic disguise; or one may see shamans in the "priests of demons" who, in the seventh century, "accomplished marvels in the air." The now well-known relationship between the blacksmith and the shaman no doubt influenced the future evolution of the Tujue: while we do not know all their history from the time when they were vassals of the Ruanruan, we know that they forged metals for them. Several characters in ancient texts perform actions that may be shamanic. The inscriptions of Hoytu Tamir depict two individuals who live at a dangerous crossroad in order to perform rites and sacrifices. The *Irq Bitig* speaks of a man dressed in a long garment and equipped with a bowl and a cup without which he could not travel far, of an old holy woman who comes back to life by licking the edge of a spoonful of grease, and of another man in a long robe who loses his mirror (a shamanic instrument). The *Oghuz Name* presents a heroic old scholar who is the prince's interpreter of dreams.

When the information is more detailed, it reveals first the divinatory arts. Theophylactus Simocattes writes, "The Turks have priests who foretell the future." Marwazi later recounts that an individual surrounded by singers and magicians (whom we see already in 576 at the court of Dilzibul when the Byzantine ambassador Zemark comes there) is summoned by the Kirghiz every year on a fixed date. He faints, goes into convulsions, and is asked to foretell the events that will take place in the year which has just begun. Kashgari, who mentions the *qam* four times, explains that he makes predictions, tells fortunes, casts spells, and pronounces a great number of incomprehensible words. Juvaini affirms that the Uighur shamans are possessed by demons who tell them all that they wish to know. Ibn Sina, to whom we owe the most remarkable ancient description of the shamanic ceremony, writes, "(in a Turkoman tribe) when they go to consult the diviner in order to receive a prophecy, he begins to run fast in every direction, panting, until he passes out. In this state, he tells what he sees in his imagination, and those who are present take down his words."

Other accounts, briefer but no less peremptory, speak of magical healing. The *Hudad al-'Alam* describes this in the following terms, "The Oghuz hold their doctors in high esteem and, whenever they see them, venerate them. These doctors guide their lives." Juvaini says literally that the shamans attend to the sick.

Bar Hebraeus affirms that Mongol shamanism has Uighur shamanism as its source. We may believe him in part,

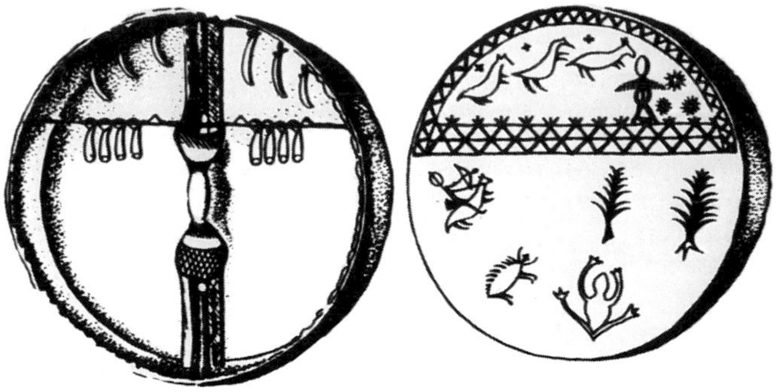

Shaman's drum. Paris, Musée de l'Homme collection. Museum photo.

because the Uighur greatly influenced the Mongols, but it would appear that their shamans were very powerful before the coming of Gengis Khan. This power would become so considerable as to force the conqueror to put to death his great shaman Teb Tenggeri (Kököchü). Male shamans (*böge, bö'e*) or female shamans (*udagan*) as shamanic pontiffs (*beki*) hold a prestigious position, playing a political role even to the point of becoming tribal leaders. Dressed in white, mounted upon white horses, covered with honors, these latter officiate as priests, preside over ceremonies of purification by fire, perform certain sacrifices, and distribute offerings to the gods. Of course, these priestly functions were monopolized by shamans of other periods as well, but it is rarer to find those who, like the Mongol shamans, infringe upon the provinces of other magicians. These practice scapulimancy, haruspicy, and possibly astrology; they are prestidigitators, they cause idols to speak, and they use the rain stone (*yada*), which renders them masters of the elements. Their principal field of action nevertheless remains shamanism. They foretell the future of newborn infants, decide which days are auspicious and which inauspicious. The magical healing that Juvaini, Rashid-ed-din, Wassaf, and Rubruck speak of is often effected by extracting from the body a piece of felt which moves like an animal, or by moistening the painful organ with magical water. The ascension into the sky is clearly attested only in the case of Teb Tenggeri, who, after his death, rises up above his tent, "once again clothed in his body." More often the spirits traffic with men by visiting them in their homes. Rubruck's description on this point is exemplary: "Cooked meat is placed at the center of the dwelling. The shaman begins to repeat his invocations. He strikes the ground violently with his drum. Finally he enters into a rage, and it becomes necessary to bind him. Then, in the darkness, the demon comes. The shaman gives him the meat to eat, and the demon responds to his questions."

Accounts of shamanic sessions become more numerous and detailed from the seventeenth century onward. They show, as would later ethnographers, that these sessions constitute a real journey which the shaman recounts step by step as he is undertaking it. He goes to search for the soul that has fled or been stolen by evil spirits, or else he drives out the spirits which have entered the body of the patient; he conducts the soul of the dead to heaven; he interrogates the Sky or the gods in order to know the future. On his path, he encounters noxious powers in the form of animals who attempt to hinder his passage, but he is helped by benevolent powers, also in the forms of animals. He is himself, with his stag or bird costume, a veritable animal. He is integrated into the world of animals and has become one of them, often by virtue of a preliminary initiation that sometimes involves ritual nudity. The dress and instruments of shamans are known to us through precise descriptions and from fragments conserved in museums. The most rudimentary of these have at least deer antlers, feathers, and wings; sometimes they have organs from other animals, such as bones, bear paws, and furs. Their essential utensils are horse-headed canes, mirrors, and especially drums decorated with designs representing the cosmos, with the two zones of the universe, the axis which joins them, and the different beings that inhabit them.

Since it is more preoccupied with daily life than with metaphysics, shamanism can easily resist the pressure of the religions which the people who practice it have come to embrace. Although destined to die out in Turkey, it would do so only after having exerted influence upon the Muslim mystic orders, on medieval literature, and on various aspects of popular life. In the Seljukid period and in the first centuries of the Ottomans, the "babas" who traveled the length and breadth of Turkey and ostensibly preached the doctrines of Islam were merely shamans in disguise. Wearing felt caps with horns on the sides, their necks adorned with bones, they carried a staff and small bells and played a drum. Barak Baba made a "terrible clamor" with this instrument.

In epics and romances, babas, heroes, and all of the saints fly up to the sky or descend through a well into the subterranean world to search for young men and women kidnapped by evil jinn or cannibals. Along the way, they fight innumerable battles with the inhabitants of upper and lower cosmic zones, helped or hindered by animals; and they meet the prophets of Islam who inhabit the heavens, who reveal to them the language spoken by the spirits, or who give them talismans against demons.

J.-P.R./d.w.

BIBLIOGRAPHY

The bibliography on shamanism in general is considerable. Almost all the works at least allude to the shamanism of Central Asia and Siberia. There are numerous bibliographic citations in the remarkable study by M. ELIADE, *Shamanism: Archaic Techniques of Ecstasy* (Princeton 1964).

See also D. BANZAROV, *Černaya vera ili šamanstva u mongolov* (Kazan 1846). N. K. CHADWICK, "Shamanism among the Tatars of Central Asia," *JRAI* 66 (1936): 75–112. V. M. MIKHAILOVSKY, "Shamanism in Siberia and European Russia," *JRAI* 24 (1894): 62–100, 126–58. G. NIORADZE, *Der Schamanismus bei den sibirischen Völkern* (Stuttgart 1925). A. OHLMARKS, *Studien zum Problem des Schamanismus* (Lund and Copenhagen 1939). A. PARTANEN, "A Description of Buriat Shamanism," *JSFO* 51 (1961). G. N. POTANIN, *Otcherki severo-zapadnij Mongolli,* 4 (Saint Petersburg 1883). J. P. ROUX, "Le chamanisme, expérience spirituelle de la vie animale," *Synthèses* 265–66 (1968): 41–46. G. SANDSCHEJEW, "Weltanschauung und Schamanismus der Alaren-Burjaten," *Ant.* 22 (1927). W. SIEROSZEWSKI, "Du chamanisme d'après les croyances des Yakoutes," *RHR* 44 (1902): 204–33, 299–338. *Studies in Shamanism,* C. M. Edsman, ed. (Stockholm 1967). *Studies in Siberian Shamanism,* M. N. Michael, ed. (Toronto 1963).

Independently of each other, Boyle and Roux have attempted to extract information about shamanism from the historical data: BOYLE, "Turkish and Mongol Shamanism in the Middle Ages," *Folklore* 83 (1972): 177–93. J. P. ROUX, "Le nom du chaman dans les textes turco-mongols," *Ant.* 53 (1958): 133–42; "Éléments chamaniques dans les textes pré-mongols," *Ant.*, 441–56; "Le chaman gengiskhanide," *Ant.* 54 (1959): 401–32; "Le chaman altaïque d'après les voyageurs européens des XVIIe et XVIIIe siècles," *Ant.* 56 (1961): 438–58.

The Sky God and the Stars among the Turks and Mongols

I. The Sky God (Tengri)

In the Chinese transcription *zhenli, tengri* represents the oldest Turco-Mongolian word that we know. Originally, it designated, on the one hand, the sky in its materiality ("the sun is in the sky"), and, on the other hand, the pan-Altaic sky god and the secondary divinities, *tengri* of time (*öd tengri*), *tengri* of the path (*yol tengri*), etc. In these latter senses, the word was used even to our time in shamanistic Central Asia and Siberia. After it came to designate the various gods of the universal religions, it became an equivalent for Allah among the Muslim Turks. The sky was later to be named after one of the adjectives applied to the sky god: *gök,* "blue."

The sky god is quite prominent in Old Turkic inscriptions and in *The Secret History of the Mongols*. He is called "high" (*üze*), which answers to cosmographic and institutional visions and at the same time emphasizes an opposition with the earth which is "below"; "blue" (Turkish *kök/gök,* Mongolian *köke*); and "strong" (*kütch*). His strength is manifested in the pressure that he exerts and even more in the delegation of his strength to the prince, jointly with the earth. Genghis Khan received his strength from the two zones of the cosmos. In the Mongolian period, the sky god's benevolent mandate was associated with this delegation. At the same time, people adopted the habit, which was not to disappear, of calling him "eternal" (*möngke,* in Mongolian).

Tengri was from the very start a national and imperial god; his people lived under him, at the center of the universe, and called him emperor (khan) or, rarely and later, father. He waged war at his will and obtained victory for his people. They were protected by him at all times; thanks to him, they avoided annihilation in times of grave danger. When the empire was extended, Tengri became the god of all the subjects of the conqueror, the god of all men: the proof of this is particularly evident under the domination of Genghis Khan.

The sovereign and high dignitaries held their power from him, were descended from him, and resembled him. They acted in his name. If they were no longer in harmony with him, there was disorder. They received his orders (*yarlik*) and echoed them. They might enter into communication with him by breaching the sky, through a voyage that the god instigated by seizing them by the top of the head, or by receiving his messengers. The common people were therefore concerned with him only indirectly and were more interested in the inferior powers. Nevertheless they received from him the viaticum of life (*qut*), sometimes represented as a gelatinous material, good fortune or chance (*ülüg*). The life and death of everyone depended on him. He chastised harshly, by killing, sometimes with lightning, and did not like those who had evil thoughts.

His creative power was not revealed until the tenth century. However, from this period, and even while Kashgari was to say, for instance, that Tengri causes plants to grow, the creator already bore another name, Balig Bayat, the Supreme Rich One or the Supreme Old One. Nothing enables us to say whether this figure was at that time distinct from Tengri, as he was to be much later.

The worship that was rendered him was not very extensive and must have chiefly concerned those in power. Among the Tujue, in the course of the enthronement ceremony for the sovereign, the latter was lifted on a carpet of felt to be presented to the Sky. The Khitan informed the Sky of the accession of a new emperor by lighting a fire. Like men, animals directed brief prayers to him. A Mongol of the thirteenth century, before leaving on a campaign, isolated himself, sought an elevated spot, dismounted, fell prostrate, and took off his cap and his sash. He prayed for twenty-four hours or three days. The same Mongols exempted from tax the pious who agreed to pray to the Sky for the longevity of the emperor. Periodically, the Sky received sacrifice; sometimes this was performed each day, sometimes each year, sometimes on fixed dates—the first, fifth, or ninth of the month—and sometimes when an important event required it. The Tujue assembled to sacrifice to the Sky in the middle ten days of the third month, on an elevation, on the bank of the Tamir or at its source. Among the T'o-pa, the sacrifice was accompanied by the circumambulation of a hillock, which was called "to go around the sky." The preferred victim was a horse; it was impaled on a slanted pole; its hide was suspended from a tree. But other animals were also immolated: oxen, dogs, sheep.

The messengers, the emanations of the Sky, are of very ancient origin. Sometimes people speak of the eagle who flies at the side of god, sometimes of enigmatic angels, or of rays of light, of dazzling maidens, of blue animals that come from him. They are today more and more numerous as Tengri recedes into inaccessible zones and tends to become otiose. Even among the Mongolian groups that always speak of *Köke Möngke Tengri,* "the Blue Eternal Sky," the celestial gods are more important than he is. He is no longer always the supreme god: he continues, however, to establish his home in the sky. His names vary with his personality. Among the Yakuts, he is called, among other names, "the White Master Creator"; among the Tatars of the Altai, "the Great One" (Ülgen) or "the Great Rich One" (Bay Ülgen). Where he exists, the other celestial gods are his daughters, his sons, or his assistants, who are also called *tengri.* There are seven or nine of them, or they may be far more numerous; there may be thirty-three or even thirty times thirty-three, whom the Buryat and others divide into the good and the evil. Elsewhere they are specialized: gods of wind, lightning, the door, vapor, anger, the four quarters, etc.

In Muslim countries, Tengri has been assimilated to Allah and has only gradually lost his primary characteristics. For a long time the Turks insisted on his lofty position, on the beauty of god, on the pressure that he exerts. They reclaimed images known from shamanism, the royal eagle who flies by the side of God, the tears that fall down from the sky to earth, the reflection of the face of God in the mirror of the lake. When Allah shows the path (*yol*) he recalls the *yol tengri,* the "god of the path" of the ancient mythology.

II. The Stars

The astrological notions of the ancient Turks seem negligible, and it is not before the beginning of the second millennium A.D. that these notions developed under Greek influence, as the vocabulary of the *Qutadgu Bilig* proves. Nevertheless, from the earliest times, the seven and nine planets (by considering Venus and Mars vesperal and matinal) and the apparent movement of the sky were at the foundation of many representations and rites. It was important that life be organized like the cosmos and unfold according to its rhythm. That is why great importance was accorded to the numbers seven and nine and to their derivatives, chosen whenever possible for funerals, the numbers of tribes, etc., or arbitrarily conceived, before the twelve months of the year placed the number twelve in competition with them. That is why multiple circumambulations around a center were performed, a repetition of the movement of the stars around the polestar, which was later regarded as the stake of the heavens to which horses are attached, or even as its navel, connected by the cosmic axis to the navel of the earth. And that is why, from the period of the Xiungnu, people waited until the moon was full to begin expeditions, and they oriented themselves in the direction of the rising sun.

The only stars that played a recognized role in the eighth century were "the Good Pleiades," *Ülker,* who were used to divide the year and occasioned the fine season, whereas Argal heralded the bad season. This was probably the source of the myths of the impregnation of the wild she-goat by the constellation, myths still known in Turkey. Another important star was Venus, *Erklik,* who was a powerful warrior destined to become a god.

From the eleventh century, a greater number of stars were included in the mythology, while animals began to populate the sky. Venus ceased to be a warrior and became a star of light, then *Cholban,* the Brilliant One, a word which was to be confounded with *Choban,* the Shepherd, of Iranian origin. The Great Bear was represented as an assembly of seven khans. Jupiter or Libra constituted the Heroes in Harmony; Sirius was the White Stallion; the Milky Way was the Path of the Bird, probably with reference to the path that souls follow going to the Sky. The Kirghiz believed that Mars bore evil influences. Certain stars were "worshiped" or "venerated," Sirius in particular (informants say that the Turks called it the Lord of Lords), Gemini, Saturn, and, naturally, the moon and the sun.

These two luminaries became the emblems of the king in the monarchies as they were becoming Islamicized, and it was perhaps as such that they often figured prominently on the cornerstones of the arches in the Seljukid monuments of Turkey. Their cult and the images to which they laid claim were, however, very ancient. The Turks and Mongols never ceased to respond to the symbol of the moon, which is born, grows, dies, and comes to life again, and to the symbol of the sun, which sets and rises. The gender of these luminaries was unstable. The creative power of the sun caused the Turks and Mongols to regard it as a female being, and the moon, in consequence, was most often male. Even today in Turkey the moon is called *Ay Dede,* "Grandfather Moon." But in the Mongolian period, the moon was said to be engendered by the sun because the moon receives its light from the sun. In return, the figures who were called Rays of the Moon were innumerable, evoking all those who are born miraculously from the power of its light. The name of the bear, *ayi,* has an entirely different etymology but had been brought into connection with the name of the moon, *ay,* because the bear had the reputation of impregnating women, and because it hibernates.

The worship rendered to the moon, well attested, was less frequent than the worship rendered to the sun. Among the Khitan, it was specified that one worships the sun but not the moon. To the star of the day, offerings were made, prayers were said when it rose, when it set, and at its fullness. Genghis Khan ascended the *Burqan Qaldun,* prayed, and prostrated himself nine times in the direction of the sun.

In the modern Altaic world, the cult of the stars has lost nothing of its relevance. The Yakuts say that the stars that move are living beings, that the planets are windows of the sky. Among the constellations venerated by the Mongols, the Great Bear, *Dolugen Ebügen,* receives sacrifices. A myth of the hunt is connected with Orion. A Turkish name of the Pleiades, misunderstood, has made them celestial apes.

J.-P.R./b.f.

Genghis Khan praying to the sun on the Kipchak steppe. Iran, Imperial Library of Tehran. Photo Forman Archive, London.

BIBLIOGRAPHY

Despite his importance, the sky god has been little studied: J. P. ROUX, "Tängri, essai sur le Ciel-Dieu des peuples altaïques," *RHR* 149:49–82, 197–230; 150:27–54, with additional notes; *RHR* 154:32–66. P. PELLIOT, "Tangrim-Tarim," *TP,* 1944, 165–85. P. W. SCHMIDT, *Der Ursprung der Gottesidee,* vol. 9 (Freiburg 1949).

Qut is included in: L. BAZIN, "Le nom propre d'homme Qorqut," *UAJ* 36:278–383. BOMBACI, "Qut-luγ. bolsun!" *UAJ* 36, nos. 3–4: 384–91. KOTWICZ, "Formules initiales des documents mongols," *RO* 10:131–37. SCHAEDER, "Über einige mitteliranische und osttürkische Abteilungen," *ZDMG* 7 (1928): 114–16.

On the stars: L. BAZIN, "Les noms turcs et mongols de la constellation des 'Pléiades,'" *AOAH* 10, no. 3 (1960): 295–97; "Über die Sternkunde in alttürkischer Zeit," *Akad. d. Wissenschaft und Literatur* 5 (1963): 571–82.

Water among the Turks and Mongols

Water is one of the four or five elements which make up the universe. Antagonistic to the fire which it extinguishes (and it is forbidden to pour any on the hearth), it is also the complement of fire, since fire comes from wood, which in turn grows with water. Water's role in fertility is well known, and it appears in certain myths of creation (a ditch in human form which fills up with water, hailstones), in certain funeral rites (funerals held under a river, near a spring). It also acquires a specific value as a special drink, comparable to milk; in the mystic Alevi-Bektashi sect of Turkey, the Water of Life (*Ab-I Hayat*) must be drunk by those who seek knowledge. But it was as a symbol of purity that water struck the Turks and Mongols most of all. In most political communities of Central Asia (pre-Slavic Bulgarians, Oghuz, eighteenth-century Mogols, modern-day Siberians and Altaians) and in certain heterodox religious communities in Turkey, it is forbidden to soil water with waste, whether by bathing or by washing laundry or household utensils. Bathing or ritual washing may therefore take on a significant meaning, which brings us back to the theme of fertility. The immersion of Turkish women who wish to become pregnant may stem from local traditions (the persistence of this rite in places visited by the Greeks in earlier times) just as easily as from those of Central Asia.

Water evidently had its "master/possessors," but this does not mean that there was a water god, although certain medieval informants speak of its worship. The accumulation of water (*Köl Irkin*, in Turkish) is for Kashgari a symbol of the great intelligence that princes were supposed to have. Its "master/possessors" are referred to as "Lords," just as are the masters of the earth in *The Secret History of the Mongols*. Earlier, among the Tujue, "the sacred lands and waters" may have been the group of the master/possessors of the sacred territory, these territories themselves or only certain ones among them. They had exceptional power.

We know of a certain number of aquatic regions, lakes, rivers, and springs that had their own cults. Among the Tujue, the spring of the Tamir (and perhaps others) was worshiped. According to Chinese sources, in the second ten days of the fifth month, people gathered on the banks of the river to sacrifice to the sky god. Among the Mongols, worship was marked by invocations to the Selenga, Onon, Kerulen, and Ili rivers. For the Yakuts, each river had its own master; the Karagasses brought him offerings so that he would give them fish. This master is sometimes imagined as a bull living in the water. The Tatars of Altai say that the prince (khan) of the Abakan River is the dispenser of rain.

J.-P.R./d.b.

BIBLIOGRAPHY

P. N. BORATAV, *Halk hikâyeleri ve halk hikâyeciliğ* (Ankara 1946); *Türk folkloru* (Istanbul 1973. See also INAN, HARVA, ROUX.

Turkish and Mongolian Eschatology: The End of the World and the Fate of Man after Death

The Turks and Mongols tell us little about the end of the world. Allusions found in the Tujue texts lead one to believe that the sky could collapse and the earth fall into ruin. But the destiny of the universe and the human race did not preoccupy them any more than did their genesis. In Turkey, Islam imposed its vision of the end, on which certain themes were grafted whose origins are unknown to us: the end of the world will be announced by such unusual events as a pact between the wolf and the lamb, the sterility of women, the shrinking of roads, and the multiplication of constructed surfaces. In the contemporary traditions of Central Asia and Siberia, Christian and Buddhist influences are perceptible and are no doubt responsible for eschatologies (the universal flood and Noah's ark).

On the other hand, the fate of man after death received great attention. Death does not put an end to life, even if rarely used expressions such as "he became nothing" in the sense of "he died" may incline one to think otherwise. The place most often indicated as the residence after death is the sky, probably because all great men, since they came from the sky, return to it, and our information is essentially connected with such men. One reaches the sky by flying up to it, perhaps by taking on the appearance of a bird. Subsequently, people spoke of a fly that leaves the body (Er Toshtük) or of a pigeon (Abu Muslim), and people made use of the formula "he became a gyrfalcon." This idea enjoyed great success for a long time among Muslim Turks. The word for flight (*utch-*) combined with the verbal suffix *maq* forms *utchmaq* ("take flight"), which was confused with the Soghdian *utchmaq*, "paradise." Thus, from the eleventh century onward, this word served to designate that particular region of the other world, which had previously been unknown. This is prefigured in the special area that was the region in which the ancestors lived and to which, according to certain pre-Tujue peoples, the dead are supposed to return: the Red Mountain of the Wu-huan, the home of the dead, might have taken the place of the Sky.

Life in the sky is similar to life on earth, which is why it is necessary to take there the greatest possible number of worldly goods, servants, and women. Hell (*tamu/tamuk*) was introduced recently under the influence of a foreign religion, and could not have been an ancient home of the dead. The notion of retribution is unknown, offenses being punished on earth. Hell and retribution have nevertheless entered greatly into more recent representations.

There is reason to think that the ruler reaches the sky by his own means, and almost ineluctably. By contrast, from an early period the aid of a shaman must have been necessary for ordinary mortals, whose fate is less certain. The failure to complete rites, the abduction of the dead person by an evil spirit, or his capture by a victorious enemy may have an influence on his eternity. The shedding of blood, which contains a soul, prohibited for members of the royal family and for sacrificial animals, and the required treatment of bones indicate that even the powerful are not entirely assured of reaching the sky without injury. It was a widely practiced custom—even in Muslim lands up to the seventeenth century—to exhume enemies in order to burn their bones. This act destroyed all of the bonds that they still maintained with the earth, and in particular the power that they maintained there. It is thus evident that the dead could also partially live in the lower world. In fact, the gift of ubiquity is general and is explained by the multiplicity of souls that every individual has. Each of these would be summoned to survive in a different place: in the tomb; in the *balbal*, a formless stone or a wooden pole set up by the slayer in order to fix his victim there; in "cushions" that take the place of the *balbal* in Mongol times when the *balbal* had disappeared; in funerary statues (which researchers have often confused with *balbal*); in idols of household gods; and in banners. Still others were able to return to their houses or wander through space in the form of unsatisfied demons. Resurrection or reincarnation are ill-defined, but seem to have been at least sporadically accepted for humans (even in Turkey, as among the Tahtaci), as they were for animals. In modern times, the abode of the dead and the visions it inspires have become further diversified. The Yakuts seem to survive in a hell "below," which may mean "to the north." Others believe that everything is reversed in the other world.

As we often see, death is a punishment, and whatever one's destiny is, the fate of the deceased is not enviable. Death is an inescapable necessity that is personified and encountered ("He found the necessity" *kergek*) when one's viaticum of life (*qut*) and one's favorable fate (*ülüg*) are exhausted and have not been "renewed" by God. In Islamic societies in Turkey, the red-winged Azrail, the angel of death, the actualization of Necessity, comes in search of the *qut*, which has become a soul. In order not to abandon it to him, the Turks of Turkey, probably like their Central Asian predecessors, enter into battle with Azrail or bargain with God or, like the Mongols, find a volunteer to die in their place (as in the episodes of the death of Tului and the death of Babur Shah in the *Kitab-i Dede Qorqut*). People seek to delay this grim deadline by every means possible. Genghis Khan goes in search of a medicine of immortality and has priests of every confession pray for his longevity.

J.-P.R./d.w.

BIBLIOGRAPHY

P. N. BORATAV, *Türk folkloru* (Istanbul 1973); "Notes sur Azraïl dans le folklore turc," *Oriens* 4 (1951). See also HARVA, RAVLOV, and IMAN, and the bibliography of the article "Turkish and Mongolian Funerary Customs."

Turkish and Mongolian Master Spirits (Ejen and Izik)

The master/possessors, also named master spirits, are known primarily through ethnography, which designates them with the Mongolo-Tungus word *ejen* or the Turkish *izik*, derived from the ancient *idhi*, which is connected with *iduq*. Today the master spirits are innumerable, since every object and every being is animated by a spirit or belongs to an invisible power.

Kashgari clearly explains what is meant by *iduq*: "Anything that is blessed/sacred. This name is given to every animal that is set free. One may not burden it with a load, or milk it, or shear its wool. It is protected by a vow made by its owner." The *Irq Bitig* offers an interesting detail when it says that the *iduq* is a white animal, which will be generally confirmed by what follows. We are quite familiar with animals "set apart, in Mongol times and after." At the same time, it is not certain that the *iduq* was originally an animal. Old Turkic inscriptions designate by this word "the earth and water," "the forest or mountain of Ötüken," "the spring" or "the springs" (of the Tamir): in other words, a series of sacred territories. These territories are sacred because they are "left free"; that is, because no transaction may be undertaken there, because an absolute respect surrounds all that is found there, including the animals that live there and the plants that grow there. We do not know whether the contagion of the numinous moves from living beings into the ground or from the ground into living beings. Documents of the Mongol period, in speaking of the "lords of the earth and of the waters," place the master spirits in higher relief, but do not resolve the problem. Rites of consecration of immaculate animals, isolated from the herd, are widely practiced at this time.

The religious manifestation of the *iduq* in the Tujue and Mongol periods is never that of an animal or a plant, but that of a place, and this undoubtedly means the master/possessor of a place. This takes place most often in conjunction with the Sky, or the Sky, Earth, and *Umay*, when the whole tribe, and not merely the leaders, are concerned. Yet we find that the Chinese masters of the earth and of the waters demonstrated violently against a prince of the family of Genghis Khan when the Mongols brought war to China.

One might envisage the master spirits as taking up residence in cairns (*obo*) set up in determined places, often on hilltops and crossroads, but it is more likely that these are particular master spirits, those of rocks—indeed, an entirely different manifestation of power.

In modern times, the *ejen* and the *izik* are not distinct animals or plants or a group of holy places but, as we have said, the animators of every object. Their importance is thus a function of the interest that a given tribe may take in a given object. They are the source of the innumerable precautions that must be taken with the tools one uses and of nearly every prohibition. It is no exaggeration to claim that they underlie all deities, mountains, springs, fire, etc. In Turkey, they could be quite easily assimilated to the jinn and, to a certain extent, to the saints whose real or imagined tombs lend *baraka* to neighboring objects.

J.-P.R./d.w.

BIBLIOGRAPHY

Idols (*ongon*) are the subject of the interesting but debatable work of ZELENINE, *Le culte des idoles en Sibérie* (Paris 1952), translated from Russian. See also: A. INAN, "Ongon ve tös kelimeleri hakkinda," *Türk tarih, arkeologya ve etnografya Dergisi*, 2 (1934): 277–85. Some describe the Master Spirits. On these, see E. LOT-FALCK, "La notion de propriété et les esprits-maîtres en Sibérie," *RHR*, 1953, 172–97. For the survivals in Turkey, see M. NICOLAS, "Les pèlerinages," in *Traditions religieuses et parareligieuses* . . . J. P. ROUX, *Traditions des nomades* . . .

The Cult of Fire Among the Turks and Mongols

So unclear is the place that fire occupied for the Turks of the seventh and eighth centuries that it was possible to doubt the existence of a cult of fire there in spite of the testimony by Theophylactus Simocattes, who said, "The Turks honor fire in an extraordinary manner." It is unlikely that no such cult existed. The fire cult is pan-Altaic and becomes clearer and clearer as more documents appear. Today, in the shamanistic milieus of Central Asia and Siberia, it is one of the principal divinities. Fire was nevertheless originally not a god but a power that played an important role.

Regarded as one of the four or five elements of the universe, fire had no known origin in the early period. The Mongols still hold it to be one of the oldest manifestations of life. It is also said to have come down from the sky, sometimes in the form of lightning, as a dangerous and inauspicious, yet sometimes beneficial, manifestation of power. Some individuals have the reputation of having discovered or tamed it. These civilizing heroes are theriomorphic among the Buryat, Teleuts, and Yakuts.

The ascensional power of fire is attested from 907 among the Khitan, who burn wood to announce to the sky the coming of a prince. Today it is exalted in hymns: "O fire! May your brilliance spread and rise up to the ninety-nine *tengri!*" The smoke goes up the axis mundi formed by the hearth, which is placed at the center of the yurt, and the upper opening of the tent; it is itself an axis mundi. As a destructive element, fire conveys with it all that it has consumed, particularly offerings, bodies, and especially the bones of the dead whose presence on earth is to be obliterated.

Fire purifies. Menander already relates how the Turks made the Byzantine ambassador Zemarchus go around a bed of coals. In the Mongol period, European travelers related that they had to pass between two fires before they could enter the camp, and that it was customary to offer tribute and gifts at such places. These travelers and other sources show that this same rite was used for mourners and for objects that the dead left behind, as well as for thieves and violators of minor taboos. Much later, other applications were found in Central Asia, Siberia, and Turkey. Among the Mongols, it is the young daughter-in-law who is purified by fire; in Turkey, people try to heal the sick by having them leap over the fireplace or pass between two fires. In Turkey, as in Siberia, rooms are fumigated with burning juniper branches to drive away spirits.

Fire is used for divination, sometimes when the colors of the flames are examined and sometimes when it roasts the scapulae of sheep. It forges weapons, giving a particular status to the smith, who is also a manipulator of iron—a luminous substance.

These principal functions—its trance, its hesitant departure, its exaltation and extension, and its powers to keep animals and spirits at a distance—give fire a very marked shamanic aspect and make it the alter ego of the shaman. Like the shaman, the Muslim Turkish saint is a master of fire and is able to walk on live coals or pick up embers in his hands.

The law code of Genghis Khan (the *yasaq*) determined the proper behavior to be observed toward fire. It is forbidden to place a knife in it, to touch it with metal—so as not to injure it or cut off its head—or to spill water on the hearth. These prohibitions are prior to the *yasaq* and are found in exactly the same form in Muslim Turkey. They prove the respect that people have for fire. The majority of medieval observers speak of the adoration or veneration of fire, describing the customs of the Ephthalites, Oghuz, Uigurs, Kimek, Pechenegs, pre-Slavic Bulgars, Khazars, etc. Some of these peoples may have practiced Zoroastrianism, but our information is too general to allow us to assign all of these phenomena to that religion. Elsewhere, certain findings are more specific: in some places people speak of a god of fire (*ot tengri*); among the Khitan, this god is especially venerated in the winter.

As a symbol of the home and guarantor of the perpetuity of the family (the term used in Central Asia for "destroy one's offspring" is "extinguish one's fire"), fire is apparently of the male gender and has had, since an early time, a high priest in the person of the youngest son, the *ejen* or *ottchigin* ("Prince of the Fire"). This son never leaves the paternal home and inherits the authority and all the possessions of the family. However, at present and even though the *ottchigin* has not disappeared either in Siberia or in the heterodox Turkish tribes, in several regions fire is a female divinity with a female priestess. It may thus be called "Mother Fire" or "Grandmother." Since 1594, we have records of young wives worshiping it. For Mongolia, it has been possible to establish a line of demarcation between north and south; on the one side fire is masculine and its priest male; on the other it is feminine and has a priestess. Prayers and offerings, consisting solely of firstfruits, are offered to this divinity by the Yakuts, Teleuts, Soyotes, Golds, etc. It causes the growth of grass and the productivity of herds. The oldest known text of prayers is thought to be the one collected by Pallas in 1768; this is sufficient to show that the fire cult is hardly perceptible at an early date. Allusions made to the performance of sacrifices are not specific enough for us to decide whether these were made for the fire itself or, through the intermediary of fire, for some other power, such as the Sky. It is undoubtedly fire that is concerned in the Khitan ceremony, later taken up by the Mongols, which consisted of burning food in the earth.

J.-P.R./d.w.

BIBLIOGRAPHY

Doubt has been cast upon the cult of fire by R. GIRAUD (*Les règnes . . .*); the cult has also been treated by N. POPPE, "Zum Feuerkultus bei den Mongolen," *Asia Major* 2 (1925), and J. P. ROUX, "Fonctions chamaniques et valeurs du feu chez les peuples altaïques," *RHR* (1976), 1:67–101. See also P. A. MOSTAERT, "A propos d'une prière au feu," *American Studies in Altaic Linguistics* (Bloomington, IN, 1962), 211–13. Numerous materials in RINTCHEN, *Les matériaux . . .*

Turkish and Mongolian Funerary Customs

The funerary customs of the Turks and Mongols show no uniformity whatsoever. Abandonment or exposure of the corpse in trees, cremation, and burial have been practiced simultaneously or in turn. It seems, nevertheless, that the former methods have persisted into modern times only among isolated and relatively undeveloped peoples, and that burial gradually supplanted cremation. A change must have taken place around 628, since the Annals of the Suei say at

Funerary stelae. From Appelgren-Kivalo, *Alt-altaische Kunstdenkmäler.* (Helsinki 1931). Paris, Bibliothèque nationale. Photo Flammarion.

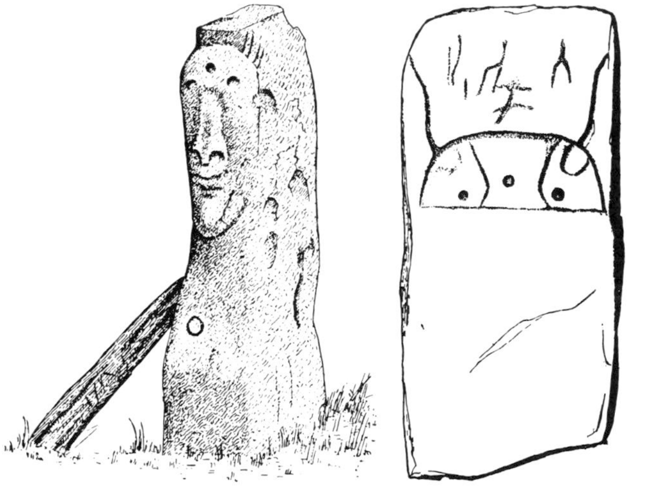

Funerary stelae. From Appelgren-Kivalo, *Alt-altaische Kunstdenkmäler.* (Helsinki 1931). Paris Bibliothèque nationale. Photo Flammarion.

this date that "In the past the custom (among the Turks) was to burn the dead. Now tombs are built for them." However, here, as elsewhere, it may have been the ashes that were interred. As for exposing the dead, this did not exclude placing the skeleton in the earth or burning it, since this was done (as was scraping the bones) in order to get rid of the flesh.

Some rites may have been common to the funerals of all the Altaic peoples: the exposing of the corpse in a mortuary tent, visits of "contemplation" paid to it, laying out the body, and wrapping it in a shroud. Similarly, they all seem to have organized their funerary rites in three periods: the day of death, the day of the funeral, and the days of commemoration.

On the day of the death, the people lamented with wild, dreadful cries, gashing their faces and ears. They walked around the funeral tent and made horses run. At this time, or later, they cut their hair, at least at an early period.

The time and place of the funeral rites were carefully chosen. The Tujue waited until the leaves fell from the trees or appeared on them; this is why, as among the Toba, Kirghiz, and others, the corpse was temporarily exposed when it was not immediately mummified. Among all of these peoples, the preference is always to bury the dead on the banks of rivers, on knolls, and in the forests. There are references to the immersion of the body or the rerouting of a watercourse so that it then passes over the sepulcher. Sometimes the place of burial was kept secret (Mongol emperors); sometimes it was indicated by a temple, an inscribed stela, *balbals,* or statues. When the sepulcher was kept secret, its builders were massacred as a precautionary measure. More often, the widows, slaves, and animals of the dead man were immolated so that they could accompany him. The custom of immolating widows was short-lived and was replaced by that of widow remarriage to the son-in-law, who was charged by her father with maintaining her. Objects were buried, burned, or placed on the tomb. When there was a temple, scenes from the life of the dead man were depicted upon it; his elegy (*agit*), sculpted upon a stela, contained a summary of his exploits or of abstract signs which included the *tamga,* or clan markings, and drawings of animals or objects.

Statues of the dead man or woman were supposed to be expressive. Quite different were the *balbals,* stones or pieces of wood stuck into the ground, representing the enemies killed by the dead man during his life or executed at his death, sometimes in great numbers. The custom of making *balbals* appears not to have survived long after the year 1000.

A great crowd, coming from a great distance, took part in the funeral. Specialized groups, such as the *sagditch,* the close friends, or the *sigiltchi,* the public mourners, played an important particular role. Around the freshly dug grave, the people would again take up their lamentations, lacerate their faces, mutilate themselves, and make the horses run. The *agit,* or elegy—which is still in use in Turkey and of which we have preserved some ancient references in short Old Turkic inscriptions—were sung or chanted. These *agit* were sometimes composed in the first person, as if the dead person himself were speaking. He proclaimed his manly virtue, his wealth, and his honor. An interesting allusion made to the accompanying ritual says that these virtues had to be proclaimed while standing up and while fasting. The sacrifice was accompanied by a communal meal, which may have been followed by orgies. The *yog* (funeral meal), which represented the most important moment in the ceremony, came to designate the obsequies themselves in the Turkish language.

The commemorations, of which we still find more than traces in Turkey—various rites can be found there that are performed in Central Asia—generally took place on the third, seventh, and fortieth days, and at the end of one year. On these days, people began to do again what had been done on the day of the funeral. Some documents say that they opened the bier to look once again at the dead man, which implies that the tomb was not completed until sometime later. Others speak of an evocation of the dead person (*ang,* in Turkish), who is supposed "to come down among his own."

If the commemorations were repeated beyond the end of the first year, they gradually became an ancestor cult.

J.-P.R./d.w.

BIBLIOGRAPHY

Funerary customs have been studied by CASTAGNÉ, *Les monuments funéraires de la steppe des Kirghizes* (Orenburg 1911). JAWORSKI, "Quelques remarques sur les coutumes funéraires turques," *RO* 4:225–61. KATANOV, "Über die Bestattungsgebräuche bei den Türkstämme," *Keleti Szemle* (Budapest 1900). KOTWICZ, "Les tombeaux dits Kereksür en Mongolie centrale," *RO* 4:60–170. NACHTINGALL, "Die erhohte Bestattung in Nord- und Hochasien," *Ant.* 48 (1953): 44–70. PASSEK and LATYNINE, "Sur la question des kammenye baby," *Eurasia septentrionalis antiqua* 4 (1929): 290–311. PAULSON, "Seelvorstellungen und Totenglaube bei nordeurasischen Völkern," *Etnos* 35, 1–2. J. P. ROUX, *La mort chez les peuples altaïques anciens et médiévaux* (Paris 1963). TOMKA, "Les termes de l'enterrement chez les peuples mongols," *AOAH,* 1965.

Heroes of the Turks and Mongols

Oghuz Khan. Manuscript from 1317. Istanbul, Topkapi Museum. Museum photo.

The range through which the numerous Turkish and Mongolian heroes are known can be either universal or local. All peoples of all tribes create legendary characters for themselves, historical or not, ancient shamans, conquerors, initiators, and ancestors to whom are attributed special powers and who are imagined to have performed marvelous feats. In extreme cases, they can become quasi deities.

There are far too many of these heroes to mention each by name. It seems that the oldest of all was A-se-na, the founder of the Tujue dynasty, known only through the Chinese transcription of a dubious word. Born of a she-wolf and a young Hiong-nu, he married the daughters of the gods of summer and winter, unknown elsewhere. The greatest of these heroes, however, must be Alp Er Tonga, "Courageous Tiger Man," still known in the eleventh century through fragments of poems collected by Kashgari. At that time, Alp Er Tonga was associated with Afrasiyab, the legendary hero of the Iranian world.

The Uighur Buqu Khan of the Tolesh tribe, born through the union of two trees, in a knothole, under the action of a ray of light, may have rivaled Alp Er Tonga in fame. The sovereign Qarakhanid, Satuk Bughra Khan, who was the first of the Turks of Central Asia to convert to Islam (960), on the recommendation of a hare, seems to have been known only among the Muslim Turks. The birth of this Camel-Prince, whose myth of origin was embellished with traditions about a lion, was accompanied by miracles, earthquakes, the appearance of springs, and the blooming of gardens. His daughter Ala Nur, Red Light, was impregnated by a ray of light, a manifestation of the lion, but identified by Muslims with Ali, the Lion of God.

Oghuz Khan, the eponymous ancestor of the Oghuz from whom the Seljukids and the Ottomans descended, probably owes his reputation to the importance of this last dynasty. Numerous *oghuz name* recounted his exploits, but few have survived until our time. We know that he married two female deities and had six children with them: Sun, Moon, Star, Sky, Mountain, and Sea. His name was understood to mean Colostrum, because he drank only the first milk of his mother, but it means Young Bull, which is what he is.

The two greatest Mongolian heroes are Genghis Khan, the founder of the thirteenth-century empire, and Geser Khan, of Tibetan origin. Both were deified. Genghis Khan was incarnated in the banner which is worshiped, and temples were erected to him. In the temple of the Eight White Tents in Ordos, he was until recently worshiped as a god of initiation. Geser Khan was the oppressor of demons and the god of shepherds and warriors.

It is probable that the episodes of the *Kitab-i Dede Qorqut* depict the various famous heroes of the Oghuz world surrounding the shaman who gives his name to this book. The memory of many of them survives today in certain regions of Turkey. Among them, one can cite Bayindir Khan, supreme ruler of the confederation, who is said by certain traditions to have been the contemporary of the Prophet. Before his conversion to Islam, he is said to have frightened Muhammad, who dug a hole into the wall and hid inside it, thus creating the first mihrab. Then there was Basat, who was fed by a lion and conquered the Cyclops, and Dumrul, whose wife wanted to give her soul to Azrail in exchange for his own and who fought with the angel of death. The Islamic saints, Old Testament characters as well as Koranic and Irano-Arabic, appropriated pre-Islamic myths, such as that of Ali, the fourth caliph of Islam who was very important in Turkey, and Abu Muslim, head of a popular Iranian movement during the Abassid era. Hizir and Ilyas, who drank the Water of Life, protected men on land and water, respectively. They are honored together during the feast of Hidrellez (Hizir-Ilyas). Hizir borrowed some of the attributes of certain nature cults connected with spring (his name means verdure) and in certain traits he resembles the Christian Saint George.

J.-P.R./d.b.

BIBLIOGRAPHY

See the articles by P. N. BORATAV in *Encyclopédie de l'Islam* (2d ed.), on Khidr-Ilyas, and *Islam Ansiklopedisi,* on Hizir. HEISSIG, *La religion* (Paris 1973).

The Turkish and Mongolian Ritual of the Blood Oath

It is among the ancient Turks that we can best understand the value that Altaic peoples attribute to blood. In fact, the uneasiness that menstrual blood and a few other images connected with blood evokes among the Siberian peoples today is secondary.

The oldest custom that we know connects blood with taking an oath. The Comans and Bulgars of the Volga swore on the blood of a dog whose throat had been cut and made alliances by drinking a few drops of their own blood from golden goblets. Similar performances existed among the Scythians, the Xiong Nu, and the Tujue, who drank blood from the gilded or skin-covered skulls of enemy chiefs. In Turkey, "to drink," *and itchmek,* remains the expression used to say "to swear." During the Mongol period, especially, we see clear evidence of a fraternal alliance between strangers who then were to treat one another as born of the same parents. These blood brothers (Turkish *kan kardesh,* Mongolian *anda,* derived from *ant,* "oath," in Turkish) exchanged blood, often by cutting their wrists. The exchange of important objects such as knucklebones and arrows could also have the same effect. This institution is very old indeed and has left behind more than mere memories in Turkey. It is already mentioned in the inscription of Begre and later by Kashgari, who states that perjury would be punished by the iron sword, "for iron is considered a sacred substance."

What must have justified these rituals and practices was the idea that blood contains the soul or one of the souls of every living being. The respect owed to princes meant that no blood could be shed when they were executed; instead, they were smothered, strangled, drowned, or trampled to death. Among the Ottomans, when members of the imperial family were executed they were strangled by a bow string around the throat. Because there was concern about the resurrection of animals, it was also forbidden to make them bleed when they were sacrificed, and even when they were hunted. When immolations took place, the sacrificer put his arm right on the victim's heart and squeezed it with his hand. Al-Umari's description of this operation during the Middle Ages corresponds almost word for word with those reported by travelers in the seventeenth and eighteenth centuries.

J.-P.R./g.h.

BIBLIOGRAPHY

On the interdiction against bloodshed, M. F. KÖPRÜLÜ, "La proibizione di versare il sangue," *Annali Istituto Univer. Orientale di Napoli,* 1940, 15–23, has given an incomplete preliminary sketch.

The Earth among the Turks and Mongols

The earth, called *yer* in the Genesis of the Orkhon, is there presented as one of the two cosmic zones, the one below formed at the same time as the sky. It may already have been a deity, as it would be later for the Khitan, Uighurs, and Mongols. The Chinese said that the Tujue had a god of the earth who appeared as a mountain, Podengringli (= But Tengri). In the inscriptions, this god gave orders jointly with the sky, but less frequently than the sky did. The same texts also use the word *yer* in the expression *iduq yer sub* ("sacred lands and waters") which defined certain numinous places animated by "master/possessors." The connections between *yer* in *iduq yer* and *yer* as a zone of the universe are not clear.

Among the Khitan, the earth was a complement of the sky; the earth, in the form of an old woman riding a gray ox, was worshiped at the same time as the sky. The earth goddess is found among the Mongols of the thirteenth century under the name of Etügen/Itügen, probably derived from Ötüken, the holy mountain of the Tujue. Marco Polo, who named her Natigay, saw her as a male deity, since he gave the deity a wife. Both husband and wife guarded the herds, grain, and earthly places. They were represented by images made of felt. At that time, the earth was regarded as male, as it was among the Buryat, who described the earth as an old man with gray hair to whom a sacrifice had to be made at the end of the harvest; but more generally the earth was regarded as female. Among the Yakuts, the earth promoted the growth of grass and the birth of babies. The Mongols prayed to her for fertility, fecundity, and the growth of the herd; they offered her milk, koumiss, and tea. A certain confusion may have arisen between the earth and other divinities, particularly between her and the goddess Umay, who also had the functions of a mother.

In Turkey, the earth is bivalent, simultaneously pure and clean, for it shakes itself to get rid of its impurities (an idea whose origin may perhaps be found in the Muslim principle of *teyemmüm,* according to which one could replace the water from ablutions with earth), and at the same time a symbol of offense, humiliation, servitude, putrefaction, and death. No memory of the ancient earth goddess would remain if there were no "earths of strength," small plots of land located on a holy site (often near a tomb) to which people come to dig up clay and eat it. This rite may, however, have another origin.

J.-P.R./g.h.

BIBLIOGRAPHY

A. E. DIEN, "A Possible Early Occurrence of Altaic Iduɣan," *CAJ* 2, 1, pp. 12–20. E. LOT-FALCK, "A propos d'Etugen, déesse mongole de la terre," *RHR* 149 (1956): 157–96. P. A. MOSTAERT, "Le mot Natigay-Nacigay chez Marco Polo," in *Oriente Poliano* (Rome 1957), pp. 95–101. PELLIOT, "Le mont Ötükän chez les anciens Turcs," *TP* (1929) 212–19. RINTCHEN, "Explication du nom Burqan Qaldun," *AOAH* 1 (1950): 189–90.

The mother goddess Umay has been singled out for study by L. BAZIN, "La déesse-mère chez les Turcs pré-islamiques," *Bull. Sté E. Renan* 2 (1953): 124–26 (continuation of *RHR*).

The Personification of Thunder among the Turks and Mongols

Storms with such spectacular manifestations as thunder and lightning deeply impressed the ancient Turks and Mongols. Kashgari said that storms were provoked by the sky god himself. A few facts show that violent and repeated thunder was considered a divine punishment which could be provoked by the violation of a taboo such as that against washing one's clothes in running water. This idea is also found in Turkey among the Tahtajis and before that in the jokes of Nasrettin Hodja. Among the Bulgars of the Volga, when lightning struck a house, no one ever approached it again; it was abandoned with all of its contents. Among Genghis Khan's Mongols, anything struck by thunder had to be purified by passing it between two fires. Later, according to Pallas, an animal struck by lightning could not be eaten.

Thunder must have been personified very early. When lightning struck, Uighurs would shoot arrows at the sky. Shooting at the sky was also practiced by the Ruanruan, Oghuz, Mongols, and Yakuts, but they did not always shoot at thunder. In Turkey, this practice made its way into the Islamized cycle of Nemrud, who wanted to kill God. More often, the target was the tree of life.

One could also pray to thunder. The Mongols would sprinkle milk and koumiss on the ground and ask the thunder to spare their cattle. Later, they sacrificed on the spot where lightning had struck, or they offered a white horse to the thunder god. In Siberia today, thunder is often given the form of a bird; the people make an image of it from wood and place it on a perch. Among the Teleuts, it is said that Ilyas is the maker of thunder. Others see it in the form of a dragon. Among the Buryat, one of the most powerful makers of thunder is Esen Sagan, who fights demons with his fiery arrows and is often thought to ward off evil spirits. Turkish traditions held that thunder materialized into stone or metal. From this metal, Köroglu was thought to have forged a saber with supernatural qualities.

J.-P.R./g.h.

BIBLIOGRAPHY

See HARVA, *Rel. Vorstellungen*. P. N. BORATAV, *Köroğlu destaru* (Istanbul 1931); *Türk folkloru* (Istanbul 1973). J. P. ROUX, *Les traditions* (Paris 1970).

Gods and Myths of the Abkhaz, the Cherkess, and the Ubykh of the Northern Caucasus

The Abkhaz and the Cherkess live to the north of the Caucasus mountains. At the beginning of the nineteenth century, before the Russian conquest, their territory extended all along the coast of the Black Sea to the Sea of Azov. The Ubykh must be included as well, being geographically, culturally, and linguistically midway between the other two groups, though they are no longer found in the Caucasus and only a few representatives remain in Turkey.

These three peoples were converted to Islam in the eighteenth century (the end result of a process which began in the fifteenth century). Their own religion disappeared relatively quickly, surviving only in certain fragmentary beliefs, which are insufficient to allow us to reconstruct the original system.

It appears that they must have worshiped, as did other Caucasians (Georgians and Ossets), a supreme god, of whom little more than a name remains. However, there is one name that does allow us to guess at some very interesting theological concepts, though these unfortunately can barely be glimpsed.

The supreme God of the Abkhaz was Anc°a. The name can be broken down as follows: *a-*, definite article; *-n-*, particle, "there," and *-c°a*, plural suffix. Literally, it means "the theres," or the group of divine parts believed to be present everywhere in the universe but united in a single Whole. This multiplicity of the One would correspond well with what we know of the Georgian supreme god, Morige. This is the purely verbal trace of a theology which may be as complex as others more famous.

Among the Ubykh and the Cherkess, the functions of the supreme God are separated and assigned to two entities, of which we know only that one was apparently benevolent toward man, while the other inspired fear. This was not a dualism of the Zoroastrian type but rather a sharing of roles reminiscent of the Indo-European dyad of sovereign gods.

For the Ubykh, the difference is not only onomastic, but seems also to have been vaguely perceived. They distinguish between a God who is invoked for blessings and a God who is invoked only in curses. The first God, who was benevolent, was Wa in the formulaic language, Waba elsewhere. This word is probably derived from a root seen in the Cherkess word *We*, "sky." The original name of God would therefore be simply "Sky," as it was among the Turks before the advent of Islam. The terrible God was Wašx°a, doubtless related to the storm, as the etymology indicates: *wa*, "sky," and *šx°a*, "gunpowder," yielding the "thundering sky."

The same division is found among the Cherkess, who once distinguished between The, today the only name given to the supreme God, and Washe, invoked exclusively for curses. His name certainly contains the word "sky," *we* or *wa*, and "big" or "high," *še*.

I. Storm Gods

The Cherkess name for storm god is the same as their word for lightning: Shyble, a pictorial term which literally means "horse-serpent." Among the Abkhaz too, the name of the god becomes confused with the name of the natural phenomenon over which he presides: Afy. As is proved by several formulaic expressions, Afy, like the supreme God Anc°a, is seen as being simultaneously one and many.

The cult dedicated to the storm god is identical, except for a few details, among the two peoples. As in Georgia and Ossetia, death by lightning was interpreted as a sign of divine favor and a good omen, whether it happened to a human being or to an animal. Both underwent the same ritual treatment. Outside the village, generally in the forest or at the end of a woods, a kind of very high scaffolding was erected, consisting for the most part of an armature of four large alder branches (or stripped young trees) stuck in the ground and attached to crosspieces of the same wood. At the top of the structure, alder branches with their leaves were arranged to form a kind of litter. The body, human or animal, was placed here and covered with leaves. Several victims, preferably white goats, had their throats cut near the scaffolding, and as soon as their heads were cut off they were fastened on top of the posts that were set in the ground. Songs, dances, and feasts went on for several days. When the ritual was completed, the area remained untouched for several days, at least three (seven in certain areas). Only at the end of this period was the corpse of the person struck by lightning, if a human, taken down and buried.

This custom, still observed at the beginning of the twentieth century, resembles the funeral practices of the inhabitants of Colchis, as described by several authors of antiquity. The northern part of Colchis coincides with the present-day territory of the Abkhaz. According to Apollonius of Rhodes, in the third century B.C., the Colchians considered it blasphemous to cremate or bury male corpses. Instead, they wrapped them in untanned cowhide and tied them high in a tree with ropes. Nicholas de Damas (first century B.C.) gives the same information: "Colchians do not bury their dead, but hang them in trees"; so does Claudius Ellien three centuries later: "Colchians sew their dead in skins and hang them in trees."

In the seventeenth century, Archangelo Lamberti noted that the Abkhaz "cut a tree trunk in the shape of a coffin, where they place the body, tying it to a treetop with vines." Other travelers observed the same practice in the eighteenth century.

According to every indication, the temporary exposure of the dead on a scaffolding of alder bushes represents the attenuation and limitation of archaic funeral rites which must originally have applied to all corpses, or at least to all dead males.

II. Blacksmith Gods

The Cherkess and the Abkhaz (unlike the Georgians) never had a sacerdotal caste. The function of a priest was performed either by the oldest member of a clan, lineage, or extended family, or, more often, by the blacksmith. Among these peoples, the god of the forge therefore had a high position and his services extended into many areas beyond those of his technical expertise.

Shashw was both one and many, as was common in Abkhaz theology. He was invoked as a single god, but various formulas of cursing treated him linguistically as plural (for example, *š'as° 'ry-lax,* "the curse of the Shashws").

The Cherkess god, Tlepsh (λ'epš'), was himself a "well-tempered" blacksmith, able to fuse metal together with his bare hands. His forehead was decorated with seven horns. At his forge he made objects, especially weapons, which had magical properties and value, but only when his work was performed with no witnesses. He plays an important role in the Nart epic (particularly among the Ossets, who call him Kurdalägon), fashioning fabulous weapons for heroes and literally tempering the metallic demigod, Batraz.

Among the two peoples, the forge is a sanctuary and the site of various cults. The Abkhaz made their most serious vows there. The Cherkess used the space to perform rituals to change the weather, usually to make rain. The blacksmith god is linked to storms through his obvious affinities with fire, and is a parallel to Shyble, the lightning spirit. He also has power over the fertility of women and the birth and raising of children, especially sons. For example, in case of a difficult birth, the woman in labor would drink water that had been used to temper a sword. The newborn infant received a kind of baptism at the forge: he was "tempered" by being immersed in water normally used by the smith to cool objects that had been heated white-hot. Among the Abkhaz, the newborn infant was left on the hearth of the forge, on the same bed of coals (fortunately cooled) where weapons and tools were usually fashioned (see the apparently strange treatment to which the Osset blacksmith god subjects young Batraz, according to Osset legend).

Long and complex rituals were performed in honor of this god. For this purpose, the Abkhaz used, not the ordinary forge, but a miniature workshop, situated in a tiny building and including all the blacksmith's tools, reproduced in miniature. The day before the main ritual, which lasted three days, the smith, accompanied by his entire family, led a kid to the toy forge and sacrificed it at sunset, "when the god is in his house." In addition, a rooster was sacrificed by a man, and a hen by a woman. During the days which followed, many shells were fired, for the smith god intercedes in the techniques of hunting and makes them successful (the divinities of the hunt preside over the game, rather than over the actual activity of hunting with dogs; see the discussion of Caucasian gods of the hunt, in section V, below).

It is noteworthy that the cult of the forge was divided into two parts: the real workshop constitutes a sanctuary for all rites not directly involved with the professional activity of the smith, while that activity gives rise to a cult which takes place in a miniature forge, set apart from the true forge.

III. Ahyn and the Cow Who Offers Herself for Sacrifice

Ahyn (*axyn,* or *axym* in some dialects) is the Cherkess patron god of animal breeding. As such, he has an important place in the pantheon of these peoples, for whom livestock played a primary economic role, to the point where several sources consider him the supreme god of the Cherkess. He is the only northern Caucasian deity to be named in the following mythological fragment:

A long time ago, at the edge of the Black Sea near Touapse, there lived a man whose daughter was of unequaled beauty. The father decided to give his daughter in marriage to the man who could jump from one mountain to the other, crossing the valley in a single bound. The only man to succeed at this test was a giant named Ahyn, thanks to his normal means of locomotion: a pole one hundred "sajēnes" long (226 meters), which he set in the valleys to propel himself from one mountain to the next. The father was horrified at the idea of such a peculiar son-in-law, but the giant pleased the young girl, and she married him.

Later, Ahyn announced his intention to visit his father-in-law. Terrified at this prospect, the father fled with all his belongings and began to stalk the giant, intending to kill him by sawing through his enormous pole while he was asleep. In the meantime, Ahyn, unsuspecting, continued along his way, accompanied by all his herds, so numerous that they entirely covered all the surrounding mountains. It was the giant's habit to sleep one week out of two; taking advantage of this long sleep, his father-in-law had no trouble sawing through Ahyn's pole in several places. When the giant awoke and tried to jump from one summit to the next, the pole broke and Ahyn sank forever beneath the waves of the river. His immense herds disappeared at once.

A sacred tree, dwelling place of a god. The horns evoke the cow that offers herself as a sacrifice.

Since that time, and, it is said, even today, to commemorate the event and to allow the Cherkess to atone for their mistake by means of a sacrifice, each year on the same date a cow appears, the cow of Ahyn. She emerges from the forest and moves toward a sacred grove. She knows where to stop and nothing and no one can interrupt her progress. Everyone follows the cow respectfully until she reaches the place where she stops of her own accord and offers herself spontaneously to her sacrificer's knife. Her throat is cut in the place she has chosen, and she is then taken to a second area to be skinned, a third to be cut up, a fourth to be cooked, and a fifth for her flesh to be eaten.

The last part of the myth, concerning "the cow who comes forth by herself" (according to the Cherkess expression), has merged with a ritual which was still practiced at the beginning of the twentieth century. The same belief, along with the cult and the practices attached to it, is widespread among the Abkhaz and the Mingrelians (inhabitants of ancient Colchis).

The legend of the god Ahyn and his death caused by the destruction of his pole includes several variations, not only among the Cherkess but also among their neighbors the Ubykh. G. Dumézil succeeded in documenting one of these variations among the Turkish Ubykh as late as 1930.

Ahyn's pole entered into other Caucasian myths, particularly the Abkhaz legends of Abrskil and the Georgian legends of Amirani; it allows us to explain certain important symbols that would be undecipherable without recourse to their Cherkess source.

IV. Shewzerysh

Shewzerysh (or Sewserysh) is especially important because of the possible links between his cult and the great hero of the Nart epic, Sosryko (Sawsyryq°e among the Cherkess and Soslan among the Ossets).

He seems to have been the protector of the grain at all stages of its production and storage. His cult was celebrated in the spring according to some sources, after the harvest or in winter according to others, and always in the presence of and by means of the knotty trunk of the young plane tree or pear tree, or a column shaped from one of these. The evening before "the night of Shewzerysh," the trunk or log of the plane tree is placed outside, in front of the door. It becomes confused with the deity himself, as it is also addressed by the name "Shewzerysh." The crucial moment of the ritual is the "entrance of the tree" into the house. This practice is reminiscent of the *arbor intrat* of Asiatic religions and the role of the pine tree in the cult of Atys (cf. Frazer, *Attis and Osiris*). This connection suggests the presence of an eschatological element which may be confirmed by the mythology of this god (if indeed this mythology belongs to him; cf. Soslan among the Ossets). The Cherkess say that he was once a man who was endowed with marvelous powers, in particular the ability to walk on water. God punished him for his excessive pride by taking away his legs.

The legend of the Nart hero, Soslan, still has definite traces of a "mythology of Shewzerysh" which has been forgotten today.

V. Gods of the Hunt

In the Caucasus, hunting was once an autonomous economic activity, and it still is today in several mountainous regions. This explains its firm grip on pagan religion and mythology.

All of the Caucasian peoples still know the "masters of game," often female, who simultaneously protect the activity of the hunters and the ecological conservation of the wild animals who are their legitimate property. Like our modern-day forestry administration, the gods of the hunt simultaneously encourage and limit the killing of wild game.

In Ossetia, the "god of the hunt" and "master of wild beasts" is the masculine spirit Aefsati (the same name is attributed to one of the Svana hunting gods, Apsat). Game is called "Aefsati's cattle" (*aefsatijy fos*). He is invoked before the hunt and is thanked after a successful hunt, before the flesh of the slain animal is consumed.

The patron of the Cherkess hunt (a goddess among the Kabards, western Cherkess) is the "forest god," Mezythe (or Mezeth in Kabard), from *mez*, "forest," and *the*, "god." His body is covered with silver, like a kind of organic armor. He has silver horns, his mustache is made of golden flames, and he is the size of an elephant. Dressed in chamois skins, he is armed with a bow of hazelwood, with dogwood arrows. Mezythe rides a gigantic boar with golden bristles, escorted by forest stags and does who are pastured and milked by the girls in his service (his own daughters, according to Abkhaz beliefs). He is fed exclusively on the blood of the animals which hunters offer him in their sacrifices.

It is important to emphasize that for all Caucasian peoples, a hunt is the equivalent of a sacrifice, each animal killed becoming a victim offered up to the master of game.

Cherkess hunters use a secret language among themselves, the "language of the forest," whose "secret" consists of adding meaningless suffixes after each open syllable.

The Abkhaz have two deities of the hunt who are related to one another by marriage: Ajrg and Azhwajpshaa. The first has daughters who are eternally young and who are dedicated to the care of the does of the forest. These daughters marry no one but the sons of Azhwajpshaa.

G.C./d.b.

BIBLIOGRAPHY

A.A., *Religioznye verovanija abxazcev,* Sbornik svedenii o kavkazskix gorcax, 5 (Tbilisi 1971). G. ÇURSIN, *Materialy po êtnografii Abxazii* (Sukhumi 1956). N. DUBROVIN, *Çerkesy (adyge)* (Krasnodar 1927). G. DUMÉZIL, *La langue des Oubykhs* (Paris 1931); *Loki* (Paris 1947); *Mythe et épopée,* 1, part 3 (Paris 1968); *Romans de Scythie et d'alentour* (Paris 1978). N. DŽANASIA, "Iz religioznyx verovanii abxazov," *Xristianskij Vostok* 4 (Saint Petersburg 1915). D. I. GULIA, *Božestva oxoty u abxazov* (Sukhumi 1926); *Kul't Kozla u abxazov* (Sukhumi 1928). S. INAL-IPA, *Abxazy* (Sukhumi 1965); *Kabardinskij fol'klor* (Moscow and Leningrad 1936). M. KOSVEN, *Etnografija i istorija Kavkaza* (Moscow 1961). L. I. LAVROV, "Doislamskie verovanija adygejcev i Kabardincev," in *Issledovanija i Materialy po voprosam pervobytnyx religioznyx verovanij* (Moscow 1959). L. L'JUL'E, *Cerkessija* (Krasnodar 1927). S. NOGMOV, *Istorija adygejskogo naroda* (Nal'čik 1947). S. X. SALAKAJA, *Abxazskij narodnyj geroičeskij êpos* (Tbilisi 1966). E. M. ŞILLING, "Religioznye verovanija narodov SSSR," *Çerkesy,* 2 (Moscow and Leningrad 1931). STAL', *Etnografičeskij očerk čerkesskogo naroda,* Kavkazskij sbornik, 21 (Tbilisi 1900).

SOULS AND THEIR AVATARS IN SIBERIA

Man has many souls. Their number varies in different populations and, within a single population, in different groups. According to the Western Tungus, as studied by G. M. Vasilevič, the Tungus have two souls: the *been,* the corporal soul which descends into the world of the dead after death, and the *omi,* the permanent vital principle which is reincarnated and thus assures the reproductive capacity of the clan. The *been* is the basis of individuality, while the *omi* is merely a clan soul. Vasilevič, contrary to other authors, does not count the *xanjan,* the shadow and the reflection in water or a mirror, as a soul.

After death, while the *been* retires along the river which descends to the lower world, the *omi* flies into the higher world and perches on the mythical tree with the other *omi* of the clan. In a few years, it redescends to the earth and drops into a tent through a smoke hole. After falling into the fire, it penetrates the womb of a woman, who becomes pregnant.

According to variants collected by other authors, the western Tungus have three souls: the *been,* the corporeal soul; the *omi,* the surviving soul; and the *maïn,* the soul-destiny of more recent creation. Certain informants conceive of the *maïn* as a thread that stretches from the head of an individual to the hand of Seveki, the master spirit of the higher world. When an evil spirit cuts the thread, the man dies. According to others, the *maïn* remains a soul exterior to the body of its owner and, under a human guise, leads the life of a hunter in the swamps of the higher world, full of game, and the adventures which it experiences are reflected in the life of the earthly hunter. In this case, as in the other, the soul does not seem to play any role after death. When a man dies, his *been* descends into the village of the dead ruled by Mangi, the chief of the ancestors. He receives the *been,* but he also desires the soul which, in the version recorded by Anisimov, carries the name of *xanjan* during the life of the individual on earth but becomes *omi* after the individual's death. Mangi thus goes to search for the *xanjan.* He catches up with it at the sources of the mythical river and forces it to turn around. But the *xanjan* suddenly transforms into a bird. He takes the name of *omi* again and flies toward the tree of the higher world from which he will redescend to be reincarnated upon the earth in his time.

It seems curious that an irregularity serves to establish the rule. Nevertheless, we can compare this *xanjan,* which carries the *omi* in essence, to the great soul of the Gilyak, which includes the small mobile soul charged with survival. However, the Gold, a Tungus group of the Amur basin, have elaborated a similar system. The *omi* becomes incarnate in a newborn child, and when the infant reaches the age of one year, it takes the name of *ergeni* (the swallow according to Lopatin, but more probably a derivation from *erga,* "breath"). When the individual dies, the *ergeni* becomes *fanja* (a phonetic variation of *xanjan*). The *fanja* descends to the world of the dead with a shaman as guide. Later, the *fanja* becomes *omi* again (it is not specified by what process this occurs) and is reincarnated. If the infant dies before it is one year old, its *omi* reascends immediately to the tree of the young birds.

The Oroč, neighbors and relatives of the Gold, have in addition a unique soul which traverses the lower world before ascending back to the higher world, from which it will descend to be reincarnated. After death, this soul (whose name is unknown) goes to the world of the dead, where it waits patiently for four generations. Then it sets out once again for the higher world. It arrives there after being transformed successively into an old man made of iron, an iron arrow, and a metallic duck, then into glass, and then into a butterfly in order to fly to the moon, which here represents the higher world. It lives several years on the moon in the territory of the old mistress of the bear or that of the tiger (this division of the moon into two halves, each having a different master spirit, is probably a survival of a dual organization among the Oroč). Fed on charcoal, the soul is transformed into a mushroom and then thrown to the earth, where it is reincarnated in a newborn child. Then the cycle begins again.

The Tungus of Manchuria have a system which is related to the Gold system. When it is still in its mother's womb, the infant is given an *omi* soul. When it is born, it receives the *erga,* "breath," which is taken here to mean not soul but rather life. During the first year the *omi* of the baby is always ready to take flight toward the higher world; that is, nursing babies are always on the edge of death in these populations. To protect the soul of the infant, it is placed in a small anthropomorphic wooden cradle called *anjan.* When the infant has grown and become conscious, one says that its *omi* is stabilized and it now possesses the *susi* soul. The *susi* is composed of three elements "unified like the nail, the skin, and the bone of a finger," say the Tungus of Manchuria.

The first element, the *fanjanga* (root *fanja/anjan*), linked to consciousness, causes death by its departure, but its ultimate fate is unknown. The second element descends into the world of the dead (according to certain informants, it some-

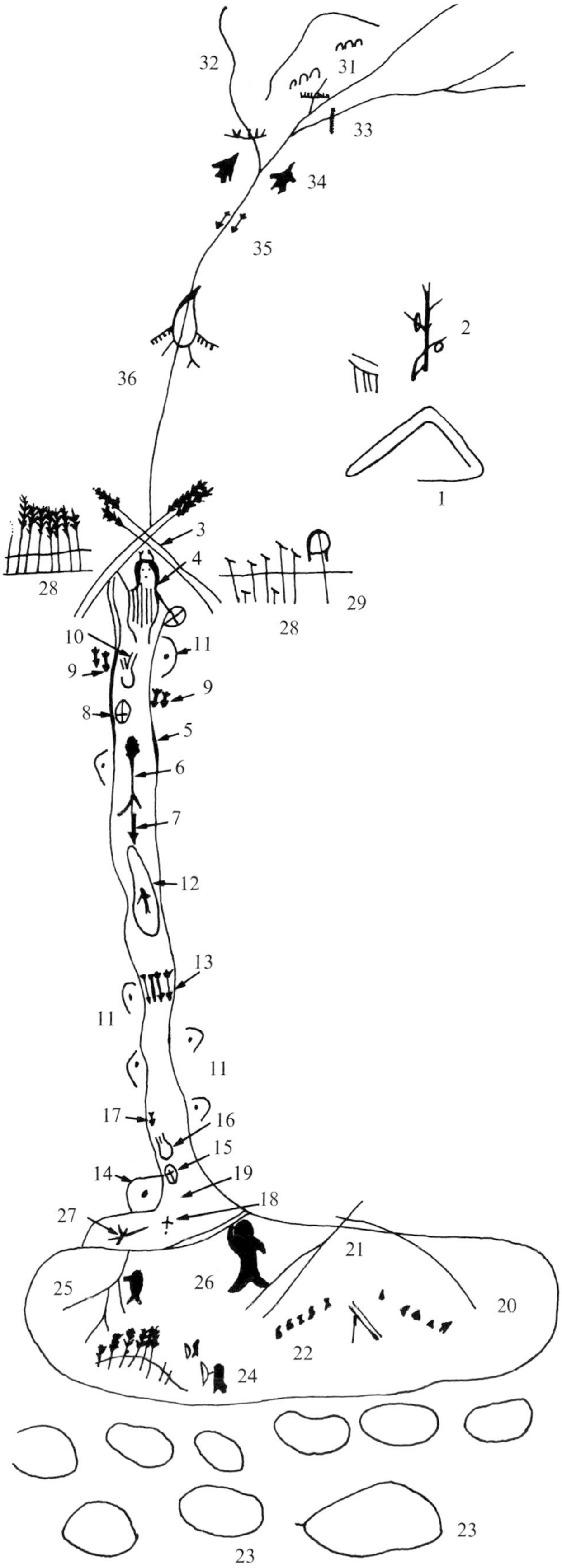

times returns to be reincarnated on earth in a human or animal form). The last element is regarded as the soul of the afterlife; it returns after death to the higher world and waits there to redescend into a new embryo. This soul is the *omi.*

In fact, what is essential among the Tungus is not the variable number of what may be called "souls" for lack of a better term, but the voyages of the soul, which continues to be reincarnated from the higher world to the earth in the middle, and passes through the lower world.

The shaman's route along the great mythic river, leading the soul of the deceased to the netherworld.

1. The abandoned tent of the deceased.
2. The platform on which the corpse of the deceased lies. The personal effects of the deceased are hung from the branches of a nearby tree so that they can accompany the deceased into the afterlife.
3. The tent of the shaman, with the items needed for the ritual.
4. Intil'gun, the old shaman of the Kordujal' clan leads the *been,* the physical soul of the deceased, into the netherworld.
5. The mythic river.
6. The spirit of the larch sweeps the path before the shaman.
7. The spirit of the loon guides the shaman.
8. The shaman's drum serves as a boat to carry him down the river.
9. The spirits that protect the shaman.
10. The physical soul of the deceased on its platform (which has now become a raft) follows the shaman.
11. The encampments of the old mistresses of the route to the netherworld. The shaman stops at each encampment to ask which path to follow.
12. The island of the old mistress of the river, where the shaman rests; he too consults her about the remainder of the route he must follow.
13. Narrow passage of the river, where the shaman has set up a barrier of protective spirits.
14. The encampment of one of the old mistresses of the route—the final stopping place on the shaman's journey. From here, he calls the inhabitants of the village of the dead, on the other side of the river, to come for the soul, but the shaman himself does not cross the estuary.
15. The shaman's drum, serving as a boat.
16. The soul of the deceased.
17. The reindeer offered as a sacrifice.
18. The loon that guides the shaman.
19. The estuary beyond which is the netherworld proper.
20. The island where the dead of the clan live.
21. The village of the dead of the clan.
22. The dead women sitting around a fire, doing various domestic tasks.
23. The nine mountains where the shaman ancestors live. Mangi, the chief of the ancestors, lives on the highest mountain.
24. The dead of the clan hunting.
25. The dead making a dam for fishing.
26. The old mistress of the village makes a sign for the dead to fetch the soul from the other side of the estuary.
27. One of the dead leaves by boat to fetch the soul.
28. The shamanistic spirits that block access to the netherworld.
29. The reindeer pelt offered as a sacrifice.
30. The *omiruk,* the reserve for the *omi* souls, the souls in the afterlife in the world above.
31. The *omi* souls.
32. The tributaries of the mythic river in the world above.
33. The barrier of protective spirits installed by the shaman in the world above to protect the *omiruk.*
34. The bird spirits that protect access to the *omiruk* by air.
35. Barrier formed by the salmon protective spirits.
36. The *omi* soul of the deceased being transformed into a bird in order to escape from Mangi, flying off to the *omiruk,* where it will wait for several generations before descending again to be reincarnated on earth.

Representation of a Tungus or Altaic shamanic ancestor, found in the Stanovoi mountains by the explorer Joseph Martin at the end of the nineteenth century. Wood, with a leather cape and yellow glass beads for eyes. Paris, Musée de l'Homme collection. Museum photo.

I. The Souls of the Dead That Have Reached the World of the Dead

The soul of the dead leaves the world of the living with regret. The route that awaits him is dangerous: a river with turbulent rapids for the Western Tungus, a dusty, rock-strewn road for the Eastern Tungus. On each of these routes, baneful spirits lie in wait to kill as the souls of the dead pass. The shaman is charged with guiding the souls through these dangers to the village of the dead. For certain groups, he is content to guide the soul from afar through directions transmitted by his bird messengers. This definitive separation of the dead from the living is one of the fundamental tasks of the shaman.

When the soul of the dead arrives in the world of the dead, he leads there a life similar to the one he knew on earth, with the difference that this new universe is cold and dark, barely illuminated by one-half of a frozen sun.

The dead keep their names and their individuality until the fourth generation. Always a little jealous of the living, they tend to be harmful to them. A Tungus of Manchuria had had eczema, his legs had swelled, and then his two horses died; he wondered who among the dead had sent him all these ills: his father, his mother, or his younger brother who had recently died? The shaman can restabilize the situation by offering a sacrifice to the angry dead in question. The dead then stop their malevolent activities and even help the shaman with advice and predictions about the future of the clan. Besides, the dead have a less evil character than the shaman's other auxiliary spirits. Thus a shaman of eastern Siberia agreed to chant on a phonographic record (in the 1920s) an invocation to the ancestral spirits, which he ended with these words: "Do not come. I am chanting only for the machine." But he refused categorically to disturb the auxiliary spirits called *séven* in the same offhanded way.

When four generations have passed, the soul of the deceased joins the swelling crowd of anonymous ancestors that have become incapable of good or evil. According to another variant, it falls into a world situated further down, the *ellamrak* for the Western Tungus, the *ela gurum* for the Eastern Tungus, and there disintegrates definitively. The Oroč explain the tragic depopulation of their group by this definitive destruction.

Nevertheless, not all the dead are reduced to impotence with time. Some very distant ancestors form the active and benevolent category of the protector spirits of the family. These spirits, of great help in daily life in warding off illnesses and aiding in the hunt, are of an ancestral origin. Indeed, the term for them among the Western Tungus—*muxdy*—comes from *mugdy*, "ancestor." *Mugdy* is itself formed from *mudge*, "trunk," for the Tungus used to place their dead in the hollowed-out trunks of trees.

Each family has at least one protector spirit, who resides in an anthropomorphic statue of wood, horn, metal, or rags. The statuette of the *Muxdy* of the Western Tungus is a stylized representation of a man. The *Džuli* of the Gold, although male, is provided with breasts prominent enough for certain Soviets to conclude that the *Džuli* was formerly female, at a supposedly matriarchal period. But in Siberia the protector spirits of the family are not necessarily masculine. Among the Ket, for example, the *Alel* are imagined in the form of old women.

The figurines are handed down in the male line in all the populations. Among the Tungus it is apparently the men who feed them. On the eve of every new moon and when he returns from a successful hunt, the senior male of a Tungus family coats the *Muxdy* with grease, blood, or marrow. The Gold master of the house, just as he leaves his family for many months of hunting in the forest, bows to the earth in front of the statue of the *Džuli* guardian spirit and asks it to watch over his return and his possessions. If, upon his return, he finds everything in good order, bowing down once again, he offers to the *Džuli* broth, alcohol, and Chinese wine.

Among the Ket, in contrast to the Tungus, the women are charged with the care of the *Alel*. Each year, at the end of summer, just before the great hunting season, the Ket women dress the statuette in a new garment of fur or cloth so that the *Alel* will continue to work at night, maintaining the fire, caressing the children and braiding their hair, sharpening the fishhooks, playing with the dogs or making them bark at the approach of danger.

The guardian spirits, like the other Siberian spirits that were kept inside a pillar, were treated according to their merits. They were honored and fed as long as their services were hoped for. At every change of camp, at the opening of the hunting and fishing season, upon the birth of a child, they were taken out of the ritual sack or sacred sleigh and were set out to be rubbed with food. On a journey, the white reindeer consecrated to the celestial spirit would transport them. But whenever these spirits did not keep their promises, and when ill fortune struck the household, they would be left without food and sometimes abused. If a Gold suffered a violent kidney pain, the *Džuli* would be taken outside and buried to the waist, and would remain in that position until the illness was healed.

II. The Souls of the Dead That Have Not Arrived at the World of the Dead

The souls of the dead that have not arrived at the world of the dead are the miserable and starving souls that wander the earth. For one reason or another, they cannot be guided to the lower world, because they have been deprived of ritual funerals.

Numerous in forests and swamps, they flutter about in the form of will-o'-the-wisps or lurk in tree trunks. When a tree is cut down, they cry: "*Onoï!* What pain!" and drive the logger mad. They whistle with the wind in the branches, creak with the ice on frozen rivers, and respond with the echo. Easily startled, they pose no danger to the brave: the crackling of a fire or the barking of a dog puts them to flight.

Much more formidable are the souls of those who have died a violent death. Those who have died from suicide, drowning, freezing, being crushed under a tree, or falling into an abyss seek to lure the hunter to a death identical to theirs. The Gold envision suicides—who are the most jealous of the happiness of the living and therefore the most dangerous—as black birds with iron feathers and metallic beaks.

These spirits generally become the master spirits of the localities in which they died. If the shaman succeeds in mastering them, they enter into the category of the *séven*, spirits who, in exchange for offerings and compliments, agree to aid the shaman. As for souls who have been led to the lower world, but who have managed to escape and to slip back again onto the earth, they lurk in hiding for the souls of the living. Their very name describes them: among the Western Tungus they are called *nevi*, "those who seek a glance."

L.D./m.s.

The Sky, the Great Celestial Divinity of Siberia

The sky, the great celestial divinity of Siberia, is the supreme divinity of all the ethnic groups of Siberia. From the summit of the sky, he superintends the proper course of the universe. For many of the groups his name originally meant "sky": Buga (Tungus), Es (Ket), Nga (Enc), Turum/Torym (Ostyak), Num (Selkup). This figure sometimes undergoes a change of status in different groups. A great celestial god for some (Ket, Enc, Eastern Tungus), he becomes a spirit-lord for others (Western Tungus), and even a collectivity of spirits (Buryat, Yakut). Nevertheless, he appears most frequently as an incarnation of the sky who superintends the mechanism of the universe without interfering in human affairs, and, ordinarily, neither prayers nor sacrifices are addressed to him.

In spite of his essentially indifferent and inaccessible character, certain groups have more or less anthropomorphized him. The Tungus offer two extreme examples. For the Eastern Tungus, Buga remains so remote that they have no idea of his appearance and even their shamans maintain no connection with him. By contrast, the Western Tungus of the Yenisey have conceived an anthropomorphic spirit who interferes in the life of men, who intervenes in their hunts, in the birth of infants, and in the reproduction of the herds of domesticated reindeer.

Under the various names of Seveki, Xovoki, Ekśeri, or Maïn, the celestial spirit of the Western Tungus governs the upper world. Further, he holds in his closed fist the ends of *maïn* threads, the soul-destiny according to some, the soul-breath according to others. Each of these threads is connected to the head of an individual, and if a malevolent spirit cuts the thread, the person dies unless a shaman succeeds in tying a knot. The celestial spirit also holds the *maïn* of plants and trees that he causes to grow by pulling from above. According to certain variants, he also casts onto the earth the souls, *omi*, of men and the souls of domesticated reindeer in the form of blades of grass and hairs, when the time has come for them to become incarnate in a baby or a fawn. Moreover, since the spirit-lords who bestow game are subordinate to him, he can thwart or favor the hunt. That is why the Western Tungus hook white ribbons to trees as an offering to the celestial spirit to obtain abundant game.

It seems that among the Western Tungus this figure exercises two functions: the function of organizer of the world and the function of dispenser of game. In this last role he evokes the Toman of the Ket, the beautiful female symbol of the south, who, each spring, climbs to the top of a cliff and shakes her white sleeves above the Yenisey. Down escapes from them and is transformed into geese, swans, and ducks, who fly north toward Ket.

The celestial spirit of the other ethnic groups is situated between these two extremes. Among the Ket, Es, under the aspect of a bearded old man, is content to inspect the universe on the longest day of summer. At that time the stars and the earth draw near to his home. He gives them his benediction with his orders for the year and wishes them a pleasant journey.

Nga, among the Enc, regulates the course of the seasons and determines the date when he will grant a favorable time for the hunt, for, it is said, if he allowed perpetually fine weather to prevail, men would take all the fish and kill all the game. Nga seems, nevertheless, a little less removed from men than his Ket homologue, for he takes the trouble to send them dreams to inform them of their destiny. Nga is married to D'ja Menjuu, the mother of vegetation, who while moving through the sky spreads out the lower part of her mantle to form the rainbow.

Organizers who ensure the equilibrium of the world, these spirits are very rarely creators. The indigenous peoples of Siberia seem to be little concerned with the creation of the world. They regard it generally as given from the very beginning. In the most widespread myth of creation, an immensity of water covers everything. In the beginning, the Tungus recount, there was water everywhere. Ekśeri, the celestial divinity, flew above the waters with his duck. Ekśeri, tired, asked his bird to dive and fetch him some mud in its bill. The duck disgorged the mud onto the surface of the water, which formed the earth.

The Tungus add that this benevolent divinity had an evil elder brother who eventually became master of the lower world and spoiled his younger brother's creation. According to a myth of the Yeniseian people, this benevolent creator fashioned human souls out of earth and stones. He put them on a board to dry under the protection of a dog who, at that time, had no fur. The elder brother succeeded in persuading the dog to let him see the souls in exchange for fur. As soon as he caught sight of them, the evil one spit on the souls, and that is why men die. On his return, the younger brother punished the dog by condemning him to feed upon ordure. In northern variants of this myth, the unfaithful guardian is a crow who allows himself to be bribed with the promise of a liver to eat.

Other Siberian pantheons, for the most part, also include a benevolent demiurge associated by close bonds of kinship with the spirit responsible for disease and death. Among the Tungus, as we have seen, it is a pair of brothers; among the Ket, Es has the malevolent Xosadam for a wife, the incarnation of the north, mistress of cold, darkness, and disease. On her lifeless island, at the northern extremity of the world, where white mosses and twisted trees grow, in the midst of gusts of wind and the doleful cries of black birds with serpent heads, the Kyns, bearers of illness and robbers of souls, Xosadam devours human souls. It is she who sends the tempests, the epidemics, and all the calamities that befall men.

As for the Enc, they make Todomé, the evil divinity of the lower world, the son of Nga, the sky. Todomé chases human souls the way hunters pursue game. Sometimes his gluttony is such that he tries to devour even his mother, D'ja Menjuu. She then ascends and asks Nga to show their son the "people for eating."

L.D./b.f.

Siberian Master Spirits and Shamanism

I. Master Spirits

Master spirits are of primary importance for the economic life of hunters; they are the masters of certain species of animals, of territories in which game lives, and of natural phenomena such as fire, lightning, etc.

As a general rule, the spirits are addressed directly, without the mediation of the shaman. However, when a master spirit manifests a particular animosity and refuses to grant game for several days or weeks at a time, the shaman directs a rite to appease and propitiate the spirit. On the occasion of certain ceremonies proper to the Western Tungus, the shaman visits the master spirits of the clan territories in order to ask for the souls of the game which the clan may slay in the course of the hunting season. The intercession of the shaman nevertheless remains reserved for exceptional cases, which has led some to think that the master spirits existed before the establishment of shamanism.

1. *The master spirit of fire.* The great majority of Siberian peoples depict the master spirit of fire, a very ancient spirit, as an old woman who is sitting bent over in the flames of the hearth. Each family jealously guards this spirit, which is essentially a clan spirit, and who lives in the center of the tent. The Tungus never allow an outsider to carry away an ember or even to light a pipe from the household fire, for in the flames of the hearth dance the souls of children who are yet to be born, who have fallen from the sky through the smoke hole and who are waiting to enter into the body of one of the women of the house. One of the most important moments of marriage among the Gold consists in the presentation of the fiancée to the "Grandmother Fire" of her new home; she is asked to grant her "a good life and many children."

As the attentive protector of the family, Grandmother Fire takes care of the herd of domesticated reindeer and patronizes the hunt. Before each meal, the mistress of the house feeds her by throwing a few pieces of meat into the fire and saying "Eat, satisfy your hunger. Give game, so that all may be satisfied." She is fed more abundantly at the beginning of the hunting and fishing seasons and when there is a big take: reindeer, elk, or bear.

To express her thanks, she counsels the hunter, shows him the path to follow, and forewarns him of his future success or failure by crackling and throwing sparks. If the fire sputters in a certain way, the hunters, certain that they will have no success, cancel their expedition. Fire helps the hunter in another, no less effective way, by purifying his traps, his weapons, and his clothes. The purification of objects with fire is regularly practiced in everyday life as well as in shamanic ritual. Fire's role as mediator with the supernatural is not limited to this: she transmits the offerings of men to other spirits, the most widespread method of sending grease or alcohol to the spirits consisting in pouring them into the fire.

Women are specially charged with caring for Grandmother Fire and making sure that she is never extinguished. At night, they leave a glowing birch log to burn. While traveling, they carry a brand from the last camp in a birch bark receptacle padded with wet moss, or else they slip a pinch of ashes into the lining of their sleeve. Before lighting the fire at a new camp, they shake the ash or the firebrand there as they ask Grandmother Fire to establish herself there. In times of war, they extinguished the fires of enemy clans and thus symbolically pledged their death.

In order to not offend Grandmother Fire, they carefully observe a series of taboos. One must never throw water or garbage into the hearth, as such things would glue her eyes together with soot. Neither should one stir up the fire too roughly or agitate a knife in the flames, for fear of wounding her. Most importantly, they are careful that tufts of hair from game do not fall into the flames. Yakut hunters are so cautious as to conceal the head of the fox under their hats in order to hide it from Grandmother Fire.

The master spirit of the fire abhors all that comes from the forest. The master spirits are in perpetual battle with them, but the antagonism is particularly virulent between the master spirit of the household fire and that of the forest. It is not that the forest dreads the fire that destroys it, as some people would explain it, but that fire, as a domestic symbol, is opposed to the forest as a symbol of the savage world and sometimes even of the world beyond. (Thus, in the forest, the realm of all kinds of spirits, the bear that the hunter

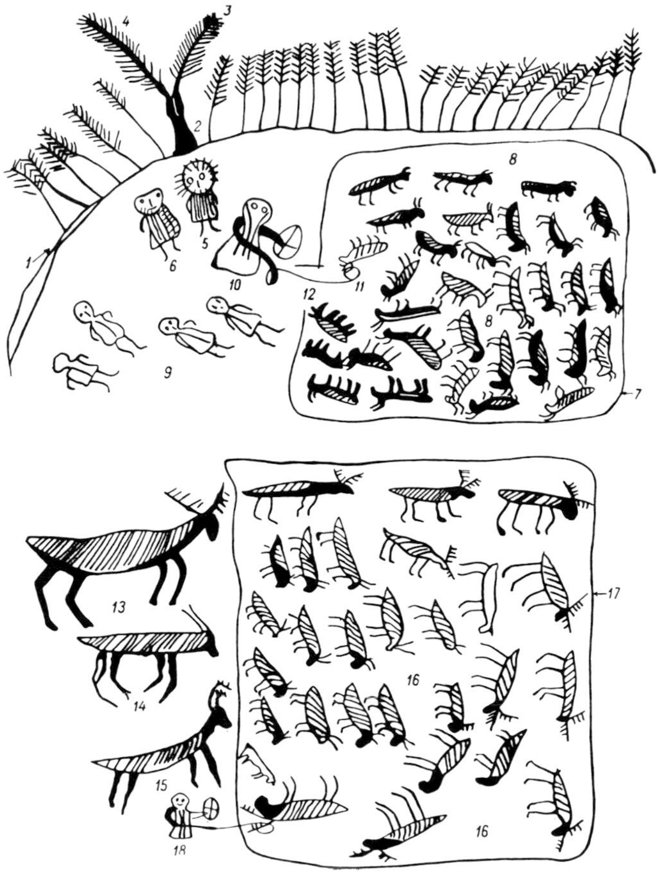

The shaman Pilja at the dwelling of the old mistress of the clan's territory (above) and at the dwelling of the old mistress of the clan (below), catching game for the hunters of the clan. (Šingkelavun ritual). Western Tungus drawing. After Anisimove, *Religija Evenkov* (1958).

Upper drawing

1. The mountain Uromi.
2. The clan's sacred tree.

3–4. The cedar (3) and the pine (4) that grow from the trunk of the sacred tree.

5. The mistress of the territory, Dunne Mušun or Dunne Enin.
6. Her old husband.
7. The stockade that encloses the Dunne's herd of deer.
8. The herd of the Dunne, made up of "souls," which, at the Dunne's command, will incarnate themselves in the reindeer and the elk of the forest.
9. The assistants of the Dunne's husband, who help him care for the herd.
10. The shaman Pilja, in the Šingkelavun ritual, lassoing the souls of the animals that the hunters will kill during the season.
11. The drum beater has been transformed into a leather lasso for the catch. The shaman will carry off the souls, which have become strands of wool and fur for the trip, in his drum.
12. The entrance to the enclosure.

Lower Drawing

13–15. The old mistress of the clan, Bugady Enintyn, represented in the form of three enormous female reindeer or elk.

16. The herd guarded on earth by the three Bugady.
17. The stockade around the enclosure.
18. The shaman Pilja lassoing the animals that his clan's Bugady has awarded him.

encounters is not an animal but a dead relative who has come to visit his descendants in a bearskin.) Although the meat of domestic reindeer may be grilled directly on the coals in the hearth, it is proper to put a receptacle between deer meat and the flames. This opposition reappears even in the killing of domestic reindeer and wild reindeer, which the Tungus do not kill in the same way, since the souls of wild reindeer come from the place of the master spirit of the forest, while those of domestic reindeer, like those of the people of the clan, are descended, under the surveillance of the celestial spirit, from territories which the clan possesses in the higher world.

2. *The master spirit of the forest.* The master spirit of the forest rules the species of animals that concern the hunters; it is he who drives into the hunter's traps a sable or fox taken in his preserves. It should be noted that the Yakut master spirit grants only animals hunted by means of traps, snares, or pitfalls, not those killed with the bow and, later, the gun.

The master spirit of the forest is named differently by different groups, but is best known in the literature by the Yakut name of Baj Bajanaj, "the rich Bajanaj." Among the Tungus he often has the name of Bainača or Bajan Ami, "the rich father." The master spirit of the Tungus forest so closely resembles his Yakut and Altaic homologues that it is believed that this personage was created at a time when these groups were still in close contact.

He appears sometimes as a bear or a sable of remarkable beauty, and sometimes as an old man dressed in sumptuous furs, who rides a reindeer, a dog, a bear, or a tiger, according to the region. The Tungus have preserved in their southern myths the memory of a master spirit of the forest who was a ravishing woman accompanied by a cortege of bears who took the place of dogs. Other Tungus myths speak of a woman who flees with the game at the slightest tinkling of metal. But this very ancient female character has disappeared from the pantheons of the nineteenth and twentieth centuries.

According to certain specialists, there were originally several master spirits, each specializing in an animal species or a type of trap, but they gradually became confused and combined into the present image of an old man who sometimes metamorphoses into a superb animal. One finds traces of these polyvalent Bajanajes among the Yakuts, where informants account for as many as seven, or sometimes eleven, Bajanajes, of which nine are brothers and two are sisters.

Possessed of a very acute sense of hearing, the master spirit of the forest demands that the departure for the hunt take place in utmost silence, and that all noise cease at the camping place. The same respectful silence should be observed at the time of offerings. On the other hand, when the hunter observes an animal caught in his trap, he should rejoice loudly and thank the Bajanaj with great bursts of laughter. In the evening in the forest, the Bajanaj comes to hear the stories told by the hunters around the fire. If the hunters succeed in making him laugh, the Bajanaj will send them abundant game the following day. This liberating power of laughter, which causes game to be released, has been attested with numerous mythic beings, from Sedna of the Eskimos, who lives at the bottom of the sea, to Gargantua of French folklore.

Being very cheerful, the Bajanaj also likes overstated praise. When he sends a musk deer, the Yakuts are supposed to act as if they think the animal is so huge that it cannot fit the frequency of tabooed words and the use of substitute terms, especially during the hunt or important rites, such as that of the bear cult. In order to combat them, the shaman uses trickery more often than strength. An Ul'č female shaman wanted to do away with a spirit who devoured all of the young children of a family. She had a wooden doll made, which she laid in the cradle. The spirit did not notice the difference and entered the doll. The shaman then simply crushed it with a hammer.

Wicked, greedy, boastful, stupid, and fearful, these spirits bear a surprisingly close resemblance to the devils that appear in our own medieval tales.

L.D./d.w.

Siberian Religion and Myths: The Example of the Tungus

I. The Peoples of Siberia

The various ethnic groups which populate Siberia belong to five great families. West of the Yenisey and in the Taimyr peninsula are the Finno-Ugric peoples, represented by the Ugrians (Xant) and the Samoyeds (Nenc, Enc, Nganasan, and Selkup). The Altaic family is made up of the Buryats, of Mongolian origin, who live around Lake Baikal, the Turks (among them the Yakut, who live on either side of the Lena, while the Altaic peoples, Tuvs, Tofalar, Šor, and Xaka populate the Altai mountains), and the Tungusic-Manchu branch (comprising Tungus [Evenk] extending from the Yenisey to the Sea of Okhotsk, Lamut [Even], Gold [Nanaj or Nanai], Ul'č, Udege, Orok, and Orochon living in the Amur River valley). The Paleo-Arctic peoples (Chukchee, Koryak, Kamchadals, and Yukaghir) wander as nomads on the northeasternmost corner of Siberia, and the Gilyaks live on the island of Sakhalin and at certain points on the opposite shore. Small groups of Eskimos are located near the Bering straits. Finally, a few Ket clans are situated on the middle Yenisey.

Though each ethnic group has elaborated its own pantheon and created its own spirits, they all have three basic categories of spirits: the great deity of the sky, the master spirits, and the shamanic spirits. They have all also developed a method of acting upon the spirits, namely, shamanism. The basic principles of this system, which make it possible to remedy the malevolent actions of the spirits and to obtain from some of them good hunting or fishing, remain similar throughout Siberia. Only the details vary: thus, the Chukchee shamans use hallucinogenic mushrooms to promote the trance, whereas in the rest of Siberia shamans attain this state without any help other than musical rhythm. Certain Paleo-Arctic shamans dress in women's clothing and live maritally with men, a practice that seems to be unknown elsewhere.

In order to illustrate Siberian beliefs, we prefer to describe the mythology of a single group, with all of its details and its particular flavor, rather than to offer an overview that would outline only the skeleton common to these mythologies. This will not, however, prevent us from occasionally mentioning other ethnic groups to point out basic resemblances.

We have chosen for this purpose a people typical of the Taiga, the Tungus. In addition to their features representative of hunters and reindeer breeders, the Tungus are the only people who are found scattered over the entire territory of Siberia, from the banks of the Yenisey to the shores of the Sea of Okhotsk by way of the forests of the Transbaikal.

Tungus shaman with his drum and his embroidered plastron made of reindeer skin. Paris, Musée de l'Homme collection. Photo Encyclopédie française/Daniel.

Before the revolution of 1917, the Tungus were hunters and breeders of reindeer and were organized into patrilineal clans. The clan was a union of relatives, all descendants of the same ancestor and possessing a common territorial hunting ground; it had a council of elders at its head. Besides the old men, three individuals enjoyed great prestige: the shaman of the clan, the civil chief who led the collective hunts, and the military chief who was in charge of the warring expeditions that were very frequent among the Tungus.

The Tungus lived in tents made of poles set into the ground in a circle and joined at the top, covered with reindeer skins in the winter and with birch bark in the summer. These two raw materials, skin and bark, were also used to make most clothing and household utensils.

Very broadly speaking, their economy might be characterized as one that depended on hunting in the winter and fishing and gathering in the summer. It is possible to distinguish three separate groups of Tungus, according to their way of life:

—the vagabond Tungus, who change their campsites in response to the vagaries of hunting and the pursuit of game;

—the nomadic Tungus, who breed reindeer and horses in the Transbaikal and go back and forth between their winter and summer campsites;

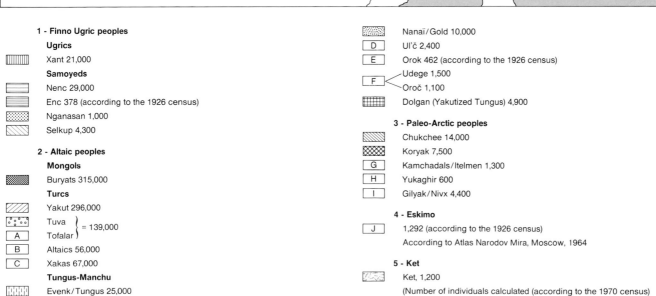

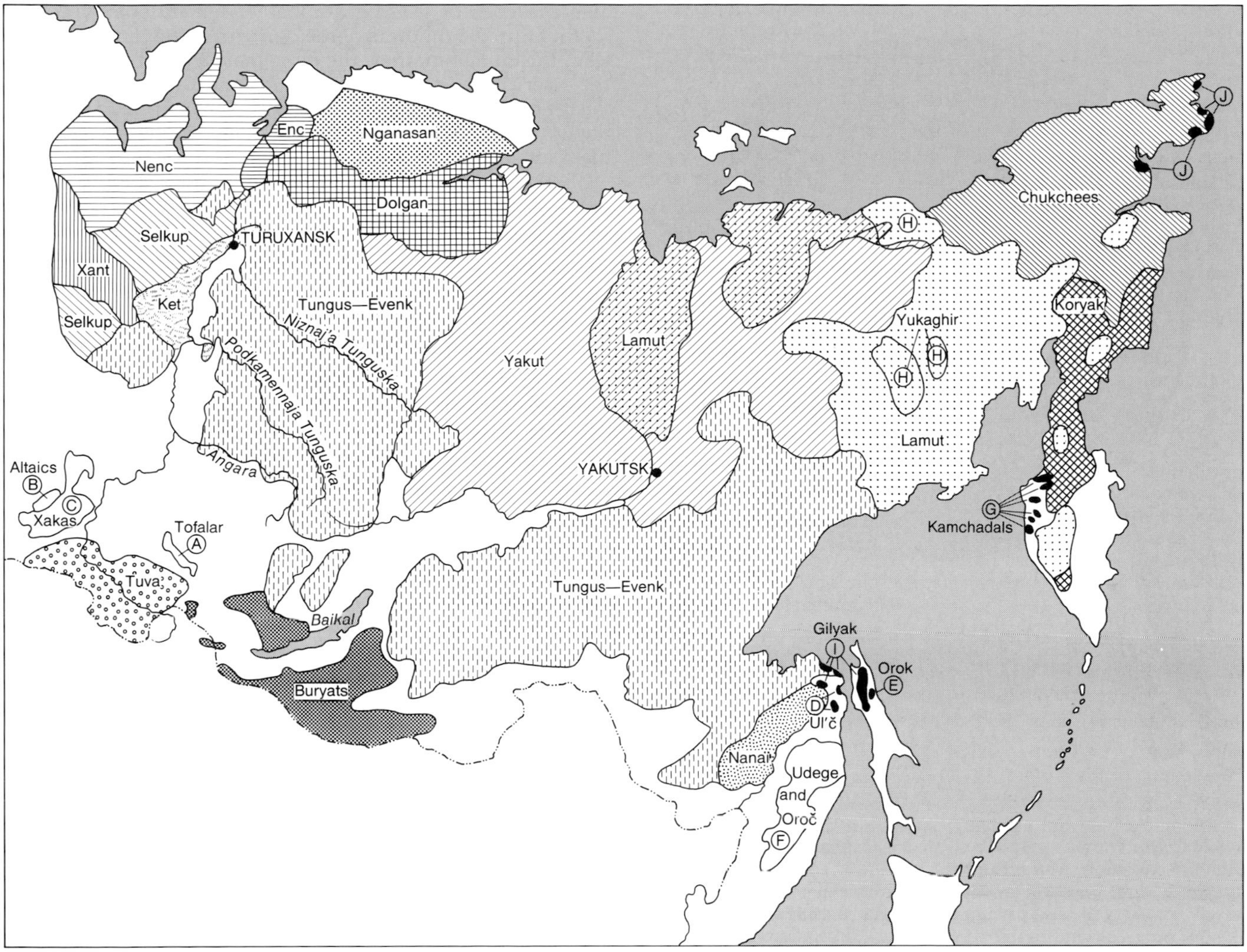

1 - Finno Ugric peoples

Ugrics

Xant 21,000

Samoyeds

Nenc 29,000

Enc 378 (according to the 1926 census)

Nganasan 1,000

Selkup 4,300

2 - Altaic peoples

Mongols

Buryats 315,000

Turcs

Yakut 296,000

Tuva } = 139,000
A Tofalar

B Altaics 56,000

C Xakas 67,000

Tungus-Manchu

Evenk/Tungus 25,000

Evenk/Lamut 12,000

Nanaï/Gold 10,000

D Ul'č 2,400

E Orok 462 (according to the 1926 census)

F Udege 1,500
Oroč 1,100

Dolgan (Yakutized Tungus) 4,900

3 - Paleo-Arctic peoples

Chukchee 14,000

Koryak 7,500

G Kamchadals/Itelmen 1,300

H Yukaghir 600

I Gilyak/Nivx 4,400

4 - Eskimo

J 1,292 (according to the 1926 census)

According to Atlas Narodov Mira, Moscow, 1964

5 - Ket

Ket, 1,200

(Number of individuals calculated (according to the 1970 census)

Märchen aus Sibirien (Jena 1940). F. LITKE (or F. LÜTKE), "Die Tschuktschen," *Archiv für die Wissenschaftliche Kunde von Russland* 3 (1843): 446–64.

(iii) Kamchadal/Itelmen

S. P. KRASHENINNIKOV, *La description du Kamtchatka,* Voyage en Sibérie 2 (Paris 1768). H. KUNIKE, *Märchen aus Sibirien* (Jena 1940).

(iv) Yukaghir

W. BOGORAS, "Tales of Yukaghir, Lamut and Russianized Natives of Eastern Siberia," *American Museum of Natural History, Anthropological Papers* 20 (New York 1918): 1–148. W. JOCHELSON, "The Jukaghir and Jukaghirized Tungus," *Memoirs of the American Museum of Natural History* 12 (New York and Leiden, part 1, 1910; part 2, 1924; part 3, 1926). H. KUNIKE, *Märchen aus Sibirien* (Jena 1940).

(v) Gilyak/Nivx

E. A. KREJNOVIČ, "Očerk kosmogoničeskix predstavlenij Giljak o. Saxalina," *Etnografija* 8, 1 (1929): 78–102. B. PILSUDSKI, "Schwangerschaft, Entbindung und Fehlgeburt bei den Bewohnern der Insel Sachalin," *Anthropos* 5 (1910): 756–74. L. ŠRENK, *Ob inorodcax Amurskogo kraja,* 3 vols. (Saint Petersburg 1883–1903). L. STERNBERG, "Die Religion der Giljaken," *Archiv fr̈ Religionswissenschaft* 8 (Leipzig 1905); *Materialy po izučeniju giljackogo jazyka i fol'klora* (Saint Petersburg 1908).

(d) The Eskimo

W. BOGORAS, "Eskimo of Siberia," *Memoirs of the American Museum of Natural History* 12 (New York 1910). E. NELSON, *The Eskimo about Bering Strait* (Washington 1900). A. OLLIVIER, "Sur les Esquimaux d'Asie," *Bulletin de la Société d'anthropologie,* 2d ser., 12 (1879). E. S. RUBCOVA, *Materialy po jazyku i fol'kloru eskimosov* (Moscow and Leningrad 1927).

(e) The Ket/Yenisey/Ostyak of Yenisey

E. A. ALEKSEENKO, *Kety: Istoriko-etnografičeskie očerki* (Leningrad 1967). V. I. ANUČIN, "Očerk šamanstva u enisejskix ostjakov," *Sbornik Muzeja Antropologii i Etnografii* 2, fasc. 2 (1914). K. DONNER, "Ethnological Notes about the Jenisey-Ostyak," *Mémoires de la Société finno-ougrienne* 66 (1933). H. FINDEISEN, "Zur Problematik des Seelenglaubens," *Europäischer Wissenschaftsdienst,* 1944; "Indochinesen in Nordsibirien," *Atlantis* 12:58–62.

Finno-Ugrian Myths and Rituals

I. The Finno-Ugrian Peoples

From the Atlantic to the Taimyr peninsula, the "archipelago" of Uralian peoples is strung across the whole of northern Europe and western Siberia as the vestiges of a continent which the increasing tide of Scandinavians, Russians, and Turko-Tartars has never ceased to wash over for the last two thousand years. Uprooted from their ancestral land by waves of backwash which stirred the people of the steppes beginning in the high Middle Ages, only the Magyar horsemen—apparently natives of present-day Bachkiria who were strongly Turkized by several centuries of contact with the Bulgars of the Volga and other southern neighbors—were able to found a state which was stable, durable, and soon to be Christian, in the heart of Europe before the year 1000. Finland—in which Swedish, although only a minority language, would remain the sole true language of the culture if not of the civilization until the end of the nineteenth century—would not obtain its independence until 1918. As for Estonia, it was only during the brief interval between the two world wars that it would escape, however briefly, from Russian power. All of the other peoples would only be independent at a period which was a prehistoric one for them—like the independence of the American Indians before the coming of the white man. All would remain more or less without writing until the revolution of 1917.

It is estimated that it was around 4000 B.C. that the two branches of the Uralic family—Samoyeds on the one hand and Finno-Ugrians on the other—separated. The Samoyeds—about 30,000 in all—are today spread over the immense stretch of tundra bordering the Arctic Ocean between the White Sea and the Taimyr peninsula; there remain only four Samoyed language groups, of which Nieniets, or Yurak, which is spoken by approximately 25,000 speakers, is by far the largest.

Several groups would successively break away from the common Finno-Ugrian: (1) At the beginning of the second millennium B.C., an Ugrian branch today represented by the Hungarians, on the one hand, and the Ugrians of the Ob—the Voguls and the Ostyaks (Mansi and Hanti)—on the other. (It should be noted that the majority of the non-Russian peoples of the Soviet Union are today officially designated by their names for themselves in their own languages. This reform, which followed the 1917 revolution, was made necessary by the often pejorative connotations attached to the names used by the Russians. Outside of the USSR, the old names borrowed from the Russians nevertheless remain in use by the majority of the Finno-Ugrians. We shall conform to this usage, indicating the indigenous ethnonym in parentheses when such is necessary.) (2) A Permian branch (from the city of Perm in the Urals) today represented by two languages: Zyrian (Komi) and Votyak (Udmurt), spoken, respectively, by 350,000 and 700,000 persons. (3) A Volgic branch, whose present-day branches, spoken in the region of the great bend of the Volga, are Cheremis (Mari) and Mordwin, with the latter subdivided into Erza Mordwin and Moksha Mordwin. There are approximately 500,000 Cheremis; the Mordwins, who number 1.3 million, are the third largest Finno-Ugrian people, after the Finns and the Hungarians, but before the Estonians. (4) Lapp, which is fragmented into numerous groups and whose position continues to give rise to much controversy. (5) The Balto-Finnic languages (previously referred to as the Finnish languages of the Baltic) of which the two largest groups are by far Finnish (4.5 million speakers), the primary language of Finland and also recognized, along with Russian, in the Karelian Republic in the USSR; and Estonian, spoken by 1 million people as their official language—alongside Russian, the federal language—of the Estonian Republic. Other Balto-Finnic languages are Veps, spoken by some 16,000 people in the Onega Lake region; Vote, spoken by certain families in the Leningrad district; and finally, Livonian, which, gone from Livonia, survives in some ten villages in Northern Kurland.

The linguistic connection uniting these different peoples in no way implies that they belong to a racial or cultural community. Ethnically the Hungarians are closer to their German, Slavic, or Latin neighbors than they are to any Finno-Ugrian people. The Finns and the Estonians more closely resemble the Scandinavians, Baltic peoples, and northern Russians—all of these being speakers of Indo-

Detail of a disk-shaped hair ornament discovered at Rakamaz; the representation is possibly of the *touroul*, the mythic bird of the ancient Hungarians. The birds it holds in its talons may be either souls that it is carrying to earth or symbols of its power. Nyíregyháza (Hungary). Josa Andras Museum. Photo Kalman Konya—Ed. Corvina, Budapest.

European languages—than they do their linguistic cousins, the Lapps. The Ugrians of the Ob and the Samoyeds are strongly Mongoloid. The hypothesis has even been advanced that the Lapps, and even the Ugrians of the Ob and the Samoyeds, may have replaced their own languages with Uralic languages.

If we also bear in mind that the Uralians, whatever their historical fortunes may have been, have nearly always been in a position of weakness and have never ceased to borrow from the ways of life, technical knowledge, beliefs, demons, and gods of their invaders and neighbors, it should not surprise us that the common foundation of Uralic mythology and religion is quite difficult to discern beneath the innumerable strata left by foreign contributions.

The task of the comparativist is made all the more difficult by the fact that we often have a very poor knowledge—or no knowledge at all—of the myths and rites of the ancient peoples under whose influence the Uralians fell. This is the case with the various Iranian peoples of the steppe—Cimmerians, Sarmatians, and Scythians—who are known to us especially through archaeological discoveries and the often unverifiable accounts of Herodotus. This is the case with the Baltic peoples, whose ancient religion has reached us only through vestiges of folklore and the hardly comprehensive testimonies of missionaries regarding their "pagan" superstitions. This is the case to a great extent with the Turko-Tartars, through the mediation of whom Islam exerted an influence upon the Cheremis and the southern Votyaks. To these one may add the possibility of a Paleoarctic substratum underlying the religions of the Lapps, Samoyeds, and Ugrians of the Ob.

II. The Sources

The documents which we have at our disposal for the study of Finno-Ugrian mythologies are relatively numerous but of very unequal antiquity, depending on whether these peoples were more or less distant from the seats of civilization. Their religion per se was first described from the outside by travelers or by missionaries charged with extirpating that religion.

The oldest written sources are also those which treat those beliefs which disappeared the earliest. The first allusions to the Hungarians appear in Arabic and Greek documents before the conquest of the Danubian homeland: these are rare, brief, and uncertain. More consistent are the testimonies contained in the Latin chronicles of the Middle Ages; much later than Christianization, they are nevertheless too often dictated by reasons of state.

The first written document on the religion of the Finns is a fairly dry and highly controversial versified compendium on the "gods" adored by the Hämians—the inhabitants of the province of Häme in western Finland—and by the Karelians. It is contained in the preface to the Finnish translation of the Psalter published in 1551 by Michael Agricola, the bishop of Turku. The first study dedicated to the religion of the ancient Finns is the *De superstitione veterum Finnorum theoretica et practica* of Chr. Lencqvist, which was published in 1782, and which was followed in 1789 by the *Mythologia fennica* of Chr. Ganander.

The Lapp religion was known fairly early, thanks mainly to Johann Scheffer of Strasburg (under his Latin name Johannes Schefferus), who, in his *Lapponia,* published in 1674 and immediately translated into German, English, French (1678), and Dutch, painted a remarkable tableau of beliefs and rites—based on his own observations but also taking into account all earlier sources—in which he devoted an entire chapter, complete with engravings, to what is today known as shamanism.

With the exception of a short hagiography of Saint Steven, apostle to the Zyrians in the fourteenth century, and of an allusion made to the customs of the Mordwins in a fifteenth-century Italian travel account, our first information about the religion of the eastern Finno-Ugrians dates mainly from the seventeenth and eighteenth centuries. In the nineteenth century, systematic studies were carried out, principally by Finns and Russians. The great name is that of Uno Harva—Holmberg before 1927—who published a series of monographs in German and Finnish whose authority still remains unquestioned. Under the title *Finno-Ugric, Siberian,* he published in English the first study of the ensemble of Finno-Ugrian religions.

Contrary to widespread general opinion outside of Finland, the *Kalevala*—that inspired compilation in which Lönnrot contributed so profoundly to the national consciousness of his people—is not a source which may be used directly in a scientific approach to ancient Finnish mythology. What Lönnrot wanted—and he succeeded magnificently—was to compose, drawing on oral poetry, an epic which would make the Finnish community proud of its traditions and which, by giving it a prehistory, would root it in history. To this end, he undoubtedly drew upon authentic folk texts, a great number of which he had collected himself in the course of his wanderings through the country. But he interpreted, interpolated, and wove them together with verses of his own making; and he restored them following the image which he himself had, influenced by the ideas of his century—notably those related to the origin of the Homeric poems—regarding a hypothetical ancestral epic of which the oral tradition would have passed on only certain sparse and corrupted fragments. He particularly eliminated all which did not appear to him to be sufficiently archaic, beginning with all that related to Christianity—introduced in Finland in its Roman Catholic form at least four centuries before the Reformation. The same reservations hold for the *Kalevipoeg*, the Estonian national epic which was compiled slightly later by Kreutzwald in imitation of the *Kalevala*.

Under its rough exterior, folklore by contrast offers researchers an exceptionally rich field of inquiry. Thanks especially to Finnish, Hungarian, and Estonian scholars, immense collections of oral texts (incantations, mythological poems, funerary lamentations, folktales, etc.) were collected throughout the Finno-Ugrian world. Customs and superstitions were—and continue to be—cataloged, analyzed, and compared. The interpretation of certain of these is not without its risks. Elements belonging to various cultural strata occur in them in a tangled form and are not always easy to isolate and date. The Finnish school has earned a deserved international reputation in this domain.

Vogul mask used in the ritual of the bear festival. Budapest, Ethnographic Museum. Photo Ferenc Cservenka.

Complementing this basic survey of written sources and oral tradition, paleolinguistics, the study of etymologies and layers of vocabulary, also affords important information which sheds light upon the depths of an even more distant past. This method has been especially applied to the Finnish (Joki, E. Itkonen, M. Kuusi) and Hungarian (Pais) spheres.

Finally, even though the culture of the Finno-Ugrian peoples was mainly based upon wood, a perishable material, it is likely that archaeology may be able to furnish us with very precious data for the reconstruction of the religious history of these peoples. It is certainly regrettable that entire regions, notably western Siberia, have been very inadequately explored. We may console ourselves by pointing out the importance of discoveries made in Hungary on several village sites and of necropolises dating from the time of the conquest.

III. Rituals and Myths of Hunting and Fishing

The rituals and myths of hunting and fishing belong to an archaic economy to which agriculture and herding—including the raising of reindeer in the great north—were added without ever wholly obliterating the manifestations of the archaic economy anywhere. The diversification of the master spirits is certainly not as great in northern Europe as in Siberia, where hunting and fishing even recently still constituted the principal, and sometimes nearly the only, sources of food.

The great keeper of game is the master of the forest. Thus we find among the Finns the names of Tapio and Hiisi which were mentioned by Agricola—the latter under the name of Hittavainen—in his double list of the gods of Häme and Karelia. The same function is fulfilled by the man of the forest, the Zyrian *vörsa-mort* or the Votyak *n'ules murt*, who was imagined to be "taller than the tallest tree" and highly enterprising with women. The Votyaks claimed that he was capable of growing and shrinking in size at will. He was also said to have only one eye. In this regard, the Cheremis and the Moksha Mordwins know of a couple made up of the Old Man and the Old Woman of the Forest. Among the Erza Mordwins, it was especially the latter who was invoked.

In a parallel fashion, all of the Finno-Ugrian peoples know of a master spirit of the water and of fish. Sometimes they even know of several, as in the case of the Cheremis, for whom every lake was until recently the domain of a particular spirit. This water spirit is generally anthropomorphic, sometimes male and sometimes female, but also capable of metamorphosing into a fish, most often the pike. It is fitting to offer it sacrifices, particularly the first catch of the fishing season. As with the Russians' *vod'anoï*, this is an often dreadful personage whose wrath is to be avoided.

The most spectacular and complex of the rituals of the hunt is certainly the bear cult, whose Finnish ritual was still being practiced in the nineteenth century and which continues even today among the Ugrians of the Ob and among the Samoyeds. The hunt, the kill, moving the animal to the village, cutting it up, and consuming it all take place according to a ceremony whose principal aim is to absolve the hunters of guilt in the eyes of the victim and to free them from guilt in their own eyes. The bear, whose real name is taboo—among the Voguls, for example, the name given to

Place of Samoyed worship. Engraving from Nordenskiöld, *Vegas färd* (1880).

the bear by men is not the same as that used by women—is often called the "man" or the "master of the forest." The dead bear is treated with deference. Women are absent during the greater part of the ceremony, probably because of the sexual power attributed to that arctic animal which most closely resembles man. The bear's skeleton is generally reconstituted and buried in order to allow for its resurrection; the skull is hung separately in a tree, outside the reach of wild animals; or else, as with the Voguls, strung from a post which is placed in the center of the village and constitutes the principal cultic site.

The worship of the bear should not be regarded as belonging exclusively to ancient Uralic culture, any more than the other rituals of the hunt. It may also be found among all of the Paleoarctic peoples of Europe, Asia, and America, and its prehistoric extension may have been much greater.

Myths and rituals of hunting and fishing are probably not the only vestiges of the ancient beliefs of these peoples. The cult of rocks, which is characteristic of the Uralic peoples of the Arctic, is undoubtedly also a legacy of the distant past. The best known example of this is the cult of the Lapps, who used to worship, under the name of *seite*, crags or mountains which were particularly outstanding for their shape, location, or size. Quite often the *seite* was to be found in a region which was said to be a part of the world of the dead.

The antiquity of various beliefs in domestic spirits is more difficult to determine. These beliefs gave rise everywhere to practices and rites which were generally very close to those which may also be found among the Scandinavians and the Russians. The house in which people live (or the nomads' tent), as well as the barn, the stable, the threshing area, and the sauna, each have their spirits. A domestic cult which is more complex than in other places is that which developed especially among the Votyaks and Cheremis. Its sanctuary is the sacrificial hut, which is connected to family and clan. Offerings destined for the spirit of the hut were generally placed unburned on the sacred board, which was regarded simultaneously as a domestic altar and the abode of the spirit. This spirit was connected with the earth.

IV. Shamanism

Shamanism, in the strict sense of the word, makes up an integral part of the Paleoarctic culture of Eurasia and America. Its prehistoric range seems to have been even wider: has it not been surmised that the famous and mysterious "staffs of command" found in certain prehistoric sites in France might have in fact been the "drumsticks" of a shamanic drum?

It was in this circumpolar culture that the widely attested shamanism of the northernmost Uralic peoples—the Lapps, Samoyeds, and Ugrians of the Ob—participated. It was, in fact, in its Lappish variant—which no longer exists today—that it was first described, although under the name of magic or sorcery.

Northern European and western Siberian shamanism hardly differ in their essentials from what is properly known as Siberian shamanism, as described elsewhere in this work. The shaman is first and foremost a mediator, healer, and diviner, capable of going into ecstasy and of communicating with the beyond. Not everyone who wants to can be a shaman, and the shamanic vocation is said to be connected to certain neurotic predispositions. Much has been said about Arctic hysteria. Shamans, however, are the exact opposite of psychopaths or the possessed. They are rather persons who "possess" spirits, whom they make their auxiliaries. If the depressive state which accompanies the first signs of a calling is troublesome and first provokes a movement of rejection on the part of the elected, the shaman later appears as an individual whose exceptional equilibrium originates from having mastered his initiatory neurosis.

We know of no Uralic shamanic customs that are analogous to those found, for example, among the Tungus. They are reduced to a minimum: a particular belt among the Lapps, a special hair style among the Samoyeds and the Ugrians of the Ob. On the other hand, the drum was indispensable. "Taking away our drums is like depriving you of your compasses," is what a Lapp is reported to have said once to the ecclesiastical authorities ordered to extirpate sorcery from the northern deserts. These drums were of different types according to the region. Four may be distinguished among the Lapps alone. The figures drawn with alder sap on the skin of the drum were more or less numerous and ordered. Sometimes two horizontal lines divided the surface into two or three "storeys," corresponding to the sky, the earth, and the subterranean world. The drum helped to provoke the shaman's ecstasy. It was also used in divination. This function explains the sometimes very high number—up to one hundred—of figures drawn on the drum. On the drum were placed—generally on the representation of the sun—a set of rings which were caused to move by striking the drumskin with a sort of drumstick made from a reindeer horn in the shape of a Y or a T. In this way one could know the future and also know to which god it was proper to sacrifice and which offerings were most acceptable. The drum was sometimes regarded as the vehicle of the shaman. The Lapp word *kannus*, which is used for a drum with an angular frame, means "spur" in Finnish.

According to our oldest sources on Lapland, adult women could not touch the drum. At the time of migrations, it was carried in the last sled, sometimes even by a different route which was far from any customary trail, in order to avoid the possibility of the great danger that might befall a woman from another community were she, in ignorance, to take the same route during the next three days.

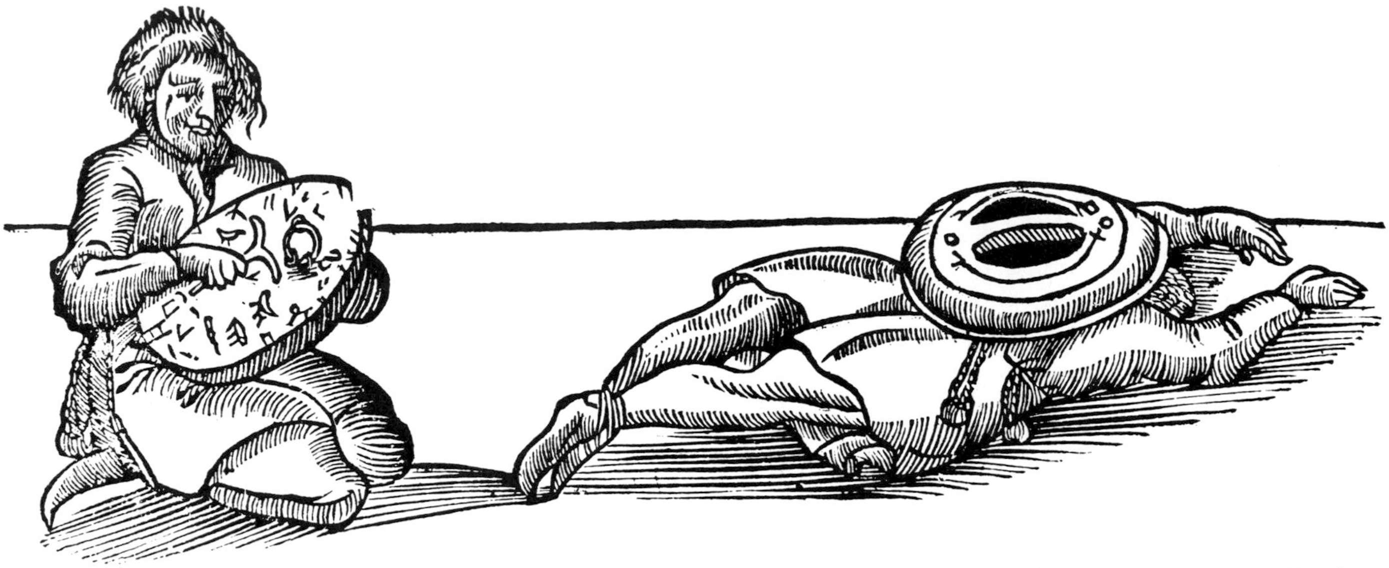

Lapp practicing divination with his shaman's drum and then throwing himself on the ground, his head almost completely covered by the drum. From Schefferus, *Lapponia* (1673).

In Lapland, the use of the drum was formerly the prerogative of the male head of the community; thus it is possible to speak of a sort of domestic shamanism. In serious or delicate cases, people nevertheless called upon individuals who were particularly known for their talents and their powers. Shamans did not, however, constitute a particular caste.

Shamanism appears to have an archaic legacy among the Uralic peoples. The same word for shaman is found in the Balto-Finnic languages (Finnish *noita,* Estonian *nõid*), in Lapp (*noaidi*), and in Vogul (*n'ait*). A number of traces of this religious complex seem be perpetuated in folklore, particularly in popular tales and in the superstitions of other Finno-Ugrian peoples, including the Hungarians. Does this give us the right to designate as shamans the *táltos* (pronounced *taltoś*) of the Magyar conquerors of the tenth century? This is uncertain, unless one takes the meaning of the word "shaman" in a very extended—perhaps over-extended—sense.

V. The Gods

We know almost nothing of the common Finno-Ugrian pantheon. It is certainly possible to find gods whose functions are more or less the same from one people to another: what archaic religion did not know of a sky god or an earth spirit? But the names of the gods—which are, moreover, often of foreign provenance—are never found in all the languages of the Finno-Ugric family. Only three names are common to at least two language groups: (1) the name of the god represented by the Finnish *Jumala* and the Lapp *Ibmel* (if the latter is not merely a borrowing, pure and simple, from the Finnish) (which today designate in both cases the god of the Christians) as well as by the Cheremis Jumo (which is unknown in Mordwin); (2) the name of the Lappish god Tiermes, who is generally identified with the Numi-Tõrem of the Ugrians of the Ob, but whose name has on numerous occasions been connected with that of the Celtic Taranis and the Scandinavian Thor; (3) the name of the Votyak god Inmar, which seems to be the same as the god Ilmari (Ilmarinen in the *Kalevala*) of the ancient Finns, although the derivation in both cases is anything but clear. Curiously, all of these are supreme gods, or at least gods of the sky or of storms. No less curious is the Indo-European word which yielded the Latin *deus* and the French *dieu,* which in Finnish is *taivas,* "sky," borrowed from a Baltic language.

According to Agricola's testimony (which uses the word *jumala* only in a Christian sense) the most important god of the ancient Finns was *Ukko* whose name means "good-man" or "old man"—a god of vegetation, rain, and thunder. His cult, together with that of Sampsa Pellervoinen—perhaps the Saint Samson of Orthodox Christianity, another divinity connected with agriculture—was celebrated in the course of a festival called "the basket of Ukko" (*Ukon vakka*) and seems to have been the occasion for orgies quite possibly of a ritual nature. Pellonpoika ("Peter-of-the-fields"?) was the god of barley and of beer. Rongoteus—whose name was, according to Haavio, a form of that of Saint Stephen the Martyr—was the god of rye. Virokannas—"John-of-the-incense"?—was the god of oats. Köndös—Saint Urban?—was the god of cleared ground. Ägräs was the god of turnips, peas, and beans. Although the etymologies which have been offered for these names are often fragile, it is likely that Agricola's list includes a number of Catholic saints who were forced into hiding by the Reformation and whose names were distorted by the popular language. It is important to stress that this is a double list: the dichotomy which opposes the "gods of the Hämeans" to the "gods of the Karelians" may be in part explained by the fact that Hämia and Karelia were, respectively, under the control of Sweden and thus of Rome, and within the sphere of influence of Novgorod and thus of Byzantium. It is nearly certain that the religion of the Balto-Finnic peoples of this period was a syncretism between ancient indigenous beliefs and the Christianity introduced by the Crusades. A similar syncretism continued into recent times, and even today it subsists here and there among the Lapps, the Votyaks, and the Ugrians of the Ob.

At times several syncretisms have succeeded one another. The Lapps incorporated several ancient Scandinavian gods into their most archaic gods, followed by—if we may allow ourselves the use of the plural—the "Christian gods."

On the first drum described by Scheffer are represented: on the higher "storey" Thor and the god the Lapps called "the Great Governor" (*Storjunkare*), each accompanied by a servant; below were Christ and the apostles; further down was the sun. No ancient god figures on the second drum (with the exception of the sun, an ambivalent figure), which shows only God the Father, Jesus, the Holy Spirit, and Saint John. On the fourth drum there are no Christian figures, but only "the god Tiuri," "the god Thor," "Thor's hammer," "the Great Governor," "a divine figure made of wood," and naturally, the sun.

What makes any comparison difficult is that it seems as if the gods of the Uralians, as a whole, had no proper names. Perhaps the supreme god was more or less the only one to dwell far enough away from men to be able to be called by his name without danger. Whatever is the case, the gods and spirits are nearly always designated by common names or by paraphrases. In other cases, the name used is often of an incontestably foreign source.

The sovereign god of the Lapps is called Tiermes only in the east. Elsewhere he is known as Radien ("the sovereign"), Veraldenradien, or Veraldenolmai ("sovereign of the world," "man of the universe"), which are names of Scandinavian origin. He is still called Atjek ("the old one, father"). Horagalles—whose name probably means "the old man of Thor"—is sometimes confused with him. The very name of Inmar, the supreme god of the Votyaks, seems to derive from the word *in/inm-*, "the sky." The same relationship exists in Finnish between the name of Ilmarinen and the word *ilma*, "air, sky." Inmar is constantly called *kildiśin*, "creator," *vordiś*, "feeder," etc.

The only thing that can be said for certain is that gods or spirits whose functions are comparable may be found among all of the Uralic peoples with few exceptions, as is also the case among their non-Uralic neighbors.

The elements and meteorological phenomena naturally have their divinities or their spirits; there are too many to list them here. Agricola mentions a "mother of the water." The Lapps honored a "man of the wind" (Pieggolmai) in olden times, who was called Ilmaris (cf. the Finnish god Ilmarinen) in the west, but who was perhaps influenced by the Scandinavian Njord. They also worshiped the sun, but, as far as we know, they never gave it a particular name.

The gods, like humans, often have families. Of course, divine couples are to be found, such as that formed among the Votyaks by *Inmar ataï* ("Inmar the father") and *Inmar anaï* ("Inmar the mother"), undoubtedly in the image of God the Father and the Mother of God. It is also undoubtedly Christian influence that gave rise here and there to the formation of trinities. Uno Harva reports that in the sacrificial formulas of the Votyaks of the old circle of Glazov, the trinity is called *Inmar-kildiśin-kuaź*, a compound in which *Inmar* means "God"; *kildiśin*, "the creator"; and *kuaź* ("air, sky, founder") designates the Holy Spirit.

The earliest sources mention a trinity among the Lapps made up of Radien-attje, "the reigning father" (a sovereign god who is identical to Ibmel), Radien-kieddi, his son, and Radien-akka, his wife, to whom is sometimes added Rananeida ("the maiden of the grass"), a goddess of renewal who is regarded as the daughter of the father god.

Just as the god of the sky is a man, the earth is everywhere "mother earth." The earth, however, was created by God. On the other hand, in every cosmogony water is considered to be the primordial and uncreated maternal element. This, as we have seen, does not stop lakes and rivers from harboring male and female water sprites, masters and mistresses of fishes to whom it is proper to pay homage. We should also point out that the Votyaks once honored a "mother sun" (*Śundy-mumy*) and a "mother thunder" (*Gudiri-mumy*), whose equivalents are not to be found elsewhere. Certain scholars, especially from the USSR, view these as traces of an ancient matriarchal society.

On the subject of the devil, Manker writes that the name of the devil in the Lapp language was a late borrowing from Finnish, and that "there does not appear to have originally been a being corresponding to the devil in Lapp mythology." This reasoning, which may be applied to all of the Finno-Ugrian peoples, is only partly convincing when one thinks of the force of vocabulary taboos regarding a character of such a dreadful nature.

VI. Agrarian Rites

The fertility of animals and plants depended upon the union of sky and earth—whose concrete manifestation was seen by the Estonians in spring lightning. Accordingly, the agrarian rites consisted primarily of prayers, offerings, and

Shaman's drum, with commentary by J. Schefferus (*Lapponia*, 1673) as follows: "Drum A: *a*, Thor; *b*, his servant; *c*, the great *Junker*; *d*, his servant; *e*, birds; *f*, stars; *g*, Christ; *h*, the apostles; *i*, a bear; *k*, a wolf; *l*, a reindeer; *m*, a bull; *n*, the sun; *o*, a lake; *p*, a fox; *q*, a squirrel; *r*, a serpent. Drum B: *a*, God the Father; *b*, men; *c*, the Holy Spirit, *d*, Saint Peter; *e*, difficult death; *f*, an oak; *g*, a squirrel; *h*, the sky; *i*, the sun; *l*, a wolf; *m*, a lavaret; *n*, a wood grouse; *o*, friendship with the wild reindeer; *p*, Anund, son of Erik, the owner of this drum, kills a fox; *q*, gifts; *r*, an otter; *s*, friendship with other Lapps; *t*, a swan; *v*, symbol allowing one to find out something about others, for example, whether someone who is ill can be cured; *x*, a bear; *y*, a pig; β, a fish; γ, a psychopomp. The T-shaped objects are the beaters for the shaman's drum." The three rings shown at the bottom of the illustration are placed on the drum and used for divination.

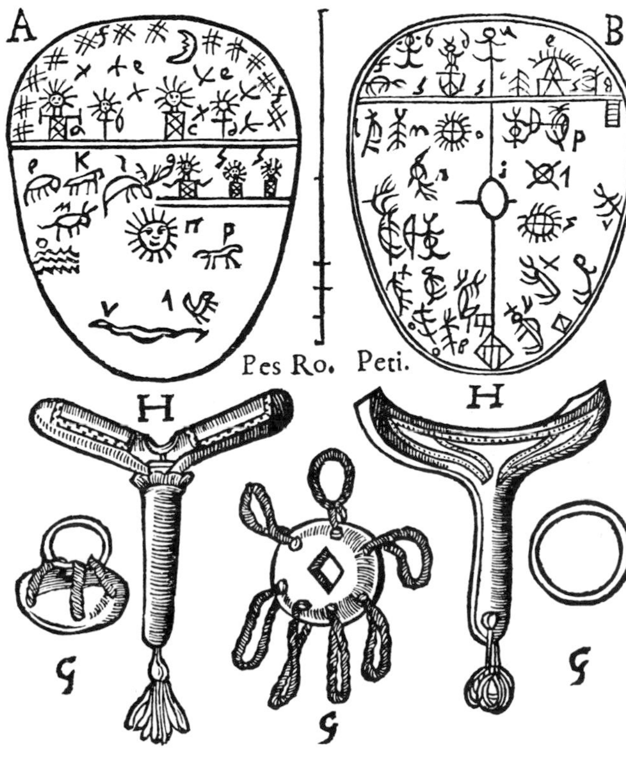

Cheremis priests kneeling in the sacred wood. Photographed by U. Harva, 1913. Helsinki, Suomalaisen Kirjallisuuden Seura. In Lehtinen and Kukkonen, *Iso Karhu–The Great Bear* (Helsinki 1980).

sacrifices addressed to the celestial powers: thunder, wind, and sun, and chthonic powers—especially the earth, but also, according to different peoples, the different "mothers" of grain, barley, cereals, and grass, or else the "father of the field"; these would later give rise to their Christian substitutes, of whom the most important were Saint George and Saint Elias.

Prayers were either simple formulas, incantations, or long mythological poems whose recitation was sometimes combined with an elaborate dramatic performance.

In a very widespread custom, white animals were sacrificed to the celestial powers, and brown or black animals to those of the earth. This custom is found not only among the agriculturalists of the forests, but also among the reindeer herders of the tundra and the nomads of the steppe who were the ancient Hungarians: the Lapps sacrificed white reindeer to the sun, and the sacrifice of a white horse is well documented among the Magyars of Árpád. The same symbolism is undoubtedly found in the milk libations offered by the Estonians to thunder gods in earlier times.

The earth was felt to be a living being. The Livonians forbade the spilling of boiling water upon it or the setting of the blade of a knife into it, for fear of wounding it. In order to remain fertile, the earth asked to be fed. The Cheremis had the custom of sacrificing a black cow to it, or sometimes a bull, whose skin and bones were then buried in order to help the springtime resurrection. In the Vyatka region, each peasant then went out into his field and placed an egg on it or poured out a spoonful of soup as he said, "Eat, earth, and bring us a good harvest."

But man could also, by means of a phenomenon of cosmic contagion, contribute to setting in motion the process of fertility. Such was the meaning of the great annual festivals that were connected to the principal moments of agricultural life: planting, bringing in the harvest, the summer and winter solstices, etc. The ritual meals and the sexual excesses which sometimes more or less licitly accompanied them—they are stigmatized by Agricola—accelerated the circulation of food, sap, and blood. In certain regions of Finland the planter was supposed to be naked. (Virgil wrote in his *Georgics*, "Make yourself naked for plowing and sowing!"). But magic worked both ways. At the feast of Saint John, the festival of the summer solstice, young girls in search of a husband rolled about naked in the fields of rye so that the night dew, by moistening their skin, would make them irresistible. Mircea Eliade believes that this custom was aimed at activating the growth of young plants. The participants seem also to have sought to appropriate the erotic power of vegetation for themselves.

VII. The Mythic Narratives

Naturally all of the Finno-Ugrian peoples know a certain number of origin myths, on the subject of which comparative studies still have been made in only a partial way. It is in the Finnish domain that these myths have been most carefully analyzed, and it is also in this domain that we have the greatest number of documents at our disposal. Popular Finnish poetry even distinguishes a particular genre, that of "birth" (*synty*), a narrative poem which related the creation *in illo tempore* of a being, an animal, an element, a substance, etc. Knowledge of the conditions in which prototypes were created gives man power over the representatives of such genera. In the *Kalevala*, Väinämöinen, the "eternal knower," recites the "birth" of iron in order to stop blood from flowing from wounds caused by iron.

The creation of the world is accounted for in an archaic myth which has innumerable variants but which in essence holds that a bird—often an eagle, but sometimes a diver—lays an egg in the primordial sea, or sometimes on an island; that the egg breaks, and that the two halves of its shell become the sky and earth, with the white and yolk giving birth to the moon and sun.

The myth known as the myth "of the great oak," a gigantic tree whose branches obscure the light of the sun, moon, and stars, and which could only be cut down by a little man who came out of the sea, is common among Balto-Finnic and Volga-Finnic peoples, but is also found among the Baltic peoples from whom it was undoubtedly borrowed. Among the Indo-Europeans, the oak is related to the god of thunder. The Baltic name of this god, Perkunas—which is also found in Perun, the name of the principal god of the Slavs, in the mysterious Scandanavian god Fjörgyn, and in the Finnish name of the devil, Perkele—may be derived from the ancient name of the oak represented by the Latin *quercus*. But the fact that the world tree was an oak for the Finnic peoples does not necessarily mean that this representation was not known to their ancestors under the form of a fir or a birch, for example, as is the case for numerous peoples further east. The memory of a mythic tree which is simultaneously the tree of life, the world tree, and the shamanic tree seems to have echoes even in popular Hungarian folktales.

Representations of the earth, sky, and heavenly bodies are most often generally the same for the Finno-Ugrians as for their neighbors. The sky is often described as a cover or as the fabric of a tent, of which one side, which was left to flap, provoked the birth of the wind by its movements. Several groups believed that the sky was lower toward the south and that only a narrow passage allowed migratory birds to return to their mythic abode, known in Finnish as *lintukotolainen*, "the house of the birds." They imagined that, at the place at which the sky met the earth, a land existed that was peopled by minuscule men; some would see in this an echo of much more southern beliefs about the Pygmies.

In the late spring, the Votyaks (Udmurts) sacrifice two sheep, a white one and a black one. First the white sheep is sacrificed to Inmar, the sky god. Photographed by U. Harva, 1911. Helsinki, Suomalaisen Kirjallisuunden Seura. In Lehtinen and Kukkonen, *Is Karhu—The Great Bear* (Helsinki 1980).

If by myths we mean a more or less sanctified archetypal representation, many legendary or marvelous accounts are not really myths. It is nevertheless often difficult to decide, since ancient myths could also survive in a degenerate form, as is often the case with folktales. On the other hand, accounts of historical acts may become obscured with time so as to become invested with all the functions of myth. How is one to classify, for example, the account of the death and resurrection of the Lemminkäinen or the cycle of the forging and abduction of the *sampo*, episodes which are well known through the *Kalevala?* Yet another problem is that of the legendary accounts of the birth of the Hungarian nation and the discovery, through the agency of a marvelous deer, of the new Danubian homeland.

VIII. The Cult of the Dead

The Finno-Ugrians, as has been shown by Ivar Paulson and others, early made the distinction between a "free soul" and a "corporal soul." The former was conceived as the extracorporal manifestation of an individual, his alter ego, which, in this life, could at certain times separate from the body and lead an independent existence, as occurs in dreams, in the shamanic trance, or in the "loss of the soul," by which a certain group of diseases were explained. The corporal soul, attached to the body for the duration of its terrestrial life, could sometimes be broken down into a "vital soul," the "breath," charged with the functions of physical life, and an "I soul," corresponding to the psyche.

The cult of the dead was practiced in various forms, apparently by all the Finno-Ugrian peoples. The free soul of the dead was supposed to lead in the beyond a life which was most often imagined as a reverse image of the terrestrial life. It was sometimes thought that the dead were rejuvenated, and that after becoming very small, they were reborn among the living. Elsewhere it was believed that the dead lived with their heads below their feet. In several Hungarian sepulchers dating from the time of the Conquest, it has been possible to ascertain that the position of the buttons on the clothing of the dead had been reversed; similarly, the sword was placed on the right side rather than on the left. We should again point out the custom—which is also well documented among the Russians—of sacrificing to the dead "backwards." The ceremonies took place, not "in the direction of the sun," but "against the sun." Thus one turned toward the west, and not the east, to say the prayers. The clothes of the participants were worn inside out and backwards.

The living were responsible for assuring the well-being of the dead through prayers, offerings, and sacrifices. The normal mode of disposal of the dead was inhumation; cemeteries have been extremely important aspects of ritual always and everywhere. Among the Karelians, the dead person was laid out in a kind of small wooden house with "windows" through which one could supply the dead person with food and other offerings. The Samoyeds and Uralians of the Ob used to have the custom of exposing their dead in trees. It is nevertheless probable that the aim of this custom was to place the remains of the dead out of the reach of wild animals while awaiting the thaw that would allow for inhumation. But the practice was connected with one that continued in Karelia into recent times: to hang the offerings for the dead in trees which were specially pruned and were regarded as sacred, trees called *karsikko* in Finnish. Among the Votyaks, all the members of the clan, that is, all the inhabitants of several villages, participated in certain ceremonies. Sacrifices in memory of the dead took place on the third, seventh, and fortieth days after the funeral. A very important ceremony took place on Holy Thursday.

It does not appear that the Finno-Ugrians had—before their first contacts with Christianity or at least with Islam—an idea of a differentiated afterlife made up of a paradise for the just and a hell for the wicked. The dead were above all physically present in their sepulchers. The tomb was the house of the dead, and the cemetery was a village whose inhabitants formed families, were married, procreated, and died; the "old one," a mythic ancestor and the first occupant of these places, held authority there.

Although the coexistence of these two representations appears contradictory, several Finno-Ugrian peoples imagined that there was also a "land of the dead," far to the north or west. The best-known example of this is *Tuonela*, which is so richly treated, as we know, in the *Kalevala*.

J.-L.M./d.w.

BIBLIOGRAPHY

A. ALFÖLDI, *Medvekultusz és anyajogú társadalmi szervezet Eurázi**ában*** (Nyk 1936); "An Ugrian Creation Myth on Early Hungarian Phalerae," *American Journal of Archaeology* 73 (1969). E. ARBMAN, "Shamanen, extatisk andebesvärjare och visionär," in Å. HULTKRANTZ, *Primitiv religion och magi* (Stockholm 1955); Underjord och heliga fjäll i de skandinaviska lapparnas tro. Arv, Bd. 16 (Uppsala 1960). P. ARISTE, Vadja rahva usund. V 36 (1932). I. I. AVDJEJEV, "Dramatičeskije predstavljenija na mjedvjež'jem prazdnike u mansi," *Sovjetskij Sjevjer*, nos. 3–4 (1935). Ö. BEKE, "Tscheremissische Texte zur Religion und Volkskunde," Oslo Etnografiske Museum, bulletin 4 (1931); "Texte zur Religion der Osttscheremissen," *Anthropos* 29 (1934). BERGSLAND and CHRISTIANSEN, "Norwegian Research on the Language and Folklore of the Lapps," *JAI*, 80 (1950). J. W. BOECLER and F. R. KREUTZWALD, *Der Ehsten abergläubische Gebräuche, Weisen und Gewohnheiten* (Saint Petersburg 1854). P. BOGAJEVSKIJ, "Očerki religioznykh predstavljenij votjakov," EO 1980 (1890). M. A. CASTRÉN, "Föreläsningar i Finsk Mytologi," *Nordiska resor och forskningar* (Helsinki 1853). V. A. ČERNJECOV, "Predstavljenija o duše u obskikh ugrov," *Issljedovanija i matjerialy po voprosam pervobytnykh religioznykh vjerovanij*, Trudy Instituta Etnografii 51 (1959). B. COLLINDER, *The Lapps* (Princeton 1949). I. DIENES, *Les Hongrois conquérants*, Corvina, ed. (Budapest 1972). V. DIÓSZEGI, "A sámánhit emlékei a magyar népi müveltségben" (Budapest 1958); a résumé of theses presented in this work has been published in German in *Acta Ethnographica* 7 (1958): 97–135; "A Pogány magyarok hitvilága" (Budapest 1967); A honfoglaló magyarság hitvilágának történeti rétegei. A világfa. Népi kultura—népi társadalom, 2–3 (1969). C. M. EDSMAN, Studier i jägarens förkristna religion: Finska björnjaktsriter, Kyrkohistorisk Årsskrift (Uppsala 1954); "Bear Rites among the Scandinavian Lapps," *Proceed. of the IXth Intern. Congress for the History of Religions* (Tokyo 1960); *Studies in Shamanism* (Stockholm 1967). M. ELIADE, *Shamanism: Archaic Techniques of Ecstasy* (Princeton 1964). J. ERDÖDI, Uráli csillagnevek és mitológiai magyarázatuk, Budapest, A Magyar Nyelvtud. Társaság kiadványai, no. 124 (1970). FJELLSTROM, *Kort berättelse om Lapparnas Björna-fänge* (Stockholm 1755). CHR. GANANDER, *Mythologia fennica* (Åbo 1789). B. GAVRILOV, "Povjer'ja, obrjady i obyčai votjakov Mamadyšskogo ujezda," *Trudy IV arkheologičeskogo sjezda* (Kazan 1891). G. GJESSING, "Sjamanistisk of Laestadiansk ekstase hos samene," SS, V (Oslo 1953). M. HAAVIO, *Suomalaiset kodinhaltiat* (Porvoo and Helsinki 1942); *Väinämöinen, Eternal Sage*, FFC 144 (1952); *Karjalan jumalat* (Porvoo and Helsinki 1959); *Heilige Haine in Ingermanland*, FFC 189 (1963); "Suomalainen mytologia," WSOY (1967). P. HAJDU, *Uráli népek* (1975), a work by a double team of Finnish and Hungarian specialists under the direction of P. Hajdu. A. HÄMÄLÄINEN, "Ihmisruumiin substanssi suomalais-ugrilaisten kansojen taikuudessa," *MSFOu* 47 (1920); Der voršud-mudor-Kult der Votjaken, ESA 6 (1931); "Das kultische Wachsfeuer der Mordwinen und Tscheremissen," *JSFOu* 32 (1937). U. HARVA (originally Uno Holmberg), "Die Wassergottheiten der finnisch-ugrischen Völker,"

MSFOu 32 (1913); "Permalaisten uskonto," *SU* 4 (1914); "Über die Jagdriten der nördlichen Völker Asiens und Europas," *JSFOu* 41 (1925); Die Religion der Tscheremissen, FFC 61 (1926); *Finno-Ugric, Siberian: The Mythology of All Races,* vol. 4 (Boston 1927); *Suomalaisten muinaisusko* (Porvoo and Helsinki 1948); *Die religiösen Vorstellungen der Mordwinen,* FFC 142 (1952); "Lappalaisten uskonto," *SU* 2 (Helsinki 1915). J. HAUTALA, "Myytit ja kvasimyytit," *Kalavalaseuran vuosikirja* 37 (Porvoo 1957). L. HONKO, Krankheitsprojektile, Untersuchung über eine urtümliche Krankheitserklärung, FFC 178 (1959); Geisterglaube in Ingermanland, 1, FFC 185 (1962); *De finsk-ugriska folks religion,* Illustreret Religionshistorie 1 (Copenhagen 1968); "Role Taking of the Shaman," *Temenos* 4 (1969). M. HOPPÁL, A mitológia mint jelrendszer, Jel és közösség (Budapest 1975). Å. HULTKRANTZ, "Swedish Research on the Religion and Folklore of the Lapps," *JAI* 85 (1955). A. IPOLYI, *Magyar Mythologia* (Eger 1854). T. I. ITKONEN, "Heidnische Religion und späterer Aberglaube bei den finnischen Lappen," *MSFOu* 87 (1946). G. JAKOVLJEV, *Religioznyje obrjady čeremis* (Kazan 1887). C. JOHANSSON, Om kultplatser och heliga områden i Torne och Lule lappmarker, Svenska Landsmål (Uppsala 1944). *Kalevala:* French translation by J. L. Perret (Stock 1931), also in English. K. KANDRA, *Magyar Mythologia* (Eger 1897). K. F. KARJALAINEN, *Die Religion der Jugra-Völker,* 1–3 (Porvoo 1922–27). R. KARSTEN, *Samefolkets religion* (Helsinki 1952). L. KETTUNEN, "Tähelepanekuid vepslaste mütoloogiast," *EK,* 1925; "Vermlannin suomalaisten uskomuksia, taruja ja taikoja," *KV* 88 (1935). M. G. KHUDJAKOV, "Kul't konja v Prikam'i," *IGAIMK* 100 (1932). J. KROHN, "Suomen suvun pakanallinen jamalanpalvelus," *SKST* 83, 1 (1894); "Suomalaisten runojen uskonto," *SU* 1 (1914); *Skandinavisk mytologi* (Helsinki 1922); *Zur finnischen Mythologie,* 1, FFC 104 (1932). M. KUUSI, *Kirjoittamaton kirjallissus,* vol. 1 of Suomen kirjallisuus, Suomenkirjallisuuden Seura/Otava (Helsinki 1963). T. LEHTISALO, *Entwurf einer Mythologie der Jurak-Samojeden* (Helsinki 1924); *Der Tod und die Wiedergeburt der künftigen Schamanen* (Helsinki 1937). CHR. E. LENCQVIST, *De superstitione veterum Fennorum theoretica et practica* (Aboae 1782). A. LOMMEL, *Shamanism: The Beginnings of Art* (New York and Toronto 1967). O. LOORITS, *Liivi rahva usund,* 3 vols. (Tartu 1926–28), includes German summary, *Der Volksglaube der Liven; Estnische Volksdichtung und Mythologie* (Tartu 1932); *Gedanken-, Tat-, und Worttabu bei den estnischen Fischern* (Tartu 1939); *Eesti rahvausundi maailmavaade* (Stockholm 1948); *Grundzüge des estnischen Volksglaubens,* 3 vols. (Lund 1949–60); *Hauptzüge und Entwicklungswege der uralischen Religion,* Folklore-Studies 17 (Tokyo 1958). EVELINE LOT-FALCK, *Les rites de chasse chez les peuples sibériens* (Paris 1953). J. LUKKARINEN, Inkeriläisten kotijumalista, SMA 26 (1912); Inkeriläisten praasnikoista, S4: 11 (1912); "Inkeriläisten vainajainpalveluksesta," *MSFOu* 35 (1914); Tietoja susi-ihmisistä Inkerissä (1914). W. MAINOV, "Les restes de la mythologie mordvine," *JSFOu* 35 (1889). E. MANKER, *Die lappische Zaubertrommel,* 2 vols. (Stockholm and Thule 1938, 1950); "Några lapska kultplatser," *Ymer* 66, 2 (1946); *Lapparnas heliga ställen* (Stockholm 1957); *Fangstgropar och Stalotomter* (Stockholm 1960). C. MÉRIOT, "Une réponse religieuse à une situation de dépersonnalisation ethnique en Laponie: Le mouvement laestadien," *Cahiers du Centre d'études et de recherches ethnologique de l'Université de Bordeaux,* 2, no. 3 (1975). H. H. MICHAEL, *Studies in Siberian Shamanism* (Toronto 1963). R. MITUSOVA, Mjedvježij prazdnik u aganskikh ostjakov Surgutskogo rajona. Tobol'skij kraj, no. 1 (1926). B. MUNKÁACSI, Seelenglaube und Totenkult der Wogulen. Keleti Szemle (1905); "Volksbräuche und Volksdichtung der Wotjaken," *MSFOu* 102 (1952). V. NALIMOV, Njekotoryje čerty iz jazyčeskogo mirosozercanija zyrjan, *EO* 57 (1903); Zagrobnyj mir po vjeronanijam zyrjan, *EO* 72–73 (1907). H. PAASONEN, "Über die ursprünglichen Seelenvorstellungen bei den finnischugrischen Völkern und die Benennungen der Seele in ihren Sprachen," *JSFOu* 26-4 (1909). D. PAIS, *A magyar ősvallás nyelvi emlékeiből,* Akadémiai kiadó (Budapest 1975). I. PAULSON, Å. HULTKRANTZ, and J. JETTMAR, *Les religions arctiques et finnoises* (Paris 1965). I. PAULSON, *Die primitiven Seelenvorstellungen der nordeurasischen Völker* (Stockholm 1958); "Die Tierknochen im Jagdritual der Nordeurasischen Völker," *ZE,* 84, 2 (1959); Seelenvorstellungen und Totenglaube bei nordeurasischen Völkern, *E,* 1960, 1–2; Schutzgeister und Gottheiten des Wildes (der Jagdtiere und Fische) in Nordeurasien, AUS-SSCR 2 (1961); *Himmel und Erde in der Agrarreligion der finnischen Völker* (Stockholm 1963); "Der Mensch im Volksglauben der finnischen Völker," *ZE* 88-1 (1963); "Seelenvorstellungen und Totenglaube der permischen und wolga-finnischen Völker," N. Vol. 9, 2 (1964); "Outline of Permian Folk Religion," *Journal of the Folklore Institute* 2 (1964); Le gibier et ses gardiens surnaturels chez les peuples ouraliens, *SFU* (1965); "Die Wassergeister als Schutzwesen der Fische im Volksglauben der finnischugrischen Völker," *AEthn,* 1966. O. PETTERSON, "Jabmek and jabmeaimo," Lunds Universitets Årsskrift, vol. 52, 6 (Lund 1957); "Tirmes-Dierbmes-Horagalles-Thor," in *Knut Lundmark och världsrymdens erövring* (Lund 1961). F. V. PLESOVSKIJ, O vozniknovjenii i razvitii kosmogoničeskikh mifov komi i udmurtov, *VKFU* (Syktyvkar 1965). G. N. PROKOFIEF, Ceremonija oživljenija bubna u ostjakov-samojedov, Izv. Leningradskogo gos. Universiteta, 2 (1929). JE. D. PROKOFIEVA, Kostjum sel'kupskogo šamana, Sbornik muzjeja antropologii i etnografii AN SSSR (1950). J. OVIGSTAD, *Kildeskrifter til den lappiske Mythologi* (Trondheim 1903, 1910); Lappische Opfersteine und heilige Berge in Norwegen, Oslo Etnografiske Museums skrifter, vol. 1, 5 (Oslo 1926). G. RANK, "Zum Problem des Sippenkultes bei den Lappen," *AV* 9 (1954); "Lapp Female Deities of the Madder-akka Group," *SS.,* 6 (Oslo 1955); *Die heilige Hinterecke im Hauskult der Völker Nordosteuropas und Nordasiens,* FFC 137 (1949). A. V. RANTASALO, *Der Ackerbau im Volksaberglauben der Finnen und Esten,* FFC 30–32 (1919–20). E. REUTERSKIÖLD, *Källskrifter till lapparnas mytologi, Bidrag till vår odlings häfder,* vol. 10 (Stockholm 1910); *De nordiska lapparnas religion* (Stockholm 1912). S. RHEEN, En kortt Relation om Lapparnes Lefwarne och Sedher, etc., Svenska Landsmål, vol. 17, 1 (Uppsala 1897). G. RÓHEIM, *Hungarian and Vogul Mythology* (Locust Valley, NY, 1954). A. SAUVAGEOT, "Mythologies des peuples de langue ouralienne," in *Mythologies des steppes, des forêts, et des îles* (Paris 1963); *Les anciens Finnois* (Paris 1961). J. SCHEFFERUS, *Lapponia* (Frankfurt 1673). TH. SEBEOK and RR. J. INGEMANN, *Studies in Cheremis: The Supernatural* (New York 1956). W. STEINITZ, "Totemismus bei den Ostjaken in Sibirien," *Ethnos,* nos. 4–5 (1938). D. STRÖMBACK, "The Realm of the Dead on the Lappish Magic Drums," in *Arctica: Essays Presented to Ake Campbell* (Uppsala 1956). A. TURUNEN, "Über die Volksdichtung und Mythologie der Wepsen," *SF* 6 (1952); *Kalevalan Sanakirja,* 1953. Z. ÚVÁRI, Az agrárkultusz kutatása a magyar és az európai folklórban (Debrecen 1969). J. VASILJEV, Übersicht über die heidnischen Gebräuche, Aberglauben und Religion der Wotjaken, *MSFOu* 18 (1902). V. M. VASILJEV, Matjerialy dlja izučenija vjerovanij i obrjadov čeremis, 10 5, 10 (1915). A. VILKUNA, *Das Verhalten der Finnen in "heiligen" Situationen,* FFC 164 (1956); Über den finnischen haltija "Geist, Schutzgeist," *AUSSSCR (SON)* 1 (1961). K. VILKUNA, Vuotuinen ajantieto, Otava (Helsinki 1968). G. VJERJEŠ-ČAGIN, Staryje obyčai i vjerovanija votjakov, *EO* 83 (1910); Votskije bogi, JAOIRS, 1911, 7. W. VON UNWERTH, *Untersuchungen über Totenkult und Odinverehrung bei Nordgermanen und Lappen* (Breslau 1911). M. WARONEN, *Vainajainpalvelus muinaisilla suomalaisilla* (Helsinki 1898). Y. WICHMANN, "Tietoja votjakkien mytologiasta," *S* 3 (1893): 6. K. B. WIKLUND, "En nyfunnen skildring av lapparnas björnfest," *MO,* 6 (1912); "Saivo: Till frågan om de nordiska beståndsdelarna i lapparnas religion," *MO,* 10 (1916). D. ZELENIN, "Tabu slov u narodov vostočnoj Jevropy i sjevjernoj Azii, I," *SMAE* 7 (1929).

PART

10

The Americas and the South Pacific

The Mythology of the Inuit of the Central Arctic 1145
Native American Myths and Rituals of North America 1152
The Creation of the World in Native American Mythology 1160
The Sun Dance among the Native Americans: The Revival of 1973 1163
Mesoamerican Religion 1165
Mesoamerican Mythic and Ritual Order 1169
Mesoamerican Creation Myths 1173
Mesoamerican Religious Conceptions of Space and Time 1176
The Sky: Sun, Moon, Stars, and Meteorological Phenomena in Mesoamerican Religions 1180
The Earth in Mesoamerican Religions 1184
Fire in Mesoamerican Mythology 1187
The Mesoamerican Image of the Human Person 1188
Cosmic Disorder, Illness, Death, and Magic in Mesoamerican Traditions 1189
Myths and Rituals of the South American Indians 1192
Indians of the South American Forest 1194
Religions and Cults of the Societies of the Andes 1201
Religious Thought and Prophetism among the Tupi-Guarani Indians of South America: The Land Without Evil 1206
Religions and Mythologies of Oceania 1208
Papua New Guinea 1224

The Mythology of the Inuit of the Central Arctic

In the mid-1970s, the population of the Inuit—spread over more than twelve thousand miles of coastline from eastern Siberia to the lands lying east of Greenland—was approximately one hundred thousand. Inuit, "the human beings" (or its variants Yuit and Suit), is the term by which they refer to themselves; but better known, since the end of the seventeenth century, is the term "Eskimo," which the French borrowed from the Algonquians; it means "eater of raw meat."[1] Those who live in Greenland, after two and a half centuries of Danish colonial presence, refer to themselves as Kālādlit.

The Inuit are distributed as follows: approximately two thousand in Siberia, thirty thousand in Alaska, twenty thousand in Canada, and fifty thousand in Greenland.

The ancestors of the Inuit (or the Proto-Eskimos) came from Asia some ten thousand years ago, crossing over the Bering Strait, which at that time connected Siberia with Alaska. Then, after they had lived in Alaska for five thousand years, their descendants (called Paleo-Eskimos) began to emigrate eastward, eventually reaching Greenland as well as the Quebec-Labrador peninsula, where the pre-Dorset and Dorset cultures would develop.

Four thousand years later (barely a thousand years ago), a new culture called the Thule developed in northern Alaska. This was characterized by its skin boats and its dogsleds. In less than four centuries, the Thule culture extended its influence to encompass all of the Arctic regions of North America, from Alaska to Greenland.

These ancestors of the Inuit were remarkably well equipped for hunting marine mammals (including the right whale), but they also hunted land mammals (especially the caribou).

This final great wave of migration which prehistory reveals to us may be viewed in connection with the great linguistic and cultural homogeneity observable from Greenland to north Alaska, though the southern Alaskan groups are different from the northern group both culturally and linguistically. Other differences appear in certain regions of the Inuit territory: the best known are those which have been observed among certain island groups (such as the Sagdlirmiut of Southampton Island) or continental groups (such as the Caribou Inuit, west of Hudson Bay), as well as among the Ammassalimmiut of Greenland, on the western edge of the Inuit zone.

I. Inuit Mythology

Inuit mythology, in anthropomorphizing the natural environment and in establishing divisions between that environment and the social milieu, reflects and serves as the foundation for social order and customs. Most beliefs and individual and collective rites, in the everyday organization of life, refer everything to that mythology.

This mythology of hunters follows an unpredictable course in which connection counts for more than explanation. A mythology of small groups, it treats social relationships at their most basic level. As a vast system of relationships and symbols, the mythology is often compared by the Inuit themselves with oneiric productions, as dreams and myths are based on the same order for them. When we realize, moreover, that death and sleep are states of the same nature for the Inuit (which explains the appearance of the dead in dreams), a panorama of mental activities and productions opens up before us.

II. Mythic History and the Emergence of Culture

It was thought for a long time that Inuit mythology contained no coherent and detailed explanation of mythic history or the emergence of culture and was essentially composed of fables about animals, heroic epics, and accounts of accidental events of no general interest.[2] We shall attempt to show that this notion does not stand up to meticulous examination and, indeed, that it arises from the fact that our Western societies are used to treating their history in a very explicit and linear fashion, while the Inuit, on the other hand, are a hunting society with an oral tradition that speaks in its own nonlinear and often indirect fashion through a mass of myths, rites, and prescriptions. Theirs is a history in which many developments are merely implied or simply defined by their absence in accounts which apparently say nothing about them.

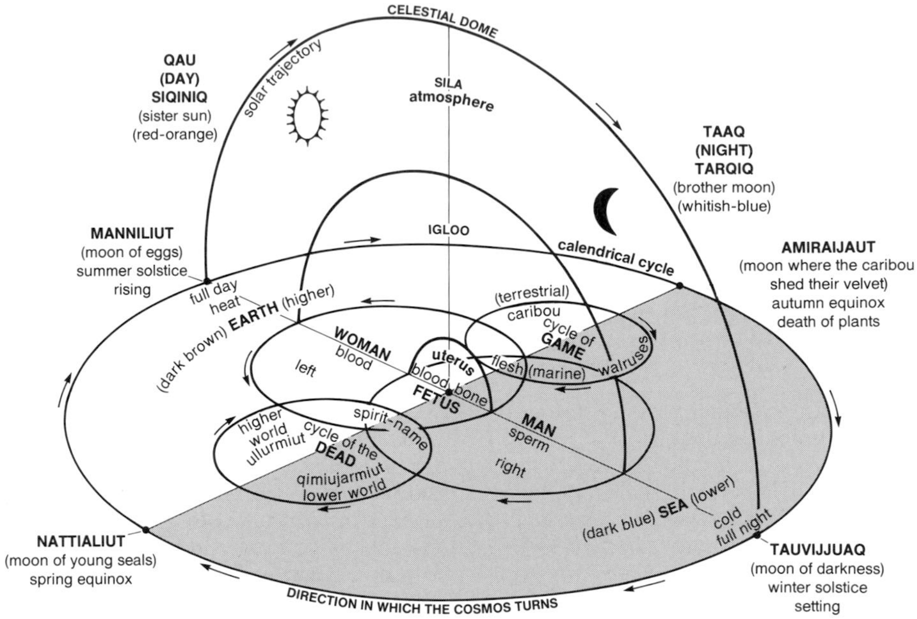

Differentiation, complementarity, and analogical construction in Inuit thought. Three-dimensional representation.

I will attempt to reconstitute their mythic history from data collected principally by K. Rasmussen in the central Arctic in 1921–24, and completed by data that I collected in the same region between 1971 and 1978.[3] A scientific analysis of this remains to be done, but the pioneering work accomplished by C. Lévi-Strauss for Native American mythologies reveals the benefits that may be derived from a systematic application of the structural method to the mythology of the Inuit.

1. *The Conception of the Universe and of Its "Prehistory"*

For the Inuit of the central Arctic, the universe in the primordial period included the earth which was, properly speaking, a sort of round disk washed by the sea. It was populated by animals and by humans who were not Inuit. It upheld, with the help of four pillars, the celestial vault which constituted another world populated with animals after the image of the earth. Just below the terrestrial disk was a cramped world in which it was impossible to stand up straight, below which was a final lower world which also replicated the earth and was populated with animals.

It then came to pass that the pillars that held up the celestial vault became dislocated and caused the earth to pitch, along with its inhabitants, which explains the presence of so many spirits beneath the terrestrial mound. A diluvian rain fell from the sky and drowned all other life.

2. *The Life-Giving Earth in the Time of the Great Blackness*

"In the time that followed there appeared two small mounds of earth from which were born two men, two adults, the first Inuit. They soon wished to reproduce, and one of them took the other to be his wife. The wife-man became pregnant and when his time came, his companion, anxious to bring the fetus out, composed a magic song:

Here is a man
Here is a penis
May he form a passage there
A great passage
Passage, passage, passage.

This song split the penis of his partner, who was transformed into a woman. All of the Inuit descend from them" (Rasmussen 1929, 252).

The first man was named Uumarnituq and the first woman Aakuluujjusi. They brought forth animals either by creating them or by bringing them back from other worlds (Saladin d'Anglure 1974).

In these earliest times it was always dark on earth. All was somber, and neither places nor animals could be made out. There were no heavenly bodies in the sky, there was no ice on the sea, neither tempest nor storm nor lightning nor winds. At the bottom of the sea, trees grew, which would sometimes wash up on the shore.

At that time the Inuit were poor and ignorant, with few hunting instruments and no knowledge of game: the only animals they hunted were the lagopus and the Arctic hare. In order to see their prey, they wet their fingertip with saliva to make it luminous, and pointed it in the air. But they often had to be content with scratching the ground and eating the earth, which at that time was their primary food. For clothing, they had only the sparse and fragile skins of birds and white foxes.

Among the first animals of this age were the crow, the white fox, the wolf, and the bear. But there was confusion between the world of animals and the world of humans. Humans could easily transform themselves into animals and animals could metamorphose into humans—to whom they thus became very close, speaking the same language, living in similar habitations, and hunting in the same way in spite of the differences between their respective habits.

There were no marine mammals, no big game, and thus no taboos. Life was without great danger but also without the real joy that follows effort and exertion.

There were no shamans in that time: people were afraid of disease and were unaware of the rules of life and of ways of arming themselves against danger and wickedness. They nevertheless discovered the protective power of amulets. First among these was the shell of the Itiq (anus) sea urchin, which one person would point toward the diseased area of the patient while farting, at the same time as another person was blowing on the diseased organ: these two acts combined all of the vital force emanating from the human body.

Among the first humans, it was not rare for women to be sterile; thus they would go out in search of "children of the earth," babies that were to be found in the ground. They had to go far away and to search for a long time to find boys, whereas there was an abundance of girls. Death did not exist, and the number of Inuit increased progressively. (After Rasmussen, 1929, 1931)

These narratives show us the essential place occupied by the earth (*nuna*) in Inuit mythological thought—not only as the generator of the human race, but also as regulator of Inuit social reproduction in the first times of humanity. On the demographic level it furnished babies to sterile women, and on the economic level it afforded essential food in a time when game was rare and difficult of access. These accounts also show us the importance of the new humanity's discovery of the magical effectiveness of breath and of the spoken word. Sexual difference is created by a song, and the first case of healing is by means of the vital breath (associated with the sea urchin).

Many natural constraints remain, however, to be overcome: the creation of woman indeed allows man to free himself in part from a dependence on mother earth for procreation, but feminine sterility is still great; the search for small game allows him to explore a new solution to the problem of provisionment, but the earth continues to be his principal food, and the endless darkness hinders any advance in hunting. A new danger threatens humanity, that of overpopulation, as death does not exist. Finally, the important role played by woman for the increase of human beings, either by procreating or by collecting the "babies of the earth" in the course of long journeys, creates a new dependence for man, who remains ignorant, poor, and nearly sedentary because of his inability to hunt.

3. Light, Death, and the Beginnings of Culture

The magical power of words was progressively explored and put to work by humans or by the metamorphosed animals who resembled them, in an attempt to surmount the obstacles that threatened the survival of the new humanity.

"One day the crow, meeting the white fox, said that he wanted light, the better to find his food. But the fox preferred the dark, the better to pillage the places where men hid their meat. The crow then cried 'qau qau qau' (light . . .), while the fox retorted 'taaq, taaq, taaq' (darkness . . .). The crow won out, and since that time day has alternated with night" (Saladin d'Anglure 1974).

"According to several myths of the central Arctic, the first Inuit lived on the island of Millijuaq in the Hudson Strait. They became so numerous that the island began to rock slowly in the sea under their weight. The people panicked until an old woman cried, 'May humans die, because there is no more room for us on earth; may they make war and disperse'; and humans became mortals, made war between themselves, and dispersed in every direction" (Rasmussen 1929, 92; Boas 1907, 173; Saladin d'Anglure: field notes).

With the appearance of the "short life" and the alternation between day and night, humans disengaged themselves further from the tutelage of the earth, which was characterized by darkness and endless life. Woman is again implicated in this process of differentiation and discontinuity, which simultaneously affirms her status and marks the dawn of culture while ensuring human survival. A variant of these two myths, from Greenland, further attributes to the same person the origin of day and of the short life.

Now that they had light, the Inuits could truly acquire technical knowledge and develop hunting. Qau, the radical which means light, is also found in compounds in the words "forehead" and "knowledge."

"At this time they had nothing to harness dogs with, and discovered that their houses (made of snow, stones, or peat),

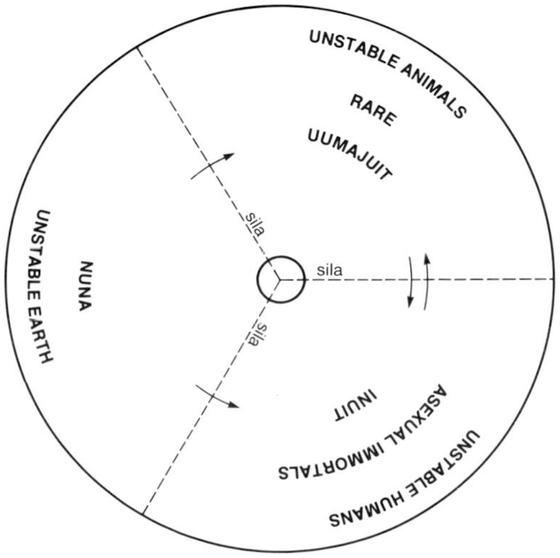

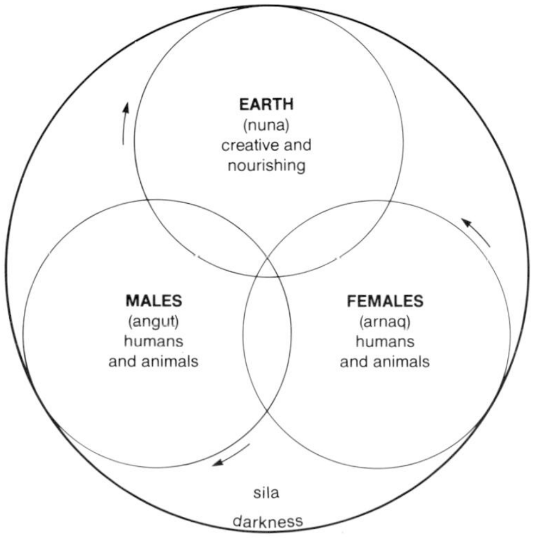

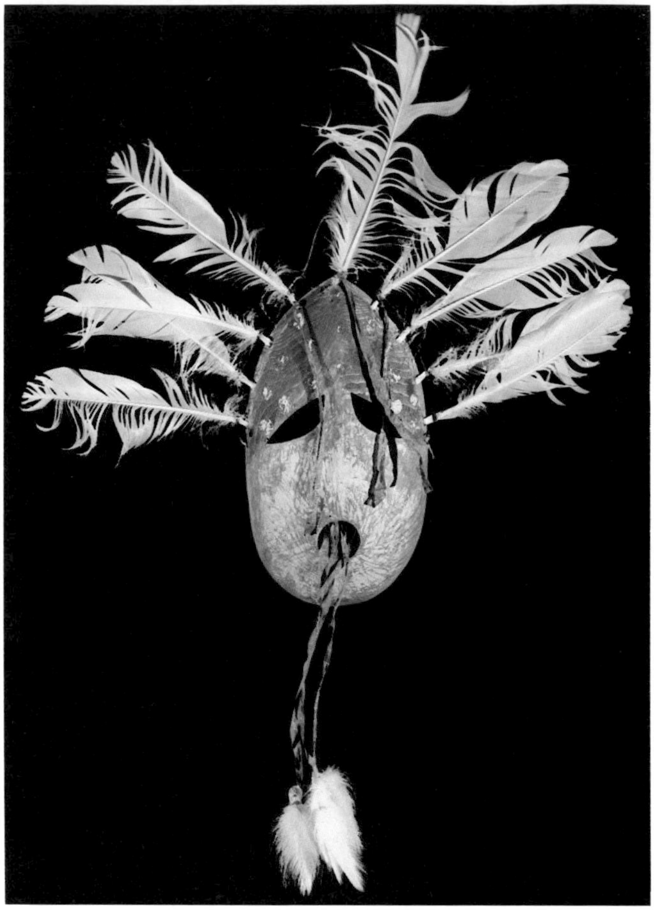

Mask, "Spirit of the Mountain." Sitka, Alaska, Sheldon Jackson College. Courtesy Amon Carter Museum, Fort Worth, Texas.

In mythic times, animals could easily turn themselves into human beings. Illustration of the myth of the woman who married an eagle and left him when she discovered his way of life. Drawing by Davidialuk Alasuaq. Povungnituk, Canada, B.S.A. collection.

which were animated by spirits and endowed with life, had the power to move about with their occupants inside by sliding over the ground when certain magic words were pronounced. They thus used them to go to places in which game was abundant. This continued until the day the Inuits complained that many children were being killed by the houses as they fell from their beds while the houses were moving—at which time the houses suddenly ceased their movement" (Rasmussen 1929; Saladin d'Anglure 1974).

Oil was not used to fuel lamps as it was possible to burn fine snow.

4. Contradictions, Human Disorders, and the Need for a Cosmic Order (Sila)

The destruction of humanity had now been averted by the appearance of death, and thus of a certain demographic equilibrium. The exploitation of game had also been rendered possible by the light of day. But no sooner were men slightly more liberated from their primary dependence on the earth than they commenced to use their new powers of antagonism and war: they brought on death and transgressed the rules they had sought to establish in order to organize their social relationships and their relationships with nature.

The sun, moon, stars, thunder, lightning, the cold wind from the north, and the warm wind from the south were all living beings, either human or animal. Their own misbehavior or the mistreatment they had suffered made them climb up into the sky, where they came to participate in the new world order, the cosmic order of Sila. Sila is at once air, ordered movement, cosmic periodicity, the rationality of the mind, and the understanding of and respect for this order.

"The sun and the moon were brother and sister. One day the brother was deceived by his mother: while he was suffering from sore eyes, she made off with his first white bear, which she ate in secret instead of sharing it in common as is the rule for the first game brought in. When his eye was healed by a dive which gave him great visual power, he caused the death of his mother by harpooning a great beluga while she was attached to the thong of his harpoon to help him in his hunt" (Rasmussen 1929).

Symbolically cutting the umbilical cord that attached him to his mother, he attached her to the beluga with the cord that was the thong of his harpoon, thus sacrificing her to his game (a social product), following the rule of the social distribution of products.

"Having become orphans, the brother and sister had many adventures until the day when, under the cover of darkness, he took advantage of her sexually. When she discovered his identity after blackening his face with soot, she reacted violently, cut off one of her breasts, and threw it at him, saying, 'If you love me so much, eat this.' Then she picked up the breast he had refused, made a torch of it, and fled into the sky, where she became the sun, Siqiniq. He pursued her with another torch—which went out—and he became the moon, Taqqiq" (Saladin d'Anglure 1974).

By her voluntary mutilation and the sacrifice of her fertility, Siqiniq established the foundation for another rule of distribution: that of exogamy or matrimonial exchange. Involuntarily incestuous, taken advantage of in a darkness which recalls the blackness—and thus the confusion and continuity—of the earliest times of the earth, Siqiniq (the sun) is now placed in a celestial position of luminosity and mobility, with an ordered trajectory and a productive seasonal periodicity.

Her severed and bloody breast, which her blood brother did not dare to consume, was never to give milk; this breast, having become a flaming torch and shining sun, would now warm humanity. Furthermore, through its symbolic representation, the oil lamp, it would illumine the microcosm constituted by the domestic family and its new rule of exogamy. By means of the cooking that it makes possible, it finally establishes a definitive separation between the bleeding woman (by virtue of her reproductive properties) and bloody meat (the game produced by the hunter). Henceforth, this separation is marked on the face of the woman in the form of a radiating facial tattoo, a sort of symbolic cooking which is effected by inserting soot from an oil lamp under a girl's skin after her first menstruation.

Her brother Taqqiq (the moon), of powerful vision and overflowing sexuality, emerges from his earthly adventure both darkened and frustrated. He nevertheless becomes a celestial instrument of this order and of its reproduction. The principal agent of the division of the calendar, he is also charged with making sterile women fertile, bringing game to unfortunate hunters, and defending orphans who have been mistreated and disfavored on earth.

"It was also a brother and a sister who were the source of thunder and lightning. They wished to avenge themselves upon the adults who had reprimanded them because of their overly noisy games. They began to produce thunder and lightning with firestones and a dried skin; when they urinate, it rains on humans" (Saladin d'Anglure 1974).

As for the winds, they are controlled by a male and a female spirit, whose attributes are described in many accounts:

> The parents of the baby giant Naarsuk were assassinated; when he was found, the people were astonished by his size and strength—he could hold up three women seated on his erect penis. He was abandoned with nothing but laced skin for clothing. He rose into the air and became the spirit-lord of the wind (the cold north wind) which rushes out when his laced swaddling clothes come unlaced. Another wind spirit, this one female, lives in a snow igloo: when the heat of her lamp makes holes in the walls, the warm southern wind blows on earth. (Rasmussen 1929, 1931; Saladin d'Anglure 1974)

All of these sidereal or atmospheric spirits, through their position and the order of their movements, constitute Sila: to move in the direction of the sun is to "act according to Sila" (Petersen 1967). Mankind progressed and began to gain control over its reproduction.

5. *The Ecological Order or the Failure of Female Autonomy*

The primordial couple, the ancestors of the Inuit, caused a number of animals to appear on earth.

"One day Aakuluujjusi took her trousers and transformed them into a caribou whose fur resembles, by its coloration, the trousers of a woman. She gave the animal sharp teeth and long tusks. Then, taking off her jacket, she made a walrus with horns on its head. But the Inuit took fright before these animals that attacked them on land and in the water: she therefore decided to interchange their horns and tusks, and kicking the forehead of the caribou she broke some of its teeth to render it inoffensive, and caused its eye sockets to bulge out to weaken its vision. She then said, 'Stay far away, like true game.' But the caribou were now too quick for the hunters, so she reversed the direction of the hair on their bellies to slow them down" (Rasmussen 1929; Saladin d'Anglure 1974).

These were the first big game animals of the Inuit, terrestrial and marine game around which they would organize their new socioeconomic life. New relationships began to be established among humans and between animals and humans, replacing the primordial confusion. It still remained to circumscribe the limits of humanity and of animality and to establish the nature of their connections. The myth of Uinigumasuittuq contributes to the resolution of these problems:

> Uinigumasuittuq ("she who did not wish to marry") lived with her parents and their dog Siarnaq. She refused all suitors. Nevertheless, one day she accorded her favors to a handsome visitor. It was their dog, metamorphosed, whom no one had recognized; he returned often and she became pregnant. The father then discovered the identity of their guest and in fury he placed the couple on an island. The girl made the dog swim back and bring food from her father's house. The father supplied them many times, but then one day he loaded the dog with rocks, causing him to drown. The girl soon gave birth to beings who were half human and half dog. On the advice of their mother, they tore their grandfather's kayak apart when he came to bring them meat; then, overwhelmed, Uinigumasuittuq sent her children away so that they might survive. The first puppies were set adrift in a southerly direction in the sole and upper leather of a boot; they disappeared in the fog amid a metallic din and became the ancestors of the white man. She sent others toward the continent to the south, and these became the ancestors of the Indians. Another group became the ancestors of the Tunit, a prehistoric people; and the final pup, sent toward the north, became the ancestor of the Ijirait, invisible beings who live on caribou.
>
> After the dispersal of those who were the originators of the human races, she returned to her father's home. But twice more she refused her suitors (a metamorphosed caribou and wolf) before she finally agreed to follow a third, a petrel who had taken a human form. He took her in his kayak, but too late she discovered his ugliness and his sarcastic laugh, which disgusted her. She then succeeded in escaping, with the complicity of her father, in a boat made of skins. But the petrel discovered her flight and stirred up a terrible storm; in panic the father threw his daughter into the water, and when she tried to hold on to the boat's sides he cut off the fingers of both of her hands and poked out her eyes. She sank into the sea, but bearded seals and ringed seals were born from her severed hands. In despair, the father let himself be covered by the tide and joined his daughter and his dog at the bottom of the sea, where they have lived ever since. They control the movements of marine game animals and punish after death all persons guilty of sexual infractions—of bestiality in particular. (Saladin d'Anglure 1974)

Several observations may be made about this new episode in the slow emergence of culture as it is conceived by the Inuit.

The first of these concerns what may be called Uinigumasuittuq's attempt at female autonomy. Since the incest taboo gave woman her trade value, it was tempting for her to take advantage of this new power, which is what she attempted to do in striving to keep control of her sexual life—first by refusing her suitors, and then by offering herself to the dog or the petrel. These two unhappy experiences culminate in a double mutilation, the first a moral one, with the loss of her children, who could survive only through dispersal and cultural division, and the second a physical one, with the loss of her hands and eyes, which separated her from culture and from her productive-reproductive functions.

Her banishment to nature brought on by her blindness, her inability to produce, and her immobilization at the bottom of the sea cannot help but recall the primordial time. Her human origin nevertheless gives her a very important role as an intermediary between humans and the new extension of nature constituted by marine animals, her creatures, as well as an intermediary between the Inuit and the new extension of humanity constituted by the new human races, her children.

The resources she brings to men give her a status which balances that of the earth: they establish her as regulator of the ecological order, but only with a heavy counterpart—the final submission of women to social rules of matrimonial exchange as established by men. Men would henceforth have free access to the women of the group, within the limits of the incest prohibition.

The differentiation between hunters and game animals leads to the exclusion of animals who have become game, both from matrimonial alliances and from sexual relationships (bestiality), and this differentiation founds the new order.

But parallel to this differentiation and to the woman's banishment to nature, there is a symmetrical and inverse rapprochement of nature toward man through the promotion of the dog. The dog is promoted to the rank of a means of production in hunting and transportation, is promoted to a personal name in addition to a species designation (a privilege which it alone shares with humans), and is finally promoted to domesticity and even a certain commensality, which confers almost magical powers upon it. When a man is seriously ill, his life may be saved by sacrificing the life of his dog, who thus carries away the ailment with him.

The acquisition of the dog as a means of production corresponds in mythic history to the acquisition of the kayak. Both are very explicit symbols of productive virility, of the social expansion of masculine sexuality. In several regions of the central Arctic, a man's right to marry depends upon the acquisition of a kayak whose prow is metaphorically designated by the name of *usuujaq* ("that which resembles a penis").

Man's access to productive mobility coincides exactly with the loss of mobility on the part of houses (and thus of women, which they symbolize), which now must fulfill their destinies as containers.

It is interesting to note further that, in a rebellious leap against her father after he had killed her dog/lover, Uinigumasuittuq attempts to destroy this male supremacy by sending her canine children out to attack the paternal kayak.

6. The End of Metamorphoses and the Recovery of Continuity

The appearance of the great distinctions—of man/woman, life/death, darkness/light, humans/game animals, and terrestrial game/marine game—beyond resolving certain crucial problems faced by the first Inuit, allows mythic thought to become conscious of the realities of the universe and to elaborate new principles which could simultaneously consolidate the cultural order and guarantee its reproduction.

With death, the short life (*inuusiq*) became the rule. It was thus believed that every living being was allotted at birth a determined time of life on earth. By means of light, shadows (*tarraq*)—doubles or reflections of living beings, without

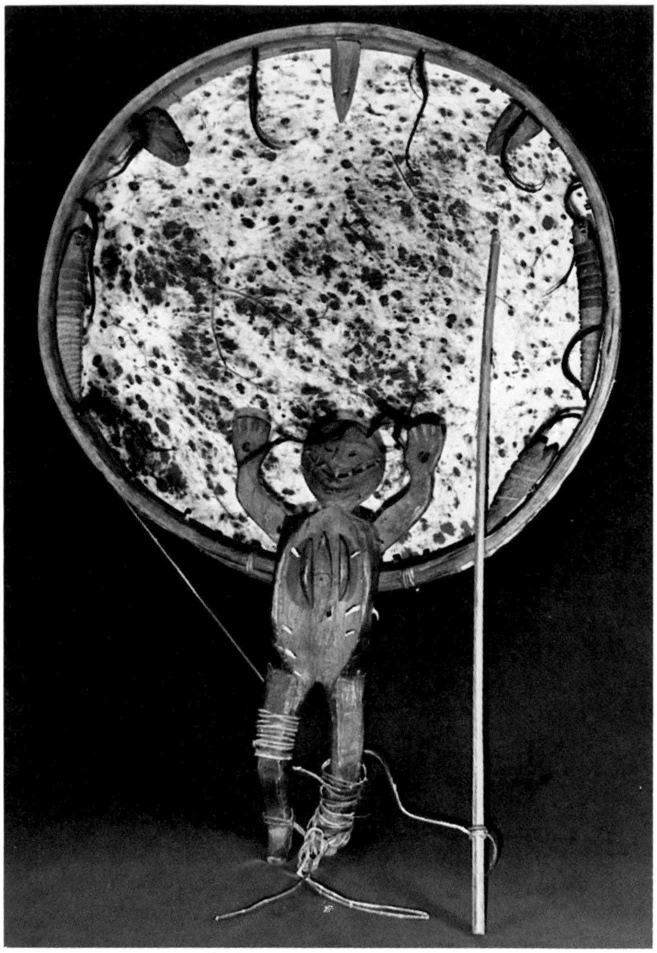

Shaman's drum. Sitka, Alaska, Sheldon Jackson Museum collection. Photo Ernest Manewal.

An Inuit (Inuk) is seized with fear on discovering a tattooed "flying head" in an old igloo. Such flying heads, half-bird and half-human, taught the Inuit the panting songs that are their language. Drawing by Davidialuk Alasuaq. Povungnituk, Canada, B.S.A. collection.

weight or materiality—were discovered, and it was supposed that these survived the body in the afterlife, in the form of souls (*tarniq*).

Finally, the differentiation between game animals and humans and between living and dead humans made possible and necessitated the classification of living beings and of their living spaces. This was done by naming: at the level of species for game animals and at the personal level for humans.

With specific names for game animals, each species was thought of as a multiple and renewable ensemble of potential resources for man.

The personal names given to humans made it possible to think of each individual as the sum of all the productive capacities and qualities of his deceased homonyms; these names also, by their absence of gender, made it possible to obliterate sexual differentiation, thus helping women to surmount the contradictions of their dependence.

So it was that the double-soul (*tarniq*) and the name-soul (*atiq*) gave a new continuity to life, beyond the limits of the present moment. Since life on earth had become short in order to make possible the continuity of human society, it once again became continuous on the level of Sila, the universal order. Culture could now reproduce itself through the reproduction of the factors and relationships of production. All that remained was to begin the appropriation of terrestrial and marine regions, the sole portions of the present that were to remain continuous and permanent. A double naming process was applied to this end, the first in order to situate the resources and activities of production and the second to preserve the memory of past people and events.

Another myth, that of Arnakpaktuq, illustrates the search for the continuity of life; it shows us how a female soul that was unsatisfied in its conjugal life decided—after a fruitless search for a better life in the womb of animals of diverse species—to live again as the son of her brother:

> A woman suffered constant ill treatment at the hands of her husband. She wanted to die, and one day while he was beating her she slipped under the blankets of her bed; the whining of a dog was heard . . . she had transformed herself into a dog. He harnessed her to his sled, but she was completely ignorant of canine hauling and was thus beaten again until she learned from the other dogs how to behave.
>
> All went well until she made a mistake; and when she was thrashed, she let out a human cry. He killed her and threw out her corpse to be devoured by wolves: she became a wolf, and, completely ignorant of the life of the wolf, she had to learn from them how to hunt. Then, as a wolf, she died, and when a caribou stepped on her corpse, she penetrated his body and became a caribou. A new and long apprenticeship thus began for her.
>
> She was harpooned by a hunter while she was crossing a lake. She was butchered and hidden in a cache for the winter, after which she was eaten and her bones thrown onto the shore next to the bones of a walrus. When the tide covered them up she passed into a walrus bone that came back to life and became a walrus. She learned to dive and to eat like a walrus, but she did not like the way they rubbed their muzzles.
>
> She died yet another time, passed into a crow that had come to rest on the corpse of the walrus, was killed by a polar bear, and fell onto the remains of a ringed seal which she entered to become a seal. She learned how to breathe through breathing holes cut into the ice in the winter, and it was at such a hole that she felt the point of a harpoon run through her head. She had been harpooned by a hunter who was none other than her brother.
>
> When her brother's wife butchered her, she entered her body and became a fetus, although up to that time her future mother (her sister-in-law) had had only miscarriages. The fetus found itself in a little house which quickly became too narrow. The time came to come out. When she was almost out, she perceived a woman's knife (*ulu*) and the point of a man's harpoon (*savik*); she first wanted to take the woman's knife, but she changed her mind, seized the point of the harpoon, and came out in the form of a baby boy. The choice she had just made changed her sex. Later the boy became a great hunter and told his story. (Saladin d'Anglure 1974)

Arnakpaktuq's tale in a sense constitutes the myth of the origins of hunting. By explaining the acquisition of the knowledge of hunting by the Inuit, it justifies the new hunter-game relationship, which excludes metamorphoses between humans and animals. It also serves as a basis for beliefs concerning the connection of identity with name, and the reincarnation or transmigration of souls. Finally, it alienates woman into a status subordinate to man, by leading her to believe either that she might have access to masculinity in a future life or that she has been a man in a past life—which allows her to see herself as transsexual, to live as a transvestite, as a boy, in her youth, and to bear the identity of a male eponym during her life (Saladin d'Anglure 1977a).

Order and continuity were thus restored in the universe, but the fragility of their balance soon necessitated the elaboration of a complex system of prescriptions and prohibitions that applied principally to the junctures in the great productive-reproductive cycles: the cycle of human life (pregnancy, childbirth, childhood, and adolescence), of souls (entering and leaving the body), and of game animals (production and consumption).

This new order was now governed by the great master-spirits of Sila (time), Taqqiq (the moon), Siqiniq (the sun), and Kannaaluk (the girl at the bottom of the sea), the dominant figures of Inuit myth and religious beliefs.

In everyday life, however, respect for this order had become too complex for the laity and too important to the socioeconomic survival of the Inuit, in which women still occupied a dominant role in the reproduction of life. It was necessary to transpose into practical life the male domination that had been established at the mythic level; it was necessary to entrust to specialists the interpretation of myths and of empirical reality; it was necessary to establish intermediaries between the visible and the invisible, between the dead and the living, between game and hunter, between men and women. This would be the function of the Angakkuq (shaman), a mainly masculine function (Meyer 1932: 422) to which women could gain access only with difficulty, except in old age. The great shamans were always men.

III. Shamanism, New Light, and Political Power

With the development of shamanism and of its practices, knowledge and power became essentially masculine privileges. An Iglulik myth tells how the first shaman, a man, came into being: A period of famine and trouble befell the Iglulik region one day. Many Inuit died of hunger and all were anxious and confused because they did not know how to face the situation. At this time a man, taking advantage of a meeting in one of their houses, asked to go behind the curtain of skins, at the front of the platform, and announced his intention to descend to the place of the mother of marine animals. No one was to watch. He dived down under the earth with the help of auxiliary spirits that had become associated with him at the time of a solitary retreat he had taken. He visited Kannaaluk and brought abundance back to men, along with game. This is how the first shaman appeared. He was later followed in this by others who gradually extended their knowledge of hidden things and elaborated a sacred language to communicate with the spirits, thus helping humanity in many ways (Rasmussen 1929).

The principal attribute of the shaman was *qaumaniq,* light, vision, the profound knowledge of things and beings; his agent was *tuurngaq,* an auxiliary spirit which could be acquired through a solitary experience of communication with the earth mother, through a visit to a cave or a stay in a deserted place. A progressive diminution of knowledge and power followed among the uninitiated, a sort of return to the chthonic origins of humanity, to the primal night of the maternal womb—to the benefit of the shaman who, substituting himself for the woman as she substituted herself for the earth, succeeded in taking control of social reproduction, thanks to his imaginary operations, and thus in ensuring male domination even as he metaphorically took over the principal female processes and characteristics of the reproduction of life.

Shamanic seances, especially those that are designed to renew communication with game, seem always to stem from scenes of pregnancy and childbirth, borrowed either from myths, like the primordial darkness relived through the extinguishing of lamps, or from reality, like the untying of the belts and laces of spectators at childbirths, the crouching posture taken on the platform of a house (a posture close to that of a woman in childbirth), or the staccato and panting cries that the shaman emits before his soul succeeds in passing through the narrow way that leads to the beyond.

In a primary phase, the shaman attempts to bring his auxiliary spirit into himself. Then, when he has succeeded, he applies himself to making his soul leave his body and to guiding it through a narrow tunnel to the light, the knowledge that allows him to repair cosmic, ecological, social, or psychological disorders provoked by humans. All shamanic rites are carried out with the left hand, the inverse of reality, in which the right hand takes priority. When laterality is used in Inuit culture to differentiate between the sexes, right is male and left is female.

As the ally and protector of men, the shaman became a public confessor, particularly of women, to whom the majority of ills were attributed and who were therefore subjected to strict prohibitions. He also had the privilege of treating the sterility of couples by intervening as sexual partner in reproduction.

The cosmic order was now controllable through the shaman, whose knowledge and power assured its effectiveness on the level of social reality.

B.S.A./d.w.

NOTES

1. Recent research by ethnolinguists suggests another meaning for the term "Eskimo": "one who speaks the language of a foreign land" (see J. Mailhot 1978).
2. After the works of Franz Boas, in particular.
3. Our research, begun on the staff of the C.N.R.S. under the direction of Professor C. Lévi-Strauss, has been continued at Laval University, Quebec, Canada. One part of the material presented here has been published in B. Saladin d'Anglure 1977a, 1977b, and 1978.
4. The works of R. Savard are a first tentative effort on this road; we cite here only his principal work (Savard 1966). Several other works on Inuit mythology have been published, some on other regions, some on themes treated in a comparative fashion, but a great deal of work remains to be done on this subject.

BIBLIOGRAPHY

F. BOAS, "The Eskimo of Baffin Land and Hudson Bay," 2 vols. (New York 1907). J. MAILHOT, "L'étymologie de 'Esquimau' revue et corrigée," *Études/Inuit/Studies* 2, no. 2 (1978): 59–69. R. PETERSEN, "Burial Forms and Death Cult among the Eskimos," *Folk* 8–9 (1967): 259–80. K. RASMUSSEN, "Intellectual Culture of the Iglulik Eskimos," in *Report of the Fifth Thule Expedition,* vol. 7 (Copenhagen 1929); "The Netsilik Eskimos, Social Life and Spiritual Culture," in *Report of the Fifth Thule Expedition,* vol. 8 (Copenhagen 1931). B. SALADIN D'ANGLURE, *La mythologie des Inuit d'Igloolik* (Ottawa 1974), a report manuscript deposited at the National Museum of Man; "Iqallijuk ou les réminiscences d'une âme—nom Inuit," in *Études/Inuit/Studies* 1, no. 1 (1977a): 33–63; "Mythe de la femme et pouvoir de l'homme chez les Inuit de l'Arctique central (Canada)," *Anthropologie et sociétés* 1, no. 3 (1977b): 79–98; "L'homme (Angut), le fils (irniq) et la lumière (qau), ou Le cercle du pouvoir masculin chez les Inuit de l'Arctique central," *Anthropologica,* n.s., 20, nos. 1–2 (1978): 101–44. R. SAVARD, *Mythologie esquimaude, analyse de textes nord-groenlandais,* Centre d'études nordiques, Travaux divers no. 14 (Quebec 1966). E. M. WEYER, *The Eskimos, Their Environment and Folkways* (New Haven 1932).

NATIVE AMERICAN MYTHS AND RITUALS OF NORTH AMERICA

The eminent mythographer Stith Thompson was right to emphasize the fact that "outside of Western civilization, few ethnic groups have been studied as much as the Indians of North America" (1946, 297). Thus, at the outset the researcher is confronted with a mass of documents, some of which date back to the conquest and even earlier if one does not contest the authenticity of the *walam olum,* for example, which recounts the origin of the Delaware people (Rafinesque 1832; Brinton, vol. 5, 1882–85).

The study of North American mythology constitutes a project all the more ambitious in that the themes that compose it are abundant and prodigiously diverse. In addition, it should be noted that no anthropologist before Claude Levi-Strauss achieved a grand synthesis of the ethnic myths of the two Americas; the difficulties involved in such an attempt seemed insurmountable. Until then some researchers were content to record tales without attaching to them any specific analysis, unless it were classical, while others, like Franz Boas, Elsie Clews Parsons, and Paul Radin, to name only a few, set about introducing a more comprehensive analysis of specific groups, specifically the Kwakiutl, the Pueblo, and the Winnebago. One might also add that North American mythology belongs to peoples whose sociological characteristics (ethnohistory, language, and culture) are sometimes totally different from and unconnected with one another. Take, for example, the Naskapi of Labrador, the Pomo of California, the Nez Percé of Idaho, and the Hopi of Arizona; at most, these tribes are united only by spatial and temporal links, that is, on the one hand the continent upon which they have lived since prehistoric times, and on the other hand the facts of conquest, which have come to transform the initial basic data in a manner both insidious and brutal.

In this regard, since Clark Wissler, anthropologists have devoted themselves to defining cultural and geographical areas which do not necessarily take into consideration the principal linguistic families. Nevertheless, these unities of an ecological type make it more possible to discern the ethnographic reality of the peoples who have lived or still live in these territories. One might define these geographical areas as cultural spaces occupied by one or more Native American groups (bands or tribes) whose activities and special characteristics are so similar that they form a kind of ethnic homogeneity in the general sense of the term. This is a purely formal definition, since notable differences may be encountered within a single ecocultural space.

I. Myth and Society

Just as certain themes recur in universal mythology, one can observe comparable subjects reflecting preoccupations common to the Native American peoples. Aside from myths that deal with sequences specific to each group and thus are original by definition, a similar way of thinking recurs continually, though the structure of the myth may be posed in a different manner. The rituals that may eventually be attached to it present a dramatization characteristic of each tribe.

In this ideological order, Native American thinkers have long reflected upon cosmogonic myths, reinventing the creation of the world and the emergence of humanity. Visionaries, they integrated cosmic space and terrestrial space into the everyday world. The original source of the myths resides in the attempt to interpret the very essence of nature and society. Moreover, the myths establish schemata which often represent opposing forces. At the beginning of a subject or in the course of its development, a myth will pose an a priori idea, such as, for example, the division of humanity into nomads and sedentary peoples, which is often founded upon historical reality. The emergence myth of the Acoma (Pueblo) shows clearly the division between hunters and agrarian peoples (Sebag 1971, 469).

Likewise, in the *walam olum*, the Delaware say that in the beginning they formed a single nation:

> And as they traveled they found that certain of them were prosperous and others vigorous. Thus, they separated, the first group becoming builders of huts, and the second hunters. The bravest, the most unified, the purest, were the hunters (Brinton 1882–85, 183).

This dualism between humans may reflect what happens among the gods. The cosmogonic myth of the Skidi Pawnee develops this antagonism in the very heart of the cosmos. This suggests that the gods are at times strangely similar to humans.

In their version of the creation of the world, there is a dichotomy between men and women. The myth relates how Tirawa, the Creator, made the stars and delegated to them a great power, giving pride of place to the Star-of-Morning. The latter, in turn, helped his younger brother, the Sun, to make the light. Tirawa chose them as the "chiefs of stars situated in the village in the East," while Star-of-Evening and Moon were named the "chief of stars situated in the village in the West." In the East were the men, and in the West, the women. After a time, the stars in the East began to desire the stars of the West. One after another the star-men went to the village of the star-women. They said that they were coming to get married. Moon, who received them, invariably responded to each one: "Very well, that is exactly what we desire. Come and follow me." But she drew them into a trap, pushing them into an abyss. Finally, Star-of-Morning fulfilled the role of mediator by marrying Star-of-Evening, while Sun married Moon. The children born of the union of these stars peopled the earth (Linton 1922, 3–5). It is on this myth that the sacrificial rite of the young captive woman is based. She was immolated in homage to Star-of-Morning. This ritual would follow upon the vision of a warrior, who then had to find his victim among an enemy tribe. Among the Pawnee, only the Skidi (Wolves) observed this practice. The last ceremony took place around 1828 (ibid., 5–16).

II. Culture Heroes and Tricksters

Once the problem of the origin of the world was resolved, it was necessary to introduce heroes into the world with the mission of guiding human beings. Indeed, it is never easy for humanity to be born after previous stays in chaotic locations, as is attested by the Zuñi myth of emergence, nor to break with the illusion of a "paradise lost," as the Navajo myth of emergence sometimes leads one to believe.

The perspicacious sages thus placed on the scene the hero, the bearer of the benefits of civilization: fire, light, water, plants, animals (sometimes including humans), language, etc. The hero is also the founder of rituals and secret societies. For one reason or another, it is often difficult to distinguish him from another demiurge, the trickster.

The culture hero often has a younger twin brother (Iroquois, Algonquin, Hopi, Apache, Navajo, Kiowa, Winnebago) with whom he quarrels to the death, like Gluskap and Malsum (Micmac, Passamaquody, Malecite), Silex and Bourgeon (Iroquois), Manabozo and Wolf (Central Algonquin).

This architect of the world belongs as much to the natural order as to the supernatural. He has a body, he lives, suffers, and can marry. Manabozo marries a muskrat, just like the Messou of the Montagnais, who, after "repairing" the world, which has been destroyed by a deluge, undertakes to repopulate the earth by means of this marriage (Le Jeune [1634] 1972, 16). The hero can have a human or an animal form, and can be man or woman, young or old, according to his disguise.

The twins represent respectively the malevolent and benevolent forces (Algonquin, Iroquois). In other cases, it is the warrior twins whose common task it is to rid the world of enemies and monsters before initiating the social order.

The parents and the grandmother of the demiurge twins usually belong to the supernatural universe. Masewi and Oyoyewi, the Hopi twins, are the sons of the sun. One of them faces north, the other south, guarantors of the equilibrium of the earth. The Great Hare of the Winnebago has for his father the west wind or the north wind, in different instances. The Kiowan culture hero, taken in by grandmother spider after the death of her mother, is himself a descendant of the sun. He is called Half-boy because he makes a double by cutting his body in two by means of a solar ring (Momaday 1974, 38 and passim). Among the Huron Iroquois and the Algonquin, the mother is a virgin who dies in childbirth, and the children are taken in by the grandmother, who has previously fallen from the sky.

The trickster often appears to be a close relative of the culture hero by elective affinity. He is one of the most popular characters in North American mythology. Portrayed with the traits of the coyote, crow, mink, jay, or magpie, this antihero takes on the mission of traversing the wide world,

Ethnic Distribution of Native American Tribes (Canada and the United States)

Ecological Areas	Geopolitical Distribution*	Principal Ethnic Groups**	Linguistic Division***
1. Western Subarctic	a) Inner Alaska, Yukon, Mackenzie	Tanana, Kutchin, Tutchone, Hare Kaska, Slave, Dogrib, Yellowknife, Carrier	Athapaskan
	b) British Columbia, Alberta, Saskatchewan, Manitoba		Sekani, Beaver, Sarsi, Chippewyan
2. Eastern Subarctic	Quebec, Ontario	Montagnais, Naskapi, Cree, Ojibwa, Algonquin	Algonkin
3. Forests on the Atlantic	New Brunswick, Quebec, Newfoundland, Prince Edward Island, Nova Scotia, Maine, New Hampshire, Vermont, Massachusetts, Connecticut, Rhode Island, New Jersey, Delaware, New York	Beothuk Micmac, Malecite, Abenaki, Penobscot, Pennacook, Mohican, Delaware, Algonquin, Powhatan, Nanticoke, Narragansett	(?) Algonkin
4. Forests on the Great Lakes	Ontario, Michigan, Indiana, Illinois, Wisconsin, Minnesota, New York	Ottawa, Ojibwa (Chippewa), Potawatomi, Miami, Menominee, Sauk, Fox, Kickapoo, Illini	Algonkin
		Wyandot (Huron), Susquehannah, Erie, Mohawk, Oneida, Onondaga, Cayuga, Seneca	Iroquoian
		Winnebago	Siouan
5. Southeast	Florida, Georgia, Alabama, Missouri, Louisiana, Carolinas, Virginia, Kentucky, Tennessee	Creek, Choctaw, Chickasaw, Seminole	Muskogean
		Natchez Cherokee, Tuscarora	Muskogean (?) Iroquoian
		Catawba, Biloxi	Siouan
		Shawnee	Algonkin
6. Plains and Prairies	a) north: Alberta, Saskatchewan, Montana, Wyoming, Colorado, Dakotas, Nebraska, Kansas	Cree, Blackfoot, Cheyenne, Arapaho	Algonkin
		Yankton, Santee and Teton Sioux, Crow, Hidatsa, Mandan, Osage, Ponca, Omaha	Siouan
	b) south: Oklahoma, Texas	Pawnee, Arikara	 Caddo
		Kiowa, Comanche	 Tanoan
		Mescalero and Lipan Apache Kiowa-Apache	Athapaskan

Ecological Areas	Geopolitical Distribution*	Principal Ethnic Groups**	Linguistic Division***
7. Southwest	Arizona, New Mexico	*Circumpueblo:*	
		Chiricahua and Jicarilla Apache	Athapaskan
		Interpueblo:	
		Navajo	Athapaskan
		Pueblo:	
		Tiwa, Tewa, Towa, Hopi	Tanoan
		Keresan	Keresan
		Zuñi	Zuñian
		Subpueblo:	
		Pima, Papago,	Tanoan
		Yuma	Yuman (Hokan)
		Havasupai, Yavapai	Hokan
8. Great Basin	Nevada, Utah, California, Oregon, Idaho, Wyoming, Colorado	Paiute (south), Paiute (north)	Uto-Tanoan
		Shoshone, Bannock, Ute	(Shoshonean)
		Mohave	Hokan
9. California	California	Maidu, Miwok, Yokuts, Wintun, Costanoan	Penutian
		Pomo, Yana, Chumash, Shasta	Hokan
		Yuki	Yukian
		Wiyot	Algonkin
10. Plateau	British Columbia, Alberta, Washington, Idaho, Oregon, Montana	Salish, Puget Sound, Okanagan, Shuswap, Thompson, Sanpoil, Kalispel, Coeur d'Alene	Salish-Wakashan
		Flathead, Pend d'Oreille, Klamath, Modoc	Penutian
		Nez-Percé	Sahaptin
11. Northwest Coast	Alaska, British Columbia, Oregon, Washington, California	Yurok	Algonkin
		Hupa, Tlingit, Haida, Eyak	Athapaskan
		Chinook	Penutian (?)
		Niska, Gitskan, Tsimshian	Tsimshian (Penutian)
		Haisla, Heiltsuk, Kwakiutl, Nootka, Bella Bella	Wakashan-Kwakiutl
		Bella Coola, Salish, Tillamook	Salish

*States or provinces, in whole or in part.

**This table does not reflect the following: (1) extinct tribes (e.g., Natchez,. Beothuk, Biloxi, Catawba); (2) exile forced by governmental policy (e.g., Dakota [19th century, to Canada], Tuscarora [18th century, New York State], and Osage, Ponca, Pawnee, Arapaho, Cheyenne, Kickapoo, Delaware, Shawnee, Wichita, Chickasaw, Choctaw, Creek, Cherokee [19th century, Oklahoma]; groups from the latter three tribes are also found in the Southeast).

***These classifications are offered merely as signposts and do not claim to be definitive.

Sources:

H. DRIVER, *Indians of North America* (5th ed., Chicago 1965).
P. DRUCKER, *Indians of the Northwest Coast* (New York 1963).
R. F. HEIZER and M. A. WHIPPLE, *The California Indians* (2d ed., Berkeley 1973).
A. L. KROEBER, *Cultural and Natural Areas of Native North America* (Berkeley 1963).
C. WISSLER, *Indians of the United States* (New York 1967).

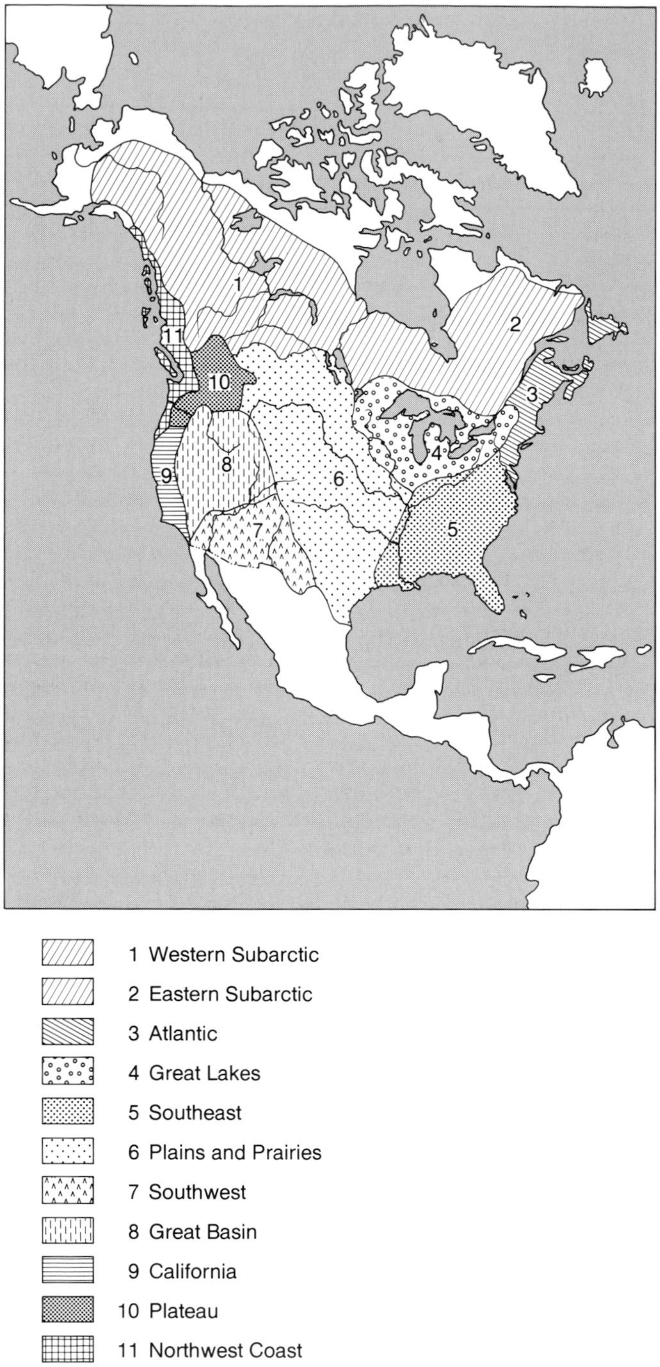

where he has numerous adventures, often crazy and erotic. He is an ambiguous character. He is both dupe and trickster, humble and pretentious, altruistic and selfish, creator and destroyer.

If it is true that people project their fantasies upon him, what should we make of this enigmatic character who joyfully violates taboos, enters forbidden places, disguises himself as woman or man according to his desires? Nevertheless, this imposter has as a double a humorist-philosopher who is under no illusions about his condition. In an episode taken from one of his extravagant pranks, the trickster (Winnebago in this case) lets himself be fooled by the branch of a tree, which he believes to be a man's arm. After conversing for a long time with the branch in question, he realizes his stupidity and makes this reflection: "In truth, it is just for this reason that people call me *wakundkaga,* the eccentric fool, and they are quite right" (Radin 1976, 14).

From an anthropological perspective, the trickster integrates himself into the reality of Native American societies. Indeed, these societies often have ceremonial institutions which do not fear the intrusion of a clown during the most serious activities. Take the case of the Navajo clown who had the "privilege of ridiculing, defying, and parodying the most important and most sacred ceremonies, characters, and costumes" (Steward 1930, 189).

We relate this example only to show that the clown of the above citation is nothing less than a public trickster who introduces into the course of the ritual elements that are used by the other, the demiurge, to contradict the natural course of events.

Nevertheless, in his grand moments the trickster brings aid and support—this is especially the case with all the heroes who have this ambivalence within them, such as Manabozo (central forest), Iktome, "The Old Man" (Plains), the Crow (Northwest Coast)—in case of famine, for example, although he himself is most often afflicted with this problem.

Alas, though the trickster is a magician-hero, he can do nothing against death. He even goes so far as to avenge himself against those who request immortality by transforming them into stone statues. He is caught in his own trap when, after he has cheerfully voted for a death without resurrection, he witnesses the death of his son.

III. The Order of the World

In another conceptual order, certain Native American tribes developed the idea of a supreme creator whose functions vary considerably according to the region. Some myths can leave the impression that the Creator whom they depict acts in a rather singular manner, in that he delegates most of his tasks to two secondary gods. He seems to do nothing or, at most, to be in a state of prodigious boredom in an eternal void. Maheo or Heammawhio, the "great chief from on high" of the Cheyenne, gives this impression somewhat: "In the beginning there was nothingness, and Maheo, Spirit from among the Spirits, lived in the void. There was nothing but Maheo, alone, in the infinitude of the void" (Marriott and Rachlin 1972, 22; Grinnell 1972, 2.88).

Olelbis, the Wintun (California) Creator, lives with two wives, to whom he delegates the creative tasks. However, this is not the case with Old Man, the Blackfoot Creator. Old Man is quite busy; he travels the earth from north to south and discusses with Old Woman the question: "Should one give humans eternity?" He forms, constructs, and prepares the terrestrial scene, neglecting neither to rest nor to amuse himself, sliding along the hillsides (Feldmann 1971, 74–79). But Old Man is more than just a debonair Creator; he also appears as a trickster from time to time. He is found with variants among the Kiowa, the Crow, and the Arapaho (Thompson 1946, 319).

Certainly, this notion of a languid and hieratic creator is purely subjective. Everything that exists bears a sacred potential. Sun and moon, planets and stars, as well as all the astronomical phenomena associated with them (eclipses, solstices, equinoxes), though the importance varies according to the tribe, have always inspired the aboriginal mythol-

An Offering of tobacco to the Bear Spirit. Cree painting. Private collection.

ogers. Prolonged contact with the earth (often identified with the mother) by means of fasting in a hole in order to provoke a vision, repeated exposure to the sun (often identified with the father), by means of dance or prayer, are so many religious ways of entering into relation with the spiritual forces of which the Creator, whatever he might be like, is an integral part.

Similarly, winds, rains, clouds, thunder, and lightning are means of communication between the terrestrial and supra terrestrial forces. A few examples will suffice to illustrate this aspect: among the Oglala, thunder could decide the career of the *heyoka* (the "contrary"). As his name indicates, the "contrary" had to interpret his thought and his acts in an inverse way. The *heyoka* would go nude in winter on the plain, pretending that it was warm; in summer, he would cover himself in a bison skin under the pretext of great cold. When he prepared his meals he would throw drops of boiling water on his legs, pretending that the water was ice cold. He would mount his horse back to front, reversing the normal position of the rider, and ride backwards—in brief, he would act against every apparent logic. Among the Cheyenne, the Society of Contraries (which had nothing to do with the *heyoka*) was composed of women and elderly men who would become part of it after they had dreamed of thunder and lightning. Among the Oglala, Hehaka Sapa (Black Elk) still relates how, during his grand vision, two men armed with lances came out of the clouds (Neihardt 1961, 22). Among the Omaha, *mixuga,* that is, the moon (considered in many myths to be a hermaphrodite) would determine the sexual future of the young adolescent who, through her instruction, could become a *berdache.* During the quest for the vision, the adolescent might see the moon appearing with a bow and arrow in one hand and a basket belt in the other. If the boy was not quick enough to seize the bow, he would then become a *berdache,* that is, a homosexual. Just like the *heyoka,* he was regarded by his tribe as a sacred being (Desy 1978).

Lakes and rivers, mountains and valleys, plants and animals are enrolled in the realm of the sacred, since they are part of the universe. Invested with a power, they may have different significations, so that men, animals, plants, or places become *poha* for the Shoshones, *wakan* for the Dakota, *xupa* for the Hidatsa, *maxpe* for the Crow, *orenda* for the Iroquois, *manitu* for the Algonquin, that is, sacred. But these terms contain, in addition, a qualitative connotation which places them in the realm of the exceptional. For all these categories, as Marcel Mauss writes, "although all the gods are *manitus,* not all the *manitus* are gods" (Mauss 1966, 112).

From another perspective, there are motifs in the myths common to Native Americans which reflect a universal mode of thought, like the myths of Orpheus or Prometheus, for example. A communal or individual mythology attempts to explain the flood, the end of the world, the universal conflagration, the sojourn of the dead, or the existence of a world beyond, except that the Navajo have no belief in a glorious immortality and have a horror of the dead. This explains why the Ghost Dance was not successful among the Navajo. It was Wovoka, along with Tavibo, a Paiute prophet, who was the instigator of this dance. The ritual, which spread like a powder trail throughout the West in 1890, is of a messianic character: "A day will come when all Indians, dead and alive, will be reunited on a purified earth in order to live in happiness, free from death, disease, and misery" (Mooney 1965, 19).

The Kiowa had a rather original conception of the afterlife (a conception quickly transformed by the missionaries): they believed that only the souls of those who had committed evil on earth would transmigrate into the abode of the owl; the others would disappear into nothingness (Marriott and Rachlin 1972, 17).

The Native American sages also reflected upon the myths that recounted the gifts of nature. These often have corollary rituals, such as the sacred pipe of the Oglala and the ceremony that is attached to it, taught by the woman "White Bison" (Brown 1972, chapter 1). Later, the sun dance will be instituted to support the ritual of the sacred pipe (ibid., chapter 5).

The acquisition of fire, corn, tobacco, and techniques of hunting and fishing are often central themes of myths. Among all the agrarian peoples, corn is the occasion for elaborate ceremonies. There are numerous myths referring to Corn Silk, goddess of the plant in question. Among peoples of the far north, tobacco served as a propitiatory offering. The Cree, the Montagnais, and the Naskapi continued to place pinches of tobacco in the skull of the bear in order to appease his spirit, which is great and benevolent. He is called, in addition, grandfather or grandmother.

The Native American sages had a final task to accomplish in order to establish the order of the world: to designate in terrestrial space signs symbolic of what had occurred in cosmogonical space; to consecrate the territory through the mediation of priests, medicine men, or shamans; in a word, to see to it that each territory would be the center of the world. Thus it is that "in the perspective of archaic societies, everything that is not 'our world' is not yet 'a world.' One makes a territory 'one's own' only by 'creating' it again, that is, by consecrating it" (Eliade 1965, 30).

But in the course of the ages, it came about that this hierophanic space branched out. The ancients knew the importance of this center and knew how far they had searched for it before it was established. The Zuñi creation myth teaches this to us very well. In a passage of this myth, the Rain Chiefs settle with their people in the Kachina village. But after a while, they begin to ask themselves if the placement of their village is in fact the center of the world. And so they gather together each night to discuss the matter and to build the altar that will confirm for them the location of the center (Parsons 1.230 and passim).

In the *hako* ceremony of the Pawnee, the circle designated by the medicine man represents the territory given by Tirawa to his people. Similarly, when one climbs to the top of a hill, the horizon one sees, where the earth and sky meet, delimits a circle of which one is the center (Alexander 1916, 97). And it is in this perspective of "sacred" territory that we are able to interpret the anger and hysteria of the Cree to the west of James Bay upon the government's decision to exploit their ancestral hunting territories for hydroelectric projects.

The religious quest for the center of the world also supports another interpretation: the constancy with which all the Native American tribes call themselves the "first men," the "human beings," the "real people." Hehaka Sapa did not err, he who ended the account of the secret rites of the Oglala with this incantation, still recited as a prayer by the Indians of today. He knows that the center of the world has been profaned among his people and that the ball—which symbolizes the earth in some way—is lost:

> In this unhappy time into which our people are plunged, we desperately seek the ball. Some no longer even attempt to capture it. Just thinking of that makes me weep. But a day will come when someone will seize it, for the end is rapidly approaching. Only then will it be returned to the center, and our people with it. (Brown 1972, 138)

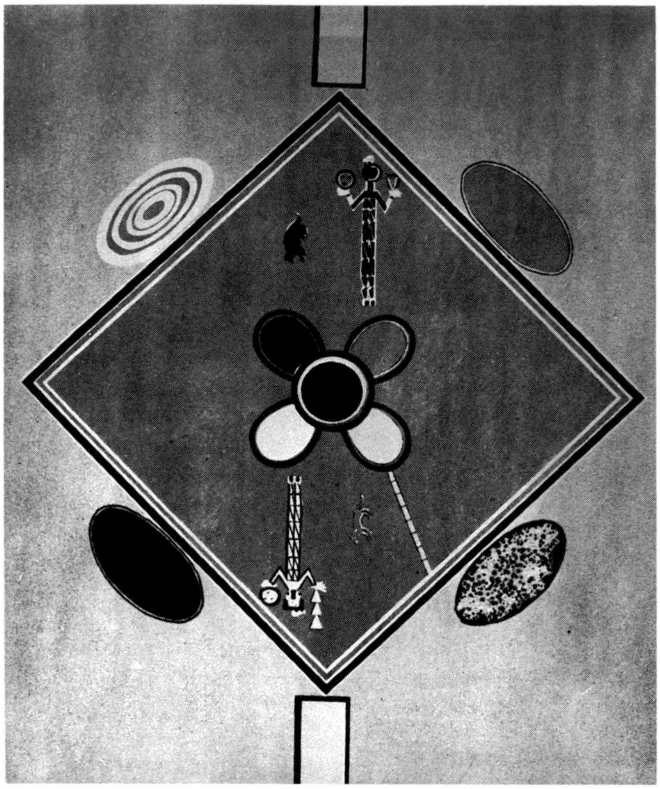

Navajo sand painting. Paris, Musée de l'Homme collection. Museum photo.

IV. Problems of Our Times

It would be a serious misunderstanding to believe that the myths and rituals of the Native American peoples belong to a finished past. Certainly, some nations famous for their sociological complexity have disappeared: the Natchez and the Mandan, to cite only two. (Following smallpox epidemics, the Mandan survivors joined the Hidatsa. Today they live on the Fort Berthold reservation in North Dakota.) On the other hand, other tribes were able to safeguard their institutions jealously, for example, the following groups: Pueblo, Lakota, Iroquois, Algonquin, Kwakiutl, and Athapaskan. In addition, the "pan-Indianism" of the last few years has made possible a revival of rituals practiced by Native Americans of various tribes, such as the creation of small spiritual communities where a mythographic erudition is held in common. The medicine men do not hesitate to travel throughout the territory just as the prophets and political visionaries of old used to do (Tecumseh [Shawnee], Pontiac [Ottawa], Cornplanter [Seneca]), as well as all the unknowns who took on the mission of bringing the "good word" to scattered groups.

For this reason, though it cannot be claimed that mythological erudition has remained the same since the conquest, or that it has not been the victim of cultural erosion, its actual power cannot be denied. Anything is possible if one keeps in mind the fact that neither the rituals nor the myths are static. As Franz Boas wrote: "Mythological universes seem destined to be annihilated when they are barely formed, so that new universes might be born from their debris" (in Lévi-Strauss 1958, 227).

Although some peoples have been able to preserve up to the present day rituals which for the most part take place far from prying eyes, we have no right to say that their function is to entertain the tourist by producing "folklore." Folklore exists, no doubt, and there are many powwows to remind us of it, but despite the fact that nothing stops it from eventually gaining respectability, it exists on a lower level, proof of a savoir faire which bears witness to the wisdom of the ancients.

We conclude this too brief analysis by turning to the museums which have acquired ethnographic collections, including certain objects invested with a sacred value centuries old.

Don Talayesva related in his book the surprise of Hopi visitors upon visiting a museum in Chicago. To their great fright and consternation, they discovered behind the display cases ceremonial masks reserved for the sole use of officials during festivals in the pueblo (Simmons 1942). What can one say to a member of the secret society of the "Black Eyes" searching desperately in the museums for the original mask that presided over the foundation of the society? (Parsons 1939). The Iroquois have also taken steps to gain possession of all the wampum (a kind of belt that related the heroic deeds of the tribe), some of which had been entrusted in 1898 to the State University of New York.

Nearer to our time, in 1973, after the events at Wounded Knee, Wallace Black Elk (grandson of Hehaka Sapa), the guardian of the sacred pipe that had belonged to Crazy Horse, his grandfather's cousin, found that the pipe had been stolen. When he spoke of it, he did so with an indescribable emotion, but he also showed great concern for the thief, whose life seemed to him to be in danger.

The descriptive function of museums gives little incentive to the amateur to gain a proper perspective of objects which, deprived of their initial function, have been transformed into "things." However much attention is given to their presentation, these objects have passed irrevocably into another world. Hans G. Gadamer writes in this regard: "One should admit, for example, that the image of an ancient deity, which was not exposed in the temple as a work of art intended for a reflective appreciation of an aesthetic kind, and which is today on display in a modern museum, contains in itself, under the form in which this image appears to us today, the world of religious experience in which it originated. The conclusion to be drawn is important: that world which is its own still becomes part of the world which is ours" (1975, 11).

We need to reestablish the tenuous bond that tied these objects—which are the bearers of signs coded in space and time—to another cultural universe. For, despite a museographic destiny, the Tlingit masks, the Mandan altars, the Navajo sand paintings, the Crow sacred pipes, the Montagnais curative beads are all intrinsically part of a mythological "becoming." In their way, these objects always carry the charge of spiritual emotion with which they were endowed at the time they were used ritually.

P.D./m.s.

BIBLIOGRAPHY

1. References in This Article

H. B. ALEXANDER, *North American*, in *The Mythology of All Races* 10 (Boston 1916). D. G. BRINTON, *The Lénâpé and Their Legends* (Philadelphia 1882–85). P. DÉSY, "L'homme-femme" (the berdaches in North America), *Libre* 3 (1978). DON TALAYESVA (see Simmons, ed., below). M. ELIADE, *The Sacred and the Profane* (New York 1959). S. FELDMANN, ed., *The Storytelling Stone* (New York 1971). H. G. GADAMER, *Truth and Method* (New York 1975); original in German. G. B. GRINNELL, *The Cheyenne Indians*, 2 vols. (Lincoln, NE, 1972). P. LE JEUNE, "Relations de ce qui s'est passé en la Nouvelle-France en l'année 1634," in *Relations des Jésuites* (Montreal 1972). C. LÉVI-STRAUSS, *Structural Anthropology* (New York 1963). R. LINTON, *The Sacrifice of the Morning Star by the Skidi Pawnee* (Chicago 1922). A. MARRIOTT and C. RACHLIN, *American Indian Mythology* (New York 1972). M. MAUSS, *Sociologie et anthropologie* (Paris 1966). N. MOMADAY and J. MOONEY, *The Ghost Dance Religion* (Chicago 1965). J. G. NEIHARDT, ed., *Black Elk Speaks* (Lincoln, NE, 1961). P. RADIN, *The Trickster* (New York 1976). N. SCOTT MOMADAY, *The Way to Rainy Mountain* (4th ed., New York 1974). L. SEBAG, *L'invention du monde chez les Indiens pueblos* (Paris 1971). L. W. SIMMONS, ed., *Sun Chief* (New Haven 1942). J. H. STEWARD, "The Ceremonial Buffoon of the American Indian," Michigan Ac. of Science (1930). S. THOMPSON, *The Folktale* (New York 1946), 297–363.

2. General Sources

H. B. ALEXANDER, *The World's Rim* (Lincoln, NE, 1953). J. DE ANGULO, *Indian Tales* (New York 1953). D. G. BRINTON, *The Myths of the New World* (New York 1876). J. CURTIN, *Creation Myths of Primitive America* (London 1899). C. HAYWOOD, *A Bibliography of North America Folklore and Folksong*, 2 vols. (2d ed., New York 1961). Å. HULTKRANTZ, *Conception of the Soul among North American Indians* (Stockholm 1953); *The North American Indian Orpheus* (Stockholm 1957). C. LÉVI-STRAUSS, *The Savage Mind* (Chicago 1966); *L'homme nu* (Paris 1971). R. H. LOWIE, "The Test Theme in North American Mythology," *Journal of American Folklore* 21 (1908). J. W. POWELL, "Sketch of the Mythology of the North American Indians," *U.S. Bureau of American Ethnology* (Washington 1879–80). C. S. RAFINESQUE SCHMALTZ, *The American Nations*, 2 vols. (Philadelphia 1832). S. THOMPSON, *Tales of the North American Indians* (Cambridge, MA, 1929). R. G. THWAITES, ed., *The Jesuit Relations and Allied Documents: Travels and Explorations of the Jesuit Missionaries in New France, 1610–1791*, 73 vols. (Cleveland 1896–1901). R. UNDERHILL, *Red Man's Religion* (3d ed., Chicago 1974).

3. Regional Sources

Northwest Coast, Plateau

M. BARBEAU, *Haida Myths* (Ottawa 1953). F. BOAS, "Ethnology of the Kwakiutl," *U.S. Bureau of American Ethnology* (Washington 1913–14); *The Religion of the Kwakiutl Indians*, 2 vols. (New York 1930). E. E. CLARK, *Indian Legends of the Pacific Northwest* (Berkeley 1933). A. H. ERNST, *The Wolf Ritual of the Northwest Coast* (Eugene 1952). T. MCILWRAITH, *The Bella Coola Indians* (Toronto 1948). E. SAPIR and M. SWADESH, *Nootka Texts* (Philadelphia 1939). J. R. SWANTON, "Tlingit Myths and Other Texts," *U.S. Bureau of American Ethnology* (Washington 1909). J. TEIT, *Traditions of the Thompson River Indians* (Boston 1898).

California

L. J. BEAN, *Mukat's People* (Berkeley 1972). J. CURTIN, *Myths of the Modocs* (Boston 1912). E. W. GIFFORD, *Central Miwok Ceremonies* (Berkeley 1955). A. L. KROEBER, *World Renewal: A Cult System of Native Northern California* (Berkeley 1926). E. M. LOEB, *Pomo Folkways* (Berkeley 1926). H. SEILER, *Cahuilla Texts* (Bloomington, IN, 1970).

Southeast

A. S. GATSCHET, *A Migration Legend of the Creek Indians*, 2 vols. (Philadelphia 1882–85). J. H. HOWARD, *The Southeastern Ceremonial Complex and Its Interpretation* (Columbia, MO, 1968). J. F. KILPATRICK and A. G. KILPATRICK, *Notebook on a Cherokee Shaman* (Washington 1970). J. MOONEY, "The Sacred Formulas of the Cherokee," *U.S. Bureau of American Ethnology*, 7th annual report (Washington 1885–86); "Myths of the Cherokee," *U.S. Bureau of American Ethnology*, 19th annual report (Washington 1897–98). J. R. SWANTON, "Religion Beliefs and Medicinal Practices of the Creek Indians," *U.S. Bureau of American Ethnology*, 42d annual report (Washington 1928); "Social and Religious Beliefs and Usages of the Chickasaw Indians," *U.S. Bureau of American Ethnology*, 44th annual report (Washington 1928).

Southwest, Great Basin, Southern Plains

A. F. BANDELIER, *The Delight Makers* (New York 1946). R. L. BUNZEL, "Introduction to Zuni Ceremonialism," *U.S. Bureau of American Ethnology* (Washington 1932). F. H. CUSHING, *Zuni Folk Tales* (New York 1901). G. GOODWIN, "Tales of the White Mountain Apaches," *Memoirs of the American Folk-Lore Society* 33 (1939). C. KLUCKHOHN, *Navaho Witchcraft* (Cambridge, MA, 1944; Boston 1967). A. MARRIOTT, *The Ten Grand Mothers* (Norman, OK, 1945). A. ORTIZ, *The Tewa World* (Chicago 1969). M. SCHEVIL LINK, *The Pollen Path* (Stanford 1956). C. L. SMITHSON, "Havasupai Religion and Mythology," *Anthropological Papers*, no. 68 (Salt Lake City 1964). H. A. TYLER, *Pueblo God and Myths* (Norman, OK, 1964). B. B. WHITING, *Paiute Sorcery* (New York 1950).

Subarctic and Forest Regions

M. BARBEAU, *Huron and Wyandot Mythology* (Ottawa 1915). REV. W. M. BEAUCHAMP, "Iroquois Folk-Lore," Empire State Historical Publications, 31 (Port Washington, NY, 1922). J. M. COOPER, "The Northern Algonquian Supreme Being," Catholic University of America, Anthropological series 2 (Washington 1934). J. N. B. HEWITT, "Iroquoian Cosmology," part 1, *U.S. Bureau of American Ethnology* (Washington 1903); part 2, ibid. (1925–26). W. J. HOFFMAN, "The Midewiwin," *U.S. Bureau of American Ethnology*, 7th annual report (Washington 1891). D. JENNESS, "The Ojibwa Indians of Parry Island," *Bull. of the Dept. of Mines* 78 (Ottawa 1935). P. RADIN, *Some Myths and Tales of the Ojibwa of Southeastern Ontario* (Ottawa 1914); *Winnebago Hero Cycles* (Baltimore 1948). R. SAVARD, *Carcajou ou le Sens du Monde*, ministère des Affaires culturelles (Quebec 1972). F. G. SPECK, *Naskapi* (Norman, OK, 1935). L. TURNER, "Ethnology of the Ungava District, Hudson Bay Territory,"

U.S. Bureau of American Ethnology (Washington 1889–90). M. L. WILLIAMS, ed., *Schoolcraft's Indian Legends* (East Lansing, MI, 1956).

Plains, Prairies

A. W. BOWERS, *Mandan Social and Ceremonial Organization* (Chicago 1950). L. BLOOMFIELD, "Sacred Stories of the Sweet Grass Cree," *Bull. of the National Museum of Canada,* no. 60 (1930). G. A. DORSEY, *The Pawnee: Mythology* (Washington 1906); *The Mythology of the Wichita* (Washington 1904). V. DUSENBERRY, *The Montana Cree: A Study in Religious Persistences* (Göteborg 1962). A. C. FLETCHER, "The Hako: A Pawnee Ceremony," *U.S. Bureau of American Ethnology,* 22d annual report (Washington 1900–1901). F. LA FLESCHE, "The Osage Tribe, Rite of the Wa-xo-be," *U.S. Bureau of American Ethnology* (Washington 1930). R. H. LOWIE, The Crow Indians (New York 1966). P. J. POWELL, *Sweet Medicine,* 2 vols. (Norman, OK, 1969). C. WISSLER, ed., *Sun Dance of the Plains Indians* (New York 1921).

The Creation of the World in Native American Mythology

I. The Woman Who Fell from the Sky

> They recognize as chief of their nation a certain woman whom they call Ataentsic, who they say fell to them from the sky. (Père Paul Le Jeune, "De la Créance, des Moeurs et Costumes des Hurons," 1636)

Ataentsic[1] lived happily above the vaults of the sky, in a land which resembled Earth. One day, when she was cultivating a field, her dog, which accompanied her, saw a bear and followed it. In order to escape from the dog's fangs, the bear, cornered at the edge of an abyss, jumped in. The dog jumped in after it, and Ataentsic, impelled by curiosity and despair, leapt in as well. Although she was pregnant, her fall into the water did her no harm.

In another version, Ataentsic, wishing to cure a very ill husband, set about cutting down a tree with curative powers. But the tree fell over a precipice and Ataentsic jumped after it. Her fall, however, was noticed by the tortoise, which "had its head out of the water; seeing her and not knowing what to do, amazed at what it saw, the tortoise called the other aquatic animals to get their advice. And behold, they all assembled forthwith. The tortoise showed them what it had seen and asked what they thought should be done. The majority brought the matter to the beaver, which through decorum took the entire question to the tortoise, which was finally of the opinion that they should set to work immediately, dive to the bottom of the water, bring up some soil, and put it onto the tortoise's back. No sooner said than done, and the woman fell very gently onto this island" (Le Jeune [1636] 1972, 101).

Soon Ataentsic gave birth to a daughter who, although she was a virgin, gave birth to the twins Taiscaron and Iskeha.[2] The two had a violent quarrel. While Iskeha armed himself with the horns of a deer, Taiscaron, convinced that a blow with a wild rose bush would take care of his brother, struck the first blow. But Iskeha mortally wounded his brother and came out the victor in the battle (ibid. 102).

It was thanks to Iskeha, their culture hero, that the Hurons learned the techniques of making fire, fishing, hunting, and navigation, as well as how to cultivate wheat and gather maple syrup (ibid. 103).

A more elaborate version of this myth is found among the Iroquois. The Seneca version tells how the daughter of the Chief of the Sky fell ill. Her father had her carried close to a nutritious tree, the only one that the celestial people possessed. He ordered that the tree be uprooted. A man who was very dissatisfied with this decision kicked the girl, knocking her into a hole. Some aquatic birds that noticed her fall placed her gently on the back of the tortoise. The sequences that follow resemble the version of the Huron. The fistful of mud brought back finally by the toad was spread out carefully upon the shell of the tortoise, and as it spread out it formed an island.

The woman who fell from the sky gave birth to a daughter. Later, when both were busy gathering potatoes, the daughter disobeyed her mother by facing the east wind. Her mother had warned her about this, saying that, if she did this, she would become impregnated by the west wind (Feldmann 1971, 56–70).

Just before giving birth, the young woman heard the twins quarreling in her womb. While the first came forward to be born through the normal channels, the second pushed out and was born through his mother's armpit. The firstborn was Juskana (Little Bud) and the second Othagwenda (Flint). The grandmother held Othagwenda responsible for the death of her daughter and bestowed all her affection upon Juskana.

These accounts contain the essentials of the themes that recur in the nations to the east and west of the Great Lakes. The special relationship of the grandmother with her grandson is an image widespread in North America (Grandmother Spider in the Southwest and Grandmother Bat in the Great Plains, for example). The grandson is the culture hero. When the grandmother falls from the sky, the earth is always covered with antediluvian waters (the deluge occurs later because of the clumsiness of some demiurge or the misdeeds of a marine monster). It is also the tortoise that serves as the support for the earth, an idea which is also found among the Mandan, according to whom the earth is carried by four tortoises.

The twins who dispute in the womb of their mother are a common figure. However, among the Ojibwa, the hero Manabozo speaks in a friendly way with his brother Wolf. They love each other so much that when Wolf accidentally drowns, Manabozo remains inconsolable. In another version, he is so furious at this death that he attempts to take on Manitu. Nevertheless, another version says that he ends up killing his brother. And Gluskap, the culture hero of the Micmac, also quarrels with his brother. The two plan to kill one another. Gluskap (called the liar or the deceiving one) emerges the victor in a combat with his brother Malsum by eliminating him in the same way that Iskeha killed Taiscaron (Mechling 1914, 44).

From this perspective, it seems clear that the legend of Dekanawida borrows freely from the myth of the origin of creation. This account—of which there are many versions—also constitutes a political attempt to explain the laws and responsibilities of the new constitutions of the League of the Iroquois (which is thought to have originated in the middle of the fifteenth century, a time which would correspond with the total solar eclipse of 1451).

According to the version of Newhouse (Fenton, *The Constitution of the Five Nations* 1971, 14 and passim, 65 and passim), the account begins with a woman of great goodness who was living alone with her daughter. Now the daughter found that she was pregnant without ever having known a man.[3] After the birth of the infant, the grandmother tried on numerous occasions to rid herself of it, but the baby always came out the victor in these trials. The old woman was astounded and adopted it. The infant was named Dekanawida. A little later, he left the two women and undertook finally to visit the neighboring peoples who were always at war. Another version says that Dekanawida undertook his circuit in a craft of white stone. It was to the people of the flint (the Hurons, or "forked tongues," according to the Iroquois) that he directed the first stage of his voyage. He overcame a trial there—a most common thing for all culture heroes—by clambering to the top of a tree situated at the edge of a ravine, which they cut down at the base. In this way he proved to the people of the flint his loyal intention to establish peace.

He continued along his path and arrived among the Ongweowe (the "true men," that is, the Iroquois). He overcame another trial by helping Ayonwatha (Hiawatha)[4] to conquer Adodaro, a kind of cannibal despot who had imposed his evil law upon the "true men" (Fenton 1971, 17).

The references to the myth of the woman who fell from the sky are rather obvious. Dekanawida is the messiah who proposes to remake the world by delivering it from chaos. Like the culture heroes, he travels magically, overcomes a whole series of trials, and battles monsters. These references are there to indicate that the legend of Dekanawida serves to support an organization of the fifteenth century (the League of the Iroquois) and originates in a historical reality: the tribes' incessant wars with one another. The myth of origin, like the legend, tells that the hero's task is to structure the world and society. It is in this sense that the myths are the reflection of society.

II. The Magpie That Came from the Earth

"My friend," asked Masauwu, "but where do you come from? You seek something, perhaps? To tell the truth, I have never heard of you. I live here alone."

"I have come out of the earth," answered the magpie.

"Is this possible?"

"Yes, I have come out of the earth."

"Oh! I have indeed heard of certain folk who live underground."

"It is from there that I come."

"But what goes on there down below?"

"Oh! You know, we have a lot of problems. . . ."

(Elsie Clews Parsons, *Pueblo Indian Religion* vol. 1, 1939, 238)

In the first world, the Hopi were like ants. In the second world, they metaphormose into new animal creatures. In the third world, they begin to resemble men a little, but they still have a long tail of which they are deeply ashamed. (The Zuñi had sticky bodies and webbed hands; they walked on one another and spat on one another.) They acted in a bizarre fashion. The young men made love to old women and the old men to young girls. The women did not want their husbands. They beat each other, cast spells upon each other, killed each other. Some people fell ill, others went mad. The chiefs expressed great dissatisfaction with this impossible situation.

As they were traveling, they arrived at a river. They decided to separate, the women to one side, the men to the other. Each group planted corn and watermelons. It seems that the men succeeded better at this task. But the deluge came. The women constructed a tower which collapsed. The men planted reeds (another version states that it was the spider woman who did this) which pierced the terrestrial crust.

Badger was the first to venture forth, but he was not able to see anything because of the dark (elsewhere it is said that the badger was too tired and had to give up his exploration). Finally the magpie flew off. In the distance she saw a house and a field of corn. A man, who had his back to the bird, did not hear her coming. When he saw the magpie, he tried to put on his mask, but it was too late. It was Masauwu,[5] (Parsons 1939, 1.236 and passim).

Among the Navajo, the present world represents the fifth level of a laborious ascension. (It is impossible to give a comprehensive account of all the sequences of this emergence myth, one of the most complete in existence. We refer the reader to the study by Gladys A. Reichard, 1950.) Three beings shared the first world, which was plunged in darkness: First Man, First Woman, and Coyote, but the place was too constricted, so that all three agreed to climb up. Two men lived in the second world, which was feebly illuminated: Sun and Moon. However, each of the four cardinal points (east = black; south = blue; west = yellow; north = white) hid a person.

Discord was established among the inhabitants of the second world after Sun attempted to seduce First Woman. Of course, Coyote, who knew everything, had the occupants of the cardinal points intervene. They decided they had to clamber up again to the higher level, where the space would be large enough to separate Sun from First Woman.

The third world resembled Earth. There were four oceans and four beautiful mountains.[6] The new arrivals were welcomed by the inhabitants of the mountain, who warned them that all would go well as long as the marine monster was left in peace. But Coyote, strong in skill, transgressed the warning. Unable to resist the incomparable beauty of the two children of the monster, he carried them off. The marine monster, furious, avenged himself by pouring the waters of the oceans (or of the great sea) into the third world. The inhabitants began to pile up the four mountains, but since that was not enough, they planted a giant reed. They were thus able to continue their climb into the fourth world. This world, though more vast than the one which preceded it, was not yet the good world. Thanks to First Woman and First Man, the "people" (as the Navajo call themselves) were able to emerge onto the Earth.

While the Huron and the Iroquois explicate the genesis of creation upon a sky-earth axis, at the other extreme, the Pueblos and the Navajo emerge laboriously from the bowels of the earth, after they have undergone physical transformations, have been put to flight by the deluge, and have successively traversed several subterranean worlds.

Between the celestial origin of the peoples of the west and the subterranean origin of the peoples of the southwest, the Creek of the southwest, the peoples of California, and the Kwakiutl of the Northwest Coast give other versions. It is Esaugetu-Emissi (the "master of breath") who has the power of creation for the Creek. These used to live in a celestial kingdom as pure spirits before they took human form. Elsewhere one finds the idea, which is quite widespread among the Californian peoples, of a creator who models from mud, or from the union of the earth (sister) and the sky (brother), in order to people the planet (Spence 1975, 122, 348 and passim).

A typical theme of the Kwakiutl, by contrast, recounts the arrival of the ancestor of the Numayma (or Nemema: the inhabitants of each village who have this ancestor in common), under the guise of an animal (bird) or a human. He might also come forth from the ocean, taking on the traits of an aquatic mammal, or emerge from the subterranean world in the form of a spirit. The ancestor immediately sets about the task of sculpting human figures from earth or wood, or bringing back to shore people who have drifted astray. As soon as he has finished his work, he shouts all around him to hear himself answered by another ancestor who is just as busy as he (Boas 1975, 304–5).

Although there is no real creation myth among the Kwakiutl, the theme of the ancestor-sculptor sets out rather nicely the synthesis of the subjects that compose the emergence of humanity and the creation of the world.

Nevertheless, there are peoples who hesitate between the high and the low and who opt for solutions different from those that we have considered. These include, for example, the Mandan, the Hidatsa, and the Arikara, all three neighboring tribes of the upper Missouri.

As Claude Lévi-Strauss has written: ". . . the myths seem troubled by the choice between a terrestrial or celestial origin. They marry the two theses, and the Hidatsa sages schematize their system by tracing a kind of Y: the two arms of the fork represent the emergence of one part of the ancestors, who lived in the bowels of the earth, and the descent from the sky of the other part; the common trunk evokes the adventures of the two groups after they came together and were associated with each other" (Lévi-Strauss 1968, 378).

In the Arikara creation myth, Nesaru was the guardian of the universe. Through a window, he was able to see a lake where two ducks swam incessantly. Then came Wolf Man and Lucky Man who sent the ducks to look for mud. With this mud, Wolf Man modeled the prairies and Lucky Man designed the valleys and the hills. Then both made an incursion underground where two spiders lived, female and male. They were hideous and dirty. The two visitors undertook to clean them. They instructed them in sexual matters, of which they were entirely ignorant. Very quickly, they set about procreating. The female spider gave birth to animals and to a race of giants. Nesaru expressed his irritation at all this. Consequently, he made the corn grow, and its grains penetrated the earth and gave birth to a race of normal people. Then he provoked the deluge which destroyed the giants but spared the others.

The survivors were unhappy in this world, for they walked upon one another. They too sought a pathway up, but did not find one. Nesaru delegated the goddess Corn to go underground with the mission of bringing them back. The people clung about her so that she was unable to find the path back. Badger began boring a tunnel. He stopped before he reached the surface because of the light; the mole relieved him, but she too was afraid of being dazzled. Finally the long-nosed mouse arrived at the surface, an achievement which was balanced by the loss of the end of her nose. Even so, the tunnel was still too narrow and the people were pushing and shoving each other at the entrance. But the thunder roared and the tunnel was enlarged. Finally all were able to emerge (Burland 1965, 84–86).

We conclude with the Arikara myth, which makes it possible to put in place the last links that compose the genesis of humanity. For the Arikara, humanity, in the final analysis, comes from grains of corn. But such ultimate recourses to solutions of replacement are usual. Among the Mandan (the bison clan), humanity takes its origin from the transformation of the prairie dog (*Cynomys sp.*). This is because neither human nor animal—nor, in some cases, plants—should be distinguished. For the Sioux sages discussed the question of who, bison or human, should eat the other.

These myths teach us a lesson about the wisdom and also the boldness of Native American thought. Whether they belong to the celestial, subterranean, or terrestrial order, these myths always keep a visual power and a spectacular dynamic which fascinates through the beauty of the word and the image that they inspire. For whatever reason, the myths of creation do not lack an acute sense of drama, humor, and passion.

P.D./m.s.

NOTES

1. Ataentsic means "old woman." She is also called Awehai (fertile Earth) or Moon. Ataentsic is not entirely devoid of the characteristics of the trickster. In certain cases she may make herself young or old. She is at once creator and seducer. In another variant she may be seduced by her grandson.

2. Taiscaron means "flint" (the blood that escapes from a wound on his flank was transformed into "firestone"), "frozen to the second degree," or "black." Iskeha means "sun," "the good," "white," "the dear little sprout," or "the young bud" (Le Jeune [1636] 1972, 102; Tooker 1962, 151).

3. Compare this story with that of the Winnebago demiurge the Great Hare, which begins in exactly the same way. See Radin 1976, 63.

4. Not to be confused with the Hiawatha of Longfellow. The author drew his inspiration from the adventures of the demiurge Manabozo (or Manabush, Chibiabo, Wenobojo).

5. Masauwu in this case is the guardian of the chthonic universe. He is also an agricultural god. He wears his mask in order to frighten the magpie. If he had been able to do it, the people of the third world would not have been able to emerge. But since he was not fast enough, Masauwu must cede the Earth and what is cultivated on it: corn, watermelon, cantaloupe, and gourds.

6. It is interesting to note that the Navajo, who are Athapaskan speakers who had emigrated from northern Canada to New Mexico and Colorado, identify the four mountains in question, situated in Arizona, as follows: Big Sheep (north), Taylor (south), Humphrey (west), and Pelado or Sierra Blanca (east). Note: among the Pueblos, the Grand Canyon of the Colorado River is often regarded as the topographic place of emergence.

BIBLIOGRAPHY

F. BOAS, *Kwakiutl Ethnography*, H. Codere, ed. (2d ed., Chicago 1975). C. BURLAND, *North American Indian Mythology* (London 1965). W. N. FENTON, ed., *Parker on the Iroquois* (Syracuse 1971). P. LE JEUNE, *Relation de ce qui s'est passé en Nouvelle-France en l'année 1636* (Montreal 1972). C. LÉVI-STRAUSS, *The Origin of Table Manners* (New York 1978). W. H. MECHLING, "Malecite Tales," *Mem. 49*, Dept. of Mines (Ottawa 1914). E. C. PARSONS, *Pueblo Indian Religion*, 2 vols. (Berkeley 1939). G. A. REICHARD, *Navaho Religion*, 2 vols. (New York 1950). L. SPENCE, *Myths and Legends of the North American Indians* (New York 1975). E. TOOKER, "An Ethnography of the Huron Indians, 1615–1649," *B.A.E.* (Washington 1964).

The Sun Dance among the Native Americans: The Revival of 1973

The founding myths of the sun dance show clearly that this ritual was introduced in order to celebrate the creation of the world or to commemorate the revival of the earth (Dorsey 1905, 46–55; Brown 1972, 3–9 and 67–100; Lévi-Strauss 1968, 163–84). As this ceremony came to be celebrated more and more, tribes added sequential features that signaled its importance from the point of view of time and space. Though the sun dance has taken on a syncretic appearance and may be performed for revolutionary ends,[1] it is important to emphasize that at the same time it embodies a strictly mythological way of thinking.[2]

While the sun dance was most elaborate among the Arapaho, Cheyenne, and Dakota, tribes such as the Comanche copied it from the Kiowa in 1874, and the Ute adopted it as late as 1890, a time that corresponds with the ghost dance of messianic inspiration, which was based in part on a myth like the myth of Orpheus.

The sun dance goes by different names: the "dance without drinking" (Cree), "the ceremony of the renewal of life" (Cheyenne, among others); the "sacred or mysterious dance" (Poncas); "to dance gazing at the sun" and sometimes "the sun gazes at the dance" (Dakota). This ritual was performed by twenty odd tribes of the Plains: Kiowa, Ute, Wind River Shoshones, Crow, Blackfeet, Sarsi, Gros Ventre, Arapaho, Cheyenne (Northern and Southern), Oglala, Ponca, Arikara, Hidatsa, Assiniboin, Sisseton, Dakota, Ojibwa, and Plains Cree (Spier 1921, 473). Conversely, the Pawnee, Wichita, Omaha, Mandan, and a few tribes of the Siouan linguistic group did not observe it. The Mandan celebrated the *O-kee-pa* (Catlin 1967 and 1973, 1.155–84), a ritual commemorating the flood, highly elaborate and complex, which, like the sun dance, lasted four days with its attending privations, fasting, and mortifications.

We must hasten to add that not all tribes practiced torture. Among those mentioned above, the Kiowa, Wind River Shoshones, and Northern Cheyenne did not use torture or used very little. Writers do not agree on this question (Spier 1921, 473; Mayhall 1971, 150).

At the time when the horse was introduced into the Plains, many tribes turned this vast territory into their permanent habitat. The Cheyenne, Gros Ventre, and Lakota groups that lived farther east in the regions bordering on the Prairies, the forests, and the Great Lakes, adapted very quickly to the Plains. The Minnesota Sioux who went to the Dakotas are the best example of this.

A ceremony like the sun dance could not help but become enriched by the new cultural and ecological circumstances. In any case, the progressive change of territory made it possible for these groups further to develop warring societies,[3] and with them there opened up a ceremonial upon which the immediate history of the tribes in question was to be inscribed.

Unlike other ceremonies reserved for specifically female or male societies,[4] the sun dance was above all tribal in character. In fact, the entire tribe—with the exception of a few "impure" individuals—was invited to participate in this grand ceremonial that took place in June or July, and sometimes in August as it does today, after the collective hunting parties which had dispersed during the winter had regrouped in a large meeting place.

Among the Dakota Sioux, the sun dance took place yearly, although it could also be performed in response to an individual wish. Such was the case with the Crow, who performed it after a warrior had expressed a desire for it when a relative had been murdered by an enemy tribe (which explains its sporadic character) (Lowie 1963, 198). This analogy between the ceremony and affairs of war was indeed clearly established, for it was customary before the ceremony began for warriors to recount their exploits.

Despite its elliptical name—given to it by European observers—and the impressive spectacle made by the dancer in his intoxicating connection with the sun (for the spectator can no longer tell with certainty who gazes at whom, the sun or the dancer), the sun dance is above all a celebration of renewal. To be sure, the sun is a prestigious and highly emblematic component in the eyes of the performer, since that performer dances for four days, bare-chested, his body exposed to the burning rays of the sun. In addition, he does this without eating and in principle without drinking, so that the pain-racked body uses the sun as its instrument of torture in order that it may touch the one called the Great Spirit.

Viewed from this perspective, the sun is above all an intermediary between Wakan Tanka (Sioux) and the dancer, as are also the thunderbird (the performer blows almost continually into a whistle shaped like the wing of an eagle), the bison (which is one of the objects of the sacred altar), the medicine man, and the dancing woman who symbolizes "the female white bison" who came to bring the sacred pipe to the Sioux. The moon serves as a counterpart to the sun; for the ceremony takes place at the time of year when the sun is at its highest point, which is also when the moon is full in June and July. This being so, although there is a special relationship between the dancer guided by the celebrant and what takes place on the spiritual level, since the vision remains the ultimate step, the performance of the sun dance is a popular event of a highly religious nature.

There are several descriptions of this ritual performed by the Indians of the Plains. We refer the reader who is interested in a step-by-step account to the works of J. O. Dorsey (1889–90), J. E. Brown (1972), G. B. Grinnell (vol. 2, 1972), J. G. Jorgensen (1972), R. H. Lowie (1915 and 1919), Skinner (1919), L. Spier (1921), J. R. Walter (1917), W. D. Wallis (1919), and C. Wissler (1918).

For our part, we were able to attend the renewal of this ceremony in 1973, an exceptional opportunity, since white men are excluded from the territory. The celebration took place on the camping grounds of a celebrated medicine man, Henry Crow Dog, at a spot called "Crow Dog's Paradise" on the Rosebud Sioux reservation in South Dakota.

We can attest to the great religious atmosphere that prevailed in the camp, in which all recording and photographic equipment had been strictly forbidden. Many very old people, who came from all the corners of South Dakota, were barely able to contain their intense emotion. The same was true of the singers seated around the ceremonial drum at the entrance of the bower. The campgrounds were heavily guarded by young "warriors" (militants who had for the most part participated in the siege of Wounded Knee). They also kept order among the spectators seated around the bower where the dance was taking place.

As in the time of the great celebration at the end of spring, the ceremony was prepared four days in advance and lasted four days straight, the last day being reserved for the corporeal offering. On this occasion, the celebrants stuck skewers under the chest muscles of the participants; the skewers were tied to a central pole by a rope (in this case, the pole was the trunk of a young poplar). Each of the approx-

Member of the Crazy Dog Society. North America. Paris, Musée de l'Homme collection. Photo P. Coze.

imately thirty participants danced until he was freed. At the end of the day, just before sunset, at the same time as the sacrifice of the dancers was taking place, the medicine man cut a piece of flesh from the shoulder or arm of those among the spectators who wished this to be done. In return, they received a small bag symbolizing the sacred altar that belongs to the sun dance.

As in times past, the bower, covered with branches, encircled the sacred space reserved for the dancers and kept the spectators cool while the sun's rays were beating down in the center where the four cardinal points were indicated: north, south, east, west. To the west of this bower, a forbidden zone was marked off in which a ceremonial tepee and a sweat tent had been erected. A little to the south was the area set aside for profane festivals and also a place where all the spectators could get food free of charge that was prepared by a group of young women.

Without wishing to claim that since 1904, when the U.S. government banned the sun dance as "immoral and barbarian," this ceremony had never been performed in its entirety, we can affirm that the ritual procedure was respected as it seldom had been since the nineteenth century. In fact, whereas the official ban goes back to 1904, local agents of the Bureau of Indian Affairs were known well before that date to have been ordered to break down the religious culture on the spot. The dance had been authorized once more in 1934, the year of the Indian Reorganization Act, which was passed in order to correct a government policy that had prevailed for one hundred years. As early as 1883, for example, orders came from Washington giving agents full power to imprison participants. So the last time the sun dance was performed was in 1883, on the Sioux reservation of the Cheyenne River in South Dakota (R. M. Utley 1972, 33). This reservation is at present a place where the ritual is once again performed.

We must unfortunately confess that quite often the sun dance is a pale copy of what it must have been in the last century. To be convinced of this, one need only see a film like *Lost Sun*, which was produced in 1961 by the Canadian Film Board. This film, shot among the Blood (Blackfoot) Indians in Alberta, far from giving the impression of being an ethnographic document, rather seeks to convince the viewer that this is an obsolete and moribund bit of "folklore." Similarly, modern descriptions in certain books leave the reader disappointed or perplexed (for instance, the chapter entitled "The Defeat of the Rodeo" in E. Schorris 1972, 137–54).

It is useful to note these facts in order to understand that the authentic revival of this ritual in our time is much more than a visual representation. The sun dance takes place on two levels simultaneously: the mythical and the real. This is the source of the symbolic and expressionistic power of such an institution.

P.D./g.h.

NOTES

1. The medicine man (*hunkpapa*) Sitting Bull had the following vision during the sun dance before the attack at the Little Big Horn: he saw dozens of white soldiers fall on the battlefield; this was the famous defeat of Custer in 1876.
2. In this regard, compare this ritual to that of the Ojibwa *midewiwin* (Landes 1968, 71–237).
3. One of the last (end of the nineteenth century) would be that of the Crazy Dogs of the Cheyenne. This society was composed of a few warriors who took an oath to die in battle; see Grinnell 1972, 2:48.
4. One of the Sioux women's societies was dedicated to the "Holy Woman Above." Among the Cheyenne women there were warriors called "Manly Hearted Women."

BIBLIOGRAPHY

See also the general bibliography.

J. E. BROWN, ed., *The Sacred Pipe* (Baltimore 1972). G. CATLIN, *O-kee-pa: A Religious Ceremony and Other Customs of the Mandans*, edited by John C. Ewers (New Haven 1967); *North American Indians*, 2 vols. (New York 1973). J. O. DORSEY, "A Study of Siouan Cults," *U.S. Bureau of American Ethnology*, 11th Annual Report (1889–90): 351–544; *The Cheyenne*, Field Columbian Museum, "Anthropological Series" 9, 1905. G. B. GRINNELL, *The Cheyenne Indians* 2 (Lincoln, NE, 1972). J. G. JORGENSEN, *The Sun Dance Religion* (Chicago 1972). R. H. LOWIE, "The Sun Dance of the Crow Indians," *A.M.N.H.* 16, part 1 (New York 1963): 1–50; *Indians of the Plains* (New York 1963). R. LANDES, *Ojibwa Religion* (Madison, WI, 1968). C. LÉVI-STRAUSS, *The Origin of Table Manners* (New York 1978) (trans. from French). M. P. MAYHALL, *The Kiowas* (2d ed., Norman, OK, 1971). E. SHORRIS, *The Death of the Great Spirit* (2d ed., New York 1972). L. SPIER, "The Sun Dance of the Plains Indians: Its Development and Diffusion," *A.M.N.H.* 16, part 7 (New York 1921). R. M. UTLEY, *The Last Days of the Sioux Nation* (7th ed., New Haven 1972). J. R. WALKER, "The Sun Dance and Other Ceremonies of the Oglala Division of the Teton Dakota," *A.M.N. H.* 16, part 2 (New York 1917): 51–221. W. D. WALLIS, "The Sun Dance of the Canadian Dakota," *A.M.N.H.* 16, part 4 (New York 1919): 317–80. C. WISSLER, "The Sun Dance of the Blackfoot Indians," *A.M.N.H.* 16, part 3 (New York 1918): 225–70.

Mesoamerican Religion

The name "Mesoamerica" refers synchronically to an area of civilization and diachronically to a collection of neighboring cultural traditions that arose in central and southern Mexico and in Guatemala, a group whose borders have varied in the course of the centuries. The term was first used in the first sense; it attempted to define the complex of "superior" civilizations that, at the beginning of the sixteenth century, stretched from north to south, starting roughly with the Rio Panuco and the Rio Sinaloa, passing through the Rio Lerma, stretching west to what is now Honduras and to the Gulf of Nicoya. Despite tremendous geographic, linguistic, and ethnic differences, this vast zone presented a cultural unity in which, among other common elements, the convergence of religious systems occupied an important position. Research into the historical depth of such a unity has made it possible to broaden the meaning of the term "Mesoamerica."

Among the developmental phases of the diverse cultures that have made up Mesoamerica, one period has traditionally been given a special rank: the period that witnessed the rise and apogee of the great metropolis of Teotihuacan on the central Mexican plateau and the vigorous growth of the great Mayan cities, a growth marked for six centuries by the uninterrupted erection of stelae bearing dates and inscriptions. The term "Classic" used for this period has produced as its consequence a system of reference for the naming of periods that preceded and followed it. The millennia that have separated the appearance of the first tribes on what was to become the territory of Mesoamerica and the beginning of the Classic Period make for a slowly evolving spectacle. But it is above all starting with the Early Preclassic Period that numerous distinctive elements of the Mesoamerican tradition appear, especially in the religious realm. The dynamics of the Olmec world may not have resulted in the standardization of the zones that came under its influence, but it does indicate without a doubt the beginnings of Mesoamerica as a reality. At the other end of the historical spectrum, the Spanish Conquest interrupted the autonomous development of the native civilizations. Isolation or contact, resistance to the invader or acceptance of him, all created disparate situations that are revealed in the study of present-day Indian societies.

Our knowledge of religious phenomena in the oldest periods comes mainly from the interpretation of archaeological vestiges. The results obtained in this way are still embryonic and often speculative. The uneven development of archaeological research has resulted in significant disproportions of space and time in the order of our understanding. The second group of sources available to the historian of religions is made up of the collection of indigenous pictographic documents that have been preserved, almost all dated in the Late Preclassic Period or in the early period of colonization. In many cases, the subject matter is mythical and ritualistic. To this set of documents one could add the numerous eyewitness accounts of the conquistadores and missionaries, the first and last ethnographers of the pre-Columbian world. Modern ethnology, finally, enables us to examine the road traveled by native cultures and to rediscover the traces of ancient visions of the world, in spite of the mutations imposed by contemporary societies.

This presentation of Mesoamerican religious thought has been sketched in the shape of eight articles: mythic and ritual order, creation, space and time, sky, earth, fire, the human being, and cosmic disorder.

Such an essay must rest on three constraints:

—the need to point out correspondences and invariables, even at the admitted risk of minimizing divergences and transformations,

—the thematic classification of phenomena that makes it possible to emphasize the birth, the development, and the result of great concepts but that can also offer an illuminating and simplified religious reality,

—finally, the preeminence given to speculative religious thought over practice, an attitude that incurs the danger of obscuring the fundamental relationships between religion and socioeconomic systems.

These initial choices, compounded by the imperfection of our knowledge, have resulted in a series of limitations and lacunae. The earliest periods and the least-known regions, western Mexico in particular, often remain in shadow. Finally, though it has been possible to deal with a maximum number of themes, it has not been possible to give certain aspects the space that they deserve. For example, the most sophisticated speculations of the philosopher-priests of Tenochtitlan have been barely touched upon.

The religious history of pre-Columbian Mesoamerica, which is known to have lasted for more than twenty centuries, challenges anyone confronting it with the fundamental problem of the unity or plurality of the religions throughout the different cultures that have been grouped together under the rubric of Mesoamerica. It also raises the equally important question of the levels of religion within each culture. Moreover, the analysis of contemporary visions of the world cannot draw any conclusions without ascertaining the impact of Catholicism on the old traditional base.

It is difficult to understand Mesoamerican religions as a unique whole without first taking into account the originality and multiplicity of the works produced by the civilization that nourished them (ceramics, statues, codices, and so forth) and the richness of the vernacular languages, of which some thirty are spoken today, each translating its own vision of the world.

The evolution of Mesoamerican social formations certainly did not follow the same paths everywhere. State societies with very strong social stratification coexisted with peasant communities with little hierarchy. Starting with the Preclassic

Structure 6 of San José Mogote (Oaxaca), one of the first stone public buildings in Mesoamerica (1350 B.C.). Photo M.A.E.F.M.

and moving from one culture to another, marked sociological differences appeared, particularly between the social complex of the high plateau and that of the Gulf Coast, and it is likely that the religious superstructures, of which we know far too little, reflect such contrasts. The phenomena of spreading and diffusion, especially evident beginning with the Olmec horizon, had only a limited impact. Indeed, they could not prevent the creation of scores of local religions, whose development was largely autonomous. But in spite of the multiplicity of processes in the construction of religious systems, common characteristics swept such multiplicity away into areas of shadow. On the eve of the Conquest, Aztec society had a caste of priests who were developing an esoteric knowledge very clearly distinguished from popular religious practice, a situation similar to that of the Mayan region during the Classic Period. Extremely strong similarities unite the ideology of the Mayan and Aztec elite on the one hand, and the simpler religion of peasant groups of these two cultures, on the other, the social stratification engendering a stratification of systems of knowledge. Furthermore, it seems that with the cult of *Itzam Na* among the Maya of the Classic Period and with the reflection of the poet-sovereign Netzahualcoyotl of Texcoco in the fifteenth century, we witness the rise of a way of thinking that opens up the possibility of monotheism. These are isolated experiences to be sure, but they indicate the potentialities attained by religious thought in Mesoamerica before the Conquest.

Because the first missionaries who arrived followed in the steps of Cortés, military order in New Spain was immediately intermingled with the moral order of Christianity.

Evangelical politics initially took the direction of an open fight against "idolatry," namely, the veneration of ancient deities and the celebration of ceremonies whose motivation profoundly baffled Christian sensibilities, such as rituals of flaying symbolizing the renewal of vegetation, or tearing out the heart in order to feed the solar deity.

But two elements were to modify permanently the ideology of the pastoral mission: on the one hand, the brutal methods of imposition of colonial power, and on the other, the shortage of manpower among the priesthood. Very rapidly, part of the clergy, who included in their ranks remarkable humanists like the Franciscan Bernardino de Sahagún or the Dominican Bartolomé de las Casas, took up the cause of the Indians against the military and the colonizers. Without losing sight of the integration of the Indians into the Christian nation, this faction of the clergy managed effectively to guarantee their defense within the missionary regions. In the central plateau, in the zone formerly occupied by the Aztecs, the collapse of the old religion was so sudden that Indian religiosity had no other recourse than to express itself through the Gospel, mixing it with bits and pieces of ancestral beliefs. The same did not hold true everywhere, and among the Maya in the south of Yucatan, fierce resistance to the invaders and their religion was sustained until the end of the seventeenth century and left scars still visible today. The superficial character of the evangelization, which spread rapidly throughout the Americas, led to inevitable rearrangements. Most often deprived of their clerics and their dogma, native groups set out to recreate their religious universe in light of the Christian religion. Each group reacted according to its own conceptual system. Some offered substantial zones of permeability, such as the multiple correspondences between the solar deity and Christ among the Huichol. Others, on the contrary, offered only resistance: the cycle of the rain gods has been largely preserved among the Maya right up to our time. The open confrontation between the two religions is still at issue, resulting in situations of rejection, as was recently the case among the Lacandon, or, more generally, in a situation of precarious equilibrium.

The Carnival at Huehuetla (Tepehua Indians). Among many present-day native groups, the Carnival serves as a refuge for traditional beliefs. Photo M.A.E.F.M.

The flexibility of Christian concepts and the absence of orthodoxy greatly facilitated the absorption of a large part of the native spiritual heritage. Thus, the idea of "diablo" or of "demonio," heavily laden with the residues of various origins and constituted in the course of the Middle Ages in the West, would allow the survival of certain native concepts of evil and human nature.

This is why the lines between the religion of the Indians and the popular faith of the mestizos (whose worship of the Virgin of Guadalupe is a living symbol of syncretism) are very often difficult to recognize. Mexican Catholicism is an institution impregnated with Indian religious feeling, and its effects can be felt even in the urban world.

Today, Catholicism is firmly rooted in Mesoamerica. Originally a symbol of domination, it has now become an instrument of the defense of the Indian faith against mestizo mercantilism and serves as a refuge for the marginal communities that are dominated by the global society.

Despite all of this, the continual shrinking of the ancient religious patrimony follows its inexorable course. Among the younger generations, contact with the Indian worldview has been broken. With the few remaining native priests and old men, a universe is in the final stage of burning out.

M.A.E.F.M./g.h.

BIBLIOGRAPHY

There are many studies of religious phenomena in Mesoamerica, and it is not possible to mention all of them here. A choice has therefore been made despite the difficulties and imperfections that such an operation entails. A detailed bibliography appears below. The publications cited are arranged in four large sections according to their nature:

I. Codices: pictographic manuscripts with their principal interpretations
II. Ancient written sources
III. Archaeology and ethnohistory: syntheses and monographs
IV. Contemporary ethnological studies

Within each section, titles are preceded by numbers. At the end of each article on Mesoamerica, numbered bibliographic citations refer to these numbers. For the present article, see, in particular, for section II: 9, 16 (22 or 44), 23, 25, 26, 27, 29, 38; section III: 6, 8, 12, 17, 19, 25, 29, 35, 38, 39, 46, 50, 51, 54, 55, 57, 62, 63, 64, 69, 72, 73, 74, 75; section IV: 21.

I. Codices: Pictographic Manuscripts with Their Principal Interpretations

(1) F. ANDERS, *Codex Tro-Cortesianus . . .* , Introduction and Summary (Graz 1967); (2) *Codex Peresianus* (codex Paris) . . . , Introduction and Summary (Graz 1968). (3) C. BURLAND, *The Selden Roll,* an ancient Mexican picture manuscript in the Bodleian Library at Oxford (Berlin 1955); (4) *Codex Laud,* Bodleian Library, Oxford (Graz 1966). (5) *Códice Ramírez,* Manuscrito del Siglo XVI entitulado "Relación del origen de los indios que habitan esta Nueva España según sus historias" (Mexico City 1944). (6) J. COOPER CLARK, *Codex Mendoza,* the Mexican manuscript known as the collection of Mendoza and preserved in the Bodleian Library, Oxford, 3 vols. (London 1938). (7) J. CORONA NUNEZ, *Antiguedades de México, basadas en la recopilación de Lord Kingsborough,* 4 vols. (Mexico City 1964–67). (8) E. FÖRSTEMAN, *Commentary on the Maya Manuscript in the Royal Public Library of Dresden, Papers of the Peabody Museum,* Harvard University, vol. 4, no. 1 (Cambridge, MA, 1906). (9) W. E. GATES, *Commentary upon the Maya-Tzeltal Perez Codex, Papers of the Peabody Museum,* Harvard University, vol. 6, no. 1 (Cambridge, MA, 1910). (10) E. T. HAMY, *Codex Telleriano Remensis,* Mexican manuscript at the Bibliothèque nationale (Paris 1899); (11) *Codex Borbonicus,* Mexican manuscript at the bibliothèque du Palais-Bourbon (Paris 1899). (12) G. KUBLER and C. GIBSON, *The Tovar Calendar,* an illustrated Mexican manuscript ca. 1858 (New Haven 1951). (13) W. LEHMANN, "Die fünf im Kindbett gestorbenen Frauen des Westens und die fünf Götter des Südens in der mexicanischen Mythologie," *Zeitschrift für Ethnologie* 37 (1905): 858–71. (14) J. F. LOUBAT, *Il manoscritto messicano-vaticano 3773,* Codex Vaticanus B (Rome 1896); (15) *Il manoscritto messicano Borgiano del Museo Etnografico della S. Congregazione di Propaganda Fide* (Rome 1898; 2d ed., Mexico City and Buenos Aires, 1963, 4 vols.); (16) *Il manoscritto messicano vaticano 3738, detto il Codice Rios* (Rome 1900) = Codex Vaticanus A or Codex Rios; (17) *Codex Fejervary-Mayer,* pre-Columbian Mexican manuscript of the Free Public Museums, Liverpool (Paris 1901). (18) *Codex Magliabecchiano XIII-3,* post-Columbian Mexican manuscript of the National Library of Florence (Rome 1904). (19) C. MARTINEZ MARIN, *Códice Laud,* Instituto National de Antropología e Historia (Mexico City 1961). (20) Z. NUTTAL, *Codex Nuttal, Facsimile of an Ancient Mexican Codex,* Peabody Museum of American Archaeology and Ethnology (Cambridge, MA, 1902). (21) F. DEL PASO Y TRONCOSO, *Descripción del Códice Cospiano,* manuscrito pictórico de los antiguos Nauas, que se conserva en la Universidad de Bolonia (Rome 1898; 2d ed. by K. A. Nowotny, Graz 1968); (22) *Descripción, historia y exposición del códice pictórico de los antiguos Nauas, que se conserva en la biblioteca de la Cámara de los Diputados de Paris* (Florence 1898). (23) E. SELER, *Das Tonalamatl der Aubinschen Sammlung,* eine altmexikanische Bilderhandschrift der Bibliothèque nationale de Paris (Berlin 1900; English trans., Berlin and London 1900–1901); (24) *Codex Fejervary-Mayer,* eine altmexikanische Bilderhandschrift der Free Public Museums in Liverpool (Berlin 1901; English trans., Berlin and London 1901–2); (25) *Codex Vaticanus no. 3773,* Codex Vaticanus B, eine altmexikanische Bilderschrift der Vatikanischen Bibliothek (Berlin 1902, 2 vols.; English trans., Berlin and London 1902–3); (26) *Codex Borgia,* eine altmexikanische Bilderschrift der Bibliothek der Congregatio de Propaganda Fide (Berlin 1904–9, 3 vols.; Spanish trans., Mexico City and Buenos Aires 1963, 4 vols.). (27) J. E. S. THOMPSON, *A Commentary on the Dresden Codex, a Maya Hieroglyphic Book* (Philadelphia 1972).

II. Ancient Written Sources

(1) F. DE ALVA IXTLILXOCHITL, *Obras históricas* (Mexico City 1891–92; 2d ed., Mexico City 1952, 2 vols.). (2) H. ALVARADO TEZOZOMOC, *Crónica mexicana escrita por D. Hernando Alvarado Tezozomoc . . . precedida del Códice Ramírez* (Mexico City 1878; 2d ed., Mexico City 1944). (3) A. BARRERA VASQUEZ, *El libro de los cantares de Dzitbalché,* una traducción con notas y una introducción (Mexico City 1965). (4) A. BARRERA VASQUEZ and S. RENDON, *El libro de los libros de Chilam Balam* (Mexico City 1948). (5) G. DE CHAVEZ, "Relación de la provincia de Meztitlán," *Boletin del Museo Nacional,* época 4, 2 (1925): 109–20. (6) *Códice Chimalpopoca, Anales de Cuauhtitlán y Leyenda de los soles,* P. F. Velazquez, trans. (Mexico City 1945). (7) CONQUISTADOR ANONIMO, *Relación de algunas cosas de la Nueva España y de la gran ciudad de Temestitán México, escrita por un compañero de Hernán Cortés,* in *Colección de documentos para la historia de México* (Mexico City 1858), 1:368–98. (8) *Costumbres, fiestas, enterramientos y diversas formas de proceder de los indios de Nueva España,* publicado por F. Gómez de Orozco, *Tlalocan* 2 (1945): 37–63. (9) F. D. DURAN, *Historia de las Indias de Nueva España y islas de Tierra Firme,* critical ed. by A. Garibay, 3 vols. (Mexico City 1967). (10) M. S. EDMONSON, *The Book of the Counsel: The Popol Vuh of the Quiche Maya of Guatemala* (New Orleans 1971). (11) G. FERNANDEZ DE OVIEDO Y VALDES, *Historia general y natural de las Indias, islas y tierra firme del mar oceano,* 4 vols. (Madrid 1851–55). (12) F. A. DE FUENTES Y GUZMAN, *Recordación Florida,* discurso historial y demostración . . . del Reyno de Guatemala, 3 vols. (Guatemala City 1932–33). (13) A. M. GARIBAY, "Relación breve de las fiestas de los dioses: Fray Bernardino de Sahagún," *Tlalocan* 2 (1948): 289–320; (14) *Veinte himnos sacros de los Nahuas,* los recogió de los nativos F. Bernardino de Sahagún (Mexico City 1958); (15) *Poesía nahuatl,* 3 vols. (Mexico City 1964–68). (16) J. GENET, *Relation des choses du Yucatan,* Spanish text and French trans., 2 vols. (Paris 1928–29), French edition incomplete. (17) *Historia de los Mexicanos por sus pinturas,* in *Nueva colección de documentos para la historia de México* (Mexico City 1891; new ed., Mexico City 1941), 3:228–63. (18) *Idolatrias y supersticiones de los Indios, Anales del Museo Nacional de México,* vol. 6 (Mexico City 1892; 2d ed., Mexico City 1953). (19) W. JIMENEZ MORENO and S. MATEOS, *Códice de Yanhuitlán* (Mexico City 1940). (20) E. DE JONGHE, *Histoyre du Méchique,* unedited French manuscript of the sixteenth century, published by de Jonghe, *Journal de la Société des Américanistes,* n.s., 2 (1905): 1–41, French trans. by A. Thevet. (21) J. LAFAYE, *Manuscrit Tovar: Origines et croyances des Indiens du Mexique,* edition based on the manuscript in the John Carter Brown Library (Graz 1972). (22) F. D. DE LANDA, *Relación de las cosas de Yucatán* (8th ed., Mexico City 1959), many earlier editions, of which two have French translations by Brasseur de Bourbourg (Paris 1864) and by Genet (Paris 1928–29). (23) F. B. DE LAS CASAS, *Apologética historia sumaria . . .* , Edmondo O'Gorman, ed., 2 vols. (Mexico City 1967). (24) M. LEON PORTILLA, *Ritos, sacerdotes y atavios de los dioses,* texts of the informants of Sahagún I (Mexico City 1958). (25) F. J. DE MENDIETA, *Historia eclesiástica indiana* (Mexico City 1870; 2d ed., Mexico City 1945, 4 vols.). (26) F. T. DE BENAVENTE MOTOLINIA, *Historia de los Indios de la Nueva España,* in *Colección de documentos para la historia de México* (Mexico City 1858; 2d ed., Mexico City 1941), 1:1–249. (27) *Memoriales o libro de las cosas de la Nueva España y de los naturales de ella,* E. O'Gorman, ed. (Mexico City 1971). (28) D. MUNOZ CAMARGO, *Historia de Tlaxcala* (Mexico City 1892; facsimile ed., Guadalajara 1966). (29) F. DEL PASO Y TRONCOSO, *Papeles de la Nueva España . . .* , 6 vols. (Madrid 1905–6). (30) *Fray Bernardino de Sahagún: Historia de las cosas de Nueva España,* vols. 5, 6, 7, and 8 (Madrid 1905–7). (31) J. B. POMAR, *Relación de Tezcoco,* in *Nueva colección de documentos para la historia de México* (Mexico City 1891), 3:1–69. (32) K. T. PREUSS and E. MENGIN, *Die mexikanische Bilderhandschrift Historia tolteca-chichimeca* (Berlin 1937–38). (33) *Procesos de indios idolatras y hechiceros, Publicaciones del Archivo General de la Nacion,* vol. 3 (Mexico City 1912). (34) G. RAYNAUD, *Les dieux, les héros et les hommes de l'ancien Guatemala d'après le livre du Conseil* (Paris 1925; 2d ed., Paris 1975). (35) A. RECINOS, *Memorial de Solola, anales de los Cakchiqueles, Título de los señores de Totonicapan* (Mexico City 1950). (36) *Relación de las ceremonias y ritos y población y gobernación de los Indios de la provincia de Mechuacán* (Morelia 1903; 2d ed., Madrid 1956). (37) R. L. ROYS, *The Book of Chilam Balam of Chumayel* (Washington 1933). (38) F. B. DE SAHAGÚN, *Historia general de las cosas de Nueva España,* anotaciones y apendices de A. M. Garibay, 4 vols. (Mexico City

1956), numerous earlier editions, including a French translation by D. Jourdanet and R. Simeon (Paris 1880); (39) *Florentine Codex,* Nahuatl text and translation into English by J. O. Anderson and C. E. Dibble, 12 vols. (Santa Fe 1950–69). (40) L. SCHULTZE-JENA, *Popol Vuh, das heilige Buch der Quiche-Indianer von Guatemala* (Berlin 1944). (41) E. SELER, *Einige Kapitel aus dem Geschichtswerke des Fray Bernardino de Sahagún aus den Aztekischen übersetzt* (Stuttgart 1927). (42) A. THEVET, see E. DE JONGHE. (43) F. J. DE TORQUEMADA, *Los veinte i un libros rituales y monarchia indiana . . . ,* 3 vols. (3d ed. facsimile, Mexico City 1943–44). (44) A. M. TOZZER, *Landa's Relación de las cosas de Yuacatán,* a translation cited with notes (Cambridge, MA, 1941).

III. Archaeology and Ethnohistory: Syntheses and Monographs

(1) F. ANDERS, *Das Pantheon der Maya* (Graz 1963). (2) *Wort- und Sachregister zu Eduard Seler, Gesammelte Abhandlungen* (Graz 1967). (3) P. ARMILLAS, "Los dioses de Teotihuacán," in *Anales del Instituto de Etnografía Americana* 6 (1945): 35–61. (4) A. BARRERA VASQUEZ, "La ceiba-cocodrilo," in *Anales del Instituto Nacional de Antropología e Historia* 7 (1974–75): 187–208. (5) T. S. BARTHEL, "Die Morgensternkult in den Darstellungen der Dresdener Maya Handschrift," *Ethnos* 17 (1952): 73–112. (6) E. BENSON, ed., *Dumbarton Oaks Conference on the Olmecs* (Washington 1967). (7) H. BERLIN, *Las antiguas creencias en San Miguel Sola, Oaxaca, México* (Hamburg 1957). (8) I. BERNAL, *El mundo olmeca* (Mexico City 1968). (9) H. BEYER, *El llamada "calendario azteca"* (Mexico City 1921). (10) "Mito y simbología del México antiguo," *México Antiguo,* vol. 10 (1965). (11) C. BOWDITCH, *The Numeration, Calendar Systems and Astronomical Knowledge of the Mayas* (Cambridge, MA, 1910). (12) C. BURLAND, *The Gods of Mexico* (London 1967). (13) P. CARRASCO, *Los Otomíes: Cultura e historia de los pueblos mesoamericanos de habla otomiana* (Mexico City 1950). (14) A. CASO, *El teocalli de la guerre sagrada* (Mexico City 1927); (15) *Las estelas zapotecas* (Mexico City 1928); (16) "El paraíso terrenal en Teotihuacán," in *Cuadernos Americanos* 6 (1942): 127–36; (17) *El pueblo del Sol* (Mexico City 1953); (18) *Los Calendarios Prehispánicos* (Mexico City 1967); (19) "Religión o Religiones mesoamericanas," in *Verhandlungen der XXXVIII Internationalen Amerikanisten Kongresses* (Munich 1971). (20) A. CASO and I. BERNAL, *Urnas de Oaxaca,* memorias del Instituto Nacional de Antropología e Historia (Mexico City 1952). (21) J. CORONA NUNEZ, *Mitología tarasca* (Mexico City 1957). (22) M. COVARRUBIAS, *Indian Art of Mexico and Central America* (New York 1957). (23) B. DAHLGREN DE JORDAN, *La Mixteca: Su cultura e historia prehispánicas* (Mexico City 1954). (24) J. FERNANDEZ, *Coatlicue: Estética del arte indígena* (Mexico City 1954). (25) K. FLANNERY, "Formative Oaxaca and the Zapotec Cosmos," *American Scientist* 64 (1976): 374–83. (26) G. FOSTER, "Nagualism in Mexico and Guatemala," *Acta Americana* 2 (1944): 85–103. (27) J. GARCIA PAYON, "Interpretación de la vida de los pueblos Matlatzincas," *México Antiguo* 6 (1942–43): 72–90, 93–119. (28) A. M. GARIBAY, *Historia de la Literatura Nahuatl,* 2 vols. (Mexico City 1953–54). (29) C. GIBSON, *The Aztecs under the Spanish Rule: A History of the Indians of the Valley of Mexico, 1519–1810* (Palo Alto, CA, 1964). (30) O. GONÇALVES DE LIMA, *El maguey y el pulque en los códices mexicanos* (Mexico City 1956). (31) Y. GONZALEZ TORRES, *El culto a los astros entre los Mexicas* (Mexico City 1975). (32) N. HAMMOND, ed., *Mesoamerican Archaeology: New Approaches* (London 1974). (33) R. HEIM and G. WASSON, *Les champignons hallucinogènes du Mexique* (Paris 1958). (34) A. HVIDTFELDT, *Teotl and Ixiptlatli: Some Central Conceptions in Ancient Mexican Religion* (Copenhagen 1958). (35) P. KIRCHHOFF, "Mesoamérica," in *Acta Americana* 1 (1943): 92–107. (36) W. KRICKEBERG, "Das mittelamerikanische Ballspiel und seine religiöse Symbolik," *Paideuma* 3 (1948): 118–98. (37) P. JORALEMON, *A Study of Olmec Iconography,* Studies in Precolumbian Arts and Archaeology (Washington 1971). (38) W. JIMENEZ MORENO, "Religión o Religiones Mesoamericanas," in *Verhandlungen des XXXVIII Internationalen Amerikanisten Kongresses* (Munich 1971). (39) J. LAFAYE, *Quetzalcoatl et Guadalupe* (Paris 1974). (40) M. LEON PORTILLA, *La Filosofía Nahuatl estudiada en sus fuentes* (2d ed., Mexico City 1959); (41) *Tiempo y Realidad en el pensamiento maya* (Mexico City 1968). (42) A. LOPEZ AUSTIN, *Augurios y abusiones,* texts of the informants of Sahagún (Mexico City 1967); (43) "Cuarenta clases de magos del mundo Nahuatl," *Estudios de cultura Nahuatl* 7 (1967): 87–117; (44) *Juegos rituales Aztecas* (Mexico City 1967); (45) *Hombre-dios: Religión y política en el mundo nahuatl* (Mexico City 1973). (46) R. MACNEISH, "Ancient Mesoamerican Civilization," *Science* 143 (1964): 531–37. (47) I. MARQUINA, *Arquitectura prehispánica* (Mexico City 1951). (48) S. W. MILES, "The Sixteenth Century Pokom-Maya," *Transactions of the American Philosophical Society,* n.s., 57 (1957): 731–81. (49) C. NAVARRETE, *The Chiapanec: History and Culture* (Provo 1966). (50) H. B. NICHOLSON, "Religion in Pre-Hispanic Central Mexico," in *Handbook of Middle American Indians* (Austin 1971), 10:395–446. (51) J. PADDOCK, *Ancient Oaxaca* (Stanford 1966). (52) K. PREUSS, "Phallishe Fruchtbarkeits-Dämonen als Träger des altmexikanischen mimischen Weltdramas," *Archiv für Anthropologie* 29 (1903): 129–88; (53) "Die Feuergötter als Ausgangpunkt zum Verständnis der mexicanischen Religion, in ihrem Zusammenhänge," *Mitteilungen der Anthropologischen Gesellschaft in Wien* 33 (1903): 129–233. (54) R. RICARD, *La conquête spirituelle du Mexique* (Paris 1933). (55) C. ROBELO, *Diccionario de mitología nahoa* (Mexico City 1951; 1st ed., Mexico City 1905–8). (56) A. RUZ LHUILLIER, *Costumbres funerarias de los antiguos mayas* (Mexico City 1968). (57) W. SANDERS and B. PRICE, *Mesoamerica: The Evolution of a Civilization* (New York 1968). (58) P. SCHELLHAS, *Representation of Deities of the Maya Manuscripts* (Cambridge, MA, 1904). (59) O. SCHONDUBE BAUMBACH, "Deidades prehispánicas en el área de Tamazula-Tuxpan-Zapotlán en el Estado de Jalisco," in *The Archaeology of West Mexico* (Ajijic 1974). (60) L. SÉJOURNÉ, *Burning Water: Thought and Religion in Ancient Mexico* (New York 1956). (61) E. SELER, *Gesammelte Abhandlungen zur Amerikanischen Sprach und Altertumskunde,* 5 vols. (Berlin 1902–23). (62) SOCIEDAD MEXICANA DE ANTROPOLOGIA, *Teotihuacan* (Mexico City 1966–72); (63) *Religión en Mesoamerica* (Mexico City 1972). (64) J. SOUSTELLE, *La penseée cosmologique des anciens Mexicains* (Paris 1940). (65) L. SPENCE, *The Gods of Mexico* (London 1923). (66) B. SPRANZ, "Göttergestalten in den mexikanischen Bilderhandschriften der Codex Borgia Gruppe: Eine ikonographische Untersuchung," *Acta Humboldtiana* (Wiesbaden 1964). (67) G. STRESSER-PEAN, "Les origines du Volador et du Comelagatoazte," in *28ᵉ Congrès International des Américanistes* (Paris 1947); (68) "La légende aztèque de la naissance du soleil et de la lune," *Annuaire de l'École pratique des Hautes Études,* 1962, 3–32. (69) S. TAX, ed., *Heritage of Conquest: The Ethnology of Middle America* (Glencoe, IL, 1952). (70) J. E. S. THOMPSON, "Sky Bearers, Colors and Directions in Maya and Mexican Religion," in *Contributions to American Archaeology* (Washington 1934); (71) "The Moon Goddess in Middle America with Notes on Related Deities," in *Contributions to American Archaeology* (Washington 1939); (72) *Maya History and Religion* (Norman 1970). (73) R. WAUCHOPE, general ed., *Handbook of Middle American Indians,* 15 vols. (Austin 1964–75). (74) G. WILLEY, *An Introduction to American Archaeology* 1: *North and Middle America* (Englewood Cliffs 1966). (75) E. WOLF, *Sons of the Shaking Earth* (Chicago 1952).

IV. Contemporary Ethnological Studies

(1) G. AGUIRRE BELTRAN, *Medicina y Magia* (Mexico City 1963). (2) R. BEALS, *Cherán, a Sierra Tarascan Village* (Washington 1946). (3) V. BRICKER, "El hombre, la carga y el camino: Antiguos conceptos mayas sobre tiempo y espacio, y el sistema zinacanteco de carbos," in *Los Zinacantecos* (Mexico City 1966), 355–72. (4) R. BUNZEL, *Chichicastenango, a Guatemalan Village* (Seattle 1959). (5) R. BURKITT, *The Hills and the Corn: A Legend of the Kekchi Indians of Guatemala* (Philadelphia: 1920). (6) P. CARRASCO, *Tarascan Folk Religion: An Analysis of Economic, Social and Religious Interactions* (New Orleans 1952). (7) H. FABREGA and D. SILVER, *Illness and Curing in Zinacantan: An Ethnomedical Analysis* (Stanford 1973). (8) G. FOSTER, "Sierra Popoloca Folklore and Beliefs," *University of California Publications in American Archaeology and Ethnology* 42 (1945): 177–250; (9) *Empire's Children: The People of Tzintzuntzan* (Washington 1948). (10) R. GIRARD, *Los Chortis ante el problema maya,* 5 vols. (Mexico City 1949). (11) C. GUITERAS HOLMES, *Perils of the Soul: The World View of a Tzotzil Indian* (Glencoe, IL, 1961). (12) E. HERMITTE, *Poder sobrenatural y control social en un pueblo maya contemporáneo* (Mexico City 1970). (13) W. R. HOLLAND, *Medicina Maya en los Altos de Chiapas* (Mexico City 1963). (14) A. ICHON, *La religion des Totonaques de la Sierra* (Paris 1969). (15) I. S. KELLY, "World View of a Highland Totonac Pueblo," in *Summa antropológica en homenaje a Roberto Weitlaner* (Mexico City 1966), 395–411. (16) O. LA FARGE, *The Yar-Bearer's People* (New Orleans 1931). (17) O. LEWIS, *Life in a Mexican Village: Tepoztlán Restudied* (Urbana 1951). (18) J. S. LINCOLN, "The Maya Calendar of the Ixil of Guatemala," in *Carnegie Institution, Contributions to American Anthropology and History,* 7, vol. 38 (1942), pp. 97–128. (19) C. LUMHOLTZ, *Symbolism of the Huichol Indians* (New York 1900); (20) *Unknown Mexico,* 2 vols. (New York 1902). (21) W. MADSEN,

Christo-Paganism: A Study of Mexican Religious Syncretism (New Orleans 1957). (22) M. OAKES, *The Two Crosses of Todos Santos: Survivals of Mayan Religious Beliefs* (New York 1951). (23) E. C. PARSONS, *Mitla, Town of the Souls* (Chicago 1936). (24) T. PREUSS, *Die Nayarit-expedition,* Die Religion der Cora Indianer (Leipzig 1912). (25) R. S. RAVICZ, *Organización Social de los Mixtecos* (Mexico City 1965). (26) R. REDFIELD, *Tepoztlán, a Mexican Village* (Chicago 1930); (27) *Folk Culture of Yucatán* (Chicago 1941). (28) R. REDFIELD and A. VILLA, *Chan Kom, a Maya Village* (Washington 1934). (29) L. REYES GARCIA, *Pasión y Muerte del Cristo Sol,* Carnaval y cuaresma en Ichcatepec (Xalapa 1960). (30) A. ROUHIER, *Monographie du peyotl* (Paris 1926). (31) A. J. RUBEL, "Ritual Relationships in Ojitlan," *American Anthropologist,* vol. 56 (1955). (32) L. SCHULTZE-JENA, *Indiana* I. *Leben, Glaube und Sprache der Quiche von Guatemala* (Jena 1933); (33) *Indiana* II: *Mythen in der Muttersprache der Pipil von Izalco in El Salvador* (Jena 1935); (34) *Indiana* III: *Bei den Azteken, Mixteken und Tlapaneken der Sierra Madre del Sur von Mexico* (Jena 1938). (35) J. SOUSTELLE, *La famille Otomí-Pame du Mexique Central* (Paris 1937). (36) G. STRESSER-PEAN, "Montagnes calcaires et sources vauclusiennes dans la religion des Indiens Huastèques," in *Revue d'histoire des religions,* vol. 141 (1952). (37) N. D. THOMAS, *Envidia, Brujeria y Organización ceremonial en un pueblo zoque* (Mexico City 1974). (38) J. E. S. THOMPSON, *Ethnology of the Mayas of Southern and Central British Honduras* (Chicago 1930). (39) A. M. TOZZER, *A Comparative Study of the Maya and the Lacandones* (London 1907). (40) A. VILLA, *The Maya of East Central Quintana Roo* (Washington 1945); (41) "Los conceptos de espacio y tiempo entre los grupos mayences contemporáneos," in *Tiempo y Realidad en el pensamiento maya,* L. Portilla, ed. (Mexico City 1968). (42) E. Z. VOGT, *Zinacantan, a Maya Community in the Highlands of Chiapas* (Cambridge 1968). (43) G. WASSON, "Ololiuhqui and the Other Hallucinogens of Mexico," in *Summa antropológica en homenaje a Roberto Weitlaner* (Mexico City 1966), 329–57. (44) R. WILLIAMS GARCIA, *Los Tepehuas* (Xalapa 1963). (45) C. WISDOM, *Los Chortis de Guatemala* (Guatemala City 1961).

Mesoamerican Mythic and Ritual Order

I. The Myths

The Mesoamerican mythology of the pre-Cortés period is known primarily through the Aztec texts of central Mexico and through the cosmogonic narrative of the Quiche transcribed in the *Popol Vuh.* For the other peoples, we have only fragmentary data which, in the case of the Maya of Yucatan, are scant indeed. Collected during the sixteenth century, these narratives are complex, often contradictory compilations abounding in details about the natural environment, the plant and animal worlds, and so forth. They have made possible the understanding or interpretation of numerous sculptures, frescoes, and various pictographs. For example, one can cite the case of a great human head sculpted in stone that was found at the site of the great temple Tenochtitlán in Mexico City. The lower edge of the neck bears bas-reliefs and thus indicates that this head was not broken off from a larger piece. The closed eyes indicate death. The face bears glyphs in the shape of small bells. Thanks to this last detail, it has been possible to identify the piece as a representation of Coyolxauhqui ("she who is painted with small bells"), a moon goddess, who according to one myth was decapitated by the sun god Huitzilopochtli.

Mythological texts from the sixteenth century have been supplemented by those that are currently being collected by ethnologists and linguists in certain regions of Mexico and Guatemala that have remained Indian. Conservation of the language is generally a precondition for maintaining the mythological tradition, but this alone is not sufficient. Relatively few myths have been preserved in the Mexican central plateau, northern Yucatan, and the highlands of Chiapas and Guatemala. On the other hand, the mountains of Nayarit, the eastern side of Mexico, and the tropical forest of eastern Chiapas and of southern Belize have provided Cora, Huichol, Huastec, Nahuatl, Tepehua, Totonac, Mixe, Popoloca, and Mayan myths.

Myths tended to die out in Mesoamerica. Not only were they driven back into the farthest reaches of the region, but they often survived only in the memories of old men, healers, or musicians, the last trustees of ancestral knowledge. They suffered the same oblivion into which certain elements of the ancient civilization have fallen: war, human sacrifice, the ritual ball game, the social hierarchy with its nobles and chiefs, and so forth. On the other hand, certain myths have annexed elements that were Spanish or biblical in origin.

Wherever they survive, myths occasionally still preserve their sacred force. They explain natural phenomena. They guarantee the bases of native morality, imposing rules of behavior and warning against the transgression of social, familial, and community norms. They provide the ideological basis for ceremonies, songs, dances, and games. They may inspire certain elements of costume. They bestow a grandeur upon the humble acts of traditional techniques like ceramics, spinning, weaving, and agriculture.

Pre-Columbian cosmogonic myths with their successive creations and destructions of the universe have become progressively impoverished. The story of a great flood, reinforced by the teaching of Christianity, is often well preserved. It has still been possible to collect myths of the birth of the sun and moon in different forms and in many regions. The myths of the morning star survive especially among the Huichol and the Cora of the Nayarit Sierra. Elsewhere, these myths are often replaced by the exploits of a young culture hero. The gods of lightning, mountains, and caves often provide important themes. Masters of animals or plants, animal guardian spirits, the dead, and ghosts still have their place in legends today.

The fusion of native beliefs and the European legacy is very common. The assimilation of Christ to the sun has concretized a whole set of ancient beliefs about presolar times and about the struggle that marked their end. This has resulted in the presence, in certain places, of representatives of pagan deities of long ago in the dance of the Moors and Christians that has become for the Indians an evocation of the birth of the sun.

Similarly, Carnival and Holy Week are often the occasion for the presentation of dramas about the ancient gods of war or the rebirth of vegetation. The dance of the Volador reenacts the journey of the souls to heaven. A whole mythic cycle comments on the return of the dead and threatens terrible punishment for those who fail to welcome them with the appropriate munificence.

II. Rituals: Elements of the Ceremonial and Typology

Rituals play an essential role in every religion. In Mesoamerica, ritual has preoccupied generations of specialists,

Coyolxauhqui, "she who is painted with small bells," Aztec goddess of the moon. Mexico City, Museum of Anthropology. Museum photo.

The dance of the Volador. Nahua Indians (Pueblo de Atla, Pahuatlan, Puebla). Photo M.A.E.F.M.

from the priestly governors of the great Olmec centers to the alcaldes of certain communities today in the highlands of Guatemala, including the thousands of religious professionals of Tenochtitlan, who were divided into thirty-eight categories according to the census of Sahagún. But ritual activity was also, and perhaps even more, the business of each individual, who not only participated in or had to attend official ceremonies organized by the hierarchy, but who was constantly compelled to perform acts or to utter words that were regarded as duties to the sacred. For the sacred pervaded the totality of the universe, and human beings experienced it at every moment of their lives. In addition, ritual obligation in Mesoamerica rested on yet another premise, that humans and gods have a common stake in the perpetuation of the world, as was articulated by the myths; and it was the celebration of this vital relationship that the rituals assured.

In Mesoamerica, the ceremonies always included a period of time and rituals of preparation that culminated in a vigil, whether it was a major or minor festival, current or pre-Columbian. Continence and fasting were the two traditional observances of these preparatory periods, the duration of which varied according to the importance of the ceremony. Sometimes reduced to a few days, they could also last an entire year, as in the case of the *teocuac* at Tenochtitlan, young men, "eaters of god," who were the incarnations of the elder brothers of Huitzilopochtli. Fasting and continence were the first two steps toward purification that had to precede any celebration. Breaking the fast or the continence was fatal, because this destroyed the force of the ritual. Purity was a prerequisite not only for the participants but also for places and objects. For purity (called *zuhuy* by the Maya) was one of the great obsessions that prevailed in Mesoamerican rituals. In certain cases, the lustration of the officiating priests by water or by incense, together with confession, was the crowning touch for the preparations.

The ritual per se was composed of at least two, often simultaneous elements: the offering and the prayer. The nature of the offering was highly variable, beginning with the ornamenting of idols and altars (notably with paper cutouts) and gifts of food or burning incense, and ending with sacrifices. The sacrifice of an animal or a human was a fundamental act of homage to the gods. For blood was the primary divine element, as is witnessed not only by the myths and their pictographic translations in the codex, but also by the ancient Mexicans' custom of annointing the mouths of idols with the "precious liquid," and perhaps by the etymology of the Yucatec term for the sacrifice: *p'a chi* ("open the mouth"). In Aztec mythology, which provides the most insistent legitimatizations of sacrifice, the sun must be revitalized each morning upon emerging from his nocturnal journey in the realm of the dead. The considerable escalation of the number of human sacrifices during the Postclassic Period should not, however, lead us to forget that we are dealing with a very ancient type of offering, which was undoubtedly practiced since Preclassic times (Izapa-Monte Alban) and had taken on multiple forms (tearing out the heart, decapitation, piercing with arrows, drowning, and so forth). Self-sacrifice, in which the celebrants extracted the blood from a part of their bodies with various types of needles, appeared in a remote period; it was, alternately or at the same time, a penitential practice or a ritual of offering. The prayers that accompanied the offerings could be prayers of petition, of thanksgiving, or of propitiation. All the prayers were geared to a material end, which was either wished for or had already been obtained. Finally, the liturgy, depending on circumstances, could be enhanced with additional activities (songs, dances, processions), which in certain cases today are the only surviving elements of ancient rituals practiced on the margins of Catholic ceremonies.

In Mesoamerica, ritual took its place in the dual framework of the community and the nuclear family. Despite numerous correspondences and sometimes actual overlapping, the public ceremony can be contrasted with the private ritual. In ancient Mexico, the organization of community rituals was the realm reserved for professional priests. Today, it is almost always the domain of the majordomos, a religious elite periodically renewed and primarily charged with the responsibility of carrying the economic burden of the cult (see below, section III). The collective ritual life in pre-Columbian and contemporary societies follows the precise rhythm of the calendar. Among the Aztecs, two great series of festivals would correspond respectively to the unfolding of the solar and ceremonial calendars; the end of each of the eighteen twenty-day periods of the solar year was marked by a specific ceremony, the nature of which was for the most part directly related to the phases of the agricultural cycle. The festivals, fixed according to the *tonalpohualli,* were the means of specific celebrations of the gods (somewhat like the cult of the saints), on the days that were associated with them. But it was the ends of the cycles, the due dates, that haunted the imagination and that certainly gave rise to the most impressive ceremonies: the festival of the *toxiuhmolpilia,* "the binding of the years," celebrated every fifty-two years during the Postclassic Period on the central high plateau, the ritual of the death and resurrection of the *baktun* among the Maya of the Classic Period. Added to this entire fixed liturgical complex were numerous episodic celebrations that concerned either a part or the whole of the community. Droughts and dearths, the inauguration of sanctuaries and departures for war, every exceptional event was and sometimes still is ritualistically treated in a spectacular manner. For theatricality is one of the peculiarities of the public rituals, a great number of which consisted in the representation of genuine religious dramas; almost every festival of the Aztec solar calendar included the reenactment of a fragment of myth such as the defeat of the moon during the month of Tititl. The dance of the Volador and the ritual ball game were great "classics" in the liturgical repertory.

But religious fervor in Mesoamerica can perhaps best be measured by the importance of individual and familial rituals. The fabric of daily life is dotted with ritual practices, whether they be domestic rituals at the altar of a home or more solemn ceremonies that accompany the great moments of an individual's life: birth, baptism, the giving of the name, marriage, death. For at every moment, the Mesoamericans turn to their gods, as we are reminded in this prayer to the "heart of the sky," taken from the *Popol Vuh:*

> Grant life and prosperity to my children, to my servants; cause to be fruitful and multiply those whose duty it is to feed you and to assure your survival and those who invoke your name on the roads, in the fields, on the banks of rivers, in the shade of trees and creepers.

The Festival of Ochpaniztli (Borbonicus Codex, p. 30). Paris, Library of the Palais-Bourbon. Library photo.

III. Rituals: Practice and Social Function

In the indigenous conceptual system, the social order was lived as a replication of the general order of the world, the latter serving to justify the former. Ritual was the means by which one periodically brought to life the profile of the social and sacred hierarchies and by which one gathered the community around the idea that the world existed only through the action of the gods. And this action was possible only as a result of the worship and the compensatory offerings made by humans in conformity with ancestral models.

Where did the ritual begin? Among today's Indians, daily life is punctuated by a series of rigid actions just as much in the relationships between relatives and in economic transactions as in the way of addressing ancient deities or pious images on the Christian home altar. This applied effort to regard life as a somewhat obsolete attachment to austere norms of behavior still rather accurately characterizes the most conservative native societies of Mesoamerica. But increasingly, as a function of the growing integration of communities into the national society, young generations disengage themselves from such constraints.

Certain essential rituals remain nonetheless, for they are necessary to the cohesion of diverse communities. Among the Otomi and the Mazahua, oratories, small chapels designed for the worship of ancestors, constitute the basic framework for the social structure of a village. The Tzeltal and the Tzotzil of Chiapas have a ceremonial organization that is notably apparent on certain festival days and that

Ball game field at Copan (Honduras). Photo M.A.E.F.M.

affirms that each individual belongs to his or her own neighborhood or barrio. As a basic subdivision of the village, this neighborhood plays multiple political and religious roles.

Similarly, in ancient Aztec society, the *calpulli* were territorial units that encompassed groups of relatives and were characterized by an eponymous deity as well as by particular rituals. Territorial subdivisions like the *calpulli* survive today among the Maya of the highlands of Chiapas, in Chinantla, and even in certain zones of central Mexico. Sometimes even a neighborhood that has become mestizo will oppose a neighborhood that has remained indigenous, each one thus maintaining its different types of religious practices.

The performance of rituals tended and still tends to reinforce the establishment. Although ancient Indian society had priestly groups distinct from other groups of leaders, the civil and religious powers were not strictly separated, because both were supposed to have originated from the same sacred source. By the tenth century, the famous Toltec sovereign Ce Acatl Topiltzin was regarded as an incarnation of the god Quetzalcoatl. Later, the Aztec during their migration would receive orders from their god Huitzilopochtli, orders that were naturally transmitted by the priests. Aztec sovereigns were sacred characters, and their names would evoke the gods. The last of them, Cuauhtemoc, actually bore the mystical name of the setting sun, "falling eagle."

After the Conquest, the Spanish administration gradually deprived the kings, chiefs, and native nobles of their powers, replacing them with dignitaries elected or appointed for limited periods of time. Thus, with the consent of the

Sunday meeting of the *governadores* of Teguerichic (Carichic). Tarahumara Indians. Photo M.A.E.F.M.

authorities, a system of political and religious responsibilities, sometimes tied to organizations of Catholic brotherhoods, was progressively developed. This system of responsibilities, which organized and regulated the munificence of individuals for the benefit of the community, enjoyed tremendous success among the Indians. It corresponded to their ideal of individual wealth that should be used for the profit of everyone. Moreover, it had antecedents in the socioreligious organization of pre-Cortés times.

Throughout the colonial period, and to this day, the same system of responsibilities, straddling both the political and the religious sectors, has played the role of a coercive instrument in local affairs, imposing the observance of festivals and exercising political authority. In the course of his life, each person must fulfill a large number of functions that will lead him progressively to take more prestigious responsibilities. Among the Maya of Chiapas and Guatemala, the system has had its most far-reaching application. Sometimes it even forces a civil servant to leave his home during his entire term of office and to reside in a ceremonial center made up of functional dwellings belonging to the community.

At the basis of this system is a multitude of minor support roles with less responsibility. These are reserved for young people, who are brought in to play the roles of police officers, deputies, and jacks-of-all-trades. They supply a permanent source of free labor that complements the periodic forced labor of the group of adult men. In this way, the system functions as a framework for socialization. But at a higher level, it also becomes the locus in which political strategies are exercised, for the highest posts, which correspond to roles in upper-level management, are few. In the past, these posts were the object of stiff competition, and this is often still the case, even though the system has entered a period of crisis.

One of the functions of the system is, therefore, economic. It tends to level out individual resources through a redistribution of wealth and through a destruction of monetary surpluses. But today the weight of the responsibilities tends to accentuate rather than even out economic inequities, for it heavily increases the indebtedness of the poor without decreasing the wealth of the rich. In addition, wealthy Indians seek to divest themselves of community responsibilities. One way to do this is to convert to Protestantism, which affirms a break with ancient religious traditions, pagan and Catholic alike. This weakening of commitment to the collective enterprise leads above all to the decline of festivals, a relatively recent phenomenon that has nevertheless spread rapidly. Lately, as in pre-Columbian times, the costs of the cult have weighed most heavily on the Indian communities. The festivals had, and still have, an essentially ostentatious character: the distribution of food and beverages, the cost of equipment, and support for dancers, fireworks, and choral societies.

Although the ancient pagan calendar still survives in a more or less altered form in certain sectors of Guatemala and southern Mexico, it no longer marks time for the succession of grandiose and often bloody festivals that the sixteenth-century chronicles describe for us. A curious exception is the important movable feast that the Quiche of Momostenango still celebrate on the day of the "eight monkeys." However, in many places, ceremonies, indeed veritable festivals, continue to be celebrated in honor of the ancient gods, but these are generally unpretentious demonstrations tied to seasons or to weather forecasting. Certain communities maintain for such use a small non-Christian temple in the form of a modest-looking house situated in an out-of-the-way place and called in Nahuatl *xochicalli* ("flower house" or "precious house"). More generally, the festivals have today become an integral part of the cycle of solemn days of the Roman Catholic church. In each village, the most important festival is generally the feast of the local patron saint. Here one almost always sees dances, some of which are indigenous in origin, such as the Volador, while others have been instituted by the missionaries, such as the dance of the shepherdesses, the dance of the Conquest, or the dance of the Moors and Christians. The festival of the patron saint is sometimes overshadowed by the festival of Holy Week, Christmas, or the Virgin of Guadalupe.

All Saints' Day, now fixed on the first of November, and the movable feast of Carnival have often preserved a large measure of native characteristics and continue to be immensely popular. When the festival reaches its final stage of decadence, its religious aspect is reduced to a simple Mass that attracts only a few of the faithful, whereas the general public crowd the square where groups of Indian dancers have been replaced by the street stalls of mestizo merchants.

In ancient Mesoamerican religion, there were pilgrimages. Some of these have been Christianized through the efforts of missionaries and continue to attract considerable crowds of Indians. The best known is that of the Virgin of Guadalupe on the site of the ancient shrine of the mother goddess. The Sacromonte and Chalma are also substitute pilgrimages. But there are still traditional pilgrimages in the most conservative regions.

M.A.E.F.M./g.h.

BIBLIOGRAPHY

See the bibliography at the end of the article "Mesoamerican Religion," and especially section I: 7, 11, 22; section II: 3, 8, 9, 13, 15, 24, 31, 35, 36, 38, 43; section III: 10, 21, 36, 45, 62, 67; section IV: 4, 6, 19, 23, 25, 26, 29, 31, 32, 33, 36, 39, 42, 44.

Mesoamerican Creation Myths

I. Creation Myths in Pre-Columbian Societies

Creation myths must have appeared at a very early period in the Mesoamerican area. One of the first pieces of evidence of their existence may be revealed in the Olmec or Olmecoid representations in the Preclassical style which show the union of a jaguar and an anthropomorphic being.

The interpretation of the symbolic content of these bas-reliefs and paintings still remains, in part, to be done. In addition, these archaic manifestations are too isolated to permit even a summary reconstruction of the oldest theogony-cosmogonies. On the other hand, the elements known from the decades before and after the Conquest present a large series of images of genesis, from which, despite the divergences in detail, it is possible to extract some important invariables. On the high plateau of central Mexico, the principal versions of the creation myths are expressed in

Jade mask of a jaguar-man (drawing by Eugenia Joyce). A major theme in Olmec art, it may illustrate one of the most ancient myths of creation in Mesoamerica. Washington, D.C., Dumbarton Oaks Collection.

Aztec sculpture (Stone of the Sun) as well as in pictographic manuscripts and texts of the sixteenth century (*Codex Vaticanus A, Historia de los Mexicanos por sus pinturas, Leyenda de los Soles, Anales de Cuauhtitlan, Codex Florentino*). These documents are relatively late but seem to be based on older, perhaps less structured, versions. A first indication of this antiquity may be the presence in the codices of fragments of myths that are clearly pre-Columbian, representative of beliefs not only of the Valley of Mexico but of all of central Mexico. Likewise, the convergence of myths collected on the high plateau in the sixteenth century and of those preserved by the Nicaraos (whose migration from central Mexico toward Nicaragua goes back to the ninth century) argues in favor of their antiquity. The second group of documents which have come down to us, and which express, in part, the ancient pre-Columbian origin, originate in the Maya region, particularly in the highlands of Guatemala (*Popol Vuh, Anales de los Cakchiqueles*). The information collected in the central and southern Maya zones is much more sparse or belongs to periods too far removed from the conquest.

In the corpus as a whole, certain common traits stand out which could have constituted a Central American mythic kernel, perhaps dating from the end of the Classical Period.

All creation proceeds from a primitive divine couple (Hunab Itzam Na and Ix Chebel Yax of the lowlands of Yucatan) or from a double principle, man and woman, sometimes incarnated in two deities, sometimes intermingled in a single deity. The latter is the case among the Aztec, who invoke Ometecuhtli, the "lord of duality," and Omecihuatl, the "lady of duality," or sometimes Ometeotl, the "deity of duality." It is from this primordial pair that all living beings have issued; it is this couple which, fundamentally, presides over the creation of the world. For this reason these original deities are designated in certain Aztec texts by the titles of "prince" and "princess of our flesh" and in the *Popol Vuh* as "Father" and "Mother of the Son," the generative cell of all life. Even the other gods descend from them: they are the firstfruits of the carnal union sometimes evoked in the codices. In the work of universal creation, certain gods of the first generation (notably Quetzalcoatl and Tezcatlipoca) played the role of special assistants, according to the tradition of central Mexico. Nevertheless, nothing that exists escapes the attention of the primitive god and his mate, who reign over the first and last sign of the days of the Aztec calendar, respectively.

The creation of the world—all the myths agree on this point—was neither an immediate reality nor the result of an evolutionary process. Rather, the history of the universe, from its very beginning, presents a succession of creations and destructions whose number and nature vary according to the sources (see table), but which have common implications. It seems, therefore, that instability is inherent in the heart of the world, either by reason of the struggle among the contradictory elements of the universe (earth, wind, fire, and water) which, in the Aztec tradition, led to the overthrow of the four previous suns and which can bring about the annihilation of the fifth, or as a result of the interventions of the gods who are concerned to improve the human race (*Popol Vuh*). Hemmed in between the past flood and the future cataclysm, the indigenous world of the sixteenth century is eminently precarious. For this reason many of the rites have as a goal a reduction of the risk of rupture, the search for preservation, for the maintenance of the cosmos. The succession of cycles has, in addition, established the union of life and death which impregnates the entire universe.

Schematic Table of the Cycles of Creation according to the Aztec and the Quiche (16th century)

Leyenda de los Soles (1558)	*Popol Vuh*
First Sun (Ocelotonatiuh) Sun of the Jaguar (with a duration of 676 years). The Universe devoured by jaguars.	*First Creation* Humanity created out of mud but without stability. Race endowed with speech but without intelligence. Impossibility of resisting the action of the water. Destruction by the gods, discontent with their work.
Second Sun (Ehecatonatiuh) Sun of the Wind (364 years). Universe destroyed by a hurricane. Survivors transformed into monkeys.	*Second Creation* Man created out of the wood of a tree (*tzite*) and woman out of a reed. Race endowed with speech, with the faculty of multiplying itself, but without soul and forgetful of the gods. Black rain of resin and rebellion of animals and domestic objects. Flood and transformation of survivors into monkeys.
Third Sun (Quiahuitonatiuh) Sun of Rain (364 years). Universe consumed by a rain of fire. Survivors transformed into turkeys.	*Third Creation* Man created out of corn. Humanity intelligent and careful about the sacred. After the destruction of the Spanish, a new world will be born.
Fourth Sun (Atonatiuh) Sun of Water (676 years). Universe drowned by a flood. Survivors changed into fish.	
Fifth Sun (Ollintonatiuh) Sun of Movement. The Universe will perish in an earthquake. (Annals of Cuauhtitlan).	

Cut paper work representing the old sun, predecessor of the present sun. San Lorenzo Achiotepec (Otomi Indians).

Finally, all the creation accounts pose, in an almost identical fashion, the problem of the relations between humans and the gods, between creatures and their creator. At the origin of humanity, a contract was established. First of all, humans owe their existence to the gods: they were created through the sacrifice of the deity. According to Leon Portilla, this is what is implied in the Aztec term *macehualli,* "that which has been merited." In the myth of central Mexico, Quetzalcoatl descends to the kingdom of the dead to seek the bones, pulverized and sprinkled with the blood of the gods, from which the human race is born. But humankind also owes to the gods the creation and the gift of the elements necessary for their survival: the creation of the sun and the moon at the cost of a collective sacrifice of the pantheon, the gift of water and plants, in the first rank of which is corn. Therefore, the beginnings of humanity are marked by a major liability to the gods. An initial debt has been contracted. The gods demand payment. They need the attentions of humans, their prayers, their offerings. "Precious water," the *chalchihuatl,* the blood of victims, is their nourishment, without which the universe goes quickly to perdition.

II. Myths of Creation in Contemporary Indigenous Societies

In the traditions of the Indians of today, the ancient conception of a series of universal cataclysms is reduced, in general, to the idea that the present world was preceded by a flood and will be destroyed in turn in the future. Nevertheless there are exceptions, especially in the Maya regions. The myth of the flood is often enriched with various details of biblical origin, among the Totonac, for example, who say that the chest that plays the role of an ark came back down to earth after forty days. Among the Maya Mopan of Belize, the son of Adam and Eve, a solar numen, provoked a deluge of water which chilled him. Among the Otomi, it is believed that the end of the present world will be caused by a rain of fire.

Here is an example of a present-day flood myth, collected by H. Lemley among the Tlapanec Indians:

> A vulture addressing a man who was working on the mountain said: "Do not work any more, for now the world is coming to its end." The vulture then said to a tree: "Get up," and to a rock, "Get up." The tree rose but not the rock. Then the vulture said to the man, "Construct a box without telling anyone, not even those in your family, or else they will begin to cry. Therefore, it is better if you say nothing." When the man had finished constructing the box, the vulture put him inside, along with a dog and a hen. A little later, the man saw through a crack in the box that it was raining and he also heard the animals that lived in the water shaking the box, with the desire, it seemed, to eat the man. He also saw that the world was filled with water. Then he noticed that the earth was so swampy that it was impossible to walk. So he put his head back inside. Later, he abandoned the box when he saw that vegetation was growing and he went to work the land. The hen changed into a vulture and flew above the land. Wherever the vulture went, mountains and valleys formed behind him.
>
> Every day the man went to work, and every afternoon when he returned from his work, he would see tortillas which had been prepared for his dinner, but he did not know who had made them.
>
> The man went to a mountaintop every day. He sat down to see who was coming to prepare the tortillas, but the dog remained in the house each time. Finally, he saw that the dog was taking off its skin, and he entered the house immediately. When he was inside, he saw a woman grinding the corn, and saw the skin of the dog in a pile on the bed. So the man took the skin of the dog and threw it into the flames to burn it, but the woman said, "Do not burn my clothes, for if the skin is burned, my children will not grow." For this reason the woman stayed, without ever taking off her skin again.

Among the Pocomam, the flood is the founding act of civilization. Before the cataclysm, the world was peopled by a cannibalistic humanity with neither faith nor law. Afterwards, it was to be the humanity of the men of the present, the progeny of a couple who escaped from the flood and were banished by God for having sinned.

In the abundance of creation themes certain preoccupations seem to impose themselves with special force, such as the cycle of corn deities, covering the area from the civilizations of the central plateau to those of Yucatan and the Guatemalan highlands with their individual variants. The culture hero (Quetzalcoatl among the Aztec) discovers corn hidden behind a crag which he penetrates through a fissure, disguised as an ant. This mountain or Tonacatepetl reappears in a Kekchi version in the form of Sakletch. In the Cakchiquel tradition, it is split apart by lightning. It is interesting to note that, among the Tepehua, the sun hidden in the mountain takes the place of the corn in the mythical account:

> The sun was sought. A lizard that was a *topil* (policeman) went to inform the authorities that, under a stone that was impossible to move, there was a strong light. A woodpecker was brought, and it opened the rock by striking it once with its beak. There, the sun was found

squatting down. All the dancers ran up. The sun said that it was going to come out and it wanted the dances always to be like this. The sun came out and it seems that a kind of glass was put in its heart so that it would not shine so much. Such is the sun now.

In this story there is an identification of corn and sun that underlies various present-day accounts without being clearly expressed.

Among the Quiche, man, a divine creation, is fashioned from corn paste. Among the Aztec, corn was rather the "Lord of our Flesh," the vital principle indispensable for survival.

In the present-day indigenous cosmologies, the vision of the sun/moon duality is an extension of the tradition of a couple with antagonistic and complementary principles, characterized as Grandfather and Grandmother (Quiche), Father and Mother (Tarascan), Son and Mother (Tzotzil) or more conventionally Husband and Wife (Yucatan, Oaxaca, central high plateau).

In a mixed version of the creation myth of the sun and the moon collected by P. Carrasco, a young boy and his sister assassinate their grandfather. Pursued by their grandmother, they reach a river, the boy first.

In order not to be held back by his sister, he took off his sandals and struck her in the face with them, smearing her face with mud so that she would not be seen and followed. They were close to the place where the earth ends, and it was then that the boy climbed first into the sky where his grandmother could not follow him. His sister took time to recover a part of her sight, after she had washed her face a bit, and it was only at the moment when the little man was about to hide on the horizon that the girl could rise into space. The spot that is seen on the moon is the mud that her brother threw. It is for that reason that it shines less than the sun.

The allegory which used to explain the appearance of the celestial bodies has more or less resisted time. In central Mexico today it takes the form of a Manichaean combat between God and the Devil, Christ and the Jews, Good and Evil. The characters change, but the structure of the account remains unchanged.

M.A.E.F.M./m.s.

BIBLIOGRAPHY

See the bibliography at the end of the article "Mesoamerican Religion," especially section II: 1, 2, 6, 17, 20, 26, 32, 34, 35, 37, 38; section III: 8, 37, 60, 61, 68; section IV: 9, 14, 44.

Mesoamerican Religious Conceptions of Space and Time

The vision of the world and the procedures of ritual life in Mesoamerica were submitted, from an early time, to a twofold principle of organization, the spatial and the temporal. Classificatory schemata (the orientation of the world and the establishment of durations of time) served, at least from the time of the recent Preclassical Period, as a framework for the religious universe. Questions and observations about space and time, far from constituting distinct preoccupations, were always closely intermingled. There are numerous proofs of the fundamental unity of these categories, be it a question, for example, of the quadripolar distribution of the signs of the days in the Aztec ceremonial calendar, of the location of the five "year bearers of the Venus cycle" between the four cardinal points and the center, or of the semantic confusion, which still exists in several Indian languages, between terms simultaneously expressing location in space and in time.

The observation of the celestial bodies and, in particular, of the apparent movement of the sun constitutes the common starting point of spatiotemporal considerations. Perhaps having an essentially economic character in the beginning (the rhythm of agricultural cycles), these become the prerogative of priestly specialists among the Olmec and the first occupants of Monte Alban. Astronomy, established as a science, is supported by an arithmetic put to religious use, and its earliest archaeological traces are dated B.C. It nevertheless remains inseparable from its astrological applications and would form the basis for the authority of the elites of the Classical Period. The collapse of the Classical civilizations (especially in the Mayan area) and then the Spanish conquest brought about the nearly total abandonment of the ancient systems of reference and of their sacred content. Though certain elements remained, they were, for the most part, transposed, and are sometimes difficult to recognize.

I. Time

From a very early date, the process of time had fascinated the peoples of Mesoamerica. Though no group seems to have arrived at a conceptualization of time in itself, abstract and undefined (as there are both multiple and singular spaces in the Indian conceptual system, so time is perceived under the form of both particular time and heterogeneous times), the flow of duration gave rise to a series of speculations and efforts to quantify it. It is even possible that certain Mayan astronomer-priests came to the conclusion that time had no beginning. Three great systems of the comprehension of time were used: two of these, the ceremonial calendar and the solar calendar, seem to have been quite widespread. The use of the third, after its invention by the Olmec, is limited to the Mayan area: it too is founded on the tropical year, but it situates each event in relationship to a date of origins (the "long count" or the computation of long durations).

The fundamental idea that seems to have governed the elaboration of these different modes of counting is the cyclic repetition of increasing units, each one submitted to the influence of one or several deities and associated with one of the directions. It is likely that the formation of these classificatory schemata was progressive (something that archaeology does not easily take account of) and that in the last centuries B.C. it caused the sudden proliferation of different calendrical systems. The computation of the long count is attested from the first century B.C. (stela 2 of Abaj Takalik, 2 of Chiapa de Corzo, C of Tres Zapotes, and 1 of El Baúl), while certain glyphs for days of the ceremonial year, as well as others representing the months of the solar year, were in use at Monte Alban from the time of the first phase of the occupation of the site, around 600 B.C.

The various modes of recording time have units and counting operations in common from one zone to another (even with their differences): twenty days follow one another without changing, designated by signs, of which two series are given as examples in the accompanying table.

Aztec (Central Mexico)	Quiche (Guatemala)
cipactli, aquatic monster	*imox* (earth)*
ehecatl, wind	*ikh*, wind
calli, house	*akhbal*, darkness, night
cuetzpallin, lizard	*kat* ?
coatl, serpent	*can*, serpent
miquiztli, death	*ceme*, death
mazatl, deer	*ceh*, deer
tochtli, rabbit	*khanil* ?
atl, water	*toh* (rain storm)*
itzcuintli, dog	*tzih*, dog
ozomatli, monkey	*batz*, monkey
malinalli, grass	*ee*, teeth
acatl, reed	*ah*, reed
ocelotl, jaguar	*balam* (jaguar)*
cuauhtli, eagle	*tzikin*, bird
cozcacuauhtli, vulture	*ahmac*, insect incarnating the spirits of the dead
ollin, earthquake	*noh* (earthquake)*
tecpatl, flint	*tihax* (obsidian knife)*
quiahuitl, rain	*canac* (rain)*
xochitl, flower	*hunahpu*, god who hunts with a blowpipe

*Obsolete.

—The ceremonial calendar (*tonalpohualli* of the Aztec, *tzolkin* of the Maya) is the result of the combination of the twenty signs for the days and the series of numbers from 1 to 13, coupled with the names of the days and repeated without interruption until the repetition of the initial day, at the end of 260 days: thus, the first day is 1 *cipactli;* the fourteenth day is named 1 *ocelotl*, the twenty-first day 8 *cipactli*, and so on, until the cycle comes back to the beginning, at the end of the 20 × 13 = 260 days.

—The solar year is composed of eighteen "months" of twenty days, to which are added five days which are considered to be inauspicious and which are designated, among the Aztec, by the general term *nemontemi*. Each year receives, as its name, the name of the initial day or the "year bearer." As a result of the time lag introduced by the five *nemontemi* in the succession of twenties, four different signs can inaugurate the year.

—The *xuihmolpilli* or Aztec "century" is the period of fifty-two years, at the end of which one day—doubly designated by its place in the ceremonial calendar and its position in the solar year—is repeated (on the conjunction of the two calendars, see the explanatory diagram).

—The Maya computation of the long count in which each date is calculated with reference to a starting point (the year 3113 B.C. according to Goodman-Martinez-Thompson) essentially uses the following units: *kin* (day), *uinal* (20 days), *tun* (360 days), *katun* (7,200 days, 20 *tuns*), *baktun* (144,000 days, 20 *katuns*).

—Two other counting cycles, although secondary, were known and often used: the lunar cycle and the Venusian year.

Time, as measured by these different systems, is never perceived as an objective and neutral element; calendars, much more than instruments for counting, always have particular religious functions. Thus there is a connection between the long count and the myths of creation, the end of the world, the primordial role of the *tonalpohualli-tzolkin* in divination, and the use of the solar calendar to mark the rhythm of the religious life of the communities. Several traditions attribute the invention of calendrical measurements to one of the gods (especially to Quetzalcoatl in his role as civilizing hero). Beyond this original bond, each part of each system is invested with one or several divinities and is affected by their combined qualities. The Maya as well as the Aztec identify the actual elements of time designation with the gods. A given day is influenced not only by one of the thirteen diurnal Lords and the nine Lords of the night, but also by the god associated with the sign itself, by the master of the group of thirteen, by the god that rules over the "month," and by the "year bearers." Furthermore, the spatial distribution of time culminates in a new play of influences, which engages directions and their properties. To clear up this tangle of connections and oppositions, there is nowhere to turn but to the knowledge of the astrologer-priests, who are the only individuals who possess the keys to this complex arithmetic. In the most complex pre-Columbian societies, in a manner parallel to that of the social hierarchies, there was a kind of dichotomy in the perception of time

"Monument" 3 from San José Mogote (Oaxaca). Dating from the sixth century B.C., this representation includes, between the legs of the figure, one of the oldest known calendric notations from Mesoamerica.

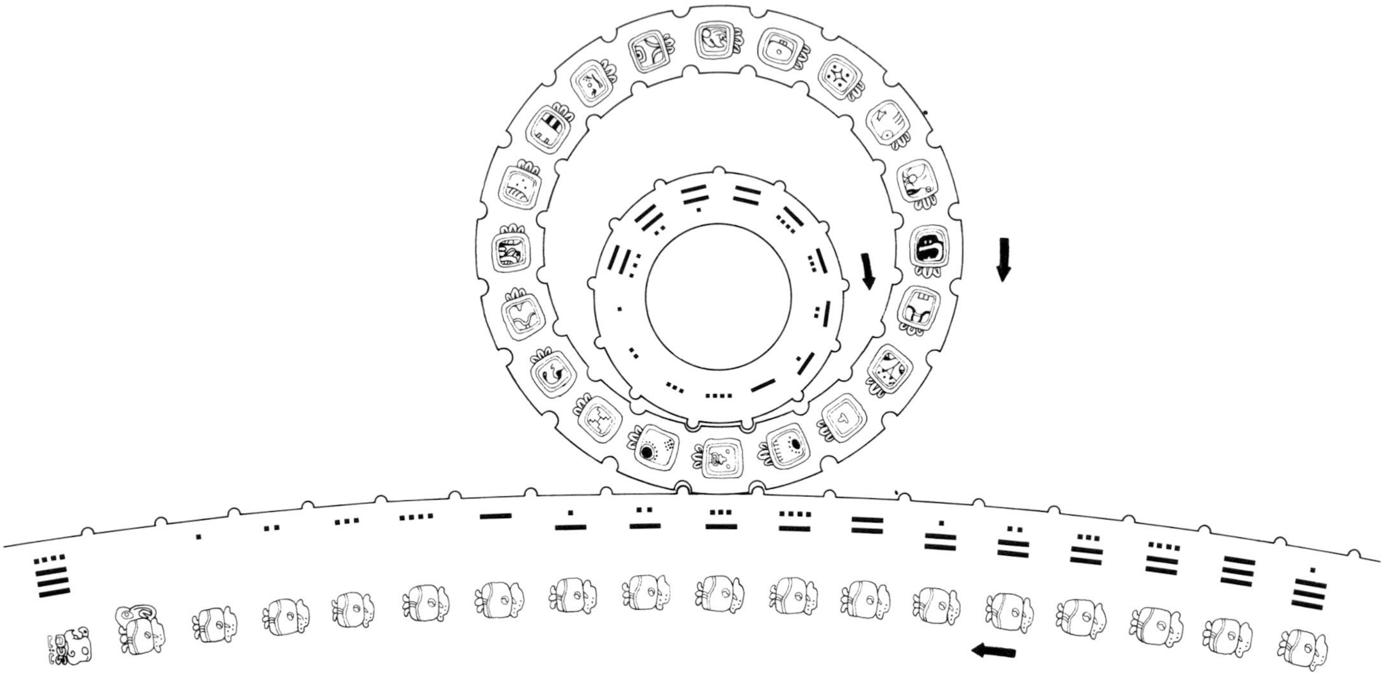

Diagram showing the conjunction of the Mayan solar and ceremonial calenders. By combining the thirteen numbers indicated on the inside circle (a dot stands for one, and a line for five) with the twenty daily glyphs in the outer circle with which they line up, 260 days can be counted. The association of each of these days with one of the 365 days of the solar year (represented on the circle of which only an arc is shown) expresses complete dates. The one indicated in the center of the diagram (reading from top to bottom) is 4 ahau 8 cumku. Adapted from *National Geographic* 148, no. 6 (December 1975).

between the elite holders of sophisticated knowledge and the members of the communities who shared a more practical knowledge (time concretized in rituals) and a blurrier knowledge (the time of myths and of the ancestors, the time of the flood or earthquake that would annihilate the world).

With the Spanish conquest, most of the ancient systems of the apprehension of time disappeared throughout nearly the whole of the Mesoamerican region. Some groups, particularly those of the Maya highlands of Mexico and of Guatemala, preserved the knowledge and practice of a few pre-Columbian elements: the Jacaltec diviners of Guatemala still deal with year bearers, groups of thirteen, groups of twenty, and inauspicious days (*hō-pic,* the "five women").

In the same way, among the Tzeltal of Oxchuc (Chiapas), the solar year, the only one known until about thirty years ago, still followed the ancient division into eighteen months of twenty days, completed by the period of the *Xma-Kaba-Kin,* the "days without name." In most cases, however, the Christian calendar is the only one used and simply co-opts certain of the functions of the ancient calendars: the five *uayeb* days were transferred to Holy Week by the Zutuhils of Santiago Atitlan and the Kekchis of Upper Verapaz, and were accompanied, as was previously the case in the Yucatan, by a cluster of rites to Mam, the god of evil. The "santos," like the festivals of the months of the old solar year, have not only acquired a privileged place in ritual life, but, in the same fashion, serve as reference points in the seasonal organization of agricultural labors. The adoption of European beliefs has often been supported by resemblances to earlier traditions (for example, the recognition of inauspicious days—Tuesday and Friday). But the presence of these disparate and disguised elements cannot mask the almost total loss of the ancient magic of time.

II. Space

The idea of a space assimilated to a stratification of layers is very ancient. The traditional view of the Maya defines the universe as a superposition of infraterrestrial and celestial worlds of unequal sizes, contained in a cubical volume and cut by a second plane, the surface of the earth. In observing the course of the sun and its displacement in the course of the year, during intersolstitial periods, the Maya took the east-west axis as the basis for their cardinal orientation of the world, discriminating between qualitatively distinct and sacralized portions of space. This religious geometry seems to have been familiar to the whole Mesoamerican world and to have served as the basis for the construction of a veritable symbolization of space.

Horizontally, space is broken up into regions endowed with specific properties, which encompass the reference points of the system of orientation: east, west, north, south, and center. In the Aztec and Maya traditions, which are the best known, each direction has a series of particularities, qualities, and powers. Among the Aztec, the east is the favorable region par excellence, as the land of the rising sun and of the rain gods; the west is the land of flowers, but also the entrance to the dark house which the setting sun and the evening star enter; the north is the endless arid plain, swept by the freezing wind that comes down from the world of the dead; the south is the land of spiny things, which forms a sort of replica of the north, but where the drought may be corrected by irrigation.

These characteristics were concretized in a personified vision of each space, with which one or several divinities were associated. Certain of these were regarded as kinds of atlantes who supported the sky—the Bacabs, for example, who were so important in ancient Mayan religion. For the Aztec, Tlaloc, the storm god, was present at the four cardinal points, but his power was especially located to the east, where Tlahuizcalpantecuhtli, the god of the morning star, and Tonatiuh, the solar god, also reigned. To the north are situated the black *Tezcatlipoca*, also named *Itztli* ("obsidian"), the white god Mixcoatl, and the goddess Itzpapalotl ("obsidian butterfly"). Quetzalcoatl was the god of the west. Huitzilopochtli and Mictlantecuhtli dominated the south. Xuihtecuhtli, the god of fire, seems to have been assigned to the center of the world.

For the ancient Maya the cardinal points were clearly associated with certain essential colors, as some of their descendants still recall. Among the Aztec, the ancient data are either poorly known or contradictory, and the modern data are faulty. The table presents the Maya data and an Aztec version. To these have been added, following Ichon, the colors of the gods of thunderbolts of the four directions among the modern Totonac.

Dominant Colors of the Directions according to Diverse Mesoamerican Traditions

Direction	Maya (Yucatan)	Tzotzil	Aztec (16th century)	Totonac
East	red	red	blue	red
West	black	black	red	blue
North	white	white	white	yellow
South	yellow	yellow	yellow	green

It is at the center that all of the properties of the directions are fused. In Mesoamerica the ceremonial space of the village is generally the middle, the point of impact of all the directions, the sacred space or "half of the world," according to present-day Indians (Chiapas, central Mexico). The village, as religious microcosm, separated clans and lineages, starting from its center, and served as a point of fusion of the community in its ritual experience. Today, the church serves as symbol of this *omphalos* at which successive levels of the celestial and infraterrestrial universe are united. Before Cortés, every religious act invoked a reference to the cardinal directions. Even today one need only observe ceremonial cycles to understand this need to orient human actions: the sacralization of the four entrances to the village and the offerings to the four directions in the cornfields of the Maya of Yucatan, and the placing of ritual material in a particular direction, generally toward the east.

The perception of the universe on the vertical plane generally contrasts, in its imprecision, with the view of horizontal spaces. These two systems of coordinates were not perceived independently of each other. They were thought to intersect at many points of contact, these being the directions. Celestial space was divided into thirteen superimposed layers, and the netherworld into nine. This conception, still held today by the Tzeltal, was shared by the Aztec, but with certain nuances (thirteen or seven heavens, according to different traditions). Though the layering of the levels of the Maya pyramid was related to a scalar conception of the universe, the characteristics proper to each of the levels would appear to have been of interest only to esoteric thought. The collections of myths offer an image of the universe whose contours are more exact for the infraterrestrial portion (the place of genesis and of dissolution) than for the celestial levels. This complex symbolism is clearly connected, at least among the Maya, to the idea of two sexually distinct worlds: a male and diurnal sky and a female and nocturnal earth, which fuse in the act of creation.

The symbolism of ascent implies the symbolism of stages, of degrees, projected in the striated vision of the mountain. These planes of the pyramid allow for a cadenced progression toward the sacred. This was also the case with the mast in the dance of the volador. The Maya and Aztec traditions speak of five cosmic trees, one at the center and four on the periphery. Descent is related to notions of regression and of an entrance into the world of the dead (tomb of the Pyramid of Inscriptions at Palenque).

III. Space and Time

In Mesoamerican civilizations, the categories of space and time are in such mutual correspondence that they constitute a single corpus of ideas. The linearity of time was, for the Maya, an idea assimilated to the diurnal course of the sun. In this primary form of computation, each unit of time represented a "burden" that was carried the length of the solar trajectory. The signs of duration are still visualized, in surviving indigenous societies, in the form of topographic elements (the past time of the ancestors entirely included in the mountain, the journey of the dead on different paths leading to another world that depends on the nature of the death, the crossing of a river, the Aztec's *Chiconauhapan*, etc.).

In Aztec religion, the *tonalpohaulli* calendar and its rhythms clearly evoked this overlapping of concepts, with the four signs of days (*acatl, tecpatl, calli, tochtli*) associated with the four cardinal directions. The day and its thirteen divinities were to coincide with the thirteen levels of the diurnal sky, and the nine divinities evoke the nine levels of the netherworld.

The successive cosmic cataclysms are directly related to the temporal idea of the cycle, since they are in essence connected with regular repetition. Furthermore, they express the total pervasion of space and the annihilation of creation.

The study of the morphological and syntactic categories of Mesoamerican languages makes it possible to emphasize this

Spatial Sense		*Temporal Sense*
TZOTZIL:		
1. *nopol*	"near"	"soon, quickly"
2. *klal*	"as far as"	"until"
3. *ts'sk'al*	"behind"	"after"
4. *b'u*	"where"	"always"
5. *yo?*	"place where"	"time when"
6. *hva'leh k'ak'al* "when the sun is at the height of a man on the horizon"		
7. *cha'va'leh k'ak'al* "when the sun is twice as high as a man on the horizon"		
OTOMI:		
1. *bę'fa*	"behind"	"next, following"
2. *bę'to*	"before"	"at the beginning of time"
3. *yatho*	"far"	"a long time ago"
4. *īgayatho*	"near"	"a short time ago"
5. *pwö*	"very far"	"a very long time ago"
6. *getā*	"near"	"at all times"
7. *nubwü pwös ra hyadi* "at the place of the sunrise; east"		"when the sun rises"
8. *nubwü yü ra hyadi* "at the place of the sunset; west"		"when the sun sets"

unity. The terminology of space and time can, in certain cases, delimit a single semantic field, as is highlighted by the two brief examples which are borrowed, respectively, from the Tzotzil (Zinacantán) and Otomi (south of Huasteca) languages.

M.A.E.F.M./d.w.

BIBLIOGRAPHY

See the bibliography at the end of the article "Mesoamerican Religion," especially section I: 8, 11, 12, 13, 17, 22, 23, 24, 27; section II: 16 (22 or 44), 38; section III: 4, 9, 11, 18, 25, 41, 64, 65, 70; section IV: 3, 15, 16, 18, 41.

The Sky: Sun, Moon, Stars, and Meteorological Phenomena in Mesoamerican Religions

I. The Sky

In Mesoamerican traditions, the sky is presented under many aspects and does not appear as a unity of substances or qualities. The division of space into seven or thirteen strata seems to be the fruit of distinctly esoteric speculations, at least in the attribution of properties to each level. The sky, more simply, is conceived as a horizontal colored band or a superimposition of bands (traditional representations from the codices), a roof (the upper part of *Itzam Na,* the "house of iguanas," an ophidian monster whose body is covered with planetary symbols), or a vault that encloses the universe. Having collapsed on the earth at the end of the last cosmic catastrophe that destroyed the world, the sky has been restored and remains supported by objects (generally trees, an ax among the Mixtec) or caryatid hero-divinities (the Bacabs of the Maya, a group of four men controlled by Quetzalcoatl and Tezcatlipoca among the Aztec). These supports maintain a permanent contact between sky and earth, but the essential connection is established at the center of the world, at the heart of the ceremonial enclosure, where the pyramid rises, where the *yaxche* tree (the sacred Mayan ceiba) grows, where the ladder ends, where the cord is suspended.

The celestial substance is never described but is perhaps evoked, in part, in the Nahuatl term *ilhuicatl* with a double semantic content ("sky" and "sea"). Like the sea, the sky is an immutable element, beyond human reach, the enclosure of the world. At the western and eastern horizons, the sky and sea meet: the setting sun plunges into the ocean infraworld, from which it reemerges when it rises. Though, among the Maya, the idea of a coupling, the source of all life, between the male sky and the female earth dominates, other traditions present an inverted image of this cosmic sexual act; for the Otomi, the celestial uterine cavity is penetrated by the mountain. The origin of this divergence lies in a dualism which is supported by both the sky and the earth. The diurnal sky, the realm of the fertilizing sun, is globally opposed to the darkness of the night dominated by the lunar star, associated with water, earth, fertility. The sun-moon antagonism gives the sky its fundamental ambivalence.

The celestial vault draws its importance from the bodies and divinities that inhabit it. It is the place of origin of atmospheric phenomena and the home of the stars, although a whole current of thought seems to have situated the clouds, the stars, and even the sun-moon pair immediately beneath the first celestial layer; but the sky is above all the residence of the major gods, even those who are non-Ouranian in appearance (Mictlantecuhtli rules over the subterranean realm of the dead but also lives in the sky: in the night of death, sky and earth are intermingled). At the top of the celestial pantheon, in the most distant spheres, the primordial divinity of duality or the creator couple reigns.

II. The Sun-Moon Pair in Pre-Columbian Religions

In creation myths, the sun and moon play an essential role among the peoples of Mesoamerica. However, while these two major luminaries seem to have occupied a preeminent place in the classical pantheon, the Postclassical Period relegated the divine beings who incarnate them to a secondary rank. This relative deposition was accompanied by the promotion of multiple divinities who were endowed with properties that were solar, lunar, or both solar and lunar. The ancient importance of the sun and moon is attested by numerous indices. At Teotihuacan, in the Tzacualli phase (A.D. 1–150), the ceremonial center was organized around pyramids dedicated, according to Aztec tradition, to the sun and to the moon. In the following period, while new elements of the pantheon were progressively set in place, the central point of the city was displaced toward the south and coincided with the temple of Quetzalcoatl. In the Mayan area, during the Classical Period, the gods of the sun and the moon occupied an important position. The solar god, invoked as Ah Kin ("the one of the sun") or Kinich Ahau ("face of the sun"), was the master of the day, fire, energy, by turns a young man and an old one, the object of veneration and fear. Ix Chel, the Yucatecan lunar goddess, presided over childbirth and procreation and ruled over diseases and medicine, but her ancient role seems to go beyond these few functions; she was also, originally, a divinity of water and earth; *caban* ("earth") was the day associated with her, and her titles of "Mistress of the Sea" and "Mistress from the Midst of the Cenote" clearly connect her with the aquatic element. In Aztec religion, the same moon-earth-water connection also held for the goddess Tlazolteotl, of Huastec origin, best known for her earthly specialization. Among the Cora and the Huichol, until our own time, the moon was a divinity of the earth and vegetation. This totalizing aspect of the two divinities makes the couple that they form an incarnation of the primary duality, an image of the old primordial couple from whom all life has sprung, a celestial transposition of the two vital principles which have been the object of the oldest religious manifestations, the Earth-Mother and the fertilizing Fire.

Not all the traditions agree in presenting the sun and moon as husband and wife. In certain cases, they are only brother and sister, but even when the lunar body appears with the traits of a male god (Tecciztecatl of the Aztec), the principle that he incarnates remains distinctly feminine: the symbol of the moon, Tecciztli, the "shellfish of the sea," also represents the woman's sexual organ. Whatever their relationship may be, therefore, the two luminaries, conceived as antithetical and complementary, serve as poles of the universe. It is on their opposition that one of the most popular schemata of distribution of the categories of thought is based, between hot and cold, light and dark, dry and wet, pure and impure. Metaphorically, eclipses result from the antagonism between the two luminaries (a marital dispute

Quetzalcoatl, feathered serpent. Paris, Musée de l'Homme collection. Photo Oster.

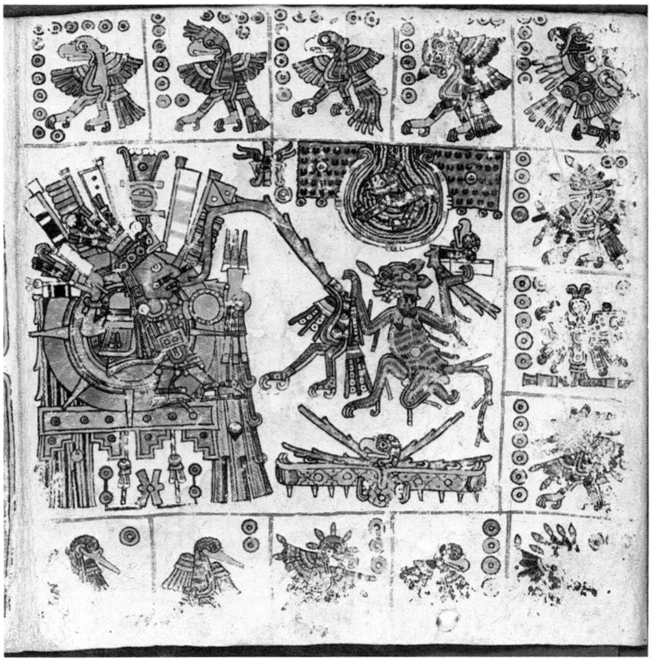

The sun and the moon in the Borgia Codex (p. 71). Vatican Library. Library Photo.

Schematic Table of Aztec Solar-Lunar Divinities

Sun	Moon
Tonatiuh, "sun." Original name: Nanahuatl, "the scurfy"; later became Teotl, "the preeminent god," or Xipilli, "the prince of turquoise." Calendrical name: Naui Olin, "four-movement" or "four quakes of the earth." Usual representation: a radiant disk. Associated animals: eagle, jaguar, wolf. Patron divinity: Tonacatecuhtli and Xiuhtecuhtli.	Metzli, "moon." Also called by his original name: Tecciztecatl, "he of the land of marine conchs" (the great marine gastropod shellfish). Calendrical name: Naui Tecpatl, "four knife of stone." Usual representation: a vase full of water, depicted in profile, containing a stone knife or a rabbit. Associated animals: shellfish, rabbit. Patron divinity: Tlaloc.
Piltzintecuhtli, "chief of princes." The sun as patron of nobles dedicated to war. Huitzilopochtli, "hummingbird of the left." Solar warrior, conqueror of the moon and the stars. God of the blue sky and more especially of the southern sky.	Coyolxauhqui, "she whose face painting represents little bells." A lunar goddess decapitated by the sun in the myth of the birth of Huitzilpochtli.
Also associated with the sun: Xiuhtecuhtli, "lord of turquoise" or "lord of the year," god of fire.	Also associated with the moon: Tlazolteotl, "goddess of impurity." Earth goddess whose nose ornament was in the form of the lunar crescent. Chalchihuitlicue, "she who has a green jadeite skirt." Ome tochtli, "two rabbits." God of intoxication and of the renewal of vegetation. His nose ornament was in the form of the crescent moon.
Formerly, the gods Tezcatlipoca, Quetzalcoatl, and Tlaloc and the goddess Chalchihuitlicue were transformed into suns (before the present sun).	

for the Indians of Yucatan). Similarly, one of the symbolic contents of the ball game (*ollamaliztli*) seems to have been the struggle of the powers included in the sun and the moon.

In the Postclassical Period, all the energy of which the two primordial stars were carriers was portioned out, distributed in several series of new gods. In the Mayan lowlands, the effacement of the lunar goddess was paralleled by the development of the role of the corn god. Among the Aztec, Tonatiuh and Tecciztecatl still personified the sun and the moon but were placed in the background. The ancient divinities were replaced by a divine company of gods, but the fascination that the old astral pair exercised was not altered. Every day, nine times a day, the priests of Tenochtitlan continued to offer their homage to the great luminary.

III. The Sun-Moon Pair in Contemporary Religions

The diversity of mythical projections about the sun and moon of the Postclassical Period was succeeded, after the Conquest, by a partial assimilation of the image of Christ to the sun and of the Virgin Mary to the moon, in the framework of Christian "dualism." This reequilibration, bipolarization, and condensation of images is common in Mesoamerica. Installed at the head of the old pantheon of former times, God hereafter governed the mass of minor divinities. However, in several indigenous traditions, Christ occupied a position subordinate to the image of the Father, and was relegated to the rank of a secondary culture hero. But on the whole, the Christ-Sun-God fusion has been complete. Certain images have had an exceptional impact on the indigenous and mestizo sensibility, such as the Virgin of Guadalupe, a receptacle of pre-Columbian beliefs about fertility, rain, and the mountains, except in the Mayan area.

The cult of the saints succeeded the polytheism of earlier times, but it consolidated the religion that came from the encounter of the two cultures, the host of male saints gravitating around the solar divinity, the female saints accompanying the lunar numen. Quite often the position of the

Terra-cotta sculpture of Tlaloc. El Zapoltal, Veracruz. Xalapa Museum. Photo M.A.E.F.M.

saints appears to be in some way intermediary between the world of humans and the world of the great divinities, with whom they are, however, occasionally conflated. Closer to the religious existence, they facilitate relations with the sacred. The Indians appeal to them, through prayer, in order to obtain an echo to their unhappiness. In Chiapas the "talking saints," veritable oracles, amplify this type of belief.

When they do not accomplish their task, the saints deserve to be punished. A special role has devolved upon the local patron saints, eponymous divinities of towns or villages whose protection they assure. This custom is proper to all of Indian and mestizo Mexico, with the possible exception of Yucatan, where the saints do not seem to have received specific worship; they were grafted onto the traditional pantheon and cohabit with other divinities. Crosses, symbols of the center of the world, are invested with a sacred power throughout the Mayan area. They are authentic divinities with whom people may communicate through the mediation of traditional priests. Substitutes or complements of the primordial divinity, they are encountered wherever the mark of the sacred is asserted: fountains, tombs, mountains, etc. Thus, the symbol of the cross, known since pre-Columbian times and associated at that time with divinities of the water, participated, after the Conquest, in solar imagery, without, however, losing its old connection with the aquatic element: around the festival of the Holy Cross, in the month of May, the anticipation of the rains culminates.

Solar and Lunar Divinities in the Present-Day Religions of Mesoamerica

Peoples	Sun	Moon
Pame	*Kunhu* sun, *dyus kunhu,* "sun god," the name by which one invokes Christ.	(Virgin of Guadalupe?)
Otomi	*Hyadi* sun, often invoked by the name of *tsidada jesu,* "our father Jesus."	*Zāna,* moon, often invoked by the name of *tsinana gwalupe,* "our mother Guadalupe."
Matlalzinca	*Insutata,* "our revered father," the name given both to the sun and to God.	*Insunene,* "our revered mother," the name given both to the moon and to the Virgin Mary.
Huastec of Ixcatepec	*Totiotsi,* "our god," the name given to Christ, assimilated to the sun.	?
Totonac	*Chichini,* sun, assimilated to Jesus Christ. He is addressed by the name of Dios. Often conflated with Saint Dominic, Saint Francis of Assisi, or Saint Lazarus.	(The Totonac considered the moon to be *malkuyu* like an evil and harmful god. They honor a mother goddess *natsi itni* who is assimilated to the Virgin Mary but who is not a lunar divinity.)
Huastec	*Ak'icha,* sun, assimilated to Dios, Christ.	*Its',* moon, assimilated, to a certain degree, to the Virgin of Guadalupe and to the Immaculate Conception.
Tzotzil of Zinacantan	*Totik k'akal,* "our father the sun," assimilated to *riosh kahval,* "God our Lord."	*Chul metik,* "divine mother," is the name given to the moon, the mother of the sun, assimilated to the Virgin Mary.

IV. The Stars and Planets

In ancient Mesoamerica, the nocturnal sky was compared poetically to the mottled fur of a jaguar or to the spangled star skirt of the goddess of primordial times. The sky also inspired astronomical observations and beliefs that remain, to a great extent, unknown.

Certain authors believe that the ancient Mexicans recognized a series of zodiacal constellations, but this remains imperfectly demonstrated. It is known that the Aztec accorded importance to the Pleiades, Orion, the Big Dipper, Scorpio, and perhaps the Southern Cross. A text of Torquemada relates that the festival of the new fire, celebrated every fifty-two years, took place on the night when the Pleiades appeared on the eastern horizon at the moment of the sun's setting, and at the hour when that constellation reached the center of the sky. The Milky Way is mentioned in the myths and appears to have been connected with the pair of primordial divinities.

It is probable that the Indians of ancient Mesoamerica had observed the planets, but the surviving texts explicitly mention only Venus, and the data drawn from the interpretation of myths and pictographic manuscripts are unreliable. It is possible that the protean god Xolotl, one of the last victims of the rising sun, represented the planet Mercury.

The importance of the planet Venus was nearly as great as the importance of the sun and the moon. The Maya had precisely calculated the cycle of its appearances. The Aztec century of 104 years, called *huehuetiliztli* ("one old age"), was equivalent to the calendrical period of correspondence between 65 Venusian years and 104 solar years.

The god of the planet Venus, Tlahuizcalpantecuhtli ("lord of the house of the dawn"), was described as an infallible archer, whose arrows of light were particularly formidable at the moment of the heliacal rising of the planet. The fact is that this god (like Xolotl, moreover) had ties with the world of the dead, from which he emerged. But he was also a beneficent god and an auxiliary of the sun. As the double star of morning and evening, Venus occupied an important place in the speculations of the ancient sacerdotal body and contributed to the complex personality of the god Quetzalcoatl.

The Indians of today have, in general, little memory of the ancient constellations, but accord importance to Venus and continue, like their ancestors, to fear the inauspicious omens announced by comets and meteorites.

V. Rain, Clouds, and Lightning

Nearly all the Mesoamerican peoples had in common the belief in a great god, the master of lightning and dispenser of rainstorms, whose residence was generally situated in the eastern ocean. This god was called Tlaloc by the Aztec, Aktsin by the Totonac, Tzahui by the Mixtec, Cocijo by the Zapotec, Nohotsyumchac by the Maya. His most ancient representations may have been those of the jaguar divinity of the Olmec at the beginning of the first millennium B.C., a half-feline, half-human figure, recognizable by his fleshy lips with drooping corners. This may have been the source of later representations of this divinity among the various Mesoamerican peoples.

All water was thought to proceed from the *teoatl* sea, "the divine water." Water was the precious element, the essential condition of plant life and agriculture. Its symbols were the green jadeite stone and the green feathers of the quetzal bird. Among the Aztec, the goddess whose skirts were adorned with jadeite, Chalchihuitlicue, associated with the moon, was the very essence of the water of the sea, lakes, rivers. The Gulf of Mexico was designated as Metztli Apan, "the place of the water of the moon." According to the Cakchiquel of Guatemala, the moon was the mistress of Lake Atitlan and ruled the sea. Everywhere, water was placed under the patronage of female divinities. A colossal statue of Teotihuacan is generally interpreted as representing the goddess of the waters.

The great god of the storm lived, according to several traditions, in the middle of the ocean, in a paradise of abundance and fertility that the Aztec called Tlalocan. He rarely stirred, and manifested himself chiefly at the beginning of the rainy season, by distant thunderclaps which seemed to fill the atmosphere and were compared to the roars of a jaguar. He had near him, at least in the dry season, his messengers, Tlalocs for the Aztec, Chacs for the Maya, who were like reductions of his own person. It was sometimes said that these were the divinized souls of men who had died by drowning, by being struck by lightning, or from dropsy. These little gods were also thought to have their residences at the four cardinal points, whence the ancient symbolism of the cosmic cross. When they came to the land of men, they took shelter in the interior of the mountains, which were thought to be filled with water, or in the chasms of the Yucatecan limestone plateau.

Chacs or Tlalocs brandished lightning in the form of resplendent arms, stone or bronze axes, and transported rainwater in pitchers or gourds, even in cloth. They were the benefactors of humanity, but if they were angry with it, they might inflict disastrous droughts or send only inauspicious rains, fogs, and mildew, entailing the loss of crops.

Children and young virgin girls were the designated victims of these divinities of the water, to whom they were assimilated after the sacrificial apotheosis. These practices were suppressed by evangelization and are now replaced by simple offerings of food and drink, which are still very common, especially when there is a drought. Indeed, beliefs concerning the divinities of rain, lightning, and water have been preserved to our time in numerous native Mesoamerican groups, not without being occasionally colored by European elements. In this way the water goddess has often become "the Siren." In Yucatan, the Maya now conceive of the Chacs as horsemen, armed with blazing swords or machetes, and their chief is Saint Michael the archangel.

Another aspect of the cult of the water is presented by its ritual and purifying role, which was often connected with "the virgin water," the *zuhuy ha* of the Maya, which issued from a spring or cavern that had not been polluted by frequent contact with humans. From its birth, the native child was (and often still is) bathed, in the company of its mother, in the steam bath commonly called Temascal. Later, water was to cleanse his body and contribute to the removal of his sins. Sometimes, in Yucatan, the corpse of the dead man was washed immediately after death and this water, mixed with a maize paste, was consumed by the parents of the dead man, who thus took on a part of his sins.

Water is the principle of life, death, and resurrection. It can temper the heat of the sun or bring forth a deluge. It is truly fruitful only when united with fire, as in the storm or the steam bath. This union of opposites was expressed by the sign *atlachinolli,* the glyph of the ritual strife that was regarded as redeeming humanity.

VI. The Winds

In Mesoamerica, the winds draw upon a complex and little-known ideology. They are, first of all, connected with the cardinal points. The present-day Maya situate their gods of the winds in the second sky and their gods of lightning in the sixth. The ancient texts about the Maya do not clearly distinguish between the *pauahtuns,* wind gods, the *bacabs,* supporters of the sky, and the *chacs,* storm gods. The present-day Totonac make the winds the companions of thunder. The Aztec and Otomi said that the wind was charged with sweeping the path of the water gods so that the latter might make rain.

Aztec tradition attributed quite diverse peculiarities to the winds, corresponding to the directions of space from which they blew. The only favorable wind was the east wind, which came from the Tlalocan. The west wind was cold, but rather benign. The north and south winds were inauspicious and destructive.

The connection between the wind and the vital breath suffices to explain why Quetzalcoatl-Ehecatl, the Aztec wind god, is depicted in the Borgia Codex as a god of life in opposition to Tezcatlipoca, who is represented with the attributes of the dead. The personality of Quetzalcoatl was extremely complex but presented aspects which were above all favorable.

But the wind might bring evil spells, introduce thorns into the human body, and contribute to the loss of the soul. These malevolent properties attributed to the wind combined with popular Spanish beliefs about "bad air" which have been assimilated everywhere without difficulty.

M.A.E.F.M./b.f.

BIBLIOGRAPHY

See the bibliography at the end of the article "Mesoamerican Religion," above, especially section I: 6, 10, 14, 15, 16, 20, 25, 26, 27; section II: 6, 9, 16 (22 or 44), 35, 37, 38; section III: 3, 5, 12, 16, 22, 31, 59, 60, 63, 64, 65, 71; section IV: 13, 14, 29, 38, 44, 45.

THE EARTH IN MESOAMERICAN RELIGIONS

I. The Earth Monster or Mother Earth

Mesoamerican mythical thought imagines the surface of the earth as having the characteristics of an animal, sometimes a monstrous animal, whose sex and nature vary according to the traditions. In the Classical Period, a creature half-cat, half-frog (depicted, notably, on numerous yokes), seems to constitute one of the first representations of the earth monster. Earlier, the jaguar, a favorite theme in Olmec iconography, also had a chthonic aspect. For the Maya of the Classical Period, the earth was the lower part (the ground floor) of the "house of the iguanas": Itzam Cab or Itzam Cab Ain ("iguana-earth," or "iguana-earth-crocodile"). The Aztec "lord of the earth," Tlaltecuhtli, appears in the form of a monstrous creature with gaping jaws, inspired by the *cipactli*, or giant crocodile, that swims in the waters created by the gods at the beginning of the world. This zoomorphic vision of the earth is still alive today: Totonac myths associate the earth, whose master is simultaneously a man and a woman, with a turtle or a caiman, whereas for their Huastec neighbors it is the great female crocodile. But all such representations generally deal only with the surface of the earth. Its deeper, essential role is only partially evoked in the images of animals through which it appears. That role is expressed, in all periods and places, in the form of multiple deities.

The cults of the earth, in its basic dual aspect, are very old. The locus of genesis and dissolution, provider of food and eater of corpses, the earth fuses the principles of life and death. The dynamic of the world is founded on this union of opposites that takes place within her womb: for all new life is born out of a previous death. Mankind was created out of bones which Quetzalcoatl went to fetch in the heart of the earth, in the realm of the dead. For the Otomi of today, sperm is a product of bone. This sense of the deeply ambiguous character of the earth is part of the most archaic expressions of religious life. During the early Preclassical Period (1300–900 B.C.), on the central plateau, an abundance of female figurines may be interpreted as a sign of a predominant fertility cult: Mother Woman and Mother Earth are thus among the first deities of whom evidence has been preserved. The cult of the dead and of the ancestors seems to be even older. The primitive and embryonic pantheon seems to be documented by the couple made up of Fire and Earth, but the Earth is associated with the night sky and the element of water. During the Aztec period, earth goddesses were for the most part still assimilated to Tonacaciuhatl, the primordial female deity. Overall, the earth remains the great feminine principle of the world, despite the existence of earthly elements of the opposite sex (male) and the presence of divine male representatives of fertility within the pantheons.

Since the Conquest, two series of beliefs and rituals have especially persisted in the cults of the earth, one connected with topographical irregularities (mountains, caves, springs, rivers), and the other with wild and cultivated plants.

II. Mountains

In the Mesoamerican world, the mountain is endowed with a remarkable accumulation of symbols.

In Tenochtitlan, one of the monthly festivals was dedicated to mountains. Each of these was modeled in miniature with amaranth paste and topped with a human head made of the same substance. The gods represented in this way were called Tepictoton ("dwarfs of the mountains") or Ehecatotontin ("dwarfs of the wind"). They were assimilated to the souls of dead people who had been drowned or struck by lightning and had then become gods of lightning or rain.

Mountains were thought to be full of water and were thus closely connected with water deities. But in Mexico and Guatemala, many mountains are active or extinct volcanoes, from which they derive their connection with divinities of fire. This is illustrated by the traditional representations of the old god of fire, the Aztec Huehueteotl, who has a brazier on his head. In the eyes of the Otomi of today, the mountain is an erect penis pointed at the sky. But the same Otomi also note that on the sides of mountains there are caves, cavities with a uterine symbolism, which often serve as cult sites. In Yucatan, there are practically no mountains, but the Maya of Guatemala also practice a cult of mountains with a frequently analogous ideology.

Thought to be hollow, the mountain is also an image of the underground world. Corn was hidden inside a mountain before it was brought to mankind. This "house of corn," Cincalco, was a dark place located to the west, as was the gate of hell. There was a god of the inside of mountains, whom the Aztec called Oztoteotl ("the god of caves") or

Coatlicue, Aztec earth goddess. Mexico City, National Museum of Anthropology. Museum photo.

Tepeyollotl ("the heart of the mountains"). His idol, once venerated in a cave near Ocuila, was replaced in popular worship by the Christ on the cross of the shrine of Chalma.

By the Preclassical Period, each town or village was mystically connected with a mountain. This is witnessed by the architecture of the pyramid, built in the middle of an agglomeration of stones and designed to attract rain like the real mountains with their surrounding agglomerations of clouds.

The great pyramid of Cholula, called Tlachihualtepetl ("the artificial mountain"), was said to have been built before the birth of the present sun, by mythical giants who sought to reach the sky. For the mountain is the special locus of communication with both the celestial world and the netherworld. The myths of the Pipils of El Salvador describe the world as a huge, hollow, cosmic mountain within which men live.

The Tzotzil of the Chiapas highlands, studied by W. Holland, venerate the sacred mountains in which the souls of the ancestors of their lineage dwell. Each of these mountains has thirteen levels, in the image of the thirteen levels of the sky and the thirteen degrees of the social hierarchy of the village. The animals that guard the highest dignitaries live near the top of the mountain, just as the principal deities live at the top of the sky. The mountain and the sky are thus in the image of human society.

III. Vegetation

In Mesoamerican religious thought, vegetation is intimately connected with water and rainstorms. The "four hundred rabbits" (Centzon Totochtin), degenerate forms of the gods of thunder, are typical vegetation deities. It is not through pure chance that, in the legends of the flood, it is a rabbit who orders the fallen trees to stand up. The "four hundred rabbits" each wore a nose ornament in the form of a crescent moon, evidence of the universal belief that certain activities connected with vegetation are dependent on the phases of the moon.

The gods of lightning are also the gods of the four cardinal points. The Maya and the Aztec share the idea that each cardinal point marked the site of a tree that supported the sky. In Mayan texts, each tree is the same color as its point on the compass. The Maya also locate in the center of the world a cosmic tree with a straight trunk, whose horizontal branches spread out over the various levels of the sky. This was a ceiba tree, known in Mayan as *yaxche* ("green tree"), indicating, among other things, the color assigned to the center of the world.

The locus of plant fertility par excellence is the eastern paradise of the great god of lightning, a paradise called Tlalocan by the Aztecs, and represented by a famous Teotihuacan fresco. This mythical place, apparently inspired by the spectacle of warm, humid lands, owed its fertility essentially to the abundance of water, whose symbolic color was the green of vegetation. Clay female figurines, which are the oldest religious representations of the Preclassical Period, are supposed to evoke the human fertility that is associated with the fertility of earth and water, the producers of vegetation.

Since its origins, corn has been the most sacred plant species in the Mesoamerican world. Mankind owes its survival to it, and the Quiche myths of the *Popol Vuh* go so far as to say that the first men worthy of the name were fashioned by the gods out of a dough made of corn. The young god of corn is often described in the myths as a civilizing hero whose birth was miraculous. This god was called Cinteotl by the Aztec, who regarded him as the son of the goddess of the earth. His calendar name was *ce xochitl* ("a flower"). But the texts sometimes speak of a female Cinteotl, and other Aztec deities of corn, Xilonen ("the ear of still green corn") and Chicomecoatl ("seven snakes"), were also goddesses, one young and the other mature. Corn joins the two sexes and passes through all the ages of life, and then through death and resurrection.

The corn deities, always exposed to many dangers, were then and still are hedged by a genuine affection. Their cult did not directly implicate human sacrifices; such sacrifices were rather addressed to the deities of earth and water, on whom the life of the plant depended. Corn was furthermore mystically associated with the sun and the planet Venus, both of whom were summoned to pass the test of the netherworld themselves.

Flowers symbolized beauty, youth, pleasure, lust, and sometimes blood. The deities of flowers among the Aztec, Xochipilli ("the prince of flowers") and Xochiquetzal, a goddess whose name may be translated "precious flower" or "precious feather," were also connected with corn, the sun, and the morning star.

The agave, a plant found in the semiarid plateaus, held a

Pyramid of the sun at Teotihuacan. Photo Guy Stresser-Pean.

"The Lord of the Forest." Otomi paper cutout. Photo M.A.E.F.M.

major place in the religion of one part of Mesoamerica. Its sweet-tasting sap had intoxicating properties when fermented, which made it the beverage of immortality in ancient Mexico. The whiteness of its sap made people compare it to milk, which is why the Aztec goddess of the agave plants, Mayauel, was said to have countless breasts like Artemis of Ephesus. But the gods of intoxication were strictly speaking the "four hundred rabbits," the gods of the vital power of plants. The principal god among these, Ome tochtli ("two-rabbit"), had become young again after a drunken sleep, which may explain why the Aztec reserved the drinking of agave wine (pulque or *octli*) for old men, at least theoretically. The Huastec sometimes absorbed the pulque in the form of an enema to bring about ritual intoxication. The Aztec poured it out in libations, notably as offerings to the god of fire.

The Mayan peoples did not use pulque. Their fermented ritual drink was a kind of mead, the efficacy of which they augmented by soaking in it a piece of bark from a tree called *balche*. The Lacandons of the Chiapas forests and some northeastern Maya still use *balche* in their ceremonies. In northwestern Mexico, the Huichol and Cora continue to use corn beer, commonly called *tesguino*.

But the Indians especially resorted to other sacred plants in order to communicate with the supernatural world. In the arid or semiarid regions of central and northern Mexico, they used peyote, a small cactus whose pulp contains mescal. The Cora and Huichol still revere this cactus as a god and surround its use with a whole ritual. In central and southern Mexico to the Isthmus of Tehuantepec, the use of hallucinogenic mushrooms was extremely widespread. The Aztec name for these mushrooms was *teonanacatl* or "divine flesh." The fact that they appeared at the moment of the rainy season evidently associated them with the gods of lightning. They are still used today, notably by Mazatec diviners, and are sometimes the occasion for veritable communion meals. But in many other regions, diviners and healers resort to modern alcoholic beverages when they commune with the gods.

Tobacco was also a ritual plant in ancient Mexico and may have served to communicate with the world of the sacred. But it was primarily used in the area of religious prophylaxis. Moreover, its smoke, like that of indigenous incense or copal (Nahuatl *copalli*), was supposed to attract clouds through sympathetic magic.

It was in connection with a vegetation cult that human sacrifice by flaying took place, a practice that goes back to the Preclassical Period. The victims of these sacrifices, men or women, were first killed by having their hearts ripped out. Then they were flayed , and a priest or devotee put on the skin of the victim in order to perform various rites. People suffering from skin diseases could treat themselves in this way on condition that they wore this funeral vestment for a full twenty days. The Aztec god of these sacrifices was called Xipe Totec, "our flayed lord." A hymn sung to him has come down to us. It refers to young corn and the new crop stimulated by the coming of the rainy season. Exegetes have thereby interpreted these rites of flaying as having been, above all, symbols of the renewal of vegetation following the sterile months of the winter dry season.

M.A.E.F.M./g.h.

BIBLIOGRAPHY

See the bibliography at the end of the article "Mesoamerican Religion," especially section I: 20, 26; section II: 6, 9. 14, 28, 34, 35, 38; section III: 4, 6, 12, 24, 30, 33, 52, 63, 65; section IV: 5, 13, 24, 30, 39, 43, 45.

Fire in Mesoamerican Mythology

In the Aztec pantheon, the god of fire, Xiuhtecuhtli, or Huehueteotl, was known as "the Lord of the Otomi," a people fascinated by the nocturnal forms of creation. This god was the one who came closest in nature to Tonacatecuhtli, the supreme masculine divinity enthroned in the summit of the sky. One of the names given to Xiuhtecuhtli designates him as living in "the turquoise pyramid," i.e., in the blue daylight sky. It was said that this was the oldest of the gods, and he was generally represented, from Preclassical times, in the form of a bent-over, wrinkled, toothless old man. But this old man carried a brazier on his head, since the god of fire was also the god of volcanoes, and most particularly of the volcano of Colima, in western Mexico.

As god of the zenith, Xiuhtecuhtli had, along with Tonacatecuhtli, chosen the hero who had become the present sun after throwing himself into a brazier. In a festival especially consecrated to him, people placed the effigy of Huehueteotl on top of a ritual greased pole. In this elevated position, the effigy of the god bore the attributes of the *cuecuex,* the divinized souls of warriors, whose deaths had rendered them worthy of inhabiting the celestial dwelling of the sun. But as the god of volcanos, fire also had a subterranean aspect which was connected with the idea of the evening sun swinging down into the chasm of night and death, to be reborn the following dawn.

As a god of ancient times, the sun was "the lord of the year." Even today, certain Otomi groups of the eastern Sierra Madre annually perform a ritual of renewing the fire. Furthermore, it was formerly through a grandiose festival of the new fire that the Aztec celebrated "the binding of the years," at the end of their "centuries" of fifty-two years, and after hours of nocturnal anguish during which the destruction of the world was feared.

As the very expression of heat, fire was associated with hot chili pepper, the symbol of masculine vital strength. Its sacred tree was the pine, whose wood supplied torches which made lighting at night possible. It was said to have the changing colors of flame, being red, yellow, or bluish. But it was also fire that produced the soot and charcoal used by certain dancers to coat their faces in evocation of ghosts risen from the land of the dead. In striking contrast, Xiuhtecuhtli was the patron of the days of *atl* ("water") in the Aztec divinatory calendar. A beautiful text collected by Sahagún describes this god in his mythic home, surrounded by water and mist. This is because its vital strength, both creative and fertilizing, was one that acted upon its opposites, like light in darkness, heat in the midst of cold, the male principle in the midst of female elements, and finally death, which gives rise to apotheosis.

The old god of fire and volcanoes, Huehueteotl. Totonac ceramic. Mexico City, National Museum of Anthropology. Museum photo.

Fire has a purificatory power. It makes possible the elimination of all stains, which explains why its bird is the vulture—eater of impurities and charged with cleaning the world—among present-day Otomi. Smoke was used in lustration rites. The ancient Maya purified themselves by walking on live coals, a rite which still survives among the Tzotzil of the highlands of Chiapas.

The vivifying and purificatory activity of fire in combination with that of water appear clearly in the multiplicity of ritual uses formerly made of the steam bath or *temascal* (Nahuatl *temascalli*) throughout the Mesoamerican culture region. Vestiges of this still remain, and in quite a few native villages the rites of birth and childbirth entail the passage of the mother and newborn child through its salvific and vivifying steam.

Finally, by virtue of its essential role in agricultural, culinary, and mechanical techniques, fire is regarded as the condition for and origin of all civilization. In every dwelling, the fireplace, which constitutes a domestic instrument and a tutelary power, must be present. It was maintained by women, but fed and fueled by men, who even today may, from time to time, offer a few drops of pulque or brandy into it as a libation.

M.A.E.F.M./d.w.

BIBLIOGRAPHY

See the bibliography at the end of the article "Mesoamerican Religion," and especially section I: 26; section II: 6, 17, 38; section III: 12, 13, 53, 65; section IV: 14, 24, 35.

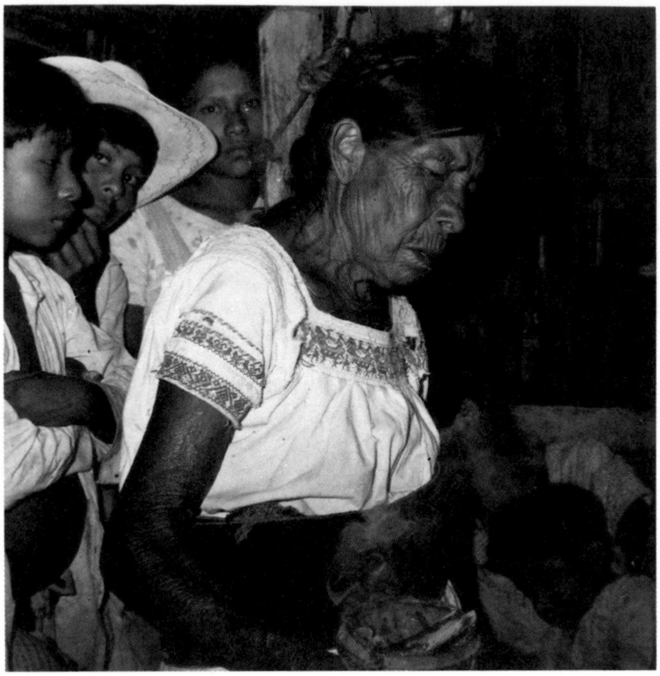

Huehuetla nurse-midwife's dance. Tepehua Indians. Photo M.A.E.F.M.

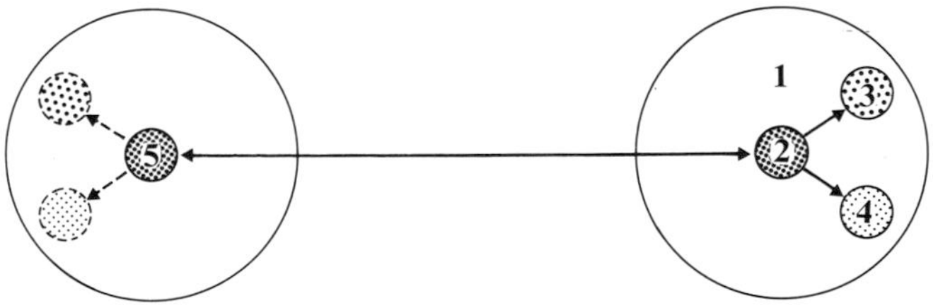

The human person and its constituent parts, from San Pedro Chenalo, Chiapas. Tzotzil Indians. Drawing M.A.E.F.M.

The Mesoamerican Image of the Human Person

Every religious system includes a set of beliefs about the human person, beliefs which determine specific types of relationships between humans and society, and between humans and the world. In the Mesoamerican domain, these beliefs and their multiple implications are really known only from the period just before the Conquest and thereafter. Our knowledge of pre-Conquest material comes from collections of oral traditions made by the first European witnesses of the indigenous world. Information for earlier periods is sporadic in nature, consisting mainly of hypothetical deductions.

The ethnohistorical and ethnological data show the individual as an assemblage of several elements. In its most highly elaborated form, for example, among the Tzotzil of Chiapas, the image of the person includes five component parts, although two or three of these are often confused. At the center of the body (1) is found the life principle, the element of dynamism and movement (2). The soul (3), an immaterial element which exists before birth and survives after death, is a kind of reflection of the life principle (the breath, the *ch'ulel* of the Tzotzil, the *listakna* of the Totonac), and dwells in all of the organs simultaneously. The concept of *yollotl* used by the ancient Nahua seems to refer both to the seat of dynamism and to its manifestations (moral values, virility, etc.). The mind (4), center of intelligence and knowledge, often constitutes a second soul, which the Aztec call *ixtli* or face. The animal double (*tonal* or *nahual*) is the last element of the structure of the individual (5). While the animal double is external to the individual, the two still have a truly consubstantial relationship. The life of a person depends on the interaction of the above components.

The funeral rituals suggest that people have long been thought to possess an element which survives the dissolution of the body. The custom of burying furniture, and sometimes sacrificed animals or people, with the dead has existed since the Preclassical Period. This custom should probably be interpreted as providing aid to whatever remains of the dead person in the world beyond. The frequent presence of miniature objects in Classical and Postclassical burials of several regions may be related to a belief in the persistence of the soul in the form of a dwarf, a belief still held by the Tzotzil and the Totonac. The notion of an animal double may also be an ancient one. In the myth of the creation of humankind, Quetzalcoatl himself calls his double, his *nahual*, to his aid.

The religious thought of Mesoamerica locks human beings into a narrow determinism from birth until after death. The individual's earthly fate depends directly on his birthday and the combined forces acting on this day. The position of Venus on this day plays a particular role in the fate of the newborn child. The nature of the animal double, which every person has, is also a function of his birthday. Finally, certain peculiarities of the newborn child are signs of his future destiny: in several traditions, for example, a tuft of hair on the head indicates a future sorcerer. Similarly, the umbilical cord is always an object of special attention, since it is endowed with magical properties. Thus inequality among people is established from the beginning; it is outside the control of individuals. To attenuate the blind and sovereign influence of the *tonalpohualli* (the calendar of divination), the Aztec had no option but to choose favorable days for naming children—but their intervention was limited to this. The attempts of the *tlamatinime* (or philosopher-sages) to influence the course of fate could only give certain people a provisional illusion of freedom. In this conception humans are merely playthings in the hands of the gods. Their appearance on earth is necessary for the perpetuation of creation, whose origin is marked by a fundamental debt to the gods. At every moment of his life, man is faced with duties which he must perform for the world of the sacred, because of the initial permanent contract which made the gods the creators of humankind and men the servants of the gods.

Even though people are subject to the law of their destiny, they move back and forth in the course of their lives between two poles which wage a constant struggle with the universe as its stake: order and disorder. For disorder is everywhere, on the cosmic level with destructive earthquakes, floods in the rainy season, volcanic eruptions; on the social level with wars and other conflicts; on the mental level with personality disorders and deviance. People on earth thus live in a precarious situation. At any moment the equilibrium of the elements which constitute the person can be shattered: the result is "espanto" (terror which can bring on loss of the soul), sickness, or death. Established in inequality by a primordial decree, people are also vulnerable to "envidia" (jealousy). But disorder is also the permanent obsession of entropy, of the fate of the world that becomes progressively degraded to end in a cosmic cataclysm. It is the struggle of antagonistic principles, the solar divinities against the lunar divinities, the "combat" between man and woman, which must nevertheless result in re-creation.

In the arsenal of myths and rites are to be found the means of taming and controlling the forces of destruction and the dangers of the deterioration of the world.

M.A.E.F.M./j.l.

BIBLIOGRAPHY

See the bibliography at the end of the article "Mesoamerican Religion," especially section II: 14; section III: 26, 28, 40, 60; section IV: 11, 12, 13, 14, 17.

Cosmic Disorder, Illness, Death, and Magic in Mesoamerican Traditions

I. Illness

To the Indians of Mesoamerica, illness was never a random occurrence; it was the sign of a disturbance of the relationship between man and the cosmos ruled by supernatural forces. Indigenous medicine therefore had two aspects: its religious nature, considered essential, which attempted to reestablish normal relationships between the patient and the gods, and its profane side, which tended to treat the simple material symptoms of the disorder.

Illness was due mainly to the punitive action of the gods, sanctioning lapses in the social or sacred order or in the rules for moral conduct or rituals. The stain of sin brought punishment sooner or later, whether it was for theft, adultery, improper use of sacred objects, failure to make offerings to the dead or to the gods, etc. Punishment could be inflicted by spirits of the earth, of the water, and especially of the air. These last were thought to transport impalpable noxious substances, often represented as tiny thorns, which could enter the body. But the action of the gods or the forces of nature might also be unleashed or directed by evil witchcraft and even by the more or less unconscious power emanating from certain individuals. One of the fatal consequences of this action is the loss of the soul, which escapes the body and is then held captive in unknown regions. This belief in the loss of the soul is still extremely widespread among the common people in Mexico and Guatemala. It is referred to in Spanish as "espanto," since it is believed to be easily triggered by emotion or shock.

The active or passive reactions of individuals to these fearful occurrences vary greatly. Individuals with strong personalities, notably those who have a strong animal as a double, easily resist supernatural aggression and are, in addition, gifted with a contingent malevolent power. Pregnant women and individuals who have the evil eye are formidable, sometimes without wanting to be. On the other hand, children have a natural weakness which makes them easy victims; they need to be surrounded with ritual precautions. Certain conditions such as bitterness (*mohina*) or apathy (*chipil*) are equally debilitating.

To the natives, the real treatment for illness is essentially a matter of religion and ritual. It consists above all in offerings and prayers to appease the wrath of supernatural beings. The cure for a disease sometimes includes sucking to extract the thorns of the disease. The reintegration of the soul into the body requires that it be sought at a great distance, brought back, and persuaded to return to its place. These are quasi-shamanistic activities which sometimes involve the use of hallucinogens.

The religious aspect of medicine, strongly linked to pagan beliefs, was evidently condemned by the Spanish authorities during the colonial period and was considered diabolic by the missionaries. It nevertheless survived, in the hands of the healers ("curanderos") who are priests, diviners, and magicians combined. Despite the reputation for witchcraft that is attached to their profession, some of them find clients not only among the rural Indians but often among the bourgeois mestizos of the city.

The other, more profane aspect of native medicine was advanced enough to merit the esteem and sometimes the admiration of the conquering Europeans. The Aztec were expert in the use of medicinal plants and knew how to let blood, set fractures, handle difficult births, etc. The Maya

Mixtec funerary vase. Zaachila, Oaxaca. Mexico City, National Anthropological Museum. Museum photo.

were no less capable. Spanish medicine, with Francisco Hernandez and others, was enriched by its contact with Indian medicine, while at the same time communicating certain new ideas in return, such as the Hippocratic opposition of hot and cold.

But the "scientific" aspect of the indigenous medicine should not allow us to forget its religious foundation, which is seen even in the properties attributed to various remedies. Indian beliefs about illness are connected with the expiatory and painful aspects of the pre-Columbian ritual, aspects which survive to this day in certain flagellations during Holy Week.

II. Magic and Sorcery

The indigenous conception of illness made traditional medicine into an activity situated at the boundaries of religion, magic, and herbalism. The healer is, above all, a magician. Even while he is addressing the gods to ask for a cure, it is faith in his personal power that creates the belief that his prayer will be answered. When he uses hallucinogenic plants to go into a trance, he is straddling the boundary between magic and religion.

Even though the Indians admit that a fault of the patient must have been at the origin of his illness, they believe no less that the onset of the pathological process is generally caused by the practice of malevolent magic. So the healer is engaged in a battle, and he will not triumph unless he is stronger than the one who cast the spells. He can then be content with curing the patient, but he may also be asked to send the malevolence back to its author, and thereby engage in an act of sorcery properly so-called. The power of the healer is thus ambivalent. It restores a person's balance but may also destroy it. In the same way, despite his protestations, the healer is often taken for a sorcerer, which at times exposes him to reprisals.

Of course, there are specialists in malevolent magic, although they do not advertise themselves as such and they exercise their activities in the strictest secrecy. The indigenous society creates a favorable atmosphere for sympathetic magic. Sorcery offers an answer to the disorder caused by natural or economic constraints and to the obligations imposed by political and religious structures. It catalyzes, amplifies, and in a way resolves the anxiety and the social tensions created by jealousy, the true instrument of coercion against individuals who transgress the communal norm of poverty. Sorcerers are sometimes considered to exercise the law of justice. On the other hand, formidable magic powers are often attributed to native dignitaries. The accusation of sorcery is readily made against neighboring villages or neighboring peoples.

Sixteenth-century texts demonstrate that the Aztec had different sorts of sorcerers and necromancers. Some could change themselves into animals. Some claimed to engage in nocturnal activities as bloodsucking vampires. Others were thieves who put their victims to sleep, using an image of the god Quetzalcoatl and the left arm of a woman who died in her first childbirth. Still others used poisons or narcotics. There was also a love magic, which used aphrodisiac plants or symbolic birds. Indians and mestizos still believe that a man who wears a dead and dried hummingbird on his person will have a greater chance of success in amorous pursuits. Another form of magic was attributed to the Huastec, who were reported to be great conjurers. Finally, let us add that the sorcery indigenous to Mexico has been enriched by numerous European borrowings since the sixteenth century. Sometimes, as among the Tarascans, Indian sorcery was completely engulfed by the sorcery of the Spanish tradition.

In modern times, the rites of the Christian religion or European recipes for countermagic are often resorted to as protection against sorcery. But the traditional native practices still have followers.

III. Death

Ancient Mesoamerican civilization had two principal types of funeral practices: burial, which seems to have been the rule in the earliest periods, and incineration, which predominated among the Aztec and Otomi at the time of the Conquest. The latter custom seems to have been connected with fire cults and celestial gods; and clearly, among the Aztec and the Otomi, the dead who had been called by the gods of lightning and rain were buried.

For Mesoamerican Indians, death represents the final rupture of the balance between the components of the self, an irreversible separation of the elements from themselves. Drunkenness, dreams, and sexual activity provided anticipatory experiences of this state. Yet this explosion of the unity constituting a human being does not seem ever to have been viewed as leading to annihilation. Even the cremated dead were given a green stone that took the place of their "heart," that is, their soul or vital element. Buried corpses were thought to conserve a part of their energy. It was said that humanity had been created from bones taken from the world of the dead, crushed, and watered with blood by Quetzalcoatl. Death is therefore the source of life, as is illustrated in the famous bas-relief of the tomb of Palenque. Furthermore, death permits the element which survives it to enter into the sacred, but under variable conditions.

The idea of free will was foreign to the Mesoamerican mentality. The destiny of each individual in existence was essentially determined by the day of his birth, according to whether it was favorable or unfavorable. In the same way, the manner of his death was decided by the gods, and his destiny in the hereafter depended on his manner of death. We have details on Aztec traditions on this subject.

Most of the dead, for example, those who died of old age or of some illness, went to the subterranean world of the gods of death, the Mictlan. In order to get there, they had to complete a long journey fraught with terrible perils: mountains that collide, winds that cut like blades, serpents, etc. Finally, they had to swim across a terrible river, which could not be done without the help of a dog. A dog was therefore sacrificed or represented in effigy during the funeral rites. This concept of a subterranean world of the dead is certainly very old and was common to the entire Mesoamerican region.

Those called by Tlaloc, the god of lightning and rain, died from lightning, drowning, and edema. They joined him in a paradise of freshness and fertility called Tlalocan. They were buried with a stick of dry wood, which, in this delightful place, would immediately become covered with flowers and leaves. The idea of this paradise is attested in a famous fresco of Teotihuacan, dating from the middle of the first millennium A.D. The idea is still held today among certain native peoples, notably the Totonac.

Children who died young, before being weaned, went to the thirteenth heaven. There they found a tree whose fruits were shaped like breasts, from which they hung. This belief was shared by the Maya. As for the Nicaraos, Nahuas who emigrated to Central America toward the middle of the ninth century A.D., we know only that they believed that the souls of these little children were destined to be reincarnated, which does not seem incompatible with certain Central American beliefs. The tree of breasts, according to many traditions, was situated in the Aztec Tlalocan or its eastern Mayan equivalent.

A final celestial apotheosis was reserved for warriors killed in combat or on the sacrificial stone, as well as for women who died in childbirth. The women were considered to have fought with courage and to have taken a prisoner when they succumbed. All of these souls were thought to take part daily in the procession of the sun, men in the eastern sky, women in the night sky. The idea of a celestial abode reserved for the souls of warriors and women who died in childbirth may have developed most during the militaristic centuries of the Postclassical Period. The Nicaraos, however, ancient emigrants to Central America, also believed that the souls of warriors became companions of the sun, in the eastern sky.

A fundamental opposition seems therefore to have existed between men who died of more or less natural causes and others. It may at first have been believed that these others had gone to a western paradise, from which they could climb up to the sky.

Whatever it was, the role of predestination in the ancient Mesoamerican beliefs about the afterlife left no room for metaphysical doubts. The almost obsessional question asked by the Aztec philosophical poets therefore seems all the more original:

> Where are we going, alas, where are we going?
>
> Is it death or life that awaits us there?
> In the hereafter, will we be given the power to live again?
> Will we again know the pleasure given by god, the giver of life?

Four centuries of Christianity have not yet brought an end to the old pre-Columbian foundation of beliefs about death. There are still Indians who create an effigy of a dog and bury it with the dead person to help him cross the underground river. In certain villages, people who die from drowning or lightning are still buried apart from the other dead because their final destinations are thought to be different.

Abodes in the Afterlife

Types of Death	Aztec	Nacaraos	Maya	Contemporary Totonac
Ordinary death	Subterranean world (after a long voyage)	Subterranean world	Subterranean world	Subterranean world (with retributional justice)
Drowned, struck by thunder, edema, etc.	Tlalocan, paradise of fertility	?	?	Aquatic realm of the God of Thunder and the Eastern Sea
Children who died young	Tree of milk in the thirteenth heaven or in Tlalocan	Possibility of reincarnation	Tree of milk in heaven	Western paradise (possibility of reincarnation)
Warriors killed in combat or in sacrifice	Celestial paradise of the rising sun	Celestial paradise of the rising sun	Celestial paradise	(Not known at present)
Women who died in childbirth	Celestial paradise of the setting sun	?	Celestial paradise	Celestial paradise

M.A.E.F.M./d.b.

BIBLIOGRAPHY

See the bibliography at the end of the article "Mesoamerican Religion," especially section II: 7, 15, 29, 33, 38; section III: 14, 16, 26, 33, 43, 56; section IV: 1, 6, 7, 13, 20, 21, 31, 37, 45.

Myths and Rituals of the South American Indians

A serious attempt to report on the Indian religions of South America would not be possible without first mentioning, however briefly, certain general facts about the cultural terrain. Evident to the specialist, they should nevertheless be included here in order to help the general reader to approach the religion: can one understand the practices and beliefs of the South American Indians without first knowing how these people live and how their societies function? Let us recall what is only apparently a truism: South America is a continent whose immense area, with rare exceptions (such as the Atacama Desert in the extreme north of Chile), was entirely populated by people at the time of the discovery of America at the end of the fifteenth century. Moreover, this population was very old, going back almost thirty millennia, as the work of prehistorians attests. And it is important to observe that, contrary to recent widespread assumptions, the density of the indigenous population was relatively high. Demographic research, notably that carried out at the University of California at Berkeley, radically undercuts the "classical" point of view according to which South America, except for its Andean part, was nearly deserted. The antiquity of the population, its size (several tens of millions), and the size of its territory gave South America suitable conditions for a very large cultural and, therefore, religious differentiation.

What are the principal sociocultural characteristics, the essential ethnological determinants of the South American peoples? The territorial extension and consequent climatic variation established a succession of ecological environments and landscapes, from the humid equatorial forest in the north (the Amazonian basin) to the Patagonian savannas and the harsh climate of Tierra del Fuego. The differences in the natural environment demand specific human adaptations and create widely contrasting cultural models: settled farmers of the Andes, migratory slash-and-burn farmers, and nomadic hunter-gatherers. But it should be noted that the cultures of hunters are, in South America, very much in the minority. Their territory corresponds, essentially, to the zones where agriculture was impossible either because of the climate (Tierra del Fuego) or because of the nature of the vegetation (the Argentinian pampas, which have no forest). But everywhere else, wherever agriculture is possible with the indigenous technology (use of fire, the stone ax, the dibble, etc.), it exists, and has existed for several millennia, as the discoveries of archaeologists and ethnobotanists demonstrate. Agriculture, therefore, embraced the greater part of the South American continent. As for the few islets of societies of hunters which capriciously interrupt the monotony of the cultural landscape, it can be shown that the absence of agriculture results not from the persistence through time of a preagricultural mode of life, but rather from a loss. The Guayaki of Paraguay and the Siriono of Bolivia practiced slash-and-burn farming, like their neighbors. But as the result of various historical circumstances, they lost it in very early periods and therefore became hunter-gatherers once again. In other words, instead of an infinite variety of cultures, there is rather an enormous homogeneous block of societies with a similar mode of production.

But on the other hand, we know that to mark a principle of order in the diversity of peoples who inhabit a given region,

Araucanian shaman. Paris, Musée de l'Homme collection. Photo Mostuy.

to subject the multiplicity of their cultures to a primary classification, one would by preference call upon linguistic criteria. And then the image of a nearly perfect cultural unity disappears, that image suggested by the almost continental recurrence of nearly identical material bases. What is, in fact, the broad linguistic picture of South America? In perhaps no other region of the world is the parceling out of languages so extreme.

The great linguistic families are counted by tens, each of them consisting of a number of dialects that are so far removed from the mother language that the people who speak them cannot understand one another. Furthermore, a considerable number of languages have been recorded that are called "isolates" because they are impossible to integrate into the principal linguistic stocks. From this extraordinary linguistic differentiation a kind of cultural atomization results. The unity of language establishes, most often, the cultural unity of a people, the "style" of its civilization, the spirit of its culture. Here or there, doubtless, there are exceptions to this "rule." Thus the Guayaki, nomadic hunters, belong, from the point of view of their language, to the Tupi-Guarani linguistic branch, which encompasses farming tribes. Such aberrant cases are very rare and arise out of historic connections which are fairly easy to establish. One essential point should be borne in mind: the millions of Tupi-Guarani, for example, occupy an immense territory and speak the same language, with variations in dialect too slight to prevent communication. Despite the great distances that separate the most far-flung groups, cultural homogeneity is remarkable in socioeconomic life as much as in ritual activities or the structure of myths. Cultural unity in no way signifies political unity: the Tupi-Guarani tribes participate in the same cultural model without constituting a "nation," since they are in a permanent state of war among themselves.

But in recognizing this affinity between language and culture and in discovering in language the principle of unity of culture, one finds oneself by that same logic constrained to accept the immediate consequences of this relationship, i.e., that there should be as many cultural configurations, and therefore systems of beliefs, as languages. Each ethnic group has a particular ensemble of beliefs, rites, and myths. The problem then is methodological: one cannot simply adopt the illusory solution of a "dictionary" which would make the interminable list of known tribes and the teeming variety of their beliefs and practices fall into order. The difficulty of choosing a method of presenting religious data comes, in large part, from the contradiction between the cultural homogeneity on the socioeconomic plane and the irreducible heterogeneity on the cultural plane. For each ethnic group has and cultivates its particular personality, between the material bases and the "point of honor." Could one not discover, nevertheless, some lines of force capable of making decisions in an identity that is too abstract, some transversalities able to regroup differences that are too specific? Precisely such a partition among the Amerindian peoples is what struck the first Europeans landing in the New World: on the one hand, the societies of the Andes subjected to the imperial powers of the mighty machine of the Inca state and, on the other hand, the tribes that populate the remainder of the continent, forest Indians, Indians of the savanna and of the pampas, "people without faith, without law, without king," as the chroniclers of the sixteenth century called them. It is not surprising to learn that this European point of view, largely founded on the ethnocentrism of those who formulated it, echoed exactly the opinion that the Incas expressed about the populations which thronged the borders of the empire: these people were to them nothing but despicable savages, just good enough, if they were successfully subdued, to pay tribute to the king. And it is hardly surprising to find that the repugnance of the Incas for these forest people had much to do with customs that the Incas thought barbarous. It was, quite often, a question of ritual practices.

It is really this line that separates the indigenous peoples of South America: the peoples of the Andes and the others, the civilized and the savages or, in terms of traditional classification, the high cultures on the one hand, the forest civilizations on the other. The cultural (and beyond that, religious) difference is rooted as much in the mode of political functioning as in the mode of economic production. In other words, there is no substantial difference—from the point of view of rituals and myths—between hunters and farmers, who together form a homogeneous cultural block in contrast with the Andean world. This opposition, otherwise stated as that of societies without states (or primitive societies) and societies with states, at least makes it possible to structure the religious space of pre-Columbian South America and at the same time to ensure an economical arrangement of the account of that space. Thus, the first part of this account will be devoted to the religious world of primitive societies, where farmers and hunters are mixed. The presentation of Andean religion will occupy the second part: this will involve distinguishing two autonomous planes, one inherent in the very old tradition of peasant communities in this region, the other much more recent, resulting from the formation and expansion of the Inca state.

This will assure the "covering" of the two domains where the spirituality of the South American Indians is developed. However, though it is consistent with the general sociocultural dimensions of these societies, the bipartition of the religious field does not offer a sufficiently exact image of its object. A number of ethnic groups that conform to the classical "primitive" model both in their mode of production and in their political institutions nevertheless deviate from this model precisely in the unusual, even puzzling, forms of their thought and religious practices. Such a deviation is pushed to its extreme by the Tupi-Guarani tribes, whose religious ethnography demands a special development which will constitute the third part of this account.

Village kraho in Brazil. Paris, Musée de l'Homme collection. Photo Arhex.

All the documents about Indian South America should be regarded as ethnographic source material. The available information is therefore quite abundant, since it began to be established at the time of the discovery. But it is at the same time incomplete: some tribes which have disappeared survive in name only. Even so, this lack is largely compensated for by the results of two decades of research in the field among populations that are hardly or not at all destroyed. Documents about primitive societies extending from the sixteenth-century chroniclers to the most recent work are at our disposal. As for the Andean religions, which were almost annihilated by the Spanish by the middle of the seventeenth century, they are known to us from the descriptions left by the companions of Pizarro and the first colonizers, to say nothing of the testimony gathered directly, soon after the Conquest, from the survivors of the Incan aristocracy.

P.C./d.f.

BIBLIOGRAPHY

The diversity of South American religions requires that the bibliographic citations be divided among the three major subjects treated in this work. See the articles "Indians of the South American Forest," "Religions and Cults of the Societies of the Andes," and "Religious Thought and Prophetism among the Tupi-Guarani Indians of South America," below.

Indians of the South American Forest

Travelers, missionaries, and ethnologists have often noted, either to their joy or to their dismay, the strong attachment of "primitive" people to their customs and traditions, or, to put it another way, their deep religiosity. Spending some time among an Amazonian society, for example, allows one to experience not only the piety of the Indians, but the way in which religious concerns so thoroughly pervade social life that the distinction between the secular and the religious seems to dissolve, and the boundary between the realm of the sacred and the domain of the profane disappears: nature, like society, is permeated with the supernatural. Thus, animals and plants may be both natural beings and supernatural agents: a falling tree that causes injury, or a snakebite, or the attack of a wild animal, or a shooting star will all be interpreted not as accidents but as the effects of deliberate aggression by supernatural powers such as forest spirits, souls of the dead, and enemy shamans. This resolute denial of both the role of chance and the discontinuity between the profane and the sacred should logically lead to the abolishment of the autonomy of the religious field, which is evident in all the individual and collective events of the ordinary life of the group. In fact, though it is never totally absent from the many facets of primitive culture, the religious dimension is affirmed as such in certain specific ritual circumstances. These will be more easily determined if we first isolate both the place and the function of the various divine figures.

I. The Gods

The European idea of religion defines the relationships between humans and gods, and more precisely, between men and God, in such a way that European evangelists and seekers were haunted, sometimes without their knowledge, by the conviction that there are no authentic religious occurrences outside monotheism. They therefore tried to discover either local versions of a great single god or the embryonic germ of the unity of the divine among the South American Indians. But ethnography shows us the vanity of this enterprise. The ritual practices of these peoples almost always take place, as we will see, without any implicit or explicit reference to a unique or central divine figure. In other words, the religious life, understood through its ritual realization, functions in a space exterior to what Western thought is accustomed to calling the realm of the divine: the "gods" are missing from the cults and rites which men celebrate because they are not intended for those celebrations. But does the absence of worship signify the absence of the gods? It used to be thought possible to discern some dominant divine figures here or there in the myths of various tribes. But who determines this dominance, who evaluates the hierarchy of these representations of the divine? Precisely those ethnologists, and more often those missionaries, who, steeped in the monotheistic illusion, imagine that their goal is achieved by the discovery of such and such a named divinity. Who are these "gods" which no cult comes to worship? Their names designate the visible celestial bodies: the sun, moon, stars, constellations metamorphosed from human beings to stars according to numerous myths; they are also named for "violent" natural phenomena: thunder, tempests, lightning. Very often the names of these gods refer not to nature but to culture: mythical founders of civilization, inventors of agriculture, culture heroes who are sometimes destined, once their earthly mission is accomplished, to become celestial bodies or animals—the Twins, the mythic heroes of the Tupi-Guarani tribes, abandon the earth in order to transform themselves into the Sun and Moon. While the Sun, "our older brother," plays a very important part in the religious thought of the modern-day Guarani, he is not the object of any special cult. In other words, all of these gods are for the most part only names, more common than personal, and as such, indicators and designators of something beyond society, the Other of culture: the cosmic alterity of the skies and the celestial bodies; the earthly alterity of nearby nature. Above all, the original alterity of culture itself, the order of law as a social (or cultural) institution, is contemporaneous not with humans but with a time before humans. It has its origin in mythic prehuman time, and society finds its foundation outside itself, in the set of rules and instructions left to them by the great ancestors or culture heroes, who were often called Father, Grandfather, or Our Father. The name of this distant and abstract god, indifferent to the destiny of humans, this god without worship, that is, deprived of the usual relationship which unites gods to humans, is the name of the law. Inscribed in the heart of the society, this law guarantees to maintain its order and asks only that men respect the tradition. This is clearly what we learn from the example of the tribes of Tierra del Fuego, among whom Americanists have sometimes been tempted to recognize the most clearly developed figures of "savage" monotheism. In fact, Temaukel of the Ona or Watahinewa of the Yahgan gather under their names the intangible norms of social life left to men by these gods and taught to adolescents during the rites of initiation. In contrast to Andean societies, the other South American peoples never depict the gods. The only noteworthy exceptions are the *zemi*, or idols of the Taino-Arawak of the Antilles, and the divine images which were housed in the temples of certain tribes of Colombia and Venezuela. But historians of religions point to influences coming from Mesoamerica, in the first case, and the Andes, in the second case: or what are called the high cultures.

A religion without gods, like that of the South American Indians, is strange: the absence is so irritating that more than one missionary has proclaimed these people to be veritable atheists. Yet they are extremely religious people: but their religious sense, rather than being individual and private, is social and collective in that it is primarily concerned with the connections between society as the world of the living and that Other, the world of the dead.

II. The Rituals of Death

From the very start, we must avoid the confusion between the cult of ancestors and the cult of the dead. Native thought distinguishes clearly between the ancient dead and the recently dead, and each of these two categories of the nonliving calls for different treatment. Between the community of the living and the community of the ancestors there has been established a diachronic relationship marked by a break in temporal continuity and a synchronic relationship marked by the desire for cultural continuity. In other words, Indian thought situates the ancestors in a time before time, a time in which the events told in the myths took place—a primordial time in which the various moments of the foundation of the culture and the institution of the society took place, the veritable time of the ancestors with whom the souls of the ancient dead mingle, anonymous and separated from the living by a great genealogical depth. In addition, the society, instituted as such in the founding act of its mythic

Departure of a family into the forest (Kayapo). Brazil. Musée de l'Homme collection. Photo Caron.

ancestors, constantly reaffirms through the voice of its leaders and shamans and by means of ritual practices its desire to persevere in its cultural identity, that is, to conform to the norms and rules which were the legacy of the ancestors and transmitted by the myths. For this reason, the ancestors are often honored with rituals in circumstances which are determined. There it is revealed that, far from being assimilated to the dead, the ancestors and their mythic acts are thought to be the very life of the society.

The relationship with the dead is quite different. They are first of all the contemporaries of the living, those who are torn from the community by age or disease, the relatives and allies of the survivors. But though death extinguishes the body, it also brings into being, into autonomous existence, that which, for lack of a better term, we call the soul. According to the particular beliefs of each culture under consideration, the number of souls may vary: sometimes a single soul, sometimes two, occasionally more. But even when there are more than one, one of them becomes the spirit of the deceased person, a kind of living dead. The funeral rites properly so-called, insofar as they concern the dead body, are essentially designed to separate the souls of the dead definitively from the living: death liberates with it a flux of evil, aggressive powers against which the living must protect themselves. Since the souls do not wish to leave the village or camp, they wander, especially at night, near relatives and friends, for whom they become sources of danger, illness, and death. Just as the ancestors, as the mythic founders of society, are marked with a positive sign and are therefore close to the community of their descendants, so the dead, as potential destroyers of this same society, are marked with a negative sign, so that the living wonder how to get rid of them.

It follows that one cannot speak of a cult of the dead among the peoples of South America: far from worshiping the dead, they are much more concerned with erasing all traces of their memory. This is why ceremonies like the "festival of the souls of the dead" of the Shipaya or the rites at which the Bororo call forth the dead (*aroe*) seem to refer more to the attempt to gain the goodwill of the ancient dead, or ancestors, than to any desire to celebrate the recent dead: with the ancestors, the community of the living tries to contract and reinforce an alliance which will guarantee its survival; against the dead, it puts various mechanisms of defense into effect as protection against their attacks.

What is done with the dead? Generally, their bodies are buried. Almost everywhere, in the area under consideration, the grave is a cylindrical hole, sometimes covered with a small roof of palms. There the body is left to decompose, usually in the fetal position, its face turned in the direction of the supposed dwelling place of souls. The almost total absence of cemeteries is due not to the periodic shifting of village sites, when the gardens become unproductive, but to the fundamental relationship of exclusion which separates the living and the dead. A cemetery is a fixed space reserved for the dead, whom one can therefore visit and who are in this way maintained permanently and in close proximity to the space of the living. But the principal concern of the Indians is to banish even the memory of the dead: how therefore could they reserve a special area, a cemetery, for them? This desire to break with the dead leads a number of these societies simply to abandon their village when someone dies, in order to put the greatest possible distance between the grave of the dead person and the space of the living. All the possessions of the deceased are burned or destroyed and a taboo cast against his name, which can never again be spoken. In short, the dead person is completely annihilated.

The belief that the dead are able to haunt the living to the point of anguish does not, however, imply a lack of emotion among the living: the various signs of mourning (shaved heads for women, for example, black paintings, prohibitions of sex or food, etc.) are not merely social, for the pain expressed is genuine. Nor is the burial of the dead perfunctory; it is done not in haste but according to the rules. For this reason, in a number of societies, the funeral rites take place in two stages. A most complex ceremonial cycle follows the burial of the dead among the Bororo: a ritual hunt, dances (among others the dance called the *mariddo,* performed by men who wear enormous rolls of leaves on their heads), and chanting for a period of approximately two weeks. The skeleton, stripped of all flesh, is then exhumed, painted with *urucu,* and decorated with feathers. Placed in a basket, it is finally carried on parade to a nearby river and thrown in. The ancient Tupi-Guarani generally buried their dead in great funeral urns buried in the ground. Like the Bororo, they then exhumed the skeletons of famous chiefs or powerful shamans. Among the Guarani, the skeleton of a great shaman became the object of a cult. In Paraguay, the Guarani still retain the custom of occasionally keeping a child's skeleton: invoked in certain circumstances, it assures mediation with the gods and thus facilitates communication between humans and divinities.

III. Cannibalism

Certain societies, however, do not bury their dead; they eat them. This type of cannibalism must be distinguished from the more widespread practice reserved by several tribes for their prisoners of war, as when the Tupi-Guarani and the Carib executed and ritually consumed their captives. The act of eating one's own dead rather than the dead of the enemy is called endocannibalism. It can take many forms. The Yanomami of the Venezuelan Amazon region burn the

Tupinamba warriors. Engraving. Paris, Musée de l'Homme collection. Museum photo.

corpse on a pyre; they collect the bony fragments that are not consumed by the fire and grind them to powder. This will later be consumed, mixed with mashed bananas, by the relatives of the deceased. The Guayaki of Paraguay, on the other hand, roast the dismembered corpse over a wood grill. The flesh, accompanied by the pith of the *pindo* palm, is eaten by the entire tribe, with the exception of the family of the dead person. The bones are broken and burned or abandoned. The apparent effect of endocannibalism is a total integration of the dead with the living, since the one absorbs the other. We might therefore think that this funeral rite is diametrically opposed to the usual attitude of the Indians, which seeks to widen the distance between the living and dead to the fullest extent possible. But the contrast is merely apparent. In fact, endocannibalism pushes the separation of the living and the dead to the limit, in that the living, by eating the dead, go so far as to deprive them of a tomb, their final attachment to space: there is no longer any possibility of contact between the two groups. Endocannibalism therefore accomplishes in the most radical manner possible the mission assigned to funeral rites.

We see therefore how mistaken is the confusion between a cult of ancestors and a cult of the dead. Among the South American tribes, not only do no cults of the dead exist, since the dead are destined for complete oblivion, but, in addition, native thinking tends to regard its relationship with the world of mythic ancestors as positively as its relationship with the world of the actual dead is negative. Society seeks union, alliance, and inclusion with its ancestors and founders, while the community of the living keeps the community of the dead in a state of separation, rupture, and exclusion. The result is that any event that threatens to change a living person for the worse is logically seen as connected to the supreme change, death viewed as the division of the person into a corpse and a hostile spirit. Illness, as it involves a risk of death, concerns not only the individual destiny of the person but also the future of the community. For this reason, therapeutic undertakings are intended, beyond the cure of the sick person, for the protection of society. This is also why the medical act, because of the theory of illness that it embodies and by which it functions, is an essentially religious practice.

IV. Shamanism and Illness

As a physician, the shaman takes his place at the center of the religious life of the group which commissions him to ensure the good health of its members. How does one become sick? What is illness? The cause is related not to a natural agent but to a supernatural origin: aggression from such and such a spirit of nature, or from the soul of a person recently dead, the attack of a shaman from an enemy group, the transgression (voluntary or involuntary) of a food or sex taboo, etc. The Indian etiology immediately associates illness, as a corporeal problem, with the world of invisible forces: the shaman's task is to determine which of these forces is responsible for the illness. But, whatever the cause of the illness, whatever the perceivable symptoms, the form of the illness is almost always the same: it consists of the provisional anticipation of what death realizes definitively: the separation of the body and soul. Good health is maintained by the coexistence of body and soul unified in the person. Illness is therefore the loss of this unity through the departure of the soul. Treating the illness and restoring the health of the person is a matter of restoring the body-soul unity of the individual: as a physician, the shaman must discover where the soul is being held prisoner, free it from the captivity in which it is being held, and bring it back to the body of the patient.

Shaman wearing a cap with small bells and holding a maraca. Musée de l'Homme collection. Photo Perrin.

The shaman. We must first resolutely discard the widespread conviction, unfortunately disseminated by certain ethnologists, that the shaman, who is essential to the life of every tribal society, is a kind of mentally ill person whom society takes charge of and saves from illness and a marginal existence by making him responsible for communication between this world and the world beyond, between the community and the supernatural. By transforming the psychopath into the physician, society is supposed to be able to integrate him while at the same time profiting from his gifts and thereby to block the probable development of his psychosis: the shaman, in this view, is no longer the physician of his tribe but a very sick person cared for by his society. Those who proffer such an absurd theory have obviously never seen a shaman.

In reality, the shaman is no different from his patients in any way save in having knowledge which he puts at their disposal. Gaining this knowledge does not depend on the personality of the shaman but on a long period of study and patient initiation. In other words, people are rarely predisposed to become shamans, so that at the outset, anyone who wishes can become a shaman. Some have this wish, some do not. Why might someone wish to become a shaman? An incident (dream, vision, strange encounter, etc.) might be interpreted as a sign that this is the path to follow, and the shaman's vocation is thereby revealed. The desire for prestige may also determine this professional choice: the reputation of a successful shaman may greatly exceed the confines of the group in which he exercises his talents. The warrior component of the shaman's activities seems to be a much greater determining factor, however; the wish to have the power of a shaman, a power which will be exerted not on humans but on the enemies of humans—the innumerable hosts of invisible powers, spirits, souls, and demons. The shaman confronts these as a warrior, and as such he hopes both to conquer them and to restore the health of the patient.

Certain tribes (for example in the Chaco) repay the shaman for his medical practices with gifts of food, fabric, feathers, ornaments, etc. Though the shaman has considerable status throughout the South American tribes, the exercise of his profession is not without its risks. As master of the life to which his powers may restore the sick, he is also master of death: these same powers are thought to confer upon him the power to attract death to others, and he is believed to be able to kill as well as cure, although not through personal malevolence or perversity. The figure of the wicked sorcerer who casts spells is rare in South America. But if a shaman suffers several successive failures in his cures, or if inexplicable events begin to occur in his society, the guilty party is quickly discovered to be the shaman himself. If he fails to cure his patients, it is said to be because he did not want to cure them. If an epidemic breaks out or a curious death takes place, the shaman has no doubt entered into an alliance with evil spirits in order to terrorize the community. He is therefore a character of uncertain fate: at times having great prestige, but at the same time responsible in advance for the ills of the group, an official scapegoat for guilt. And let us not underestimate the risk the shaman runs—the usual penalty is death.

As a general rule, shamans are men. Certain exceptions are known, however: among the tribes of the Chaco (Abipon, Mocovi, Toba, etc.), for example, or among the Mapuche of Chile, or the Guajiro of Venezuela, this function is often filled by women, who distinguish themselves no less than their male counterparts. Once the candidate is assured of a shamanic vocation, the young person undertakes his professional training. The training is of variable duration (from several weeks to several years) and is generally acquired under the direction of another shaman who has been established for a long time, although it may be the soul of a dead shaman who undertakes the teaching of the novice (as among the Campa of Peru). Among the Carib of Suriname, there are schools for shamans. The instruction of shaman apprentices takes the form of an initiation: since the illnesses which they plan to treat are due to the effects of supernatural powers upon the body, they must acquire the various means to deal with these forces in order to control, manipulate, and neutralize them. The shaman's preparation is thus designed to help him acquire the protection of one or more spirit guardians who will be his auxiliaries in his therapeutic endeavors. The goal of the apprenticeship is to put the soul of the novice in direct contact with the world of the spirits. This often leads to what is called a trance: the moment when the young person knows that the invisible forces have recognized him as a shaman, knows the identity of his spirit guardian, and receives the chant which will thereafter accompany all his cures. To allow the soul initiatory access to the supernatural world, the body must be abolished in some way. For this reason the shaman's training includes asceticism of the body: through prolonged fasting, continual sleep deprivation, isolation in the forest or the brush, massive absorption of smoke or tobacco juice (Tupi-Guarani, Chaco tribes, etc.) or hallucinogenic drugs (Amazonian northwest), the apprentice reaches such a state of physical exhaustion and bodily ruin that he seems almost to experience death. At that time, the soul, freed from its earthly weight, its bodily burden lightened, at last finds itself on the same footing with the supernatural: at the ultimate moment of the trance, in the vision sent to him from the invisible world, the young apprentice is initiated into the knowledge which will henceforth make him a shaman.

V. Therapies, Travel, Drugs

As we have seen, native thought states that illness (with the exclusion of all the diseases introduced into the Americas from Europe) is a rupture of the soul-body unity of the individual, and the cure is the restoration of this unity. It follows that the shaman, as a physician, is a traveler: he must go out in search of the soul which is being held captive by the evil spirits. Aided by his auxiliary spirit, he undertakes a long voyage of exploration in the invisible world, fights the keepers of the soul, and restores it to the body of his patient. For each cure, therefore, the initiatory voyage which first helped the shaman to acquire his powers must be repeated: the shaman must put himself in a trance state, exalting his spirit and lightening his body. Moreover, the treatment or the preparation for this voyage hardly ever takes place without the consumption of large quantities of tobacco, either smoked or drunk as juice, or of various drugs, cultivated above all in the west and northwest Amazon regions where the Indians use them extensively. For certain groups, such as the Guarani, the soul, as a principle of individuation which makes the living body a person, is identified with the proper name: the soul is the name. A particularly serious illness may be diagnosed as an inadequacy in the name of the sick person: the error in naming is therefore the cause of the illness, as the patient does not possess the soul name which is right for him. The shaman must therefore undertake a voyage to discover the true name of the patient. When the gods have communicated it to him, he tells it to the patient and his relatives. The patient's recovery is proof that he has succeeded in finding the right name.

While his spirit is searching for the lost soul (sometimes traveling a great distance, even to the sun), the shaman dances and sings around the patient, who is either seated in a chair or stretched out on the ground. In many societies, the shaman marks the rhythm of his dancing and chanting with a rattle (maraca), which is both a musical instrument and the voice of the spirits with whom he is conversing. Depending on the nature of the problem diagnosed (the identity of the spirit who has captured the soul), the shaman may also need to metamorphose himself in order to effect a cure: sometimes he transforms himself into a jaguar, serpent, or bird. From time to time, he interrupts his movement to blow on the patient (often tobacco smoke), massage him, or suck the painful area. Everywhere the breath and the saliva of the shaman are reputed to have great power. When the lost soul has been reintegrated into the sick body, the patient is healed and the cure is ended. The shaman often proves his success by exhibiting, at the end of the cure, a foreign substance which he has succeeded in extracting from the patient's body: a thorn, small stone, feather, etc., which he has kept in his mouth. The absence of the soul and the presence of a foreign body are not two different causes of the illness. Much more often, it seems, in the place vacated by the capture of the soul the evil spirits leave an object which, by its very presence, attests to the absence of the soul. The reinsertion

Sacred hut where provisions for feast days are kept. Orinoco Guaraúnos region (Venezuela). Paris, Musée de l'Homme collection. Museum photo.

of the soul is therefore, by the same logic, publicly indicated by the extraction of a perceptible, palpable object which guarantees the reality of his cure to the patient and proves the competence of the shaman.

Although essential, the therapeutic role is not the only function of the shaman. We have already indicated the difficulty in drawing a clear line between the social and the religious, the profane and the sacred, the ordinary and the supernatural among Indian cultures. This means that the shaman's intervention is constantly called for by the different events which punctuate both individual lives and the life of the community. He is called upon to interpret dreams and visions, to decide whether a sign is favorable or not (for example when a war expedition is being planned against an enemy tribe). In this last case, the shaman may act as a sorcerer or caster of spells: he is capable of sending maladies down upon the enemies which will weaken or even kill them. In short, there is no ritual activity of importance in which the shaman does not play a decisive role.

VI. Rites and Ceremonies

The religious life of the societies under consideration cannot be reduced to the ritualization of their relationship to the dead or to illness. Of equal importance is the celebration of life, not only in its natural manifestations (the birth of a child), but also in its more properly social aspects (rites of passage). In accordance with the profound religious sense of these peoples, the religious sphere takes into account and pervades the great stages of individual destiny in order to deploy them in sociorituaI events.

Birth. The birth of a child is much more than a biological matter. It concerns not only the father and mother of the newborn child but the entire community, precisely because of its implications and its religious effects. The coming into existence of an additional member of the group upsets the cosmic order. The surplus life, through the imbalance it creates, provokes the awakening of all sorts of powers from which the group must protect the child, as they are the powers of death and hostile to all new life. This attempt at protection is expressed (before and after the birth) in numerous rites of purification, food taboos, sexual prohibitions, ritual hunts, songs, dances, etc., all of which are performed in the certainty that the infant's life would be threatened by death if they were not done. The couvade, practiced by all the Tupi-Guarani tribes, has particularly attracted the attention of observers: the father of the child, from the time of childbirth, lies in his hammock and fasts there until the umbilical cord falls off; unless he does so, the mother and the child risk serious danger. Among the Guayaki, a birth, through the cosmic disorder it causes, threatens not only the child but his father: under penalty of being devoured by a jaguar, he must go into the forest and kill a wild animal. The death of the child is, of course, attributed to man's defeat by these evil powers.

Initiation. It is not surprising that there is a structural analogy between the rites associated with birth and those which sanction the passage of boys and girls to adulthood. The passage is immediately comprehensible on two levels: first it marks the social recognition of the biological maturity of individuals who can no longer be considered children; then it expresses the group's acceptance of the entrance of the new adults into its midst and of the full and complete participation of these young people in society. But the break with the world of childhood is recognized in native thought and expressed in the ritual as a death and rebirth: to become an adult means to die to childhood and to be born to social life, since from that moment on, girls and boys may freely express their sexuality. This is why the rites of passage, like the rites of birth, take place in an extremely dramatic atmosphere. The community of adults at first pretends to withhold recognition of the new members, resists accepting them as equals, making as if to see them as rivals or enemies. But the community also wishes, through the ritual practice, to show the young people that their pride in attaining the age of adulthood is at the cost of an irremedial loss, the loss of the carefree, happy world of childhood. In a great many South American societies, therefore, the rites of passage include a component of very painful physical testing, a dimension of cruelty and pain which makes this passage an unforgettable event: tattooing, scarification, whippings, stinging by wasps or ants, etc., which the young initiates must endure in the strictest silence: they faint, but without a sound. This pseudodeath, this provisional death (unconsciousness deliberately induced by the masters of the ritual), shows clearly the structural identity which Indian belief establishes between birth and passage: that of a rebirth, a repetition of the first birth which must therefore be preceded by a symbolic death.

VII. Myth and Society

We know, on the other hand, that the rites of passage are also identified as rituals of initiation. Every initiatory step is

Mask worn during the banana festival. Tapirare. Paris, Musée de l'Homme collection. Museum photo.

designed to bring the postulant from a state of ignorance to a state of knowledge; its goal is to conduct him to the revelation of a truth, to the communication of knowledge. What knowledge do the rituals of the South American Indians communicate to the young people, which truth do they reveal, to what understanding do they initiate them? The teaching involved in the initiatory rites does not concern the interpersonal relationship which unites master and disciple, nor is it a matter of an individual adventure. What is involved is the social per se, society in itself, on the one hand, and the young people who will belong fully to this same society, on the other. In other words, the rites of passage, as initiatory rites, are intended to communicate to the young people a knowledge of the society that is preparing to welcome them. This says little: the knowledge acquired through initiation is not, in fact, knowledge *about* the society, and therefore knowledge exterior to it. It is necessarily the knowledge *of* the society itself, a knowledge that is immanent to it and, as such, constitutes the very substance of the society, its substantial Self, that which it is in itself. In the initiatory rite, the young people receive from society—represented by the organizers of the ritual—the knowledge of what is, in its being, society, what constitutes it, institutes it as itself: the universe of its laws and standards, the ethico-political universe of its law. The teaching of this law, and, consequently, the requirement of fidelity to this law, will assure the continuity and permanence of the very being of society.

VIII. Myth and Foundation

But what is the origin of the law as a foundation for society, who promulgated it, who was its legislator? Native belief, we have already seen, saw the relationship between society and its foundation (that is, between society and native belief itself) as a relationship of exteriority. Or, in other words, society, though perhaps self-reproducing, is not self-founding. The function of assuring the self-reproduction of society, the repetition of its Self, in accordance with the rules and standards traditionally in force, has particularly devolved upon the rites of initiation. But the founding act of the social, the institution of the society, comes from the presocial or metasocial: this is the work of those who preceded men, in a time before human time, the work of the ancestors. And myth, as a story of the great deed that founded society, the deed of the ancestors, constitutes the foundation of society, the storehouse of its maxims, standards, and laws, the very sum of knowledge transmitted to the young people during the ritual of initiation.

In summary, then, the initiatory dimension of rites of passage lies in the truth toward which the initiates are led; this truth acknowledges the foundation of society, under the auspices of its organic law, and this self-knowledge of the society affirms its own origin in the founding deed of its ancestors, who are chronicled in its myths. This is why the ancestors are necessarily, implicitly or explicitly, involved and present on the level of the concrete process of the moments of the ritual. They are the ones from whom the young people are preparing to receive their instruction. Major figures in every rite of initiation, the ancestors are the real object of worship in the rites of passage: the true worship of the mythic ancestors or culture heroes consists in the rites of initiation which have for so long held a central importance in the religious life of the Amerindian peoples.

Among the Yahgan of Tierra del Fuego, the special moment in religious life was the initiation rite of girls and boys: it consisted essentially of teaching the initiates the traditional rules of the society, instituted in mythic times by Watahinewa, the culture hero and great ancestor. Among the Bororo, the souls (*aroe*) are invited by a particular group of shamans (*aroettaware*) to participate in certain ceremonies, including the initiation of the young, whose passage to adulthood and entrance into the social world is thus supervised under the aegis of the founding ancestors. In the same way, the Cubeo of Brazil link the initiation of boys to the invocation of the ancestors, represented on this occasion by great trumpets, elsewhere by calabash maracas. It is also most probable that among the tribes of the northwest Amazon (Tucano, Witoto, Yagua, Tucuno, etc.) or the Upper Xingu (Kamayura, Aweto, Bacairi, etc.) or the Araguaia (Caraja, Javae) who represent their gods in the form of masks worn by male dancers, these masks, like the musical instruments, symbolize not only the spirits of the forest or the rivers, but also the ancestors.

The tribal societies of South America are completely absorbed in their religious and ritual lives which function as an unceasing affirmation of the community Self. Each ceremony is a new occasion to remember that if society is good, viable, it is by virtue of the respect for standards established long ago by the ancestors. We therefore understand why the reference to the ancestors is logically implied in the initiatory rites: the mythic discourse, the word of the ancestors and the ancestors alone, guarantees the perpetuity of society and its eternal repetition.

P.C./d.b.

BIBLIOGRAPHY

E. BIOCCA, *Yanoama* (London 1969), in several languages. A. BUTT, "Réalité et idéal dans la pratique chamanique," *L'homme,* 2, no. 3 (1962). P. CLASTRES, *Chronique des Indiens Guayaki* (Paris 1972). A. COLBACCHINI and C. ALBISETTI, *Os Bororos Orientais* (São Paulo 1942). M. DOBRIZHOFER, *An Account of the Abipones* (London 1822), in several languages, originally in Latin. R. GIRARD, *Les Indiens de l'Amazonie péruvienne* (Paris 1963), originally in Spanish. J. GUMILLA, *El Orinoco Ilustrado y Defendido* (Caracas 1963). M. GUSINDE, *Die Feuerland-Indianer,* 3 vols. (Vienna 1931–39). *Handbook of South American Indians,* Smithsonian Institution, vols. 1, 3, 4 (Washington 1946). F. HUXLEY, *Affable Savages* (London 1956). C. LÉVI-STRAUSS, *Mythologiques,* 4 vols. (Paris 1966–71). J. LIZOT, *Le cercle des feux* (Paris 1976). P. LOZANO, *Descripcion corografica del Gran Chaco Gualamba* (Tucuman 1941). A. METRAUX, *Religions et magies indiennes d'Amérique du Sud* (Paris 1967). M. PERRIN, *Le chemin des Indiens morts* (Paris 1976). G. REICHEL-DOLMATOFF, *Amazonian Cosmos* (Chicago 1971). L. SEBAG, "Le Chamanisme ayoreo," *L'homme,* 5, nos. 1 and 2.

Religions and Cults of the Societies of the Andes

In entering the Andean world, one reaches a cultural horizon, a religious space which is very different from that of the inhabitants of the forests. For these people, although in large part farmers, the specific importance of the natural food resources remains very considerable: hunting, fishing, gathering. Nature as such is not abolished by gardens, and the forest tribes rely as much on wild fauna and plants as on cultivated plants. Their technology is by no means deficient—it would suffice for them to increase the surface of the cultivated land; but less effort is required for the "predatory" exploitation of the ecological environment, which is often very generous (game, fish, roots, berries, and fruits). The techno-ecological relationship that the Andean peoples maintain with their natural environment follows another line altogether: they are all farmers and almost exclusively farmers, in the sense that wild resources count very little for them. That is, the Indians of the Andes establish a relationship with the earth which is infinitely more intense than that of the Amazonian Indians. For them the earth is really the nourishing mother, and naturally that has a profound effect upon religious life and ritual practice. From the point of view of the real and symbolic occupation of space, the forest Indians are people of territory, while those of the Andes are people of the land: they are, in other words, peasants.

This rooting in the land is very ancient in the Andes, where agriculture is attested from the third millennium B.C. Its exceptional development is exemplified by the very advanced specialization of its cultural techniques, the abundance of irrigation works, and the astonishing variety of vegetable species. These species were obtained by selection and adapted to different ecological levels, which are tiered from sea level to the high central plain. Andean societies are distinguished on the South American horizon by a characteristic that is elsewhere absent: they are hierarchical, stratified, divided along a vertical axis of political power. Aristocracies or religious and military castes reign over a mass of peasants who have to pay them tribute. This division of the social body into dominators and dominated is very old in the Andes, as archaeological research has established. The Chavín civilization, dating from the beginning of the first millennium B.C., shows that the habitat had already become urban and that social life was organized around temples, ritual sites, and places of pilgrimage, under the aegis of priests. The history of the Andes appears to be, from this epoch, a succession of empires strongly tinged by theocratism, of which the last and best known was that of the Incas. For the pre-Incan Andean religions, only fragmentary information remains, furnished by the funerary contents of tombs, the surviving monuments, the textiles and the ceramics, etc. The Inca period, which extended from the thirteenth century to the arrival of the Spanish, is naturally better known, thanks to abundant archaeological documents but also from the descriptions of chroniclers and the reports of missionaries who systematically undertook to wipe out the idolatry and convert the Indians to Christianity.

The establishment and the expansion of the Inca empire, as could be expected, modified the religious face of the Andes without, however, profoundly altering it. In fact, the political imperialism of the Incas was at the same time cultural and particularly religious, since the subjected peoples were forced not only to recognize the authority of the emperor but to accept the religion of their conquerors. Yet the Incas tried hardly at all to substitute their own body of beliefs for that of the populations which were integrated into the empire: they never tried to wipe out local cults or rites. That is why two great religious systems are found in the Andes at this period: the religion of the Incas, properly speaking, whose diffusion kept pace with political expansion, and the local religions, which thrived long before the rise of the Inca state.

I. The Popular Religion

The popular religion clearly expresses the relationship of the Andean Indians to the world: it is essentially a religion of peasants, an agrarian religion, whether it belongs to the people of the seacoast or the inhabitants of the plateau. The principal preoccupation of the Andean Indians was to reconcile all the forces which presided over the regular repetition of the cycle of seasons and assured the abundance of harvests and the fertility of herds of llamas. This is surely why, beyond local peculiarities, pan-Andean cults and beliefs encompass the seacoast and the plateau, or the Quechua and the Aymara and the Mochica.

II. The Gods

The natural elements that rule over the daily life of these peasant peoples (the sun and the moon, often thought of as brother and sister and simultaneously as spouses; the evening and morning stars; the rainbow; the Pacha-Mama, mother earth . . .) are exalted to the status of divine powers. All these divine figures were the objects of cults and of imposing ceremonies, as we will see. The essential Andean agricultural plant, corn, is represented by numerous images of gold, silver, or stone: they are the *sara-mama*, corn mothers, from whom the abundance of the harvest is expected. These divinities are honored with offerings, libations (drinks of fermented corn), or sacrifices (particularly the immolation of llamas, whose blood is sprinkled on the cornfields and anoints the faces of the participants in the ritual).

III. The Cults of Ancestors and of the Dead

The cults of the ancestors and of the dead show the distance which separates the forest tribes from the Andean peoples. Among the former, as has been noted, the ancestors are not the dead who are the contemporaries of the living, but mythical founders of society. In the Andes, by contrast, the socioreligious life of the community rests in large part on the cult of both the ancestors and the dead: the latter were the descendants of the former, and Andean thought, in contrast with Amazonian thought, strives to mark the continuity between the world of the living and the world of the dead, a continuity of the peasant community which occupies the same soil under the protection of its gods and of its dead. The mythical ancestor was frequently represented by a rock, *markayok*, venerated as much as the place, *pakarina*, through which the ancestor came out from the subterranean world. Each community or *ayllu* thus had its ancestor and worshiped him: *markayok* and *pakarina*, attesting to the permanence and the identity, through time, of the *ayllu*, established the solidarity of the families that comprised the community.

While the funerary rites of the forest Indians tend to abolish the dead, to cast them into oblivion, the Andean Indians, by contrast, place them in cemeteries: the tombs were grouped in the shelter of caverns, or in a kind of cave built in the form of a tower, or in holes dug into cliffs. They continued to participate in the collective life, because relatives came to visit them to consult them, regular offerings maintained their well-being, and sacrifices were offered to them. Far from forgetting their dead, the Indians of the Andes did everything possible so that the dead would not forget the living but would guard their prosperity: a relationship of alliance and of inclusion, not one of exclusion and hostility as in the forest. This is why, as the Spanish priests charged with wiping out idolatry said, the real dead, in the form of skeletons or of mummies (*malqui*), were, like the mythical dead, the objects of cults and veneration: in certain ceremonial circumstances, they were ornamented with precious feathers and textiles.

The Huaca

Huaca is the name that the Indians gave to every being or natural object supposed to contain a supernatural force. The sacred stones representing the ancestors were *huaca*, as were the mummified dead. But *huaca* were also the idols and the sites where they were found, a mountain or a plant, a spring or a grotto, a child born malformed, a temple, a constellation, or a tomb. On a journey, the special sites, such as a mountain pass or a stopping point, were marked by piles of stones, *apacheta*, which travelers also regarded as *huaca*: they added their own rock to it and offered a quid of coca in sacrifice. Space was thus entirely quartered off by the supernatural, and the system of the *huaca* constituted a kind of sacred coding of the world.

To the group of the *huaca* belong not only the points of contact between spatial expanse and the sphere of the

Mochican vase with a representation of a human sacrifice. Paris, Musée de l'Homme collection. Museum photo.

sacred, but also objects, figurines, and amulets which represent the tutelary powers of each family. These are the *conopa:* sometimes rocks in strange forms or colors, sometimes carved or molded statuettes in the form of a llama or an ear of corn. The familial *conopa* remain under cover in houses whose occupants they protect from disease, or they are buried in fields, guaranteeing their fertility. The communal *conopa* (those of the *ayllu*) were, at certain times of the year, taken out of their hiding places: homage was given, sacrifices of llamas or coca were offered, and prayers were addressed to them.

There was in each community at least one curer or shaman. He was often designated by the thunder god, who struck him with the thunderbolt. Besides his therapeutic functions, he fulfilled the office of diviner. But, unlike the forest tribes, shamanism in the Andes was not the center of religious life. That was developed in a set of ritual practices all of which tended to ask the gods, the ancestors, the dead (all the forces that were called *huaca*) to assure the well-being of the *ayllu* by guaranteeing the prosperity of mother earth. This eminently agrarian religion expresses the profound investment of the peasant in his soil, which it is the mission of the diviners to guard.

IV. Inca Religion

In its origin and its substance, Inca religion does not differ profoundly from the so-called popular religion. In the thirteenth century A.D., the Incas were a small tribe of the region of Cuzco. Farmers and herders, their religious and ritual life was rooted, like those of all the peasant communities of the coast or the plateau, in a desire for the repetition of cosmic order, for the eternal return of this order, and in the hope that through the rituals that celebrated them and the sacrifices that were offered to them, the divine forces, the ancestors, and the dead would guarantee to humans the fertility of the earth and the permanence of society. For reasons which remain mysterious, the Inca tribe inaugurated in the thirteenth century a march of conquest which was stopped only by the arrival of the Spanish. But during this relatively short period, the Incas greatly expanded the boundaries of their empire (which numbered between twelve and fifteen million inhabitants in 1530) and built an astonishing power machine, a state apparatus which still amazes us by the "modernity" of its institutions.

The imperial society, inscribed in a rigorously hierarchical pyramid, expresses first the radical division between the triumphant aristocracy of the Incas and the masses of people, ethnic groups, and tribes integrated into the empire whose power they recognized by the tribute they paid. At the summit of this hierarchy the monarch reigned; the Inca, simultaneously the chief of his ethnic group, the master of the empire, and the representative on earth of the principal divine power. It would be a mistake to believe that the politico-military expansionism of the Incas was accompanied by religious proselytism, so that they imposed their own system upon the peoples whom they subjugated, by eliminating the traditional beliefs and rituals of the conquered people. First of all, in its essential outlines the religion of the Incas scarcely differed from that of their tributaries: moreover, their enterprise of domination aimed only to obtain the obedience of their subjects and not, as did the Spanish, to wipe out their "idolatry." In fact, they let the traditional religious "code" survive, in order to superimpose upon it a "supercode" consisting of their own religion: freedom of religion was left to the vassals of the Incas, on condition that, in addition, they recognize and honor the gods of their conquerors.

The conquerors, as their power gradually increased, proceeded to renovate their old system of beliefs by exalting certain figures of their pantheon, by giving a grandiose character to their festivals and traditional ceremonies, by conferring a considerable sociopolitical weight upon the religion through the institution of a numerous and highly hierarchical clergy, through the construction of temples and multiple sites of cults, and through the allocation to the clergy of an important part of the tribute paid to the Incas by their subjects.

V. The Cult of the Sun

The solar star, Inti, stands out as a major figure of the Inca pantheon by virtue of a double logic: that of the tradition which for a long time had made the sun a pan-Peruvian divinity; and that of the sociopolitical innovation which, through the institution of an imperial system, incorporated practically all the archaic despotisms and led to the identification of the master of the empire with the sun. This is why the sun became the principal Inca god, as the great founding ancestor of the royal lineage: the emperors were the children of the sun. Also, the worship of the sun had the value of both a dynastic ancestor cult and an official religion imposed on everyone: it was through the cult of the sun that Inca religion became a state religion.

When the Incas obtained the submission of an ethnic group, they immediately took a number of administrative measures (a census of the population, of resources, etc.) and religious measures: the conquered people had to integrate the cult of Inti into their religious system. This involved setting up a ritual infrastructure consisting of the temples that had to be built, the clergy destined to officiate at them, and, of course, the gift of important resources to the clergy which would ensure their subsistence and allow them to perform the sacrifices required for the worship of the sun. We know that for each subjugated community the Incas established a tripartition of the lands: one part remained at the disposition of the *ayllu,* another was allocated to the state, and the third was consecrated to the sun. The construction of numerous temples of the sun built in the provinces followed the model of the most famous among them, that of the imperial capital, Coricancha, the true religious and political center of the empire and the site of the cult and pilgrimage, where the mummies of past emperors were found. The wall enclosing Coricancha had a rectangular plan and was four hundred meters long. All along the carefully executed masonry ran a band of fine golden plates thirty to forty centimeters high. Coricancha sheltered diverse sanctuaries filled with golden or silver offerings and the lodgings of the numerous personnel designated for the service of the temple. There was also a garden planted with stalks of golden corn. By working ritually in this garden, the Inca himself opened the season of sowing in the empire.

Besides the hierarchical group of priests, diviners, and servants, the personnel of each sun temple included a group of women, the virgins of the sun, the *Aclla,* chosen from the entire empire by royal functionaries, who selected them for their grace and beauty. Assembled and educated in convent-like institutions (*aclla-huasi*), they learned to make luxurious fabrics of vicuña or alpaca, offered in enormous quantities during sacrifices; they prepared the *chicha,* a drink of fermented corn which was required for all ceremonies. Though they were, like the vestal virgins, pledged to absolute chastity, the Inca nevertheless chose from among them his concubines or women whom he gave as gifts to great men of the empire whom he wished to recompense. A certain number of them were sacrificed in times of crisis: the succession of a new emperor, the serious illness or death of the Inca, an earthquake, etc. Four thousand persons, it is said, composed the personnel of Coricancha, of whom more than fifteen hundred were virgins of the sun. In each temple, the virgins were subject to the authority of a matron, Mama Cuna, regarded as the wife of the sun. At the summit of the religious hierarchy of the empire was the great priest of the sun, the Vilca Oma, the uncle or brother of the emperor, who lived ascetically in Coricancha where he directed the religious life of the empire.

VI. The Cult of Viracocha

Viracocha was an anthropomorphic divine figure, both very ancient and pan-Peruvian, since he was known and honored both by the Aymara and by the Quechua. Throughout the often obscure myths that are dedicated to Viracocha, one can make out the image of the eternal god, creator of all

Kenko ceremonial hemicycle. Paris, Musée de l'Homme collection. Photo Metais.

Cuzco. On the right, the Accla Huasi (Convent of the Virgins), and on the left, the Amaru Kancha (Temple of Huayna Capac). Paris, Musée de l'Homme collection. Museum photo.

things (sky and earth, sun and moon, day and night), and of the civilizing hero. When he had created and destroyed several successive humanities, he engendered the people of the present day, to whom he assigned their respective territories, and taught the arts which would make it possible for them to live and the norms whose observance would assure social and cosmic good order. Once his duty was accomplished, Viracocha, on arriving at the seacoast, transformed his coat into a boat and disappeared forever, heading west. From the time of their first contacts with the Spanish, the Indians called them *viracochas*.

The Incas imposed the cult of their ethnic god, the sun, upon their entire empire. By an inverse course, they transformed Viracocha, a pan-Andean figure, into a tribal god. It was under the reign of the great emperor Pachacuti (who reigned from 1438 to 1471) that this alteration in the hierarchy of the Inca pantheon can be precisely fixed, at the end of which Inti ceded the central position to Viracocha, although the emperor remained the descendant of the sun. The preeminence accorded to Viracocha may have been the cumulative effect of several factors: the theological work of priests seeking a more fundamental religious presence than that of anything visible, even the sun; the personal belief of Pachacuti himself, whom Viracocha, in a dream, helped to win an essential military victory over the Chanca; and, the final factor, the logic immanent, perhaps, in every despotic system, such that its theocratic vocation tends occasionally to be realized in the affirmation and institution of monotheism.

In any case, this was the course Pachacuti followed when he built a temple at Cuzco to Viracocha, where the god was represented in the form of a solid gold statue, "the size of a ten-year-old child." In each provincial capital, a sanctuary was built to Viracocha, tended by a clergy consecrated to his exclusive service and with resources destined to assure the maintenance of the temple and the priests. The cult of Viracocha—ancient Lord, distant Lord, very excellent Lord—never became a popular cult, like that of the sun. Perhaps the Incas did not maintain it because, among other things, they were anxious to institute a more abstract, more esoteric cult, a cult less rooted in the perceptible world than were the popular cults, in order to mark, even on a religious plane, the specific feature of their dominant caste. This is why the cult of Viracocha, unlike the popular cults, did not survive for a single instant the fall of the empire.

VII. The Cult of Thunder and the *Huaca*

Illapa, thunder, was also a pan-Andean figure of the Inca pantheon. Master of the storm, of hail, of lightning, and of rain, he produced his rumbling in the sky by snapping his sling. The Andean peoples, as farmers, were very attentive to the activities of Illapa, whom they begged to grant them sufficient rain and to whom they offered large sacrifices in the event of drought. The agrarian character of Andean societies explains the superior position, after Viracocha and Inti, of Illapa in the Inca pantheon.

For the caste of the Incas, as for the peasant masses, the *huaca* constituted a sacred "grid" of space. To the popular network of the *huaca*, the Incas added their own system, defined in sanctified places by a real or imaginary bond between the person of the emperor and any place through which he passed or of which he dreamed. Whatever they were, the *huaca* were venerated and honored by sacrifices (corn beer, coca, llamas, and chosen children and women, whose hearts were offered to the divinity). The city of Cuzco alone, it is said, contained five hundred of them. The *huaca* of the empire were dispersed along imaginary axes, the *ceque*, which started at Coricancha and reached out, like rays, to the boundaries of the empire. The proliferation of divinities, lesser and greater, is the indication, in the Andes, of an inundation of space and time by the sacred. The punctuation of time by ritual practices corresponds to the marking of space by the *huaca*.

VIII. Festivals and Ceremonies

Rare or unforeseen events were the occasion for important ceremonial demonstrations: eclipses of the moon or sun, earthquakes and droughts called for solemn sacrifices to appease the anger of the gods. Everything that affected the person of the emperor had repercussions for the well-being of the empire: as the son of the sun, he occupied the point of contact between the world of the gods and the world of humans, in such a way that the collective destiny of the people depended directly upon the personal destiny of the Inca. On the other hand, to transgress the norms of social life was to offend the emperor and therefore to incite the anger of the gods. This is why the enthronement of a new Inca, the death of the emperor, his illnesses, and his military defeats called into question the health of the empire itself and the survival of the people: numerous human sacrifices (children, prisoners of war, and virgins of the sun) attempted to reestablish the altered social and cosmic order in favor of humans.

These exceptional circumstances, in which sinister disproportions gaped in the "prose of the world," called for a ritual response improvised in some way. But there was also an annual cycle of religious ceremonies which followed the movement of social life very closely, a movement articulated principally in the agrarian cycle: sowing, harvest, solstices, and payments of tribute. Although the year was divided into twelve lunar months, it was the movement of the sun in the sky that preoccupied the Indians of the Andes. Each month was marked by a particular festival which determined the moment of planting, harvesting, dividing the fields, preparing them for sowing, etc. These festivals took place in the temples and, usually, on public grounds reserved for this purpose, notably on the public square of Cuzco, where all the figures of the Inca pantheon were then exhibited, including the mummies of past emperors. In this regular ceremonial cycle, three festivals stand out for their importance and their magnificence: two of them correspond to the solstices, while the third was originally a lunar festival.

The southern winter solstice (June 21) was dedicated to the Inti Raymi, a celebration of the sun and at the same time a glorification of her son on earth, the Inca himself. For this reason all the high functionaries and local chiefs of the country were summoned to the ceremony at Cuzco. The emperor, surrounded by all his relatives and the court, waited in the large square of his capitol for the first light of the solar star to appear. All then knelt and the Inca offered the sun a drink of *chicha* in a silver vase. Like all great festivals, the Inti Raymi was accompanied by libations, sacrifices, songs, and dances. During the period of the southern summer solstice (December 21), the Capac Raymi took place, also a solar festival but in addition dedicated to the performance of initiation rites which marked the young nobles' passage to adulthood. While among the peasant masses this passage was not ritually marked, it was, by contrast, the occasion for great ceremonies in the dominant caste: entrance into adulthood and entrance into the aristocracy of the lords. Like all initiatory rituals, the *huarachicoy* (*huara* is the loincloth given to the young people at the end of the ritual) consisted in, beyond sacrifices to the gods, physical ordeals (flagellations, contests, fasting, and races), exhortations to follow the example of the ancestors, and so forth. With the loincloths of adults they were given weapons and their ears were pierced to be adorned with disks. In the *huarachicoy,* the accent was placed less on the passage to adulthood than on the full entrance into the aristocracy and on the necessity for absolute fidelity in service to the Inca.

The third great Incan ceremony took place in September. The *sitowa* was an undertaking of general purification of the capital from which evils were expelled. At the appearance of the new moon, the crowd, assembled in the large square, cried out, "Illnesses, disasters, misfortunes, leave this land!" On the four principal roads leading to the four regions into which the empire was divided, four groups of one hundred armed warriors rushed forth, driving back the evils before them. In the city, the inhabitants shook out their clothes at the entrance of their homes. Songs, dances, and processions cadenced the night. At dawn, everyone took a purifying bath in the rivers. The gods and the emperors participated in the *sitowa* because their statues and mummies were exhibited on the square. White llamas were offered to them in sacrifice and a dough of corn meal specially prepared for this occasion was dipped in the blood of these animals. The gods and the mummies were anointed with this dough, the *sanku,* and all the inhabitants of Cuzco ate a piece of it.

In this society, impregnated with religiosity, every enterprise, individual or collective, humble or imperial, had to be preceded by an inquiry into the will of the supernatural powers. This is the source of the very important role of the diviners, who would observe the disposition of coca leaves thrown on the ground, the trickle of saliva running between fingers, the entrails of sacrificed animals, the lungs of llamas into which one blew in order to interpret the pattern of blood vessels. Since every disorder in such a world could only arise from some transgression (voluntary or involuntary) of some interdiction, it was also incumbent on the diviners to discover the guilty and to purify them. When circumstances demanded it, collective and public sessions of confession took place, designed to reestablish the sociocosmic order which was troubled by the sins that had been committed. The temples of Pachacamac and Lima, traditional pilgrimage sites, were the homes of oracles famous throughout the empire, whom the emperors themselves did not hesitate to consult. Despite the efforts of the Church, a number of native rites, syncretically mixed with the Christian cult, survive today among the Aymara of Bolivia and the Quechua of Peru.

P.C./d.f.

BIBLIOGRAPHY

L. BAUDIN, *L'empire socialiste des Inka* (Paris 1928). G. H. S. BUSCHNELL, *Le Pérou* (Grenoble 1958), French trans. F. A. ENGEL, *Le monde précolombien des Andes* (Paris 1972). GARCILASO DE LA VEGA, *Comentarios reales de los Incas* (Buenos Aires 1943). GUAMAN POMA DE AYALA, *Nueva Coronica y Buen Gobierno* (Paris 1936). A. METRAUX, *Les Incas* (Paris 1962). J. MURRA, *Formaciones economicas y politicas del mundo andino* (Lima 1975). F. PEASE, *Los Ultimos Incas del Cuzco* (Lima 1972); in French, *Les derniers Incas du Cuzco* (Tours 1974). J. H. ROWE, "Inca Culture at the Time of the Spanish Conquest," in *Handbook of South American Indians,* 2 (Washington 1946). N. WACHTEL, *La vision des vaincus* (Paris 1971). R. T. ZUIDEMA, *The Ceque System in the Social Organization of Cuzco* (Leiden 1962).

Religious Thought and Prophetism among the Tupi-Guarani Indians of South America: The Land Without Evil

Despite its brevity, this essay on the religions of the societies of the forest and the Andes will nevertheless endeavor to include their essential characteristics in constructing a faithful picture of the religious beliefs and practices of the South American peoples. The religiosity of the forest societies appears to be both public and collective. It is sung, danced, and acted out; as the sacred totally permeates the social, so, inversely, the social totally penetrates the religious. To say that religious sentiment exists primarily in its public expression does not minimize in any way the intensity of individual devotion. Like all tribal peoples, the Indians of South America have shown and continue to show an exemplary steadfastness in their fidelity to their myths and rituals. Nevertheless, the personal equation of religious life tends to be dwarfed by the collective dimension, which explains the enormous importance of ritual practice. The exceptions to this general rule merely make it stand out even more. During the second half of the nineteenth century, various scholars collected from among populations now extinct, who then lived along the lower and middle courses of the Amazon, a set of texts that differ significantly from the "classical" corpus of myths. The religious, indeed the mystical, uneasiness contained in these texts suggests the existence in these societies, not of narrators of myths, but of philosophers or intellectuals dedicated to the task of personal reflection, in sharp contrast to the ritual exuberance of other forest societies. Rare as this may be in South America, this idiosyncrasy was carried to the extreme by the Tupi-Guarani.

The term Tupi-Guarani covers a great many tribes that belong to the same linguistic group and share great cultural homogeneity. These populations occupied a very large territory: in the south, the Guarani lived from the Paraguay River in the west to the Atlantic coast in the east. The Tupi inhabited the same coast up to the mouth of the Amazon in the north and extended deep inland for an indeterminate distance. These Indians numbered several million. As far as economic life and social organization are concerned, the Tupi-Guarani conformed to the model that prevailed throughout the forest area: slash-and-burn farming, hunting, fishing, villages made up of several large collective houses. A notable fact among these Indians is their population density, substantially higher than that of the neighboring populations; communities could assemble two thousand or more people. Although all of these tribes have long since disappeared, with the exception of about five thousand Guarani who survive in Paraguay, they are nevertheless among the best known on the South American continent. The coastal Tupi were the first Indians to establish contact with Europeans at the dawn of the sixteenth century. Travelers and missionaries of various nationalities have left an abundant literature about these people that is rich in observations of all sorts, especially in the area of beliefs and customs.

As with all the tribal societies of the continent, the religious life of the Tupi-Guarani centered on shamanism. The *paje,* shaman-medicine men, performed there the same tasks as elsewhere and ritual life was always conducted, in whatever the circumstances (initiation, the execution of a prisoner of war, burials, etc.), in accordance with norms that ensured social cohesion at all times. The norms and rules of life were imposed on humankind by culture heroes (Maira, Monan, Sun, Moon, etc.) or by mythical ancestors. Up to this point, the Tupi-Guarani do not differ at all from the other forest societies. Yet the chronicles of French, Portuguese, and Spanish travelers bear witness to a difference so considerable that it gives the Tupi-Guarani an absolutely original place in the spectrum of South American indigenous tribes. Indeed, the newcomers confronted religious phenomena of such an abundance and nature that they were completely incomprehensible to the Europeans.

What did the religion involve? Besides the incessant wars among the various tribes, these people were profoundly driven by a powerful movement of strictly religious origin and intention. Of course, the Europeans could only see the pagan manifestation of the devil in all of this and viewed the makers of this movement as Satan's henchmen. Serious errors in judgment were made in response to the strange phenomenon of Tupi-Guarani prophetism. It was interpreted until recently as a kind of messianism, as the common response of many primitive peoples to a grave crisis resulting from the contact with Western civilization. Messianism was thus a reaction to culture shock. But it was a serious misunderstanding of the radically different nature of Tupi-Guarani prophetism to reduce it to the level of messianism, for the simple and incontrovertible reason that it had been an Indian practice long before the whites ever arrived, possibly toward the middle of the fifteenth century. At issue therefore is an indigenous phenomenon that owes nothing to contact with the West, and that furthermore was not even directed at the whites. We are dealing with a prophetism for which ethnology has discovered no equivalent anywhere else.

I. Prophets

Ill-equipped to understand the phenomenon of prophetism, the first chroniclers were, however, careful enough not to confuse the shamans with certain enigmatic individuals who were prominent in that society, the *karai.* These had nothing to do with therapy, which was reserved for *paje* only. Nor did they fulfill any specialized ritual function. They were neither priests of a traditional cult nor founders of a new cult. Neither shamans, nor priests, who then were the *karai?* These men were exclusively devoted to the spoken word. Speaking was their sole activity. Men of discourse (the content of whose discourse will be discussed below), they were committed to giving speeches everywhere they went, and not just in their own community. The *karai* moved about all the time from village to village, haranguing the Indians who would listen. This nomadic vocation of the prophets was all the more astonishing because the local groups, sometimes allied into federations of several villages, waged war on one another mercilessly. But the *karai* were allowed to circulate with impunity from one camp to another. They ran no risks, and were fervently welcomed everywhere. The people went so far as to clear the foliage from the roads to the village, and they would run ahead to meet them and escort them into the village in a procession. No matter where they came from, the *karai* were never regarded as enemies.

How was this possible? In tribal society, the individual is first defined as belonging to a kin group and a local community. A person is thus put in a genealogical chain of relatives and in a network of allies. Among the Tupi-Guarani, where descent is patrilineal, one belonged to the lineage of one's father. Yet this is the strange statement that the *karai* made about themselves: they asserted that they had no father but were the sons of a woman and a deity. Here the megalomaniac fantasy by which the prophets made themselves divine

Guarani shaman's pipe. Paris, Musée de l'Homme collection. Photo J. Oster.

Guarani calabash. Paris, Musée de l'Homme collection. Photo J. Oster.

is less significant than their denial and refusal of a father. Proclaiming the absence of a father was tantamount to denying that one belonged to a lineage, and by extension, to society. To make such a statement in this type of society is to incur a charge of incomparable subversion, because it denies the very framework of primitive society, the bonds of blood.

It is obvious that the nomadism of the *karai* stemmed from their not belonging to any community whatsoever, and not from some fantasy on their part or a lust for travel. They were from nowhere and by definition could not settle anywhere, since they were not members of any lineage. This explains why they could not be taken for representatives of an enemy group when entering any village. To be an enemy meant to be set within a social structure, which was precisely not the case for the *karai*. And this is also why, being from nowhere, they were in a way from everywhere and at home everywhere. In other words, their semidivinity, their partial nonhumanity, removed them from human society and compelled them to live in accordance with their nature as "beings from afar." But at the same time it assured them total security during their travels from one tribe to another. The Indians felt no hostility toward them as they would toward a stranger, because they considered them to be gods and not men, which is another way of saying that far from taking the *karai* to be madmen, the Indians never questioned the coherence of what the *karai* said and were ready to accept their words.

II. The Discourse of the Prophets

What did the *karai* talk about? The nature of their discourse was commensurate with their status vis-à-vis society. It was discourse beyond discourse, as they themselves were beyond society. Or to put it another way, what they uttered before the fascinated and enchanted Indian crowds was a discourse that broke with traditional discourse, a discourse that developed outside the system of ancient norms, rules, and values bequeathed and imposed by the gods and the mythical ancestors. That is why the prophetic phenomenon that stirred these people is so perplexing to us. Here we have a tribal society that tends to persevere by resolutely maintaining conservative norms that have prevailed since the dawn of human time, and from this society emerge enigmatic men who proclaim the end of such norms, the end of the world that depends on such norms and is committed to respect them.

The prophetic discourse of the *karai* may be summarized in one assertion and one promise. They relentlessly asserted the fundamentally evil character of the world, and they expressed the certainty that the conquest of a good world was possible. "The world is evil! The earth is ugly!" they said. "Let us leave it!" they concluded. Their absolutely pessimistic assessment of the world met with general approval from the Indians who listened to them. As a result, despite its complete difference from the usual discourse that holds all tribal society together—the discourse of repetition and not of difference, the discourse of faithfulness to tradition and not the discourse that is an overture to innovation—the discourse of the *karai* did not sound to the Indians like sick discourse, like a madman's delirium, since it rang out as the expression of a truth that they were fully expecting, like a new prose articulating the new form, the evil form, of the world. In summary, it was not the discourse of the prophet that was sick, but the world they were speaking about, the society in which they lived. The unhappiness of living in this world was rooted for them in the evil that was destroying society, and the novelty of their discourse was exclusively connected with the change that had gradually come to light in social life to alter it and disfigure it.

Where did this change come from and how did it take effect? We shall not attempt to give a genealogy of the difference in this society, but only to shed light on its principal effect: the appearance of prophets and of the discourse that spoke of the immanence of evil. The radicalism of the discourse was a measure of the depth of the evil that it unveiled. Tupi-Guarani society was quite simply experiencing the pressure of various forces and was in the process of ceasing to be a "primitive" society, i.e., a society that refused change and difference. The discourse of the *karai* stated the demise of the society. What sickness had corrupted the Tupi-Guarani to this point? The answer lies in a combination of factors: demographic (heavy population increase), sociological (a tendency to concentrate the population in large villages instead of the usual dispersion), and political (the emergence of powerful chiefs). As a result of all this, this society experienced the most deadly innovation: that of social division and inequality. A deep malaise was gnawing at these tribes, the sign of a grave crisis. The *karai* recognized this malaise and announced that it was the presence of evil and misfortune in society, the ugliness and mendacity of the world. The prophets were more sensitive than others to the slow transformations that were taking effect around them. They were the first to become clearly aware of these transformations, and they undertook to proclaim what everyone felt more or less confusedly, but the *karai* proclaimed it with such force that their discourse did not sound like the aberrations of madmen. There was complete agreement between the Indians and the prophets who told them that the world had to be changed.

III. The Land without Evil

The emergence of the prophets and their discourse that identified the world as a place of evil and unhappiness resulted from historical circumstances peculiar to the Tupi-Guarani: a reaction to a deep crisis, the symptom of a grave sickness of the social body, a premonition of the death of the society. By way of remedy in the face of this menace, the *karai* exhorted the Indians to abandon *ywy mba'emegua,* the evil earth, in order to join *ywy mara eÿ,* the land without evil. This is in fact the dwelling place of the gods, the place where arrows go hunting by themselves, where corn grows without human care, a territory of divine beings free of all alienation, a territory that, before the destruction of the first humanity by the universal flood, was a place shared in common by men and gods. Thus the return to the mythical past provided the prophets with the means to escape the present world. But the radicalism of their desire to rupture with evil was not limited to the promise of a world free of worry; it further empowered their discourse with a charge to destroy all norms and rules, for the total subversion of the old order. The call to abandon all rules left no exceptions. It explicitly included the ultimate basis of human society, the rule of the exchange of women, the law prohibiting incest: "Henceforth," they said, "you may give your women to whomever you please!"

Where was the Land without Evil located? Here again the unlimited mysticism of the prophets appeared in its full scope. The myth of paradise on earth is common to almost all cultures, and mankind may attain this paradise only after death. But for the *karai,* the Land without Evil was a real, concrete place, accessible here and now, i.e., without passing through the trial of death. According to the myths, it was generally situated to the east, toward the rising sun. From the end of the fifteenth century, the great religious migrations of the Tupi-Guarani were devoted to finding it. Led by their prophets, Indians by the thousands abandoned their villages and gardens, fasted and danced relentlessly, became nomads like their prophets, and proceeded to move eastward in search of the land of the gods. On reaching the seacoast, they discovered their major obstacle, the sea. Beyond it, surely, lay the Land without Evil. On the other hand, certain tribes thought that they might find it to the west, toward the setting sun. More than ten thousand Indians accordingly set out from the mouth of the Amazon at the beginning of the sixteenth century. Ten years later, the three hundred who were left reached Peru, already occupied by the Spanish. The rest had died of privation, hunger, and exhaustion. The prophetism of the *karai* was an assertion of the deadly risk that society ran, but it also expressed in its practical effect—religious migration—a will for subversion which went as far as the desire to die and even mass suicide.

Prophetism did not vanish with the coastal Tupi. It has persisted among the Guarani of Paraguay, whose last migration in quest of the Land without Evil took place in 1947, when a few score of Mbya Indians went to the region of Santos in Brazil. The migratory flux has dried up among the last remaining Guarani, but their mystical vocation continues to inspire their *karai.* The prophets, no longer able to lead their people to the Land without Evil, engage constantly in inner voyages that take them on the path of a search in thought, a task of reflecting on their own myths. It is a path of strictly metaphysical speculation, as is attested by the texts and sacred chants that can still be heard from their mouths today. Like their ancestors five centuries ago, they know that the world is evil and they wait for the end to come. They no longer seek access to the Land without Evil but expect the world to be destroyed by fire and by the great celestial jaguar, who will spare the Guarani Indians alone among contemporary humanity. Their immense, pathetic pride maintains them in the certainty that they are the Chosen and that, sooner or later, the gods will summon them to join them. In their eschatological expectation of the end of the world, the Guarani Indians know that their kingdom will come and that the Land without Evil will be their true dwelling place.

P.C./g.h.

BIBLIOGRAPHY

C. D'ABBEVILLE, *Histoire de la Mission des Pères Capucins en l'Isle de Maragnon . . .* (Graz 1963). L. CADOGAN, *Ayvu Rapyta: Textos miticos de los Mbya-Guarani del Guaira* (São Paulo 1959). F. CARDIM, *Tratados da terra e gente do Brasil* (Rio de Janeiro 1925). *Cartas dos Primeiros Jesuitas do Brasil,* 3 vols., S. Leite, ed. (São Paulo 1954). H. CLASTRES, *La terre sans mal* (Paris 1975). P. CLASTRES, *Le grand parler: Mythes et chants sacrés des Indiens Guarani* (Paris 1974). Y. D'EVREUX, *Voyage dans le Nord du Brésil, fair durant les années 1613 et 1614* (Leipzig and Paris 1864). J. DE LÉRY, *Histoire d'un voyage fait en la terre du Brésil,* 2 vols. (Paris 1880). P. LOZANO, *Historia de la conquista del Paraguay . . .* , 5 vols. (Buenos Aires 1873). A. METRAUX, *La religion des Tupinamba et ses rapports avec celle des autres tribus tupi-guarani* (Paris 1928). R. DE MONTOYA, *Conquista espiritual . . .* (Bilbao 1892). C. NIMUENDAJU, *Leyenda de la Creacion y Juicio final del Mundo . . .* (São Paulo 1944), for the Spanish trans. A. SEPP, *Viagem as Missoes Jesuiticas . . .* (São Paulo 1972). G. SOARES DE SOUZA, *Tratado descriptivo do Brasil em 1587* (São Paulo 1971). H. STADEN, *Vera Historia . . .* (Buenos Aires 1944), for the Spanish trans. A. THEVET, "La cosmographie universelle: Histoire de deux voyages," in *Les Français en Amérique,* vol. 2 (Paris 1953).

Religions and Mythologies of Oceania

During the last century, Oceania has been a popular field of ethnological inquiry because of the variability of its social and symbolic systems. This variability has justified the great amount of theoretical reflection devoted to Oceania in preference to the continental civilizations with their large populations. Each Oceanian culture is of such complexity that an observer may convince himself that he is a specialist in it after a few years, only to discover twenty years later that he has yet to uncover the greater part of its secrets.

It is easy to yield to the temptation of classifying the elements of knowledge obtained by several generations of amateur observers and alleged specialists. This classical procedure, intellectually convenient, casts a mantle of modesty over reality, a reality that is less brilliant than it appears to be. It is thus appropriate first of all to examine it closely.

The first observers—adventurers who married locally and settled down to a bourgeois old age, or missionaries who devoted their lives to the Pacific—made up the ruling class on archipelago after archipelago, from the early part of the nineteenth century. They established the ideology of the time, which justified domination by a presupposed racial superiority. After they had consolidated their power, they assumed a protective role, very much like the love of a father for children he deems incapable of progressing intellectually beyond adolescence, since they are in the grip of primitive impulses.

Such a priori assumptions did not inspire respect for the tradition or facilitate the collection of data. The Oceanians quickly found out what the souls of their temporary masters were made of. Even if they realized that people might be interested in their tradition, they saw to it that each of their interlocutors would get only what he was capable of understanding and appreciating. The filter through which knowledge had to pass differed depending on whether they were dealing with a strict Protestant, a curious trader in exotic goods, a military man, or a civil servant who was cultivated, secular, and accessible to romanticism, and thus more likely to be respectful of what could be confided to him.

In the eighteenth century, the Polynesians were thought to be children of nature, unaware of evil. It was not until the social revolution brought about in England by the terrible conditions at the beginning of the Industrial Revolution that Protestant missionaries could introduce the notion of sin and decide to found on the islands a universe that would be free of sin. At the same time, the Romantic movement in literature, espousing the cause of ancient European paganism, had its influence on the first regiments, both military and civilian, of the nascent European colonization. Polynesian priests and sages were identified with Celtic bards and druids. Sir Walter Scott, at the height of his glory in England and continental Europe, was thus indirectly responsible for these events.

Understanding the material benefit that would result from having their culture accepted at the level where Western intellectuals would put it, the Polynesians furnished the information necessary to encourage that movement. And in application of the principle that one must avail oneself of someone inferior in order to establish oneself as superior, they participated actively in everything that at that time designated Melanesia as a locus of barbarism. This barbarism was defined by contrast with a Polynesia closely related to the classical civilizations which were, as they were known through books, the basis of Western education. Setting aside elements of spectacle—ceremonies in uncovered enclosures paved with stones called *marae*—the sociopolitical structures of eastern and western Polynesia feature nothing essentially different from what one can find in at least half of Melanesia.

Extending the idea of Polynesia's greater value than the rest of the Pacific, the first specialists eagerly studied the Polynesian migrations that brought with them a superior civilization and that could reach Melanesia only indirectly, to dominate it. That Te Rangi Hiroa, better known as Sir Peter H. Buck, was the principal proponent of this idea—in his *Vikings of the Sunrise,* the Polynesians come from Asia by way of Micronesia—shows clearly to what extent the idea had been integrated into the modern struggle for the survival and integrity of the people speaking Polynesian languages. The young generation of Polynesian university students express new feelings when they challenge that thesis in their attempt to establish a political solidarity with Melanesia. This new awareness, born of the current conditions of increased independence for their countries, comes at the end of an evolution that in the course of nearly two centuries of contact has made the Polynesians the accomplices of European colonization in Melanesia: they supplied preachers, petty officers, and even soldiers.

Thus the Polynesians, first brought from afar or taken from groups who had remained Polynesians established on the outer reaches of Melanesia (Vila in Vanuatu) and later Melanesian groups, given preference by Christian missions and then by governments, were the first informants of the Europeans. They have been for the most part men and women well trained in the white man's techniques of subtle manipulation and accustomed to telling him only what he wanted to hear.

Only a few persons who have risen above the ordinary—through the benefits of intellectual training in a university or elsewhere, a training on the average better than most get—have ever attempted to go beyond the easy way in order to bear witness to the Oceanian cultures themselves. R. M. Codrington, head of the College of the Melanesian Mission, an Anglican establishment on Norfolk Island, gave notebooks to his Melanesian students from Aoba and from the Banks Islands in the southern and central Solomons when they went away on vacation on the missionary ship *Southern Cross.* He would ask them to write about what they knew of their own cultures and to write it, at their leisure, in the language of Mota Island, the lingua franca transcribed and chosen by the mission. These written materials served as the foundation for a comprehensive work. If ever these notebooks could be found today, they would certainly be worthy of a separate publication. The same technique of obtaining information was used by Codrington's younger colleagues, the Reverend G. E. Fox and the Reverend W. G. Ivens, to establish the materials for their classical monographs on the Solomon Islands.

Maurice Leenhardt went even farther. He lived at a time when there was neither training nor teaching in ethnology in France, except for a few armchair scholars, beginning with Sir James Frazer, who were interested in the comparison of exotic institutions and beliefs. At this time, when Marcel Mauss was just barely beginning to show his genius, Maurice Leenhardt applied the classical doctrine of Protestant churches, that is, evangelizing by way of the sacred texts, and worked for many years to codify and write the language of the Valley of Huailu in east central New Caledonia. He published a printed journal in which various authors attempted to write short analyses of their own society at the same time that Leenhardt distributed a questionnaire, also printed, with questions derived from the traditional lexicon and, consequently, from vernacular concepts. The files established on the basis of these questionnaires represent true ethnological studies. This encouraged various Melanesian authors to express themselves spontaneously about what they felt was worth keeping alive in their culture, yielding texts of remarkable beauty written in a language that was archaic and sometimes difficult to understand. Half a century later, one linguistic group after another pursued the same methods of research, now modernized, under the aegis of André Haudricourt, and ensured the collection and publication of a corpus in a vernacular; this massive collection, which continues to reveal an extraordinary richness, will make possible an almost entirely new analysis of the symbolic systems of the region. All of this tends to prove that we still have almost everything left to learn and that it would be appropriate, if only for the sake of efficacy, to put the control of such research operations in the hands of the Oceanians, since in any case nothing will ever be known unless they have sanctioned it.

To this point of view can be added the results of a new mode of behavior, among the younger generation, of all those who, in increasing numbers, want to know if it is appropriate to let Europeans continue to intervene in their affairs. For some indefinite time to come, the very existence of Western specialists will be the object of a considerable and sometimes definitive dispute. We will have to adjust to this and realize that Oceania, far from being completely acculturated, has barely unlocked its secrets.

How did European analysts apprehend these symbolic universes that appeared so strange to them and that they attempted to reduce to what they knew, or what they thought they knew?

I. The Biblical Bias

The first filter was that of the teaching of the Bible, especially the Old Testament and most especially the books of Judges and Kings. The first generation of Europeans who settled in the Pacific, missionaries, officials, and traders, British for the most part, had been brought up on the scriptures. Missionary preaching at that time tended to use those parts of the Bible that were most accessible, and found the texts narrating the process of the constitution of the kingdom of David and Solomon most suitable for preaching. As the missions dreamt of Christian kingdoms, and the Oceanians dreamt of the white man's means of power, each of them saw in these texts a quasi-pedagogical model for the conquest of a power sanctified by God. The concepts that could be directly assimilated by the Oceanians were, therefore, concepts of a political power justified through religion; and they were able to find illuminating parallels in their own reinterpreted traditions. Thus, both sides simplified both the analysis of the factors that constituted European political power and the real possibilities that Oceanian societies had of rivaling that power. This situation between Europeans and Oceanians, however dialectical it may have been, was one of the greatest factors in determining, during the last century, the modalities of their contact and, during the first half of the twentieth century, the modalities of the lack of understanding by European observers of fragments of knowledge brought to them for political ends of which they were not always conscious.

We may thus be able to understand today why the description of Polynesian systems was so poor for so long and why even the classical monographs published by the Bernice Pauahi Bishop Museum in Hawaii present descriptions in the form of critical catalogs, the result of an ill-adapted questionnaire, which never make possible any understanding of how the society functions or of what is represented by the beliefs that were seemingly identified. It was not until 1930 that the Rockefeller Foundation launched an effort through the University of Sydney to put together in a matter of a few years an efficient team of researchers committed to a coherent program uncluttered by romantic a prioris, who would obtain results that were truly analytical and hence comparable, with the purpose of identifying the structure of the societies that were studied. Since 1945, this effort has been undertaken again in a more diversified way by various Australian and New Zealand universities, and particularly by the Australian National University at Canberra. In recent years, national universities have been established (the University of Papua New Guinea at Port Moresby) and also multinational universities (the University of the South Pacific at Suva, Fiji), in which the disciplines of the humanities and the social sciences take on a new aspect and students often vigorously challenge traditional British social anthropology. This is where tomorrow's synthesis will be worked out in the service of the independent nations of the Pacific. We will have to reckon with these new centers of knowledge and with these non-European colleagues who have different motivations from ours and who have greater direct access to their own societies. They are already indifferent to our favored theories, but are grateful for any means of making available to them the documents that have been collected by us or our predecessors.

II. The Classical Bias

The second filter was that of the classical education received by the European elite. All tradition was understood in the light of Greek and Latin mythology, and all rituals were appreciated on the basis of our meager understanding of the religions of antiquity. Gradually, new comparative concepts were introduced, derived from the results of Mediterranean scholarship or archaeology. This reasoning by analogy was doubly compounded, in its relative inefficiency, by the enduring idea, still held today by certain Marxists, that all civilizations can be placed in chronological sequence. Since the beliefs of antiquity had supposedly culminated in Christianity and then in modern-day unbelief, the Oceanian systems had to find their place in some linear evolution, as primitive systems. It never dawned on the least of our great forebears (and too many of our current colleagues still act in the same way) that these societies were from the very first the result of a millennia-long adaptation to their environment, that they were far from being static, and that—having become increasingly complex and refined, following a dialectic process, from crisis to crisis, in conditions that we know little about—they represent extraordinarily diversified models resulting from a constant quest that was material and especially spiritual. While the technologies, all too well adapted to their ends, remained relatively stable, and only relatively so, the spirit of invention ran riot on the intellectual plane. The Pacific represents a true experimental laboratory, one that has no equal, in which, every few kilometers, the will for autonomy found in each local group has pushed that group to constitute itself as an independent cultural unity and to play with its institutions and with the concepts peculiar to its tradition so as to arrive each time at a specific synthesis.

This assertion demands the only method suitable to the circumstances, that is, to collect all possible data meticulously, without allowing a single point to escape us, in order to create an exhaustive inventory. We are far from our goal. Such an enterprise depends entirely on the goodwill of the Oceanians and can only be envisioned today if they have full control of it.

III. The First Elements of Understanding—Maurice Leenhardt

And yet, despite all this, at every instant we must be satisfied with our knowledge such as it is and pose the problem of the functional quality of the concepts that are employed.

Of course, well-bred people quickly abandoned the demonic image that the first missionaries assigned to individuals designated by local tradition, though they allowed the term "devil" or *tepolo* to survive in the languages that

Apuema masks (*pwemwa*) made of carved wood, wicker, hair, and feathers, worn by men during festivals. New Caledonia. Paris, Musée de l'Homme collection. Museum photo.

incorporated a lingua franca lexicon received from the nineteenth century. These terms, which hold research back, are maintained in their negative formulation by the Melanesian and Polynesian clergies formed by Catholic and Protestant missions.

To avoid resorting to the term "devil," British authors adopted the term "spirit," designating a disembodied person; but the French translation of this term (*esprit*) sounds bad, and the literal French translation of the expanded term "spiritual world" sounds even worse (*monde spirituel,* a theological phrase in the French context) and is better translated by *monde des esprits* ("world of spirits").

It was necessary to define these "spirits" by qualifying the word spirit with certain terms that were meant to make it more specific and closer to perceived reality, for example, ancestral spirit, protective spirit, totemic spirit, guardian spirit, child spirit, etc. Despite attempts at precision in definitions elaborated out of local data, these terms, chosen to facilitate comparison, are somewhat of a blindman's bluff and hardly recover vernacular concepts. No satisfying theory that could stand the test of time was developed from these Western terms.

attempts to describe the rituals of the aborigines of central Australia has not yet been the object of a renewed analysis, so complex and interwoven are the symbolic systems that appear in it, and the vernacular texts that would make truly productive work possible are lacking.

VII. The Contact between the Living and the Dead

The reference to modalities of contact between the living and the dead offers us a special key to the way in which this contact is experienced. One of the great themes is the descent into the land of the dead, which is found on the everyday level at least in New Caledonia and Vanuatu, and apparently to some extent everywhere else. In the first instance, who among Melanesian Catholics or Protestants would confess to having taken such a compromising journey? There are, however, some rare cases that bring to life the very rich mythology that is still widespread. They depict the chief grieving over the sudden death of his young wife; he proceeds to seek her in the underwater world of the dead, braving the perils and avatars of the route, assisted by a protecting bird or even by the guardian of the barrier that marks the entrance to the world ruled by Tein Pijopatch, whose body is spotted, covered with eyes. There dwell the dead, who in contrast with the living eat lizards instead of meat, bamboo shoots instead of cane sugar, excrement instead of root vegetables; who, unlike the living, dance clockwise and play ball by throwing a bitter orange. On the way to the underwater world, the identity of the deceased is verified by a being who feels the lobe of the left ear and pierces it, causing great pain if the lobe is not already pierced. Through trickery, some people are said to have succeeded in retrieving their wives from the state of death and have brought them back to life. The story is also told of the chief who died but remained in love and who tried in vain to deceive his wife and to make her believe that he was still alive.

Elsewhere, in Vanuatu, the voyage can be frequent; it is an exploit of seers, male or female. I say seers because simple mortals do not know how to find the way, which follows one of the deep roots of one of the gigantic banyan trees that shade the squares where people dance. The journey still takes place today. It explains missing persons and the birth of children with physical characteristics different from what they ought to be. It assures every person of the sustained protection of the dead for the benefit of the living. Messages are received from the beyond, messages which may contain instructions or merely offer the interpretation of a strange fact, the inspiration for a song, or, more rarely, a prophecy. On Tana there is an inversion of the myth of Orpheus: it is the seer who becomes infatuated with a woman from the underground land of Ipay, brings her back with him, and loses her because he does not respect the prohibition that she imposes, that he should not unite sexually with his earthly wife or eat hot food before a certain time lapses. She does, however, leave him a new cultural element, a clone of a yam, for example, as proof of her carnal existence.

There seems to be an uncrossable frontier here. The union between a dead person and a living person can only be ephemeral. In the first theme, union between spouses could be reestablished because the husband made his wife come back from beyond death. In New Caledonia, sexual union between a living person and a dead person is possible, since the dead may appear at any moment in a deceptive form. They can be recognized at night: they snore, their joints become dislocated, or the body disappears, leaving only the head visible. But who are these visitors from the beyond?

Ceremonial headdress included in the so-called Nalawan cycle. Paris, Musée national des arts africains et océaniens. Museum photo.

VIII. The Active Dead

This problem leads to the topic of the dead who become active, who are often malevolent and anonymous, because they do not belong to one's lineage, but who may in extreme cases bear a name. And it is at this point also that the reference to the term "god" arises. The first British missionary observers did not want to use this term, not because they were troubled by their memories of Olympus, but because they had to select from within the vernacular lexicon a term that would fit well with the more recent notion of a demiurge or culture hero, so as to translate the name of Jehovah.

Once the choice was made, it was necessary to introduce a semantic extension to their customs and to reject all language habits that might have tended to favor the previous meaning of the word. Hence they chose the term "spirit."

Maurice Leenhardt proceeded from another point of view, which consisted in introducing the Greek and Hebrew terms into the written language—through the translation of the Bible—and into the spoken language, rather than looking for equivalents that might be more than approximate and perhaps spiritually dangerous. In the second phase of his career, when he was involved in research and university teaching, he was less constrained than others and adopted the term "god," which finally made it possible to pose the problem of the deification of the dead. But the Melanesian pastors that he had trained preached in their language and the choice did not embarrass them. If one takes "god" in the generally accepted sense of a personage situated beyond the sensible world, capable of appearing with human traits, endowed with a power superior to our physical norms and therefore made the object of worship involving prayers and offerings, the term is qualified to represent what happens to the dead person once the breath has left his body.

But then we are confronted by the distinction that Codrington was forced to make among the spirits: between those who had been humans and those who had never been humans. There is the crowd of anonymous dead who can be called forth on a deserted spot, among the Big Nambas on the northern end of Malekula Island in Vanuatu, that may be asked where a marauding hog might be, or a wife who has run away from her husband. This contact is established on both sides of a temporary wall made of interwoven reeds where a square opening has been arranged through which a bamboo passes, or a bundle of the central veins of coconut palm leaves, held on the side of the living by three men whose eyes are closed, while the crowd of men dances around it before stopping to ask the questions; the answer comes in a movement from top to bottom to say yes or a movement forward and backward to say no. Precautions must be taken. A dissatisfied inquirer who had discharged his gun on the other side of the line to show his anger died a few days later of an uncontrollable swelling of his stomach.

There are also the dead people in one's own lineage; a list of them is recited in a traditional order in invocations, but one prays particularly to the most recent and the closest, the one who has just died, the father or grandfather. In New Caledonia they do this while speaking into the steam of a yam cooking in a pot, after pulling out the plug of leaves; in Vanuatu they do it while continually spitting out a fine rain of kava, which they produce by chewing the kava root or drinking a beverage made from it. In north Malekula they do it while spitting continually in the direction of the skulls of dead people placed on a flat stone on the floor of the men's hut; or, on Tana, on the edge of the square for dancing, after wailing in the particular modulations that are the signature of one who drinks and prays, they address themselves to the dead, to the ones they know, the ones whose existence beside them they are not anxious to test too closely. But, as they said to me on Tana, "How can you stop the dead from talking?"

IX. The Gods

If the dead are the gods, who then are those gods who are not from among the dead because they have never been human? Are they dead people from long ago whose historicity has been forgotten? This attractive hypothesis does not stand up, since the same individuals are valued over a considerable area, by dozens of lineages, even across linguistic barriers. That the facts cannot be very well reduced to our patterns of thinking is especially demonstrated by the obvious ambiguity of this category. There are, however, gods who are placed at the beginnings of certain genealogies, such as Tein Kanaké, Dui Daulo, and Bwae Bealo in the area where the Paici language is spoken in New Caledonia, but we do not know very well what they are: genuine ancestors who have been deified—though they are placed at the origin of too many lines of descent for this to be credible—or culture heroes placed in the position of ancestors in order to affirm an identity among lines of descent that may have had different origins. The problem remains wholly unresolved. José Garanger discovered the skeleton of Roy Mata in an extraordinary group burial on the island of Retoka near the southeasternmost tip of Efate in Vanuatu. We have not yet been able to find the remains of New Caledonian heroes, and no one can tell us where to look for them.

Gomawe, by contrast, in New Caledonia, exists at the origin, when the earth appeared above the water and when humans appeared on earth. On Huailu, he is said to have the technique of a potter, because he molded bodies out of a mixture of clay and water. The great myth of the Paici says that he has Bumè pull one of his teeth so that he can offer it to the rays of the moon. He places it on the rock sticking out of the water on top of the mountain Tyaumyê. From each tooth a worm emerges, which is transformed into a human being through a series of operations, implicit or explicit according to different versions.

Whether or not Gomawe is the originator of humankind, he appears in multiple forms: sea serpent, lizard, bubbles at the bottom of a waterfall, a dead log floating downstream, or in human forms, among them the god whose extensible phallus seeks out at a distance the sexual organs of pregnant women. Everywhere he places his foot is the origin of a spring, that is, of life. He is all sorts of characters who are identified with one another, and, at the end of the list, he is master of the realm of the dead and is represented both by his feathered mask and by the face carved on the heads on coins (which must not leave the "sacred basket" of the clan) or carved high on the handle of the "monstrance ax." He is accompanied by less popular characters, like Kapwangwa Kapwityalo, who watches over the game of bitter oranges during the death dances; Hway Hway, the keeper of the barrier gate; Dangginy, the bird that crosses from the living to the dead, serves as messenger, and helps widowers who are looking for their wives who died in the flower of youth. All of these beings are male. But there is also a female deity, Toririhnan, mistress of the thunderstorm and flooding, which she brings by blowing her nose with her finger, and who is known throughout the northern part of the island for having tried to substitute herself for the pregnant wife of a chief by drowning the woman and filling her own belly with pieces of pottery. The legitimate wife, carried by the current to the sea, landed on a distant island where she gave birth to two sons and raised them; and when they grew up to be strong and brave, she returned with them and was recognized. The usurper was shut up in her cabin, and the cabin was then set on fire. It is said that she perished in the flames, but that, nevertheless, she continues to reside on the mountain above Hienghene and that from the clouds she continues to regulate precipitation.

One of the criteria for the existence of a deity, in common

terms, is the presentation of gifts and prayers addressed to the deity. Generally speaking, prayers are not addressed to the gods we have just mentioned. Consequently, there is no major organized worship. But each god belongs to a well-localized group, and rarely to several groups; each god is thus the object of an adaptation, which eventually involves offerings and prayers. After a century and a half of colonial repression and Christianization, there is still no evidence that there were rituals on behalf of these beings, but this must nevertheless have been the case in a certain number of instances.

X. The Firstfruits of the Harvest and the Invisible World

This brings us to a seemingly general phenomenon: the link, which Maurice Leenhardt established at a different level, between the genesis of life, both human fertility and the fertility of the soil, and at least some of the beings that we have just discussed. Pragmatically speaking, we are referring to the firstfruits of the yam harvest, yams being everywhere the subject of public and private rituals, establishing a chain of partial or compensatory allegiances. To whom are prayers addressed in a remote spot and on the occasion of the first yam, in New Caledonia? Whom do you thank for a yam or a white chicken in Vanuatu?

Here we touch upon an essential factor in the Oceanian symbolic worlds. The relationship between the yearly harvest, which may turn out to be good, bad, or indifferent, and the invisible world that takes responsibility for it is always manifest in a precise location, nearby or distant, in an abandoned grave, in the middle of the fields, or outside the fields. This location is still respected today and is where a designated individual, usually the youngest son, who could be called a priest, will go to pray at the first symbolic sign of the harvest to come. It is of no concern to us here with whom he decides to eat this first yam. But whom does he address?

Our criteria for classification again turn out to be inoperative. The man of the firstfruits invokes all sorts of things and people. It could be the sun, a lizard, a sea serpent, as well as Tein Pijopatch or Toririhnan. The Ihuwa, from Lounakiyamapën to Tana, make a pandanus basket called *nat pwatil* ("belly of man"), which contains smaller baskets, each one representing one of the internal organs, and place within it representative fragments of each form of food, wrapped in leaves or lianas regarded as heavy. The first basket is said to contain famine, *numus,* which one must feed in order to prevent it from coming out and spreading all over the country. Famine is thus a power held in awe, but not personified.

At Seniang, in the southwestern part of Malekula, according to information supplied by the late A. B. Deacon, which we verified in the field more than twenty years ago, the altar of the clan also serves as a charnel house—the dry skulls, cleaned out by ants, are used in the making of mannequins known as *rambaramb.* A stone there carries in it the deity to whom people pray; the priest designates it by a proper name for those deities that are represented as humans (the culture hero Ambat or one of his brothers, the ogress Nevinbumbaau, her husband Temes Malau or their son Mansip), by the term that corresponds to the symbol of the deity's power (the cycad when the being who is invoked provokes the death of a man on request), or by the term that indicates its efficacy—*namar* (famine). It also seems that the rituals known as *nerew* can take place at the onset of the agricultural season as well as at its end, especially when one can reverse the process and provoke famine among one's neighbors instead of being content with merely protecting one's own people from famine.

The rituals of the *xoro* on the Big Nambas plateau on northwest Malekula call on a mythical power, the *xoro,* of which we know nothing except that it occurs at the time of the firstfruits to sponsor the new year: the fire previously extinguished in the hearths is renewed, the old pandanus mats, women's skirts, and men's penis coverings are replaced by new ones; and, thirty days after the first of the six days of obligatory sexual abstinence, the prophets who will forecast events in the coming year are revealed. The *nal* ritual, parallel to that of the *xoro* but on behalf of neighbors, is no more specific about the individual that is invoked, except that the invocations are made to the moon and the prophets are determined on the basis of an invasion of harmless land snakes of the python family into the house of the masters of the ritual.

In Australia, the ritual sites owe their existence to a group of individuals who are regarded as the entire group of ancestors of all men, never individually as the ancestor of any one descent line. On each of these sites, people will come to pray just before the rainy season. This prayer can be a symbolic gesture with or without words, but it can also consist in the restoration of paintings that represent the gods, together with the animals, plants, or atmospheric elements that one wants to multiply or to deter, as conditions dictate. The link between the beings that are present at the origin of things and the animals, plants, or other beings is more or less clear. It is clearer for the so-called historical rituals, which trace the high deeds and wanderings of the divine beings, though still without ever making explicit the connection with the rituals of multiplication. Is this connection implicit in each case? This is quite possible, but in the absence of analyzable vernacular texts, it is difficult to decide.

XI. Mythical Cycles

The mythical cycles are not always present in an obvious way. Some have the appearance of a coherent whole. None of them seems to provide the exclusive basis for any symbolic system that is fully understood. There seems to be some sort of measured rhythm, but one that is not strictly observed.

The very notion of a mythical cycle is imprecise, however. There may be a corpus of myths that can be recited individually or in a single stretch over a period of several consecutive days and dealing with the same social group. There may also be an apparent, fleeting coherence across several groups, through the appearance of parallel versions of the same themes, or closely related themes, in different places. There may also be a coherent cycle, clearly affirmed, that seems to have spilled over the boundaries of the group that is its principal owner. Finally, there are quasi-universal themes, or those that are simply regularly attested. All of these have been the objects of more publications than anything else we have seen, because they correspond more closely to our ways of thinking. But the cycles are inscribed in a highly diversified manner within global structures that are different in each case. Since these are too numerous for us to cite them all, a few examples will suffice.

On the island of Makura, which belongs to the Shepherd Islands in Vanuatu, the story is told of Sakora, who set out in a dugout canoe in a northeasterly direction to look for the origin of the sun. He finally arrived on the island of Merig, populated exclusively by women who lived together, each receiving at night the visit of a flying fox, or fruit bat, who

Tararamanu. Drawing by Saunitiku. From C. E. Fox, *Threshold of the Pacific* (London: Kegan Paul, 1924).

Two Maam males (evil spirits) dancing with a Maam female. Namatbara painter, Crocker Island, Arnhem Land, Australia. Paris, Musée national des arts africains et océaniens (K. Kupka collection). Museum photo.

served as her husband. Sakora offered to replace the fruit bats; he killed them and introduced the women to true sexual experience, at the same time making them pregnant. At the end of several years, Sakora tired of this role and returned home, carried through the air by the Tuarere, winged women who fly from island to island to fish, swim, or comb their hair. He kept one of these as his wife by means of a trick, hiding her wings. After a quarrel between their children and the father, she found her wings again, put them on, and flew back to her sisters.

A journey to the island of Merig, the smallest and one of the most isolated of the Banks Islands, can yield many surprises. A genealogical inventory, together with a land survey, quickly shows that there is a microsociety of sixty inhabitants with a special tradition. All the husbands come from the outside, at the age when isolation becomes bearable. All the landowners are women, whose children, boys and girls, all go into exile at each generation, leaving to the mother only one or two girls who will in turn receive a husband who has come from afar. Myth and reality are virtually identical. Merig is indeed the island of women. Moreover, its inhabitants claim an origin myth that is a variant of the myth collected on the island of Makura, the theme of which turns out to be known throughout the region.

This single example touches upon one of the problems in the study of mythical cycles, namely, the problem of cross-fertilization. Should this be called a cycle? The theme of winged women is attested all the way from Denmark to Vanuatu. What about in places beyond this constellation? It would be more unusual to find an instance where the theme did *not* occur. I know of no such negative example in New Caledonia or in Tana, in the southern part of Vanuatu.

Attempts have already been made to map the distribution of themes. The results are no more convincing than the *Kulturkreise* of the German and Austrian schools before 1930. This leads one to presuppose migration movements for which at the moment we have no possible proof. Why is the theme of the journey of food—tubers, fruit, edible leaves—found simultaneously in Tana (the route moving from the southeast to the west), in Vanuatu, and on Maré in the Loyalty Islands (the route moving from the west to the east)? Why is the theme of the chief's daughter married to the sun, which is attested on Uvea (Ciau, the daughter of Bahit), so infrequent?

The theme of the intermeshed arrows that make up a bridge is used on Pentecost Island, in the story of a husband who goes to find his wife, a winged woman who has run away from him, and on north Malekula, in the story of a man who goes looking for a fat sow of his that escapes; he finally finds her at Elephant Point, after she has given birth to a human baby boy.

The Polynesian myth of Mauitikitiki-a-Taranga, a girl who miscarries, is abandoned to the sea, and is saved by the effect of the sea foam, is the myth of the trickster, who tricks all the gods, ties up the sun and disrupts its orbit, pulls islands out of the sea by fishing them out with a mother-of-pearl hook, and succeeds (in the form of a bird) in stealing the fire in the underworld. He finally dies while attempting to steal eternal life from the goddess Hine-nui-te-po by entering her through her vagina; but one of the birds accompanying him bursts out laughing and awakens the goddess, who contracts her sphincter, thus strangling Maui and assuring that men will not escape death.

There are innumerable versions of the life and death of Mauitikitiki. The Melanesian texts, at least those that we have collected on Vanuatu, are no less literary and no less labyrinthine than those that come from classical Polynesia. But in all the literature specially devoted to Mauitikitiki in Polynesia, there is no serious implication that she was the object of a cult. By contrast, in Vanuatu, on Emae in the Shepherd Islands and on the southwesternmost tip of Tana, Mwatikitiki (Mauitikitiki) still receives offerings of yams or white hens and is addressed in prayer. Current information thus strongly confirms what the first missionaries had learned from their Polynesian evangelists. Katharine Luomala, a specialist in the mythology of Maui, thinks that the myth spread from Polynesia to central Vanuatu and from southern Vanuatu to the Santa Cruz Islands. One could reverse this argument and suggest that nothing is certain except that the myth of Mauitikitiki is common to both zones and that a secularized narrative that turned into a symbolic and literary construct, deprived of any local support, could just as well have originated in the south of the Melanesian arc. We do not have the means of solving this problem at this time. It would also seem that the emergence of a class of priests, interpreters and amplifiers of the tradition, is a phenomenon observed essentially in eastern Polynesia and on the outer perimeter of Polynesia. They may well have made use of a Maui myth and turned it into something of their own. Our inadequate knowledge of Tahiti and the Windward Islands has nonetheless given us two versions of the myth of Maui. In one, which is scholarly, Maui is full of virtues; in the other, which is popular, Maui retains the image of a trickster.

The Tangaloa cycle varies widely. In Aniwa and the east coast, facing Tana, Tangaloa is only a kindly snake, who is put to death; this results in the origin of the first coconut tree, which grows out of the burnt corpse of the snake. The Tahitian cosmographic myths make him into a demiurge, while still other variants view him only as the god of the ocean. The people of the Wallis Islands strip Maui of his role of fisherman of the islands and give this role to Tangaloa.

"Ta'aroa (the one and only) was the ancestor of all the gods. He created everything. Since time immemorial the great Ta'aroa, the original, has existed. Ta'aroa grew by himself in solitude. He was his own parent, having neither father nor mother. Ta'aroa had countless forms, but there was only one Ta'aroa up above, down below, and in the night. Ta'aroa was confined in his shell and in the night for thousands of years."

These fragments of a text on the creation of the world, dictated in 1822, give a faint idea of the imagery and ambiguity that make it possible for a theological interpretation to substitute for the myth a cosmogonic poem that sets the criteria of a literary tradition.

Statue representing the god Tangaroa. Island of Rurútu, Austral Islands, French Polynesia. London, British Museum. Museum photo.

The reigning chief Paiore of the Tuamotu island of Anaa drew a sketch that the resident administrator Caillot obtained, a sketch that laid out his conception of superimposed earths and skies. The primordial egg, in which Tangaroa had enclosed himself, according to Tahitian tradition, contained Te tumu (the foundation) and Te papa (the stratified rock). The egg broke open, giving birth to three superimposed platforms. On the lower platform, Te tumu and Te papa created humans, animals, and plants. It took three attempts to obtain a viable man and woman, whose children increased in number and took up the task of raising the platform that was above them; then they moved onto it with animals and plants by making an opening through this second platform, the first sky, which they first softened by means of a fire. They then repeated the same process with the third platform and settled upon it too, leaving above them the superimposed skies. But Tangaroa set fire to the earthly world and for this deed was banished to an underground world.

We could go on indefinitely, taking each of the figures from Polynesian mythology, relating its avatars, and demonstrating a gigantic "system of transformation," to use Lévi-Strauss's terms. The schematization of the transitions of every possible theme from one divine individual to another, or from one particular acceptance to another, would be of interest only to a few specialized readers. There has already been an attempt to put these themes into a thematic index, though no tool of any demonstrated usefulness has been derived from it. There is, nevertheless, a consensus that the collection has a coherence. This is certainly the case if we think of the last period, at least in Tahiti, during which it was attested that the cult of Oro, the god of war, replaced the cult of cosmogonic deities, divine rivalry thus masking local power struggles through the rivalries between clans of priests and theologians.

There are also other cycles that we have treated as incomplete cosmogonies, wrongly, since this term, however attractive it may be, masks a value judgment and some chronological implication: a transition from one cosmogony (the incomplete one) to the other (completed) or vice versa. In fact, the solution chosen was the wrong one. The attractive cosmogony corresponds to a social support whose function is to reproduce it or cause it to evolve, namely, a class of priests seeking independence with respect to political power. The quasi cosmogonies that are found in Melanesia can have much more diversified functions.

The Paici tradition in north central New Caledonia places the origin of men on Mount Tyaumyê and attributes it to Bumê's intervention. The different available versions of the myth end with the explanation of the origin of the regional clans and their split into two intermarrying phratries, who incidentally share between them the useful universe, including animal and plant forms, atmospheric elements, and the regional gods endowed with a civil status. The practice of exchanging sisters and circulating shell coins is instituted in the myth, with variants as to the identity of the first partners. Demographically and linguistically speaking, this mythical cycle enjoys the support of the overwhelming majority on the island, united through flexible and multiple ties designed to form a loose military confederation that at times put up successful resistance to the intruding French military forces.

The first known mythical cycle in New Caledonia is the cycle of the lizard, published in 1830 by Maurice Leenhardt. In varying versions, it tells the story of a chief who goes to bring in his snares and picks up a fabulous lizard, who settles down on the chief's back. When it falls asleep and slides off to the ground during the night, the man quickly takes flight and the lizard pursues him. The chief meets people on his flight, all of whom first offer to help the chief to victory, but then are frightened away. After covering all of New Caledonia, from east to west and from north to south, the fleeing chief finally meets the one whose function is to speak to the lizard and return his protecting animal to its kindly role at the edge of the forest. A detailed examination of the characters who appear in the course of this narrative reveals that they were not chosen indiscriminately, and that they belong to one of the networks of related individuals who share the great earth among themselves, each having their branches on the nearby Loyalty Islands.

Unlike New Caledonia, where the sea had to recede from the heights so that man could be born, Vanuatu raised the problem of the origins of the sea, which existed only in the form of a secret condiment in the food of the culture hero, Barkolkol, Tagaro, Qat, or Mwatikitiki, who appropriated it for himself. A friend or relative who solves the mystery and wants to steal the condiment lifts the stone and lets the sea pass through. A version collected in Tana depicts the biblical Noah, who was robbed of his salt water and went east in a dugout. One day he returned and brought his descendants the power that until then had been reserved for whites. This reinterpretation of the Old Testament is not new. MacDonald recorded on Efate, at the dawn of Christianization, a tradition claiming that Mauitikitiki's grandson, Tamakaia, stole the sea from his grandfather by opening the gates that enclosed it, built himself a dugout out of banana peels, and left for England, where he was known as Jehovah. Similarly, the dugout which is Noah's ark is found above a mountain pass at the north end of a mountain range culminating in Mount Panié in New Caledonia. These Christianized versions contain recognizable attempts of syncretism at the start of European contact, but they have their limits. In general, the Old and New Testaments were treated as myths to be added to the existing body of myths without ever raising the slightest questions about the actual existence of holy places or about the historicity of the individuals of the Christian pantheon. Maurice Leenhardt had noted earlier the people's surprise when soldiers wrote in 1917 that they were passing through a place close to Palestine. I myself noticed fifty years later the bewilderment of all of my wife's Melanesian relatives when she told them about her trip to Jerusalem. They had never entertained the thought that anything they were taught in church could actually exist.

A frequent theme is that of the five fingers that become real characters: Mauitikitiki-a-Taranga and her brothers in the versions of the myth of Maui in which Maui is not alone. In southeast Malekula, A. B. Deacon recorded the myth of Ambat and his brothers who were trapped one after another by the ogress Nevinbumbaau and were stuck in a ditch until Ambat came to free them. The same brothers later attempted to kill their youngest brother Ambat because they envied him his beautiful wife Lindanda, who learned of her husband's death when she saw blood on the comb he had left her. She escaped from the brothers, who thought they had won. Thus the gods and civilizing heroes can die. This does not prevent Ambat from receiving offerings and prayers at the *nembrbrkon,* a sacred place dedicated to him on the island of Tomman. There is no historicity in the death of the gods, nor do they have to be considered ancestors in the biological sense, nor are the real dead prevented from becoming gods. A very broad liberalism prevails. It is up to each local society to constitute the set of characters, myths, and symbols it deems appropriate for itself.

Other classical cycles should be mentioned, starting with

the cycle of the rainbow snake in northern Australia. Lloyd Warner has pointed out the connection between the initiation rites of young men from the northeasternmost corner of Arnhem Land and the image of the snake Yurlunggur coiled up in his water holes. The snake rises to the sky and falls back to earth because he experiences unbearable pain after he swallows the Wawilak sisters who belong to the same moiety as he does. This all happens because they danced at the edge of his water hole during their menstrual period, and their menstrual blood flowed into his shelter and awakened in him a violent incestuous desire. Interpretations that do not always fit with the myth have been given by this same author and by Lévi-Strauss, Karel Kupka, and myself. The relative artificiality of these analyses comes from their applications to texts written in English and not in the local vernacular. Throughout the region the rituals connected with the rainbow snake are designed to ensure normal rainfall and consequently the food and the survival of human society.

Another Australian cycle tells of the search for red ocher. In the myth, this quest is connected with the proliferation of fat emus. A couple of emus were hunted by dogs for several hundred miles, to Parochilna, where they dug into the ground and became deposits of red ocher. This story is the origin of the journey made by young men along the same road, where they are received by each of the local groups who share the myth. In the course of several days, the initiation of young men to the myth is accomplished by means of colorful games in which they participate and which reenact the details of the story told. The novices are received by those who have made the journey and have brought back red ocher, which on this occasion entitles them to theoretically incestuous sexual relations with women from their own exogamous moiety.

XII. Incest

Much has been written for a long time about the incest taboo. A recurrent theme of many myths is the theme of desired or consummated incest. The consequences vary. Certain lines of descent are known to have incestuous origins. They derive from this a special status at the very least, if not outright pride. Bronislaw Malinowski was one of the first to record a myth dealing with incest. There is the myth of Inuvayla'u, whose penis moved like a snake on the ground or under water and penetrated the vulva of his brother's wives, or the wives of his uterine nephews. His actions go unpunished for a long time, as the women do not dare to speak up. When the truth comes out, the hero castrates himself and goes into exile. In a myth that takes place in Kumilabwa, a sister accidentally spills on herself some drops of a coconut oil that was prepared as a love potion for her own brother. Overcome by the magic force, she sets out in search of her brother, who is swimming, takes off her skirt on the way, and forces him to have intercourse with her. The two of them hide in a cave and die there. A mint leaf grows out of their chests. Since then, this same mint is the basic ingredient for love potions, and the myth is used to justify incest, which does occur.

XIII. Myths of Origin

Myths are easily made up of models. Myths of origin are the most obvious example. They are everywhere and of all kinds. Almost every institution is based on a myth of origin. One of the simplest ones, common in initiation cycles, is the myth claiming that the techniques for making masks or musical instruments were invented by a woman. Some men took her by surprise, robbed her of her invention, killed her, and saw to it that no woman could ever again have access to such knowledge.

Local villages and groups also claim to have a myth of origin. Some of these myths represent complex sets that cover an entire region, with more or less detailed variants depending on the place of the village or group within the system. One of the most developed myths is the myth of the *lue jajiny,* the two girls at the origin of most chiefdoms in the district of Lösi, i.e., the southern part of the island of Lifou, the central island of the Loyalty Islands. According to some, they came out of the hole of Masalo; according to others, they came from the northern district, where they are supposed to have participated in an abortive attempt to set up a single political system. They were welcomed by the *wananathin,* the oldest inhabitants of the region, who had peculiar features: long hair, double-jointedness, and, in the women, pendulous breasts. The younger of the two shows respect for her hosts, prepares meals for them, and unites with them sexually. Of the two, she is the first to have children, who will later enjoy political preeminence in the area. The older of the two follows suit with some delay. She too has children, who spread to the interior and the east coast. They are at the origins of the elder chiefdoms, called *anga haetra,* as opposed to the others, called *angete lösi,* and they challenge the preeminence of the Bula chiefs, who were patrilineal descendants of the younger sister. The origin from a hole, i.e., in an ancient grotto with a caved-in roof, is generally thought to refer to an origin from outside of the island. Maurice Leenhardt shares this opinion. This kind of information is often regarded as the "secret" of the lineages in question, and in any case there is a corresponding prohibition against mentioning it in public. There is no graver insult in Oceania than treating someone as a stranger, which implies denying his rights to the earth, unless it happens that the person concerned has a particular status derived from his foreign origin, or unless he belongs to a clan dispersed over several islands, a clan whose members have preserved their mutual bonds, refusing to hide their origins under a veil of modesty.

Douglas Oliver has recorded, from the Siuai of Bougainville, the myth of origin of the Ta, through two sisters, Noika and Korina, who together, inside a cave, initiated some of the elements of the local culture, the making of pearls from shells and the invention of magic formulas governing growth, welfare, and prosperity rites. After their marriage, they separated because of a quarrel; one left with her people, the other one stayed. The various incidents are strictly localized: the origin of a food taboo, the birth of a nonhuman child: an arboreal rat that becomes the symbol of the matrilineal descendants of the two sisters and crops up repeatedly in the story. Douglas Oliver was the first author to recognize the value of these localities (*urinno,* sacred places) as signs of the land tenure being claimed.

The myth of Ciau, the daughter of Bahit, the northern chief of the island of Uvea (Loyalty Islands), has long been a puzzle to me. She had the habit of going with her attendants to a beach of white sand and shell called Hony and there bleaching her hair. One day as she was washing her hair with seawater, two fish came and stationed themselves, one under each armpit, and whisked her away to the tiny island of Sëunö Oüdet, the island where the sun goes to rest every evening. There she finds the sun's mother, who welcomes her and hides her lest she be burned by the rays of her son. The sun arrives, finds her, marries her, and gives her a child. One day when the brat misbehaves, the father gets angry

and insults his wife by calling her a foreigner. The next day the young woman takes her son and goes off into the sea. The two fish return, take her under the armpits, and bring her back to Hony. She is joyously welcomed at Wekiny, at the court of her father Bahit. But the sun soon arrives demanding his son (not his wife), and arrests his movement over the country. Everything in sight dries up and burns. The earth cracks and the people must seek refuge underground. They decide to reunite sun and son. One man builds a pyre of green wood, to produce a lot of smoke, in a locality called Webelu; he places the child on it and sets it on fire. The smoke then carries the child toward the sun, who then continues its course. This man's descendant in each generation receives the name of Hoi (he gives allegiance to Wasau, the younger lineage of Bahit). He is the master of rain and sun and looks after their rituals at Webelu, and the function of the myth of Ciau is to justify his worship. Twenty pages full of highly literary text to give substance to a privilege that could have been expressed in a few lines! How many Polynesian texts lost, when they were collected, the few key words that would have allowed us to understand their raison d'être? Perhaps all of them.

This last text is connected with the cycle of the Xetiwaan, as they are known on the Loyalty Islands (elsewhere they are known as Naatyuwe or Tyidopwaan, depending on the linguistic group, and on Kunié as Ketiware). These people, who are verbally abused when they are not present, claim a common place of origin, which concerted scholarship indicates might be Tonga. Such is at least the working hypothesis. Their outstanding feature is their refusal to be integrated into the existing political system unless they can hide behind assumed traditional names and unless they are regarded everywhere as the masters of the rituals that guarantee the control of rain and the sun. At the same time, the Xetiwaan take pride in their special relationship with the shark: it does not attack them and they never eat its meat. The elder of the Xetiwaan, Xetiwaan Inangoj from the southeastern coast of Lifou, boasts of a *watenge ne ea,* a magic for navigation, which is in keeping with his origin. The Xetiwaan are thought to have considerable powers when it comes to the sea. Xetawaan Dromau of Tingeting, in the Wetr region of northern Lifou, is supposed to have changed into increasingly smaller fish to seek out inside the stomach of a whale the magical hook *wageledra* lost by Zangzang, the lord of the land at Tingeting.

XIV. Ogres and Ogresses

Ogres and ogresses, already seen in connection with Nevinbumbaau and Ambat's brothers, are a recurring theme with an important connotation. The people that the Europeans thought to be cannibals do not practice cannibalism to any significant extent. Whether it is Tramsëmwas on Tana, Mutuama on Efate, or Kahwikahok in northern New Caledonia, the outline is basically the same. The country is laid waste by the cannibal and only one elderly couple remains, or a woman with one or two sons. They manage to hide so well that the sons grow up to be adults and become adept at martial skills: they carefully hide weapons along the road on which they anticipate having to retreat before the advancing enemy, whom they finally overcome. The former population

Votive picket, tied to the priest by a thin rope made of fibers from the coconut outer shell, during the invocation. Paris, Musée des arts africains et océaniens. Museum photo.

returns. It is either liberated from the enclosure that served as a food storage area, or they resume normal life as soon as the cannibal's stomach has been opened.

Raymond Mayer reports the story of the ogress Lona (from the Uvea of the Wallis Islands). The sole survivor of the land is Pikipikilauifi, a little girl hidden by her parents in a chestnut tree. She meets Mele, Lona's daughter, who plays with her without telling her mother (Lona) in order to protect her little friend. Lona sees it all from the house, takes Pikipikilauifi by surprise, and eats her, but Mele's despair and anger drives Lona to vomit the swallowed child and die.

The country is eventually said to have been divided up into localized social categories by the avengers, heroes who succeeded in killing the cannibal and in putting in place those whose lives they restored. The hero may have come from the outside, as in the case of Mwatikitiki (Mauitikitiki).

XV. Pictorial Representations

The *Adoro ni Matawa* of San Cristobal in the Solomon Islands are among those rare individuals for whom we have pictorial representations. According to Maekabia, who hails from the village of Fagani and whose interpretation was cited by C. E. Fox, Tararamanu is a god of the open sea without any home, not even on shore. He appeared to three brothers as they were fishing for bonito with a long bamboo fishing rod. As their dugout was drifting and they were catching nothing, they saw a red rainbow across the island of Ugi. The rainbow disappeared and was followed by a shower and then by a white trail crossing the horizon "like a white-barked tree in the forest," lighting up like a fire, and driving before them a shoal of leaping bonitos. The three brothers then brought back a miraculous catch. Tararamanu was in the apparition; one of the three brothers was possessed by him and Tararamanu spoke through his voice as follows: "You call your dugout Wakio. You shall not do this again, but rather name it like my own dugout Sautatare-i-roburo (pursuer of bonitos to where they live). There you shall build an altar to me and I shall give you fish. You shall offer sacrifice to me in the dugout and at the village altar." His will was done, and Tararamanu gave them all sorts of fish in abundance, but he would shoot arrows at whomever he did not like.

The lack of visual representations of heroes and gods from the Oceanian pantheon causes us much trouble. Some great Polynesian gods are exceptions to this rule, but rarely. There is a statue of Tangaroa, for instance, showing, in this case, the marks of his role as a demiurge, with creatures stuck to his body and other separable figurines inside his hollow back. This unique piece is in the British Museum.

If we take an inventory of sculpted pieces that unmistakably represent a mythical character, when all doubtful cases are eliminated, the list is short: Kalaipahoa, the Hawaiian god of evil deeds, who came from Oahu, as seen in a piece in the Bernice Pauahi Bishop Museum; Tangaroa Upao Vahu, the sea god in the act of creating humans, sculpted on Rurutu; Kukailimoku, a representation of a human face made of hard wickerwork covered with a tight net, each knot tying a cluster of feathers, the Hawaiian god of war, of which there are several other known representations; Kuula, a god in the shape of a Hawaiian fish, rendered in the form of a stone fish brought along for fishing; small gods in the form of humans,

Wooden statue of the god Ku. Hawaii. London, British Museum. Museum photo.

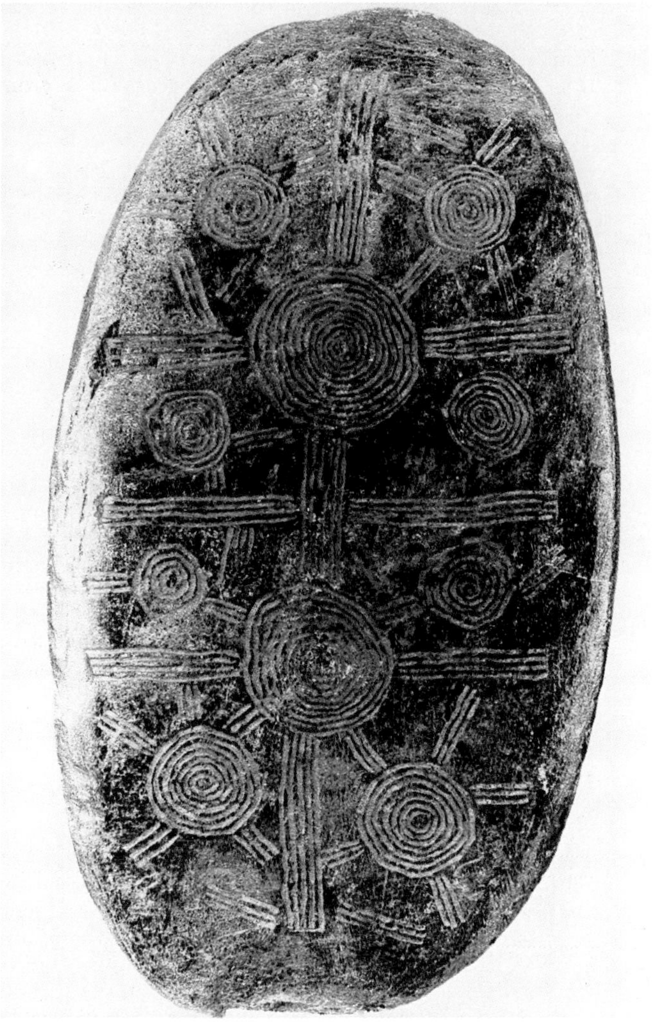

Tjurunga. Schist plate with engravings symbolizing events of the past in the lives of ancestors and each one of their adventures. Paris, Musée national des arts africains et océaniens (Guiart). Museum photo.

with erect penises, vertical with respect to the body, brought along by fishermen from Rarotonga and placed in the prow of dugouts; the "goddesses" of the island of Lifuka in the Tonga Islands; the lizard men of Easter Island. The "staff gods" of Rarotonga seem rather tempting examples but less certain: one main head dominates secondary heads, the whole enclosed in tapa cloth.

A New Zealand peg with a rope of plant fibers, topped by a human head with its tongue sticking out, served as an altar of repose offered to the particular god invoked; they had to roll out the rope held at one end by the seated priest, after they painted the whole thing in ocher and decorated it with feathers; one example found in the Auckland War Memorial Museum had been used in the worship of Maru, the god of war. The reason why the personalities and practices so many gods of war survived is because Europeans were fascinated by them: first to get them out of circulation and second to take pleasure in showing them off as their possessions in Europe. Beyond that, there was such a belief that any human figure was an idol to be destroyed or confiscated that no one took the trouble to note its exact meaning. The image of the ancestor, the only standing sculpture to have survived the Moriori culture on the Chatham Islands, gives no hints other than the fact that it was fear-inspiring, but the fear may have originated from the location of the sculpture, which was struck in the ground inside a cemetery.

Other forms of divine representation were apparently as satisfactory: fine braids on Tikopia, tapa, packets of fibers made from coconut shells (the god Oro on Tahiti), red feathers, adzes; this explains why a great number of sculptures had only ornamental or architectural functions, and why sculpted divine representations do not correspond to a systematic solution.

Melanesia is no better in this respect, with the exception of masks. In New Caledonia, masks represent the master of the land of the dead, Tein Pijopatch. In Vanuatu, in the Seniang region, southeast of Malekula, and probably on the southern coast of this same island, masks are known to represent the ogress Nevimbumbaau, her husband, and her son, but never the civilizing hero Ambat. Elsewhere human figures represent symbols of the social status of individuals or groups. In the rest of Melanesia, these instances are rather rare, unless one does what Codrington, Fox, and Father Patrick O'Reilly did, that is, give people paper and pencil and ask them to draw characters from their pantheon.

Aboriginal Australia is more open from this standpoint, whether it be the paintings on bark in Arnhem Land studied by Karel Kupka or the engraved schist plates, finished in ocher and emu grease, which represent the peregrinations of the ancestors in "the dream time."

XVI. Recent Messianic Movements

A word should be said about the messianic movements which have strewn the Pacific since the arrival of the Europeans, both in Polynesia and in Melanesia. The neopagan rebellion, called the Rebellion of the Mamaias, at the turn of the century in Tahiti, is not well documented. It had a parallel on Samoa. Fiji has experienced several such movements, of which the first is particularly well known, the Tuka, based on the worship of the dead and on the refusal to be dominated by noble Christian converts who lived on the coasts. The other movements await approval for study.

The New Guinea and Melanesian cargo cults received greater publicity in the years after the war. Also based on a return to the cult of the dead and the refusal of direct domination by whites, administrators, traders, and missionaries, they took various forms and succeeded in molding political movements in recent years (Bougainville). The common denominator was the notion that the white man's means of power arrived in cargo ships, and that the only way to gain satisfaction was by resorting to the dead and to ancient deities, since the whites did not want to share. Treated with contempt by European settlers and viewed as irrational movements, these cargo cults began very early. They have had concrete results, politically and economically, and play a part in the many forms of resistance put up by Oceanians to white domination. Only the well-known cases have been reported, and the thinking that was expressed in spectacular behaviors may have been very general, public demonstrations taking place at points of maximum tension. Moreover, if we take the example of Sumatra, where forms of messianism go back a long way, and if we see one or two instances, such as archaeological proof of the myth of Roy Mata in Vanuatu, as an initiating culture change, it seems possible that prophetic movements in Oceania were an accepted form of social, religious, and political change, whenever a new level of awareness was attained and no other solution was at hand.

J.G./g.h.

BIBLIOGRAPHY

Giving a bibliography has become a senseless rite, unless the bibliography is analytic and exhaustive and thus represents a useful tool for the work of other researchers. The list given below is composed of landmarks and so that the great names may not be forgotten. The bibliography of the subject treated includes many hundreds of titles, of which each ought to be the object of an analysis of contents in order to be truly useful. The Oceanians would probably prefer to maintain their oral traditions in place of such an exhausting exercise.

A. BASTIAN, *Die heilige Sage der Polynesier Kosmogonie und Theogonie* (Leipzig 1881). R. BERNDT, *Kunapipi: A Study of an Australian Aboriginal Religious Cult* (Melbourne 1951). E. BEST, *Maori Religion and Mythology* (Wellington 1924). K. O. L. BURRIDGE, *Mambu* (London 1960). E. CAILLOT, *Mythes, légendes et traditions des Polynésiens* (Paris 1914). R. H. CODRINGTON, *The Melanesians: Studies in Their Anthropology and Folklore* (Oxford 1891). A. B. DEACON, *Malekula: A Vanishing People in the New Hebrides,* Camilla Wedgwood, ed. (London 1934). A. P. ELKIN, *The Australian Aborigines: How to Understand Them* (Sydney 1945); "The Rainbow Serpent Myth in North Western Australia," *Oceania* 1 (1930): 349–52. W. ELLIS, *Polynesian Researches during a Residence of Nearly Eight Years in the Society and in the Sandwich Islands,* 2 vols. (London 1829). R. FIRTH, *The Work of the Gods in Tikopia,* 2 vols. (London 1940). R. P. M. GAGNÉRE, *Étude ethnologique sur la religion des Néo-Calédoniens* (Saint-Louis 1905). J. GUIART, *Un siècle et demi de contacts culturels à Tanna, Nouvelles-Hébrides* (Paris 1956); *Structure de la chefferie en Mélanésie du Sud,* travaux et mémoires de l'Institut d'ethnologie, vol. 66 (Paris 1963). J.-J. GUIART, M.-S. LAGRANGE, and M. RENAUD, *Système des titres dans les Nouvelles-Hébrides centrales: D'Efate aus îles Shepherds,* mémoires de l'Institut d'ethnologie, vol. 10 (Paris 1973). C. E. FOX, *The Threshold of the Pacific* (London 1924). C. HANDY, *Polynesian Religion* (Honolulu 1927). T. HENRY, *Ancient Tahiti, Compiled from Notes of J. M. Orsmond* (Honolulu 1928). H. LAVAL, *Mangareva: L'histoire ancienne d'un peuple polynésien* (Braine-le-Comte 1938). P. LAWRENCE, *Road Belong Cargo* (London 1964). P. LAWRENCE and M. J. MEGGITT, eds., *Gods, Ghosts and Men in Melanesia* (London 1965). J. W. LAYARD, *Stone Men of Malekula: Vao* (London 1942). M. LEENHARDT, *Do Kamo* (Paris 1947); *Notes d'ethnologie néo-calédonienne,* mémoires et travaux de l'Institut d'ethnologie, vol. 8 (Paris 1930).

Papua New Guinea

Papua New Guinea appears to be a vast mosaic of different cultures teeming with different local religious phenomena. It is nonetheless possible to identify certain common cultural constants that may serve to define, at the heart of this diversity, a New Guinean model of mythological and ritual representations.

I. Mythology

Religious ideology distinguishes within the cosmic order two features that are simultaneously separate and linked together: the sensory and the intelligible, separate because they are marked by opposing characteristics, but linked together in that one (the sensory world) draws from the other (the intelligible world) the causes and principles of its coherence. The conception of empirical order integrates this contradiction, which is assumed to be a necessary contradiction between the two simultaneous instances of the thought process and which recovers the obsessional theme of the relationship between what is generated and what is becoming. The thing that is sensory shares with the thing that is intelligible the same definitional equivocation, the same ontological uncertainty. Because it is produced by a transcendental power that human beings claim they cannot control, visible reality can disappear by the same volition that caused it to appear in the first place. The transcendence that is thus liable to manifest itself positively or negatively beyond man's control is paradoxical, in that as myth it appears as a force that is self-sufficient, while as ritual it appears as a force that is instituted, the end result of a human product (Guidieri 1978).

The sensory aspect, constituted by the immanent reality of the natural environment, economic resources, and living creatures, is most often conceived as the anthropomorphized projection of the supernatural world that represents the intelligible side of the universe. This latter, intelligible aspect includes the invisible realm of supernatural creatures: mythical heroes, occult forces, demons, celestial deities, spirits of the dead, ancestors, and so forth, whose existence, attested by mythical discourse, justifies the whole body of religious beliefs and practices. The themes of these beliefs and practices can be grouped around two types of entities: independent spirits and ancestral spirits.

The independent spirits, whose existence the mythology traces back to the very founding of the universe and whose origins are strictly supernatural, have prospered (and continue to progenerate) in the human environment by exerting the regulatory powers that have been (or are now) more or less invested in them. This category of entities is the one that is involved in most myths of creation, notably the stories of the origins of the first men and of the natural or cultural laws that govern their universe. The question of the genesis of the physical world and the birth of supernatural heroes seems to have been practically banished from mythological discourse, which prefers to narrate the actions performed by the heroes of the early times and to describe those times, which is useful for justifying the current state of things.

Thus, for the most part, the myths posit the existence of the earth—flat, dry, and uninhabited—before the existence of the principal deities who created the first human beings, endowed the universe with the natural attributes it is known to have (rivers, mountains, forests, animals, etc.), and established the norms of social and cultural institutions. Consequently, the exemplary deeds of the founding spirits performed in mythical times must provide the sole referential criteria for current human behavior, for which what is traditional therefore becomes mandatory.

This ideal of conformity to what is said to have existed is reinforced by the general observation that phratries, clans, or subclans often have exclusive possession of a whole set of secret myths that evoke the bonds of linear descent that unite the group to its ancestral deities. These deities are generally said to have a power of metamorphosis that is ultimately able to accomplish their petrification into things of nature (trees, rocks, plants, and so forth). This characteristic aptitude of spirits to transform themselves by assuming the most diverse

Skull rack with two skulls covered with molding showing the features of the deceased. Melanesia, New Guinea. Paris, Musée de l'Homme (Madeleine Rousseau collection). Museum photo.

Mask made of rough bark and painted black and white. Papua New Guinea (Bay of Kerewa). Paris, Musée de l'Homme collection. Museum photo.

shapes familiar to humans explains the human feeling of utter confusion between objective reality and mythical reality, which are conceived as fundamentally similar and interdependent. In New Guinea, people experience at the very core of their person this cosmogonic duality that they assimilate within themselves in terms of the dichotomy between body and soul. Every human being is endowed with a "soul" present inside the body diffusely and without form. The soul can leave the body temporarily during sleep or permanently when the person dies. Thus, dreams are seen as the manifestation of such flights of the soul and its encounters with supernatural creatures from an intangible world to which people in their state of wakefulness have no direct access.

The spirits of the dead are defined as the immaterial components of humans that survive after death and persist indefinitely in the universe in a disembodied form. Ideas about the exact destination of souls and the location of the land of the dead sometimes appear rather ill-defined, though there is a general consensus that the ancestors' place of residence is to the west or underground. The route that leads to that place is strewn with obstacles, dangers, and trials to overcome, whose description forms the substance of the myth. The fate of the soul and the things that can happen to it are tied to the earthly personality and the circumstances surrounding the death of the dead person. For instance, among the Baktaman of central New Guinea, a violent death in combat or as the result of an accident makes it impossible for the spirit to live in the land of the dead, which can be attained only through a nonviolent death. That is why in the human environment, in addition to the independent spirits that haunt the forests, the rivers, and the air, there are also souls of the dead who have no homeland, who wander about interfering in the lives of human beings. The nature of this interference, sometimes positive and sometimes (more often) negative, depends on the culture; sometimes it is connected with the wholly anthropomorphic character of the spirit, sometimes with the powers inherent in its ancestral status, and sometimes with the degree of its interest in the affairs of the living. In certain cases (the Huli of the southern highlands), the influence of the spirits increases with their antiquity and varies with their sex, malevolence apparently being a specific feature of female spirits. In other cases, by contrast (the Kyaka of the western highlands), less power is attributed to remote ancestors—even if they are founding ancestors—than to the spirits of the recent dead, whose good or evil influence is the shared lot of both sexes.

Both types of entities, the independent spirits and the spirits of the dead, share a common dimension: ancestry. Ancestry is innate in the first instance, inherently given to the spirit since the beginning of its existence; it is acquired, in the second instance, at the end of a liturgical process of transformation. The mythological and the genealogical are therefore defined in New Guinean thought as the two aspects of memory fit to ensure the intangibility and durability of representations of belief. But discourse is not the only place where memory can find its actualization, and the question of ancestry inevitably leads to a consideration of the rituals in which such subjects of representations are invoked in a dramatic mode.

II. From Myth to Cult

The independent spirits correspond to the initiation rites whose object is to reveal the mystery of such spirits. The spirits of the dead correspond to the funerary cults performed on the occasion of a death.

Initiation rites share with other rites the explicit ultimate objective of enhancing fertility, fecundity, growth, success, and efficacy; appeasing the spirits; promoting the wealth of the clan and the strength and courage of its members; ensuring success in combat and trade; protecting men from the risk of impurity through contact with women; and, notably, teaching ethical principles and social values to novices, as shown by the example of initiation among the Kamano, Usurufa, Jate, and Fore in the eastern highlands: "You must not steal another man's pig or steal his fire. You must not do these things. But you may kill men. If a man uses sorcery against another, you may kill him. You must become strong, you must be big to do these things. You must look after your gardens. You must build enclosures for them and plant crops in them. You must not eat anything from a woman's hand. If a woman offers you food, refuse; if you do not, you will lose your strength and become sickly. You must not eat anything from the hands of young men, because they have copulated with their wives; if you do so, your body will be nothing but flesh and bones . . ." (Berndt 1962).

But it is in the latent, esoteric content of the initiation rituals rather than in this manifest end that it is possible to understand their import: they aim to furnish a tangible proof of the existence of a transcendental reality, to render perceptible what is unintelligible and thereby to allow the spirit of the novice to set in motion the process of the acquisition of belief. This objective is met by means of a ritual object that serves as a simulacrum or material "double" of the entity that is its referent. Depending on the culture, such objects vary in number and nature: flutes among the Mundugumor and Iatmul south of Sepik, Kamano, Usurufa, Flore, Siane, Chimbu, Kuma, and Gahuku-Gama in the highlands; bullroarers among the Marind Anim of West Irian, Arapesh, Abelam of Sepik, Kamano, Fore, and Orokaiva, Koko, Elema of Papua New Guinea; gongs among the Arapesh, Abelam, Tchambuli; masks among the Iatmul, Tchambuli, Kerewa, Namau, Elema, Turamarubi of Papua New Guinea; stones among the Mbowang, Kyaka, Enga, Huli, and Mendi of the highlands, and so forth.

Through the simulacrum, the reification of the transcendent spirit takes place. Through the object, the invisible presence is brought forth to be seen, to be perceived in a mystical way. The mystery revealed in the initiation is that of the incarnation of the subject into the object (of the idea into the thing); the object turns out to be nothing but an illusion, the screen of an immaterial world beyond, of an idea that transcends it and for which it stands as an incarnate allusion. For the novice, who expects to encounter the supernatural creature that has been foretold and given an extravagant and terrifying representation by his naive imagination, coming face to face with the simulacra is a decisive event. Wavering between his inability to sustain the childish belief to which the initiation has just dealt a brutal blow and the commensurate impossibility of giving it up altogether (Guidieri 1977), the new initiate can find a conceivable (and livable) compromise only in a belief transformed into the mystical rather than empirical existence of the spiritual entity as it is incarnate in the ritual object. This object, through which he comes to know the spirit model, is the instrument of the process of the acquisition of belief, at the end of which the novice gains access to the higher status of adult believer and male mystifier. Endowed this time with a new and real knowledge, he is expected not only to believe but to make others believe, to comfort in their cunning and ignorance, through his own deceitful talk, the women with whom he previously shared the inferior status of the credulous uninitiated. This demonstrates the principle of hierarchical opposition of the sexes, for which the ritual process seems to be the periodic reiteration.

In most cultures where myths justify the origins of ceremonial practices, the story begins with a description of the time when women had a dominant role and possessed sacred objects that they had discovered or created; it then goes on to conclude by evoking the inversion of the situation, by which men acquire through cunning or force not just power but also a monopoly over objects. Thus, for example, the Kamano and Fore myth of the sacred flutes:

> Jugumishanta and Morufonu [the ancestral founding couple] were living at Koripika. Jugumishanta built a small segregation-hut where she slept by herself, her husband having built a large house for himself. At her place Jugumishanta planted wild ginger. She cut a length of bamboo and bored a hole in its surface, making a flute, and this she hid in the ginger foliage. Later she took it out and, hiding it in her skirt, left the camp. Reaching a secluded place, she began to play the flute; and from his own hut her husband heard its cry. "What is this that cries?" he said. "I would like to see it, but perhaps it

Marind Anim actors impersonating Dema spirits and carrying their bullroarers and drums. Southern New Guinea. Amsterdam, Kon. Instituut v/d Tropen. Institute photo.

would kill and eat me." So he thought to himself, and was afraid. Day after day Jugumishanta played her flute, and her husband became increasingly curious. Returning one night, she plucked out some pubic hair and placed it in the barrel of the flute; this would enable it to cry out if handled by someone other than herself; she then hid it in the ginger foliage. Later, when she went out to work in her garden, Morufonu made sure she was out of sight. Then he went down to her house and following her footprints eventually found the ginger bush and the flute. He dug up the ginger and took it back to his own house, where he planted it and prepared to play the flute; but the flute was playing by itself, warning Jugumishanta. As he lifted it to his mouth, the pubic hair within the flute touched him, and he immediately began to grow facial and body hair. [This explains why men are much hairier than women.—Berndt's note.] When Jugumishanta heard her flute, she ran back to her house and finding it and her ginger gone came to Morufonu and asked him, "Who stole my flute?" Morufonu replied, "I heard something playing outside your hut, and I grew angry. I came down and found it. You couldn't play it properly, but I do it well. You must not look at it now, it is something belonging to me." He then placed the flute in the ginger foliage; it "turned" [became transformed—Berndt's note] and grew into a clump of bamboos with ginger growing at its base, seen today at Koripika. . . . Now men cut branches and make flutes, playing them in the bush at night during the pig festival so that pigs will increase. During the night, too, they enter the village, decorated with branches of foliage, playing their flutes, while women, children, and young boys fasten their doors and stay in their houses. Moon after moon the flutes are played, increasing the pigs and making them grow larger, improving and advancing the crops, until finally pigs are killed and a festival is held. If a woman looks at a flute, she is killed; if a young boy is caught looking at the players, his nose is bled. (Berndt, pp. 50–51)

The majority of the mythical narrations about the origins of ritual objects thus tell the story of a dispossession (confiscation) in which the women are the victims and the men are the winners, appropriating for themselves the Kuma flutes or the Marind and Elema bullroarers. This turn of events in mythical times explains why in the current norms of New Guinea cultures, and Melanesian culture in general, women are excluded from the sacred domain of ritual practices, the fundamental meaning of which rests on the mystery of the object. On the basis of this mystery, forever denied to the knowledge of women, males assert the legitimacy of their supremacy in the sexual order. The presence of the simulacrum, reserved exclusively for manipulation by men, signifies the concrete and indisputable proof of their superiority (a peculiar proof, entirely self-contained, since it never needs to be made to the interested parties). But such superiority, so fragile because it is artificially founded on a mystifying discourse addressed to women, is not acquired once and for all. It is a precarious virtue which needs to be reaffirmed at

"Murup" mask made of painted wood, worn by men at festivals. New Guinea, Sepik. Paris, Musée de l'Homme collection. Museum photo.

Male sculpture made of wood, seeds, and human hair; eyes and ear ornaments made of mother-of-pearl; designs in black on brown background (sacred flute ornament). New Guinea. Paris, Musée de l'Homme collection.

regular intervals. Through ritual representation, males have the means of this reaffirmation. On such occasions, the ideology of contrasts, which in these cultures makes a woman a figure of impurity and a man a container, not impure but empty—and therefore vulnerable because threatened in his integrity by an opposite identity—finds its spectacular expression in ritual. Several features of this dramatization make up the characteristic constants tied to the communal theme of male sexual anxiety. The treatment given to this obsession which is focused on the female principle of fertility and procreation is brought about through the rejection and/or imitation of this principle. In rites of initiation, rejection is the actual practice of all New Guinean society, whether it takes the form of nose bleeding (Kuma, Chimbu, Kamano, Fore, Usurufa, Jate, Siane, Gahuku-Gama), of an incision on the penis (Kamano, Fore, Siane, Kuma, Arapesh, Abelam, Wogeo), or deep scarifications (Iatmul, Tchambuli). In all cases, the practice aims at draining from the body the substance most likely to endure and convey contamination: blood. The discharge is liberating in that it allows the male to rid himself of the female impurity, notably transmitted by the mother, and at the same time to put an end to his nonadult status. Thus freed from the negative forces that were stifling the male identity inside him, the initiate can at last aspire to the revelation of the cultural attributes of masculinity (flutes, gongs, masks, bullroarers) and gain access to his new status. Yet ethnographic evidence shows that what Bettelheim calls the "envy" of femininity remains in men despite all the acts designed to widen the gap that separates men from the feminine pole. Imitation, which appeared quite explicitly in the transvestite rites of the Iatmul, Kuma, Mbowang, and Arapesh, achieves the clearest symbolism when blood is regarded not only as a substance but as a dynamic entity that has a particular function: it is the process that becomes relevant for manifesting the difference. Thus the bleeding of certain organs or, in other cultures, circumcision and subincision, express not only the desire to eliminate from oneself any trace of female impurity but also an attempt by men to reproduce fictitiously upon themselves the exemplary periodicity of the specifically female mechanism of menstruation. Alongside this theme of cyclic movement there also appears, in the rituals of Papua New Guinea, the theme of giving birth, which finds its psychoanalytic equivalent in the initiatory symbolism of the death and rebirth of the novice (Allen 1967).

In all cases, however, liturgical artifice offers the male identity anxiety only a solution of temporary compromise that must be reiterated if it is to be effective. The ritual setting is the time and place of this reiteration. Beyond that, males merely have to protect themselves individually, by acts of purification, against the dangers of daily sexual promiscuity with women.

It should be noted that the antagonistic relationship between the sexes, characteristic of Melanesia in general, reaches an unparalleled dimension in Papua New Guinea (where this opposition has not been resolved), through the generation of a striking proliferation of models that represent sexuality (Guidieri 1975).

In funerary rites, the central referent is no longer the deified mythical subject but the formerly human entity that death projects outside the world of the living, the entity to whom one resorts in order to attain a particular status. A man who dies does not immediately acquire the name (and consequently the function) of an ancestor. Being an ancestor, in other words, is not a favor from death but a virtue which is earned in the process of transformation that death sets in motion.

When an individual has stopped living, the nonsubstantial part of his being escapes from the body and undertakes the journey that will take it to the land of the dead. The route to that place is particularly perilous, according to numerous myths, strewn with a succession of obstacles to be overcome and sufferings to be endured that make the journey look like a true initiation, and only at its end does he acquire the status of a completed dead person, that is, an ancestor.

Thus, in the conceptual thought of Papua New Guinea, death is defined not as the endpoint of a process of growth leading to annihilation but rather as the starting point of a new symmetrical evolution. In this evolution, the living have a role to play, since by their liturgical action they help the dead reach the final goal of transformation. The rites surrounding the corpse constitute the earthly equivalent of the occult course traversed by the soul moving toward its destiny, and they furnish an objective representation of the dead man's trajectory. They enact this trajectory, make it visible, that is, conceivable. Thus, in the example of Marind Anim, after the funeral the tomb is opened twice. The first time, shortly after death, the substance that is exuded by the decomposing body is extracted from the exhumed corpse, in imitation of the homologous practice that is performed on the soul as it travels on its initiatory road toward becoming an ancestor. This practice, consisting of tearing out the entrails of the soul, is a torment inflicted by a deity whose name, Adak ("to make a gash," or "to press"), evokes precisely the actions performed by the celebrants in order to collect the liquids from the corpse. At the end of these operations, the tomb is closed again; the dead man has become an ancestor. About one year later, the tomb is opened for the second time, and the bones of the dead man, now free of their flesh, are washed and painted red before they are arranged at the bottom of the tomb, which this time is closed forever. This process effectively "doubles" the mythical action in the same way that the supernatural events experienced by the soul in order to achieve its accession to ancestry "double" the actual initiation imposed on the male in order for him to become a complete adult (Van Baal 1966).

The other specific element of the funerary cults consists of bringing into place among the ritual objects that are the instruments of the liturgical process not only simulacra but relics, that is, the imperishable remains of one who has definitively attained the status of individuality. The memory that is actualized in the mortuary rite is therefore a memory that does not obliterate the anthropomorphic origin of the deified transcendence that is the ancestor. Such an entity, which can only be an identity, is assured of its temporal connection with the present by means of the genealogical discourse that shores up the memory of the living by conceptualizing it.

Mortuary rites, like initiation rites, function in both the visible and the invisible dimensions, but according to inverse modalities. While the initiation process aimed to make transcendance reach deep inside the immanent, through the intervention of artificial objects, the funerary liturgy orchestrates the accession of the immanent to the transcendant, by means of natural objects. It consecrates the transfiguration of the temporary and the perishable into the idea of the immutable.

In both cases, ritual produces transcendance and plays a role in that extraordinary moment when the Papuan brings his thought to its fullest expression.

M.Ba./g.h

BIBLIOGRAPHY

ALLEN, *Male Cults and Secret Initiations in Melanesia* (Melbourne 1967). F. BARTH, *Ritual and Knowledge among the Baktaman of New-Guinea* (New Haven 1975). G. BATESON, *Naven* (Stanford 1971); "Music in New-Guinea," *The Eagle,* vol. 48 (1935). R. M. BERNDT, *Excess and Restraint* (Chicago 1962). B. BETTELHEIM, *Symbolic Wounds,* rev. ed. (New York 1962). GLASSE, SALISBURY, BERNDT, MEGGITT, and BULMER, *Gods, Ghosts and Men in Melanesia* (Oxford 1965). R. GUIDIERI, "Note sur le rapport mâle/femelle en Mélanésie," *L'Homme,* 15, 2 (1975); *Introduction à l'anthropologie des croyances,* course of the Department of Ethnology at the University of Paris-X (Nanterre 1975–78). O. MANNONI, *Clefs pour l'imaginaire ou l'autre scène* (Paris 1969). M. MEAD, *Sex and Temperament in Three Primitive Societies* (London 1935). NEVERMANN, WORMS, and PETRI, *Les religions du Pacifique et de l'Australie* (Paris 1968). M. STRATHERN, *Women in Between: Female Role in a Male Role, Mount Hagen, New-Guinea* (London 1972). J. VAN BAAL, "The Cult of the Bull-Roarer in Australia and Southern New-Guinea," in *Bijdragen . . . ,* 119.2; *Dema: Description and Analysis of Marind-Anim Culture, South New-Guinea* (The Hague 1966). F. E. WILLIAMS, "Natives of the Purari Delta," *Anthropological Report,* no. 5 (Papua 1924); "Bull-Roarers in the Papuan Gulf," *Anthropological Report,* no. 17 (Papua 1936); *Orokaiva Society* (Oxford 1930); *Drama of Orokolo* (Oxford 1940).

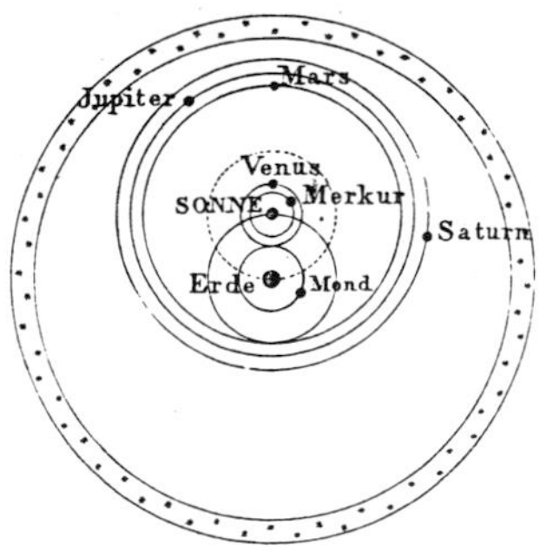

Epilogue: The Contemporary Need for Myths—a Testimonial

On a woodcut from Dürer's studio, the cosmos is represented by three circular spaces: in the center is the earth that is our place and its sky studded with stars; on the edge is the luminous space in which God reigns alone; and separating them both, a circle of dark fire. Between the divine kingdom and the human world there is no passage. Such was undoubtedly the initial state of creation. The tragic abandonment of the human species is balanced by the solitude of the deity. But it was man's task to bore a hole through the circle of dark fire. It is a long adventure, the last phase of which the Gnostic Clement of Alexandria has clearly depicted for us: "The knowledge of what we are and of what we have become, of the place from which we came and the place into which we have fallen, of the objective toward which we hasten and of what we are redeemed from, of the nature of our birth and our rebirth." On this path of knowledge, men separated from the divine have undertaken first to make the divine descend among them.

Thus the gods were born from the tears of mankind; men invented myths to console themselves, for the gods were all silence and opacity. They had no regard for the strangeness of our condition, and any compassion for our sufferings was alien to them. All creatures therefore had to force them to exist fully and to manifest themselves; a single path presented itself to the human imagination: to forge a history for them so that they might be engulfed in time and space like living creatures and, like us, be both actors and spectators in the savage theater of life and death. This foundation of mythic adventures was not achieved haphazardly. Well before the first rigors of reason defined our earthly existence as a line staked out by our birth and our demise, men had a premonition of those disastrous abysses which are the upstream and downstream flow of our belonging to the earth. Since these forever impenetrable areas of nothingness nurture anxiety and madness, there remains only one way out, which is to restore time's circular deployment, to enclose fate within a sequence of events either lived or dreamed, closely intertwined and eternally tied together by the miracle of metamorphoses. That is, furthermore, what plant life shows us: from the tiny fruit rotting in the mud is born the luxuriant bough, whose seed will return into the depths of the earth when the season comes.

This mythical imagination appears as a revolt against the basic perversity of matter, against creation's profound indifference toward us. It is a way to force nature to recognize our necessity, for the only justification for our long and painful history is that we are not in any sense a useless suffering nor the last link of an itinerary destined for destruction; we mortals are what makes nature immortal. If matter is perverse, if nature is indifferent, and as indifferent to itself as it is to our human destiny, it is because they are unaware of the heart that underlies them and gives them life. In their blindness, they are unaware of what makes them act within the vast unfurling of time.

I. The Hidden Creation

It is incumbent upon human inventiveness to reveal the heart that hides what mythic dreaming calls the Word, the Logos, the breath of life. This revelation is the object of myths. Through them, men reveal to creation what, in its depths, makes it live. The projection of the human spirit toward nature is not a game: it is born of the certainty, inherent in our condition, that the Word hidden within matter is also the word hidden within our being. And all revelation concerning the secret energy of nature is a revelation concerning our own essence.

Thus, far from being an explanation of the organization and the movement of the universe, mythology appears as a voyage toward knowledge, as an ever fresh approach to a knowledge of which the ephemeral character of our existence will allow us to discover only fragments. Far from shedding light on this mystery, myths are, on the contrary, designed to deepen it. An image common to all mythical representations introduces us to this nocturnal expedition: the image of the cave.

The first habitat of the human being, who alone in the entire realm of the living finds himself at birth bereft of everything and constrained to seek help from his environment, the cave is also the image of the maternal dwelling from which we are torn to be thrown into the harsh light of day. But the cave is a place of mixed associations in which all the opposing figures of our condition coexist: the white of the sky and the black of the earth, the dryness of the rock wall and the wetness of the spring. It is open like a shelter, yet closed like a tomb. The cave is the very image of our endurance; it is the fortress within which both life and death are enclosed. It is in a cave that Aphrodite reveals to human beings the mystery of love, but it is also in a cave that the Buddha meditates for millennia to give rise to as yet unimagined worlds.

We are inside the cave, as Plato says. All we can know of the world is that there is fire below us and above us, that there is also air outside, water inside, and the earth. But existence in the cave is tolerable only if we see it as the center of the universe; thus the blind, unknowable forces that whirl about far from the cave are directed around it, and for us. Such is the meaning of mythologies: to give the house of men its true dimension, to make our dwelling the Temple. In this way, depending on its time and place, every tribe invents what is necessary for its own coherence. Every element of creation is a sound or a word, and out of the totality of elements a language must be made which is audible to everyone, for if words go off on their own wandering paths, creation has no aim and slips toward absurdity and suicide.

These mythological dramas cannot be enclosed in the strictures of rational analysis. All attempts of contemporary scholarship to account for the enormous load of mythical materials carried along by the human past may lock up heroic adventures in the frozen compartments of learning. The vast inventories are like greenhouses in which wild plants have been imprisoned: their lively shoots break through the glass and proliferate skyward far from the guardians' watchful eyes, or their roots sink cunningly into the darkness of the virgin soil. It is better to regard myths as theater that is meant to carry a different message at each performance. The text of the play can remain the same, but each performance constitutes a different event because the acting conditions, the actors, the spectators, and also the immediate story of which they are the witnesses have changed.

II. The Masks of Mystery

If we look at these cosmogonies as integral parts of life as it was experienced in its intensity or endured in its daily round by the peoples of long ago, if we restore their movement and the passionate charge that was once theirs in the city, we can see that they were felt to be "revelations of being," that they allowed each participant in the community to become an active witness of those energies which by their confrontations and connections determined the metamorphoses of creation. The image at the center of archaic ritual celebrations is an image whose emotional force we can still entirely grasp, because, whether provoked or refuted, it remains at the core of our existence. It is the image of sacrifice. The sacrificial theme is directly involved in the most innocent contemplation of natural life, in which mortal and nascent forms, destruction and change, putrefaction and desiccation are endlessly exchanged. At the community level, any form of sacrifice is an alliance with the moving landscapes of nature, a humble participation in the vast holocaust which is the very condition of the survival of creation. In primitive communities, human blood is an object of exchange with the gods, just as gold is an object of exchange among the powerful in mercantile societies. Any blood that is shed is a tribute paid to the fertility of the earth; it is the promise of things to come. The values attached to particular kinds of blood, female blood, animal blood, the blood of certain special plants, are inscribed within this general concern with a pact between men and the powers of the Elsewhere. The gods must also take this pact very seriously since, if they fail to keep their word, men can exclude them from their kingdoms and make dead gods of them, never again to be celebrated in ritual.

Mythical representation has abandoned the wide stage of the tribe to be devoted entirely to each being in all his intimacy. The gods are no longer shared by a multitude. They have become the exclusive property of anyone who invents them. What once functioned on the collective level is now achieved on the personal level. Although today the only nameable progress is one that frees the individual from the constraints of the social body and hands him over totally to his true identity, imagination allows each person to explore the depth of his hidden source and to nurture his own mythology. But since we are not born of nothing, since we are but one parcel of the immense experience accumulated in time and space by our fellow creatures, the mythological corpus is revealed to be a treasure cave in which we mine riches meant especially for us.

For the divine adventures reported by myths are not the errant or aberrant fruits of a primordial imagination led astray by enthusiasm or the anxiety of solitude. On the contrary, they mirror the adventures experienced by men in a universe laden with meaning, a universe in which human destinies take their positions on a more general stage on which all the figures of creation, those of the plant, mineral, and animal kingdoms alike, play their roles. The stories present the dialogue between living beings and the basic mystery of life that no rational knowledge could ever hope to bring to light and of which the fundamental incarnations are birth, dreams, love, and death.

This dialogue, however, since the earliest days of our species, has been able to change its outer face as the material field of our history has undergone its own changes. The dialogue has not changed its nature. It has no object other than to open our eyes to the back country that is beyond words, beyond explicit communication, but where true fusion is achieved between the beings that we are in our turbulent individuality and the being of the world.

Images of fire provide the classic illustration. All mythologies give them a key place in their accounts of the origin. Two characteristics are common to all these mythical narratives. On the one hand, the stories dramatize an artisan's imagination, which is the very condition of the survival of the species. On the other hand, they put flesh on the heroic energies that made the mystery of fire familiar and gave it its place in the community. The artisan's imagination, for which men have often sought a model in animal society or in the secret lives of plants and stones, functions the same way in modern times as it did in antiquity. Only the instruments with which we invest reality have changed. Instead of having a direct relationship with fire, we usually experience it in the secondary form transmitted to us abstractly by machines.

The figures that serve as masks for the mystery have lost, perhaps provisionally, the carnal resonance that people bestowed on them in earlier times and have instead donned conceptual garments. But the garments of modern rationality do not delve into the depth of the enigma, and the loss of divine flesh makes us experience it as an impoverishment, conducive to solitude.

Rubens, *The Festival of the Gods*. Prague, Narodni Galeri. Photo Prokop Paul.

The permanence of our intimate tie with fire has been underscored by Gaston Bachelard in the single evocation of the flame of a candle. Before a candle or the brightly burning log in the fireplace, the daydreams of a child of today are just like those of the Neolithic, just like those of Mary Magdalene, whom Georges de la Tour painted in the humble smock of a peasant girl of seventeenth-century Lorraine. The universe experienced and the universe represented are confused in the uncertain territory of our inalienable intimacy. In the depths of our being, inaccessible to social constraint, sheltered from the curse that reduces us to being merely another person among others, the amalgam of forces unfolds, and the confrontation or the connection of these forces writes the history of life. We must turn for a moment to the imagery of Paracelsus when he describes each human creature as a microcosm that reflects the totality of the macrocosm, that is, all that the cosmos bears within itself as a creative spark, as a passion to exist, as anguish, as contradiction, as uncertainty.

To return to the realm of fire, this macrocosm, whose imagination has no bounds, figures in all the accounts that have nurtured the dreams of human tribes since the beginning. Its memory retains others, those that history has buried under its ruins, those that the eyes that we have now do not yet know how to excavate, and beyond memory are all the narratives yet to come. Although we are microcosms, we have the potential to recreate the totality of these accounts in ourselves, but our nature is fragmented and immature. As Michelet pointed out, we are far from being complete; we are, as the Greeks said, "not sufficiently cooked." We can therefore explore only a very small part of the timber yards of the imagination during our personal itineraries.

But however partial our course, our elementary connection with the flame of a log fire introduces us to the sum total of the values in which daily existence is invested. Through fire, time is manifested. The evening fireplace stands against the heat of the sun; the winter hearth protects against the harshness of the cold. Beyond this temporal relationship, fire defines our dietary mode, that is, our feelings about our own bodies. Within the secret of the unconscious, the presence of Eros is also experienced as a secret permanence of fire, while Thanatos is perceived as the absence of all igneous elements.

In archaic societies where cosmogony is directly implicated in the essential moments in the life of the tribe, the various representations of fire govern a certain number of daily rituals and practices and roughly define the boundaries that separate the forbidden from the permitted. These rituals and practices make ancient societies into communities invested with the sacred. Into this fabric of the sacred is woven a series of ties between man and the universe. It is through these ties that men are protected from anguish and solitude. When the boundaries of the sacred collapse, when the ties that bind creatures to the sky and the earth are annihilated, men are reduced to their own company, and the foundations of the community are based merely on ethics. The primordial image of life, the only one that can be the point of convergence of all ancient mythologies, is replaced by images of good and evil, underground figures that leave a living creature helpless before the opacity of his development.

By nature, ethics reduce the mental field of individuals to the measure of city life or throw individuals into what Ronald Laing calls "ontological insecurity," an insecurity that arises as soon as the being feels or anticipates that a part of him is moving far from the play of social requirements. Anyone who wishes to recuperate his being in its fullness must found his own sacredness, create his own myths and rituals. He must experience a new birth, he must be reborn to

Athena (*continued*) 1:546; and Christianity, 2:661; in literature, 2:788
Athenaea, 1:386
Athenaeus, 1:629
Athenagorus, 1:668, 1:669, 1:670
Athens, Greece, 1:330, 1:340–46, 1:355, 1:425
Athirat, 1:188, 1:189, 1:191, 1:209, 1:211, *1:212,* 1:214–15
Athribis, 1:93
Athtar, 1:190, 1:192, 1:211–12, 1:215
Athtart, 1:190, 1:214
Atiedii Brethren, 1:523, 1:539
Atiq, 2:1151
Atjek, 2:1137
Atlantis, 1:355; myth of, 1:386, 1:355, 1:357
Atlas, 1:371
Ātman, 2:800, 2:818–19, 2:822
Atonatiuh, 2:1174
Atrahasīs, 1:149–51, 1:158, 1:173–76, 1:180
Atreus, 1:403–4, 1:408, 1:508; in literature, 2:787
Atreus, house of, 1:403–4, 1:446
Attis, 1:217, *1:626;* in literature, 2:784; to Naassenes, 2:676
Attus Navius, 1:585
Atum, 1:92–93
Atymnios, 1:335
Atys, 2:1115
Auðumla, 1:286
Augurelli, Giovanni Aurelio, 2:702, 2:712
Augurs and augury, 1:532–33, 1:584–87, 1:593–94, 1:605–6; among Germano-Nordic peoples, 1:290; in pre-Roman Italy, 1:523, 1:539
Augustine, Saint, 1:341, 1:601, 1:617, 1:619, 1:636, 2:656, 2:664, 2:667, 2:668, 2:691, 2:694, 2:710, 2:735, 2:751
Augustus, 1:593, 1:606–11, *1:608, 1:610,* 1:618
Aule, 1:519
Aulus Gellius, 1:550, 1:603, 1:627, 1:628, 1:635, 1:645
Aunam, 1:227
Aurelius Cotta (Lucius), 1:598–99, 1:614
Aurora. *See* Eos
Aurva, 2:875
Auson, 1:546
Ausonius, 1:255
Australia. *See* Oceania
Austroasiatic and Austronesian peoples, 2:977, 2:981–85, 2:990–95
Autochthon, 1:341, 1:342–43, 1:345, 1:354–58, 1:391, 1:393, 1:497
Autogenēs, 1:681
Autolycos, 1:421, 1:497
Autonoë, 1:433, 1:461
Autun, 1:251, 1:268
Auxesia, 1:335
Avalokiteśvara, 2:895, 2:901, 2:902, 2:903, 2:905, 2:907–8, *2:908,* 2:1083, 2:1085
Avatars, *Avatāra,* 2:829–31, 2:834–39, 2:849–52, 2:854–56, 2:859–64, 2:928–29
Aventia, 2:733
Aventinus, Johannes Turmair, 1:136
Avesta, 2:878–79, 2:891–93
Avidyā, 2:820
Avyakta, 2:818
Aweto, 2:1200
Äxsärtägkats, 1:317
Axym, Axyn. *See* Ahyn
Ay Ata, Ay Atam, 2:1095
Ay Dede, 2:1106
Ayisit, 2:1092
Aymara, 2:1201, 2:1203, 2:1205
Ayonwatha, 2:1161
Ay-wa, 2:1095
Azeri, 2:1098
Azhwajpshaa, 2:1116
'Azizu, 1:204
Azrafil, 2:1095
Azrail, 2:1095, 2:1108
Aztecs, 2:1165–80, 2:1181, 2:1182–83, 2:1184–91

B

Ba, 1:96, 1:97–99, 1:111, 2:1019, 2:1021
Baader, Franz Xaver von, 2:765
Ba'al, *1:183, 1:187,* 1:188–89, 1:191, 1:194–200, 1:206–15, *1:207,* 1:228
Baalat, 1:193–95
Baalat Gebal, 1:194
Ba'al Hammon, 1:198–99
Ba'al Sapon, 1:199
Ba'al-Shamain, 1:200–202
Baalshamen, 1:191, 1:194–95
Ba'alshamîn, 1:205
Ba'al Tsur, 1:194
Babalawo, 1:54
Babas, 2:1104
Babel, 2:649; and Christianity, 2:660; in literature, 2:785
Babito, 1:79
Babylon, Mesopotamia, 1:151, 1:143–44, 1:156–57, 1:161, 1:179–81
Bacabs, 2:1178–79, 2:1180
Bacairi, 2:1200
Bacchae, 1:459–60, 1:462
Bacchus, in art and literature, 2:694, 2:700
Bacchylide, 1:466, 1:482
Bac Dau, 2:996
Bacwezi, 1:78–81
Baghdad, 1:192
Bagong, 2:954, *2:955*
Bahau, 2:933
Bahima, 1:78
Bahit, 2:1217
Bahnar, 2:977, 2:979, 2:984, 2:993
Bahram. *See* Verethraghna
Bainača, Bajan Ami, 2:1122
Baj Bajanaj, 2:1122
Baka, 2:863
Baktaman, 2:1226
Baktun, 2:1171
Balain, 2:716
Balar, 1:257, 1:259
Balarāma, 2:833, 2:839, 2:859–60
Balbal, 2:1108, 2:1110
Baldr, 1:285
Bali, 2:858. *See also* Insular Southeast Asia
Balig Bayat, 2:1105
Balitok, 2:940
Balius, 1:474
Ballanche, Pierre Simon, 2:752, 2:759, 2:765, 2:768, 2:769, 2:772–73, 2:775
Baloz, 1:307
Balsäg, 1:318
Balsamon, Theodorus, 2:673
Baltic peoples, 1:301, 1:305–6
Balzac, Honoré de, 2:757–58, 2:765, 2:766, 2:769, 2:770, 2:777
Bamana, 1:27
Bambara, *1:26,* 1:29, 1:30–31, 1:33–35 passim, 1:37, 1:39, 1:41, 1:44, 1:45, *1:48,* 1:49, 1:50, 1:52
Bāṇāsura, 2:862
Banbha, 1:258, 1:260
Banier, Abbé, 2:728
Banit, 1:203
Banowati, 2:957
Bantu-speaking peoples, 1:62–81, *1:66*
Banyani (Dada), 1:58
Banyiginya, 1:79
Banzaburo, 2:1052
Bao, 2:1212
Baour-Lormian, Pierre, 2:768
Barak, 2:1099, 2:1104
Barastyr, 1:317
Barbari, Jacopo de', 2:700
Barbelo, 2:680
Bard, *bard(d),* 1:242, 1:250
Bar Hebraeus, 2:1103
Barnaud, Nicolas, 2:703
Baro Devel, 2:720
Barrès, Maurice, 2:761
Baršamin, 1:320
Bartolomé de Las Casas, 2:1166
Baruch, 2:686–88
Basat, 2:1099
Bashkir, 2:1092, 2:1099
Basmil, 2:1089
Basseri, 1:21–22
Bastet, 1:128
Batak, 2:931, 2:933, 2:934, 2:935, 2:940, 2:948, 2:949, 2:957
Batala, 2:938
Batara Guru, 2:935, 2:937, 2:940, 2:941, *2:941,* 2:953, 2:954
Batara Ismaya, 2:954
Batara Kala, 2:948
Batara Lattu, 2:941, 2:944
Batraz, 1:317–18, 2:1114
Batutsi, 1:78
Batwa, 1:78
Baubo, 1:128
Baudelaire, Charles, 2:754, 2:759, 2:761, 2:770, 2:779
Baudihillie, 1:287
Bauwa Danö, 2:937, 2:940
Bawin Jata Balawang Bulan, 2:937–38
Bayard, 2:689
Bayindir Khan, 2:1111
Bayol, cave of, Ardèche, 1:18
Bayusuta, 2:956
Beaune, Côte-d'Or, 1:253
Beauvais, Oise, 1:257
Beckford, William, 2:769
Bedoyo ketawang, 2:940
Bedwyr, 1:265
Been, 2:1116
Begawan Maenaka, 2:956
Begoe, 1:535
Beher, 1:192
Beiling, 2:1027–28
Bekhtek, 2:946
Bektash, Hadji, 2:1098
Bel (Bol), 1:204–5
Bel'astar, 1:204
Belatucadros, 1:249
Belen, Belenos, 1:267, 2:735
Bêlet-ilî, 1:174–76
Beli, 1:263
Belinus, 1:250
Bellerophon, 1:387, 1:401–3, *1:402,* 1:418, 1:432, 1:480; and Christianity, 2:656, 2:661, 2:663
Belleros, 1:401
Bellini, Giovanni, 2:700, 2:701
Beltekalli, 1:226
Bemba, 1:67
Bendigeidfran, 1:260–61
Benserade, Isaac de, 2:725
Benzaiten, 2:900, 2:905
Béranger, Pierre Jean de, 2:777
Berbiguier de Terre Neuve du Thym (Alexis-Vincent-Charles), 2:772
Beregyni, 1:297
Bergelmir, 1:282
Berlioz, Hector, 2:769
Bernard, Thalès, 2:754
Bernard de Chartres, 2:696
Bernardino de Sahagún, 2:1166
Bernard of Clairvaux, Saint, 2:715
Bernifal, cave of, Dordogne, 1:18
Bérolade, François, 2:703
Berossos, 1:153, 2:681
Béroul, 2:717
Berserkir, 1:287
Ber shishvlish, 1:314
Bersuire, Pierre, 2:698
Besorongola, 2:966
Bethel, 1:203
Betkil, 1:315
Bey Börek, 2:1100
Bhadrapāla, 2:904
Bhagavat, 2:928
Bhagīratha, 2:876
Bhairava, *2:815,* 2:821, *2:824,* 2:826, 2:839, 2:850, 2:855
Bhakti, 2:821, 2:839, 2:850, 2:855
Bharata, 2:834–36, 2:838

Bhima, Bima: in India, 2:830–31, 2:836–38, 2:860–61, 2:863; in insular Southeast Asia, 2:936, 2:956
Bhīsma, 2:829–30, 2:832–33, *2:833*, 2:860
Bhrgu, 2:858
Bhṛkutī, 2:1083
Bhū, 2:841
Bhujon, 2:926
Bhuvajan, 2:926
Bia, 1:371, 1:375, 1:377
Bībhatsu, 2:860
Bible, 1:184, 1:185, 2:650
Bidadari, 2:957, 2:959–60
Bifrost, 1:281
Bigan, 2:1024
Big Nambas, 2:1215
Bihogo, 1:78
Bimān Chan, 2:925
Bimbisāra, 2:1087
Bindus Neptunus, 1:250
Binego, 1:80–81
Bingyi, 2:1013
Binu, *1:43*, 1:51–52, *1:51*
Binu, Seru, 1:33–34
Binzuru, 2:904
Bishamon, 2:905
Bit-Adini, 1:200
Bith, 1:258
Bitinhi, 1:226
Bius, 2:948
Blackfoot, 2:1156, 2:1163, 2:1164
Blacksmith: among Austroasiatics and Austronesians, 2:990, 2:991; among the Baltic peoples, 1:305; in China, 2:1032–33; in Crete and Mycenae, 1:335; among the Georgians, 1:313, 1:315; among the Germano-Nordic peoples, 1:304; in Greece, 1:384–86, 1:414; among the insular Celts, 1:263; in literature, 2:785; in Northern Caucasus, 2:1114; among the Ossets, 1:318; in Rome, 1:646; among the Slavs, 1:298, 1:300, 1:302, 1:304; in Southeast Asia, 2:917; in southern Africa (Bantu), 1:71, 1:73; in Tibet, 2:1080; in Ugarit, 1:208; in West Africa, 1:36, 1:38, 1:39–42; among the Yoruba, 1:57
Blaí, 1:270
Blake, William, 2:755, 2:756–58, 2:768, 2:769, 2:786
Blaze de Bury, Henri, 2:770
Blodeuwedd, 1:263
Blok, Aleksandr Aleksandrovitch, 2:758
Blood, 2:1164
Blood, symbolism of, 2:1232; for Gypsies, 2:721; in Indochina, 2:985; in Papua New Guinea, 2:1229; in southern Africa (Bantu), 1:69, 1:72–73; for Turks and Mongols, 2:1112; in West Africa, 1:37, 1:41, 1:43
Blót, 1:289–90
Blumauer, Aloys, 2:726
Bobo, 1:49
Boccaccio, 1:133, 1:135, 2:699
Bóchra, 1:258
Bodhidharma, 2:905
Bodhisattva, 2:895
Bödreng, 2:985
Boeotus, 1:382
Boğazköy. *See* Hattuša
Bogomiles, 2:674
Böhme, Jakob, 2:754, 2:774
Bohort, 2:715
Bol. *See* Bel
Bolards, Côte d'Or, 1:268
Bolzani, Giovanni Piero Valeriano, 2:707
Bon, feast of, 2:1037, 2:1046, 2:1051, 2:1068–69
Bona Dea, 2:560
Bonpo, 2:1076, 2:1077, 2:1078, 2:1080, 2:1088
Bonus Eventus, 1:565
Boqiang, 2:1014
Boreas, 1:345, 1:510
Boriats, 1:317
Bormanicus, 1:249
Born, Ignaz von, 1:142
Boron, Robert de, 2:715
Börö N'adu, 2:940, 2:948
Bororo, 2:1195–96, 2:1200
Bosatsu, 2:1049
Bötau, 2:990
Botticelli, 2:700
Boubrōstis, 1:454
Bouilhet, Louis, 2:776
Boulanger, Nicolas, 2:753
Boulimia *(Boulimos)*, 1:454
Boun Teto Ti-K'i, 2:920
Bouphonia, 1:425, 1:427, 1:432
Bouray, Essonne, 1:253
Bourgeon, 2:1153
Bourges, Elémir, 1:761
Bouriège, Aude, 1:253
Bouvet, Joachim, 2:707–8
Bouzugion, 1:454
Bow, symbolism of, 2:1071
Bozo, 1:29, 1:30–31, 1:34–35, 1:37, 1:39, 1:41, 1:49, 1:52
Bracesco da Iorci Novi, Giovanni, 2:702
Brag-srin-mo, 2:1082
Braḥ Bisnukar, 2:917
Braḥ Chan, 2:924–26
Braḥ Dhar(a)ni, 2:926
Braḥ Isūr, 2:927
Braḥ Iśvara, 2:927
Braḥ Khê, 2:924
Braḥ Khet Mālā, 2:917
Brahmā, 2:811–13, 2:818–23, 2:824–26, 2:828–29, 2:834, 2:841, 2:852–55, 2:861, 2:867, 2:870–71, 2:874, 2:875–76, 2:896
Brahmaloka, 2:822, 2:825
Brahman, *brahman*, 2:800, 2:813–14, 2:818, 2:819–20, 2:822–23, 2:824–25, 2:840, 2:855
Brahmānī, 2:824
Brahmans, brahmanism: in India, 2:800–802, 2:807, 2:810, 2:813–14, 2:816–17, 2:819, 2:822–23, 2:827–29, 2:841, 2:842, 2:846, 2:848, 2:849, 2:851–52, 2:855, 2:873, 2:874; in Southeast Asia, 2:915
Brahmaśakti, 2:845
Braḥ Narāy, 2:928
Braḥ Thoṅ, 2:924
Bran, 1:261, 1:262
Branwen, 1:262
Brassempouy, Landes, 1:19
Bratasena, 2:956
Brauron, *Brauronia*, 1:432, 1:445, 1:474
Brazil, 1:53, 1:55, 1:56, 1:57, 1:58, 1:59, 1:60, 1:61
Bṛhannalā, 2:832
Bṛhaspati, 2:826, 2:835, 2:814
Briang, 2:985
Briareus, 1:372
Bricriu, 1:271
Bricta, Brixta, 1:254
Brieng, 2:985
Brigantia, 1:249
Brighid, 1:259
Britomarpis, 1:332, 1:335
Bromalia, 2:673
Brontes, 1:372
Browning, Robert, 2:769
Bruno, Giordano, 1:138
Brutus, in art and literature, 2:694
Bryaxis, 1:123
Bua'kasalle, 2:948
Budai heshang, 2:905–7
Buddhi, 2:819, 2:865, 2:897
Buddhism, 2:893–95; in China, 2:898–910; in insular Southeast Asia, 2:931, 2:936; in Japan, 2:898–910 passim, 2:1038–40, 2:1047–50, 2:1056–57, 2:1062–63; among Mongols, 2:1090; in Southeast Asia, 2:915, 2:923–24, 2:925, 2:929–31; in Tibet, 2:898–910 passim, 2:1076, 2:1082–85, 2:1087
Budsene, Denmark, *1:290*
Buga, 2:1119
Bugady Enintyn, 2:1123, 2:1125
Bugan, 2:940
Buganda, 1:77, 1:78, 1:79–80
Bugis, 2:934, 2:935, 2:941, 2:944, 2:949, 2:953
Buha, 1:78
Buhaya, 1:78
Bukuku, 1:78
Bula, 2:1220
Bulanda, 1:72
Bulgars, 2:1098, 2:1107, 2:1112, 2:1113
Bulopwe, 1:72
Bumè, 2:1215, 2:1219
Bummo, 1:32
Bunaq, 2:931, 2:934, 2:941–42
Bung, 2:983
Bunyoro, 1:76, 1:78–79, 1:81
Bunzi, 1:65, 1:71
Bupfumu, 1:72
Buqu Khan, 2:1100, 2:1111
Burak, 2:1099
Burisrawa, 2:957
Burma. *See* Southeast Asia
Burqan Qaldun, 2:1103, 2:1106
Burundi, 1:78, 1:80
Buryat, 2:1090, 2:1095, 2:1100, 2:1102, 2:1109, 2:1112, 2:1113, 2:1119, 2:1128
Bush, 2:982–83
Bush, grandmother, 2:982
Bushi, 1:78
Busiris, 1:443
Busoga, 1:78
Bu-ston, 2:1085, 2:1087
But, 2:989
But Tengri, 2:1103
Butukala, 2:952
Butyakengo, 2:720
Buzhou, Mount, 2:1029
Bwae Bealo, 2:1215
Byblos, Phoenicia, 1:182, 1:193–95, 1:436, *1:194*, *1:195*
Byin-te, 2:1080
Byron, George Gordon Noël, Lord, 2:755, 2:756, 2:767–68, 2:769, 2:770, 2:777

C

Cabal, 1:265
Cabala, 2:704–6, 2:712
Caban, 2:1180
Cabirī, 1:385–86
Cacu, 1:531
Cacus, 1:519, 1:531, 1:618; in art and literature, 2:694
Cadmus, 1:378, 1:390, 1:404–5, 1:459–60, 1:499
Caeculus, 1:645
Caeneus (Caenis), 1:471–72
Caere, Italy, 1:525, 1:590
Caesar, Julius, 1:242, 1:243, 1:245, 1:246, 1:259, 1:267, 1:276, 1:278, 1:282, 1:565, 1:627
Čaghan ebügen, 2:907
Cahen, Isidore, 2:768–69
Cahusac, Louis de, 1:142
Cai, 1:266
Caile Vipinas, 1:519
Caílte, 1:273
Cain: for the Perates, 2:682; in literature, 2:768
Cakchiquels, 2:1183
Calaïs, 1:474
Calchas, 1:446, 1:640
Calendar: in China, 2:1021–22; in Christianity, 2:673; among continental Celts, 1:246, 1:255–56; in Crete and Mycenae, 1:332; among Etruscans, 1:529; in Japan, 2:1067; in Mesoamerica, 2:1176–77, 2:1179, 2:1183, 2:1189; in Rome, 1:573, 1:582–83, 1:602; among Turks and Mongols, 2:1097, 2:1098, in West Africa (Mande), 1:49–50
Calligeneia, 1:454
Callimachus, 1:385, 1:438, 1:439–40, 1:445, 1:446, 1:454, 1:508

Calliope, 1:492
Callisto, 1:393, 1:432
Calu, 1:520, 1:526
Calydon, Greece, 1:429, 1:447
Calypso, 1:410, 2:678
Cambodia. *See* Southeast Asia
Campa, 2:1198
Camulos, 1:249
Canaanites, 1:184
Cancong, 2:1027
Candamius, 1:249
Candra Kirana, 2:943
Candramas, 2:807, 2:814
Cannibalism. *See* Anthropophagy
Canopus, 1:122; in art and literature, 1:136
Cantari, Vincenzo, 1:138
Capac Raymi, 2:1205
Capua, Italy, 1:523, 1:526
Caradawg, 1:262, 1:264
Caraja, 2:1200
Cardinal points, symbolism of: in China, 2:1013–14; in India, 2:807, 2:825; in Korea, 2:1074; in Madagascar, 2:962, 2:969, 2:973; in Mesoamerica, 2:1178–79, 2:1185; in North America, 2:1161; in West Africa (Mande), 1:31, 1:43
Cargo cults, 2:1212, 2:1223–24
Caria, 1:229
Carib, 2:1196, 2:1198
Caristia, 1:604
Carlyle, Thomas, 2:755, 2:777
Carmen Arvale, 1:603–4
Carmentalia, 1:600
Carmina Marciana, 1:588
Carna, 1:577–78
Carneades, 1:597
Carneus, 1:126
Carthage, 1:182, 1:197–99
Caryatids, 1:475
Cassandra, 1:412
Castor, *1:561;* in art and literature, 2:694; among continental Celts, 1:255; in Rome, 1:463, 1:562–62, 1:572–73, 1:574
Castrioti, Georges (Gjergi), called Scanderbeg, 1:308
Caswallawn, 1:262
Catha, 1:534
Cathars, Cathar heresy, 2:690, 2:692
Cathbad, 1:270–71
Cato the Elder, 1:550, 1:567, 1:570, 1:589, 1:594, 1:597–98, 1:603, 1:604, 1:612, 1:622, 1:625, 1:636
Cato Uticensis, 1:597
Caucasus, Northern, 2:1113–16, *2:1115*
Ca(u)tha, 1:520
Cavafy, Constantine, 2:759, 2:787–88
Cavern, grotto, symbolism of: in China, 2:1033–34; in Crete and Mycenae, 1:335-36; in Greece, 1:506; in Japan, 2:1046; in the Maghreb, 1:87; in Mesoamerica, 2:1184–85; in Plato, 1:355, 1:358, 2:1231; prehistoric, 1:12–20; in pre-Islamic Iran, 2:892
Caxton, William, 2:715, 2:718
Caylus, 1:140
Cazotte, Jacques, 2:772
Cecrops, 1:341, 1:343, *1:344,* 1:381, 1:395, 1:410
Cedalion, 1:385, 1:500
Céitinn (Keating), 1:274
Ceja, 2:919
Cel, 1:534
Celbes of Carysta, 2:680
Celi, 1:526
Celmis, 1:384
Celsus, 2:656, 2:658, 2:660–61, 2:669, 2:680
Celtic art, 1:251–53
Celts, continental, 1:242–57, *1:252, 1:253, 1:254,* 1:267, 1:268–70, 1:272–73, 1:274–80, 1:516
Celts, Iberian, 1:249
Celts, insular, 1:250, 1:257–67, 1:270–71, 1:273–74; in literature, 2:783–87
Censorinus, 1:535, 1:573, 1:617
Centaurs, 1:451–52, *1:451,* 1:472, 1:491
Centzon Totochtin, 2:1185
Cephalus (Kephalos), 1:420–21
Cerberus, 1:406, 1:480, 1:501, 1:532, 1:633
Cercyon, 1:342, 1:382
Ceres, 1:521–22, 1:559, 1:561–62, 1:563, 1:564, 1:565, 1:567, 1:609, 1:611–13, *1:612,* 1:633; in art and literature, 2:694, 2:696
Cerfo, 1:522, 1:538–39
Cerialia, 1:559, 1:578, 1:583, 1:612
Cernunnos, 1:251–52, 1:257, 1:268–70, *1:269*
Cerularius, Michel, 2:673
Cesair, 1:257–58
Cet de Connacht, 1:271
Ceto, 1:380, 1:381, 1:473
Ce xochitl, 2:1185
Chacs, 2:1183
Chadrapha, 1:204
Chagar Bazar, Mesopotamia, 1:227
Chalcheia, 1:386
Chalchihuitlicue, 2:1181, 2:1183
Cham, 2:977, 2:979–80, 2:990, 2:993
Chamalières, Puy-de-Dôme, 1:246
Chamisso de Boncourt, Adalbert von, 2:766
Champa, 2:990
Chan, 2:925
Chancelade, Dordogne, 1:20
Chang Sha, China, 2:1007
Changxi (Changyi), 2:1011
Chaos: in China, 2:1008–9; in Greece, 1:369–71, 1:380, 1:382, 1:405, 1:464–65, 1:469
Charites, 1:396, 1:453
Charon, 1:532, 2:674
Charshamba Karisi, 2:1096
Charun, 1:525, 1:532
Chateaubriand, François René, 2:753–54, 2:768, 2:776, 2:777
Chaucer, Geoffrey, 2:784
Chechens, 1:311
Chénier, André, 2:730, 2:773
Chen-Wu, 2:995
Cheremis, 2:1134–35, 2:1138, *2:1138*
Cherkess, 1:315, 1:317–18, 2:1113–16
Chernichovsky, Saul, 2:762
Cheyenne, 2:1156, 2:1163
Chiang, 2:1084
Chichini, 2:1182
Chicomecoatl, 2:1185
Chidkür, 2:1096
Chigil, 2:1103
Chikō, 2:1048
Chimbu, 2:1226, 2:1229
Chimera, 1:530
China, 2:1007–34; Buddhism in, 2:893–95
Chinju-gami, 2:1064
Chinkonsai, 2:1043
Chinnamastā, 2:856
Chiron, 1:442, 1:444, 1:449, 1:451–52; in art and literature, 2:694
Chisangzi, 2:1036
Chistāt, 2:887
Chiyou, 2:1020–21, 2:1029, 2:1032
Cholban, 2:1106
Chompré, Pierre, 2:723
Chongli, 2:1009
Chors, 1:300
Chorzar, 2:681
Chos, 2:1076
Chou Ta-kuan, 2:924
Chrétien de Troyes, 1:240, 1:265–66, 1:267, 2:715
Christ. *See* Jesus
Christianity: analogies with paganism, 2:655–65; in Armenia, 1:319; Euhemerism, 2:666–71; among Finno-Ugrians, 2:1136–37; in France, 2:734–35; in Georgia, 1:308; among Germano-Nordic peoples, 1:282; in Greek church, 2:671–75; among Gypsies, 2:719; in insular Southeast Asia, 2:932, 2:933, 2:936; in medieval West, 2:688–92; in Mesoamerica, 2:1166, 2:1173, 2:1181–82; in Oceania, 2:1209, 2:1219; in Rome, 1:125, 1:556–57, 1:600–601, 1:619; in South America, 2:1205; in southern Africa (Bantu), 1:64; survival of myths in, 2:649–55, 2:692–701; among Yoruba, 1:53–61 passim
Christmas, rites of, 2:736, *2:747,* 2:749–52
Christopher, Saint, 2:656
Chrysaor, 1:382, 1:473
Chryse, 1:414
Chrysippus, 1:403, 1:404, 1:508, 1:511
Chthōn, 1:406
Chtonios, 1:404
Chu Dông-tu, 2:1001
Chukchee, 2:1128
Chul metik, 2:1182
Cian, 1:257
Ciau, 2:1217, 2:1220–21
Cicero, 1:132, 1:455, 1:466, 1:471, 1:472, 1:533, 1:549, 1:550, 1:552, 1:555, 1:570, 1:575, 1:582, 1:584–96 passim, 1:598–60, 1:605, 1:606, 1:612, 1:613–15, *1:614,* 1:616, 1:619, 1:621, 1:623, 1:628, 1:635, 1:636, 1:637, 1:638, 1:642, 1:646, 2:666, 2:668, 2:670, 2:697, 2:710
Cilen(s), 1:520
Cilydd, 1:264
Cincalco, 2:1184
Cinteotl, 2:1185
Cinyras, 1:435
Circe, 1:443, 1:444, 1:546; in art and literature, 2:700
Circumcision, 1:37–39, 1:41, 1:67, 1:69, 2:936
Claudel, Paul, 2:762–63
Cleanthes, 2:678
Clementia Augusta, 2:609
Clement of Alexandria, 1:133, 1:439, 2:656–61, 2:663–64, 2:667–68, 2:670–71, 2:672, 2:683, 2:771, 2:1231
Clio, 1:492
Clito, 1:355
Clusium, Italy, 1:524–25
Clymene, 1:371, 1:375
Clytemnestra, 1:404, 1:408, 1:421, 1:446
Cnossos, Crete, *1:331,* 1:332, 1:333, 1:336, *1:336,* 1:337, 1:338–39, *1:338*
Coatlicue, *2:1185*
Cocalus, 1:388
Cocijo, 2:1183
Cockaigne, 2:689
Cocytus, 1:414
Coeus, 1:371, 1:372, 1:375, 1:465
Coleridge, Samuel Taylor, 2:755, 2:756, 2:766
Coligny (Ain), 1:246, 1:256
Columella, 2:630
Comaitho, 1:446
Comana of Cappadocia, 1:227–28
Comanche, 2:1163
Cumans, 2:1089, 2:1098, 2:1112
Combarelles, cave of, 1:15, 1:18
Compitalia, 2:622
Comte, Auguste, 2:752
Conall Cernach, 1:271
Conchobar, 1:270–71
Concordia, 1:599
Confucius, 1:1033, 2:1035
Conisalus, 2:629
Conlaí, 1:270
Connacht(a) (Connaught), Ireland, 1:240, 1:258–59, 1:271, 1:274
Conopa, 2:1202
Consentes, 1:520

Constantine Porphyrogenetus, 1:280
Consualia, 1:559, 1:583
Consus, 1:559–60, 1:635
Conti, Natale, 1:136
Coras, 2:1169, 2:1180,2:1186
Coricancha, Andes, 2:1203, 2:1204
Cormac mac Airt, King, 1:274
Corn. *See* Grain
Cornelius Balbus, Lucius, 2:615
Corn silk, 2:1157
Cornutus, 2:695
Coronis, of Thessaly, 1:440, 1:449
Corybantes, 1:335
Cosmas of Prague, 1:296
Cosmogony, 1:4; of Austroasiatics and Austronesians, 2:981–85; of the Chinese, 2:1008–10, 2:1010–11, 2:1027; of the Finno-Ugrians, 2:1138–40; of the Georgians, 1:308–9; of the Germano-Nordic peoples, 1:285–86; of the Greeks, 1:366–75, 1:379–84; of India, 2:806–7, 2:817–24; of insular Southeast Asia, 2:932–33; of the Inuit, 2:1145–46; of the Maghreb, 1:87–88; of the Mesopotamians, 1:155–62; of the Nilotic peoples, 1:82; of Oceania, 2:1218–19; of the Pharaohnic Egyptians, 1:91–95; of Southeast Asia, 2:929–31; of southern Africans (Bantu), 1:62–64, 1:76–77; of the Tibetans, 2:1078, 2:1079–82; of the Turks and Mongols, 2:1090, 2:1095–96; in Ugarit, 1:213–15; of the Vietnamese, 2:996–1001; of western Africa (Mande), 1:37–39, 1:39–41
Cottus, 1:372
Cougnac (Lot), 1:18
Court de Gébelin, 1:773–84, 2:753–54
Cousin, Victor, 2:754
Coventina, 1:249
Coyolxauhqui, *2:1170*, 2:1181
Coyote, 2:1161
Creation, creator, 1:4, 1:45; of China, 2:1008–10, 2:1016, 2:1025; of Christianity, 2:650, 2:659–60; of Egypt, 1:91–95, 1:95–100; among the Finno-Ugrians, 2:1138–40; of Georgia, 1:308; of Germano-Nordic peoples, 1:281, 1:285–86; of Greece, 1:390–95; among Gypsies, 2:720–21; of India, 2:812–13, 2:817–23; of Indochina, 2:983; of insular Southeast Asia, 2:937–40; of Madagascar, 2:967; of the Maghreb, 1:85, 1:87–88; of Mesoamerica, 2:1184, 2:1185; of Mesopotamia, 1:148–52, 1:174–76; among nomads, 1:21; of North America, 2:1153, 2:1156–57, 2:1158, 2:1160–62; of Oceania, 2:1218–19; of Papua New Guinea, 2:1224–27; of pre-Islamic Iran, 2:888–89; of Siberia, 2:1105; of Southeast Asia, 2:916–18; of southern Africa (Bantu), 1:78–81; of Tibet, 2:1079–82; among Turks and Mongols, 2:1095–96; of Ugarit, 1:225; of Vietnam, 2:996–1001; 1:225; of West Africa (Mande), 1:30–32, 1:33–34, 1:36–37, 1:37–39, 1:39–41, 1:42–44; of Western Semites, 1:188; among Yoruba, 1:54–57. *See also* Origin
Cree, 2:1157–58, *2:1157*, 2:1163
Creek, 2:1161
Crenides, 1:505
Creon, 1:404, 1:405
Crete, 1:330–40
Cretheus, 1:442
Creusa, 1:410, 1:443
Critias, 1:340
Critolaus, 1:597
Crius, 1:371, 1:375, 1:465
Crommyon, 1:342
Cronus. *See* Kronos
Crow, 2:1156, 2:1163
Cuba, 1:53, 1:55, 1:56, 1:60, 1:61
Cubeo, 2:1200
Cú Chulainn, 1:266, 1:270–71; in literature, 2:783
Cuḍalai MāḍaN, 2:845–46, *2:846*
Culann, 1:270
Culhwch, 1:264, 1:265
Culsu, 1:526, 2:523, 2:532, 2:534
Cultural heroes, 1:332; Albanian, 1:307–8; of ancient Switzerland, 2:733–34; Austroasiatic and Austronesian, 2:988–89, 2:990; Chinese, 2:1023, 2:1027–28; in Greece, 1:341–42, 1:393–95, 1:415–18, 1:451–52, 1:478–84, 1:485; of the insular Celts, 1:270–71; of insular Southeast Asia, 2:934–35, 2:936, 2:941–47, 2:1077; Korean, 2:1070–71; in Madagascar, 2:963–65; Mesopotamian, 1:154; of the nomads, 1:21; North American, 2:1153–56, 2:1160–61; in Oceania, 2:1215, 2:1216; of the Ossets, 1:317; in pre-Roman Italy, 1:541, 1:546; Siberian, 2:1124; southern African, 1:62–63, 1:64, 1:73, 1:79–81; South American, 2:1194, 2:1200; of the Turks and Mongols, 2:1111; Vietnamese, 2:1001–3
Culture, civilization, 1:5; of China, 2:1027; of Greece, 1:343, 1:395–403, 1:445–49, 1:451–52, 1:452–55, 1:460; of Mesopotamia, 1:159–60; of Siberia, 2:1120; of South America, 2:1194
Čumong, 2:1070–74
Cuôi, 2:997, 2:999
Cuong Bao, 2:1000
Cupra, 1:522, 1:538
Curetes, 1:335, 1:381, 2:681
Cusan. *See* Culsu
Cushites, 1:115–20
Custennin, 1:264, 1:266
Cybele, 1:216–17, 1:251, 1:554, 1:563, 1:571, 2:607; continental Celts, 1:243; in literature, 2:779, 2:785; Naassenes, 2:676
Cyclopes, 1:335, 1:371, 1:377, 1:495–96, 2:646
Cycnus, 1:414
Cynosura, 1:335
Cyprus, 1:197
Cyrene, 1:400–401
Cyriacus of Ancona, 2:699
Cyril of Alexandria, 1:436, 2:663
Cytherea, 1:465
Cytissorus, 1:443
Czechs, 1:300
Czerneboch, 1:301

D

Dactyls, 1:335, 1:384, 1:453
Dada (Banyani), 1:58
Daedalus, 1:335, 1:337, 1:388–90, 1:546; in art and literature, 2:694, 2:785
Daeli, 2:940
Daemons. *See* Demons
Daenā, 2:888, 2:891
Dagan, 1:190, 1:206, 1:215
Dagara, 1:34
Daghdha, 1:259
Dagit, 1:226
Daikoku, *2:897*, 2:898, 2:904, 2:905, 2:907
Daimons. *See* Demons
Dainichi Nyorai, 2:1039, 2:1049, 2:1050, 2:1057
Daji, 2:1024
Dajjāl, 1:87
Dak, 1:83
Daki(t), 1:226
Dakota, 2:1163
Dakṣa, 2:816, 2:817, 2:835, 2:869
Dalang, 2:954
Dali, 1:314, 1:315
Damar Wulan, 2:960
Damascius, 1:465, 1:185, 1:187, 1:189, 1:360, 2:886
Damascus, Kingdom of, 1:200
Dambhodbhava, 2:853
Damgalnunna, 1:146, 1:158
Damia, 1:560
Damkina, 1:146, 1:158, 1:161, 1:221, 1:224, 1:226
Damnameneus, 1:384
Damophiles, 1:562
Dampu Awang, 2:945
Danaë, 1:458, 1:509; in Christian works, 2:661, 2:667
Danaids, 1:400–403, 1:490
Danajaya, 2:957
Danann, 1:259–60, 1:263
Danaus, 1:387, 1:424, 1:490
Dangginy, 2:1215
D'Annunzio, Gabriele, 2:758, 2:760
Dante, 1:644, 2:656, 2:665, 2:696
Da Nuo, 2:1031
Danzhu, 2:1030
Daoan, 2:904
Daoism, 2:1028–31, 2:1033, 2:1034–37
Daojun, 2:1036
Daoxuan, 2:899–900
Daphne, 1:335, *2:730;* in literature, 2:696
Da Ponte, Lorenzo, 2:770
Dapuritoyo Potiniya, 1:332
Dara Cempaka Tempurong Alang, 2:943
Darafify (Darafely), 2:973
Darío, Rubén, 2:958, 2:962
Darkness: for Gnostics, 2:683; in Greece, 1:369–70, 1:413; in pre-Islamic Iran, 2:885–86; in Tibet, 2:1081, 2:1082
Daru Dakidu, 1:226
Daruma, 2:905
Darzamat, 1:306
Daśaratha, 2:827, 2:834, 2:835, 2:856, 2:957
Dasheng, 2:902
Dassoucy, 2:726
Dattaratha, 2:918
Dattātreya, 2:824
Datu Laukku, 2:939
Datu nPayompo Yangi Sambira-nya, 2:943
Datu nTo Kasoyao, 2:943
Datu nTo Mato Eo, 2:943
Datu nTo Wawo Yangi, 2:943
Daunians, 1:540
Daunus, 1:540
David, 2:656
Davit, 1:321
Dayang Raca, 2:940
Dayang Sumbi, 2:960
Daye, 2:1016
Dayichin tengri, 2:1092
Daylight (Hēmerē), 1:369
Dažbog, 1:300–301
Ddau, 2:990
Ddöi, 2:983–84
Dea Dia, 1:555, 1:573, 1:603–5
Death: for Aramaeans, 1:202–3; for Baltic peoples, 1:305; in China, 2:1012, 2:1033–34; in Egypt, 1:97–99, 1:111–15; for Germano-Nordic peoples, 1:290, 1:291; in Greece, 1:405–12, 1:423, 1:453, 1:455, 1:491; for Gypsies, 2:720–21; for Indo-Europeans, 1:236–37; in insular Southeast Asia, 2:952; for Inuit, 2:1145; in Japan, 2:1041–42, 2:1043, 1:1045–47, 2:1051, 2:1052, 2:1054; in Madagascar, 2:967, 2:969–70; in the Maghreb, 1:85, 1:87; in Mesoamerica, 2:1190–91; in Mesopotamia, 1:180–81;

Death (*continued*)
for Nilotic peoples, 1:84; in Oceania, 2:1214–15; in Papua New Guinea, 2:1225–26, 2:1229; in pre-Islamic Iran, 2:887–88; in pre-Roman Italy, 1:525–26; in Rome, 1:623–24; in Siberia, 2:1116–19; in South America, 2:1194–96; in southern Africa (Bantu), 1:67, 1:68–69; in Tibet, 2:1088; for Turks and Mongols, 2:1090; in Ugarit, 1:210–12; in Vietnam, 2:998–99; in West Africa (Mande), 1:37, 1:45–49. *See also* Ancestors, cult of; Funerary rites; Underworld
Débata Asi-Asi, 2:937
Deb Pranam, 2:926
De Brosse, Charles, 1:141
Decima, Italy, 1:525; Castel di, 1:545
Deianira, 1:482–83, *2:693;* in art and literature, 2:694
Deichtine, 1:270, 1:271
Deimos, 1:414
Deioneus, 1:490
Deirdre, 1:271; in literature, 2:783
Deir el Bahari, 1:109
Deiva, Deïvaï, 1:305
Dejberg, Denmark, 1:281
Dekanawida, 2:1160
Del, 2:719
Delaware Indians, 2:1153
Del Bene (Bartolomeo and Alphonse), 2:712
Della Riviera, Cesare, 2:702, 2:703, 2:709, 2:705
Delphyne, 1:378
Demeter, 1:376, 1:380–81, 1:395–97, 1:403, 1:406, 1:409–11, 1:431, 1:452–56, *1:453, 1:455,* 1:508, 1:612–13; in literature, 2:787–90. *See also* Perates; Phoenicians and Punics
Demetra, Saint, 2:674
Demetrius Chomatianus, 2:673
Demodocus, 1:492, 1:494–95
Demogorgon, in literature, 2:708, 2:768
Demons, daemons, daimons, demonology: Albanian, 1:307–8; in art and literature, 2:771–72; Baltic, 1:305–6; Chinese, 2:1028–31; of Christianity, 2:661, 2:672, 2:674; Etruscan, 1:525–26, 1:530–32; Georgian, 1:308–9, 1:313–14; Germano-Nordic, 1:294–95; of Gnostics, 2:677, 2:685–86, 2:687–88; Gypsy, 2:719–22; of India, 2:826–27, 2:829, 2:842–45, 2:867–68; insular Southeast Asian, 2:944; Japanese, 2:1037, 2:1047–48, 2:1051, 2:1059–61; of Madagascar, 2:964–65; of the Maghreb, 1:85, 1:87; Mesopotamian, 1:159–60, 1:162–65; pre-Islamic Iranian, 2:884–85; Slavic, 1:298; Southeast Asian, 2:918; Tibetan, 2:1080–82, 2:1083–84, 2:1087; of the Turks and Mongols, 2:1096; Vietnamese, 2:1002–3
Demophon, 1:454, 1:455
Demosthenes, 1:343
Demoustier, C. A., 2:725
Dendera, Egypt, 1:108–9
Dengyō Daishi, 2:1057
Denicales, 1:582
De Quincey, Thomas, 2:755
Dercetius, 1:249
Despoina, 1:381, 1:411, 1:412
Deucalion, 1:391, 1:394–95, 1:447; in Christianity, 2:656; in literature, 2:706
Deva, 2:826–27, 2:884–85, 2:927
Devakī, 2:861–62
Devasenā, 2:867–69
Devatā, 2:926–27
Devel, 2:719
De Vere, Aubrey Thomas, 2:776
Devī, 2:861, 2:869–72
Devil, 2:1210
Devotio, 1:550, 1:552, 1:559, 1:560, 1:589
Dewa Anta, 2:953
Dewa Ruci, 2:956
Dewa Wenang, 2:953
Dewi Anjani, 2:957
Dewi Arimbi, 2:956
Dewi Danuh, 2:952
Dewi Drupadi, 2:955
Dewi Nagagini, 2:956
Dewi Nawang Sasih, 2:953
Dewi Sri, 2:952–53
Dewi Srikandi, 2:957
Dewi Srimendang, 2:957
Dewi Sumbadra, 2:957
Dewi Ulupi, 2:957
Dharanī, 2:926
Dharma, Dharmarājā, 2:807, 2:816, 2:826, 2:829–33, 2:840, 2:850–52, 2:853, 2:855, 2:866, 2:873, 2:875
Dharmakāya, 2:895
Dharmatala, 2:905
Dhṛṣṭadyumna, 2:830, 2:832
Dhṛtarāṣṭra, 2:829–33, 2:860
Dhu-Ghabat, 1:192
Dhu-Shara (Dusares), 1:192–93
Di, 2:1018–20
Diagoras of Melos, 2:667
Diana, 1:521, 1:544, 1:554, *1:560,* 1:561, 1:564, 1:565, 1:608, 1:615–16
Dian Cécht, 1:257, 1:259
Diarmaid, 1:274
Dicte, 1:336
Dictynna, 1:332, 1:336, 1:337
Dido, 1:641
Dier, 2:982
Digenis Acritas, 2:787, 2:788
Dike, 1:408
Dīkṣā, 2:813, 2:832
Di Ku, 2:1010, 2:1016, 2:1021, 2:1026
Dinglinger, Melchior, 1:141
Dinka, 1:81–84
Dio Cassius, 1:242, 1:585, 1:605, 1:625
Diö-Diung-Yung-Hmeng, 2:983
Diodorus of Sicily, 1:134, 1:135, 1:139, 1:185, 1:245, 1:246, 1:255, 1:338, 1:339, 1:410, 1:412, 1:436, 1:437, 1:444, 1:461, 1:479, 1:480, 1:481, 1:483, 1:484, 1:546, 1:548, 1:618, 1:629, 2:666
Diodotus, 1:613
Diogenes, 1:597
Diogenes Laertius, 1:472
Diola, 1:29
Diomedes, 1:417–18, 1:480, 1:540, 1:541, 1:546, 1:547
Dione, 1:380, 1:466, 1:467, 1:469
Dionysia, 1:461
Dionys(i)us, Saint, 2:674
Dionysius of Halicarnassus, 1:502, 1:526, 1:531, 1:542, 1:546, 1:547, 1:562, 1:565, 1:603, 1:612, 1:618, 1:624, 1:629, 1:635
Dionysus, 1:329, 1:332, 1:333, 1:359, 1:395, 1:421, 1:427, 1:432–33, 1:453, 1:456–63, *1:457, 1:458, 1:459, 1:460, 1:462, 1:463,* 1:465–66, 1:471, 1:491, 1:494, 1:505, 1:629; and Christianity, 2:661, 2:663, 2:673–74; in literature, 2:756, 2:781–82, 2:788
Dioscuri, 1:463–64, *1:464,* 1:476–77, *1:550,* 1:573, 1:574; among continental Celts, 1:255; and Christianity, 2:663, 2:672; in literature, 2:766
Diotima, 1:467, 1:469, 1:470
(D)iove, (D)iuve, 1:521, 1:522, 1:538
Dipaṃkara, 2:906
Dipisiyoi, 1:332
Disciplina Etrusca, 1:528–29, 1:533–36
Dísir, 1:285
Dis Pater, 1:276, 1:278, 1:608
Diva Angerona, 1:552
Divination: in the Andes, 2:1205; among Austroasiatics and Austronesians, 2:993; Baltic, 1:305–6; among continental Celts, 1:242, 1:246; Etruscan, 1:528–29, 1:532–35; Germano-Nordic, 1:304; in Greece, 1:450, 1:471; among Gypsies, 1:721; Japanese, 2:1040, 2:1055, 2:1057–58, 2:1067–68; Mesoamerican, 2:1178, 2:1186–87; in pre-Roman Italy, 1:532–33, 1:539; Roman, 1:584–94, 1:605–6; Slavic, 1:299, 1:304; in southern Africa (Bantu), 1:62, 1:78–79; among Turks and Mongols, 2:1103–4, 2:1109; Ugarit, 1:215; Yoruban, 1:61. *See also* Augurs and augury; Magic
Divinization of sovereigns, 2:667–68; in Japan, 2:1040; in Mesoamerica, 2:1172; in Rome, 1:554–56, 1:559, 1:609–11; among Turks and Mongols, 2:1111
Diviriks, 1:305
Divs, 2:1103
Diwata, 2:938
Diwya, 1:332
Di Xun, 2:1010–11, 2:1021
D'ja Menjuu, 2:1119–20
dMu, 2:1081, 2:1086–87
Dogon, 1:25–27, *1:26,* 1:29–30, 1:30–45, *1:38, 1:46,* 1:49–52
Dolon, 1:417, 1:418–19, *1:418*
Dolugen Ebügen, 2:1106
Domnall the Bellicose, 1:270
Domovoï, 1:298
Dōn, 1:262–63, 1:265
Donar. *See* Thor
Donbyttyr, 1:317
Dong-gsum mi-la sngon-mo, 2:1081
Dong Huang Taiyi, 2:1018
Dongwanggong, 2:1013, 2:1017
Don Juan, in literature, 2:755, 2:770–71
Donn, 1:260
Doonte, 2:1122
Dopota, 1:332
Dora, 2:944
Dorion, 1:333
Doris, 1:375, 1:380
Dōsojin, 2:1044
Dostoyevski, Fiodor Mikhailovitch, 2:766
Double: in Egypt, 1:96–97; in literature, 2:766–67; in Mesoamerica, 2:1188–89
Draupadī, 2:830–33, 2:835–36, 2:869
Driang, 2:985
Dri-dmu tri-btsan, 2:1086
Dri-gum btsan-po (Gri-gum btsan-po), 2:1088
Drit, 2:982–83, 2:986–87, 2:988–89, 2:990
Droṇa, 2:830, 2:831, 2:832, 2:860, 2:868
Druids, 1:242, 1:246, 1:250
Druj, 2:885, 2:887–88, 2:891, 2:893
Drupada, 2:830–31
Drvāspā, 2:891
Dryads, 1:505
Du Guangting, 2:1017–18
Duḥśāgana, 2:831
Dui Daulo, 2:1215
Dumas, Alexandre, 2:767, 2:770
Dumrul, 2:1111
Dumuzi, 1:147
Dung-Dai, 2:983
Dungu, 1:79
Dunhuang, China, 2:899, 2:901, 2:903, 2:908, 2:1075, 2:1082
Dunne Enin, 2:1122–23
Dupuis, Charles-François, 2:753
Dura-Europos, Syria, 1:204
Durgā, *2:870,* 2:871, *2:871, 2:872, 2:935;* in insular Southeast Asia, 2:952, 2:957

Durna, 2:956
Duryodhana, 2:829–33, 2:837, 2:860, 2:863
Dusares. *See* Dhu-Shara
Dussieux, Louis, 2:755
Duval, Robert, 2:702
Duyu, 2:1027
Dvāpara, 2:829, 2:850, 2:861
Dvāpara Yuga, 2:850
Dvorniki, 1:298
Dyaus, 2:829
Dyfed, 1:241, 1:260–64, 1:265
Dylan, 1:263
Dyongu Seru, 1:33–34, 1:47–48
Dyus kunhu, 2:1182
Dzhuar, 1:311
Džuli, 2:1118
Dzwars, 1:316

E

Ea, 1:145–54, 1:157–59, 1:160–61, 1:163, 1:165, 1:172–80, 1:221, 1:224, 1:225–26, 1:228
Earth, spirits of: in China, 2:1014, 2:1023; in Southeast Asia, 2:918–24
Earth, symbolism and divinities of: in Albania, 1:307; in the Andes, 2:1201, 2:1202; in art and literature, 2:694, 2:699, 2:715, 2:771–72, 2:780–81, 2:784–86; in China, 2:1008–9, 2:1010, 2:1019–20; in Egypt, 1:103, 1:129; for Finno-Ugrians, 2:1137–38, 2:1139; for Germano-Nordic peoples, 1:282, 1:285, 1:287–88; for Gnostics, 2:687–88; in Greece, 1:369, 1:371–73, 1:380–81, 1:390, 1:393–95, 1:399, 1:405–6, 1:450, 1:453–55, 1:464–65, 1:468, 1:494; for Hurrites, 1:226; in India, 2:807, 2:873–75; in insular Southeast Asia, 2:933–35, 2:938, 2:952; for Inuit, 2:1147; in Madagascar, 2:962–68; in Mesoamerica, 2:1179, 2:1180, 2:1184–87; in Mesopotamia, 1:155–58, 1:173; in North America, 2:1161–62; in Rome, 1:613; in Southeast Asia, 2:926; in southern Africa (Bantu), 1:64–65, 1:68–69, 1:71–72; for the Tupi-Guarani, 2:1208; for Turks and Mongols, 2:1092, 2:1095–96, 2:1112; in Vietnam, 2:996–97, 2:1002; in West Africa (Mande), 1:37, 1:42–43
Ea-šarri, 1:225
Ebbon, 1:302
Ebbou, 1:14
Ébher, 1:260
Ebisu, 2:905
Echidna, 1:382, 1:442, 1:490
Echion, 1:404
Echo, 1:492, *1:493*, 1:494, 1:506
Eckhart, Meister, 2:754
Edem, 2:687–88
Eden, 2:682, 2:683–85
Edern, 1:266
Edfu, Egypt, 1:91, *1:92*, 1:93, *1:101*, 1:107, 1:108, 1:109, *1:110*
Edshu, 1:37
Efrog, 1:266
Egidio da Viterbo, 2:704–5, 2:707, 2:710
Egypt, 1:91–94, *1:94*, 1:95–99, 1:100–105, 1:106–10, 1:111–15, 1:121–27; in literature, 1:131–42. *See also* Meroe
Ehecatl, 2:1184
Ehecatonatiuh, 2:1174
Ehecatotontin, 2:1184
Eichendorff, Joseph von, 2:776
Eichō Sōzu, 2:1050
Eiduia, Idyia, 1:380, 1:442
Eileithyia, 1:337
Eileithyiae, 1:511, 1:608
Eilhart von Oberg, 2:717
Eita, 1:520
Ejen, 2:1108, 2:1109
Ekseri, 2:1119
El (Il), 1:189, 1:192, 1:200, 1:209, *1:210*, 1:211–15, 1:226
Ela gurum, 2:1118
Elam, 1:147
El Amarna, Egypt, 1:225
Elatha, 1:257
El Castillo, Spain, 1:16, *1:17*, 1:18
Elema, 2:1226
Elephantine (island), Egypt, 1:101, 1:109, 1:203
Eleusis, 1:453, 1:455
Eleuthiya, 1:332
Eligius, Saint, 1:254, 2:735
Eliot, T. S., 2:715, 2:780, 2:783–85
Elkesai, Elchasaïsm, 2:653
Elkin (Yelkin), 2:1096
Ellamrak, 2:1118
Ellien, Claudius, 2:1114
Elohim, 2:687–88
El Pendo, Spain, *1:17*
El Valle, Spain, *1:17*
'Elyon, 1:200
Emar (Meskene), Syria, 1:184, 1:190, 1:225, 1:226, 1:227
Embla, 1:281
Emhain-Mhacha, 1:270–71
Emher, 1:270
Emma, 2:1048
Empedocles, 1:349, 1:391, 1:399, 1:410, 1:465, 2:771
Enareis, 1:471
Enbilulu, 1:147
Enc, 2:1119–20, 2:1128
Enceladus, 1:400
Endovellicus, 1:249
Endu Dara Tincin Temaga, 2:943
Endu Sudan Galiggan Tincin Mas, 2:943
Endymion, 1:478; for Naassenes, 2:675–76
Enga, 2:1226
Engur, 1:146
Enid, 1:266
Eni Mahanahi, 1:229
Enki, 1:145–54, *1:153*, 1:156, 1:157, 1:163–65, 1:172–81
Enkidu, 1:155–56, 1:159, 1:175
Enkimdu, 1:147
Enlil, 1:145, 1:145–46, 1:148, 1:149, 1:152, 1:155–56, 1:157, 1:161, 1:172–74, 1:176, 1:179–81, 1:227
Ennius, 1:575, 1:585–86, 1:598, 1:599, 2:666, 2:667, 2:669, 2:694
En no Gyōja, 2:908, 2:1037, 1:1050, 2:1057, 2:1062–63, *2:1063*
En no Ozunu, 2:1062–63
E no Ozunu, 2:1057
Entala, 2:938
Entremont, Bouches-du-Rhône, 1:245
Enūma eliš, 1:3, 1:155–56, 1:157, 1:158, 1:159, 1:172
Enyalios, 1:332
Enyo, 1:333
Eochaidh Bres, 1:257–59
Eos (Aurora), 1:371, 1:375, 1:378, 1:510
Epaphus, 1:490
Epeus, 1:546
Ephialtes, 1:468
Ephorus, 1:548
Epicasta, 1:498
Epicurus and Epicureanism, 1:598–99, 1:613, 1:614
Epidaurus, Greece, 1:450
Epigoni, 1:405
Epimelides, 1:505
Epimetheus, 1:371, 1:394, 1:423–24
Epiphanius, 2:677, 2:679, 2:680
Epiur, 1:519, 1:531, *1:532*
Epona, 1:249–50, 1:272, *1:272*, 2:733
Eponymous Ones, 1:345–46
Equirria, 1:583, 1:624
Equus october, 1:621
Er, 1:321
Erbin, 1:266
Erc, 1:258
Erde. *See* Jörð
Erebus, 1:369, 1:410, 1:413, 1:464
Erec, 1:267
Erechtheus, 1:341, *1:342*, 1:343, *1:344*, 1:345, 1:386, 1:388, 1:390, 1:393, 1:411
Éremhon, 1:260
Ereškigal, 1:152, 1:178, 1:180, 1:227, 2:686
Erga, 2:1116
Ergeni, 2:1116
Erichthonius. *See* Erechtheus
Eridu, Mesopotamia, 1:146, *1:148*, 1:156, 1:157, 1:172
Erigone, 1:459
Erikepaios, 1:465, 1:470
Erinlè, 1:61
Erinu (Erinys), 1:332, 1:414
Erinyes (Furies), 1:373–74, 1:404, 1:439, 1:465; in literature, 1:408, 1:491, 2:787
Ériu, 1:257, 1:259–60
Erklik (Erlik), 2:1092, 2:1106
Erlang, 2:1028
Eros, 1:370–71, 1:373, 1:378, 1:380, 1:432, 1:464–72, *1:466*, *1:467*, 1:485, 1:632–34, *2:684*; in art and literature, 1:355, 1:358, 2:694, 2:698; in Christianity, 2:662; to Gnostics, 2:678, 2:681, 2:682–85
Erra, 1:158, 1:163, 1:178–81
Ertemi, 1:229
Er Töshtük, 2:1099, 2:1107
Erymanthean Boar, 1:420
Erysichthon, 1:454
Erytheïs, 1:490
Eryx, Mount (in Sicily), 1:637–38
Eryximachus, 1:466–67, 1:469
Es, 2:1119–20
Esagil, 1:157, 1:167–68
Ešarra, 1:160
Esau, 2:682
Esaugetu-Emissi, 2:1161
Eschatiai, Eschatia, 1:445–46, 1:502
Eschatology: in Christianity, 2:652; Etruscan, 1:529; Indo-European, 1:236–37; insular Southeast Asian, 2:958–59; in the Maghreb, 1:87; pre-Islamic Iranian, 2:887–89; among Turks and Mongols, 2:1107–8
Esen Sagan, 2:1113
Eshmun, 1:195–97, 1:199
Eshu (Èlègbara), 1:55, *1:59*
Eskimos, 2:1128, 2:1145–52
Esna, Egypt, 1:91, 1:92, 1:107, 1:109
Esus, 1:242–43, 1:244, 1:272–73, *1:273*, 1:279
Etana, 1:176
Eteocles, 1:404–5
Ethausva, 1:531
Ether (Aithēr), 1:369
Ethereo (Giacom' Antonio Gromo), 2:703
Ethniu, 1:257
Etruscans, 1:516–17 passim, 1:518–19, 1:520–21, 1:525–26, 1:526–29, 1:530–32, 1:532–33, 1:533–35, 1:549, 1:552, 1:588–89, 1:627
Etügen (Itügen), 2:1112
Etüken, 2:1103
Eudora, 1:380
Eudoxus de Cnidos, 1:213
Euhemerus, Euhemerism, 1:132, 2:666–68, 2:694
Eumaeus, 1:384, 1:486, 1:497
Eumolpus, 1:341, 1:345, 1:382, 1:455
Eunapius, 1:275, 1:360
Eupalamus, 1:388
Euphrates the Peratic, 2:680
Euripides, 1:336, 1:343, 1:345, 1:384, 1:391, 1:392, 1:398, 1:404, 1:410, 1:413, 1:414, 1:427, 1:438, 1:440, 1:441, 1:448, 1:450, 1:459, 1:476, 1:477, 1:479–80, 1:481, 1:482, 1:484, 1:503–5, 1:507, 2:660
Europa, 1:334, 1:335, 1:379, 1:410, 1:458, *1:472*, 1:473,

Gregory of Nyssa, 2:650
Gregory of Tours, 1:133
Gregory the Great, 2:696
Gri-gum btsan-po, 2:1088
Grillparzer, Franz, 2:767, 2:777
Grimm, Jakob and Wilhelm, 2:736
Gronw, 1:263
Gros Ventre, 2:1163
Grotto. *See* Cavern; Labyrinth
gShen-za ne'u-chung, 2:1082
gTsugs, 2:1081
Guadalupe, Virgin of, 2:1166, 2:1173, 2:1181–82
Guajiro, 2:1198
Guanyin, 2:895, 2:900–902, 2:904, 2:906–7
Guanzizai, 2:907
Guarani, 2:1196, *2:1207*, 2:1208
Guardians. *See* Gate, Guardian of the; Spirits
Guayaki, 2:1192, 2:1197
Gubbio (Iguvium), Italy, 1:522, 1:522–24, *1:523*, 1:536, 1:539, 1:587
Gudiri-mumy, 2:1137
Guðr. *See* Gunnr
Guérin, Maurice de, 2:774
Guha, 2:868
Gūhra, 2:681
Guhyaka, 2:899
Guhyapada, 2:908
Gui, 2:1021
Gui (demons), 2:1028–31
Guigniaut, Joseph-Daniel, 2:754
Guiji, Mount, 2:1034
Guinevere, 2:715
Guizi mu, 2:899
Gulšeš, 1:219
Gulu, 1:79
Gulzanniges, 1:219
Gun, 2:1023, 2:1024, 2:1029
Gundestrup, Bowl of (in Denmark), 1:243–44, *1:244*, *1:247*, 1:251, 1:253, 1:256, 1:268, 1:278, 1:279, 1:280, 1:282
Gung-btsun, 2:1078
Gungnir, 1:287
Gung-rgyal, 2:1086
Gunnr, 1:287
Gunung Agung, 2:953
Guopu, 2:1027, 2:1036
Guriang Tunggal, 2:961
Guri ri Selleng, 2:944
Gurmanche, 1:32, 1:35–36
Guruda, 2:942
Guru Tatea Bulan, 2:940
Gu Sou, 2:1022
Gustehem, 2:946
Gwalchmai, Gauvain, 1:266, 1:267
Gwawl, 1:261–62
Gwenhwyfar, 1:265
Gwern, 1:262
Gwydion, 1:261, 1:262–63, 1:264
Gwynedd, 1:240, 1:262–63, 1:264, 1:266
Gwynn ap Nudd, 1:264, 1:265, 1:274
Gydyrty-kom, 1:317
Gyes, 1:372
Gyges (Gyes), 1:355, 1:357, 1:372
Gyllu, 2:674
Gymir, 1:288
Gyōgi, 2:1042, 2:1057
Gypsies, 2:718–22

H

Ha, 2:908
Haba no kuni, 2:1046
Habantali, 1:221
Habiru, 1:219
Hachiman, 2:1059
Hadad, Haddu, 1:189, 1:190–91, 1:200–203
Hadephagia, 1:453
Hades, 1:376, 1:381, 1:389, 1:391, 1:405–6, 1:407–12, *1:407*, *1:411*, 1:412–14, 1:449, 1:480, 1:481, 1:525; in literature, 2:788
Hadji Bektash, 2:1091
Haemon, 1:405
Hafgan, 1:261, 1:262
Hainuwele, 2:952–53
Haitraitra, 2:970–71
Hajib Nadjar, 2:1102
Hako, 2:1158
Half-boy, 2:1154
Halil, 1:307
Halki, 1:221
Ha-lu-ma-da', 2:1083
Hamann, Johann Georg, 2:754, 2:773
Hama. *See* Laash and Hama
Hämosu, 2:1070, 2:1073
Hämyts, 1:317
Hanchan, 2:907
Hanfeizi, 2:1022
Hantidaššu, 1:221
Hanumān, *2:835*, *2:838*; in India, 2:835, 2:836, 2:837–38, 2:864, 2:957; in Indonesia, 2:956
Hanyeri, Turkey, 1:222
Haoma, 1:235–36, 2:883–84, 2:892
Harentas, 1:522
Hari, 2:853
Hārītī, 2:899, 2:900, 2:904, 2:907, 2:908
Harmon, 1:387
Harmonia, 1:499
Harpies, 1:474, 1:490
Harpocrates, 1:121, 1:124, 1:128; in literature, 1:138, 1:141
Haruspicy, 1:528–29, 1:532–33, 1:533, 1:570, 1:587–90, 1:593–94
Hašameli, 1:221
Hašamili, 1:219
Hasan, 2:947
Hasanuddin, 2:947
Hašawanza Kammama, 1:219–20
Ha-shan, 2:905–6, 2:907
Haššuššara, 1:220
Hathor, 1:103, 1:105, 1:110, 1:121; in Greece, 1:121–22; in literature, 1:135, 1:141
Hat'i, 1:309, 1:310, 1:311
Hatti, 1:216, 1:218, 1:219, 1:220–21
Hattuša (Boğazköy), Turkey, 1:184, 1:216, 1:220, 1:223, *1:223*, 1:225, 1:226, 1:227, 1:228
Haurot and Maurot, 1:320
Hawwa, 1:229
Hayagrīva, 2:854, 2:895
Hazzi, Mount, 1:219, 1:221, 1:226
He, 2:906–7, 2:1021–22
Heammawhio, 2:1156
Hebat, 1:217, 1:221, 1:223, 1:224, 1:225, 1:226, 1:227–29
Hebe, 1:399–400, 1:478, 1:481
Hebel, Johann Peter, 2:772
Hebo, 2:1013
Hecataeus of Abdera, 2:666
Hecate, 1:128, 1:138, 1:375, 1:409, 1:442, 1:444, 1:486; for Gnostics, 2:685–86, *2:686*
Hector, 1:416–17, 1:486, 1:505
Hecatoncheires. *See* Hundred-Handeds
Hehaka Sapa, 2:1157, 2:1158–59
Heimarmene, 2:685, 2:687
Heimdallr, 1:281, 1:291, 1:294
Heine, Heinrich, 2:766, 2:779
Hel, 1:286, 1:295
Helen, 1:342, 1:387, 1:408, 1:410, 1:474–78, *1:476*, *1:477*, 1:494; for Gnostics, 2:677; in art and literature, 2:694, 2:758–59, 2:774–75, 2:789
Heliades, 1:509
Heliopolis, 1:91, 1:92–94, *1:92*, 1:103
Helios, 1:375, 1:478, *1:478*, 1:509
Hellè, 1:442
Hellen, 1:394–95
Hellotis, 1:334, 1:335
Helmold von Bosan, 1:296, 1:298, 1:302
Hēmerē, 1:369
Heng, 2:908
Hengnge, 2:1011
Hephaesteia, 1:386
Hephaestus, 1:326, 1:341, 1:343, 1:345, 1:355, 1:384–87, *1:385*, 1:388–89, 1:390, 1:392–93, 1:399, 1:465, 1:488, 1:511; to Perates, 2:681
Hera, 1:332, 1:376, 1:379, 1:381, 1:384–85, 1:387, 1:396–401, 1:407, 1:410, 1:424, 1:428, 1:431, 1:438, 1:442, 1:443, 1:444, 1:459, 1:478, 1:480, 1:490, 1:546
Heracles, 1:335, 1:342, 1:345, 1:378, *1:379*, 1:389, 1:410, 1:420, 1:437, 1:440, 1:451, 1:453, 1:478–84, 1:490; in Christianity, 2:656, 2:660, 2:663, 2:672, 2:673; to Gnostics, 2:678–79, 2:688
Heraclitus, 2:671, 2:695
Herbord, 1:296, 1:298
Hercle, *1:517*, *1:518*, 1:519, 1:520, 1:531, 1:618
Hercules, 1:554, 1:555, 1:556, 1:564, 1:565, 1:569, 1:615, 1:618–19, *1:619*, *2:699*; in art and literature, 1:618–19, 2:693, 2:694, 2:697, 2:702, 2:706, 2:708, 2:711–12; to continental Celts, 1:275, 1:276
Herder, Johann Gottfried, 2:729, 2:730, 2:754–55, 2:768, 2:773
Herekle, 1:522, 1:538
Herero, 1:63
Herfjöturr, 1:287
Hermaion, 1:486
Hermaphroditus, hermaphroditism, 1:399, 1:471, *1:471*, *2:679*; among the Germano-Nordic peoples, 1:288; among the Gnostics, 2:680, 2:683
Hermes, 1:332, 1:359, 1:378, 1:396, 1:398–99, 1:405, 1:407–8, 1:411–12, 1:423, 1:442, 1:459, 1:466, 1:471, 1:480, 1:485–89, *1:486*, *1:487*, *1:488*, *1:489*, 1:502, 1:503, *1:503*, 1:504, *1:504*, 1:506, 1:509; Cults of Isis, 1:128; to the Gnostics, 2:664, 2:676, 2:677, 2:678, 2:681
Hermes Trismegistus, 1:134, 2:667. *See also* Thoth
Hermeticism, 2:706–11
Hermias, 2:677
Hermoðr, 1:287
Hermogenes, 2:677
Hermopolis, Egypt, 1:91–92, 1:93, 1:115, 1:203
Herne, 1:270
Herodias, in literature, 2:758, 2:780
Herodotus, 1:117, 1:121, 1:122, 1:128, 1:132, 1:134, 1:185, 1:298, 1:304, 1:318, 1:329, 1:332, 1:341, 1:345, 1:413, 1:421, 1:436–37, 1:440, 1:443, 1:471, 1:477, 1:480, 1:527, 1:546, 2:660, 2:668, 2:877, 2:880, 2:882
Herse, 1:341
Heshang, 2:905
Heshang Gong, 2:1008
Hesiod, 1:347–48, 1:352, 1:367–75 passim, 1:375–78 passim, 1:380, 1:382–83, 1:385, 1:386, 1:387, 1:390–95 passim, 1:399, 1:405–10 passim, 1:412–14 passim, 1:422–23, 1:439, 1:447, 1:460, 1:464–72 passim, 1:473, 1:478–84 passim, 1:485, 1:486, 1:488, 1:494, 1:510, 1:511, 1:546, 2:660, 2:677, 2:888
Hespere, 1:490
Hesperides, 1:480, 1:490
Hesteau de Nuysement, Clovis, 2:703
Hestia, 1:333, 1:362, 1:376, 1:384, 1:488, 1:490
Hešui, 1:226
Hesychius, 1:185, 1:385

Heyoka, 2:1157
Heywood, Thomas, 2:771
Hia, 2:940. *See also* Xia
Hiawatha, 2:1161
Hidatsa, 2:1157, 2:1158, 2:1162, 2:1163
Hidrellez, 2:1111
Hiei, Mount (in Japan), 2:1039
Hienghene, 2:1215
Hierapolis, Syria, 1:202
Hierogamy: in Crete and Mycenae, 1:338; in Greece, 1:455; among Phoenicians and Punics, 1:196; in southern Africa (Bantu), 1:71–75; in Ugarit, 1:214; among the Western Semites, 1:189
Hiisi, 2:1134
Hilanzipa, Hilašši, 1:219
Hildr, 1:287
Hima, 1:79
Himeros, 1:371, 1:432, 1:465, 2:682
Hīnayāna, 2:893–94
Hinduism: in India, 2:893–95; in insular Southeast Asia, 2:931, 2:933, 2:936
Hine-nui-te-po, 2:1218
Hippius, 1:381
Hippocrates, 1:437
Hippodamia, 1:398, 1:403, 1:451; in the art of the Middle Ages, 2:694
Hippolytus, 1:381, 1:408, 1:421, 1:432, 1:448–49, 1:492
Hippolytus of Rome, 2:652, 2:657, 2:664
Hippomenes, 1:396; in literature, 2:706
Hippo of Melos, 2:667
Hippys, 1:547
Hipta, 1:229
Hiranyakaśipu, 2:826, 2:854–55, 2:860–61, 2:875
Hitokotonushi, 2:1062
Hittites, 1:216, 1:217, 1:218–22, 1:222–23, 1:224–25, 1:227–29
Hizir, 2:1098, 2:1111
H'Kroah, 2:982
Hlökk, 1:287
Ho, 2:1074
Hodong, 2:1071
Hödr, 1:285
Hoenir, 1:287, 1:291, 1:295
Hoffmann, E. T. A., 2:754, 2:755, 2:766, 2:767, 2:772
Hohenburg, Herwart von, 1:139
Hölderlin, Friedrich, 2:731, 2:771, 2:773, 2:778–79, 2:781–82
Holkot, Robert, 2:696
Holo, 1:522
Holzhausen, Bavaria, 1:246
Homadhenu, 2:857, 2:873
Homer, 1:326, 1:329, 1:352–53, *1:363*, 1:366–67, 1:380, 1:384–90 passim, 1:391–95 passim, 1:402, 1:410, 1:412–14, 1:415, 1:428–31, 1:436, 1:440, 1:445, 1:449, 1:451, 1:453, 1:455, 1:459, 1:467, 1:478–84 passim, 1:485–89 passim, 1:494–98 passim, 1:586, 2:659, 2:660, 2:664
Hondo, 1:522
Hōnen, 2:1040
Honji-Suijaku, 2:1049–50
Ho Phi, 2:919
Hopi, 2:1153, 2:1161
Horace, 1:561, 1:562, 1:575, 1:586–87, 1:603, 1:609–10, 1:617, 1:620, 1:627, 1:629, 1:631, 1:636, 1:642
Horagalles, 2:1137
Horai, 1:375, 1:478
Horapollo, 1:103
Horatius Cocles, 1:549
Hordai, Egypt, 1:100
Horon, 1:215
Hortlak, 2:1096
Horus, 1:93, 1:96, *1:102*, 1:103, 1:107, 1:109–10, 1:117, 1:118, 1:122, 1:128–30, 1:138–41
Horus Apollo, 2:699
Hotei, 2:905
Hou Ji, Houzi, 2:1016, 2:1023
Hoytu Tamir, 2:1103
Hraesvelgr, 1:282
Hrist, 1:287
Hri-yang, 2:993
Hrungnir, 1:282
Hrymir, 1:282
Hu, 1:92, 2:1009
Huaca, 2:1202, 2:1204
Huagai, 2:1009
Huandou, 2:1030
Huang, 2:1018–19
Huangdi (the Yellow Emperor), 2:1015, 2:1020–21, *2:1021*, 2:1029–30, 2:1032, 2:1035
Huanxitian, 2:902, 2:904, 2:906
Huarachicoy, 2:1205
Huastec, 2:1182, 2:1184, 2:1186
Huaxu, 2:1016
Hubešna (Kybistra), 1:221
Huehueteotl, 2:1184, 2:1187, *2:1187*
Hughes, Ted, 2:786
Hugo, Victor, 2:752, 2:754, 2:755, 2:756, 2:759, 2:767, 2:769, 2:770–71, 2:773, 2:777–78
Huichol, 2:1166, 2:1169, 2:1180, 2:1186
Huitzilopochtli, 2:1169, 2:1172, 2:1179, 2:1181
Huli, 2:1226
Hulla, 1:221, 1:226
Hullara, 1:221
Hulu, 2:940
Humbaba, 1:181
Hunab Itzam Na, 2:1174
Hundred-Handeds (Hecatoncheires), 1:372, 1:377, 1:481
Hundun, 2:1009, 2:1027, 2:1029
Hung, 2:996
Hungarians, 2:1132–33, 2:1138
Hung vuong, 2:1002
Hunter-gatherers. *See* Nomads
Hunting, symbolism and divinities of: among Finno-Ugrians, 2:1134–35; in Georgia, 1:314, 1:315; in Greece, 1:402, 1:418–19, 1:433, 1:445–49, 1:451, 1:500, 1:504; in India, 2:814; in insular Southeast Asia, 2:948, 2:952; among Inuit, 2:1150; in Mesopotamia, 1:181; in Northern Caucasus, 2:1115–16; in Siberia, 2:1120–22; in southern Africa (Bantu), 1:67, 1:72–73; among Turks and Mongols, 2:1098, 2:1101; among Yoruba, 1:60–61
Huo, 2:906–7
Huohe, 2:906–7
Huotou jingang, 2:903
Hurons, 2:1154, 2:1160, 2:1161
Hurri, 1:219, 1:221, 1:226
Hurrians, 1:216, 1:219, 1:221, 1:224, 1:225–27, 1:227–29
Husayn, 2:947
Husiatyn, Galicia, *1:296*
Hutellurra, 1:224–26
Hutena, 1:224–26
Huwaššanna, 1:221
Huysmans, Joris-Karl, 2:758, 2:761
Hway Hway, 2:1215
Hyacinthia, 1:475, 1:476, 1:477
Hyacinthus, 1:335, 1:399, 1:439, 1:475
Hyadi, 2:1182
Hydriads, 1:505
Hyginus, 1:334, 1:387, 1:400, 1:433, 1:444
Hylas, 1:507
Hyllus, 1:482
Hyperboreans, 1:438, 1:439
Hyperion, 1:371–72, 1:375, 1:465
Hypermestra, 1:400, 1:472
Hypnos, 1:405, 1:407, *1:407*, *1:482*, 1:496
Hypseus, 1:401

I

Ia, 1:335
Iachtanabas, 2:685
Iahsar, 1:312
Ialdabaoth, 2:682
Iamblichus, 1:360, 1:507, 2:700
Iampelasoamananoro, 2:969
Iapetus, 1:371, 1:375, 1:422, 1:465
Iapyges, 1:540–41
Iapyx, 1:540, 1:546
Iasion, 1:335, 1:454
Iatmul, 2:1226, 2:1229
Iban, 2:933, 2:935, 2:938, 2:940, 2:943, 2:948
Iberian Celts. *See* Celts, Iberian
Ibicwezi, 1:80
Ibmel, 2:1136
Ibn al-Kalbi, 1:192
Ibn Fadhlan, Ahmad, 1:280, 1:284, 1:290, 2:1092
Ibn Hisham, 1:192
Ibn Sina, 2:1103
Ibonia, 2:961–62, 2:967, 2:968–70
Ibsen, Henrik, 2:776
Ibualama, 1:61
Ibu Pertiwi, 2:952
Ibycus, 1:466
Icarius, 1:459
Icarus, 1:388; in literature, 2:785, 2:787
Ida, 1:335, 1:337
Ida, Mount, 1:333, 1:335, 1:336, 2:1103
Iddawc, 1:264
Idomeneus, 1:546
Iðunn, 1:295
Iduq, 2:1108
Idyia, Eiduia, 1:380, 1:442
Iessaul, 1:311
Ifa, 1:55, 1:61
Ifaranomby, 2:970–71
Ifugao, 2:933, 2:934, 2:939, 2:940
Igbo, 1:54
Igigi, 1:173, 1:174, 1:175, 1:176
Igomori matsuri, 2:1064
Iguvium. *See* Gubbio
Ijirait, 2:1149
Ikotofetsy, 2:974
Iktome, 2:1156
Il. *See* El
Ilah, 1:192
Ilaliyanteš, 1:219
Ilāni māti, 1:177
Illapa, 2:1204
Ilmari, Ilmaris, 2:1136, 2:1137
Iltara, 1:227
Ilyas, *2:1111*, 2:1113
Ilythia, 1:546
Imahaka, 2:974
Imaitsoanala, 2:970, 2:973
Imam Bonjol, 2:947
Imamkulu, Turkey, 1:222
Imana, 1:80
Imandwa, 1:80
Imbahitrila, 2:963–64
Imerina, 2:970, 2:973
Inachus, 1:391, 1:393, 1:424
Inada Dao, 2:940
Inada Samadulo Hosi, 2:937
Inada Samihara Luwo, 2:937
Inai, 2:1045
Inakhos. *See* Inachos
Inanna, 1:147–48, *1:153*, 1:172
Inar. *See* Hašawanza Kammama
Inara, 1:222
Incarnation. *See* Avatars
Incas, 2:1201–5, *2:1204*
Incest: in China, 2:1025; in Georgia, 1:310–11; in Greece, 1:404–5, 1:498–500; in India, 2:814–15, 2:824; in Indochina, 2:984; in insular Southeast Asia, 2:940; for Inuit, 2:1148; in Madagascar, 2:969; in Oceania, 2:1220; in pre-Islamic Iran, 2:889; in southern Africa (Bantu), 1:70, 1:73, 1:75; in West Africa, 1:42
Incosatana, 1:75
Indai Jebua, 2:941
Indech mac Dé Domhnann, 1:257
India, 1:23–39 passim, 2:799–877, 2:896–98

Indochina, 2:976–95; Buddhism in, 2:893–95. *See also* Vietnam
Indo-Europeans, 1:233–39, 2:877–90 passim
Indonesia. *See* Insular Southeast Asia
Indra, 2:802, 2:806–7, 2:814, 2:826, 2:829, 2:835, 2:856, 2:858, 2:863–64, 2:867, 2:893, 2:929; in Southeast Asia, 2:916–17
Indrajaya, 2:961
Indrajit, 2:838
Ingegneri, Angelo, 2:703
Initiation, rites of: in Crete and Mycenae, 1:337; for Germano-Nordic peoples, 1:293; in Greece, 1:341–42, 1:421, 1:446, 1:451, 1:452, 1:455, 1:471, 1:474–78; for Indo-Europeans, 1:236; in literature, 2:741–43, 2:786; in Japan, 2:1045, 2:1069; in Madagascar, 2:964–65; in Oceania, 2:1220; in Papua New Guinea, 2:1226–29; in pre-Islamic Iran, 2:882, 2:883; in Rome, 1:620, 1:634; in South America, 2:1199–1201, 2:1205; in southern Africa (Bantu), 1:67–68, 1:69, 1:73; for Turks and Mongols, 2:1101; in West Africa (Mande), 1:25–27, 1:30–32, 1:37–39, 1:41, 1:45
Inlé, 1:61
Inmar, 2:1137
Ino, 1:335, 1:384, 1:442, 1:443, 1:459, 1:461
Inoko, 2:1069
Insular Southeast Asia, 2:931–61, *2:953;* Buddhism in, 2:893–95
Insunene, 2:1182
Insutata, 2:1182
Interpretatio Romana, 1:555
Inti, 2:1203
Inti Raymi, 2:1205
Intshwala, 1:68, 1:73–75
Inuit, 2:1145–52, *2:1146*
Inuvayla' u, 2:1220
Involuti (gods), 1:520
Io, 1:410, 1:442, 1:490; in art and literature, 1:133, 1:135, 1:138, 2:706; in Christianity, 2:667
Iobates, 1:402–3
Iocasta, 1:404–5, 1:498–99
Iodama, 1:410
Iolaus, 1:481
Iole, 1:482
Ion, 1:345
Iouktas, Mount (in Crete), 1:336
Iov-, 1:553
Ipay, 2:1214
Ipemedeya, 1:332
Iphigenia, 1:404, 1:408, 1:446; in literature, 2:787
Iphinoe, 1:388
Ippen, 2:1040, 2:1050
Irbitig, 1:227
Ireland. *See* Celts, insular
Irenaeus, 2:677, 2:679
Irik, 2:938
Iris, 1:474, 1:490
Irminsul, 1:281, 1:304
Iroquois, 2:1153, 2:1157, 2:1158, 2:1160, 2:1161
Irungu, 1:79
Isaac of Antioch, 1:185
Išara, 1:217, 1:224, 1:226, 1:227, 1:229
Isaza, 1:78
Isia, 1:122
Isiacs (cults), 1:121–31, 1:634; in Greece and the Roman Empire, 1:594, 1:600–601
Isidore of Alexandria, 1:361
Isidore of Seville, 1:281, 2:667, 2:694
Isilakolona, 2:964
Isim, 1:146
Isimbwa, 1:78
Isis, *1:118, 1:121, 1:124, 1:129, 1:132, 1:137, 1:139, 1:601, 2:775;* in Christianity, 2:672; in Egypt, 1:91, 1:92, 1:93, 1:103, 1:104, 1:109, 1:117–18, 1:121–23; among Gnostics, 2:676, 2:679, 2:680, 2:681; in Greece, 1:121–22, 1:125; in Greek and Coptic papyruses, 1:128–31; in literature, 1:133, 1:135–40, 2:774–75; in Rome, 1:122, 1:125, 1:556, 1:609, 1:634
Iškalli, 1:226
Iskandar Zulkarnain, 2:946
Iskeha, 2:1160
Iškur, 1:145, 1:147
Islam: in insular Southeast Asia, 2:931–32, 2:936, 2:945–47; in Iran, 2:880; in Madagascar, 2:971, 2:972–73; in the Maghreb, 1:84, 1:87; in northern Caucasus, 2:1113; for Turks and Mongols, 2:1090–93, 2:1111
Isolde. *See* Tristan and Isolde
Israel, 2:687
Israfil, 2:1095
Istakhri, 2:1097
Ištanu, 1:220
Ištar, 1:181, 1:221, 1:223, 1:224, 1:226, 1:227, 1:229
Isturitz, Basses-Pyrénées, *1:13,* 1:19
Išum, 1:181
Isyllus, 1:450
Italus, 1:546
Italy, pre-Roman, 1:515–48. *See also* Rome
Ith, 1:260
Ithyphallus, 1:629
It Matromna, 2:938
Itoerambolafotsy, 2:965
Itoga, 2:1103
Its', 2:1182
Itsukushima Myōjin, 2:1059
Itügen, 2:1103, 2:1112
Itzam Na, 2:1166, 2:1180
Itzpapalotl, 2:1179
Itztli, 2:1179
Iupater, 1:521
Ivan Kupalo, 1:298
Iwsa'as, 1:92
Ix Chebel Yax, 2:1174
Ix Chel, 2:1180
Ixion, 1:490–91
Iyarri, 1:221
Izäd, 1:316
Izanagi, 2:1038, 2:1044
Izanami, 2:1038, 2:1044, 2:1046
Izik, 2:1108

J

Jablonski, Paul Ernst, 1:141
Jacaltecs, 2:1178
Jacob of Saroug, 1:185
Jade Emperor, 2:997, 2:999–1000
Jadi, 2:1096
Jaka Tarub, 2:959–60, *2:960*
Jamadagni, 2:856–57
Jambhala, 2:899, 2:903, 2:907
'Jamd-byangs, 2:1078
Janaka: in India, 2:835–36, 2:839; in insular Southeast Asia, 2:957
Janaloka, 2:821
Janārdana, 2:823
Janus, 1:552–53, 1:565, 1:567, 1:577, 1:607, 1:619–20, *1:620,* 1:638
Japan, 2:1037–70, *2:1056, 2:1058;* Buddhism in, 2:893–95
Jara, 2:833
Jarai, 2:977, *2:978,* 2:979, 2:980, 2:981–95, *2:984, 2:987, 2:992, 2:993*
Jarāsandha, 2:831, 2:860–62
Jarilo, 1:298
Jarovit, 1:301
Jason, 1:414, 1:442–44, *1:443;* in art and literature, 2:702, 2:703
Jata, 2:935, 2:937–38
Jaṭāyu, 2:837
Jate, 2:1226
Jaucourt, Louis de, 2:722–24
Java. *See* Insular Southeast Asia
Jayabaya, 2:958–59, *2:959*
Jean de Sponde, 2:713
Jebrail, 2:1095
Jehovah, in literature, 2:767, 2:769
Jen Fang, 2:1007
Jerome, Saint, 1:600, 2:656, 2:665
Jerome of Prague, 1:302
Jesus, *2:650,* 2:651–52, 2:654, 2:662, 2:663, 2:1169; among Gnostics, 2:679, 2:682, 2:688; in literature, 2:768
Jhang Hua, 2:1008
Jiandi, 2:1016
Jiangyuan, 2:1016
Jiantan, 2:907
Jian tuo, 2:899
Jie, 2:1023–24
Jigoku, 2:1048
Jimmu Tennō, 2:1038
Jing, 2:1030–31
Jingang, 2:900, 2:902, 2:907
Jingū Kōgō, 2:1042
Jinn, 1:87, 1:192, 1:204, 2:1096, 2:1108
Jiulong, 2:1028
Jiuzi mu, 2:899
Jizō, 2:1048
Job, *2:770,* in literature, 2:768–69
Jōdo, 2:1040, 2:1048
John Chrysostom, Saint, 2:775
John Garland, 2:696
John Italos, 2:673
John of Salisbury, 2:696
John "The Grammarian," 2:673
Jōkan, 2:1050
Jonah, 2:663
Jones, David, 2:786
Jörð, 1:285, 1:287
Jörmungandr, 1:281, 1:294
Joseph, 2:656, 2:660
Jouy, Victor-Joseph Étienne de, 2:776
Joyce, James, 2:783, 2:785–86
Judas, 2:689
Jugumishanta, 2:1226–27
Julian the Apostate, 1:555, 2:696, 2:775–77
Julian the Hospitable, Saint, 2:688
Julii, 1:555
Julius Africanus, 1:128
Julus Ascanius, 1:555, 1:563
Jumala, 2:1136
Jumo, 2:1136
Juni-sama, 2:1052
Juno, 1:552, 1:553, 1:560, 1:562–64, *1:562, 1:564,* 1:565, 1:567, 1:576, 1:608, 1:620–21, *1:621, 1:622,* 1:627, 1:634, *2:696, 2:697;* in literature, 1:640, 2:696, 2:702, 2:703
Jupiter, *1:255,* 1:542–43, 1:544, 1:552–53, 1:561, 1:562, 1:563–64, *1:564,* 1:565, 1:567–68, 1:575, 1:576–77, 1:608, 1:610, 1:621–22, *1:622,* 1:627, 1:633, 1:635; in art and literature, 1:640–42, 2:694, 2:695, 2:696, 2:697, 2:700, 2:706, 2:707, 2:767, 2:768; for continental Celts, 1:249, 1:254, 1:278
Jurasmat, 1:302, 1:306
Juskana, 2:1160
Justin the Gnostic, 1:185, 1:548, 2:656, 2:659–63 passim, 2:678–79, 2:686–88
Justitia Augusta, 1:609
Juturna, 1:641
Juvaini, 2:1103, 2:1104
Juvenal, 1:594

K

Ka, 1:96–99
Kabigat, 2:939, 2:940
Kabunian, 2:938–39
Kabyles, 1:84–88
Kacilmic, 1:307
Kadag, 1:309
Kadaklan, 2:939

Kadar, 2:1123
Kadrū, 2:804–5
Kadzhi, 1:313
Kaf Dagi, Caucasus, 2:1103
Kagoro (Bacwezi), 1:80
Kagoros, 1:29
Kahwikahok, 2:1221
Kai, 1:4
Kaikeyī, 2:834, 2:836
Kailāśa, 2:822
Kaiming, 2:1028
Kaiṭabha, 2:870
Kakia, 1:483
Kakinomoto Hitomaru, 2:1042
KAL (gods), 1:221, 1:222, 1:223, 1:226
Kāla, 2:821, 2:859, 2:861
Kalaipahoa, 2:1222
Kalala Ilunga, 1:68, 1:70, 1:72
Kālanemi, 2:861
Kalanga, 1:70
Kali, 2:829, 2:850, 2:861
Kālī (divinity of India), 2:817, 2:871–72, 2:874
Kalinga, 2:938
Kali Yuga, 2:850
Kalkal, 1:174
Kalkin, 2:850
Kalmuks, 2:1090, 2:1100
Kalogheroi, 2:673
Kalpa, 2:820, 2:821–22, 2:850
Kaluti, 1:226
Kalvos, Andreas, 1:787–88
Kāma, 2:816, 2:825, 2:836, 2:868, 2:896
Kāmabhūmi, 2:929
Kama blō, 1:31, 1:32, 1:50
Kāmadhenu, 2:873
Kamano, 2:1226, 2:1229
Kamayura, 2:1200
Kambu, 2:926
Kamchadal, 2:1128
Kami, 2:1037, 2:1038, 2:1041, 2:1042, 2:1049–50, 2:1062
Kami-waza, 2:1066
Kammama, 1:220
Kaṃsa, 2:860–62, 2:869–70
Kaneš (Kültepe), Turkey, 1:220, 1:221
Kangiten, *2:902*
Kaniyar, 2:845
Kankanay, 2:939
Kannaaluk, 2:1151
Kannia (Mitropolis), Crete, 1:337
Kan-non (Kannon), 2:895, 2:901, 2:902, 2:904, 2:1048
Kantu, 1:78
Kao Pien, 2:995
Kapilā, 2:873, 2:876
Kapwangwa Kapwityalo, 2:1215
Karagasses, 2:1100, 2:1107
Karai, 2:1206–8
Karaiyadi MādaN, 2:845
Karajaoglan, 2:1102
Kara Kondjolos, 2:1096
Kara Koyunlu, 2:1099, 2:1102
Kara-Kura, 2:1096
Kargamiš, 1:226, 1:227, 1:229
Kariba Myōjin, 2:1052
Karkanxhol, 1:307
Karma (Karme), 1:335
Karman, 2:820, 2:825
Karṇa, 2:831–32, 2:837, 2:860, 2:862
Kārtavīrya, 2:856–57
Kartini, 2:947
Kārttikeya, 2:896, 2:901
Karzi, 1:221
Kashgari, 2:1092, 2:1096, 2:1097, 2:1098, 2:1101, 2:1103, 2:1105, 2:1107, 2:1108, 2:1111, 2:1112, 2:1113
Kassonke, 1:29
Kastamuni, 2:1091
Kaśyapa, 2:857, 2:874
Katahzipuri, 1:219
Katallā, 1:307
Katonda, 1:79
Katrinia (Piskokephalo), Crete, 1:337
Katsuragi, Mount (in Japan), 2:1051, 2:1062–63
Kattahha, 1:221
Katu. *See* Kö-Du
Kaukaï, 1:305
Kaundinya, 2:924
Kaurava (Kurawa): in India, 2:829, 2:832; in insular Southeast Asia, 2:955, 2:956
Kauśalyā, 2:834
Kawa, 1:117, 1:120
Kayon, 2:933
Kazak, 2:1090, 2:1102
Kazantzakis, Nikos, 2:790
Kaz Dagi (Mount of Geese), Turkey, 2:1091, 2:1103
Kazi Dawa Samdup, 2:903
K'Du kon Bo, 2:994
Keating. *See* Céitinn
Keats, John, 2:755, 2:774
Kekchis, 2:1178
Kekrops. *See* Cecrops
Kenduri arwah, 2:951
Kengyō, 2:1039
Keos, 1:333
Kere, 1:538
Keres, 1:374, 1:405, 1:480
Kerewa, 2:1226
Këshetë, 1:307
Keśin, 2:867
Ket, 2:1118, 2:1119, 2:1128
Kha, 2:976
Khalkha, 2:1090
Khara, 2:837
Khazars, 2:1079, 2:1089
Khepri, 1:94
Khitan, 2:1089, 2:1099, 2:1100, 2:1102, 2:1103, 2:1106, 2:1109, 2:1112
Khmers. *See* Southeast Asia
Khnum, 1:91, 1:92, 1:95, 1:102, 1:107, *1:108*, 1:109
Không Lo, 2:996
Khonsu, 1:104
Khri-rgyal-ba, 2:1086
Khun, 2:916
Khun Borom, 2:916
Khutsauty Khutsau, 1:316
Khvarenah, 2:887
Khyab-pa lag-ring, 2:1081–82
Khyong shang, 2:918
Kiao, 2:1002–3
Kibuka, 1:79
Kigwa, 1:80
Kijoten, 2:900
Kikimora, 1:298
Kimpasi, 1:70
Kingship. *See* Royalty
Kingu, 1:3, 1:158–60, 1:172, 1:175, 1:178
Kinich Ahau, 2:1180
Kinnari, 2:926, *2:927*
Ki no Tsurayuki, 2:1042
Kinpu, Mount (in Japan), *2:1056*, 2:1062–63
Kintu, 1:79
Kiowa, 2:1153, 2:1156, 2:1163
Kiranga, 1:80
Kircher, Athanasius, 1:139–40, 2:705, 2:709–10
Kirghiz, 2:1089, 2:1090, 2:1099, 2:1102, 2:1103, 2:1106, 2:1110
Kišar, 1:159
Kishi, 2:1095
Kisula, 1:70
Kitomi, 1:71
Kivanga, 1:64
Kizzuwatna, 1:217, 1:221, 1:222, 1:227
Kleist, Heinrich von, 2:755, 2:766–67, 2:774
Kling, 2:986
Klinger, Friedrich Maximilian von, 2:769
Klopstock, Friedrich Gottlieb, 2:752
Klu, *klu-mo*, 2:1079–80
Klu rgyal-mo srid-pa gtan-la phab-pa, 2:1080
Kōbō Daishi, 2:1039, 2:1057, 2:1069
Kodai, *2:843*, 2:844, *2:844*, 2:847
Kö-Du, Katu, 2:981, 2:994
Kofinas, Mount (in Crete), 1:336
Kögmen, 2:1102
Kojiki, 2:1051
Koko, 2:1226
Koma, 2:1052
Komo, 1:68, 1:73
Komo (society), 1:32, 1:36, 1:39, 1:41, 1:44, 1:45
Komori Myōjin, 2:1051
Köndös, 2:1136
Kongo, 1:64–65, 1:70, 1:71, 1:73
Kong-tse, 2:1078
Konkō-kyō, 2:1040
K'op'ala, 1:312–13
Kore, 1:199, 1:381, 1:406, 1:453, 1:409–12, *1:455*
Korea, 2:1070–75, *2:1070–72*, *2:1074*; Buddhism in, 2:893–95
Korina, 2:1220
Köroglu, 2:1113
Koryak, 2:1128
Koshōgatsu, 2:1067
Kostienki, USSR, 1:19
Kötang, 2:990
Kothar, 1:208, 1:209, 1:215
Kotharat, 1:214
Kotoage, 2:1041
Kotodama, 2:1041, 2:1054
Koubebe, 1:217
Kouros, 1:438, 1:439
Kouros (god), 1:333
Kōya, Mount (in Japan), 2:1039, 2:1046, 2:1048, 2:1052
Kramat, *2:935*, 2:936
Kratos, 1:371, 1:375, 1:377
Kreuzer, Frederick, 2:754
Kri Koro, 1:31
Krishna. *See* Kṛṣṇa
Krodha, 2:816
Kronos, Kronides, 1:335, 1:355, 1:369, 1:371–73, 1:375–78, *1:376*, 1:379, 1:380, 1:381, 1:385, 1:386, 1:399, 1:405, 1:463, 1:465, 1:490, 1:511; to Gnostics, 2:677, 2:681, 2:682
Kṛpa, 2:830, 2:832–33, 2:868
Kṛpī, 2:868
Kṛṣṇa, 2:816, 2:823, 2:829–33, 2:835, 2:839, 2:850–52, 2:853, 2:859–64, *2:859*, *2:860*, *2:862*, *2:863*, 2:897, 2:928
Kṛtavarman, 2:832
Kṛtavīrya, 2:875
Kṛta Yuga, 2:850
Kṛttika, 2:867–68, 2:896
Kruṅ Bāli, 2:926
Kṣatriya, 2:801–2, 2:807, 2:827, 2:828, 2:836, 2:852, 2:856–58, 2:859–63
Kshatra, 2:886
Ku, *2:1222*
Kuba, 1:67, 1:68, *1:68*, 1:73
Kubaba, 1:217, 1:226, 1:229
Kubele. *See* Koubebe
Kubera, 2:835, 2:900
Kūbu, 1:160
Kuçedër, 1:307
Kūkai, 2:1040, 2:1048, 2:1052
Kukailimoku, 2:1220
Kulitta, 1:224, 1:226
Kulla, 1:147, 1:156–57
Kulshedër, 1:307
Kuma, 2:1226, 2:1227, 2:1229
Kumano Gongen, 2:1059
Kumāra, 2:867–68, 2:896, 2:903
Kumarbi, 1:224, 1:226, 1:227, 1:228
Kummi, 1:228
Kŭmwa, 2:1071
Kuṇḍali Yaksa, 2:903
Kunhu, 2:1182
Kuniyawanni, 1:221
Kunlun, 2:1009, 2:1012–13, 2:1017, 2:1033
Kuntadi, 2:957
Kuntī: in India, 2:829, 2:831, 2:833; in insular Southeast Asia (Dewi Kunti), 2:956
Kurawa. *See* Kaurava
Kurdalaegon, 1:316, 1:318, 2:1114
Kure, 1:401
Kurke, 1:306
Kurozumi-kyō, 2:1040
Kurukṣetra, 2:875
Kurumba, 1:27
Kuśa, 2:839
Kù-sig, 1:157
Kušuh, 1:217, 1:224, 1:226
Kuula, 2:1222
Kuvēra, 2:899, 2:900–901, 2:903, 2:907, 2:918
Kuwaššaš, 1:219

Kuzanišu, 1:220
Kvasir, 1:287
K'viria, 1:308, 1:311
Kwakiutl, 2:1152, 2:1158, 2:1161
Kwore, 1:32, 1:36, 1:39, 1:41, 1:44
Kyaka, 2:1226
Kybistra. *See* Hubešna
Kyns, 2:1120
Kyomya, 1:78

L

Laash and Hama, kingdom of, 1:200
Labdacus, 1:403–5, 1:499, 1:500
Labensky, Jean, 2:771
Labyrinth: in China, 2:1033–34; in Greece, 1:335, 1:337, 1:342, 1:388–89; in literature, 2:706, 2:785
Lacandons, 2:1166, 2:1186
Lac Long-Quān, 2:1002
Lactantius, 1:133, 1:134, 1:631, 2:659, 2:666, 2:667, 2:669, 2:694, 2:698, 2:771
Ladon, 1:490
Ladra, 1:258
Lady Au-Co, 2:1002
LaFontaine, Jean de, 2:728
La Galigo, 2:942, 2:944
Laḫamu, 1:159, 1:161, 1:172
Laḫmu, 1:159, 1:161, 1:172
Laigin (Leinster), Ireland, 1:241, 1:258, 1:265, 1:271
Laigne Lethan-glas, 1:258
Laima, 1:306
Laius, 1:404–5, 1:499, 1:500
Lakish, Israel, 1:183
Lakṣmaṇa, 2:835, 2:836–37, 2:957
Lakṣmī, 2:841, 2:854, *2:855,* 2:869, 2:874
Lallariya, 1:221
Lamaholot, 2:938
La Marche, Olivier de, 1:136
Lamartine, Alphonse de, 2:752, 2:754, 2:756, 2:768, 2:769, 2:775, 2:777
Lamashtu, 1:3
Lamberti, Archangelo, 2:1114
Lamennais, Félicité Robert de, 2:754
Lamos, 1:382
La Motte-Fouqué, Friedrich de, 2:772
Lancelot, 1:267, 2:715
Lang, 2:987
Lanite, 2:952
Laodamas, 1:404–5
Laojun, 2:1036
Laomedon, 1:438
Laos. *See* Southeast Asia
Laozi, 1:1029, 2:1009, *2:1035,* 2:1034–36
La Pasiega, Spain, 1:16
Lapps, 2:1132, 2:1133, 2:1135–38 passim, *2:1136, 2:1137*
Lara, 1:622
Laran. *See* Larun
Larentia, 1:635
Lares and Lases, 1:520, 1:565, *1:574,* 1:575, 1:604, 1:610, *1:618,* 1:622–23, *1:622,* 1:625; in literature, 2:788
Laro, 1:58
Larun (Laran), 1:526
Lasa, 1:531
Lasa Vecu, 1:519, 1:531
Lascaux, Dordogne, 1:13–16, *1:17,* 1:19
Las Chimeneas, Spain, 1:15
Lases. *See* Lares
Lasha Giorgi, 1:311
Lashari, 1:310, 1:313–14
La Tenritatta, 2:944
Latins, 1:515, 1:544–45, 1:552
Latinus, 1:546, 1:640
La Toge'langi', 2:941, 2:953
Latona, 1:564, 1:565, *1:565,* 1:602
Lato Phytia, 1:335
Latouche, Henri de, 2:766
Lature Danö, 2:937, 2:940
Latvians, 1:302, 1:305–6
Laugerie-Basse, Dordogne, 1:19
Laukamat, 1:302, 1:306
Laukosargas, 1:306
Lauma, 1:305
Lava, 2:839
Lavinium, Italy, 1:545, 1:546–47, 1:572, 1:573, 1:574, 1:623, 1:629
Lawrence, D. H., 2:783, 2:786
Layamon, 1:265, 2:714
Learchus, 1:442, 1:444
Lebe Seru, 1:33–34
Leconte de Lisle (pseudonym for Charles Marie Leconte), 2:758, 2:759
Lectisternium, 1:563–65
Leda, 1:458, 1:463; in Renaissance art, 2:700
Le Fèvre de la Boderie, Guy, 2:705, 2:712, 2:773
Lei, 2:907
Leimōn, 1:410
Leino, Armas Eino Leopold, 2:758
Leinster. *See* Laigin
Leinth, 1:526
Lele, 1:68, 1:70
Lelwani, 1:221, 1:227
Lemba, 1:65
Lemo nTonda, 2:942–43
Lemures, 1:568, 1:643
Lemuria, 1:568, 1:582, 1:643
Lenaea, 1:461
Lēnai, 1:461
Lenau, Nikolaus, 2:769, 2:770
Lenggang perut, 2:949
Lenoir, Alexandre, 1:142, 2:754
Lenus, 1:249
Leo of Pella, 2:667, 2:668
Leopardi, Giacomo, 2:755
Leo the Philosopher, 2:673
Lera Wulan, 2:933, 2:938
Lerna, source of, 1:400
Leroux, Pierre, 2:754, 2:769
Lešii, 1:298
Lespugue, Haute-Garonne, 1:19
Letha(m), 1:520, 1:526, 1:534
Leto, 1:128, 1:216, 1:334, 1:375, 1:438, 1:439
Leucetios, 1:249
Leucippe, 1:355, 1:472
Leucippides, 1:476
Leucothea, 1:335, 1:384, 1:442, 1:546
Levavasseur, 2:770
Leviathan, 2:651
Lewis, Matthew Gregory, 2:767, 2:769
Lha-rgod thog-pa, 2:1080
Liath, 1:258
Libanius, 1:396, 2:775
Libenice, Bohemia, 1:246
Liber, 1:561, 1:562, 1:563, 1:565, 1:568, 1:612
Libera, 1:561, 1:562, 1:563, 1:565, 1:612
Li Bing, 2:1028
Lidaiya, 2:929
Liêu Hanh, 2:999
Líf, 1:286
Líf Þrasir, 1:286
Light: for Gnostics, 2:683; in Greece, 1:369, 1:370, 1:464–65; for Inuit, 2:1147, 2:1152; in pre-Islamic Iran, 2:886; in Tibet, 2:1081, 2:1082
Lightning. *See* Thunder
Lihyanites, 1:192
Līlā, 2:861
Liluri, 1:226
Liman Sena, 2:956
Lindanda, 2:1219
Linga, *2:808, 2:811,* 2:812–13, 2:824, 2:825, 2:841–42, 2:927
Ling Bao, 2:1033–34
Ling-dkar, 2:1078
Linjun, 2:1027
Linthaut, Henri de, 2:706
Linwu dong tian, 2:1033, 2:1034
Liparus, 1:546
Lippi, Filippo, 1:136
Lishi, 2:900, 2:902, 2:907
Literature: of insular Southeast Asia, 2:959–61; of Middle Ages and Renaissance, 2:692–705, 2:711–12; of sixteenth and seventeenth centuries, 2:706–11; of seventeenth and eighteenth centuries, 2:722–32; of eighteenth and nineteenth centuries (romanticism), 2:752–58, 2:765–72, 2:774–77; of nineteenth and twentieth centuries, 1:5–10, 2:758–64, 2:772–74, 2:783–95. *See also* Poetry
Lithuanians, 1:302, 1:305–6
Liu Xiang, 2:1011, 2:1036
Livy, 1:185, 1:520, 1:526, 1:535, 1:544, 1:545, 1:547, 1:548, 1:550–52 passim, 1:555, 1:561–65 passim, 1:570, 1:575, 1:577, 1:578, 1:583, 1:586, 1:588, 1:590–91, 1:599, 1:602–3, 1:605, 1:606, 1:612, 1:615–28 passim, 1:635–46 passim
Llefelys, 1:263–64
Lleu, 1:259, 1:262, 1:263
Lludd, 1:263–64
Llwyd, 1:262, 1:264
Llŷr, 1:262, 1:263, 1:265
Lmalayekkat, 1:87
Loango, kingdom of, 1:70–71
Loch Lethglas, 1:259, 1:264
Lóðurr, 1:287, 1:295
Loeghaire Buadhach, 1:271
Logun Èdè, 1:61
Loki, 1:285, 1:286, 1:294–95
Lona, 2:1222
Lo-ngam, 2:1088
Longus, 1:505
Long-vuong, 2:1000
Lönnrot, Elias, 2:1133–34
Lopemat, 1:306
Loptr, 1:285, 1:295
Lorrain, Jean, 2:758, 2:760
Loucetios. *See* Leucetios
Loudera, 1:542
Loutrophoria, 1:400
Lovecraft, H. P., 2:792–93
Lovedu, 1:68
Lowalangi, 2:937, 2:940
Loxias, 1:440
Lua Mater, 1:552
Luang pho, 2:915, 2:930
Luba, 1:67–68, 1:70–71, 1:72–73
Lubi, 1:307
Lucan, 1:242, 1:243, 1:246, 1:273, 1:278, 1:279, 1:550, 2:656
Lucaria, 1:583, 1:628
Luceres, 1:552
Lucian of Samosate, 1:185, 1:195, 1:202, 1:244, 1:275, 1:432, 1:433, 1:435, 1:631, 2:772
Lucifer, 2:660
Lucilius Balbus, 1:598–99
Lucius, Afranius, 1:634
Lucretius, 1:535, 1:550, 1:599
Lucumon, 1:552, 1:589
Lue jajiny, 2:1220
Lueji, 1:67, 1:72
Lugh, 1:258, 1:259, 1:263, 1:264, 1:279, 2:733
Lugoves, 1:259
Łukaszewka, Moldavia (USSR), 1:270
Lulahi, 1:219, 1:221
Lull, Raymond, 2:708
Lullû, 1:159, 1:160
Lumawig, 2:938
Luna, 1:565
Lunda, 1:67–68, 1:72
Luo, goddess of the (Luoshen), 2:1013, 2:1018
Luo Mewöna, 2:937, 2:940
Luong pho, 2:930
Lupercalia, 1:551, 1:560, 1:574, 1:578, 1:600, 1:607, 1:616–17
Lupercus (luperci), 1:551, 1:616–17
Lussa, 1:482
Lu Thai, 2:929
Luther, Martin, 2:696
Lutung Kasarung, 2:961
Luwians, 1:216, 1:217, 1:219, 1:221

Lycaon, 1:443
Lycia, 1:229
Lycophron, 1:450, 1:548, 2:663
Lycurgus, 1:458, 1:459, 1:476
Lycus, 1:404, 1:547
Lydus, 1:602
Lympha, 1:565
Lynceus, 1:400
Lysias, 1:343

M

Ma, 1:554
Maa, 2:977, 2:981
Maajan, 2:949
Maam, *2:1217*
Ma'at, 1:92, 1:97, 1:107, *1:108*
Mabinogi, 1:240–41, 1:260–65
Mabitu, 2:952
Mabon, 1:265
Mabonagrain, 1:267
Mac Cécht, 1:260
Mac Cuill, 1:260
Mac Greíne, 1:260
Macha, 1:270
Machado, Manuel, 2:758
Machaon, 1:449
Mac-mai, 2:985
MacPherson, James, 2:752
Macrobius, 1:138, 1:471, 1:534, 1:557, 1:562, 1:573, 1:582, 1:590, 1:602, 1:612, 1:616, 1:618, 1:619, 1:622, 1:631, 1:640, 2:698, 2:771
Madagascar, 2:961–76
Madeleine, La, Dordogne, 1:19
Madhu, 2:870
Mādrī, 2:829
Maelgwn, 1:264
Maenads, Maenadism, 1:456, 1:457, 1:461; in art and literature, 2:700, 2:787
Maeterlinck, Maurice, 2:758
Maghreb, 1:84–88
Magic: in Albania, 1:307–8; in Asia Minor, 1:217; in China, 2:1031; for continental Celts, 1:253; in Egypt, 1:128–31; for Finno-Ugrians, 2:1135–36; for Germano-Nordic peoples, 1:282–84, 1:286–87, 1:288, 1:291, 1:292–93; for Gnostics, 2:685–86; for Greece, 1:384, 1:385, 1:444; for Gypsies, 2:720, 2:721–22; for insular Celts, 1:240, 1:259, 1:261–63, 1:264, 1:274; in Japan, 2:1037–40 passim, 2:1042–43, 2:1055, 2:1056–58, 2:1062–63; in Korea, 2:1071–72; in Mesoamerica, 2:1190; in Mesopotamia, 1:164; for prehistoric peoples, 1:12–13, 1:16–18; in pre-Islamic Iran, 2:880, 2:890, 2:892; in Rome, 1:578–79; for Slavs, 1:298; in southern Africa (Bantu), 1:64; in Tibet, 2:1081–82; for Turks and Mongols, 2:1089, 2:1103–4
Magna Mater, 1:554, 1:563, 1:600
Mah, 1:177
Mahābala, 2:902
Mahābhārata (MBh), 2:816–17, 2:829–34, 2:850–51
Mahādeva: in India, 2:816, 2:896, 2:903; in insular Southeast Asia, 2:953
Mahākāla, *2:897*, 2:898–99, 2:900–901, 2:903, 2:904, 2:905–8 passim
Mahākalpa, 2:819, 2:820, 2:821, 2:850, 2:852
Mahālakṣmī, 2:869
Mahāmāyā, 2:871
Mahān (ātmā), 2:818–19, 2:820
Maharaja Buno, 2:940
Maharloka, 2:821
Mahatala, 2:935, 2:937–38
Mahāyāna, 2:906, 2:929
Mahāyuga, 2:820, 2:850
Maheo, 2:1156
Maheśvara, 2:896, 2:898, *2:900*, 2:901, 2:902
Mahiṣa, Mahiṣi, 2:849, 2:867, 2:868, 2:871
Mahrem, 1:192
Mahungu, 1:65
Maia, 1:485, 1:627, 1:645
Maier, 2:701, 2:708, 2:711, 2:755
Maïn *(maïn)*, 2:1116, 2:1119
Ma'in, 1:192
Maistre, Joseph de, 2:753
Maitreya, 2:904, 2:905, 2:1048
Malakbel, 1:204, 1:205
Malatya, Turkey, 1:222, 1:223
Malavis(ch), 1:531
Malay, 2:930
Malayo-Polynesians. *See* Austroasiatic and Austronesian peoples
Malaysia. *See* Insular Southeast Asia
Malecite, 2:1153
Malia, Crete, 1:338, 1:339
Malik Ibrahim, 2:945, *2:946*
Malineus, 1:332
Malinke, 1:29–34, 1:37, 1:39, 1:41, 1:44, 1:45, 1:49, 1:50, 1:52
Maliya, 1:220, 1:229
Malkat-Shamain, 1:203
Malkuyu, 2:1182
Mallarmé, Stéphane, 2:759–62, 2:779–80, 2:785
Mallet, Paul-Henri, 2:752
Malory, Sir Thomas, 2:714–15, 2:718
Malsum, 2:1153, 2:1160
Mam, 2:1178
Mama Cuna, 2:1203
Mamallapuram, India, 2:877
Mamers (Mamertini), 1:517, 1:522, 1:538, 1:543
Mami, 1:175, 1:178
Mamuralia, 1:602
Man, first. *See* Creation; Origin, myths of
Manabozo, 2:1153, 2:1156, 2:1160
Manah, Manyu, 2:888
Manannán mac Lir, 1:259, 1:261, 1:262
Manas, 2:819
Manasa, 1:332
Manat, 1:192, 1:193, 1:204
Manawydan, 1:261, 1:262, 1:265, 1:267
Mandan, 2:1158, 2:1160, 2:1162, 2:1163
Mande (Manding), 1:27, 1:29–39, *1:31*, 1:41, 1:49, 1:50
Mandu-daki, 2:957
Mandudari, 2:957
Mandulis, 1:120
Manes, 1:520, 1:534, 1:559, 1:623–24
Mangala, 1:33
Mangalabulan, 2:937, 2:940
Mangi, 2:1116, 2:1124, 2:1125
Mang-ling, 2:981, 2:984–85
Mangu, 1:34
Mania, 1:520, 1:526, 1:622
Manichaeans, Manichaeism, 2:886
Mani Kabunga, 1:71
Manikmaya, 2:954
Manimekhala, 2:918, 2:926
Mani Vunda, 1:71
Mañjuśrī, 2:898, 2:899, 2:900, 2:901, 2:904, 2:907
Mannucci, Aldo, 2:699
Mansip, 2:1216
Mansur Halladj, 2:1102
Mantegna, Andrea, 2:699, 2:701
Mantus, 1:520, 1:526
Manu, 2:853–54
Manyanga, 1:65
Manyu, 2:814
Manzoni, Alessandro, 2:777
Map, Walter, 2:715
Maponus, 1:249
Mapuche, 2:1198
Māra, 2:919, 2:926
Marae, 2:1209
Marchangy, Louis de, 2:753
Marcius, 1:588, 1:603
Marduk, 1:3, 1:145, 1:146, 1:151, 1:154, 1:155, 1:157, 1:158–61, 1:165, 1:167–68, 1:171, 1:172, 1:178–81
Mare, 1:397, 1:432
Mares, 1:519
Margana, 2:957
Marhaši, 1:147
Mari, Mesopotamia, 1:182, 1:184, 1:190–91, 1:225, 1:227
Mārīca, 2:837
Marind Anim, 2:1226, *2:1227*
Marini, Giambattista, 2:725
Marinus, 1:361
Marinus Barletius, 1:308
Maris, 1:519, 1:520
Marivaux, 2:726
Marka, 1:41, 1:49, 1:52
Markayok, 2:1202
Marmadi, 2:946
Marmaya, 2:946
Marōdo-gami, 2:1068–69
Marriage: in France, 2:746–49; in Georgia, 1:309, 1:314; in Greece, 1:341, 1:395–403, 1:409–10, 1:423, 1:424, 1:454, 1:476–77, 1:485, 1:490; in India, 2:829; in insular Southeast Asia, 2:949; in Madagascar, 2:972; in Mesopotamia, 1:176; in pre-Islamic Iran, 2:882; in Tibet, 2:1078, 2:1088; in Ugarit, 1:214; in West Africa (Mande), 1:34
Mars, 1:537–38, 1:542–43, *1:544*, 1:552–53, 1:563–65, 1:568, 1:575, 1:576–77, 1:603–5, 1:608, 1:624–25, *1:625*, 1:635, 1:636, 1:637, *1:637*; in art and literature of the Middle Ages and Renaissance, 2:695, 2:700; to continental Celts, 1:249, 1:279, 1:733
Marsilio Ficino, 1:133–34, 2:700, 2:773
Marsyas, *1:491*, *2:701*; in Greece, 1:491; in Renaissance art, 2:700; in Rome, 1:519
Mart-, 1:553
Martial, 1:602, 1:631
Martianus Capella, 1:133, 1:534, 2:698
Martu, 1:147
Maru, 2:1223
Marwazi, 2:1103
Mary, Virgin: for Gypsies, 2:720; in literature, 2:774–75
Masalo, 2:1220
Masauwu, 2:1161
Masculine principle: for Austroasiatics and Austronesians, 2:983, 2:990; in China, 2:1014; for Gnostics, 2:676, 2:682–85, 2:686–87; in Greece, 1:341, 1:379, 1:390, 1:392, 1:399, 1:467–68, 1:470–72; in India, 2:806, 2:842, 2:849; in insular Southeast Asia, 2:933–35, 2:938, 2:952; in the Maghreb, 1:85; in Mesoamerica, 2:1179, 2:1187; in Papua New Guinea, 2:1227–28; for prehistoric peoples, 1:12–14, 1:16, 1:19–20; in southern Africa (Bantu), 1:67, 1:69. *See also* Androgyne
Mas-d'Azil, Ariège, 1:12, *1:17*
Masewi, 2:1153
Mashira, 1:80
Masks: in China, 2:1029, 2:1031; in Greece, 1:456, 1:461; in Oceania, 2:1220, 2:1223; in Papua New Guinea, 2:1229; in South America, 2:1200; in Southeast Asia, 2:916; in southern Africa (Bantu), 1:64; in Tibet, 2:906; in West Africa, 1:26–27, 1:32, 1:39, 1:45–49, 1:50
Mater Larum, 1:622
Mater Matuta, 1:551–52, 1:577
Math, 1:261, 1:262–63
Matha, 1:261
Matholwch, 1:262
Mathonwy, 1:261, 1:262
Mathu, 1:261

Matlaltzinca, 2:1182
Māṭrs, 2:867
Matralia, 1:551–52, 1:577, 1:583
Matres, 1:249
Matronalia, 1:620
Matsuri, 2:1063–64, 2:1067
Matsya, 2:853–54
Mau Ipi Guloq, 2:934, 2:941–42
Mauitikitiki (Mwatikitiki), 2:1217–18, 2:1219, 2:1222
Maurot. *See* Haurot and Maurot
Mavilly, Côte-d'Or, 1:257, 1:280
Maximus of Ephesus, 1:360
Maximus of Turin, 2:657–58
Maximus of Tyre, 1:507
Maximus the Confessor, 2:656
Māyā *(māyā),* 2:802, 2:861, 2:865, 2:896
Maya Danawa, 2:948
Ma Yăn, 2:995
Mayas, 1:1167–91, *2:1178*
Mayauel, 2:1186
Mayombe, 1:64–65
Mazahua, 2:1171
Mazatecs, 2:1186
Mazdā. *See* Ahura Mazdā
Mbandwa, 1:79
Mbata, 1:65, 1:70, 1:71–72
Mbenza, 1:64–65
Mbidi Kiluwe, 1:67, 1:70, 1:72, 1:73
Mbowang, 2:1226, 2:1229
Mbumba, 1:65–67, 1:71
Mbuti, 1:21
Me, 1:147–48
Mean, 1:531
Meath. *See* Midhe
Mēchanē, mēchanēma, 1:406–8, 1:496
Medea, 1:442–43, 1:444–45, 1:510; in literature, 2:702, 2:703
Meder. *See* Beher
Medes, 2:877, 2:880
Medhbh, 1:270–71
Medrawd, 1:264, 1:265
Medusa, 1:382, 1:408, 1:410, 1:473, *1:473,* 1:480, 1:509; in art of the Middle Ages, 2:697
Mefitis, 1:522, 1:538, 1:539
Megara Hyblaea, Sicily, 1:534
Megiddo, Israel, 1:183
Méher. *See* Mithra
Meiden, 1:306
Melanesia. *See* Oceania
Melanion, 1:421
Melanippus, 1:446
Melanthus, 1:329
Mele, 2:1222
Méléagant (Melwas), 1:267
Meleager, 1:414, 1:418, 1:419, 1:421, 1:447–48
Meles, 1:472
Melesagoras, 1:507
Melete, 1:492
Melia, 1:391, 1:393
Meliai, 1:373–74, 1:391
Melicertes, 1:442, 1:444, 1:459
Melissa, 1:395
Melissai, 1:335, 1:396, 1:433, 1:454
Melqart (Milqart), 1:194, 1:196, *1:196,* 1:197, 1:200
Meluhha, 1:147
Mélusine, 2:689, 2:735, 2:745, *2:745*
Melwas, 1:265
Memnon, 2:708
Memory, *See* Mnemosyne
Memphis, Egypt, 1:91, 1:92, 1:93
Mēn, 1:217; to Perates, 2:681
Menakā, 2:828
Menak Jingga, 2:960
Menander, 1:196, 1:330, 2:1109
Ménard, Louis, 2:754, 2:758, 2:768, 2:771, 2:776
Mencius, 2:1023, 2:1025
Mendi, 2:1226
Mene, 1:128, 2:685
Menechmes, in literature, 2:766
Menelaus, 1:404, 1:417, 1:446, 1:477; in Christianity, 2:660
Menerva, 1:520
Menesthus, 1:546
Menggin, 2:943
Mennens, Guillaume, 2:712
Menoeceus, 1:404
Menoetius, 1:371
Mens, 1:565, 1:587, 1:599
Mentor, 1:387
Menuthis, in literature, 1:136
Menzana, 1:522, 1:540
Mera, 2:926
Mercury, *1:255, 1:560,* 1:564–65, 1:625–27, *1:626;* in art and literature, 2:697, 2:698, 2:700; for continental Celts, 1:252–53, 1:254, 1:275, 1:279
Merig, island, 2:1216–17
Mérimée, Prosper, 2:770
Merina, 2:962, *2:963, 2:970,* 2:973
Merlin, 2:689
Mermnades, 1:355
Meroe, 1:115–20
Mertronnus, 1:276
Meru, Mount, 2:930
Méry, Joseph, 2:769
Me Sar, 2:923
Mesh, 1:120
Meskene. *See* Emar
Meskhenet, 1:99, 1:104
Mesoamerica, 2:1165–91, *2:1181*
Mesopotamia, 1:142–81, *1:158, 1:160, 1:161*
Messapians, 1:540
Messapus, 1:540
Messianism: in Indochina, 2:985; in insular Southeast Asia, 2:958–59; in Oceania, 2:1212, 2:1223–24
Messou, 2:1153
Metabus, 1:546
Metapontum, 1:534, 1:546, 1:547
Metapontus, 1:546
Methodius of Olympus, 2:657
Metiadousa, 1:388
Metion, Metionidae, 1:388
Metis, 1:367, 1:376–77, 1:378, 1:380, 1:382, 1:386–87, 1:399, 1:414, 1:444, 1:463, 1:465, 1:511
Mētis, 1:376–78, 1:387–88, 1:390, 1:406–9, 1:414, 1:418, 1:422, 1:444, 1:449, 1:485–89, 1:494–98
Metztli, 2:1183
Mē Ya Ngam, 2:916
Mezamat, 1:306
Mezurashizuka, Japan, 2:1045, 2:1047
Mezythe, 2:1115
Mezzulla, 1:220, 1:226
mGon-po Ben, 2:898
Mher, 1:321
Miaoshan, 2:907
Michael (archangel), 2:1095
Michelangelo, 2:700
Michelet, Jules, 2:693, 2:756, 2:765, 2:767, 2:768
Mi che-riṅ, 2:907
Mickiewicz, Adam, 2:778
Micmac, 2:1153, 2:1160
Mictlan, 2:1191
Mictlantecuhtli, 2:1179, 2:1180
Midas, 1:491
Mider, 1:259
Miðgarðr, 1:281, 1:286, 1:294
Miðgarðsormr, 1:294, 1:295
Midhe (Meath), 1:240
Mifei, 2:1018
Mihir, Mihr. *See* Mithra
Mihrnigar, 2:946
Miji jingang, 2:899–900, 2:903
Mikal, 1:197
Mikenu, 2:1045
Mikkyō, 2:894, 2:1039
Miko, 2:1066, *2:1069*
Míl, sons of, 1:257–60
Milkashtart, 1:194, 1:196
Miluo, 2:905–8
Milosz, Oscar Vladislas de Lubicz, 2:761–63
Milqart. *See* Melqart
Milton, John, 2:752–53, 2:755, 2:757, 2:767, 2:768
Mímir, 1:281, 1:294
Min, 1:101, 1:109
Minahasa, 2:933, 2:934
Minderer, Raymond, 2:708
Minerva, 1:520, 1:553, 1:563–64, 1:565, *1:622,* 1:627, *1:627,* 1:628; in art and literature, 1:640, 1:700, *2:706;* for continental Celts, 1:254
Mingrelians, 2:1115
Ming-tang, 2:1010
Minki, 1:227
Min Mahagiri, 2:918
Minoikon Hieron, Kato Simi, Crete, 1:337
Minos, 1:335, 1:337–39, 1:388–90, 1:404, 1:473, 1:510, 1:546
Minotaur, 1:335, 1:337, 1:342, 1:345, 1:382, 1:388–89; in literature, 2:706–7
Minucius Felix, 2:659, 2:667, 2:668, 2:669, 2:670
Minyanka, 1:29, 1:30–32, 1:37, 1:41, 1:44, 1:45
Miroku, 2:1039, 2:1048
Mist, 1:287
Mitanni, 1:225, 1:226, 1:227
Mithra, *1:556,* 2:877–78, 2:887, 2:888, 2:890–91, 2:891–92, 2:893; in Christianity, 2:662, 2:674; for continental Celts, 1:243; in Rome, 1:557
Mitra, 2:802, 2:886
Miwa, Mount, 2:1051
Mixcoatl, 2:1179
Mixtecs, 2:1180, 2:1183, *2:1190*
Mixuga, 2:1157
Mjöllnir, 1:285
Mlacuch, 1:531
Mneme, 1:492
Mnemosyne, 1:371–72, 1:375, 1:414, 1:465, 1:492
Mnong, 2:977, *2:978,* 2:981
Mochica, 2:1201, *2:1202*
Mocovi, 2:1198
Mogons, 1:249
Mohinī, 2:848
Moï, 2:976
Moirai, 1:128, *1:368,* 1:375, 1:378, 1:396, 1:405, 1:406, 1:447, 1:480, 1:491; to Perates, 2:681
Mokoš, 1:297, 1:300
Molos, 1:414
Molu, 2:678
Momata Tibu, 2:943
Moncapat, 2:933
Mondred, 2:714
Mongols. *See* Turks and Mongols
Mōn-Khmer. *See* Austroasiatic and Austronesian peoples
Monsters. *See* Animals; Demons
Montagnais, 2:1153, 2:1157
Monte Albān, Mexico, 2:1176
Montebelluna, Italy, 1:522
Monte Circeo, Italy, 1:12
Montfaucon, Bernard de, 1:140
Moon, symbolism and divinities of: in the Andes, 2:1201; in art and literature, 2:694, 2:783; in Asia Minor, 1:217; for the Baltic peoples, 1:305; in China, 2:1010–11, 2:1020; in Crete and Mycenae, 1:336; in Egypt, 1:103, 1:105, 1:128, 1:130; in Georgia, 1:309; for the Germano-Nordic peoples, 1:282; for the Gnostics, 2:685–86; in Greece, 1:371, 1:468, 1:471, 1:478; for the Hittites, 1:224; for the Hurrites, 1:226; in India, 2:803, 2:807, 2:897; in Indochina, 2:985; for the Indo-Europeans, 1:238; in insular Southeast Asia, 2:933, 2:937–38, 2:940, 2:943, 2:952; for the Inuit, 2:1148–49; in Korea, 2:1070; in Mesoamerica, 2:1175–76, 2:1180–82; in North America, 2:1153, 2:1157, 2:1161, 2:1163; for the Palmyrenes, 1:205; in pre-Roman Italy, 1:520; in Rome, 1:620; in

South America, 2:1194; in Southeast Asia, 2:924–26; in southern Africa (Bantu), 1:64, 1:67, 1:68–69, 1:70, 1:73, 1:74–75; for the Turks and Mongols, 2:1091–92, 2:1095, 2:1106; in Ugarit, 1:214; in Vietnam, 2:997; in West Africa (Mande), 1:50
Mordwins, 2:1134
Moréas, Jean, 2:759
Moreau, Gustave, 2:758, 2:765
Morgan Le Fay (Morgana), 2:689, 2:735
Morges, 1:546
Morige, 1:310
Morisot, Claude Barthélémy, 2:703
Moritasgus, 1:267
Morufonu, 2:1226–27
Moses, 2:649, 2:659, 2:660, 2:661, 2:681; in literature, 2:759
Moses of Khorene, 1:320, 1:321
Mot, 1:210–12
Mother goddesses: of the Baltic, 1:306; of China, 2:1015–18, 2:1023; of the continental Celts, 1:249, 1:251; of Crete and Mycenae, 1:333, 1:334; of Egypt, 1:103; of the Germano-Nordic peoples, 1:285; of the Gnostics, 2:680; of Greece, 1:122, 1:453; of the Hittites, 1:228–29; of the Maghreb, 1:84–87; of Mesopotamia, 1:148–49; of pre-Roman Italy, 1:546; of Rome, 1:551–52
Moulo, 2:721
Mountain, symbolism and divinities of: in China, 2:1012–13; in Crete and Mycenae, 1:335–37; for Hittites, 1:218; in India, 2:869–70; in insular Southeast Asia, 2:938, 2:952–53; in Japan, 2:1038, 2:1045–46, 2:1051–53, 2:1056–58, 2:1059, 2:1064; in Korea, 2:1073–74; in Mesoamerica, 2:1179, 2:1184–85; in Southeast Asia, 2:918, 2:920, 2:921; in Tibet, 2:1086; for Turks and Mongols, 2:1096, 2:1102–3; in Vietnam, 2:1002–3
Mount Alban (in Rome), 1:544, 1:561, 1:615
Mouso Koroni, 1:38–39
Moye, 2:1032
Mozart, Wolfgang Amadeus, 1:141, 2:770, 2:773, 2:774
Mozi, 2:1029
Mrga, 2:814
Mšecké Žehrovice, Bohemia, 1:246
Mts'evar, 1:314
Mucius Scaevola, 1:549
Mugasa, 1:80
Mugenyi, 1:78
Muhammad Hanafiah, 2:946–47
Muj, 1:307–8
Mukannišum, 1:154
Mukara, 1:318
Mukasa, 1:79
Mula Jadi na Bolon, 2:937, 2:940
Mulua Dapie Bulane, 2:952
Mulua Satene, 2:952
Mummu, 1:158, 1:159
Mumu (Munster), Ireland, 1:240, 1:241, 1:257, 1:258, 1:265, 1:271
Muṇḍam, 2:845
Munḍugumor, 2:1226
Mungonge, 1:66, 1:67–68
Munki, 1:227
Munster. *See* Mumu
Munthuch, 1:531
Murut, 2:933
Musawwaret Es-Sufra, 1:116–20
Mušdamma, 1:147
Muses, 1:435, 1:368, 1:375, 1:472, 1:492
Múspellsheimr, 1:286
Musset, Alfred de, 2:766, 2:770
Musubi, 2:1042
Mut, 1:103, 1:104
Mutuama, 2:1221
Mutusi, 1:80
Muxa, 2:1122
Muxdy, 2:1118
Mu-ye, 2:1103
Mwatikitiki. *See* Mauitikitiki
Mweel, 1:73
Mycenae, 1:329, 1:330–40, 1:403–4
Myrrha, 1:434
Myrtilus, 1:508

N

Naarsuk, 2:1149
Naas, 2:675, 2:678, 2:687–88
Naassenes, 2:652, 2:664, 2:675–76
Naatyuwe, 2:1221
Nabaloi, 2:938–39
Nabarbi, 1:225
Nabataeans, 1:182, 1:193
Nabu, 1:203, 1:204
Naga (Meroe), 1:116–18
Nāgā, nāgī, 2:823, 2:926; Southeast Asia, 2:924
Naga Padoha, 2:937, 2:940
Nag Hammadi, Egypt, 2:677, 2:678, *2:679*, 2:680, *2:684*
Nago-Yoruba, 1:52
Nahr Ibrahim, 1:435
Nahuas, 2:1188, 2:1191
Naiads, 1:505
Na-khi, 2:1077
Nakula: India, 2:831; Indonesia, 2:957
Nal, 2:1216
Nalagaréng, 2:954, *2:955*
Nama Koro, 1:32, 1:39, 1:41, 1:44, 1:45
Namar, 2:1216
Namau, 2:1226
Nambi, 1:79
Nammu, 1:148–49, 1:156, 1:174
Namni, Mount, 1:226
Namsara, Napsara, 1:227
Nam Tao, 2:996
Nana Buruku, 1:60
Nana e votrës, 1:307
Nanahuatl, 2:1181
Nanai (goddess), 1:204
Nanaï, Nanaj, 2:1128
Nanda, 2:861, 2:870
Nandikeśvara, 2:902
Nandin, 2:904
Nanna, *1:144*, 1:145, 1:147
Nanše, 1:147
Nantosueta, Nantosvelta, 1:276, 1:277
Naoise, 1:271
Naojote, 2:882
Napata, 1:115–16
Napoleon, myth of, 2:777–78, *2:777*
Napsara. *See* Namsara
Nár, 1:282
Nara (ancient god), 1:227
Nara (ṛṣi), 2:830, 2:852–53, 2:860
Nārada, 2:853, 2:861, 2:864, 2:876
Narakāsura, 2:862
Narasiṃha, 2:850, 2:854–56, *2:855*, 2:858, 2:872, 2:875
Nārāyaṇa, 2:820, 2:821, 2:823, 2:830, 2:838, 2:841, 2:850, 2:852–53, 2:860, 2:928
Narcissus, 1:492–94, *2:493;* in literature, 2:673, 2:766–67
Nartamongä, 1:317
Narts, 1:317–19, 2:741, 2:747
Naskapi, 2:1153, 2:1157
Nasrettin Hodja, 2:1113
Nat, 2:915, 2:918–19, *2:921*
Natchez, 2:1158
Nathum, 1:526
Natigay, 2:1103, 2:1112
Natinusna. *See* Nathum
Nat pwatil, 2:1216
Natrpiyemi, 1:229
Natsi itni, 2:1182
Nature, cults of: in the Baltics, 1:305–6; among the continental Celts, 1:246, 1:247, 1:249; among Germano-Nordic peoples, 1:218–82, 1:289–90, 1:304; in Japan, 2:1038, 2:1056–58; in literature, 2:761–63, 2:784; in the Maghreb, 1:87; in Mesoamerica, 2:1184–87; among nomads, 1:22; in North America, 2:1157; in Siberia, 2:1122; among the Slavs, 1:298–99, 1:302–4; in southern Africa (Bantu), 1:62
Naui Olin, 2:1181
Naui Tecpatl, 2:1181
Naumann, Johann Gottlieb, 1:142
Navajo, Navaho, 1:4, 2:1155, 2:1156, 2:1157, *2:1158*
Navigium Isidis, 1:125
Nawangsih, 2:959
Nawangwulan, 2:959, *2:960*
Naweji, 1:72
Ndahura, 1:78
Ndembu, 1:70, 1:72
Ndibu, 1:65
N'domo, 1:39, 1:45
Ndu, 2:981–83, 2:985, 2:993
Neanderthal man, 1:11
Neak-tā, 2:915, 2:918, 2:920–24, *2:922, 2:923*
Nebo, 1:204
Nechta Scéne, 1:270
Neckham, Alexander, 2:697, 2:698
Nehalennia, 1:274, 1:284
Neit, 1:259
Neith, 1:92, 1:93
Nekhbet, 1:103
Nelides, 1:547
Nembrbrkon, 2:1219
Nemburnyawa, 2:956
Nembutsu, 2:1039–40
Nemean lion, 1:420
Nemesis, 1:128, 1:374, 1:405, 1:492, 1:494
Nemetona, 1:249
Nemhedh, 1:257–58
Nemrod, Perates, 2:682
Nemus Dianae, 1:544
Nenc, 2:1128
Nenchū gyōji, 2:1067–70
Nennius, 1:265
Ne no kuni, 2:1044–46
Neoplatonists. *See* Philosophy
Nephele (cloud), 1:442, 1:443
Nephthys, 1:91, 1:92–93, 1:118, 1:122, 1:130, 1:131
Neptunalia, 1:583, 1:627–28
Neptune, 1:564–65, 1:568, 1:627, *1:628;* in art and literature, 1:639, 1:640, 2:694, 2:696
Nerab, 1:200, 1:202
Nereids, 1:375, 1:380, 1:381; Christianity, 2:674
Nereus, 1:375, 1:380, 1:381, 1:382, 1:510
Nerew, 2:1216
Nergal: Aramaeans and Palmyrenes, 1:200, 1:204; Mesopotamia, 1:152, 1:163, 1:178–81, 1:224
Nerthus, 1:284, 1:291
Nerval, Gérard de, 2:754, 2:756–58, 2:766, 2:768, 2:769, 2:772, 2:773, 2:774, 2:777
Nesaru, 2:1162
Ness, 1:271
Nessus, 1:452, 1:482–83, *2:693;* medieval art, 2:694
Netherworld. *See* Underworld
Nethuns, 1:520, 1:534
Neuri, 1:304
Nevi, 2:1119
Nevimbumbaao, Nevinbumbaau, 2:1216, 2:1223
New Caledonia. *See* Oceania
New Hebrides. *See* Oceania
New Testament, 2:651–54
Nez Percé, 2:1153
Nga, 2:1119–20
Ngada, 2:948
Ngaju, 2:931, 2:933, 2:937, 2:940, 2:947, 2:949
Nganasan, 2:1128
Ngoc Hoang, 2:997, 2:999

Nguni, 1:68
Niaux, Ariège, 1:13, 1:14–18, *1:17*
Nicagoras of Cyprus, 2:667
Nicander of Colophon, 1:245
Nicaraos, 2:1191
Nicholas de Damas, 2:1114
Nið, 1:293, 1:304
Nidaba, 1:147
Nidrā, 2:869
Nietzsche, Friedrich, 2:756, 2:760, 2:763
Niflheimr, 1:286
Nifutsuhime, 2:1052
Night, 1:367, 1:369, 1:370, 1:374, 1:378, 1:405, 1:406–9, 1:439, 1:463, 1:464, 1:465, 1:480, 1:490, 1:494, 1:511
Nigidius Figulus, 1:535, 1:550, 1:599, 1:608
Nihongi, 2:1051–52
Nikkal, 1:200, 1:214, 1:217, 1:224, 1:225, 1:226
Nikko, 2:1052
Nikon, 2:673
Nil, Saint, 1:185
Nilotic peoples, 1:81–84
Ninatta, 1:224, 1:226
Ning Feng Zu, Ning Feng Zi, 2:1033, 2:1036
Ningirsu, 1:152, 1:159
Ninhursag, 1:145–47, 1:157
Ninigi, 2:1038
Ninisinna, 1:147
Ninkasi, 1:146
Nin-KUR, 1:146
Ninlil, 1:227
Ninmah, 1:148–49, 1:174
Ninmug, 1:147
Nin-sar, 1:146
Nintu, 1:175
Ninurta, 1:152, 1:173–74, 1:177–78, 1:181, 1:226
Ni-Ō, 2:908
Niobe, 1:393, 1:405; in Christianity, 2:656; in literature, 2:759
Niraikanai, 2:1045
Nirmāṇakāya, 2:895
Niru Khani (Kokkini Khani), Crete, 1:337
Nisaba, 1:145, 1:226
Nissyen, 1:262
Niśumbha, 2:871
Niwatakawaca, 2:957
Njörðr, 1:284, 1:288, 1:291
Nkhimba, 1:65
Nkisi, 1:65
Nkita, 1:64–65, 1:70
Nkongolo, 1:67–68, 1:72, 1:73
Nkula, 1:72
Noah, 2:656
Nodier, Charles, 2:753, 2:767, 2:772, 2:775
Nodons, 1:249
Nohotsyumchac, 2:1183
Noika, 2:1220
Nomads, nomadism, 1:21–22, 1:192, 2:718–19
Nommo, 1:27, *1:33*, 1:34, 1:35, 1:37, 1:38, 1:39–41, 1:42–44,d 1:47, 1:49–50, 1:52
Nonadeï, 1:306
Nonius, 1:612
Nonnos, 1:217, 1:378, 1:387, 1:400, 1:630
Nopina, 1:335
Nordics. *See* Germano-Nordic peoples
Noreia, 1:250
Norns, 1:285, 1:294
North America, 2:1152–64. *See also* Eskimos
Nortia, 1:520
Notus, 1:510
Novalis (Friedrich von Hardenberg), 2:754–55, 2:756, 2:766, 2:772, 2:773, 2:774
Novgorod-the-Great, 1:300
Nsaku, 1:71
Ntandu, 1:65, 1:70
Nuadhu airgedlámh, 1:259, 1:261, 1:271, 1:274
Nubadig, 1:225, 1:226
Nudd, 1:266
Nudimmud, 1:156, 1:159
N'ules murt, 2:1134
Num, 2:1119
Numa, 1:545, 1:551, 1:582, 1:586, 1:605–6
Numancia, Spain, 1:268
Numenius of Apamea, 2:660, 2:683
Numi-Tōrem, 2:1136
Numus, 2:1216
Nuna, 2:1147
Nunusaku, 2:952
Nupi, 1:335
Nuset e malit, 1:307
Nushku, 1:200
Nusku, 1:174
Nusyirwan, 2:946
Nut, 1:91, 1:92, 1:103, 1:118
Nüwa, 2:1008, 2:1009, 2:1016, 2:1019–20, 2:1025, 2:1029
Nuxiu, 2:1016
Nuysement, Clovis Hesteau de, 2:706, 2:708, 2:711
Nuzi (Kirkuk), 1:225, 1:226, 1:227
Nya, 1:32, 1:39, 1:44
Nyabingi, 1:81
Nyabirungu, 1:79
Nyag-khri btsan-po, 2:1086
Nyamata, 1:78
Nyamiyonga, 1:76, 1:78
Nyamuzinda, 1:76
Nyamwezi, 1:76
Nycteis (Night), 1:404
Nycteus, 1:404
Nyikango, 1:83–84
Nyi Pohaci, 2:953
Nymphē, 1:396, 1:400
Nymphs, 1:335, 1:371, 1:373, 1:383, 1:396, 1:410, 1:459, 1:465, 1:504–5, 1:506, 1:507–8, 1:509
Nyut, 2:982
Nyx. *See* Night
Nzambi, 1:65
Nzinga Nkuwu, 1:71
Nzondo, 1:64–67, 1:70

O

Oannes, 1:153
Oba, 1:56, 1:59
Oba Igbo, 1:54
Obaluaye. *See* Shapannan
Obatala (Orishanla, Oshala), 1:53, 1:54–55, 1:58
Oblivion, 1:414
Oceania, 2:1208–24
Oceanids, 1:379, 1:380, 1:381, 1:410
Oceanus, 1:366–67, 1:371, 1:375, 1:377, 1:379–80, 1:382, 1:413, 1:465, 1:478; and Christianity, 2:660
Ocelotonatiuh, 2:1174
Öd, 2:1091
Oðinn, 1:281, 1:282–84, 1:286–87, 1:291, 1:292–93, 1:294
Ödlek, 2:1091
Óðr, 1:288
Oduduwa, 1:53, 1:54, 1:57
Odysseus, 1:387–88, 1:409, 1:417, 1:418–19, 1:421, 1:430, 1:443, 1:482, 1:486, 1:492, 1:494–98, *1:495, 1:496, 1:498*, 1:545, 1:546; in Christianity, 2:657–58; for Gnostics, 2:677–78; in literature, 2:759, 2:780, 2:785, 2:787, 2:789, 2:790
Oedipus, 1:405, 1:410, 1:421, 1:480, 1:498–500, *1:500, 2:723*; in literature, 2:790
Oelasus, 1:404
Oeneus, 1:447–49
Oenomaus, 1:414, 1:508
Oenopion, 1:500
Oenotrus, 1:546
Oghma, 1:259
Oghuz, 2:1089, 2:1090, 2:1098, 2:1101, 2:1103, 2:1107, 2:1111, 2:1113
Oghuz Khan, 2:1099, 2:1111, *2:1111*
Oglala, 2:1157, 2:1163
Ogmios, 1:244, 1:274–75
Ogo, 1:33–34, 1:36, 1:37–38, 1:39–40, 1:42, 1:47, 1:49–50
Ogun, 1:53, 1:55, *1:55*, 1:57, 1:60
O-hirume, 2:1052
Ohrmazd. *See* Ahura Mazdā
Oisín, 1:273
Øjazi, 1:282
Ojibwa, 2:1160, 2:1163
Ojin Tennô, 2:1042
O-kee-pa, 2:1163
Ôkuninushi, 2:1038, 2:1041, 2:1042, 2:1043, 2:1045
Olaus Magnus, 2:733, 2:734
'O-lde spu-rgyal, 2:1077, 2:1086
Old Man, 2:1156
Old Prussians, 1:302, 1:305–6
Old Testament, 2:649–51, 2:653–54
Olelbis, 2:1156
Olen, 1:399
Ollintonatiuh, 2:1174
Olloudios, 1:249
Olmec, *2:1174*, 2:1176, 2:1183, 2:1184
Olodumaré, 1:52, 1:54
Olokun, 1:60
Olorun, 1:52
Olwen, 1:264, 1:265
Olympiodorus, 1:414
Oma, 2:1052
Omaha, 2:1157, 2:1163
Omecihuatl, 2:1174
Omen, 1:590–93
Ometecuhtli, 2:1174
Ometeotl, 2:1174
Ome tochtli, 2:1181, 2:1186
Omi, 2:1116, 2:1119
Omine (mountain), Japan, 2:1057
Ômisoka, 2:1069
Omolu, *1:57*. *See also* Shapannan
Omononushi, 2:1068
Omphale, 2:678
Ompunta Tuan Bubi na Bolon, 2:937
Ona, 2:1194
Oname matsuri, 2:1042
Ongon, 2:1092
Ong Troi, 2:999
Oni, 1:53
Ontake, Mount, 2:1051
Onuris, 1:117, *1:117*
Opalia, 1:583
Ophiens, ophites, 2:680
Opiconsivia, 1:560, 1:583
Ops Consiva, 1:552, 1:560, 1:576
Oranyan, 1:57–58
Orcus, 1:565
Ordo, 2:1090
Orë, 1:307
Oreiads, 1:505
Oreithuia, Oreithyia, 1:345, 1:410
Orestes, 1:408, 1:412, 1:421, 1:440, 1:508
Orestheus, 1:447
Origen, 1:434, 2:650, 2:658, 2:660, 2:662, 2:669, 2:672, 2:680
Origin, myths of, 1:4, 1:5; among the Austroasiatics and Austronesians, 2:983–85; in China, 2:1027, 2:1028; of Christianity, 2:650; among Eskimos, 2:1145–51; among Finno-Ugrians, 2:1138–40; in Greece, 1:341–46, 1:390–95, 1:465; among insular Celts, 1:257–60; in insular Southeast Asia, 2:933–35, 2:938–40, 2:940–41, 2:952–53; in Korea, 2:1070–71; in Madagascar, 2:971; in Mesopotamia, 1:3, 1:148–52, 1:155–61, 1:175; among Nilotic peoples, 1:82–83; in Oceania, 2:1215, 2:1217, 2:1220–21; in Papua New Guinea, 2:1224–27; in pre-Roman Italy, 1:542–44; in Southeast Asia, 2:916–18; in southern Africa (Bantu), 1:64, 1:68, 1:71, 1:78–81; in Tibet, 2:1077–79, 2:1079–82, 2:1082–86; among Turks and Mongols, 2:1099–1101, 2:1107; in Vietnam, 2:996–1001, 1001–2; in West Africa (Mande), 1:35–36, 1:42–44. *See also* Creation

Orion, 1:419–21, 1:446, 1:500–501, 1:510
Orisha, 1:52–55
Orishanla. *See* Obatala, Oshala
Orisha Popo, 1:54
Oro, 2:1219, 2:1223
Oroč, Orochon, 2:1116, 2:1118, 2:1128
Orok, 2:1128
Orokaiva, 2:1226
Oromazdès. *See* Ahura Mazdā
Orosius, Paulus, 2:610, 2:694
Orpheus, orphism, 1:352–53, 1:427, 1:444, 1:461–63, 1:465–66, 1:469–71, 1:501, *2:501, 2:654, 2:713, 2:774;* in art and literature, 1:360, 2:694, 2:706–7, 2:712–13, 2:772–74, 2:781; in Christianity, 2:660; among Gnostics, 2:683
Orthanes, 2:629
Ortho, 1:128
Orthopolis, 1:454
Orthus, 1:480
Osanyin, *1:59,* 1:61
Oschophoria, 1:337
Oshaguiyan, 1:55
Oshala (Orishanla), 1:55
Oshalufan, 1:55
Oshalufon, 1:54–55
Ôshôgatsu, 2:1067
Oshosi, 1:57, 1:58, 1:60–61
Oshumaré, *1:57,* 1:60
Oshun, 1:53, *1:53,* 1:55, 1:56, *1:56,* 1:58–59, 1:61
Osiris, 1:91–93, 1:104–5, *1:106,* 1:109, 1:112–15, 1:117–18, 1:122, 1:128–31, *1:134, 1:137;* among Gnostics, 2:676, 2:679, 2:681; in literature, 1:134–42, 2:710, 2:784; among Phoenicians and Punics, 1:195; in Rome, 1:122, 1:125
Osman, 2:1102
Osore, Mount (in Japan), 2:1046, *2:1047,* 2:1051
Ossets, 1:315, 1:316–19
Ossian, 1:273; in literature, 2:752, 2:783
Ostyak, 2:1119, 2:1122
Othagwenda, 2:1160
Ot Kayam, 2:949
Ötken, 2:1103
Ot Pari, 2:949
Otomi, 2:1171, 2:1175, *2:1175,* 2:1180, 2:1182, 2:1184, *2:1186,* 2:1187–88, 2:1190
Ottawa, 2:1158
Ottchigin, 2:1109
Ötüken, 2:1102–3, 2:1112
Otus, 1:468
Ouranos, 1:369, 1:371–74, 1:375–76, 1:379, 1:380–81, 1:385–86, 1:391, 1:463, 1:464–66
Ourmes, 2:720
Ouroboros, *2:681,* 2:682
Oursitori, 2:720
Ovid, 1:132, 1:382, 1:387, 1:395, 1:435, 1:471–72, 1:491, 1:493, 1:548, 1:551, 1:552, 1:563, 1:565, 1:573–79 passim, 1:583, 1:587, 1:600, 1:602, 1:612, 1:615, 1:617, 1:618, 1:619, 1:620, 1:622, 1:624, 1:627, 1:628, 1:629, 1:631, 1:635, 1:636, 1:638, 1:645, 2:656, 2:693, 2:696
Owain, 1:264, 1:265–67
Owen, Saint, 2:735
Oya, 1:56, 1:58
Oyo Alafin, 1:53, *1:53,* 1:56
Oyoyewi, 2:1155
Oztoteotl, 2:1184

P

Pacha-Mama, 2:1201
Pactolus, 1:403
Pade, 1:332
Padrita (Pedrite), 1:229
Paean, 1:440
Paiawon, 1:332
Paici, 2:1215, 2:1219
Pairra, 1:226
Paiute, 2:1157
Pakarina, 2:1202
Pala, 1:216, 1:219
Palamaon, 1:388
Palamas, Kōstes, 2:788
Pale Fox, The, 1:33, 1:38, 1:39–40, 1:43, 1:47
Paleo-Arctic peoples, 2:1128
Pales, 1:560, 1:568, 1:578, 1:639
Palguna, 2:957
Pallantids, 1:342
Pallas, 1:371, 1:375, 1:410, *1:560, 2:697;* in sixteenth- to seventeenth-century literature, 2:710
Palmyrenes, 1:182, 1:202–6, *1:205*
Pamade, 2:957
Pame, 2:1182
Pan, 1:378, 1:478, 1:502–8, *1:503, 1:504, 1:505, 1:506, 1:507,* 1:565, 1:633; in literature, 2:700, 2:705, 2:708, 2:767, 2:788
Panaetius, 2:614
Panathenaea, 1:343
Pañcajana, 2:862
Pañcamukha, 2:824–26
Pancanaka, 2:956
Pañcaśikha, 2:899
Pañcika, 2:899, 2:901, 2:909
Pandareus, 1:453
Pāṇḍava: in India, 2:829–33, 2:835, 2:839, 2:859–63; in Indonesia (Pandawa), 2:955–57
Pandora, 1:387, 1:389, 1:390, 1:392–94, *1:392, 1:394,* 1:411, 1:423, 1:485; and Christianity, 2:662; in literature, 2:768
Pandrosos, 1:341
Pāṇḍu, 2:829, 2:831
Paṇḍuputra, 2:957
Pangu, 2:1009, 2:1010, 2:1027, 2:1035
Panhu, 2:1026–27
Panié (mountain), 2:1219
Pañji, 2:936, *2:942,* 2:943
Pao jengki, 2:944
Paoxi, 2:1019–20. *See also* Fuxi
Papua New Guinea, 2:1224–30
Paracelsus, 2:754, 2:1233
Paradise: Christianity, 2:649–50, 2:654; China, 2:1013; Gnostics, 2:682–85, 2:687; India, 2:822; Indo-Europeans, 1:234, 1:236; Japan, 2:1039–40, 2:1048; Mesoamerica, 2:1191; pre-Islamic Iran, 2:882, 2:887–89. *See also* Afterlife
Parāma, 2:916
Paraplex, 2:685
Paraśurāma, 2:830, 2:836, 2:856–58, 2:862, 2:874
Parcae, 1:608
Parentalia, 2:623
Pārijāta, 2:864
Parikṣit: India, 2:833; Indonesia (Parikesit), 2:955, 2:957
Parilia, 2:560, 2:568, 2:583, 2:673
Parion, 1:472
Paris, 1:387, 1:398, 1:408, 1:416
Parjanya, 2:835
Parmenides, 1:347–48, 1:351, 1:465, 1:467
Parnsag, 2:688
Parny (Evariste Désiré de Forges, vicomte de), 2:753
Parsifal, 2:784
Parsis, 1:234, 1:236, 2:878, 2:880, 2:881, 2:883, 2:888, 2:890
Parta, 2:957
Parthenos, 1:400
Partholón, 1:258
Parvata, 2:869
Pārvatī, 2:845, 2:861, 2:864–66, 2:869, 2:896–98, 2:904
Pasaya, 1:332
Pasiphaë, 1:338, 1:388, 1:389
Passage, rites of. *See* Death; Initiation; Marriage
Passamaquoddy, 2:1155
Pásu, 2:814–15
Paśupati, 2:842, 2:861, 2:904
Pater, Walter, 2:761
Patoto'e, 2:941
Patroclus, 1:417; in literature, 2:788
Pauahtuns, 2:1183
Paul, Saint, 2:651–53, 2:655, 2:656, 2:658, 2:663, 2:710
Paulicians, 2:674
Paulus-Festus, 1:530, 1:534, 1:542, 1:552, 1:568, 1:572, 1:577, 1:586, 1:588, 1:605, 1:606, 1:612–13, 1:615, 1:617, 1:618, 1:619, 1:620, 1:622, 1:623, 1:625, 1:627, 1:628, 1:635, 1:638, 1:645
Pausanias, 1:335, 1:341–46, 1:387, 1:388, 1:391, 1:401, 1:409–12 passim, 1:413, 1:424, 1:425, 1:432, 1:446, 1:447, 1:450, 1:466–67, 1:469, 1:472, 1:480, 1:483, 1:493, 1:499, 1:502–5 passim, 1:525, 1:532, 1:680
Pawnee, 2:1155, 2:1158, 2:1163
Pax Augusta, 1:609
Pazuzu, *1:163*
Pé, Damoiselle, 2:980, 2:986
Pecheneg, 2:1089
Pech-Merle, 1:13, *1:15,* 1:16–17, *1:17,* 1:18
Pedrite. *See* Padrita
Pegasus, 1:382, 1:387, 1:401–2, 1:432, 1:473
Peithō, 1:380, 1:396, 1:408, 1:488
Peladan, Joséphin, *2:762,* 2:765
Pelasgos, 1:393–94
Peleus, 1:451–52, *1:452,* 1:510, *1:510;* in literature, 2:788
Pelias, 1:442–45
Pelles, 2:716
Pellonpoika, 2:1136
Pelopia, 1:404
Pelops, 1:398, 1:403, 1:404, 1:508–9
Pemba, 1:33–34, 1:37, 1:39
Penates, 1:521, 1:565, 1:628–29, *1:629*
Pen Dao Gong, 2:945
Pende, 1:67–68, 1:73
Penelope, 1:388, 1:497, 1:504; in literature, 2:785
Penglai, 2:1012
Penia, 2:683
Pentheus, 1:404, 1:421, 1:459, 1:461, 1:493–94
Perates, 2:680–82
Përbindsh, 1:307
Percival, 2:715
Peredur, 1:265, 1:266, 1:267
Pérès, J. B., 2:778
Peresa, 1:332
Peri, 2:1096, 2:1103
Perkele, 2:1139
Perkun, 1:300, 1:303, 1:306
Perkunas, 1:300, 1:302, 1:302–5, 1:306
Pernety, Antoine Joseph, 2:701, 2:702, 2:708, 2:711
Perrault, Charles, 2:746
Persaeus of Citium, 2:666, 2:668, 2:670
Persephone, 1:342, 1:381, 1:406, *1:407,* 1:409–12, *1:411,* 1:431, 1:434, 1:453, 1:454, 1:463, 1:494; in literature, 2:787–90. *See also* Kore
Perses, 1:375
Perseus, 1:408, 1:473, 1:480, 1:509, *2:723;* and Christianity, *1:509,* 2:661, 2:663
Persians, 2:877
Perun, 1:297, 1:300, 1:302–5
Perwa, 1:220
Peryń, 1:300
Petara, 2:938
Peter of Dusburg, 1:302
Peter the Venerable, 2:704
Petra, 1:193
Petrarch, 1:136, 2:698–99
Pětruk, 2:954–55, *2:955*
Petrus Bonus Lombardus, 2:702
Petrus Comestor, 2:694
Petrus Magnus (Pierre Victor Palma Cayet), 2:712
Petsofas, Mount (in Crete), 1:336
Peucetians, 1:540
Peucetius, 1:540, 1:546
Pēy-kōvil, 2:843

Peyote, 2:1186
Phaedra, 1:332, 1:448, 1:492, 1:507
Phaethon, 1:509, 2:660, 2:696; in literature, 2:706
Phanes, 1:463, 1:465, *1:467*, 1:470–71, 1:511, 2:683
Pha-wang drel-dkar, 2:1080
Phaya Then, 2:916
Phedre (Phaedrus), 1:466, 1:467, 1:469, 1:613
Pherecydes, 1:465
Phersipnai, 1:520, 1:525, 1:532
Phi, 2:915, 2:918, 2:919–20, *2:922*
Philae, Egypt, 1:107, 1:109, 1:118
Philargyrius, 2:664
Philiorimos, Mount (in Crete), 1:336
Philippines. *See* Insular Southeast Asia
Philistus of Syracuse, 1:548
Philochorus, 1:471
Philoctetes, 1:421, 1:502, 1:546
Philonoë, *1:402*, 1:403
Philo of Alexandra, 2:649, 2:650, 2:771
Philo of Byblos, 1:185, 1:187, 1:189, 1:227
Philo of Larissa, 1:613
Philosophy, in Greece: from Hesiod to Proclus, 1:346–52; of Plato, 1:352–60; of Neoplatonists, 1:360–66
Philosophy, in Rome, 1:597–600
Philostratus, 1:494
Philotes, 1:370, 1:405, 1:487
Phineus, 1:474
Phlegon, 1:470
Phlegyas, 1:414, 1:449, 1:450
Phnong, 2:976
Phobus, 1:414
Phoebe, 1:371, 1:375, 1:465
Phoenicians, 1:182, 1:185–86, 1:193–99
Phoenix, 1:314, 1:431, 1:472, 1:473, 2:677; in art and literature, 2:708–9, 2:760
Phoibos. *See* Apollo
Pholus, 1:451, 1:452
Phorcys, 1:380, 1:381, 1:382, 1:473
Phoroneus, 1:381, 1:391, 1:394, 1:424
Phra Bang, 2:930
Phra Keo, 2:930
Phrasimede, 1:388
Phra Taksin, 2:920
Phrixus, 1:442, 1:443
Phusis, 1:455, 2:676
Phyva, 2:1081
Piacenza, Italy, 1:520, 1:534, *1:534*, 1:535
Pico della Mirandola, Gianfrancesco, 2:700, 2:702, 2:704, 2:709, 2:712, 2:771
Pieggolmai, 2:1137
Piero di Cosimo, 2:700
Pietas Augusta, 1:609
Pignoria, Lorenzo, 1:139
Pikipikilauifi, 2:1222
Piltzintecuhtli, 2:1181
Pindal, Cave of, Spain, *1:14*
Pindar, 1:126, 1:387, 1:389, 1:395, 1:401, 1:406, 1:413, 1:440, 1:441, 1:444, 1:449, 1:466, 1:478–81 passim, 1:505, 1:508
Piṇḍola, 2:901, 2:904
Pintorrichio, 1:135
Pipils, 2:1185
Pipituna, 1:332
Piranesi, 1:141
Pirinkir, 1:226
Pirithous, 1:342, 1:451
P'irkusha, 1:312
Pisanello (called Antonio Pisano), 2:699
Pisasaphi, 1:224, 1:226
Pithanu, 1:226
Pittheus, 1:401, 1:403
Pizamar, 1:301
Placenta, 1:30, 1:35–37, 1:40, 1:42–43
Plaisance, *1:534*. *See also* Piacenza
Plan Carpin, Jean de, 2:1096
Plancy, Collin de, 2:772
Plato, 1:132, 1:321, 1:340–45 passim, 1:348–51, 1:352–60, 1:362–65, 1:366, 1:384–89 passim, 1:390–94 passim, 1:397, 1:411–12, 1:413–14, 1:419, 1:434, 1:437–41 passim, 1:466–72 passim, 1:502, 2:683, 2:710, 2:1231
Plautus, 1:569, 1:575, 1:586, 1:617, 1:620, 1:621, 1:622, 1:626, 1:629, 1:636
Pleiades, 1:500, 1:510
Plemnaeus, 1:454
Pliny the Elder, 1:185, 1:246, 1:472, 1:519, 1:525, 1:531, 1:533, 1:542, 1:544, 1:547, 1:548, 1:553, 1:555, 1:559, 1:562, 1:568, 1:586–91 passim, 1:597–98, 1:606, 1:613, 1:619, 2:683
Pliny the Younger, 1:556
Plotinus, 1:360–63, *1:361*, 1:634, 2:651, 2:672, 1:673, 1:678, 1:685, 1:700
Plutarch, 1:112, 1:122, 1:124, 1:128, 1:134, 1:135, 1:185, 1:195, 1:244, 1:341, *1:364*, 1:385, 1:389, 1:396, 1:398, 1:403, 1:424, 1:434, 1:436, 1:447, 1:464, 1:479, 1:485, 1:503, 1:511, 1:553, 1:634, 2:669, 2:671, 2:679, 2:733
Pluto, *Ploutōn*, 1:380, 1:449
Pluto (king of the Styx), 1:569, 1:608
Plutus, 1:406, 1:454
Podalirius, 1:449
Podarge, 1:474
Podengringli, P'o-teng-ning-li, 2:1102, 2:1112
Poe, Edgar Allen, 2:766
Poetry, 2:778–83; among Germano-Nordic peoples, 1:287, 1:288; in Greece, 1:358; among insular Celts, 1:250
Pohuo, 2:1027
Poinai, 1:128
Pô-Klong-Garai, 2:980
Pokomam, 2:1175
Polabians, 1:302
Polemius Silvius, 1:600
Poliziano, 1:135
Pollux, 1:463, *1:561*, 1:562, 1:574; among continental Celts, 1:255; in medieval art, 2:694
Polonius (Jean Labensky), 2:771
Polybius, 1:185, 1:506, 1:597–98, 1:635
Polydora, 1:380
Polydorus, 1:404
Polynesia. *See* Oceania
Polyphemus, 1:382, 1:495
Polyphonte, 1:397
Polytechnus, 1:453
Pomana, 2:720, 2:721
Pomo, 2:1153
Pomono, 1:522
Pomponius Mela, 1:243
Ponca, 2:1163
Pong Mula Tau, 2:939
Pontifex maximus, 1:552, 1:560, 1:576
Pontus, 1:371, 1:373, 1:375, 1:380, 1:382
Popeştil, Romania, 1:270
Popol Vuh, 2:1169, 2:1171, 2:1174, 2:1185
Poppa, Mount (in Burma), 2:918
Porevit, 1:301
Porka, 2:938, 2:948
Poros, 1:367, 1:371, 2:683
Porphyry, 1:360–63, 1:425, 1:427, 1:531, 2:672, 2:678, 2:700
Porsenna, 1:519
Portel, Ariège, 1:20
Portion of the Gods: in Greece, 1:422–23; in India, 2:815
Portunalia, 1:583
Posedaon, 1:332
Poseidon, 1:341, 1:355, 1:375, 1:376, 1:380–82, *1:383*, 1:385, 1:387, 1:400, 1:401–2, *1:401*, 1:405, *1:407*, 1:410, 1:424, 1:432, 1:473, 1:508
Posidaeya, 1:332
Posidas, 1:332
Posidonius, 1:243, 1:246, 2:613
Possession: among Georgians, 1:309–10, 313–14; in Greece, 1:458–61, 1:507; in India, 2:843–44, 2:846; in southern Africa (Bantu), 1:79; among the Yoruba, 1:53. *See also* Shaman and shamanism
Postel, Guillaume, 2:705, 2:708–9, 2:771
Potao, 2:982, 2:990–91, *2:991*
P'o-teng-ning-li, Podengringli, 2:1102, 2:1112
Pō Tolo, 1:49
Pound, Ezra, 2:783–85
Poussin, Nicolas, 1:494
Powys, province of, 1:262, 1:264, 1:266
Prabu Palgundi, 2:957
Prabu Pandu, 2:956
Pradakṣiṇā, 2:824, 2:925
Pradhāna, 2:818
Praeneste, Italy, 1:545, 1:590, 1:627, 1:645
Prahlāda, 2:826, 2:855–56, 2:858
Prajāpati, 2:802, 2:814–17, 2:824, 2:826
Prajñavarman, 2:1085
P'ra Khap'ung, 2:920
Prakṛti, 2:806, 2:818
Pralaya, 2:816, 2:817, 2:821–23
Prasenajit, 2:1087
Praxiteles, 1:472
Predmost, Moravia, 1:19
Prehistoric art, 1:11–20
Prehistory, 1:11–20
Pre-Islamic Iran, 1:233–39 passim, 2:877–93
Prevelakis, Pandelis, 2:790
Priam, 1:407, 1:486, *1:540*
Priapus, 1:431, 1:629–32, *1:630*, *1:631*, *1:632*; in Renaissance art, 2:700; among Gnostics, 2:686
Prince of the Center, 2:962, 2:965, 2:968–70
Pripegala, 1:302
Proclus, 1:349–52, 1:360–65, 1:385, 1:531, 2:673, 2:700
Procopius of Caesarea, 1:127, 1:295, 1:297
Procris, 1:421
Procrustes, 1:342
Prodicus, 1:483–84, 2:666
Proetus, 1:402
Prohm, 2:926
Prometheus, 1:371, 1:376, 1:384, 1:390–95 passim, 1:422–24, 1:427, 1:484; in literature, 2:755, 2:756, 2:759, 2:763, 2:767–68, 2:790
Pronoia, 1:130, 2:682–85
Propertius, 1:554, 1:615
Proserpina, 1:633. *See also* Persephone
Prostitution. *See* Sacred prostitution
Protagoras, 1:357, 1:358
Proteleia, 1:396
Proteus, 1:382
Protogonos, 1:465, 1:470
Proven, 1:302, 1:304
Pṛthā, 2:830
Pryderi, 1:260–62, 1:263, 1:265, 1:267
Psellus, Michael, 1:531, 2:673, 2:686, 2:771
Pseudo-Apollodorus, 1:376, 1:378
Pseudo-Dionysius the Areopagite, 2:656
Pseudo-Nonnus, 1:629
Pseudo-Scylax, 1:548
Psyche, 1:632–34, *1:633*; in art and literature, 2:694, 2:700, 2:758; among Gnostics, 2:678, 2:683, 2:684–85
Ptah, 1:92, 1:95, 1:203; in literature, 1:138, 1:141
Ptuj, Slovenia, 1:296

Puang Basi-Basian, 2:939
Puang Matua, 2:939
Puang Tudang, 2:939
Pueblos, 2:1153, 2:1158, 2:1161
Pulanggeni, 2:957
Pulu Bunzi, 1:65, 1:70
Punan, 2:949
Pu Ngoe Nga Ngoe, *2:917*
Punics, 1:182, 1:186, 1:193–200
Purbararang, 2:961
Purbasari, 2:961
Pure/Impure: in China, 2:903; in Christianity, 2:655; in Greece, 1:425, 1:439–40; among the Gypsies, 2:721; in India, 2:810, 2:811, 2:813–14, 2:827, 2:841–42, 2:846–49, 2:851–52, 2:856, 2:858, 2:865–66, 2:896, 2:903; in Indochina, 2:984; in Japan, 2:1044, 2:1045, 2:1065; in Mesoamerica, 2:1170, 2:1187–88; in Papua New Guinea, 2:1229; in southern Africa (Bantu), 1:68; in Tibet, 2:903; among Turks and Mongols, 2:1109; in West Africa (Mande), 1:33–34, 1:35–36, 1:38, 1:39–40, 1:44
Purich, 1:531
Puruṣa, 2:806–7, 2:818, 2:819, 2:821, 2:840, 2:849, 2:853, 2:874
Pushkin, Alexander Sergeivitch, 2:770
Pu Thao Yoe, 2:916
Puy-du-Touge, Haute Garonne, 1:251
Pu Yoe Ya Yoe, 2:916
Pwyll, 1:260–62, 1:264, 1:265, 1:266
Pyanopsia, 1:478
Pylos, 1:331, 1:332, 1:333
Pyrgi, 1:520, 1:574
Pyriphlegethon, 1:413–14
Pyrrha, 1:391, 1:394–95
Pyrrhe, Pyrrhus, in literature, 2:706
Pythagoras, 1:427, 1:492, 2:710
Pythia, 1:425–26, 1:440

Q

Qa, 2:1084
Qadshu, 1:191
Qalatch, 2:1099
Qarakhanids, 2:1098, 2:1099, 2:1111
Qarluq, 2:1089, 2:1097, 2:1103
Qataban, 1:191
Qatna, 1:182, 1:184, 1:227
Qaumaniq, 2:1152
Qazilik Tag, 2:1103
Qielan, 2:906, 2:907
Qingmian jingang, 2:903
Qingyi Shen, 2:1027
Qin Shi Huangdi, 2:1018
Qiongqi, 2:1029
Qipchaq, 2:1089, 2:1095, 2:1101
Qiu Yuan, 2:1007
Quadriviae (goddesses of the crossroads), 1:250, *1:251*
Quai, 2:997, 2:1001
Quanfengguo, 2:1027
Quanrong, 2:1027
Quechua, 2:1201, 2:1203, 2:1205
Querasiya, 1:332
Quetzalcoatl, 2:1172, 2:1174–75, 2:1177, 2:1179, 2:1180, *2:1181*, 2:1183, 2:1184, 2:1190, 2:1191
Quiahuitonatiuh, 2:1174
Quiche, 2:1169–73, 2:1174, 2:1176, 2:1177
Quinctiales, 1:617
Quinet, Edgar, 2:754, 2:755, 2:768, 2:769, 2:770
Quinquatrus, 1:583, 1:624, 1:627
Quintus Aucler, 1:585, 2:773
Quirinalia, 1:635
Quirinus, 1:552–53, 1:563–65, 1:575, 1:576–77, 1:620, 1:634–35, *1:635*
Quirites, 1:552
Qūq, 2:68–82
Quraysh, 1:192
Q'ursha, 1:315
Qut, 2:1095, 2:1105, 2:1108

R

Ra, 1:93, 1:96
Raban Maur, 2:698
Rabbe, Alphonse, 2:774
Rabelais, François, 2:689, 2:696, 2:735, 2:745
Rabenimiehaka, 2:964
Radcliffe, Ann, 2:767
Raden Inu Kertapati, 2:943
Raden Pancawala, 2:955
Raden Puntadewa, 2:955
Raden Rahmat, 2:945
Radha, 2:862, *2:863*
Radien, 2:1137
Radogoszcz, Rethra, 1:300
Rāga, 2:896
Ragana, 1:305
Ragnarök, 1:286, 1:295
Rahab, 2:650
Rahū, 2:904, 2:925
Rai/lanitra, 2:967
Raja Isumbaon, 2:940
Raja Odap-Odap, 2:940
Raja Pinangkabo, 2:937
Rajas, 2:818–19, 2:820
Rakib-El, 1:200
Rakoube, 2:973
Rākṣasas, 2:826, 2:829, 2:831, 2:835, 2:837
Raktabīja, 2:872
Ralambo, 2:973
Rāma, 2:829, 2:834–39, 2:850–51, *2:851*, 2:856–57, 2:926, 2:928–29, 2:957, 2:958
Rāma-Hvāstra, 2:893
Rama Jāmadagnya, 2:856–57
Ramanongavato, 2:963–65
Ra/masy, 2:973
Rāmāyana, 2:834–39; in Indonesia, 2:957
Rambaramb, 2:1216
Rambhā, 2:828
Rameau, Jean-Philippe, 1:142
Ramini, Raminias, 2:961–62, 2:973
Ramnes, 1:552
Ramsey, Michael Andrew, 1:141
Rán, 1:288
Ranakombe, 2:962, 2:965, 2:968, 2:971–72
Rananeida, 2:1137
Ranoro, 2:970, 2:973
Raphaël, 2:699, 2:700
Rarasati, 2:957
Rashap, 1:190, 1:193, 1:197, 1:199, 1:200, 1:215
Rashid-ed-din, 2:1092, 2:1104
Rashnu, 2:888, 2:892
Ras Shamra. *See* Ugarit
Ratu adil, 2:959
Ratu Kidul, 2:936, 2:939
Rāvana, 2:826, 2:834, 2:836–38, 2:860, 2:929, 2:957
Raymonden, Dordogne, *1:17*
Ra/Zatovo, 2:964
Rcīka, 2:828, 2:856
Ṙeba, 2:948
Rebel, Myth of the, 2:767–71
Rebell, Hugues, 2:763
Rebirth: in China, 2:1033–34; in Egypt, 1:112–15; in India, 2:819, 2:822–23, 2:875; in Japan, 2:1047–48. *See also* Reincarnation
Rediculus, 1:559
Régnier, Henri de, 2:759
Reincarnation: among the Baltic peoples, 1:305; among the Indo-Europeans, 1:237; in Japan, 2:1044–49; in Mesoamerica, 2:1191
Reitia, 1:522, 1:542
Religio, 1:549–50
Remi d'Auxerre, 2:698
Remmang ri Langi', 2:944
Rémus, 1:585, 1:617
Renenut, 1:99, 1:104
Renewal, 2:886, 2:888–89
Renouncer, renunciation, 2:819, 2:822–23, 2:825, 2:832, 2:836, 2:838, 2:841, 2:845, 2:847–49, 2:852, 2:853, 2:863, 2:896–98
Renukā, 2:856–57
Rescial, 1:531
Rešef, 1:200, 1:222
Resi Bisma, 2:957
Rex sacrorum, 1:553, 1:565, 1:576
Rhadamanthys, 1:335, 1:339, 1:473, 1:510
Rhadé, 2:977, 2:980
Rhea, 1:335, 1:380, 1:405, 1:490, 1:511; to Gnostics, 2:676, 2:681
Rhe(i)a, 1:335, 1:338, 1:371, 1:375, 1:376
Rhesus, 1:417
Rhiannon, 1:261–62, 1:264, 1:265, 1:267
Rhodus, 1:382
Rhonabwy, 1:264
Rhun, 1:264
Ricciardi, Antonio, 2:702
Riccio, 2:700
Richter, Jean-Paul, 2:766, 2:768
Ridewall, John, 2:696, 2:698
Rigisamus, 1:249
Rilke, Rainer Maria, 2:781
Rimbaud, Arthur, 2:763
Rin-chen dar-lu, 2:1080
Rindr, 1:287
Riosh Kahval, 2:1182
Rioug, 2:933
Ripa, Cesare, 1:138
Rit. *See* Drit
Rites and rituals: in Albania, 1:307; in ancient Switzerland, 2:733–34; Aramaean, 1:202; Armenian, 1:319–20; Austroasiatic and Austronesian, 2:991, 2:994–95; among the Baltic peoples, 1:306; in China, 2:1031, 2:1033; among the continental Celts, 1:242–48; in Crete and Mycenae, 1:333, 1:336–37; in Egypt, 1:106–11, 1:125; Finno-Ugrian, 2:1134–38; in France, 2:746–52; in Georgia, 1:309–12; Germano-Nordic, 1:290; in Greece, 1:460–61, 1:474–77, 1:490; Gypsy, 2:720–22; in India, 2:802, 2:803–5, 2:813–15, 2:844, 2:847–48; Indo-European, 1:234–36; insular Southeast Asian, 2:936, 2:944–45, 2:947–49, 2:949–52, 2:953–57; in Japan, 2:1039, 2:1042–43, 2:1046, 2:1053–54, 2:1057–58, 2:1063–70; Mesoamerican, 2:1169–73, 2:1183, 2:1186, 2:1187–88; in Mesopotamia, 1:156–57; Nilotic, 1:83; North American, 2:1157–58, 2:1163–64; in northern Caucasus, 2:1113–16; in Oceania, 2:1213–16; among the Palmyrenes, 1:205; in Papua New Guinea, 2:1226–29; Phoenician and Punic, 1:196, 1:198–99; pre-Islamic Arab and Nabataean, 1:192–93; in pre-Islamic Iran, 2:880–84; in pre-Roman Italy, 1:522–24, 1:525–26, 1:528, 1:534, 1:536–39, 1:541, 1:542–44; in Rome, 1:122, 1:544, 1:551–53, 1:568–70, 1:582–83, 1:603–5, 1:612–13, 1:615–17, 1:618–19, 1:620–21, 1:624, 1:627–28, 1:629, 1:635, 1:638, 1:645–46; Siberian, 2:1118–19, 2:1120; Slavic, 1:298–99; South American, 2:1195–97, 2:1199–1201, 2:1201–5; Southeast Asian, 2:919–20, 2:923–24, 2:925; in southern Africa (Bantu), 1:72–75, 1:76–77; in Tibet, 2:1088; among the Turks and Mongols, 2:1091, 2:1101–2, 2:1105, 2:1109, 2:1110, 2:1112; in Ugarit, 1:213–14; in Vietnam, 2:1002–3; in

Rites and rituals (*continued*)
West Africa (Mande), 1:30–32, 1:35–37, 1:41, 1:51–52, 1:55–61; among the Western Semites, 1:189; among the Yoruba, 1:55–61
Ritona, 1:275
Ritual theater: in Greece, 1:421, 1:432–33, 1:458–61; in insular Southeast Asia, 2:933, 2:936, 2:943, 2:953–57; in Japan, 2:1049, 2:1066; in Siberia, 2:1125; in Southeast Asia, 2:929
Rizal, 2:947
rMa, 2:1080
rNam-rgyal, 2:1078
rNgam-rje btsan-po, 2:1081
Robigalia, 1:583
Robigo (Robigus), 1:552, 1:565, 1:635
Rod, 1:297, 1:300
Rody, 1:297
Roglai, 2:981, 2:994
Rohinī, 2:861
Rok, 2:989
Rollin, Charles, 2:722–24
Rome, 1:121–27 passim, 1:544–45, 1:548–613, *1:606, 1:610*, 1:615–29, 1:634–35, 1:636–38, 1:639–46
Romulus, 1:545, 1:552, 1:564, 1:585, 1:593, 1:603, 1:605, 1:609, 1:617, 1:625, 1:635
Rong Chen Gong, 2:1037
Rong Dog, 2:1026–27
Rongoteus, 2:1136
Roquepertuse, Bouches-du-Rhône, 1:243, 1:252, 1:253
Roro Kidul, 2:939, *2:939*
Rosmerta, 1:275
Rossano di Vaglio, Italy, 1:521, 1:522, 1:539
Roucadour (Lot), 1:18
Rouffignac, Dordogne, 1:15
Rousalia, 2:673
Rousseau, Jean-Jacques, 2:728, 2:729
Royalty: Austroasiatic and Austronesian, 2:990–91; in China, 2:1018–24; in Egypt, 1:103–4, 1:106–7, 1:109–10; among the Germano-Nordic peoples, 1:284, 1:292; in Greece, 1:382, 1:403–5, 1:414–15, 1:416, 1:421, 1:463, 1:478, 1:481, 1:511; Hurrian, 1:228–29; in India, 2:807, 2:816–17, 2:827–29, 2:829–33, 2:834, 2:836–37, 2:841, 2:848–49, 2:850–52, 2:854, 2:858, 2:859–64, 2:874–75; Indo-European, 1:237–39; among insular Celts, 1:260–65; in Madagascar, 2:961–76; in Mesopotamia, 1:145, 1:146, 1:160, 1:172–81; Nilotic, 1:83; Plato on, 1:358; in pre-Islamic Iran, 2:890; in Rome, 1:551–53; in southern Africa (Bantu), 1:63–64, 1:67–68; in Tibet, 2:1086–88
Roy Mata, 2:1215, 2:1223
Röyot, 2:984
Rožanica, 1:297
Rožanicy, 1:297–98
Ṛṣi, 2:799–800, 2:836, 2:852–53
Ṙuanruan, 2:1089, 2:1103, 2:1113
Rubruck, 2:1104
Rucika, 2:900
Rudra, 2:802, 2:811–17, 2:819, 2:821, 2:823, 2:825, 2:832–33, 2:835–36, 2:839–42, 2:867–69, 2:896
Rudrāṇī, 2:867
Rufinus, 1:136
Ruganzu Ndori, 1:81
Rügen, 1:296, 1:300, 1:301
Ruhanga, 1:78
Ruhinda, 1:78
Rujevit, 1:301
Rukmakala, 2:956
Rukminī, 2:860, 2:863–64
Rukmuka, 2:956
Rusalkí, 1:298
Ruse. *See Métis*
Rutilius Namatianus, 2:600
Rwanda, 1:76, 1:77, 1:78, 1:79–81
Ryangombe, 1:80–81
Ryuhwa, 2:1070

S

Saba, Sabaeans, 1:192
Śabalā, 2:827, 2:873
Sabellian-Umbrians, 1:517, 1:521–22, 1:536–39
Sabines, 1:552
Sabinus, 1:519
Sacher-Masoch, Leopold, 2:760
Śacī, 2:830–33, 2:864
Sacred prostitution: in Armenia, 1:320; among Western Semites, 1:189, 1:435
Sacrifice: in Albania, 1:307; in the Andes, 2:1202, 2:1204–5; in Armenia, 1:319, 1:320; for Austroasiatics and Austronesians, 2:994; for Baltic peoples, 1:306; in China, 2:1027; in Christianity, 2:649, 2:651; for continental Celts, 1:242–43, 1:273, 1:278; in Crete and Mycenae, 1:333, 1:336; for Finno-Ugrians, 2:1138, 2:1140; in Georgia, 1:310, 1:311–12, 1:313; for Germano-Nordic peoples, 1:289–90, 1:304; in Greece, 1:342, 1:396, 1:419, 1:421, 1:422–27, 1:430, 1:444–45, 1:457–88, 1:461–62, 1:487, 1:490, 1:510; in India, 2:803–5, 2:806–7, 2:811–13, 2:819, 2:821–23, 2:825, 2:832–33, 2:840–42, 2:843–46, 2:851–52, 2:857–58, 2:865–66, 2:871–72, 2:873, 2:874; for Indo-Europeans, 1:234–36; in insular Southeast Asia, 2:934, 2:948, 2:952; in Japan, 2:1057; in North America, 2:1153, 2:1163–64; in northern Caucasus, 2:1114–15; for pre-Islamic Arabs and Nabataeans, 1:192, 1:193; in pre-Islamic Iran, 2:880–81, 2:882, 2:883, 2:892; in pre-Roman Italy, 1:552–24, 1:536, 1:539, 1:543; in Mesoamerica, 2:1170–71, 2:1183, 2:1185, 2:1187; for Phoenicians and Punics, 1:197, 1:198–99; in Rome, 1:561, 1:567–71, 1:589, 1:603–4, 1:612, 1:620, 1:624, 1:629, 1:638, 1:645; for Slavs, 1:304; in Southeast Asia, 2:923; in southern Africa (Bantu), 1:73–75, 1:79; for Turks and Mongols, 2:1105, 2:1110; in Vietnam, 2:1001, 2:1003; in West Africa (Mande), 1:39–41, 1:42–44, 1:47, 1:49, 1:51–52; for the Yoruba, 1:60
Sadewa, 2:936, 2:957
Sādhaka, 2:820
Safa, 1:317
Safaites, 1:192
Sagara, Sāgaras, 2:875–76
Sagdlirmiut, 2:1145
Saghmto, 1:311
Sagittarius, 2:709
Sahadeva, 2:831, 2:862
Sahagún, 2:1187
Saichō, 2:1040
Śailajā, 2:861
Saint-Blaise, Bouches-du-Rhône, 1:243
Saint-Martin, Louis-Claude de, 2:772
Saint-Pol Roux (called Paul Pierre Roux), 2:762–63
Sakka, 2:929
Sakletch, 2:1175
Sakon, 1:199
Sakora, 2:1216–17
Śakti, *y*Śāktism, 2:806, 2:869
Śakuni, 2:829, 2:831
Śākyamuni, 2:901, 2:905, 2:907, 2:1087
Salacia, 1:628
Šalaš, 1:226
Salii, 1:553, 1:577, 1:624, 1:635
Sallust, 1:362–63, 2:651, 2:696
Salmacis, 1:471
Salome, in literature, 2:758
Saluhua, 2:952
Šaluš, 1:226
Salus Augusta, 1:609
Śālva, 2:860
Salvian, 1:254
Śalya, 2:832
Samal, kingdom of, 1:200
Samantabhadra, 2:906
Šamaš, 1:159, 1:165, 1:180
Sambhogakāya, 2:895
Samdzimari, 1:310, 1:313–14
Sames, 1:293
Saṃgha, Saṃgharama, 2:907
Samoyeds, 2:1128–29, 2:1132–33, 2:1134–35, *2:1135*, 2:1140
Sampo, 2:944–45
Sampsa Pellervoinen, 2:1136
Samson, 2:656, 2:660
Sanchoniathon, 1:185
Sand, George, 2:746, 2:769, 2:774
Šandaš, 1:217
Sang Hyang Bayu, 2:956
Sanghyang Sri, 2:953
Sang Hyang Tunggal, 2:954, 2:961
Sang Hyang Widi Wasa, *2:938*
Sangiang Serri, 2:941, 2:953
Sang Kuriang, *2:960–61*
Sanglin, 2:1015, 2:1016, 2:1025
Sanhuang (Three August Ones), 2:1018–20
Śankara, 2:903
Saṅkarṣaṇa, 2:861
San-ku-nichi, 2:1069
San Miao, 2:1029–30
Ṣaṇmukha, 2:866
Sannazaro, Jacopo, 2:704
Sannyāsin. See Renouncer, renunciation
Šanšalla, Šanšila, 1:219
Ṣapon, 1:196, 1:210
Sappho, 1:466, 1:470
Šara, 1:177
Sarakolle, 1:41
Sara-mama, 2:1202
Sarasvatī, 2:824, 2:875, 2:900, 2:905, 2:908
Sarotama, 2:957
Šarpa, Mount, 1:221
Sarpedon, 1:335, 1:416, 1:473, 1:481, *1:482;* in literature, 2:788
Sarruma, 1:222, 1:224, 1:226, 1:228
Sarsi, 2:1163
Sarvatāt, 2:886, 2:887
Śāstā, 2:846–49
Sasthi, 2:868
Satan, 2:652, 2:654, 2:672, 2:690, 2:691; in literature, 2:756, 2:767, 2:775
Satana, 1:318, 2:747–48
Śatarūpā, 2:824
Satī, 2:869
Satres, 1:520
Śatrughna, 2:834, 2:836
Sattva, 2:818–19, 2:823
Satuk Bughra Khan, 2:1111
Saturn, in art and literature, 2:696, 2:698, 2:707
Saturnalia, 1:603
Satyabhāmā, 2:864
Satyavatī, 2:856–57, 2:874
Satyavrata, 2:854
Sau-dzwar, 1:317
Sauromatae, 1:436
Šauška, 1:224, 1:225, 1:226, 1:227–28
Sautatare-i-roburo, 2:1222
Sāvitrī, 2:824–25
Sawerigading, 2:934, 2:941, 2:944
Sawsyrqwa, 1:318
Sawsyryq°e, 1:318, 2:1115
Saxo Grammaticus, 1:296, 1:299, 1:301, 1:304
Scanderbeg. *See* Castrioti, Georges (Gjergi)
Scarab, symbolism of: in Isis cults, 1:128; in literature, 2:709–10

Scarron, Paul, 2:726
Scáthach, 1:270
Schefferus, Johannes, 2:1133
Schelling, Friedrich Wilhelm Joseph von, 2:752, 2:755
Schikaneder, Emmanuel, 1:142, 2:773, 2:774
Schiller, Friedrich von, 2:731, 2:754, 2:767, 2:771
Schlegel, August Wilhelm, 2:755, 2:766
Schlegel, Friedrich, 2:731, 2:754–55
Schubert, Friedrich, 2:770
Scilla, 1:532
Sciphius, 1:381
Sciron, 1:382
Scopas, 1:473
Scot, Michael, 2:697
Scott, Sir Walter, 2:772
Scythians, 2:1112
Sebek, 1:109
Sebiumeker, 1:117, *1:117*, 1:118, 1:120
Sedna, 2:1122
Seferis, George, 2:789–90
Sefire, 1:200–201
Segomo, 1:249
Seiðr, 1:291, 1:293
Seite, 2:1135
Sekhmet, 1:104; in art and literature, 1:138
Selene, 1:128, 1:375, 1:478; and Gnostics, 2:676, 2:685
Selkup, 2:1119, 2:1128
Selvans, 1:520, 1:534
Semar, 2:936, 2:954–55, *2:955*
Sembodra, 2:944
Semele, 1:457, 1:458, 1:460
Semiramis, 1:321
Semites, Western, 1:182–91
Semones, 1:575, 1:604, 1:625
Sena, 2:956
Senancour, Étienne Pivert de, 2:777
Senanku, 1:34
Senapati, 2:939
Senāyaka, 2:901
Senboth, 1:258
Sencha, 1:270
Seneca, 1:520, 1:528, 1:534, 2:1158
Sengjia heshang, 2:902
Sentona, 1:250
Senufo, 1:32, 1:41
Septimontium, 1:551
Seragunting, 2:934, 2:943
Serapis, *1:122*, 1:123–24, *1:124*, *1:133*; in Christianity, 2:660; in Greece, 1:122, 1:124; in literature, 1:136, 1:141; in Rome, 1:609, 1:124, 1:126
Šeri, 1:219, 1:227
Serpent, symbolism of: in Albania, 1:307; for Austroasiatics and Austronesians, 2:993; in China, 2:1027, 2:1028, 2:1029; in Christianity, 2:649–50, 2:658; for continental Celts, 1:249; in Crete and Mycenae, 1:337, 1:338; in Georgia, 1:313; for Germano-Nordic peoples, 1:294, 1:304; for Gnostics, 2:675, 2:678, 2:682, 2:685; in Greece, 1:450; for Hittites, 1:223; in India, 2:823, 2:926, 2:928; in Indochina, 2:984; in insular Southeast Asia, 2:933, 2:937, 2:938, 2:940, 2:953, 2:956; in literature, 2:702; in Oceania, 2:1218, 2:1220; in pre-Roman Italy, 1:532; in Southeast Asia, 2:926, 2:928; in southern Africa (Bantu), 1:65, 1:67, 1:68; for Turks and Mongols, 2:1098; in Vietnam, 2:998, 2:1001; for Yoruba, 1:60
Servius Danielis, 1:387, 1:471, 1:526, 1:533, 1:534, 1:542, 1:552, 1:560, 1:612, 1:616, 1:617, 1:624, 1:628–29, 1:635, 1:636, 1:645, 2:698
Servius Tullius, 1:531, 1:545, 1:553, 1:615, 1:640, 1:645
Śeṣa, 2:823, 2:833, 2:841, 2:854, 2:860, 2:870
Sese nTaola, 2:935, 2:942–43
Set, 2:989
Seth, 1:91, 1:92, 1:93, 1:97, *1:102*, 1:104–5, 1:122; in literature, 1:134, 1:138, 1:140
Sethlans, 1:520
Settut, 1:85
Seveki, 2:1116, 2:1119, 2:1124
Seven, symbolism of: for Austroasiatics and Austronesians, 2:988–89; for Yoruba, 1:57
Séven, 2:1118, 2:1119, 2:1127
Sewserysh. *See* Shewzerysh
Sex, sexuality: in Egypt, 1:92; for Germano-Nordic peoples, 1:288, 1:291; for Gnostics, 2:682–85; in Greece, 1:395, 1:421, 1:434–35, 1:451, 1:468–72, 1:475, 1:499–500, 1:504, 1:629–32; in India, 2:841, 2:842, 2:875, 2:896–98; in Mesoamerica, 2:1180; in Papua New Guinea, 2:1229; in southern Africa (Bantu), 1:69; in Vietnam, 2:997; in West Africa, 1:38–39; for Western Semites, 1:189. *See also* Androgyne
Sextus Empiricus, 1:353, 2:661
sGam-po dkar-po, 2:907
Shadrapha, 1:199
Shahar, 1:200, 1:202, 1:213
Shākyamuni, 2:1039, 2:1040
Shalim, 1:213
Shalman, 1:204
Shaman and shamanism: among Austroasiatics and Austronesians, 2:987–88, 2:993; among Germano-Nordic peoples, 1:292–93; among Inuit, 2:1151–52; in Japan, 2:1042, 2:1057, 2:1062–63; in Korea, 2:1073; in North America, 2:1157–58; in Siberia, 2:1117–18, 2:1120–28; in South America, 2:1197–99, 2:1202; among Turks and Mongols, 2:1089, 2:1091, 2:1097, 2:1102, 2:1103–4
Shamash, 1:200
Shamu, 1:191
Shang. *See* Yin
Shangdi, 2:1018
Shang Huang, 2:1018
Shango, *1:54*, 1:55–59
Shanxiao, 2:1030
Shapannan (Obaluaye, Omolu), *1:57*, 1:60
Shapash, 1:211, 1:212, 1:215
Shashw, 2:1114
Shawnee, 2:1154
Shay al-qawm, 1:193
Shelley, Percy Bysshe, 2:755, 2:756, 2:759, 2:768, 2:769–70, 2:774
Shem, 1:182
Shennong, 2:1019, 2:1020, *2:1020*
Shentao, 2:1029, 2:1031
Shewzerysh (Sewserysh), 2:1115
Sheyyad Hamza, 2:1091
Shibari Jizō, 2:1054
Shichi go san, 2:1069
Shide, 2:907
Shiism, 2:947
Shilluk, 1:81–84
Shimbi, 1:70
Shingon, 2:1039, 2:1040, 2:1049
Shinran, 2:1040
Shinto, 2:1038, 2:1040, 2:1049–50
Shin Upago, 2:918
Shipaya, 2:1195
Shoshone, 2:1157, 2:1163
Shouxing, 2:907
Shtojzavalle, 1:307
Shu, 1:91, 1:92, 1:94, 1:100, *1:102*, 1:103, 1:104, 1:117
Shugendō, 2:1051–52, 2:1056–58, 2:1062–63
Shun (Zhuen), 2:1010, 2:1022–23, *2:1023*, 2:1024–25, 2:1029
Shyble, 2:1113, 2:1114
Sia, 1:92, 1:97
Siane, 2:1226, 2:1229
Siarnaq, 2:1149
Siberia, 2:1107, 2:1113, 2:1116–32
Sibitti, 1:178–79
Si Boru Deak Parujar, 2:940
Si Boru Ihat Manisia, 2:940
Sibyl, *Sibylline Books*, 1:535, 1:560, 1:562, 1:579, 1:587–88, 1:591, 1:593–94, 1:603, 1:608, 1:612, *1:626*, 1:643; in art and literature, 1:626, 2:694, 2:784, 2:788, in Christianity, 2:664–65
Sicilus, 1:546
Siddhi, *Siddhi*, 2:820, 2:865, 2:897
Sidon, 1:183, 1:195–96
Sif, 1:295
Sighvatr Þorðarson, 1:289
Signs, graphic: prehistory, 1:16–18; in West Africa, 1:30–32, 1:35–36, 1:37, 1:44, 1:50, 1:51–52
Sigui, 1:30, 1:36, 1:41, 1:47–48, 1:50
Sigurðr, 1:285
Sikelianos, Angelos, 2:788–89
Sila, 2:1148–49, 2:1151
Silai, 2:935
Silenus, 1:432
Silewe Nazarata, 2:937
Silex, 2:1153
Silius Italicus, 1:185
Siliwangi, 2:953
Silvanus, 1:565, 1:636, 1:639; among continental Celts, 1:255
Sima Qian, 2:1012–13 passim, 2:1019, 2:1020, 2:1024, 2:1034–35
Simbi, 1:64–65, 1:70
Simbolon Manik, 2:939
Šimegi, 1:224, 1:226
Simonides, 1:466
Simon Magus, 2:677, 2:678
Simpang Impang, 2:941
Simplicius, 1:434
Simurgh, 1:297, 1:298, 1:300
Sin (god), 1:192, 1:200, 1:217
Šingkelavun, 2:1123
Sing-könga, 2:987
Sinis, 1:342
Sintians, 1:385
Sioux, 2:1163–64
Siproïtes, 1:472
Sipylus, Mount, 1:216
Siqiniq, 2:1148, 2:1151
Si Raja Batak, 2:940
Si Raja Ihat Manisia, 2:940
Sirao, 2:940
Sirens, 1:335, 1:409, 1:410–12, 1:488, 1:545; in Christianity, 2:657–58; in literature, 2:710
Siriono, 2:1192
Sirona, 1:250, 1:275
Sisseton, 2:1163
Śiśupāla, 2:860, 2:862
Sisyphus, 1:406, 1:414
Sītā, 2:835–37, 2:838–39, 2:869, 2:926, 2:957
Sito, 1:453
Sitopotiniya, 1:332, 1:334
Sitowa, 2:1205
Siu. *See* Menggin
Siuai, 2:1220
Shiva, among the Slavs, 1:302. *See also* Śiva
Śiva, 2:812–13, 2:819, 2:824–26, 2:839–42, 2:845, 2:846, 2:848, 2:864–66, 2:875–77, 2:896–98, 2:903, 2:927–28; in insular Southeast Asia, 2:953
Shouxing, 2:907
Shu, 1:91, 1:92, 1:94, 1:100, *1:102*, 1:103, 1:104, 1:117
Shun (Zhuen), 2:1010, 2:1022–23, *2:1023*, 2:1024–25, 2:1029
Skaði, 1:288, 1:295
Skanda, 2:824, 2:849, 2:864, 2:866–69, 2:899–901, *2:900*, 2:906
sKar-ma yol-sde, 2:1086–87
Skiðblaðnir, 1:291
Skidi, 2:1153
Skira, 1:478
Skirnír, 1:288

Skotino (Pediados), Crete, 1:337
Skotos (obscurity), 1:367
Skrýmnir, 1:282
Sky, symbolism and divinities of: in art and literature, 2:699; in China, 2:1008–9, 2:1010–15, 2:1019, 2:1033; in Egypt, 1:103; among Finno-Ugrians, 2:1137, 2:1139; in Greece, 1:369, 1:371, 1:381, 1:463–64; among Hurrians, 1:226; in Indochina, 2:983; in insular Southeast Asia, 2:933–34, 2:938, 2:952–53; in Japan, 2:1047; in Korea, 2:1072; in Madagascar, 2:962–70; in Mesoamerica, 2:1179–84; in Mesopotamia, 1:155–56, 1:160–61, 1:173; in North America, 2:1162; in pre-Roman Italy, 1:520; in Siberia, 2:1119–20; in southern Africa (Bantu), 1:65, 1:68, 1:71–72; among Turks and Mongols, 2:1090–92, 2:1095–96, 2:1105–7; in Vietnam, 2:996, 2:997, 2:999–1000
Slametan, 2:951–52
Slavs, 1:295–305
Sleipnir, 1:295
Smertrios, 1:244, 1:276
Smṛti (tradition), 2:799–803, 2:808–10
Snorri Sturluson, 1:280–86 passim, 1:289, 1:290, 1:291, 1:292, 1:294
Soba, 1:116
Socrates, 1:353, 1:364, 1:391, 1:467–69 passim, 1:507
Sode-mogisama, 2:1042
Sodom and Gomorrah, 2:660
Sōkō, 2:908
Soko no kuni, 2:1045, 2:1046
Sŏk T'alhä, 2:1073
Sol, 1:565
Sol Invictus, 1:556
Soma, *soma*, 1:236, 2:802, 2:803–6; in Southeast Asia, 2:924–25
Song Yu, 2:1030
Soninke, 1:29, 1:37, 1:41, 1:49, 1:52
Sonrhaï, 1:27
Son-Tinh, 2:1003
Sopatros, 1:425–26
Sopdu, 1:103
Sophia, 2:679–80; in literature, 2:774–75
Sophocles, 1:386, 1:405, 1:406, 1:408, 1:410, 1:411, 1:412, 1:421, 1:480, 1:481, 1:482, 1:483, 1:486, 1:498, 1:499
Šor, 2:1128
Sorbayati, 2:940
Soripada, 2:937
Sortes, 1:590
Soslan, 1:318, 2:1115
Sosryko. *See* Sozryko
Sothis, 1:128
Soul, the: to Aramaeans and Palmyrenes, 1:202–3, 1:205; in China, 1:1030; to Eskimos, 2:1150–51; to Etruscans, 1:525–26; in Greece, 1:355–56, 1:357, 1:492; to Gypsies, 2:720–21; to Indo-Europeans, 1:236–37; to Indonesians, 2:949, 2:951; in Japan, 2:1041–44, 2:1051–52; to Mesoamericans, 2:1188, 2:1190–91; in Norse religion, 1:292–93; in Papua New Guinea, 2:1225–26, 2:1229; in pre-Islamic Iran, 2:888–89; in Siberia, 2:1116–28; in South America, 2:1195, 2:1197, 2:1198–99; in Western Africa, 1:34. *See also* Gnostics
Soumet, Alexandre, 2:753, 2:754
South America, 2:1192–1208, *2:1193*
Southeast Asia, 2:913–31, *2:914, 2:915, 2:929. See also* Insular Southeast Asia
Sozryko, 1:318, 2:741, 2:1115
Spain. *See* Celts, Iberian
Sparta, Greece, 1:329, 1:330, 1:404, 1:445, 1:447, 1:474–78
Spengler, Oswald, 2:783
Spenta Manyu, 2:885–88, 2:891, 2:893
Sphynx, 1:411, 1:499, *1:500*
Spiess, Henri, 1:142
Spirit, 2:1211
Spirits, genies: Albanian, 1:307; Baltic, 1:305; Chinese, 2:1013–14, 2:1028–29; Finno-Ugrian, 2:1134–35; Germano-Nordic, 1:294–95; Gypsy, 2:719, 2:720–21; in literature, 2:771–72; in the Maghreb, 1:87; Mesoamerican, 2:1189; among Nilotic peoples, 1:81; among nomads, 1:21; North American, 2:1156–57; among Ossets, 1:317; in Papua New Guinea, 2:1224–26; pre-Islamic Iranian, 2:884, 2:891; Siberian, 2:1118–19, 2:1120–28, 2:1130; Slavic, 1:295–302; Southeast Asian, 2:917–18, 2:918–24; in southern Africa (Bantu), 1:64–65, 1:70–71, 1:77–78, 1:79; Tibetan, 2:1084; among Turks and Mongols, 2:1107, 2:1108
Spor, 1:298
Springtime. See *Ver sacrum*
Sraosha, 2:888, 2:892
Sré, 2:977, 2:979, 2:981–85, *2:982*, 2:985–87, 2:988, 2:990, 2:992–95
Śrī, 2:811, 2:830–32, 2:836–39, 2:840, 2:841, 2:854, 2:862, 2:864, 2:867, 2:869, 2:874, 2:900, 2:928, 2:952, 2:953
Srid-lcam 'phrul-mo-che, 2:1078
Srid-pa'i rgyal-mo, 2:1080
Srin-mo, 1:1084
Śruti (revelation), 2:799–801, 2:809–10
Staël, Madame de, 2:752–53, 2:768
Stars. *See* Astrology
Stata Mater, 1:645
Statius, 1:615
Stendhal, 2:755, 2:777
Stephanus of Byzantium, 1:385
Steropes, 1:372
Stesichorus, 1:546, 2:677
Steven, Saint, 2:1133
Steven the Younger, 2:673
Sthāṇu, 2:841–42
Stheneboea, 1:402
Stheno, 1:473
Stobeus, 2:678
sTobs-chung, 2:1087
sTon-pa gShen-rab, 2:1081
Strabo, 1:185, 1:243, 1:246, 1:270, 1:312, 1:319, 1:385, 1:437, 1:443, 1:542, 1:546, 1:547, 1:629, 2:729
Strewings *(stibadeia)*, 1:456
Stribing, 1:305
Stribog, 1:300
Sturla Þhórðarson, 1:284
Styx, 1:371, 1:377, 1:378, 1:380, 1:413, 1:490, 1:633
Sualtaim (Sualtach Sídech), 1:270
Subhadrā, 2:831, 2:832
Subrahmanya, 2:845–46, 2:849, 2:864, 2:866, *2:868*, 2:896
Sucellus, 1:249, 1:276–78, *1:277, 2:734*
Su Dongpo, 2:1034
Śūdra, 2:807, 2:849
Sue, Eugène, 2:767
Suetonius, 1:385, 1:591, 1:592, 1:594, 1:603, 1:609, 1:616, 1:635, 2:658
Sugrīva, 2:835, 2:837, 2:838
Suidas, 1:128, 1:185, 2:702
Suiren, 2:1019
Śukrācārya, 2:826, 2:858
Sukunabikona, 2:1042, 2:1043, 2:1045, 2:1051
Sula, 1:250
Suleviae, 1:250
Sulis, 1:249
Sumba, 2:935
Śumbha, 2:871
Sumbolon, 1:487
Sumer, 1:142–45, 1:147–49, 1:172
Sumitrā, 2:834
Sum-pa mkhan-po, 2:1087–88
Sumu, 2:1127
Sumuqan, 1:147
Sun, symbolism and divinities of, 2:1234; in the Andes, 2:1203–5; in Armenia, 1:320; in art and literature, 2:694, 2:761–63; in Asia Minor, 1:216; for Baltic peoples, 1:305; in China, 2:1010–11, 2:1020, 2:1021, 2:1024, 2:1034; in Christianity, 2:653–54; in Crete and Mycenae, 1:336; in Egypt, 1:93, 1:103, 1:105, 1:109–10, 1:112, 1:1115; for Finno-Ugrians, 2:1137; in France, 2:750–52; in Georgia, 1:309, 1:313; for Germano-Nordic peoples, 1:281–82, 1:284, 1:304; in Greece, 1:371, 1:439, 1:468, 1:478, 1:509; for Hurrites, 1:226; in India, 2:807; in Indochina, 2:984–85; for Indo-Europeans, 1:238; in insular Southeast Asia, 2:933, 2:937–38, 2:940, 2:943, 2:952, 2:953; for Inuit, 2:1148–49; in Japan, 2:1038; in Korea, 2:1070–71; in Madagascar, 2:969; in Meroe, 1:119, 1:120; in Mesoamerica, 2:1174–76, 2:1177, 2:1180–82, 2:1187; in North America, 2:1153, 2:1161, 2:1163–64; in Oceania, 2:1220–21; for Palmyrenes, 1:205; for pre-Islamic Iran, 2:892; in pre-Roman Italy, 1:520; in Rome, 1:556–57; for Slavs, 1:298, 1:301, 1:304; in South America, 2:1194; in Southeast Asia, 2:924–25; in southern Africa (Bantu), 1:64, 1:67–69, 1:73–75; for Turks and Mongols, 2:1092, 2:1106; in Ugarit, 1:211; in Vietnam, 2:997–98; in West Africa (Mande), 1:49–50
Sunahśepa, 2:828
Sunan Ambu, 2:961
Sunan Ampel, 2:945
Sunan Bayat, 2:946
Sunan Bonang, 2:945
Sunan Drajat, 2:945
Sunan Giri, 2:945
Sunan Gunung Jati, 2:946
Sunan Kali Jaga, 2:945
Sunan Panggung, 2:946
Sun Dance, 2:1163–64
Šundy-mumy, 2:1137
Sungir, USSR, 1:12
Suovetaurilia, 1:568, 1:603, 1:605, *1:624*, 1:625
Suparṇī, 2:804–5
Superiors (gods), 1:520
Sur(i), 1:526
Surong Gunting, 2:943. *See also* Seragunting
Śūrpanakhā, 2:837
Surtr, 1:285
Sūrya: in India, 2:802, 2:807, 2:831, 2:835, 2:837, *2:925;* in insular Southeast Asia, 2:953
Suryavaṅ, 2:925
Susano-o, 2:1038, 2:1043, 2:1044–45, 2:1066, 2:1068
Suseri-hime, 2:1041
Susi, 2:1116
Suttungr, 1:287
Suttunius, 1:249
Šuwaliyat, 1:226
Suyudana, 2:957
Svāhā, 2:867
Svanetians, 1:314
Svarog, 1:298–301
Svarožic, 1:298–301
Sventovit (Sviatovit), 1:298, 1:301
Swazi, 1:68, 1:73, 1:75

Swinburne, Algernon Charles, 2:758, 2:760, 2:765
Switzerland, ancient, 2:733–34
Syaikh Burhanuddin, 2:946
Sylvanus. *See* Silvanus
Symplegades, 1:444
Synesius, 1:360
Syrdon, 1:317–19
Syria, 1:182, 1:184, 1:190–91, 1:200–206
Syrianus, 1:363, 1:365

T

Ta, 2:1219
Ta'aroa, 2:1218
Tabari, 1:192
Tabula Agnonensis, 1:537, 1:539
Tacitus, 1:136, 1:242, 1:246, 1:255, 1:280, 1:281, 1:284, 1:290, 1:291, 1:547, 1:587, 1:627, 1:645
Tages, 1:519, 1:528, 1:530, 1:531, 1:533, 1:535, 1:588
Tahtajis, 2:1113
Taichō, 2:1057
Taino-Arawak, 2:1194
Taiscaron, 2:1160
Taishan, 2:1012
Taishi-kō, 2:1069
Tajimamori, 2:1046
Takama no hara, 2:1044, 2:1046–47
Takeuchi no Sukune, 2:1043
Takitu, Takitum, 1:224, 1:226
TakkaN, 2:845
Taksin, 2:929
Ta'lab, 1:191
Talafsa, 1:86
Talaina peithō, 1:405
Talavāy MāḍaN, 2:845, 2:848
Talitha, 1:531
Talon (Talos), 1:335
Talos, 1:473
Tama, 2:1037, 2:1041–44
Tamakaia, 2:1219
Tamar, 1:310, 1:311, 1:313
Tamas, 2:818, 2:819, 2:823
Tambon Haruei Bungai, 2:938
Tan, 1:335
Tanabata, 2:1068
Tana Ekan, 2:938
Tang, 2:989
Tangaloa, 2:1218
Tangaroa, *2:1218,* 2:1219, 2:1222
Tangaroa Upao Vahu, 2:1222
Tangun, 2:1070–71, 2:1072
Tanit, 1:198–99
Ta no kami, 2:1051, 2:1064
Tantalus, 1:403, 1:414, 1:454, 1:508; in literature, 2:787
Tantrism, 2:872, 2:894–95, 2:899
Tan Viên, 2:998, 2:1000, 2:1003
Tao Angong, 2:1032
Taotie, 2:1029
Taowu, 2:1029
Tapas, 2:827–28, 2:855
Tapele, 2:952
Tapio, 2:1134
Tapkina, 1:225
Tapoloka, 2:821
Taqqiq, 2:1148, 2:1149, 2:1151
Tara, 1:258
Tārā, 2:902, 2:1083, 2:1085
Tāraka, 2:867
Taranis, 1:243, 1:244, 1:248, 1:278
Tararamanu, *2:1217,* 2:1222
Tarasca, 2:689, *2:735*
Tarchon, 1:519, 1:533, 1:535
Tarhunda, 1:222
Tarhun(t), 1:217
Tarkondas, 1:217
Tarniq, 2:1151
Tarquinii, Italy, 1:525, 1:546
Tarquinius Superbus, 1:545, 1:553, 1:587, 1:594
Tarquinius the Elder, 1:545, 1:553, 1:585, 1:589
Tarquitius, 1:534, 1:535, 1:588
Tarqunt-, 1:229
Tartarus, 1:369, 1:375, 1:377–78, 1:406, 1:412–14, 1:447
Taru, 1:221, 1:224
Tarvos Trigaranus (bull with three cranes), 1:273, 1:279, *1:279*
Tasaday, 2:936
Täso, 2:1071
Tāṭakā, 2:835
Tatars, 2:1090, 2:1099, 2:1102, 2:1105
Tate, Mount (in Japan), 2:1046
Tatian, 2:659, 2:660, 2:662, 2:667, 2:668
Tatius, 1:552
Taurin, 1:244
Tauri(t), 1:220
Tavibo, 2:1157
Tchambuli, 2:1226, 2:1229
Tchao, 2:1099
Teb Tenggeri, 2:1104
Tecciztecatl, 2:1180–81
Tecciztli, 2:1180
Technē, 1:387–89, 1:488
Tecmor, 1:367, 1:371
Tefnut, 1:91, 1:92, 1:94, 1:117
Tefro, 1:522
Tein Kanaké, 2:1215
Tein Pijopatch, 2:1214, 2:1216, 2:1223
Tekton, 1:387
Telavel, 1:302, 1:305
Telchines, 1:385
Telemachus, 1:387, 1:439, 1:497; in literature, 2:785
Telephassa, 1:473
Telephus, 1:546
Teleuts, 2:1109, 2:1113
Telipinu, 1:221
Tell Açana (Alalakh), Syria, 1:191, 1:226
Tell el Amarna, Egypt, 1:184, 1:188, 1:193
Tellem, 1:27–28
Tell Hariri, 1:190
Tell Mishrife (Qatna), 1:191
Tell Ta'Anekh, 1:184, 1:191
Tellus, 1:565, 1:608, 1:612, 1:613
Telos, 1:397
Temaukel, 2:1194
Temes Malau, 2:1216
Tempon Telon, 2:947
Tendai, 2:1039, 2:1040, 2:1050
Tengere Kaira Kan, 2:1095
Tengri, 2:1091–92, 2:1101, 2:1105
Tengu, 2:1037, 2:1052, 2:1059–61, *2:1059,* 2:1060, 2:1061
Tenochtitlan, 2:1165, 2:1169, 2:1170
Tenri-kyō, 2:1040
Tenu, 1:225, 1:226
Teotl, 2:1181
Te papa, 2:1219
Tepegöz, 2:1091, 2:1100
Tepehuas, *2:1166,* 2:1175
Tepeyollotl, 2:1185
Tepictoton, 2:1184
Tepolo, 2:1210–11
Terence, 1:620
Terrasson, Jean, 1:141–42, 2:173
Tertullian, 1:276, 1:635, 2:654, 2:655, 2:658, 2:659, 2:660, 2:661, 2:662, 2:668, 2:669
Teryel/teryalin, 1:85, 1:87
Tešup (Tešub), 1:219, 1:222, 1:224–25, 1:226, 1:227–29, *1:228*
Tethra, 1:270
Tethys, 1:366–67, 1:371, 1:375, 1:379, 1:465; in Christianity, 2:660
Te tumu, 2:1219
Tetun, 2:934
Teutates, 1:243, 1:248, 1:249, 1:279–80
Teyrnon, 1:261–62
Tezcatlipoca, 2:1174, 2:1179, 2:1180, 2:1184
Thailand. *See* Southeast Asia
Thalassa (Gnostics), 2:681
Thalatth-Omorka, 2:681
Thales, 1:366
Thalia, 1:492
Thalna, 1:531
Thammuz, 1:434
Thamudians, 1:192
Thamyris, 1:492
Thana (Thanr), 1:531
Thanatos, 1:405–9, *1:407,* 1:480, *1:482*
Than-nong, 2:1002
Thanr. *See* Thana
Thargelia, 1:478
Thauma, 1:489
Thaumas, 1:474, 1:490
Thaumatopoiia, 1:488
The, 2:1113
Thea, 1:371, 1:375, 1:465
Thebes, Greece, 1:329, 1:404, 1:459–60, 1:498–99
Themis, 1:371–72, 1:375, 1:465, 1:494
Themisto, 1:444
Theocritus, 1:436, 1:476, 1:504, 1:507, 1:508
Theodore bar Konai, 2:681, 2:688
Theodore of Cyrene, 2:667
Theodorus of Asine, 1:360
Theodulf, 2:696
Theogamia, 1:397–98
Theogony, in Greece, 1:375–78
Theophilus of Antioch, 2:656, 2:659, 2:667, 2:668
Theophrastus, 1:334, 1:425, 1:427
Theophylactus Simocattes, 2:1096, 2:1103, 2:1109
Theoscenia, 1:464
Theotokas, George, 2:790
Thesan, 1:520
Theseus, 1:337, 1:341–42, 1:345–46, 1:381, 1:382, 1:388–89, 1:403, 1:420, 1:448–49, 1:451, 1:460, 1:475, *1:476, 1:477,* 1:479; in literature, 2:706, 2:790
Thesmophoria, 1:396, 1:409, 1:431, 1:433, 1:454
Thespiae, Greece, 1:472
Thetis, 1:335, 1:382, 1:385, 1:413, 1:459, 1:510, *1:510;* in art and literature, 2:694, 2:788
The'u-brang, 2:1086
Theuth. *See* Thoth
Thiasos (Dionysus), 1:432, 1:456, 1:457, 1:631; in Palmyra, 1:205
Thien Lôi, 2:1000
Thietmar of Merseburg, 1:281, 1:296, 1:300
Thomas, 2:717, 2:718
Thonga, 1:68, 1:70, 1:71
Thopç, 1:307
Thor, 1:285, 1:286–87, 1:292, 1:295, 1:302–3, 2:1136, 2:1137
Thoth, 1:101, 1:105, 1:109, 1:128, 1:131; in Christianity, 2:672; in literature, 1:132, 1:133–36, 1:355, 1:358, 2:785
Thraētaona, 2:893
Thucydides, 1:415, 1:548, 2:667
Thunder, symbolism and divinities of: in the Andes, 2:1202; in Asia Minor, 1:217; for Baltic peoples, 1:306; for continental Celts, 1:278; for Etruscans, 1:520, 1:528–29, 1:532–33; for Finno-Ugrians, 2:1136; in Georgia, 1:312–13; for Germano-Nordic peoples, 1:285; in Greece, 1:372, 1:381; for Hittites, 1:222; for Hurrites, 1:227–28; in Indochina, 2:985; for Indo-Europeans, 1:238; for Inuit, 2:1148–49; in Mesoamerica, 2:1183, 2:1185, 2:1186, 2:1191; in North America, 2:1157; in northern Caucasus, 2:1113–14; for Ossets, 1:316, 1:317; for Palmyrenes, 1:205; in Rome, 1:592, 1:593–94, 1:621; for Slavs, 1:300; in South America, 2:1194, 2:1202, 2:1204; in southern Africa (Bantu), 1:76; for Turks and Mongols, 2:1113; in Ugarit, 1:210; in Vietnam, 2:999–1000; for Yoruba, 1:55–56
Thunor. *See* Thor
Thu'o'ng, 2:976

Thuong-dê, 2:999
Thuy-tê, 2:1000
Thuy-Tinh, 2:1003
Thyestes, 1:403–4, 1:408, 1:508
Tiamat, 1:3, 1:151, 1:155–56, 1:158–61, 1:172, 1:178
Tiandi, 2:1010
Tibet, 2:1075–88. *See also* Buddhism
Tibiran, grotto at, Hautes-Pyrénées, 1:18
Tibullus, 1:594, 1:612, 1:617
Tieck, Louis, 2:754, 2:755, 2:772
Tiermes, 2:1136, 2:1137
Tigillum Sororium, 1:583, 1:624
Tilmun, 1:146, 1:147, 1:157
Timaeus of Tauromenium, 1:548
Timagoras, 1:472
Timeus, 1:255, 1:354
Tinguian, 1:939
Tinia, 1:520, 1:531, *1:532*, 1:534, 1:553
Tintoretto, 2:700
Tiphys, 1:387
Tirawa, 2:1153, 2:1158
Tiresias, 1:399, 1:405, 1:409, 1:459–60, 1:471, 1:494, 1:507, 1:531, 2:764
Ti-se (Kailāśa), 2:1080
Tisnawati, 2:953
Titans, 1:369, 1:371–72, 1:375–78, 1:379, 1:380, 1:381, 1:384, 1:391, 1:392, 1:399, 1:422–24, 1:427, 1:461–62, 1:465–66, 1:481, 1:506
Tithenidia, 1:475
Titian, 2:700
Titiens, 1:552
Tityus, 1:439
Tiv(r), 1:520
Tiwah, 2:947
Tiyabenti, 1:225, 1:226, 1:229
Tjarnaglofi, 1:301
Tlachihualtepetl, 2:1185
Tlahuizcalpantecuhtli, 2:1179, 2:1183
Tlaloc, 2:1179, 2:1181, *2:1182*, 2:1183, 2:1191
Tlalocan, 2:1183, 2:1185, 2:1191
Tlalocs, 2:1183
Tlaltecuhtli, 2:1184
Tlapanes, 2:1175
Tlazolteotl, 2:1180, 2:1181
Tlepolemus, 1:416
Tlepsh, 1:1114
Toba (Mesoamerican tribe), 2:1198
Toba (Mongolian people), 2:1089, 2:1105, 2:1110
Todomé, 2:1120
Tofalar, 2:1128
Tōkan-ya, 2:1069
Tokoyo no kuni, 2:1045, 2:1046
Tölish, 2:1089
Tolkien, John Ronald Reuel, 2:791–92
Tollius, Jacob, 2:701, 2:703
Tollund, Denmark, *1:289*
Tolstoy, Lev Nikolayevich, 2:778
Toman, 2:1119
Tonacaciuhatl, 2:1184
Tonacatecuhtli, 2:1181, 2:1187
Tonacatepetl, 2:1176
Tonatiuh, 2:1179, 2:1181
Tongmyŏng, 2:1070
Tong shang, 2:918
Tonu, 1:32
Ton Yuquq, 2:1096, 2:1098
Toquz Oghuz, 2:1089
Tor. *See* Thor
Tora, 1:522
Toraja, 2:931, 2:933, 2:934, 2:935, 2:936, 2:939, 2:942, 2:948, 2:949, *2:951*
Toranda Ue, 2:943
Toririhnan, 2:1215, 2:1216
Toro, 1:78
Torokuku mBetu'e, 2:943
Torquemada, Juan de, 2:1183
Torre, Spain, *1:17*, 1:20
Tor Tignosa, Italy, 1:572
Torym, 2:1119
Totemism: in Albania, 1:307; for Baltic peoples, 1:306; in Oceania, 2:1212–13; in pre-Roman Italy, 1:536; in Siberia, 2:1130; for Turks and Mongols, 2:1091, 2:1092, 2:1098; in West Africa, 1:51–52
Totik k'akal, 2:1182
Totiotsi, 2:1182
Totonac, 2:1175, 2:1179, 2:1182, 2:1183, 2:1184, 2:1188, 2:1191
Toutatis. *See* Teutates
Toxiuhmolpilia, 2:1171
Toya matsuri, 2:1064–65
Toymu, 1:32
Tradition. *See Smṛti*
Tragedy, 1:353
Trailokyavijaya, 2:903
Tramsëmwas, 2:1221
Tranol, 2:923
Transmigration, 2:821–22
Trdat, 1:320
Trebatius, 1:550, 1:569
Trebo, 1:522
Tree, symbolism of the: for Baltic peoples, 1:305; in China, 2:1023, 2:1036; in Crete and Mycenae, 1:334; for Finno-Ugrians, 2:1138–39; in Georgia, 1:313; for Germano-Nordic peoples, 1:281, 1:286, 1:290, 1:294, 1:304; for Gnostics, 2:683, 2:684, 2:687; in Greece, 1:341, 1:343, 1:424, 1:447, 1:490; for Gypsies, 2:719, 2:720; in India, 2:845–46, 2:864; in insular Southeast Asia, 2:933, 2:937–38, 2:940, 2:944, 2:954; in Korea, 2:1072; in the Maghreb, 1:86, 1:87; in Mesoamerica, 2:1179, 2:1185–86, 2:1187; in northern Caucasus, 2:1115; for insular Celts, 1:262; in Siberia, 2:1117, 2:1124; in southern Africa (Bantu), 1:64, 1:80; for Turks and Mongols, 2:1096, 2:1098, 2:1101–2; in West Africa, 1:43
Tretā Yuga, 2:850
Trickster: Norse, 1:295; in North America, 2:1153–56; in Oceania, 2:1217–18
Trigartas, 2:832
Triglav, 1:301
Trimo, 2:964, 2:967
Trimūrti, 2:812, 2:819–21
Triopas, 1:454
Triptolemus, 1:395, 1:565
Triśaṅku, 2:828
Trismosin, Salomon, 2:701, 2:712
Tristan and Isolde, 2:717–18, *2:717*, 2:760
Triton, 1:380, 1:382, *1:383*
Triviae (goddesses of crossroads), 1:250, *1:251*
Trivikrama, 2:858
Troit, 1:265
Trojan War, 1:389, 1:415–16, 1:446, 1:546
Trokondas, 1:217
Trong, 2:986, 2:987
Trophonius, 1:439, 1:450
Trundholm, Denmark, 1:281, *1:283*
Tsagan Ebügen, 2:1092
Tscholkwe, 1:28
Tshang-pa, 2:1078
Tshekish angelwez, 1:314
Tshibinda Ilunga, 1:67, 1:72, *1:74*
Tshilimbulu, 1:67
Tshitimukulu, 1:67
Tshitomi, 1:71
Tsidada jesu, 2:1182
Tsinana gwalupe, 2:1182
Tsuntas house, Mycenae, 1:333
Tswana, 1:70
Tuan, 1:258
Tuarere, 2:1217
Tuatha Dé Danann, 1:240, 1:258–60, 1:270, 1:271, 1:274
Tuathal, 1:273
Tubilustrium, 1:583, 1:624
Tubo, 2:1030
Tucano, Tucuno, 2:1200
Tuchulcha, 1:525, 1:532
Tudi, 2:907
Tuhuši, 1:227
Tujue, 2:1089, 2:1097, 2:1098, 2:1099, 2:1102, 2:1103, 2:1105, 2:1107, 2:1108, 2:1110, 2:1111, 2:1112
Tuka, 2:1223
Tumburu, 2:898
Tung fang Sho, 2:1008
Tungus, 2:1116–32, *2:1117*, *2:1118*, *2:1121*, *2:1123*, *2:1124*, *2:1126*, *2:1127*, *2:1128*
Tuonela, 2:1140
Tupi-Guarani, 2:1192, 2:1194, 2:1196, 2:1198, 2:1206–8
Tup-šimāti, 1:176–78
Turamarubi, 2:1226
Turan, 1:520, 1:531
Türgesh, 2:1089
Turks and Mongols, 2:1089–1113, 2:1128
Turms, 1:520
Turnus, 1:641
Turum, 2:1119
Tushan, 2:1016, 2:1025
Tutyr, 1:316
Tuurngaq, 2:1152
Tuvs, 2:1128
Tuwala Lia Matai, 2:952
Twa, 1:80
Twins: in Greece, 1:463–64; in India, 2:834; in insular Southeast Asia, 2:933; in literature, 2:766–67; in North America, 2:1153–54, 2:1160; in pre-Islamic Iran, 2:885–86, 2:889; in South America, 2:1194; in southern Africa (Bantu), 1:64, 1:65, 1:69, 1:70–71; in West Africa (Mande), 1:33–35, 1:37–43
Twrch Trwyth, 1:265
Tyaumyê, Mount, 2:1215, 2:1219
Tychon, 1:629
Tydeus, 1:417
Tyidopwaan, 2:1221
Tyndareos, 1:404, 1:463
Typheus (Typhon), 1:130, 1:377–78, *1:377*, 1:399, 1:510, 1:634; among Gnostics, 1:685
Týr, 1:281–82, 1:284, 1:291, 1:292, 1:295
Tyre, 1:184, 1:194, 1:195, 1:196
Tyrrhenus, 1:546
Tzahui, 2:1183
Tzeltal, 2:1171, 2:1178, 2:1179
Tzetzes, 1:548
Tzotzil, 2:1171, 2:1176, 2:1179–80, 2:1182, 2:1185, 2:1188

U

Uathach, 1:270
Ubusuna-gami, 2:1064
Ubykh, 2:1113–16
Ucchusma, 2:902–3, 2:906, 2:907–8
Udayana, 2:1087
Udege, 2:1128
UD.SIG$_5$, 1:221
Ugarit, 1:182–85, *1:183*, *1:184*, 1:187, *1:187*, 1:188–89, 1:190, 1:206–15, *1:209*, *1:214*, 1:217, 1:224, 1:225, 1:226, 1:227–28
Ugrasena, 2:860, 2:862
Ugrians, 2:1132–40 passim, 2:1128
Uighurs, 2:1089, 2:1098, 2:1100, 2:1101, 2:1103, 2:1111, 2:1112, 2:1113
Uinigumasuittuq, 2:1149–50
Uisliu, 1:271
Uji-gami, 2:1051, 2:1064
Ukko, 2:1136
Ulaidh (Ulster), 1:240, 1:258, 1:270–71
Ul'č, 2:1128
Ülgen, 2:1102, 2:1105
Uliliyantigeš, 1:219
Ülker, 2:1106
Ullr, 1:291–92, 1:303
Ulster. *See* Ulaidh
Üllüg, 2:1105, 2:1108
Umā, 2:866, 2:896–97, 2:901, 2:902, *2:914*, 2:927; in insular Southeast Asia, 2:952

Umari, Ibn Fadl Allah Al-, 2:1112
Umay, 2:1089, 2:1091, 2:1108, 2:1112
Umbu, 1:226
Ummânu, 1:153–54
Umm el Amad, 1:183
Underworld: in China, 2:1033; in Greece, 1:409–10, 1:412–14, 1:510; to Indo-Europeans, 1:236; in Japan, 2:1039–40, 2:1048; in Mesopotamia, 1:152, 1:155, 1:180; in pre-Roman Italy, 1:520, 1:525–26; for Turks and Mongols, 2:1095–96, 2:1107–8; in Vietnam, 2:1000. *See also* Afterlife
Uni, 1:517, *1:518*, 1:520, 1:523, 1:546, 2:621
Unkei, 2:1061
'U-pe-ra, 2:1086
Upu Lero, 2:933, 2:938
Upu Nusa, 2:933, 2:938
Ur, Mesopotamia, *1:144*, 1:147
Urashim Taro, 2:1046
Urðorbrunnr, 1:294
Urðr, 1:288
Urien, 1:264
Urinno, 2:1220
Ursitory, 2:720
Uršui, 1:226
Uruk, 1:172
Uryzmäg, 2:748
Uṣas, 2:802, 2:814
Uṣil, 1:520
Usmū, 1:146
Usuk Sangbamban, 2:939
Ušumgallū, 1:158, 1:160
Usurufa, 2:1226, 2:1229
Ute, 2:1163
Útgarðr, 1:286
Uttarā, 2:832, 2:833
Uttara-Kuru, 2:867
Uttu, 1:147
Utu, 1:147
Uumarnituq, 2:1146

V

Vahagn, 1:320
Vai, Vay. *See* Vayu
Vaikuṇṭha, 2:822
Väinämöinen, 2:1138
Vairocana, 2:906
Vaiṣṇavī, 2:872
Vaiśravaṇa, 2:899, 2:900–901, 2:902, 2:903, 2:905, 2:906, 2:907, 2:908, 2:909
Vaiśya, 2:807
Vajra, 2:902–3, 2:907
Vajraḍaka, 2:903–4
Vajragarbha, 2:903
Vajrapāni, 2:898, 2:899, 2:900, 2:902–4, 2:907–9
Vajra-yakṣa, 2:902, 2:903
Valaršak, 1:320
Val Camonica, Italy, 1:256, 1:268
Valentinus, 2:677
Valeriano, Piero, 1:138, 2:699
Valerius Flaccus, 1:443, 1:444
Valerius Maximus, 1:567
Valerius Probus, 1:611
Valéry, Paul, 2:758
Valhöll, 1:286, 1:287
Väli, 1:287
Vālin, 2:835, 2:837
Valkyries, 1:287
Valkyrjur, 1:287
Valli, 2:869
Vālmīki, 2:834, 2:839
Valois, Nicolas, 2:708
Vāmana, 2:858–59
Van Gorp, Joannes Goropius Becanus, 2:712
Vanir, 1:287, 1:291–92, 1:293
Vanth, 1:520, 1:525, 1:532
Vanuhi Dāītyā (Veh Dātīg), 2:891
Varahran. *See* Verethraghna
Varangians (Varegs), 1:292, 1:300, 1:303
Varṇa, 2:807, 2:849, 2:857
Varro, 1:519, 1:520, 1:542, 1:551–67 passim, 1:573, 1:582, 1:586, 1:599, 1:602, 1:604, 1:605, 1:606, 1:612, 1:616, 1:618, 1:619, 1:620, 1:622, 1:628, 1:629, 1:634, 1:635, 1:636, 1:639, 1:641, 1:645
Varuṇa, 2:802, 2:826, 2:835; in pre-Islamic Iran, 2:890
Varuṇī, 2:928
Vasiṣṭha, 2:824, 2:827–29, 2:835–36, 2:853, 2:856
Vāsudeva, 2:823, 2:854, 2:861, 2:870
Vasuki, 2:928
Vauquelin des Yveteaux, Jean, 2:702
Vāyu, 2:802, 2:807, 2:814, 2:820, 2:830, 2:835, 2:837, 2:860
Vayu (Vay, Vai), 2:887, 2:892–93
Vazimba, 2:962, 2:973
Vecuvia, 1:519, 1:531
Veda, 2:799–803
Vegetarianism, 2:810, 2:838, 2:841, 2:847–49, 2:858
Vegoia, 1:519, 1:528, 1:530, 1:531, 1:533, 1:534, 1:535
Veh Dātīg. *See* Vanuhi Dāītyā
Veii, Italy, 1:563
Veive (Veiovis), 1:523, 1:526, 1:532
Vejamat, 1:306
Veletes, 1:300
Velleius, 1:598, 1:599, 1:614
Veltune-Voltumna, 1:519, 1:520
Venda, 1:67
Veneti, 1:296–97, 1:515, 1:521, 1:541–42
Venilia, 1:628
Venus, 1:553–54, *1:554*, 1:555, 1:563–65, 1:587, 1:608, 1:625, 1:632–33, 1:636–38, *1:637*, 1:640, 1:641, 1:646; in art and literature, 2:693–94, 2:695, 2:697, *2:697*, 2:698, 2:700, *2:700*, 2:707, 2:760
Veraldenolmai, Veraldenradien, 2:1137
Verethraghna, 2:892, 2:893
Vergicius, 1:135
Verlaine, Paul, 2:759, 2:761
Verrius Flaccus, 1:568
Ver sacrum, 1:517, 1:536, 1:537, 1:542–44
VērvaiputtiraN, 2:845
Vesona, 1:522
Vesperna, 1:572
Vessantara, 2:929
Vesta, 1:551, *1:553*, 1:560, 1:564, 1:565, 1:629, 1:638, *1:639*, 1:645; in fourteenth- to seventeenth-century literature, 2:710–11
Vestalia, 1:638
Vestal virgins, 1:551, 1:569, 1:602, 1:607, 1:638
Vetis-Veiovis, 1:520, 1:526, 1:534
Viard, J., 2:770
Vibhīṣaṇa, 2:826, 2:838
Vicitravīrya, 2:860
Vico, Eneas, 1:139
Vico, Giambattista, 2:729, 2:753, 2:785
Viðarr, 1:287
Vidura, 2:829–30, 2:833
Vieille-Toulouse, Haute-Garonne, 1:257
Vietnam, 2:995–1003
Vigenère, Blaise de, 2:703, 2:705, 2:710, 2:711
Vighnāntaka, 2:902
Vighneśvara, 2:865–66, 2:896
Vigny, Alfred de, 2:752, 2:754, 2:755, 2:756, 2:768, 2:775, 2:776, 2:777
Vilca Oma, 2:1203
Vili, 1:65
Villars, Abbé of, 2:771
Villedieu, Alexander of, 2:693
Vinalia, 1:583, 1:621, 1:637
Vināyaka, 2:865, 2:898, 2:901, 2:902, 2:903
Vincent de Beauvais, 2:691, 2:694
Vindonnus, 1:267
Violence, nonviolence, 2:813–17, 2:836, 2:838, 2:846, 2:848, 2:849, 2:852, 2:858
Vīrabhadra, 2:817, 2:846
Viracocha, 2:1203–4
Virāta, 2:832
Virbius, 1:616
Virgil, 1:501, 1:519, 1:548, 1:559, 1:560, 1:575, 1:579, 1:603, 1:612, 1:616, 1:617, 1:618, 1:627, 1:628, 1:630, 1:635, 1:636, 1:639–45, 1:646–47, 2:664–65, 2:667, 2:696, 2:710, 2:788, 2:1138
Virgins. *See* Mary; Vestal virgins
Virokannas, 2:1136
Virotutis, 1:267
Virtus, 1:599
Viṣṇu, 2:806, 2:811–15, 2:816, 2:819, 2:820, 2:821, 2:822, 2:825–27, *2:825*, 2:829, 2:830, 2:834–38, 2:839–42, 2:848, 2:849–54, *2:851*, 2:856–59, 2:861, 2:864, 2:865–67, 2:870–72, 2:876, 2:896; in Southeast Asia, 2:918, 2:927–29
Viśvakarman: in India, 2:835; in Southeast Asia, 2:917–18
Viśvāmitra, 2:827–29, 2:835–36, 2:853, 2:856–57, 2:867
Viśvāvasu, 2:805
Vitore, 1:307
Vitruvius, 1:533, 1:624, 1:645
Vivahvant, 2:889
Vivasvat, 2:854
Vodjanoi, 1:298
Vofiono-, 1:553
Vofionus, 1:635
Voguls, 2:1132, 2:1134–35, *2:1134*
Vohu Manyu, 2:885, 2:886
Volador, dance of the, *2:1170*, 2:1171, 2:1173
Volcanalia, 1:583, 1:645–46
Volcanus. *See* Vulcan
Volos, 1:298, 1:300–301, 1:303
Volta, *1:518*, 1:519, 1:530
Voltaire, 2:727
Voltumna, 1:520
Volturnalia, 1:583
Völundr, 1:282, 1:284, 1:285
Vörsa-mort, 2:1134
Vossius, 2:729
Vota, 2:673
Votyaks, 2:1134–40 passim, *2:1139*
Vrysinas, Mount (in Crete), 1:336
Vulcan, 1:564, 1:565, 1:608, 1:638, 1:645–46; in art of the Middle Ages, 2:698; among continental Celts, 1:254, *1:256*; in sixteenth- and seventeenth-century literature, 2:706
Vulca of Veii, 1:553, 1:562
Vyāsa, 2:816, 2:853, 2:875

W

Wa, Waba, 2:1113
Wace, 1:265, 2:714, 2:715
Wace house, Mycenae, 1:333
Wad-Ban-Naga, 1:116
Wadd, 1:192
Wageledra, 2:1221
Wagner, Richard, 2:715, 2:718, 2:759–60, 2:761, 2:765
Wakan Tanka, 2:1163
Wakio, 2:1222
Wales. *See* Celts, insular
Waleys, Thomas, 2:696
Wali Sanga, 2:945
Wamara, 1:78, 1:80
Wananathin, 2:1220
Wang, 2:1019
Wang Chong, 2:1007, 2:1028–29, 2:1036
Wang Di, 2:1027–28
Wang Jia, 2:1008
Wangliang, 2:1030
Wang lingguan, 2:902
Wanhuei, 2:902, 2:907
Wanzo, 1:38–39

War, symbolism and deities of: among the Austroasiatics and Austronesians, 2:991; among the continental Celts, 1:279–80; among the Germano-Nordics, 1:285–86, 1:291–92; in Greece, 1:375–78, 1:386–87, 1:402–3, 1:415–18, 1:418–19, 1:419–21, 1:436–37, 1:446–48, 1:505–6; in India, 2:807, 2:816–17, 2:827–28, 2:830–33, 2:837, 2:838, 2:851–52, 2:854, 2:856, 2:898; among the Indo-Europeans, 1:238; among the insular Celts, 1:262–63, 1:270–71; in Madagascar, 2:965; in Mesopotamia, 1:160, 1:177–81; among the Narts, 1:317; in pre-Islamic Iran, 2:892; in Rome, 1:624–25; among the Slavs, 1:301; in southern Africa (Bantu), 1:72
Wasau, 2:1221
Wašhe, 2:1113
Washulassas, 1:219
Wassaf, 2:1104
Wastyrdzhi, 1:316
Wašx°a, 2:1113
Watahinewa, 2:1194, 2:1200
Watenge ne ea, 2:1221
Water, symbolism and divinities of, 2:1231; in Armenia, 1:319; in art and literature, 2:699, 2:771–72; in Asia Minor, 1:217; for Austroasiatics and Austronesians, 2:990–91; in China, 2:1011–14, 2:1018, 2:1027–28; in Christianity, 2:650–53; in Crete and Mycenae, 1:334, 1:336–37; in Egypt, 1:109, 1:125; for Finno-Ugrians, 2:1134–35, 2:1137; for Georgians, 1:309, 1:315; for Germano-Nordics, 1:291; for Gnostics, 2:688; in Greece, 1:366–67, 1:379–84, 1:400–401, 1:413–14, 1:424, 1:425; for Gypsies, 2:719; for Hittites, 2:218; in insular Southeast Asia, 2:938, 2:952–53; in Japan, 2:1051; in Korea, 2:1071–72, 2:1073; in Madagascar, 2:968; in Mesoamerica, 2:1180, 2:1183, 2:1187–88; in Mesopotamia, 1:146, 1:155–56, 1:157–58, 1:173–74; for Ossets, 1:317; in pre-Islamic Iran, 2:891; in pre-Roman Italy, 1:539; in Rome, 1:627–28; in Siberia, 2:1122; for Slavs, 1:298; in southern Africa (Bantu), 1:62, 1:64–65, 1:68–69, 1:70; for Turks and Mongols, 2:1107; in Vietnam, 2:1101–3; in West Africa (Mande), 1:40; for Yoruba, 1:59–60
Watsilla, 1:316
Wawilak, 2:1220
Wayang, *2:927*, 2:933, 2:936, 2:943, 2:946, 2:953–57, *2:954*, *2:955*, *2:956*, 2:959, 2:960
Wê, Wê-ila, 1:175
Webelu, 2:1221
We Cudai, 2:944
Wê-ila. *See* Wê
Weituo, 2:899–901, 2:903–4, *2:905*, 2:906–9
Welkhanos, 1:335
Welle ri Lino, 2:944
Wemale, 2:952
Wends, 1:297
We Nyili' Timo, 2:941
We O'dangriu, 2:953
We Opu Sengngeng, 2:941
We Pinrakati, 2:944
Werkudara, 2:956
Wer-ma, 2:1080
Werner, Zacharias, 2:767
We Tenriabeng, 2:941, 2:944
We Tenridio, 2:944
Whirlpool, 2:982
White Goddess, in literature, 2:786
Wichita, 2:1163
Wigan, 2:940
Wildness, savagery, 1:5–6; among Austroasiatics and Austronesians, 2:992; in China, 2:1027; in Georgia, 1:311; in Greece, 1:343, 1:395–403, 1:417, 1:419–21, 1:425–27, 1:444, 1:445–49, 1:451–52, 1:453–55, 1:458, 1:460, 1:462, 1:486; in the Maghreb, 1:85; in Mesopotamia, 1:159, 1:180–81; in Siberia, 2:1120–21
Willendorf, Austria, 1:19
William (Wilhelm) Tell, 2:733–34
Winckelmann, Johann Joachim, 2:730, 2:765
Wind: in Greece, 1:510; in India, 2:807, 2:860; in Mesoamerica, 2:1183–84; in Mesopotamia, 1:155–56, 1:160
Winnebago, 2:1153, 2:1154, 2:1156
Wintun, 2:1156
Wirulaka, 2:918
Wirupakkha, 2:918
Witoto, 2:1200
Wodan, 1:286–87
Wolf, 2:1153, 2:1160
Wolfram von Eschenbach, 2:715
Woot, 1:73
Wordsworth, William, 2:755, 2:756
World. *See* Cosmogony; Creation
Wotanaz, 1:286–87
Wovoka, 2:1157
Wu, 2:1024
Wudi (the Five Emperors), 2:1018, 2:1020–24, 2:1036
Wuding Lishi, 2:1028
Wuhuan, 2:1089, 2:1102
Wuro, 1:49
Wurtz, Wendel, 2:778
Wurunkatte, 1:221
Wusun, 2:1089, 2:1099
Wu Yue, 2:1012

X

Xakas, 2:1128
Xanjan, 2:1116
Xant, 2:1128
Xanthus, 1:329, 1:474
Xargi, 2:1124, 2:1125
Xeglun, 2:1124
Xenika, 1:456
Xenodice, 1:332
Xenophanes of Colophon, 1:352–53, 2:671
Xenophon, 1:483, 2:320
Xetiwaan Dromau, 2:1221
Xetiwaan Inangoj, 2:1221
Xi, 2:907, 2:1021–22
Xia, 2:1018. *See also* Hia
Xianbi, 2:1089, 2:1100
Xiang, 2:1022–23
Xiangliu, 2:1029
Xianren, 2:1036
Xianyuan, 2:1020
Xie, 2:1016
Xihe, 2:907, 2:1010, 2:1022
Xi Huang, 2:1018–19
Xilonen, 2:1185
Xiong Nu, 2:1089, 2:1099, 2:1112
Xipe Totec, 2:1187
Xipilli, 2:1181
Xiwang Mu, 2:907, 2:1013, 2:1016–17, *2:1017*
Xiuhtecuhtli, 2:1181, 2:1187
Xochipilli, 2:1185
Xochiquetzal, 2:1185
Xolotl, 2:1183
Xoro, 2:1216
Xorz, 1:300
Xosadam, 2:1120
Xovoki, 2:1119
Xuandu, 2:1033
Xuannü, 2:1021
Xuanzang, 2:907

Y

Yab-lha bdag-drug, 2:1078
Yadu, 2:859
Yagua, 2:1200
Yahgan, 2:1194, 2:1200
Yahweh, 2:650–51, 2:653
Yai-dam-du, 2:985
Yakṣas, 2:898–99, 2:926
Yakuts, 2:1090–91, 2:1092, 2:1096, 2:1098, 2:1100, 2:1102, 2:1105, 2:1106, 2:1107, 2:1108, 2:1109, 2:1113, 2:1119, 2:1120, 2:1122, 2:1127, 2:1128
Yala, 1:32
Yam, 1:208–9, 1:212
Yama: in India, 2:830, 2:875, 2:895; in Iran, 89, 2:893
Yamabushi, 2:1037, 2:1040, 2:1056–58, 2:1059–61, 2:1062–63
Yama no kami, 2:1051–52, 2:1064
Yama no shinbo, 2:1052
Yamāntaka, 2:895
Yamasse, 1:58
Yamato-takeru, 2:1041, 2:1046
Yamunā, 2:875
Yan, 2:1016
Yandi, 2:1020, 2:1036
Yang (Indochina), 2:981, 2:984, 2:992–95
Yang, paddy, 2:981, 2:993
Yang and ying, 2:1008–9, 2:1011, 2:1014, 2:1019–20, 2:1025, 2:1082
Yang-In, 2:980
Yang-La, Mount, 2:984
Yang-Pō-Nagar, 2:980
Yanomami, 2:1196–97
Yansan, 1:58
Yao, 2:1010, 2:1018, 2:1021–22, *2:1022*, 2:1023, 2:1029
Ya'-Pum. *See* Bush
Yaqut, 1:192
Yarhibol, 1:205
Yarikh, 1:190, 1:214
Yasa, 1:40
Yasigui, 1:33–34, 1:38, 1:47
Yaśodā, 2:861, 2:870
Yayāti, 2:859
Yazatas, 2:887, 2:891
Yazid, 2:947
Yazılıkaya, 1:218, 1:222, 1:223, 1:224–25, *1:224*, 1:226, 1:228
Yeats, William Butler, 2:759, 2:783–84
Yek, 2:1096
Yelkin, 2:1096
Yemanja, *1:56*, 1:60
Yemma-t n dunnit, 1:84–85
Ye-smon rgyal-po, 2:1079, 2:1081, 2:1084, 2:1085
Yeye Mowo, 1:55
Yeyeponda, 1:61
Yggdrasill, 1:281, 1:286, 1:294, 1:304
Yijing, 2:899
Yima, 2:1079
Yin. *See* Yang and yin
Yin (dragon), 2:1021
Yin (Shang), 2:1018
Yingzhou, 2:1012
Yi the archer, 2:1010–11, 2:1013, 2:1017, 2:1018
Yi Yin, 2:1025
Ymir, 1:282, 1:286
Yniwl, 1:266
Yoga, 2:818–22, 2:841
Yoganidrā, 2:871
Yogeśvarī, 2:869
Yogi, 2:817, 2:818–19, 2:840–41, 2:852
Yol Tengri, 2:1092
Yombe, 1:64–65, 1:70, 1:71
Yomi no kuni, 2:1044–48
Yoni, 2:812, 2:841
Yör, 2:1096
Yoruba, 1:35, 1:37, 1:52–62
Yoruk, 2:1102
Yoshino, Mount, 2:1051
Yoshitsune, 2:1060
Young, Edward, 2:752, 2:768
Youth, 1:399–400
Yspaddaden, 1:264
Yuanshi Tianzun, 2:1036
Yudhiṣṭhira: in India, 2:830–33, 2:836–37; in insular Southeast Asia, 2:955–56
Yuga, 2:849–50

Yukaghir, 2:1128
Yulei, 2:907, 2:1029, 2:1031
Yunhua furen, 2:1017–18
Yūpa, 2:811–13
Yuqiang, 2:1012, 2:1014
Yuri, 2:1072
Yurlunggur, 2:1220
Yu the Great, 2:1007, 2:1009–10, 2:1012, 2:1015, 2:1023, *2:1024*, 2:1029–31, 2:1032, 2:1033, 2:1034
Yuxiao, 2:1027

Z

Zababa, 1:221, 1:224, 1:226
Zabarwa, 1:219
Za-byed, 2:903
Zagreus, 1:333
Zainal Abidin, 2:947
Zaltieri, Bolognino, 1:138, 1:140
Zan (Zen), 1:335
Zāna, 2:1182
Zanahary, 2:967
Zanë, 1:307
Zangzang, 2:1221
Zao bosatsu, 2:1063
Zaō Gongen, 2:1050, 2:1059
Zapotecs, 2:1183
Zappana, 1:221
Zarathustra, 1:235–36, 1:319, 2:878–90 passim, 2:891, 2:892, 2:893
Zatovo, 2:968
Zchokke, Heinrich, 2:767
Zemi, 2:1194
Zempat, 1:306
Zendjirli, 1:200
Zeno of Sidon, 1:613
Zephyr, 1:399, 1:474, 1:510
Zetes, 1:474
Zethus, 1:404
Zeus, 1:234, 1:330–36 passim, 1:355, 1:371–75 passim, *1:372*, 1:376–78, *1:376*, *1:377*, 1:379–82, 1:385, 1:386, 1:392, 1:393, 1:396, 1:398, 1:399, 1:405–11 passim, *1:407*, 1:414, 1:422–23, 1:424, 1:428, 1:438, 1:439, 1:440–41, 1:442, 1:443, 1:444, 1:449, 1:450, 1:456–63 passim, 1:465–69 passim, 1:473, 1:474, 1:478, 1:480–89 passim, 1:490–91, 1:492, 1:494, 1:506, 1:509, 1:510, 1:511, 2:764; in Christianity, 2:662–63, 2:666–69 passim; among Gnostics, 2:667; in literature, 2:778
Zhao Yu, 2:1025
Zhikai, 2:1050
Zhou, 2:1018
Zhouxin, 2:1024
Zhuanxu, 2:1009, 2:1021, 2:1030
Zhuge Liang, 2:1034
Zhumang, 2:1016
Zhurong, 2:1019
Zhuwang, 2:1028
Zibarwa. *See* Zabarwa
Zinthrepus, 1:531
Zipna, 1:531
Zirna, 1:531
Zithariya, 1:221
Zoroaster. *See* Zarathustra
Zoroastrians, Zoroastrianism, 1:234, 1:235–36, 1:320, 2:878–90 passim, 2:890–92
Zorrilla y Moral, José, 2:755, 2:771
Zou Yan, 2:1015
Zradasht, 1:320
Zuangzi (Zhuang Zi), 2:1009, 2:1036
Zulu, 1:67, 1:68–69, 1:70, 1:75
Zuñi, 2:1161
Zurvān, 2:886
Zutuhils, 2:1178
Zvoruna, 1:306
Zyrians, 2:1134